KU-712-027

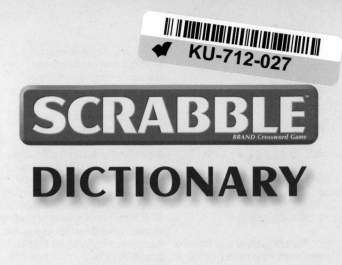

SCRABBLE
BRAND Crossword Game

DICTIONARY

Collins

HarperCollins Publishers
Westerhill Road
Bishopbriggs
Glasgow
G64 2QT

Second Edition 2012

Reprint 10 9 8 7 6 5 4 3 2 1 0

© HarperCollins Publishers 2008, 2012

ISBN 978-0-00-749773-7

Collins® is a registered trademark of HarperCollins Publishers Limited

Scrabble® is a registered trademark of J.W. Spear & Sons Ltd, a subsidiary of Mattel, Inc. © 2012 Mattel

www.collinslanguage.com

A catalogue record for this book is available from the British Library

Typeset by Davidson Publishing Solutions, Glasgow

Printed in Great Britain by Clays Ltd, St Ives plc

Acknowledgements
We would like to thank those authors and publishers who kindly gave permission for copyright material to be used in the Collins Corpus. We would also like to thank Times Newspapers Ltd for providing valuable data.

All rights reserved. No part of this book may be reproduced, stored in a retrieval system, or transmitted in any form or by any means, electronic, mechanical, photocopying, recording or otherwise, without the prior permission in writing of the publisher. This book is sold subject to the conditions that it shall not, by way of trade or otherwise, be lent, re-sold, hired out or otherwise circulated without the publisher's prior consent in any form of binding or cover other than that in which it is published and without a similar condition including this condition being imposed on the subsequent purchaser.

Entered words that we have reason to believe constitute trademarks have been designated as such. However, neither the presence nor absence of such designation should be regarded as affecting the legal status of any trademark.

HarperCollins does not warrant that www.collinsdictionary.com, www.collinslanguage.com or any other website mentioned in this title will be provided uninterrupted, that any website will be error free, that defects will be corrected, or that the website or the server that makes it available are free of viruses or bugs. For full terms and conditions please refer to the site terms provided on the website.

Contents

Editorial Staff   iv

Introduction   v

Two-letter Words   xiii

Abbreviations used in this Dictionary   xvii

Scrabble Dictionary   1

EDITORIAL STAFF

EDITORS
Gerry Breslin
Lorna Gilmour
Robert Groves
Andrew Holmes
Persephone Lock

COMPUTING SUPPORT
Thomas Callan

FOR THE PUBLISHER
Lucy Cooper
Kerry Ferguson
Elaine Higgleton

Introduction

Collins Scrabble Dictionary – Every Word Counts

The *Collins Scrabble Dictionary* is the ideal reference book for people who play Scrabble for enjoyment, in a social or family setting. This dictionary doesn't include every word eligible for Scrabble, but does contain the most commonly used of the 270,000 words in *Collins Official Scrabble Words 2011*, the definitive Scrabble wordlist. The concise definitions in the *Scrabble Dictionary* allow players to check the meaning of words, as well as to use the book for settling arguments during games.

The *Collins Scrabble Dictionary* contains words of up to 7 letters in length. However, references to longer words playable in Scrabble are included. These longer words output in bold, and are introduced by a chevron symbol (>). Because this dictionary is designed for family play, it does not include offensive terms. Such words are, on the other hand, included in the *Collins Official Scrabble Words 2011*, the complete wordlist for tournaments and club competitions, along with words of 8–15 letters.

In the *Collins Scrabble Dictionary*, all words are listed in alphabetical order, rather than some being grouped at the base form as in a conventional dictionary. Where words are inflections of a base form, only the base form has a definition, but the inflections are listed alphabetically as individual entries for easy reference during a game. A black triangle symbol (▶) is used to refer readers to another related entry in the dictionary.

Two-letter words

A sound knowledge of the 124 two-letter words is crucial to success in Scrabble, not least because they are so useful in enabling 'tagging plays', as explained below in the Forming Words section. For this reason, these are supplied in a separate list on pages 13–16 as well as being included in the body of the text.

Special Scrabble Words

To help family players learn and use some of the most useful words in the game, the *Collins Scrabble Dictionary* includes a number of special panel entries, drawing attention to more than 200 words of particular interest or utility. For the most part these are words which are less likely to form part of a novice player's natural vocabulary, and the emphasis is on particularly useful three-letter words, on high probability seven-letter bonus words, on words that are especially useful when you have either too many vowels on your rack or too many consonants, and on selected shorter words that use the high value consonants **J**, **K**, **Q**, **X** and **Z**. But just for fun we have also featured a few of the unusual and exciting words of the kind that Scrabble players dream about. Realistically, you may well never get the chance to play words like **ZOOTAXY**, **TZADDIQ** and **QUETZAL**. But imagine the thrill (and the score!) if you did...

There are also panel entries at the start of every letter section, which offer advice on useful words beginning with that letter.

The *Collins Scrabble Dictionary* is designed to be useful to new players and Scrabble veterans alike – we hope you enjoy using it!

Forming Words

The key to successful Scrabble is constant awareness of the opportunities for forming words on the board. The obvious way to play a new word is to place it so that it intersects with a word already on the board through a common letter:

			D_2		
			O_1		
	L_1	U_1	C_3	K_5	
			T_1		
			O_1		
			R_1		

The common letter is known as a floater, in this case the floater being **C**. Skilful players are occasionally able to play through two or more floaters, whether the floating letters are adjacent or (even more difficult!) separated. A good deal of Scrabble skill revolves around using floaters, and on denying the use of floaters to your opponent.

Other methods of forming words, however, create more than one new word in the process, giving a higher score. The two main ways of doing this are 'hooking' and 'tagging'.

Hooking

Hooking involves 'hanging' one word on another – the word already on the board acts as a 'hook' on which the other word can be hung – changing the first word in the process. When you form a word by hooking, you add a letter to the beginning or end of a word on the board, transforming it into a longer word as you do so:

| C_3 | O_1 | M_3 | E_1 | T_1 | |

C_3	O_1	M_3	E_1	T_1	S_1
					E_1
					R_1
					P_3
					E_1
					N_1
					T_1

In this example, you get the points for **COMETS** as well as for **SERPENTS**. Plurals ending in **S** provide some of the most obvious – and useful – end-hooks. But there are plenty of other end-hooks as well. There are also lots of useful front-hooks. Consider the following example:

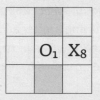

	O_1	X_8

If you happened to have **C**, **E**, **F**, **I**, **K** and **L** among the letters on your rack, you could play the following, taking full advantage of the valuable **X** played by your opponent:

Here you get the 13 points for **FOX** as well as those for **FICKLE**. So you can see that hooking is generally a much more profitable method of word-formation than simply playing a word through one that is already on the board.

Obviously, not all words provide hooks. Some words cannot form other words by having a letter added to either their front or their back; these are known as 'blockers', as they prevent other players from adding words by hooking.

Tagging

Playing a word parallel to one already on the board,
so that one or more tiles are in contact, is known as tagging.
Tagging is more difficult than hooking because you need to
form one additional word for each tile in contact with the
word on the board. In most circumstances, these will be
two-letter words, which is why these words are so vital to the
game. The more two-letter words you know, the greater your
opportunities for fitting words onto the board through
tagging – and of running up some impressive scores!
Very skilful players have even been known to make 7-letter
parallel plays!

For example, consider the following situation (your opponent
has started the game with **SHAM** and you have **E,E,H,I,S,T**
and **X** on your rack):

You could play **HEXES** so that it also forms **SH**, **HE**, **AX** and **ME**
(all valid two-letter words), thus adding the scores for these
three words to the points you make from **HEXES**:

	S_1	H_4	A_1	M_3	
	H_4	E_1	X_8	E_1	S_1

A particular advantage of tagging is that it allows you to benefit from valuable tiles twice in one go, as in the example above where **X** is used in both **HEXES** and **AX**.

Other Word Forming Techniques

There are other ways of forming new words from letters already on the board. For example, it is sometimes possible to 'infill' between existing letters, or to extend existing words at the front or back by the addition of more than one letter. Thus, if your opponent opens with **COVER**, placing the **C** on the double-letter square, you may be able to prefix it with **DIS** making **DISCOVER** and earning a triple-word score. But hooking and tagging are by far the most common techniques.

Two-letter Words

Where many inexperienced Scrabble players go wrong is that they think the longer a word is, the better it is to know, as it's likely to score more. In fact, the key to a good Scrabble vocabulary is a good knowledge of short words.

The reason for that is you can use the short words to 'hook' the word you want to play on to the board, allowing you to play parallel to another word, rather than always going through it crosswise. That way you will usually make more than one word each shot, gaining you a higher score.

8 POINTS = BAD PLAY   **25 POINTS = GOOD PLAY**

Notice how by using the same letters from your rack, you have scored seventeen more points. But notice also that little word **FA** which enabled you to fit the play in. And there we have the first, essential thing you have to know to improve

your game: **all the allowable two letter words**.
Yes, all of them.

There are 124 of these to learn, but to make the list more manageable, you can divide them into three groups:

1.   The ones you already know.

2.   The ones you already know, but may not have realized were words.

3.   The ones you probably don't know.

There are thirty-seven two-letter words which most people would know and which would appear in most dictionaries:

AH	AM	AN	AS	AT	AX	AY	BE	BY	DO	EH
GO	HA	HE	HI	HO	IF	IN	IS	IT	LA	LO
MA	ME	MY	NO	OF	OH	ON	OR	OX	PA	SO
TO	UP	US	WE							

So straight away you only have eighty-seven new ones to learn. But it's not even as bad as that, because now we move on to the second group: the ones you know, but don't know you know.

These include:

Contractions

AD (advertisement)	**PO** (chamberpot)
BI (bisexual)	**RE** (regarding)
MO (moment)	**TA** (thank you)
OP (operation)	

Interjections and exclamations

AW	ER	HM	MM	OI	OW	OY
SH	ST	UH	UM	UR	YA	YO

Letters of the alphabet

AR	EF	EL	EM	EN	ES	EX

Then add in **ID** (the psychiatric term), **PI** (the Greek letter and mathematical term), and **YE** (the old form of **YOU**), and that's another thirty-one taken care of with no trouble at all.

Fifty-six to go. These are the ones you probably don't know, so let's set them out where you can get the measure of them:

AA	AB	AE	AG	AI	AL	BA	BO	CH	DA	DE
DI	EA	ED	EE	ET	FA	FE	FY	GI	GU	IO
JA	JO	KA	KI	KO	KY	LI	MI	MU	NA	NE
NU	NY	OB	OD	OE	OM	OO	OS	OU	PE	QI
SI	TE	TI	UG	UN	UT	WO	XI	XU	YU	ZA
ZO									

If all this looks a bit gobbledygookish, you may be surprised to know that even some of these are more familiar to you than you might realize. An **AB** is an abdominal muscle, as in toning up your abs and your pecs. **MU**, **NU**, and **XI** are Greek letters (and **PE** and **TE** are letters from our alphabet). **OM** is what Buddhists chant as part of their prayers.

Having said that, it can't be denied that some of the definitions are genuinely obscure. To go from start to finish, **AA** is a word from Hawaiian, meaning a rough volcanic rock. And a **ZO** is a Himalayan cross-breed of a yak and a cow, also spelt **ZHO**, **DZO**, **DZHO**, or **DSO**.

Now, where else but in Scrabble can you go from Hawaii to the Himalayas in one step? Have a look at the two-letter words every so often. Once you're happy with the first two groups (i.e. the common ones, the contractions, the interjections, the letters, plus **ID**, **PI**, and **YE**), have a real go at mastering the unusual ones. They really are the essential first step to improving your game.

Abbreviations used in this Dictionary

adj	adjective
adv	adverb
conj	conjunction
det	determiner
interj	interjection
n	noun
pl	plural
prep	preposition
pron	pronoun
vb	verb

Aa

A forms a two-letter word when followed by any one of **A, B, D, E, G, H, I, L, M, N, R, S, T, W, X** and **Y** - 16 letters out of 26 - so it's a really useful tile. There are also a number of short high-scoring words beginning with **A**. **Axe** (10 points) and **adze** (14 points) are good examples, but don't forget their US variants, **ax** (9 points) and **adz** (13 points). Also remember their plurals and the verb form **axed** (12 points). **Aye** (6) and **ay** (5) are handy for tight corners.

AA n volcanic rock consisting of angular blocks of lava with a very rough surface

AAH vb exclaim in pleasure or surprise

AAHED ▸ aah

AAHING ▸ aah

AAHS ▸ aah

AAL n Asian shrub or tree
An **aal** is an East Indian shrub, useful for getting rid of annoying multiples of A.

AALII n bushy sapindaceous shrub with small greenish flowers and sticky foliage
An **aalii** is a tropical tree, great for getting rid of surplus As and Is.

AALIIS ▸ aalii

AALS ▸ aal

AARGH ▸ argh

AARRGH ▸ argh

AARRGHH ▸ argh

AARTI n Hindu ceremony in which lights with wicks soaked in ghee are lit and offered up to one or more deities

AARTIS ▸ aarti

AAS ▸ aa

AB n abdominal muscle

ABA n type of cloth from Syria, made of goat hair or camel hair

ABAC n mathematical diagram

ABACA n Philippine plant, related to the banana

ABACAS ▸ abaca

ABACI ▸ abacus

ABACK adv towards the back; backwards

ABACS ▸ abac

ABACTOR n cattle thief

ABACUS n beads on a wire frame, used for doing calculations

ABAFT adv closer to the rear of (a ship) ▷ adj closer to the stern of a ship

ABAKA n abaca

ABAKAS ▸ abaka

ABALONE n edible sea creature with a shell lined with mother of pearl

ABAMP same as
> abampere

ABAMPS ▸ abamp

ABAND vb abandon

ABANDED ▸ aband

ABANDON vb desert or leave (one's wife, children, etc) ▷ n lack of inhibition

ABANDS ▸ aband

ABAS ▸ aba

ABASE vb humiliate or degrade (oneself)

ABASED ▸ abase

ABASER ▸ abase

ABASERS ▸ abase

ABASES ▸ abase

ABASH vb cause to feel ill at ease, embarrassed, or confused

ABASHED adj embarrassed and ashamed

ABASHES ▸ abash

ABASIA n disorder affecting ability to walk

ABASIAS ▸ abasia

ABASING ▸ abase

ABASK adv in pleasant warmth

ABATE vb make or become less strong

ABATED ▸ abate

ABATER ▸ abate

ABATERS ▸ abate

ABATES ▸ abate

ABATING ▸ abate

ABATIS n rampart of felled trees bound together, placed with their branches outwards

ABATOR n person who effects an abatement

ABATORS ▸ abator

ABATTIS same as ▸ abatis

ADATTU adj dejected

ABATURE n trail left by hunted stag

ABAXIAL adj facing away from the axis, as the surface of a leaf

ABAXILE adj away from the axis

ABAYA n Arab outer garment

ABAYAS ▸ abaya

ABB n yarn used in weaving

ABBA n title for a bishop in the Coptic Church

ABBACY n office or jurisdiction of an abbot or abbess

ABBAS ▸ abba

ABBE n French abbot

ABBED adj displaying well-developed abdominal muscles

ABBES ▸ abbe

ABBESS n nun in charge of a convent

ABBEY n dwelling place of, or a church belonging to, a community of monks or nuns

A

ABBEYS ▸ abbey
ABBOT n head of an abbey of monks
ABBOTCY ▸ abbot
ABBOTS ▸ abbot
ABBS ▸ abb
ABCEE n alphabet
ABCEES ▸ abcee
ABDABS n highly nervous state
ABDOMEN n part of the body containing the stomach and intestines
ABDUCE vb abduct
ABDUCED ▸ abduce
ABDUCES ▸ abduce
ABDUCT vb carry off, kidnap
ABDUCTS ▸ abduct
ABEAM adj at right angles to the length of a ship or aircraft
ABEAR vb bear or behave
ABEARS ▸ abear
ABED adv in bed
ABEIGH adv aloof
ABELE n white poplar tree
ABELES ▸ abele
ABELIA n garden plant with pink or white flowers
ABELIAN ▸ abelia
ABELIAS ▸ abelia
ABET vb help or encourage in wrongdoing
ABETS ▸ abet
ABETTAL ▸ abet
ABETTED ▸ abet
ABETTER ▸ abet
ABETTOR ▸ abet
ABEYANT > abeyance
ABFARAD n cgs unit of capacitance in the electromagnetic system
ABHENRY n cgs unit of inductance in the electromagnetic system
ABHOR vb detest utterly
ABHORS ▸ abhor
ABID ▸ abide
ABIDDEN ▸ abide
ABIDE vb endure, put up with
ABIDED ▸ abide
ABIDER ▸ abide
ABIDERS ▸ abide
ABIDES ▸ abide
ABIDING adj lasting ▷ n action of one who abides
ABIES n fir tree
ABIETIC adj as in **abietic acid** a yellowish powder used in lacquers, varnishes, and soap
ABIGAIL n maid for a lady

ABILITY n competence, power
ABIOSES ▸ abiosis
ABIOSIS n absence of life
ABIOTIC ▸ abiosis
ABITUR n German final-year school examination
ABITURS ▸ abitur
ABJECT adj utterly miserable ▷ vb throw down
ABJECTS ▸ abject
ABJOINT vb cut off
ABJURE vb deny or renounce on oath
ABJURED ▸ abjure
ABJURER ▸ abjure
ABJURES ▸ abjure
ABLATE vb remove by ablation
ABLATED ▸ ablate
ABLATES ▸ ablate
ABLATOR n heat shield of a space vehicle, which melts or wears away during re-entry into the earth's atmosphere
ABLAUT n vowel gradation, esp in Indo-European languages
ABLAUTS ▸ ablaut
ABLAZE adj burning fiercely ▷ adv on fire
ABLE adj capable, competent ▷ vb enable
ABLED adj having a range of physical powers as specified
ABLEISM n discrimination against disabled or handicapped people
ABLEIST ▸ ableism
ABLER ▸ able
ABLES ▸ able
ABLEST ▸ able
ABLET n freshwater fish
ABLETS ▸ ablet
ABLING ▸ able
ABLINGS adv possibly
ABLINS adv Scots word meaning perhaps
ABLOOM adj in flower
ABLOW adj blooming
ABLUENT n substance used for cleansing
ABLUSH adj blushing
ABLUTED adj washed thoroughly
ABLY adv competently or skilfully
ABMHO n unit of electrical conductance
ABMHOS ▸ abmho

ABOARD adv on, in, onto, or into (a ship, train, or plane) ▷ adj on, in, onto, or into (a ship, plane, or train)
ABODE n home, dwelling ▷ vb forebode
ABODED ▸ abode
ABODES ▸ abode
ABODING ▸ abode
ABOHM n cgs unit of resistance in the electromagnetic system: equivalent to 10^{-9} ohm
ABOHMS ▸ abohm
ABOIL adj boiling
ABOLISH vb do away with
ABOLLA n Roman cloak
ABOLLAE ▸ abolla
ABOLLAS ▸ abolla
ABOMA n South American snake
ABOMAS ▸ aboma
ABOMASA > abomasum
ABOMASI > abomasus
ABOON Scots word for ▸ above
ABORAL adj away from or opposite the mouth
ABORD vb accost
ABORDED ▸ abord
ABORDS ▸ abord
ABORE ▸ abear
ABORNE adj Shakespearean form of auburn
ABORT vb have an abortion or perform an abortion on ▷ n premature termination or failure of (a space flight, military operation, etc)
ABORTED ▸ abort
ABORTEE n woman having an abortion
ABORTER ▸ abort
ABORTS ▸ abort
ABORTUS n aborted fetus
ABOUGHT ▸ aby
ABOULIA same as ▸ abulia
ABOULIC ▸ aboulia
ABOUND vb be plentiful
ABOUNDS ▸ abound
ABOUT adv nearly, approximately
ABOUTS prep about
ABOVE adv over or higher (than) ▷ n something that is or appears above
ABOVES ▸ above
ABRADE vb scrape away or wear down by friction
ABRADED ▸ abrade
ABRADER ▸ abrade
ABRADES ▸ abrade
ABRAID vb awake

ABRAIDS ▸ abraid
ABRAM adj auburn
ABRASAX same as
  ▸ **abraxas**
ABRAXAS n ancient charm composed of Greek letters: believed to have magic powers; from the second century AD personified by Gnostics as a deity
ABRAY vb awake
ABRAYED ▸ abray
ABRAYS ▸ abray
ABRAZO n embrace
ABRAZOS ▸ abrazo
ABREACT vb alleviate (emotional tension) through abreaction
ABREAST adj side by side
ABREGE n abridgment
ABREGES ▸ abrege
ABRI n shelter or place of refuge, esp in wartime
ABRIDGE vb shorten by using fewer words
ABRIM adj full to the brim
ABRIN n poisonous compound
ABRINS ▸ abrin
ABRIS ▸ abri
ABROACH adj (of a cask, barrel, etc) tapped
ABROAD adv in a foreign country ▷ adj (of news, rumours, etc) in general circulation ▷ n foreign place
ABROADS ▸ abroad
ABROOKE vb bear or tolerate
ABROSIA n condition involving refusal to eat
ABRUPT adj sudden, unexpected ▷ n abyss
ABRUPTS ▸ abrupt
ABS ▸ ab
ABSCESS n inflamed swelling containing pus ▷ vb form a swelling containing pus
ABSCIND vb cut off
ABSCISE vb separate or be separated by abscission
ABSCISS n cutting off
ABSCOND vb leave secretly
ABSEIL vb go down a steep drop by a rope fastened at the top and tied around one's body ▷ n instance of abseiling
ABSEILS ▸ abseil
ABSENCE n being away
ABSENT adj not present

▷ vb stay away
ABSENTS ▸ absent
ABSEY n alphabet
ABSEYS ▸ absey
ABSINTH same as
  ▸ **absinthe**
ABSIT n overnight leave from college
ABSITS ▸ absit
ABSOLVE vb declare to be free from blame or sin
ABSORB vb soak up (a liquid)
ABSORBS ▸ absorb
ABSTAIN vb choose not to do something
ABSURD adj incongruous or ridiculous ▷ n conception of the world, esp in Existentialist thought, as neither designed nor predictable but irrational and meaningless
ABSURDS ▸ absurd
ABTHANE n ancient Scottish church territory
ABUBBLE adj bubbling
ABULIA n pathological inability to take decisions
ABULIAS ▸ abulia
ABULIC ▸ abulia
ABUNA n male head of Ethiopian family
ABUNAS ▸ abuna
ABUNE Scots word for
  ▸ **above**
ABURST adj bursting
ABUSAGE n wrong use
ABUSE vb use wrongly ▷ n prolonged ill-treatment
ABUSED ▸ abuse
ABUSER ▸ abuse
ABUSERS ▸ abuse
ABUSES ▸ abuse
ABUSING ▸ abuse
ABUSION n wrong use or deception
ABUSIVE adj rude or insulting
ABUT vb be next to or touching
ABUTS ▸ abut
ABUTTAL same as
  ▸ **abutment**
ABUTTED ▸ abut
ABUTTER n owner of adjoining property
ABUZZ adj noisy, busy with activity etc
ABVOLT n cgs unit of potential difference in the electromagnetic system
ABVOLTS ▸ abvolt

ABWATT n cgs unit of power in the electromagnetic system, equal to the power dissipated when a current of 1 abampere flows across a potential difference of 1 abvolt: equivalent to 10^{-7} watt
ABWATTS ▸ abwatt
ABY vb pay the penalty for

> If someone plays this word, remember that it can be expanded to **baby** and **gaby** and also to **abye** and **abys**.

ABYE same as ▸ **aby**
ABYEING ▸ abye
ABYES ▸ abye
ABYING ▸ aby
ABYS ▸ aby
ABYSM archaic word for
  ▸ **abyss**
ABYSMAL adj extremely bad, awful
ABYSMS ▸ abysm
ABYSS n very deep hole or chasm
ABYSSAL adj of or belonging to the ocean depths, esp below 2000 metres (6500 feet)
ABYSSES ▸ abyss
ACACIA n tree or shrub with yellow or white flowers
ACACIAS ▸ acacia
ACADEME n place of learning
ACADEMY n society to advance arts or sciences
ACAI n berry found in Brazilian rainforest
ACAIS ▸ acai
ACAJOU n type of mahogany used by cabinet-makers in France
ACAJOUS ▸ acajou
ACALEPH n invertebrate of the former taxonomic group which included the jellyfishes
ACANTH n acanthus
ACANTHA n thorn or prickle
ACANTHI > acanthus
ACANTHS ▸ acanth
ACAPNIA n lack of carbon dioxide
ACARI ▸ acarus
ACARIAN ▸ acarus
ACARID n member of the group of small arachnids which includes the ticks and mites ▷ adj of or relating to these arachnids

A

ACARIDS ▸ acarid
ACARINE n acarid
ACAROID adj resembling a mite or tick
ACARUS n type of mites which is a serious pests of stored flour, grain, etc
ACATER n buyer of provisions
ACATERS ▸ acater
ACATES n provisions
ACATOUR n buyer of provisions
ACCA n academic
ACCABLE adj dejected or beaten
ACCAS ▸ acca
ACCEDE vb consent or agree (to)
ACCEDED ▸ accede
ACCEDER ▸ accede
ACCEDES ▸ accede
ACCEND vb set alight
ACCENDS ▸ accend
ACCENT n distinctive style of pronunciation of a local, national, or social group ▷ vb place emphasis on
ACCENTS ▸ accent
ACCEPT vb receive willingly
ACCEPTS ▸ accept
ACCESS n means of or right to approach or enter ▷ vb obtain (data) from a computer
ACCIDIA same as ▸ accidie
ACCIDIE n spiritual sloth
ACCINGE vb put a belt around
ACCITE vb summon
ACCITED ▸ accite
ACCITES ▸ accite
ACCLAIM vb applaud, praise ▷ n enthusiastic approval
ACCLOY vb choke or clog
ACCLOYS ▸ accloy
ACCOAST vb accost
ACCOIED ▸ accoy
ACCOIL n welcome ▷ vb gather together
ACCOILS ▸ accoil
ACCOMPT vb account
ACCORD n agreement, harmony ▷ vb fit in with
ACCORDS ▸ accord
ACCOST vb approach and speak to, often aggressively ▷ n greeting
ACCOSTS ▸ accost
ACCOUNT n report, description ▷ vb judge to be
ACCOURT vb entertain

ACCOY vb soothe
ACCOYED ▸ accoy
ACCOYLD ▸ accoil
ACCOYS ▸ accoy
ACCRETE vb grow or cause to grow together
ACCREW vb accrue
ACCREWS ▸ accrew
ACCRUAL n act of accruing
ACCRUE vb increase gradually
ACCRUED ▸ accrue
ACCRUES ▸ accrue
ACCURSE vb curse
ACCURST same as ▸ accursed
ACCUSAL n accusation
ACCUSE vb charge with wrongdoing
ACCUSED n person or people accused of a crime in a court
ACCUSER ▸ accuse
ACCUSES ▸ accuse
ACE n playing card with one symbol on it ▷ adj excellent ▷ vb serve an ace in racquet sports
ACED ▸ ace
ACEDIA same as ▸ accidie
ACEDIAS ▸ acedia
ACEQUIA n irrigation ditch
ACER n type of tree cultivated for its brightly coloured foliage
ACERATE same as ▸ acerated
ACERB adj bitter
ACERBER ▸ acerb
ACERBIC adj harsh or bitter
ACEROLA n cherry-like fruit
ACEROSE adj shaped like a needle, as pine leaves
ACEROUS same as ▸ acerose
ACERS ▸ acer
ACES ▸ ace
ACETA ▸ acetum
ACETAL n 1,1-diethoxyethane, a colourless volatile liquid used as a solvent and in perfumes
ACETALS ▸ acetal
ACETATE n salt or ester of acetic acid
ACETIC adj of or involving vinegar
ACETIFY vb become or cause to become acetic acid or vinegar
ACETIN n type of acetate
ACETINS ▸ acetin

ACETONE n colourless liquid used as a solvent
ACETOSE same as ▸ acetous
ACETOUS adj containing, producing, or resembling acetic acid or vinegar
ACETUM n solution that has dilute acetic acid as solvent
ACETYL n of, consisting of, or containing the monovalent group CH_3CO-
ACETYLS ▸ acetyl
ACH interj Scots expression of surprise
ACHAGE n pain
ACHAGES ▸ achage
ACHAR n spicy pickle made from mango
ACHARNE adj furiously violent
ACHARS ▸ achar
ACHARYA n prominent religious teacher and spiritual guide
ACHATES same as ▸ acates
ACHE n dull continuous pain ▷ vb be in or cause continuous dull pain
ACHED ▸ ache
ACHENE n dry one-seeded indehiscent fruit with the seed distinct from the fruit wall. It may be smooth, as in the buttercup, or feathery, as in clematis
ACHENES ▸ achene
ACHENIA > achenium
ACHES ▸ ache
ACHIER ▸ achy
ACHIEST ▸ achy
ACHIEVE vb gain by hard work or ability
ACHING ▸ ache
ACHINGS ▸ ache
ACHIOTE n annatto
ACHIRAL adj of a tuber producing arrowroot
ACHKAN n man's coat in India
ACHKANS ▸ achkan
ACHOLIA n condition involving lack of bile secretion
ACHOO interj sound of a sneeze
ACHY adj affected by a continuous dull pain
ACICULA n needle-shaped part, such as a spine, prickle, or crystal
ACID n one of a class of compounds, corrosive and sour when dissolved in

water, that combine with a base to form a salt ▷ *adj* containing acid

ACIDER ▶ **acid**

ACIDEST ▶ **acid**

ACIDIC *adj* containing acid

ACIDIER ▶ **acid**

ACIDIFY *vb* convert into acid

ACIDITY *n* quality of being acid

ACIDLY ▶ **acid**

ACIDS ▶ **acid**

ACIDY ▶ **acid**

ACIFORM *adj* shaped like a needle

ACINAR *adj* of small sacs

ACING ▶ **ace**

ACINI ▶ **acinus**

ACINIC ▶ **acinus**

ACINOSE ▶ **acinus**

ACINOUS ▶ **acinus**

ACINUS *n* any of the terminal saclike portions of a compound gland

ACKEE *n* tropical African tree cultivated in the Caribbean for its edible fruit

ACKEES ▶ **ackee**

ACKER *same as* ▶ **acca**

ACKERS ▶ **acker**

ACKNEW ▶ **acknow**

ACKNOW *vb* recognize

ACKNOWN ▶ **acknow**

ACKNOWS ▶ **acknow**

ACLINIC *adj* unbending

ACMATIC *adj* highest or ultimate

ACME *n* highest point of achievement or excellence

ACMES ▶ **acme**

ACMIC *same as* ▶ **acmatic**

ACMITE *n* chemical with pyramid-shaped crystals

ACMITES ▶ **acmite**

ACNE *n* pimply skin disease

ACNED *adj* marked by acne

ACNES ▶ **acne**

ACNODAL ▶ **acnode**

ACNODE *n* point whose coordinates satisfy the equation of a curve although it does not lie on the curve

ACNODES ▶ **acnode**

ACOCK *adv* cocked

ACOLD *adj* feeling cold

ACOLYTE *n* follower or attendant

ACOLYTH *n* acolyte

ACONITE *n* poisonous plant with hoodlike flowers

ACORN *n* nut of the oak tree

ACORNED *adj* covered with acorns

ACORNS ▶ **acorn**

ACOUCHI *n* South American rodent with a white-tipped tail

ACOUCHY *same as* ▶ **acouchi**

ACQUEST *n* something acquired

ACQUIRE *vb* gain, get

ACQUIS *n as in* **acquis communautaire** body of law accumulated by the European Union

ACQUIST *n* acquisition

ACQUIT *vb* pronounce (someone) innocent

ACQUITE *vb* acquit

ACQUITS ▶ **acquit**

ACRASIA *n* lack of willpower

ACRASIN *n* chemical produced by slime moulds

ACRATIC ▶ **acrasia**

ACRAWL *adv* crawling

ACRE *n* measure of land, 4840 square yards (4046.86 square metres)

ACREAGE *n* land area in acres ▷ *adj* of or relating to a large allotment of land, esp in a rural area

ACRED *adj* having acres of land

ACRES ▶ **acre**

ACRID *adj* pungent, bitter

ACRIDER ▶ **acrid**

ACRIDIN *n* acridine

ACRIDLY ▶ **acrid**

ACROBAT *n* person skilled in gymnastic feats requiring agility and balance

ACROGEN *n* any flowerless plant, such as a fern or moss, in which growth occurs from the tip of the main stem

ACROMIA > **acromion**

ACRONIC *adj* acronical

ACRONYM *n* word formed from the initial letters of other words, such as NASA

ACROSS *adv* from side to side (of)

ACROTER *n* plinth bearing a statue, etc, at either end or at the apex of a pediment

ACROTIC *adj* of a surface

ACRYLIC *adj* (synthetic fibre, paint, etc) made from acrylic acid ▷ *n* man-made fibre used for clothes and blankets

ACRYLYL *n* type of monovalent group

ACT *n* thing done ▷ *vb* do something

ACTA *n* minutes of meeting

ACTABLE ▶ **act**

ACTANT *n* (in valency grammar) a noun phrase functioning as the agent of the main verb of a sentence

ACTANTS ▶ **actant**

ACTED ▶ **act**

ACTIN *n* protein that participates in many kinds of cell movement, including muscle contraction, during which it interacts with filaments of a second protein, myosin

ACTINAL *adj* of or denoting the oral part of a radiate animal, such as a jellyfish, sea anemone, or sponge, from which the rays, tentacles, or arms grow

ACTING *n* art of an actor ▷ *adj* temporarily performing the duties of

ACTINGS ▶ **acting**

ACTINIA *n* type of sea anemone common in rock pools

ACTINIC *adj* (of radiation) producing a photochemical effect

ACTINON *same as* > **actinide**

ACTINS ▶ **actin**

ACTION *n* process of doing something ▷ *vb* put into effect

ACTIONS ▶ **action**

ACTIVE *adj* moving, working ▷ *n* active form of a verb

ACTIVES ▶ **active**

ACTON *n* jacket or jerkin, originally of quilted cotton, worn under a coat of mail

ACTONS ▶ **acton**

ACTOR *n* person who acts in a play, film, etc

ACTORLY *adj* of or relating to an actor

ACTORS ▶ **actor**

ACTRESS *n* woman who acts in a play, film, broadcast, etc

ACTS ▶ **act**

ACTUAL *adj* existing in reality

ACTUALS *pl n* commercial commodities that can be

A

bought and used

ACTUARY n statistician who calculates insurance risks

ACTUATE vb start up (a device)

ACTURE n action

ACTURES ▸ acture

ACUATE adj sharply pointed

ACUITY n keenness of vision or thought

ACULEI ▸ aculeus

ACULEUS n prickle or spine, such as the thorn of a rose

ACUMEN n ability to make good judgments

ACUMENS ▸ acumen

ACUSHLA n Irish endearment

ACUTE adj severe ▷ n accent (') over a letter to indicate the quality or length of its sound, as in café

ACUTELY ▸ acute

ACUTER ▸ acute

ACUTES ▸ acute

ACUTEST ▸ acute

ACYCLIC adj not cyclic

ACYL n member of the monovalent group of atoms RCO-

ACYLATE vb introduce an acyl group into a compound

ACYLOIN n organic chemical compound

ACYLS ▸ acyl

AD n advertisement

ADAGE n wise saying, proverb

ADAGES ▸ adage

ADAGIAL ▸ adage

ADAGIO adv (piece to be played) slowly and gracefully ▷ n movement or piece to be performed slowly

ADAGIOS ▸ adagio

ADAMANT adj unshakable in determination or purpose ▷ n any extremely hard or apparently unbreakable substance

ADAPT vb alter for new use or new conditions

ADAPTED ▸ adapt

ADAPTER same as ▸ adaptor

ADAPTOR n device for connecting several electrical appliances to a single socket

ADAPTS ▸ adapt

ADAW vb subdue

ADAWED ▸ adaw

ADAWING ▸ adaw

ADAWS ▸ adaw

ADAXIAL adj facing towards the axis, as the surface of a leaf that faces the stem

ADAYS adv daily

ADD vb combine (numbers or quantities)

ADDABLE ▸ add

ADDAX n N African light-coloured antelope with ribbed spiralled horns

ADDAXES ▸ addax

ADDED ▸ add

ADDEDLY ▸ add

ADDEEM vb adjudge

ADDEEMS ▸ addeem

ADDEND n any of a set of numbers that is to be added

ADDENDA > addendum

ADDENDS ▸ addend

ADDER n small poisonous snake

ADDERS ▸ adder

ADDIBLE adj addable

ADDICT n person who is unable to stop taking drugs ▷ vb cause (someone or oneself) to become dependent (on something, esp a narcotic drug)

ADDICTS ▸ addict

ADDIES ▸ addy

ADDING n act or instance of addition ▷ adj of, for, or relating to addition

ADDINGS ▸ adding

ADDIO interj farewell ▷ n cry of addio

ADDLE vb make or become confused or muddled ▷ adj indicating a confused or muddled state

ADDLED ▸ addle

ADDLES ▸ addle

ADDLING ▸ addle

ADDOOM vb adjudge

ADDOOMS ▸ addoom

ADDRESS n place where a person lives ▷ vb mark the destination, as on an envelope

ADDREST ▸ address

ADDS ▸ add

ADDUCE vb mention something as evidence or proof

ADDUCED ▸ adduce

ADDUCER ▸ adduce

ADDUCES ▸ adduce

ADDUCT vb (of a muscle) to draw or pull (a leg, arm, etc)

towards the median axis of the body ▷ n compound formed by direct combination of two or more different compounds or elements

ADDUCTS ▸ adduct

ADDY n e-mail address

ADEEM vb cancel

ADEEMED ▸ adeem

ADEEMS ▸ adeem

ADENINE n purine base present in tissues of all living organisms as a constituent of the nucleic acids DNA and RNA and of certain coenzymes

ADENOID adj of or resembling a gland

ADENOMA n tumour, usually benign, occurring in glandular tissue

ADENYL n enzyme

ADENYLS ▸ adenyl

ADEPT n very skilful (person) ▷ adj proficient in something requiring skill

ADEPTER ▸ adept

ADEPTLY ▸ adept

ADEPTS ▸ adept

ADERMIN n vitamin

ADHAN n call to prayer

ADHANS ▸ adhan

ADHARMA n wickedness

ADHERE vb stick (to)

ADHERED ▸ adhere

ADHERER ▸ adhere

ADHERES ▸ adhere

ADHIBIT vb administer or apply

ADIEU n goodbye

This French word for farewell is very appropriate when you want to say goodbye to a surplus of vowels. And remember that its plural can be either **adieus** or **adieux**.

ADIEUS ▸ adieu

ADIEUX ▸ adieu

ADIOS sentence substitute Spanish for goodbye

ADIPIC adj as in **adipic acid** colourless crystalline solid used in the preparation of nylon

ADIPOSE adj of or containing fat ▷ n animal fat

ADIPOUS adj made of fat

ADIPSIA n complete lack of thirst

ADIT n almost horizontal shaft into a mine, for access or drainage

ADITS ▸ **adit**

ADJIGO n SW Australian yam plant with edible tubers

ADJIGOS ▸ **adjigo**

ADJOIN vb be next to

ADJOINS ▸ **adjoin**

ADJOINT n type of mathematical matrix

ADJOURN vb close (a court) at the end of a session

ADJUDGE vb declare (to be)

ADJUNCT n something incidental added to something else

ADJURE vb command (to do)

ADJURED ▸ **adjure**

ADJURER ▸ **adjure**

ADJURES ▸ **adjure**

ADJUROR ▸ **adjure**

ADJUST vb adapt to new conditions

ADJUSTS ▸ **adjust**

ADLAND n advertising industry and the people who work in it

ADLANDS ▸ **adland**

ADMAN n man who works in advertising

ADMASS n mass advertising

ADMEN ▸ **adman**

ADMIN n administration

ADMINS ▸ **admin**

ADMIRAL n highest naval rank

ADMIRE vb regard with esteem and approval

ADMIRED ▸ **admire**

ADMIRER ▸ **admire**

ADMIRES ▸ **admire**

ADMIT vb confess, acknowledge

ADMITS ▸ **admit**

ADMIX vb mix or blend

ADMIXED ▸ **admix**

ADMIXES ▸ **admix**

ADMIXT ▸ **admix**

ADNATE adj growing closely attached to an adjacent part or organ

ADNEXA pl n organs adjoining the uterus

ADNEXAL ▸ **adnexa**

ADNOUN n adjective used as a noun

ADNOUNS ▸ **adnoun**

ADO n fuss, trouble

ADOBE n sun-dried brick

ADOBES ▸ **adobe**

ADOBO n Philippine dish

ADOBOS ▸ **adobo**

ADONIS n beautiful young man

ADONISE vb adorn

ADONIZE vb adorn

ADOORS adv at the door

ADOPT vb take (someone else's child) as one's own

ADOPTED adj having been adopted

ADOPTEE n one who has been adopted

ADOPTER n person who adopts

ADOPTS ▸ **adopt**

ADORE vb love intensely

ADORED ▸ **adore**

ADORER ▸ **adore**

ADORERS ▸ **adore**

ADORES ▸ **adore**

ADORING ▸ **adore**

ADORN vb decorate, embellish

ADORNED ▸ **adorn**

ADORNER ▸ **adorn**

ADORNS ▸ **adorn**

ADOS ▸ **ado**

ADOWN adv down

ADOZE adv asleep

ADPRESS vb press together

ADRAD adj afraid

ADREAD vb dread

ADREADS ▸ **adread**

ADRED adj filled with dread

ADRENAL adj near the kidneys ▷ n adrenal gland

ADRIFT adv drifting

ADROIT adj quick and skilful

ADRY adj dry

ADS ▸ **ad**

ADSORB vb (of a gas or vapour) condense and form a thin film on a surface

ADSORBS ▸ **adsorb**

ADSUKI same as ▸ **adzuki**

ADSUKIS ▸ **adsuki**

ADSUM sentence substitute I am present

ADUKI same as ▸ **adzuki**

ADUKIS ▸ **aduki**

ADULATE vb flatter or praise obsequiously

ADULT adj fully grown, mature ▷ n adult person or animal

ADULTLY ▸ **adult**

ADULTS ▸ **adult**

ADUNC adj hooked

ADUST vb dry up or darken by heat

ADUSTED ▸ **adust**

ADUSTS ▸ **adust**

ADVANCE vb go or bring forward ▷ n forward movement ▷ adj done or happening before an event

ADVECT vb move horizontally in air

ADVECTS ▸ **advect**

ADVENE vb add as extra

ADVENED ▸ **advene**

ADVENES ▸ **advene**

ADVENT n arrival

ADVENTS ▸ **advent**

ADVERB n word that adds information about a verb, adjective, or other adverb

ADVERBS ▸ **adverb**

ADVERSE adj unfavourable

ADVERT n advertisement ▷ vb draw attention (to)

ADVERTS ▸ **advert**

ADVEW vb look at

ADVEWED ▸ **advew**

ADVEWS ▸ **advew**

ADVICE n recommendation as to what to do

ADVICES ▸ **advice**

ADVISE vb offer advice to

ADVISED adj considered, thought-out

ADVISEE n person receiving advice

ADVISER n person who offers advice, e.g. on careers to students or school pupils

ADVISES ▸ **advise**

ADVISOR same as ▸ **adviser**

ADWARD vb award

ADWARDS ▸ **adward**

ADWARE n type of computer software that collects information about a user's browsing patterns in order to display relevant advertisements in his or her Web browser

ADWARES ▸ **adware**

ADWOMAN n woman working in advertising

ADWOMEN ▸ **adwoman**

ADYTA ▸ **adytum**

ADYTUM n most sacred place of worship in an ancient temple from which the laity was prohibited

ADZ same as ▸ **adze**

This is the American spelling of **adze**, and is one of the essential short words to know for using the Z.

ADZE n tool with an arched

A

blade at right angles to the handle ▷ *vb* use an adze
ADZED ▶ adze
ADZES ▶ adze
ADZING ▶ adze
ADZUKI *n* type of leguminous plant with yellow flowers and pods containing edible brown seeds
ADZUKIS ▶ adzuki
AE *determiner* one
AECIA ▶ aecium
AECIAL ▶ aecium
AECIDIA > aecidium
AECIUM *n* globular or cup-shaped structure in some rust fungi in which aeciospores are produced
AEDES *n* type of mosquito which transmits yellow fever and dengue
AEDILE *n* magistrate of ancient Rome in charge of public works, games, buildings, and roads
AEDILES ▶ aedile
AEDINE *adj* of a species of mosquito
AEFALD *adj* single
AEFAULD *adj* single
AEGIS *n* sponsorship, protection
AEGISES ▶ aegis
AEMULE *vb* emulate
AEMULED ▶ aemule
AEMULES ▶ aemule
AENEOUS *adj* brass-coloured or greenish-gold
AENEUS *n* aquarium fish
AEOLIAN *adj* of or relating to the wind
AEON *n* immeasurably long period of time

Meaning a long period of time, this little word often gets played as a rack-balancing move when you have too many vowels. And it has a partner **eoan**, meaning of the dawn: beware though that this, unlike **aeon**, does not take a plural S.

AEONIAN *adj* everlasting
AEONIC ▶ aeon
AEONS ▶ aeon
AERATE *vb* put gas into (a liquid), as when making a fizzy drink
AERATED ▶ aerate
AERATES ▶ aerate

AERATOR ▶ aerate
AERIAL *adj* in, from, or operating in the air ▷ *n* metal pole, wire, etc, for receiving or transmitting radio or TV signals
AERIALS ▶ aerial
AERIE *a variant spelling (esp US) of* ▶ **eyrie**

This word for an eagle's nest is a great one for dealing with a surplus of vowels. And it has several variants: **aery, aiery, ayrie, eyrie** and **eyry**.

AERIED *adj* in a very high place
AERIER ▶ aery
AERIES ▶ aerie
AERIEST ▶ aery
AERIFY *vb* change or cause to change into a gas
AERILY ▶ aery
AERO *n* of or relating to aircraft or aeronautics
AEROBAT *n* person who does stunt flying
AEROBE *n* organism that requires oxygen to survive
AEROBES ▶ aerobe
AEROBIA > aerobium
AEROBIC *adj* designed for or relating to aerobics
AEROBOT *n* unmanned aircraft used esp in space exploration
AEROGEL *n* colloid that has a continuous solid phase containing dispersed gas
AEROS ▶ aero
AEROSAT *n* communications satellite
AEROSOL *n* pressurized can from which a substance can be dispensed as a fine spray
AERUGO *(esp of old bronze) another name for >* **verdigris**
AERUGOS ▶ aerugo
AERY *adj* lofty, insubstantial, or visionary
AESC *n* rune
AESCES ▶ aesc
AESIR *n* chief of the Norse gods
AETHER *same as* ▶ **ether**
AETHERS ▶ aether
AFALD *adj* single
AFAR *adv* at, from, or to a great distance ▷ *n* great distance
AFARA *n* African tree
AFARAS ▶ afara
AFARS ▶ afar

AFAWLD *adj* single
AFEAR *vb* frighten
AFEARD *an archaic or dialect word for* ▶ **afraid**
AFEARED *same as* ▶ **afeard**
AFEARS ▶ afear
AFF *adv* off
AFFABLE *adj* friendly and easy to talk to
AFFABLY ▶ affable
AFFAIR *n* event or happening
AFFAIRE *n* love affair
AFFAIRS *pl n* personal or business interests
AFFEAR *vb* frighten
AFFEARD ▶ affear
AFFEARE *vb* frighten
AFFEARS ▶ affear
AFFECT *vb* act on, influence ▷ *n* emotion associated with an idea or set of ideas
AFFECTS ▶ affect
AFFEER *vb* assess
AFFEERS ▶ affeer
AFFIANT *n* person who makes an affidavit
AFFICHE *n* poster or advertisement, esp one drawn by an artist, as for the opening of an exhibition
AFFIED ▶ affy
AFFIES ▶ affy
AFFINAL ▶ affine
AFFINE *adj* of, characterizing, or involving transformations which preserve collinearity, esp in classical geometry, those of translation, rotation and reflection in an axis ▷ *n* relation by marriage
AFFINED *adj* closely related
AFFINES ▶ affine
AFFIRM *vb* declare to be true
AFFIRMS ▶ affirm
AFFIX *vb* attach or fasten ▷ *n* word or syllable added to a word to change its meaning
AFFIXAL ▶ affix
AFFIXED ▶ affix
AFFIXER ▶ affix
AFFIXES ▶ affix
AFFLICT *vb* give pain or grief to
AFFLUX *n* flowing towards a point
AFFOORD *vb* consent
AFFORCE *vb* strengthen
AFFORD *vb* have enough

A

money to buy
AFFORDS ▸ **afford**
AFFRAP vb strike
AFFRAPS ▸ **affrap**
AFFRAY n noisy fight, brawl ▷ vb frighten
AFFRAYS ▸ **affray**
AFFRET n furious attack
AFFRETS ▸ **affret**
AFFRONT n insult ▷ vb hurt someone's pride or dignity
AFFY vb trust
AFFYDE ▸ **affy**
AFFYING ▸ **affy**
AFGHAN n type of biscuit
AFGHANI n standard monetary unit of Afghanistan, divided into 100 puli
AFGHANS ▸ **afghan**
AFIELD adj away from one's usual surroundings or home
AFIRE adj on fire
AFLAJ ▸ **falaj**
AFLAME adj burning
AFLOAT adj floating ▷ adv floating
AFOOT adj happening, in operation ▷ adv happening
AFORE adv before
AFOUL adj in or into a state of difficulty, confusion, or conflict (with)
AFRAID adj frightened
AFREET n powerful evil demon or giant monster
AFREETS ▸ **afreet**
AFRESH adv again, anew
AFRIT same as ▸ **afreet**
AFRITS ▸ **afrit**
AFRO n bush-like frizzy hairstyle
AFRONT adv in front
AFROS ▸ **afro**
AFT adv at or towards the rear of a ship or aircraft ▷ adj at or towards the rear of a ship or aircraft
AFTER adv at a later time
AFTERS n sweet course of a meal
AFTMOST adj furthest towards rear
AFTOSA n foot-and-mouth disease
AFTOSAS ▸ **aftosa**
AG n agriculture
AGA n title of respect, often used with the title of a senior position
AGACANT adj irritating
AGAIN adv once more

AGAINST prep in opposition or contrast to
AGAMA n type of small terrestrial lizard which inhabits warm regions of the Old World
AGAMAS ▸ **agama**
AGAMETE n reproductive cell, such as the merozoite of some protozoans, that develops into a new form without fertilization
AGAMI n South American bird
AGAMIC adj asexual
AGAMID same as ▸ **agama**
AGAMIDS ▸ **agamid**
AGAMIS ▸ **agami**
AGAMOID n lizard of the agamid type
AGAMONT another name for ▸ **schizont**
AGAMOUS adj without sex
AGAPAE ▸ **agape**
AGAPAI ▸ **agape**
AGAPE adj (of the mouth) wide open ▷ n love feast among the early Christians
AGAPEIC ▸ **agape**
AGAPES ▸ **agape**
AGAR n jelly-like substance obtained from seaweed and used as a thickener in food
AGARIC n fungus with gills on the underside of the cap, such as a mushroom
AGARICS ▸ **agaric**
AGAROSE n gel used in chemistry
AGARS ▸ **agar**
AGAS ▸ **aga**
AGAST adj aghast
AGATE n semiprecious form of quartz with striped colouring ▷ adv on the way
AGATES ▸ **agate**
AGATISE same as ▸ **agatize**
AGATIZE vb turn into agate
AGATOID adj like agate
AGAVE n tropical American plant with tall flower stalks and thick leaves
AGAVES ▸ **agave**
AGAZE adj gazing at something
AGAZED adj amazed
AGE n length of time a person or thing has existed ▷ vb make or grow old
AGED adj old
AGEDLY ▸ **aged**
AGEE adj awry, crooked, or ajar ▷ adv awry

AGEING n fact or process of growing old ▷ adj becoming or appearing older
AGEINGS ▸ **ageing**
AGEISM n discrimination against people on the grounds of age
AGEISMS ▸ **ageism**
AGEIST ▸ **ageism**
AGEISTS ▸ **ageism**
AGELAST n someone who never laughs
AGELESS adj apparently never growing old
AGELONG adj lasting for a very long time
AGEMATE n person the same age as another person
AGEN archaic form of ▸ **again**
AGENCY n organization providing a service
AGENDA n list of things to be dealt with, esp at a meeting
AGENDAS same as ▸ **agenda**
AGENDUM same as ▸ **agenda**
AGENE n chemical used to whiten flour
AGENES ▸ **agene**
AGENISE same as ▸ **agenize**
AGENIZE vb whiten using agene
AGENT n person acting on behalf of another ▷ vb act as an agent
AGENTED ▸ **agent**
AGENTRY n acting as agent
AGENTS ▸ **agent**
AGER n something that ages
AGERS ▸ **ager**
AGES ▸ **age**
AGEUSIA n lack of the sense of taste
AGGADA n explanation in Jewish literature
AGGADAH same as ▸ **aggada**
AGGADAS ▸ **aggada**
AGGADIC adj of aggada
AGGADOT ▸ **aggada**
AGGER n earthwork or mound forming a rampart, esp in a Roman military camp
AGGERS adj aggressive
AGGIE n American agricultural student
AGGIES ▸ **aggie**
AGGRACE vb add grace to

AGGRADE vb build up the level of (any land surface) by the deposition of sediment

AGGRATE vb gratify

AGGRESS vb attack first or begin a quarrel

AGGRI adj of African beads

AGGRO n aggressive behaviour

AGGROS ▸ aggro

AGGRY adj of African beads

AGHA same as ▸ aga

AGHAS ▸ agha

AGHAST adj overcome with amazement or horror

AGILA n eaglewood

AGILAS ▸ agila

AGILE adj nimble, quick-moving

AGILELY ▸ agile

AGILER ▸ agile

AGILEST ▸ agile

AGILITY ▸ agile

AGIN prep against, opposed to

AGING same as ▸ ageing

AGINGS ▸ aging

AGINNER n someone who is against something

AGIO n difference between the nominal and actual values of a currency

AGIOS ▸ agio

AGISM same as ▸ ageism

AGISMS ▸ agism

AGIST vb care for and feed (cattle or horses) for payment

AGISTED ▸ agist

AGISTER n person who grazes cattle for money

AGISTOR n person who grazes cattle for money

AGISTS ▸ agist

AGITA n acid indigestion

AGITANS adj as in **paralysis agitans** Parkinson's disease

AGITAS ▸ agita

AGITATE vb disturb or excite

AGITATO adv (to be performed) in an agitated manner

AGITPOP n use of pop music to promote political propaganda

AGLARE adj glaring

AGLEAM adj glowing

AGLEE same as ▸ agley

AGLET n metal sheath or tag at the end of a shoelace, ribbon, etc

AGLETS ▸ aglet

AGLEY adj awry

AGLOO same as ▸ aglu

AGLOOS ▸ agloo

AGLOW adj glowing

AGLU n breathing hole made in ice by a seal

AGLUS ▸ aglu

AGLY Scots word for ▸ wrong

AGLYCON n chemical compound

AGMA n symbol used to represent a velar nasal consonant

AGMAS ▸ agma

AGNAIL another name for > hangnail

AGNAILS ▸ agnail

AGNAME n name additional to first name and surname

AGNAMED adj having an agname

AGNAMES ▸ agname

AGNATE adj related by descent from a common male ancestor ▹ n male or female descendant by male links from a common male ancestor

AGNATES ▸ agnate

AGNATIC ▸ agnate

AGNISE vb acknowledge

AGNISED ▸ agnise

AGNISES ▸ agnise

AGNIZE vb acknowledge

AGNIZED ▸ agnize

AGNIZES ▸ agnize

AGNOMEN n fourth name or second cognomen occasionally acquired by an ancient Roman

AGNOSIA n loss or diminution of the power to recognize familiar objects or people, usually as a result of brain damage

AGNOSIC ▸ agnosia

AGO adv in the past

AGOG adj eager or curious

AGOGE n ancient Greek tempo

AGOGES ▸ agoge

AGOGIC n musical accent

AGOGICS ▸ agogic

AGOING adj moving

AGON n (in ancient Greece) a festival at which competitors contended for prizes. Among the best known were the Olympic, Pythian, Nemean, and Isthmian Games

AGONAL adj of agony

AGONE an archaic word for ▸ ago

AGONES ▸ agon

AGONIC adj forming no angle

AGONIES ▸ agony

AGONISE same as ▸ agonize

AGONIST n any muscle that is opposed in action by another muscle

AGONIZE vb worry greatly

AGONS ▸ agon

AGONY n extreme physical or mental pain

AGOOD adv seriously or earnestly

AGORA n marketplace in Athens, used for popular meetings, or any similar place of assembly in ancient Greece

AGORAE ▸ agora

AGORAS ▸ agora

AGOROT ▸ agora

AGOROTH n agorot

AGOUTA n Haitian rodent

AGOUTAS ▸ agouta

AGOUTI n rodent of Central and South America and the Caribbean with long legs and hooflike claws, valued for its meat

AGOUTIS ▸ agouti

AGOUTY n agouti

AGRAFE same as ▸ agraffe

AGRAFES ▸ agrafe

AGRAFFE n fastening consisting of a loop and hook, formerly used in armour and clothing

AGRAPHA > agraphon

AGRASTE ▸ aggrace

AGRAVIC adj of zero gravity

AGREE vb be of the same opinion

AGREED adj determined by common consent

AGREES ▸ agree

AGREGE n winner in examination for university teaching post

AGREGES ▸ agrege

AGRIA n appearance of pustules

AGRIAS ▸ agria

AGRIN adv grinning

AGRISE vb fill with fear

AGRISED ▸ agrise

AGRISES ▸ agrise

AGRIZE vb fill with fear

AGRIZED ▸ agrize

AGRIZES ▸ agrize

AGROUND adv onto the

bottom of shallow water
▷ *adj* on or on the ground
or bottom, as in shallow
water

AGRYZE *vb* fill with fear

AGRYZED ▶ **agryze**

AGRYZES ▶ **agryze**

AGS ▶ **ag**

AGUE *n* periodic fever with
shivering

AGUED *adj* suffering from
fever

AGUES ▶ **ague**

AGUISE *vb* dress

AGUISED ▶ **aguise**

AGUISES ▶ **aguise**

AGUISH ▶ **ague**

AGUIZE *vb* dress

AGUIZED ▶ **aguize**

AGUIZES ▶ **aguize**

AGUNA *n* (in Jewish law)
woman whose husband
will not grant her a divorce

AGUNAH ▶ **aguna**

AGUNOT ▶ **aguna**

AGUTI *n* agouti

AGUTIS ▶ **aguti**

AH *interj* exclamation
expressing surprise, joy etc
▷ *vb* say ah

AHA *interj* exclamation
expressing triumph,
surprise, etc, according to
the intonation of the
speaker

AHCHOO *interj* sound made
by someone sneezing

AHEAD *adv* in front

AHEAP *adv* in a heap

AHED ▶ **ah**

AHEIGHT *adv* at height

AHEM *interj* clearing of the
throat in order to attract
attention

AHENT *adv* behind

AHI *n* yellowfin tuna

> You will be surprised how
> many times you want to
> catch this Hawaiian fish!

AHIGH *adv* at height

AHIMSA *n* (in Hindu,
Buddhist, and Jainist
philosophy) the law of
reverence for, and
nonviolence to, every form
of life

AHIMSAS ▶ **ahimsa**

AHIND *adv* behind

AHING ▶ **ah**

AHINT *adv* behind

AHIS ▶ **ahi**

AHOLD *n* holding

AHOLDS ▶ **ahold**

AHORSE *adv* on horseback

AHOY *interj* hail used to call
a ship

AHS ▶ **ah**

AHULL *adv* with sails furled

AHUNGRY *adj* very hungry

AHURU *n* type of small pink
cod of SW Pacific waters

AHURUS ▶ **ahuru**

AI *n* shaggy-coated
slow-moving animal of
South America

AIA *n* female servant in East

AIAS ▶ **aia**

AIBLINS *Scots word for*
▶ **perhaps**

AID *n* (give) assistance or
support ▷ *vb* help
financially or in other ways

AIDA *n* cotton fabric with a
natural mesh

AIDANCE *n* help

AIDANT *adj* helping

AIDAS ▶ **aida**

AIDE *n* assistant

AIDED ▶ **aid**

AIDER ▶ **aid**

AIDERS ▶ **aid**

AIDES ▶ **aide**

AIDFUL *adj* helpful

AIDING ▶ **aid**

AIDLESS *adj* without help

AIDMAN *n* military medical
assistant

AIDMEN ▶ **aidman**

AIDOI *adj* of the genitals

AIDOS *Greek word for*
▶ **shame**

AIDS ▶ **aid**

AIERIES ▶ **aiery**

AIERY *n* eyrie

AIGA *n* Maori word for
family

AIGAS ▶ **aiga**

AIGHT *adv* all right

AIGLET *same as* ▶ **aglet**

AIGLETS ▶ **aiglet**

AIGRET *same as* > **aigrette**

AIGRETS ▶ **aigret**

AIKIDO *n* Japanese system
of self-defence employing
similar principles to judo,
but including blows from
the hands and feet

AIKIDOS ▶ **aikido**

AIKONA *interj* South African
expression meaning no

AIL *vb* trouble, afflict

AILANTO *n* Asian tree

AILED ▶ **ail**

AILERON *n* movable flap on
an aircraft wing which
controls rolling

AILETTE *n* shoulder armour

AILING *adj* sickly

AILMENT *n* illness

AILS ▶ **ail**

AIM *vb* point (a weapon or
missile) or direct (a blow or
remark) at a target ▷ *n*
aiming

AIMED ▶ **aim**

AIMER ▶ **aim**

AIMERS ▶ **aim**

AIMFUL *adj* with purpose or
intention

AIMING ▶ **aim**

AIMLESS *adj* having no
purpose

AIMS ▶ **aim**

AIN *same as* ▶ **ayin**

AINE *adj* French word for
elder (male)

> This is a word of French
> origin meaning elder,
> one of those words that
> doesn't score much but is
> useful to remember
> when you have too many
> vowels and are trying to
> balance your rack. And it
> can be extended to
> **ainee**, the feminine
> form.

AINEE *adj* French word for
elder (female)

AINGA *n* Maori word for
village

AINGAS ▶ **ainga**

AINS ▶ **ain**

AINSELL *n* Scots word
meaning own self

AIOLI *n* garlic mayonnaise

AIOLIS ▶ **aioli**

AIR *n* mixture of gases
forming the earth's
atmosphere ▷ *vb* make
known publicly

AIRBAG *n* safety device in a
car, consisting of a bag that
inflates automatically in an
accident to protect the
driver or passenger

AIRBAGS ▶ **airbag**

AIRBASE *n* centre from
which military aircraft
operate

AIRBOAT *n* shallow-
draught boat powered by
an aeroplane engine on a
raised structure for use in
swamps

AIRBUS *n* commercial
passenger aircraft

AIRCON *n* air conditioner

AIRCONS ▶ **aircon**

A

AIRCREW n crew of an aircraft

AIRDATE n date of a programme broadcast

AIRDROP n delivery of supplies, troops, etc, from an aircraft by parachute ▷ vb deliver (supplies, etc) by an airdrop

AIRED ▶ air

AIRER n device on which clothes are hung to dry

AIRERS ▶ airer

AIREST ▶ air

AIRFARE n money for an aircraft ticket

AIRFLOW n flow of air in a wind tunnel or past a moving aircraft, car, train, etc

AIRFOIL same as ▶ aerofoil

AIRGAP n gap between parts in an electrical machine

AIRGAPS ▶ airgap

AIRGLOW n faint light from the upper atmosphere in the night sky, esp in low latitudes

AIRGUN n gun fired by compressed air

AIRGUNS ▶ airgun

AIRHEAD n person who is stupid or incapable of serious thought

AIRHOLE n hole that allows the passage of air

AIRIER ▶ airy

AIRIEST ▶ airy

AIRILY adv in a light-hearted and casual manner

AIRING n exposure to air for drying or ventilation

AIRINGS ▶ airing

AIRLESS adj stuffy

AIRLIFT n transport of troops or cargo by aircraft when other routes are blocked ▷ vb transport by airlift

AIRLIKE ▶ air

AIRLINE n company providing scheduled flights for passengers and cargo

AIRLOCK n air bubble blocking the flow of liquid in a pipe

AIRMAIL n system of sending mail by aircraft ▷ adj of, used for, or concerned with airmail ▷ vb send by airmail

AIRMAN n member of the air force

AIRMEN ▶ airman

AIRN Scots word for ▶ iron

AIRNED ▶ airn

AIRNING ▶ airn

AIRNS ▶ airn

AIRPARK n car park at airport

AIRPLAY n broadcast performances of a record on radio

AIRPORT n airfield for civilian aircraft, with facilities for aircraft maintenance and passengers

AIRPOST n system of delivering mail by air

AIRPROX n near collision involving aircraft

AIRS pl n manners put on to impress people

AIRSHED n air over a particular geographical area

AIRSHIP n lighter-than-air self-propelled aircraft

AIRSHOT n (in golf) shot that misses the ball completely, but counts as a stroke

AIRSHOW n occasion when an air base is open to the public and a flying display and, usually, static exhibitions are held

AIRSICK adj nauseated from travelling in an aircraft

AIRSIDE n part of an airport nearest the aircraft

AIRSTOP n helicopter landing-place

AIRT n direction or point of the compass, esp the direction of the wind ▷ vb direct

AIRTED ▶ airt

AIRTH same as ▶ airt

AIRTHED ▶ airth

AIRTHS ▶ airth

AIRTIME n time allocated to a particular programme, topic, or type of material on radio or television

AIRTING ▶ airt

AIRTS ▶ airt

AIRWARD adj into air

AIRWAVE n radio wave used in radio and television broadcasting

AIRWAY n air route used regularly by aircraft

AIRWAYS ▶ airway

AIRWISE adv towards the air

AIRY adj well-ventilated

AIS ▶ ai

AISLE n passageway separating seating areas in a church, theatre, etc, or row of shelves in a supermarket

AISLED ▶ aisle

AISLES ▶ aisle

AISLING Irish word for ▶ dream

AIT n islet, esp in a river

AITCH n letter h or the sound represented by it

AITCHES ▶ aitch

AITS ▶ ait

AITU n half-human half-divine being

▌ This Polynesian word for a demigod is frequently played to dispose of an excess of vowels.

AITUS ▶ aitu

AIVER n a working horse

AIVERS ▶ aiver

AIZLE n Scots word for hot ashes

AIZLES ▶ aizle

AJAR adv (of a door) partly open ▷ adj not in harmony

AJEE same as ▶ agee

▌ This Scots word meaning ajar is often useful for disposing of the J. It has an alternative spelling agee.

AJIVA n Jainist term for non-living thing

AJIVAS ▶ ajiva

AJOWAN n plant related to caraway

AJOWANS ▶ ajowan

AJUGA n garden plant

AJUGAS ▶ ajuga

AJUTAGE n nozzle

AJWAN n plant related to caraway

AJWANS ▶ ajwan

AKA n type of New Zealand vine

▌ This New Zealand vine is one of the key short words when it comes to using the K.

AKAS ▶ aka

AKATEA n New Zealand vine with white flowers

AKATEAS ▶ akatea

AKE vb old spelling of ache

AKEAKE n New Zealand tree

AKEAKES ▸ akeake
AKED ▸ ake
AKEDAH n binding of Isaac in Bible
AKEDAHS ▸ akedah
AKEE same as ▸ ackee
AKEES ▸ akee
AKELA n adult leader of a pack of Cub Scouts
AKELAS ▸ akela
AKENE same as ▸ achene
AKENES ▸ akene
AKENIAL ▸ achene
AKES ▸ ake
AKHARA n (in India) gymnasium
AKHARAS ▸ akhara
AKIMBO adj as in **with arms akimbo** with hands on hips and elbows projecting outwards
AKIN adj related by blood
AKING ▸ ake
AKIRAHO n small New Zealand shrub with white flowers
AKITA n large powerfully-built dog of a Japanese breed with erect ears, a typically full white coat, and a large full tail carried curled over its back
AKITAS ▸ akita
AKKAS slang word for ▸ money
AKRASIA n weakness of will
AKRATIC ▸ akrasia
AKVAVIT same as ▸ aquavit
AL same as ▸ aal
ALA n wing or flat winglike process or structure, such as a part of some bones and cartilages
ALAAP n part of raga in Indian music
ALAAPS ▸ alaap
ALACK archaic or poetic word for ▸ alas
ALAE ▸ ala
ALALIA n complete inability to speak
ALALIAS ▸ alalia
ALAMEDA n public walk or promenade lined with trees, often poplars
ALAMO n poplar tree
ALAMODE n soft light silk used for shawls and dresses, esp in the 19th century
ALAMORT adj exhausted and downcast
ALAMOS ▸ alamo

ALAN n member of ancient European nomadic people
ALAND vb come onto land
ALANDS ▸ aland
ALANE Scots word for ▸ alone
ALANG n type of grass in Malaysia
ALANGS ▸ alang
ALANIN n alanine
ALANINE n nonessential aliphatic amino acid that occurs in many proteins
ALANINS ▸ alanin
ALANNAH interj my child: used as a term of address or endearment ▷ n cry of alannah
ALANS ▸ alan
ALANT n flowering plant used in herbal medicine
ALANTS ▸ alant
ALANYL n chemical found in proteins
ALANYLS ▸ alanyl
ALAP n Indian vocal music without words
ALAPA n part of raga in Indian music
ALAPAS ▸ alapa
ALAPS ▸ alap
ALAR adj relating to, resembling, or having wings or alae
ALARM n sudden fear caused by awareness of danger ▷ vb fill with fear
ALARMED ▸ alarm
ALARMS ▸ alarm
ALARUM n alarm, esp a call to arms ▷ vb raise the alarm
ALARUMS ▸ alarum
ALARY adj of, relating to, or shaped like wings
ALAS adv unfortunately, regrettably
ALASKA n dessert made of cake and ice cream
ALASKAS ▸ alaska
ALASTOR n avenging demon
ALATE adj having wings or winglike extensions ▷ n winged insect
ALATED adj having wings
ALATES ▸ alate
ALATION n state of having wings
ALAY vb allay
ALAYED ▸ alay
ALAYING ▸ alay
ALAYS ▸ alay

ALB n long white robe worn by a Christian priest
ALBA n song of lament
ALBAS ▸ alba
ALBATA n variety of German silver consisting of nickel, copper, and zinc
ALBATAS ▸ albata
ALBE old word for ▸ albeit
ALBEDO n ratio of the intensity of light reflected from an object, such as a planet, to that of the light it receives from the sun
ALBEDOS ▸ albedo
ALBEE archaic form of ▸ albeit
ALBEIT conj even though
ALBERGO n Italian word for inn
ALBERT n kind of watch chain usually attached to a waistcoat
ALBERTS ▸ albert
ALBINAL ▸ albino
ALBINIC ▸ albino
ALBINO n person or animal with white skin and hair and pink eyes
ALBINOS ▸ albino
ALBITE n colourless, milky-white, yellow, pink, green, or black mineral
ALBITES ▸ albite
ALBITIC ▸ albite
ALBIZIA n mimosa
ALBS ▸ alb
ALBUGO n opacity of the cornea
ALBUGOS ▸ albugo
ALBUM n book with blank pages for keeping photographs or stamps in
ALBUMEN ▸ albumin
ALBUMIN n protein found in blood plasma, egg white, milk, and muscle
ALBUMS ▸ album
ALCADE same as ▸ alcalde
ALCADES ▸ alcade
ALCAIC n verse consisting of strophes with four tetrametric lines
ALCAICS ▸ alcaic
ALCAIDE n commander of a fortress or castle
ALCALDE n (in Spain and Spanish America) the mayor or chief magistrate in a town
ALCAYDE n alcaide
ALCAZAR n any of various palaces or fortresses built in

Spain by the Moors

ALCHEMY n medieval form of chemistry concerned with trying to turn base metals into gold and to find the elixir of life

ALCHERA n (in the mythology of Australian Aboriginal peoples) mythical Golden Age of the past

ALCHYMY old spelling of ▸ **alchemy**

ALCID n bird of the auk family

ALCIDS ▸ **alcid**

ALCO same as ▸ **alko**

ALCOHOL n colourless flammable liquid present in intoxicating drinks

ALCOOL n form of pure grain spirit distilled in Quebec

ALCOOLS ▸ **alcool**

ALCOPOP n alcoholic drink that tastes like a soft drink

ALCORZA n Spanish sweet

ALCOS ▸ **alco**

ALCOVE n recess in the wall of a room

ALCOVED adj with or in an alcove

ALCOVES ▸ **alcove**

ALDEA n Spanish village

ALDEAS ▸ **aldea**

ALDER n tree related to the birch

ALDERN adj made of alder wood

ALDERS ▸ **alder**

ALDOL n colourless or yellowish oily liquid

ALDOLS ▸ **aldol**

ALDOSE n sugar that contains the aldehyde group or is a hemiacetal

ALDOSES ▸ **aldose**

ALDRIN n brown to white poisonous crystalline solid

ALDRINS ▸ **aldrin**

ALE n kind of beer

ALEC same as ▸ **aleck**

ALECK n irritatingly oversmart person

ALECKS ▸ **aleck**

ALECOST another name for > **costmary**

ALECS ▸ **alec**

ALEE adj on or towards the lee

ALEF n first letter of Hebrew alphabet

ALEFS ▸ **alef**

ALEFT adv at or to left

ALEGAR n malt vinegar

ALEGARS ▸ **alegar**

ALEGGE vb alleviate

ALEGGED ▸ **alegge**

ALEGGES ▸ **alegge**

ALEMBIC n anything that distils or purifies, esp an obsolete vessel used for distillation

ALENCON n elaborate lace worked on a hexagonal mesh

ALENGTH adv at length

ALEPH n first letter in the Hebrew alphabet

ALEPHS ▸ **aleph**

ALEPINE n type of cloth

ALERCE n wood of the sandarac tree

ALERCES ▸ **alerce**

ALERION n eagle in heraldry

ALERT adj watchful, attentive ▷ n warning of danger ▷ vb warn of danger

ALERTED ▸ **alert**

ALERTER ▸ **alert**

ALERTLY ▸ **alert**

ALERTS ▸ **alert**

ALES ▸ **ale**

ALETHIC adj of or relating to such philosophical concepts as truth, necessity, possibility, contingency, etc

ALEURON n outer protein-rich layer of certain seeds, esp of cereal grains

ALEVIN n young fish, esp a young salmon or trout

ALEVINS ▸ **alevin**

ALEW n cry to call hunting hounds

ALEWIFE n North American fish

ALEWS ▸ **alew**

ALEXIA n disorder of the central nervous system characterized by impaired ability to read

ALEXIAS ▸ **alexia**

ALEXIC ▸ **alexia**

ALEXIN n complement

ALEXINE same as ▸ **alexin**

ALEXINS ▸ **alexin**

ALEYE vb allay

ALEYED ▸ **aleye**

ALEYES ▸ **aleye**

ALEYING ▸ **aleye**

ALF n uncultivated Australian

ALFA n type of grass

ALFAKI n expert in Muslim law

ALFAKIS ▸ **alfaki**

ALFALFA n kind of plant used to feed livestock

ALFAQUI n expert in Muslim law

ALFAS ▸ **alfa**

ALFEREZ n Spanish standard-bearer

ALFORJA n saddlebag made of leather or canvas

ALFREDO adj cooked with a cheese and egg sauce

ALFS ▸ **alf**

ALGA n unicellular or multicellular organism formerly classified as a plant

ALGAE ▸ **alga**

ALGAL ▸ **alga**

ALGAS ▸ **alga**

ALGATE adv anyway

ALGATES adv anyway

ALGEBRA n branch of mathematics using symbols to represent numbers

ALGESES ▸ **algesis**

ALGESIA n capacity to feel pain

ALGESIC ▸ **algesia**

ALGESIS n feeling of pain

ALGETIC ▸ **algesia**

ALGID adj chilly or cold

ALGIN n gelatinous solution obtained as a by-product in the extraction of iodine from seaweed

ALGINIC adj as in **alginic acid** powdery substance extracted from kelp

ALGINS ▸ **algin**

ALGOID adj resembling or relating to algae

ALGOR n chill

ALGORS ▸ **algor**

ALGUM n type of wood mentioned in Bible

ALGUMS ▸ **algum**

ALIAS adv also known as ▷ n false name

ALIASES ▸ **alias**

ALIBI n plea of being somewhere else when a crime was committed ▷ vb provide someone with an alibi

ALIBIED ▸ **alibi**

ALIBIES ▸ **alibi**

ALIBIS ▸ **alibi**

ALIBLE adj nourishing

ALICANT n wine from Alicante in Spain

ALIDAD same as ▸ **alidade**

ALIDADE *n* surveying instrument used in plane-tabling for drawing lines of sight on a distant object and taking angular measurements

ALIDADS ▷ **alidad**

ALIEN *adj* foreign ▷ *n* foreigner ▷ *vb* transfer (property, etc) to another

ALIENED ▷ **alien**

ALIENEE *n* person to whom a transfer of property is made

ALIENER ▷ **alien**

ALIENLY ▷ **alien**

ALIENOR *n* person who transfers property to another

ALIENS ▷ **alien**

ALIF *n* first letter of Arabic alphabet

ALIFORM *adj* wing-shaped

ALIFS ▷ **alif**

ALIGHT *vb* step out of (a vehicle) ▷ *adj* on fire ▷ *adv* on fire

ALIGHTS ▷ **alight**

ALIGN *vb* bring (a person or group) into agreement with the policy of another

ALIGNED ▷ **align**

ALIGNER ▷ **align**

ALIGNS ▷ **align**

ALIKE *adj* like, similar ▷ *adv* in the same way

ALIMENT *n* something that nourishes or sustains the body or mind ▷ *vb* support or sustain

ALIMONY *n* allowance paid under a court order to a separated or divorced spouse

ALINE *a rare spelling of* ▷ **align**

ALINED ▷ **aline**

ALINER ▷ **aline**

ALINERS ▷ **aline**

ALINES ▷ **aline**

ALINING ▷ **aline**

ALIPED *n* animal, like the bat, whose toes are joined by a membrane that serves as a wing ▷ *adj* (of bats and similar animals) having the digits connected by a winglike membrane

ALIPEDS ▷ **aliped**

ALIQUOT *adj* of or denoting an exact divisor of a number ▷ *n* exact divisor

ALISMA *n* marsh plant

ALISMAS ▷ **alisma**

ALISON *same as* ▷ **alyssum**

ALISONS ▷ **alison**

ALIST *adj* leaning over

ALIT *rare past tense and past participle of* ▷ **alight**

ALIUNDE *adj* from a source extrinsic to the matter, document, or instrument under consideration

ALIVE *adj* living, in existence

ALIYA *n* immigration to Holy Land

ALIYAH *n* immigration to the Holy Land

ALIYAHS ▷ **aliyah**

ALIYAS ▷ **aliya**

ALIYOS *n* remission of sin in Jewish faith

ALIYOT ▷ **aliyah**

ALIYOTH ▷ **aliyah**

ALIZARI *n* madder from Middle East

ALKALI *n* substance which combines with acid and neutralizes it to form a salt

ALKALIC *adj* (of igneous rocks) containing large amounts of alkalis, esp sodium and potassium

ALKALIN *adj* leaning over

ALKALIS ▷ **alkali**

ALKANE *n* any saturated hydrocarbon with the general formula C_nH_{2n+2}

ALKANES ▷ **alkane**

ALKANET *n* European plant whose roots yield a red dye

ALKENE *n* type of unsaturated hydrocarbon

ALKENES ▷ **alkene**

ALKIE *same as* ▷ **alky**

ALKIES ▷ **alky**

ALKINE *n* alkyne

ALKINES ▷ **alkine**

ALKO *n* heavy drinker or alcoholic

ALKOS ▷ **alko**

ALKOXY *adj* of type of chemical compound containing oxygen

ALKY *n* heavy drinker or alcoholic

ALKYD *n* synthetic resin

ALKYDS ▷ **alkyd**

ALKYL *n* of or containing the monovalent group C_nH_{2n+1}

ALKYLIC ▷ **alkyl**

ALKYLS ▷ **alkyl**

ALKYNE *n* any unsaturated aliphatic hydrocarbon

ALKYNES ▷ **alkyne**

ALL *adj* whole quantity or number (of) ▷ *adv* wholly, entirely ▷ *n* entire being, effort, or property

ALLAY *vb* reduce (fear or anger)

ALLAYED ▷ **allay**

ALLAYER ▷ **allay**

ALLAYS ▷ **allay**

ALLEDGE *vb* allege

ALLEE *n* avenue

ALLEES ▷ **allee**

ALLEGE *vb* state without proof

ALLEGED *adj* stated but not proved

ALLEGER ▷ **allege**

ALLEGES ▷ **allege**

ALLEGGE *vb* alleviate

ALLEGRO *adv* (piece to be played) in a brisk lively manner ▷ *n* piece or passage to be performed in a brisk lively manner

ALLEL *n* form of gene

ALLELE *n* any of two or more genes that are responsible for alternative characteristics, such as smooth or wrinkled seeds in peas

ALLELES ▷ **allele**

ALLELIC ▷ **allele**

ALLELS ▷ **allel**

ALLERGY *n* extreme sensitivity to a substance, which causes the body to react to it

ALLEY *n* narrow street or path

ALLEYED *adj* having alleys

ALLEYS ▷ **alley**

ALLHEAL *n* any of several plants reputed to have healing powers, such as selfheal and valerian

ALLICE *n* species of fish

ALLICES ▷ **allice**

ALLICIN *n* chemical found in garlic

ALLIED *adj* joined, as by treaty, agreement, or marriage

ALLIES ▷ **ally**

ALLIS *n* species of fish

ALLISES ▷ **allis**

ALLIUM *n* type of plant of the family including the onion, garlic, shallot, leek, and chive

ALLIUMS ▷ **allium**

ALLNESS *n* being all

ALLOBAR *n* form of element

ALLOD *same as* > **allodium**
ALLODIA > **allodium**
ALLODS ▸ **allod**
ALLONGE *n* paper extension to bill of exchange
ALLONS *interj* French word meaning let's go
ALLONYM *n* name, often one of historical significance or that of another person, assumed by a person, esp an author
ALLOT *vb* assign as a share or for a particular purpose
ALLOTS ▸ **allot**
ALLOVER *n* fabric completely covered with a pattern
ALLOW *vb* permit
ALLOWED ▸ **allow**
ALLOWS ▸ **allow**
ALLOXAN *n* chemical found in uric acid
ALLOY *n* mixture of two or more metals ▷ *vb* mix (metals)
ALLOYED ▸ **alloy**
ALLOYS ▸ **alloy**
ALLS ▸ **all**
ALLSEED *n* any of several plants that produce many seeds, such as knotgrass
ALLUDE *vb* refer indirectly to
ALLUDED ▸ **allude**
ALLUDES ▸ **allude**
ALLURE *n* attractiveness ▷ *vb* entice or attract
ALLURED ▸ **allure**
ALLURER ▸ **allure**
ALLURES ▸ **allure**
ALLUVIA > **alluvium**
ALLY *vb* unite or be united, esp formally, as by treaty, confederation, or marriage ▷ *n* country, person, or group allied with another
ALLYING ▸ **ally**
ALLYL *n* of, consisting of, or containing the monovalent group CH_2:$CHCH_2^-$
ALLYLIC ▸ **allyl**
ALLYLS ▸ **allyl**
ALLYOU *pron* all of you
ALMA *n* Egyptian dancing girl
ALMAH *n* Egyptian dancing girl
ALMAHS ▸ **almah**
ALMAIN *n* German dance
ALMAINS ▸ **almain**
ALMANAC *n* yearly calendar with detailed information

on anniversaries, phases of the moon, etc
ALMAS ▸ **alma**
ALME *n* Egyptian dancing girl
ALMEH *n* Egyptian dancing girl
ALMEHS ▸ **almeh**
ALMEMAR *n* (in Ashkenazic usage) the raised platform in a synagogue on which the reading desk stands
ALMERY *n* cupboard for church vessels
ALMES ▸ **alme**
ALMIRAH *n* cupboard
ALMNER *n* almoner
ALMNERS ▸ **almoner**
ALMOND *n* edible oval-shaped nut which grows on a small tree
ALMONDS ▸ **almond**
ALMONDY ▸ **almond**
ALMONER *n* formerly, a hospital social worker
ALMONRY *n* house of an almoner, usually the place where alms were given
ALMOST *adv* very nearly
ALMOUS *Scots word for* ▸ **alms**
ALMS *pl n* gifts to the poor
ALMSMAN *n* person who gives or receives alms
ALMSMEN ▸ **almsman**
ALMUCE *n* fur-lined hood or cape formerly worn by members of certain religious orders, more recently by canons of France
ALMUCES ▸ **almuce**
ALMUD *n* Spanish unit of measure
ALMUDE *n* Spanish unit of measure
ALMUDES ▸ **almude**
ALMUDS ▸ **almud**
ALMUG *n* type of wood mentioned in Bible
ALMUGS ▸ **almug**
ALNAGE *n* measurement in ells
ALNAGER *n* inspector of cloth
ALNAGES ▸ **alnage**
ALNICO *n* alloy of various metals including iron, nickel, and cobalt
ALNICOS ▸ **alnico**
ALOD *n* feudal estate with no superior
ALODIA ▸ **alodium**

ALODIAL ▸ **alodium**
ALODIUM *same as* > **allodium**
ALODS ▸ **alod**
ALOE *n* plant with fleshy spiny leaves
ALOED *adj* containing aloes
ALOES *another name for* > **eaglewood**
ALOETIC ▸ **aloe**
ALOFT *adv* in the air ▷ *adj* in or into a high or higher place
ALOGIA *n* inability to speak
ALOGIAS ▸ **alogia**
ALOHA *a Hawaiian word for* ▸ **hello**
ALOHAS ▸ **aloha**
ALOIN *n* bitter crystalline compound derived from various species of aloe: used as a laxative and flavouring agent
ALOINS ▸ **aloin**
ALONE *adv* without anyone or anything else
ALONELY ▸ **alone**
ALONG *adv* forward
ALONGST *adv* along
ALOO *n* (in Indian cookery) potato
ALOOF *adj* distant or haughty in manner
ALOOFLY ▸ **aloof**
ALOOS ▸ **aloo**
ALOUD *adv* in an audible voice ▷ *adj* in a normal voice
ALOW *adj* in or into the lower rigging of a vessel, near the deck
ALOWE *Scots word for* ▸ **ablaze**
ALP *n* high mountain
ALPACA *n* Peruvian llama
ALPACAS ▸ **alpaca**
ALPACCA *same as* ▸ **alpaca**
ALPEEN *n* Irish cudgel
ALPEENS ▸ **alpeen**
ALPHA *n* first letter in the Greek alphabet
ALPHAS ▸ **alpha**
ALPHORN *n* wind instrument used in the Swiss Alps, consisting of a very long tube of wood or bark with a cornet-like mouthpiece
ALPHYL *n* univalent radical
ALPHYLS ▸ **alphyl**
ALPINE *adj* of high mountains ▷ *n* mountain plant

ALPINES ▸ alpine
ALPS ▸ alp
ALREADY *adv* before the present time
ALRIGHT *adj* all right
ALS ▸ al
ALSIKE *n* clover native to Europe and Asia
ALSIKES ▸ alsike
ALSO *adv* in addition, too
ALSOON *same as* ▸ alsoone
ALSOONE *adv* as soon
ALT *n* octave directly above the treble staff
ALTAR *n* table used for Communion in Christian churches
ALTARS ▸ altar
ALTER *vb* make or become different
ALTERED ▸ alter
ALTERER ▸ alter
ALTERN *adj* alternate
ALTERNE *n* neighbouring but different plant group
ALTERS ▸ alter
ALTESSE *n* French word for highness
ALTEZA *n* Spanish word for highness
ALTEZAS ▸ alteza
ALTEZZA *n* Italian word for highness
ALTHAEA *n* plant such as the hollyhock, having tall spikes of showy white, yellow, or red flowers
ALTHEA *same as* ▸ althaea
ALTHEAS ▸ althea
ALTHO *conj* short form of although
ALTHORN *n* valved brass musical instrument belonging to the saxhorn or flügelhorn families
ALTO *n* (singer with) the highest adult male voice ▷ *adj* denoting such an instrument, singer, or voice
ALTOIST *n* person who plays the alto saxophone
ALTOS ▸ alto
ALTS ▸ alt
ALU ▸ aloo
ALUDEL *n* pear-shaped vessel, open at both ends, formerly used with similar vessels for collecting condensates, esp of subliming mercury
ALUDELS ▸ aludel
ALULA *n* tuft of feathers

attached to the first digit of a bird
ALULAE ▸ alula
ALULAR ▸ alula
ALULAS ▸ alula
ALUM *n* double sulphate of aluminium and potassium
ALUMIN *n* aluminium oxide
ALUMINA *n* aluminium oxide
ALUMINE *n* French word for alumina
ALUMINS ▸ alumin
ALUMISH *adj* like alum
ALUMIUM *old name for* > aluminium
ALUMNA *n* female graduate of a school, college, etc
ALUMNAE ▸ alumna
ALUMNI ▸ alumnus
ALUMNUS *n* graduate of a college
ALUMS ▸ alum
ALUNITE *n* white, grey, or reddish mineral
ALURE *n* area behind battlements
ALURES ▸ alure
ALUS ▸ alu
ALVEARY *n* beehive
ALVEOLE *n* alveolus
ALVEOLI > alveolus
ALVINE *adj* of or relating to the intestines or belly
ALWAY *same as* ▸ always
ALWAYS *adv* at all times
ALYSSUM *n* garden plant with small yellow or white flowers
AM *see* ▸ be
AMA *n* vessel for water
AMABILE *adj* sweet
AMADODA *pl n* grown men
AMADOU *n* spongy substance made from certain fungi, used as tinder to light fires and in medicine to stop bleeding
AMADOUS ▸ amadou
AMAH *n* (in the East, formerly) a nurse or maidservant
AMAHS ▸ amah
AMAIN *adv* with great strength, speed, or haste
AMAKOSI ▸ inkhosi
AMALGAM *n* blend or combination
AMANDLA *n* political slogan calling for power to the Black population
AMANITA *n* type of fungus
AMARANT *n* amaranth

AMARNA *adj* pertaining to the reign of the Pharaoh Akhenaton
AMARONE *n* strong dry red Italian wine
AMAS ▸ ama
AMASS *vb* collect or accumulate
AMASSED ▸ amass
AMASSER ▸ amass
AMASSES ▸ amass
AMATE *vb* match
AMATED ▸ amate
AMATES ▸ amate
AMATEUR *n* person who engages in a sport or activity as a pastime rather than as a profession ▷ *adj* not professional
AMATING ▸ amate
AMATION *n* lovemaking
AMATIVE *a rare word for* ▸ amorous
AMATOL *n* explosive mixture of ammonium nitrate and TNT, used in shells and bombs
AMATOLS ▸ amatol
AMATORY *adj* relating to romantic or sexual love
AMAUT *n* hood on an Inuit woman's parka for carrying a child
AMAUTS ▸ amaut
AMAZE *vb* surprise greatly, astound
AMAZED ▸ amaze
AMAZES ▸ amaze
AMAZING *adj* causing wonder or astonishment
AMAZON *n* any tall, strong, or aggressive woman
AMAZONS ▸ amazon
AMBACH *same as* ▸ ambatch
AMBAGE *n* ambiguity
AMBAGES ▸ ambage
AMBAN *n* Chinese official
AMBANS ▸ amban
AMBARI *same as* ▸ ambary
AMBARIS ▸ ambari
AMBARY *n* tropical Asian plant that yields a fibre similar to jute
AMBASSY *n* embassy
AMBATCH *n* tree or shrub of the Nile Valley, valued for its light-coloured wood
AMBEER *n* saliva coloured by tobacco juice
AMBEERS ▸ ambeer
AMBER *n* clear yellowish

A

fossil resin ▷ *adj*
brownish-yellow
AMBERED *adj* fixed in
amber
AMBERS ▶ **amber**
AMBERY *adj* like amber
AMBIENT *adj* surrounding
▷ *n* ambient music
AMBIT *n* limits or boundary
AMBITS ▶ **ambit**
AMBITTY *adj* crystalline and
brittle
AMBLE *vb* walk at a leisurely
pace ▷ *n* leisurely walk or
pace
AMBLED ▶ **amble**
AMBLER ▶ **amble**
AMBLERS ▶ **amble**
AMBLES ▶ **amble**
AMBLING *n* walking at a
leisurely pace
AMBO *n* either of two raised
pulpits from which the
gospels and epistles were
read in early Christian
churches
AMBOINA *same as*
▶ **amboyna**
AMBONES ▶ **ambo**
AMBOS ▶ **ambo**
AMBOYNA *n* mottled
curly-grained wood of an
Indonesian tree, used in
making furniture
AMBRIES ▶ **ambry**
AMBROID *same as*
> **amberoid**
AMBRY *n* recessed
cupboard in the wall of a
church near the altar, used
to store sacred vessels, etc
AMBSACE *n* double ace, the
lowest throw at dice
AMBUSH *n* act of waiting in
a concealed position to
make a surprise attack ▷ *vb*
attack from a concealed
position
AME *n* soul
AMEARST *old form of*
▶ **amerce**
AMEBA *same as* ▶ **amoeba**
AMEBAE ▶ **ameba**
AMEBAN ▶ **ameba**
AMEBAS ▶ **ameba**
AMEBEAN *same as*
> **amoebean**
AMEBIC ▶ **ameba**
AMEBOID *same as*
> **amoeboid**
AMEER *n* (formerly) the
ruler of Afghanistan
AMEERS ▶ **ameer**

AMELIA *n* congenital
absence of arms or legs
AMELIAS ▶ **amelia**
AMEN *n* term used at the
end of a prayer or religious
statement ▷ *vb* say amen
AMENAGE *vb* tame
AMEND *vb* make small
changes to correct or
improve (something)
AMENDE *n* public apology
and reparation made to
satisfy the honour of the
person wronged
AMENDED ▶ **amend**
AMENDER ▶ **amend**
AMENDES ▶ **amende**
AMENDS *n* recompense or
compensation given or
gained for some injury,
insult, etc
AMENE *adj* pleasant
AMENED ▶ **amen**
AMENING ▶ **amen**
AMENITY *n* useful or
enjoyable feature
AMENS ▶ **amen**
AMENT *n* mentally deficient
person
AMENTA ▶ **amentum**
AMENTAL ▶ **amentum**
AMENTIA *n* severe mental
deficiency, usually
congenital
AMENTS ▶ **ament**
AMENTUM *same as* ▶ **ament**
AMERCE *vb* punish by a fine
AMERCED ▶ **amerce**
AMERCER ▶ **amerce**
AMERCES ▶ **amerce**
AMES ▶ **ame**
AMESACE *same as*
▶ **ambsace**
AMI *n* male friend
AMIA *n* species of fish
AMIABLE *adj* friendly,
pleasant-natured
AMIABLY ▶ **amiable**
AMIAS ▶ **amia**
AMICE *n* rectangular piece
of white linen worn by
priests around the neck and
shoulders under the alb or,
formerly, on the head
AMICES ▶ **amice**
AMICI ▶ **amicus**
AMICUS *n* Latin for friend
AMID *prep* in the middle of,
among ▷ *n* amide
AMIDASE *n* enzyme
AMIDE *n* any organic
compound containing the
group –$CONH_2$

AMIDES ▶ **amide**
AMIDIC ▶ **amide**
AMIDIN *n* form of starch
AMIDINE *n* crystalline
compound
AMIDINS ▶ **amidin**
AMIDO *adj* containing
amide
AMIDOL *n* chemical used in
developing photographs
AMIDOLS ▶ **amidol**
AMIDONE *n* pain-killing
drug
AMIDS *same as* ▶ **amid**
AMIDST *same as* ▶ **amid**
AMIE *n* female friend
AMIES ▶ **amie**
AMIGA *n* Spanish female
friend
AMIGAS ▶ **amiga**
AMIGO *n* friend
AMIGOS ▶ **amigo**
AMILDAR *n* manager in
India
AMIN *same as* ▶ **amine**
AMINE *n* organic base
formed by replacing one or
more of the hydrogen
atoms of ammonia by
organic groups
AMINES ▶ **amine**
AMINIC ▶ **amine**
AMINITY *n* amenity
AMINO *n* of, consisting of,
or containing the group of
atoms -NH_2
AMINS ▶ **amin**
AMIR *n* (formerly) the ruler
of Afghanistan
AMIRATE ▶ **amir**
AMIRS ▶ **amir**
AMIS ▶ **ami**
AMISES ▶ **ami**
AMISS *adv* wrongly, badly
▷ *adj* wrong, faulty ▷ *n* evil
deed
AMISSES ▶ **amiss**
AMITIES ▶ **amity**
AMITY *n* friendship
AMLA *n* species of Indian
tree
AMLAS ▶ **amla**
AMMAN *same as* ▶ **amtman**
AMMANS ▶ **amman**
AMMETER *n* instrument for
measuring electric current
AMMINE *n* compound that
has molecules containing
one or more ammonia
molecules bound to
another molecule, group,
or atom by coordinate
bonds

AMMINES ▸ ammine

AMMINO adj containing ammonia molecules

AMMIRAL old word for ▸ **admiral**

AMMO n ammunition

AMMON n Asian wild sheep

AMMONAL n explosive made by mixing TNT, ammonium nitrate, and aluminium powder

AMMONIA n strong-smelling alkaline gas containing hydrogen and nitrogen

AMMONIC adj of or concerned with ammonia or ammonium compounds

AMMONO adj using ammonia

AMMONS ▸ ammon

AMMOS ▸ ammo

AMNESIA n loss of memory

AMNESIC ▸ amnesia

AMNESTY n general pardon for offences against a government ▷ vb overlook or forget (an offence)

AMNIA ▸ amnion

AMNIC adj relating to amnion

AMNIO n amniocentesis

AMNION n innermost of two membranes enclosing an embryo

AMNIONS ▸ amnion

AMNIOS ▸ amnio

AMNIOTE n any vertebrate animal, such as a reptile, bird, or mammal, that possesses an amnion, chorion, and allantois during embryonic development

AMOEBA n microscopic single-celled animal able to change its shape

AMOEBAE ▸ amoeba

AMOEBAN ▸ amoeba

AMOEBAS ▸ amoeba

AMOEBIC ▸ amoeba

AMOK n state of murderous frenzy, originally observed among Malays

AMOKS ▸ amok

AMOKURA n type of white tropical sea bird with a red beak and long red tail feathers

AMOLE n American plant

AMOLES ▸ amole

AMOMUM n plant of ginger family

AMOMUMS ▸ amomum

AMONG prep in the midst of

AMONGST same as ▸ **among**

AMOOVE vb stir someone's emotions

AMOOVED ▸ amoove

AMOOVES ▸ amoove

AMORAL adj without moral standards

AMORANT > amorance

AMORCE n small percussion cap

AMORCES ▸ amorce

AMORET n sweetheart

AMORETS ▸ amoret

AMORINI ▸ amorino

AMORINO same as > **amoretto**

AMORISM ▸ amorist

AMORIST n lover or a writer about love

AMOROSA n lover

AMOROSO adv (to be played) lovingly ▷ n rich sweetened sherry of a dark colour

AMOROUS adj feeling, showing, or relating to sexual love

AMORT adj in low spirits

AMOSITE n form of asbestos

AMOTION n act of removing

AMOUNT n extent or quantity ▷ vb be equal or add up to

AMOUNTS ▸ amount

AMOUR n (secret) love affair

AMOURS ▸ amour

AMOVE vb stir someone's emotions

AMOVED ▸ amove

AMOVES ▸ amove

AMOVING ▸ amove

AMOWT same as ▸ **amaut**

AMOWTS ▸ amowt

AMP n ampere ▷ vb excite or become excited

AMPASSY n ampersand

AMPED ▸ amp

AMPERE n basic unit of electric current

AMPERES ▸ ampere

AMPHORA n two-handled ancient Greek or Roman jar

AMPING ▸ amp

AMPLE adj more than sufficient

AMPLER ▸ ample

AMPLEST ▸ ample

AMPLIFY vb increase the strength of (a current or sound signal)

AMPLY adv fully or generously

AMPOULE n small sealed glass vessel containing liquid for injection

AMPS ▸ amp

AMPUL n ampoule

AMPULE same as ▸ **ampoule**

AMPULES ▸ ampule

AMPULLA n dilated end part of certain tubes in the body

AMPULS ▸ ampul

AMPUTEE n person who has had a limb amputated

AMREETA same as ▸ **amrita**

AMRIT n sanctified solution of sugar and water used in the Amrit Ceremony

AMRITA n ambrosia of the gods that bestows immortality

AMRITAS ▸ amrita

AMRITS ▸ amrit

AMTMAN n magistrate in parts of Europe

AMTMANS ▸ amtman

AMTRAC n amphibious tracked vehicle

AMTRACK n amphibious tracked vehicle

AMTRACS ▸ amtrac

AMU n unit of mass

AMUCK same as ▸ **amok**

AMUCKS ▸ amuck

AMULET n something carried or worn as a protection against evil

AMULETS ▸ amulet

AMUS ▸ amu

AMUSE vb cause to laugh or smile

AMUSED ▸ amuse

AMUSER ▸ amuse

AMUSERS ▸ amuse

AMUSES ▸ amuse

AMUSIA n inability to recognize musical tones

AMUSIAS ▸ amusia

AMUSIC ▸ amusia

AMUSING adj mildly entertaining

AMUSIVE adj deceptive

AMYGDAL n almond

AMYL n of, consisting of, or containing any of eight isomeric forms of the monovalent group $C_5H_{11}-$

AMYLASE n enzyme, present in saliva, that helps to change starch into sugar

A

AMYLENE *another name (no longer in technical usage) for* ▶ **pentene**

AMYLIC *adj* of or derived from amyl

AMYLOID *n* complex protein resembling starch, deposited in tissues in some degenerative diseases ▷ *adj* starchlike

AMYLOSE *n* minor component (about 20 per cent) of starch, consisting of long unbranched chains of glucose units. It is soluble in water and gives an intense blue colour with iodine

AMYLS ▶ **amyl**

AMYLUM *another name for* ▶ **starch**

AMYLUMS ▶ **amylum**

AN *adj* form of **a** used before vowels, and sometimes before 'h' ▷ *n* an additional consideration or condition, as in 'ifs and ans'

ANA *adv* (of ingredients in a prescription) in equal quantities ▷ *n* collection of reminiscences, sketches, etc, of or about a person or place

ANABAS *n* type of fish

ANADEM *n* garland for the head

ANADEMS ▶ **anadem**

ANAEMIA *n* deficiency in the number of red blood cells

ANAEMIC *adj* having anaemia

ANAGOGE *n* allegorical or spiritual interpretation, esp of sacred works such as the Bible

ANAGOGY *same as* ▶ **anagoge**

ANAGRAM *n* word or phrase made by rearranging the letters of another word or phrase

ANAL *adj* of the anus

ANALGIA *same as* > **analgesia**

ANALITY *n* quality of being psychologically anal

ANALLY ▶ **anal**

ANALOG *same as* > **analogue**

ANALOGA > **analogon**

ANALOGS ▶ **analog**

ANALOGY *n* similarity in some respects

ANALYSE *vb* make an analysis of (something)

ANALYST *n* person skilled in analysis

ANALYTE *n* substance that is being analyzed

ANALYZE *same as* ▶ **analyse**

ANAN *interj* expression of failure to understand

ANANA *n* pineapple

> More than two As on your rack is not good news, but fortunately there are a number of short words that use three of them, of which this word for the pineapple plant is one.

ANANAS *n* plant related to the pineapple

ANANKE *n* unalterable necessity

ANANKES ▶ **ananke**

ANAPEST *same as* > **anapaest**

ANAPHOR *n* word referring back to a previous word

ANARCH *n* instigator or personification of anarchy

ANARCHS ▶ **anarch**

ANARCHY *n* lawlessness and disorder

ANAS ▶ **ana**

ANATA *n* (in Theravada Buddhism) the belief that since all things are constantly changing, there can be no such thing as a permanent, unchanging self

ANATAS ▶ **anata**

ANATASE *n* rare blue or black mineral

ANATMAN *same as* ▶ **anata**

ANATOMY *n* science of the structure of the body

ANATTA *n* annatto

ANATTAS ▶ **anatta**

ANATTO *same as* ▶ **annatto**

ANATTOS ▶ **anatto**

ANAXIAL *adj* asymmetrical

ANBURY *n* soft spongy tumour occurring in horses and oxen

ANCE *dialect form of* ▶ **once**

ANCHO *n* chili pepper

ANCHOR *n* heavy hooked device attached to a boat by a cable and dropped overboard to fasten the ship to the sea bottom ▷ *vb* fasten with or as if with an anchor

ANCHORS *pl n* brakes of a motor vehicle

ANCHOS ▶ **ancho**

ANCHOVY *n* small strong-tasting fish

ANCHUSA *n* Eurasian plant with rough hairy stems and leaves and blue flowers

ANCIENT *adj* dating from very long ago ▷ *n* member of a civilized nation in the ancient world, esp a Greek, Roman, or Hebrew

ANCILE *n* mythical Roman shield

ANCILIA ▶ **ancile**

ANCILLA *n* Latin word for servant

ANCLE *old spelling of* ▶ **ankle**

ANCLES ▶ **ancle**

ANCOME *n* inflammation

ANCOMES ▶ **ancome**

ANCON *n* projecting bracket or console supporting a cornice

ANCONAL ▶ **ancon**

ANCONE *same as* ▶ **ancon**

ANCONES ▶ **ancone**

ANCORA *adv* Italian for encore

ANCRESS *n* female anchorite

AND *n* additional matter or problem

ANDANTE *adv* (piece to be played) moderately slowly ▷ *n* passage or piece to be performed moderately slowly

ANDIRON *n* iron stand for supporting logs in a fireplace

ANDRO *n* type of sex hormone

ANDROID *n* robot resembling a human ▷ *adj* resembling a human being

ANDROS ▶ **andro**

ANDS ▶ **and**

ANDVILE *old form of* ▶ **anvil**

ANE *Scots word for* ▶ **one**

ANEAR *adv* nearly ▷ *vb* approach

ANEARED ▶ **anear**

ANEARS ▶ **anear**

ANEATH *Scots word for* ▶ **beneath**

ANELACE *same as* ▶ **anlace**

ANELE *vb* anoint, esp to give extreme unction to

ANELED ▶ **anele**

ANELES ▶ **anele**

ANELING ▶ **anele**

ANELLI pl n pasta shaped like small rings

ANEMIA n anaemia

ANEMIAS ▸ anemia

ANEMIC same as ▸ anaemic

ANEMONE n plant with white, purple, or red flowers

ANENST dialect word for ▸ against

ANENT prep lying against

ANERGIA n anergy

ANERGIC ▸ anergy

ANERGY n lack of energy

ANERLY Scots word for ▸ only

ANEROID adj not containing a liquid ▸ n barometer that does not contain liquid

Referring to a kind of barometer, this is one of the most commonly played of all 7-letter bonus words.

ANES ▸ ane

ANESTRA > anestrus

ANESTRI > anestrus

ANETHOL n substance derived from oil of anise

ANETIC adj medically soothing

ANEURIN a less common name for ▸ thiamine

ANEW adv once more

ANGA n a part in Indian music

ANGAKOK n Inuit shaman

ANGARIA n species of shellfish

ANGARY n right of a belligerent state to use the property of a neutral state or to destroy it if necessary, subject to payment of full compensation to the owners

ANGAS ▸ anga

ANGEKOK n Inuit shaman

ANGEL n spiritual being believed to be an attendant or messenger of God ▸ vb provide financial support for

ANGELED ▸ angel

ANGELIC adj very kind, pure, or beautiful

ANGELS ▸ angel

ANGELUS n series of prayers recited in the morning, at midday, and in the evening, commemorating the Annunciation and Incarnation

ANGER n fierce displeasure or extreme annoyance ▸ vb make (someone) angry

ANGERED ▸ anger

ANGERLY adv old form of angrily

ANGERS ▸ anger

ANGICO n South American tree

ANGICOS ▸ angico

ANGINA n heart disorder causing sudden severe chest pains

ANGINAL ▸ angina

ANGINAS ▸ angina

ANGIOMA n tumour consisting of a mass of blood vessels or lymphatic vessels

ANGLE n space between or shape formed by two lines or surfaces that meet ▸ vb bend or place (something) at an angle

ANGLED ▸ angle

ANGLER n person who fishes with a hook and line

ANGLERS ▸ angler

ANGLES ▸ angle

ANGLICE adv in English

ANGLIFY same as > anglicize

ANGLING n art or sport of fishing with a hook and line

ANGLIST same as ▸ anglicist

ANGLO n White inhabitant of the US not of Latin extraction

ANGLOS ▸ anglo

ANGOLA same as ▸ angora

ANGORA n variety of goat, cat, or rabbit with long silky hair

ANGORAS ▸ angora

ANGRIER ▸ angry

ANGRIES ▸ angry

ANGRILY ▸ angry

ANGRY adj full of anger ▸ n angry person

ANGST n feeling of anxiety

ANGSTS ▸ angst

ANGSTY adj displaying or feeling angst, esp in a self-conscious manner

ANGUINE adj of, relating to, or similar to a snake

ANGUISH n great mental pain ▸ vb afflict or be afflicted with anguish

ANGULAR adj (of a person) lean and bony

ANHINGA n type of bird

ANI n tropical American bird

with black plumage, a long square-tipped tail, and a hooked bill

ANICCA n (in Theravada Buddhism) the belief that all things, including the self, are impermanent and constantly changing: the first of the three basic characteristics of existence

ANICCAS ▸ anicca

ANICUT n dam in India

ANICUTS ▸ anicut

ANIGH adv near

ANIGHT adv at night

ANIL n West Indian shrub, from which indigo is obtained

ANILE adj of or like a feeble old woman

ANILIN n aniline

ANILINE n colourless oily liquid obtained from coal tar and used for making dyes, plastics, and explosives

ANILINS ▸ anilin

ANILITY ▸ anile

ANILS ▸ anil

ANIMA n feminine principle as present in the male unconscious

ANIMACY n state of being animate

ANIMAL n living creature with specialized sense organs and capable of voluntary motion, esp one other than a human being ▸ adj of animals

ANIMALS ▸ animal

ANIMAS ▸ anima

ANIMATE vb give life to ▸ adj having life

ANIMATO adv (to be performed) in a lively manner

ANIME n type of Japanese animated film with themes and styles similar to manga comics

ANIMES ▸ anime

ANIMI ▸ animus

ANIMIS ▸ animi

ANIMISM n belief that natural objects possess souls

ANIMIST ▸ animism

ANIMUS n hatred, animosity

ANION n ion with negative charge

ANIONIC ▸ anion

ANIONS ▸ anion

ANIS ▸ ani

ANISE n plant with liquorice-flavoured seeds

ANISEED n liquorice-flavoured seeds of the anise plant

ANISES ▸ anise

ANISIC ▸ anise

ANISOLE n colourless pleasant-smelling liquid used as a solvent

ANKER n old liquid measure for wine

ANKERS ▸ anker

ANKH n T-shaped cross with a loop on the top, which symbolized eternal life in ancient Egypt

ANKHS ▸ ankh

ANKLE n joint between the foot and leg ▷ vb move

ANKLED ▸ ankle

ANKLES ▸ ankle

ANKLET n ornamental chain worn round the ankle

ANKLETS ▸ anklet

ANKLING ▸ ankle

ANKLONG n Asian musical instrument

ANKLUNG n Asian musical instrument

ANKUS n stick used, esp in India, for goading elephants

ANKUSES ▸ ankus

ANKUSH n Indian weapon

ANLACE n medieval short dagger with a broad tapering blade

ANLACES ▸ anlace

ANLAGE n organ or part in the earliest stage of development

ANLAGEN ▸ anlage

ANLAGES ▸ anlage

ANLAS same as ▸ anlace

ANLASES ▸ anlas

ANN n old Scots word for a widow's pension

ANNA n former Indian coin worth one sixteenth of a rupee

ANNAL n recorded events of one year

ANNALS ▸ annal

ANNAS ▸ anna

ANNAT n singular of annates

ANNATES pl n first year's revenue of a see, an abbacy, or a minor benefice, paid to the pope

ANNATS ▸ annat

ANNATTA n annatto

ANNATTO n small tropical American tree with red or pinkish flowers and seeds that yield a dye

ANNEAL vb toughen (metal or glass) by heating and slow cooling ▷ n act of annealing

ANNEALS ▸ anneal

ANNELID n type of worm with a segmented body, such as an earthworm

ANNEX vb seize (territory)

ANNEXE n extension to a building

ANNEXED ▸ annex

ANNEXES ▸ annexe

ANNICUT n dam in India

ANNO adv Latin for in the year

ANNONA n American tree or shrub

ANNONAS ▸ annona

ANNOY vb irritate or displease

ANNOYED ▸ annoy

ANNOYER ▸ annoy

ANNOYS ▸ annoy

ANNS ▸ ann

ANNUAL adj happening once a year ▷ n plant that completes its life cycle in a year

ANNUALS ▸ annual

ANNUITY n fixed sum paid every year

ANNUL vb declare (something, esp a marriage) invalid

ANNULAR adj ring-shaped ▷ n ring finger

ANNULET n moulding in the form of a ring, as at the top of a column adjoining the capital

ANNULI ▸ annulus

ANNULS ▸ annul

ANNULUS n area between two concentric circles

ANOA n type of small cattle

ANOAS ▸ anoa

ANOBIID n any type of beetle

ANODAL ▸ anode

ANODE n positive electrode in a battery, valve, etc

ANODES ▸ anode

ANODIC ▸ anode

ANODISE same as ▸ anodize

ANODIZE vb coat (metal) with a protective oxide film by electrolysis

ANODYNE n something that relieves pain or distress ▷ adj relieving pain or distress

ANOESES ▸ anoesis

ANOESIS n feeling without understanding

ANOETIC ▸ anoesis

ANOINT vb smear with oil as a sign of consecration

ANOINTS ▸ anoint

ANOLE n type of lizard

ANOLES ▸ anole

ANOLYTE n part of electrolyte around anode

ANOMALY n something that deviates from the normal, irregularity

ANOMIC ▸ anomie

ANOMIE n lack of social or moral standards

ANOMIES ▸ anomie

ANOMY same as ▸ anomie

ANON adv in a short time, soon

ANONYM n anonymous person or publication

ANONYMA n promiscuous woman

ANONYMS ▸ anonym

ANOPIA n inability to see

ANOPIAS ▸ anopia

ANOPSIA n squint in which the eye turns upwards

ANORAK n light waterproof hooded jacket

ANORAKS ▸ anorak

ANOREXY old name for ▸ anorexia

ANOSMIA n loss of the sense of smell, usually as the result of a lesion of the olfactory nerve, disease in another organ or part, or obstruction of the nasal passages

ANOSMIC ▸ anosmia

ANOTHER adj one more

ANOUGH adj enough

ANOW adj old form of enough

ANOXIA n lack or absence of oxygen

ANOXIAS ▸ anoxia

ANOXIC ▸ anoxia

ANS pl n as in **ifs and ans** things that might have happened, but which did not

ANSA n either end of Saturn's rings

ANSAE ▸ ansa

ANSATE adj having a handle or handle-like part

ANSATED adj ansate

ANSWER n reply to a question, request, letter, etc ▷ vb give an answer (to)

ANSWERS ▸ answer

ANT n small insect living in highly-organized colonies

ANTA n pilaster attached to the end of a side wall or sometimes to the side of a doorway

ANTACID n substance that counteracts acidity, esp in the stomach ▷ adj having the properties of this substance

ANTAE ▸ anta

ANTAR old word for ▸ **cave**

ANTARA n South American panpipes

ANTARAS ▸ antara

ANTARS ▸ antar

ANTAS ▸ anta

ANTBEAR n aardvark

ANTBIRD n any of various dull-coloured passerine birds that typically feed on ants

ANTE n player's stake in poker ▷ vb place (one's stake) in poker

ANTED ▸ ante

ANTEED ▸ ante

ANTEFIX n carved ornament at the eaves of a roof to hide the joint between the tiles

ANTEING ▸ ante

ANTENNA n insect's feeler

ANTES ▸ ante

ANTHEM n song of loyalty, esp to a country ▷ vb provide with an anthem

ANTHEMS ▸ anthem

ANTHER n part of a flower's stamen containing pollen

ANTHERS ▸ anther

ANTHILL n mound of soil, leaves, etc, near the entrance of an ants' nest, carried and deposited there by the ants while constructing the nest

ANTHOID adj resembling a flower

ANTHRAX n dangerous disease of cattle and sheep, communicable to humans

ANTI n opposed (to) ▷ n opponent of a party, policy, or attitude

ANTIAIR adj countering attack by aircraft or missile

ANTIAR another name for ▸ **upas**

ANTIARS ▸ antiar

ANTIBUG adj acting against computer bugs

ANTIC n actor in a ludicrous or grotesque part ▷ adj fantastic

ANTICAL adj (of the position of plant parts) in front of or above another part

ANTICAR adj opposed to cars

ANTICK vb perform antics

ANTICKE adj old form of antique

ANTICKS ▸ antick

ANTICLY adv grotesquely

ANTICS pl n absurd acts or postures

ANTIENT old spelling of ▸ **ancient**

ANTIFAT adj acting to remove or prevent fat

ANTIFLU adj acting against influenza

ANTIFOG adj preventing the buildup of moisture on a surface

ANTIFUR adj opposed to the wearing of fur garments

ANTIGAY adj hostile to homosexuals

ANTIGEN n substance causing the blood to produce antibodies

ANTIGUN adj opposed to the possession of guns

ANTIJAM adj preventing jamming

ANTILOG n number whose logarithm to a given base is a given number

ANTIMAN adj opposed to men

ANTING n placing or rubbing of ants by birds on their feathers. The body fluids of the ants are thought to repel parasites

ANTINGS ▸ anting

ANTIPOT adj opposed to illegal use of marijuana

ANTIQUE n object of an earlier period, valued for its beauty, workmanship, or age ▷ adj made in an earlier period ▷ vb give an antique appearance to

ANTIRED adj of a particular colour of antiquark

ANTIS ▸ anti

ANTISAG adj preventing sagging

ANTISEX adj opposed to sexual activity

ANTITAX adj opposed to taxation

ANTIWAR adj opposed to war

ANTLER n branched horn of a male deer

ANTLERS ▸ antler

ANTLIA n butterfly proboscis

ANTLIAE ▸ antlia

ANTLIKE adj of or like an ant or ants

ANTLION n type of insect resembling a dragonfly, mostly found in tropical regions

ANTONYM n word that means the opposite of another

ANTRA ▸ antrum

ANTRAL ▸ antrum

ANTRE n cavern or cave

ANTRES ▸ antre

ANTRUM n natural cavity, esp in a bone

ANTRUMS ▸ antrum

ANTS ▸ ant

ANTSIER ▸ antsy

ANTSY adj restless, nervous, and impatient

ANURAL adj without a tail

ANURAN n type of tailless amphibian with very long hind legs specialized for hopping, such as frogs and toads

ANURANS ▸ anuran

ANURIA n complete suppression of urine formation, often as the result of a kidney disorder

ANURIAS ▸ anuria

ANURIC ▸ anuria

ANUROUS adj lacking a tail

ANUS n opening at the end of the alimentary canal, through which faeces are discharged

ANUSES ▸ anus

ANVIL n heavy iron block on which metals are hammered into particular shapes ▷ vb forge on an anvil

ANVILED ▸ anvil

ANVILS ▸ anvil

ANXIETY n state of being anxious

A

ANXIOUS *adj* worried and tense

ANY *adj* one or some, no matter which ▷ *adv* at all

ANYBODY *n* any person at random

ANYHOW *adv* anyway

ANYMORE *adv* at present

ANYON *n* (in mathematics) projective representation of a Lie group

ANYONE *pron* any person ▷ *n* any person at random

ANYONES ▸ **anyone**

ANYONS ▸ **anyon**

ANYROAD *a northern English dialect word for* ▸ **anyway**

ANYTIME *adv* at any time

ANYWAY *adv* at any rate, nevertheless

ANYWAYS *nonstandard word for* ▸ **anyway**

ANYWHEN *adv* at any time

ANYWISE *adv* in any way or manner

ANZIANI *n* Italian word for councillors

AORIST *n* tense of the verb in classical Greek and in certain other inflected languages, indicating past action without reference to whether the action involved was momentary or continuous

AORISTS ▸ **aorist**

AORTA *n* main artery of the body, carrying oxygen-rich blood from the heart

AORTAE ▸ **aorta**

AORTAL ▸ **aorta**

AORTAS ▸ **aorta**

AORTIC ▸ **aorta**

AOUDAD *n* N African wild mountain sheep with curved horns and long hair covering the neck and forelegs

AOUDADS ▸ **aoudad**

APACE *adv* swiftly

APACHE *n* Parisian gangster or ruffian

APACHES ▸ **apache**

APADANA *n* ancient Persian palace hall

APAGE *interj* Greek word meaning go away

APAGOGE *n* reduction to absurdity

APAID ▸ **apay**

APANAGE *same as* > **appanage**

APAREJO *n* kind of packsaddle made of stuffed leather cushions

APART *adv* to pieces or in pieces

APATHY *n* lack of interest or enthusiasm

APATITE *n* pale green to purple mineral, found in igneous rocks

APAY *vb* old word meaning satisfy

APAYD ▸ **apay**

APAYING ▸ **apay**

APAYS ▸ **apay**

APE *n* tailless monkey such as the chimpanzee or gorilla ▷ *vb* imitate

APEAK *adj* in a vertical or almost vertical position

APED ▸ **ape**

APEDOM *n* state of being an ape

APEDOMS ▸ **apedom**

APEEK *adv* nautical word meaning vertically

APEHOOD *n* state of being ape

APELIKE ▸ **ape**

APEMAN *n* extinct primate thought to have been the forerunner of true humans

APEMEN ▸ **apeman**

APEPSIA *n* digestive disorder

APEPSY *n* apepsia

APER *n* person who apes

APERCU *n* outline

APERCUS ▸ **apercu**

APERIES ▸ **apery**

APERS ▸ **aper**

APERT *adj* open

APERY *n* imitative behaviour

APES ▸ **ape**

APETALY > **apetalous**

APEX *n* highest point

APEXES ▸ **apex**

APGAR *n as in* **apgar score** system for determining the condition of an infant at birth

APHAGIA *n* refusal or inability to swallow

APHAKIA *n* absence of the lens of an eye, congenital or otherwise

APHASIA *n* disorder of the central nervous system that affects the ability to speak and understand words

APHASIC ▸ **aphasia**

APHELIA > **aphelion**

APHESES ▸ **aphesis**

APHESIS *n* gradual disappearance of an unstressed vowel at the beginning of a word

APHETIC ▸ **aphesis**

APHID *n* small insect which sucks the sap from plants

APHIDES ▸ **aphis**

APHIDS ▸ **aphid**

APHIS *n* type of aphid such as the blackfly

APHONIA *n* loss of the voice caused by damage to the vocal tract

APHONIC *adj* affected with aphonia ▷ *n* person affected with aphonia

APHONY *same as* ▸ **aphonia**

APHOTIC *adj* characterized by or growing in the absence of light

APHTHA *n* small ulceration on a mucous membrane, as in thrush, caused by a fungal infection

APHTHAE ▸ **aphtha**

APHYLLY > **aphyllous**

APIAN *adj* of, relating to, or resembling bees

APIARY *n* place where bees are kept

APICAL *adj* of, at, or being an apex ▷ *n* sound made with the tip of the tongue

APICALS ▸ **apical**

APICES *plural of* ▸ **apex**

APICIAN *adj* of fine or dainty food

APICULI > **apiculus**

APIECE *adv* each

APIEZON *adj as in* **apiezon oil** oil left by distillation

APING ▸ **ape**

APIOL *n* substance formerly used to assist menstruation

APIOLS ▸ **apiol**

APISH *adj* stupid or foolish

APISHLY ▸ **apish**

APISM *n* behaviour like an ape

APISMS ▸ **apism**

APLANAT *n* aplanatic lens

APLASIA *n* congenital absence or abnormal development of an organ or part

APLENTY *adv* in plenty

APLITE *n* light-coloured fine-grained acid igneous rock with a sugary texture, consisting of quartz and feldspars

A

APLITES ▸ **aplite**
APLITIC ▸ **aplite**
APLOMB n calm self-possession
APLOMBS ▸ **aplomb**
APNEA same as ▸ **apnoea**
APNEAL ▸ **apnea**
APNEAS ▸ **apnea**
APNEIC ▸ **apnea**
APNOEA n temporary inability to breathe
APNOEAL ▸ **apnoea**
APNOEAS ▸ **apnoea**
APNOEIC ▸ **apnoea**
APO n type of protein
APOCARP n apocarpous gynoecium or fruit
APOCOPE n omission of the final sound or sounds of a word
APOD n animal without feet
APODAL adj (of snakes, eels, etc) without feet
APODE n animal without feet
APODES ▸ **apode**
APODOUS same as ▸ **apodal**
APODS ▸ **apod**
APOGAMY n type of reproduction, occurring in some ferns, in which the sporophyte develops from the gametophyte without fusion of gametes
APOGEAL ▸ **apogee**
APOGEAN ▸ **apogee**
APOGEE n point of the moon's or a satellite's orbit that is farthest from the earth
APOGEES ▸ **apogee**
APOGEIC ▸ **apogee**
APOLLO n strikingly handsome youth
APOLLOS ▸ **apollo**
APOLOG same as > **apologue**
APOLOGS ▸ **apolog**
APOLOGY n expression of regret for wrongdoing
APOLUNE n point in a lunar orbit when a spacecraft is at its greatest distance from the moon
APOMICT n organism, esp a plant, produced by apomixis
APOOP adv on the poop deck
APOPLEX vb afflict with apoplexy
APORIA n doubt, real or professed, about what to do or say

APORIAS ▸ **aporia**
APORT adj on or towards the port side
APOS ▸ **apo**
APOSTIL n marginal note
APOSTLE n one of the twelve disciples chosen by Christ to preach his gospel
APOTHEM n perpendicular line or distance from the centre of a regular polygon to any of its sides
APOZEM n medicine dissolved in water
APOZEMS ▸ **apozem**
APP n application program
APPAID ▸ **appay**
APPAIR vb old form of impair
APPAIRS ▸ **appair**
APPAL vb dismay, terrify
APPALL same as ▸ **appal**
APPALLS ▸ **appall**
APPALS ▸ **appal**
APPALTI ▸ **appalto**
APPALTO n Italian word for contact
APPARAT n Communist Party organization in the former Soviet Union and other states
APPAREL n clothing ▷ vb clothe, adorn, etc
APPAY old word for ▸ **satisfy**
APPAYD ▸ **appay**
APPAYS ▸ **appay**
APPEACH old word for ▸ **accuse**
APPEAL vb make an earnest request ▷ n earnest request
APPEALS ▸ **appeal**
APPEAR vb become visible or present
APPEARS ▸ **appear**
APPEASE vb pacify (a person) by yielding to his or her demands
APPEL n stamp of the foot, used to warn of one's intent to attack
APPELS ▸ **appel**
APPEND vb join on, add
APPENDS ▸ **append**
APPERIL old word for ▸ **peril**
APPLAUD vb show approval of by clapping one's hands
APPLE n round firm fleshy fruit that grows on trees
APPLES ▸ **apple**
APPLET n computing program that runs within a page on the World Wide Web

APPLETS ▸ **applet**
APPLEY adj resembling or tasting like an apple
APPLIED adj (of a skill, science, etc) put to practical use
APPLIER ▸ **apply**
APPLIES ▸ **apply**
APPLY vb make a formal request
APPOINT vb assign to a job or position
APPORT n production of objects by apparently supernatural means at a spiritualists' seance
APPORTS ▸ **apport**
APPOSE vb place side by side or near to each other
APPOSED ▸ **appose**
APPOSER ▸ **appose**
APPOSES ▸ **appose**
APPRESS vb press together
APPRISE vb make aware (of)
APPRIZE same as ▸ **apprise**
APPRO n approval
APPROOF old word for ▸ **trial**
APPROS ▸ **appro**
APPROVE vb consider good or right
APPS ▸ **app**
APPUI n support
APPUIED ▸ **appuy**
APPUIS ▸ **appui**
APPULSE n very close approach of two celestial bodies so that they are in conjunction but no eclipse or occultation occurs
APPUY vb support
APPUYED ▸ **appuy**
APPUYS ▸ **appuy**
APRAXIA n disorder of the central nervous system caused by brain damage and characterized by impaired ability to carry out purposeful muscular movements
APRAXIC ▸ **apraxia**
APRES prep French word for after
APRICOT n yellowish-orange juicy fruit like a small peach ▷ adj yellowish-orange
APRON n garment worn over the front of the body to protect the clothes ▷ vb equip with an apron
APRONED ▸ **apron**
APRONS ▸ **apron**

APROPOS *adv* appropriate(ly)

APROTIC *adj* (of solvents) neither accepting nor donating hydrogen ions

APSARAS *n* Hindu water sprite

APSE *n* arched or domed recess, esp in a church

APSES ▸ apse

APSIDAL ▸ apsis

APSIDES ▸ apsis

APSIS *n* either of two points lying at the extremities of the elliptical orbit of a planet or satellite

APSO *n* Tibetan terrier

APSOS ▸ apso

APT *adj* having a specified tendency ▷ *vb* be fitting

APTAMER *n* artificially-created DNA or RNA molecule with therapeutic properties

APTED ▸ apt

APTER ▸ apt

APTERAL *adj* (esp of a classical temple) not having columns at the sides

APTERIA ▸ apterium

APTERYX *n* kiwi (the bird)

APTEST ▸ apt

APTING ▸ apt

APTLY ▸ apt

APTNESS ▸ apt

APTOTE *n* noun without inflections

APTOTES ▸ aptote

APTOTIC ▸ aptote

APTS ▸ apt

APYRASE *n* enzyme

AQUA *n* water

> This Latin word for water, together with its plural **aquae** or **aquas**, comes up over and over again.

AQUAE ▸ aqua

AQUAFER *n* aquifer

AQUAFIT *n* type of aerobic exercise done in water

AQUARIA ▸ aquarium

AQUAS ▸ aqua

AQUATIC *adj* living in or near water ▷ *n* marine or freshwater animal or plant

AQUAVIT *n* grain- or potato-based spirit from the Scandinavian countries, flavoured with aromatic seeds and spices, esp caraway

AQUEOUS *adj* of, like, or containing water

AQUIFER *n* deposit of rock, such as sandstone, containing water that can be used to supply wells

AQUILON *n* name for the north wind

AQUIVER *adv* quivering

AR *n* letter R

ARAARA *another name for* **> trevally**

ARAARAS ▸ araara

ARABA *n* Asian carriage

> This word for a kind of Russian wagon is another of the short words that can help you to deal with a surplus of As.

ARABAS ▸ araba

ARABESK *same as* **> arabesque**

ARABIC *adj as in* **gum arabic** gum exuded by certain acacia trees

ARABICA *n* high-quality coffee bean

ARABIN *n* essence of gum arabic

ARABINS ▸ arabin

ARABIS *n* type of plant which forms low-growing mats with downy grey foliage and white flowers

ARABISE *vb* make or become Arab

ARABIZE *vb* make or become Arab

ARABLE *adj* suitable for growing crops on ▷ *n* arable land or farming

ARABLES ▸ arable

ARACHIS *n* Brazilian plant

ARAISE *vb* old form of raise

ARAISED ▸ araise

ARAISES ▸ araise

ARAK *same as* **▸ arrack**

ARAKS ▸ arak

ARALIA *n* type of plant grown in greenhouses or as a house plant for its decorative evergreen foliage

ARALIAS ▸ aralia

ARAME *n* Japanese edible seaweed

ARAMES ▸ arame

ARAMID *n* synthetic fibre

ARAMIDS ▸ aramid

ARANEID *n* type of arachnid of the order which comprises the spiders

ARAR *n* African tree

ARAROBA *n* Brazilian leguminous tree

ARARS ▸ arar

ARAYSE *vb* old form of raise

ARAYSED ▸ arayse

ARAYSES ▸ arayse

ARB *short for* **> arbitrage**

ARBA *n* Asian carriage

ARBAS ▸ arba

ARBITER *n* person empowered to judge in a dispute

ARBLAST *n* arbalest

ARBOR *n* revolving shaft or axle in a machine

ARBORED *adj* having arbors

ARBORES ▸ arbor

ARBORET *n* old name for an area planted with shrubs

ARBORIO *n as in* **arborio rice** variety of round-grain rice used for making risotto

ARBORS ▸ arbor

ARBOUR *n* glade sheltered by trees

ARBOURS ▸ arbour

ARBS ▸ arb

ARBUTE *old name for* **▸ arbutus**

ARBUTES ▸ arbute

ARBUTUS *n* evergreen shrub with strawberry-like berries

ARC *n* part of a circle or other curve ▷ *vb* form an arc

ARCADE *n* covered passageway lined with shops ▷ *vb* provide with an arcade

ARCADED ▸ arcade

ARCADES ▸ arcade

ARCADIA *n* traditional idealized rural setting

ARCANA *n* either of the two divisions of a pack of tarot cards

ARCANAS ▸ arcana

ARCANE *adj* mysterious and secret

ARCANUM *n* profound secret or mystery known only to initiates

ARCED ▸ arc

ARCH *n* curved structure supporting a bridge or roof ▷ *vb* (cause to) form an arch ▷ *adj* superior, knowing

ARCHAEA *n* order of prokaryotic microorganisms

ARCHAEI > archaeus

ARCHAIC *adj* ancient

ARCHEAN > archaean
ARCHED *adj* provided with or spanned by an arch or arches
ARCHEI ▸ archeus
ARCHER *n* person who shoots with a bow and arrow
ARCHERS ▸ archer
ARCHERY *n* art or sport of shooting with a bow and arrow
ARCHES ▸ arch
ARCHEST ▸ arch
ARCHEUS *n* spirit believed to inhabit a living thing
ARCHFOE *n* chief enemy
ARCHIL *a variant spelling of* ▸ orchil
ARCHILS ▸ archil
ARCHINE *n* Russian unit of length equal to about 71 cm
ARCHING ▸ arch
ARCHIVE *n* collection of records or documents ▷ *vb* store (documents, data, etc) in an archive or other repository
ARCHLET *n* small arch
ARCHLY ▸ arch
ARCHON *n* (in ancient Athens) one of the nine chief magistrates
ARCHONS ▸ archon
ARCHWAY *n* passageway under an arch
ARCING ▸ arc
ARCINGS ▸ arc
ARCKED ▸ arc
ARCKING ▸ arc
ARCMIN *n* 1/60 of a degree of an angle
ARCMINS ▸ arcmin
ARCO *adv* musical direction meaning with bow ▷ *n* bow of a stringed instrument
ARCOS ▸ arco
ARCS ▸ arc
ARCSEC *n* 1/3600 of a degree of an angle
ARCSECS ▸ arcsec
ARCSINE *n* trigonometrical function
ARCTIC *adj* very cold ▷ *n* high waterproof overshoe with buckles
ARCTICS ▸ arctic
ARCTIID *n* type of moth of the family which includes the ermine and tiger moths
ARCTOID *adj* like a bear
ARCUATE *adj* shaped or bent like an arc or bow

ARCUS *n* circle around the cornea of the eye
ARCUSES ▸ arcus
ARD *n* primitive plough
ARDEB *n* unit of dry measure used in Egypt and other Middle Eastern countries. In Egypt it is approximately equal to 0.195 cubic metres
ARDEBS ▸ ardeb
ARDENCY ▸ ardent
ARDENT *adj* passionate
ARDOR *same as* ▸ ardour
ARDORS ▸ ardor
ARDOUR *n* passion
ARDOURS ▸ ardour
ARDRI *n* Irish high king
ARDRIGH *n* Irish high king
ARDRIS ▸ ardri
ARDS ▸ ard
ARDUOUS *adj* hard to accomplish, strenuous
ARE *n* unit of measure, 100 square metres ▷ *vb* used as the singular form with *you*
AREA *n* part or region
AREACH *vb* old form of reach
AREAD *vb* old word meaning declare
AREADS ▸ aread
AREAE ▸ area
AREAL ▸ area
AREALLY ▸ area
AREAR *n* old form of arrear
AREAS ▸ area
AREAWAY *n* passageway between parts of a building or between different buildings
ARECA *n* tall SE Asian palm tree with white flowers and orange or red egg-shaped nuts
ARECAS ▸ areca
ARED ▸ aread
AREDD ▸ aread
AREDE *vb* old word meaning declare
AREDES ▸ arede
AREDING ▸ arede
AREFIED ▸ arefy
AREFIES ▸ arefy
AREFY *vb* dry up
AREG *a plural of* ▸ erg
AREIC *adj* relating to area
ARENA *n* seated enclosure for sports events
ARENAS ▸ arena
ARENE *n* aromatic hydrocarbon
ARENES ▸ arene

ARENITE *n* any arenaceous rock
ARENOSE *adj* sandy
ARENOUS *adj* sandy
AREOLA *n* small circular area, such as the coloured ring around the human nipple
AREOLAE ▸ areola
AREOLAR ▸ areola
AREOLAS ▸ areola
AREOLE *n* space outlined on a surface, such as an area between veins on a leaf or on an insect's wing
AREOLES ▸ areole
AREPA *n* Colombian cornmeal cake
AREPAS ▸ arepa
ARERE *adv* old word meaning backwards
ARES ▸ are
ARET *vb* old word meaning entrust
ARETE *n* sharp ridge separating two cirques or glacial valleys in mountainous regions
ARETES ▸ arete
ARETS ▸ aret
ARETT *vb* old word meaning entrust
ARETTED ▸ arett
ARETTS ▸ arett
AREW *adv* old word meaning in a row
ARF *n* barking sound
ARFS ▸ arf
ARGAL *same as* ▸ argali
ARGALA *n* Indian stork
ARGALAS ▸ argala
ARGALI *n* large wild sheep of central Asia, the male of which has massive curving horns
ARGALIS ▸ argali
ARGALS ▸ argal
ARGAN *n* Moroccan tree
ARGAND *n* lamp with a hollow circular wick
ARGANDS ▸ argand
ARGANS ▸ argan
ARGENT *n* silver
ARGENTS ▸ argent
ARGH *interj* cry of pain
ARGHAN *n* agave plant
ARGHANS ▸ arghan
ARGIL *n* clay, esp potters' clay
ARGILS ▸ argil
ARGLE *vb* quarrel
ARGLED ▸ argle
ARGLES ▸ argle

A

ARGLING ▸ argle

ARGOL n crude potassium hydrogentartrate, deposited as a crust on the sides of wine vats

ARGOLS ▸ argol

ARGON n inert gas found in the air

ARGONON n inert gas

ARGONS ▸ argon

ARGOSY n large merchant ship

ARGOT n slang or jargon

ARGOTIC ▸ argot

ARGOTS ▸ argot

ARGUE vb try to prove by giving reasons

ARGUED ▸ argue

ARGUER ▸ argue

ARGUERS ▸ argue

ARGUES ▸ argue

ARGUFY vb argue or quarrel, esp over something trivial

ARGUING ▸ argue

ARGULI ▸ argulus

ARGULUS n parasite on fish

ARGUS n any of various brown butterflies

ARGUSES ▸ argus

ARGUTE adj shrill or keen

ARGYLE adj made of knitted or woven material with a diamond-shaped pattern of two or more colours ▷ n sock made of this

ARGYLES ▸ argyle

ARGYLL n sock with diamond pattern

ARGYLLS ▸ argyll

ARGYRIA n staining of skin by exposure to silver

ARHAT n Buddhist, esp a monk who has achieved enlightenment and at death passes to nirvana

ARHATS ▸ arhat

ARIA n elaborate song for solo voice, esp one from an opera

ARIARY n currency of Madagascar

ARIAS ▸ aria

ARID adj parched, dry

ARIDER ▸ arid

ARIDEST ▸ arid

ARIDITY ▸ arid

ARIDLY ▸ arid

ARIEL n type of Arabian gazelle

ARIELS ▸ ariel

ARIETTA n short relatively uncomplicated aria

ARIETTE same as ▸ arietta

ARIGHT adv rightly

ARIKI n first-born male or female in a notable family

ARIKIS ▸ ariki

ARIL n appendage on certain seeds, such as those of the yew and nutmeg, developed from or near the funicle of the ovule and often brightly coloured and fleshy

ARILED adj having an aril

ARILLI ▸ arillus

ARILLUS n aril

ARILS ▸ aril

ARIOSE adj songlike

ARIOSI ▸ arioso

ARIOSO n recitative with the lyrical quality of an aria

ARIOSOS ▸ arioso

ARIOT adv riotously

ARIPPLE adv in ripples

ARISE vb come about

ARISEN ▸ arise

ARISES ▸ arise

ARISH n field that has been mown

ARISHES ▸ arish

ARISING ▸ arise

ARISTA n stiff bristle such as the awn of some grasses and cereals

ARISTAE ▸ arista

ARISTAS ▸ arista

ARISTO n aristocrat

ARISTOS ▸ aristo

ARK n boat built by Noah, which survived the Flood ▷ vb place in an ark

ARKED ▸ ark

ARKING ▸ ark

ARKITE n passenger in ark

ARKITES ▸ arkite

ARKOSE n sandstone consisting of grains of feldspar and quartz cemented by a mixture of quartz and clay minerals

ARKOSES ▸ arkose

ARKOSIC ▸ arkose

ARKS ▸ ark

ARLE vb make downpayment

ARLED ▸ arle

ARLES ▸ arle

ARLING ▸ arle

ARM n either of the upper limbs from the shoulder to the wrist ▷ vb supply with weapons

ARMADA n large number of warships

ARMADAS ▸ armada

ARMBAND n band of material worn round the arm, such as one bearing an identifying mark, etc, or a black one indicating mourning

ARMED adj equipped with or supported by arms, armour, etc

ARMER ▸ arm

ARMERS ▸ arm

ARMET n close-fitting medieval visored helmet with a neck guard

ARMETS ▸ armet

ARMFUL n as much as can be held in the arms

ARMFULS ▸ armful

ARMHOLE n opening in a garment through which the arm passes

ARMIES ▸ army

ARMIGER n person entitled to bear heraldic arms, such as a sovereign or nobleman

ARMIL n bracelet

ARMILLA n bracelet

ARMILS ▸ armil

ARMING n act of taking arms or providing with arms

ARMINGS ▸ arming

ARMLESS ▸ arm

ARMLET n band worn round the arm

ARMLETS ▸ armlet

ARMLIKE ▸ arm

ARMLOAD n amount carried in the arms

ARMLOCK vb grip someone's arms

ARMOIRE n large cabinet, originally used for storing weapons

ARMOR same as ▸ armour

ARMORED same as ▸ armoured

ARMORER same as ▸ armourer

ARMORS ▸ armor

ARMORY same as ▸ armoury

ARMOUR n metal clothing formerly worn to protect the body in battle ▷ vb equip or cover with armour

ARMOURS ▸ armour

ARMOURY n place where weapons are stored

ARMPIT n hollow under the arm at the shoulder

ARMPITS ▸ armpit

ARMREST *n* part of a chair or sofa that supports the arm

ARMS ▸ **arm**

ARMSFUL ▸ **armful**

ARMURE *n* silk or wool fabric with a small cobbled pattern

ARMURES ▸ **armure**

ARMY *n* military land forces of a nation

ARNA *n* Indian water buffalo

ARNAS ▸ **arna**

ARNATTO *n* annatto

ARNICA *n* N temperate or arctic plant typically having yellow flowers

ARNICAS ▸ **arnica**

ARNOTTO *n* annatto

ARNUT *n* plant with edible tubers

ARNUTS ▸ **arnut**

AROBA *n* Asian carriage

AROBAS ▸ **aroba**

AROHA *n* love, compassion, or affection

AROHAS ▸ **aroha**

AROID *n* type of plant of the family which includes the arum, calla, and anthurium

AROIDS ▸ **aroid**

AROINT *vb* drive away

AROINTS ▸ **aroint**

AROLLA *n* European pine tree

AROLLAS ▸ **arolla**

AROMA *n* pleasant smell

AROMAS ▸ **aroma**

AROSE *past tense of* ▸ **arise**

AROUND *adv* on all sides (of)

AROUSAL ▸ **arouse**

AROUSE *vb* stimulate, make active

AROUSED ▸ **arouse**

AROUSER ▸ **arouse**

AROUSES ▸ **arouse**

AROW *adv* in a row

AROYNT *vb* old word meaning to drive away

AROYNTS ▸ **aroynt**

ARPA *n* website concerned with structure of the internet

ARPAS ▸ **arpa**

ARPEN *n* old French measure of land

ARPENS ▸ **arpen**

ARPENT *n* former French unit of length equal to 190 feet (approximately 58 metres)

ARPENTS ▸ **arpent**

ARRACK *n* alcoholic drink distilled from grain or rice

ARRACKS ▸ **arrack**

ARRAH *interj* Irish exclamation

ARRAIGN *vb* bring (a prisoner) before a court to answer a charge

ARRANGE *vb* plan

ARRANT *adj* utter, downright

ARRAS *n* tapestry wall-hanging

ARRASED *adj* having an arras

ARRASES ▸ **arras**

ARRAY *n* impressive display or collection ▷ *vb* arrange in order

ARRAYAL ▸ **array**

ARRAYED ▸ **array**

ARRAYER ▸ **array**

ARRAYS ▸ **array**

ARREAR *n* singular of arrears

ARREARS *pl n* money owed

ARRECT *adj* pricked up

ARREEDE *vb* old word meaning declare

ARREST *vb* take (a person) into custody ▷ *n* act of taking a person into custody

ARRESTS ▸ **arrest**

ARRET *n* judicial decision

ARRETS ▸ **arret**

ARRIAGE *n* Scottish feudal service

ARRIBA *interj* exclamation of pleasure or approval

ARRIDE *vb* old word meaning gratify

ARRIDED ▸ **arride**

ARRIDES ▸ **arride**

ARRIERE *adj* French word meaning old-fashioned

ARRIERO *n* Spanish word for mule driver

ARRIS *n* sharp edge at the meeting of two surfaces at an angle with one another, as at two adjacent sides of a stone block

ARRISES ▸ **arris**

ARRISH *n* corn stubble

ARRIVAL *n* arriving

ARRIVE *vb* reach a place or destination

ARRIVED ▸ **arrive**

ARRIVER ▸ **arrive**

ARRIVES ▸ **arrive**

ARROBA *n* unit of weight used in some Spanish-speaking countries

ARROBAS ▸ **arroba**

ARROW *n* pointed shaft shot from a bow

ARROWED *adj* having an arrow pattern

ARROWS ▸ **arrow**

ARROWY *adj* like an arrow

ARROYO *n* steep-sided stream bed that is usually dry except after heavy rain

ARROYOS ▸ **arroyo**

ARS ▸ **ar**

ARSENAL *n* place where arms and ammunition are made or stored

ARSENIC *n* toxic grey element ▷ *adj* of or containing arsenic

ARSENO *adj* containing arsenic

ARSHEEN *n* old measure of length in Russia

ARSHIN *n* old measure of length in Russia

ARSHINE *n* old measure of length in Russia

ARSHINS ▸ **arshin**

ARSINE *n* colourless poisonous gas used in the manufacture of organic compounds, to dope transistors, and as a military poisonous gas

ARSINES ▸ **arsine**

ARSINO *adj* containing arsine

ARSIS *n* (in classical prosody) the long syllable or part on which the ictus falls in a metrical foot

ARSON *n* crime of intentionally setting property on fire

ARSONS ▸ **arson**

ART *n* creation of works of beauty, esp paintings or sculpture

ARTAL *a plural of* ▸ **rotl**

ARTEL *n* (in the former Soviet Union) a cooperative union or organization, esp of producers, such as peasants

ARTELS ▸ **artel**

ARTERY *n* one of the tubes carrying blood from the heart

ARTFUL *adj* cunning, wily

ARTI *n* ritual performed in homes and temples in which incense and light are

A

offered to a deity
ARTIC n articulated vehicle
ARTICLE n written piece in a magazine or newspaper ⊳ vb bind by a written contract
ARTICS ▸ artic
ARTIER ▸ arty
ARTIES ▸ arty
ARTIEST ▸ arty
ARTILY ▸ arty
ARTIS ▸ arti
ARTISAN n skilled worker, craftsman
ARTIST n person who produces works of art, esp paintings or sculpture
ARTISTE n professional entertainer such as a singer or dancer
ARTISTS ▸ artist
ARTLESS adj free from deceit or cunning
ARTS ▸ art
ARTSIER ▸ artsy
ARTSIES ▸ artsy
ARTSMAN old word for > **craftsman**
ARTSMEN ▸ artsman
ARTSY adj interested in the arts ⊳ n person interested in the arts
ARTWORK n all the photographs and illustrations in a publication
ARTY adj having an affected interest in art ⊳ n person interested in art
ARUGOLA n salad plant
ARUGULA another name for ▸ **rocket**
ARUHE n edible root of a fern
ARUHES ▸ aruhe
ARUM n type of plant with arrow-shaped leaves and a typically white spathe
ARUMS ▸ arum
ARUSPEX variant spelling of > **haruspex**
ARVAL adj of ploughed land
ARVO n afternoon
ARVOS ▸ arvo
ARY dialect form of ▸ **any**
ARYL n of, consisting of, or containing an aromatic group
ARYLS ▸ aryl
AS adv used to indicate amount or extent in comparisons ⊳ n ancient Roman unit of weight

ASANA n any of various postures in yoga
ASANAS ▸ asana
ASAR ▸ as
ASARUM n dried strong-scented root of the wild ginger plant: a flavouring agent and source of an aromatic oil used in perfumery, formerly used in medicine
ASARUMS ▸ asarum
ASCARED adj afraid
ASCARID n type of parasitic nematode worm, such as the common roundworm
ASCARIS n ascarid
ASCAUNT adv old word meaning slantwise
ASCEND vb go or move up
ASCENDS ▸ ascend
ASCENT n ascending
ASCENTS ▸ ascent
ASCESES ▸ ascesis
ASCESIS n exercise of self-discipline
ASCETIC adj (person) abstaining from worldly pleasures and comforts ⊳ n person who abstains from worldly comforts and pleasures
ASCI ▸ ascus
ASCIAN n person living in the tropics
ASCIANS ▸ ascian
ASCIDIA > ascidium
ASCITES n accumulation of serous fluid in the peritoneal cavity
ASCITIC ▸ ascites
ASCONCE adv old form of askance
ASCOT n cravat with wide square ends, usually secured with an ornamental stud
ASCOTS ▸ ascot
ASCRIBE vb attribute, as to a particular origin
ASCUS n saclike structure that produces (usually) eight ascospores during sexual reproduction in ascomycetous fungi such as yeasts and mildews
ASDIC an early form of ▸ **sonar**
ASDICS ▸ asdic
ASEA adv towards the sea
ASEITY n existence derived from itself, having no other source

ASEPSES ▸ asepsis
ASEPSIS n aseptic condition
ASEPTIC adj free from harmful bacteria ⊳ n aseptic substance
ASEXUAL adj without sex
ASH n powdery substance left when something is burnt ⊳ vb reduce to ashes
ASHAKE adv shaking
ASHAME vb make ashamed
ASHAMED adj feeling shame
ASHAMES ▸ ashame
ASHCAKE n cornmeal bread
ASHCAN n large metal dustbin
ASHCANS ▸ ashcan
ASHED ▸ ash
ASHEN adj pale with shock
ASHERY n place where ashes are made
ASHES ▸ ash
ASHET n shallow oval dish or large plate
ASHETS ▸ ashet
ASHFALL n dropping of ash from a volcano
ASHIER ▸ ashy
ASHIEST ▸ ashy
ASHINE adv old word meaning shining
ASHING ▸ ash
ASHIVER adv shivering
ASHKEY n winged fruit of the ash
ASHKEYS ▸ ashkey
ASHLAR n square block of hewn stone used in building ⊳ vb build with ashlars
ASHLARS ▸ ashlar
ASHLER same as ▸ ashlar
ASHLERS ▸ ashler
ASHLESS ▸ ash
ASHMAN n man who shovels ashes
ASHMEN ▸ ashman
ASHORE adv towards or on land ⊳ adj on land, having come from the water
ASHRAF ▸ sherif
ASHRAM n religious retreat where a Hindu holy man lives
ASHRAMA n stage in Hindu spiritual life
ASHRAMS ▸ ashram
ASHTRAY n receptacle for tobacco ash and cigarette butts
ASHY adj pale greyish
ASIAGO n either of two

A

varieties (ripened or fresh) of a cow's-milk cheese produced in NE Italy
ASIAGOS ▸ asiago
ASIDE adv one side ▷ n remark not meant to be heard by everyone present
ASIDES ▸ aside
ASINICO n old Spanish word for fool
ASININE adj stupid, idiotic
ASK vb say or write (something) in a form that requires an answer
ASKANCE adv with an oblique glance ▷ vb turn aside
ASKANT same as ▸ **askance**
ASKANTS ▸ askant
ASKARI n (in East Africa) a soldier or policeman
ASKARIS ▸ askari
ASKED ▸ ask
ASKER ▸ ask
ASKERS ▸ ask
ASKESES ▸ askesis
ASKESIS n practice of self-discipline
ASKEW adj one side, crooked
ASKING ▸ ask
ASKINGS ▸ ask
ASKLENT Scots word for ▸ **aslant**
ASKOI ▸ askos
ASKOS n ancient Greek vase
ASKS ▸ ask
ASLAKE vb slake
ASLAKED ▸ aslake
ASLAKES ▸ aslake
ASLANT adv at a slant (to), slanting (across)
ASLEEP adj sleeping
ASLOPE adj sloping
ASLOSH adj awash
ASMEAR adj smeared
ASOCIAL n person who avoids social contact
ASP n small poisonous snake
ASPECT n feature or element ▷ vb look at
ASPECTS ▸ aspect
ASPEN n kind of poplar tree ▷ adj trembling
ASPENS ▸ aspen
ASPER n former Turkish monetary unit, a silver coin, worth 1/120 of a piastre
ASPERGE vb sprinkle
ASPERS ▸ asper
ASPERSE vb spread false rumours about

ASPHALT n black hard tarlike substance used for road surfaces etc ▷ vb cover with asphalt
ASPHYXY n > asphyxia
ASPIC n savoury jelly used to coat meat, eggs, fish, etc
ASPICK old word for ▸ **asp**
ASPICKS ▸ aspick
ASPICS ▸ aspic
ASPIDIA > aspidium
ASPINE old word for ▸ **aspen**
ASPINES ▸ aspine
ASPIRE vb yearn (for), hope (to do or be)
ASPIRED ▸ aspire
ASPIRER ▸ aspire
ASPIRES ▸ aspire
ASPIRIN n drug used to relieve pain and fever
ASPIS n horned viper
ASPISES ▸ aspis
ASPISH adj like an asp
ASPORT vb old word meaning take away
ASPORTS ▸ asport
ASPOUT adv spouting
ASPRAWL adv sprawling
ASPREAD adv spreading
ASPRO n associate professor at an academic institution
ASPROS ▸ aspro
ASPROUT adv sprouting
ASQUAT adv squatting
ASQUINT adj with a glance from the corner of the eye, esp a furtive one
ASRAMA n stage in Hindu spiritual life
ASRAMAS ▸ asrama
ASS n donkey
ASSAGAI same as ▸ **assegai**
ASSAI adv (usually preceded by a musical direction) very ▷ n Brazilian palm tree with small dark purple fleshy edible fruit
ASSAIL vb attack violently
ASSAILS ▸ assail
ASSAIS ▸ assai
ASSAM n (in Malaysia) tamarind as used in cooking
ASSAMS ▸ assam
ASSART vb clear ground for cultivation
ASSARTS ▸ assart
ASSAULT n violent attack ▷ vb attack violently
ASSAY n analysis of a substance, esp a metal, to ascertain its purity ▷ vb

make such an analysis
ASSAYED ▸ assay
ASSAYER ▸ assay
ASSAYS ▸ assay
ASSEGAI n slender spear used in S Africa ▷ vb spear with an assegai
ASSENT n agreement or consent ▷ vb agree or consent
ASSENTS ▸ assent
ASSERT vb declare forcefully
ASSERTS ▸ assert
ASSES ▸ ass
ASSESS vb judge the worth or importance of
ASSET n valuable or useful person or thing
ASSETS ▸ asset
ASSEVER vb old form of asseverate
ASSEZ adv (as part of a musical direction) fairly
ASSIEGE vb old form of besiege
ASSIGN vb appoint (someone) to a job or task ▷ n person to whom property is assigned
ASSIGNS ▸ assign
ASSIST vb give help or support ▷ n pass by a player which enables another player to score a goal
ASSISTS ▸ assist
ASSIZE n sitting of a legislative assembly or administrative body
ASSIZED ▸ assize
ASSIZER n weights and measures official
ASSIZES ▸ assize
ASSLIKE ▸ ass
ASSOIL vb absolve
ASSOILS ▸ assoil
ASSORT vb arrange or distribute into groups of the same type
ASSORTS ▸ assort
ASSOT vb old word meaning make infatuated
ASSOTS ▸ assot
ASSOTT vb besot
ASSUAGE vb relieve (pain, grief, thirst, etc)
ASSUME vb take to be true without proof
ASSUMED adj false
ASSUMER ▸ assume
ASSUMES ▸ assume
ASSURE vb promise or guarantee

A

ASSURED adj confident ▷ n beneficiary under a life assurance policy
ASSURER ▶ assure
ASSURES ▶ assure
ASSUROR ▶ assure
ASSWAGE old spelling of ▶ assuage
ASTABLE adj not stable
ASTARE adv staring
ASTART old word for ▶ start
ASTARTS ▶ astart
ASTASIA n inability to stand
ASTATIC adj not static
ASTATKI n fuel derived from petroleum
ASTEISM n use of irony
ASTELIC ▶ astely
ASTELY n lack of central cylinder in plants
ASTER n plant with daisy-like flowers
ASTERIA n gemstone with starlike light effect
ASTERID n variety of flowering plant
ASTERN adv at or towards the stern of a ship ▷ adj at or towards the stern of a ship
ASTERS ▶ aster
ASTERT vb start
ASTERTS ▶ astert
ASTHENY same as ▶ asthenia
ASTHMA n illness causing difficulty in breathing
ASTHMAS ▶ asthma
ASTHORE n Irish endearment
ASTILBE n E Asian and N American plant cultivated for its ornamental spikes of pink or white flowers
ASTIR adj out of bed
ASTONE vb old form of ▶ astonish
ASTONED ▶ astone
ASTONES ▶ astone
ASTONY vb old form of ▶ astonish
ASTOOP adv stooping
ASTOUND vb overwhelm with amazement
ASTRAL adj of stars ▷ n oil lamp
ASTRALS ▶ astral
ASTRAND adv on shore
ASTRAY adv off the right path
ASTRICT vb bind, confine, or constrict

ASTRIDE adv with a leg on either side (of) ▷ adj with a leg on either side
ASTROID n hypocycloid having four cusps
ASTRUT adv old word meaning in a protruding way
ASTUN vb old form of astonish
ASTUNS ▶ astun
ASTUTE adj perceptive or shrewd
ASTUTER ▶ astute
ASTYLAR adj without columns or pilasters
ASUDDEN adv old form of suddenly
ASUNDER adv into parts or pieces ▷ adj into parts or pieces
ASWARM adj filled, esp with moving things
ASWAY adv swaying
ASWIM adv floating
ASWING adv swinging
ASWIRL adv swirling
ASWOON adv swooning
ASYLA ▶ asylum
ASYLEE n person who is granted asylum
ASYLEES ▶ asylee
ASYLUM n refuge or sanctuary
ASYLUMS ▶ asylum
AT n Laotian monetary unit worth one hundredth of a kip
ATAATA n grazing marine gastropod
ATAATAS ▶ ataata
ATABAL n N African drum
ATABALS ▶ atabal
ATABEG n Turkish ruler
ATABEGS ▶ atabeg
ATABEK n Turkish ruler
ATABEKS ▶ atabek
ATABRIN n drug formerly used for treating malaria
ATACTIC adj (of a polymer) having a random sequence of the stereochemical arrangement of groups on carbon atoms in the chain
ATAGHAN same as ▶ yataghan
ATALAYA n watchtower in Spain
ATAMAN n elected leader of the Cossacks
ATAMANS ▶ ataman
ATAP n palm tree of S Asia
ATAPS ▶ atap

ATARAXY same as ▶ ataraxia
ATAVIC ▶ atavism
ATAVISM n recurrence of a trait present in distant ancestors
ATAVIST ▶ atavism
ATAXIA n lack of muscular coordination
ATAXIAS ▶ ataxia
ATAXIC ▶ ataxia
ATAXICS ▶ ataxia
ATAXIES ▶ ataxy
ATAXY same as ▶ ataxia
ATE past tense of ▶ eat
ATEBRIN n drug formerly used to treat malaria
ATELIC adj of action without end
ATELIER n workshop, artist's studio
ATEMOYA n tropical fruit tree
ATES n shop selling confectionary
ATHAME n (in Wicca) witch's ceremonial knife, usually with a black handle, used in rituals rather than for cutting or carving
ATHAMES ▶ athame
ATHANOR n alchemist's furnace
ATHEISE vb speak atheistically
ATHEISM n belief that there is no God
ATHEIST ▶ atheism
ATHEIZE vb speak atheistically
ATHEOUS adj without a belief in god
ATHIRST adj having an eager desire
ATHLETA n old form of ▶ athlete
ATHLETE n person trained in or good at athletics
ATHODYD another name for ▶ ramjet
ATHRILL adv feeling thrills
ATHROB adv throbbing
ATHWART adv transversely
ATIGI n type of parka worn by the Inuit in Canada
ATIGIS ▶ atigi
ATILT adj in a tilted or inclined position
ATIMIES ▶ atimy
ATIMY n loss of honour
ATINGLE adv tingling
ATISHOO n sound of a sneeze

ATLAS *n* book of maps

ATLASES ▸ atlas

ATLATL *n* Native American throwing stick

ATLATLS ▸ atlatl

ATMA *same as* ▸ atman

ATMAN *n* personal soul or self

ATMANS ▸ atman

ATMAS ▸ atma

ATOC *n* skunk

ATOCIA *n* inability to have children

ATOCIAS ▸ atocia

ATOCS ▸ atoc

ATOK *n* skunk

ATOKAL *adj* having no children

ATOKE *n* part of a worm

ATOKES ▸ atoke

ATOKOUS *adj* having no children

ATOKS ▸ atok

ATOLL *n* ring-shaped coral reef enclosing a lagoon

ATOLLS ▸ atoll

ATOM *n* smallest unit of matter which can take part in a chemical reaction

ATOMIC *adj* of or using atomic bombs or atomic energy

ATOMICS *n* science of atoms

ATOMICS ▸ atomy

ATOMISE *same as* ▸ atomize

ATOMISM *n* ancient philosophical theory that the ultimate constituents of the universe are atoms

ATOMIST ▸ atomism

ATOMIZE *vb* reduce to atoms or small particles

ATOMS ▸ atom

ATOMY *n* atom or minute particle

ATONAL *adj* (of music) not written in an established key

ATONE *vb* make amends (for sin or wrongdoing)

ATONED ▸ atone

ATONER ▸ atone

ATONERS ▸ atone

ATONES ▸ atone

ATONIA *n* lack of normal muscle tone

ATONIAS ▸ atonia

ATONIC *adj* (of a syllable, word, etc) carrying no stress ▷ *n* unaccented or unstressed syllable, word

ATONICS ▸ atonic

ATONIES ▸ atony

┃ The plural of **atony**, this is another of the most frequently played 7-letter bonus words that it is essential to know.

ATONING ▸ atone

ATONY *n* lack of normal tone or tension, as in muscles

ATOP *adv* on top

ATOPIC *adj* of or relating to hereditary hypersensitivity to certain allergens

ATOPIES ▸ atopy

ATOPY *n* hereditary tendency to be hypersensitive to certain allergens

ATRESIA *n* absence of or unnatural narrowing of a body channel

ATRESIC ▸ atresia

ATRETIC ▸ atresia

ATRIA ▸ atrium

ATRIAL ▸ atrium

ATRIP *adj* (of an anchor) no longer caught on the bottom

ATRIUM *n* upper chamber of either half of the heart

ATRIUMS ▸ atrium

ATROPHY *n* wasting away of an organ or part ▷ *vb* (cause to) waste away

ATROPIA *n* atropine

ATROPIN *same as* ▸ atropine

ATS ▸ at

ATT *n* old Siamese coin

ATTABOY *sentence substitute* expression of approval or exhortation

ATTACH *vb* join, fasten, or connect

ATTACHE *n* a specialist attached to a diplomatic mission

ATTACK *vb* launch a physical assault (against) ▷ *n* act of attacking

ATTACKS ▸ attack

ATTAIN *vb* achieve or accomplish (a task or aim)

ATTAINS ▸ attain

ATTAINT *vb* pass judgment of death or outlawry upon (a person) ▷ *n* dishonour

ATTAP *n* palm tree of South Asia

ATTAPS ▸ attap

ATTAR *n* fragrant oil made from roses

ATTARS ▸ attar

ATTASK *old word for* ▸ criticize

ATTASKS ▸ attask

ATTASKT ▸ attask

ATTEMPT *vb* try, make an effort ▷ *n* effort or endeavour

ATTEND *vb* be present at

ATTENDS ▸ attend

ATTENT *old word for* ▸ attention

ATTENTS ▸ attent

ATTEST *vb* affirm the truth of, be proof of

ATTESTS ▸ attest

ATTIC *n* space or room within the roof of a house

ATTICS ▸ attic

ATTIRE *n* fine or formal clothes ▷ *vb* dress, esp in fine elegant clothes

ATTIRED ▸ attire

ATTIRES ▸ attire

ATTONCE *adv* old word for at once

ATTONE *vb* old word meaning appease

ATTONED ▸ attone

ATTONES ▸ attone

ATTORN *vb* acknowledge a new owner of land as one's landlord

ATTORNS ▸ attorn

ATTRACT *vb* arouse the interest or admiration of

ATTRAP *vb* adorn

ATTRAPS ▸ attrap

ATTRIST *vb* old word meaning to sadden

ATTRIT *vb* wear down or dispose of gradually

ATTRITE *vb* wear down

ATTRITS ▸ attrit

ATTUENT *adj* carrying out attuition

ATTUITE *vb* perceive by attuition

ATTUNE *vb* adjust or accustom (a person or thing)

ATTUNED ▸ attune

ATTUNES ▸ attune

ATUA *n* spirit or demon

ATUAS ▸ atua

ATWAIN *adv* old word meaning into two parts

ATWEEL *Scots word for* ▸ well

ATWEEN *an archaic or Scots word for* ▸ between

ATWIXT *old word for* ▸ between

ATYPIC *adj* not typical

A

AUA *n* yellow-eye mullet
This Maori word for a kind of mullet is very often played to balance a rack by getting rid of a surplus of vowels.

AUAS ▸ **aua**

AUBADE *n* song or poem appropriate to or greeting the dawn

AUBADES ▸ **aubade**

AUBERGE *n* inn or tavern

AUBURN *adj* (of hair) reddish-brown ▷ *n* moderate reddish-brown colour

AUBURNS ▸ **auburn**

AUCEPS *n* old word meaning person who catches hawks

AUCTION *n* public sale in which articles are sold to the highest bidder ▷ *vb* sell by auction

AUCUBA *n* Japanese laurel

AUCUBAS ▸ **aucuba**

AUDAD *n* wild African sheep

AUDADS ▸ **audad**

AUDIAL *adj* of sound

AUDIBLE *adj* loud enough to be heard ▷ *n* change of playing tactics called by the quarterback when the offence is lined up at the line of scrimmage ▷ *vb* call an audible

AUDIBLY ▸ **audible**

AUDIENT *n* person who hears

AUDILE *n* person who possesses a faculty for auditory imagery that is more distinct than his visual or other imagery ▷ *adj* of or relating to such a person

AUDILES ▸ **audile**

AUDING *n* practice of listening to try to understand

AUDINGS ▸ **auding**

AUDIO *adj* of sound or hearing ▷ *n* of or relating to sound or hearing

AUDIOS ▸ **audio**

AUDIT *n* official examination of business accounts ▷ *vb* examine (business accounts) officially

AUDITED ▸ **audit**

AUDITEE *n* one who is audited

AUDITOR *n* person qualified to audit accounts

AUDITS ▸ **audit**

AUE *interj* Maori exclamation
This is another of those Maori words, an exclamation of pain or distress, so useful for getting rid of surplus vowels. But remember that unlike **aua** it does not take an S.

AUF *old word for* ▸ **oaf**

AUFGABE *n* word used in psychology to mean task

AUFS ▸ **auf**

AUGEND *n* number to which another number, the addend, is added

AUGENDS ▸ **augend**

AUGER *n* tool for boring holes

AUGERS ▸ **auger**

AUGHT *adv* in any least part ▷ *n* less common word for nought (zero)

AUGHTS ▸ **aught**

AUGITE *n* black or greenish-black mineral

AUGITES ▸ **augite**

AUGITIC ▸ **augite**

AUGMENT *vb* increase or enlarge ▷ *n* (in Greek and Sanskrit grammar) a vowel or diphthong prefixed to a verb to form a past tense

AUGUR *vb* be a sign of (future events) ▷ *n* (in ancient Rome) a religious official who observed and interpreted omens and signs to help guide the making of public decisions

AUGURAL ▸ **augur**

AUGURED ▸ **augur**

AUGURER *old word for* ▸ **augur**

AUGURS ▸ **augur**

AUGURY *n* foretelling of the future

AUGUST *adj* dignified and imposing ▷ *n* auguste

AUGUSTE *n* type of circus clown who usually wears battered ordinary clothes and is habitually maladroit or unlucky

AUGUSTS ▸ **august**

AUK *n* northern sea bird with short wings and black-and-white plumage

AUKLET *n* type of small auk

AUKLETS ▸ **auklet**

AUKS ▸ **auk**

AULA *n* hall

AULAS ▸ **aula**

AULD *a Scots word for* ▸ **old**

AULDER ▸ **auld**

AULDEST ▸ **auld**

AULIC *adj* relating to a royal court

AULNAGE *n* measurement in ells

AULOI ▸ **aulos**

AULOS *n* ancient Greek pipes

AUMAIL *old word for* ▸ **enamel**

AUMAILS ▸ **aumail**

AUMBRY *same as* ▸ **ambry**

AUMIL *n* manager in India

AUMILS ▸ **aumil**

AUNE *n* old French measure of length

AUNES ▸ **aune**

AUNT *n* father's or mother's sister

AUNTER *old word for* ▸ **adventure**

AUNTERS ▸ **aunter**

AUNTIE *n* aunt

AUNTIES ▸ **aunty**

AUNTLY *adj* of or like an aunt

AUNTS ▸ **aunt**

AUNTY *same as* ▸ **auntie**

AURA *n* distinctive air or quality of a person or thing

AURAE ▸ **aura**

AURAL *adj* of or using the ears or hearing

AURALLY ▸ **aural**

AURAR *plural of* ▸ **eyrir**

AURAS ▸ **aura**

AURATE *n* salt of auric acid

AURATED *adj* combined with auric acid

AURATES ▸ **aurate**

AUREATE *adj* covered with gold, gilded

AUREI ▸ **aureus**

AUREITY *n* attributes of gold

AURELIA *n* large jellyfish

AUREOLA *same as* ▸ **aureole**

AUREOLE *n* halo

AURES ▸ **auris**

AUREUS *n* gold coin of the Roman Empire

AURIC *adj* of or containing gold in the trivalent state

AURICLE *n* upper chamber of the heart

AURIFY *vb* turn into gold

AURIS n medical word for ear

AURIST a former name for > **audiology**

AURISTS ▸ **aurist**

AUROCHS n recently extinct European wild ox

AURORA n bands of light sometimes seen in the sky in polar regions

AURORAE ▸ **aurora**

AURORAL ▸ **aurora**

AURORAS ▸ **aurora**

AUROUS adj of or containing gold, esp in the monovalent state

AURUM n gold

AURUMS ▸ **aurum**

AUSFORM vb temper steel

AUSPEX same as ▸ **augur**

AUSPICE n patronage or guidance

AUSTERE adj stern or severe

AUSTRAL adj southern ▷ n former monetary unit of Argentina equal to 100 centavos, replaced by the peso

AUSUBO n tropical tree

AUSUBOS ▸ **ausubo**

AUTARCH n absolute ruler

AUTARKY n policy of economic self-sufficiency

AUTEUR n director whose creative influence on a film is so great as to be considered its author

AUTEURS ▸ **auteur**

AUTHOR n writer of a book etc ▷ vb write or originate

AUTHORS ▸ **author**

AUTISM n disorder characterized by lack of response to people and limited ability to communicate

AUTISMS ▸ **autism**

AUTIST n autistic person

AUTISTS ▸ **autist**

AUTO n automobile ▷ vb travel in an automobile

AUTOBUS n motor bus

AUTOCAR n motor car

AUTOCUE n electronic television prompting device

AUTOED ▸ **auto**

AUTOING ▸ **auto**

AUTOMAN n car manufacturer

AUTOMAT n vending machine

AUTOMEN ▸ **automan**

AUTONYM n writing

published under the real name of an author

AUTOPEN n mechanical device used to produce imitation signatures

AUTOPSY n examination of a corpse to determine the cause of death

AUTOPUT n motorway in the former Yugoslavia

AUTOS ▸ **auto**

AUTOVAC n vacuum pump in a car petrol tank

AUTUMN n season between summer and winter

AUTUMNS ▸ **autumn**

AUTUMNY adj like autumn

AUXESES ▸ **auxesis**

AUXESIS n growth in animal or plant tissues resulting from an increase in cell size without cell division

AUXETIC n something that promotes growth

AUXIN n any of various plant hormones, such as indoleacetic acid, that promote growth and control fruit and flower development. Synthetic auxins are widely used in agriculture and horticulture

AUXINIC ▸ **auxin**

AUXINS ▸ **auxin**

AVA adv at all ▷ n Polynesian shrub

AVAIL vb be of use or advantage (to) ▷ n use or advantage

AVAILE old word for ▸ **lower**

AVAILED ▸ **avail**

AVAILES ▸ **availe**

AVAILS ▸ **avail**

AVAL adj of a grandparent

AVALE old word for ▸ **lower**

AVALED ▸ **avale**

AVALES ▸ **avale**

AVALING ▸ **avale**

AVANT prep before

AVANTI interj forward!

AVARICE n greed for wealth

AVAS ▸ **ava**

AVAST sentence substitute stop! cease!

AVATAR n appearance of a god in animal or human form

AVATARS ▸ **avatar**

AVAUNT sentence substitute go away! depart! ▷ vb go away; depart

AVAUNTS ▸ **avaunt**

AVE n expression of welcome or farewell

AVEL same as ▸ **ovel**

AVELLAN adj of hazelnuts

AVELS ▸ **avel**

AVENGE vb take revenge in retaliation for (harm done) or on behalf of (a person harmed)

AVENGED ▸ **avenge**

AVENGER ▸ **avenge**

AVENGES ▸ **avenge**

AVENIR n future

AVENIRS ▸ **avenir**

AVENS n any of several temperate or arctic rosaceous plants

AVENSES ▸ **avens**

AVENTRE old word for ▸ **thrust**

AVENUE n wide street

AVENUES ▸ **avenue**

AVER vb state to be true

AVERAGE n typical or normal amount or quality ▷ adj usual or typical ▷ vb calculate the average of

AVERRED ▸ **aver**

AVERS ▸ **aver**

AVERSE adj disinclined or unwilling

AVERT vb turn away

AVERTED ▸ **avert**

AVERTER ▸ **avert**

AVERTS ▸ **avert**

AVES ▸ **ave**

AVGAS n aviation fuel

AVGASES ▸ **avgas**

AVIAN adj of or like a bird ▷ n bird

AVIANS ▸ **avian**

AVIARY n large cage or enclosure for birds

AVIATE vb pilot or fly in an aircraft

AVIATED ▸ **aviate**

AVIATES ▸ **aviate**

AVIATIC adj pertaining to aviation

AVIATOR n pilot of an aircraft

AVID adj keen or enthusiastic

AVIDER ▸ **avid**

AVIDEST ▸ **avid**

AVIDIN n protein, found in egg-white, that combines with biotin to form a stable compound that cannot be absorbed, leading to a biotin deficiency in the consumer

A

AVIDINS ▸ avidin
AVIDITY n quality or state of being avid
AVIDLY ▸ avid
AVIETTE n aeroplane driven by human strength
AVIFORM adj like a bird
AVINE adj of birds
AVION n aeroplane
AVIONIC > avionics
AVIONS ▸ avion
AVISE old word for ▸ advise
AVISED ▸ avise
AVISES ▸ avise
AVISING ▸ avise
AVISO n boat carrying messages
AVISOS ▸ aviso
AVITAL adj of a grandfather
AVIZE old word for ▸ advise
AVIZED ▸ avize
AVIZES ▸ avize
AVIZING ▸ avize
AVO n Macao currency unit
AVOCADO n pear-shaped tropical fruit with a leathery green skin and yellowish-green flesh
AVOCET n long-legged wading bird with a long slender upward-curving bill
AVOCETS ▸ avocet
AVODIRE n African tree
AVOID vb prevent from happening
AVOIDED ▸ avoid
AVOIDER ▸ avoid
AVOIDS ▸ avoid
AVOS ▸ avo
AVOSET n avocet
AVOSETS ▸ avoset
AVOUCH vb vouch for
AVOURE old word for ▸ avowal
AVOURES ▸ avoure
AVOUTRY old word for > adultery
AVOW vb state or affirm
AVOWAL ▸ avow
AVOWALS ▸ avow
AVOWED ▸ avow
AVOWER ▸ avow
AVOWERS ▸ avow
AVOWING ▸ avow
AVOWRY old word for ▸ avowal
AVOWS ▸ avow
AVOYER n former Swiss magistrate
AVOYERS ▸ avoyer
AVRUGA n herring roe with a smoky flavour, sometimes used as a less expensive alternative to caviar
AVRUGAS ▸ avruga
AVULSE vb take away by force
AVULSED ▸ avulse
AVULSES ▸ avulse
AVYZE old word for ▸ advise
AVYZED ▸ avyze
AVYZES ▸ avyze
AVYZING ▸ avyze
AW same as ▸ all
AWA adv away
AWAIT vb wait for
AWAITED ▸ await
AWAITER ▸ await
AWAITS ▸ await
AWAKE vb emerge or rouse from sleep ▷ adj not sleeping
AWAKED ▸ awake
AWAKEN vb awake
AWAKENS ▸ awaken
AWAKES ▸ awake
AWAKING ▸ awake
AWARD vb give (something, such as a prize) formally ▷ n something awarded, such as a prize
AWARDED ▸ award
AWARDEE ▸ award
AWARDER ▸ award
AWARDS ▸ award
AWARE adj having knowledge, informed
AWARER ▸ aware
AWAREST ▸ aware
AWARN vb old form of warn
AWARNED ▸ awarn
AWARNS ▸ awarn
AWASH adv washed over by water ▷ adj washed over by water
AWATCH adv watching
AWATO n New Zealand caterpillar
AWATOS ▸ awato
AWAVE adv in waves
AWAY adv from a place ▷ adj not present ▷ n game played or won at an opponent's ground
AWAYDAY n day trip taken for pleasure
AWAYES old word for ▸ away
AWAYS ▸ away
AWDL n traditional Welsh poem
AWDLS ▸ awdl
AWE n wonder and respect mixed with dread ▷ vb fill with awe
AWEARY old form of ▸ weary
AWED ▸ awe
AWEE adv for a short time
AWEEL interj Scots word meaning well
AWEIGH adj (of an anchor) no longer hooked onto the bottom
AWEING ▸ awe
AWELESS ▸ awe
AWES ▸ awe
AWESOME adj inspiring awe
AWETO n New Zealand caterpillar
AWETOS ▸ aweto
AWFUL adj very bad or unpleasant ▷ adv very
AWFULLY adv in an unpleasant way
AWFY adv (Scots) awfully, extremely
AWHAPE old word for ▸ amaze
AWHAPED ▸ awhape
AWHAPES ▸ awhape
AWHATO n New Zealand caterpillar
AWHATOS ▸ awhato
AWHEEL adv on wheels
AWHEELS same as ▸ awheel
AWHETO n New Zealand caterpillar
AWHETOS ▸ awheto
AWHILE adv for a brief time
AWHIRL adv whirling
AWING ▸ awe
AWK n type of computer programming language

> This computer language provides a useful high-scoring outlet for what can be the awkward letters W and K.

AWKS ▸ awk
AWKWARD adj clumsy or ungainly
AWL n pointed tool for piercing wood, leather, etc
AWLBIRD n woodpecker
AWLESS ▸ awe
AWLS ▸ awl
AWLWORT n type of small stemless aquatic plant of the N hemisphere, with slender sharp-pointed leaves and minute white flowers
AWMOUS Scots word for ▸ alms
AWMRIE n cupboard for church vessels
AWMRIES ▸ awmrie
AWMRY n cupboard for

A

church vessels

AWN *n* any of the bristles growing from the flowering parts of certain grasses and cereals

AWNED ▸ **awn**

AWNER *n* machine for removing awns

AWNERS ▸ **awner**

AWNIER ▸ **awny**

AWNIEST ▸ **awny**

AWNING *n* canvas roof supported by a frame to give protection against the weather

AWNINGS ▸ **awning**

AWNLESS ▸ **awn**

AWNS ▸ **awn**

AWNY *adj* having awns

AWOKE *past tense of* ▸ **awake**

AWOKEN ▸ **awake**

AWOL *n* person who is absent without leave

AWOLS ▸ **awol**

AWORK *adv* old word meaning at work

AWRACK *adv* in wrecked condition

AWRONG *adv* old word meaning wrongly

AWRY *adj* with a twist to one side, askew

AWSOME *adj* old form of awesome

AX *same as* ▸ **axe**

AXAL *adj* of an axis

AXE *n* tool with a sharp blade for felling trees or chopping wood ▷ *vb* dismiss (employees), restrict (expenditure), or terminate (a project)

AXEBIRD *n* nightjar of northern Queensland and New Guinea with a cry that sounds like a chopping axe

AXED ▸ **axe**

AXEL *n* jump in which the skater takes off from the forward outside edge of one skate, makes one and a half, two and a half, three and a half turns in the air, and lands on the backward outside edge of the other skate

AXELS ▸ **axel**

AXEMAN *n* man who wields an axe, esp to cut down trees

AXEMEN ▸ **axeman**

AXENIC *adj* (of a biological culture or culture medium) free from other microorganisms

AXES ▸ **axis**

AXIAL *adj* forming or of an axis

AXIALLY ▸ **axial**

AXIL *n* angle where the stalk of a leaf joins a stem

AXILE *adj* of, relating to, or attached to the axis

AXILLA *n* area on the undersurface of a bird's wing corresponding to the armpit

AXILLAE ▸ **axilla**

AXILLAR *same as* ▸ **axillary**

AXILLAS ▸ **axilla**

AXILS ▸ **axil**

AXING ▸ **axe**

AXINITE *n* crystalline substance

AXIOM *n* generally accepted principle

AXIOMS ▸ **axiom**

AXION *n* type of hypothetical elementary particle

AXIONS ▸ **axion**

AXIS *n* (imaginary) line round which a body can rotate or about which an object or geometrical figure is symmetrical

AXISED *adj* having an axis

AXISES ▸ **axis**

AXITE *n* type of gunpowder

AXITES ▸ **axite**

AXLE *n* shaft on which a wheel or pair of wheels turns

AXLED *adj* having an axle

AXLES ▸ **axle**

AXLIKE ▸ **ax**

AXMAN *same as* ▸ **axeman**

AXMEN ▸ **axman**

AXOID *n* type of curve

AXOIDS ▸ **axoid**

AXOLOTL *n* aquatic salamander of central America

AXON *n* long threadlike extension of a nerve cell that conducts nerve impulses from the cell body

AXONAL ▸ **axon**

AXONE *same as* ▸ **axon**

AXONEME *n* part of cell consisting of proteins

AXONES ▸ **axone**

AXONIC ▸ **axon**

AXONS ▸ **axon**

AXSEED *n* crown vetch

AXSEEDS ▸ **axseed**

AY *adv* ever ▷ *n* expression of agreement

AYAH *n* (in parts of the former British Empire) a native maidservant or nursemaid

AYAHS ▸ **ayah**

AYE *n* affirmative vote or voter ▷ *adv* always

AYELP *adv* yelping

AYES ▸ **aye**

AYGRE old word for ▸ **eager**

AYIN *n* 16th letter in the Hebrew alphabet

AYINS ▸ **ayin**

AYONT *adv* beyond

AYRE old word for ▸ **air**

AYRES ▸ **ayre**

AYRIE old word for ▸ **eyrie**

AYRIES ▸ **ayrie**

AYS ▸ **ay**

AYU *n* small Japanese fish

This small Japanese fish comes up more times than you might think, being an extension of both **ay** and **yu**, which illustrates how important it is to know those little 'hook' words.

AYUS ▸ **ayu**

AYWORD *n* old word meaning byword

AYWORDS ▸ **ayword**

AZALEA *n* garden shrub grown for its showy flowers

AZALEAS ▸ **azalea**

AZAN *n* call to prayer five times a day, usually by a muezzin from a minaret

AZANS ▸ **azan**

AZERTY *n* common European version of typewriter keyboard layout with the characters a, z, e, r, t, and y positioned on the top row of alphabetic characters at the left side of the keyboard

AZIDE *n* type of chemical compound

AZIDES ▸ **azide**

AZIDO *adj* containing an azide

AZIMUTH *n* arc of the sky between the zenith and the horizon

AZINE *n* any organic compound having a six-membered ring containing at least one nitrogen atom

AZINES ▸ **azine**

A

AZIONE *n* musical drama
AZIONES ▸ **azione**
AZLON *n* fibre made from protein
AZLONS ▸ **azlon**
AZO *adj* of, consisting of, or containing the divalent group -N:N-

> **Azo** is a chemical term that you will want to play very often, but remember that it does not take an S. It does however take an N to form **azon**.

AZOIC *adj* without life
AZOLE *n* organic five-membered ring compound containing one or more atoms in the ring, the number usually being specified by a prefix
AZOLES ▸ **azole**
AZOLLA *n* tropical water fern
AZOLLAS ▸ **azolla**
AZON *n* type of drawing paper

AZONAL *adj* not divided into zones
AZONIC *adj* not confined to a zone
AZONS ▸ **azon**
AZOTE *an obsolete name for* ▸ **nitrogen**
AZOTED ▸ **azote**
AZOTES ▸ **azote**
AZOTH *n* panacea postulated by Paracelsus
AZOTHS ▸ **azoth**
AZOTIC *adj* of, containing, or concerned with nitrogen
AZOTISE *same as* ▸ **azotize**
AZOTIZE *vb* combine or treat with nitrogen or a nitrogen compound
AZOTOUS *adj* containing nitrogen
AZUKI *same as* ▸ **adzuki**
AZUKIS ▸ **azuki**
AZULEJO *n* Spanish porcelain tile

> An **azulejo** is a kind of brightly coloured tile, beautiful in its combination of the J and Z.

AZURE *n* (of) the colour of a clear blue sky ▹ *adj* deep blue
AZUREAN *adj* azure
AZURES ▸ **azure**
AZURINE *n* blue dye
AZURITE *n* azure-blue mineral associated with copper deposits
AZURN *old word for* ▸ **azure**
AZURY *adj* bluish
AZYGIES ▸ **azygy**
AZYGOS *n* biological structure not in a pair
AZYGOUS *adj* developing or occurring singly
AZYGY *n* state of not being joined in a pair
AZYM *n* unleavened bread
AZYME *n* unleavened bread
AZYMES ▸ **azyme**
AZYMITE *n* member of a church using unleavened bread in the Eucharist
AZYMOUS *adj* unleavened
AZYMS ▸ **azym**

Bb

B forms a two-letter word before every vowel except **U** - and with **Y** as well. With a **B** in your rack, you can play lots of short words that will give you relatively high scores. The best of these are **box** (12 points), **bez** (14 points) and **biz** (14 points), but don't forget **bay** (8), **by** (7), **bow** (8), **boy** (8), **buy** (8) and **bye** (8).

BA n symbol for the soul in Ancient Egyptian religion

BAA vb make the characteristic bleating sound of a sheep ▷ n cry made by a sheep

BAAED ▸ baa

BAAING ▸ baa

BAAINGS ▸ baa

BAAL n any false god or idol

BAALIM ▸ baal

BAALISM ▸ baal

BAALS ▸ baal

BAAS South African word for ▸ boss

BAASES ▸ baas

BAASKAP n (in South Africa) control by Whites of non-Whites

BABA n small cake of leavened dough, sometimes mixed with currants and usually soaked in rum

BABACO n greenish-yellow egg-shaped fruit

BABACOS ▸ babaco

BABALAS adj drunk

BABAS ▸ baba

BABASSU n Brazilian palm tree with hard edible nuts that yield an oil used to make soap, margarine, etc

BABBITT vb line (a bearing) or face (a surface) with Babbitt metal or a similar soft alloy

BABBLE vb talk excitedly or foolishly ▷ n muddled or foolish speech

BABBLED ▸ babble

BABBLER n person who babbles

BABBLES ▸ babble

BABBLY ▸ babble

BABE n baby

BABEL n confused mixture of noises or voices

BABELS ▸ babel

BABES ▸ babe

BABESIA n parasite causing infection in cattle

BABICHE n thongs or lacings of rawhide

BABIED ▸ baby

BABIER ▸ baby

BABIES ▸ baby

BABIEST ▸ baby

BABKA n cake

BABKAS ▸ babka

BABLAH n type of acacia

BABLAHS ▸ bablah

BABOO same as ▸ babu

BABOOL n type of acacia

BABOOLS ▸ babool

BABOON n large monkey with a pointed face and a long tail

BABOONS ▸ baboon

BABOOS ▸ baboo

BABOOSH same as ▸ babouche

BABU n title or form of address used in India

BABUCHE same as ▸ babouche

BABUDOM ▸ babu

BABUISM ▸ babu

BABUL n N African and Indian tree with small yellow flowers, which is a source of gum arabic, tannin, and hardwood

BABULS ▸ babul

BABUS ▸ babu

BABY n very young child or animal ▷ adj comparatively small of its type ▷ vb treat as a baby

BABYING ▸ baby

BABYISH ▸ baby

BABYSAT ▸ babysit

BABYSIT vb look after a child in its parents' absence

BAC n baccalaureate

BACALAO n dried salt cod

BACCA n berry

BACCAE ▸ bacca

BACCARA same as ▸ baccarat

BACCARE same as ▸ backare

BACCAS ▸ bacca

BACCATE adj like a berry in form, texture, etc

BACCHIC adj riotously drunk

BACCHII ▸ bacchius

BACCIES ▸ baccy

BACCO n tobacco

BACCOES ▸ bacco

BACCOS ▸ bacco

BACCY n tobacco

BACH same as ▸ batch

BACHA n Indian English word for young child

BACHAS ▸ bacha

BACHCHA n Indian English word for young child

BACHED ▸ bach

BACHES ▸ bach

BACHING ▸ bach

BACHS ▸ bach

BACILLI ▸ bacillus

BACK n rear part of the human body, from the neck to the pelvis ▷ vb (cause to) move backwards ▷ adj situated behind ▷ adv at, to, or towards the rear

BACKARE interj instruction to keep one's distance; back off

BACKBIT ▸ backbite

BACKED adj having a back or backing

B

BACKER n person who gives financial support

BACKERS ▸ backer

BACKET n shallow box

BACKETS ▸ backet

BACKFIT vb overhaul nuclear power plant

BACKHOE n digger ▷ vb dig with a backhoe

BACKIE n ride on the back of someone's bicycle

BACKIES ▸ backie

BACKING n support

BACKLIT adj illuminated from behind

BACKLOG n accumulation of things to be dealt with

BACKLOT n area outside a film or television studio used for outdoor filming

BACKOUT n instance of withdrawing (from an agreement, etc)

BACKRA n white person

BACKRAS ▸ backra

BACKS ▸ back

BACKSAW n small handsaw stiffened along its upper edge by a metal section

BACKSET n reversal

BACKSEY n sirloin

BACKUP n support or reinforcement

BACKUPS ▸ backup

BACLAVA same as ▸ baklava

BACON n salted or smoked pig meat

BACONER n pig that weighs between 83 and 101 kg, from which bacon is cut

BACONS ▸ bacon

BACS ▸ bac

BACULA ▸ baculum

BACULUM n bony support in the penis of certain mammals, esp the carnivores

BAD adj not good ▷ n unfortunate or unpleasant events collectively ▷ adv badly

BADDER ▸ bad

BADDEST ▸ bad

BADDIE n bad character in a story, film, etc, esp an opponent of the hero

BADDIES ▸ baddy

BADDISH ▸ bad

BADDY same as ▸ baddie

BADE ▸ bid

BADGE n emblem worn to show membership, rank, etc ▷ vb put a badge on

BADGED ▸ badge

BADGER n nocturnal burrowing mammal of Europe, Asia, and N America with a black and white head ▷ vb pester or harass

BADGERS ▸ badger

BADGES ▸ badge

BADGING ▸ badge

BADIOUS adj chestnut; brownish-red

BADLAND > badlands

BADLY adv poorly

BADMAN n hired gunman, outlaw, or criminal

BADMASH n evil-doer ▷ adj naughty or bad ▷ n hooligan

BADMEN ▸ badman

BADNESS ▸ bad

BADS ▸ bad

BADWARE n software designed to harm a computer system

BAEL n type of spiny Indian tree

BAELS ▸ bael

BAETYL n magical meteoric stone

BAETYLS ▸ baetyl

BAFF vb strike ground with golf club

BAFFED ▸ baff

BAFFIES pl n slippers

BAFFING ▸ baff

BAFFLE vb perplex or puzzle ▷ n device to limit or regulate the flow of fluid, light, or sound

BAFFLED ▸ baffle

BAFFLER ▸ baffle

BAFFLES ▸ baffle

BAFFS ▸ baff

BAFFY n golf club

BAFT n coarse fabric

BAFTS ▸ baft

BAG n flexible container with an opening at one end ▷ vb put into a bag

BAGARRE n brawl

BAGASS same as ▸ bagasse

BAGASSE n pulp remaining after the extraction of juice from sugar cane or similar plants: used as fuel and for making paper, etc

BAGEL n hard ring-shaped bread roll

BAGELS ▸ bagel

BAGFUL n amount (of something) that can be held in a bag

BAGFULS ▸ bagful

BAGGAGE n suitcases packed for a journey

BAGGED ▸ bag

BAGGER n person who packs groceries

BAGGERS ▸ bagger

BAGGIE n plastic bag

BAGGIER ▸ baggy

BAGGIES ▸ baggy

BAGGILY ▸ baggy

BAGGING ▸ bag

BAGGIT n unspawned salmon

BAGGITS ▸ baggit

BAGGY same as ▸ bagie

BAGH n (in India and Pakistan) a garden

BAGHS ▸ bagh

BAGIE n turnip

BAGIES ▸ bagie

BAGLESS adj (esp of a vacuum cleaner) not containing a bag

BAGLIKE ▸ bag

BAGMAN n travelling salesman

BAGMEN ▸ bagman

BAGNIO n brothel

BAGNIOS ▸ bagnio

BAGPIPE vb play the bagpipes

BAGS ▸ bag

BAGSFUL ▸ bagful

BAGUET same as > baguette

BAGUETS ▸ baguet

BAGUIO n hurricane

BAGUIOS ▸ baguio

BAGWASH n laundry that washes clothes without drying or pressing them

BAGWIG n 18th-century wig with hair pushed back into a bag

BAGWIGS ▸ bagwig

BAGWORM n type of moth

BAH interj expression of contempt or disgust

BAHADA same as ▸ bajada

BAHADAS ▸ bahada

BAHADUR n title formerly conferred by the British on distinguished Indians

BAHT n standard monetary unit of Thailand, divided into 100 satang

BAHTS ▸ baht

BAHU n (in India) daughter-in-law

BAHUS ▸ bahu

BAHUT n decorative cabinet

BAHUTS ▸ bahut

BAIL n money deposited

with a court as security for a person's reappearance in court ▷ vb pay bail for (a person)

BAILED ▸ bail

BAILEE n person to whom the possession of goods is transferred under a bailment

BAILEES ▸ bailee

BAILER ▸ bail

BAILERS ▸ bail

BAILEY n outermost wall or court of a castle

BAILEYS ▸ bailey

BAILIE n (in Scotland) a municipal magistrate

BAILIES ▸ bailie

BAILIFF n sheriff's officer who serves writs and summonses

BAILING ▸ bail

BAILLI n magistrate

BAILLIE same as ▸ bailie

BAILLIS ▸ bailli

BAILOR n person who retains ownership of goods but entrusts possession of them to another under a bailment

BAILORS ▸ bailor

BAILOUT n instance of helping (a person, organization, etc) out of a predicament

BAILS ▸ bail

BAININ n Irish collarless jacket made of white wool

BAININS ▸ bainin

BAINITE n mixture of iron and iron carbide found in incompletely hardened steels, produced when austenite is transformed at temperatures between the pearlite and martensite ranges

BAIRN n child

BAIRNLY ▸ bairn

BAIRNS ▸ bairn

BAIT n piece of food on a hook or in a trap to attract fish or animals ▷ vb put a piece of food on or in (a hook or trap)

BAITED ▸ bait

BAITER ▸ bait

BAITERS ▸ bait

BAITH adj both

BAITING ▸ bait

BAITS ▸ bait

BAIZA n Omani unit of currency

BAIZAS ▸ baiza

BAIZE n woollen fabric used to cover billiard and card tables ▷ vb line or cover with such fabric

BAIZED ▸ baize

BAIZES ▸ baize

BAIZING ▸ baize

BAJADA n sloping surface formed from rock deposits

BAJADAS ▸ bajada

BAJAN n freshman at Aberdeen University

BAJANS ▸ bajan

BAJRA n Indian millet

BAJRAS ▸ bajra

BAJREE same as ▸ bajra

BAJREES ▸ bajree

BAJRI same as ▸ bajra

BAJRIS ▸ bajri

BAJU n Malay jacket

BAJUS ▸ baju

BAKE vb cook by dry heat as in an oven ▷ n party at which the main dish is baked

BAKED ▸ bake

BAKEN ▸ bake

BAKEOFF n baking competition

BAKER n person whose business is to make or sell bread, cakes, etc

BAKERS ▸ baker

BAKERY n place where bread, cakes, etc are baked or sold

BAKES ▸ bake

BAKGAT adj fine, excellent, marvellous

BAKING n process of cooking bread, cakes, etc ▷ adj (esp of weather) very hot and dry

BAKINGS ▸ baking

BAKKIE n small truck

BAKKIES ▸ bakkie

BAKLAVA n rich cake of Middle Eastern origin consisting of thin layers of pastry filled with nuts and honey

BAKLAWA same as ▸ baklava

BAKRA n White person, esp one from Britain ▷ adj (of people) White, esp British

BAKRAS ▸ bakra

BAL n balmoral

BALADIN n dancer

BALANCE n stability of mind or body ▷ vb weigh in a balance

BALAS n red variety of spinel, used as a gemstone

BALASES ▸ balas

BALATA n tropical American tree yielding a latex-like sap

BALATAS ▸ balata

BALBOA n standard currency unit of Panama, divided into 100 centesimos

BALBOAS ▸ balboa

BALCONY n platform on the outside of a building with a rail along the outer edge

BALD adj having little or no hair on the scalp ▷ vb make bald

BALDED ▸ bald

BALDER ▸ bald

BALDEST ▸ bald

BALDIE ▸ baldy

BALDIER ▸ baldy

BALDIES ▸ baldy

BALDING adj becoming bald

BALDISH ▸ bald

BALDLY ▸ bald

BALDRIC n wide silk sash or leather belt worn over the right shoulder to the left hip for carrying a sword, etc

BALDS ▸ bald

BALDY adj bald ▷ n bald person

BALE same as ▸ bail

BALED ▸ bale

BALEEN n whalebone

BALEENS ▸ baleen

BALEFUL adj vindictive or menacing

BALER ▸ bail

BALERS ▸ bail

BALES ▸ bale

BALING ▸ bale

BALISE n electronic beacon used on a railway

BALISES ▸ balise

BALISTA same as > ballista

BALK vb stop short, esp suddenly or unexpectedly ▷ n roughly squared heavy timber beam

BALKED ▸ balk

BALKER ▸ balk

BALKERS ▸ balk

BALKIER ▸ balky

BALKILY ▸ balky

BALKING ▸ balk

BALKS ▸ balk

BALKY adj inclined to stop abruptly and unexpectedly

BALL n round or nearly round object, esp one used in games ▷ vb form into a ball

B

B

BALLAD n narrative poem or song ▷ vb sing or write a ballad

BALLADE n verse form consisting of three stanzas and an envoy, all ending with the same line

BALLADS ▸ ballad

BALLAN n species of fish

BALLANS ▸ ballan

BALLANT vb write a ballad

BALLAST n substance, such as sand, used to stabilize a ship when it is not carrying cargo ▷ vb give stability or weight to

BALLAT vb write a ballad

BALLATS ▸ ballat

BALLED ▸ ball

BALLER n ball-game player

BALLERS ▸ baller

BALLET n classical style of expressive dancing based on conventional steps

BALLETS ▸ ballet

BALLIES ▸ bally

BALLING ▸ ball

BALLIUM same as ▸ bailey

BALLON n light, graceful quality

BALLONS ▸ ballon

BALLOON n inflatable rubber bag used as a plaything or decoration ▷ vb fly in a balloon

BALLOT n method of voting ▷ vb vote or ask for a vote from

BALLOTS ▸ ballot

BALLOW n heavy club

BALLOWS ▸ ballow

BALLUTE n inflatable balloon parachute

BALLY another word for ▸ ballyhoo

BALM n aromatic substance used for healing and soothing ▷ vb apply balm to

BALMED ▸ balm

BALMIER ▸ balmy

BALMILY ▸ balmy

BALMING ▸ balm

BALMS ▸ balm

BALMY adj (of weather) mild and pleasant

BALNEAL adj of or relating to baths or bathing

BALONEY n foolish talk; nonsense

BALOO n bear

BALOOS ▸ baloo

BALS ▸ bal

BALSA n very light wood from a tropical American tree

BALSAM n type of fragrant balm ▷ vb embalm

BALSAMS ▸ balsam

BALSAMY ▸ balsam

BALSAS ▸ balsa

BALTI n spicy Indian dish served in a metal dish

BALTIC adj very cold

BALTIS ▸ balti

BALU same as ▸ baloo

BALUN n device for coupling two electrical circuit elements, such as an aerial and its feeder cable, where one is balanced and the other is unbalanced

BALUNS ▸ balun

BALUS ▸ balu

BAM vb cheat

BAMBI n born-again middle-aged biker: an affluent middle-aged man who rides a powerful motorbike

BAMBINI ▸ bambino

BAMBINO n young child, esp an Italian one

BAMBIS ▸ bambi

BAMBOO n tall treelike tropical grass with hollow stems

BAMBOOS ▸ bamboo

BAMMED ▸ bam

BAMMER ▸ bam

BAMMERS ▸ bam

BAMMING ▸ bam

BAMPOT n fool

BAMPOTS ▸ bampot

BAMS ▸ bam

BAN vb prohibit or forbid officially ▷ n official prohibition

BANAK n type of Central American tree

BANAKS ▸ banak

BANAL adj ordinary and unoriginal

BANALER ▸ banal

BANALLY ▸ banal

BANANA n yellow crescent-shaped fruit

BANANAS adj crazy

BANC n as in **in banc** sitting as a full court

BANCO n call made in gambling games

BANCOS ▸ banco

BANCS ▸ banc

BAND n group of musicians playing together ▷ vb unite

BANDA n African thatched hut

BANDAGE n piece of material used to cover a wound or wrap an injured limb ▷ vb cover with a bandage

BANDAID adj (of a solution or remedy) temporary

BANDANA same as > bandanna

BANDAR n species of monkey

BANDARI n Indian English word for female monkey

BANDARS ▸ bandar

BANDAS ▸ banda

BANDBOX n lightweight usually cylindrical box for hats

BANDEAU n narrow ribbon worn round the head

BANDED ▸ band

BANDER ▸ band

BANDERS ▸ band

BANDH n (in India) a general strike

BANDHS ▸ bandh

BANDIED ▸ bandy

BANDIER ▸ bandy

BANDIES ▸ bandy

BANDING n practice of grouping schoolchildren according to ability to ensure a balanced intake at different levels of ability to secondary school

BANDIT n robber, esp a member of an armed gang

BANDITO n Mexican bandit

BANDITS ▸ bandit

BANDOG n ferocious dog

BANDOGS ▸ bandog

BANDOOK same as ▸ bundook

BANDORA same as ▸ bandore

BANDORE n 16th-century plucked musical instrument resembling a lute but larger and fitted with seven pairs of metal strings

BANDROL same as > banderole

BANDS ▸ band

BANDSAW n power saw with continuous blade

BANDURA n type of lute

BANDY adj having legs curved outwards at the knees ▷ vb exchange (words) in a heated manner

BANE n person or thing that causes misery or distress ▷ vb cause harm or distress to (someone)

BANED ▶ bane

BANEFUL adj destructive, poisonous, or fatal

BANES ▶ bane

BANG vb make a short explosive noise

BANGED ▶ bang

BANGER n old decrepit car

BANGERS ▶ banger

BANGING ▶ bang

BANGKOK n type of straw hat

BANGLE n bracelet worn round the arm or the ankle

BANGLED ▶ bangle

BANGLES ▶ bangle

BANGS ▶ bang

BANI ▶ ban

BANIA same as ▶ banyan

BANIAN same as ▶ banyan

BANIANS ▶ banian

BANIAS ▶ bania

BANING ▶ bane

BANISH vb send (someone) into exile

BANJAX vb ruin; destroy
| Meaning to ruin or confound, this is a great word to remember, with its high-scoring combination of J and X

BANJO n guitar-like musical instrument with a circular body

BANJOES ▶ banjo

BANJOS ▶ banjo

BANK n institution offering services such as the safekeeping and lending of money ▷ vb deposit (cash or cheques) in a bank

BANKED ▶ bank

BANKER n manager or owner of a bank

BANKERS ▶ banker

BANKET n gold-bearing conglomerate found in South Africa

BANKETS ▶ banket

BANKING same as ▶ bank

BANKIT same as
> banquette

BANKITS ▶ bankit

BANKS ▶ bank

BANKSIA n Australian evergreen tree or shrub

BANNED ▶ ban

BANNER n long strip of cloth displaying a slogan, advertisement, etc ▷ vb (of a newspaper headline) to display (a story) prominently ▷ adj outstandingly successful

BANNERS ▶ banner

BANNET n bonnet

BANNETS ▶ bannet

BANNING ▶ ban

BANNOCK n round flat cake made from oatmeal or barley

BANNS pl n public declaration, esp in a church, of an intended marriage

BANOFFI same as
> banoffee

BANQUET n elaborate formal dinner ▷ vb hold or take part in a banquet

BANS same as ▶ banns

BANSELA same as ▶ bonsela

BANSHEE n (in Irish folklore) female spirit whose wailing warns of a coming death

BANSHIE same as ▶ banshee

BANT n string ▷ vb tie with string

BANTAM n small breed of chicken

BANTAMS ▶ bantam

BANTED ▶ bant

BANTENG n wild ox

BANTER vb tease jokingly ▷ n teasing or joking conversation

BANTERS ▶ banter

BANTIES ▶ banty

BANTING ▶ bant

BANTS ▶ bant

BANTY n bantam

BANYA n traditional Russian steam bath

BANYAN n Indian tree whose branches grow down into the soil forming additional trunks

BANYANS ▶ banyan

BANYAS ▶ banya

BANZAI interj patriotic cheer, battle cry, or salutation

BANZAIS ▶ banzai

BAOBAB n African tree with a thick trunk and angular branches

BAOBABS ▶ baobab

BAP n large soft bread roll

BAPS ▶ bap

BAPTISE same as ▶ baptize

BAPTISM n Christian religious ceremony in which a person is immersed in or sprinkled with water as a sign of being cleansed from sin and accepted into the Church

BAPTIST n one who baptizes

BAPTIZE vb perform baptism on

BAPU n spiritual father

BAPUS ▶ bapu

BAR n rigid usually straight length of metal, wood, etc, that is longer than it is wide or thick, used esp as a barrier or as a structural or mechanical part ▷ vb fasten or secure with a bar

BARACAN same as
> barracan

BARAZA n place where public meetings are held

BARAZAS ▶ baraza

BARB n cutting remark ▷ vb provide with a barb or barbs

BARBAL adj of a beard

BARBATE adj having tufts of long hairs

BARBE n Waldensian missionary

BARBED ▶ barb

BARBEL n long thin growth that hangs from the jaws of certain fishes, such as the carp

BARBELL n long metal rod to which heavy discs are attached at each end for weightlifting

BARBELS ▶ barbel

BARBER n person who cuts men's hair and shaves beards ▷ vb cut the hair of

BARBERS ▶ barber

BARBES ▶ barbe

BARBET n type of small tropical brightly coloured bird with short weak wings and a sharp stout bill

BARBETS ▶ barbet

BARBIE short for > barbecue

BARBIES ▶ barbie

BARBING ▶ barb

BARBOLA n small models of flowers, etc made from plastic paste

BARBS ▶ barb

BARBULE n very small barb

BARBUT n open-faced helmet

BARBUTS ▶ barbut

BARBY > barbecue

B

BARCA n boat
BARCAS ▸ barca
BARCHAN n crescent-shaped shifting sand dune, convex on the windward side and steeper and concave on the leeward
BARCODE n machine-readable code printed on goods
BARD n poet ▷ vb place a piece of pork fat on
BARDASH n kept boy in a homosexual relationship
BARDE same as ▸ bard
BARDED ▸ barde
BARDES ▸ barde
BARDIC ▸ bard
BARDIE n type of Australian grub
BARDIER ▸ bard
BARDIES ▸ bardie
BARDING ▸ bard
BARDISM ▸ bard
BARDO n (in Tibetan Buddhism) the state of the soul between its death and its rebirth
BARDOS ▸ bardo
BARDS ▸ bard
BARDY ▸ bard
BARE adj unclothed, naked ▷ vb uncover
BARED ▸ bare
BAREFIT > barefoot
BAREGE n light silky gauze fabric made of wool ▷ adj made of such a fabric
BAREGES ▸ barege
BARELY adv only just
BARER ▸ bare
BARES ▸ bare
BAREST ▸ bare
BARF vb vomit ▷ n act of vomiting
BARFED ▸ barf
BARFING ▸ barf
BARFLY n person who frequents bars
BARFS ▸ barf
BARFUL adj presenting difficulties
BARGAIN n agreement establishing what each party will give, receive, or perform in a transaction ▷ vb negotiate the terms of an agreement
BARGE n flat-bottomed boat used to transport freight ▷ vb push violently
BARGED ▸ barge
BARGEE n person in charge

of a barge
BARGEES ▸ bargee
BARGES ▸ barge
BARGEST same as > barghest
BARGING ▸ barge
BARGOON Canadian word for ▸ bargain
BARHOP vb visit several bars in succession
BARHOPS ▸ barhop
BARIC adj of or containing barium
BARILLA n impure mixture of sodium carbonate and sodium sulphate obtained from the ashes of certain plants, such as the saltworts
BARING ▸ bare
BARISH adj quite thinly covered
BARISTA n person who makes and sells coffee in a coffee bar
BARITE n colourless or white mineral consisting of barium sulphate in orthorhombic crystalline form, occurring in sedimentary rocks and with sulphide ores: a source of barium
BARITES ▸ barite
BARIUM n soft white metallic element
BARIUMS ▸ barium
BARK vb (of a dog) make its typical loud abrupt cry
BARKAN same as ▸ barchan
BARKANS ▸ barkan
BARKED ▸ bark
BARKEEP n barkeeper
BARKEN vb become dry with a bark-like outer layer
BARKENS ▸ barken
BARKER n person at a fairground who calls loudly to passers-by in order to attract customers
BARKERS ▸ barker
BARKHAN same as ▸ barchan
BARKIER ▸ barky
BARKING adj mad ▷ adv extremely
BARKS ▸ bark
BARKY adj having the texture or appearance of bark
BARLESS ▸ bar
BARLEY n tall grasslike plant cultivated for grain

▷ sentence substitute cry for truce or respite from the rules of a game
BARLEYS ▸ barley
BARLOW n type of strong knife
BARLOWS ▸ barlow
BARM n yeasty froth on fermenting malt liquors
BARMAID n woman who serves in a pub
BARMAN same as > bartender
BARMEN ▸ barman
BARMIE same as ▸ barmy
BARMIER ▸ barmy
BARMKIN n protective wall around castle
BARMPOT n foolish or deranged person
BARMS ▸ barm
BARMY adj insane
BARN n large building on a farm used for storing grain ▷ vb keep in a barn
BARNED ▸ barn
BARNET n hair
BARNETS ▸ barnet
BARNEY n noisy fight or argument ▷ vb argue or quarrel
BARNEYS ▸ barney
BARNIER ▸ barny
BARNING ▸ barn
BARNS ▸ barn
BARNY adj reminiscent of a barn
BAROCCO same as ▸ baroque
BAROCK same as ▸ baroque
BAROCKS ▸ barock
BAROLO n red Italian wine
BAROLOS ▸ barolo
BARON n member of the lowest rank of nobility
BARONET n commoner who holds the lowest hereditary British title
BARONG n broad-bladed cleaver-like knife used in the Philippines
BARONGS ▸ barong
BARONNE n baroness
BARONS ▸ baron
BARONY n domain or rank of a baron
BAROQUE n highly ornate style of art, architecture, and music from the late 16th to the early 18th century ▷ adj ornate in style
BARP n hillock or bank of stones

B

BARPS ▸ barp

BARQUE n sailing ship, esp one with three masts

BARQUES ▸ barque

BARRA n barramundi

BARRACE n record of teams entering a sports contest

BARRACK vb criticize loudly or shout against (a team or speaker)

BARRAGE n continuous delivery of questions, complaints, etc ▸ vb attack or confront with a barrage

BARRAS ▸ barra

BARRAT n fraudulent dealings

BARRATS ▸ barrat

BARRE n rail at hip height used for ballet practice ▸ vb execute guitar chords by laying the index finger over some or all of the strings so that the pitch of each stopped string is simultaneously raised ▸ adv by using the barre

BARRED ▸ bar

BARREED ▸ barree

BARREL n cylindrical container with rounded sides and flat ends ▸ vb put in a barrel

BARRELS ▸ barrel

BARREN adj (of a woman or female animal) incapable of producing offspring

BARRENS pl n (in North America) a stretch of usually level land that is sparsely vegetated or barren

BARRES ▸ barre

BARRET n small flat cap resembling a biretta

BARRETS ▸ barret

BARRICO n small container for liquids

BARRIE adj very good

BARRIER n anything that prevents access, progress, or union ▸ vb create or form a barrier

BARRIES ▸ barry

BARRING ▸ bar

BARRIO n Spanish-speaking quarter in a town or city, esp in the US

BARRIOS ▸ barrio

BARRO adj embarrassing

BARROOM n room or building where alcoholic drinks are served over a counter

BARROW n wheelbarrow

BARROWS ▸ barrow

BARRY n mistake or blunder

BARS ▸ bar

BARTEND vb serve drinks from a bar

BARTER vb trade (goods) in exchange for other goods ▸ n trade by the exchange of goods

BARTERS ▸ barter

BARTON n farmyard

BARTONS ▸ barton

BARTSIA n type of semiparasitic plant

BARWARE n glasses, etc used in a bar

BARWOOD n red wood from small African tree

BARYE n unit of pressure in the cgs system equal to one dyne per square centimetre. 1 barye is equivalent to 1 microbar

BARYES ▸ barye

BARYON n elementary particle that has a mass greater than or equal to that of the proton

BARYONS ▸ baryon

BARYTA same as ▸ barite

BARYTAS ▸ baryta

BARYTE same as ▸ baryta

BARYTES ▸ baryte

BARYTIC ▸ baryta

BARYTON n bass viol with sympathetic strings as well as its six main strings

BAS ▸ ba

BASAL adj of, at, or constituting a base

BASALLY ▸ basal

BASALT n dark volcanic rock

BASALTS ▸ basalt

BASAN n sheepskin tanned in bark

BASANS ▸ basan

BASANT n Pakistani spring festival

BASANTS ▸ basant

BASCULE n drawbridge that operates by a counterbalanced weight

BASE n bottom or supporting part of anything ▸ vb use as a basis (for) ▸ adj dishonourable or immoral

BASED ▸ base

BASEEJ pl n Iranian volunteer militia

BASELY ▸ base

BASEMAN n fielder positioned near a base

BASEMEN ▸ baseman

BASEN Spencerian spelling of ▸ basin

BASENJI n small smooth-haired breed of dog of African origin having a tightly curled tail and an inability to bark

BASER ▸ base

BASES ▸ basis

BASEST ▸ base

BASH vb hit violently or forcefully ▸ n heavy blow

BASHAW n important or pompous person

BASHAWS ▸ bashaw

BASHED ▸ bash

BASHER ▸ bash

BASHERS ▸ bash

BASHES ▸ bash

BASHFUL adj shy or modest

BASHING ▸ bash

BASHLIK n Caucasian hood

BASHLYK same as ▸ bashlik

BASHO n grand tournament in sumo wrestling

BASIC adj of or forming a base or basis ▸ n fundamental principle, fact, etc

BASICS ▸ basic

BASIDIA > basidium

BASIFY vb make basic

BASIJ ▸ baseej

BASIL n aromatic herb used in cooking

BASILAR adj of or situated at a base

BASILIC > basilica

BASILS ▸ basil

BASIN n round open container

BASINAL ▸ basin

BASINED ▸ basin

BASINET n close-fitting medieval helmet of light steel usually with a visor

BASING ▸ base

BASINS ▸ basin

BASION n (in anatomy) midpoint on the forward border of the foramen magnum

BASIONS ▸ basion

BASIS n fundamental principles etc from which something is started or developed

BASK vb lie in or be exposed to something, esp pleasant warmth

BASKED ▸ bask

B

BASKET n container made of interwoven strips of wood or cane

BASKETS ▸ basket

BASKING ▸ bask

BASKS ▸ bask

BASMATI n variety of long-grain rice with slender aromatic grains, used for savoury dishes

BASNET same as ▸ basinet

BASNETS ▸ basnet

BASOCHE n society of medieval French lawyers who performed comic plays

BASON same as ▸ basin

BASONS ▸ bason

BASQUE n tight-fitting bodice for women

BASQUED ▸ basque

BASQUES ▸ basque

BASS vb speak or sing in a low pitch

BASSE same as ▸ bass

BASSED ▸ bass

BASSER ▸ bass

BASSES ▸ bass

BASSEST ▸ bass

BASSET n long low smooth-haired breed of hound with short strong legs and long ears ▷ vb outcrop

BASSETS ▸ basset

BASSETT same as ▸ basset

BASSI ▸ basso

BASSIER ▸ bassy

BASSING ▸ bass

BASSIST n player of a double bass, esp in a jazz band

BASSLY ▸ bass

BASSO n singer with a bass voice

BASSOON n low-pitched woodwind instrument

BASSOS ▸ basso

BASSY adj manifesting strong bass tones

BAST n fibrous material obtained from the phloem of jute, hemp, flax, lime, etc, used for making rope, matting, etc

BASTA interj enough; stop

BASTE vb moisten (meat) during cooking with hot fat

BASTED ▸ baste

BASTER ▸ baste

BASTERS ▸ baste

BASTES ▸ baste

BASTI n (in India) a slum inhabited by poor people

BASTIDE n small isolated house in France

BASTILE same as ▸ bastille

BASTING n loose temporary stitches

BASTION n projecting part of a fortification

BASTIS ▸ basti

BASTLE n fortified house

BASTLES ▸ bastle

BASTO n ace of clubs in certain card games

BASTOS ▸ basto

BASTS ▸ bast

BASUCO n cocaine-based drug

BASUCOS ▸ basuco

BAT n any of various types of club used to hit the ball in certain sports ▷ vb strike with or as if with a bat

BATABLE ▸ bat

BATATA n sweet potato

BATATAS ▸ batata

BATAVIA n variety of lettuce with smooth pale green leaves

BATBOY n boy who works at baseball games

BATBOYS ▸ batboy

BATCH n group of people or things dealt with at the same time ▷ vb group (items) for efficient processing

BATCHED ▸ batch

BATCHER ▸ batch

BATCHES ▸ batch

BATE vb (of hawks) to jump violently from a perch or the falconer's fist, often hanging from the leash while struggling to escape

BATEAU n light flat-bottomed boat used on rivers in Canada and the northern US

BATEAUX ▸ bateau

BATED ▸ bate

BATES ▸ bate

BATFISH n type of angler fish with a flattened scaleless body

BATFOWL vb catch birds by temporarily blinding them with light

BATGIRL n girl who works at baseball games

BATH n large container in which to wash the body ▷ vb wash in a bath

BATHE vb swim in open water for pleasure

BATHED ▸ bathe

BATHER ▸ bathe

BATHERS pl n swimming costume

BATHES ▸ bathe

BATHING ▸ bathe

BATHMAT n mat to stand on after a bath

BATHMIC > bathmism

BATHOS n sudden ludicrous change in speech or writing from a serious subject to a trivial one

BATHS ▸ bath

BATHTUB n bath, esp one not permanently fixed

BATHYAL adj denoting or relating to an ocean depth of between 200 and 2000 metres (about 100 and 1000 fathoms), corresponding to the continental slope

BATIK n process of printing fabric using wax to cover areas not to be dyed ▷ vb treat material with this process

BATIKED ▸ batik

BATIKS ▸ batik

BATING ▸ bate

BATISTE n fine plain-weave cotton fabric: used esp for shirts and dresses

BATLER n flat piece of wood for beating clothes, etc before washing

BATLERS ▸ batler

BATLET same as ▸ batler

BATLETS ▸ batlet

BATLIKE ▸ bat

BATMAN n officer's servant in the armed forces

BATMEN ▸ batman

BATON n thin stick used by the conductor of an orchestra ▷ vb carry or wave a baton

BATONED ▸ baton

BATONS ▸ baton

BATOON same as ▸ baton

BATOONS ▸ batoon

BATS ▸ bat

BATSMAN n person who bats or specializes in batting

BATSMEN ▸ batsman

BATT ▸ bat

BATTA n soldier's allowance

BATTAS ▸ batta

BATTEAU same as ▸ bateau

BATTED ▸ bat

BATTEL vb make fertile

BATTELS ▸ battel

BATTEN n strip of wood fixed to something, esp to hold it in place ▷ vb strengthen or fasten with battens

BATTENS ▸ batten

BATTER vb hit repeatedly ▷ n mixture of flour, eggs, and milk, used in cooking

BATTERO n heavy club

BATTERS ▸ batter

BATTERY n device that produces electricity in a torch, radio, etc ▷ adj kept in series of cages for intensive rearing

BATTIER ▸ batty

BATTIES ▸ batty

BATTIK same as ▸ batik

BATTIKS ▸ battik

BATTILL old spelling of ▸ battle

BATTING ▸ bat

BATTLE n fight between large armed forces ▷ vb struggle

BATTLED ▸ battle

BATTLER ▸ battle

BATTLES ▸ battle

BATTS ▸ batt

BATTU adj (in ballet) involving a beating movement

BATTUE n beating of woodland or cover to force game to flee in the direction of hunters

BATTUES ▸ battue

BATTUTA n (in music) a beat

BATTUTO n (in Italian cookery) selection of chopped herbs

BATTY adj eccentric or crazy ▷ n bottom; bum

BATWING adj shaped like the wings of a bat, as a black tie, collar, etc

BAUBEE same as ▸ bawbee

BAUBEES ▸ baubee

BAUBLE n trinket of little value

BAUBLES ▸ bauble

BAUCHLE vb shuffle along

BAUD n unit used to measure the speed of transmission of electronic data

BAUDRIC same as ▸ baldric

BAUDS ▸ baud

BAUERA n small evergreen Australian shrub

BAUERAS ▸ bauera

BAUK same as ▸ balk

BAUKED ▸ bauk

BAUKING ▸ bauk

BAUKS ▸ bauk

BAULK ▸ balk

BAULKED ▸ balk

BAULKER ▸ balk

BAULKS ▸ balk

BAULKY same as ▸ balky

BAUR n humorous anecdote; joke

BAURS ▸ baur

BAUSOND adj (of animal) dappled with white spots

BAUXITE n claylike substance that is the chief source of aluminium

BAVIN n impure limestone

BAVINS ▸ bavin

BAWBEE n former Scottish silver coin

BAWBEES ▸ bawbee

BAWBLE same as ▸ bauble

BAWBLES ▸ bawble

BAWCOCK n fine fellow

BAWD n person who runs a brothel, esp a woman

BAWDIER ▸ bawdy

BAWDIES ▸ bawdy

BAWDILY ▸ bawdy

BAWDKIN same as > baldachin

BAWDRIC n heavy belt to support sword

BAWDRY n obscene talk or language

BAWDS ▸ bawd

BAWDY adj (of writing etc) containing humorous references to sex ▷ n obscenity or eroticism, esp in writing or drama

BAWL vb shout or weep noisily ▷ n loud shout or cry

BAWLED ▸ bawl

BAWLER ▸ bawl

BAWLERS ▸ bawl

BAWLEY n small fishing boat

BAWLEYS ▸ bawley

BAWLING ▸ bawl

BAWLS ▸ bawl

BAWN n fortified enclosure

BAWNEEN same as ▸ bainin

BAWNS ▸ bawn

BAWR same as ▸ baur

BAWRS ▸ bawr

BAWSUNT adj black and white in colour

BAWTIE n name for a dog

BAWTIES ▸ bawtie

BAWTY same as ▸ bawtie

BAXTER old variant of ▸ baker

BAXTERS ▸ baxter

BAY n wide semicircular indentation of a shoreline ▷ vb howl in deep tones

BAYAMO n Cuban strong wind

BAYAMOS ▸ bayamo

BAYARD n bay horse

BAYARDS ▸ bayard

BAYE vb bathe

BAYED ▸ bay

BAYES ▸ baye

BAYING ▸ bay

BAYLE n barrier

BAYLES ▸ bayle

BAYMAN n fisherman

BAYMEN ▸ bayman

BAYONET n sharp blade that can be fixed to the end of a rifle ▷ vb stab with a bayonet

BAYOU n (in the southern US) a sluggish marshy tributary of a lake or river

BAYOUS ▸ bayou

BAYS ▸ bay

BAYT same as ▸ bate

BAYTED ▸ bayt

BAYTING ▸ bayt

BAYTS ▸ bayt

BAYWOOD n light soft wood of a tropical American mahogany tree

BAYYAN n Islamic declaration

BAYYANS ▸ bayyan

BAZAAR n sale in aid of charity

BAZAARS ▸ bazaar

BAZAR same as ▸ bazaar

BAZARS ▸ bazar

BAZAZZ same as ▸ pizzazz

BAZOO a US slang word for ▸ mouth

BAZOOKA n portable rocket launcher that fires an armour-piercing projectile

BAZOOS ▸ bazoo

BAZOUKI same as > bouzouki

BAZZAZZ ▸ pizzazz

BE vb exist or live

BEACH n area of sand or pebbles on a shore ▷ vb run or haul (a boat) onto a beach

BEACHED ▸ beach

BEACHES ▸ beach

BEACHY adj with gentle sandy slopes

BEACON n fire or light on a hill or tower, used as a

B

warning ▷ *vb* guide or warn
BEACONS ▸ **beacon**
BEAD *n* small piece of plastic, wood, etc, pierced for threading on a string to form a necklace etc ▷ *vb* decorate with beads
BEADED ▸ **bead**
BEADER *n* person making things with beads
BEADERS ▸ **beader**
BEADIER ▸ **beady**
BEADILY ▸ **beady**
BEADING *n* strip of moulding used for edging furniture
BEADLE *n* (formerly) a minor parish official who acted as an usher
BEADLES ▸ **beadle**
BEADMAN *same as* > **beadsman**
BEADMEN ▸ **beadman**
BEADS ▸ **bead**
BEADY *adj* small, round, and glittering
BEAGLE *n* small hound with short legs and drooping ears ▷ *vb* hunt with beagles, normally on foot
BEAGLED ▸ **beagle**
BEAGLER *n* person who hunts with beagles
BEAGLES ▸ **beagle**
BEAK *n* projecting horny jaws of a bird ▷ *vb* strike with the beak
BEAKED ▸ **beak**
BEAKER *n* large drinking cup
BEAKERS ▸ **beaker**
BEAKIER ▸ **beak**
BEAKS ▸ **beak**
BEAKY ▸ **beak**
BEAM *n* broad smile ▷ *vb* smile broadly
BEAMED ▸ **beam**
BEAMER *n* full-pitched ball bowled at the batsman's head
BEAMERS ▸ **beamer**
BEAMIER ▸ **beam**
BEAMILY ▸ **beam**
BEAMING ▸ **beam**
BEAMISH *adj* smiling
BEAMLET *n* small beam
BEAMS ▸ **beam**
BEAMY ▸ **beam**
BEAN *n* seed or pod of various plants, eaten as a vegetable or used to make coffee etc ▷ *vb* strike on the head

BEANBAG *n* small cloth bag filled with dried beans and thrown in games
BEANED ▸ **bean**
BEANERY *n* cheap restaurant
BEANIE *n* close-fitting woollen hat
BEANIES ▸ **beany**
BEANING ▸ **bean**
BEANO *n* celebration or party
BEANOS ▸ **beano**
BEANS ▸ **bean**
BEANY *same as* ▸ **beanie**
BEAR *vb* support or hold up (something) ▷ *n* type of omnivorous mammal with a large head, long shaggy coat, and strong claws
BEARCAT *n* lesser panda
BEARD *n* hair growing on the lower parts of a man's face ▷ *vb* oppose boldly
BEARDED ▸ **beard**
BEARDIE *n* another name for bearded loach
BEARDS ▸ **beard**
BEARDY *adj* having a beard
BEARE *same as* ▸ **bear**
BEARED ▸ **bear**
BEARER *n* person who carries, presents, or upholds something
BEARERS ▸ **bearer**
BEARES ▸ **beare**
BEARHUG *n* wrestling hold in which the arms are locked tightly round an opponent's chest and arms
BEARING ▸ **bear**
BEARISH *adj* like a bear
BEARS ▸ **bear**
BEAST *n* large wild animal ▷ *vb* torture someone using excessive physical exercise
BEASTED ▸ **beast**
BEASTIE *n* small animal
BEASTLY *adj* unpleasant or disagreeable ▷ *adv* extremely
BEASTS ▸ **beast**
BEAT *vb* strike with or as if with a series of violent blows; dash or pound repeatedly (against) ▷ *n* stroke or blow ▷ *adj* totally exhausted
BEATBOX *n* drum machine simulated by a human voice
BEATEN ▸ **beat**
BEATER *n* device used for beating

BEATERS ▸ **beater**
BEATH *vb* dry; heat
BEATHED ▸ **beath**
BEATHS ▸ **beath**
BEATIER ▸ **beaty**
BEATIFY *vb* declare (a dead person) to be among the blessed in heaven: the first step towards canonization
BEATING ▸ **beat**
BEATNIK *n* young person in the late 1950s who rebelled against conventional attitudes etc
BEATS ▸ **beat**
BEATY *adj* (of music) having a strong rhythm
BEAU *n* boyfriend or admirer
BEAUFET *same as* ▸ **buffet**
BEAUFIN *same as* ▸ **biffin**
BEAUISH *adj* vain and showy
BEAUS ▸ **beau**
BEAUT *n* person or thing that is outstanding or distinctive ▷ *adj* good or excellent ▷ *interj* exclamation of joy or pleasure
BEAUTS ▸ **beaut**
BEAUTY *n* combination of all the qualities of a person or thing that delight the senses and mind ▷ *interj* expression of approval or agreement ▷ *vb* make beautiful
BEAUX ▸ **beau**
BEAVER *n* amphibious rodent with a big flat tail ▷ *vb* work steadily or assiduously
BEAVERS ▸ **beaver**
BEAVERY *n* place for keeping beavers
BEBEERU *n* tropical American tree
BEBLOOD *vb* stain with blood
BEBOP *same as* ▸ **bop**
BEBOPS ▸ **bebop**
BEBUNG *n* vibrato effect on clavichord
BEBUNGS ▸ **bebung**
BECALL *vb* use insulting words about someone
BECALLS ▸ **becall**
BECALM *vb* make calm
BECALMS ▸ **becalm**
BECAME ▸ **become**
BECAP *vb* put cap on
BECAPS ▸ **becap**
BECASSE *n* woodcock**

BECAUSE *conj* on account of the fact that; on account of being; since

BECHALK *vb* mark with chalk

BECHARM *vb* delight

BECK *n* stream ▷ *vb* attract someone's attention by nodding or gesturing

BECKE *same as* ▶ **beak**

BECKED ▶ **beck**

BECKES ▶ **becke**

BECKET *n* clevis forming part of one end of a sheave, used for securing standing lines by means of a thimble

BECKETS ▶ **becket**

BECKING ▶ **beck**

BECKON *vb* summon with a gesture ▷ *n* summoning gesture

BECKONS ▶ **beckon**

BECKS ▶ **beck**

BECLASP *vb* embrace

BECLOAK *vb* dress in cloak

BECLOG *vb* put clogs on

BECLOGS ▶ **beclog**

BECLOUD *vb* cover or obscure with a cloud

BECLOWN *vb* clown around

BECOME *vb* come to be

BECOMES ▶ **become**

BECRAWL *vb* crawl all over

BECRIME *vb* make someone guilty of a crime

BECROWD *vb* crowd with something

BECRUST *vb* cover with crust

BECURL *vb* curl

BECURLS ▶ **becurl**

BECURSE *vb* curse

BECURST ▶ **becurse**

BED *n* piece of furniture on which to sleep ▷ *vb* plant in a bed

BEDAD *interj* by God (oath)

BEDAMN *vb* damn

BEDAMNS ▶ **bedamn**

BEDASH *vb* sprinkle with liquid

BEDAUB *vb* smear with something sticky or dirty

BEDAUBS ▶ **bedaub**

BEDAWIN *same as* ▶ **bedouin**

BEDAZE *vb* daze

BEDAZED ▶ **bedaze**

BEDAZES ▶ **bedaze**

BEDBATH *n* washing of a sick person in bed

BEDBUG *n* small blood-sucking wingless insect that infests dirty houses

BEDBUGS ▶ **bedbug**

BEDDED ▶ **bed**

BEDDER *n* (at some universities) a college servant employed to keep students' rooms in order

BEDDERS ▶ **bedder**

BEDDING ▶ **bed**

BEDE *n* prayer

BEDECK *vb* cover with decorations

BEDECKS ▶ **bedeck**

BEDEL *archaic spelling of* ▶ **beadle**

BEDELL ▶ **beadle**

BEDELLS ▶ **bedell**

BEDELS ▶ **bedel**

BEDEMAN *same as* ▶ **beadsman**

BEDEMEN ▶ **bedeman**

BEDERAL *same as* ▶ **bedral**

BEDES ▶ **bede**

BEDEVIL *vb* harass, confuse, or torment

BEDEW *vb* wet or cover with or as if with drops of dew

BEDEWED ▶ **bedew**

BEDEWS ▶ **bedew**

BEDFAST *an archaic word for* ▶ **bedridden**

BEDGOWN *n* night dress

BEDHEAD *n* untidy state of hair, esp caused by sleeping

BEDIDE ▶ **bedye**

BEDIGHT *vb* array or adorn ▷ *adj* adorned or bedecked

BEDIM *vb* make dim or obscure

BEDIMS ▶ **bedim**

BEDIRTY *vb* make dirty

BEDIZEN *vb* dress or decorate gaudily or tastelessly

BEDLAM *n* noisy confused situation

BEDLAMP *n* bedside light

BEDLAMS ▶ **bedlam**

BEDLESS ▶ **bed**

BEDLIKE *adj* like a bed

BEDMATE *n* person who shares a bed

BEDOUIN *n* member of any of the nomadic tribes of Arabs inhabiting the deserts of Arabia, Jordan, and Syria, as well as parts of the Sahara

BEDPAN *n* shallow bowl used as a toilet by bedridden people

BEDPANS ▶ **bedpan**

BEDPOST *n* vertical support on a bedstead

BEDRAIL *n* rail or board along the side of a bed that connects the headboard with the footboard

BEDRAL *n* minor church official

BEDRALS ▶ **bedral**

BEDRAPE *vb* adorn

BEDRID *same as* ▶ **bedridden**

BEDRITE ▶ **bedright**

BEDROCK *n* solid rock beneath the surface soil

BEDROLL *n* portable roll of bedding, such as a sleeping bag, used esp for sleeping in the open

BEDROOM *n* room used for sleeping ▷ *adj* containing references to sex

BEDROP *vb* drop on

BEDROPS ▶ **bedrop**

BEDROPT ▶ **bedrop**

BEDRUG *vb* drug excessively

BEDRUGS ▶ **bedrug**

BEDS ▶ **bed**

BEDSIDE *n* area beside a bed ▷ *adj* placed at or near the side of the bed

BEDSIT *n* furnished sitting room with a bed

BEDSITS ▶ **bedsit**

BEDSORE *n* ulcer on the skin, caused by a lengthy period of lying in bed due to illness

BEDTICK *n* case containing stuffing in mattress

BEDTIME *n* time when one usually goes to bed

BEDU *adj* relating to beduins

BEDUCK *vb* duck under water

BEDUCKS ▶ **beduck**

BEDUIN *same as* ▶ **bedouin**

BEDUINS ▶ **beduin**

BEDUMB *vb* make dumb

BEDUMBS ▶ **bedumb**

BEDUNCE *vb* cause to look or feel foolish

BEDUNG *vb* spread with dung

BEDUNGS ▶ **bedung**

BEDUST *vb* cover with dust

BEDUSTS ▶ **bedust**

BEDWARD *adj* towards bed

BEDWARF *vb* hamper growth of

BEDYDE ▶ **bedye**

BEDYE *vb* dye

B

BEDYED ▸ bedye

BEDYES ▸ bedye

BEE n insect that makes wax and honey

BEEBEE n air rifle

BEEBEES ▸ beebee

BEECH n tree with a smooth greyish bark

BEECHEN ▸ beech

BEECHES ▸ beech

BEECHY ▸ beech

BEEDI n Indian cigarette

BEEDIE ▸ beedi

BEEDIES ▸ beedi

BEEF n flesh of a cow, bull, or ox ▷ vb complain

BEEFALO n cross between cow and buffalo

BEEFED ▸ beef

BEEFIER ▸ beefy

BEEFILY ▸ beefy

BEEFING ▸ beef

BEEFS ▸ beef

BEEFY adj like beef

BEEGAH same as ▸ bigha

BEEGAHS ▸ beegah

BEEHIVE n structure in which bees live

BEELIKE ▸ bee

BEELINE n most direct route between two places ▷ adj make a beeline for (something)

BEEN ▸ be

BEENAH n understanding; insight

BEENAHS ▸ beenah

BEENTO n person who has resided in Britain, esp during part of his education ▷ adj of, relating to, or characteristic of such a person

BEENTOS ▸ beento

BEEP n high-pitched sound, like that of a car horn ▷ vb (cause to) make this noise

BEEPED ▸ beep

BEEPER ▸ beep

BEEPERS ▸ beep

BEEPING ▸ beep

BEEPS ▸ beep

BEER n alcoholic drink brewed from malt and hops

BEERAGE n brewing industry

BEERIER ▸ beery

BEERILY ▸ beery

BEERS ▸ beer

BEERY adj smelling or tasting of beer

BEES ▸ bee

BEESOME same as ▸ bisson

BEESWAX n wax secreted by bees, used in polishes etc ▷ vb polish with such wax

BEET n plant with an edible root and leaves ▷ vb improve or make better

BEETED ▸ beet

BEETFLY n type of fly which is a common pest of beets and mangel-wurzels

BEETING ▸ beet

BEETLE n insect with a hard wing cover on its back ▷ adj overhang or jut ▷ vb scuttle or scurry

BEETLED ▸ beetle

BEETLER n one who operates a beetling machine

BEETLES ▸ beetle

BEETS ▸ beet

BEEVES ▸ beef

BEEYARD n place where bees are kept

BEEZER n person or chap ▷ adj excellent

BEEZERS ▸ beezer

BEFALL vb happen to (someone)

BEFALLS ▸ befall

BEFANA n Italian gift-bearing good fairy

BEFANAS ▸ befana

BEFELD ▸ befall

BEFELL ▸ befall

BEFFANA same as ▸ befana

BEFIT vb be appropriate or suitable for

BEFITS ▸ befit

BEFLAG vb decorate with flags

BEFLAGS ▸ beflag

BEFLEA vb infect with fleas

BEFLEAS ▸ beflea

BEFLECK vb fleck

BEFLUM vb fool; deceive

BEFLUMS ▸ beflum

BEFOAM vb cover with foam

BEFOAMS ▸ befoam

BEFOG vb surround with fog

BEFOGS ▸ befog

BEFOOL vb make a fool of

BEFOOLS ▸ befool

BEFORE adv indicating something earlier in time, in front of, or preferred to ▷ prep preceding in space or time

BEFOUL vb make dirty or foul

BEFOULS ▸ befoul

BEFRET vb fret about something

BEFRETS ▸ befret

BEG vb solicit (money, food, etc), esp in the street

BEGAD interj emphatic exclamation

BEGALL vb make sore by rubbing

BEGALLS ▸ begall

BEGAN ▸ begin

BEGAR n compulsory labour

BEGARS ▸ begar

BEGAT ▸ beget

BEGAZE vb gaze about or around

BEGAZED ▸ begaze

BEGAZES ▸ begaze

BEGEM vb decorate with gems

BEGEMS ▸ begem

BEGET vb cause or create

BEGETS ▸ beget

BEGGAR n person who begs, esp one who lives by begging ▷ vb be beyond the resources of

BEGGARS ▸ beggar

BEGGARY n extreme poverty or need

BEGGED ▸ beg

BEGGING ▸ beg

BEGHARD n member of a Christian brotherhood that was founded in Flanders in the 13th century and followed a life based on that of the Beguines

BEGIFT vb give gift or gifts to

BEGIFTS ▸ begift

BEGILD vb gild

BEGILDS ▸ begild

BEGILT ▸ begild

BEGIN vb start

BEGINNE same as > beginning

BEGINS ▸ begin

BEGIRD vb surround

BEGIRDS ▸ begird

BEGIRT ▸ begird

BEGLAD vb make glad

BEGLADS ▸ beglad

BEGLOOM vb make gloomy

BEGNAW vb gnaw at

BEGNAWS ▸ begnaw

BEGO vb harrass; beset

BEGOES ▸ bego

BEGOING ▸ bego

BEGONE ▸ bego

BEGONIA n tropical plant with waxy flowers

BEGORAH same as ▸ begorra

BEGORED adj smear with gore

BEGORRA interj emphatic exclamation, regarded as a characteristic utterance of Irishmen

BEGOT past participle of ▸ beget

BEGRIM same as ▸ begrime

BEGRIME vb make dirty

BEGRIMS ▸ begrim

BEGROAN vb groan at

BEGS ▸ beg

BEGUILE vb cheat or mislead

BEGUIN another name for ▸ beghard

BEGUINE n S American dance

BEGUINS ▸ beguin

BEGULF vb overwhelm

BEGULFS ▸ begulf

BEGUM n Muslim woman of high rank

BEGUMS ▸ begum

BEGUN past participle of ▸ begin

BEGUNK vb delude; trick

BEGUNKS ▸ begunk

BEHALF n interest, part, benefit, or respect

BEHAVE vb act or function in a particular way

BEHAVED ▸ behave

BEHAVER ▸ behave

BEHAVES ▸ behave

BEHEAD vb remove the head from

BEHEADS ▸ behead

BEHELD ▸ behold

BEHEST n order or earnest request

BEHESTS ▸ behest

BEHIGHT vb entrust

BEHIND adv indicating position to the rear, lateness, responsibility, etc ▷ n buttocks ▷ prep in or to a position further back than ▷ adj in a position further back

BEHINDS ▸ behind

BEHOLD vb look (at)

BEHOLDS ▸ behold

BEHOOF n advantage or profit

BEHOOFS ▸ behoof

BEHOOVE same as ▸ behove

BEHOTE same as ▸ behight

BEHOTES ▸ behote

BEHOVE vb be necessary or fitting for

BEHOVED ▸ behove

BEHOVES ▸ behove

BEHOWL vb howl at

BEHOWLS ▸ behowl

BEIGE adj pale brown ▷ n very light brown, sometimes with a yellowish tinge, similar to the colour of undyed wool

BEIGEL same as ▸ bagel

BEIGELS ▸ beigel

BEIGES ▸ beige

BEIGIER ▸ beige

BEIGNE same as ▸ beignet

BEIGNES ▸ beigne

BEIGNET n square deep-fried pastry served hot and sprinkled with icing sugar

BEIGY ▸ beige

BEIN adj financially comfortable

BEING ▸ be

BEINGS ▸ be

BEINKED adj daubed with ink

BEJADE vb jade; tire

BEJADED ▸ bejade

BEJADES ▸ bejade

BEJANT same as ▸ bajan

BEJANTS ▸ bejant

BEJESUS interj exclamation of surprise ▷ n as in **the bejesus** mild expletive

BEJEWEL vb decorate with or as if with jewels

BEKAH n half shekel

BEKAHS ▸ bekah

BEKISS vb smother with kisses

BEKNAVE vb treat as a knave

BEKNOT vb tie a knot or knots in

BEKNOTS ▸ beknot

BEKNOWN adj known about

BEL n unit for comparing two power levels or measuring the intensity of a sound, equal to 10 decibels

BELABOR same as > belabour

BELACE vb decorate with lace

BELACED ▸ belace

BELACES ▸ belace

BELADY vb call a lady

BELAH n Australian tree which yields a useful timber

BELAHS ▸ belah

BELAMY n close friend

BELAR same as ▸ belah

BELARS ▸ belar

BELATE vb cause to be late

BELATED adj late or too late

BELATES ▸ belate

BELAUD vb praise highly

BELAUDS ▸ belaud

BELAY vb secure a line to a pin or cleat ▷ n attachment (of a climber) to a mountain by tying the rope off round a rock spike, piton, nut, etc, to safeguard the party in the event of a fall

BELAYED ▸ belay

BELAYER ▸ belay

BELAYS ▸ belay

BELCH vb expel wind from the stomach noisily through the mouth ▷ n act of belching

BELCHED ▸ belch

BELCHER ▸ belch

BELCHES ▸ belch

BELDAM n old woman, esp an ugly or malicious one

BELDAME same as ▸ beldam

BELDAMS ▸ beldam

BELEAP vb leap over

BELEAPS ▸ beleap

BELEAPT ▸ beleap

BELEE vb put on sheltered side

BELEED ▸ belee

BELEES ▸ belee

BELFRY n part of a tower where bells are hung

BELGA n former Belgian monetary unit worth five francs

BELGARD n kind gaze

BELGAS ▸ belga

BELIE vb show to be untrue

BELIED ▸ belie

BELIEF n faith or confidence

BELIEFS ▸ belief

BELIER ▸ belie

BELIERS ▸ belie

BELIES ▸ belie

BELIEVE vb accept as true or real

BELIKE adv perhaps

BELIVE adv speedily

BELL n hollow, usu metal, cup-shaped instrument that emits a ringing sound when struck ▷ vb utter (such a sound)

BELLBOY n man or boy employed in a hotel, club, etc, to carry luggage and answer calls for service

BELLE n beautiful woman, esp the most attractive woman at a function

B

BELLED ▸ bell
BELLEEK n kind of thin fragile porcelain with a lustrous glaze
BELLES ▸ belle
BELLHOP same as ▸ bellboy
BELLIED ▸ belly
BELLIES ▸ belly
BELLING ▸ bell
BELLMAN n man who rings a bell, esp (formerly) a town crier
BELLMEN ▸ bellman
BELLOCK vb shout
BELLOW vb make a low deep cry like that of a bull ▷ n loud deep roar
BELLOWS pl n instrument for pumping a stream of air into something
BELLS ▸ bell
BELLY n part of the body of a vertebrate which contains the intestines ▷ vb (cause to) swell out
BELON n type of oyster
BELONG vb be the property of
BELONGS ▸ belong
BELONS ▸ belon
BELOVE vb love
BELOVED adj dearly loved ▷ n person dearly loved
BELOVES ▸ belove
BELOW adv at or to a position lower than, under ▷ prep at or to a position lower than
BELOWS same as ▸ bellows
BELS ▸ bel
BELT n band of cloth, leather, etc, worn usu around the waist ▷ vb fasten with a belt
BELTED ▸ belt
BELTER n outstanding person or event
BELTERS ▸ belter
BELTING n material used to make a belt or belts ▷ adj excellent
BELTMAN n (formerly) the member of a beach life-saving team who swam out with a line attached to his belt
BELTMEN ▸ beltman
BELTS ▸ belt
BELTWAY n people and institutions located in the area bounded by the Washington Beltway, taken to be politically and socially

out of touch with the rest of America and much given to political intrigue
BELUGA n large white sturgeon of the Black and Caspian Seas, from which caviar and isinglass are obtained
BELUGAS ▸ beluga
BELYING ▸ belie
BEMA n speaker's platform in the assembly in ancient Athens
BEMAD vb cause to become mad
BEMADAM vb call a person madam
BEMADS ▸ bemad
BEMAS ▸ bema
BEMATA ▸ bema
BEMAUL vb maul
BEMAULS ▸ bemaul
BEMAZED adj amazed
BEMBEX n type of wasp
BEMBIX same as ▸ bembex
BEMEAN a less common word for ▸ demean
BEMEANS ▸ bemean
BEMEANT ▸ bemean
BEMEDAL vb decorate with medals
BEMETE vb measure
BEMETED ▸ bemete
BEMETES ▸ bemete
BEMIRE vb soil with or as if with mire
BEMIRED ▸ bemire
BEMIRES ▸ bemire
BEMIST vb cloud with mist
BEMISTS ▸ bemist
BEMIX vb mix thoroughly
BEMIXED ▸ bemix
BEMIXES ▸ bemix
BEMIXT ▸ bemix
BEMOAN vb express sorrow or dissatisfaction about
BEMOANS ▸ bemoan
BEMOCK vb mock
BEMOCKS ▸ bemock
BEMOIL vb soil with mud
BEMOILS ▸ bemoil
BEMOUTH vb endow with a mouth
BEMUD vb cover with mud
BEMUDS ▸ bemud
BEMUSE vb confuse
BEMUSED adj puzzled or confused
BEMUSES ▸ bemuse
BEN n mountain peak ▷ adv in ▷ adj inner
BENAME an archaic word for ▸ name

BENAMED ▸ bename
BENAMES ▸ bename
BENCH n long seat ▷ vb put a person on a bench
BENCHED ▸ bench
BENCHER n member of the governing body of one of the Inns of Court, usually a judge or a Queen's Counsel
BENCHES ▸ bench
BENCHY adj (of a hillside) hollowed out in benches
BEND vb (cause to) form a curve ▷ n curved part
BENDAY vb (printing) reproduce using Benday technique
BENDAYS ▸ benday
BENDED ▸ bend
BENDEE same as ▸ bendy
BENDEES ▸ bendee
BENDER n drinking bout
BENDERS ▸ bender
BENDIER ▸ bendy
BENDING ▸ bend
BENDLET n narrow diagonal stripe on heraldic shield
BENDS ▸ bend
BENDY adj flexible or pliable ▷ n okra
BENDYS ▸ bendy
BENE n blessing
BENEATH prep below ▷ adv below
BENEFIC adj a rare word for beneficent
BENEFIT n something that improves or promotes ▷ vb do or receive good
BENEMPT a past participle of ▸ name
BENES ▸ bene
BENET vb trap (something) in a net
BENETS ▸ benet
BENGA n type of Kenyan popular music featuring guitars
BENGAS ▸ benga
BENI n sesame plant
BENIGHT vb shroud in darkness
BENIGN adj showing kindliness
BENIS ▸ beni
BENISON n blessing, esp a spoken one
BENJ another word for ▸ bhang
BENJES ▸ benj
BENNE another name for ▸ sesame

BENNES ▸ benne
BENNET n Eurasian and N African plant with yellow flowers
BENNETS ▸ bennet
BENNI n sesame
BENNIES ▸ benny
BENNIS ▸ benni
BENNY n amphetamine tablet, esp benzedrine: a stimulant
BENOMYL n fungicide, derived from imidazole, used on cereal and fruit crops: suspected of being carcinogenic
BENS ▸ ben
BENT adj not straight ▷ n personal inclination, propensity, or aptitude
BENTHAL ▸ benthos
BENTHIC ▸ benthos
BENTHON same as ▸ benthos
BENTHOS n animals and plants living at the bottom of a sea or lake
BENTIER ▸ benty
BENTO n thin lightweight box divided into compartments, which contain small separate dishes comprising a Japanese meal
BENTOS ▸ bento
BENTS ▸ bent
BENTY adj covered with bentgrass
BENUMB vb make numb or powerless
BENUMBS ▸ benumb
BENZAL n transparent crystalline substance
BENZALS ▸ benzal
BENZENE n flammable poisonous liquid used as a solvent, insecticide, etc
BENZIL n yellow compound radical
BENZILS ▸ benzil
BENZIN same as ▸ benzine
BENZINE n volatile liquid used as a solvent
BENZINS ▸ benzin
BENZOIC adj of, containing, or derived from benzoic acid or benzoin
BENZOIN n gum resin obtained from various Javanese and Sumatran trees, used in ointments, perfume, etc
BENZOL n crude form of

benzene, containing toluene, xylene, and other hydrocarbons, obtained from coal tar or coal gas and used as a fuel
BENZOLE same as ▸ benzol
BENZOLS ▸ benzol
BENZOYL n of, consisting of, or containing the monovalent group C_6H_5CO-
BENZYL n of, consisting of, or containing the monovalent group $C_6H_5CH_2-$
BENZYLS ▸ benzyl
BEPAINT vb dye; paint
BEPAT vb pat
BEPATS ▸ bepat
BEPEARL vb decorate with pearls
BEPELT vb pelt energetically
BEPELTS ▸ bepelt
BEPITY vb feel great pity for
BEPROSE vb (of poetry) reduce to prose
BEPUFF vb puff up
BEPUFFS ▸ bepuff
BEQUEST n legal gift of money or property by someone who has died
BERAKE vb rake thoroughly
BERAKED ▸ berake
BERAKES ▸ berake
BERATE vb scold harshly
BERATED ▸ berate
BERATES ▸ berate
BERAY vb soil; defile
BERAYED ▸ beray
BERAYS ▸ beray
BERBERE n hot-tasting Ethiopian paste made from garlic, cayenne pepper, coriander, and other spices, often used in stews
BERBICE n as in berbice chair large armchair with long arms that can be folded inwards to act as leg rests
BERCEAU n arched trellis for climbing plants
BERDASH same as > berdache
BERE n barley
BEREAVE vb deprive (of) something or someone valued, esp through death
BEREFT adj deprived
BERES ▸ bere
BERET n round flat close-fitting brimless cap
BERETS ▸ beret
BERETTA n type of pistol

BERG n iceberg
BERGAMA n type of Turkish rug
BERGEN n large rucksack with a capacity of over 50 litres
BERGENS ▸ bergen
BERGERE n type of French armchair
BERGS ▸ berg
BERGYLT n large northern marine food fish
BERHYME vb mention in poetry
BERIME same as ▸ berhyme
BERIMED ▸ berime
BERIMES ▸ berime
BERK n stupid person
BERKO adj berserk
BERKS ▸ berk
BERLEY n bait scattered on water to attract fish ▷ vb scatter (bait) on water
BERLEYS ▸ berley
BERLIN n fine wool yarn used for tapestry work, etc
BERLINE same as ▸ berlin
BERLINS ▸ berlin
BERM n narrow grass strip between the road and the footpath in a residential area ▷ vb create a berm
BERME same as ▸ berm
BERMED ▸ berm
BERMES ▸ berme
BERMING ▸ berm
BERMS ▸ berm
BEROB vb rob
BEROBED adj wearing a robe
BEROBS ▸ berob
BERRET same as ▸ beret
BERRETS ▸ berret
BERRIED ▸ berry
BERRIES ▸ berry
BERRY n small soft stoneless fruit ▷ vb bear or produce berries
BERSEEM n Mediterranean clover grown as a forage crop and to improve the soil
BERSERK adj frenziedly violent or destructive ▷ n member of a class of ancient Norse warriors who worked themselves into a frenzy before battle and fought with insane fury and courage
BERTH n bunk in a ship or train ▷ vb dock (a ship)
BERTHA n wide deep capelike collar, often of

B

lace, usually to cover up a low neckline
BERTHAS ▸ bertha
BERTHE n type of lace collar
BERTHED ▸ berth
BERTHES ▸ berthe
BERTHS ▸ berth
BERYL n hard transparent mineral
BERYLS ▸ beryl
BES same as ▸ **beth**
BESAINT vb give saint status to
BESANG ▸ besing
BESAT ▸ besit
BESAW ▸ besee
BESCOUR vb scour thoroughly
BESEE vb provide for; mind
BESEECH vb ask earnestly
BESEEKE same as ▸ **beseech**
BESEEM vb be suitable for
BESEEMS ▸ beseem
BESEEN ▸ besee
BESEES ▸ besee
BESES ▸ bes
BESET vb trouble or harass constantly
BESETS ▸ beset
BESHAME vb cause to feel shame
BESHINE vb illuminate
BESHONE ▸ beshine
BESHOUT vb shout about
BESHREW vb wish evil on
BESIDE prep at, by, or to the side of
BESIDES prep in addition ▷ adv in addition
BESIEGE vb surround with military forces
BESIGH vb sigh for
BESIGHS ▸ besigh
BESING vb sing about joyfully
BESINGS ▸ besing
BESIT vb suit; fit
BESITS ▸ besit
BESLAVE vb treat as slave
BESLIME vb cover with slime
BESMEAR vb smear over
BESMILE vb smile on
BESMOKE vb blacken with smoke
BESMUT vb blacken with smut
BESMUTS ▸ besmut
BESNOW vb cover with snow
BESNOWS ▸ besnow
BESOIN n need
BESOINS ▸ besoin

BESOM n broom made of twigs ▷ vb sweep with a besom
BESOMED ▸ besom
BESOMS ▸ besom
BESORT vb fit
BESORTS ▸ besort
BESOT vb make stupid or muddled
BESOTS ▸ besot
BESPAKE ▸ bespoke
BESPAT ▸ bespit
BESPATE ▸ bespit
BESPEAK vb indicate or suggest
BESPED ▸ bespeed
BESPEED vb get on with (doing something)
BESPICE vb flavour with spices
BESPIT vb cover with spittle
BESPITS ▸ bespit
BESPOKE adj (esp of a suit) made to the customer's specifications
BESPORT vb amuse oneself
BESPOT vb mark with spots
BESPOTS ▸ bespot
BESPOUT vb speak pretentiously
BEST adj most excellent of a particular group etc ▷ adv in a manner surpassing all others ▷ n utmost effort ▷ vb defeat
BESTAD same as ▸ **bestead**
BESTAIN vb stain
BESTAR vb decorate with stars
BESTARS ▸ bestar
BESTEAD vb serve; assist
BESTED ▸ best
BESTI Indian English word for ▸ **shame**
BESTIAL adj brutal or savage
BESTICK vb cover with sharp points
BESTILL vb cause to be still
BESTING ▸ best
BESTIR vb cause (oneself) to become active
BESTIRS ▸ bestir
BESTIS ▸ besti
BESTORM vb assault
BESTOW vb present (a gift) or confer (an honour)
BESTOWS ▸ bestow
BESTREW vb scatter or lie scattered over (a surface)
BESTRID > **bestride**
BESTROW same as ▸ **bestrew**
BESTS ▸ best

BESTUCK ▸ bestick
BESTUD vb set with, or as with studs
BESTUDS ▸ bestud
BESUNG ▸ besing
BESWARM vb swarm over
BET n agreement between two parties that a sum of money or other stake will be paid by the loser to the party who correctly predicts the outcome of an event ▷ vb make or place a bet with (a person or persons)
BETA n second letter in the Greek alphabet, a consonant, transliterated as b
BETAINE n sweet-tasting alkaloid that occurs in the sugar beet
BETAKE vb as in **betake oneself** go
BETAKEN ▸ betake
BETAKES ▸ betake
BETAS ▸ beta
BETAXED adj burdened with taxes
BETCHA interj bet you
BETE same as ▸ **beet**
BETED ▸ bete
BETEEM vb accord
BETEEME same as ▸ **beteem**
BETEEMS ▸ beteem
BETEL n Asian climbing plant, the leaves and nuts of which can be chewed
BETELS ▸ betel
BETES ▸ bete
BETH n second letter of the Hebrew alphabet transliterated as b
BETHANK vb thank
BETHEL n seaman's chapel
BETHELS ▸ bethel
BETHINK vb cause (oneself) to consider or meditate
BETHORN vb cover with thorns
BETHS ▸ beth
BETHUMB vb (of books) wear by handling
BETHUMP vb thump hard
BETID ▸ betide
BETIDE vb happen (to)
BETIDED ▸ betide
BETIDES ▸ betide
BETIGHT ▸ betide
BETIME vb befall
BETIMED ▸ betime
BETIMES ▸ betime
BETING ▸ bete

BETISE n folly or lack of perception

BETISES ▸ betise

BETITLE vb give title to

BETOIL vb tire through hard work

BETOILS ▸ betoil

BETOKEN vb indicate or signify

BETON n concrete

BETONS ▸ beton

BETONY n North American plant

BETOOK the past tense of ▸ betake

BETOSS vb toss about

BETRAY vb hand over or expose (one's nation, friend, etc) treacherously to an enemy

BETRAYS ▸ betray

BETREAD vb tread over

BETRIM vb decorate

BETRIMS ▸ betrim

BETROD ▸ betread

BETROTH vb promise to marry or to give in marriage

BETS ▸ bet

BETTA n fighting fish

BETTAS ▸ betta

BETTED ▸ bet

BETTER adj more excellent than others ▷ adv in a more excellent manner ▷ pl n one's superiors ▷ vb improve upon

BETTERS ▸ better

BETTIES ▸ betty

BETTING ▸ bet

BETTONG n short-nosed rat kangaroo

BETTOR n person who bets

BETTORS ▸ bettor

BETTY n type of short crowbar

BETWEEN adv indicating position in the middle, alternatives, etc ▷ prep at a point intermediate to two other points in space, time, etc

BETWIXT adv between

BEURRE n butter

BEURRES ▸ beurre

BEVEL n slanting edge ▷ vb slope

BEVELED ▸ bevel

BEVELER ▸ bevel

BEVELS ▸ bevel

BEVER n snack

BEVERS ▸ bever

BEVIES ▸ bevy

BEVOMIT vb vomit over

BEVOR n armour protecting lower part of face

BEVORS ▸ bevor

BEVUE n careless error

BEVUES ▸ bevue

BEVVIED ▸ bevvy

BEVVIES ▸ bevvy

BEVVY n alcoholic drink ▷ vb drink alcohol

BEVY n flock or group

BEWAIL vb express great sorrow over

BEWAILS ▸ bewail

BEWARE vb be on one's guard (against)

BEWARED ▸ beware

BEWARES ▸ beware

BEWEARY vb cause to be weary

BEWEEP vb express grief through weeping

BEWEEPS ▸ beweep

BEWENT ▸ bego

BEWEPT ▸ beweep

BEWET vb make wet

BEWETS ▸ bewet

BEWHORE vb treat as a whore

BEWIG vb adorn with a wig

BEWIGS ▸ bewig

BEWITCH vb attract and fascinate

BEWORM vb fill with worms

BEWORMS ▸ beworm

BEWORRY vb beset with worry

BEWRAP vb wrap up

BEWRAPS ▸ bewrap

BEWRAPT ▸ bewrap

BEWRAY an obsolete word for ▸ betray

BEWRAYS ▸ bewray

BEY n (in the Ottoman empire) a title given to senior officers, provincial governors, and certain other officials

> A **bey** was an official in the Ottoman empire. If someone plays this remember that you can of course put an O in front of it to make **obey**.

BEYLIC n province ruled over by a bey

BEYLICS ▸ beylic

BEYLIK same as ▸ beylic

BEYLIKS ▸ beylik

BEYOND prep at or to a point on the other side of ▷ adv at or to the far side of something ▷ n unknown, esp life after death

BEYONDS ▸ beyond

BEYS ▸ bey

BEZ n part of deer's horn

> This word for the tine of a deer's horn is one of the essential short words for using the Z.

BEZANT n medieval Byzantine gold coin

BEZANTS ▸ bezant

BEZAZZ another word for ▸ pizzazz

BEZEL n sloping edge of a cutting tool

BEZELS ▸ bezel

BEZES ▸ bez

BEZIL archaic word for > alcoholic

BEZILS ▸ bezil

BEZIQUE n card game for two or more players

> This card game played with two decks of cards combines the Q and Z and would make a wonderful bonus word.

BEZOAR n hard mass, such as a stone or hairball, in the stomach and intestines of animals, esp ruminants, and man: formerly thought to be an antidote to poisons

BEZOARS ▸ bezoar

BEZZANT same as ▸ bezant

BEZZAZZ ▸ bezazz

BEZZLE vb drink to excess

BEZZLED ▸ bezzle

BEZZLES ▸ bezzle

BHAGEE same as ▸ bhaji

BHAGEES ▸ bhagee

BHAI n Indian form of address for a man

BHAIS ▸ bhai

BHAJAN n singing of devotional songs and hymns

BHAJANS ▸ bhajan

BHAJEE same as ▸ bhaji

BHAJEES ▸ bhajee

BHAJI n Indian deep-fried savoury of chopped vegetables in spiced batter

BHAJIA ▸ bhaji

BHAJIS ▸ bhaji

BHAKTA n Hindu term for devotee of God

BHAKTAS ▸ bhakta

BHAKTI n loving devotion to God leading to nirvana

BHAKTIS ▸ bhakti

BHANG n preparation of Indian hemp used as a narcotic and intoxicant

B

BHANGRA n type of traditional Punjabi folk music combined with elements of Western pop music

BHANGS ▸ bhang

BHARAL n wild Himalayan sheep with a bluish-grey coat and round backward-curving horns

BHARALS ▸ bharal

BHAT n currency of Thailand

BHAVAN n (in India) a large house or building

BHAVANS ▸ bhavan

BHAWAN same as ▸ bhavan

BHAWANS ▸ bhawan

BHEESTY ▸ bhishti

BHEL same as ▸ bael

BHELS ▸ bhel

BHIKHU n fully ordained Buddhist monk

BHIKHUS ▸ bhikhu

BHINDI same as ▸ bindhi

BHINDIS ▸ bhindi

BHISHTI n (formerly in India) a water-carrier

BHISTEE same as ▸ bhishti

BHISTI same as ▸ bhishti

BHISTIE same as ▸ bhishti

BHISTIS ▸ bhisti

BHOONA ▸ bhuna

BHOONAS ▸ bhoona

BHOOT same as ▸ bhut

BHOOTS ▸ bhoot

BHUNA n Indian sauce

BHUNAS ▸ bhuna

BHUT n Hindu term for type of ghost

BHUTS ▸ bhut

BI short for > bisexual

BIALI same as ▸ bialy

BIALIES ▸ bialy

BIALIS ▸ biali

BIALY n type of bagel

BIALYS ▸ bialy

BIAS n mental tendency, esp prejudice ▷ vb cause to have a bias ▷ adj slanting obliquely ▷ adv obliquely

BIASED ▸ bias

BIASES ▸ bias

BIASING ▸ bias

BIASSED ▸ bias

BIASSES ▸ bias

BIAXAL same as ▸ biaxial

BIAXIAL adj (esp of a crystal) having two axes

BIB same as ▸ bibcock

BIBASIC adj with two bases

BIBB n wooden support on a mast for the trestletrees

BIBBED ▸ bib

BIBBER n drinker

BIBBERS ▸ bibber

BIBBERY n drinking to excess

BIBBING ▸ bib

BIBBLE n pebble

BIBBLES ▸ bibble

BIBBS ▸ bibb

BIBCOCK n tap with a nozzle bent downwards

BIBELOT n attractive or curious trinket

BIBFUL n as in spill a bibful to divulge secrets

BIBFULS ▸ bibful

BIBLE n any book containing the sacred writings of a religion

BIBLES ▸ bible

BIBLESS ▸ bib

BIBLIKE ▸ bib

BIBLIST same as > biblicist

BIBS ▸ bib

BICARB n bicarbonate of soda

BICARBS ▸ bicarb

BICCIES ▸ biccy

BICCY n biscuit

BICE n medium blue colour

BICEP same as ▸ biceps

BICEPS n muscle with two origins, esp the muscle that flexes the forearm

BICES ▸ bice

BICHIR n African freshwater fish with an elongated body

BICHIRS ▸ bichir

BICHORD adj having two strings for each note

BICKER vb argue over petty matters ▷ n petty squabble

BICKERS ▸ bicker

BICKIE short for ▸ biscuit

BICKIES ▸ bickie

BICOLOR same as > bicolour

BICORN adj having two horns or hornlike parts

BICORNE same as ▸ bicorn

BICORNS ▸ bicorn

BICRON n billionth part of a metre

BICRONS ▸ bicron

BICYCLE n vehicle with two wheels, one behind the other, pedalled by the rider ▷ vb ride a bicycle

BID vb offer (an amount) in attempting to buy something, esp in competition with others as at an auction ▷ n offer of a specified amount, as at an auction

BIDARKA n canoe covered in animal skins, esp sealskin, used by the Inuit of Alaska

BIDDEN ▸ bid

BIDDER ▸ bid

BIDDERS ▸ bid

BIDDIES ▸ biddy

BIDDING ▸ bid

BIDDY n woman, esp an old gossipy one

BIDE vb stay or continue

BIDED ▸ bide

BIDENT n instrument with two prongs

BIDENTS ▸ bident

BIDER ▸ bide

BIDERS ▸ bide

BIDES ▸ bide

BIDET n low basin for washing the genital area

BIDETS ▸ bidet

BIDI same as ▸ beedi

BIDING ▸ bide

BIDINGS ▸ bide

BIDIS ▸ bidi

BIDON n oil drum

BIDONS ▸ bidon

BIDS ▸ bid

BIELD n shelter ▷ vb shelter or take shelter

BIELDED ▸ bield

BIELDS ▸ bield

BIELDY adj sheltered

BIEN adv well

BIENNIA > biennium

BIER n stand on which a corpse or coffin rests before burial

BIERS ▸ bier

BIFACE n prehistoric stone tool

BIFACES ▸ biface

BIFF n blow with the fist ▷ vb give (someone) such a blow

BIFFED ▸ biff

BIFFER n someone, such as a sportsperson, who has a reputation for hitting hard

BIFFERS ▸ biffer

BIFFIES ▸ biffy

BIFFIN n variety of red cooking apple

BIFFING ▸ biff

BIFFINS ▸ biffin

BIFFO n fighting or aggressive behaviour ▷ adj aggressive

BIFFOS ▸ biffo

BIFFS ▸ biff

BIFFY n outdoor toilet

BIFID adj divided into two by

a cleft in the middle
BIFIDLY ▸ **bifid**
BIFILAR *adj* having two parallel threads, as in the suspension of certain measuring instruments
BIFLEX *adj* bent or flexed in two places
BIFOCAL *adj* having two different focuses
BIFOLD *adj* that can be folded in two places
BIFORM *adj* having or combining the characteristics of two forms, as a centaur
BIFTAH *n* ▸ **bifter**
BIFTAHS ▸ **biftah**
BIFTER *n* cannabis cigarette
BIFTERS ▸ **bifter**
BIG *adj* of considerable size, height, number, or capacity ▹ *adv* on a grand scale ▹ *vb* build
BIGA *n* chariot drawn by two horses
BIGAE ▸ **biga**
BIGAMY *n* crime of marrying a person while still legally married to someone else
BIGENER *n* hybrid between individuals of different genera
BIGEYE *n* type of tropical or subtropical red marine fish with very large eyes and rough scales
BIGEYES ▸ **bigeye**
BIGFEET ▸ **bigfoot**
BIGFOOT *n* yeti ▹ *vb* throw one's weight around
BIGG *n* type of barley
BIGGED ▸ **big**
BIGGER ▸ **big**
BIGGEST ▸ **big**
BIGGETY *same as* ▸ **biggity**
BIGGIE *n* something big or important
BIGGIES ▸ **biggie**
BIGGIN *n* plain close-fitting cap, often tying under the chin, worn in the Middle Ages and by children in the 17th century
BIGGING ▸ **big**
BIGGINS ▸ **biggin**
BIGGISH ▸ **big**
BIGGITY *adj* conceited
BIGGON *same as* ▸ **biggin**
BIGGONS ▸ **biggon**
BIGGS ▸ **bigg**
BIGGY *same as* ▸ **biggie**

BIGHA *n* in India, unit for measuring land
BIGHAS ▸ **bigha**
BIGHEAD *n* conceited person
BIGHORN *n* large wild mountain sheep of N America and NE Asia, the male of which has massive curved horns
BIGHT *n* long curved shoreline ▹ *vb* fasten or bind with a bight
BIGHTED ▸ **bight**
BIGHTS ▸ **bight**
BIGLY ▸ **big**
BIGNESS ▸ **big**
BIGOS *n* Polish stew
BIGOSES ▸ **bigos**
BIGOT *n* person who is intolerant, esp regarding religion or race
BIGOTED ▸ **bigot**
BIGOTRY *n* attitudes, behaviour, or way of thinking of a bigot
BIGOTS ▸ **bigot**
BIGS ▸ **big**
BIGTIME *adj* important
BIGWIG *n* important person
BIGWIGS ▸ **bigwig**
BIJOU *adj* (of a house) small but elegant ▹ *n* something small and delicately worked

> A **bijou** is a French word for a jewel, and it is indeed a jewel to play, getting rid of awkward letters for a good score. And remember that the plural can be **bijous** or **bijoux**.

BIJOUS ▸ **bijou**
BIJOUX ▸ **bijou**
BIKE *same as* ▸ **bicycle**
BIKED ▸ **bike**
BIKER *n* person who rides a motorcycle
BIKERS ▸ **biker**
BIKES ▸ **bike**
BIKEWAY *n* cycle lane
BIKIE *n* member of a motorcycle gang
BIKIES ▸ **bikie**
BIKING ▸ **bike**
BIKINGS ▸ **bike**
BIKINI *n* woman's brief two-piece swimming costume
BIKINIS ▸ **bikini**
BIKKIE *slang word for* ▸ **biscuit**
BIKKIES ▸ **bikkie**

BILAYER *n* part of cell membrane
BILBIES ▸ **bilby**
BILBO *n* (formerly) a sword with a marked temper and elasticity
BILBOA *same as* ▸ **bilbo**
BILBOAS ▸ **bilboa**
BILBOES ▸ **bilbo**
BILBOS ▸ **bilbo**
BILBY *n* Australian marsupial with long pointed ears and grey fur
BILE *n* bitter yellow fluid secreted by the liver ▹ *vb* boil
BILED ▸ **bile**
BILES ▸ **bile**
BILEVEL *n* hairstyle with two different lengths
BILGE *n* nonsense ▹ *vb* (of a vessel) to take in water at the bilge
BILGED ▸ **bilge**
BILGES ▸ **bilge**
BILGIER ▸ **bilge**
BILGING ▸ **bilge**
BILGY ▸ **bilge**
BILIAN *n* type of tree used for its wood
BILIANS ▸ **bilian**
BILIARY *adj* of bile, the ducts that convey bile, or the gall bladder ▹ *n* disease found in dogs
BILIMBI *n* type of fruit-bearing tree
BILING ▸ **bile**
BILIOUS *adj* sick, nauseous
BILK *vb* cheat, esp by not paying ▹ *n* swindle or cheat
BILKED ▸ **bilk**
BILKER ▸ **bilk**
BILKERS ▸ **bilk**
BILKING ▸ **bilk**
BILKS ▸ **bilk**
BILL *n* money owed for goods or services supplied ▹ *vb* to send or present an account for payment to (a person)
BILLBUG *n* type of weevil
BILLED ▸ **bill**
BILLER *n* stem of a plant
BILLERS ▸ **biller**
BILLET *vb* assign a lodging to (a soldier) ▹ *n* accommodation for a soldier in civil lodgings
BILLETS ▸ **billet**
BILLIE *same as* ▸ **billy**
BILLIES ▸ **billy**
BILLING *n* relative

B

importance of a performer or act as reflected in the prominence given in programmes, advertisements, etc

BILLION n one thousand million ▷ determiner amounting to a billion

BILLMAN n person who uses a billhook

BILLMEN ▸ billman

BILLON n alloy consisting of gold or silver and a base metal, usually copper, used esp for coinage

BILLONS ▸ billon

BILLOW n large sea wave ▷ vb rise up or swell out

BILLOWS ▸ billow

BILLOWY adj full of or forming billows

BILLS ▸ bill

BILLY n metal can or pot for cooking on a camp fire

BILLYO n as in **like billyo** phrase used to emphasize or intensify something

BILLYOH same as ▸ **billyo**

BILLYOS ▸ billyo

BILOBAR same as > **bilobate**

BILOBED same as > **bilobate**

BILSTED n American gum tree

BILTONG n strips of dried meat

BIMA same as ▸ **bema**

BIMAH same as ▸ **bema**

BIMAHS ▸ bimah

BIMANAL same as > **bimanous**

BIMAS ▸ bima

BIMBLE n as in **bimble box** type of dense Australian tree

BIMETAL n material made from two sheets of metal

BIMODAL adj having two modes

BIMORPH n assembly of two piezoelectric crystals cemented together so that an applied voltage causes one to expand and the other to contract, converting electrical signals into mechanical energy. Conversely, bending can generate a voltage: used in loudspeakers, gramophone pick-ups, etc

BIN n container for rubbish or for storing grain, coal,

etc ▷ vb put in a rubbish bin

BINAL adj twofold

BINARY adj composed of, relating to, or involving two ▷ n something composed of two parts or things

BINATE adj occurring in two parts or in pairs

BIND vb make secure with or as if with a rope ▷ n annoying situation

BINDER n firm cover for holding loose sheets of paper together

BINDERS ▸ binder

BINDERY n bookbindery

BINDHI same as ▸ **bindi**

BINDHIS ▸ bindhi

BINDI n decorative dot worn in the middle of the forehead, esp by Hindu women

BINDING ▸ bind

BINDIS ▸ bindi

BINDLE n small packet

BINDLES ▸ bindle

BINDS ▸ bind

BINE n climbing or twining stem of any of various plants, such as the woodbine or bindweed

BINER n clip used by climbers

BINERS ▸ biner

BINES ▸ bine

BING n heap or pile, esp of spoil from a mine

BINGE n bout of excessive indulgence, esp in drink ▷ vb indulge in a binge (esp of eating or drinking)

BINGED ▸ binge

BINGER n person who is addicted to crack cocaine

BINGERS ▸ binger

BINGES ▸ binge

BINGIES ▸ bingy

BINGING ▸ binge

BINGLE n minor crash or upset, as in a car or on a surfboard ▷ vb layer (hair)

BINGLED ▸ bingle

BINGLES ▸ bingle

BINGO n gambling game in which numbers are called out and covered by the players on their individual cards ▷ sentence substitute cry by the winner of a game of bingo

BINGOES ▸ bingo

BINGOS ▸ bingo

BINGS ▸ bing

BINGY Australian slang for ▸ **stomach**

BINIOU n small high-pitched Breton bagpipe

BINIOUS ▸ biniou

BINIT n (computing) early form of bit

BINITS ▸ binit

BINK n ledge

BINKS ▸ bink

BINMAN another name for ▸ **dustman**

BINMEN ▸ binman

BINNED ▸ bin

BINNING ▸ bin

BINOCLE n binocular-style telescope

BINOCS > binocular

BINS ▸ bin

BIO short for > **biography**

BIOBANK n large store of human samples for medical research

BIOCHIP n small glass or silicon plate containing an array of biochemical molecules or structures, used as a biosensor or in gene sequencing

BIOCIDE n substance used to destroy living things

BIODATA n information regarding an individual's education and work history, esp in the context of a selection process

BIODOT n temperature-sensitive device stuck to the skin in order to monitor stress

BIODOTS ▸ biodot

BIOFACT n item of biological information

BIOFILM n thin layer of living organisms

BIOFUEL n gaseous, liquid, or solid substance of biological origin that is used as a fuel ▷ vb fuel (a vehicle, etc) using biofuel

BIOG short form of > **biography**

BIOGAS n gaseous fuel produced by the fermentation of organic waste

BIOGEN n hypothetical protein assumed to be the basis of the formation and functioning of body cells and tissues

BIOGENS ▸ biogen

BIOGENY n principle that a living organism must originate from a parent form similar to itself

BIOGS ▸ biog

BIOHERM n mound of material laid down by sedentary marine organisms, esp a coral reef

BIOLOGY n study of living organisms

BIOMASS n total number of living organisms in a given area

BIOME n major ecological community, extending over a large area and usually characterized by a dominant vegetation

BIOMES ▸ biome

BIONIC adj having a part of the body that is operated electronically

BIONICS n study of biological functions in order to develop electronic equipment that operates similarly

BIONOMY n laws of life

BIONT n living thing

BIONTIC ▸ biont

BIONTS ▸ biont

BIOPHOR n hypothetical material particle

BIOPIC n film based on the life of a famous person

BIOPICS ▸ biopic

BIOPSIC ▸ biopsy

BIOPSY n examination of tissue from a living body ▸ vb perform a biopsy on

BIOPTIC ▸ biopsy

BIOS ▸ bio

BIOTA n plant and animal life of a particular region or period

BIOTAS ▸ biota

BIOTECH n biotechnology

BIOTIC adj of or relating to living organisms ▸ n living organism

BIOTICS ▸ biotic

BIOTIN n vitamin of the B complex, abundant in egg yolk and liver

BIOTINS ▸ biotin

BIOTITE n black or dark green mineral of the mica group

BIOTOPE n small area, such as the bark of a tree, that supports its own distinctive community

BIOTRON n climate-control chamber

BIOTYPE n group of genetically identical plants within a species, produced by apomixis

BIPACK n obsolete filming process

BIPACKS ▸ bipack

BIPARTY adj involving two parties

BIPED n animal with two feet ▸ adj having two feet

BIPEDAL adj having two feet

BIPEDS ▸ biped

BIPLANE n aeroplane with two sets of wings, one above the other

BIPOD n two-legged support or stand

BIPODS ▸ bipod

BIPOLAR adj having two poles

BIPRISM n prism having a highly obtuse angle to facilitate beam splitting

BIRCH n tree with thin peeling bark ▸ vb flog with a birch

BIRCHED ▸ birch

BIRCHEN ▸ birch

BIRCHES ▸ birch

BIRCHIR ▸ bichir

BIRD n creature with feathers and wings, most types of which can fly ▸ vb hunt for birds

BIRDDOG n dog used or trained to retrieve game birds

BIRDED ▸ bird

BIRDER n birdwatcher

BIRDERS ▸ birder

BIRDIE n score of one stroke under par for a hole ▸ vb play (a hole) in one stroke under par

BIRDIED ▸ birdie

BIRDIES ▸ birdie

BIRDING ▸ bird

BIRDMAN n man concerned with birds, such as a fowler or ornithologist

BIRDMEN ▸ birdman

BIRDS ▸ bird

BIREME n ancient galley having two banks of oars

BIREMES ▸ bireme

BIRETTA n stiff square cap worn by the Catholic clergy

BIRIANI same as ▸ biryani

BIRK n birch tree ▸ adj consisting or made of birch

BIRKEN adj relating to the birch tree

BIRKIE n spirited or lively person ▸ adj lively

BIRKIER ▸ birkie

BIRKIES ▸ birkie

BIRKS ▸ birk

BIRL same as ▸ burl

BIRLE same as ▸ burl

BIRLED ▸ birl

BIRLER ▸ birl

BIRLERS ▸ birl

BIRLES ▸ birle

BIRLING ▸ birl

BIRLINN n small Scottish book

BIRLS ▸ birl

BIRO n tradename of a kind of ballpoint pen

BIROS ▸ biro

BIRR vb make or cause to make a whirring sound ▸ n whirring sound

BIRRED ▸ birr

BIRRING ▸ birr

BIRRS ▸ birr

BIRSE n bristle

BIRSES ▸ birse

BIRSIER ▸ birsy

BIRSLE vb roast

BIRSLED ▸ birsle

BIRSLES ▸ birsle

BIRSY adj bristly

BIRTH n process of bearing young ▸ vb give birth to

BIRTHED ▸ birth

BIRTHS ▸ birth

BIRYANI n any of a variety of Indian dishes made with rice, highly flavoured and coloured with saffron or turmeric, mixed with meat or fish

BIS adv twice ▸ sentence substitute encore! again!

BISCUIT n small flat dry sweet or plain cake ▸ adj pale brown

BISE n cold dry northerly wind in Switzerland and the neighbouring parts of France and Italy, usually in the spring

BISECT vb divide into two equal parts

BISECTS ▸ bisect

BISES ▸ bise

BISH n mistake

BISHES ▸ bish

BISHOP n clergyman who governs a diocese ▸ vb make a bishop

B

BISHOPS ▸ bishop
BISK *a less common spelling of* **▸ bisque**
BISKS ▸ bisk
BISMAR *n* type of weighing scale
BISMARS ▸ bismar
BISMUTH *n* pinkish-white metallic element
BISNAGA *n* type of cactus
BISOM ▸ besom
BISOMS ▸ bisom
BISON *same as* **▸ buffalo**
BISONS ▸ bison
BISQUE *n* thick rich soup made from shellfish
BISQUES ▸ bisque
BISSON *adj* blind
BIST *a form of the second person singular of* **▸ be**
BISTATE *adj* involving two states
BISTER *same as* **▸ bestir**
BISTERS ▸ bister
BISTORT *n* Eurasian plant with a spike of small pink flowers
BISTRE *n* transparent water-soluble brownish-yellow pigment made by boiling the soot of wood, used for pen and wash drawings
BISTRED ▸ bistre
BISTRES ▸ bistre
BISTRO *n* small restaurant
BISTROS ▸ bistro
BIT *n* small piece, portion, or quantity
BITABLE ▸ bite
BITCH *n* female dog, fox, or wolf ▷ *vb* complain or grumble
BITCHED ▸ bitch
BITCHEN *same as* > **bitching**
BITCHES ▸ bitch
BITCHY *adj* spiteful or malicious
BITE *vb* grip, tear, or puncture the skin, as with the teeth or jaws ▷ *n* act of biting
BITER ▸ bite
BITERS ▸ bite
BITES ▸ bite
BITING ▸ bite
BITINGS ▸ bite
BITLESS *adj* without a bit
BITMAP *n* picture created by colour or shading on a visual display unit ▷ *vb* create a bitmap of
BITMAPS ▸ bitmap

BITO *n* African and Asian tree
BITONAL *adj* consisting of black and white tones
BITOS ▸ bito
BITOU *n as in* **bitou bush** type of sprawling woody shrub
BITS ▸ bit
BITSER *n* mongrel dog
BITSERS ▸ bitser
BITSIER ▸ bitsy
BITSY *adj* very small
BITT *n* one of a pair of strong posts on the deck of a ship for securing mooring and other lines ▷ *vb* secure (a line) by means of a bitt
BITTE *interj* you're welcome
BITTED ▸ bitt
BITTEN ▸ bite
BITTER *adj* having a sharp unpleasant taste ▷ *n* beer with a slightly bitter taste ▷ *adv* very ▷ *vb* make or become bitter
BITTERN *n* wading marsh bird with a booming call
BITTERS *pl n* bitter-tasting spirits flavoured with plant extracts
BITTIE *n* small piece
BITTIER ▸ bitty
BITTIES ▸ bittie
BITTING ▸ bitt
BITTOCK *n* small amount
BITTOR *n* bittern
BITTORS ▸ bittor
BITTOUR *same as* **▸ bittor**
BITTS ▸ bitt
BITTUR *same as* **▸ bittor**
BITTURS ▸ bittur
BITTY *adj* lacking unity, disjointed
BITUMED *adj* covered with bitumen
BITUMEN *n* black sticky substance obtained from tar or petrol
BIVALVE *adj* (marine mollusc) with two hinged segments to its shell ▷ *n* sea creature, such as an oyster or mussel, that has a shell consisting of two hinged valves and breathes through gills
BIVIA ▸ bivium
BIVINYL *another word for* > **butadiene**
BIVIOUS *adj* offering a choice of two different ways

BIVIUM *n* parting of ways
BIVOUAC *n* temporary camp in the open air ▷ *vb* camp in a bivouac
BIVVIED ▸ bivvy
BIVVIES ▸ bivvy
BIVVY *n* small tent or shelter ▷ *vb* camp in a bivouac
BIZ *n* business
BIZARRE *adj* odd or unusual ▷ *n* bizarre thing
BIZARRO *n* bizarre person
BIZAZZ *same as* > **pizazz**
BIZE *n* dry, cold wind in France
BIZES ▸ bize
BIZNAGA *same as* **▸ bisnaga**
BIZONAL ▸ bizone
BIZONE *n* place comprising two zones
BIZONES ▸ bizone
BIZZES ▸ biz
BIZZIES ▸ bizzy
BIZZO *n* empty and irrelevant talk or ideas
BIZZOS ▸ bizzo
BIZZY *n* policeman
BLAB *vb* reveal (secrets) indiscreetly
BLABBED ▸ blab
BLABBER *vb* talk without thinking ▷ *n* person who blabs
BLABBY *adj* talking too much; indiscreet
BLABS ▸ blab
BLACK *adj* of the darkest colour, like coal ▷ *n* darkest colour ▷ *vb* make black
BLACKED ▸ black
BLACKEN *vb* make or become black
BLACKER ▸ black
BLACKLY ▸ black
BLACKS ▸ black
BLAD *same as* **▸ blaud**
BLADDED ▸ blad
BLADDER *n* sac in the body where urine is held
BLADE *n* cutting edge of a weapon or tool
BLADED ▸ blade
BLADER *n* person skating with in-line skates
BLADERS ▸ blader
BLADES ▸ blade
BLADIER ▸ blady
BLADING *n* act or instance of skating with in-line skates
BLADS ▸ blad
BLADY *adj as in* **blady grass**

coarse leafy Australasian grass

BLAE adj bluish-grey

BLAER ▸ blae

BLAES n hardened clay or shale, esp when crushed and used to form the top layer of a sports pitch: bluish-grey or reddish in colour

BLAEST ▸ blae

BLAFF n West Indian stew

BLAFFS ▸ blaff

BLAG vb obtain by wheedling or cadging ▸ n robbery, esp with violence

BLAGGED ▸ blag

BLAGGER ▸ blag

BLAGS ▸ blag

BLAGUE n pretentious but empty talk

BLAGUER ▸ blague

BLAGUES ▸ blague

BLAH n worthless or silly talk ▸ adj uninteresting ▸ vb talk nonsense or boringly

BLAHED ▸ blah

BLAHING ▸ blah

BLAHS ▸ blah

BLAIN n blister, blotch, or sore on the skin

BLAINS ▸ blain

BLAISE same as ▸ blaes

BLAIZE same as ▸ blaes

BLAM n representation of the sound of a bullet being fired

BLAME vb consider (someone) responsible ▸ n responsibility for something that is wrong

BLAMED euphemistic word for ▸ damned

BLAMER ▸ blame

BLAMERS ▸ blame

BLAMES ▸ blame

BLAMING ▸ blame

BLAMS ▸ blam

BLANCH vb become white or pale

BLANCO n whitening substance ▸ vb whiten (something) with blanco

BLANCOS ▸ blanco

BLAND adj dull and uninteresting ▸ n bland thing ▸ vb as in **bland out** to become bland

BLANDED ▸ bland

BLANDER ▸ bland

BLANDLY ▸ bland

BLANDS ▸ bland

BLANK adj not written on ▸ n empty space ▸ vb cross out, blot, or obscure

BLANKED ▸ blank

BLANKER ▸ blank

BLANKET n large thick cloth used as covering for a bed ▸ adj applying to a wide group of people, situations, conditions, etc ▸ vb cover as with a blanket

BLANKLY ▸ blank

BLANKS ▸ blank

BLARE vb sound loudly and harshly ▸ n loud harsh noise

BLARED ▸ blare

BLARES ▸ blare

BLARING ▸ blare

BLARNEY n flattering talk ▸ vb cajole with flattery

BLART vb sound loudly and harshly

BLARTED ▸ blart

BLARTS ▸ blart

BLASE adj indifferent or bored through familiarity

BLASH n splash

BLASHES ▸ blash

BLASHY adj windy and rainy

BLAST n explosion ▸ vb blow up (a rock etc) with explosives ▸ interj expression of annoyance

BLASTED adv extreme or extremely ▸ adj blighted or withered

BLASTER ▸ blast

BLASTIE n ugly creature

BLASTS ▸ blast

BLASTY adj gusty

BLAT vb cry out or bleat like a sheep

BLATANT adj glaringly obvious

BLATE adj shy; ill at ease

BLATER ▸ blate

BLATEST ▸ blate

BLATHER vb speak foolishly ▸ n foolish talk

BLATS ▸ blat

BLATT n newspaper

BLATTED ▸ blat

BLATTER n, vb prattle

BLATTS ▸ blatt

BLAUBOK n South African antelope

BLAUD vb slap

BLAUDED ▸ blaud

BLAUDS ▸ blaud

BLAW vb blow

BLAWED ▸ blaw

BLAWING ▸ blaw

BLAWN ▸ blaw

BLAWORT n harebell

BLAWS ▸ blaw

BLAY n small river fish

BLAYS ▸ blay

BLAZAR n type of active galaxy

BLAZARS ▸ blazar

BLAZE n strong fire or flame ▸ vb burn or shine brightly

BLAZED ▸ blaze

BLAZER n lightweight jacket, often in the colours of a school etc

BLAZERS ▸ blazer

BLAZES pl n hell

BLAZING ▸ blaze

BLAZON vb proclaim publicly ▸ n coat of arms

BLAZONS ▸ blazon

BLEACH vb make or become white or colourless ▸ n bleaching agent

BLEAK adj exposed and barren ▸ n type of slender silvery European fish found in slow-flowing rivers

BLEAKER ▸ bleak

BLEAKLY ▸ bleak

BLEAKS ▸ bleak

BLEAKY same as ▸ bleak

BLEAR vb make (eyes or sight) dim with or as if with tears ▸ adj bleary

BLEARED ▸ blear

BLEARER ▸ blear

BLEARS ▸ blear

BLEARY adj with eyes dimmed, as by tears or tiredness

BLEAT vb (of a sheep, goat, or calf) utter its plaintive cry ▸ n cry of sheep, goats, and calves

BLEATED ▸ bleat

BLEATER ▸ bleat

BLEATS ▸ bleat

BLEB n fluid-filled blister on the skin

BLEBBY ▸ bleb

BLEBS ▸ bleb

BLED ▸ bleed

BLEE n complexion; hue

BLEED vb lose or emit blood

BLEEDER n despicable person

BLEEDS ▸ bleed

BLEEP n high-pitched signal or beep ▸ vb make such a noise

BLEEPED ▸ bleep

BLEEPER n small portable

B

radio receiver that makes a bleeping signal

BLEEPS ▸ **bleep**

BLEES ▸ **blee**

BLELLUM n babbler; blusterer

BLEMISH n defect or stain ▹ vb spoil or tarnish

BLENCH vb shy away, as in fear

BLEND vb mix or mingle (components or ingredients) ▹ n mixture

BLENDE n mineral consisting mainly of zinc sulphide

BLENDED ▸ **blend**

BLENDER n electrical appliance for puréeing vegetables etc

BLENDES ▸ **blende**

BLENDS ▸ **blend**

BLENNY n small fish with a tapering scaleless body

BLENT a past participle of ▸ **blend**

BLERT n foolish person

BLERTS ▸ **blert**

BLESBOK n S African antelope with a deep reddish-brown coat and a white blaze between the eyes

BLESS vb make holy by means of a religious rite

BLESSED ▸ **bless**

BLESSER ▸ **bless**

BLESSES ▸ **bless**

BLEST ▸ **bless**

BLET n state of softness or decay in certain fruits, such as the medlar, brought about by overripening ▹ vb go soft

BLETHER same as ▸ **blather**

BLETS ▸ **blet**

BLETTED ▸ **blet**

BLEW ▸ **blow**

BLEWART same as ▸ **blawort**

BLEWITS n type of edible fungus with a pale brown cap and a bluish stalk

BLEY same as ▸ **blay**

BLEYS ▸ **bley**

BLIGHT n person or thing that spoils or prevents growth ▹ vb cause to suffer a blight

BLIGHTS ▸ **blight**

BLIGHTY n home country; home leave

BLIKSEM interj South

African expression of surprise

BLIMEY interj exclamation of surprise or annoyance

BLIMP n small airship

BLIMPS ▸ **blimp**

BLIMY same as ▸ **blimey**

BLIN Scots word for ▸ **blind**

BLIND adj unable to see ▹ vb deprive of sight ▹ n covering for a window

BLINDED ▸ **blind**

BLINDER same as ▸ **blind**

BLINDLY ▸ **blind**

BLINDS ▸ **blind**

BLING adj flashy ▹ n ostentatious jewellery

BLINGER ▸ **bling**

BLINGS ▸ **bling**

BLINGY same as ▸ **bling**

BLINI pl n Russian pancakes made of buckwheat flour and yeast

BLINIS same as ▸ **blini**

BLINK vb close and immediately reopen (the eyes) ▹ n act of blinking

BLINKED ▸ **blink**

BLINKER vb provide (a horse) with blinkers ▹ n flashing light for sending messages, as a warning device, etc, such as a direction indicator on a road vehicle

BLINKS ▸ **blink**

BLINNED ▸ **blin**

BLINS ▸ **blin**

BLINTZ n thin pancake folded over a filling usually of apple, cream cheese, or meat

BLINTZE same as ▸ **blintz**

BLINY same as ▸ **blini**

BLIP n spot of light on a radar screen indicating the position of an object ▹ vb produce such a noise

BLIPPED ▸ **blip**

BLIPS ▸ **blip**

BLISS n perfect happiness ▹ vb make or become perfectly happy

BLISSED ▸ **bliss**

BLISSES ▸ **bliss**

BLIST archaic form of ▸ **blessed**

BLISTER n small bubble on the skin ▹ vb (cause to) have blisters

BLIT vb move or copy (a block of data) from one location to another in a

computer's memory

BLITE n type of herb

BLITES ▸ **blite**

BLITHE adj casual and indifferent

BLITHER same as ▸ **blether**

BLITS ▸ **blit**

BLITTED ▸ **blit**

BLITTER n circuit that transfers large amounts of data within a computer's memory

BLITZ n violent and sustained attack by aircraft ▹ vb attack suddenly and intensively

BLITZED ▸ **blitz**

BLITZER ▸ **blitz**

BLITZES ▸ **blitz**

BLIVE same as ▸ **belive**

BLOAT vb cause to swell, as with liquid or air ▹ n abnormal distention of the abdomen in cattle, sheep, etc, caused by accumulation of gas in the stomach

BLOATED adj swollen, as with a liquid, air, or wind

BLOATER n salted smoked herring

BLOATS ▸ **bloat**

BLOB n soft mass or drop ▹ vb put blobs, as of ink or paint, on

BLOBBED ▸ **blob**

BLOBBY ▸ **blob**

BLOBS ▸ **blob**

BLOC n people or countries combined by a common interest

BLOCK n large solid piece of wood, stone, etc ▹ vb obstruct or impede by introducing an obstacle

BLOCKED adj functionally impeded by amphetamine

BLOCKER n person or thing that blocks

BLOCKIE n owner of a small property, esp a farm

BLOCKS ▸ **block**

BLOCKY adj like a block, esp in shape and solidity

BLOCS ▸ **bloc**

BLOG n journal written on-line and accessible to users of the internet ▹ vb write a blog

BLOGGED ▸ **blog**

BLOGGER ▸ **blog**

BLOGS ▸ **blog**

BLOKART n single-seat

three-wheeled vehicle propelled by the wind

BLOKE *n* man

BLOKES ▸ **bloke**

BLOKEY *same as* ▸ **blokeish**

BLOKIER ▸ **blokey**

BLOKISH *same as* ▸ **blokeish**

BLOND *adj* (of men's hair) of a light colour ▷ *n* person, esp a man, having light-coloured hair and skin

BLONDE *n* fair-haired (person) ▷ *adj* (of hair) fair

BLONDER ▸ **blonde**

BLONDES ▸ **blonde**

BLONDS ▸ **blond**

BLOOD *n* red fluid that flows around the body ▷ *vb* initiate (a person) to war or hunting

BLOODED *adj* (of horses, cattle, etc) of good breeding

BLOODS ▸ **blood**

BLOODY *adj* covered with blood ▷ *adv* extreme or extremely ▷ *vb* stain with blood

BLOOEY *adj* out of order; faulty

BLOOIE *same as* ▸ **blooey**

BLOOK *n* book published on a blog

BLOOKS ▸ **blook**

BLOOM *n* blossom on a flowering plant ▷ *vb* (of flowers) open

BLOOMED *adj* (of a lens) coated with a thin film of magnesium fluoride or some other substance to reduce the amount of light lost by reflection

BLOOMER *n* stupid mistake

BLOOMS ▸ **bloom**

BLOOMY *adj* having a fine whitish coating on the surface, such as on the rind of a cheese

BLOOP *vb* (baseball) hit a ball into air beyond infield

BLOOPED ▸ **bloop**

BLOOPER *n* stupid mistake

BLOOPS ▸ **bloop**

BLOOSME *same as* ▸ **blossom**

BLORE *n* strong blast of wind

BLORES ▸ **blore**

BLOSSOM *n* flowers of a plant ▷ *vb* (of plants) flower

BLOT *n* spot or stain ▷ *vb* cause a blemish in or on

BLOTCH *n* discoloured area or stain ▷ *vb* become or cause to become marked by such discoloration

BLOTCHY *adj* covered in or marked by blotches

BLOTS ▸ **blot**

BLOTTED ▸ **blot**

BLOTTER *n* sheet of blotting paper

BLOTTO *adj* extremely drunk

BLOTTY *adj* covered in blots

BLOUBOK *same as* ▸ **blaubok**

BLOUSE *n* woman's shirtlike garment ▷ *vb* hang or cause to hang in full loose folds

BLOUSED ▸ **blouse**

BLOUSES ▸ **blouse**

BLOUSON *n* short loose jacket with a tight waist

BLOUSY *adj* loose; blouse-like

BLOW *vb* (of air, the wind, etc) move ▷ *n* hard hit

BLOWBY *n* leakage of gas past the piston of an engine at maximum pressure

BLOWBYS ▸ **blowby**

BLOWED ▸ **blow**

BLOWER *n* mechanical device, such as a fan, that blows

BLOWERS ▸ **blower**

BLOWFLY *n* fly that lays its eggs in meat

BLOWGUN *same as* ▸ **blowpipe**

BLOWIE *n* bluebottle

BLOWIER ▸ **blowy**

BLOWIES ▸ **blowy**

BLOWING *n* moving of air

BLOWN ▸ **blow**

BLOWOFF *n* discharge of a surplus fluid

BLOWOUT *n* sudden loss of air in a tyre

BLOWS ▸ **blow**

BLOWSE *n* large, red-faced woman

BLOWSED *same as* ▸ **blowsy**

BLOWSES ▸ **blowse**

BLOWSY *adj* fat, untidy, and red-faced

BLOWUP *n* fit of temper

BLOWUPS ▸ **blowup**

BLOWY *adj* windy

BLOWZE *same as* ▸ **blowse**

BLOWZED *same as* ▸ **blowsy**

BLOWZES ▸ **blowze**

BLOWZY *same as* ▸ **blowsy**

BLUB *a slang word for* ▸ **blubber**

BLUBBED ▸ **blub**

BLUBBER *n, vb* sob without restraint ▷ *adj* swollen or fleshy ▷ *n* fat of whales, seals, etc

BLUBS ▸ **blub**

BLUCHER *n* high shoe with laces over the tongue

BLUDE *Scots form of* ▸ **blood**

BLUDES ▸ **blude**

BLUDGE *vb* evade work ▷ *n* easy task

BLUDGED ▸ **bludge**

BLUDGER *n* person who scrounges

BLUDGES ▸ **bludge**

BLUDIE *Scots form of* ▸ **bloody**

BLUDIER ▸ **bludie**

BLUDY *same as* ▸ **bludie**

BLUE *n* colour of a clear unclouded sky ▷ *adj* of the colour blue ▷ *vb* make or become blue

BLUECAP *another name for* ▸ **bluetit**

BLUED ▸ **blue**

BLUEFIN *another name for* ▸ **tunny**

BLUEGUM *n* tall fast-growing widely cultivated Australian tree with aromatic leaves, bark that peels off in shreds, and hard timber

BLUEING ▸ **blue**

BLUEISH *same as* ▸ **bluish**

BLUEJAY *n* common N American jay with bright blue plumage and greyish-white underparts

BLUELY ▸ **blue**

BLUER ▸ **blue**

BLUES *pl n* type of music

BLUEST ▸ **blue**

BLUESY ▸ **blues**

BLUET *n* N American plant with small four-petalled blue flowers

BLUETIT *n* small European bird with a blue crown, wings, and tail and yellow underparts

BLUETS ▸ **bluet**

BLUETTE *n* short, brilliant piece of music

BLUEY *adj* bluish ▷ *n* informal Australian word meaning blanket

BLUEYS ▸ **bluey**

BLUFF *vb* pretend to be

B

confident in order to influence (someone) ▷ *n* act of bluffing ▷ *adj* good-naturedly frank and hearty
BLUFFED ▸ bluff
BLUFFER ▸ bluff
BLUFFLY ▸ bluff
BLUFFS ▸ bluff
BLUGGY *same as* ▸ **bloody**
BLUID *Scots word for* ▸ **blood**
BLUIDS ▸ bluid
BLUIDY ▸ bluid
BLUIER ▸ bluey
BLUIEST ▸ bluey
BLUING ▸ blue
BLUINGS ▸ blue
BLUISH *adj* slightly blue
BLUME *Scots word for* ▸ **bloom**
BLUMED ▸ blume
BLUMES ▸ blume
BLUMING ▸ blume
BLUNDER *n* clumsy mistake ▷ *vb* make a blunder
BLUNGE *vb* mix (clay or a similar substance) with water in order to form a suspension for use in ceramics
BLUNGED ▸ blunge
BLUNGER *n* large vat in which the contents, esp clay and water, are mixed by rotating arms
BLUNGES ▸ blunge
BLUNK *vb* ruin; botch
BLUNKED ▸ blunk
BLUNKER ▸ blunk
BLUNKS ▸ blunk
BLUNT *adj* not having a sharp edge or point ▷ *vb* make less sharp ▷ *n* cannabis cigarette
BLUNTED ▸ blunt
BLUNTER ▸ blunt
BLUNTLY ▸ blunt
BLUNTS ▸ blunt
BLUR *vb* make or become vague or less distinct ▷ *n* something vague, hazy, or indistinct
BLURB *n* promotional description, as on the jacket of a book ▷ *vb* describe or recommend in a blurb
BLURBED ▸ blurb
BLURBS ▸ blurb
BLURRED ▸ blur
BLURRY ▸ blur
BLURS ▸ blur
BLURT *vb* utter suddenly

and involuntarily
BLURTED ▸ blurt
BLURTER ▸ blurt
BLURTS ▸ blurt
BLUSH *vb* become red in the face, esp from embarrassment or shame ▷ *n* reddening of the face
BLUSHED ▸ blush
BLUSHER *n* cosmetic for giving the cheeks a rosy colour
BLUSHES ▸ blush
BLUSHET *n* modest young woman
BLUSTER *vb* speak loudly or in a bullying way ▷ *n* empty threats or protests
BLYPE *n* piece of skin peeled off after sunburn
BLYPES ▸ blype
BO *interj* exclamation uttered to startle or surprise someone, esp a child in a game ▷ *n* fellow, buddy
BOA *n* large nonvenomous snake
BOAB *short for* ▸ **baobab**
BOABS ▸ boab
BOAK *same as* ▸ **boke**
BOAKED ▸ boak
BOAKING ▸ boak
BOAKS ▸ boak
BOAR *n* uncastrated male pig
BOARD *n* long flat piece of sawn timber ▷ *vb* go aboard (a train, aeroplane, etc)
BOARDED ▸ board
BOARDER *n* person who pays rent in return for accommodation in someone else's home
BOARDS ▸ board
BOARISH *adj* coarse, cruel, or sensual
BOARS ▸ boar
BOART *same as* ▸ **bort**
BOARTS ▸ boart
BOAS ▸ boa
BOAST *vb* speak too proudly about one's talents etc ▷ *n* bragging statement
BOASTED ▸ boast
BOASTER ▸ boast
BOASTS ▸ boast
BOAT *n* small vehicle for travelling across water ▷ *vb* travel in a boat
BOATED ▸ boat
BOATEL *n* waterside hotel

catering for boating people
BOATELS ▸ boatel
BOATER *n* flat straw hat
BOATERS ▸ boater
BOATFUL ▸ boat
BOATIE *n* boating enthusiast
BOATIES ▸ boatie
BOATING *n* rowing, sailing, or cruising in boats as a form of recreation
BOATMAN *n* man who works on, hires out, or repairs boats
BOATMEN ▸ boatman
BOATS ▸ boat
BOB *vb* move or cause to move up and down repeatedly, as while floating in water ▷ *n* short abrupt movement, as of the head
BOBA *n* type of Chinese tea
BOBAC *same as* ▸ **bobak**
BOBACS ▸ bobac
BOBAK *n* type of marmot
BOBAKS ▸ bobak
BOBAS ▸ boba
BOBBED ▸ bob
BOBBER *n* type of float for fishing
BOBBERS ▸ bobber
BOBBERY *n* mixed pack of hunting dogs, often not belonging to any of the hound breeds ▷ *adj* noisy or excitable
BOBBIES ▸ bobby
BOBBIN *n* reel on which thread is wound
BOBBING ▸ bob
BOBBINS ▸ bobbin
BOBBISH ▸ cheery
BOBBITT *vb* sever the penis of
BOBBLE *n* small ball of material, usu for decoration ▷ *vb* (of a ball) to bounce erratically because of an uneven playing surface
BOBBLED ▸ bobble
BOBBLES ▸ bobble
BOBBLY *adj* (of fabric) covered in small balls; worn
BOBBY *n* policeman
BOBCAT *n* N American feline mammal with reddish-brown fur with dark spots or stripes, tufted ears, and a short tail
BOBCATS ▸ bobcat
BOBECHE *n* candle drip-catcher

BOBLET n two-man bobsleigh

BOBLETS ▶ boblet

BOBOL n fraud carried out by one or more persons with access to public funds in collusion with someone in a position of authority ▷ vb commit a bobol

BOBOLS ▶ bobol

BOBOTIE n dish of curried mince

BOBS ▶ bob

BOBSLED same as ▶ bobsleigh

BOBSTAY n strong stay between a bowsprit and the stem of a vessel for holding down the bowsprit

BOBTAIL n docked tail ▷ adj having the tail cut short ▷ vb dock the tail of

BOBWIG n type of short wig

BOBWIGS ▶ bobwig

BOCAGE n wooded countryside characteristic of northern France, with small irregular-shaped fields and many hedges and copses

BOCAGES ▶ bocage

BOCCA n mouth

BOCCAS ▶ bocca

BOCCE same as ▶ boccie

BOCCES ▶ bocce

BOCCI same as ▶ boccie

BOCCIA same as ▶ boccie

BOCCIAS ▶ boccia

BOCCIE n Italian version of bowls played on a lawn smaller than a bowling green

BOCCIES ▶ boccie

BOCCIS ▶ bocci

BOCK a variant spelling of ▶ boke

BOCKED ▶ bock

BOCKEDY adj (of a structure, piece of furniture, etc) unsteady

BOCKING ▶ bock

BOCKS ▶ bock

BOD n person

BODACH n old man

BODACHS ▶ bodach

BODDLE same as ▶ bodle

BODDLES ▶ boddle

BODE vb portend or presage

BODED ▶ bode

BODEFUL adj portentous

BODEGA n building in a Spanish-speaking country that sells wine

BODEGAS ▶ bodega

BODES ▶ bode

BODGE vb make a mess of

BODGED ▶ bodge

BODGER adj worthless or second-rate

BODGERS ▶ bodger

BODGES ▶ bodge

BODGIE n unruly or uncouth young man, esp in the 1950s ▷ adj inferior

BODGIER ▶ bodgie

BODGIES ▶ bodgie

BODGING ▶ bodge

BODHI as in **bodhi tree** holy tree of Buddhists

BODHRAN n shallow one-sided drum popular in Irish and Scottish folk music

BODICE n upper part of a dress

BODICES ▶ bodice

BODIED ▶ body

BODIES ▶ body

BODIKIN n little body

BODILY adj relating to the body ▷ adv by taking hold of the body

BODING ▶ bode

BODINGS ▶ bode

BODKIN n blunt large-eyed needle

BODKINS ▶ bodkin

BODLE n small obsolete Scottish coin

BODLES ▶ bodle

BODRAG n enemy attack

BODRAGS ▶ bodrag

BODS ▶ bod

BODY n entire physical structure of an animal or human

BODYING ▶ body

BOEP n South African word for a big belly

BOEPS ▶ boep

BOERBUL n crossbred mastiff used esp as a watchdog

BOET n brother

BOETS ▶ boet

BOEUF n as in **boeuf bourgignon** casserole of beef, vegetables, herbs, etc, cooked in red wine

BOFF n boffin ▷ vb hit

BOFFED ▶ boff

BOFFIN n scientist or expert

BOFFING ▶ boff

BOFFINS ▶ boffin

BOFFO adj very good

BOFFOLA n great success

BOFFOS ▶ boffo

BOFFS ▶ boff

BOG n wet spongy ground ▷ vb mire or delay

BOGAN n youth who dresses and behaves rebelliously

BOGANS ▶ bogan

BOGART vb monopolize or keep (something, esp a marijuana cigarette) to oneself selfishly

BOGARTS ▶ bogart

BOGBEAN same as ▶ buckbean

BOGEY n evil or mischievous spirit ▷ vb play (a hole) in one stroke over par

BOGEYED ▶ bogey

BOGEYS ▶ bogey

BOGGARD same as ▶ boggart

BOGGART n ghost or poltergeist

BOGGED ▶ bog

BOGGER n lavatory

BOGGERS ▶ bogger

BOGGIER ▶ bog

BOGGING ▶ bog

BOGGISH ▶ bog

BOGGLE vb be surprised, confused, or alarmed

BOGGLED ▶ boggle

BOGGLER ▶ boggle

BOGGLES ▶ boggle

BOGGY ▶ bog

BOGIE same as ▶ bogey

BOGIED ▶ bogie

BOGIES ▶ bogy

BOGLAND n area of wetland

BOGLE n rhythmic dance performed to ragga music ▷ vb to perform such a dance

BOGLED ▶ bogle

BOGLES ▶ bogle

BOGLING ▶ bogle

BOGMAN n body of a person found preserved in a peat bog

BOGMEN ▶ bogman

BOGOAK n oak or other wood found preserved in peat bogs; bogwood

BOGOAKS ▶ bogoak

BOGONG n large nocturnal Australian moth

BOGONGS ▶ bogong

BOGS ▶ bog

BOGUS adj not genuine

BOGUSLY ▶ bogus

BOGWOOD same as ▶ bogoak

B

BOGY same as ▸ **bogey**

BOGYISM same as
> **bogeyism**

BOGYMAN same as
> **bogeyman**

BOGYMEN ▸ **bogyman**

BOH same as ▸ **bo**

BOHEA n black Chinese tea,
once regarded as the
choicest, but now as an
inferior grade

BOHEAS ▸ **bohea**

BOHEMIA n area
frequented by
unconventional (esp
creative) people

BOHO short for > **bohemian**

BOHOS ▸ **boho**

BOHRIUM n element
artificially produced in
minute quantities

BOHS ▸ **boh**

BOI n lesbian who dresses
like a boy

BOIL vb (cause to) change
from a liquid to a vapour so
quickly that bubbles are
formed ▷ n state or action
of boiling

BOILED ▸ **boil**

BOILER n piece of
equipment which provides
hot water

BOILERS ▸ **boiler**

BOILERY n place where
water is boiled to extract
salt

BOILING adj very hot ▷ n
sweet

BOILOFF n quantity of
liquified gases lost in
evaporation

BOILS ▸ **boil**

BOING vb rebound making a
noise

BOINGED ▸ **boing**

BOINGS ▸ **boing**

BOINK same as ▸ **boing**

BOINKED ▸ **boink**

BOINKS ▸ **boink**

BOIS ▸ **boi**

BOITE n artist's portfolio

BOITES ▸ **boite**

BOK n S African antelope

This useful K word,
meaning an antelope,
can take quite a number
of front extensions,
forming words like
**blesbok, reitbok,
rhebok,** and even, if you
are lucky, **jambok** or
sjambok.

BOKE vb retch or vomit
▷ n retch

BOKED ▸ **boke**

BOKES ▸ **boke**

BOKING ▸ **boke**

BOKO slang word for ▸ **nose**

BOKOS ▸ **boko**

BOKS ▸ **bok**

BOLA n missile used by
gauchos and Indians of
South America, consisting
of two or more heavy balls
on a cord. It is hurled at a
running quarry, such as an
ox or rhea, so as to entangle
its legs

BOLAR adj relating to clay

BOLAS same as ▸ **bola**

BOLASES ▸ **bolas**

BOLD adj confident and
fearless ▷ n boldface

BOLDEN vb make bold

BOLDENS ▸ **bolden**

BOLDER ▸ **bold**

BOLDEST ▸ **bold**

BOLDLY ▸ **bold**

BOLDS ▸ **bold**

BOLE n tree trunk

BOLERO n (music for)
traditional Spanish dance

BOLEROS ▸ **bolero**

BOLES ▸ **bole**

BOLETE n type of fungus

BOLETES ▸ **bolete**

BOLETI ▸ **boletus**

BOLETUS n type of fungus,
often edible, with a brownish
umbrella-shaped cap

BOLIDE n large
exceptionally bright
meteor that often explodes

BOLIDES ▸ **bolide**

BOLINE n (in Wicca) a knife,
usually sickle-shaped and
with a white handle, used
for gathering herbs and
carving symbols

BOLINES ▸ **boline**

BOLIVAR n standard
monetary unit of
Venezuela, equal to 100
céntimos

BOLIVIA n type of woollen
fabric

BOLL n rounded seed
capsule of cotton, flax, etc
▷ vb form into a boll

BOLLARD n short thick post
used to prevent the
passage of motor vehicles

BOLLED ▸ **boll**

BOLLEN ▸ **boll**

BOLLING ▸ **boll**

BOLLS ▸ **boll**

BOLO n large single-edged
knife, originating in the
Philippines

BOLOGNA n type of
sausage

BOLONEY a variant spelling
of ▸ **baloney**

BOLOS ▸ **bolo**

BOLSHIE adj difficult or
rebellious ▷ n any political
radical

BOLSHY same as ▸ **bolshie**

BOLSON n desert valley
surrounded by mountains,
with a shallow lake at the
centre

BOLSONS ▸ **bolson**

BOLSTER vb support or
strengthen ▷ n long
narrow pillow

BOLT n sliding metal bar for
fastening a door etc ▷ vb
run away suddenly

BOLTED ▸ **bolt**

BOLTER ▸ **bolt**

BOLTERS ▸ **bolt**

BOLTING ▸ **bolt**

BOLTS ▸ **bolt**

BOLUS same as ▸ **bole**

BOLUSES ▸ **bolus**

BOMA n enclosure, esp a
palisade or fence of thorn
bush, set up to protect a
camp, herd of animals, etc

BOMAS ▸ **boma**

BOMB n container fitted
with explosive material
▷ vb attack with bombs

BOMBARD vb attack with
heavy gunfire or bombs ▷ n
ancient type of cannon that
threw stone balls

BOMBAST n pompous
language ▷ vb speak
pompous language

BOMBAX n type of S
American tree

BOMBE n dessert of ice
cream lined or filled with
custard, cake crumbs, etc
▷ adj (of furniture) having a
projecting swollen shape

BOMBED ▸ **bomb**

BOMBER n aircraft that
drops bombs

BOMBERS ▸ **bomber**

BOMBES ▸ **bombe**

BOMBING ▸ **bomb**

BOMBLET n small bomb

BOMBO n inferior wine

BOMBORA n submerged
reef

BOMBOS ▸ bombo
BOMBS ▸ bomb
BOMBYX n type of moth
BOMMIE n outcrop of coral reef
BOMMIES ▸ bommie
BON adj good
BONA n goods
BONACI n type of fish
BONACIS ▸ bonaci
BONAMIA n parasite
BONANZA n sudden good luck or wealth
BONASUS n European bison
BONBON n sweet
BONBONS ▸ bonbon
BONCE n head
BONCES ▸ bonce
BOND n something that binds, fastens or holds together ▸ vb bind
BONDAGE n slavery
BONDED adj consisting of, secured by, or operating under a bond or bonds
BONDER same as > bondstone
BONDERS ▸ bonder
BONDING n process by which individuals become emotionally attached to one another
BONDMAN same as > bondsman
BONDMEN ▸ bondman
BONDS ▸ bond
BONDUC n type of North American tree
BONDUCS ▸ bonduc
BONE n any of the hard parts in the body that form the skeleton ▸ vb remove the bones from (meat for cooking etc)
BONED ▸ bone
BONER n blunder
BONERS ▸ boner
BONES ▸ bone
BONESET n N American plant with flat clusters of small white flowers
BONEY same as ▸ bony
BONEYER ▸ boney
BONFIRE n large outdoor fire
BONG n deep reverberating sound, as of a large bell ▸ vb make a deep reverberating sound
BONGED ▸ bong
BONGING ▸ bong
BONGO n small drum played with the fingers

BONGOES ▸ bongo
BONGOS ▸ bongo
BONGS ▸ bong
BONHAM n piglet
BONHAMS ▸ bonham
BONIATO n sweet potato
BONIE same as ▸ bonny
BONIER ▸ bony
BONIEST ▸ bony
BONING ▸ bone
BONINGS ▸ bone
BONISM n doctrine that the world is good, although not the best of all possible worlds
BONISMS ▸ bonism
BONIST ▸ bonism
BONISTS ▸ bonism
BONITA slang term for ▸ heroin
BONITAS ▸ bonita
BONITO n small tunny-like marine food fish
BONITOS ▸ bonito
BONJOUR interj hello
BONK vb have sex with
BONKED ▸ bonk
BONKERS adj crazy
BONKING ▸ bonk
BONKS ▸ bonk
BONNE n housemaid or female servant
BONNES ▸ bonne
BONNET n metal cover over a vehicle's engine ▸ vb place a bonnet on
BONNETS ▸ bonnet
BONNIE same as ▸ bonny
BONNIER ▸ bonny
BONNIES ▸ bonny
BONNILY ▸ bonny
BONNOCK n thick oatmeal cake
BONNY adj beautiful ▸ adv agreeably or well
BONOBO n type of anthropoid ape of central W Africa
BONOBOS ▸ bonobo
BONSAI n ornamental miniature tree or shrub
BONSELA n small gift of money
BONSOIR interj good evening
BONUS n something given, paid, or received above what is due or expected
BONUSES ▸ bonus
BONXIE n great skua
BONXIES ▸ bonxie
BONY adj having many bones

BONZA same as ▸ bonzer
BONZE n Chinese or Japanese Buddhist priest or monk
BONZER adj excellent
BONZES ▸ bonze
BOO interj shout of disapproval ▸ vb shout 'boo' to show disapproval
BOOAI ▸ boohai
BOOAIS ▸ booai
BOOAY ▸ boohai
BOOAYS ▸ booay
BOOB n foolish mistake ▸ vb make a foolish mistake ▸ adj of poor quality, similar to that provided in prison
BOOBED ▸ boob
BOOBIES ▸ booby
BOOBING ▸ boob
BOOBIRD n person who boos
BOOBISH ▸ booby
BOOBOO n blunder
BOOBOOK n small spotted Australian brown owl
BOOBOOS ▸ booboo
BOOBS ▸ boob
BOOBY n foolish person
BOOCOO same as > beaucoup
BOOCOOS ▸ boocoo
BOODIE n type of kangaroo
BOODIED ▸ boody
BOODIES ▸ boody
BOODLE n money or valuables, esp when stolen, counterfeit, or used as a bribe ▸ vb give or receive money corruptly or illegally
BOODLED ▸ boodle
BOODLER ▸ boodle
BOODLES ▸ boodle
BOODY vb sulk
BOOED ▸ boo
BOOFIER ▸ boofy
BOOFY adj muscular and strong but stupid
BOOGER n dried mucous from the nose
BOOGERS ▸ booger
BOOGEY same as ▸ boogie
BOOGEYS ▸ boogey
BOOGIE vb dance to fast pop music ▸ n session of dancing to pop music
BOOGIED ▸ boogie
BOOGIES ▸ boogie
BOOGY same as ▸ boogie
BOOH same as ▸ boo
BOOHAI n as in up the boohai thoroughly lost
BOOHAIS ▸ boohai

B

BOOHED ▶ booh
BOOHING ▶ booh
BOOHOO vb sob or pretend to sob noisily ▷ n distressed or pretended sobbing
BOOHOOS ▶ boohoo
BOOHS ▶ booh
BOOING ▶ boo
BOOJUM n American tree
BOOJUMS ▶ boojum
BOOK n number of pages bound together between covers ▷ vb reserve (a place, passage, etc) in advance
BOOKED ▶ book
BOOKEND n one of a pair of usually ornamental supports for holding a row of books upright
BOOKER ▶ book
BOOKERS ▶ book
BOOKFUL ▶ book
BOOKIE short for > **bookmaker**
BOOKIER ▶ booky
BOOKIES ▶ bookie
BOOKING n reservation, as of a table or seat
BOOKISH adj fond of reading
BOOKLET n thin book with paper covers
BOOKMAN n learned person
BOOKMEN ▶ bookman
BOOKOO same as ▶ **boocoo**
BOOKOOS ▶ bookoo
BOOKS ▶ book
BOOKSIE same as ▶ **booksy**
BOOKSY adj inclined to be bookish or literary
BOOKY adj bookish
BOOL n bowling bowl ▷ vb play bowls
BOOLED ▶ bool
BOOLING ▶ bool
BOOLS ▶ bool
BOOM vb make a loud deep echoing sound ▷ n loud deep echoing sound
BOOMBOX n portable stereo system
BOOMED ▶ boom
BOOMER n large male kangaroo
BOOMERS ▶ boomer
BOOMIER ▶ boomy
BOOMING ▶ boom
BOOMKIN n short boom projecting from the deck of a ship, used to secure the main-brace blocks or to

extend the lower edge of the foresail
BOOMLET n small boom in business, birth rate, etc
BOOMS ▶ boom
BOOMY adj characterized by heavy bass sound
BOON n something extremely useful, helpful, or beneficial
BOONER n young working-class person from Canberra
BOONERS ▶ booner
BOONIES short form of > **boondocks**
BOONS ▶ boon
BOOR n rude or insensitive person
BOORD obsolete spelling of ▶ **board**
BOORDE obsolete spelling of ▶ **board**
BOORDES ▶ boorde
BOORDS ▶ boord
BOORISH adj ill-mannered, clumsy, or insensitive
BOORKA same as ▶ **burka**
BOORKAS ▶ boorka
BOORS ▶ boor
BOOS ▶ boo
BOOSE same as ▶ **booze**
BOOSED ▶ boose
BOOSES ▶ boose
BOOSHIT adj very good
BOOSING ▶ boose
BOOST n encouragement or help ▷ vb improve
BOOSTED ▶ boost
BOOSTER n small additional injection of a vaccine
BOOSTS ▶ boost
BOOT n outer covering for the foot that extends above the ankle ▷ vb kick
BOOTCUT adj (of trousers) slightly flared at the bottom of the legs to fit over boots
BOOTED adj wearing boots
BOOTEE n baby's soft shoe
BOOTEES ▶ bootee
BOOTERY n shop where boots and shoes are sold
BOOTH n small partly enclosed cubicle
BOOTHS ▶ booth
BOOTIE n Royal Marine
BOOTIES ▶ booty
BOOTING ▶ boot
BOOTLEG adj produced, distributed, or sold illicitly

▷ vb make, carry, or sell (illicit goods) ▷ n something made or sold illicitly, such as alcohol during Prohibition in the US
BOOTS ▶ boot
BOOTY n valuable articles obtained as plunder
BOOZE n (consume) alcoholic drink ▷ vb drink alcohol, esp in excess
BOOZED ▶ booze
BOOZER n person who is fond of drinking
BOOZERS ▶ boozer
BOOZES ▶ booze
BOOZEY same as ▶ **boozy**
BOOZIER ▶ boozy
BOOZILY ▶ boozy
BOOZING ▶ booze
BOOZY adj inclined to or involving excessive drinking of alcohol
BOP vb dance to pop music ▷ n form of jazz with complex rhythms and harmonies
BOPEEP n quick look; peek
BOPEEPS ▶ bopeep
BOPPED ▶ bop
BOPPER ▶ bop
BOPPERS ▶ bop
BOPPING ▶ bop
BOPS ▶ bop
BOR n neighbour
BORA n Aboriginal ceremony
BORACES ▶ borax
BORACIC same as ▶ **boric**
BORAGE n Mediterranean plant with star-shaped blue flowers
BORAGES ▶ borage
BORAK n rubbish
BORAKS ▶ borak
BORAL n type of fine powder
BORALS ▶ boral
BORANE n any compound of boron and hydrogen, used in the synthesis of other boron compounds and as high-energy fuels
BORANES ▶ borane
BORAS ▶ bora
BORATE n salt or ester of boric acid. Salts of boric acid consist of BO_3 and BO_4 units linked together ▷ vb treat with borax, boric acid, or borate
BORATED ▶ borate
BORATES ▶ borate

BORAX n soluble white mineral occurring in alkaline soils and salt deposits

BORAXES ▸ borax

BORAZON n extremely hard form of boron nitride

BORD obsolete spelling of ▸ board

BORDAR n smallholder who held cottage in return for menial work

BORDARS ▸ bordar

BORDE obsolete spelling of ▸ board

BORDEL same as ▸ bordello

BORDELS ▸ bordel

BORDER n dividing line between political or geographical regions ▷ vb provide with a border

BORDERS ▸ border

BORDES ▸ borde

BORDS ▸ bord

BORDURE n outer edge of a shield, esp when decorated distinctively

BORE vb make (someone) weary by being dull

BOREAL adj of or relating to the north or the north wind

BOREAS n name for the north wind

BORED ▸ bore

BOREDOM n state of being bored

BOREE same as ▸ myall

BOREEN n country lane or narrow road

BOREENS ▸ boreen

BOREES ▸ boree

BOREL adj unlearned

BORER n machine or hand tool for boring holes

BORERS ▸ borer

BORES ▸ bear

BORGO n small attractive medieval village

BORGOS ▸ borgo

BORIC adj of or containing boron

BORIDE n compound in which boron is the most electronegative element, esp a compound of boron and a metal

BORIDES ▸ boride

BORING n act or process of making or enlarging a hole ▷ adj dull

BORINGS ▸ boring

BORK vb dismiss from job unfairly

BORKED ▸ bork

BORKING ▸ bork

BORKS ▸ bork

BORM vb smear with paint, oil, etc

BORMED ▸ borm

BORMING ▸ borm

BORMS ▸ borm

BORN adj possessing certain qualities from birth

BORNA n as in borna disease viral disease found in mammals, esp horses

BORNE ▸ bear

BORNEOL n white solid terpene alcohol

BORNITE n mineral consisting of a sulphide of copper and iron that tarnishes to purple

BORNYL n as in bornyl alcohol white solid alcohol from a Malaysian tree

BORNYLS ▸ bornyl

BORON n element used in hardening steel

BORONIA n Australian aromatic flowering shrub

BORONIC ▸ boron

BORONS ▸ boron

BOROUGH n town or district with its own council

BORREL adj ignorant

BORRELL same as ▸ borrel

BORROW vb obtain (something) temporarily

BORROWS ▸ borrow

BORS ▸ bor

BORSCH same as ▸ borscht

BORSCHT n Russian soup based on beetroot

BORSHCH same as ▸ borscht

BORSHT same as ▸ borscht

BORSHTS ▸ borsht

BORSIC n strong light composite material of boron fibre and silicon carbide used in aviation

BORSICS ▸ borsic

BORSTAL n (formerly in Britain) prison for young criminals

BORT n inferior grade of diamond used for cutting and drilling or, in powdered form, as an industrial abrasive

BORTIER ▸ bort

BORTS ▸ bort

BORTSCH same as ▸ borscht

BORTY ▸ bort

BORTZ same as ▸ bort

BORTZES ▸ bortz

BORZOI n tall dog with a long silky coat

BORZOIS ▸ borzoi

BOS ▸ bo

BOSBOK same as > bushbuck

BOSBOKS ▸ bosbok

BOSCAGE n mass of trees and shrubs

BOSH n empty talk, nonsense

BOSHBOK same as > bushbuck

BOSHES ▸ bosh

BOSHTA same as ▸ boshter

BOSHTER adj excellent

BOSIE n (in cricket) another term for googly

BOSIES ▸ bosie

BOSK n small wood of bushes and small trees

BOSKAGE same as ▸ boscage

BOSKER adj excellent

BOSKET n clump of small trees or bushes

BOSKETS ▸ bosket

BOSKIER ▸ bosky

BOSKS ▸ bosk

BOSKY adj containing or consisting of bushes or thickets

BOSOM n chest of a person, esp the female breasts ▷ adj very dear ▷ vb embrace

BOSOMED ▸ bosom

BOSOMS ▸ bosom

BOSOMY adj (of a woman) having large breasts

BOSON n any of a group of elementary particles, such as a photon or pion, that has zero or integral spin and obeys the rules of Bose-Einstein statistics

BOSONIC ▸ boson

BOSONS ▸ boson

BOSQUE same as ▸ bosk

BOSQUES ▸ bosque

BOSQUET same as ▸ bosket

BOSS n raised knob or stud ▷ vb employ, supervise, or be in charge of ▷ adj excellent

BOSSBOY n Black African foreman of a gang of workers

BOSSDOM n bosses collectively

BOSSED ▸ boss

BOSSER ▸ boss

BOSSES ▸ boss

B

BOSSEST ▸ boss
BOSSET n either of the rudimentary antlers found in young deer
BOSSETS ▸ bosset
BOSSIER ▸ bossy
BOSSIES ▸ bossy
BOSSILY ▸ bossy
BOSSING n act of shaping malleable metal, such as lead cladding, with mallets to fit a surface
BOSSISM n domination or the system of domination of political organizations by bosses
BOSSY same as ▸ **boss**
BOSTON n card game for four, played with two packs
BOSTONS ▸ boston
BOSTRYX n phenomenon in which flowers develop on one side only
BOSUN same as > **boatswain**
BOSUNS ▸ bosun
BOT n larva of a botfly, which typically develops inside the body of a horse, sheep, or man
BOTA n leather container
BOTANIC same as > **botanical**
BOTANY n study of plants
BOTARGO n relish consisting of the roe of mullet or tunny, salted and pressed into rolls
BOTAS ▸ bota
BOTCH vb spoil through clumsiness ▷ n badly done piece of work or repair
BOTCHED ▸ botch
BOTCHER ▸ botch
BOTCHES ▸ botch
BOTCHY adj clumsily done or made
BOTE n compensation given for injury or damage to property
BOTEL same as ▸ **boatel**
BOTELS ▸ botel
BOTES ▸ bote
BOTFLY n type of stout-bodied hairy fly, the larvae of which are parasites of man, sheep, and horses
BOTH pron two considered together ▷ adj two considered together ▷ determiner two
BOTHAN n unlicensed drinking house
BOTHANS ▸ bothan
BOTHER vb take the time or trouble ▷ n trouble, fuss, or difficulty ▷ interj exclamation of slight annoyance
BOTHERS ▸ bother
BOTHIE same as ▸ **bothy**
BOTHIES ▸ bothy
BOTHOLE n hole made by the larva of the botfly
BOTHRIA > bothrium
BOTHY n hut used for temporary shelter
BOTNET n network of infected computers
BOTNETS ▸ botnet
BOTONE adj having lobes at the ends
BOTONEE same as ▸ **botone**
BOTS n digestive disease of horses and some other animals caused by the presence of botfly larvae in the stomach
BOTT same as ▸ **bot**
BOTTE n thrust or hit
BOTTED ▸ bot
BOTTEGA n workshop; studio
BOTTES ▸ botte
BOTTIES ▸ botty
BOTTINE n light boot for women or children
BOTTING ▸ bot
BOTTLE n container for holding liquids ▷ vb put in a bottle
BOTTLED ▸ bottle
BOTTLER n exceptional person or thing
BOTTLES ▸ bottle
BOTTOM n lowest, deepest, or farthest removed part of a thing ▷ adj lowest or last ▷ vb provide with a bottom
BOTTOMS ▸ bottom
BOTTONY same as ▸ **botone**
BOTTS ▸ bott
BOTTY n diminutive for bottom
BOTULIN n potent toxin produced by a bacterium in imperfectly preserved food, etc, which causes botulism
BOUBOU n long flowing garment worn by men and women in Mali, Nigeria, Senegal, and some other parts of Africa
BOUBOUS ▸ boubou
BOUCHE n notch cut in top corner of shield
BOUCHEE n small pastry case filled with a savoury mixture, served hot with cocktails or as an hors d'oeuvre
BOUCHES ▸ bouche
BOUCLE n looped yarn giving a knobbly effect ▷ adj of or designating such a yarn or fabric
BOUCLEE n support for a cue in billiards formed by doubling the first finger so that its tip is aligned with the thumb at its second joint, to form a loop through which the cue may slide
BOUCLES ▸ boucle
BOUDIN n French version of a black pudding
BOUDINS ▸ boudin
BOUDOIR n woman's bedroom or private sitting room
BOUFFE n type of light or satirical opera common in France during the 19th century
BOUFFES ▸ bouffe
BOUGE vb move
BOUGED ▸ bouge
BOUGES ▸ bouge
BOUGET n budget
BOUGETS ▸ bouget
BOUGH n large branch of a tree
BOUGHED ▸ bough
BOUGHS ▸ bough
BOUGHT ▸ buy
BOUGHTS ▸ buy
BOUGIE n long slender semiflexible cylindrical instrument for inserting into body passages, such as the rectum or urethra, to dilate structures, introduce medication, etc
BOUGIES ▸ bougie
BOUGING ▸ bouge
BOUILLI n stew
BOUK n bulk; volume
BOUKS ▸ bouk
BOULDER n large rounded rock ▷ vb convert into boulders
BOULE same as ▸ **boulle**
BOULES n game, popular in France, in which metal bowls are thrown to land as close as possible to a target ball

BOULLE adj denoting or relating to a type of marquetry of patterned inlays of brass and tortoiseshell, occasionally with other metals such as pewter, much used on French furniture from the 17th century ▷ n something ornamented with such marquetry

BOULLES ▸ **boulle**

BOULT same as ▸ **bolt**

BOULTED ▸ **boult**

BOULTER ▸ **bolt**

BOULTS ▸ **boult**

BOUN vb prepare to go out

BOUNCE vb (of a ball etc) rebound from an impact ▷ n act of rebounding

BOUNCED ▸ **bounce**

BOUNCER n person employed at a disco etc to remove unwanted people

BOUNCES ▸ **bounce**

BOUNCY adj lively, exuberant, or self-confident

BOUND ▸ **bind**

BOUNDED adj (of a set) having a bound, esp where a measure is defined in terms of which all the elements of the set, or the differences between all pairs of members, are less than some value, or else all its members lie within some other well-defined set

BOUNDEN adj morally obligatory

BOUNDER n morally reprehensible person

BOUNDS pl n limit

BOUNED ▸ **boun**

BOUNING ▸ **boun**

BOUNS ▸ **boun**

BOUNTY n generosity

BOUQUET n bunch of flowers

BOURBON n whiskey made from maize

BOURD n prank

BOURDER n prankster

BOURDON n 16-foot organ stop of the stopped diapason type

BOURDS ▸ **bourd**

BOURG n French market town, esp one beside a castle

BOURGS ▸ **bourg**

BOURKHA same as ▸ **burka**

BOURLAW same as ▸ **byrlaw**

BOURN n (in S Britain) stream

BOURNE same as ▸ **bourn**

BOURNES ▸ **bourne**

BOURNS ▸ **bourn**

BOURREE n traditional French dance in fast duple time

BOURSE n stock exchange of continental Europe, esp Paris

BOURSES ▸ **bourse**

BOURSIN n tradename of a smooth white creamy cheese, often flavoured with garlic

BOUSE vb raise or haul with a tackle

BOUSED ▸ **bouse**

BOUSES ▸ **bouse**

BOUSIER ▸ **bousy**

BOUSING ▸ **bouse**

BOUSY adj drunken; boozy

BOUT n period of activity or illness

BOUTADE n outburst

BOUTON n knob-shaped contact between nerve fibres

BOUTONS ▸ **bouton**

BOUTS ▸ **bout**

BOUVIER n large powerful dog of a Belgian breed, having a rough shaggy coat: used esp for cattle herding and guarding

BOVATE n obsolete measure of land

BOVATES ▸ **bovate**

BOVID n type of ruminant, hollow-horned mammal such as sheep, goats, cattle, antelopes, and buffalo

BOVIDS ▸ **bovid**

BOVINE n domesticated bovine mammal

BOVINES ▸ **bovine**

BOVVER n rowdiness, esp caused by gangs of teenage youths

BOVVERS ▸ **bovver**

BOW vb lower (one's head) or bend (one's knee or body) as a sign of respect or shame ▷ n movement made when bowing

BOWAT n lamp

BOWATS ▸ **bowat**

BOWBENT adj bent; bow-like

BOWED adj lowered, bent forward, or curved

BOWEL n intestine, esp the large intestine ▷ vb remove the bowels

BOWELED ▸ **bowel**

BOWELS ▸ **bowel**

BOWER n shady leafy shelter ▷ vb surround as with a bower

BOWERED ▸ **bower**

BOWERS ▸ **bower**

BOWERY ▸ **bower**

BOWES ▸ **bough**

BOWET same as ▸ **bowat**

BOWETS ▸ **bowet**

BOWFIN n primitive N American freshwater bony fish with an elongated body and a very long dorsal fin

BOWFINS ▸ **bowfin**

BOWGET obsolete variant of ▸ **budget**

BOWGETS ▸ **bowget**

BOWHEAD n type of large-mouthed arctic whale

BOWIE n as in **bowie knife** type of hunting knife

BOWING n technique of using the bow in playing a violin, viola, cello, or related instrument

BOWINGS ▸ **bowing**

BOWKNOT n decorative knot usually having two loops and two loose ends

BOWL n round container with an open top ▷ vb roll smoothly along the ground

BOWLDER same as ▸ **boulder**

BOWLED ▸ **bowl**

BOWLEG n a leg curving outwards like a bow between the ankle and the thigh

BOWLEGS ▸ **bowleg**

BOWLER n player who sends (a ball) towards the batsman

BOWLERS ▸ **bowler**

BOWLESS ▸ **bow**

BOWLFUL same as ▸ **bowl**

BOWLIKE ▸ **bow**

BOWLINE n line used to keep the sail taut against the wind

BOWLING n game in which bowls are rolled at a group of pins

BOWLS n game played on a very smooth area of grass in which opponents roll biased wooden bowls as near a small bowl (the jack) as possible

BOWMAN n archer

BOWMEN ▸ bowman

BOWNE same as ▸ boun

BOWNED ▸ bowne

BOWNES ▸ bowne

BOWNING ▸ bowne

BOWPOT same as > boughpot

BOWPOTS ▸ bowpot

BOWR n muscle

BOWRS ▸ bowr

BOWS ▸ bow

BOWSAW n saw with a thin blade in a bow-shaped frame

BOWSAWS ▸ bowsaw

BOWSE same as ▸ bouse

BOWSED ▸ bowse

BOWSER n tanker containing fuel for aircraft, military vehicles, etc

BOWSERS ▸ bowser

BOWSES ▸ bowse

BOWSEY ▸ bowsie

BOWSEYS ▸ bowsey

BOWSHOT n distance an arrow travels from the bow

BOWSIE n low-class, mean or obstreperous person

BOWSIES ▸ bowsie

BOWSING ▸ bowse

BOWWOW n imitation of the bark of a dog ▷ vb make a noise like a dog

BOWWOWS ▸ bowwow

BOWYANG n band worn round trouser leg below knee

BOWYER n person who makes or sells archery bows

BOWYERS ▸ bowyer

BOX n container with a firm flat base and sides ▷ vb put into a box

BOXBALL n street ball game

BOXCAR n closed railway freight van

BOXCARS ▸ boxcar

BOXED ▸ box

BOXEN ▸ box

BOXER n person who participates in the sport of boxing

BOXERS ▸ boxer

BOXES ▸ box

BOXFISH another name for > trunkfish

BOXFUL same as ▸ box

BOXFULS ▸ box

BOXHAUL vb bring (a

square-rigger) onto a new tack by backwinding the foresails and steering hard round

BOXIER ▸ boxy

BOXIEST ▸ boxy

BOXILY ▸ boxy

BOXING n sport of fighting with the fists

BOXINGS ▸ boxing

BOXLIKE ▸ box

BOXPLOT n (in statistics) type of graph

BOXROOM n small room in which boxes, cases, etc may be stored

BOXTIES n Irish potato cakes

BOXTY n type of Irish potato pancake

BOXWOOD n hard yellow wood of the box tree, used to make tool handles, etc

BOXY adj squarish or chunky

BOY n male child ▷ vb act the part of a boy in a play

BOYAR n member of an old order of Russian nobility, ranking immediately below the princes: abolished by Peter the Great

BOYARD same as ▸ boyar

BOYARDS ▸ boyard

BOYARS ▸ boyar

BOYAU n connecting trench

BOYAUX ▸ boyau

BOYCHIK n young boy

BOYCOTT vb refuse to deal with (an organization or country) ▷ n instance of boycotting

BOYED ▸ boy

BOYF n boyfriend

BOYFS ▸ boyf

BOYG n troll-like mythical creature

BOYGS ▸ boyg

BOYHOOD n state or time of being a boy

BOYING ▸ boy

BOYISH adj of or like a boy in looks, behaviour, or character, esp when regarded as attractive or endearing

BOYKIE n chap or fellow

BOYKIES ▸ boykie

BOYLA n Australian Aboriginal word for magician

BOYLAS ▸ boyla

BOYO n boy or young man:

often used in direct address

BOYOS ▸ boyo

BOYS ▸ boy

BOYSIER ▸ boysy

BOYSY adj suited to or typical of boys or young men

BOZO n man, esp a stupid one

BOZOS ▸ bozo

BRA same as > brassiere

BRAAI vb grill or roast (meat) over open coals

BRAAIED ▸ braai

BRAAIS ▸ braai

BRAATA n small portion added to a purchase of food by a market vendor, to encourage the customer to return

BRAATAS same as ▸ braata

BRABBLE rare word for > squabble

BRACCIA ▸ braccio

BRACCIO n former unit of measurement; length of man's arm

BRACE n object fastened to something to straighten or support it ▷ vb steady or prepare (oneself) for something unpleasant

BRACED ▸ brace

BRACER n person or thing that braces

BRACERO n Mexican World War II labourer

BRACERS ▸ bracer

BRACES pl n pair of straps worn over the shoulders for holding up the trousers

BRACH n bitch hound

BRACHAH n blessing

BRACHES ▸ brach

BRACHET same as ▸ brach

BRACHIA > brachium

BRACHOT > brachah

BRACHS ▸ brach

BRACING adj refreshing and invigorating ▷ n system of braces used to strengthen or support

BRACK same as > barmbrack

BRACKEN n large fern

BRACKET n pair of characters used to enclose a section of writing ▷ vb put in brackets

BRACKS ▸ brack

BRACT n leaf at the base of a flower

BRACTED ▸ bract

BRACTS ▸ bract

BRAD n small tapered nail with a small head

BRADAWL n small boring tool

BRADDED ▸ brad

BRADOON same as ▸ bridoon

BRADS ▸ brad

BRAE n hill or slope

BRAES ▸ brae

BRAG vb speak arrogantly and boastfully ▷ n boastful talk or behaviour

BRAGGED ▸ brag

BRAGGER ▸ brag

BRAGGY adj boastful

BRAGLY ▸ brag

BRAGS ▸ brag

BRAHMA n heavy breed of domestic fowl with profusely feathered legs and feet

BRAHMAN n member of highest Hindu caste

BRAHMAS ▸ brahma

BRAHMIN same as ▸ brahman

BRAID vb interweave (hair, thread, etc) ▷ n length of hair etc that has been braided ▷ adj broad ▷ adv broadly

BRAIDE adj given to deceit

BRAIDED adj (of a river or stream) flowing in several shallow interconnected channels separated by banks of deposited material

BRAIDER ▸ braid

BRAIDS ▸ braid

BRAIL n one of several lines fastened to the leech of a fore-and-aft sail to aid in furling it ▷ vb furl (a fore-and-aft sail) using brails

BRAILED ▸ brail

BRAILLE n system of writing for the blind consisting of raised dots that can be interpreted by touch ▷ vb print or write using this method

BRAILS ▸ brail

BRAIN n soft mass of nervous tissue in the head ▷ vb hit (someone) hard on the head

BRAINED ▸ brain

BRAINS ▸ brain

BRAINY adj clever

BRAIRD vb appear as shoots

BRAIRDS ▸ braird

BRAISE vb cook slowly in a covered pan with a little liquid

BRAISED ▸ braise

BRAISES ▸ braise

BRAIZE same as ▸ braise

BRAIZES ▸ braize

BRAK n crossbred dog ▷ adj (of water) slightly salty

BRAKE same as ▸ bracken

BRAKED ▸ brake

BRAKES ▸ brake

BRAKIER ▸ braky

BRAKING ▸ brake

BRAKS ▸ brak

BRAKY adj brambly

BRALESS ▸ bra

BRAMBLE n Scots word for blackberry

BRAMBLY ▸ bramble

BRAME n powerful feeling of emotion

BRAMES ▸ brame

BRAN n husks of cereal grain

BRANCH n secondary stem of a tree ▷ vb (of stems, roots, etc) divide, then develop in different directions

BRANCHY ▸ branch

BRAND n particular product ▷ vb mark with a brand

BRANDED adj identifiable as being the product of a particular manufacturer or marketing company

BRANDER ▸ brand

BRANDS ▸ brand

BRANDY n alcoholic spirit distilled from wine ▷ vb give brandy to

BRANE n hypothetical component of string theory

BRANES ▸ brane

BRANGLE vb quarrel noisily

BRANK vb walk with swaggering gait

BRANKED ▸ brank

BRANKS pl n (formerly) iron bridle used to restrain scolding women

BRANKY adj ostentatious

BRANLE n old French country dance performed in a linked circle

BRANLES ▸ branle

BRANNED ▸ bran

BRANNER n person or machine that treats metal with bran

BRANNY adj having the appearance or texture of bran

BRANS ▸ bran

BRANSLE another word for ▸ brantle

BRANT n type of small goose of northern coastal regions, with dark grey plumage and a short neck

BRANTLE n French country dance

BRANTS ▸ brant

BRAS ▸ bra

BRASCO n lavatory

BRASCOS ▸ brasco

BRASERO n metal grid for burning coals

BRASES ▸ bra

BRASH adj offensively loud, showy, or self-confident ▷ n loose rubbish, such as broken rock, hedge clippings, etc ▷ vb assault

BRASHED ▸ brash

BRASHER ▸ brash

BRASHES ▸ brash

BRASHLY ▸ brash

BRASHY adj loosely fragmented

BRASIER same as ▸ brazier

BRASIL same as ▸ brazil

BRASILS ▸ brasil

BRASS n alloy of copper and zinc ▷ vb make irritated or annoyed

BRASSED ▸ brass

BRASSES ▸ brass

BRASSET same as > brassart

BRASSIE n former name for a club, a No. 2 wood, originally having a brass-plated sole and with a shallower face than a driver to give more loft

BRASSY same as ▸ brassie

BRAST same as ▸ burst

BRASTS ▸ brast

BRAT n unruly child

BRATS ▸ brat

BRATTLE vb make a rattling sound

BRATTY ▸ brat

BRAUNCH old variant of ▸ branch

BRAVA n professional assassin

BRAVADO n showy display of self-confidence ▷ vb behave with bravado

BRAVAS ▸ brava

BRAVE adj having or showing courage, resolution, and daring ▷ n Native American warrior ▷ vb confront with

resolution or courage
BRAVED ▸ **brave**
BRAVELY ▸ **brave**
BRAVER ▸ **brave**
BRAVERS ▸ **brave**
BRAVERY ▸ **brave**
BRAVES ▸ **brave**
BRAVEST ▸ **brave**
BRAVI ▸ **bravo**
BRAVING ▸ **brave**
BRAVO *interj* well done! ▷ *n*
cry of 'bravo' ▷ *vb* cry or
shout 'bravo'
BRAVOED ▸ **bravo**
BRAVOES ▸ **bravo**
BRAVOS ▸ **bravo**
BRAVURA *n* display of
boldness or daring
BRAVURE ▸ **bravura**
BRAW *adj* fine or excellent,
esp in appearance or dress
▷ *pl n* best clothes
BRAWER ▸ **braw**
BRAWEST ▸ **braw**
BRAWL *n* noisy fight ▷ *vb*
fight noisily
BRAWLED ▸ **brawl**
BRAWLER ▸ **brawl**
BRAWLIE *adj* in good health
BRAWLS ▸ **brawl**
BRAWLY ▸ **braw**
BRAWN *n* physical strength
BRAWNED ▸ **brawn**
BRAWNS ▸ **brawn**
BRAWNY *adj* muscular and
strong
BRAWS *n* fine apparel
BRAXIES ▸ **braxy**
BRAXY *n* acute and usually
fatal bacterial disease of
sheep
BRAY *vb* (of a donkey) utter
its loud harsh sound ▷ *n*
donkey's loud harsh sound
BRAYED ▸ **bray**
BRAYER ▸ **bray**
BRAYERS ▸ **bray**
BRAYING ▸ **bray**
BRAYS ▸ **bray**
BRAZA *n* Spanish unit of
measurement
BRAZAS ▸ **braza**
BRAZE *vb* join (two metal
surfaces) with brass ▷ *n*
high-melting solder or alloy
used in brazing
BRAZED ▸ **braze**
BRAZEN *adj* shameless and
bold ▷ *vb* face and
overcome boldly or
shamelessly
BRAZENS ▸ **brazen**
BRAZER ▸ **braze**

BRAZERS ▸ **braze**
BRAZES ▸ **braze**
BRAZIER *n* portable
container for burning
charcoal or coal
BRAZIL *n* red wood
obtained from various
tropical leguminous trees,
used for cabinetwork
BRAZILS ▸ **brazil**
BRAZING ▸ **braze**
BREACH *n* breaking of a
promise, obligation, etc
▷ *vb* break (a promise, law,
etc)
BREAD *n* food made by
baking a mixture of flour
and water or milk ▷ *vb*
cover (food) with
breadcrumbs before
cooking
BREADED ▸ **bread**
BREADS ▸ **bread**
BREADTH *n* extent of
something from side to side
BREADY *adj* having the
appearance or texture of
bread
BREAK ▸ **bracken**
BREAKER *n* large wave
BREAKS ▸ **bracken**
BREAKUP *n* separation or
disintegration
BREAM *n* Eurasian
freshwater fish with a
compressed body covered
with silvery scales ▷ *vb*
clean debris (from the
bottom of a vessel)
BREAMED ▸ **bream**
BREAMS ▸ **bream**
BREARE *same as* ▸ **brier**
BREARES ▸ **breare**
BREAST *n* either of the (two
soft fleshy milk-secreting
glands on a woman's chest
▷ *vb* reach the summit of
BREASTS ▸ **breast**
BREATH *n* taking in and
letting out of air during
breathing
BREATHE *vb* take in oxygen
and give out carbon dioxide
BREATHS ▸ **breath**
BREATHY *adj* (of the
speaking voice)
accompanied by an audible
emission of breath
BRECCIA *n* rock consisting
of angular fragments
embedded in a finer matrix,
formed by erosion, impact,
volcanic activity, etc

BRECHAM *n* straw
horse-collar
BRECHAN *same as*
▸ **brecham**
BRED *n* person who lives in
a small remote place
BREDE *archaic spelling of*
▸ **braid**
BREDED ▸ **brede**
BREDES ▸ **brede**
BREDIE *n* meat and
vegetable stew
BREDIES ▸ **bredie**
BREDING ▸ **brede**
BREDREN ▸ **brethren**
BREDRIN > **brethren**
BREDS ▸ **bred**
BREE *n* broth, stock, or juice
BREECH *n* buttocks ▷ *vb* fit
(a gun) with a breech
BREED *vb* produce new or
improved strains of
(domestic animals or
plants) ▷ *n* group of
animals etc within a
(species that have certain
clearly defined
characteristics
BREEDER *n* person who
breeds plants or animals
BREEDS ▸ **breed**
BREEKS *pl n* trousers
BREEM *same as* ▸ **breme**
BREENGE *vb* lunge forward
▷ *n* violent movement
BREER *another word for*
▸ **braird**
BREERED ▸ **breer**
BREERS ▸ **breer**
BREES ▸ **bree**
BREESE *same as* ▸ **breeze**
BREESES ▸ **breese**
BREEST ▸ **breast**
BREESTS ▸ **breast**
BREEZE *n* gentle wind ▷ *vb*
move quickly or casually
BREEZED ▸ **breeze**
BREEZES ▸ **breeze**
BREEZY *adj* windy
BREGMA *n* point on the top
(of the skull where the
coronal and sagittal sutures
meet: in infants this
corresponds to the anterior
fontanelle
BREHON *n* (formerly) judge
in Ireland
BREHONS ▸ **brehon**
BREI *vb* speak with a uvular
r, esp in Afrikaans
BREID *n* bread
BREIDS ▸ **breid**
BREIING ▸ **brei**

BREINGE same as ▸ **breenge**
BREIS ▸ **brei**
BREIST Scots word for ▸ **breast**
BREISTS ▸ **breist**
BREKKY slang word for > **breakfast**
BREME adj well-known
BREN n type of machine gun
BRENNE vb burn
BRENNES ▸ **brenne**
BRENS ▸ **bren**
BRENT n type of goose ▹ adj steep
BRENTER ▸ **brent**
BRENTS ▸ **brent**
BRER n brother: usually prefixed to a name
BRERE same as ▸ **brier**
BRERES ▸ **brere**
BRERS ▸ **brer**
BRETON n hat with an upturned brim and a rounded crown
BRETONS ▸ **breton**
BREVE n accent (˘), placed over a vowel to indicate that it is short or is pronounced in a specified way
BREVES ▸ **breve**
BREVET n document entitling a commissioned officer to hold temporarily a higher military rank without the appropriate pay and allowances ▹ vb promote by brevet
BREVETE adj patented
BREVETS ▸ **brevet**
BREVIER n (formerly) size of printer's type approximately equal to 8 point
BREVIS same as ▸ **brewis**
BREVITY n shortness
BREW vb make (beer etc) by steeping, boiling, and fermentation ▹ n beverage produced by brewing
BREWAGE n product of brewing
BREWED ▸ **brew**
BREWER ▸ **brew**
BREWERS ▸ **brew**
BREWERY n place where beer etc is brewed
BREWING n quantity of a beverage brewed at one time
BREWIS n bread soaked in broth, gravy, etc
BREWPUB n pub that

incorporates a brewery on its premises
BREWS ▸ **brew**
BREWSKI n beer
BREY same as ▸ **brei**
BREYED ▸ **brey**
BREYING ▸ **brey**
BREYS ▸ **brey**
BRIAR n S European shrub with a hard woody root (briarroot)
BRIARD n medium-sized dog of an ancient French sheep-herding breed having a long rough coat of a single colour
BRIARDS ▸ **briard**
BRIARED ▸ **briar**
BRIARS ▸ **briar**
BRIARY ▸ **briar**
BRIBE vb offer or give something to someone to gain favour, influence, etc ▹ n something given or offered as a bribe
BRIBED ▸ **bribe**
BRIBEE n one who is bribed
BRIBEES ▸ **bribee**
BRIBER ▸ **bribe**
BRIBERS ▸ **bribe**
BRIBERY n process of giving or taking bribes
BRIBES ▸ **bribe**
BRIBING ▸ **bribe**
BRICHT Scots word for ▸ **bright**
BRICK n (rectangular block of) baked clay used in building ▹ vb build, enclose, or fill with bricks
BRICKED ▸ **brick**
BRICKEN adj made of brick
BRICKIE n bricklayer
BRICKLE same as ▸ **brittle**
BRICKS ▸ **brick**
BRICKY same as ▸ **brickie**
BRICOLE n shot in which the cue ball touches a cushion after striking the object ball and before touching another ball
BRIDAL adj of a bride or a wedding ▹ n wedding or wedding feast
BRIDALS ▸ **bridal**
BRIDE n woman who has just been or is about to be married
BRIDED ▸ **bride**
BRIDES ▸ **bride**
BRIDGE n structure for crossing a river etc ▹ vb build a bridge over (something)

BRIDGED ▸ **bridge**
BRIDGES ▸ **bridge**
BRIDIE n semicircular pie containing meat and onions
BRIDIES ▸ **bridie**
BRIDING ▸ **bride**
BRIDLE n headgear for controlling a horse ▹ vb show anger or indignation
BRIDLED ▸ **bridle**
BRIDLER ▸ **bridle**
BRIDLES ▸ **bridle**
BRIDOON n horse's bit: small snaffle used in double bridles
BRIE same as ▸ **bree**
BRIEF adj short in duration ▹ n condensed statement or written synopsis ▹ vb give information and instructions to (a person)
BRIEFED ▸ **brief**
BRIEFER ▸ **brief**
BRIEFLY ▸ **brief**
BRIEFS pl n men's or women's underpants without legs
BRIER same as ▸ **briar**
BRIERED ▸ **brier**
BRIERS ▸ **brier**
BRIERY ▸ **brier**
BRIES ▸ **brie**
BRIG n two-masted square-rigged ship
BRIGADE n army unit smaller than a division ▹ vb organize into a brigade
BRIGAND n bandit
BRIGHT adj emitting or reflecting much light ▹ adv brightly
BRIGHTS pl n high beam of the headlights of a motor vehicle
BRIGS ▸ **brig**
BRIGUE vb solicit
BRIGUED ▸ **brigue**
BRIGUES ▸ **brigue**
BRIK n Tunisian deep-fried spicy pastry filled with fish or meat and sometimes an egg
BRIKI same as ▸ **cezve**
BRIKIS ▸ **briki**
BRIKS ▸ **brik**
BRILL n type of European flatfish popular as a food fish
BRILLER ▸ **brill**
BRILLO n tradename for a type of scouring pad impregnated with a detergent

B

BRILLOS ▸ brillo
BRILLS ▸ brill
BRIM *n* upper rim of a vessel ▷ *vb* fill or be full to the brim
BRIMFUL *adj* completely filled with
BRIMING *n* phosphorescence of sea
BRIMMED ▸ brim
BRIMMER *n* vessel, such as a glass or bowl, filled to the brim
BRIMS ▸ brim
BRIN *n* thread of silk from silkworm
BRINDED *adj* streaky or patchy
BRINDLE *n* brindled animal
BRINE *n* salt water ▷ *vb* soak in or treat with brine
BRINED ▸ brine
BRINER ▸ brine
BRINERS ▸ brine
BRINES ▸ brine
BRING *vb* carry, convey, or take to a designated place or person
BRINGER ▸ bring
BRINGS ▸ bring
BRINIER ▸ briny
BRINIES ▸ briny
BRINING ▸ brine
BRINISH ▸ brine
BRINJAL *n* dark purple tropical fruit, cooked and eaten as a vegetable
BRINK *n* edge of a steep place
BRINKS ▸ brink
BRINNY *n* stone, esp when thrown
BRINS ▸ brin
BRINY *adj* very salty
BRIO *n* liveliness
BRIOCHE *n* soft roll or loaf made from a very light yeast dough, sometimes mixed with currants
BRIONY *same as* ▸ **bryony**
BRIOS ▸ brio
BRIQUET *same as* > **briquette**
BRIS *n* ritual circumcision of male babies, usually at eight days old, regarded as the formal entry of the child to the Jewish community
BRISANT ▸ brisance
BRISE *n* type of jump
BRISES ▸ bris
BRISK *adj* lively and quick ▷ *vb* enliven
BRISKED ▸ brisk

BRISKEN *vb* make or become more lively or brisk
BRISKER ▸ brisk
BRISKET *n* beef from the breast of a cow
BRISKLY ▸ brisk
BRISKS ▸ brisk
BRISKY *another word for* ▸ **brisk**
BRISS *same as* ▸ **bris**
BRISSES ▸ bris
BRISTLE *n* short stiff hair ▷ *vb* (cause to) stand up like bristles
BRISTLY ▸ bristle
BRISTOL *n as in* **bristol board** type of heavy cardboard
BRISURE *n* mark of cadency in heraldry
BRIT *n* young of a herring, sprat, or similar fish
BRITH *same as* ▸ **bris**
BRITHS ▸ brith
BRITS ▸ brit
BRITSKA *same as* ▸ **britzka**
BRITT *n* young herring or sprat
BRITTLE *adj* hard but easily broken ▷ *n* crunchy sweet made with treacle and nuts
BRITTLY ▸ brittle
BRITTS ▸ britt
BRITZKA *n* long horse-drawn carriage with a folding top over the rear seat and a rear-facing front seat
BRIZE *same as* ▸ **breeze**
BRIZES ▸ brize
BRO *n* family member
BROACH *vb* introduce (a topic) for discussion ▷ *n* spit for roasting meat
BROAD *adj* having great breadth or width ▷ *n* woman
BROADAX *same as* > **broadaxe**
BROADEN *vb* make or become broad or broader
BROADER ▸ broad
BROADLY ▸ broad
BROADS ▸ broad
BROCADE *n* rich fabric woven with a raised design ▷ *vb* weave with such a design
BROCAGE *another word for* > **brokerage**
BROCARD *n* basic principle of civil law
BROCH *n* (in Scotland) a

circular dry-stone tower large enough to serve as a fortified home
BROCHAN *n* type of thin porridge
BROCHE *adj* woven with a raised design, as brocade
BROCHED ▸ broche
BROCHES ▸ broche
BROCHO *same as* ▸ **brachah**
BROCHOS ▸ brocho
BROCHS ▸ broch
BROCK *n* badger
BROCKED *adj* having different colours
BROCKET *n* small tropical American deer with small unbranched antlers
BROCKIT *same as* ▸ **brocked**
BROCKS ▸ brock
BROCOLI *same as* > **broccoli**
BROD *vb* prod
BRODDED ▸ brod
BRODDLE *vb* poke or pierce (something)
BRODKIN *same as* > **brodekin**
BRODS ▸ brod
BROG *n* bradawl
BROGAN *n* heavy laced, usually ankle-high, work boot
BROGANS ▸ brogan
BROGGED ▸ brog
BROGH *same as* ▸ **broch**
BROGHS ▸ brogh
BROGS ▸ brog
BROGUE *n* sturdy walking shoe
BROGUES ▸ brogue
BROIDER *archaic word for* > **embroider**
BROIL *vb* cook by direct heat under a grill ▷ *n* process of broiling
BROILED ▸ broil
BROILER *n* young tender chicken for roasting
BROILS ▸ broil
BROKAGE *another word for* > **brokerage**
BROKE *vb* negotiate or deal
BROKED ▸ broke
BROKEN ▸ bracken
BROKER *n* agent who buys or sells goods, securities, etc ▷ *vb* act as a broker (in)
BROKERS ▸ broker
BROKERY *n* work done by a broker
BROKES ▸ broke
BROKING ▸ broke
BROLGA *n* large grey

Australian crane with a trumpeting call

BROLGAS ▸ brolga

BROLLY *n* umbrella

BROMAL *n* yellowish oily synthetic liquid formerly used medicinally as a sedative and hypnotic

BROMALS ▸ bromal

BROMATE *same as* > **brominate**

BROME *n* type of grass

BROMES ▸ brome

BROMIC *adj* of or containing bromine in the trivalent or pentavalent state

BROMID *same as* ▸ **bromide**

BROMIDE *n* chemical compound used in medicine and photography

BROMIDS ▸ bromid

BROMIN *same as* ▸ **bromine**

BROMINE *n* dark red liquid element that gives off a pungent vapour

BROMINS ▸ bromin

BROMISE *same as* ▸ **bromize**

BROMISM *n* poisoning caused by the excessive intake of bromine or compounds containing bromine

BROMIZE *vb* treat with bromine

BROMMER *n* S African word for bluebottle

BROMO *n* something that contains bromide

BROMOS ▸ bromo

BRONC *same as* ▸ **bronco**

BRONCHI > **bronchus**

BRONCHO *same as* ▸ **bronco**

BRONCO *n* (in the US) wild or partially tamed pony

BRONCOS ▸ bronco

BRONCS ▸ bronc

BROND *n* old form of brand

BRONDS ▸ brond

BRONZE *n* alloy of copper and tin ▷ *adj* made of, or coloured like, bronze ▷ *vb* (esp of the skin) make or become brown

BRONZED ▸ bronze

BRONZEN *adj* made of or the colour of bronze

BRONZER *n* cosmetic applied to the skin to simulate a sun tan

BRONZES ▸ bronze

BRONZY ▸ bronze

BROO *n* brow of hill

BROOCH *n* ornament with a pin, worn fastened to clothes ▷ *vb* decorate with a brooch

BROOD *n* number of birds produced at one hatching ▷ *vb* (of a bird) sit on or hatch eggs

BROODED ▸ brood

BROODER *n* enclosure or other structure, usually heated, used for rearing young chickens or other fowl

BROODS ▸ brood

BROODY *adj* moody and sullen

BROOK *n* small stream ▷ *vb* bear or tolerate

BROOKED ▸ brook

BROOKIE *n* brook trout

BROOKS ▸ brook

BROOL *n* low roar

BROOLS ▸ brool

BROOM *n* long-handled sweeping brush ▷ *vb* sweep with a broom

BROOMED ▸ broom

BROOMS ▸ broom

BROOMY *adj* covered with growth of broom

BROOS ▸ broo

BROOSE *n* race at country wedding

BROOSES ▸ broose

BROS ▸ bro

BROSE *n* oatmeal or pease porridge, sometimes with butter or fat added

BROSES ▸ brose

BROSIER ▸ brosy

BROSY *adj* smeared with porridge

BROTH *n* soup, usu containing vegetables

BROTHEL *n* house where men pay to have sex with prostitutes

BROTHER *n* boy or man with the same parents as another person ▷ *interj* exclamation of amazement, disgust, surprise, disappointment, etc ▷ *vb* treat someone like a brother

BROTHS ▸ broth

BROTHY *adj* having appearance or texture of broth

BROUGH *same as* ▸ **broch**

BROUGHS ▸ brough

BROUGHT ▸ bring

BROUZE *same as* ▸ **broose**

BROUZES ▸ brouze

BROW *n* part of the face (from the eyes to the hairline)

BROWED *adj* having a brow

BROWN *n* colour of earth or wood ▷ *adj* (of bread) made from wheatmeal or wholemeal flour ▷ *vb* make or become brown

BROWNED ▸ brown

BROWNER ▸ brown

BROWNIE *n* small square nutty chocolate cake

BROWNS ▸ brown

BROWNY ▸ brown

BROWS ▸ brow

BROWSE *vb* look through (a book or articles for sale) in a casual manner ▷ *n* instance of browsing

BROWSED ▸ browse

BROWSER *n* software package that enables a user to read hypertext, esp on the Internet

BROWSES ▸ browse

BROWST *n* brewing (of ale, tea)

BROWSTS ▸ browst

BROWSY ▸ browse

BRR *same as* ▸ **brrr**

▌ This is useful if your consonant-heavy rack is giving you the shivers. And if you are even colder, **brrr** is available.

BRRR *interj* used to suggest shivering

BRU *South African word for* ▸ **friend**

BRUCHID *n* type of beetle

BRUCIN *same as* ▸ **brucine**

BRUCINE *n* bitter poisonous alkaloid resembling strychnine

BRUCINS ▸ brucin

BRUCITE *n* white translucent mineral

BRUCKLE *adj* brittle

BRUGH *n* large house

BRUGHS ▸ brugh

BRUHAHA *same as* > **bruhaha**

BRUIN *n* name for a bear, used in children's tales, fables, etc

BRUINS ▸ bruin

BRUISE *n* discoloured area on the skin caused by an injury ▷ *vb* cause a bruise on

B

BRUISED ▸ bruise
BRUISER n strong tough person
BRUISES ▸ bruise
BRUIT vb report ▷ n abnormal sound heard within the body during auscultation, esp a heart murmur
BRUITED ▸ bruit
BRUITER ▸ bruit
BRUITS ▸ bruit
BRULE n shortened form of the archaic word for a mixed-race person of Canadian Indian and White (usually French-Canadian) ancestry
BRULES ▸ brule
BRULOT n coffee-based alcoholic drink, served flaming
BRULOTS ▸ brulot
BRULYIE same as ▸ **brulzie**
BRULZIE n noisy dispute
BRUMAL adj of, characteristic of, or relating to winter
BRUMBY n wild horse
BRUME n heavy mist or fog
BRUMES ▸ brume
BRUMMER same as ▸ **brommer**
BRUMOUS ▸ brume
BRUNCH n breakfast and lunch combined ▷ vb eat brunch
BRUNET adj dark brown
BRUNETS ▸ brunet
BRUNG ▸ bring
BRUNT n main force or shock of a blow, attack, etc ▷ vb suffer the main force or shock of a blow, attack, etc
BRUNTED ▸ brunt
BRUNTS ▸ brunt
BRUS ▸ bru
BRUSH n device made of bristles, wires, etc used for cleaning, painting, etc ▷ vb clean, scrub, or paint with a brush
BRUSHED adj treated with a brushing process to raise the nap and give a softer and warmer finish
BRUSHER ▸ brush
BRUSHES ▸ brush
BRUSHUP n the act or an instance of tidying one's appearance
BRUSHY adj like a brush
BRUSK same as ▸ **brusque**

BRUSKER ▸ brusk
BRUSQUE adj blunt or curt in manner or speech
BRUSSEN adj bold
BRUST same as ▸ **burst**
BRUSTS ▸ brust
BRUT adj (of champagne or sparkling wine) very dry ▷ n very dry champagne
BRUTAL adj cruel and vicious
BRUTE n brutal person ▷ adj wholly instinctive or physical, like an animal
BRUTED ▸ brute
BRUTELY ▸ brute
BRUTER n diamond cutter
BRUTERS ▸ bruter
BRUTES ▸ brute
BRUTIFY less common word for ▸ **brutalize**
BRUTING n diamond cutting
BRUTISH adj of or like an animal
BRUTISM n stupidity; vulgarity
BRUTS ▸ brut
BRUX vb grind one's teeth
BRUXED ▸ brux
BRUXES ▸ brux
BRUXING ▸ brux
BRUXISM n habit of grinding the teeth, esp unconsciously
BRYONY n wild climbing hedge plant
BUAT same as ▸ **bowat**
BUATS ▸ buat
BUAZE n fibrous African plant
BUAZES ▸ buaze
BUB n youngster
BUBA another name for ▸ **yaws**
BUBAL n any of various antelopes, esp an extinct N African variety of hartebeest
BUBALE n large antelope
BUBALES ▸ bubale
BUBALIS same as ▸ **bubal**
BUBALS ▸ bubal
BUBAS ▸ buba
BUBBA n ordinary American person
BUBBAS ▸ bubba
BUBBLE n ball of air in a liquid or solid ▷ vb form bubbles
BUBBLED ▸ bubble
BUBBLER n drinking fountain in which the water

is forced in a stream from a small vertical nozzle
BUBBLES ▸ bubble
BUBBLY adj excited and lively ▷ n champagne
BUBINGA n reddish-brown wood from African tree
BUBKES n very small amount
BUBKIS n nothing
BUBO n inflammation and swelling of a lymph node, esp in the armpit or groin
BUBOED ▸ bubo
BUBOES ▸ bubo
BUBONIC ▸ bubo
BUBS ▸ bub
BUBU same as ▸ **boubou**
BUBUKLE n red spot on skin
BUBUS ▸ bubu
BUCARDO n type of Spanish mountain goat, recently extinct
BUCCAL adj of or relating to the cheek
BUCCINA n curved Roman horn
BUCHU n S African shrub whose leaves are used as an antiseptic and diuretic
BUCHUS ▸ buchu
BUCK n male of the goat, hare, kangaroo, rabbit, and reindeer ▷ vb (of a horse etc) jump with legs stiff and back arched
BUCKED ▸ buck
BUCKEEN n (in Ireland) poor young man who aspires to the habits and dress of the wealthy
BUCKER ▸ buck
BUCKERS ▸ buck
BUCKET vb open-topped roughly cylindrical container ▷ vb rain heavily
BUCKETS ▸ bucket
BUCKEYE n N American tree with erect clusters of white or red flowers and prickly fruits
BUCKIE n whelk or its shell
BUCKIES ▸ buckie
BUCKING ▸ buck
BUCKISH ▸ buck
BUCKLE n clasp for fastening a belt or strap ▷ vb fasten or be fastened with a buckle
BUCKLED ▸ buckle
BUCKLER n small round shield worn on the forearm ▷ vb defend

BUCKLES ▸ buckle

BUCKO n lively young fellow: often a term of address

BUCKOES ▸ bucko

BUCKOS ▸ bucko

BUCKRAM n cotton or linen cloth stiffened with size, etc, used in lining or stiffening clothes, bookbinding, etc ▷ vb stiffen with buckram

BUCKS ▸ buck

BUCKSAW n woodcutting saw having its blade set in a frame and tensioned by a turnbuckle across the back of the frame

BUCKSOM same as ▸ **buxom**

BUCKU same as ▸ **buchu**

BUCKUS ▸ bucku

BUCOLIC adj of the countryside or country life ▷ n pastoral poem

BUD n swelling on a plant that develops into a leaf or flower ▷ vb produce buds

BUDDED ▸ bud

BUDDER ▸ bud

BUDDERS ▸ bud

BUDDHA n person who has achieved a state of perfect enlightenment

BUDDHAS ▸ buddha

BUDDIED ▸ buddy

BUDDIER ▸ buddy

BUDDIES ▸ buddy

BUDDING ▸ buddy

BUDDLE n sloping trough in which ore is washed ▷ vb wash (ore) in a buddle

BUDDLED ▸ buddle

BUDDLES ▸ buddle

BUDDY n friend ▷ vb act as a friend to ▷ adj friendly

BUDGE vb move slightly ▷ n lambskin dressed for the fur to be worn on the outer side

BUDGED ▸ budge

BUDGER ▸ budge

BUDGERO same as > budgerow

BUDGERS ▸ budge

BUDGES ▸ budge

BUDGET n financial plan for a period of time ▷ vb plan the expenditure of (money or time) ▷ adj cheap

BUDGETS ▸ budget

BUDGIE n short form of budgerigar

BUDGIES ▸ budgie

BUDGING ▸ budge

BUDLESS ▸ bud

BUDLIKE ▸ bud

BUDMASH ▸ badmash

BUDO n combat and spirit in martial arts

BUDOS ▸ budo

BUDS ▸ bud

BUDWORM n pest that eats tree leaves and buds

BUFF n soft flexible undyed leather ▷ adj dull yellowish-brown ▷ vb clean or polish with soft material

BUFFA ▸ buffo

BUFFALO n member of the cattle tribe with upward-curving horns, mostly found in game reserves in S and E Africa ▷ vb confuse

BUFFE ▸ buffo

BUFFED ▸ buff

BUFFEL adj as in **buffel grass** grass used for pasture in Africa, India, and Australia

BUFFER same as ▸ **buff**

BUFFERS ▸ buffer

BUFFEST ▸ buff

BUFFET n counter where drinks and snacks are served ▷ vb knock against or about

BUFFETS ▸ buffet

BUFFI ▸ buffo

BUFFIER ▸ buffy

BUFFING ▸ buff

BUFFO n (in Italian opera of the 18th century) comic part, esp one for a bass

BUFFOON n clown or fool

BUFFOS ▸ buffo

BUFFS ▸ buff

BUFFY adj having appearance or texture of buff

BUFO n type of toad

BUFOS ▸ bufo

BUG n insect ▷ vb irritate

BUGABOO n imaginary source of fear

BUGBANE n European plant whose flowers are reputed to repel insects

BUGBEAR n thing that causes obsessive anxiety

BUGEYE n oyster-dredging boat

BUGEYES ▸ bugeye

BUGGAN n evil spirit

BUGGANE same as ▸ **buggan**

BUGGANS ▸ buggan

BUGGED ▸ bug

BUGGERY n anal intercourse

BUGGIER ▸ buggy

BUGGIES ▸ buggy

BUGGIN same as ▸ **buggan**

BUGGING ▸ bug

BUGGINS ▸ buggin

BUGGY n light horse-drawn carriage having two or four wheels ▷ adj infested with bugs

BUGLE n instrument like a small trumpet ▷ vb play or sound (on) a bugle

BUGLED ▸ bugle

BUGLER ▸ bugle

BUGLERS ▸ bugle

BUGLES ▸ bugle

BUGLET n small bugle

BUGLETS ▸ buglet

BUGLING ▸ bugle

BUGLOSS n hairy Eurasian plant with clusters of blue flowers

BUGONG same as ▸ **bogong**

BUGONGS ▸ bugong

BUGOUT n act of running away

BUGOUTS ▸ bugout

BUGS ▸ bug

BUGSEED n form of tumbleweed

BUGSHA same as ▸ **buqsha**

BUGSHAS ▸ bugsha

BUGWORT another name for ▸ bugbane

BUHL same as ▸ **boulle**

BUHLS ▸ buhl

BUHR ▸ burr

BUHRS ▸ burr

BUHUND n type of Norwegian dog

BUHUNDS ▸ buhund

BUIBUI n piece of black cloth worn as a shawl by Muslim women, esp on the E African coast

BUIBUIS ▸ buibui

BUIK same as ▸ **book**

BUIKS ▸ buik

BUILD vb make, construct, or form by joining parts or materials ▷ n shape of the body

BUILDED ▸ build

BUILDER n person who constructs houses and other buildings

BUILDS ▸ build

BUILDUP n gradual approach to a climax or critical point

BUILT ▸ build

B

BUIRDLY adj well-built
BUIST vb brand sheep with identification mark
BUISTED ▸ buist
BUISTS ▸ buist
BUKE same as ▸ book
BUKES ▸ buke
BUKKAKE n type of sexual practice
BUKSHEE n person in charge of paying wages
BUKSHI same as ▸ bukshee
BUKSHIS ▸ bukshi
BULB n onion-shaped root which grows into a flower or plant ▷ vb form into the shape of a bulb
BULBAR adj of or relating to a bulb, esp the medulla oblongata
BULBED ▸ bulb
BULBEL same as ▸ bulbil
BULBELS ▸ bulbel
BULBIL n small bulblike organ of vegetative reproduction growing in leaf axils or on flower stalks of plants such as the onion and tiger lily
BULBILS ▸ bulbil
BULBING ▸ bulb
BULBLET n small bulb at base of main bulb
BULBOUS adj round and fat
BULBS ▸ bulb
BULBUL n songbird of tropical Africa and Asia, with brown plumage and often a distinct crest
BULBULS ▸ bulbul
BULGE n swelling on a normally flat surface ▷ vb swell outwards
BULGED ▸ bulge
BULGER ▸ bulge
BULGERS ▸ bulge
BULGES ▸ bulge
BULGHUR same as ▸ bulgur
BULGIER ▸ bulge
BULGINE same as ▷ bullgine
BULGING ▸ bulge
BULGUR n kind of dried cracked wheat
BULGURS ▸ bulgur
BULGY ▸ bulge
BULIMIA n disorder characterized by compulsive overeating followed by vomiting
BULIMIC ▸ bulimia
BULIMUS ▸ bulimia
BULIMY ▸ bulimia
BULK n volume, size, or

magnitude of something ▷ vb cohere or cause to cohere in a mass
BULKAGE ▸ bulk
BULKED ▸ bulk
BULKER n ship that carries unpackaged cargo, usually consisting of a single dry commodity, such as coal or grain
BULKERS ▸ bulker
BULKIER ▸ bulky
BULKILY ▸ bulky
BULKING n expansion of excavated material to a volume greater than that of the excavation from which it came
BULKS ▸ bulk
BULKY adj very large and massive, esp so as to be unwieldy
BULL adj any male bovine animal, esp one that is sexually mature
BULLA n leaden seal affixed to a papal bull, having a representation of Saints Peter and Paul on one side and the name of the reigning pope on the other
BULLACE n small Eurasian tree of which the damson is the cultivated form
BULLAE ▸ bulla
BULLARY n boilery for preparing salt
BULLATE adj puckered or blistered in appearance
BULLBAT another name for ▷ nighthawk
BULLDOG n thickset dog with a broad head and a muscular body
BULLED ▸ bull
BULLER vb make bubbling sound
BULLERS ▸ buller
BULLET n small piece of metal fired from a gun ▷ vb move extremely quickly
BULLETS ▸ bullet
BULLIED ▸ bully
BULLIER ▸ bully
BULLIES ▸ bully
BULLING ▸ bull
BULLION n gold or silver in the form of bars
BULLISH adj like a bull
BULLOCK n castrated bull ▷ vb work hard and long
BULLOSA adj as in epidermolysis bullosa

type of genetic skin disorder
BULLOUS adj blistered
BULLPEN n large cell where prisoners are confined together temporarily
BULLS ▸ bull
BULLY n person who hurts, persecutes, or intimidates weaker people ▷ vb hurt, intimidate, or persecute (a weaker or smaller person), esp to make him do something ▷ adj dashing
BULRUSH n tall stiff reed
BULSE n purse or bag for diamonds
BULSES ▸ bulse
BULWARK n wall used as a fortification ▷ vb defend or fortify with or as if with a bulwark
BUM n buttocks or anus ▷ vb get by begging ▷ adj of poor quality
BUMALO same as ▸ bummalo
BUMBAG n small bag attached to a belt and worn round the waist
BUMBAGS ▸ bumbag
BUMBAZE vb confuse; bewilder
BUMBLE vb speak, do, or move in a clumsy way ▷ n blunder or botch
BUMBLED ▸ bumble
BUMBLER ▸ bumble
BUMBLES ▸ bumble
BUMBO n drink with gin or rum, nutmeg, lemon juice, etc
BUMBOAT n any small boat used for ferrying supplies or goods for sale to a ship at anchor or at a mooring
BUMBOS ▸ bumbo
BUMELIA n thorny shrub
BUMF n official documents or forms
BUMFS ▸ bumf
BUMKIN same as ▸ bumpkin
BUMKINS ▸ bumkin
BUMMALO n Bombay duck
BUMMED ▸ bum
BUMMEL n stroll
BUMMELS ▸ stroll
BUMMER n unpleasant or disappointing experience
BUMMERS ▸ bummer
BUMMEST ▸ bum
BUMMING ▸ bum
BUMMLE Scots variant of

▸ **bumble**

BUMMLED ▸ bummle

BUMMLES ▸ bummle

BUMMOCK n submerged mass of ice projecting downwards

BUMP vb knock or strike with a jolt ▹ n dull thud from an impact or collision

BUMPED ▸ bump

BUMPER n bar on the front and back of a vehicle to protect against damage ▹ adj unusually large or abundant ▹ vb toast with a bumper

BUMPERS ▸ bumper

BUMPH same as ▸ bumf

BUMPHS ▸ bumph

BUMPIER ▸ bumpy

BUMPILY ▸ bumpy

BUMPING ▸ bump

BUMPKIN n awkward simple country person

BUMPS ▸ bump

BUMPY adj having an uneven surface

BUMS ▸ bum

BUMSTER adj (of trousers) cut low so as to reveal the top part of the buttocks

BUN n small sweet bread roll or cake

BUNA n synthetic rubber formed by polymerizing butadiene or by copolymerizing it with such compounds as acrylonitrile or styrene

BUNAS ▸ buna

BUNCE n windfall; boom ▹ vb charge someone too much money

BUNCED ▸ bunce

BUNCES ▸ bunce

BUNCH n number of things growing, fastened, or grouped together ▹ vb group or be grouped together in a bunch

BUNCHED ▸ bunch

BUNCHES pl n hairstyle in which hair is tied into two sections on either side of the head at the back

BUNCHY adj composed of or resembling bunches

BUNCING ▸ bunce

BUNCO n swindle, esp one by confidence tricksters ▹ vb swindle

BUNCOED ▸ bunco

BUNCOS ▸ bunco

BUND n embankment or German federation ▹ vb form into an embankment

BUNDE ▸ bund

BUNDED ▸ bund

BUNDH same as ▸ bandh

BUNDHS ▸ bundh

BUNDIED ▸ bundy

BUNDIES ▸ bundy

BUNDING ▸ bund

BUNDIST ▸ bund

BUNDLE n number of things gathered loosely together ▹ vb cause to go roughly or unceremoniously

BUNDLED ▸ bundle

BUNDLER ▸ bundle

BUNDLES ▸ bundle

BUNDOOK n rifle

BUNDS ▸ bund

BUNDT n type of sweet cake

BUNDTS ▸ bundt

BUNDU n largely uninhabited wild region far from towns

BUNDUS ▸ bundu

BUNDY n time clock at work ▹ vb register arrival or departure from work on a time clock

BUNG n stopper for a cask etc ▹ vb close with a bung

BUNGED ▸ bung

BUNGEE n strong elastic cable

BUNGEES ▸ bungee

BUNGER n firework

BUNGERS ▸ bunger

BUNGEY same as ▸ bungee

BUNGEYS ▸ bungey

BUNGIE same as ▸ bungee

BUNGIES ▸ bungy

BUNGING ▸ bung

BUNGLE vb spoil through incompetence ▹ n blunder or muddle

BUNGLED ▸ bungle

BUNGLER ▸ bungle

BUNGLES ▸ bungle

BUNGS ▸ bung

BUNGY ▸ bungee

BUNIA same as ▸ bunnia

BUNIAS ▸ bunia

BUNION n inflamed swelling on the big toe

BUNIONS ▸ bunion

BUNJE same as ▸ bungee

BUNJEE same as ▸ bungee

BUNJEES ▸ bunjee

BUNJES ▸ bunje

BUNJIE same as ▸ bungee

BUNJIES ▸ bunjie

BUNJY same as ▸ bungee

BUNK n narrow shelflike bed ▹ vb prepare to sleep

BUNKED ▸ bunk

BUNKER n sand-filled hollow forming an obstacle on a golf course ▹ vb drive (the ball) into a bunker

BUNKERS ▸ bunker

BUNKING ▸ bunk

BUNKO same as ▸ bunco

BUNKOED ▸ bunko

BUNKOS ▸ bunko

BUNKS ▸ bunk

BUNKUM n nonsense

BUNKUMS ▸ bunkum

BUNN same as ▸ bun

BUNNET same as ▸ bonnet

BUNNETS ▸ bunnet

BUNNIA n Hindu shopkeeper

BUNNIAS ▸ bunnia

BUNNIES ▸ bunny

BUNNS ▸ bunn

BUNNY n child's word for a rabbit

BUNRAKU n Japanese form of puppet theatre in which the puppets are usually about four feet high, with moving features as well as limbs and each puppet is manipulated by up to three puppeteers who remain onstage

BUNS pl n buttocks

BUNSEN n as in bunsen burner gas burner used in scientific labs

BUNSENS ▸ bunsen

BUNT vb (of an animal) butt (something) with the head or horns ▹ n act or an instance of bunting

BUNTAL n straw obtained from leaves of the talipot palm

BUNTALS ▸ buntal

BUNTED ▸ bunt

BUNTER n batter who deliberately taps ball lightly

BUNTERS ▸ bunter

BUNTIER ▸ bunt

BUNTING n decorative flags

BUNTS ▸ bunt

BUNTY ▸ bunt

BUNYA n tall dome-shaped Australian coniferous tree

BUNYAS ▸ bunya

BUNYIP n legendary monster said to live in swamps and lakes

BUNYIPS ▸ bunyip

BUOY n floating marker

B

anchored in the sea ▷ *vb* prevent from sinking

BUOYAGE *n* system of buoys

BUOYANT *adj* able to float

BUOYED ▶ buoy

BUOYING ▶ buoy

BUOYS ▶ buoy

BUPKES *same as* ▶ bubkes

BUPKIS ▶ bubkis

BUPKUS *same as* ▶ bubkes

BUPPIE *n* affluent young Black person

BUPPIES ▶ buppy

BUPPY *same as* ▶ buppie

BUQSHA *n* former Yemeni coin

BUQSHAS ▶ buqsha

BUR ▶ burr

BURA *same as* ▶ buran

BURAN *n* blizzard, with the wind blowing from the north and reaching gale force

BURANS ▶ buran

BURAS ▶ bura

BURB *n* suburb

BURBLE *vb* make a bubbling sound ▷ *n* bubbling or gurgling sound

BURBLED ▶ burble

BURBLER ▶ burble

BURBLES ▶ burble

BURBLY *adj* burbling

BURBOT *n* freshwater fish of the cod family that has barbels around its mouth

BURBOTS ▶ burbot

BURBS ▶ burb

BURD *Scots form of* ▶ bird

BURDASH *n* fringed sash worn over coat

BURDEN *n* heavy load ▷ *vb* put a burden on

BURDENS ▶ burden

BURDIE *Scots form of* ▶ birdie

BURDIES ▶ burdie

BURDOCK *n* weed with prickly burrs

BURDS ▶ burd

BUREAU *n* office that provides a service

BUREAUS ▶ bureau

BUREAUX ▶ bureau

BURET *same as* ▶ burette

BURETS ▶ buret

BURETTE *n* glass tube for dispensing known volumes of fluids

BURG *n* fortified town

BURGAGE *n* (in England) tenure of land or tenement

in a town or city, which originally involved a fixed money rent

BURGEE *n* triangular or swallow-tailed flag flown from the mast of a merchant ship for identification and from the mast of a yacht to indicate its owner's membership of a particular yacht club

BURGEES ▶ burgee

BURGEON *vb* develop or grow rapidly ▷ *n* bud of a plant

BURGER *n* hamburger

BURGERS ▶ burger

BURGESS *n* (in England) citizen or freeman of a borough

BURGH *n* Scottish borough

BURGHAL ▶ burgh

BURGHER *n* citizen

BURGHS ▶ burgh

BURGHUL *same as* ▶ bulgur

BURGLAR *n* person who enters a building to commit a crime, esp theft ▷ *vb* burgle

BURGLE *vb* break into (a house, shop, etc)

BURGLED ▶ burgle

BURGLES ▶ burgle

BURGOO *n* porridge

BURGOOS ▶ burgoo

BURGOUT *same as* ▶ burgoo

BURGS ▶ burg

BURHEL *same as* ▶ bharal

BURHELS ▶ burhel

BURIAL *n* burying of a dead body

BURIALS ▶ burial

BURIED ▶ bury

BURIER *n* person or thing that buries

BURIERS ▶ burier

BURIES ▶ bury

BURIN *n* steel chisel used for engraving metal, wood, or marble

BURINS ▶ burin

BURITI *n* type of palm tree

BURITIS ▶ buriti

BURK *same as* ▶ berk

BURKA *same as* ▶ burqa

BURKAS ▶ burka

BURKE *vb* murder in such a way as to leave no marks on the body, usually by suffocation

BURKED ▶ burke

BURKER ▶ burke

BURKERS ▶ burke

BURKES ▶ burke

BURKHA *n* all-enveloping garment worn by Muslim women

BURKHAS ▶ burkha

BURKING ▶ burke

BURKITE ▶ burke

BURKS ▶ burk

BURL *n* small knot or lump in wool ▷ *vb* remove the burls from (cloth)

BURLAP *n* coarse fabric woven from jute, hemp, or the like

BURLAPS ▶ burlap

BURLED ▶ burl

BURLER ▶ burl

BURLERS ▶ burl

BURLESK *same as* > burlesque

BURLEY *same as* ▶ berley

BURLEYS ▶ burley

BURLIER ▶ burly

BURLILY ▶ burly

BURLING ▶ burl

BURLS ▶ burl

BURLY *adj* (of a person) broad and strong

BURN *vb* be or set on fire ▷ *n* injury or mark caused by fire or exposure to heat

BURNED ▶ burn

BURNER *n* part of a stove or lamp that produces the flame

BURNERS ▶ burner

BURNET *n* type of rose

BURNETS ▶ burnet

BURNIE *n* sideburn

BURNIES ▶ burnie

BURNING ▶ burn

BURNISH *vb* make smooth and shiny by rubbing ▷ *n* shiny finish

BURNOUS *n* long circular cloak with a hood, worn esp by Arabs

BURNOUT *n* failure of a mechanical device from excessive heating

BURNS ▶ burn

BURNT ▶ burn

BUROO *n* government office from which unemployment benefit is distributed

BUROOS ▶ buroo

BURP *n* belch ▷ *vb* belch

BURPED ▶ burp

BURPEE *n* type of physical exercise movement

BURPEES ▶ burpee

BURPING ▶ burp

BURPS ▸ burp

BURQA n long enveloping garment worn by Muslim women in public, covering all but the wearer's eyes

This Arab woman's garment, illustrates the fact that Q doesn't always have to be followed by U. It has several variants including **burka** and **burkha**.

BURQAS ▸ burqa

BURR n small power-driven hand-operated rotary file, esp for removing burrs or for machining recesses ▸ vb form a rough edge on (a workpiece)

BURRED ▸ burr

BURREL same as ▸ bharal

BURRELL same as ▸ bharal

BURRELS ▸ burrel

BURRER n person who removes burrs

BURRERS ▸ burrer

BURRHEL same as ▸ burrel

BURRIER ▸ burry

BURRING ▸ burr

BURRITO n tortilla folded over a filling of minced beef, chicken, cheese, or beans

BURRO n donkey, esp one used as a pack animal

BURROS ▸ burro

BURROW n hole dug in the ground by a rabbit etc ▸ vb dig holes in the ground

BURROWS ▸ burrow

BURRS ▸ burr

BURRY adj full of or covered in burs

BURS ▸ burr

BURSA n small fluid-filled sac that reduces friction between movable parts of the body, esp at joints

BURSAE ▸ bursa

BURSAL ▸ bursa

BURSAR n treasurer of a school, college, or university

BURSARS ▸ bursar

BURSARY n scholarship

BURSAS ▸ bursa

BURSATE ▸ bursa

BURSE n flat case used at Mass as a container for the corporal

BURSEED n type of plant

BURSERA adj of a type of gum tree

BURSES ▸ burse

BURST vb break or cause to break open or apart suddenly and noisily, esp from internal pressure ▸ n sudden breaking open or apart ▸ adj broken apart

BURSTED ▸ burst

BURSTEN ▸ burst

BURSTER ▸ burst

BURSTS ▸ burst

BURTHEN archaic word for ▸ burden

BURTON n type of hoisting tackle

BURTONS ▸ burton

BURWEED n any of various plants that bear burs, such as the burdock

BURY vb place in a grave

BURYING ▸ bury

BUS n large motor vehicle for carrying passengers between stops ▸ vb travel by bus

BUSBAR n electrical conductor, maintained at a specific voltage and capable of carrying a high current, usually used to make a common connection between several circuits in a system

BUSBARS ▸ busbar

BUSBIES ▸ busby

BUSBOY n waiter's assistant

BUSBOYS ▸ busboy

BUSBY n tall fur hat worn by some soldiers

BUSED ▸ bus

BUSERA n Ugandan alcoholic drink made from millet: sometimes mixed with honey

BUSERAS ▸ busera

BUSES ▸ bus

BUSGIRL n waiter's assistant

BUSH n dense woody plant, smaller than a tree ▸ vb fit a bush to (a casing or bearing)

BUSHED adj extremely tired

BUSHEL n obsolete unit of measure equal to 8 gallons (36.4 litres) ▸ vb alter or mend (a garment)

BUSHELS ▸ bushel

BUSHER ▸ bush

BUSHERS ▸ bush

BUSHES ▸ bush

BUSHFLY n small black Australian fly that breeds in faeces and dung

BUSHIDO n feudal code of the Japanese samurai, stressing self-discipline, courage and loyalty

BUSHIE same as ▸ bushy

BUSHIER ▸ bushy

BUSHIES ▸ bushy

BUSHILY ▸ bushy

BUSHING same as ▸ bush

BUSHMAN n person who lives or travels in the bush

BUSHMEN ▸ bushman

BUSHPIG n wild brown or black forest pig of tropical Africa and Madagascar

BUSHTIT n small grey active North American songbird

BUSHWA n nonsense

BUSHWAH same as ▸ bushwa

BUSHWAS ▸ bushwa

BUSHY adj (of hair) thick and shaggy ▸ n person who lives in the bush

BUSIED ▸ busy

BUSIER ▸ busy

BUSIES ▸ busy

BUSIEST ▸ busy

BUSILY adv in a busy manner

BUSING ▸ bus

BUSINGS ▸ bus

BUSK vb act as a busker ▸ n strip of whalebone, wood, steel, etc, inserted into the front of a corset to stiffen it

BUSKED ▸ busk

BUSKER ▸ busk

BUSKERS ▸ busk

BUSKET n bouquet

BUSKETS ▸ busket

BUSKIN n (formerly) sandal-like covering for the foot and leg, reaching the calf and usually laced

BUSKING ▸ busk

BUSKINS ▸ buskin

BUSKS ▸ busk

BUSKY same as ▸ bosky

BUSLOAD n number of people bus carries

BUSMAN n person who drives a bus

BUSMEN ▸ busman

BUSS archaic or dialect word for ▸ kiss

BUSSED ▸ bus

BUSSES ▸ bus

BUSSING ▸ bus

BUSSU n type of palm tree

BUSSUS ▸ bussu**

B

BUST n chest of a human being, esp a woman's bosom ▷ vb burst or break

BUSTARD n bird with long strong legs, a heavy body, a long neck, and speckled plumage

BUSTED ▸ bust

BUSTEE same as ▸ basti

BUSTEES ▸ bustee

BUSTER n person or thing destroying something as specified

BUSTERS ▸ buster

BUSTI same as ▸ basti

BUSTIC n type of small American tree

BUSTICS ▸ bustic

BUSTIER n close-fitting strapless women's top

BUSTING ▸ bust

BUSTIS ▸ busti

BUSTLE vb hurry with a show of activity or energy ▷ n energetic and noisy activity

BUSTLED ▸ bustle

BUSTLER ▸ bustle

BUSTLES ▸ bustle

BUSTS ▸ bust

BUSTY adj (of a woman) having a prominent bust

BUSUUTI n long garment with short sleeves and a square neckline, worn by Ugandan women, esp in S Uganda

BUSY adj actively employed ▷ vb keep (someone, esp oneself) busy

BUSYING ▸ busy

BUT prep except ▷ adv only ▷ n outer room of a two-roomed cottage: usually the kitchen

BUTANE n gas used for fuel

BUTANES ▸ butane

BUTANOL n colourless substance

BUTCH adj markedly or aggressively masculine ▷ n lesbian who is noticeably masculine

BUTCHER n person who slaughters animals or sells their meat ▷ vb kill and prepare (animals) for meat

BUTCHES ▸ butch

BUTE n drug used illegally to dope horses

BUTENE n pungent colourless gas

BUTENES ▸ butene

BUTEO n type of American hawk

BUTEOS ▸ buteo

BUTES ▸ bute

BUTLE vb act as butler

BUTLED ▸ butle

BUTLER n chief male servant ▷ vb act as a butler

BUTLERS ▸ butler

BUTLERY n butler's room

BUTLES ▸ butle

BUTLING ▸ butle

BUTMENT same as > abutment

BUTS ▸ but

BUTT n thicker or blunt end of something, such as the end of the stock of a rifle ▷ vb strike or push with the head or horns

BUTTALS n abuttal

BUTTE n isolated steep flat-topped hill

BUTTED ▸ butt

BUTTER n edible fatty yellow solid made form cream ▷ vb put butter on

BUTTERS ▸ butter

BUTTERY n (in some universities) room in which food and drink are sold to students ▷ adj containing, like, or coated with butter

BUTTES ▸ butte

BUTTIES ▸ butty

BUTTING ▸ butt

BUTTLE vb act as butler

BUTTLED ▸ buttle

BUTTLES ▸ buttle

BUTTOCK n either of the two fleshy masses that form the human rump ▷ vb perform a kind of wrestling manoeuvre on a person

BUTTON n small disc or knob sewn to clothing, which can be passed through a slit in another piece of fabric to fasten them ▷ vb fasten with buttons

BUTTONS n page boy

BUTTONY ▸ button

BUTTS ▸ butt

BUTTY n sandwich

BUTUT n Gambian monetary unit worth one hundredth of a dalasi

BUTUTS ▸ butut

BUTYL adj of or containing any of four isomeric forms of the group C_4H_9- ▷ n of,

consisting of, or containing any of four isomeric forms of the group C_4H_9-

BUTYLS ▸ butyl

BUTYRAL n type of resin

BUTYRIC adj as in butyric acid type of acid

BUTYRIN n colourless liquid ester or oil found in butter. It is formed from butyric acid and glycerine

BUTYRYL n radical of butyric acid

BUVETTE n roadside café

BUXOM adj (of a woman) healthily plump and full-bosomed

BUXOMER ▸ buxom

BUXOMLY ▸ buxom

BUY vb acquire by paying money for ▷ n thing acquired through payment

BUYABLE ▸ buy

BUYBACK n repurchase by a company of some or all of its shares from an investor, who acquired them by putting venture capital into the company when it was formed

BUYER n customer

BUYERS ▸ buyer

BUYING n as in panic buying the buying up of large quantities of something feared to be scarce

BUYINGS ▸ buying

BUYOFF n purchase

BUYOFFS ▸ buyoff

BUYOUT n purchase of a company, esp by its former management or staff

BUYOUTS ▸ buyout

BUYS ▸ buy

BUZUKI same as > bouzouki

BUZUKIA ▸ buzuki

BUZUKIS ▸ buzuki

BUZZ n rapidly vibrating humming sound ▷ vb make a humming sound

BUZZARD n bird of prey of the hawk family

BUZZCUT n very short haircut

BUZZED ▸ buzz

BUZZER n electronic device that produces a buzzing sound as a signal

BUZZERS ▸ buzzer

BUZZES ▸ buzz

BUZZIER ▸ buzzy

BUZZING ▸ buzz

BUZZWIG *n* bushy wig

BUZZY *adj* making a buzzing sound

BWANA *n* (in E Africa) master, often used as a respectful form of address

BWANAS ▶ bwana

BWAZI *same as* **▶ buaze**

BWAZIS ▶ bwazi

BY *prep* indicating the doer of an action, nearness, movement past, time before or during which, etc ▷ *adv* near ▷ *n* a pass to the next round (of a competition, etc)

BYCATCH *n* unwanted fish and other sea animals caught in a fishing net along with the desired kind of fish

BYCOKET *n* former Italian high-crowned hat

BYDE *same as* **▶ bide**

BYDED ▶ byde

BYDES ▶ byde

BYDING ▶ byde

BYE *n* situation where a player or team wins a round by having no opponent ▷ *interj* goodbye ▷ *sentence substitute* goodbye

BYELAW *n* rule made by a local authority for the regulation of its affairs or management of the area it governs

BYELAWS ▶ byelaw

BYES ▶ bye

BYGONE *adj* past

BYGONES ▶ bygone

BYKE ▶ bicycle

BYKED ▶ bicycle

BYKES ▶ bicycle

BYKING ▶ bicycle

BYLANE *n* side lane or alley off a road

BYLANES ▶ bylane

BYLAW *n* rule made by a local authority

BYLAWS ▶ bylaw

BYLINE *n* line under the title of a newspaper or magazine article giving the author's name ▷ *vb* give a byline to

BYLINED ▶ byline

BYLINER ▶ byline

BYLINES ▶ byline

BYLIVE *same as* **▶ belive**

BYNAME *n* nickname

BYNAMES ▶ byname

BYNEMPT ▶ bename

BYPASS *n* main road built to avoid a city ▷ *vb* go round or avoid

BYPAST ▶ bypass

BYPATH *n* little-used path or track, esp in the country

BYPATHS ▶ bypath

BYPLACE *n* private place

BYPLAY *n* secondary action or talking carried on apart while the main action proceeds, esp in a play

BYPLAYS ▶ byplay

BYRE *n* shelter for cows

BYREMAN *n* man who works in byre

BYREMEN ▶ byreman

BYRES ▶ byre

BYRL *same as* **▶ birl**

BYRLADY *interj* short for By Our Lady

BYRLAW *same as* **▶ bylaw**

BYRLAWS ▶ byrlaw

BYRLED ▶ byrl

BYRLING ▶ byrl

BYRLS ▶ byrl

BYRNIE *n* archaic word for coat of mail

BYRNIES ▶ byrnie

BYROAD *n* secondary or side road

BYROADS ▶ byroad

BYROOM *n* private room

BYROOMS ▶ byroom

BYS ▶ by

BYSSAL *adj* of mollusc's byssus

BYSSI ▶ byssus

BYSSINE *adj* made from flax

BYSSOID *adj* consisting of fine fibres

BYSSUS *n* mass of strong threads secreted by a sea mussel or similar mollusc that attaches the animal to a hard fixed surface

BYTALK *n* trivial conversation

BYTALKS ▶ bytalk

BYTE *n* group of bits processed as one unit of data

BYTES ▶ byte

BYWAY *n* minor road

BYWAYS ▶ byway

BYWONER *n* poor tenant-farmer

BYWORD *n* person or thing regarded as a perfect example of something

BYWORDS ▶ byword

BYWORK *n* work done outside usual working hours

BYWORKS ▶ bywork

BYZANT *same as* **▶ bezant**

BYZANTS ▶ byzant

Cc

C can be a tricky letter to use, especially as it only forms a single two-letter word **ch**. But if you remember this, you won't waste time racking your brains for two-letter words. There are, however, plenty of good three-letter words beginning with **C**. **Cox** scores 12 points, while **caw, cow** and **coy** are each worth 8 and **caz, coz** and **cuz** are worth 14. It's also a good idea to remember the short words starting with **C** that don't contain any vowels: **cly** and **cwm** as well as **ch**.

CAA *a Scots word for* ▸ **call**

CAAED ▸ **caa**

CAAING ▸ **caa**

CAAS ▸ **caa**

CAB *n* taxi ▷ *vb* take a taxi

CABA *same as* ▸ **cabas**

CABAL *n* small group of political plotters ▷ *vb* form a cabal

CABALA *a variant spelling of* > **kabbalah**

CABALAS ▸ **cabala**

CABALS ▸ **cabal**

CABANA *n* tent used as a dressing room by the sea

CABANAS ▸ **cabana**

CABARET *n* dancing and singing show in a nightclub

CABAS *n* reticule

CABBAGE *n* vegetable with a large head of green leaves ▷ *vb* steal

CABBAGY ▸ **cabbage**

CABBALA *a variant spelling of* > **kabbalah**

CABBED ▸ **cab**

CABBIE *n* taxi driver

CABBIES ▸ **cabbie**

CABBING ▸ **cab**

CABBY *same as* ▸ **cabbie**

CABER *n* tree trunk tossed in competition at Highland games

CABERS ▸ **caber**

CABEZON *n* large food fish of N American Pacific coastal waters, with greenish flesh

CABILDO *n* Spanish municipal council

CABIN *n* compartment in a ship or aircraft ▷ *vb* confine in a small space

CABINED ▸ **cabin**

CABINET *n* piece of furniture with drawers or shelves

CABINS ▸ **cabin**

CABLE *n* strong thick rope; a wire or bundle of wires that conduct electricity ▷ *vb* send (someone) a message by cable

CABLED ▸ **cable**

CABLER *n* cable broadcasting company

CABLERS ▸ **cabler**

CABLES ▸ **cable**

CABLET *n* small cable, esp a cable-laid rope that has a circumference of less than 25 centimetres (ten inches)

CABLETS ▸ **cablet**

CABLING ▸ **cable**

CABMAN *n* driver of a cab

CABMEN ▸ **cabman**

CABOB *vb* roast on a skewer

CABOBS ▸ **cabob**

CABOC *n* type of Scottish cheese

CABOCS ▸ **caboc**

CABOMBA *n* type of aquatic plant

CABOOSE *n* guard's van on a train

CABOVER *adj* of or denoting a truck or lorry in which the cab is over the engine

CABRE *adj* heraldic term designating an animal rearing

CABRIE *n* pronghorn antelope

CABRIES ▸ **cabrie**

CABRIO *short for* > **cabriolet**

CABRIOS ▸ **cabrio**

CABRIT *n* pronghorn antelope

CABRITS ▸ **cabrit**

CABS ▸ **cab**

CACA *n* heroin

CACAO *same as* ▸ **cocoa**

CACAOS ▸ **cocoa**

CACAS ▸ **caca**

CACHACA *n* white Brazilian rum made from sugar cane

CACHE *n* hidden store of weapons or treasure ▷ *vb* store in a cache

CACHED ▸ **cache**

CACHES ▸ **cache**

CACHET *n* prestige, distinction ▷ *vb* apply a commemorative design to an envelope, as a first-day cover

CACHETS ▸ **cachet**

CACHEXY *same as* > **cachexia**

CACHING ▸ **cache**

CACHOU *same as* ▸ **catechu**

CACHOUS ▸ **catechu**

CACIQUE *n* American Indian chief in a Spanish-speaking region

CACKIER ▸ **cacky**

CACKLE *vb* laugh shrilly ▷ *n* cackling noise

CACKLED ▸ **cackle**

CACKLER ▸ **cackle**

CACKLES ▸ **cackle**

CACKY *adj* of or like excrement

CACODYL *n* oily poisonous liquid with a strong garlic smell

CACOEPY *n* bad or mistaken pronunciation

CACOLET n seat fitted to the back of a mule

CACONYM n erroneous name

CACOON n large seed of the sword-bean

CACOONS ▸ cacoon

CACTI ▸ cactus

CACTOID adj resembling a cactus

CACTUS n fleshy desert plant with spines but no leaves

CACUMEN n apex

CAD n dishonourable man

CADAGA n eucalyptus tree of tropical and subtropical Australia with a smooth green trunk

CADAGAS ▸ cadaga

CADAGI same as ▸ **cadaga**

CADAGIS ▸ cadagi

CADAVER n corpse

CADDICE same as ▸ **caddis**

CADDIE n person who carries a golfer's clubs ▷ vb act as a caddie

CADDIED ▸ caddie

CADDIES ▸ caddie

CADDIS n type of coarse woollen yarn, braid, or fabric

CADDISH ▸ cad

CADDY same as ▸ **caddie**

CADDYSS same as ▸ **caddis**

CADE n juniper tree ▷ adj (of a young animal) left by its mother and reared by humans, usually as a pet

CADEAU n present

CADEAUX ▸ cadeau

CADEE old form of ▸ **cadet**

CADEES ▸ cadee

CADELLE n type of beetle that feeds on flour, grain, and other stored foods

CADENCE n rise and fall in the pitch of the voice ▷ vb modulate musically

CADENCY same as ▸ **cadence**

CADENT adj having cadence

CADENZA n complex solo passage in a piece of music

CADES ▸ cade

CADET n young person training for the armed forces or police

CADETS ▸ cadet

CADGE vb get (something) by taking advantage of someone's generosity

CADGED ▸ cadge

CADGER n person who cadges

CADGERS ▸ cadger

CADGES ▸ cadge

CADGIER ▸ cadgy

CADGING ▸ cadge

CADGY adj cheerful

CADI n judge in a Muslim community

CADIE n messenger

CADIES ▸ cadie

CADIS ▸ cadi

CADMIC ▸ cadmium

CADMIUM n bluish-white metallic element used in alloys

CADRANS n instrument used in gemcutting

CADRE n small group of people selected and trained to form the core of a political organization or military unit

CADRES ▸ cadre

CADS ▸ cad

CADUAC n windfall

CADUACS ▸ caduac

CADUCEI > caduceus

CAECA ▸ caecum

CAECAL ▸ caecum

CAECUM n pouch at the beginning of the large intestine

CAEOMA n aecium in some rust fungi that has no surrounding membrane

CAEOMAS ▸ caeoma

CAERULE same as ▸ **cerule**

CAESAR n any emperor, autocrat, dictator, or other powerful ruler

CAESARS ▸ caesar

CAESE interj Shakespearean interjection

CAESIUM n silvery-white metallic element used in photocells

CAESTUS same as ▸ **cestus**

CAESURA n pause in a line of verse

CAFARD n feeling of severe depression

CAFARDS ▸ cafard

CAFE n small or inexpensive restaurant serving light refreshments

CAFES ▸ cafe

CAFF n café

CAFFEIN same as > **caffeine**

CAFFILA n caravan train

CAFFS ▸ caff

CAFILA same as ▸ **caffila**

CAFILAS ▸ cafila

CAFTAN same as ▸ **kaftan**

CAFTANS ▸ caftan

CAG same as ▸ **cagoule**

CAGANER n figure of a squatting defecating person, a traditional character in Catalan Christmas crèche scenes

CAGE n enclosure of bars or wires, for keeping animals or birds ▷ vb confine in a cage

CAGED ▸ cage

CAGEFUL n amount which fills a cage to capacity

CAGER n basketball player

CAGERS ▸ cager

CAGES ▸ cage

CAGEY adj reluctant to go into details

CAGIER ▸ cagey

CAGIEST ▸ cagey

CAGILY ▸ cagey

CAGING ▸ cage

CAGMAG adj done shoddily ▷ vb chat idly

CAGMAGS ▸ cagmag

CAGOT n member of a class of French outcasts

CAGOTS ▸ cagot

CAGOUL same as ▸ **cagoule**

CAGOULE n lightweight hooded waterproof jacket

CAGOULS ▸ cagoul

CAGS ▸ cag

CAGY same as ▸ **cagey**

CAHIER n notebook

CAHIERS ▸ cahier

CAHOOT n partnership

CAHOOTS ▸ cahoot

CAHOW n Bermuda petrel

CAHOWS ▸ cahow

CAID n Moroccan district administrator

CAIDS ▸ caid

CAILLE n quail

CAILLES ▸ caille

CAIMAC same as > **caimacam**

CAIMACS ▸ caimac

CAIMAN same as ▸ **cayman**

CAIMANS ▸ caiman

CAIN n (in Scotland and Ireland) payment in kind, usually farm produce paid as rent

CAINS ▸ cain

CAIQUE n long narrow light rowing skiff used on the Bosporus

CAIQUES ▸ caique

CAIRD n travelling tinker

CAIRDS ▸ caird

C

CAIRN n mound of stones erected as a memorial or marker

CAIRNED adj marked by a cairn

CAIRNS ▸ **cairn**

CAIRNY adj covered with cairns

CAISSON > **cofferdam**

CAITIFF n cowardly or base person ▷ adj cowardly

CAITIVE n captive

CAJAPUT same as ▸ **cajuput**

CAJEPUT same as ▸ **cajuput**

CAJOLE vb persuade by flattery

CAJOLED ▸ **cajole**

CAJOLER ▸ **cajole**

CAJOLES ▸ **cajole**

CAJON n Peruvian wooden box used as a drum

CAJONES ▸ **cajon**

CAJUN n music of the Cajun people, combining blues and European folk music

CAJUPUT n small tree or shrub native to the East Indies and Australia, with whitish flowers and leaves

CAKE n sweet food baked from a mixture of flour, eggs, etc ▷ vb form into a hardened mass or crust

CAKED ▸ **cake**

CAKES ▸ **cake**

CAKEY ▸ **cake**

CAKIER ▸ **cake**

CAKIEST ▸ **cake**

CAKING ▸ **cake**

CAKINGS ▸ **cake**

CAKY ▸ **cake**

CALALOO same as ▸ **calalu**

CALALU n edible leaves of various plants, used as greens or in making thick soups

CALALUS ▸ **calalu**

CALAMAR n any member of the squid family

CALAMI ▸ **calamus**

CALAMUS n tropical Asian palm, some species of which are a source of rattan and canes

CALANDO adv (to be performed) with gradually decreasing tone and speed

CALASH n horse-drawn carriage with low wheels and a folding top

CALATHI > **calathus**

CALCAR n spur or spurlike process, as on the leg of a

bird or the corolla of a flower

CALCARS ▸ **calcar**

CALCED adj wearing shoes

CALCES ▸ **calx**

CALCIC adj of, containing, or concerned with lime or calcium

CALCIFY vb harden by the depositing of calcium salts

CALCINE vb oxidize (a substance) by heating

CALCITE n colourless or white form of calcium carbonate

CALCIUM n silvery-white metallic element found in bones, teeth, limestone, and chalk

CALCULI > **calculus**

CALDERA n large basin-shaped crater at the top of a volcano, formed by the collapse or explosion of the cone

CALDRON same as > **cauldron**

CALECHE same as ▸ **calash**

CALEFY vb to make warm

CALENDS pl n first day of each month in the ancient Roman calendar

CALESA n horse-drawn buggy

CALESAS ▸ **calesa**

CALF n young cow, bull, elephant, whale, or seal

CALFS ▸ **calf**

CALIBER same as ▸ **calibre**

CALIBRE n person's ability or worth

CALICES ▸ **calix**

CALICHE n bed of sand or clay in arid regions cemented by calcium carbonate, sodium chloride, and other soluble minerals

CALICLE same as ▸ **calycle**

CALICO n white cotton fabric

CALICOS ▸ **calico**

CALID adj warm

CALIF same as ▸ **caliph**

CALIFS ▸ **calif**

CALIGO n speck on the cornea causing poor vision

CALIGOS ▸ **caligo**

CALIMA n Saharan dust-storm

CALIMAS ▸ **calima**

CALIPEE n yellow glutinous edible part of the turtle

found next to the lower shell, considered a delicacy

CALIPER same as > **calliper**

CALIPH n Muslim ruler

CALIPHS ▸ **caliph**

CALIVER n type of musket

CALIX n cup

CALK same as ▸ **caulk**

CALKED ▸ **calk**

CALKER ▸ **calk**

CALKERS ▸ **calk**

CALKIN ▸ **calk**

CALKING ▸ **calk**

CALKINS ▸ **calk**

CALKS ▸ **calk**

CALL vb name ▷ n cry, shout

CALLA n S African plant with a white funnel-shaped spathe enclosing a yellow spadix

CALLAIS n green stone found as beads and ornaments in the late Neolithic and early Bronze Age of W Europe

CALLAN same as ▸ **callant**

CALLANS ▸ **callan**

CALLANT n youth

CALLAS ▸ **calla**

CALLBOY n person who notifies actors when it is time to go on stage

CALLED ▸ **call**

CALLEE n computer function being used

CALLEES ▸ **callee**

CALLER n person or thing that calls, esp a person who makes a brief visit ▷ adj (of food, esp fish) fresh

CALLERS ▸ **caller**

CALLET n scold

CALLETS ▸ **callet**

CALLID adj cunning

CALLING n vocation, profession

CALLOP n edible Australian freshwater fish, often golden or pale yellow in colour

CALLOPS ▸ **callop**

CALLOSE n carbohydrate, a polymer of glucose, found in plants, esp in the sieve tubes

CALLOUS adj showing no concern for other people's feelings ▷ vb make or become callous

CALLOW adj young and inexperienced ▷ n someone young and inexperienced

CALLOWS ▸ callow
CALLS ▸ call
CALLUNA n type of heather
CALLUS n area of thick hardened skin ▷ vb produce or cause to produce a callus
CALM adj not agitated or excited ▷ n peaceful state ▷ vb make or become calm
CALMANT n sedative
CALMED ▸ calm
CALMER ▸ calm
CALMEST ▸ calm
CALMIER ▸ calmy
CALMING ▸ calm
CALMLY ▸ calm
CALMS ▸ calm
CALMY adj tranquil
CALO n military servant
CALOMEL n colourless tasteless powder
CALORIC adj of heat or calories ▷ n hypothetical elastic fluid formerly postulated as the embodiment of heat
CALORIE n unit of measurement for the energy value of food
CALORY same as ▸ calorie
CALOS ▸ calo
CALOTTE n skullcap worn by Roman Catholic clergy
CALOYER n monk of the Greek Orthodox Church, esp of the Basilian Order
CALP n type of limestone
CALPA n Hindu unit of time
CALPAC n large black brimless hat made of sheepskin or felt, worn by men in parts of the Near East
CALPACK same as ▸ calpac
CALPACS ▸ calpac
CALPAIN n type of enzyme
CALPAS ▸ calpa
CALPS ▸ calp
CALQUE ▸ caulk
CALQUED ▸ calque
CALQUES ▸ calque
CALTHA n marsh marigold
CALTHAS ▸ caltha
CALTRAP same as ▸ caltrop
CALTROP n floating Asian plant
CALUMBA n Mozambiquan root used for medicinal purposes
CALUMET n peace pipe
CALUMNY n false or malicious statement
CALVARY n representation

of Christ's crucifixion, usually sculptured and in the open air
CALVE vb give birth to a calf
CALVED ▸ calve
CALVER vb prepare fish for cooking
CALVERS ▸ calver
CALVES ▸ calf
CALVING ▸ calve
CALX n powdery metallic oxide formed when an ore or mineral is roasted
CALXES ▸ calx
CALYCES ▸ calyx
CALYCLE n cup-shaped structure, as in the coral skeleton
CALYPSO n West Indian song with improvised topical lyrics
CALYX n outer leaves that protect a flower bud
CALYXES ▸ calyx
CALZONE n folded pizza filled with cheese, tomatoes, etc
CALZONI ▸ calzone
CAM n device that converts a circular motion to a to-and-fro motion ▷ vb furnish (a machine) with a cam
CAMA n hybrid offspring of a camel and a llama
CAMAIEU n cameo
CAMAIL n neck and shoulders covering of mail worn with and laced to the basinet
CAMAILS ▸ camail
CAMAN n wooden stick used to hit the ball in shinty
CAMANS ▸ caman
CAMARON n shrimp
CAMAS same as ▸ camass
CAMASES ▸ camas
CAMASH same as ▸ camass
CAMASS n type of North American plant
CAMBER n slight upward curve to the centre of a surface ▷ vb form or be formed with a surface that curves upwards to its centre
CAMBERS ▸ camber
CAMBIA ▸ cambium
CAMBIAL ▸ cambium
CAMBISM ▸ cambist
CAMBIST n dealer or expert in foreign exchange
CAMBIUM n meristem that

increases the girth of stems and roots by producing additional xylem and phloem
CAMBOGE n type of gum resin
CAMBREL same as ▸ gambrel
CAMBRIC n fine white linen fabric
CAME ▸ come
CAMEL n humped mammal that can survive long periods without food or water in desert regions
CAMELIA same as > camellia
CAMELID adj of or relating to camels ▷ n any animal of the camel family
CAMELOT n supposedly idyllic period or age
CAMELRY n troops mounted on camels
CAMELS ▸ camel
CAMEO n brooch or ring with a profile head carved in relief ▷ vb to appear in a brief role
CAMEOED ▸ cameo
CAMEOS ▸ cameo
CAMERA n apparatus used for taking photographs or pictures for television or cinema
CAMERAE ▸ camera
CAMERAL adj of or relating to a judicial or legislative chamber
CAMERAS ▸ camera
CAMES ▸ canvas
CAMESE same as ▸ camise
CAMESES ▸ camese
CAMION n lorry, or, esp formerly, a large dray
CAMIONS ▸ camion
CAMIS n light robe
CAMISA n smock
CAMISAS ▸ camisa
CAMISE n loose light shirt, smock, or tunic originally worn in the Middle Ages
CAMISES ▸ camise
CAMISIA n surplice
CAMLET n tough waterproof cloth
CAMLETS ▸ camlet
CAMMED ▸ cam
CAMMIE n webcam award
CAMMIES ▸ cammie
CAMMING ▸ cam
CAMO n short for camouflage

C

CAMOGIE n form of hurling played by women

CAMOODI a Caribbean name for ▸ **anaconda**

CAMORRA n secret criminal group

CAMOS ▸ camo

CAMOTE n type of sweet potato

CAMOTES ▸ camote

CAMP vb stay in a camp ▷ adj effeminate or homosexual ▷ adj (place for) temporary lodgings consisting of tents, huts, or cabins

CAMPANA n bell or bell shape

CAMPED ▸ camp

CAMPER n person who lives or temporarily stays in a tent, cabin, etc

CAMPERS ▸ camper

CAMPERY n campness

CAMPEST ▸ camp

CAMPHOL another word for ▸ borneol

CAMPHOR n aromatic crystalline substance used medicinally and in mothballs

CAMPI ▸ campo

CAMPIER ▸ campy

CAMPILY ▸ campy

CAMPING ▸ camp

CAMPION n red, pink, or white wild flower

CAMPLE vb to argue

CAMPLED ▸ cample

CAMPLES ▸ cample

CAMPLY ▸ camp

CAMPO n level or undulating savanna country, esp in the uplands of Brazil

CAMPONG n in Malaysia, a village

CAMPOS ▸ campo

CAMPOUT n camping trip

CAMPS ▸ camp

CAMPUS n grounds of a university or college ▷ vb to restrict a student to campus, as a punishment

CAMPY adj effeminate

CAMS ▸ cam

CAMSHO adj crooked

CAMUS n type of loose robe

CAMUSES ▸ camus

CAMWOOD n W African leguminous tree whose hard wood was formerly used to make a red dye

CAN vb be able to ▷ n metal container for food or liquids

CANADA n canada goose

CANADAS ▸ canada

CANAKIN same as ▸ cannikin

CANAL n artificial waterway ▷ vb dig a canal through

CANALED ▸ canal

CANALS ▸ canal

CANAPE n small piece of bread or toast with a savoury topping

CANAPES ▸ canape

CANARD n false report

CANARDS ▸ canard

CANARY n small yellow songbird often kept as a pet ▷ vb perform a dance called the canary

CANASTA n card game like rummy, played with two packs

CANBANK n container for receiving cans for recycling

CANCAN n lively high-kicking dance performed by a female group

CANCANS ▸ cancan

CANCEL vb stop (something that has been arranged) from taking place ▷ n new leaf or section of a book replacing a defective one, one containing errors, or one that has been omitted

CANCELS ▸ cancel

CANCER n serious disease resulting from a malignant growth or tumour

CANCERS ▸ cancer

CANCHA n toasted maize

CANCHAS ▸ cancha

CANDELA n unit of luminous intensity

CANDENT adj emitting light as a result of being heated to a high temperature

CANDID adj honest and straightforward ▷ n unposed photograph

CANDIDA n yeastlike parasitic fungus which causes thrush

CANDIDS ▸ candid

CANDIE n South Indian unit of weight

CANDIED adj coated with sugar

CANDIES ▸ candy

CANDIRU n parasitic freshwater catfish of the Amazon region

CANDLE n stick of wax enclosing a wick, which is burned to produce light ▷ vb test by holding up to a candle

CANDLED ▸ candle

CANDLER ▸ candle

CANDLES ▸ candle

CANDOCK n type of water lily, or horsetail

CANDOR same as ▸ candour

CANDORS ▸ candor

CANDOUR n honesty and straightforwardness

CANDY n sweet or sweets ▷ vb make sweet

CANE n stem of the bamboo or similar plant ▷ vb beat with a cane

CANED ▸ cane

CANEH n Hebrew unit of length

CANEHS ▸ caneh

CANELLA n fragrant cinnamon-like inner bark of a W Indian tree, used as a spice and in medicine

CANER ▸ cane

CANERS ▸ cane

CANES ▸ cane

CANFUL n amount a can will hold

CANFULS ▸ canful

CANG same as ▸ cangue

CANGLE vb to wrangle

CANGLED ▸ cangle

CANGLES ▸ cangle

CANGS ▸ cang

CANGUE n (formerly in China) a large wooden collar worn by petty criminals as a punishment

CANGUES ▸ cangue

CANID n animal of the dog family

CANIDS ▸ canid

CANIER ▸ cany

CANIEST ▸ cany

CANIKIN same as ▸ cannikin

CANINE adj of or like a dog ▷ n sharp pointed tooth between the incisors and the molars

CANINES ▸ canine

CANING n beating with a cane as a punishment

CANINGS ▸ caning

CANKER n ulceration, ulcerous disease ▷ vb infect or become infected with or as if with canker

CANKERS ▸ canker
CANKERY adj like a canker
CANN vb direct a ship's steering
CANNA n type of tropical plant with broad leaves, cultivated for its red or yellow showy flowers
CANNACH n cotton grass
CANNAE vb can not
CANNAS ▸ canna
CANNED ▸ can
CANNEL n type of dull coal
CANNELS ▸ cannel
CANNER n person or organization whose job is to can foods
CANNERS ▸ canner
CANNERY n factory where food is canned
CANNIE same as ▸ canny
CANNIER ▸ canny
CANNILY ▸ canny
CANNING ▸ can
CANNOLI n Sicilian pudding of pasta shells filled with sweetened ricotta
CANNON n gun of large calibre ▷ vb to collide (with)
CANNONS ▸ cannon
CANNOT vb can not
CANNS ▸ cann
CANNULA n narrow tube for insertion into a bodily cavity, as for draining off fluid, introducing medication, etc
CANNY adj shrewd, cautious ▷ adv quite
CANOE n light narrow open boat propelled by a paddle or paddles ▷ vb use a canoe
CANOED ▸ canoe
CANOER ▸ canoe
CANOERS ▸ canoe
CANOES ▸ canoe
CANOLA n cooking oil extracted from a variety of rapeseed developed in Canada
CANOLAS ▸ canola
CANON n priest serving in a cathedral
CANONIC same as ▸ canonical
CANONRY n office, benefice, or status of a canon
CANONS ▸ canon
CANOPIC adj of ancient Egyptian vase
CANOPY n covering above a bed, door, etc ▷ vb cover

with or as if with a canopy
CANS ▸ can
CANSFUL ▸ canful
CANSO n love song
CANSOS ▸ canso
CANST vb form of 'can' used with the pronoun thou or its relative form
CANT n insincere talk ▷ vb use cant ▷ adj oblique
CANTAL n French cheese
CANTALA n tropical American plant, the agave
CANTALS ▸ cantal
CANTAR variant form of ▸ kantar
CANTARS ▸ cantar
CANTATA n musical work consisting of arias, duets, and choruses
CANTATE n 98th psalm sung as a nonmetrical hymn
CANTDOG same as ▸ canthook
CANTED ▸ cant
CANTEEN n restaurant attached to a workplace or school
CANTER vb move at gait between trot and gallop
CANTERS ▸ canter
CANTEST ▸ cant
CANTHAL ▸ canthus
CANTHI ▸ canthus
CANTHUS n inner or outer corner or angle of the eye, formed by the natural junction of the eyelids
CANTIC ▸ cant
CANTICO vb to dance as part of an act of worship
CANTIER ▸ canty
CANTILY ▸ canty
CANTINA n bar or wine shop, esp in a Spanish-speaking country
CANTING ▸ cant
CANTION n song
CANTLE n back part of a saddle that slopes upwards ▷ vb to set up, or stand, on high
CANTLED ▸ cantle
CANTLES ▸ cantle
CANTLET n piece
CANTO same as ▸ cantus
CANTON n political division of a country, esp Switzerland ▷ vb divide into cantons
CANTONS ▸ canton
CANTOR n man employed

to lead services in a synagogue
CANTORS ▸ cantor
CANTOS ▸ canto
CANTRAP same as ▸ cantraip
CANTRED n district comprising a hundred villages
CANTREF same as ▸ cantred
CANTRIP n magic spell ▷ adj (of an effect) produced by black magic
CANTS ▸ cant
CANTUS n medieval form of church singing
CANTY adj lively
CANULA same as ▸ cannula
CANULAE ▸ canula
CANULAR adj shaped like a cannula
CANULAS ▸ canula
CANVAS n heavy coarse cloth used for sails and tents, and for oil painting ▷ vb to cover with, or be applied to, canvas
CANVASS vb try to get votes or support (from) ▷ n canvassing
CANY adj cane-like
CANYON n deep narrow valley
CANYONS ▸ canyon
CANZONA n type of 16th- or 17th-century contrapuntal music, usually for keyboard, lute, or instrumental ensemble
CANZONE n Provençal or Italian lyric, often in praise of love or beauty
CANZONI ▸ canzone
CAP n soft close-fitting covering for the head ▷ vb cover or top with something
CAPA n type of Spanish cloak
CAPABLE adj having the ability (for)
CAPABLY ▸ capable
CAPAS ▸ capa
CAPE n short cloak ▷ vb to cut and remove the hide of an animal
CAPED ▸ cape
CAPELAN another word for ▸ capelin
CAPELET n small cape
CAPELIN n type of small marine food fish occurring in northern and Arctic seas

C

CAPER n high-spirited prank ▷ vb skip about

CAPERED ▶ **caper**

CAPERER ▶ **caper**

CAPERS pl n pickled flower buds of a Mediterranean shrub used in sauces

CAPES ▶ **cape**

CAPEX n capital expenditure

CAPEXES ▶ **capex**

CAPFUL n quantity held by a (usually bottle) cap

CAPFULS ▶ **capful**

CAPH n letter of the Hebrew alphabet

CAPHS ▶ **caph**

CAPI ▶ **capo**

CAPIAS n (formerly) a writ directing a sheriff or other officer to arrest a named person

CAPING ▶ **cape**

CAPITA ▶ **caput**

CAPITAL n chief city of a country ▷ adj involving or punishable by death

CAPITAN another name for ▶ **hogfish**

CAPITOL n (in America) building housing the state legislature

CAPIZ n bivalve shell of a mollusc found esp in the Philippines, used in jewellery, ornaments, lampshades, etc

CAPIZES ▶ **capiz**

CAPLE n horse

CAPLES ▶ **caple**

CAPLESS ▶ **cap**

CAPLET n medicinal tablet, usually oval in shape, coated in a soluble substance

CAPLETS ▶ **caplet**

CAPLIN same as ▶ **capelin**

CAPLINS ▶ **caplin**

CAPO n device fitted across the strings of a guitar or similar instrument so as to raise the pitch

CAPON n castrated cock fowl fattened for eating

CAPONS ▶ **capon**

CAPORAL n strong coarse dark tobacco

CAPOS ▶ **capo**

CAPOT n winning of all the tricks by one player ▷ vb score a capot (against)

CAPOTE n long cloak or soldier's coat, usually with a hood

CAPOTES ▶ **capote**

CAPOTS ▶ **capot**

CAPOUCH same as ▶ **capuche**

CAPPED ▶ **cap**

CAPPER ▶ **cap**

CAPPERS ▶ **cap**

CAPPING ▶ **cap**

CAPRATE n any salt of capric acid

CAPRIC adj (of a type of acid) smelling of goats

CAPRICE same as > **capriccio**

CAPRID n any member of the goat family

CAPRIDS ▶ **caprid**

CAPRIFY vb induce figs to ripen

CAPRINE adj of or resembling a goat

CAPRIS pl n women's tight-fitting trousers

CAPROCK n layer of rock that overlies a salt dome

CAPROIC adj as in **caproic acid** oily acid found in milk

CAPS ▶ **cap**

CAPSID n outer protein coat of a mature virus

CAPSIDS ▶ **capsid**

CAPSIZE vb (of a boat) overturn accidentally

CAPSTAN n rotating cylinder round which a ship's rope is wound

CAPSULE n soluble gelatine case containing a dose of medicine ▷ adj very concise ▷ vb to contain within a capsule

CAPTAIN n commander of a ship or civil aircraft ▷ vb be captain of

CAPTAN n type of fungicide

CAPTANS ▶ **captan**

CAPTION n title or explanation accompanying an illustration ▷ vb provide with a caption

CAPTIVE n person kept in confinement ▷ adj kept in confinement ▷ vb to take prisoner

CAPTOR n person who captures a person or animal

CAPTORS ▶ **captor**

CAPTURE vb take by force ▷ n capturing

CAPUCHE n large hood or cowl, esp that worn by Capuchin friars

CAPUERA same as

> **capoeira**

CAPUL same as ▶ **caple**

CAPULS ▶ **capul**

CAPUT n main or most prominent part of an organ or structure

CAR n motor vehicle designed to carry a small number of people

CARABAO n water buffalo

CARABID n type of usu dark-coloured beetle such as the bombardier and other ground beetles

CARABIN same as ▶ **carbine**

CARACAL n lynx with reddish fur, which inhabits deserts of N Africa and S Asia

CARACK same as ▶ **carrack**

CARACKS ▶ **carack**

CARACOL same as > **caracole**

CARACT n sign or symbol

CARACTS ▶ **caract**

CARACUL n black loosely curled fur obtained from the skins of newly born lambs of the karakul sheep

CARAFE n glass bottle for serving water or wine

CARAFES ▶ **carafe**

CARAMBA n Spanish interjection similar to 'wow!'

CARAMEL n chewy sweet made from sugar and milk ▷ vb to turn into caramel

CARANNA n gumlike substance

CARAP n crabwood

CARAPAX n carapace

CARAPS ▶ **carap**

CARAT n unit of weight of precious stones

CARATE n tropical disease

CARATES ▶ **carate**

CARATS ▶ **carat**

CARAUNA same as ▶ **caranna**

CARAVAN n large enclosed vehicle for living in, designed to be towed by a car or horse ▷ vb travel or have a holiday in a caravan

CARAVEL n two- or three-masted sailing ship, esp one with a broad beam, high poop deck, and lateen rig that was used by the Spanish and Portuguese in the 15th and 16th centuries

CARAWAY n plant whose

seeds are used as a spice

CARB n carbohydrate

CARBARN n streetcar depot

CARBEEN n Australian eucalyptus tree with drooping branches and grey bark

CARBENE n neutral divalent free radical, such as methylene: CH_2

CARBIDE n compound of carbon with a metal

CARBIES ▸ carby

CARBINE n light automatic rifle

CARBO n carbohydrate

CARBON n nonmetallic element occurring as charcoal, graphite, and diamond, found in all organic matter

CARBONS ▸ carbon

CARBORA n former name for the koala

CARBOS ▸ carbo

CARBOY n large bottle with a protective casing

CARBOYS ▸ carboy

CARBS ▸ carb

CARBY n short for carburettor

CARCAKE n (formerly, in Scotland) a cake traditionally made for Shrove Tuesday

CARCASE ▸ carcass

CARCASS n dead body of an animal ▸ vb to make a carcass of

CARCEL n French unit of light

CARCELS ▸ carcel

CARD n piece of thick stiff paper or cardboard used for identification, reference, or sending greetings or messages ▸ vb comb out fibres of wool or cotton before spinning

CARDAN n as in **cardan joint** type of universal joint

CARDECU n old French coin (a quarter of a crown)

CARDED ▸ card

CARDER ▸ card

CARDERS ▸ card

CARDI n cardigan

CARDIA n lower oesophageal sphincter

CARDIAC adj of the heart ▸ n person with a heart disorder

CARDIAE ▸ cardia

CARDIAS ▸ cardia

CARDIE short for ▸ **cardigan**

CARDIES ▸ cardie

CARDING ▸ card

CARDIO adj exercising heart ▸ n cardiovascular exercise

CARDIOS ▸ cardio

CARDIS ▸ cardi

CARDON n variety of cactus

CARDONS ▸ cardon

CARDOON n thistle-like S European plant with spiny leaves, purple flowers, and an edible leafstalk

CARDS ▸ card

CARDUUS n thistle

CARDY same as ▸ **cardie**

CARE vb be concerned ▸ n careful attention, caution

CARED ▸ care

CAREEN vb tilt over to one side

CAREENS ▸ careen

CAREER n series of jobs in a profession or occupation that a person has through their life ▸ vb rush in an uncontrolled way ▸ adj having chosen to dedicate his or her life to a particular occupation

CAREERS ▸ career

CAREFUL adj cautious in attitude or action

CAREME n period of Lent

CAREMES ▸ careme

CARER n person who looks after someone who is ill or old, often a relative

CARERS ▸ carer

CARES ▸ care

CARESS n gentle affectionate touch or embrace ▸ vb touch gently and affectionately

CARET n symbol indicating a place in written or printed matter where something is to be inserted

CARETS ▸ caret

CAREX n any member of the sedge family

CARFARE n fare that a passenger is charged for a ride on a bus, etc

CARFAX n place where principal roads or streets intersect, esp a place in a town where four roads meet

CARFOX same as ▸ **carfax**

CARFUL n maximum number of people a car will hold

CARFULS ▸ carful

CARGO n goods carried by a ship, aircraft, etc ▸ vb to load

CARGOED ▸ cargo

CARGOES ▸ cargo

CARGOS ▸ cargo

CARHOP n waiter or waitress at a drive-in restaurant ▸ vb work as a carhop

CARHOPS ▸ carhop

CARIAMA another word for ▸ **seriema**

CARIBE n piranha

CARIBES ▸ caribe

CARIBOU n large N American reindeer

CARICES ▸ carex

CARIED adj (of teeth) decayed

CARIERE obsolete word for ▸ **career**

CARIES n tooth decay

CARINA n keel-like part or ridge, as in the breastbone of birds or the fused lower petals of a leguminous flower

CARINAE ▸ carina

CARINAL adj keel-like

CARINAS ▸ carina

CARING adj feeling or showing care and compassion for other people ▸ n practice or profession of providing social or medical care

CARINGS ▸ caring

CARIOCA n Brazilian dance similar to the samba

CARIOLE n small open two-wheeled horse-drawn vehicle

CARIOSE same as ▸ **carious**

CARIOUS adj (of teeth or bone) affected with caries

CARITAS n divine love; charity

CARJACK vb attack (a car driver) to rob them or to steal the car ▸ vb to steal a car, by force, from a person who is present

CARK vb break down

CARKED ▸ cark

CARKING ▸ cark

CARKS ▸ cark

CARL another word for ▸ **churl**

CARLE same as ▸ **carl**

CARLES ▸ carle
CARLESS ▸ car
CARLIN ▸ carling
CARLINE same as ▸ **carling**
CARLING n fore-and-aft beam in a vessel, used for supporting the deck, esp around a hatchway or other opening
CARLINS ▸ carling
CARLISH adj churlish
CARLOAD n amount that can be carried by a car
CARLOCK n type of Russian isinglass
CARLOT n boor
CARLOTS ▸ carlot
CARLS ▸ carl
CARMAN n man who drives a car or cart
CARMEN ▸ carman
CARMINE adj vivid red ▹ n vivid red colour, sometimes with a purplish tinge
CARN n cairn
CARNAGE n extensive slaughter of people
CARNAL adj of a sexual or sensual nature ▹ vb act in a carnal manner
CARNALS ▸ carnal
CARNET n customs licence permitting motorists to take their cars across certain frontiers
CARNETS ▸ carnet
CARNEY same as ▸ **carny**
CARNEYS ▸ carney
CARNIE same as ▸ **carny**
CARNIED ▸ carny
CARNIER ▸ carny
CARNIES ▸ carny
CARNIFY vb (esp of lung tissue, as the result of pneumonia) to be altered so as to resemble skeletal muscle
CARNOSE adj fleshy
CARNS ▸ carn
CARNY vb coax or cajole or act in a wheedling manner ▹ n person who works in a carnival ▹ adj sly
CARNYX n bronze Celtic war trumpet
CAROACH same as ▸ **caroche**
CAROB n pod of a Mediterranean tree, used as a chocolate substitute
CAROBS ▸ carob
CAROCH same as ▸ **caroche**
CAROCHE n stately

ceremonial carriage used in the 16th and 17th centuries
CAROL n joyful Christmas hymn ▹ vb sing carols
CAROLED ▸ carol
CAROLER ▸ carol
CAROLI ▸ carolus
CAROLS ▸ carol
CAROLUS n any of several coins struck in the reign of a king called Charles, esp an English gold coin from the reign of Charles I
CAROM n shot in which the cue ball is caused to contact one object ball after another ▹ vb to carambole
CAROMED ▸ carom
CAROMEL vb to turn into caramel
CAROMS ▸ carom
CARON n inverted circumflex
CARONS ▸ caron
CAROTID n either of the two arteries supplying blood to the head ▹ adj of either of these arteries
CAROTIN same as ▹ **carotene**
CAROUSE vb have a merry drinking party
CARP n large freshwater fish ▹ vb complain, find fault
CARPAL n wrist bone
CARPALE same as ▸ **carpal**
CARPALS ▸ carpal
CARPED ▸ carp
CARPEL n female reproductive organ of a flowering plant
CARPELS ▸ carpel
CARPER ▸ carp
CARPERS ▸ carp
CARPET n heavy fabric for covering floors ▹ vb cover with a carpet
CARPETS ▸ carpet
CARPI ▸ carpus
CARPING adj tending to make petty complaints ▹ n petty complaint
CARPOOL vb (of a group of people) to share the use of a single car to travel to work or school
CARPORT n shelter for a car, consisting of a roof supported by posts
CARPS ▸ carp
CARPUS n set of eight bones of the wrist

CARR n area of bog or fen in which scrub, esp willow, has become established
CARRACK n galleon sailed in the Mediterranean as a merchantman in the 15th and 16th centuries
CARRACT same as ▸ **carrack**
CARRAT same as ▸ **carat**
CARRATS ▸ carrat
CARRECT same as ▸ **carrack**
CARREL n small individual study room or private desk, often in a library, where a student or researcher can work undisturbed
CARRELL same as ▸ **carrel**
CARRELS ▸ carrel
CARRICK n as in **carrick bend** type of knot
CARRIED ▸ carry
CARRIER n person or thing that carries something
CARRIES ▸ carry
CARRION n dead and rotting flesh
CARROCH same as ▸ **caroche**
CARROM ▸ carom
CARROMS ▸ carrom
CARRON n as in **carron oil** ointment of limewater and linseed oil
CARROT n long tapering orange root vegetable
CARROTS ▸ carrot
CARROTY adj (of hair) reddish-orange
CARRS ▸ carr
CARRY vb take from one place to another
CARRYON n fuss or commotion
CARS ▸ car
CARSE n riverside area of flat fertile alluvium
CARSES ▸ carse
CARSEY slang word for ▸ **toilet**
CARSEYS ▸ carsey
CARSICK adj nauseated from riding in a car
CART n open two-wheeled horse-drawn vehicle for carrying goods or passengers ▹ vb carry, usu with some effort
CARTA n charter
CARTAGE n process or cost of carting
CARTAS ▸ carta
CARTE n fencing position
CARTED ▸ cart
CARTEL n association of

competing firms formed to fix prices

CARTELS ▸ cartel

CARTER ▸ cart

CARTERS ▸ cart

CARTES ▸ carte

CARTFUL n amount a cart can hold

CARTING ▸ cart

CARTON n container made of cardboard or waxed paper ▷ vb enclose (goods) in a carton

CARTONS ▸ carton

CARTOON n humorous or satirical drawing ▷ vb to depict in a cartoon

CARTOP adj designed to be transported on top of a vehicle

CARTS ▸ cart

CARTWAY n way by which carts travel

CARVE vb cut to form an object

CARVED ▸ carve

CARVEL same as ▸ **caravel**

CARVELS ▸ carvel

CARVEN an archaic or literary past participle of ▸ **carve**

CARVER n carving knife

CARVERS ▸ carver

CARVERY n restaurant where customers pay a set price for unrestricted helpings of carved meat and other food

CARVES ▸ carve

CARVIES ▸ carvy

CARVING n figure or design produced by carving stone or wood

CARVY n caraway seed

CARWASH n drive-through structure containing automated equipment for washing cars

CASA n house

CASABA n kind of winter muskmelon having a yellow rind and sweet juicy flesh

CASABAS ▸ casaba

CASAS ▸ casa

CASAVA same as ▸ **cassava**

CASAVAS ▸ casava

CASBAH n citadel of a N African city

CASBAHS ▸ casbah

CASCADE n waterfall ▷ vb flow or fall in a cascade

CASCARA n bark of a N American shrub, used as a laxative

CASCO n Argentinian homestead

CASCOS ▸ casco

CASE n instance, example ▷ vb inspect (a building) with the intention of burgling it

CASEASE n proteolytic enzyme formed by certain bacteria that activates the solution of albumin and casein in milk and cheese

CASEATE vb undergo caseation

CASED ▸ case

CASEFY vb make or become similar to cheese

CASEIC adj relating to cheese

CASEIN n a phosphoprotein, precipitated from milk by the action of rennin, forming the basis of cheese: used in the manufacture of plastics and adhesives

CASEINS ▸ casein

CASEMAN n in printing, a person who sets and corrects type

CASEMEN ▸ caseman

CASEMIX n mix or type of patients treated by a hospital or medical unit

CASEOSE n peptide produced by the peptic digestion of casein

CASEOUS adj of or like cheese

CASERN n (formerly) a billet or accommodation for soldiers in a town

CASERNE same as ▸ **casern**

CASERNS ▸ casern

CASES ▸ case

CASETTE same as > **cassette**

CASEVAC vb evacuate (a casualty) from a combat zone, usu by air

CASH n banknotes and coins ▷ adj of, for, or paid in cash ▷ vb obtain cash for

CASHAW n winter squash

CASHAWS ▸ cashaw

CASHBOX n box for holding cash

CASHED ▸ cash

CASHES ▸ cash

CASHEW n edible kidney-shaped nut

CASHEWS ▸ cashew

CASHIER n person responsible for handling cash in a bank, shop, etc

▷ vb dismiss with dishonour from the armed forces

CASHING ▸ cash

CASHOO n catechu

CASHOOS ▸ cashoo

CASING n protective case, covering

CASINGS ▸ casing

CASINI ▸ casino

CASINO n public building or room where gambling games are played

CASINOS ▸ casino

CASITA n small house

CASITAS ▸ casita

CASK n barrel used to hold alcoholic drink ▷ vb to put into a cask

CASKED ▸ cask

CASKET n small box for valuables ▷ vb to put into a casket

CASKETS ▸ casket

CASKIER ▸ casky

CASKING ▸ cask

CASKS ▸ cask

CASKY adj (of wine) having a musty smell due to resting too long in the cask

CASPASE n type of enzyme

CASQUE n helmet or a helmet-like process or structure, as on the bill of most hornbills

CASQUED ▸ casque

CASQUES ▸ casque

CASSABA same as ▸ **casaba**

CASSATA n ice cream, originating in Italy, usually containing nuts and candied fruit

CASSAVA n starch obtained from the roots of a tropical American plant, used to make tapioca

CASSENA same as ▸ **cassina**

CASSENE same as ▸ **cassina**

CASSIA n tropical plant whose pods yield a mild laxative

CASSIAS ▸ cassia

CASSINA n American tree

CASSINE same as ▸ **cassina**

CASSINO n card game for two to four players in which players pair cards from their hands with others exposed on the table

CASSIS n blackcurrant cordial

CASSOCK n long tunic, usu black, worn by priests

CASSONE n highly-decorated Italian dowry chest

CASSPIR n armoured military vehicle

CAST n actors in a play or film collectively ▷ vb select (an actor) to play a part in a play or film

CASTE n any of the hereditary classes into which Hindu society is divided

CASTED adj having a caste

CASTER n person or thing that casts

CASTERS ▸ caster

CASTES ▸ caste

CASTING ▸ cast

CASTLE n large fortified building, often built as a ruler's residence ▷ vb (in chess) move (the king) two squares laterally on the first rank and place the nearest rook on the square passed over by the king

CASTLED adj like a castle in construction

CASTLES ▸ castle

CASTOCK n kale stalk

CASTOFF n person or thing that has been discarded or abandoned

CASTOR same as ▸ caster

CASTORS ▸ castor

CASTORY n dye derived from beaver pelts

CASTRAL adj relating to camps

CASTS ▸ cast

CASUAL adj careless, nonchalant ▷ n occasional worker

CASUALS ▸ casual

CASUIST n person, esp a theologian, who attempts to resolve moral dilemmas by the application of general rules and the careful distinction of special cases

CASUS n event

CAT n small domesticated furry mammal ▷ vb flog with a cat-'o-nine-tails

CATALO same as ▸ cattalo

CATALOG same as > catalogue

CATALOS ▸ catalo

CATALPA n tree of N America and Asia with bell-shaped whitish flowers

CATAPAN n governor in the Byzantine Empire

CATARRH n excessive mucus in the nose and throat, during or following a cold

CATASTA n platform on which slaves were presented for sale

CATAWBA n type of red North American grape

CATBIRD n North American songbird whose call resembles the mewing of a cat

CATBOAT n sailing vessel with a single mast, set well forward and often unstayed, and a large sail, usually rigged with a gaff

CATCALL n derisive whistle or cry ▷ vb utter such a call (at)

CATCH vb seize, capture ▷ n device for fastening a door, window, etc

CATCHED rarely used past tense of ▸ catch

CATCHEN same as ▸ catch

CATCHER n person or thing that catches, esp in a game or sport

CATCHES ▸ catch

CATCHT same as ▸ catched

CATCHUP a variant spelling (esp US) of ▸ ketchup

CATCHY adj (of a tune) pleasant and easily remembered

CATCLAW n type of shrub; black bead

CATCON n catalytic converter

CATCONS ▸ catcon

CATE n delicacy

CATECHU n astringent resinous substance obtained from certain tropical plants, used in medicine, tanning, and dyeing

CATELOG obsolete word for > catalogue

CATENA n connected series, esp of patristic comments on the Bible

CATENAE ▸ catena

CATENAS ▸ catena

CATER vb provide what is needed or wanted, esp food or services

CATERAN n (formerly) a member of a band of

brigands and marauders in the Scottish highlands

CATERED ▸ cater

CATERER n person whose job is to provide food for social events such as parties and weddings

CATERS ▸ cater

CATES pl n choice dainty food

CATFACE n deformity of the surface of a tree trunk, caused by fire or disease

CATFALL n line used as a tackle for hoisting an anchor to the cathead

CATFISH n fish with whisker-like barbels round the mouth

CATFLAP n small flap in a door to let a cat go through

CATGUT n strong cord used to string musical instruments and sports rackets

CATGUTS ▸ catgut

CATHEAD n fitting at the bow of a vessel for securing the anchor when raised

CATHECT vb to invest mental or emotional energy in

CATHODE n negative electrode, by which electrons leave a circuit

CATHOLE n hole in a ship through which ropes are passed

CATHOOD n state of being a cat

CATION n positively charged ion

CATIONS ▸ cation

CATJANG n tropical shrub

CATKIN n drooping flower spike of certain trees

CATKINS ▸ catkin

CATLIKE ▸ cat

CATLIN same as ▸ catling

CATLING n long double-edged surgical knife for amputations

CATLINS ▸ catlin

CATMINT n Eurasian plant with scented leaves that attract cats

CATNAP vb doze ▷ n short sleep or doze

CATNAPS ▸ catnap

CATNEP same as ▸ catmint

CATNEPS ▸ catnep

CATNIP same as ▸ catmint

CATNIPS ▸ catmint

CATS ▸ cat
CATSKIN n skin and/or fur of a cat
CATSPAW n person used by another as a tool
CATSUIT n one-piece usually close-fitting trouser suit
CATSUP a variant (esp US) of ▸ **ketchup**
CATSUPS ▸ catsup
CATTABU n cross between common cattle and zebu
CATTAIL n reed mace
CATTALO n hardy breed of cattle developed by crossing the American bison with domestic cattle
CATTED ▸ cat
CATTERY n place where cats are bred or looked after
CATTIE same as ▸ **catty**
CATTIER ▸ catty
CATTIES ▸ catty
CATTILY ▸ catty
CATTING ▸ cat
CATTISH ▸ cat
CATTLE pl n domesticated cows and bulls
CATTY adj spiteful ▹ n unit of weight, used esp in China, equal to about one and a half pounds or about 0.67 kilogram
CATWALK n narrow pathway or platform
CATWORM n type of carnivorous worm about 10cm (4in) long, often dug for bait
CAUCUS n local committee or faction of a political party ▹ vb hold a caucus
CAUDA n area behind the anus of an animal
CAUDAD adv towards the tail or posterior part
CAUDAE ▸ cauda
CAUDAL adj at or near an animal's tail
CAUDATE adj having a tail or a tail-like appendage ▹ n lizard-like amphibian
CAUDEX n thickened persistent stem base of some herbaceous perennial plants
CAUDLE n hot spiced wine drink made with gruel, formerly used medicinally ▹ vb make such a drink
CAUDLED ▸ caudle
CAUDLES ▸ caudle

CAUDRON Spenserian spelling of ▸ **cauldron**
CAUF n cage for holding live fish in the water
CAUGHT ▸ catch
CAUK n type of barite
CAUKER n one who caulks
CAUKERS ▸ cauker
CAUKS ▸ cauk
CAUL n membrane sometimes covering a child's head at birth
CAULD a Scots word for ▸ **cold**
CAULDER ▸ cauld
CAULDS ▸ cauld
CAULES ▸ caulis
CAULINE adj relating to or growing from a plant stem
CAULIS n main stem of a plant
CAULK vb fill in (cracks) with paste etc
CAULKED ▸ caulk
CAULKER ▸ caulk
CAULKS ▸ caulk
CAULOME n plant's stem structure, considered as a whole
CAULS ▸ caul
CAUM same as ▸ **cam**
CAUMED ▸ caum
CAUMING ▸ caum
CAUMS ▸ caum
CAUP n type of quaich
CAUPS ▸ caup
CAUSA n reason or cause
CAUSAE ▸ causa
CAUSAL adj of or being a cause ▹ n something that suggests a cause
CAUSALS ▸ causal
CAUSE n something that produces a particular effect ▹ vb be the cause of
CAUSED ▸ cause
CAUSEN old infinitive of ▸ **cause**
CAUSER ▸ cause
CAUSERS ▸ cause
CAUSES ▸ cause
CAUSEY n cobbled street ▹ vb cobble
CAUSEYS ▸ causey
CAUSING ▸ cause
CAUSTIC adj capable of burning by chemical action ▹ n caustic substance
CAUTEL n craftiness
CAUTELS ▸ cautel
CAUTER n cauterising instrument
CAUTERS ▸ cauter

CAUTERY n coagulation of blood or destruction of body tissue by cauterizing
CAUTION n care, esp in the face of danger ▹ vb warn, advise
CAUVES ▸ cauf
CAVA n Spanish sparkling wine produced by a method similar to that used for champagne
CAVALLA n type of tropical fish
CAVALLY same as ▸ **cavalla**
CAVALRY n part of the army orig. on horseback, but now often using fast armoured vehicles
CAVAS ▸ cava
CAVASS n Turkish armed police officer
CAVE n hollow in the side of a hill or cliff ▹ vb hollow out
CAVEAT n warning ▹ vb to introduce a caveat
CAVEATS ▸ caveat
CAVED ▸ cave
CAVEL n drawing of lots among miners for an easy and profitable place at the coalface
CAVELS ▸ cavel
CAVEMAN n prehistoric cave dweller
CAVEMEN ▸ caveman
CAVER ▸ caving
CAVERN n large cave ▹ vb shut in or as if in a cavern
CAVERNS ▸ cavern
CAVERS ▸ caving
CAVES ▸ cave
CAVETTI ▸ cavetto
CAVETTO n concave moulding, shaped to a quarter circle in cross section
CAVIAR n salted sturgeon roe, regarded as a delicacy
CAVIARE same as ▸ **caviar**
CAVIARS ▸ caviar
CAVIE n hen coop
CAVIER same as ▸ **caviar**
CAVIERS ▸ cavier
CAVIES ▸ cavy
CAVIL vb make petty objections ▹ n petty objection
CAVILED ▸ cavil
CAVILER ▸ cavil
CAVILS ▸ cavil
CAVING n sport of exploring caves
CAVINGS ▸ caving

CAVITY n hollow space

CAVORT vb skip about

CAVORTS ▸ cavort

CAVY n type of small S American rodent with a thickset body and a very small tail

CAW n cry of a crow, rook, or raven ▷ vb make this cry

CAWED ▸ caw

CAWING ▸ caw

CAWINGS ▸ caw

CAWK same as ▸ cauk

CAWKER n metal projection on a horse's shoe to prevent slipping

CAWKERS ▸ cawker

CAWKS ▸ cawk

CAWS ▸ caw

CAXON n type of wig

CAXONS ▸ caxon

CAY n low island or bank composed of sand and coral fragments

CAYENNE n very hot condiment, bright red in colour, made from dried capsicums

CAYMAN n S American reptile similar to an alligator

CAYMANS ▸ cayman

CAYS ▸ cay

CAYUSE n small American Indian pony used by cowboys

CAYUSES ▸ cayuse

CAZ short for ▸ casual

> Caz is slang for casual, and is one of the essential short words for using the Z.

CAZIQUE same as ▸ cacique

> This word means an American Indian chief, and its plural **caziques** was once played as a 9-timer (that is, a word spanning two triple-word squares) earning the highest score for a single word ever officially recorded in a game of Scrabble, 392 points.

CEAS same as ▸ caese

CEASE vb bring or come to an end

CEASED ▸ cease

CEASES ▸ cease

CEASING ▸ cease

CEAZE obsolete spelling of ▸ seize

CEAZED ▸ ceaze

CEAZES ▸ ceaze

CEAZING ▸ ceaze

CEBID n any member of the Cebidae family of New World monkeys

CEBIDS ▸ cebid

CEBOID same as ▸ cebid

CEBOIDS ▸ ceboid

CECA ▸ cecum

CECAL ▸ cecum

CECALLY ▸ cecum

CECILS pl n fried meatballs

CECITIS n inflammation of the c(a)ecum

CECITY n rare word for blindness

CECUM same as ▸ caecum

CEDAR n evergreen coniferous tree ▷ adj made of the wood of a cedar tree

CEDARED adj covered with cedars

CEDARN adj relating to cedar

CEDARS ▸ cedar

CEDARY adj like cedar

CEDE vb surrender (territory or legal rights)

CEDED ▸ cede

CEDER ▸ cede

CEDERS ▸ cede

CEDES ▸ cede

CEDI n standard monetary unit of Ghana, divided into 100 pesewas

CEDILLA n character placed under a c in some languages, to show that it is pronounced s, not k

CEDING ▸ cede

CEDIS ▸ cedi

CEDRATE n citron

CEDRINE adj relating to cedar

CEDULA n form of identification in Spanish-speaking countries

CEDULAS ▸ cedula

CEE n third letter of the alphabet

CEES ▸ cee

CEIBA n type of tropical tree

CEIBAS ▸ ceiba

CEIL vb line (a ceiling) with plaster, boarding, etc

CEILED ▸ ceil

CEILER ▸ ceil

CEILERS ▸ ceil

CEILI variant spelling of ▸ ceilidh

CEILIDH n informal social gathering for singing and dancing, esp in Scotland

CEILING n inner upper surface of a room ▷ vb make a ceiling

CEILIS ▸ ceili

CEILS ▸ ceil

CEL short for ▸ celluloid

CELADON n type of porcelain having a greyish-green glaze: mainly Chinese

CELEB n celebrity

CELEBS ▸ celeb

CELERY n vegetable with long green crisp edible stalks

CELESTA n instrument like a small piano in which key-operated hammers strike metal plates

CELESTE same as ▸ celesta

CELIAC same as ▸ coeliac

CELIACS ▸ celiac

CELL n smallest unit of an organism that is able to function independently

CELLA n inner room of a classical temple, esp the room housing the statue of a deity

CELLAE ▸ cella

CELLAR n underground room for storage ▷ vb store in a cellar

CELLARS ▸ cellar

CELLED adj cellular

CELLI ▸ cello

CELLING n formation of cells

CELLIST ▸ cello

CELLO n large low-pitched instrument of the violin family

CELLOS ▸ cello

CELLOSE n a disaccharide obtained by the hydrolysis of cellulose by cellulase

CELLS ▸ cell

CELLULE n very small cell

CELOM same as ▸ coelom

CELOMIC ▸ celom

CELOMS ▸ celom

CELOSIA same as > cockscomb

CELOTEX n tradename for a type of insulation board

CELS ▸ cel

CELT n stone or metal axelike instrument with a bevelled edge

CELTS ▸ celt

CEMBALI ▸ cembalo

CEMBALO n harpsichord

CEMBRA *n* Swiss pine
CEMBRAS ▸ **cembra**
CEMENT *n* fine grey powder mixed with water and sand to make mortar or concrete ▷ *vb* join, bind, or cover with cement
CEMENTA > **cementum**
CEMENTS ▸ **cement**
CENACLE *n* supper room, esp one on an upper floor
CENDRE *adj* ash-blond
CENOTE *n* (esp in the Yucatán peninsula) a natural well formed by the collapse of an overlying limestone crust: often used as a sacrificial site by the Mayas
CENOTES ▸ **cenote**
CENS *n* type of annual property rent
CENSE *vb* burn incense near or before (an altar, shrine, etc)
CENSED ▸ **cense**
CENSER *n* container for burning incense
CENSERS ▸ **censer**
CENSES ▸ **cense**
CENSING ▸ **cense**
CENSOR *n* person authorized to examine films, books, etc, to ban or cut anything considered obscene or objectionable ▷ *vb* ban or cut parts of (a film, book, etc)
CENSORS ▸ **censor**
CENSUAL ▸ **census**
CENSURE *n* severe disapproval ▷ *vb* criticize severely
CENSUS *n* official count of a population ▷ *vb* to conduct a census
CENT *n* hundredth part of a monetary unit such as the dollar or euro
CENTAGE *n* rate per hundred
CENTAI ▸ **centas**
CENTAL *n* unit of weight equal to 100 pounds (45.3 kilograms)
CENTALS ▸ **cental**
CENTARE *same as* > **centiare**
CENTAS *n* monetary unit of Lithuania, worth one hundredth of a litas
CENTAUR *n* mythical creature with the head, arms, and torso of a man,

and the lower body and legs of a horse
CENTAVO *n* monetary unit worth one hundredth of the main unit of currency in Portugal and many Latin American countries
CENTER *same as* ▸ **centre**
CENTERS ▸ **center**
CENTILE *n* one of 99 actual or notional values of a variable dividing its distribution into 100 groups with equal frequencies
CENTIME *n* monetary unit worth one hundredth of a franc
CENTIMO *n* monetary unit of Costa Rica, Paraguay, Peru, and Venezuela. It is worth one hundredth of their respective standard currency units
CENTNER *n* unit of weight equivalent to 100 pounds (45.3 kilograms)
CENTO *n* piece of writing, esp a poem, composed of quotations from other authors
CENTOS ▸ **cento**
CENTRA ▸ **centrum**
CENTRAL *adj* of, at, or forming the centre ▷ *n* workplace serving as a telecommunications facility
CENTRE *n* middle point or part ▷ *vb* put in the centre of something
CENTRED *adj* mentally and emotionally confident, focused, and well-balanced
CENTRES ▸ **centre**
CENTRIC *adj* being central or having a centre
CENTRUM *n* main part or body of a vertebra
CENTRY *obsolete variant of* ▸ **sentry**
CENTS ▸ **cent**
CENTU *n* Lithuanian money unit
CENTUM *adj* denoting or belonging to the Indo-European languages in which original velar stops (k) were not palatalized ▷ *n* hundred
CENTUMS ▸ **centum**
CENTURY *n* period of 100 years

CEORL *n* freeman of the lowest class in Anglo-Saxon England
CEORLS ▸ **ceorl**
CEP *another name for* ▸ **porcino**
CEPAGE *n* grape variety or type of wine
CEPAGES ▸ **cepage**
CEPE *another spelling of* ▸ **cep**
CEPES ▸ **cepe**
CEPHEID *n* type of variable star with a regular cycle of variations in luminosity
CEPS ▸ **cep**
CERAMAL *same as* ▸ **cermet**
CERAMIC *n* hard brittle material made by heating clay to a very high temperature ▷ *adj* made of ceramic
CERASIN *n* meta-arabinic acid
CERATE *n* hard ointment or medicated paste consisting of lard or oil mixed with wax or resin
CERATED *adj* (of certain birds, such as the falcon) having a cere
CERATES ▸ **cerate**
CERATIN *same as* ▸ **keratin**
CERCAL *adj* of or relating to a tail
CERCI ▸ **cercus**
CERCIS *n* type of tree or shrub of the genus which includes the redbud and Judas tree
CERCUS *n* one of a pair of sensory appendages at the tip of the abdomen of some insects and other arthropods
CERE *n* soft waxy swelling, containing the nostrils, at the base of the upper beak of a parrot ▷ *vb* wrap (a corpse) in a cerecloth
CEREAL *n* grass plant with edible grain, such as oat or wheat
CEREALS ▸ **cereal**
CEREBRA > **cerebrum**
CERED ▸ **cere**
CEREOUS *adj* waxlike
CERES ▸ **cere**
CERESIN *n* white wax extracted from ozocerite
CEREUS *n* type of tropical American cactus
CERGE *n* large altar candle
CERGES ▸ **cerge**

CERIA n ceric oxide

CERIAS ▸ ceria

CERIC adj of or containing cerium in the tetravalent state

CERING ▸ cere

CERIPH same as ▸ serif

CERIPHS ▸ ceriph

CERISE adj cherry-red ▷ n moderate to dark red colour

CERISES ▸ cerise

CERITE n hydrous silicate of cerium

CERITES ▸ cerite

CERIUM n steel-grey metallic element

CERIUMS ▸ cerium

CERMET n any of several materials consisting of a metal matrix with ceramic particles disseminated through it. They are hard and resistant to high temperatures

CERMETS ▸ cermet

CERNE obsolete variant of > encircle

CERNED ▸ cerne

CERNES ▸ cerne

CERNING ▸ cerne

CERO n type of large spiny-finned food fish of warm American coastal regions of the Atlantic

CEROON n hide-covered bale

CEROONS ▸ ceroon

CEROS ▸ cero

CEROTIC adj as in cerotic acid white insoluble odourless wax

CEROUS adj of or containing cerium in the trivalent state

CERRADO n vast area of tropical savanna in Brazil

CERRIAL adj relating to the cerris

CERRIS n Turkey oak

CERT n certainty

CERTAIN adj positive and confident

CERTES adv with certainty

CERTIE n as in by my certie assuredly

CERTIFY vb confirm, attest to

CERTS ▸ cert

CERTY n as in by my certy assuredly

CERULE adj sky-blue

CERUMEN n soft brownish-yellow wax secreted by glands in the auditory canal of the external ear

CERUSE n white lead

CERUSES ▸ ceruse

CERVEZA n Spanish word for beer

CERVID n type of ruminant mammal such as the deer, characterized by the presence of antlers

CERVIDS ▸ cervid

CERVINE adj resembling or relating to a deer

CERVIX n narrow entrance of the womb

CESIOUS same as ▸ caesious

CESIUM same as ▸ caesium

CESIUMS ▸ cesium

CESS n any of several special taxes, such as a land tax in Scotland ▷ vb tax or assess for taxation

CESSE obsolete variant of ▸ cease

CESSED ▸ cess

CESSER n coming to an end of a term interest or annuity

CESSERS ▸ cesser

CESSES ▸ cess

CESSING ▸ cess

CESSION n ceding

CESSPIT same as > cesspool

CESTA n in jai alai, the basket used to throw and catch the pelota

CESTAS ▸ cesta

CESTI ▸ cestus

CESTODE n type of parasitic flatworm such as the tapeworms

CESTOI ▸ cestos

CESTOID adj (esp of tapeworms and similar animals) ribbon-like in form ▷ n ribbon-like worm

CESTOS same as ▸ cestus

CESTUI n "the one (who)"; legal term, used in certain phrases, to designate a person

CESTUIS ▸ cestui

CESTUS n girdle of Aphrodite (Venus) decorated to cause amorousness

CESURA a variant spelling of ▸ caesura

CESURAE ▸ cesura

CESURAL ▸ cesura

CESURAS ▸ cesura

CESURE same as ▸ caesura

CESURES ▸ cesure

CETANE n colourless liquid hydrocarbon, used as a solvent

CETANES ▸ cetane

CETE n group of badgers

CETES ▸ cete

CETYL n univalent alcohol radical

CETYLS ▸ cetyl

CEVICHE n Peruvian seafood dish

CEZVE n small metal pot for brewing coffee

CEZVES ▸ cezve

CH pron obsolete from of I

CHA n tea

CHABLIS n dry white French wine

CHABOUK n type of whip

CHABUK same as ▸ chabouk

CHABUKS ▸ chabuk

CHACE obsolete variant of ▸ chase

CHACED ▸ chace

CHACES ▸ chace

CHACHKA n cheap trinket

CHACING ▸ chace

CHACK vb to bite

CHACKED ▸ chack

CHACKS ▸ chack

CHACMA n type of baboon with coarse greyish hair, occurring in S and E Africa

CHACMAS ▸ chacma

CHACO same as ▸ shako

CHACOES ▸ chaco

CHACOS ▸ chaco

CHAD n small pieces removed during the punching of holes in punch cards, printer paper, etc

CHADAR same as ▸ chuddar

CHADARS ▸ chadar

CHADDAR same as ▸ chuddar

CHADDOR same as ▸ chuddar

CHADO n Japanese tea ceremony

CHADOR same as ▸ chuddar

CHADORS ▸ chador

CHADOS ▸ chado

CHADRI n shroud which covers the body from head to foot, usually worn by females in Islamic countries

CHADS ▸ chad

CHAEBOL n large, usually family-owned, business group in South Korea

CHAETA n any of the

chitinous bristles on the body of such annelids as the earthworm and the lugworm: used in locomotion

CHAETAE ▸ **chaeta**

CHAETAL ▸ **chaeta**

CHAFE vb make sore or worn by rubbing

CHAFED ▸ **chafe**

CHAFER n large beetle

CHAFERS ▸ **chafer**

CHAFES ▸ **chafe**

CHAFF n grain husks ▷ vb tease good-naturedly

CHAFFED ▸ **chaff**

CHAFFER vb haggle

CHAFFS ▸ **chaff**

CHAFFY ▸ **chaff**

CHAFING ▸ **chafe**

CHAFT n jaw

CHAFTS ▸ **chaft**

CHAGAN n Mongolian royal or imperial title

CHAGANS ▸ **chagan**

CHAGRIN n annoyance and disappointment ▷ vb embarrass and annoy

CHAI n tea, esp as made in India with added spices

CHAIN n flexible length of connected metal links ▷ vb restrict or fasten with or as if with a chain

CHAINE adj (of a dance turn) producing a full rotation for every two steps taken ▷ vb produce a full rotation for every two steps taken

CHAINED ▸ **chain**

CHAINES ▸ **chaine**

CHAINS ▸ **chain**

CHAIR n seat with a back, for one person ▷ vb preside over (a meeting)

CHAIRED ▸ **chair**

CHAIRS ▸ **chair**

CHAIS ▸ **chai**

CHAISE n light horse-drawn carriage

CHAISES ▸ **chaise**

CHAKRA n (in yoga) any of the seven major energy centres in the body

CHAKRAS ▸ **chakra**

CHAL n in Romany, person or fellow

CHALAH same as ▸ **challah**

CHALAHS ▸ **chalah**

CHALAN vb (in India) to cause an accused person to appear before a magistrate

CHALANS ▸ **chalan**

CHALAZA n one of a pair of spiral threads of albumen holding the yolk of a bird's egg in position

CHALCID n type of tiny hymenopterous insect whose larvae are parasites of other insects

CHALDER n former Scottish dry measure

CHALEH same as ▸ **challah**

CHALEHS ▸ **chaleh**

CHALET n kind of Swiss wooden house with a steeply sloping roof

CHALETS ▸ **chalet**

CHALICE n large goblet

CHALK n soft white rock consisting of calcium carbonate ▷ vb draw or mark with chalk

CHALKED ▸ **chalk**

CHALKS ▸ **chalk**

CHALKY ▸ **chalk**

CHALLA same as ▸ **challah**

CHALLAH n bread, usually in the form of a plaited loaf, traditionally eaten by Jews to celebrate the Sabbath

CHALLAN same as ▸ **chalan**

CHALLAS ▸ **challa**

CHALLIE same as ▸ **challis**

CHALLIS n lightweight plain-weave fabric of wool, cotton, etc, usually with a printed design

CHALLOT ▸ **challah**

CHALLY same as ▸ **challis**

CHALONE n any internal secretion that inhibits a physiological process or function

CHALOT ▸ **chalah**

CHALOTH ▸ **chalah**

CHALS ▸ **chal**

CHALUPA n Mexican dish

CHALUTZ n member of an organization of immigrants to Israeli agricultural settlements

CHAM an archaic word for ▸ **khan**

CHAMADE n (formerly) a signal by drum or trumpet inviting an enemy to a parley

CHAMBER n hall used for formal meetings ▷ vb act lasciviously

CHAMBRE adj (of wine) at room temperature

CHAMETZ n leavened food which may not be eaten

during Passover

CHAMFER same as ▸ **chase**

CHAMISA n American shrub

CHAMISE same as ▸ **chamiso**

CHAMISO n fourwing saltbush

CHAMLET same as ▸ **camlet**

CHAMMY same as ▸ **chamois**

CHAMOIS n small mountain antelope or a pice of leather from its skin, used for polishing ▷ vb polish with a chamois

CHAMOIX same as ▸ **chamois**

CHAMP vb chew noisily

CHAMPAC n type of tree of India and the E Indies, whose yellow flowers yield an oil used in perfumes

CHAMPAK same as ▸ **champac**

CHAMPED ▸ **champ**

CHAMPER ▸ **champ**

CHAMPS ▸ **champ**

CHAMPY adj (of earth) churned up (by cattle, for example)

CHAMS ▸ **cham**

CHANA n (in Indian cookery) chickpeas

CHANAS ▸ **chana**

CHANCE n likelihood probability ▷ vb risk, hazard

CHANCED ▸ **chance**

CHANCEL n part of a church containing the altar and choir

CHANCER n unscrupulous or dishonest opportunist who is prepared to try any dubious scheme for making money or furthering his own ends

CHANCES ▸ **chance**

CHANCEY same as ▸ **chancy**

CHANCRE n small hard growth which is the first sign of syphilis

CHANCY adj uncertain, risky

CHANG n loud discordant noise

CHANGA interj in Indian English, an expression of approval or agreement

CHANGE n becoming different ▷ vb make or become different

CHANGED ▸ **change**

CHANGER ▸ **change**

CHANGES ▸ change

CHANGS ▸ chang

CHANK n shell of several types of sea conch, used to make bracelets

CHANKS ▸ chank

CHANNEL n band of broadcasting frequencies ▹ vb direct or convey through a channel

CHANNER n gravel

CHANOYO same as ▸ chado

CHANOYU same as ▸ chado

CHANSON n song

CHANT vb utter or sing (a slogan or psalm) ▹ n rhythmic or repetitious slogan

CHANTED ▸ chant

CHANTER n (on bagpipes) pipe on which the melody is played

CHANTEY the usual US spelling of ▸ shanty

CHANTIE n chamber pot

CHANTOR same as ▸ chanter

CHANTRY n endowment for the singing of Masses for the soul of the founder or others designated by him

CHANTS ▸ chant

CHANTY same as ▸ shanty

CHAO n Vietnamese rice porridge

CHAOS n complete disorder or confusion

CHAOSES ▸ chaos

CHAOTIC ▸ chaos

CHAP n man or boy ▹ vb (of the skin) to make or become raw and cracked, esp by exposure to cold

CHAPATI n (in Indian cookery) flat thin unleavened bread

CHAPE n metal tip or trimming for a scabbard

CHAPEAU n hat

CHAPEL n place of worship with its own altar, within a church

CHAPELS ▸ chapel

CHAPES ▸ chape

CHAPESS n woman

CHAPKA same as ▸ czapka

CHAPKAS ▸ chapka

CHAPLET n garland for the head ▹ vb create a garland

CHAPMAN n travelling pedlar

CHAPMEN ▸ chapman

CHAPPAL n one of a pair of sandals, usually of leather, worn in India

CHAPPED ▸ chap

CHAPPIE n man or boy

CHAPPY adj (of skin) chapped

CHAPS ▸ chap

CHAPT adj chapped

CHAPTER n division of a book ▹ vb divide into chapters

CHAR vb blacken by partial burning ▹ n charwoman

CHARA n type of green freshwater algae

CHARACT n distinctive mark

CHARADE n absurd pretence

CHARAS another name for ▸ hashish

CHARD n variety of beet with large succulent leaves and thick stalks, used as a vegetable

CHARDS ▸ chard

CHARE same as ▸ char

CHARED ▸ char

CHARES ▸ char

CHARET obsolete variant of ▸ chariot

CHARETS ▸ charet

CHARGE vb ask as a price ▹ n price charged

CHARGED ▸ charge

CHARGER n device for charging an accumulator

CHARGES ▸ charge

CHARIER ▸ chary

CHARILY adv cautiously

CHARING ▸ char

CHARIOT n two-wheeled horse-drawn vehicle used in ancient times in wars and races ▹ vb to ride in a chariot

CHARISM same as > charisma

CHARITY n organization that gives help, such as money or food, to those in need

CHARK vb to char

CHARKA same as ▸ charkha

CHARKAS ▸ charka

CHARKED ▸ chark

CHARKHA n (in India) a spinning wheel, esp for cotton

CHARKS ▸ chark

CHARLEY n as in charley horse muscle stiffness after strenuous exercise

CHARLIE n fool

CHARM n attractive quality ▹ vb attract, delight

CHARMED adj delighted or fascinated

CHARMER n attractive person

CHARMS ▸ charm

CHARNEL adj ghastly ▹ n ghastly thing

CHARPAI same as ▸ charpoy

CHARPIE n lint pieces used to make surgical dressings

CHARPOY n bedstead of woven webbing or hemp stretched on a wooden frame on four legs, common in India

CHARQUI n meat, esp beef, cut into strips and dried

CHARR same as ▸ char

CHARRED ▸ char

CHARRO n Mexican cowboy

CHARROS ▸ charro

CHARRS ▸ charr

CHARRY adj of or relating to charcoal

CHARS ▸ char

CHART n graph, table, or diagram showing information ▹ vb plot the course of

CHARTA n charter

CHARTAS ▸ charta

CHARTED ▸ chart

CHARTER n document granting or demanding certain rights ▹ vb hire by charter

CHARTS ▸ chart

CHARY adj wary, careful

CHAS ▸ cha

CHASE vb run after quickly in order to catch or drive away ▹ n chasing, pursuit

CHASED ▸ chase

CHASER n milder drink drunk after another stronger one

CHASERS ▸ chaser

CHASES ▸ chase

CHASING ▸ chase

CHASM n deep crack in the earth ▹ vb create a chasm

CHASMAL ▸ chasm

CHASMED ▸ chasm

CHASMIC ▸ chasm

CHASMS ▸ chasm

CHASMY adj full of chasms

CHASSE n one of a series of gliding steps in ballet in which the same foot always leads ▷ *vb* perform either of these steps

CHASSED ▸ **chasse**

CHASSES ▸ **chasse**

CHASSIS *n* frame, wheels, and mechanical parts of a vehicle

CHASTE *adj* abstaining from sex outside marriage or altogether

CHASTEN *vb* subdue by criticism

CHASTER ▸ **chaste**

CHAT *n* informal conversation ▷ *vb* have an informal conversation

CHATBOT *n* computer program in the form of a virtual e-mail correspondent that can reply to messages from computer users

CHATEAU *n* French castle

CHATON *n* in jewellery, a stone with a reflective metal foil backing

CHATONS ▸ **chaton**

CHATS ▸ **chat**

CHATTA *n* umbrella

CHATTAS ▸ **chatta**

CHATTED ▸ **chat**

CHATTEL *n* item of movable personal property

CHATTER *vb* speak quickly and continuously about unimportant things ▷ *n* idle talk

CHATTI *n* (in India) an earthenware pot

CHATTIS ▸ **chatti**

CHATTY *adj* (of a person) fond of friendly, informal conversation

CHAUFE *obsolete variant of* ▸ **chafe**

CHAUFED ▸ **chaufe**

CHAUFER *same as* > **chauffer**

CHAUFES ▸ **chaufe**

CHAUFF *obsolete variant of* ▸ **chafe**

CHAUFFS ▸ **chauff**

CHAUMER *n* chamber

CHAUNCE *archaic variant of* ▸ **chance**

CHAUNGE *archaic variant of* ▸ **change**

CHAUNT *a less common variant of* ▸ **chant**

CHAUNTS ▸ **chaunt**

CHAUVIN *n* chauvinist

CHAVE *vb* old dialect term for "I have"

CHAW *vb* chew (tobacco), esp without swallowing it ▷ *n* something chewed, esp a plug of tobacco

CHAWED ▸ **chaw**

CHAWER ▸ **chaw**

CHAWERS ▸ **chaw**

CHAWING ▸ **chaw**

CHAWK *n* jackdaw

CHAWKS ▸ **chawk**

CHAWS ▸ **chaw**

CHAY *n* plant of the madder family

CHAYA *same as* ▸ **chay**

CHAYAS ▸ **chaya**

CHAYOTE *n* tropical American climbing plant with edible pear-shaped fruit enclosing a single huge seed

CHAYS ▸ **chay**

CHAZAN *same as* ▸ **cantor**

CHAZANS ▸ **chazan**

CHAZZAN *same as* ▸ **chazan**

CHAZZEN *same as* ▸ **chazzan**

CHE *pron* dialectal form meaning "I"

CHEAP *adj* costing relatively little ▷ *adv* at very little cost ▷ *n* bargain ▷ *vb* take the cheapest option

CHEAPED ▸ **cheap**

CHEAPEN *vb* lower the reputation of

CHEAPER ▸ **cheap**

CHEAPIE *n* something inexpensive

CHEAPLY ▸ **cheap**

CHEAPO *n* very cheap and possibly shoddy thing

CHEAPOS ▸ **cheapo**

CHEAPS ▸ **cheap**

CHEAPY *same as* ▸ **cheapie**

CHEAT *vb* act dishonestly to gain profit or advantage ▷ *n* person who cheats

CHEATED ▸ **cheat**

CHEATER ▸ **cheat**

CHEATS ▸ **cheat**

CHEBEC *n* type of boat

CHEBECS ▸ **chebec**

CHECHIA *n* Berber skullcap

CHECK *vb* examine or investigate ▷ *n* control designed to ensure accuracy

CHECKED ▸ **check**

CHECKER *same as* ▸ **chequer**

CHECKS ▸ **check**

CHECKUP *n* thorough medical examination ▷ *vb*

investigate or make an inquiry into (a person's character, evidence, etc), esp when suspicions have been aroused

CHECKY *adj* having squares of alternating tinctures or furs

CHEDDAR *n* type of smooth hard yellow or whitish cheese

CHEDER *n* (in Western countries) elementary religious education classes, usually outside normal school hours

CHEDERS ▸ **cheder**

CHEDITE *same as* ▸ **cheddite**

CHEEK *n* either side of the face below the eye ▷ *vb* speak impudently to

CHEEKED ▸ **cheek**

CHEEKS ▸ **cheek**

CHEEKY *adj* impudent, disrespectful

CHEEP *n* young bird's high-pitched cry ▷ *vb* utter a cheep

CHEEPED ▸ **cheep**

CHEEPER ▸ **cheep**

CHEEPS ▸ **cheep**

CHEER *vb* applaud or encourage with shouts ▷ *n* shout of applause or encouragement

CHEERED ▸ **cheer**

CHEERER ▸ **cheer**

CHEERIO *interj* goodbye ▷ *n* small red cocktail sausage ▷ *sentence substitute* farewell greeting

CHEERLY *adv* cheerful or cheerfully

CHEERO *same as* ▸ **cheerio**

CHEEROS ▸ **cheero**

CHEERS *interj* drinking toast ▷ *sentence substitute* drinking toast

CHEERY *adj* cheerful

CHEESE *n* food made from coagulated milk curd ▷ *vb* stop

CHEESED ▸ **cheese**

CHEESES ▸ **cheese**

CHEESY *adj* like cheese

CHEETAH *n* large fast-running spotted African wild cat

CHEF *n* cook in a restaurant ▷ *vb* to work as a chef

CHEFDOM *n* state or condition of being a chef

CHEFED ▸ **chef**

CHEFFED ▸ chef
CHEFING ▸ chef
CHEFS ▸ chef
CHEGOE *same as* **▸ chigger**
CHEGOES ▸ chigger
CHEKA *n* secret police set up in Russia in 1917
CHEKAS ▸ cheka
CHEKIST *n* member of the cheka
CHELA *n* disciple of a religious teacher
CHELAE ▸ chela
CHELAS ▸ chela
CHELATE *n* coordination compound in which a metal atom or ion is bound to a ligand at two or more points on the ligand, so as to form a heterocyclic ring containing a metal atom ▷ *adj* of or possessing chelae ▷ *vb* form a chelate
CHELLUP *n* noise
CHELOID *a variant spelling of* **▸ keloid**
CHELONE *n* hardy N American plant grown for its white, rose, or purple flower spikes
CHELP *vb* (esp of women or children) to chatter or speak out of turn
CHELPED ▸ chelp
CHELPS ▸ chelp
CHEMIC *vb* to bleach ▷ *n* chemist
CHEMICS ▸ chemic
CHEMISE *n* woman's loose-fitting slip
CHEMISM *n* chemical action
CHEMIST *n* shop selling medicines and cosmetics
CHEMMY *n* gambling card game
CHEMO *n* short form of chemotherapy
CHEMOS ▸ chemo
CHENAR *n* oriental plane tree
CHENARS ▸ chenar
CHENET *another word for* **▸ genip**
CHENETS ▸ chenet
CHENIX *n* ancient measure, slightly more than a quart
CHEQUE *n* written order to one's bank to pay money from one's account
CHEQUER *n* piece used in Chinese chequers ▷ *vb* make irregular in colour or character

CHEQUES ▸ cheque
CHEQUY *same as* **▸ checky**
CHER *adj* dear or expensive
CHERE *feminine variant of* **▸ cher**
CHERISH *vb* cling to (an idea or feeling)
CHEROOT *n* cigar with both ends cut flat
CHERRY *n* small red or black fruit with a stone ▷ *adj* deep red ▷ *vb* to cheer
CHERT *n* microcrystalline form of silica usually occurring as bands or layers of pebbles in sedimentary rock. Formula: SiO_2. Varieties include flint, lyddite (Lydian stone)
CHERTS ▸ chert
CHERTY ▸ chert
CHERUB *n* angel, often represented as a winged child
CHERUBS ▸ cherub
CHERUP *same as* **▸ chirrup**
CHERUPS ▸ cherup
CHERVIL *n* aniseed-flavoured herb
CHESIL *n* gravel or shingle
CHESILS ▸ chesil
CHESNUT *rare variant of* **> chestnut**
CHESS *n* game for two players with 16 pieces each, played on a chequered board of 64 squares
CHESSEL *n* mould used in cheese-making
CHESSES ▸ chess
CHEST *n* front of the body, from neck to waist ▷ *vb* to hit with the chest, as with a ball in football
CHESTED ▸ chest
CHESTS ▸ chest
CHESTY *adj* symptomatic of chest disease
CHETAH *same as* **▸ cheetah**
CHETAHS ▸ chetah
CHETH *same as* **▸ heth**
CHETHS ▸ cheth
CHETNIK *n* member of a Serbian nationalist paramilitary group
CHETRUM *n* monetary unit in Bhutan
CHEVAL *n as in* **cheval glass** full-length mirror that can swivel
CHEVEN *n* chub
CHEVENS ▸ cheven
CHEVET *n* semicircular or

polygonal east end of a church, esp a French Gothic church, often with a number of attached apses
CHEVETS ▸ chevet
CHEVIED ▸ chevy
CHEVIES ▸ chevy
CHEVIN *same as* **▸ cheven**
CHEVINS ▸ chevin
CHEVIOT *n* type of British sheep reared for its wool
CHEVRE *n* any cheese made from goats' milk
CHEVRES ▸ chevre
CHEVRET *n* type of goats' cheese
CHEVRON *n* V-shaped pattern, esp on the sleeve of a military uniform to indicate rank ▷ *vb* make a chevron
CHEVY *same as* **▸ chivy**
CHEW *vb* grind (food) between the teeth ▷ *n* act of chewing
CHEWED ▸ chew
CHEWER ▸ chew
CHEWERS ▸ chew
CHEWET *n* type of meat pie
CHEWETS ▸ chewet
CHEWIE *n* chewing gum
CHEWIER ▸ chewy
CHEWIES ▸ chewy
CHEWING ▸ chew
CHEWINK *n* towhee
CHEWS ▸ chew
CHEWY *adj* requiring a lot of chewing ▷ *n* dog's rubber toy
CHEZ *prep* at the home of
CHI *n* 22nd letter of the Greek alphabet, a consonant, transliterated as *ch* or rarely *kh*

| **Chi** is a letter of the Greek alphabet, and can also be spelt **khi**.

CHIA *n* plant of the mint family
CHIACK *vb* tease or banter ▷ *n* good-humoured banter
CHIACKS ▸ chiack
CHIANTI *n* dry red Italian wine
CHIAO *n* Chinese coin equal to one tenth of one yuan
CHIAS ▸ chia
CHIASM *same as* **▸ chiasma**
CHIASMA *n* cross-shaped connection produced by the crossing over of pairing chromosomes during meiosis

CHIASMI > **chiasmus**

CHIASMS ▸ **chiasma**

CHIAUS *same as* ▸ **chouse**

CHIB *vb* in Scots English, stab or slash with a sharp weapon ▷ *n* sharp weapon

CHIBBED ▸ **chib**

CHIBOL *n* spring onion

CHIBOLS ▸ **chibol**

CHIBOUK *n* Turkish tobacco pipe with an extremely long stem

CHIBS ▸ **chib**

CHIC *adj* stylish, elegant ▷ *n* stylishness, elegance

CHICA *n* Spanish young girl

CHICANA *n* female chicano

CHICANE *n* obstacle in a motor-racing circuit ▷ *vb* deceive or trick by chicanery

CHICANO *n* American citizen of Mexican origin

CHICAS ▸ **chica**

CHICER ▸ **chic**

CHICEST ▸ **chic**

CHICH *another word for* > **chickpea**

CHICHA *n* Andean drink made from fermented maize

CHICHAS ▸ **chicha**

CHICHES ▸ **chickpea**

CHICHI *adj* affectedly pretty or stylish ▷ *n* quality of being affectedly pretty or stylish

CHICHIS ▸ **chichi**

CHICK *n* baby bird

CHICKEE *n* opensided, thatched building on stilts

CHICKEN *n* domestic fowl ▷ *adj* cowardly ▷ *vb* to lose one's nerve

CHICKS ▸ **chick**

CHICLE *n* gumlike substance obtained from the sapodilla

CHICLES ▸ **chicle**

CHICLY ▸ **chic**

CHICO *n* spiny chenopodiaceous shrub

CHICON *same as* ▸ **chicory**

CHICONS ▸ **chicon**

CHICORY *n* plant whose leaves are used in salads

CHICOS ▸ **chico**

CHICS ▸ **chic**

CHID ▸ **chide**

CHIDDEN ▸ **chide**

CHIDE *vb* rebuke, scold

CHIDED ▸ **chide**

CHIDER ▸ **chide**

CHIDERS ▸ **chide**

CHIDES ▸ **chide**

CHIDING ▸ **chide**

CHIEF *n* head of a group of people ▷ *adj* most important

CHIEFER ▸ **chief**

CHIEFLY *adv* especially ▷ *adj* of or relating to a chief or chieftain

CHIEFRY *same as* > **chiefery**

CHIEFS ▸ **chief**

CHIEL *n* young man

CHIELD *same as* ▸ **chiel**

CHIELDS ▸ **chiel**

CHIELS ▸ **chiel**

CHIFFON *n* fine see-through fabric ▷ *adj* made of chiffon

CHIGGER *n* parasitic larva of any of various mites, which causes intense itching of human skin

CHIGNON *n* knot of hair pinned up at the back of the head ▷ *vb* make a chignon

CHIGOE *same as* ▸ **chigger**

CHIGOES ▸ **chigoe**

CHIGRE *same as* ▸ **chigger**

CHIGRES ▸ **chigre**

CHIK *n* slatted blind

CHIKARA *n* Indian seven-stringed musical instrument

CHIKHOR *same as* ▸ **chukar**

CHIKOR *same as* ▸ **chukar**

CHIKORS ▸ **chikor**

CHIKS ▸ **chik**

CHILD *n* young human being, boy or girl ▷ *vb* to give birth

CHILDE *n* young man of noble birth

CHILDED ▸ **child**

CHILDER *dialect variant of* > **children**

CHILDES ▸ **childe**

CHILDLY ▸ **child**

CHILDS ▸ **child**

CHILE *a variant spelling of* ▸ **chilli**

CHILES ▸ **chile**

CHILI *same as* ▸ **chilli**

CHILIAD *n* group of one thousand

CHILIES ▸ **chili**

CHILIS ▸ **chili**

CHILL *n* feverish cold ▷ *vb* make (something) cool or cold ▷ *adj* unpleasantly cold

CHILLED ▸ **chill**

CHILLER *n* cooling or refrigerating device

CHILLI *n* small red or green hot-tasting capsicum pod, used in cooking

CHILLIS ▸ **chilli**

CHILLS ▸ **chill**

CHILLUM *n* short pipe, usually of clay, used esp for smoking cannabis

CHILLY *adj* moderately cold

CHIMAR *same as* ▸ **chimere**

CHIMARS ▸ **chimar**

CHIMB *same as* ▸ **chime**

CHIMBLY *same as* ▸ **chimney**

CHIMBS ▸ **chime**

CHIME *n* musical ringing sound of a bell or clock ▷ *vb* make a musical ringing sound

CHIMED ▸ **chime**

CHIMER ▸ **chime**

CHIMERA *n* unrealistic hope or idea

CHIMERE *n* sleeveless red or black gown, part of a bishop's formal dress though not a vestment

CHIMERS ▸ **chime**

CHIMES ▸ **chime**

CHIMING ▸ **chime**

CHIMLA *same as* ▸ **chimney**

CHIMLAS ▸ **chimla**

CHIMLEY *same as* ▸ **chimney**

CHIMNEY *n* hollow vertical structure for carrying away smoke from a fire ▷ *vb* to climb two vertical, parallel, chimney-like rock faces

CHIMO *interj* Inuit greeting and toast

CHIMP *n* chimpanzee

CHIMPS ▸ **chimp**

CHIN *n* part of the face below the mouth ▷ *vb* hit someone in the chin

CHINA *n* fine earthenware or porcelain

CHINAR *same as* ▸ **chenar**

CHINARS ▸ **chenar**

CHINAS ▸ **china**

CHINCH *another name for a* ▸ **bedbug**

CHINCHY *adj* tightfisted

CHINDIT *n* Allied soldier fighting behind the Japanese lines in Burma during World War II

CHINE *same as* ▸ **chime**

CHINED ▸ **chine**

CHINES ▸ **chine**

CHINESE *adj* of or relating to China

CHINING ▸ chine

CHINK n small narrow opening ▷ vb make a light ringing sound

CHINKED ▸ chink

CHINKS ▸ chink

CHINKY ▸ chink

CHINNED ▸ chin

CHINO n durable cotton twill cloth

CHINONE n benzoquinone

CHINOOK n warm dry southwesterly wind blowing down the eastern slopes of the Rocky Mountains

CHINOS pl n trousers made of a kind of hard-wearing cotton

CHINS ▸ chin

CHINTS obsolete variant of ▸ chintz

CHINTZ n printed cotton fabric with a glazed finish

CHINTZY adj of or covered with chintz

CHINWAG n chat

CHIP n strip of potato, fried in deep fat ▷ vb break small pieces from

CHIPPED ▸ chip

CHIPPER vb chirp or chatter

CHIPPIE same as ▸ chippy

CHIPPY n fish-and-chip shop ▷ adj resentful or oversensitive about being perceived as inferior

CHIPS ▸ chip

CHIPSET n highly integrated circuit on the motherboard of a computer that controls many of its data transfer functions

CHIRAL > chirality

CHIRK vb to creak, like a door ▷ adj spritely; high-spirited

CHIRKED ▸ chirk

CHIRKER ▸ chirk

CHIRKS ▸ chirk

CHIRL vb to warble

CHIRLED ▸ chirl

CHIRLS ▸ chirl

CHIRM n chirping of birds ▷ vb (esp of a bird) to chirp

CHIRMED ▸ chirm

CHIRMS ▸ chirm

CHIRO n an informal name for chiropractor

CHIROS ▸ chiro

CHIRP vb (of a bird or insect) make a short high-pitched sound ▷ n chirping sound

CHIRPED ▸ chirp

CHIRPER ▸ chirp

CHIRPS ▸ chirp

CHIRPY adj lively and cheerful

CHIRR vb (esp of certain insects, such as crickets) to make a shrill trilled sound ▷ n sound of chirring

CHIRRE same as ▸ chirr

CHIRRED ▸ chirr

CHIRREN n dialect form of children

CHIRRES ▸ chirre

CHIRRS ▸ chirr

CHIRRUP vb (of some birds) to chirp repeatedly ▷ n chirruping sound

CHIRT vb to squirt

CHIRTED ▸ chirt

CHIRTS ▸ chirt

CHIRU n Tibetan antelope with a dense woolly pinkish-brown fleece, prized as the source of shahtoosh wool

CHIRUS ▸ chiru

CHIS ▸ chi

CHISEL n metal tool with a sharp end for shaping wood or stone ▷ vb carve or form with a chisel

CHISELS ▸ chisel

CHIT n short official note, such as a receipt ▷ vb to sprout

CHITAL n type of deer

CHITALS ▸ chital

CHITIN n tough substance forming the outer layer of the bodies of arthropods

CHITINS ▸ chitin

CHITLIN n pig intestine cooked and served as a dish

CHITON n (in ancient Greece and Rome) a loose woollen tunic worn knee length by men and full length by women

CHITONS ▸ chiton

CHITS ▸ chit

CHITTED ▸ chit

CHITTER vb twitter or chirp

CHITTY adj childish ▷ vb sprout

CHIV n knife ▷ vb stab (someone)

CHIVARI same as > charivari

CHIVE n small Eurasian purple-flowered plant whose long slender hollow leaves are used in cooking ▷ vb file or cut off

CHIVED ▸ chive

CHIVES same as ▸ chive

CHIVIED ▸ chivy

CHIVIES ▸ chivy

CHIVING ▸ chive

CHIVS ▸ chiv

CHIVVED ▸ chiv

CHIVVY same as ▸ chivy

CHIVY vb harass or nag ▷ n hunt

CHIZ n cheat ▷ vb cheat

CHIZZ same as ▸ chiz

CHIZZED ▸ chiz

CHIZZES ▸ chiz

CHLAMYS n woollen cloak worn by ancient Greek soldiers

CHLORAL n colourless oily liquid with a pungent odour, made from chlorine and acetaldehyde and used in preparing chloral hydrate and DDT

CHLORIC adj of or containing chlorine in the pentavalent state

CHLORID n type of chlorine compound

CHLORIN same as > chlorine

CHOANA n posterior nasal aperture

CHOANAE ▸ choana

CHOBDAR n in India and Nepal, king's macebearer or attendant

CHOC short form of > chocolate

CHOCCY n chocolate ▷ adj made of, tasting of, smelling of, or resembling chocolate

CHOCHO same as ▸ chayote

CHOCHOS ▸ chocho

CHOCK n block or wedge used to prevent a heavy object from moving ▷ vb secure by a chock ▷ adv as closely or tightly as possible

CHOCKED ▸ chock

CHOCKER adj full up

CHOCKO same as ▸ choco

CHOCKOS ▸ choco

CHOCKS ▸ chock

CHOCO n member of the Australian army

CHOCOS ▸ choco

CHOCS ▸ choc

CHOCTAW n turn from the inside edge of one skate to the outside edge of the other or vice versa

CHODE ▸ chide

CHOENIX same as ▸ chenix**

CHOG n core of a piece of fruit

CHOGS ▸ chog

CHOICE n choosing ▷ adj of high quality

CHOICER ▸ choice

CHOICES ▸ choice

CHOIR n organized group of singers, esp in church ▷ vb to sing in chorus

CHOIRED ▸ choir

CHOIRS ▸ choir

CHOKE vb hinder or stop the breathing of (a person) by strangling or smothering ▷ n device controlling the amount of air that is mixed with the fuel in a petrol engine

CHOKED adj disappointed or angry

CHOKER n tight-fitting necklace

CHOKERS ▸ choker

CHOKES ▸ choke

CHOKEY n a slang word for prison ▷ adj involving, caused by, or causing choking

CHOKEYS ▸ chokey

CHOKIER ▸ chokey

CHOKIES ▸ chokey

CHOKING ▸ choke

CHOKO n pear-shaped fruit of a tropical American vine, eaten as a vegetable

CHOKOS ▸ choko

CHOKRA n in India, a boy or young man

CHOKRAS ▸ chokra

CHOKRI n in India, a girl or young woman

CHOKRIS ▸ chokri

CHOKY same as ▸ **chokey**

CHOLA n Hispanic girl

CHOLAS ▸ chola

CHOLATE n salt of cholic acid

CHOLENT n meal usually consisting of a stew of meat, potatoes, and pulses prepared before the Sabbath on Friday and left to cook until eaten for Sabbath lunch

CHOLER n bad temper

CHOLERA n serious infectious disease causing severe vomiting and diarrhoea

CHOLERS ▸ choler

CHOLI n short-sleeved bodice, as worn by Indian women

CHOLIC adj as in **cholic acid** crystalline acid found in bile

CHOLINE n colourless viscous soluble alkaline substance present in animal tissues, esp as a constituent of lecithin: used as a supplement to the diet of poultry and in medicine for preventing the accumulation of fat in the liver

CHOLIS ▸ choli

CHOLLA n type of spiny cactus of the southwestern US and Mexico, with cylindrical stem segments

CHOLLAS ▸ cholla

CHOLO n chicano gangster

CHOLOS ▸ cholo

CHOLTRY n caravanserai

CHOMETZ same as ▸ **chametz**

CHOMMIE n (in informal South African English) friend

CHOMP vb chew noisily ▷ n act or sound of chewing in this manner

CHOMPED ▸ chomp

CHOMPER ▸ chomp

CHOMPS ▸ chomp

CHON n North and South Korean monetary unit worth one hundredth of a won

CHONDRE another word for > **chondrule**

CHONDRI > **chondrus**

CHOOF vb go away

CHOOFED ▸ choof

CHOOFS ▸ choof

CHOOK n hen or chicken ▷ vb make the sound of a hen of chicken

CHOOKED ▸ chook

CHOOKIE same as ▸ **chook**

CHOOKS ▸ chook

CHOOM n Englishman

CHOOMS ▸ choom

CHOON n slang term for music that one likes

CHOONS ▸ choon

CHOOSE vb select from a number of alternatives

CHOOSER ▸ choose

CHOOSES ▸ choose

CHOOSEY same as ▸ **choosy**

CHOOSY adj fussy, hard to please

CHOP vb cut with a blow from an axe or knife ▷ n cutting or sharp blow

CHOPIN same as ▸ **chopine**

CHOPINE n sandal-like shoe on tall wooden or cork bases popular in the 18th century

CHOPINS ▸ chopin

CHOPPED ▸ chop

CHOPPER n helicopter ▷ vb travel by helicopter

CHOPPY adj (of the sea) fairly rough

CHOPS ▸ chop

CHORAGI > choragus

CHORAL adj of a choir

CHORALE n slow stately hymn tune

CHORALS ▸ choral

CHORD n straight line joining two points on a curve ▷ vb provide (a melodic line) with chords

CHORDA n in anatomy, a cord

CHORDAE ▸ chorda

CHORDAL ▸ chord

CHORDED ▸ chord

CHORDEE n painful penile erection, a symptom of gonorrhoea

CHORDS ▸ chord

CHORE n routine task ▷ vb to carry out chores

CHOREA n disorder of the nervous system characterized by uncontrollable brief jerky movements

CHOREAL ▸ chorea

CHOREAS ▸ chorea

CHORED ▸ chore

CHOREE n trochee

CHOREES ▸ choree

CHOREGI > choregus

CHOREIC ▸ chorea

CHORES ▸ chore

CHOREUS same as ▸ **choree**

CHORIA ▸ chorion

CHORIAL ▸ chorion

CHORIC adj of, like, for, or in the manner of a chorus, esp of singing, dancing, or the speaking of verse

CHORINE n chorus girl

CHORING ▸ chore

CHORION n outer of two membranes that form a sac around the embryonic reptile, bird, or mammal

CHORISM ▸ chorisis

CHORIST n choir member

CHORIZO n kind of highly seasoned pork sausage of Spain or Mexico

C

CHOROID adj resembling the chorion, esp in being vascular ▷ n brownish vascular membrane of the eyeball between the sclera and the retina

CHORRIE n dilapidated old car

CHORTEN n Buddhist shrine

CHORTLE vb chuckle in amusement ▷ n amused chuckle

CHORUS n large choir ▷ vb sing or say together

CHOSE ► choose

CHOSEN ► choose

CHOSES ► choose

CHOTA adj (in British Empire Indian usage) small

CHOTT a variant spelling of ► shott

CHOTTS ► chott

CHOU n type of cabbage

CHOUGH n large black Eurasian and N African bird of the crow family

CHOUGHS ► chough

CHOUSE vb to cheat

CHOUSED ► chouse

CHOUSER ► chouse

CHOUSES ► chouse

CHOUSH n Turkish messenger

CHOUT n blackmail

CHOUTS ► chout

CHOUX ► chou

CHOW n thick-coated dog with a curled tail, orig. from China ▷ vb eat

CHOWDER n thick soup containing clams or fish ▷ vb to make a chowder of

CHOWED ► chow

CHOWING ► chow

CHOWK n marketplace or market area

CHOWKS ► chowk

CHOWRI n fly-whisk

CHOWRIS ► chowri

CHOWRY same as ► chowri

CHOWS ► chow

CHOWSE same as ► chouse

CHOWSED ► chowse

CHOWSES ► chowse

CHRISM n consecrated oil used for anointing in some churches

CHRISMA > chrismon

CHRISMS ► chrism

CHRISOM same as ► chrism

CHRISTY n skiing turn for stopping or changing

direction quickly

CHROMA n attribute of a colour that enables an observer to judge how much chromatic colour it contains irrespective of achromatic colour present

CHROMAS ► chroma

CHROME n anything plated with chromium ▷ vb plate with chromium ▷ vb to chromium-plate ▷ adj of or having the appearance of chrome

CHROMED ► chrome

CHROMEL n nickel-based alloy containing about 10 per cent chromium, used in heating elements

CHROMES ► chrome

CHROMIC adj of or containing chromium in the trivalent state

CHROMO n picture produced by the process of making coloured prints by lithography

CHROMOS ► chromo

CHROMY ► chrome

CHROMYL n of, consisting of, or containing the divalent radical CrO_2

CHRONIC adj (of an illness) lasting a long time ▷ n chronically-ill patient

CHRONON n unit of time equal to the time that a photon would take to traverse the diameter of an electron: about 10^{-24} seconds

CHUB n European freshwater fish of the carp family

CHUBBY adj plump and round

CHUBS ► chub

CHUCK vb throw ▷ n cut of beef from the neck to the shoulder

CHUCKED ► chuck

CHUCKER n person who throws something

CHUCKIE n small stone

CHUCKLE vb laugh softly ▷ n soft laugh

CHUCKS ► chuck

CHUCKY same as ► chuckie

CHUDDAH same as ► chuddar

CHUDDAR n large shawl or veil worn by Muslim or Hindu women that covers

them from head to foot

CHUDDER same as ► chuddar

CHUDDY n chewing gum

CHUFA n type of sedge of warm regions of the Old World, with nutlike edible tubers

CHUFAS ► chufa

CHUFF vb (of a steam engine) move while making a puffing sound ▷ n puffing sound of or as if of a steam engine ▷ adj boorish

CHUFFED adj very pleased

CHUFFER ► chuff

CHUFFS ► chuff

CHUFFY adj boorish and surly

CHUG n short dull sound like the noise of an engine ▷ vb operate or move with this sound

CHUGGED ► chug

CHUGGER ► chug

CHUGS ► chug

CHUKAR n common Indian partridge with red legs and bill and a black-barred sandy plumage

CHUKARS ► chukar

CHUKKA n period of play in polo

CHUKKAR same as ► chukka

CHUKKAS ► chukka

CHUKKER same as ► chukka

CHUKOR same as ► chukar

CHUKORS ► chukor

CHUM n close friend ▷ vb be or become an intimate friend (of)

CHUMASH n printed book containing one of the Five Books of Moses

CHUMLEY same as ► chimney

CHUMMED ► chum

CHUMMY adj friendly ▷ n chum

CHUMP n stupid person ▷ vb chew noisily

CHUMPED ► chump

CHUMPS ► chump

CHUMS ► chum

CHUNDER vb vomit ▷ n vomit

CHUNK n thick solid piece ▷ vb to break up into chunks

CHUNKED ► chunk

CHUNKS ► chunk

CHUNKY adj (of a person)

broad and heavy
CHUNNEL n rail tunnel beneath the English Channel, linking England and France
CHUNNER same as ▸ **chunter**
CHUNTER vb mutter or grumble incessantly in a meaningless fashion
CHUPATI same as > **chupatti**
CHUPPA same as ▸ **chuppah**
CHUPPAH n canopy under which a marriage is performed
CHUPPAS ▸ **chuppa**
CHUPPOT ▸ **chuppah**
CHUR interj expression of agreement
CHURCH n building for public Christian worship ▷ vb bring (someone, esp a woman after childbirth) to church for special ceremonies
CHURCHY adj like a church, church service, etc
CHURL n surly ill-bred person
CHURLS ▸ **churl**
CHURN n machine in which cream is shaken to make butter ▷ vb stir (cream) vigorously to make butter
CHURNED ▸ **churn**
CHURNER ▸ **churn**
CHURNS ▸ **churn**
CHURR same as ▸ **chirr**
CHURRED ▸ **churr**
CHURRO n Spanish dough stick snack
CHURROS ▸ **churro**
CHURRS ▸ **churr**
CHURRUS n hemp resin
CHUSE obsolete variant of ▸ **choose**
CHUSES ▸ **chuse**
CHUSING ▸ **chuse**
CHUT interj expression of surprise or annoyance ▷ vb make such an expression
CHUTE n steep slope down which things may be slid ▷ vb to descend by a chute
CHUTED ▸ **chute**
CHUTES ▸ **chute**
CHUTING ▸ **chute**
CHUTIST ▸ **chute**
CHUTNEE same as ▸ **chutney**
CHUTNEY n pickle made from fruit, vinegar, spices, and sugar
CHUTZPA same as

> **chutzpah**
CHYACK same as ▸ **chiack**
CHYACKS ▸ **chyack**
CHYLDE archaic word for ▸ **child**
CHYLE n milky fluid formed in the small intestine during digestion
CHYLES ▸ **chyle**
CHYLIFY vb to be turned into chyle
CHYLOUS ▸ **chyle**
CHYME n thick fluid mass of partially digested food that leaves the stomach
CHYMES ▸ **chyme**
CHYMIC same as ▸ **chemic**
CHYMICS ▸ **chymic**
CHYMIFY vb to form into chyme
CHYMIST same as ▸ **chemist**
CHYMOUS ▸ **chyme**
CHYND adj chined
CHYPRE n perfume made from sandalwood
CHYPRES ▸ **chypre**
CHYTRID n variety of fungus
CIAO an informal word for ▸ **hello**
CIBOL same as ▸ **chibol**
CIBOLS ▸ **cibol**
CIBORIA > **ciborium**
CIBOULE same as ▸ **chibol**
CICADA n large insect that makes a high-pitched drone
CICADAE ▸ **cicada**
CICADAS ▸ **cicada**
CICALA same as ▸ **cicada**
CICALAS ▸ **cicala**
CICALE ▸ **cicala**
CICELY n type of plant
CICERO n measure for type that is somewhat larger than the pica
CICEROS ▸ **cicero**
CICHLID n type of tropical freshwater fish popular in aquariums
CICOREE same as ▸ **chicory**
CICUTA n spotted hemlock
CICUTAS ▸ **cicuta**
CID n leader
CIDARIS n sea urchin
CIDE Shakespearean variant of ▸ **decide**
CIDED ▸ **cide**
CIDER n alcoholic drink made from fermented apple juice
CIDERS ▸ **cider**
CIDERY ▸ **cider**

CIDES ▸ **cide**
CIDING ▸ **cide**
CIDS ▸ **cid**
CIEL same as ▸ **ceil**
CIELED ▸ **ciel**
CIELING ▸ **ciel**
CIELS ▸ **ciel**
CIERGE same as ▸ **cerge**
CIERGES ▸ **cierge**
CIG same as > **cigarette**
CIGAR n roll of cured tobacco leaves for smoking
CIGARET same as > **cigarette**
CIGARS ▸ **cigar**
CIGGIE same as > **cigarette**
CIGGIES ▸ **ciggie**
CIGGY > **cigarette**
CIGS ▸ **cig**
CILIA ▸ **cilium**
CILIARY adj of or relating to cilia
CILIATE n type of protozoan
CILICE n haircloth fabric or garment
CILICES ▸ **cilice**
CILIUM n short thread projecting from a cell, whose rhythmic beating causes movement
CILL a variant spelling (used in the building industry) for ▸ **sill**
CILLS ▸ **cill**
CIMAR same as ▸ **cymar**
CIMARS ▸ **cimar**
CIMELIA n (especially, ecclesiastical) treasures
CIMEX n type of heteropterous insect, esp the bedbug
CIMICES ▸ **cimex**
CIMIER n crest of a helmet
CIMIERS ▸ **cimier**
CINCH n easy task ▷ vb fasten a girth around (a horse)
CINCHED ▸ **cinch**
CINCHES ▸ **cinch**
CINCT adj encircled
CINDER n piece of material that will not burn, left after burning coal ▷ vb burn to cinders
CINDERS ▸ **cinder**
CINDERY ▸ **cinder**
CINE n as in **cine camera** camera able to film moving pictures
CINEAST same as > **cineaste**
CINEMA n place for showing films
CINEMAS ▸ **cinema**
CINEOL n colourless oily

liquid with a camphor-like odour and a spicy taste

CINEOLE same as ▶ cineol

CINEOLS ▶ cineol

CINEREA n grey matter of the brain and nervous system

CINERIN n either of two organic compounds used as insecticides

CINES ▶ cine

CINGULA > cingulum

CINQUE n number five in cards, dice, etc

CINQUES ▶ cinque

CION same as ▶ scion

CIONS ▶ cion

CIPHER n system of secret writing ▷ vb put (a message) into secret writing

CIPHERS ▶ cipher

CIPHONY n ciphered telephony; process of enciphering audio information, producing encrypted speech

CIPOLIN n Italian marble with alternating white and green streaks

CIPPI ▶ cippus

CIPPUS n pillar bearing an inscription

CIRCA prep approximately, about

CIRCAR n in India, part of a province

CIRCARS ▶ circar

CIRCLE n perfectly round geometric figure, line, or shape ▷ vb move in a circle (round)

CIRCLED ▶ circle

CIRCLER ▶ circle

CIRCLES ▶ circle

CIRCLET n circular ornament worn on the head

CIRCLIP n flat spring ring split at one point so that it can be sprung open, passed over a shaft or spindle, and allowed to close into a closely fitting annular recess to form a collar on the shaft. A similar design can be closed to pass into a bore and allowed to spring out into an annular recess to form a shoulder in the bore

CIRCS pl n circumstances

CIRCUIT n complete route

or course, esp a circular one ▷ vb make or travel in a circuit around (something)

CIRCUS n (performance given by) a travelling company of acrobats, clowns, performing animals, etc

CIRCUSY ▶ circus

CIRE adj (of fabric) treated with a heat or wax process to make it smooth ▷ n such a surface on a fabric

CIRES ▶ cire

CIRL n bird belonging to the bunting family

CIRLS ▶ cirl

CIRQUE n steep-sided semicircular hollow found in mountainous areas

CIRQUES ▶ cirque

CIRRATE adj bearing or resembling cirri

CIRRI ▶ cirrus

CIRROSE same as ▶ cirrate

CIRROUS same as ▶ cirrate

CIRRUS n high wispy cloud

CIRSOID adj resembling a varix

CIS adj having two groups of atoms on the same side of a double bond

CISCO n whitefish, esp the lake herring of cold deep lakes of North America

CISCOES ▶ cisco

CISCOS ▶ cisco

CISSIER ▶ cissy

CISSIES ▶ cissy

CISSING n appearance of pinholes, craters, etc, in paintwork due to poor adhesion of the paint to the surface

CISSOID n geometric curve whose two branches meet in a cusp at the origin and are asymptotic to a line parallel to the y-axis

CISSUS n type of climbing plant sometimes grown in a greenhouse or house plant for its shiny green or mottled leaves

CISSY same as ▶ sissy

CIST n wooden box for holding ritual objects used in ancient Rome and Greece ▷ vb make a cist

CISTED ▶ cist

CISTERN n water tank, esp one that holds water for flushing a toilet

CISTIC adj cist-like

CISTRON n section of a chromosome that encodes a single polypeptide chain

CISTS ▶ cist

CISTUS n type of plant

CIT n pejorative term for a town dweller

CITABLE ▶ cite

CITADEL n fortress in a city

CITAL n court summons

CITALS ▶ cital

CITATOR n legal publication listing cases and statutes, their history and current status

CITE vb quote, refer to

CITED ▶ cite

CITER ▶ cite

CITERS ▶ cite

CITES ▶ cite

CITESS n female cit

CITHARA n stringed musical instrument of ancient Greece and elsewhere, similar to the lyre and played with a plectrum

CITHER same as ▶ cittern

CITHERN ▶ cittern

CITHERS ▶ cither

CITHREN same as ▶ cithara

CITIED adj having cities

CITIES ▶ city

CITIFY vb cause to conform to or adopt the customs, habits, or dress of city people

CITING ▶ cite

CITIZEN n native or naturalized member of a state or nation

CITO adv swiftly

CITOLA n type of medieval stringed instrument

CITOLAS ▶ citola

CITOLE a rare word for ▶ cittern

CITOLES ▶ citole

CITRAL n yellow volatile liquid with a lemon-like odour, found in oils of lemon grass, orange, and lemon and used in perfumery

CITRALS ▶ citral

CITRATE n any salt or ester of citric acid

CITRIC adj of or derived from citrus fruits or citric acid

CITRIN n vitamin P

CITRINE n brownish-yellow variety of quartz: a gemstone

CITRINS ▶ citrin

CITRON n lemon-like fruit of a small Asian tree

CITRONS ▶ citron

CITROUS same as ▶ **citrus**

CITRUS n type of tropical or subtropical tree or shrub of the genus which includes the orange, lemon, lime, and grapefruit

CITRUSY same as > **citrussy**

CITS ▶ cit

CITTERN n medieval stringed instrument resembling a lute but having wire strings and a flat back

CITY n large or important town

CITYFY same as ▶ **citify**

CIVE same as ▶ **chive**

CIVES ▶ cive

CIVET n spotted catlike African mammal

CIVETS ▶ civet

CIVIC adj of a city or citizens

CIVICS n study of the rights and responsibilities of citizenship

CIVIE same as ▶ **civvy**

CIVIES ▶ civie

CIVIL adj relating to the citizens of a state as opposed to the armed forces or the Church

CIVILLY ▶ civil

CIVILS ▶ civil

CIVISM n good citizenship

CIVISMS ▶ civism

CIVVIES ▶ civvy

CIVVY n civilian

CIZERS archaic spelling of > **scissors**

CLABBER vb to cover with mud

CLACH n stone

CLACHAN n small village

CLACHS ▶ clach

CLACK n sound made by two hard objects striking each other ▷ vb make this sound

CLACKED ▶ clack

CLACKER n object that makes a clacking sound

CLACKS ▶ clack

CLAD vb bond a metal to (another metal), esp to form a protective coat

CLADDED adj covered with cladding

CLADDER ▶ clad

CLADDIE another name for

▶ **korari**

CLADE n group of organisms considered as having evolved from a common ancestor

CLADES ▶ clade

CLADISM ▶ cladist

CLADIST n proponent of cladistics: a method of grouping animals that makes use of lines of descent rather than structural similarities

CLADODE n flattened stem resembling and functioning as a leaf, as in butcher's-broom

CLADS ▶ clad

CLAES Scots word for ▶ **clothes**

CLAG n sticky mud ▷ vb stick, as mud

CLAGGED ▶ clag

CLAGGY adj stickily clinging, as mud

CLAGS ▶ clag

CLAIM vb assert as a fact ▷ n assertion that something is true

CLAIMED ▶ claim

CLAIMER ▶ claim

CLAIMS ▶ claim

CLAM n edible shellfish with a hinged shell ▷ vb gather clams

CLAMANT adj noisy

CLAMBE old variant of ▶ **climb**

CLAMBER vb climb awkwardly ▷ n climb performed in this manner

CLAME archaic variant of ▶ **claim**

CLAMES ▶ claim

CLAMMED ▶ clam

CLAMMER n person who gathers clams

CLAMMY adj unpleasantly moist and sticky

CLAMOR same as ▶ **clamour**

CLAMORS ▶ clamor

CLAMOUR n loud protest ▷ vb make a loud noise or outcry

CLAMP n tool with movable jaws for holding things together tightly ▷ vb fasten with a clamp

CLAMPED ▶ clamp

CLAMPER n spiked metal frame fastened to the sole of a shoe to prevent slipping on ice ▷ vb to tread heavily

CLAMPS ▶ clamp

CLAMS ▶ clam

CLAN n group of families with a common ancestor, esp among Scottish Highlanders

CLANG vb make a loud ringing metallic sound ▷ n ringing metallic sound

CLANGED ▶ clang

CLANGER n obvious mistake

CLANGOR same as > **clangour**

CLANGS ▶ clang

CLANK n harsh metallic sound ▷ vb make such a sound

CLANKED ▶ clank

CLANKS ▶ clank

CLANKY adj making clanking sounds

CLANS ▶ clan

CLAP vb applaud by hitting the palms of one's hands sharply together ▷ n act or sound of clapping

CLAPNET n net that can be closed instantly by pulling a string

CLAPPED ▶ clap

CLAPPER n piece of metal inside a bell, which causes it to sound when struck against the side ▷ vb make a sound like a clapper

CLAPS ▶ clap

CLAPT ▶ clap

CLAQUE n group of people hired to applaud

CLAQUER same as > **claqueur**

CLAQUES ▶ claque

CLARAIN n one of the four major lithotypes of banded coal

CLARET n dry red wine from Bordeaux ▷ adj purplish-red ▷ vb to drink claret

CLARETS ▶ claret

CLARIES ▶ clary

CLARIFY vb make (a matter) clear and unambiguous

CLARINI ▶ clarino

CLARINO adj of or relating to a high passage for the trumpet in 18th-century music ▷ n high register of the trumpet

CLARION n obsolete high-pitched trumpet ▷ adj clear and ringing ▷ vb proclaim loudly

CLARITY n clearness

CLARKIA n N American plant cultivated for its red, purple, or pink flowers

CLARO n mild light-coloured cigar

CLAROES ▸ claro

CLAROS ▸ claro

CLART vb to dirty

CLARTED ▸ clart

CLARTS pl n lumps of mud, esp on shoes

CLARTY adj dirty, esp covered in mud

CLARY n European plant with aromatic leaves and blue flowers

CLASH vb come into conflict ▸ n fight, argument

CLASHED ▸ clash

CLASHER ▸ clash

CLASHES ▸ clash

CLASP n device for fastening things ▸ vb grasp or embrace firmly

CLASPED ▸ clasp

CLASPER ▸ clasp

CLASPS ▸ clasp

CLASPT old inflection of ▸ clasp

CLASS n group of people sharing a similar social position ▸ vb place in a class

CLASSED ▸ class

CLASSER ▸ class

CLASSES ▸ classis

CLASSIC adj being a typical example of something ▸ n author, artist, or work of art of recognized excellence

CLASSIS n governing body of elders or pastors

CLASSON n elementary atomic particle

CLASSY adj stylish and elegant

CLAST n fragment of a clastic rock

CLASTIC adj (of sedimentary rock, etc) composed of fragments of pre-existing rock that have been transported some distance from their points of origin ▸ n clast

CLASTS ▸ clast

CLAT n irksome or troublesome task ▸ vb to scrape

CLATCH vb to move making a squelching sound

CLATS ▸ clat

CLATTED ▸ clat

CLATTER n (make) a rattling noise ▸ vb make a rattling noise, as when hard objects hit each other

CLAUCHT vb to seize by force

CLAUGHT same as ▸ claucht

CLAUSAL ▸ clause

CLAUSE n section of a legal document

CLAUSES ▸ clause

CLAUT same as ▸ clat

CLAUTED ▸ claut

CLAUTS ▸ claut

CLAVATE adj shaped like a club with the thicker end uppermost

CLAVE n one of a pair of hardwood sticks struck together to make a hollow sound, esp to mark the beat of Latin-American dance music

CLAVER vb talk idly ▸ n idle talk

CLAVERS ▸ claver

CLAVES ▸ clave

CLAVI ▸ clavus

CLAVIE n tar-barrel traditionally set alight in Moray in Scotland on Hogmanay

CLAVIER n any keyboard instrument

CLAVIES ▸ clavie

CLAVIS n key

CLAVUS n corn on the toe

CLAW n sharp hooked nail of a bird or beast ▸ vb tear with claws or nails

CLAWED ▸ claw

CLAWER ▸ claw

CLAWERS ▸ claw

CLAWING ▸ claw

CLAWS ▸ claw

CLAXON same as ▸ klaxon

CLAXONS ▸ claxon

CLAY n fine-grained earth, soft when moist and hardening when baked, used to make bricks and pottery ▸ vb cover or mix with clay

CLAYED ▸ clay

CLAYEY ▸ clay

CLAYIER ▸ clay

CLAYING ▸ clay

CLAYISH ▸ clay

CLAYPAN n layer of stiff impervious clay situated just below the surface of

the ground, which holds water after heavy rain

CLAYS ▸ clay

CLEAN adj free from dirt or impurities ▸ vb make (something) free from dirt ▸ adv completely

CLEANED ▸ clean

CLEANER n person or thing that removes dirt

CLEANLY adv easily or smoothly ▸ adj habitually clean or neat

CLEANS ▸ clean

CLEANSE vb make clean

CLEANUP n process of cleaning up or eliminating something

CLEAR adj free from doubt or confusion ▸ adv in a clear or distinct manner ▸ vb make or become clear

CLEARED ▸ clear

CLEARER ▸ clear

CLEARLY adv in a clear, distinct, or obvious manner

CLEARS ▸ clear

CLEAT n wedge ▸ vb supply or support with a cleat or cleats

CLEATED ▸ cleat

CLEATS ▸ cleat

CLEAVE vb split apart ▸ n split

CLEAVED ▸ cleave

CLEAVER n butcher's heavy knife with a square blade

CLEAVES ▸ cleave

CLECHE adj (in heraldry) voided so that only a narrow border is visible

CLECK vb (of birds) to hatch ▸ n piece of gossip

CLECKED ▸ cleck

CLECKS ▸ cleck

CLECKY ▸ cleck

CLEEK n large hook, such as one used to land fish ▸ vb to seize

CLEEKED ▸ cleek

CLEEKIT ▸ cleek

CLEEKS ▸ cleek

CLEEP same as ▸ clepe

CLEEPED ▸ cleep

CLEEPS ▸ cleep

CLEEVE n cliff

CLEEVES ▸ cleeve

CLEF n symbol at the beginning of a stave to show the pitch

CLEFS ▸ clef

CLEFT ▸ cleave

CLEFTED ▸ cleave

CLEFTS ▸ cleave

CLEG another name for a **> horsefly**

CLEGS ▸ cleg

CLEIK same as **▸ cleek**

CLEIKS ▸ cleek

CLEM vb be hungry or cause to be hungry

CLEMENT adj (of weather) mild

CLEMMED ▸ clem

CLEMS ▸ clem

CLENCH vb close or squeeze (one's teeth or fist) tightly ▷ n firm grasp or grip

CLEOME n type of herbaceous or shrubby plant cultivated for its clusters of white or purplish flowers

CLEOMES ▸ cleome

CLEPE vb call by the name of

CLEPED ▸ clepe

CLEPES ▸ clepe

CLEPING ▸ clepe

CLEPT ▸ clepe

CLERGY n priests and ministers as a group

CLERIC n member of the clergy

CLERICS ▸ cleric

CLERID n beetle that preys on other insects

CLERIDS ▸ clerid

CLERISY n learned or educated people

CLERK n employee in an office, bank, or court who keeps records, files, and accounts ▷ vb work as a clerk

CLERKED ▸ clerk

CLERKLY adj of or like a clerk ▷ adv in the manner of a clerk

CLERKS ▸ clerk

CLERUCH n settler in a cleruchy

CLEUCH same as **▸ clough**

CLEUCHS ▸ cleuch

CLEUGH same as **▸ clough**

CLEUGHS ▸ cleugh

CLEVE same as **▸ cleeve**

CLEVER adj intelligent, quick at learning

CLEVES ▸ cleeve

CLEVIS n U-shaped component of a shackle for attaching a drawbar to a plough or similar implement

CLEW n ball of thread, yarn, or twine ▷ vb coil or roll into a ball

CLEWED ▸ clew

CLEWING ▸ clew

CLEWS ▸ clew

CLICHE n expression or idea that is no longer effective because of overuse ▷ vb use a cliché (in speech or writing)

CLICHED ▸ cliche

CLICHES ▸ cliche

CLICK n short sharp sound ▷ vb make this sound

CLICKED ▸ click

CLICKER ▸ click

CLICKET vb make a click

CLICKS ▸ click

CLIED ▸ cly

CLIENT n person who uses the services of a professional person or company

CLIENTS ▸ client

CLIES ▸ cly

CLIFF n steep rock face, esp along the sea shore ▷ vb scale a cliff

CLIFFED ▸ cliff

CLIFFS ▸ cliff

CLIFFY ▸ cliff

CLIFT same as **▸ cliff**

CLIFTED ▸ cliff

CLIFTS ▸ cliff

CLIFTY ▸ cliff

CLIMATE n typical weather conditions of an area ▷ vb acclimatize

CLIMAX n most intense point of an experience, series of events, or story ▷ vb reach a climax

CLIMB vb go up, ascend ▷ n climbing

CLIMBED ▸ climb

CLIMBER n person or thing that climbs

CLIMBS ▸ climb

CLIME n place or its climate

CLIMES ▸ clime

CLINAL ▸ cline

CLINCH vb settle (an argument or agreement) decisively ▷ n movement in which one competitor holds on to the other to avoid punches

CLINE n continuous variation in form between members of a species having a wide variable geographical or ecological range

CLINES ▸ cline

CLING vb hold tightly or stick closely ▷ n tendency of cotton fibres in a sample to stick to each other

CLINGED ▸ cling

CLINGER ▸ cling

CLINGS ▸ cling

CLINGY ▸ cling

CLINIC n building where outpatients receive medical treatment or advice

CLINICS ▸ clinic

CLINK n (make) a light sharp metallic sound ▷ vb make a light sharp metallic sound

CLINKED ▸ clink

CLINKER n fused coal left over in a fire or furnace ▷ vb form clinker during burning

CLINKS ▸ clink

CLINT n section of a limestone pavement separated from adjacent sections by solution fissures

CLINTS ▸ clint

CLIP vb cut with shears or scissors ▷ n short extract of a film

CLIPART n large collection of simple drawings stored in a computer

CLIPE same as **▸ clype**

CLIPED ▸ clipe

CLIPES ▸ clipe

CLIPING ▸ clipe

CLIPPED ▸ clip

CLIPPER n fast commercial sailing ship

CLIPPIE n bus conductress

CLIPS ▸ clip

CLIPT old inflection of **▸ clip**

CLIQUE n small exclusive group ▷ vb to form a clique

CLIQUED ▸ clique

CLIQUES ▸ clique

CLIQUEY adj exclusive, confined to a small group

CLIQUY same as **▸ cliquey**

CLIT > clitoris

CLITIC adj (of a word) incapable of being stressed, usually pronounced as if part of the word that follows or precedes it ▷ n clitic word

CLITICS ▸ clitic

CLITS ▸ clit

CLITTER vb to stridulate

CLIVERS same as **> cleavers**

CLIVIA n plant belonging to the Amaryllid family

CLIVIAS ▸ clivia

CLOACA n cavity in most

animals, except higher mammals, into which the alimentary canal and the genital and urinary ducts open

CLOACAE ▸ **cloaca**

CLOACAL ▸ **cloaca**

CLOACAS ▸ **cloaca**

CLOAK n loose sleeveless outer garment ▷ vb cover or conceal

CLOAKED ▸ **cloak**

CLOAKS ▸ **cloak**

CLOAM adj made of clay or earthenware ▷ n clay or earthenware pots, dishes, etc, collectively

CLOAMS ▸ **cloam**

CLOBBER vb hit ▷ n belongings, esp clothes

CLOCHE n cover to protect young plants

CLOCHES ▸ **cloche**

CLOCK n instrument for showing the time ▷ vb record (time) with a stopwatch

CLOCKED ▸ **clock**

CLOCKER ▸ **clock**

CLOCKS ▸ **clock**

CLOD n lump of earth ▷ vb pelt with clods

CLODDED ▸ **clod**

CLODDY ▸ **clod**

CLODLY ▸ **clod**

CLODS ▸ **clod**

CLOFF n cleft of a tree

CLOFFS ▸ **cloff**

CLOG vb obstruct ▷ n wooden or wooden-soled shoe

CLOGGED ▸ **clog**

CLOGGER n clogmaker

CLOGGY ▸ **clog**

CLOGS ▸ **clog**

CLOISON n partition

CLOKE same as ▸ **cloak**

CLOKED ▸ **cloke**

CLOKES ▸ **cloke**

CLOKING ▸ **cloke**

CLOMB a past tense and past participle of ▸ **climb**

CLOMP same as ▸ **clump**

CLOMPED ▸ **clomp**

CLOMPS ▸ **clomp**

CLON same as ▸ **clone**

CLONAL ▸ **clone**

CLONE n animal or plant produced artificially from the cells of another animal or plant, and identical to the original ▷ vb produce as a clone

CLONED ▸ **clone**

CLONER ▸ **clone**

CLONERS ▸ **clone**

CLONES ▸ **clone**

CLONIC ▸ **clonus**

CLONING ▸ **clone**

CLONISM n series of clonic spasms

CLONK vb make a loud dull thud ▷ n loud thud

CLONKED ▸ **clonk**

CLONKS ▸ **clonk**

CLONS ▸ **clon**

CLONUS n type of convulsion characterized by rapid contraction and relaxation of a muscle

CLOOP n sound made when a cork is drawn from a bottle

CLOOPS ▸ **cloop**

CLOOT n hoof

CLOOTIE adj as in **clootie dumpling** kind of dumpling

CLOOTS ▸ **cloot**

CLOP vb make or move along with a sound as of a horse's hooves striking the ground ▷ n sound of this nature

CLOPPED ▸ **clop**

CLOPS ▸ **clop**

CLOQUE n fabric with an embossed surface

CLOQUES ▸ **cloque**

CLOSE vb shut ▷ n end, conclusion ▷ adj near ▷ adv closely, tightly ▷ n passageway leading to a tenement building

CLOSED ▸ **close**

CLOSELY ▸ **close**

CLOSER ▸ **close**

CLOSERS ▸ **close**

CLOSES ▸ **close**

CLOSEST ▸ **close**

CLOSET n cupboard ▷ adj private, secret ▷ vb shut (oneself) away in private

CLOSETS ▸ **closet**

CLOSEUP n photo taken close to subject

CLOSING ▸ **close**

CLOSURE n closing ▷ vb (in a deliberative body) to end (debate) by closure

CLOT n soft thick lump formed from liquid ▷ vb form soft thick lumps

CLOTBUR n burdock

CLOTE n burdock

CLOTES ▸ **clote**

CLOTH n (piece of) woven fabric

CLOTHE vb put clothes on

CLOTHED ▸ **clothe**

CLOTHES n garments

CLOTHS ▸ **cloth**

CLOTS ▸ **clot**

CLOTTED ▸ **clot**

CLOTTER vb to clot

CLOTTY adj full of clots

CLOTURE n closure in the US Senate ▷ vb end (debate) in the US Senate by cloture

CLOU n crux; focus

CLOUD n mass of condensed water vapour floating in the sky ▷ vb become cloudy

CLOUDED ▸ **cloud**

CLOUDS ▸ **cloud**

CLOUDY adj having a lot of clouds

CLOUGH n gorge or narrow ravine

CLOUGHS ▸ **clough**

CLOUR vb to thump or dent

CLOURED ▸ **clour**

CLOURS ▸ **clour**

CLOUS ▸ **clou**

CLOUT n hard blow ▷ vb hit hard

CLOUTED ▸ **clout**

CLOUTER ▸ **clout**

CLOUTS ▸ **clout**

CLOVE n tropical evergreen myrtaceous tree

CLOVEN ▸ **cleave**

CLOVER n plant with three-lobed leaves

CLOVERS ▸ **clover**

CLOVERY ▸ **clover**

CLOVES ▸ **clove**

CLOVIS n as in **clovis point** flint projectile dating from the 10th millennium bc

CLOW n clove

CLOWDER n collective term for a group of cats

CLOWN n comic entertainer in a circus ▷ vb behave foolishly

CLOWNED ▸ **clown**

CLOWNS ▸ **clown**

CLOWS ▸ **clow**

CLOY vb make weary or cause weariness through an excess of something initially pleasurable or sweet

CLOYE vb to claw

CLOYED ▸ **cloy**

CLOYES ▸ **cloye**

CLOYING adj sickeningly sweet

CLOYS ▸ cloy

CLOZE *adj as in* **cloze test** test of the ability to understand text

CLOZES ▸ cloze

CLUB *n* association of people with common interests ▷ *vb* hit with a club

CLUBBED ▸ club

CLUBBER *n* person who regularly frequents nightclubs and similar establishments

CLUBBY *adj* sociable, esp effusively so

CLUBMAN *n* man who is an enthusiastic member of a club or clubs

CLUBMEN ▸ clubman

CLUBS ▸ club

CLUCK *n* low clicking noise made by a hen ▷ *vb* make this noise

CLUCKED ▸ cluck

CLUCKS ▸ cluck

CLUCKY *adj* wishing to have a baby

CLUDGIE *n* toilet

CLUE *n* something that helps to solve a mystery or puzzle ▷ *vb* help solve a mystery or puzzle

CLUED ▸ clue

CLUEING ▸ clue

CLUES ▸ clue

CLUING ▸ clue

CLUMBER *n* type of thickset spaniel

CLUMP *n* small group of things or people ▷ *vb* walk heavily

CLUMPED ▸ clump

CLUMPER ▸ clump

CLUMPS ▸ clump

CLUMPY ▸ clump

CLUMSY *adj* lacking skill or physical coordination

CLUNCH *n* hardened clay

CLUNG ▸ cling

CLUNK *n* dull metallic sound ▷ *vb* make such a sound

CLUNKED ▸ clunk

CLUNKER *n* dilapidated old car or other machine

CLUNKS ▸ clunk

CLUNKY *adj* making a clunking noise

CLUPEID *n* type of widely distributed soft-finned fish, typically with oily flesh, such as the herrings,

sardines, and shad

CLUSIA *n* tree of the tropical American genus Clusia

CLUSIAS ▸ clusia

CLUSTER *n* small close group ▷ *vb* gather in clusters

CLUTCH *vb* grasp tightly ▷ *n* device enabling two revolving shafts to be connected and disconnected, esp in a motor vehicle

CLUTCHY *adj* (of a person) tending to cling

CLUTTER *vb* scatter objects about (a place) untidily ▷ *n* untidy mess

CLY *vb* to steal or seize

> A little word meaning to seize or steal, this can be useful when you are short of vowels.

CLYING ▸ cly

CLYPE *vb* tell tales ▷ *n* person who tells tales

CLYPEAL ▸ clypeus

CLYPED ▸ clype

CLYPEI ▸ clypeus

CLYPES ▸ clype

CLYPEUS *n* cuticular plate on the head of some insects between the labrum and the frons

CLYPING ▸ clype

CLYSTER *a former name for an* ▸ **enema**

CNEMIAL ▸ cnemis

CNEMIS *n* shin or tibia

CNIDA *n* nematocyst

CNIDAE ▸ cnida

COACH *n* long-distance bus ▷ *vb* train, teach

COACHED ▸ coach

COACHEE *n* person who receives training from a coach, esp in business or office practice

COACHER ▸ coach

COACHES ▸ coach

COACHY *n* coachman ▷ *adj* resembling or pertaining to a coach

COACT *vb* to act together

COACTED ▸ coact

COACTOR ▸ coact

COACTS ▸ coact

COADMIT *vb* to admit together

COAEVAL *n* contemporary

COAGENT > **coagency**

COAGULA > **coagulum**

COAITA *n* spider monkey

COAITAS ▸ coaita

COAL *n* black rock consisting mainly of carbon, used as fuel ▷ *vb* take in, or turn into coal

COALA *same as* ▸ **koala**

COALAS ▸ coala

COALBIN *n* bin for holding coal

COALBOX *n* box for holding coal

COALED ▸ coal

COALER *n* ship, train, etc, used to carry or supply coal

COALERS ▸ coaler

COALIER ▸ coal

COALIFY *vb* to turn into coal

COALING ▸ coal

COALISE *vb* to form a coalition

COALIZE *same as* ▸ **coalise**

COALMAN *n* man who delivers coal

COALMEN ▸ coalman

COALPIT *n* pit from which coal is extracted

COALS ▸ coal

COALY ▸ coal

COAMING *n* raised frame round a ship's hatchway for keeping out water

COANNEX *vb* to annex with something else

COAPT *vb* to secure

COAPTED ▸ coapt

COAPTS ▸ coapt

COARB *n* spiritual successor

COARBS ▸ coarb

COARSE *adj* rough in texture

COARSEN *vb* make or become coarse

COARSER ▸ coarse

COAST *n* place where the land meets the sea ▷ *vb* move by momentum, without the use of power

COASTAL ▸ coast

COASTED ▸ coast

COASTER *n* small mat placed under a glass

COASTS ▸ coast

COAT *n* outer garment with long sleeves ▷ *vb* cover with a layer

COATE *same as* ▸ **quote**

COATED *adj* covered with an outer layer, film, etc

COATEE *n* short coat, esp for a baby

COATEES ▸ coatee

COATER *n* machine that applies a coating to something

C

COATERS ▸ coater
COATES ▸ coate
COATI n type of omnivorous mammal of Central and S America, with a long flexible snout and a brindled coat
COATING n covering layer
COATIS ▸ coati
COATS ▸ coat
COAX vb persuade gently
COAXAL same as ▸ coaxial
COAXED ▸ coax
COAXER ▸ coax
COAXERS ▸ coax
COAXES ▸ coax
COAXIAL adj (of a cable) transmitting by means of two concentric conductors separated by an insulator
COAXING ▸ coax
COB n stalk of an ear of maize ▷ vb beat, esp on the buttocks
COBAEA n tropical American climbing shrub grown for its large trumpet-shaped purple or white flowers
COBAEAS ▸ cobaea
COBALT n brittle silvery-white metallic element
COBALTS ▸ cobalt
COBB same as ▸ cob
COBBED ▸ cob
COBBER n friend
COBBERS ▸ cobber
COBBIER ▸ cobby
COBBING ▸ cob
COBBLE n cobblestone ▷ vb pave (a road) with cobblestones
COBBLED ▸ cobble
COBBLER n shoe mender
COBBLES pl n coal in small rounded lumps
COBBS ▸ cobb
COBBY adj short and stocky
COBIA n large dark-striped game fish of tropical and subtropical seas
COBIAS ▸ cobia
COBLE n small single-masted flat-bottomed fishing boat
COBLES ▸ coble
COBLOAF n round loaf of bread
COBNUT another name for ▸ hazelnut
COBNUTS ▸ cobnut
COBRA n venomous

hooded snake of Asia and Africa
COBRAS ▸ cobra
COBRIC ▸ cobra
COBS ▸ cob
COBURG n rounded loaf with a cross cut on the top
COBURGS ▸ coburg
COBWEB n spider's web
COBWEBS ▸ cobweb
COBZA n Romanian lute
COBZAS ▸ cobza
COCA n dried leaves of a S American shrub which contain cocaine
COCAIN same as ▸ cocaine
COCAINE n addictive drug used as a narcotic and as an anaesthetic
COCAINS ▸ cocain
COCAS ▸ coca
COCCAL ▸ coccus
COCCI ▸ coccus
COCCIC ▸ coccus
COCCID n type of homopterous insect of the family which includes the scale insects
COCCIDS ▸ coccid
COCCO n taro
COCCOID ▸ coccus
COCCOS ▸ cocco
COCCOUS ▸ coccus
COCCUS n any spherical or nearly spherical bacterium, such as a staphylococcus
COCCYX n bone at the base of the spinal column
COCH obsolete variant of ▸ coach
COCHAIR vb to chair jointly
COCHES ▸ coch
COCHIN n large breed of domestic fowl
COCHINS ▸ cochin
COCHLEA n spiral tube in the internal ear, which converts sound vibrations into nerve impulses
COCK n male bird, esp of domestic fowl ▷ vb draw back (the hammer of a gun) to firing position
COCKADE n feather or rosette worn on a hat as a badge
COCKED ▸ cock
COCKER n devotee of cockfighting ▷ vb pamper or spoil by indulgence
COCKERS ▸ cocker
COCKET n document issued by a customs officer

COCKETS ▸ cocket
COCKEYE n eye affected with strabismus or one that squints
COCKIER ▸ cocky
COCKIES ▸ cocky
COCKILY ▸ cocky
COCKING ▸ cock
COCKISH adj wanton
COCKLE n edible shellfish ▷ vb fish for cockles
COCKLED ▸ cockle
COCKLER n person employed to gather cockles
COCKLES ▸ cockle
COCKNEY n native of London, esp of its East End ▷ adj characteristic of cockneys or their dialect
COCKPIT n pilot's compartment in an aircraft
COCKS ▸ cock
COCKSHY n target aimed at in throwing games
COCKSY adj cocky
COCKUP n something done badly ▷ vb ruin or spoil
COCKUPS ▸ cockup
COCKY adj conceited and overconfident ▷ n farmer whose farm is regarded as small or of little account
COCO n coconut palm
COCOA n powder made from the seed of the cacao tree
COCOAS ▸ cocoa
COCOMAT n mat made from coconut fibre
COCONUT n large hard fruit of a type of palm tree
COCOON n silky protective covering of a silkworm ▷ vb wrap up tightly for protection
COCOONS ▸ cocoon
COCOPAN n (in South Africa) a small wagon running on narrow-gauge railway lines used in mines
COCOS ▸ coco
COCOTTE n small fireproof dish in which individual portions of food are cooked
COCOYAM n either of two food plants of West Africa, the taro or the yantia, both of which have edible underground stems
COCTILE adj made by exposing to heat
COCTION n boiling
COD n large food fish of the

North Atlantic ▷ *adj* having the character of an imitation or parody ▷ *vb* make fun of

CODA *n* final part of a musical composition

CODABLE *adj* capable of being coded

CODAS ▷ **coda**

CODDED ▷ **cod**

CODDER *n* cod fisherman or his boat

CODDERS ▷ **codder**

CODDING ▷ **cod**

CODDLE *vb* pamper, overprotect ▷ *n* stew made from ham and bacon scraps

CODDLED ▷ **coddle**

CODDLER ▷ **coddle**

CODDLES ▷ **coddle**

CODE *n* system of letters, symbols, or prearranged signals by which messages can be communicated secretly or briefly ▷ *vb* put into code

CODEC *n* set of equipment that encodes an analogue speech or video signal into digital form for transmission purposes and at the receiving end decodes the digital signal into a form close to its original

CODECS ▷ **codec**

CODED ▷ **code**

CODEIA *n* codeine

CODEIAS ▷ **codeia**

CODEIN *same as* ▷ **codeine**

CODEINA *obsolete variant of* ▷ **codeine**

CODEINE *n* drug used as a painkiller

CODEINS ▷ **codein**

CODEN *n* unique six-character code assigned to a publication for identification purposes

CODENS ▷ **coden**

CODER *n* person or thing that codes

CODERS ▷ **coder**

CODES ▷ **code**

CODETTA *n* short coda

CODEX *n* volume of manuscripts of an ancient text

CODFISH *n* cod

CODGER *n* old man

CODGERS ▷ **codger**

CODICES ▷ **codex**

CODICIL *n* addition to a will

CODIFY *vb* organize (rules or procedures) systematically

CODILLA *n* coarse tow of hemp and flax

CODILLE *n* in the card game ombre, term indicating that the game is won

CODING ▷ **code**

CODINGS ▷ **code**

CODIST *n* codifier

CODISTS ▷ **codist**

CODLIN *same as* ▷ **codling**

CODLING *n* young cod

CODLINS ▷ **codlin**

CODON *n* unit that consists of three adjacent bases on a DNA molecule and that determines the position of a specific amino acid in a protein molecule during protein synthesis

CODONS ▷ **codon**

CODRIVE *vb* take alternate turns driving a car with another person

CODROVE ▷ **codrive**

CODS ▷ **cod**

COED *adj* educating both sexes together ▷ *n* school or college that educates both sexes together

COEDIT *vb* edit (a book, newspaper, etc) jointly

COEDITS ▷ **coedit**

COEDS ▷ **coed**

COEHORN *n* type of small artillery mortar

COELIAC *adj* of or relating to the abdomen ▷ *n* person who has coeliac disease

COELOM *n* body cavity of many multicellular animals, situated in the mesoderm and containing the digestive tract and other visceral organs

COELOME *same as* ▷ **coelom**

COELOMS ▷ **coelom**

COEMPT *vb* buy up something in its entirety

COEMPTS ▷ **coempt**

COENACT *vb* to enact jointly

COENURE *variant form of* > **coenurus**

COENURI > **coenurus**

COEQUAL *n* equal ▷ *adj* of the same size, rank, etc

COERCE *vb* compel, force

COERCED ▷ **coerce**

COERCER ▷ **coerce**

COERCES ▷ **coerce**

COERECT *vb* to erect together

COESITE *n* polymorph of silicon dioxide

COEVAL *n* contemporary ▷ *adj* contemporary

COEVALS ▷ **coeval**

COEXERT *vb* to exert together

COEXIST *vb* exist together, esp peacefully despite differences

COFF *vb* buy

COFFED ▷ **coff**

COFFEE *n* drink made from the roasted and ground seeds of a tropical shrub ▷ *adj* medium-brown

COFFEES ▷ **coffee**

COFFER *n* chest, esp for storing valuables ▷ *vb* store

COFFERS > **cofferdam**

COFFIN *n* box in which a corpse is buried or cremated ▷ *vb* place in or as in a coffin

COFFING ▷ **coff**

COFFINS ▷ **coffin**

COFFLE *n* (esp formerly) a line of slaves, beasts, etc, fastened together ▷ *vb* to fasten together in a coffle

COFFLED ▷ **coffle**

COFFLES ▷ **coffle**

COFFRET *n* small coffer

COFFS ▷ **coff**

COFOUND *vb* to found jointly

COFT ▷ **coff**

COG *n* one of the teeth on the rim of a gearwheel ▷ *vb* roll (cast-steel ingots) to convert them into blooms

COGENCE ▷ **cogent**

COGENCY ▷ **cogent**

COGENER *n* congener

COGENT *adj* forcefully convincing

COGGED ▷ **cog**

COGGER *n* deceiver

COGGERS ▷ **cogger**

COGGIE *n* quaich or drinking cup

COGGIES ▷ **coggie**

COGGING ▷ **cog**

COGGLE *vb* wobble or rock

COGGLED ▷ **coggle**

COGGLES ▷ **coggle**

COGGLY ▷ **coggle**

COGIE *same as* ▷ **coggie**

COGIES ▷ **cogie**

COGITO *n* philosophical theory that one must exist

because one is capable of thought

COGITOS ▸ cogito

COGNAC n French brandy

COGNACS ▸ cognac

COGNATE adj derived from a common original form ▷ n cognate word or language

COGNISE same as ▸ **cognize**

COGNIZE vb perceive, become aware of, or know

COGON n type of coarse tropical grass used for thatching

COGONS ▸ cogon

COGS ▸ cog

COGUE n wooden pail or drinking vessel

COGUES ▸ cogue

COGWAY n rack railway

COGWAYS ▸ cogway

COHAB n cohabitor

COHABIT vb live together as husband and wife without being married

COHABS ▸ cohab

COHEAD vb to head jointly

COHEADS ▸ cohead

COHEIR n person who inherits jointly with others

COHEIRS ▸ coheir

COHEN ▸ kohen

COHENS ▸ cohen

COHERE vb hold or stick together

COHERED ▸ cohere

COHERER n electrical component formerly used to detect radio waves, consisting of a tube containing loosely packed metal particles. The waves caused the particles to cohere, thereby changing the current through the circuit

COHERES ▸ cohere

COHIBIT vb to restrain

COHO n type of Pacific salmon

COHOE same as ▸ **coho**

COHOES ▸ coho

COHOG n quahog, an edible clam

COHOGS ▸ cohog

COHORN same as ▸ **coehorn**

COHORNS ▸ coehorn

COHORT n band of associates

COHORTS ▸ cohort

COHOS ▸ coho

COHOSH n type of North American plant

COHOST vb to host jointly

COHOSTS ▸ cohost

COHUNE n tropical American feather palm whose large nuts yield an oil similar to coconut oil

COHUNES ▸ cohune

COIF vb arrange the hair of ▷ n close-fitting cap worn in the Middle Ages

COIFED adj wearing a coif

COIFFE vb to coiffure

COIFFED ▸ coif

COIFFES ▸ coiffe

COIFING ▸ coif

COIFS ▸ coif

COIGN vb wedge ▷ n quoin

COIGNE same as ▸ **coign**

COIGNED ▸ coign

COIGNES ▸ coigne

COIGNS ▸ coign

COIL vb wind in loops ▷ n something coiled

COILED ▸ coil

COILER ▸ coil

COILERS ▸ coil

COILING ▸ coil

COILS ▸ coil

COIN n piece of metal money ▷ vb invent (a word or phrase)

COINAGE n coins collectively

COINED ▸ coin

COINER ▸ coin

COINERS ▸ coin

COINFER vb infer jointly

COINING ▸ coin

COINOP adj (of a machine) operated by putting a coin in a slot

COINS ▸ coin

COINTER vb to inter together

COIR n coconut fibre, used for matting

COIRS ▸ coir

COIT n buttocks

COITAL ▸ coitus

COITION same as ▸ **coitus**

COITS ▸ coit

COITUS n sexual intercourse

COJOIN vb to conjoin

COJOINS ▸ cojoin

COJONES pl n testicles

COKE n solid fuel left after gas has been distilled from coal ▷ vb become or convert into coke

COKED ▸ coke

COKES n fool

COKESES ▸ cokes

COKIER ▸ coky

COKIEST ▸ coky

COKING ▸ coke

COKY adj like coke

COL n high mountain pass

COLA n dark brown fizzy soft drink

COLAS ▸ cola

COLBIES ▸ colby

COLBY n type of mild-tasting hard cheese

COLBYS ▸ colby

COLD adj lacking heat ▷ n lack of heat

COLDER ▸ cold

COLDEST ▸ cold

COLDIE n cold can or bottle of beer

COLDIES ▸ coldie

COLDISH ▸ cold

COLDLY ▸ cold

COLDS ▸ cold

COLE same as ▸ **cabbage**

COLEAD vb to lead together

COLEADS ▸ colead

COLED ▸ colead

COLES ▸ cole

COLETIT n coal tit

COLEUS n Old World plant cultivated for its variegated leaves, typically marked with red, yellow, or white

COLEY same as ▸ **coalfish**

COLEYS ▸ coley

COLIBRI n hummingbird

COLIC n severe pains in the stomach and bowels

COLICIN n bacteriocidal protein

COLICKY adj relating to or suffering from colic

COLICS ▸ colic

COLIES ▸ coly

COLIN n quail

COLINS ▸ colin

COLITIC ▸ colitis

COLITIS n inflammation of the colon

COLL vb to embrace

COLLAGE n art form in which various materials or objects are glued onto a surface ▷ vb to make a collage

COLLAR n part of a garment round the neck ▷ vb seize, arrest

COLLARD n variety of the cabbage with a crown of edible leaves

COLLARS ▸ collar

COLLATE vb gather together, examine, and put

in order

COLLECT vb gather together ▷ n short prayer

COLLED ▸ coll

COLLEEN n girl

COLLEGE n place of higher education

COLLET n (in a jewellery setting) a band or coronet-shaped claw that holds an individual stone ▷ vb mount in a collet

COLLETS ▸ collet

COLLIDE vb crash together violently

COLLIE n silky-haired sheepdog

COLLIED ▸ colly

COLLIER n coal miner

COLLIES ▸ colly

COLLING n embrace

COLLINS n tall fizzy iced drink made with gin, vodka, rum, etc, mixed with fruit juice, soda water, and sugar

COLLOID n suspension of particles in a solution ▷ adj of or relating to the gluelike translucent material found in certain degenerating tissues

COLLOP n small slice of meat

COLLOPS ▸ collop

COLLS ▸ coll

COLLUDE vb act in collusion

COLLY n soot or grime, such as coal dust ▷ vb begrime

COLOBI ▸ colobus

COLOBID ▸ colobus

COLOBUS n type of leaf-eating arboreal Old World monkey of W and central Africa, with a slender body, long silky fur, and a long tail

COLOG n logarithm of the reciprocal of a number

COLOGNE n mild perfume

COLOGS ▸ colog

COLON n punctuation mark (:)

COLONE same as ▸ colon

COLONEL n senior commissioned army or air-force officer

COLONES ▸ colone

COLONI ▸ colonus

COLONIC adj of or relating to the colon ▷ n irrigation of the colon by injecting large amounts of fluid high into the colon

COLONS ▸ colon

COLONUS n ancient Roman farmer

COLONY n group of people who settle in a new country but remain under the rule of their homeland

COLOR same as ▸ colour

COLORED US spelling of > coloured

COLORER ▸ color

COLORS ▸ color

COLORY same as ▸ coloury

COLOSSI > colossus

COLOUR n appearance of things as a result of reflecting light ▷ vb apply colour to

COLOURS ▸ colour

COLOURY adj possessing colour

COLS ▸ col

COLT n young male horse ▷ vb to fool

COLTAN n metallic ore found esp in the E Congo, consisting of columbite and tantalite and used as a source of tantalum

COLTANS ▸ coltan

COLTED ▸ colt

COLTER same as ▸ coulter

COLTERS ▸ coulter

COLTING ▸ colt

COLTISH adj inexperienced

COLTS ▸ colt

COLUGO n flying lemur

COLUGOS ▸ colugo

COLUMEL n in botany, the central column in a capsule

COLUMN n pillar ▷ vb create a column

COLUMNS ▸ column

COLURE n either of two great circles on the celestial sphere, one of which passes through the celestial poles and the equinoxes and the other through the poles and the solstices

COLURES ▸ colure

COLY n S African arboreal bird with a soft hairlike plumage, crested head, and very long tail

COLZA n oilseed rape, a Eurasian plant with bright yellow flowers

COLZAS ▸ colza

COMA n state of deep unconsciousness

COMADE ▸ comake

COMAE ▸ coma

COMAKE vb to make together

COMAKER ▸ comake

COMAKES ▸ comake

COMAL ▸ coma

COMARB same as ▸ coarb

COMARBS ▸ comarb

COMART n covenant

COMARTS ▸ comart

COMAS ▸ coma

COMATE adj having tufts of hair ▷ n companion

COMATES ▸ comate

COMATIC ▸ coma

COMATIK same as ▸ komatik

COMB n toothed implement for arranging the hair ▷ vb use a comb on

COMBAT vb fight, struggle ▷ n fight or struggle

COMBATS ▸ combat

COMBE same as ▸ comb

COMBED ▸ comb

COMBER n long curling wave

COMBERS ▸ comber

COMBES ▸ combe

COMBI n combination boiler

COMBIER ▸ comby

COMBIES ▸ comby

COMBINE vb join together ▷ n association of people or firms for a common purpose

COMBING ▸ comb

COMBIS ▸ combi

COMBLE n apex; zenith

COMBLES ▸ comble

COMBO n small group of jazz musicians

COMBOS ▸ combo

COMBS ▸ comb

COMBUST adj (of a star or planet) invisible for a period between 24 and 30 days each year due to its proximity to the sun ▷ vb burn

COMBY adj comb-like ▷ n combination boiler

COME vb move towards a place, arrive

COMEDIC adj of or relating to comedy

COMEDO the technical name for > blackhead

COMEDOS ▸ comedo

COMEDY n humorous play, film, or programme

COMELY adj nice-looking

C

COMER n person who comes
COMERS ▸ comer
COMES ▸ come
COMET n heavenly body with a long luminous tail
COMETH ▸ come
COMETIC ▸ comet
COMETS ▸ comet
COMFIER ▸ comfy
COMFIT n sugar-coated sweet
COMFITS ▸ comfit
COMFORT n physical ease or wellbeing ▹ vb soothe, console
COMFREY n tall plant with bell-shaped flowers
COMFY adj comfortable
COMIC adj humorous, funny ▹ n comedian
COMICAL adj amusing
COMICE n kind of pear
COMICES ▸ comice
COMICS ▸ comic
COMING ▸ come
COMINGS ▸ come
COMIQUE n comic actor
COMITAL adj relating to a count or earl
COMITIA n ancient Roman assembly that elected officials and exercised judicial and legislative authority
COMITY n friendly politeness, esp between different countries
COMIX n comic books in general
COMM n as in **comm badge** small wearable badge-shaped radio transmitter and receiver
COMMA n punctuation mark (,)
COMMAND vb order ▹ n authoritative instruction that something must be done
COMMAS ▸ comma
COMMATA ▸ comma
COMMEND vb praise
COMMENT n remark ▹ vb make a comment
COMMER same as ▸ comer
COMMERE n female compere
COMMERS ▸ commer
COMMIE adj communist
COMMIES ▸ commie
COMMIS n apprentice waiter or chef ▹ adj (of a waiter or chef) apprentice
COMMIT vb perform (a

crime or error)
COMMITS ▸ commit
COMMIX a rare word for ▸ mix
COMMIXT ▸ commix
COMMO short for ▸ communist
COMMODE n seat with a hinged flap concealing a chamber pot
COMMODO same as ▸ comodo
COMMON adj occurring often ▹ n area of grassy land belonging to a community ▹ vb sit at table with strangers
COMMONS n people not of noble birth viewed as forming a political order
COMMOS ▸ commo
COMMOT n in medieval Wales, a division of land
COMMOTE same as ▸ commot
COMMOTS ▸ commot
COMMOVE vb disturb
COMMS pl n communications
COMMUNE n group of people who live together and share everything ▹ vb feel very close (to)
COMMUTE vb travel daily to and from work ▹ n journey made by commuting
COMMY same as ▸ commie
COMODO adv (to be performed) at a convenient relaxed speed
COMOSE another word for ▸ comate
COMOUS adj hairy
COMP n person who sets and corrects type ▹ vb set or correct type
COMPACT adj closely packed ▹ n small flat case containing a mirror and face powder ▹ vb pack closely together
COMPAGE obsolete form of ▸ compages
COMPAND vb (of a transmitter signal) to compress before, and expand after, transmission
COMPANY n business organization ▹ vb associate or keep company with someone
COMPARE vb examine (things) and point out the resemblances or differences

COMPART vb to divide into parts
COMPAS n rhythm in flamenco
COMPASS n instrument for showing direction, with a needle that points north ▹ vb encircle or surround
COMPAST adj rounded
COMPEAR vb in Scots law, to appear in court
COMPED ▸ comp
COMPEER n person of equal rank, status, or ability ▹ vb to equal
COMPEL vb force (to be or do)
COMPELS ▸ compel
COMPEND n compendium
COMPER n person who regularly enters competitions in newspapers, magazines, etc, esp competitions offering consumer goods as prizes
COMPERE n person who presents a stage, radio, or television show ▹ vb be the compere of
COMPERS ▸ comper
COMPETE vb try to win or achieve (a prize, profit, etc)
COMPILE vb collect and arrange (information), esp to make a book
COMPING ▸ comp
COMPLEX adj made up of parts ▹ n whole made up of parts ▹ vb to form a complex
COMPLIN same as ▸ compline
COMPLOT n plot or conspiracy ▹ vb plot together
COMPLY vb act in accordance (with)
COMPO n mixture of materials, such as mortar, plaster, etc ▹ adj intended to last for several days
COMPONE same as ▸ compony
COMPONY adj made up of alternating metal and colour, colour and fur, or fur and metal
COMPORT vb behave (oneself) in a specified way
COMPOS ▸ compo
COMPOSE vb put together
COMPOST n decayed plants used as a fertilizer ▹ vb make (vegetable matter) into compost
COMPOT same as ▸ compote

COMPOTE n fruit stewed with sugar

COMPOTS ▸ compot

COMPS ▸ comp

COMPT obsolete variant of ▸ count

COMPTED ▸ compt

COMPTER n formerly, a prison

COMPTS ▸ count

COMPUTE vb calculate, esp using a computer ▹ n calculation

COMRADE n fellow member of a union or socialist political party

COMS pl n one-piece woollen undergarment with long sleeves and legs

COMTE n European nobleman

COMTES ▸ comte

COMUS n wild party

COMUSES ▸ comus

CON vb deceive, swindle ▹ n convict ▹ prep with

CONACRE n farming land let for a season or for eleven months ▹ vb to let conacre

CONARIA > conarium

CONATUS n effort or striving of natural impulse

CONCAVE adj curving inwards ▹ vb make concave

CONCEAL vb cover and hide

CONCEDE vb admit to be true

CONCEDO interj I allow; I concede (a point)

CONCEIT n too high an opinion of oneself ▹ vb like or be able to bear (something, such as food or drink)

CONCENT n concord, as of sounds, voices, etc

CONCEPT n abstract or general idea

CONCERN n anxiety, worry ▹ vb worry (someone)

CONCERT n musical entertainment

CONCH same as ▸ concha

CONCHA n any bodily organ or part resembling a shell in shape, such as the external ear

CONCHAE ▸ concha

CONCHAL ▸ concha

CONCHAS ▸ concha

CONCHE vb (in chocolate-making) to use a conche (machine which mixes and smooths the chocolate mass)

CONCHED ▸ conche

CONCHES ▸ conche

CONCHIE n conscientious objector

CONCHO n American metal ornament

CONCHOS ▸ concho

CONCHS ▸ conch

CONCHY same as ▸ conchie

CONCISE adj brief and to the point ▹ vb mutilate

CONCOCT vb make up (a story or plan)

CONCORD n state of peaceful agreement, harmony ▹ vb to agree

CONCREW vb to grow together

CONCUPY n concupiscence

CONCUR vb agree

CONCURS ▸ concur

CONCUSS vb injure (the brain) by a fall or blow

COND old inflection of ▸ con

CONDEMN vb express disapproval of

CONDER n person who directs the steering of a vessel

CONDERS ▸ conder

CONDIE n culvert; tunnel

CONDIES ▸ condie

CONDIGN adj (esp of a punishment) fitting

CONDO n condominium

CONDOES ▸ condo

CONDOLE vb express sympathy with someone in grief, pain, etc

CONDOM n rubber sheath worn on the penis or in the vagina during sexual intercourse to prevent conception or infection

CONDOMS ▸ condom

CONDONE vb overlook or forgive (wrongdoing)

CONDOR n large vulture of S America

CONDORS ▸ condor

CONDOS ▸ condo

CONDUCE vb lead or contribute (to a result)

CONDUCT n management of an activity ▹ vb carry out (a task)

CONDUIT n channel or tube for fluid or cables

CONDYLE n rounded projection on the articulating end of a bone, such as the ball portion of a ball-and-socket joint

CONE n object with a circular base, tapering to a point ▹ vb shape like a cone or part of a cone

CONED ▸ cone

CONES ▸ cone

CONEY same as ▸ cony

CONEYS ▸ coney

CONF n online forum

CONFAB n conversation ▹ vb converse

CONFABS ▸ confab

CONFECT vb prepare by combining ingredients

CONFER vb discuss together

CONFERS ▸ confer

CONFESS vb admit (a fault or crime)

CONFEST adj admitted

CONFIDE vb tell someone (a secret)

CONFINE vb keep within bounds ▹ n limit

CONFIRM vb prove to be true

CONFIT n preserve

CONFITS ▸ confit

CONFIX vb to fasten

CONFLUX n merging or folowing togther, especially of rivers

CONFORM vb comply with accepted standards or customs

CONFS ▸ conf

CONFUSE vb mix up

CONFUTE vb prove wrong

CONGA n dance performed by a number of people in single file ▹ vb dance the conga

CONGAED ▸ conga

CONGAS ▸ conga

CONGE n permission to depart or dismissal, esp when formal ▹ vb to take one's leave

CONGEAL vb (of a liquid) become thick and sticky

CONGED ▸ conge

CONGEE same as ▸ conge

CONGEED ▸ congee

CONGEES ▸ congee

CONGER n large sea eel

CONGERS ▸ conger

CONGES ▸ conge

CONGEST vb crowd or become crowded to excess

CONGII ▸ congius

CONGIUS n unit of liquid measure equal to 1 Imperial gallon

CONGO same as ▸ congou

CONGOES ▸ congou

CONGOS ▸ congo

CONGOU n kind of black tea from China

CONGOUS ▸ congou

CONGREE vb to agree

CONGRUE vb to agree

CONI ▸ conus

CONIA same as ▸ coniine

CONIAS ▸ coniine

CONIC adj having the shape of a cone

CONICAL adj cone-shaped

CONICS n branch of geometry concerned with the parabola, ellipse, and hyperbola

CONIDIA > conidium

CONIES ▸ cony

CONIFER n cone-bearing tree, such as the fir or pine

CONIINE n colourless poisonous soluble liquid alkaloid found in hemlock

CONIMA n gum resin from the conium hemlock tree

CONIMAS ▸ conima

CONIN same as ▸ coniine

CONINE same as ▸ coniine

CONINES ▸ conine

CONING ▸ cone

CONINS ▸ conin

CONIUM n N temperate umbelliferous plant, esp hemlock

CONIUMS ▸ conium

CONJECT vb to conjecture

CONJEE vb prepare as, or in, a conjee (a gruel of boiled rice and water)

CONJEED ▸ conjee

CONJEES ▸ conjee

CONJOIN vb join or become joined

CONJURE vb perform tricks that appear to be magic

CONJURY n magic

CONK n nose ▷ vb strike (someone) on the head or nose

CONKED ▸ conk

CONKER n nut of the horse chestnut

CONKERS n game played with conkers tied on strings

CONKIER ▸ conky

CONKING ▸ conk

CONKS ▸ conk

CONKY adj affected by the timber disease, conk

CONN same as ▸ con

CONNATE adj existing in a person or thing from birth

CONNE same as ▸ con

CONNECT vb join together

CONNED ▸ con

CONNER same as ▸ conder

CONNERS ▸ conner

CONNES ▸ conne

CONNIE n tram or bus conductor

CONNIES ▸ connie

CONNING ▸ con

CONNIVE vb allow (wrongdoing) by ignoring it

CONNOTE vb (of a word, phrase, etc) to imply or suggest (associations or ideas) other than the literal meaning

CONNS ▸ conn

CONOID n geometric surface formed by rotating a parabola, ellipse, or hyperbola about one axis ▷ adj conical, cone-shaped

CONOIDS ▸ conoid

CONQUER vb defeat

CONS ▸ con

CONSEIL n advice

CONSENT n agreement, permission ▷ vb permit, agree to

CONSIGN vb put somewhere

CONSIST vb be composed (of)

CONSOL n consolidated annuity, a British government bond

CONSOLE vb comfort in distress ▷ n panel of controls for electronic equipment

CONSOLS pl n irredeemable British government securities carrying annual interest rates of two and a half or four per cent

CONSORT vb keep company (with) ▷ n husband or wife of a monarch

CONSPUE vb spit on with contempt

CONSTER obsolete variant of > construe

CONSUL n official representing a state in a foreign country

CONSULS ▸ consul

CONSULT vb go to for advice or information

CONSUME vb eat or drink

CONTACT n communicating ▷ vb get in touch with ▷ interj (formerly) a call made by the pilot to indicate that an aircraft's ignition is switched on and that the engine is ready for starting by swinging the propeller

CONTAIN vb hold or be capable of holding

CONTE n tale or short story, esp of adventure

CONTECK n contention

CONTEMN vb regard with contempt

CONTEND vb deal with

CONTENT n meaning or substance of a piece of writing ▷ adj satisfied with things as they are ▷ vb make (someone) content

CONTES ▸ conte

CONTEST n competition or struggle ▷ vb dispute, object to

CONTEXT n circumstances of an event or fact

CONTO n former Portuguese monetary unit worth 1000 escudos

CONTORT vb twist out of shape

CONTOS ▸ conto

CONTOUR n outline ▷ vb shape so as to form or follow the contour of something

CONTRA n counter-argument

CONTRAS ▸ contra

CONTRAT old form of > contract

CONTROL n power to direct something ▷ vb have power over

CONTUND vb to pummel

CONTUSE vb injure (the body) without breaking the skin

CONURE n small American parrot

CONURES ▸ conure

CONUS n any of several cone-shaped structures, such as the conus medullaris, the lower end of the spinal cord

CONVECT vb to circulate hot air by convection

CONVENE vb gather or summon for a formal meeting

CONVENT n building where nuns live ▷ vb to summon

CONVERT vb change in form, character, or function ▷ n person who has converted to a different belief or religion

CONVEX adj curving outwards ▷ vb make convex

CONVEY vb communicate (information)

CONVEYS ▸ convey

CONVICT vb declare guilty ▷ n person serving a prison sentence ▷ adj convicted

CONVIVE vb to feast together

CONVO n conversation

CONVOKE vb call together

CONVOS ▸ convo

CONVOY n group of vehicles or ships travelling together ▷ vb escort while in transit

CONVOYS ▸ convoy

CONY n rabbit

COO vb (of a dove or pigeon) make a soft murmuring sound ▷ n sound of cooing ▷ interj exclamation of surprise, awe, etc

COOCOO old spelling of ▸ **cuckoo**

COOED ▸ coo

COOEE interj call to attract attention ▷ vb utter this call ▷ n calling distance

COOEED ▸ cooee

COOEES ▸ cooee

COOER ▸ coo

COOERS ▸ coo

COOEY same as ▸ **cooee**

COOEYED ▸ cooey

COOEYS ▸ cooey

COOF n simpleton

COOFS ▸ coof

COOING ▸ coo

COOINGS ▸ coo

COOK vb prepare (food) by heating ▷ n person who cooks food

COOKED ▸ cook

COOKER n apparatus for cooking heated by gas or electricity

COOKERS ▸ cooker

COOKERY n art of cooking

COOKEY same as ▸ **cookie**

COOKEYS ▸ cookey

COOKIE n biscuit

COOKIES ▸ cookie

COOKING ▸ cook

COOKOFF n cookery competition

COOKOUT n party where a meal is cooked and eaten out of doors

COOKS ▸ cook

COOKTOP n flat unit for cooking in saucepans or the top part of a stove

COOKY same as ▸ **cookie**

COOL adj moderately cold ▷ vb make or become cool ▷ n coolness

COOLANT n fluid used to cool machinery while it is working

COOLED ▸ cool

COOLER n container for making or keeping things cool

COOLERS ▸ cooler

COOLEST ▸ cool

COOLIE n unskilled Oriental labourer

COOLIES ▸ coolie

COOLING n as in **regenerative cooling** a method of cooling rocket combustion chambers

COOLISH ▸ cool

COOLLY ▸ cool

COOLS ▸ cool

COOLTH n coolness

COOLTHS ▸ coolth

COOLY same as ▸ **coolie**

COOM n waste material, such as dust from coal, grease from axles, etc ▷ vb to blacken

COOMB same as ▸ **comb**

COOMBE ▸ comb

COOMBES ▸ coombe

COOMBS ▸ coomb

COOMED ▸ coom

COOMIER ▸ coomy

COOMING ▸ coom

COOMS ▸ coom

COOMY adj grimy

COON n raccoon

COONCAN n card game for two players, similar to rummy

COONDOG n dog trained to hunt raccoons

COONS ▸ coon

COONTIE n evergreen plant of S Florida, with large dark green leathery leaves

COONTY same as ▸ **coontie**

COOP n cage or pen for poultry ▷ vb confine in a restricted area

COOPED ▸ coop

COOPER n person who makes or repairs barrels ▷ vb make or mend (barrels, casks, etc)

COOPERS ▸ cooper

COOPERY same as > **cooperage**

COOPING ▸ coop

COOPS ▸ coop

COOPT vb add (someone) to a group by the agreement of the existing members

COOPTED ▸ coopt

COOPTS ▸ coopt

COORIE same as ▸ **courie**

COORIED ▸ coorie

COORIES ▸ coorie

COOS ▸ coo

COOSEN same as ▸ **cozen**

COOSENS ▸ coosen

COOSER n stallion

COOSERS ▸ cooser

COOSIN same as ▸ **cozen**

COOSINS ▸ coosin

COOST Scots form of ▸ **cast**

COOT n small black water bird

COOTCH n hiding place ▷ vb hide

COOTER n type of freshwater turtle

COOTERS ▸ cooter

COOTIE ▸ louse

COOTIES ▸ cootie

COOTS ▸ coot

COP same as ▸ **copper**

COPAIBA n resin obtained from certain tropical S American trees, used in varnishes and ointments

COPAIVA same as ▸ **copaiba**

COPAL n resin used in varnishes

COPALM n aromatic brown resin obtained from the sweet gum tree

COPALMS ▸ copalm

COPALS ▸ copal

COPAY n amount payable for treatment by person with medical insurance

COPAYS ▸ copay

COPE vb deal successfully (with) ▷ n large ceremonial cloak worn by some Christian priests

COPECK same as ▸ **kopeck**

COPECKS ▸ copeck

COPED ▸ cope

COPEN n shade of blue

COPENS ▸ copen

COPEPOD n type of minute crustacean of marine and fresh waters, which is an important constituent of plankton

COPER n horse-dealer ▷ vb smuggle liquor to deep-sea fishermen

COPERED ▸ coper

COPERS ▸ coper

C

COPES ▸ **cope**
COPIED ▸ **copy**
COPIER n machine that copies
COPIERS ▸ **copier**
COPIES ▸ **copy**
COPIHUE n Chilean bellflower
COPILOT n second pilot of an aircraft
COPING n sloping top row of a wall
COPINGS ▸ **coping**
COPIOUS adj abundant, plentiful
COPITA n tulip-shaped sherry glass
COPITAS ▸ **copita**
COPLOT vb plot together
COPLOTS ▸ **coplot**
COPOUT n act of avoiding responsibility
COPOUTS ▸ **copout**
COPPED ▸ **copper**
COPPER n soft reddish-brown metal ▷ adj reddish-brown ▷ vb coat or cover with copper
COPPERS ▸ **copper**
COPPERY ▸ **copper**
COPPICE n small group of trees growing close together ▷ vb trim back (trees or bushes) to form a coppice
COPPIES ▸ **coppy**
COPPIN n ball of thread
COPPING ▸ **copper**
COPPINS ▸ **coppin**
COPPLE n hill rising to a point
COPPLES ▸ **copple**
COPPRA same as ▸ **copra**
COPPRAS ▸ **coppra**
COPPY n small wooden stool
COPRA n dried oil-yielding kernel of the coconut
COPRAH same as ▸ **copra**
COPRAHS ▸ **coprah**
COPRAS ▸ **copra**
COPS ▸ **copper**
COPSE same as ▸ **coppice**
COPSED ▸ **copse**
COPSES ▸ **copse**
COPSHOP n police station
COPSIER ▸ **copsy**
COPSING ▸ **copse**
COPSY adj having copses
COPTER n helicopter
COPTERS ▸ **copter**
COPULA n verb used to link the subject and

complement of a sentence
COPULAE ▸ **copula**
COPULAR ▸ **copula**
COPULAS ▸ **copula**
COPY n thing made to look exactly like another ▷ vb make a copy of
COPYBOY n formerly, in journalism, boy who carried copy and ran errands
COPYCAT n person who imitates or copies someone ▷ vb to imitate with great attention to detail
COPYING ▸ **copy**
COPYISM n slavish copying
COPYIST n person who makes written copies
COQUET vb behave flirtatiously
COQUETS ▸ **coquet**
COQUINA n soft limestone consisting of shells, corals, etc, that occurs in parts of the US
COQUITO n Chilean palm tree yielding edible nuts and a syrup
COR interj exclamation of surprise, amazement, or admiration
CORACLE n small round boat of wicker covered with skins
CORAL n hard substance formed from the skeletons of very small sea animals ▷ adj orange-pink
CORALLA > **corallum**
CORALS ▸ **coral**
CORAM prep before, in the presence of
CORANTO same as > **courante**
CORBAN n gift to God
CORBANS ▸ **corban**
CORBE obsolete variant of ▸ **corbel**
CORBEAU n blackish green colour
CORBEIL n carved ornament in the form of a basket of fruit, flowers, etc
CORBEL n stone or timber support sticking out of a wall ▷ vb lay (a stone or brick) so that it forms a corbel
CORBELS ▸ **corbel**
CORBES ▸ **corbe**
CORBIE n raven or crow
CORBIES ▸ **corbie**
CORBINA n type of North

American whiting
CORBY same as ▸ **corbie**
CORCASS n in Ireland, marshland
CORD n thin rope or thick string ▷ adj (of fabric) ribbed ▷ vb bind or furnish with a cord or cords
CORDAGE n lines and rigging of a vessel
CORDATE adj heart-shaped
CORDED adj tied or fastened with cord
CORDER ▸ **cord**
CORDERS ▸ **cord**
CORDIAL adj warm and friendly ▷ n drink with a fruit base
CORDING ▸ **cord**
CORDITE n explosive used in guns and bombs
CORDOBA n standard monetary unit of Nicaragua, divided into 100 centavos
CORDON n chain of police, soldiers, etc, guarding an area ▷ vb put or form a cordon (around)
CORDONS ▸ **cordon**
CORDS pl n trousers made of corduroy
CORE n central part of certain fruits, containing the seeds ▷ vb remove the core from
CORED ▸ **core**
COREIGN vb to reign jointly
CORELLA n white Australian cockatoo
COREMIA > **coremium**
CORER ▸ **core**
CORERS ▸ **core**
CORES ▸ **core**
CORF n wagon or basket used formerly in mines
CORGI n short-legged sturdy dog
CORGIS ▸ **corgi**
CORIA ▸ **corium**
CORIES ▸ **cory**
CORING ▸ **core**
CORIOUS adj leathery
CORIUM n deep inner layer of the skin, beneath the epidermis, containing connective tissue, blood vessels, and fat
CORIUMS ▸ **corium**
CORIVAL same as > **corrival**
CORIXID n type of water bug
CORK n thick light bark of a

Mediterranean oak ▷ *vb* seal with a cork ▷ *adj* made of cork

CORKAGE *n* restaurant's charge for serving wine bought elsewhere

CORKED *adj* (of wine) spoiled through having a decayed cork

CORKER *n* splendid or outstanding person or thing

CORKERS ▸ corker

CORKIER ▸ corky

CORKING *adj* excellent

CORKIR *n* lichen from which red or purple dye is made

CORKIRS ▸ corkir

CORKS ▸ cork

CORKY *same as* ▸ **corked**

CORM *n* bulblike underground stem of certain plants

CORMEL *n* new small corm arising from the base of a fully developed one

CORMELS ▸ cormel

CORMOID *adj* like a corm

CORMOUS ▸ corm

CORMS ▸ corm

CORMUS *n* corm

CORN *n* cereal plant such as wheat or oats ▷ *vb* feed (animals) with corn, esp oats

CORNAGE *n* rent fixed according to the number of horned cattle pastured

CORNCOB *n* core of an ear of maize, to which the kernels are attached

CORNEA *n* transparent membrane covering the eyeball

CORNEAE ▸ cornea

CORNEAL ▸ cornea

CORNEAS ▸ cornea

CORNED *adj* (esp of beef) cooked and then preserved or pickled in salt or brine, now often canned

CORNEL *n* type of plant such as the dogwood and dwarf cornel

CORNELS ▸ cornel

CORNER *n* area or angle where two converging lines or surfaces meet ▷ *vb* force into a difficult or inescapable position

CORNERS ▸ corner

CORNET *same as* ▸ **cornett**

CORNETS ▸ cornet

CORNETT *n* musical instrument consisting of a straight or curved tube of wood or ivory having finger holes like a recorder and a cup-shaped mouthpiece like a trumpet

CORNFED *adj* fed on corn

CORNFLY *n* small fly whose larvae cause swollen, gouty stems in cereal crops

CORNI ▸ corno

CORNICE *n* decorative moulding round the top of a wall ▷ *vb* furnish or decorate with or as if with a cornice

CORNIER ▸ corny

CORNIFY *vb* turn soft tissue hard

CORNILY ▸ corny

CORNING ▸ corn

CORNIST *n* horn-player

CORNO *n* French horn

CORNROW *n* hairstyle in which the hair is plaited in close parallel rows ▷ *vb* style the hair in a cornrow

CORNS ▸ corn

CORNU *n* part or structure resembling a horn or having a hornlike pattern, such as a cross section of the grey matter of the spinal cord

CORNUA ▸ cornu

CORNUAL ▸ cornu

CORNUS *n* any member of the genus Cornus, such as dogwood

CORNUTE *adj* having or resembling cornua ▷ *vb* to make a cuckold of

CORNUTO *n* cuckold

CORNY *adj* unoriginal or oversentimental

CORODY *n* (originally) the right of a lord to receive free quarters from his vassal

COROLLA *n* petals of a flower collectively

CORONA *n* ring of light round the moon or sun

CORONAE ▸ corona

CORONAL *n* circlet for the head ▷ *adj* of or relating to a corona or coronal

CORONAS ▸ corona

CORONEL *n* iron head of a tilting spear

CORONER *n* official responsible for the investigation of violent,

sudden, or suspicious deaths

CORONET *n* small crown

CORONIS *n* in Greek grammar, symbol placed over a contracted syllable

COROZO *n* tropical American palm whose seeds yield a useful oil

COROZOS ▸ corozo

CORPORA ▸ corpus

CORPS *n* military unit with a specific function

CORPSE *n* dead body ▷ *vb* laugh or cause to laugh involuntarily or inopportunely while on stage

CORPSED ▸ corpse

CORPSES ▸ corpse

CORPUS *n* collection of writings, esp by a single author

CORRADE *vb* (of rivers, streams, etc) to erode (land) by the abrasive action of rock particles

CORRAL *n* enclosure for cattle or horses ▷ *vb* put in a corral

CORRALS ▸ corral

CORREA *n* Australian evergreen shrub with large showy tubular flowers

CORREAS ▸ correa

CORRECT *adj* free from error, true ▷ *vb* put right

CORRIDA *the Spanish word for* > **bullfight**

CORRIE *same as* ▸ **cirque**

CORRIES ▸ corrie

CORRODE *vb* eat or be eaten away by chemical action or rust

CORRODY *same as* ▸ **corody**

CORRUPT *adj* open to or involving bribery ▷ *vb* make corrupt

CORS ▸ cor

CORSAC *n* type of fox of central Asia

CORSACS ▸ corsac

CORSAGE *n* small bouquet worn on the bodice of a dress

CORSAIR *n* pirate

CORSE *n* corpse

CORSES ▸ corse

CORSET *n* women's close-fitting undergarment worn to shape the torso ▷ *vb* dress or enclose in, or as in, a corset

C

CORSETS ▸ corset

CORSEY n pavement or pathway

CORSEYS ▸ corsey

CORSIVE n corrodent

CORSLET same as ▸ **corselet**

CORSNED n ordeal whereby an accused person had to eat a morsel of bread; swallowing it freely indicated innocence; choking, guilt

CORSO n promenade

CORSOS ▸ corso

CORTEGE n funeral procession

CORTEX n outer layer of the brain or other internal organ

CORTILE n open, internal courtyard

CORTILI ▸ cortile

CORTIN n adrenal cortex extract containing cortisone and other hormones

CORTINA n weblike part of certain mushrooms

CORTINS ▸ cortin

CORULER n joint ruler

CORVEE n day's unpaid labour owed by a feudal vassal to his lord

CORVEES ▸ corvee

CORVES ▸ corf

CORVET same as ▸ **curvet**

CORVETS ▸ corvet

CORVID n any member of the crow family

CORVIDS ▸ corvid

CORVINA same as ▸ **corbina**

CORVINE adj of, relating to, or resembling a crow

CORVUS n type of ancient hook

CORY n catfish belonging to the South American Corydoras genus

CORYLUS n hazel genus

CORYMB n flat-topped flower cluster with the stems growing progressively shorter towards the centre ▷ vb be corymb-like

CORYMBS ▸ corymb

CORYPHE n coryphaeus

CORYZA n acute inflammation of the mucous membrane of the nose, with discharge of mucus

CORYZAL ▸ coryza

CORYZAS ▸ coryza

COS same as ▸ **cosine**

COSE vb get cosy

COSEC same as ▸ **cosecant**

COSECH n hyperbolic cosecant

COSECHS ▸ cosech

COSECS ▸ cosec

COSED ▸ cose

COSES ▸ cose

COSET n mathematical set

COSETS ▸ coset

COSEY n tea cosy

COSEYS ▸ cosey

COSH n heavy blunt weapon ▷ vb hit with a cosh

COSHED ▸ cosh

COSHER vb pamper or coddle

COSHERS ▸ cosher

COSHERY n Irish chief's right to lodge at his tenants' houses

COSHES ▸ cosh

COSHING ▸ cosh

COSIE same as ▸ **cosy**

COSIED ▸ cosy

COSIER n cobbler

COSIERS ▸ cosier

COSIES ▸ cosy

COSIEST ▸ cosy

COSIGN vb to sign jointly

COSIGNS ▸ cosign

COSILY ▸ cosy

COSINE n (in trigonometry) ratio of the length of the adjacent side to that of the hypotenuse in a right-angled triangle

COSINES ▸ cosine

COSING ▸ cose

COSMEA n plant of the genus Cosmos

COSMEAS ▸ cosmea

COSMIC adj of the whole universe

COSMID n segment of DNA

COSMIDS ▸ cosmid

COSMIN same as ▸ **cosmine**

COSMINE n substance resembling dentine, forming the outer layer of cosmoid scales

COSMINS ▸ cosmin

COSMISM n Russian cultural and philosophical movement

COSMIST ▸ cosmism

COSMOID adj (of the scales of coelacanths and lungfish) consisting of two inner bony layers and an outer layer of cosmine

COSMOS n universe

COSS another name for ▸ **kos**

COSSACK n Slavonic warrior-peasant who served in the Russian cavalry under the tsars

COSSES ▸ coss

COSSET vb pamper ▷ n any pet animal, esp a lamb

COSSETS ▸ cosset

COSSIE n informal name for a swimming costume

COSSIES ▸ cossie

COST n amount of money, time, labour, etc, required for something ▷ vb have as its cost

COSTA n riblike part, such as the midrib of a plant leaf

COSTAE ▸ costa

COSTAL n strengthening rib of an insect's wing

COSTALS ▸ costal

COSTAR n actor who shares the billing with another ▷ vb share the billing with another actor

COSTARD n English variety of apple tree

COSTARS ▸ costar

COSTATE adj having ribs

COSTE vb to draw near

COSTEAN vb to mine for lodes

COSTED ▸ cost

COSTER n person who sells fruit, vegetables etc from a barrow

COSTERS ▸ coster

COSTES ▸ coste

COSTING n as in **marginal costing** a method of cost accounting

COSTIVE adj having or causing constipation

COSTLY adj expensive

COSTREL n flask, usually of earthenware or leather

COSTS ▸ cost

COSTUME n style of dress of a particular place or time, or for a particular activity ▷ vb provide with a costume

COSTUS n Himalayan herb with an aromatic root

COSY adj warm and snug ▷ n cover for keeping things warm ▷ vb to make oneself snug and warm

COSYING ▸ cosy

COT n baby's bed with high sides ▷ vb entangle or become entangled

COTAN *same as* > **cotangent**

COTANS > **cotangent**

COTE ▸ **cot**

COTEAU *n* hillside

COTEAUX ▸ **coteau**

COTED ▸ **cot**

COTERIE *n* exclusive group, clique

COTES ▸ **cote**

COTH *n* hyperbolic cotangent

COTHS ▸ **coth**

COTHURN *same as* > **cothurnus**

COTIDAL *adj* (of a line on a tidal chart) joining points at which high tide occurs simultaneously

COTING ▸ **cot**

COTINGA *n* tropical American bird such as the umbrella bird and the cock-of-the-rock, with a broad slightly hooked bill

COTISE *same as* ▸ **cottise**

COTISED ▸ **cotise**

COTISES ▸ **cotise**

COTLAND *n* grounds that belong to a cotter

COTS ▸ **cot**

COTT *same as* ▸ **cot**

COTTA *n* short form of surplice

COTTAE ▸ **cotta**

COTTAGE *n* small house in the country ▷ *vb* engage in homosexual activity in a public lavatory

COTTAR *same as* ▸ **cotter**

COTTARS ▸ **cottar**

COTTAS ▸ **cotta**

COTTED ▸ **cot**

COTTER *n* pin or wedge used to secure machine parts ▷ *vb* secure (two parts) with a cotter

COTTERS ▸ **cottier**

COTTID *n* type of fish typically with a large head, tapering body, and spiny fins

COTTIDS ▸ **cottid**

COTTIER *same as* ▸ **cotter**

COTTING ▸ **cot**

COTTISE *n* type of heraldic decoration ▷ *vb* (in heraldry) decorate with a cottise

COTTOID *adj* resembling a fish of the genus Cottus

COTTON *n* white downy fibre covering the seeds of a tropical plant ▷ *vb* take a liking

COTTONS ▸ **cotton**

COTTONY ▸ **cotton**

COTTOWN *Scots variant of* ▸ **cotton**

COTTS ▸ **cott**

COTTUS *n* type of fish with four yellowish knobs on its head

COTWAL *n* Indian police officer

COTWALS ▸ **cotwal**

COTYLAE ▸ **cotyle**

COTYLE *n* cuplike cavity

COTYLES ▸ **cotyle**

COTYPE *n* additional type specimen from the same brood as the original type specimen

COTYPES ▸ **cotype**

COUCAL *n* type of ground-living bird of Africa, S Asia, and Australia, with long strong legs

COUCALS ▸ **coucal**

COUCH *n* piece of upholstered furniture for seating more than one person ▷ *vb* express in a particular way

COUCHE *adj* in heraldry (of a shield), tilted

COUCHED ▸ **couch**

COUCHEE *n* reception held late at night

COUCHER ▸ **couch**

COUCHES ▸ **couch**

COUDE *adj* (of a reflecting telescope) having plane mirrors positioned to reflect light from the primary mirror along the axis onto a detector

COUGAN *n* drunk and rowdy person

COUGANS ▸ **cougan**

COUGAR *n* puma

COUGARS ▸ **cougar**

COUGH *vb* expel air from the lungs abruptly and noisily ▷ *n* act or sound of coughing

COUGHED ▸ **cough**

COUGHER ▸ **cough**

COUGHS ▸ **cough**

COUGUAR *same as* ▸ **cougar**

COULD ▸ **can**

COULDST *vb* form of 'could' used with the pronoun *thou* or its relative form

COULEE *n* flow of molten lava

COULEES ▸ **coulee**

COULIS *n* thin purée of vegetables or fruit, usually served as a sauce surrounding a dish

COULOIR *n* deep gully on a mountain side, esp in the French Alps

COULOMB *n* SI unit of electric charge

COULTER *n* blade at the front of a ploughshare

COUNCIL *n* group meeting for discussion or consultation ▷ *adj* of or by a council

COUNSEL *n* advice or guidance ▷ *vb* give guidance to

COUNT *vb* say numbers in order ▷ *n* counting

COUNTED ▸ **count**

COUNTER *n* long flat surface in a bank or shop, on which business is transacted ▷ *vb* oppose, retaliate against ▷ *adv* in the opposite direction

COUNTRY *n* nation

COUNTS ▸ **count**

COUNTY *n* (in some countries) division of a country ▷ *adj* upper-class

COUP *n* successful action ▷ *vb* turn or fall over

COUPE *n* sports car with two doors and a sloping fixed roof

COUPED ▸ **coup**

COUPEE *n* (in dance) a forward movement on one leg, with the other slightly bent and raised

COUPEES ▸ **coupee**

COUPER *n* dealer

COUPERS ▸ **couper**

COUPES ▸ **coupe**

COUPING ▸ **coup**

COUPLE *n* two people who are married or romantically involved ▷ *vb* connect, associate

COUPLED ▸ **couple**

COUPLER *n* link or rod transmitting power between two rotating mechanisms or a rotating part and a reciprocating part

COUPLES ▸ **couple**

COUPLET *n* two consecutive lines of verse, usu rhyming and of the same metre

COUPON *n* piece of paper

C

entitling the holder to a discount or gift

COUPONS ▷ **coupon**

COUPS ▷ **coup**

COUPURE n entrenchment made by beseiged forces behind a breach in their defences

COUR obsolete variant of ▷ **cover**

COURAGE n ability to face danger or pain without fear

COURANT n courante ▷ adj (of an animal) running

COURB vb to bend

COURBED ▷ **courb**

COURBS ▷ **courb**

COURD obsolete variant of ▷ **covered**

COURE obsolete variant of ▷ **cover**

COURED ▷ **coure**

COURES ▷ **coure**

COURIE vb nestle or snuggle

COURIED ▷ **courie**

COURIER n person employed to look after holiday-makers ▷ vb send (a parcel, letter, etc) by courier

COURIES ▷ **courie**

COURING ▷ **cour**

COURLAN another name for ▷ **limpkin**

COURS ▷ **cour**

COURSE n series of lessons or medical treatment ▷ vb (of liquid) run swiftly

COURSED ▷ **course**

COURSER n swift horse

COURSES another word for ▷ **menses**

COURT n body which decides legal cases ▷ vb try to gain the love of

COURTED ▷ **court**

COURTER n suitor

COURTLY adj ceremoniously polite

COURTS ▷ **court**

COUSIN n child of one's uncle or aunt

COUSINS ▷ **cousin**

COUTA n traditional Australian sailing boat

COUTAS ▷ **couta**

COUTEAU n large two-edged knife used formerly as a weapon

COUTER n armour designed to protect the elbow

COUTERS ▷ **couter**

COUTH adj refined ▷ n refinement

COUTHER ▷ **couth**

COUTHIE adj sociable

COUTHS ▷ **couth**

COUTHY same as ▷ **couthie**

COUTIL n type of tightly-woven twill cloth

COUTILS ▷ **coutil**

COUTURE n high-fashion designing and dressmaking ▷ adj relating to high fashion design and dress-making

COUVADE n custom in certain cultures of treating the husband of a woman giving birth as if he were bearing the child

COUVERT another word for ▷ **cover**

COUZIN n South African word for a friend

COUZINS ▷ **couzin**

COVARY vb vary together maintaining a certain mathematical relationship

COVE n small bay or inlet ▷ vb form an architectural cove in

COVED ▷ **cove**

COVELET n small cove

COVEN n meeting of witches

COVENS ▷ **coven**

COVENT same as ▷ **convent**

COVENTS ▷ **covent**

COVER vb place something over, to protect or conceal ▷ n anything that covers

COVERED ▷ **cover**

COVERER ▷ **cover**

COVERS ▷ **cover**

COVERT adj concealed, secret ▷ n thicket giving shelter to game birds or animals

COVERTS ▷ **covert**

COVERUP n concealment of a mistake, crime, etc

COVES ▷ **cove**

COVET vb long to possess (what belongs to someone else)

COVETED ▷ **covet**

COVETER ▷ **covet**

COVETS ▷ **covet**

COVEY n small flock of grouse or partridge

COVEYS ▷ **covey**

COVIN n conspiracy between two or more persons to act to the detriment or injury of another

COVING same as ▷ **cove**

COVINGS ▷ **coving**

COVINS ▷ **covin**

COVYNE same as ▷ **covin**

COVYNES ▷ **covyne**

COW n mature female of cattle and of certain other mammals, such as the elephant or seal ▷ vb intimidate, subdue

COWAGE n tropical climbing plant whose bristly pods cause severe itching and stinging

COWAGES ▷ **cowage**

COWAL n shallow lake or swampy depression supporting vegetation

COWALS ▷ **cowal**

COWAN n drystone waller

COWANS ▷ **cowan**

COWARD n person who lacks courage ▷ vb show (someone) up to be a coward

COWARDS ▷ **coward**

COWBANE n N temperate poisonous marsh plant with clusters of small white flowers

COWBELL n bell hung around a cow's neck

COWBIND n any of various bryony plants, esp the white bryony

COWBIRD n American oriole with a dark plumage and short bill

COWBOY n (in the US) ranch worker who herds and tends cattle, usu on horseback ▷ vb work or behave as a cowboy

COWBOYS ▷ **cowboy**

COWED ▷ **cow**

COWEDLY ▷ **cow**

COWER vb cringe in fear

COWERED ▷ **cower**

COWERS ▷ **cower**

COWFISH n type of trunkfish with hornlike spines over the eyes

COWFLAP n cow dung

COWFLOP n foxglove

COWGIRL n female cowboy

COWHAGE same as ▷ **cowage**

COWHAND same as ▷ **cowboy**

COWHEEL n heel of a cow, used as cooking ingredient

COWHERB n European plant with clusters of pink flowers

COWHERD n person employed to tend cattle

COWHIDE n hide of a cow ▷ vb to lash with a cowhide whip

COWIER ▶ cowy

COWIEST ▶ cowy

COWING ▶ cow

COWISH adj cowardly

COWITCH another name for ▶ cowage

COWK vb retch or feel nauseated

COWKED ▶ cowk

COWKING ▶ cowk

COWKS ▶ cowk

COWL same as ▶ cowling

COWLED adj wearing a cowl

COWLICK n tuft of hair over the forehead

COWLING n cover on an engine

COWLS ▶ cowl

COWMAN n man who owns cattle

COWMEN ▶ cowman

COWP same as ▶ coup

COWPAT n pool of cow dung

COWPATS ▶ cowpat

COWPEA n type of tropical climbing plant producing long pods with edible pealike seeds

COWPEAS ▶ cowpea

COWPED ▶ cowp

COWPIE n cowpat

COWPIES ▶ cowpie

COWPING ▶ cowp

COWPLOP n cow dung

COWPOKE n cowboy

COWPOX n disease of cows, the virus of which is used in the smallpox vaccine

COWPS ▶ cowp

COWRIE n brightly-marked sea shell

COWRIES ▶ cowrie

COWRITE vb to write jointly

COWROTE ▶ cowrite

COWRY same as ▶ cowrie

COWS ▶ cow

COWSHED n byre

COWSKIN same as ▶ cowhide

COWSLIP n small yellow wild European flower

COWTREE n South American tree that produces latex

COWY adj cowlike

COX n coxswain ▷ vb act as cox of (a boat)

COXA n technical name for the hipbone or hip joint

COXAE ▶ coxa

COXAL ▶ coxa

COXALGY same as ▶ coxalgia

COXCOMB same as ▶ cockscomb

COXED ▶ cox

COXES ▶ cox

COXIB n anti-inflammatory drug used to treat osteoarthritis

COXIBS ▶ coxib

COXIER ▶ coxy

COXIEST ▶ coxy

COXING ▶ cox

COXITIS n inflammation of the hip joint

COXLESS ▶ cox

COXY adj cocky

COY adj affectedly shy or modest ▷ vb to caress

COYDOG n cross between a coyote and a dog

COYDOGS ▶ coydog

COYED ▶ coy

COYER ▶ coy

COYEST ▶ coy

COYING ▶ coy

COYISH ▶ coy

COYLY ▶ coy

COYNESS ▶ coy

COYOTE n prairie wolf of N America

COYOTES ▶ coyote

COYPOU same as ▶ coypu

COYPOUS ▶ coypou

COYPU n beaver-like aquatic rodent native to S America, bred for its fur

COYPUS ▶ coypu

COYS ▶ coy

COZ archaic word for ▶ cousin

| Coz is an old word for **cousin**, and a good one to know for using the Z.

COZE vb to chat

COZED ▶ coze

COZEN vb cheat, trick

COZENED ▶ cozen

COZENER ▶ cozen

COZENS ▶ cozen

COZES ▶ coze

COZEY n tea cosy

COZEYS ▶ cozey

COZIE same as ▶ cozey

COZIED ▶ cosy

COZIER n cobbler

COZIERS ▶ cozier

COZIES ▶ cozey

COZIEST ▶ cozy

COZILY ▶ cozy

COZING ▶ coze

COZY ▶ cosy

COZYING ▶ cozy

COZZES ▶ coz

CRAAL vb to enclose in a craal (or kraal)

CRAALED ▶ craal

CRAALS ▶ craal

CRAB n edible shellfish with ten legs, the first pair modified into pincers

CRABBED ▶ crab

CRABBER n crab fisherman

CRABBIT adj bad-tempered

CRABBY adj bad-tempered

CRABS ▶ crab

CRACK vb break or split partially ▷ n sudden sharp noise ▷ adj first-rate, excellent

CRACKED adj damaged by cracking ▷ n sharp noise

CRACKER n thin dry biscuit

CRACKET n low stool, often one with three legs

CRACKLE vb make small sharp popping noises ▷ n crackling sound

CRACKLY adj making a cracking sound

CRACKS ▶ crack

CRACKUP n physical or mental breakdown

CRACKY adj full of cracks

CRACOWE n medieval shoe with a sharply pointed toe

CRADLE n baby's bed on rockers ▷ vb hold gently as if in a cradle

CRADLED ▶ cradle

CRADLER ▶ cradle

CRADLES ▶ cradle

CRAFT n occupation requiring skill with the hands ▷ vb make skilfully

CRAFTED ▶ craft

CRAFTER n person doing craftwork

CRAFTS ▶ craft

CRAFTY adj skilled in deception

CRAG n steep rugged rock

CRAGGED same as ▶ craggy

CRAGGY adj having many crags

CRAGS ▶ crag

CRAIC n Irish word meaning fun

CRAICS ▶ craic

CRAIG a Scots word for ▶ crag

CRAIGS ▶ craig

CRAKE n bird of the rail family, such as the corncrake ▷ vb to boast

CRAKED ▶ crake**

CRAKES ▸ crake

CRAKING ▸ crake

CRAM vb force into too small a space ▷ n act or condition of cramming

CRAMBE n any plant of the genus Crambe

CRAMBES ▸ crambe

CRAMBO n word game in which one team says a rhyme or rhyming line for a word or line given by the other team

CRAMBOS ▸ crambo

CRAME n merchant's booth or stall

CRAMES ▸ crame

CRAMESY same as > cramoisy

CRAMMED ▸ cram

CRAMMER n person or school that prepares pupils for an examination

CRAMP n painful muscular contraction ▷ vb affect with a cramp

CRAMPED adj closed in

CRAMPER n spiked metal plate used as a brace for the feet in throwing the stone

CRAMPET n cramp iron

CRAMPIT same as ▸ crampet

CRAMPON n spiked plate strapped to a boot for climbing on ice ▷ vb climb using crampons

CRAMPS ▸ cramp

CRAMPY adj affected with cramp

CRAMS ▸ cram

CRAN n unit of capacity used for measuring fresh herring, equal to 37.5 gallons

CRANAGE n use of a crane

CRANCH vb to crunch

CRANE n machine for lifting and moving heavy weights ▷ vb stretch (one's neck) to see something

CRANED ▸ crane

CRANES ▸ crane

CRANIA ▸ cranium

CRANIAL adj of or relating to the skull

CRANING ▸ crane

CRANIUM n skull

CRANK n arm projecting at right angles from a shaft, for transmitting or converting motion ▷ vb turn with a crank ▷ adj (of a

sailing vessel) easily keeled over by the wind

CRANKED ▸ crank

CRANKER ▸ crank

CRANKLE vb to bend or wind

CRANKLY adj vigorously

CRANKS ▸ crank

CRANKY same as ▸ crank

CRANNOG n ancient Celtic lake or bog dwelling dating from the late Bronze Age to the 16th century AD

CRANNY n narrow opening ▷ vb to become full of crannies

CRANS ▸ cran

CRANTS n garland carried in front of a maiden's bier

CRAP n rubbish, nonsense ▷ vb defecate

CRAPAUD n frog or toad

CRAPE same as ▸ crepe

CRAPED ▸ crape

CRAPES ▸ crape

CRAPIER ▸ crape

CRAPING ▸ crape

CRAPLE same as ▸ grapple

CRAPLES ▸ craple

CRAPOLA n rubbish

CRAPPED ▸ crap

CRAPPIE n N American freshwater fish)

CRAPPY adj worthless, lousy

CRAPS ▸ crap

CRAPY ▸ crape

CRARE n type of trading vessel

CRARES ▸ crare

CRASES ▸ crasis

CRASH n collision involving a vehicle or vehicles ▷ vb (cause to) collide violently with a vehicle, a stationary object, or the ground ▷ adj requiring or using great effort in order to achieve results quickly

CRASHED ▸ crash

CRASHER ▸ crash

CRASHES ▸ crash

CRASIS n fusion or contraction of two adjacent vowels into one

CRASS adj stupid and insensitive

CRASSER ▸ crass

CRASSLY ▸ crass

CRATCH n rack for holding fodder for cattle, etc

CRATE n large wooden container for packing goods ▷ vb put in a crate

CRATED ▸ crate

CRATER n bowl-shaped opening at the top of a volcano ▷ vb make or form craters

CRATERS ▸ crater

CRATES ▸ crate

CRATHUR n ▸ cratur

CRATING ▸ crate

CRATON n stable part of the earth's continental crust or lithosphere that has not been deformed significantly for many millions, even hundreds of millions, of years

CRATONS ▸ craton

CRATUR n whisky or whiskey

CRATURS ▸ cratur

CRAUNCH same as ▸ crunch

CRAVAT n man's scarf worn like a tie ▷ vb wear a cravat

CRAVATS ▸ cravat

CRAVE vb desire intensely

CRAVED ▸ crave

CRAVEN adj cowardly ▷ n coward ▷ vb to make cowardly

CRAVENS ▸ craven

CRAVER ▸ crave

CRAVERS ▸ crave

CRAVES ▸ crave

CRAVING n intense desire or longing

CRAW n pouchlike part of a bird's oesophagus

CRAWDAD n crayfish

CRAWL vb move on one's hands and knees ▷ n crawling motion or pace

CRAWLED ▸ crawl

CRAWLER n servile flatterer

CRAWLS ▸ crawl

CRAWLY adj feeling or causing a sensation like creatures crawling on one's skin

CRAWS ▸ craw

CRAY n crayfish

CRAYER same as ▸ crare

CRAYERS ▸ crayer

CRAYON n a stick or pencil of coloured wax or clay ▷ vb draw or colour with a crayon

CRAYONS ▸ crayon

CRAYS ▸ cray

CRAZE n short-lived fashion or enthusiasm ▷ vb make mad

CRAZED adj wild and uncontrolled

CRAZES ▸ craze

CRAZIER ▸ crazy

CRAZIES ▸ crazy

CRAZILY ▸ crazy

CRAZING ▸ craze
CRAZY adj ridiculous ▹ n crazy person ▹ n crazy person
CREACH same as ▸ **creagh**
CREACHS ▸ creach
CREAGH n foray
CREAGHS ▸ creagh
CREAK n (make) a harsh squeaking sound ▹ vb make or move with a harsh squeaking sound
CREAKED ▸ creak
CREAKS ▸ creak
CREAKY ▸ creak
CREAM n fatty part of milk ▹ adj yellowish-white ▹ vb beat to a creamy consistency
CREAMED ▸ cream
CREAMER n powdered milk substitute for use in coffee
CREAMS ▸ cream
CREAMY adj resembling cream in colour, taste, or consistency
CREANCE n long light cord used in falconry
CREANT adj formative
CREASE n line made by folding or pressing ▹ vb crush or line
CREASED ▸ crease
CREASER ▸ crease
CREASES ▸ crease
CREASY ▸ crease
CREATE vb make, cause to exist
CREATED ▸ create
CREATES ▸ create
CREATIC adj relating to flesh or meat
CREATIN same as ▸ **creatine**
CREATOR n person who creates
CRECHE n place where small children are looked after while their parents are working, shopping, etc
CRECHES ▸ creche
CRED n short for credibility
CREDAL ▸ creed
CREDENT adj believing or believable
CREDIT n system of allowing customers to receive goods and pay later ▹ vb enter as a credit in an account
CREDITS pl n list of people responsible for the production of a film, programme, or record

CREDO n creed
CREDOS ▸ credo
CREDS ▸ cred
CREE vb to soften grain by boiling or soaking
CREED n statement or system of (Christian) beliefs or principles
CREEDAL ▸ creed
CREEDS ▸ creed
CREEING ▸ cree
CREEK n narrow inlet or bay
CREEKS ▸ creek
CREEKY adj abounding in creeks
CREEL n wicker basket used by anglers ▹ vb to fish using creels
CREELED ▸ creel
CREELS ▸ creel
CREEP vb move quietly and cautiously ▹ n creeping movement
CREEPED ▸ creep
CREEPER n creeping plant ▹ vb train a plant to creep
CREEPIE n low stool
CREEPS ▸ creep
CREEPY adj causing a feeling of fear or disgust
CREES ▸ cree
CREESE ▸ kris
CREESED ▸ creese
CREESES ▸ creese
CREESH vb to lubricate
CREESHY adj greasy
CREM n crematorium
CREMANT adj (of wine) moderately sparkling
CREMATE vb burn (a corpse) to ash
CREME n cream ▹ adj (of a liqueur) rich and sweet
CREMES ▸ creme
CREMINI n variety of mushroom
CREMONA same as ▸ **cromorna**
CREMOR n cream
CREMORS ▸ cremor
CREMS ▸ crem
CREMSIN same as ▸ **cremosin**
CRENA n cleft or notch
CRENAS ▸ crena
CRENATE adj having a scalloped margin, as certain leaves
CRENEL n any of a set of openings formed in the top of a wall or parapet and having slanting sides, as in a battlement ▹ vb to crenelate

CRENELS ▸ crenel
CREOLE n language developed from a mixture of languages ▹ adj of or relating to a creole
CREOLES ▸ creole
CREOSOL n colourless or pale yellow insoluble oily liquid with a smoky odour and a burning taste
CREPE n fabric or rubber with a crinkled texture ▹ vb cover or drape with crepe ▹ vb to crimp or frizz
CREPED ▸ crepe
CREPES ▸ crepe
CREPEY same as ▸ **crepy**
CREPIER ▸ crepy
CREPING ▸ crepe
CREPON n thin material made of fine wool and/or silk
CREPONS ▸ crepon
CREPS pl n slang term for training shoes
CREPT ▸ creep
CREPY adj (esp of the skin) having a dry wrinkled appearance like crepe
CRESOL n aromatic compound derived from phenol, existing in three isomeric forms: found in coal tar and creosote and used in making synthetic resins and as an antiseptic and disinfectant
CRESOLS ▸ cresol
CRESS n plant with strong-tasting leaves, used in salads
CRESSES ▸ cress
CRESSET n metal basket mounted on a pole in which oil or pitch was burned for illumination
CRESSY ▸ cress
CREST n top of a mountain, hill, or wave ▹ vb come to or be at the top of
CRESTA adj as in cresta run high-speed tobogganing down a steep narrow passage of compacted snow and ice
CRESTAL ▸ crest
CRESTED ▸ crest
CRESTON n hogback
CRESTS ▸ crest
CRESYL n tolyl
CRESYLS ▸ cresyl
CRETIC n metrical foot consisting of three syllables,

the first long, the second short, and the third long

CRETICS ▸ **cretic**

CRETIN n stupid person

CRETINS ▸ **cretin**

CRETISM n lying

CRETONS pl n spread made from pork fat and onions

CREVICE n narrow crack or gap in rock

CREW n people who work on a ship or aircraft ▷ vb serve as a crew member (on)

CREWCUT n very short haircut

CREWE n type of pot

CREWED ▸ **crew**

CREWEL n fine worsted yarn used in embroidery ▷ vb to embroider in crewel

CREWELS ▸ **crewel**

CREWES ▸ **crewe**

CREWING ▸ **crew**

CREWMAN n member of a ship's crew

CREWMEN ▸ **crewman**

CREWS ▸ **crew**

CRIA n baby llama, alpaca, or vicu

CRIANT adj garish

CRIAS ▸ **cria**

CRIB n piece of writing stolen from elsewhere ▷ vb copy (someone's work) dishonestly

CRIBBED ▸ **crib**

CRIBBER ▸ **crib**

CRIBBLE vb to sift

CRIBLE adj dotted

CRIBS ▸ **crib**

CRICK n muscle spasm or cramp in the back or neck ▷ vb cause a crick in

CRICKED ▸ **crick**

CRICKET n outdoor game played with bats, a ball, and wickets by two teams of eleven ▷ vb play cricket

CRICKEY same as ▸ **crikey**

CRICKS ▸ **crick**

CRICKY same as ▸ **crikey**

CRICOID adj of or relating to the ring-shaped lowermost cartilage of the larynx ▷ n this cartilage

CRIED ▸ **cry**

CRIER n (formerly) official who made public announcements

CRIERS ▸ **crier**

CRIES ▸ **cry**

CRIKEY interj expression of surprise

CRIM short for ▸ **criminal**

CRIME n unlawful act ▷ vb charge with a crime

CRIMED ▸ **crime**

CRIMEN n crime

CRIMES ▸ **crime**

CRIMINA ▸ **crimen**

CRIMINE interj expression of surprise

CRIMING ▸ **crime**

CRIMINI ▸ **crimine**

CRIMINY interj cry of surprise

CRIMMER a variant spelling of ▸ **krimmer**

CRIMP vb fold or press into ridges ▷ n act or result of crimping

CRIMPED ▸ **crimp**

CRIMPER ▸ **crimp**

CRIMPLE vb crumple, wrinkle, or curl

CRIMPS ▸ **crimp**

CRIMPY ▸ **crimp**

CRIMS ▸ **crim**

CRIMSON adj deep purplish-red ▷ n deep or vivid red colour ▷ vb make or become crimson

CRINAL adj relating to the hair

CRINATE adj having hair

CRINE vb to shrivel

CRINED ▸ **crine**

CRINES ▸ **crine**

CRINGE vb flinch in fear ▷ n act of cringing

CRINGED ▸ **cringe**

CRINGER ▸ **cringe**

CRINGES ▸ **cringe**

CRINGLE n eye at the edge of a sail, usually formed from a thimble or grommet

CRINING ▸ **crine**

CRINITE adj covered with soft hairs or tufts ▷ n sedimentary rock

CRINKLE n wrinkle, crease, or fold ▷ vb become slightly creased or folded

CRINKLY adj wrinkled ▷ n old person

CRINOID n type of primitive echinoderm with delicate feathery arms radiating from a central disc, such as feather stars and sea lilies

CRINOSE adj hairy

CRINUM n type of mostly tropical plant with straplike leaves and clusters of lily-like flowers

CRINUMS ▸ **crinum**

CRIOLLO n native or

inhabitant of Latin America of European descent, esp of Spanish descent ▷ adj of, relating to, or characteristic of a criollo or criollos

CRIOS n multicoloured woven woollen belt traditionally worn by men in the Aran Islands

CRIOSES ▸ **crios**

CRIPE same as ▸ **cripes**

CRIPES interj expression of surprise

CRIPPLE n offensive word for a person who is lame or disabled ▷ vb make lame or disabled

CRIS same as ▸ **kris**

CRISE n crisis

CRISES ▸ **crisis**

CRISIC adj relating to a crisis

CRISIS n crucial stage, turning point

CRISP adj fresh and firm ▷ n very thin slice of potato fried till crunchy ▷ vb make or become crisp

CRISPED same as ▸ **crispate**

CRISPEN vb to make crisp

CRISPER n compartment in a refrigerator for storing salads, vegetables, etc, in order to keep them fresh

CRISPIN n cobbler

CRISPLY ▸ **crisp**

CRISPS ▸ **crisp**

CRISPY adj hard and crunchy

CRISSA ▸ **crissum**

CRISSAL ▸ **crissum**

CRISSUM n area or feathers surrounding the cloaca of a bird

CRISTA n structure resembling a ridge or crest, such as that formed by folding of the inner membrane of a mitochondrion

CRISTAE ▸ **crista**

CRIT abbreviation of ▸ **criticism**

CRITH n unit of weight for gases

CRITHS ▸ **crith**

CRITIC n professional judge of any of the arts

CRITICS ▸ **critic**

CRITS ▸ **crit**

CRITTER a dialect word for ▸ **creature**

CRITTUR same as ▸ **critter**

CRIVENS interj expression of surprise

CROAK vb (of a frog or crow) give a low hoarse cry ▷ n low hoarse sound

CROAKED ▶ **croak**

CROAKER n animal, bird, etc, that croaks

CROAKS ▶ **croak**

CROAKY ▶ **croak**

CROC short for ▶ **crocodile**

CROCEIN n any one of a group of red or orange acid azo dyes

CROCHE n knob at the top of a deer's horn

CROCHES ▶ **croche**

CROCHET vb make by looping and intertwining yarn with a hooked needle ▷ n work made in this way

CROCI ▶ **crocus**

CROCINE adj relating to the crocus

CROCK n earthenware pot or jar ▷ vb become or cause to become weak or disabled

CROCKED adj injured

CROCKET n carved ornament in the form of a curled leaf or cusp, used in Gothic architecture

CROCKS ▶ **crock**

CROCS ▶ **croc**

CROCUS n flowering plant

CROFT n small farm worked by one family in Scotland ▷ vb farm land as a croft

CROFTED ▶ **croft** vb

CROFTER n owner or tenant of a small farm, esp in Scotland or northern England

CROFTS ▶ **croft**

CROG vb ride on a bicycle as a passenger

CROGGED ▶ **crog**

CROGGY n ride on a bicycle as a passenger

CROGS ▶ **crog**

CROJIK n triangular sail

CROJIKS ▶ **crojik**

CROMACK same as ▶ **crummock**

CROMB same as ▶ **crome**

CROMBEC n African Old World warbler with colourful plumage

CROMBED ▶ **cromb**

CROMBS ▶ **cromb**

CROME n hook ▷ vb use a crome

CROMED ▶ **crome**

CROMES ▶ **crome**

CROMING ▶ **crome**

CRONE n witchlike old woman

CRONES ▶ **crone**

CRONET n hair which grows over the top of a horse's hoof

CRONETS ▶ **cronet**

CRONIES ▶ **crony**

CRONISH ▶ **crone**

CRONK adj unfit

CRONKER ▶ **cronk**

CRONY n close friend

CROODLE vb to nestle close

CROOK n dishonest person ▷ vb bend or curve

CROOKED adj bent or twisted

CROOKER ▶ **crook**

CROOKS ▶ **crook**

CROOL vb spoil

CROOLED ▶ **crool**

CROOLS ▶ **crool**

CROON vb sing, hum, or speak in a soft low tone ▷ n soft low singing or humming

CROONED ▶ **croon**

CROONER ▶ **croon**

CROONS ▶ **croon**

CROOVE n animal enclosure

CROOVES ▶ **croove**

CROP n cultivated plant ▷ vb cut very short

CROPFUL n quantity that can be held in the craw

CROPPED ▶ **crop**

CROPPER n person who cultivates or harvests a crop

CROPPIE same as ▶ **croppy**

CROPPY n rebel in the Irish rising of 1798

CROPS ▶ **crop**

CROQUET n game played on a lawn in which balls are hit through hoops ▷ vb drive away (another player's ball) by hitting one's own ball when the two are in contact

CROQUIS n rough sketch

CRORE n (in Indian English) ten million

CRORES ▶ **crore**

CROSIER n staff surmounted by a crook or cross, carried by bishops as a symbol of pastoral office ▷ vb bear or carry such a cross

CROSS vb move or go across (something) ▷ n structure, symbol, or mark of two intersecting lines ▷ adj angry, annoyed

CROSSE n light staff with a triangular frame to which a network is attached, used in playing lacrosse

CROSSED ▶ **cross**

CROSSER ▶ **cross**

CROSSES ▶ **cross**

CROSSLY ▶ **cross**

CROST ▶ **cross**

CROTAL n any of various lichens used in dyeing wool, esp for the manufacture of tweeds

CROTALA ▶ **crotalum**

CROTALS ▶ **crotal**

CROTCH n part of the body between the tops of the legs ▷ vb have crotch (usu of a piece of clothing) removed

CROTON n type of shrub or tree, the seeds of which yield croton oil

CROTONS ▶ **croton**

CROTTLE same as ▶ **crotal**

CROUCH vb bend low with the legs and body close ▷ n this position

CROUP n throat disease of children, with a cough ▷ vb have croup

CROUPE same as ▶ **croup**

CROUPED ▶ **croup**

CROUPER obsolete variant of ▶ **crupper**

CROUPES ▶ **croupe**

CROUPON n type of highly-polished flexible leather

CROUPS ▶ **croup**

CROUPY ▶ **croup**

CROUSE adj lively, confident, or saucy

CROUT n sauerkraut

CROUTE n small round of toasted bread on which a savoury mixture is served

CROUTES ▶ **croute**

CROUTON n small piece of fried or toasted bread served in soup

CROUTS ▶ **crout**

CROW n large black bird with a harsh call ▷ vb (of a cock) make a shrill squawking sound

CROWBAR n iron bar used as a lever ▷ vb use a crowbar to lever (something)

CROWD n large group of people or things ▷ vb gather together in large numbers

CROWDED ▸ crowd

CROWDER ▸ crowd

CROWDIE n porridge of meal and water

CROWDS ▸ crowd

CROWDY same as ▸ **crowdie**

CROWEA n Australian shrub with pink flowers

CROWEAS ▸ crowea

CROWED ▸ crow

CROWER ▸ crow

CROWERS ▸ crow

CROWING ▸ crow

CROWN n monarch's headdress of gold and jewels ▷ vb put a crown on the head of (someone) to proclaim him or her monarch

CROWNED ▸ crown

CROWNER n promotional label consisting of a shaped printed piece of card or paper attached to a product on display

CROWNET n coronet

CROWNS ▸ crown

CROWS ▸ crow

CROZE n recess cut at the end of a barrel or cask to receive the head

CROZER n machine which cuts grooves in cask staves

CROZERS ▸ crozer

CROZES ▸ croze

CROZIER same as ▸ **crosier**

CRU n (in France) a vineyard, group of vineyards, or wine-producing region

CRUBEEN n pig's trotter

CRUCES ▸ crux

CRUCIAL adj very important

CRUCIAN n European fish with a dark-green back, a golden-yellow undersurface, and reddish dorsal and tail fins, popular in aquariums

CRUCIFY vb put to death by fastening to a cross

CRUCK n one of a pair of curved wooden timbers supporting the end of the roof in certain types of building

CRUCKS ▸ cruck

CRUD n sticky or encrusted substance ▷ interj expression of disgust, disappointment, etc ▷ vb cover with a sticky or encrusted substance

CRUDDED ▸ crud

CRUDDLE vb to curdle

CRUDDY adj dirty or unpleasant

CRUDE adj rough and simple ▷ n crude oil

CRUDELY ▸ crude

CRUDER ▸ crude

CRUDES ▸ crude

CRUDEST ▸ crude

CRUDITY ▸ crude

CRUDS ▸ crud

CRUDY adj raw

CRUE obsolete variant of ▸ **crew**

CRUEL adj delighting in others' pain

CRUELER ▸ cruel

CRUELLS same as ▸ **cruels**

CRUELLY ▸ cruel

CRUELS n disease of cattle and sheep

CRUELTY n deliberate infliction of pain or suffering

CRUES ▸ crew

CRUET n small container for salt, pepper, etc, at table

CRUETS ▸ cruet

CRUISE n sail for pleasure ▷ vb sail from place to place for pleasure

CRUISED ▸ cruise

CRUISER n fast warship

CRUISES ▸ cruise

CRUISIE same as ▸ **cruizie**

CRUIVE n animal enclosure

CRUIVES ▸ cruive

CRUIZIE n oil lamp

CRULLER n light sweet ring-shaped cake, fried in deep fat

CRUMB n small fragment of bread or other dry food ▷ vb prepare or cover (food) with breadcrumbs ▷ adj (esp of pie crusts) made with a mixture of biscuit crumbs, sugar, etc

CRUMBED ▸ crumb

CRUMBER ▸ crumb

CRUMBLE vb break into fragments ▷ n pudding of stewed fruit with a crumbly topping

CRUMBLY adj easily crumbled or crumbling

CRUMBS interj expression of dismay or surprise

CRUMBUM n rogue

CRUMBY adj full of crumbs

CRUMEN n deer's larmier or tear-pit

CRUMENS ▸ crumen

CRUMMIE n cow with a crumpled horn

CRUMMY adj of poor quality ▷ n lorry that carries loggers to work from their camp

CRUMP vb thud or explode with a loud dull sound ▷ n crunching, thudding, or exploding noise ▷ adj crooked

CRUMPED ▸ crump

CRUMPER ▸ crump

CRUMPET n round soft yeast cake, eaten buttered

CRUMPLE vb crush, crease ▷ n untidy crease or wrinkle

CRUMPLY ▸ crumple

CRUMPS ▸ crump

CRUMPY adj crisp

CRUNCH vb bite or chew with a noisy crushing sound ▷ n crunching sound

CRUNCHY ▸ crunch

CRUNK n form of hip-hop music originating in the Southern US

CRUNKED adj excited or intoxicated

CRUNKLE Scots variant of ▸ **crinkle**

CRUNKS ▸ crunk

CRUNODE n point at which two branches of a curve intersect, each branch having a distinct tangent

CRUOR n blood clot

CRUORES ▸ cruor

CRUORS ▸ cruor

CRUPPER n strap that passes from the back of a saddle under a horse's tail

CRURA ▸ crus

CRURAL adj of or relating to the leg or thigh

CRUS n leg, esp from the knee to the foot

CRUSADE n medieval Christian war to recover the Holy Land from the Muslims ▷ vb take part in a crusade

CRUSADO n former gold or silver coin of Portugal bearing on its reverse the figure of a cross

CRUSE n small earthenware jug or pot

CRUSES ▸ cruse

CRUSET n goldsmith's crucible

CRUSETS ▸ cruset

CRUSH vb compress so as to injure, break, or crumple ▷ n dense crowd

CRUSHED ▸ crush

CRUSHER ▸ crush

CRUSHES ▸ crush

CRUSIAN same as ▸ **crucian**

CRUSIE same as ▸ **cruizie**

CRUSIES ▸ crusie

CRUSILY adj (in heraldry) strewn with crosses

CRUST n hard outer part of something, esp bread ▷ vb cover with or form a crust

CRUSTA n hard outer layer

CRUSTAE ▸ crusta

CRUSTAL adj of or relating to the earth's crust

CRUSTED ▸ crust

CRUSTS ▸ crust

CRUSTY adj having a crust ▷ n dirty type of punk or hippy whose lifestyle involves travelling and squatting

CRUSY same as ▸ **cruizie**

CRUTCH n long sticklike support with a rest for the armpit, used by a lame person ▷ vb support or sustain (a person or thing) as with a crutch

CRUVE same as ▸ **cruive**

CRUVES ▸ cruve

CRUX n crucial or decisive point

CRUXES ▸ crux

CRUZADO same as ▸ **crusado**

CRUZIE same as ▸ **cruizie**

CRUZIES ▸ cruzie

CRWTH n ancient stringed instrument of Celtic origin similar to the cithara but bowed in later types

▌ This old Celtic musical instrument makes a fine tune when your rack is all consonants.

CRWTHS ▸ crwth

CRY vb shed tears ▷ n fit of weeping

CRYBABY n person, esp a child, who cries too readily

CRYING ▸ cry

CRYINGS ▸ cry

CRYOGEN n substance used to produce low temperatures

CRYONIC > cryonics

CRYPT n vault under a church, esp one used as a burial place

CRYPTAL ▸ crypt

CRYPTIC adj obscure in meaning, secret

CRYPTO n person who is a secret member of an organization or sect

CRYPTON n krypton

CRYPTOS ▸ crypto

CRYPTS ▸ crypt

CRYSTAL n (single grain of) a symmetrically shaped solid formed naturally by some substances ▷ adj bright and clear

CSARDAS n type of Hungarian folk dance

CTENE n locomotor organ found in ctenophores (or comb jellies)

CTENES ▸ ctene

CTENOID adj toothed like a comb, as the scales of perches

CUATRO n four-stringed guitar

CUATROS ▸ cuatro

CUB n young wild animal such as a bear or fox ▷ adj young or inexperienced ▷ vb give birth to cubs

CUBAGE same as ▸ **cubature**

CUBAGES > cubature

CUBANE n rare octahedral hydrocarbon

CUBANES ▸ cubane

CUBBED ▸ cub

CUBBIER ▸ cubby

CUBBIES ▸ cubby

CUBBING ▸ cub

CUBBISH ▸ cub

CUBBY n a cubbyhole ▷ adj short and plump

CUBE n object with six equal square sides ▷ vb cut into cubes

CUBEB n SE Asian woody climbing plant with brownish berries

CUBEBS ▸ cubeb

CUBED ▸ cube

CUBER ▸ cube

CUBERS ▸ cube

CUBES ▸ cube

CUBHOOD n state of being a cub

CUBIC adj having three dimensions ▷ n cubic equation

CUBICA n fine shalloon-like fabric

CUBICAL adj of or related to volume

CUBICAS ▸ cubica

CUBICLE n enclosed part of a large room, screened for privacy

CUBICLY ▸ cubic

CUBICS ▸ cubic

CUBING ▸ cube

CUBISM n style of art in which objects are represented by geometrical shapes

CUBISMS ▸ cubism

CUBIST ▸ cubism

CUBISTS ▸ cubism

CUBIT n old measure of length based on the length of the forearm

CUBITAL adj of or relating to the forearm

CUBITI ▸ cubitus

CUBITS ▸ cubit

CUBITUS n elbow

CUBLESS adj having no cubs

CUBOID adj shaped like a cube ▷ n geometric solid whose six faces are rectangles

CUBOIDS ▸ cuboid

CUBS ▸ cub

CUCKING adj as in **cucking stool** stool to which suspected witches, etc, were tied and pelted or ducked into water as punishment

CUCKOLD n man whose wife has been unfaithful ▷ vb be unfaithful to (one's husband)

CUCKOO n migratory bird with a characteristic two-note call, which lays its eggs in the nests of other birds ▷ adj insane or foolish ▷ interj imitation or representation of the call of a cuckoo ▷ vb repeat over and over

CUCKOOS ▸ cuckoo

CUD n partially digested food which a ruminant brings back into its mouth to chew again

CUDBEAR another name for ▸ **orchil**

CUDDEN n young coalfish

CUDDENS ▸ cudden

CUDDIE same as ▸ **cuddy**

CUDDIES ▸ cuddy

CUDDIN same as ▸ **cudden**

CUDDINS ▸ cuddin

CUDDLE n hug ▷ vb hold (another person or thing) close or (of two people, etc) to hold each other close, as for affection, comfort, or warmth

CUDDLED ▸ cuddle

C

CUDDLER ▸ cuddle
CUDDLES ▸ cuddle
CUDDLY ▸ cuddle
CUDDY *n* small cabin in a boat
CUDGEL *n* short thick stick used as a weapon ▷ *vb* use a cudgel
CUDGELS ▸ cudgel
CUDS ▸ cud
CUDWEED *n* type of temperate woolly plant with clusters of whitish or yellow flowers
CUE *n* signal to an actor or musician to begin speaking or playing ▷ *vb* give a cue to
CUED ▸ cue
CUEING > **foldback**
CUEINGS ▸ cueing
CUEIST *n* snooker or billiards player
CUEISTS ▸ cueist
CUES ▸ cue
CUESTA *n* long low ridge with a steep scarp slope and a gentle back slope, formed by the differential erosion of strata of differing hardness
CUESTAS ▸ cuesta
CUFF *n* end of a sleeve ▷ *vb* hit with an open hand
CUFFED ▸ cuff
CUFFIN *n* man
CUFFING ▸ cuff
CUFFINS ▸ cuffin
CUFFLE *vb* scuffle
CUFFLED ▸ cuffle
CUFFLES ▸ cuffle
CUFFO *adv* free of charge
CUFFS ▸ cuff
CUIF *same as* ▸ **coof**
CUIFS ▸ cuif
CUING ▸ cue
CUIRASS *n* piece of armour, of leather or metal covering the chest and back ▷ *vb* equip with a cuirass
CUISH *same as* ▸ **cuisse**
CUISHES ▸ cuish
CUISINE *n* style of cooking
CUISSE *n* piece of armour for the thigh
CUISSER *same as* ▸ **cooser**
CUISSES ▸ cuisse
CUIT *n* ankle
CUITER *vb* to pamper
CUITERS ▸ cuiter
CUITS ▸ cuit
CUITTLE *vb* to wheedle
CUKE *n* cucumber
CUKES ▸ cuke

CULCH *n* mass of broken stones, shells, and gravel that forms the basis of an oyster bed
CULCHES ▸ culch
CULCHIE *n* rough or unsophisticated country-dweller from outside Dublin
CULET *n* flat face at the bottom of a gem
CULETS ▸ culet
CULEX *n* type of mosquito
CULEXES ▸ culex
CULICES ▸ culex
CULICID *n* type of dipterous insect of the family which comprises the mosquitoes
CULL *vb* choose, gather ▷ *n* culling
CULLAY *n* soapbark tree
CULLAYS ▸ cullay
CULLED ▸ cull
CULLER *n* person employed to cull animals
CULLERS ▸ culler
CULLET *n* waste glass for melting down to be reused
CULLETS ▸ cullet
CULLIED ▸ cully
CULLIES ▸ cully
CULLING ▸ cull
CULLION *n* rascal
CULLIS *same as* > **coulisse**
CULLS ▸ cull
CULLY *n* pal ▷ *vb* to trick
CULM *n* coal-mine waste ▷ *vb* to form a culm or grass stem
CULMED ▸ culm
CULMEN *n* summit
CULMINA ▸ culmen
CULMING ▸ culm
CULMS ▸ culm
CULOTTE > **culottes**
CULPA *n* act of neglect
CULPAE ▸ culpa
CULPRIT *n* person guilty of an offence or misdeed
CULT *n* specific system of worship ▷ *adj* very popular among a limited group of people
CULTCH *same as* ▸ **culch**
CULTER *same as* ▸ **coulter**
CULTERS ▸ culter
CULTI ▸ cultus
CULTIC *adj* of or relating to a religious cult
CULTIER ▸ culty
CULTISH *adj* intended to appeal to a small group of fashionable people

CULTISM ▸ cult
CULTIST ▸ cult
CULTS ▸ cult
CULTURE *n* ideas, customs, and art of a particular society ▷ *vb* grow (bacteria) for study
CULTUS *another word for* ▸ **cult**
CULTY *same as* ▸ **cultish**
CULVER *an archaic or poetic name for* ▸ **pigeon**
CULVERS ▸ culver
CULVERT *n* drain under a road or railway
CUMARIC ▸ cumarin
CUMARIN *same as* > **coumarin**
CUMBENT *adj* lying down
CUMBER *vb* obstruct or hinder ▷ *n* hindrance or burden
CUMBERS ▸ cumber
CUMBIA *n* Colombian style of music
CUMBIAS ▸ cumbia
CUMEC *n* unit of volumetric rate of flow
CUMECS ▸ cumec
CUMIN *n* sweet-smelling seeds of a Mediterranean plant, used in cooking
CUMINS ▸ cumin
CUMMER *n* gossip
CUMMERS ▸ cummer
CUMMIN *same as* ▸ **cumin**
CUMMINS ▸ cummin
CUMQUAT *same as* ▸ **kumquat**
CUMSHAW *n* (used, esp formerly, by beggars in Chinese ports) a present or tip
CUMULET *n* variety of domestic fancy pigeon, pure white or white with light red markings
CUMULI ▸ cumulus
CUMULUS *n* thick white or dark grey cloud
CUNDIES ▸ cundy
CUNDUM *n* early form of condom
CUNDUMS ▸ cundum
CUNDY *n* sewer
CUNEAL *same as* > **cuneiform**
CUNEATE *adj* wedge-shaped: cuneate leaves are attached at the narrow end
CUNEI ▸ cuneus
CUNETTE *n* small trench dug in the main ditch of a fortification**

CUNEUS n small wedge-shaped area of the cerebral cortex

CUNNER n fish of the wrasse family

CUNNERS ▶ cunner

CUNNING adj clever at deceiving ▷ n cleverness at deceiving

CUP n small bowl-shaped drinking container with a handle ▷ vb form (one's hands) into the shape of a cup

CUPCAKE n small cake baked in a cup-shaped foil or paper case

CUPEL n refractory pot in which gold or silver is refined ▷ vb refine (gold or silver) by means of cupellation

CUPELED ▶ cupel

CUPELER ▶ cupel

CUPELS ▶ cupel

CUPFUL n amount a cup will hold

CUPFULS ▶ cupful

CUPGALL n gall found on oakleaves

CUPHEAD n type of bolt or rivet with a cup-shaped head

CUPID n figure representing the Roman god of love

CUPIDS ▶ cupid

CUPLIKE ▶ cup

CUPMAN n drinking companion

CUPMEN ▶ cupman

CUPOLA n domed roof or ceiling ▷ vb to provide with a cupola

CUPOLAR ▶ cupola

CUPOLAS ▶ cupola

CUPPA n cup of tea

CUPPAS ▶ cuppa

CUPPED ▶ cup

CUPPER same as ▶ cuppa

CUPPERS ▶ cupper

CUPPIER ▶ cuppy

CUPPING ▶ cup

CUPPY adj cup-shaped

CUPRIC adj of or containing copper in the divalent state

CUPRITE n red secondary mineral

CUPROUS adj of or containing copper in the monovalent state

CUPRUM an obsolete name for ▶ copper

CUPRUMS ▶ cuprum

CUPS ▶ cup

CUPSFUL ▶ cupful

CUPULA n dome-shaped structure, esp the sensory structure within the semicircular canals of the ear

CUPULAE ▶ cupula

CUPULAR same as > cupulate

CUPULE n cup-shaped part or structure, such as the cup around the base of an acorn

CUPULES ▶ cupule

CUR n mongrel dog

CURABLE adj capable of being cured

CURABLY ▶ curable

CURACAO n orange-flavoured liqueur

CURACOA same as ▶ curacao

CURACY n work or position of a curate

CURAGH same as ▶ currach

CURAGHS ▶ curagh

CURARA same as ▶ curare

CURARAS ▶ curara

CURARE n poisonous resin of a S American tree, used as a muscle relaxant in medicine

CURARES ▶ curare

CURARI same as ▶ curare

CURARIS ▶ curari

CURAT n cuirass

CURATE n clergyman who assists a parish priest ▷ vb be in charge of (an art exhibition or museum) ▷ vb to act as a curator

CURATED ▶ curate

CURATES ▶ curate

CURATOR n person in charge of a museum or art gallery

CURATS ▶ curat

CURB n something that restrains ▷ vb control, restrain

CURBED ▶ curb

CURBER ▶ curb

CURBERS ▶ curb

CURBING the US spelling of ▶ kerbing

CURBS ▶ curb

CURCH n woman's plain cap or kerchief

CURCHEF same as ▶ curch

CURCHES ▶ curch

CURCUMA n type of tropical Asian tuberous plant

CURD n coagulated milk, used to make cheese ▷ vb turn into or become curd

CURDED ▶ curd

CURDIER ▶ curd

CURDING ▶ curd

CURDLE vb turn into curd, coagulate

CURDLED ▶ curdle

CURDLER ▶ curdle

CURDLES ▶ curdle

CURDS ▶ curd

CURDY ▶ curd

CURE vb get rid of (an illness or problem) ▷ n (treatment causing) curing of an illness or person

CURED ▶ cure

CURER ▶ cure

CURERS ▶ cure

CURES ▶ cure

CURET same as ▶ curette

CURETS ▶ curet

CURETTE n surgical instrument for scraping tissue from body cavities ▷ vb scrape with a curette

CURF n type of limestone

CURFEW n law ordering people to stay inside their homes after a specific time at night

CURFEWS ▶ curfew

CURFS ▶ curf

CURIA n papal court and government of the Roman Catholic Church

CURIAE ▶ curia

CURIAL ▶ curia

CURIAS ▶ curia

CURIE n standard unit of radioactivity

CURIES ▶ curie

CURIET n cuirass

CURIETS ▶ curiet

CURING ▶ cure

CURIO n rare or unusual object valued as a collector's item

CURIOS ▶ curio

CURIOSA n curiosities

CURIOUS adj eager to learn or know

CURITE n oxide of uranium and lead

CURITES ▶ curite

CURIUM n radioactive element artificially produced from plutonium

CURIUMS ▶ curium

CURL n curved piece of hair ▷ vb make (hair) into curls or (of hair) grow in curls

CURLED ▶ curl

CURLER n pin or small tube for curling hair

CURLERS ▶ curler

CURLEW n long-billed wading bird

CURLEWS ▶ curlew

CURLI pl n curled hairlike processes on the surface of the E. coli bacterium, by means of which it adheres to and infects wounds

CURLIER ▶ curly

CURLIES pl n as in **have by the short and curlies** have completely in one's power

CURLILY ▶ curly

CURLING n game like bowls, played with heavy stones on ice

CURLS ▶ curl

CURLY adj tending to curl

CURN n grain (of corn etc)

CURNEY same as ▶ **curny**

CURNIER ▶ curny

CURNS ▶ curn

CURNY adj granular

CURPEL same as ▶ **crupper**

CURPELS ▶ curpel

CURR vb to purr

CURRACH a Scots or Irish name for ▶ **coracle**

CURRAGH same as ▶ **currach**

CURRAN n black bun

CURRANS ▶ curran

CURRANT n small dried grape

CURRED ▶ curr

CURRENT adj of the immediate present ▷ n flow of water or air in one direction

CURRIE same as ▶ **curry**

CURRIED ▶ curry

CURRIER n person who curries leather

CURRIES ▶ curry

CURRING ▶ curr

CURRISH adj of or like a cur

CURRS ▶ curr

CURRY n Indian dish of meat or vegetables in a hot spicy sauce ▷ vb prepare (food) with curry powder

CURS ▶ cur

CURSAL ▶ cursus

CURSE vb swear (at) ▷ n swearword

CURSED ▶ curse

CURSER ▶ curse

CURSERS ▶ curse

CURSES ▶ curse

CURSI ▶ cursus

CURSING ▶ curse

CURSIVE n (handwriting) done with joined letters ▷ adj of handwriting or print in which letters are joined in a flowing style

CURSOR n movable point of light that shows a specific position on a visual display unit

CURSORS ▶ cursor

CURSORY adj quick and superficial

CURST ▶ curse

CURSUS n Neolithic parallel earthworks

CURT adj brief and rather rude

CURTAIL vb cut short

CURTAIN n piece of cloth hung at a window or opening as a screen ▷ vb provide with curtains

CURTAL adj cut short ▷ n animal whose tail has been docked

CURTALS ▶ curtal

CURTANA n unpointed sword carried before an English sovereign at a coronation as an emblem of mercy

CURTATE adj shortened

CURTAXE same as > curtalaxe

CURTER ▶ curt

CURTEST ▶ curt

CURTESY n widower's life interest in his wife's estate

CURTLY ▶ curt

CURTSEY same as ▶ **curtsy**

CURTSY n woman's gesture of respect made by bending the knees and bowing the head ▷ vb make a curtsy

CURULE adj (in ancient Rome) of the highest rank, esp one entitled to use a curule chair

CURVATE adj curved

CURVE n continuously bending line with no straight parts ▷ vb form or move in a curve

CURVED ▶ curve

CURVES ▶ curve

CURVET n horse's low leap with all four feet off the ground ▷ vb make such a leap

CURVETS ▶ curvet

CURVEY same as ▶ **curvy**

CURVIER ▶ curve

CURVING ▶ curve

CURVITY n curvedness

CURVY ▶ curve

CUSCUS n large Australian nocturnal possum

CUSEC n unit of flow equal to 1 cubic foot per second

CUSECS ▶ cusec

CUSH n cushion

CUSHAT n wood pigeon

CUSHATS ▶ cushat

CUSHAW same as ▶ **cashaw**

CUSHAWS ▶ cushaw

CUSHES ▶ cush

CUSHIE same as ▶ **cushat**

CUSHIER ▶ cushy

CUSHIES ▶ cushie

CUSHILY ▶ cushy

CUSHION n bag filled with soft material, to make a seat more comfortable ▷ vb lessen the effects of

CUSHTY interj exclamation of pleasure, agreement, approval, etc

CUSHY adj easy

CUSK n type of food fish of northern coastal waters, with a single long dorsal fin

CUSKS ▶ cusk

CUSP n pointed end, esp on a tooth

CUSPAL ▶ cusp

CUSPATE adj having a cusp or cusps

CUSPED same as ▶ **cuspate**

CUSPID n tooth having one point

CUSPIDS ▶ cuspid

CUSPIER ▶ cuspy

CUSPIS n in anatomy, tapering structure

CUSPS ▶ cusp

CUSPY adj (of a computer program) well-designed and user-friendly

CUSS n curse, oath ▷ vb swear (at)

CUSSED adj obstinate

CUSSER same as ▶ **cooser**

CUSSERS ▶ cusser

CUSSES ▶ cuss

CUSSING ▶ cuss

CUSSO n tree of the rose family

CUSSOS ▶ cusso

CUSTARD n sweet yellow sauce made from milk and eggs

CUSTOCK same as ▶ **castock**

CUSTODE n custodian

CUSTODY n protective care

CUSTOM n long-established

activity or action ▷ *adj* made to the specifications of an individual customer

CUSTOMS *n* duty charged on imports or exports

CUSTOS *n* superior in the Franciscan religious order

CUSTREL *n* knave

CUSUM *n* analysis technique used in statistics

CUSUMS ▸ cusum

CUT *vb* open up, penetrate, wound, or divide with a sharp instrument ▷ *n* act of cutting

CUTAWAY *adj* (of a drawing or model) having part of the outside omitted to reveal the inside ▷ *n* man's coat cut diagonally from the front waist to the back of the knees

CUTBACK *n* decrease or reduction ▷ *vb* shorten by cutting

CUTBANK *n* steep banking at a bend in a river

CUTCH *same as* ▸ catechu

CUTCHA *adj* crude

CUTCHES ▸ cutch

CUTDOWN *n* decrease

CUTE *adj* appealing or attractive

CUTELY ▸ cute

CUTER ▸ cute

CUTES ▸ cutis

CUTESIE *same as* ▸ cutesy

CUTEST ▸ cute

CUTESY *adj* affectedly cute or coy

CUTEY *same as* ▸ cutie

CUTEYS ▸ cutey

CUTICLE *n* skin at the base of a fingernail or toenail

CUTIE *n* person regarded as appealing or attractive, esp a girl or woman

CUTIES ▸ cutie

CUTIKIN *same as* > cootikin

CUTIN *n* waxy waterproof substance, consisting of derivatives of fatty acids, that is the main constituent of the plant cuticle

CUTINS ▸ cutin

CUTIS *a technical name for the* ▸ skin

CUTISES ▸ cutis

CUTLAS *same as* ▸ cutlass

CUTLASS *n* curved one-edged sword formerly used by sailors

CUTLER *n* maker of cutlery

CUTLERS ▸ cutler

CUTLERY *n* knives, forks, and spoons

CUTLET *n* small piece of meat like a chop

CUTLETS ▸ cutlet

CUTLINE *n* caption

CUTOFF *n* limit or termination

CUTOFFS ▸ cutoff

CUTOUT *n* something that has been cut out from something else

CUTOUTS ▸ cutout

CUTOVER *n* transitional period in IT system changeover, during which old and new systems are working concurrently

CUTS ▸ cut

CUTTAGE *n* propagation by using parts taken from growing plants

CUTTER *n* person or tool that cuts

CUTTERS ▸ cutter

CUTTIER ▸ cutty

CUTTIES ▸ cutty

CUTTING ▸ cut

CUTTLE *vb* to whisper

CUTTLED ▸ cuttle

CUTTLES ▸ cuttle

CUTTO *n* large knife

CUTTOE *same as* ▸ cutto

CUTTOES ▸ cutto

CUTTY *adj* short or cut short ▷ *n* something cut short, such as a spoon or short-stemmed tobacco pipe

CUTUP *n* joker or prankster

CUTUPS ▸ cutup

CUTWORK *n* openwork embroidery in which the pattern is cut away from the background

CUTWORM *n* caterpillar of various types of moth, a pest of young crop plants in N America

CUVEE *n* individual batch or blend of wine

CUVEES ▸ cuvee

CUVETTE *n* shallow dish or vessel for holding liquid

CUZ *n* cousin

> Cuz is another word for cousin, great for using the Z.

CUZZES ▸ cuz

CUZZIE *n* close friend or family member

CUZZIES ▸ cuzzie

CWM *same as* ▸ cirque

> Cwm is a Welsh word meaning a valley, a useful one to remember because it doesn't contain any vowels.

CWMS ▸ cwm

CWTCH *vb* be snuggled up

> This delightful Welsh word meaning to cuddle is not likely to come up, but might just help you out of a tight spot one day when your rack is all consonants.

CWTCHED ▸ cwtch

CWTCHES ▸ cwtch

CYAN *n* highly saturated green-blue that is the complementary colour of red and forms, with magenta and yellow, a set of primary colours ▷ *adj* of this colour

CYANATE *n* any salt or ester of cyanic acid

CYANIC *adj as in* **cyanic acid** colourless poisonous volatile liquid acid

CYANID *same as* ▸ cyanide

CYANIDE *n* extremely poisonous chemical compound ▷ *vb* treat with cyanide

CYANIDS ▸ cyanid

CYANIN *same as* ▸ cyanine

CYANINE *n* blue dye used to extend the sensitivity of photographic emulsions to colours other than blue and ultraviolet

CYANINS ▸ cyanin

CYANISE *vb* to turn into cyanide

CYANITE *a variant spelling of* ▸ kyanite

CYANIZE *same as* ▸ cyanise

CYANO *adj* containing cyanogen

CYANS ▸ cyan

CYATHI ▸ cyathus

CYATHIA > cyathium

CYATHUS *n* ancient measure of wine

CYBER *adj* involving computers

CYBORG *n* (in science fiction) a living being whose powers are enhanced by computer implants

CYBORGS ▸ cyborg

CYBRID *n* cytoplasmic hybrid (hybrid resulting from the fusion of a cytoplast and a whole cell)

CYBRIDS ▸ cybrid

CYCAD n type of tropical or subtropical plant with an unbranched stem and fernlike leaves crowded at the top

CYCADS ▸ cycad

CYCAS n palm tree of the genus Cycas

CYCASES ▸ cycas

CYCASIN n glucoside, toxic to mammals, occurring in cycads

CYCLASE n enzyme which acts as a catalyst in the formation of a cyclic compound

CYCLE vb ride a bicycle ▷ n bicycle

CYCLED ▸ cycle

CYCLER same as ▸ cyclist

CYCLERS ▸ cyclist

CYCLERY n business dealing in bicycles and bicycle accessories

CYCLES ▸ cycle

CYCLIC adj recurring or revolving in cycles

CYCLIN n type of protein

CYCLING ▸ cycle

CYCLINS ▸ cyclin

CYCLISE same as ▸ cyclize

CYCLIST n person who rides a bicycle

CYCLIZE vb be cyclical

CYCLO n type of rickshaw

CYCLOID adj resembling a circle ▷ n curve described by a point on the circumference of a circle as the circle rolls along a straight line

CYCLONE n violent wind moving round a central area

CYCLOPS n type of copepod characterized by having one eye

CYCLOS ▸ cyclo

CYCLUS n cycle

CYDER same as ▸ cider

CYDERS ▸ cyder

CYESES ▸ cyesis

CYESIS the technical name for ▸ pregnancy

CYGNET n young swan

CYGNETS ▸ cygnet

CYLICES ▸ cylix

CYLIX same as ▸ kylix

CYMA n moulding with a double curve, part concave and part convex

CYMAE ▸ cyma

CYMAR n woman's short fur-trimmed jacket, popular in the 17th and 18th centuries

CYMARS ▸ cymar

CYMAS ▸ cyma

CYMATIA > cymatium

CYMBAL n percussion instrument consisting of a brass plate which is struck against another or hit with a stick

CYMBALO another name for > dulcimer

CYMBALS ▸ cymbal

CYME n flower cluster which has a single flower on the end of each stem and of which the central flower blooms first

CYMENE n colourless insoluble liquid with an aromatic odour that exists in three isomeric forms

CYMENES ▸ cymene

CYMES ▸ cyme

CYMLIN same as ▸ cymling

CYMLING n pattypan squash

CYMLINS ▸ cymlin

CYMOID adj resembling a cyme or cyma

CYMOL same as ▸ cymene

CYMOLS ▸ cymol

CYMOSE adj having the characteristics of a cyme

CYMOUS adj relating to a cyme

CYNIC n person who believes that people always act selfishly ▷ adj of or relating to Sirius, the Dog Star

CYNICAL adj believing that people always act selfishly

CYNICS ▸ cynic

CYPHER same as ▸ cipher

CYPHERS ▸ cypher

CYPRES n legal doctrine stating that a testator's intentions should be carried out as closely as possible

CYPRESS n evergreen tree with dark green leaves

CYPRIAN n prostitute or dancer

CYPRID n cypris

CYPRIDS ▸ cyprid

CYPRINE adj relating to carp

CYPRIS n member of the genus Cypris (small bivalve freshwater crustaceans)

CYPRUS same as ▸ cypress

CYPSELA n dry one-seeded fruit of the daisy and related plants, which resembles an achene but is surrounded by a calyx sheath

CYST n (abnormal) sac in the body containing fluid or soft matter

CYSTEIN same as > cysteine

CYSTIC adj of, relating to, or resembling a cyst

CYSTID n cystidean

CYSTIDS ▸ cystid

CYSTINE n sulphur-containing amino acid

CYSTOID adj resembling a cyst or bladder ▷ n tissue mass, such as a tumour, that resembles a cyst but lacks an outer membrane

CYSTS ▸ cyst

CYTASE n cellulose-dissolving enzyme

CYTASES ▸ cytase

CYTE n biological cell

CYTES ▸ cyte

CYTISI ▸ cytisus

CYTISUS n any plant of the broom genus, Cytisus

CYTODE n mass of protoplasm without a nucleus

CYTODES ▸ cytode

CYTOID adj resembling a cell

CYTON n main part of a neuron

CYTONS ▸ cyton

CYTOSOL n solution of proteins and metabolites inside a biological cell, in which the organelles are suspended

CZAPKA n leather and felt peaked military helmet of Polish origin

CZAPKAS ▸ czapka

CZAR same as ▸ tsar

CZARDAS n Hungarian national dance of alternating slow and fast sections

CZARDOM ▸ czar

CZARINA variant spellings (esp US) of ▸ tsarina

CZARISM a variant spelling (esp US) of ▸ tsarism

CZARIST ▸ czarism

CZARS ▸ czar

Dd

D forms a two-letter word before every vowel except **U**. There are plenty of good three-letter words beginning with **D**, particularly those with a **Y** or **W**: **day, dye** and **dew** are worth 7 points each, for example. And don't forget **dex** and **dux** for 11 points each and the invaluable **dzo** for 13 points.

DA *n* Burmese knife

DAAL *n* (in Indian cookery) split pulses

DAALS ▶ daal

DAB *vb* pat lightly ▷ *n* small amount of something soft or moist

DABBA *n* in Indian cookery, round metal box used to transport hot food

DABBAS ▶ dabba

DABBED ▶ dab

DABBER *n* pad used by printers for applying ink by hand

DABBERS ▶ dabber

DABBING ▶ dab

DABBITY *n* temporary tattoo

DABBLE *vb* be involved in something superficially

DABBLED ▶ dabble

DABBLER ▶ dabble

DABBLES ▶ dabble

DABS ▶ dab

DABSTER *n* incompetent or amateurish worker

DACE *n* small European freshwater fish

DACES ▶ dace

DACHA *n* country cottage in Russia

DACHAS ▶ dacha

DACITE *n* volcanic rock

DACITES ▶ dacite

DACK *vb* remove the trousers from (someone) by force

DACKED ▶ dack

DACKER *vb* walk slowly

DACKERS ▶ dacker

DACKING ▶ dack

DACKS ▶ dack

DACOIT *n* (in India and Myanmar) a member of a gang of armed robbers

DACOITS ▶ dacoit

DACOITY *n* (in India and Myanmar) robbery by an armed gang

DACRON *n* US tradename for a synthetic polyester fibre or fabric characterized by lightness and crease resistance

DACRONS ▶ dacron

DACTYL *n* metrical foot of three syllables, one long followed by two short

DACTYLI > dactylus

DACTYLS ▶ dactyl

DAD *n* father ▷ *vb* act or treat as a father

DADA *n* nihilistic artistic movement of the early 20th century

DADAH *n* illegal drugs

DADAHS ▶ dadah

DADAISM *same as* ▶ **dada**

DADAIST ▶ dada

DADAS ▶ dada

DADDED ▶ dad

DADDIES ▶ daddy

DADDING ▶ dad

DADDLE *vb* walk unsteadily

DADDLED ▶ daddle

DADDLES ▶ daddle

DADDOCK *n* core of a dead tree

DADDY *n* father

DADGUM *mild form of* ▶ **damned**

DADO *n* lower part of an interior wall, below a rail, decorated differently from the upper part ▷ *vb* provide with a dado

DADOED ▶ dado

DADOES ▶ dado

DADOING ▶ dado

DADOS ▶ dado

DADS ▶ dad

DAE *a Scots word for* ▶ **do**

DAEDAL *adj* skilful or intricate

DAEING ▶ dae

DAEMON *same as* ▶ **demon**

DAEMONS ▶ daemon

DAES ▶ dae

DAFF *vb* frolic

DAFFED ▶ daff

DAFFIER ▶ daffy

DAFFIES ▶ daffy

DAFFILY ▶ daffy

DAFFING ▶ daff

DAFFS ▶ daff

DAFFY *another word for* ▶ **daft**

DAFT *adj* foolish or crazy

DAFTAR *Indian word for* ▶ **office**

DAFTARS ▶ daftar

DAFTER ▶ daft

DAFTEST ▶ daft

DAFTIE *n* foolish person

DAFTIES ▶ daftie

DAFTLY ▶ daft

DAG *n* character ▷ *vb* cut daglocks from sheep

DAGABA *n* shrine for Buddhist relics

DAGABAS ▶ dagaba

DAGGA *n* cannabis

DAGGAS ▶ dagga

DAGGED ▶ dag

DAGGER ▶ dag

DAGGERS ▶ dag

DAGGIER ▶ daggy

DAGGING ▶ dag

DAGGLE *vb* trail through water

DAGGLED ▶ daggle

DAGGLES ▶ daggle

DAGGY *adj* amusing

DAGLOCK *n* dung-caked

D

lock of wool around the hindquarters of a sheep

DAGOBA n dome-shaped shrine containing relics of the Buddha or a Buddhist saint

DAGOBAS ▸ dagoba

DAGS ▸ dag

DAGWOOD n European shrub

DAH n long sound used in combination with the short sound in the spoken representation of Morse and other telegraphic codes

DAHL same as ▸ **dhal**

DAHLIA n brightly coloured garden flower

DAHLIAS ▸ dahlia

DAHLS ▸ dahl

DAHOON n evergreen shrub

DAHOONS ▸ dahoon

DAHS ▸ dah

DAIDLE vb waddle about

DAIDLED ▸ daidle

DAIDLES ▸ daidle

DAIKER vb walk slowly

DAIKERS ▸ daiker

DAIKO n Japanese drum

DAIKON another name for ▸ **mooli**

DAIKONS ▸ daikon

DAIKOS ▸ daiko

DAILIES ▸ daily

DAILY adj occurring every day or every weekday ▷ adv every day ▷ n daily newspaper

DAIMEN adj occasional

DAIMIO same as ▸ **daimyo**

DAIMIOS ▸ daimio

DAIMOKU n Nichiren Buddhist chant

DAIMON same as ▸ **demon**

DAIMONS ▸ daimon

DAIMYO n (in Japan) one of the territorial magnates who dominated much of the country from about the 11th to the 19th century

DAIMYOS ▸ daimyo

DAINE vb condescend

DAINED ▸ daine

DAINES ▸ daine

DAINING ▸ daine

DAINT adj dainty

DAINTY adj delicate or elegant ▷ n small cake or sweet

DAIRIES ▸ dairy

DAIRY n place for the processing or sale of milk and its products ▷ adj of

milk or its products

DAIS n raised platform in a hall, used by a speaker

DAISES ▸ dais

DAISIED ▸ daisy

DAISIES ▸ daisy

DAISY n small wild flower with a yellow centre and white petals

DAK n system of mail delivery or passenger transport by relays of bearers or horses stationed at intervals along a route

A **dak** is an old mail or transport system, often useful for disposing of the K.

DAKER vb walk slowly

DAKERED ▸ daker

DAKERS ▸ daker

DAKOIT same as ▸ **dacoit**

DAKOITI same as ▸ **dakoit**

DAKOITS ▸ dakoit

DAKOITY n armed robbery

DAKS an informal name for > **trousers**

DAL same as ▸ **decalitre**

DALAPON n herbicide

DALASI n standard monetary unit of The Gambia, divided into 100 bututs

DALASIS ▸ dalasi

DALE n (esp in N England) valley

DALED same as ▸ **daleth**

DALEDH n letter of Hebrew alphabet

DALEDHS ▸ daledh

DALEDS ▸ daled

DALES ▸ dale

DALETH n fourth letter of the Hebrew alphabet, transliterated as d or, when final, dh

DALETHS ▸ daleth

DALGYTE another name for ▸ **bilby**

DALI n type of tree

DALIS ▸ dali

DALLE ▸ **dalles**

DALLES pl n stretch of a river between high rock walls, with rapids and dangerous currents

DALLIED ▸ dally

DALLIER ▸ dally

DALLIES ▸ dally

DALLOP n semisolid lump

DALLOPS ▸ dallop

DALLY vb waste time

DALS ▸ dal

DALT n foster child

DALTON n atomic mass unit

DALTONS ▸ dalton

DALTS ▸ dalt

DAM n barrier built across a river to create a lake ▷ vb build a dam across (a river)

DAMAGE vb harm, spoil ▷ n harm to a person or thing

DAMAGED ▸ damage

DAMAGER ▸ damage

DAMAGES pl n money awarded as compensation for injury or loss

DAMAN n the Syrian rock hyrax

DAMANS ▸ daman

DAMAR same as ▸ **dammar**

DAMARS ▸ dammar

DAMASK n fabric with a pattern woven into it, used for tablecloths etc ▷ vb ornament (metal) by etching or inlaying, usually with gold or silver

DAMASKS ▸ damask

DAMBROD n draughtboard

DAME n woman

DAMES ▸ dame

DAMFOOL adj foolish

DAMIANA n herbal medicine

DAMMAR n any of various resins obtained from SE Asian trees used for varnishes, lacquers, bases for oil paints, etc

DAMMARS ▸ dammar

DAMME interj exclamation of surprise

DAMMED ▸ dam

DAMMER same as ▸ **dammar**

DAMMERS ▸ dammer

DAMMING ▸ dam

DAMMIT interj exclamation of surprise

DAMN interj exclamation of annoyance ▷ adj extreme(ly) ▷ vb condemn as bad or worthless

DAMNED adj condemned to hell ▷ adv extreme or extremely

DAMNER n person who damns

DAMNERS ▸ damner

DAMNIFY vb cause loss or damage to (a person)

DAMNING ▸ damn

DAMNS ▸ damn

DAMOSEL same as ▸ **damsel**

DAMOZEL same as ▸ **damsel**

DAMP adj slightly wet ▷ n slight wetness, moisture ▷ vb make damp
DAMPED ▷ damp
DAMPEN vb reduce the intensity of
DAMPENS ▷ dampen
DAMPER n movable plate to regulate the draught in a fire
DAMPERS ▷ damper
DAMPEST ▷ damp
DAMPIER ▷ dampy
DAMPING n moistening or wetting
DAMPISH ▷ damp
DAMPLY ▷ damp
DAMPS ▷ damp
DAMPY adj damp
DAMS ▷ dam
DAMSEL n young woman
DAMSELS ▷ damsel
DAMSON n small blue-black plumlike fruit
DAMSONS ▷ damson
DAN n in judo, any of the 10 black-belt grades of proficiency
DANAZOL n type of drug
DANCE vb move the feet and body rhythmically in time to music ▷ n series of steps and movements in time to music
DANCED ▷ dance
DANCER ▷ dance
DANCERS ▷ dance
DANCES ▷ dance
DANCEY adj of, relating to, or resembling dance music
DANCIER ▷ dancey
DANCING ▷ dance
DANCY adj (of music) appropriate for dancing
DANDER n stroll ▷ vb stroll
DANDERS ▷ dander
DANDIER ▷ dandy
DANDIES ▷ dandy
DANDIFY vb dress like or cause to resemble a dandy
DANDILY ▷ dandy
DANDLE vb move (a child) up and down on one's knee
DANDLED ▷ dandle
DANDLER ▷ dandle
DANDLES ▷ dandle
DANDY n man who is overconcerned with the elegance of his appearance ▷ adj very good
DANELAW n Danish law and customs of northern, central, and eastern parts

of Anglo-Saxon England
DANG a euphemistic word for ▷ damn
DANGED ▷ dang
DANGER n possibility of being injured or killed ▷ vb in archaic usage, endanger
DANGERS ▷ danger
DANGING ▷ dang
DANGLE vb hang loosely ▷ n act of dangling or something that dangles
DANGLED ▷ dangle
DANGLER ▷ dangle
DANGLES ▷ dangle
DANGLY ▷ dangle
DANGS ▷ dang
DANIO n type of brightly coloured tropical freshwater fish popular in aquariums
DANIOS ▷ danio
DANISH n sweet pastry
DANK adj unpleasantly damp and chilly ▷ n unpleasant damp and chilliness
DANKER ▷ dank
DANKEST ▷ dank
DANKISH ▷ dank
DANKLY ▷ dank
DANKS ▷ dank
DANNIES ▷ danny
DANNY n hand (used esp when addressing children)
DANS ▷ dan
DANSEUR n male ballet dancer
DANT vb intimidate
DANTED ▷ dant
DANTING ▷ dant
DANTON same as ▷ daunton
DANTONS ▷ danton
DANTS ▷ dant
DAP vb fish with a natural or artificial fly on a floss silk line so that the wind makes the fly bob on and off the surface of the water
DAPHNE n ornamental Eurasian shrub with shiny evergreen leaves and clusters of small bell-shaped flowers
DAPHNES ▷ daphne
DAPHNIA n type of water flea with a rounded body in a transparent shell
DAPHNID n water flea
DAPPED ▷ dap
DAPPER adj (of a man) neat in appearance ▷ n

fisherman or -woman who uses a bobbing bait
DAPPERS ▷ dapper
DAPPING ▷ dap
DAPPLE vb mark or become marked with spots or patches of a different colour ▷ n mottled or spotted markings ▷ adj marked with dapples or spots
DAPPLED ▷ dapple
DAPPLES ▷ dapple
DAPS ▷ dap
DAPSONE n antimicrobial drug used to treat leprosy and certain types of dermatitis
DAQUIRI n rum cocktail
DARAF n unit of elastance equal to a reciprocal farad
DARAFS ▷ daraf
DARB n something excellent
DARBAR n hall in Sikh temple
DARBARS ▷ darbar
DARBIES > handcuffs
DARBS ▷ darb
DARCIES ▷ darcy
DARCY n unit expressing the permeability coefficient of rock
DARCYS ▷ darcy
DARE vb be courageous enough to try (to do something) ▷ n challenge to do something risky
DARED ▷ dare
DAREFUL adj daring
DARER ▷ dare
DARERS ▷ dare
DARES ▷ dare
DARESAY vb venture to say
DARG n day's work
DARGA n Muslim shrine
DARGAH n tomb of a Muslim saint
DARGAHS ▷ dargah
DARGAS ▷ darga
DARGLE n wooded hollow
DARGLES ▷ dargle
DARGS ▷ darg
DARI n variety of sorghum
DARIC n gold coin of ancient Persia
DARICS ▷ daric
DARING adj willing to take risks ▷ n courage to do dangerous things
DARINGS ▷ daring
DARIOLE n small cup-shaped mould used for

D

making individual sweet or savoury dishes

DARIS ▸ **dari**

DARK adj having little or no light ▷ n absence of light ▷ vb in archaic usage, darken

DARKED ▸ **dark**

DARKEN vb make or become dark or darker

DARKENS ▸ **darken**

DARKER ▸ **dark**

DARKEST ▸ **dark**

DARKING ▸ **dark**

DARKISH ▸ **dark**

DARKLE vb grow dark

DARKLED ▸ **darkle**

DARKLES ▸ **darkle**

DARKLY ▸ **dark**

DARKNET n covert communication network on the Internet

DARKS ▸ **dark**

DARLING n much-loved person ▷ adj much-loved

DARN vb mend (a garment) with a series of interwoven stitches ▷ n patch of darned work

DARNED adj damned

DARNEL n weed that grows in grain fields

DARNELS ▸ **darnel**

DARNER ▸ **darn**

DARNERS ▸ **darn**

DARNING ▸ **darn**

DARNS ▸ **darn**

DAROGHA n in India, manager

DARRAIN vb clear of guilt

DARRAYN vb clear of guilt

DARRE vb dare

DARRED ▸ **darre**

DARRES ▸ **darre**

DARRING ▸ **darre**

DARSHAN n Hindu blessing

DART n small narrow pointed missile that is thrown or shot, esp in the game of darts ▷ vb move or direct quickly and suddenly

DARTED ▸ **dart**

DARTER n type of aquatic bird of tropical and subtropical inland waters, with a long slender neck and bill

DARTERS ▸ **darter**

DARTING ▸ **dart**

DARTLE vb move swiftly

DARTLED ▸ **dartle**

DARTLES ▸ **dartle**

DARTRE n skin disease

DARTRES ▸ **dartre**

DARTS n game in which darts are thrown at a dartboard

DARZI n tailor in India

DARZIS ▸ **darzi**

DAS ▸ **da**

DASH vb move quickly ▷ n sudden quick movement

DASHED ▸ **dash**

DASHEEN another name for ▸ **taro**

DASHEKI n upper garment

DASHER n one of the boards surrounding an ice-hockey rink

DASHERS ▸ **dasher**

DASHES ▸ **dash**

DASHI n clear stock made from dried fish and kelp

DASHIER ▸ **dashy**

DASHIKI n large loose-fitting buttonless upper garment worn esp by Blacks in the US, Africa, and the Caribbean

DASHING adj stylish and attractive

DASHIS ▸ **dashi**

DASHPOT n device for damping vibrations

DASHY adj showy

DASSIE n type of hoofed rodent-like animal

DASSIES ▸ **dassie**

DASTARD n contemptible sneaking coward

DASYPOD n armadillo

DASYURE n small marsupial of Australia, New Guinea, and adjacent islands

DATA n information consisting of observations, measurements, or facts

DATABLE ▸ **date**

DATABUS n computing term

DATAL adj slow-witted ▷ n day labour

DATALS ▸ **datal**

DATARIA n Roman Catholic office

DATARY n head of the dataria, the papal office that assesses candidates for benefices reserved to the Holy See

DATCHA same as ▸ **dacha**

DATCHAS ▸ **datcha**

DATE n specified day of the month ▷ vb mark with the date

DATED adj old-fashioned

DATEDLY ▸ **dated**

DATER n person who dates

DATERS ▸ **dater**

DATES ▸ **date**

DATING n any of several techniques, such as radioactive dating, dendrochronology, or varve dating, for establishing the age of rocks, palaeontological or archaeological specimens, etc

DATINGS ▸ **dating**

DATIVAL ▸ **dative**

DATIVE adj denoting a case of nouns, pronouns, and adjectives used to express the indirect object ▷ n this grammatical case

DATIVES ▸ **dative**

DATO n chief of any of certain Muslim tribes in the Philippine Islands

DATOS ▸ **dato**

DATTO n Datsun car

DATTOS ▸ **datto**

DATUM n single piece of information in the form of a fact or statistic

DATUMS ▸ **datum**

DATURA n type of chiefly Indian plant with large trumpet-shaped flowers, prickly pods, and narcotic properties

DATURAS ▸ **datura**

DATURIC ▸ **datura**

DAUB vb smear or spread quickly or clumsily ▷ n crude or badly done painting

DAUBE n braised meat stew

DAUBED ▸ **daub**

DAUBER ▸ **daub**

DAUBERS ▸ **daub**

DAUBERY n act or an instance of daubing

DAUBES ▸ **daube**

DAUBIER ▸ **daub**

DAUBING ▸ **daub**

DAUBRY n unskilful painting

DAUBS ▸ **daub**

DAUBY ▸ **daub**

DAUD n lump or chunk of something ▷ vb (in dialect) whack

DAUDED ▸ **daud**

DAUDING ▸ **daud**

DAUDS ▸ **daud**

DAULT n foster child

D

DAULTS ▸ dault
DAUNDER vb stroll
DAUNER vb stroll
DAUNERS ▸ dauner
DAUNT vb intimidate
DAUNTED ▸ daunt
DAUNTER ▸ daunt
DAUNTON vb dishearten
DAUNTS ▸ daunt
DAUPHIN n (formerly) eldest son of the king of France
DAUR a Scots word for ▸ **dare**
DAURED ▸ daur
DAURING ▸ daur
DAURS ▸ daur
DAUT vb fondle
DAUTED ▸ daut
DAUTIE n darling
DAUTIES ▸ dautie
DAUTING ▸ daut
DAUTS ▸ daut
DAVEN vb pray
DAVENED ▸ daven
DAVENS ▸ daven
DAVIDIA n Chinese shrub
DAVIES ▸ davy
DAVIT n crane, usu one of a pair, at a ship's side, for lowering and hoisting a lifeboat
DAVITS ▸ davit
DAVY n miner's safety lamp
DAW n an archaic, dialect, or poetic name for a jackdaw ▹ vb old word for dawn

This is another name for a **jackdaw**. It is worth remembering that not only does this little word take D, K, N, S and T at the back, to make **dawd, dawk, dawn, daws** and **dawt**, but you can put an A on the front of it to make **adaw**.

DAWAH n practice of educating non-Muslims about the message of Islam
DAWAHS ▸ dawah
DAWBAKE n foolish or slow-witted person
DAWBRY n unskilful painting
DAWCOCK n male jackdaw
DAWD vb thump
DAWDED ▸ dawd
DAWDING ▸ dawd
DAWDLE vb walk slowly, lag behind
DAWDLED ▸ dawdle
DAWDLER ▸ dawdle
DAWDLES ▸ dawdle

DAWDS ▸ dawd
DAWED ▸ daw
DAWEN ▸ daw
DAWING ▸ daw
DAWISH ▸ daw
DAWK same as ▸ **dak**
DAWKS ▸ dawk
DAWN n daybreak ▹ vb begin to grow light
DAWNED ▸ dawn
DAWNER vb stroll
DAWNERS ▸ dawner
DAWNEY adj (of a person) dull or slow
DAWNING ▸ dawn
DAWNS ▸ dawn
DAWS ▸ daw
DAWT vb fondle
DAWTED ▸ dawt
DAWTIE n darling
DAWTIES ▸ dawtie
DAWTING ▸ dawt
DAWTS ▸ dawt
DAY n period of 24 hours
DAYAN n senior rabbi, esp one who sits in a religious court
DAYANIM ▸ dayan
DAYANS ▸ dayan
DAYBED n narrow bed with a head piece and sometimes a foot piece and back, for day use
DAYBEDS ▸ daybed
DAYBOAT n small sailing boat with no sleeping accommodation
DAYBOOK n book in which the transactions of each day are recorded as they occur
DAYBOY n boy who attends a boarding school daily, and returns home each evening
DAYBOYS ▸ dayboy
DAYCARE n occupation, treatment, or supervision during the working day for people who might be at risk if left on their own, or whose usual carers need daytime relief
DAYCH vb thatch
DAYCHED ▸ daych
DAYCHES ▸ daych
DAYFLY another name for ▸ **mayfly**
DAYGIRL n a girl who attends boarding school during the day but returns home in the evening
DAYGLO n fluorescent colours

DAYGLOW n fluorescent colours
DAYLILY n any of various plants having lily-like flowers that typically last only one day before being succeeded by others
DAYLIT > daylight
DAYLONG adv lasting the entire day
DAYMARE n bad dream during the day
DAYMARK n navigation aid
DAYNT adj dainty
DAYPACK n small rucksack
DAYROOM n communal living room in a residential institution
DAYS adv during the day, esp regularly
DAYSACK n rucksack
DAYSIDE n side of a planet nearest the sun
DAYSMAN n umpire
DAYSMEN ▸ daysman
DAYSTAR a poetic word for ▸ **sun**
DAYTALE n day labour
DAYTIME n time from sunrise to sunset
DAYWEAR n clothes for everyday or informal wear
DAYWORK n daytime work
DAZE vb stun, by a blow or shock ▹ n state of confusion or shock
DAZED ▸ daze
DAZEDLY ▸ daze
DAZER ▸ daze
DAZERS ▸ daze
DAZES ▸ daze
DAZING ▸ daze
DAZZLE vb impress greatly ▹ n bright light that dazzles
DAZZLED ▸ dazzle
DAZZLER ▸ dazzle
DAZZLES ▸ dazzle
DE prep of or from
DEACON n ordained minister ranking immediately below a priest ▹ vb make a deacon of
DEACONS ▸ deacon
DEAD adj no longer alive ▹ n period during which coldness or darkness is most intense ▹ adv extremely ▹ vb in archaic usage, die or kill
DEADBOY ▸ deadman
DEADED ▸ dead
DEADEN vb make less intense

D

DEADENS ▸ **deaden**
DEADER ▸ **dead**
DEADERS ▸ **dead**
DEADEST ▸ **dead**
DEADEYE n either of a pair of disclike wooden blocks, supported by straps in grooves around them, between which a line is rove so as to draw them together to tighten a shroud
DEADING ▸ **dead**
DEADLY adj likely to cause death ▷ adv extremely
DEADMAN n heavy plate, wall, or block buried in the ground that acts as an anchor for a retaining wall, sheet pile, etc, by a tie connecting the two
DEADMEN ▸ **deadman**
DEADPAN adv showing no emotion or expression ▷ adj deliberately emotionless ▷ n deadpan expression or manner
DEADS ▸ **dead**
DEAF adj unable to hear
DEAFEN vb make deaf, esp temporarily
DEAFENS ▸ **deafen**
DEAFER ▸ **deaf**
DEAFEST ▸ **deaf**
DEAFISH ▸ **deaf**
DEAFLY ▸ **deaf**
DEAIR vb reove air from
DEAIRED ▸ **deair**
DEAIRS ▸ **deair**
DEAL n agreement or transaction ▷ vb inflict (a blow) on ▷ adj of fir or pine
DEALATE adj (of ants and other insects) having lost their wings, esp by biting or rubbing them off after mating ▷ n insect that has shed its wings
DEALER n person whose business involves buying and selling
DEALERS ▸ **dealer**
DEALING ▸ **deal**
DEALS ▸ **deal**
DEALT ▸ **deal**
DEAN n chief administrative official of a college or university faculty ▷ vb punish (a student) by sending them to the dean
DEANED ▸ **dean**
DEANER n shilling
DEANERS ▸ **deaner**

DEANERY n office or residence of a dean
DEANING ▸ **dean**
DEANS ▸ **dean**
DEAR n someone regarded with affection ▷ adj much-loved
DEARE vb harm
DEARED ▸ **deare**
DEARER ▸ **dear**
DEARES ▸ **deare**
DEAREST ▸ **dear**
DEARIE same as ▸ **deary**
DEARIES ▸ **deary**
DEARING ▸ **deare**
DEARLY adv very much
DEARN vb hide
DEARNLY ▸ **dearn**
DEARNS ▸ **dearn**
DEARS ▸ **dear**
DEARTH n inadequate amount, scarcity
DEARTHS ▸ **dearth**
DEARY n term of affection: now often sarcastic or facetious
DEASH vb remove ash from
DEASHED ▸ **deash**
DEASHES ▸ **deash**
DEASIL adv in the direction of the apparent course of the sun ▷ n motion in this direction
DEASILS ▸ **deasil**
DEASIUL n motion towards the sun
DEASOIL n motion towards the sun
DEATH n permanent end of life in a person or animal
DEATHLY adv like death ▷ adj resembling death
DEATHS ▸ **death**
DEATHY ▸ **death**
DEAVE vb deafen
DEAVED ▸ **deave**
DEAVES ▸ **deave**
DEAVING ▸ **deave**
DEAW n dew
DEAWIE ▸ **deaw**
DEAWS ▸ **deaw**
DEAWY ▸ **deaw**
DEB n debutante
DEBACLE n disastrous failure
DEBAG vb remove the trousers from (someone) by force
DEBAGS ▸ **debag**
DEBAR vb prevent, bar
DEBARK vb remove the bark from (a tree)
DEBARKS ▸ **debark**

DEBARS ▸ **debar**
DEBASE vb lower in value, quality, or character
DEBASED ▸ **debase**
DEBASER ▸ **debase**
DEBASES ▸ **debase**
DEBATE n discussion ▷ vb discuss formally
DEBATED ▸ **debate**
DEBATER ▸ **debate**
DEBATES ▸ **debate**
DEBAUCH vb make (someone) bad or corrupt, esp sexually ▷ n instance or period of extreme dissipation
DEBBIER ▸ **debby**
DEBBIES ▸ **debby**
DEBBY n debutante ▷ adj of, or resembling a debutante
DEBE n tin
DEBEAK vb remove part of the beak of poultry to reduce the risk of such habits as feather-picking or cannibalism
DEBEAKS ▸ **debeak**
DEBEARD vb remove beard from mussel
DEBEL vb beat in war
DEBELS ▸ **debel**
DEBES ▸ **debe**
DEBILE adj lacking strength
DEBIT n acknowledgment of a sum owing by entry on the left side of an account ▷ vb charge (an account) with a debt
DEBITED ▸ **debit**
DEBITOR n person in debt
DEBITS ▸ **debit**
DEBONE vb remove bones from
DEBONED ▸ **debone**
DEBONER ▸ **debone**
DEBONES ▸ **debone**
DEBOSH vb debauch
DEBOSS vb carve a design into
DEBOUCH vb move out from a narrow place to a wider one ▷ n outlet or passage, as for the exit of troops
DEBRIDE vb remove dead tissue from
DEBRIEF vb receive a report from (a soldier, diplomat, etc) after an event
DEBRIS n fragments of something destroyed
DEBS ▸ **deb**

DEBT n something owed, esp money

DEBTED adj in debt

DEBTEE n person owed a debt

DEBTEES ▸ debtee

DEBTOR n person who owes money

DEBTORS ▸ debtor

DEBTS ▸ debt

DEBUD same as ▸ disbud

DEBUDS ▸ debud

DEBUG vb find and remove defects in (a computer program) ▷ n something, esp a computer program, that locates and removes defects in a device, system, etc

DEBUGS ▸ debug

DEBUNK vb expose the falseness of

DEBUNKS ▸ debunk

DEBUR vb remove burs from (a piece of machined metal)

DEBURR vb remove burrs from (a workpiece)

DEBURRS ▸ deburr

DEBURS ▸ debur

DEBUS vb unload (goods) or (esp of troops) to alight from a motor vehicle

DEBUSED ▸ debus

DEBUSES ▸ debus

DEBUT n first public appearance of a performer ▷ vb make a debut

DEBUTED ▸ debut

DEBUTS ▸ debut

DEBYE n unit of electric dipole moment

DEBYES ▸ debye

DECAD n ten years

DECADAL ▸ decade

DECADE n period of ten years

DECADES ▸ decade

DECADS ▸ decad

DECAF n decaffeinated coffee ▷ adj decaffeinated

DECAFF n decaffeinated coffee

DECAFFS ▸ decaff

DECAFS ▸ decaf

DECAGON n geometric figure with ten faces

DECAL vb transfer (a design) by decalcomania

DECALED ▸ decal

DECALOG same as > decalogue

DECALS ▸ decal

DECAMP vb depart secretly or suddenly

DECAMPS ▸ decamp

DECANAL adj of or relating to a dean or deanery

DECANE n liquid alkane hydrocarbon

DECANES ▸ decane

DECANI adv be sung by the decanal side of a choir

DECANT vb pour (a liquid) from one container to another

DECANTS ▸ decant

DECAPOD n creature, such as a crab, with five pairs of walking limbs ▷ adj of, relating to, or belonging to these creatures

DECARB vb decoke

DECARBS ▸ decarb

DECARE n ten ares or 1000 square metres

DECARES ▸ decare

DECAY vb become weaker or more corrupt ▷ n process of decaying

DECAYED ▸ decay

DECAYER ▸ decay

DECAYS ▸ decay

DECCIE n decoration

DECCIES ▸ deccie

DECEASE n death

DECEIT n behaviour intended to deceive

DECEITS ▸ deceit

DECEIVE vb mislead by lying

DECENCY n conformity to the prevailing standards of what is right

DECENT adj (of a person) polite and morally acceptable

DECERN vb decree or adjudge

DECERNS ▸ decern

DECIARE n one tenth of an are or 10 square metres

DECIBEL n unit for measuring the intensity of sound

DECIDE vb (cause to) reach a decision

DECIDED adj unmistakable

DECIDER n point, goal, game, etc, that determines who wins a match or championship

DECIDES ▸ decide

DECIDUA n specialized mucous membrane that lines the uterus of some mammals during pregnancy: is shed, with the placenta, at parturition

DECILE n one of nine actual or notional values of a variable dividing its distribution into ten groups with equal frequencies: the ninth decile is the value below which 90% of the population lie

DECILES ▸ decile

DECIMAL n fraction written in the form of a dot followed by one or more numbers ▷ adj relating to or using powers of ten

DECIME n a former French coin

DECIMES ▸ decime

DECK n area of a ship that forms a floor ▷ vb dress or decorate

DECKED adj having a wooden deck or platform

DECKEL same as ▸ deckle

DECKELS ▸ deckel

DECKER ▸ deck

DECKERS ▸ deck

DECKING n wooden platform in a garden

DECKLE n frame used to contain pulp on the mould in the making of handmade paper

DECKLED ▸ deckle

DECKLES ▸ deckle

DECKO n look ▷ vb have a look

DECKOED ▸ decko

DECKOS ▸ decko

DECKS ▸ deck

DECLAIM vb speak loudly and dramatically

DECLARE vb state firmly and forcefully

DECLASS vb lower in social status or position

DECLAW vb remove claws from

DECLAWS ▸ declaw

DECLINE vb become smaller, weaker, or less important ▷ n gradual weakening or loss

DECO adj as in art deco style of art, jewellery, design, etc

DECOCT vb extract the essence from (a substance) by boiling

DECOCTS ▸ decoct

DECODE vb convert from code into ordinary language

DECODED ▸ decode

DECODER ▸ **decode**
DECODES ▸ **decode**
DECOKE n decarbonize
DECOKED ▸ **decoke**
DECOKES ▸ **decoke**
DECOLOR vb bleach
DECOR n style in which a room or house is decorated
DECORS ▸ **decor**
DECORUM n polite and socially correct behaviour
DECOS ▸ **deco**
DECOY n person or thing used to lure someone into danger ▷ vb lure away by means of a trick
DECOYED ▸ **decoy**
DECOYER ▸ **decoy**
DECOYS ▸ **decoy**
DECREE n law made by someone in authority ▷ vb order by decree
DECREED ▸ **decree**
DECREER ▸ **decree**
DECREES ▸ **decree**
DECREET n final judgment or sentence of a court
DECREW vb decrease
DECREWS ▸ **decrew**
DECRIAL ▸ **decry**
DECRIED ▸ **decry**
DECRIER ▸ **decry**
DECRIES ▸ **decry**
DECROWN vb depose
DECRY vb express disapproval of
DECRYPT vb decode (a message) with or without previous knowledge of its key
DECTET n ten musicians
DECTETS ▸ **dectet**
DECUMAN n large wave
DECUPLE vb increase by ten times ▷ n amount ten times as large as a given reference ▷ adj increasing tenfold
DECURIA n group of ten
DECURVE vb curve downwards
DECURY n (in ancient Rome) a body of ten men
DEDAL same as ▸ **daedal**
DEDANS n open gallery at the server's end of the court
DEDIMUS n legal term
DEDUCE vb reach (a conclusion) by reasoning from evidence
DEDUCED ▸ **deduce**
DEDUCES ▸ **deduce**
DEDUCT vb subtract

DEDUCTS ▸ **deduct**
DEE a Scots word for ▸ **die**
DEED n something that is done ▷ vb convey or transfer (property) by deed ▷ adj Scots form of dead
DEEDED ▸ **deed**
DEEDER ▸ **deed**
DEEDEST ▸ **deed**
DEEDFUL adj full of exploits
DEEDIER ▸ **deedy**
DEEDILY ▸ **deedy**
DEEDING ▸ **deed**
DEEDS ▸ **deed**
DEEDY adj hard-working
DEEING ▸ **dee**
DEEJAY n disc jockey ▷ vb work or act as a disc jockey
DEEJAYS ▸ **deejay**
DEEK vb look at
DEELY adj as in **deely boppers** hairband with two bobbing antennae-like attachments
DEEM vb consider, judge
DEEMED ▸ **deem**
DEEMING ▸ **deem**
DEEMS ▸ **deem**
DEEN n din
DEENS ▸ **deen**
DEEP adj extending or situated far down, inwards, backwards, or sideways ▷ n any deep place on land or under water
DEEPEN vb make or become deeper or more intense
DEEPENS ▸ **deepen**
DEEPER ▸ **deep**
DEEPEST ▸ **deep**
DEEPIE n 3D film
DEEPIES ▸ **deepie**
DEEPLY ▸ **deep**
DEEPS ▸ **deep**
DEER n large wild animal, the male of which has antlers
DEERE adj serious
DEERFLY n insect related to the horsefly
DEERLET n ruminant mammal
DEERS ▸ **deer**
DEES ▸ **dee**
DEET n insect-repellent
DEETS ▸ **deet**
DEEV n mythical monster
DEEVE vb deafen
DEEVED ▸ **deeve**
DEEVES ▸ **deeve**
DEEVING ▸ **deeve**
DEEVS ▸ **deev**
DEEWAN n chief of a village in India

DEEWANS ▸ **deewan**
DEF adj very good
DEFACE vb deliberately spoil the appearance of
DEFACED ▸ **deface**
DEFACER ▸ **deface**
DEFACES ▸ **deface**
DEFAME vb attack the good reputation of
DEFAMED ▸ **defame**
DEFAMER ▸ **defame**
DEFAMES ▸ **defame**
DEFANG vb remove the fangs of
DEFANGS ▸ **defang**
DEFAST adj defaced
DEFASTE adj defaced
DEFAT vb remove fat from
DEFATS ▸ **defat**
DEFAULT n failure to do something ▷ vb fail to fulfil an obligation
DEFEAT vb win a victory over ▷ n defeating
DEFEATS ▸ **defeat**
DEFECT n imperfection, blemish ▷ vb desert one's cause or country to join the opposing forces
DEFECTS ▸ **defect**
DEFENCE n resistance against attack
DEFEND vb protect from harm or danger
DEFENDS ▸ **defend**
DEFENSE same as ▸ **defence**
DEFER vb delay (something) until a future time
DEFERS ▸ **defer**
DEFFER ▸ **def**
DEFFEST ▸ **def**
DEFFLY archaic word meaning the same as ▸ **deftly**
DEFFO interj definitely: an expression of agreement or consent
DEFI n challenge
DEFIANT adj marked by resistance or bold opposition, as to authority
DEFICIT n amount by which a sum of money is too small
DEFIED ▸ **defy**
DEFIER ▸ **defy**
DEFIERS ▸ **defy**
DEFIES ▸ **defy**
DEFILE vb treat (something sacred or important) without respect ▷ n narrow valley or pass
DEFILED ▸ **defile**
DEFILER ▸ **defile**
DEFILES ▸ **defile**

DEFINE vb state precisely the meaning of
DEFINED ▸ **define**
DEFINER ▸ **define**
DEFINES ▸ **define**
DEFIS ▸ **defi**
DEFLATE vb (cause to) collapse through the release of air
DEFLEA vb remove fleas from
DEFLEAS ▸ **deflea**
DEFLECT vb (cause to) turn aside from a course
DEFLEX vb turn downwards
DEFO interj (slang) definitely
DEFOAM vb remove foam from
DEFOAMS ▸ **defoam**
DEFOCUS vb put out of focus
DEFOG vb clear of vapour
DEFOGS ▸ **defog**
DEFORCE vb withhold (property, esp land) wrongfully or by force from the rightful owner
DEFORM vb put out of shape or spoil the appearance of
DEFORMS ▸ **deform**
DEFOUL vb defile
DEFOULS ▸ **defoul**
DEFRAG vb defragment
DEFRAGS ▸ **defrag**
DEFRAUD vb cheat out of money, property, etc
DEFRAY vb provide money for (costs or expenses)
DEFRAYS ▸ **defray**
DEFROCK vb deprive (a priest) of priestly status
DEFROST vb make or become free of ice
DEFROZE > **defreeze**
DEFT adj quick and skilful in movement
DEFTER ▸ **deft**
DEFTEST ▸ **deft**
DEFTLY ▸ **deft**
DEFUEL vb remove fuel from
DEFUELS ▸ **defuel**
DEFUNCT adj no longer existing or operative ▷ n deceased person
DEFUND vb stop funds to
DEFUNDS ▸ **defund**
DEFUSE vb remove the fuse of (an explosive device)
DEFUSED ▸ **defuse**
DEFUSER ▸ **defuse**
DEFUSES ▸ **defuse**

DEFUZE same as ▸ **defuse**
DEFUZED ▸ **defuze**
DEFUZES ▸ **defuze**
DEFY vb resist openly and boldly
DEFYING ▸ **defy**
DEG vb water (a plant, etc)
DEGAGE adj unconstrained in manner
DEGAME n tree of South and Central America
DEGAMES ▸ **degame**
DEGAMI same as ▸ **degame**
DEGAMIS ▸ **degami**
DEGAS vb remove gas from (a container, vacuum tube, liquid, adsorbent, etc)
DEGASES ▸ **degas**
DEGAUSS n demagnetize
DEGERM vb remove germs from
DEGERMS ▸ **degerm**
DEGGED ▸ **deg**
DEGGING ▸ **deg**
DEGLAZE vb dilute meat sediments in (a pan) in order to make a sauce or gravy
DEGOUT n disgust
DEGOUTS ▸ **degout**
DEGRADE vb reduce to dishonour or disgrace
DEGRAS n emulsion used for dressing hides
DEGREE n stage in a scale of relative amount or intensity
DEGREED adj having a degree
DEGREES ▸ **degree**
DEGS ▸ **deg**
DEGU n small S American rodent
DEGUM vb remove gum from
DEGUMS ▸ **degum**
DEGUS ▸ **degu**
DEGUST vb taste, esp with care or relish
DEGUSTS ▸ **degust**
DEHISCE vb (of the seed capsules of some plants) to burst open spontaneously
DEHORN vb remove or prevent the growth of the horns of (cattle, sheep, or goats)
DEHORNS ▸ **dehorn**
DEHORT vb dissuade
DEHORTS ▸ **dehort**
DEI ▸ **deus**
DEICE vb to free or be freed of ice

DEICED ▸ **deice**
DEICER ▸ **deice**
DEICERS ▸ **deice**
DEICES ▸ **deice**
DEICIDE n act of killing a god
DEICING ▸ **deice**
DEICTIC adj proving by direct argument
DEID a Scots word for ▸ **dead**
DEIDER ▸ **deid**
DEIDEST ▸ **deid**
DEIDS ▸ **deid**
DEIF a Scots word for ▸ **deaf**
DEIFER ▸ **deif**
DEIFEST ▸ **deif**
DEIFIC adj making divine or exalting to the position of a god
DEIFIED ▸ **deify**
DEIFIER ▸ **deify**
DEIFIES ▸ **deify**
DEIFORM adj having the form or appearance of a god
DEIFY vb treat or worship as a god
DEIGN vb agree (to do something), but as if doing someone a favour
DEIGNED ▸ **deign**
DEIGNS ▸ **deign**
DEIL a Scots word for ▸ **devil**
DEILS ▸ **deil**
DEINDEX vb cause to become no longer index-linked
DEISEAL n clockwise motion
DEISM n belief in God but not in divine revelation
DEISMS ▸ **deism**
DEIST ▸ **deism**
DEISTIC ▸ **deism**
DEISTS ▸ **deism**
DEITIES ▸ **deity**
DEITY n god or goddess
DEIXES ▸ **deixis**
DEIXIS n use or reference of a deictic word
DEJECT vb have a depressing effect on ▷ adj downcast
DEJECTA pl n waste products excreted through the anus
DEJECTS ▸ **deject**
DEJEUNE n lunch
DEKARE n unit of measurement equal to ten ares
DEKARES ▸ **dekare**
DEKE vb (in ice hockey or box lacrosse) to draw (a

D

defending player) out of position by faking a shot or movement ▷ *n* such a shot or movement

DEKED ▸ **deke**

DEKEING ▸ **deke**

DEKES ▸ **deke**

DEKING ▸ **deke**

DEKKO *n* look ▷ *vb* have a look

DEKKOED ▸ **dekko**

DEKKOS ▸ **dekko**

DEL *n* differential operator

DELAINE *n* sheer wool or wool and cotton fabric

DELAPSE *vb* be inherited

DELATE *vb* (formerly) to bring a charge against

DELATED ▸ **delate**

DELATES ▸ **delate**

DELATOR ▸ **delate**

DELAY *vb* put off to a later time ▷ *n* act of delaying

DELAYED ▸ **delay**

DELAYER ▸ **delay**

DELAYS ▸ **delay**

DELE *n* sign indicating that typeset matter is to be deleted ▷ *vb* mark (matter to be deleted) with a dele

DELEAD *vb* remove lead from

DELEADS ▸ **delead**

DELEAVE *vb* separate copies

DELEBLE *adj* able to be deleted

DELED ▸ **dele**

DELEING ▸ **dele**

DELENDA *pl n* items for deleting

DELES ▸ **dele**

DELETE *vb* remove (something written or printed)

DELETED ▸ **delete**

DELETES ▸ **delete**

DELF *n* kind of earthenware

DELFS ▸ **delf**

DELFT *n* tin-glazed earthenware, typically having blue designs on white

DELFTS ▸ **delft**

DELI *n* delicatessen

DELIBLE *adj* able to be deleted

DELICE *n* delicacy

DELICES ▸ **delice**

DELICT *n* wrongful act for which the person injured has the right to a civil remedy

DELICTS ▸ **delict**

DELIGHT *n* (source of) great pleasure ▷ *vb* please greatly

DELIME *vb* remove lime from

DELIMED ▸ **delime**

DELIMES ▸ **delime**

DELIMIT *vb* mark or lay down the limits of

DELIRIA > **delirium**

DELIS ▸ **deli**

DELISH *adj* delicious

DELIST *vb* remove from a list

DELISTS ▸ **delist**

DELIVER *vb* carry (goods etc) to a destination

DELL *n* small wooded hollow

DELLIES ▸ **delly**

DELLS ▸ **dell**

DELLY *n* delicatessen

DELO *an informal word for* > **delegate**

DELOPE *vb* shoot into the air

DELOPED ▸ **delope**

DELOPES ▸ **delope**

DELOS ▸ **delo**

DELOUSE *vb* rid (a person or animal) of lice

DELPH *n* kind of earthenware

DELPHIC *adj* obscure or ambiguous

DELPHIN *n* fatty substance from dolphin oil

DELPHS ▸ **delph**

DELS ▸ **del**

DELT *n* deltoid muscle

DELTA *n* fourth letter in the Greek alphabet

DELTAIC ▸ **delta**

DELTAS ▸ **delta**

DELTIC ▸ **delta**

DELTOID *n* thick muscle forming the rounded contour of the outer edge of the shoulder and acting to raise the arm ▷ *adj* shaped like a Greek capital delta

DELTS ▸ **delt**

DELUDE *vb* deceive

DELUDED ▸ **delude**

DELUDER ▸ **delude**

DELUDES ▸ **delude**

DELUGE *n* great flood ▷ *vb* flood

DELUGED ▸ **deluge**

DELUGES ▸ **deluge**

DELUXE *adj* rich, elegant, superior, or sumptuous

DELVE *vb* research deeply (for information)

DELVED ▸ **delve**

DELVER ▸ **delve**

DELVERS ▸ **delve**

DELVES ▸ **delve**

DELVING ▸ **delve**

DEMAGOG *same as* > **demagogue**

DEMAIN *n* demesne

DEMAINE *n* demesne

DEMAINS ▸ **demain**

DEMAN *vb* reduce the workforce of (a plant, industry, etc)

DEMAND *vb* request forcefully ▷ *n* forceful request

DEMANDS ▸ **demand**

DEMANS ▸ **deman**

DEMARK *vb* demarcate

DEMARKS ▸ **demark**

DEMAST *vb* remove the mast from

DEMASTS ▸ **demast**

DEMAYNE *n* demesne

DEME *n* (in preclassical Greece) the territory inhabited by a tribe

DEMEAN *vb* lower (oneself) in dignity, status, or character

DEMEANE *n* demesne

DEMEANS ▸ **demean**

DEMENT *vb* deteriorate mentally, esp because of old age

DEMENTI *n* denial

DEMENTS ▸ **dement**

DEMERGE *vb* separate a company from another with which it was previously merged

DEMERIT *n* fault, disadvantage ▷ *vb* deserve

DEMERSE *vb* immerse

DEMES ▸ **deme**

DEMESNE *n* land surrounding a house

DEMETON *n* insecticide

DEMIC *adj* of population

DEMIES ▸ **demy**

DEMIGOD *n* being who is part mortal, part god

DEMIREP *n* woman of bad repute, esp a prostitute

DEMISE *n* eventual failure (of something successful) ▷ *vb* transfer for a limited period

DEMISED ▸ **demise**

DEMISES ▸ **demise**

DEMISS *adj* humble

DEMIST *vb* remove condensation from (a windscreen)

DEMISTS ▸ demist

DEMIT *vb* resign (an office, position, etc)

DEMITS ▸ demit

DEMIVEG *n* person who eats poultry and fish, but no red meat ▷ *adj* denoting a person who eats poultry and fish, but no red meat

DEMO *n* demonstration, organized expression of public opinion ▷ *vb* demonstrate

DEMOB *vb* demobilize

DEMOBS ▸ demob

DEMODE *adj* out of fashion

DEMODED *adj* out of fashion

DEMOED ▸ demo

DEMOING ▸ demo

DEMON *n* evil spirit

DEMONIC *adj* evil

DEMONRY ▸ demon

DEMONS ▸ demon

DEMOS *n* people of a nation regarded as a political unit

DEMOSES ▸ demos

DEMOTE *vb* reduce in status or rank

DEMOTED ▸ demote

DEMOTES ▸ demote

DEMOTIC *adj* of the common people ▷ *n* demotic script of ancient Egypt

DEMOUNT *vb* remove (a motor, gun, etc) from its mounting or setting

DEMPT ▸ deem

DEMUR *vb* raise objections or show reluctance ▷ *n* act of demurring

DEMURE *adj* quiet, reserved, and rather shy ▷ *vb* archaic for look demure ▷ *n* archaic for demure look

DEMURED ▸ demure

DEMURER ▸ demure

DEMURES ▸ demure

DEMURS ▸ demur

DEMY *n* size of printing paper, 17½ by 22½ inches (444.5 × 571.5 mm)

DEN *n* home of a wild animal ▷ *vb* live in or as if in a den

DENAR *n* standard monetary unit of Macedonia, divided into 100 deni

DENARI ▸ denar

DENARII > denarius

DENARS ▸ denar

DENARY *adj* calculated by tens

DENAY *vb* deny

DENAYED ▸ denay

DENAYS ▸ denay

DENDRON *same as* > dendrite

DENE *n* narrow wooded valley

DENES ▸ dene

DENET *vb* remove from the Net Book Agreement

DENETS ▸ denet

DENGUE *n* viral disease transmitted by mosquitoes, characterized by headache, fever, pains in the joints, and a rash

DENGUES ▸ dengue

DENI *n* monetary unit of the Former Yugoslav Republic of Macedonia, worth one hundredth of a denar

DENIAL *n* statement that something is not true

DENIALS ▸ denial

DENIED ▸ deny

DENIER *n* unit of weight used to measure the fineness of nylon or silk

DENIERS ▸ denier

DENIES ▸ deny

DENIM *n* hard-wearing cotton fabric, usu blue

DENIMED *adj* wearing denim

DENIMS *pl n* jeans or overalls made of denim

DENIS ▸ deni

DENIZEN *n* inhabitant ▷ *vb* make a denizen

DENNED ▸ den

DENNET *n* carriage for one horse

DENNETS ▸ dennet

DENNING ▸ den

DENOTE *vb* be a sign of

DENOTED ▸ denote

DENOTES ▸ denote

DENS ▸ den

DENSE *adj* closely packed

DENSELY ▸ dense

DENSER ▸ dense

DENSEST ▸ dense

DENSIFY *vb* make or become dense

DENSITY *n* degree to which something is filled or occupied

DENT *n* hollow in the surface of something,

made by hitting it ▷ *vb* make a dent in

DENTAL *adj* of teeth or dentistry ▷ *n* dental consonant

DENTALS ▸ dental

DENTARY *n* lower jawbone with teeth

DENTATE *adj* having teeth or teethlike notches

DENTED ▸ dent

DENTEL *n* architectural term

DENTELS ▸ dentel

DENTEX *n* large predatory fish of Mediterranean and E Atlantic waters, with long sharp teeth and powerful jaws

DENTIL *n* one of a set of small square or rectangular blocks evenly spaced to form an ornamental row, usually under a classical cornice on a building, piece of furniture, etc

DENTILS ▸ dentil

DENTIN *same as* ▸ **dentine**

DENTINE *n* hard dense tissue forming the bulk of a tooth

DENTING ▸ dent

DENTINS ▸ dentin

DENTIST *n* person qualified to practise dentistry

DENTOID *adj* resembling a tooth

DENTS ▸ dent

DENTURE *n* false tooth

DENUDE *vb* remove the covering or protection from

DENUDED ▸ denude

DENUDER ▸ denude

DENUDES ▸ denude

DENY *vb* declare to be untrue

DENYING ▸ deny

DEODAND *n* (formerly) a thing that had caused a person's death and was forfeited to the crown for a charitable purpose: abolished 1862

DEODAR *n* Himalayan cedar with drooping branches

DEODARA *same as* ▸ **deodar**

DEODARS ▸ deodar

DEODATE *n* offering to God

DEONTIC *adj* of or relating to such ethical concepts as obligation and permissibility

DEORBIT vb go out of orbit

DEOXY adj having less oxygen than a specified related compound

DEPAINT vb depict

DEPART vb leave

DEPARTS ▸ depart

DEPECHE n message

DEPEND vb put trust (in)

DEPENDS ▸ depend

DEPERM vb demagnetize

DEPERMS ▸ deperm

DEPICT vb produce a picture of

DEPICTS ▸ depict

DEPLANE vb disembark from an aeroplane

DEPLETE vb use up

DEPLORE vb condemn strongly

DEPLOY vb organize (troops or resources) into a position ready for immediate action

DEPLOYS ▸ deploy

DEPLUME vb deprive of feathers

DEPONE vb declare (something) under oath

DEPONED ▸ depone

DEPONES ▸ depone

DEPORT vb remove forcibly from a country

DEPORTS ▸ deport

DEPOSAL n deposition; giving of testimony under oath

DEPOSE vb remove from an office or position of power

DEPOSED ▸ depose

DEPOSER ▸ depose

DEPOSES ▸ depose

DEPOSIT vb put down ▷ n sum of money paid into a bank account

DEPOT n building where goods or vehicles are kept when not in use ▷ adj (of a drug or drug dose) designed for gradual release from the site of an injection so as to act over a long period

DEPOTS ▸ depot

DEPRAVE vb make morally bad

DEPRESS vb make sad

DEPRIVE vb prevent from (having or enjoying)

DEPSIDE n any ester formed by the condensation of the carboxyl group of one phenolic carboxylic acid with the hydroxyl group of another, found in plant cells

DEPTH n distance downwards, backwards, or inwards

DEPTHS ▸ depth

DEPUTE vb appoint (someone) to act on one's behalf ▷ n deputy

DEPUTED ▸ depute

DEPUTES ▸ depute

DEPUTY n person appointed to act on behalf of another

DEQUEUE vb remove (an item) from a queue of computing tasks

DERAIGN vb contest (a claim, suit, etc)

DERAIL vb cause (a train) to go off the rails ▷ n device designed to make rolling stock or locomotives leave the rails to avoid a collision or accident

DERAILS ▸ derail

DERANGE vb disturb the order or arrangement of

DERAT vb remove rats from

DERATE vb assess the value of (some types of property, such as agricultural land) at a lower rate than others for local taxation

DERATED ▸ derate

DERATES ▸ derate

DERATS ▸ derat

DERAY vb go mad

DERAYED ▸ deray

DERAYS ▸ deray

DERBIES ▸ derby

DERBY n bowler hat

DERE vb injure

DERED ▸ dere

DERES ▸ dere

DERHAM same as ▸ **dirham**

DERHAMS ▸ derham

DERIDE vb treat with contempt or ridicule

DERIDED ▸ deride

DERIDER ▸ deride

DERIDES ▸ deride

DERIG vb remove equipment, e.g. from stage set

DERIGS ▸ derig

DERING ▸ dere

DERIVE vb take or develop (from)

DERIVED ▸ derive

DERIVER ▸ derive

DERIVES ▸ derive

DERM same as ▸ **derma**

DERMA n beef or fowl intestine used as a casing for certain dishes, esp kishke

DERMAL adj of or relating to the skin

DERMAS ▸ derma

DERMIC ▸ dermis

DERMIS another name for ▸ **corium**

DERMOID adj of or resembling skin ▷ n congenital cystic tumour whose walls are lined with epithelium

DERMS ▸ derm

DERN n concealment

DERNFUL adj sorrowful

DERNIER adj last

DERNLY adv sorrowfully

DERNS ▸ dern

DERO n tramp or derelict

DEROS ▸ dero

DERRICK n simple crane ▷ vb raise or lower the jib of (a crane)

DERRIES ▸ derry

DERRIS n E Indian woody climbing plant

DERRO n vagrant

DERROS ▸ derro

DERRY n derelict house, esp one used by tramps, drug addicts, etc

DERTH same as ▸ **dearth**

DERTHS ▸ derth

DERV n diesel oil, when used for road transport

DERVISH n member of a Muslim religious order noted for a frenzied whirling dance

DERVS ▸ derv

DESALT vb desalinate

DESALTS ▸ desalt

DESAND vb remove sand from

DESANDS ▸ desand

DESCALE vb remove a hard coating from inside (a kettle or pipe)

DESCANT n tune played or sung above a basic melody ▷ adj denoting the highest member in a family of musical instruments ▷ vb compose or perform a descant (for a piece of music)

DESCEND vb move down (a slope etc)

DESCENT n descending

DESCRY vb catch sight of

DESEED vb to remove the seeds from (eg a fruit)

DESEEDS ▸ deseed
DESERT n region with little or no vegetation because of low rainfall ▷ vb abandon (a person or place) without intending to return
DESERTS ▸ desert
DESERVE vb be entitled to or worthy of
DESEX n desexualize
DESEXED ▸ desex
DESEXES ▸ desex
DESHI same as ▸ **desi**
DESI adj in Indian English, indigenous or local
DESIGN vb work out the structure or form of (something), by making a sketch or plans ▷ n preliminary drawing
DESIGNS ▸ design
DESINE same as ▸ **design**
DESINED ▸ desine
DESINES ▸ desine
DESIRE vb want very much ▷ n wish, longing
DESIRED ▸ desire
DESIRER ▸ desire
DESIRES ▸ desire
DESIST vb stop (doing something)
DESISTS ▸ desist
DESK n piece of furniture with a writing surface and drawers
DESKILL vb mechanize or computerize (a job) thereby reducing the skill required to do it
DESKING n desks and related furnishings in a given space, eg an office
DESKMAN n police officer in charge in police station
DESKMEN ▸ deskman
DESKS ▸ desk
DESKTOP adj (of a computer) small enough to use at a desk ▷ n denoting a computer system, esp for word processing, that is small enough to use at a desk
DESMAN n either of two molelike amphibious mammals
DESMANS ▸ desman
DESMID n type of mainly unicellular freshwater green alga
DESMIDS ▸ desmid
DESMINE n type of mineral
DESMOID adj resembling a

tendon or ligament ▷ n very firm tumour of connective tissue
DESNOOD vb remove the snood of a turkey poult to reduce the risk of cannibalism
DESORB vb change from an adsorbed state on a surface to a gaseous or liquid state
DESORBS ▸ desorb
DESOXY same as ▸ **deoxy**
DESPAIR n total loss of hope ▷ vb lose hope
DESPISE vb regard with contempt
DESPITE prep in spite of ▷ n contempt ▷ vb show contempt for
DESPOIL vb plunder
DESPOND vb lose heart or hope
DESPOT n person in power who acts unfairly or cruelly
DESPOTS ▸ despot
DESSE n desk
DESSERT n sweet course served at the end of a meal
DESSES ▸ desse
DESTAIN vb remove stain from
DESTINE vb set apart or appoint (for a certain purpose or person, or to do something)
DESTINY n future marked out for a person or thing
DESTOCK vb (of a retailer) to reduce the amount of stock held or cease to stock certain products
DESTROY vb ruin, demolish
DESUGAR vb remove sugar from
DESYNE same as ▸ **design**
DESYNED ▸ desyne
DESYNES ▸ desyne
DETACH vb disengage and separate
DETAIL n individual piece of information ▷ vb list fully
DETAILS ▸ detail
DETAIN vb delay (someone)
DETAINS ▸ detain
DETECT vb notice
DETECTS ▸ detect
DETENT n locking piece of a mechanism, often spring-loaded to check the movement of a wheel in one direction only
DETENTE n easing of tension between nations

DETENTS ▸ detent
DETENU n prisoner
DETENUE n female prisoner
DETENUS ▸ detenu
DETER vb discourage (someone) from doing something by instilling fear or doubt
DETERGE vb wash or wipe away
DETERS ▸ deter
DETEST vb dislike intensely
DETESTS ▸ detest
DETICK vb remove ticks from
DETICKS ▸ detick
DETINUE n action brought by a plaintiff to recover goods wrongfully detained
DETORT vb pervert
DETORTS ▸ detort
DETOUR n route that is not the most direct one ▷ vb deviate or cause to deviate from a direct route or course of action
DETOURS ▸ detour
DETOX n treatment to rid the body of poisonous substances ▷ vb undergo treatment to rid the body of poisonous substances, esp alcohol and drugs
DETOXED ▸ detox
DETOXES ▸ detox
DETRACT vb make (something) seem less good
DETRAIN vb leave or cause to leave a railway train, as passengers, etc
DETRUDE vb force down or thrust away or out
DETUNE vb change pitch of (stringed instrument)
DETUNED ▸ detune
DETUNES ▸ detune
DEUCE vb score deuce in tennis ▷ n score of forty all
DEUCED adj damned
DEUCES ▸ deuce
DEUCING ▸ deuce
DEUS n god
DEUTON old form of > **deuteron**
DEUTONS ▸ deuton
DEUTZIA n shrub with clusters of pink or white flowers
DEV same as ▸ **deva**
⏐ **Dev** is a Sanskrit word for a good spirit; related words are **deev** and **deva**

DEVA n (in Hinduism and Buddhism) divine being or god

DEVALL vb stop

DEVALLS ▸ devall

DEVALUE vb reduce the exchange value of (a currency)

DEVAS ▸ deva

DEVEIN vb remove vein from

DEVEINS ▸ devein

DEVEL same as ▸ **devvel**

DEVELED ▸ devel

DEVELOP vb grow or bring to a later, more elaborate, or more advanced stage

DEVELS ▸ devel

DEVEST variant spelling of ▸ **divest**

DEVESTS ▸ devest

DEVIANT adj (person) deviating from what is considered acceptable behaviour ▹ n person whose behaviour deviates from what is considered to be acceptable

DEVIATE vb differ from others in belief or thought

DEVICE n machine or tool used for a specific task

DEVICES ▸ device

DEVIL n evil spirit ▹ vb prepare (food) with a highly flavoured spiced mixture

DEVILED ▸ devil

DEVILET n young devil

DEVILRY n mischievousness

DEVILS ▸ devil

DEVIOUS adj insincere and dishonest

DEVISAL n act of inventing, contriving, or devising

DEVISE vb work out (something) in one's mind ▹ n disposition of property by will

DEVISED ▸ devise

DEVISEE n person to whom property, esp realty, is devised by will

DEVISER ▸ devise

DEVISES ▸ devise

DEVISOR n person who devises property, esp realty, by will

DEVLING n young devil

DEVOICE vb make (a voiced speech sound) voiceless

DEVOID adj completely lacking (in)

DEVOIR n duty

DEVOIRS ▸ devoir

DEVOLVE vb pass (power or duties) or (of power or duties) be passed to a successor or substitute

DEVON n bland processed meat in sausage form, eaten cold in slices

DEVONS ▸ devon

DEVORE n velvet fabric with a raised pattern created by disintegrating some of the pile with chemicals

DEVORES ▸ devore

DEVOT n devotee

DEVOTE vb apply or dedicate to a particular purpose

DEVOTED adj showing loyalty or devotion

DEVOTEE n person who is very enthusiastic about something

DEVOTES ▸ devote

DEVOTS ▸ devot

DEVOUR vb eat greedily

DEVOURS ▸ devour

DEVOUT adj deeply religious

DEVS ▸ dev

DEVVEL vb strike with blow

DEVVELS ▸ devvel

DEW n drops of water that form on the ground at night from vapour in the air ▹ vb moisten with or as with dew

DEWAN n (formerly in India) the chief minister or finance minister of a state ruled by an Indian prince

DEWANI n post of dewan

DEWANIS ▸ dewani

DEWANNY same as ▸ **dewani**

DEWANS ▸ dewan

DEWAR n as in **dewar flask** type of vacuum flask

DEWARS ▸ dewar

DEWATER vb remove water from

DEWAX vb remove wax from

DEWAXED ▸ dewax

DEWAXES ▸ dewax

DEWCLAW n nonfunctional claw on a dog's leg

DEWDROP n drop of dew

DEWED ▸ dew

DEWFALL n formation of dew

DEWFULL obsolete form of ▸ **due**

DEWIER ▸ dewy

DEWIEST ▸ dewy

DEWILY ▸ dewy

DEWING ▸ dew

DEWITT vb kill, esp hang unlawfully

DEWITTS ▸ dewitt

DEWLAP n loose fold of skin hanging under the throat in dogs, cattle, etc

DEWLAPS ▸ dewlap

DEWLAPT ▸ dewlap

DEWLESS ▸ dew

DEWOOL vb remove wool from

DEWOOLS ▸ dewool

DEWORM vb rid of worms

DEWORMS ▸ deworm

DEWS ▸ dew

DEWY adj moist with or as with dew

DEX n dextroamphetamine

⬛ Short for Dexedrine®, a stimulant drug, this is another of the key words to know for using the X. It can be extended to **dexy** or **dexie**.

DEXES ▸ dex

DEXIE n pill containing dextroamphetamine

DEXIES ▸ dexie

DEXTER adj of or on the right side of a shield, etc, from the bearer's point of view ▹ n small breed of red or black beef cattle, originally from Ireland

DEXTERS ▸ dexter

DEXTRAL adj of, relating to, or located on the right side, esp of the body

DEXTRAN n polysaccharide produced by the action of bacteria on sucrose: used as a substitute for plasma in blood transfusions

DEXTRIN n sticky substance obtained from starch, used as a thickening agent in food

DEXTRO adj dextrorotatory or rotating to the right

DEXY same as ▸ **dexie**

DEY n title given to commanders or (from 1710) governors of the Janissaries of Algiers (1671–1830)

DEYS ▸ dey

DEZINC vb remove zinc from

DEZINCS ▸ dezinc

DHAK n tropical Asian tree with bright red flowers,

which yields a red resin used as an astringent

DHAKS ▸ dhak

DHAL n curry made from lentils or beans

DHALS ▸ dhal

DHAMMA same as ▸ **dharma**

DHAMMAS ▸ dhamma

DHANSAK n any of a variety of Indian dishes consisting of meat or vegetables braised with water or stock and lentils

DHARMA n moral law or behaviour

DHARMAS ▸ dharma

DHARMIC ▸ dharma

DHARNA n (in India) a method of obtaining justice, as the payment of a debt, by sitting, fasting, at the door of the person from whom reparation is sought

DHARNAS ▸ dharna

DHIMMI n non-Muslim living in a state governed by sharia law

DHIMMIS ▸ dhimmi

DHOBI n (in India, Malaya, East Africa, etc, esp formerly) a washerman

DHOBIS ▸ dhobi

DHOL n type of Indian drum

DHOLE n fierce canine mammal of the forests of central and SE Asia, with a reddish-brown coat and rounded ears

DHOLES ▸ dhole

DHOLL same as ▸ **dhal**

DHOLLS ▸ dholl

DHOLS ▸ dhol

DHOOLY same as ▸ **doolie**

DHOORA same as ▸ **durra**

DHOORAS ▸ dhoora

DHOOTI same as ▸ **dhoti**

DHOOTIE same as ▸ **dhoti**

DHOOTIS ▸ dhooti

DHOTI n long loincloth worn by men in India

DHOTIS ▸ dhoti

DHOURRA same as ▸ **durra**

DHOW n Arab sailing ship

DHOWS ▸ dhow

DHURNA same as ▸ **dharna**

DHURNAS ▸ dhurna

DHURRA same as ▸ **durra**

DHURRAS ▸ dhurra

DHURRIE same as ▸ **durrie**

DHUTI same as ▸ **dhoti**

DHUTIS ▸ dhuti

DI ▸ deus

DIABASE n altered dolerite

DIABLE n type of sauce

DIABLES ▸ diable

DIABOLO n game in which one throws and catches a spinning top on a cord fastened to two sticks held in the hands

DIACID n lead plaster

DIACIDS ▸ diacid

DIACT n two-rayed

DIADEM n crown ▷ vb adorn or crown with or as with a diadem

DIADEMS ▸ diadem

DIADROM n complete course of pendulum

DIAGRAM n sketch showing the form or workings of something ▷ vb show in or as if in a diagram

DIAGRID n diagonal structure network

DIAL n face of a clock or watch ▷ vb operate the dial or buttons on a telephone in order to contact (a number)

DIALECT n form of a language spoken in a particular area

DIALED ▸ dial

DIALER ▸ dial

DIALERS ▸ dial

DIALING ▸ dial

DIALIST n dial-maker

DIALLED ▸ dial

DIALLEL n interbreeding among a group of parents

DIALLER ▸ dial

DIALOG same as ▸ **dialogue**

DIALOGS ▸ dialog

DIALS ▸ dial

DIALYSE vb separate by dialysis

DIALYZE same as ▸ **dialyse**

DIAMIDE n compound containing two amido groups

DIAMIN same as ▸ **diamine**

DIAMINE n any chemical compound containing two amino groups in its molecules

DIAMINS ▸ diamin

DIAMOND n exceptionally hard, usu colourless, precious stone ▷ adj (of an anniversary) the sixtieth ▷ vb stud or decorate with diamonds

DIAMYL adj with two amyl groups

DIANDRY n practice of having two husbands

DIANE adj as in steak diane kind of steak

DIANOIA n perception and experience regarded as lower modes of knowledge

DIAPASE same as ▸ **diapason**

DIAPER n nappy ▷ vb decorate with a geometric pattern

DIAPERS ▸ diaper

DIAPIR n anticlinal fold in which the brittle overlying rock has been pierced by material, such as salt, from beneath

DIAPIRS ▸ diapir

DIAPSID n reptile with two holes in rear of skull

DIARCH adj (of a vascular bundle) having two strands of xylem

DIARCHY n government by two states, individuals, etc

DIARIAL ▸ diary

DIARIAN ▸ diary

DIARIES ▸ diary

DIARISE same as ▸ **diarize**

DIARIST n person who writes a diary

DIARIZE vb record in diary

DIARY n (book for) a record of daily events, appointments, or observations

DIASCIA n S African plant, usu with pink flowers

DIASTEM same as ▸ **diastema**

DIASTER n stage in cell division at which the chromosomes are in two groups at the poles of the spindle before forming daughter nuclei

DIATOM n microscopic unicellular alga

DIATOMS ▸ diatom

DIATRON n circuit that uses diodes

DIAXON n bipolar cell

DIAXONS ▸ diaxon

DIAZIN same as ▸ **diazine**

DIAZINE n organic compound

DIAZINS ▸ diazin

DIAZO adj of, or relating to the reproduction of documents using the bleaching action of ultraviolet radiation on diazonium salts ▷ *n* document produced by this method

DIAZOES ▶ **diazo**

DIAZOLE *n* type of organic compound

DIAZOS ▶ **diazo**

DIB *vb* fish by allowing the bait to bob and dip on the surface

DIBASIC *adj* (of an acid, such as sulphuric acid, H_2SO_4) containing two acidic hydrogen atoms

DIBBED ▶ **dib**

DIBBER *same as* ▶ **dibble**

DIBBERS ▶ **dibber**

DIBBING ▶ **dib**

DIBBLE *n* small hand tool used to make holes in the ground for seeds or plants ▷ *vb* make a hole in (the ground) with a dibble

DIBBLED ▶ **dibble**

DIBBLER ▶ **dibble**

DIBBLES ▶ **dibble**

DIBBS *n* money

DIBBUK *variant spelling of* ▶ **dybbuk**

DIBBUKS ▶ **dibbuk**

DIBS ▶ **dib**

DIBUTYL *adj* with two butyl groups

DICAMBA *n* type of weedkiller

DICAST *n* (in ancient Athens) a juror in the popular courts chosen by lot from a list of citizens

DICASTS ▶ **dicast**

DICE *n* small cube each of whose sides has a different number of spots (1 to 6), used in games of chance ▷ *vb* cut (food) into small cubes

DICED ▶ **dice**

DICER ▶ **dice**

DICERS ▶ **dice**

DICES ▶ **dice**

DICEY *adj* dangerous or risky

DICH *interj* archaic expression meaning "may it do"

DICHORD *n* two-stringed musical instrument

DICHT *vb* wipe

DICHTED ▶ **dicht**

DICHTS ▶ **dicht**

DICIER ▶ **dicey**

DICIEST ▶ **dicey**

DICING ▶ **dice**

DICINGS ▶ **dice**

DICKENS *n* euphemism for devil

DICKER *vb* trade (goods) by bargaining ▷ *n* petty bargain or barter

DICKERS ▶ **dicker**

DICKEY *same as* ▶ **dicky**

DICKEYS ▶ **dickey**

DICKIE *same as* ▶ **dicky**

DICKIER ▶ **dicky**

DICKIES ▶ **dicky**

DICKTY *same as* ▶ **dicky**

DICKY *n* false shirt front ▷ *adj* shaky or weak

DICLINY ▶ **diclinous**

DICOT *n* type of flowering plant

DICOTS ▶ **dicot**

DICOTYL *n* a type of flowering plant; dicotyledon

DICT *vb* dictate

DICTA ▶ **dictum**

DICTATE *vb* say aloud for someone else to write down ▷ *n* authoritative command

DICTED ▶ **dict**

DICTIER ▶ **dicty**

DICTING ▶ **dict**

DICTION *n* manner of pronouncing words and sounds

DICTS ▶ **dict**

DICTUM *n* formal statement

DICTUMS ▶ **dictum**

DICTY *adj* conceited; snobbish

DICYCLY ▶ **dicyclic**

DID ▶ **do**

DIDACT *n* instructive person

DIDACTS ▶ **didact**

DIDAKAI *same as* ▶ **didicoy**

DIDAKEI *same as* ▶ **didicoy**

DIDDER *vb* shake with fear

DIDDERS ▶ **didder**

DIDDIER ▶ **diddy**

DIDDIES ▶ **diddy**

DIDDLE *vb* swindle

DIDDLED ▶ **diddle**

DIDDLER ▶ **diddle**

DIDDLES ▶ **diddle**

DIDDLEY *n* worthless amount

DIDDLY *n* worthless amount

DIDDY *n* female breast or nipple ▷ *adj* of or relating to a diddy

DIDICOI *same as* ▶ **didicoy**

DIDICOY *n* (in Britain) one

of a group of caravan-dwelling roadside people who live like Gypsies but are not true Romanies

DIDIE *same as* ▶ **didy**

DIDIES ▶ **didy**

DIDO *n* antic

DIDOES ▶ **dido**

DIDOS ▶ **dido**

DIDST *form of the past tense of* ▶ **do**

DIDY *n* woman's breast

DIE *vb* (of a person, animal, or plant) cease all biological activity permanently ▷ *n* shaped block used to cut or form metal

DIEB *n* N African jackal

DIEBACK *n* disease of trees and shrubs characterized by death of the young shoots, which spreads to the larger branches: caused by injury to the roots or attack by bacteria or fungi ▷ *vb* (of plants) to suffer from dieback

DIEBS ▶ **dieb**

DIED ▶ **die**

DIEDRAL *same as* ▶ **dihedral**

DIEDRE *n* large shallow groove or corner in a rock face

DIEDRES ▶ **diedre**

DIEHARD *n* person who resists change or who holds on to an outdated attitude

DIEING ▶ **die**

DIEL *n* 24-hour period

DIENE *n* hydrocarbon that contains two carbon-to-carbon double bonds in its molecules

DIENES ▶ **diene**

DIEOFF *n* process of dying in large numbers

DIEOFFS ▶ **dieoff**

DIES ▶ **die**

DIESEL *vb* drive diesel-fueled vehicle ▷ *n* diesel engine

DIESELS ▶ **diesel**

DIESES ▶ **diesis**

DIESIS *n* (in ancient Greek theory) any interval smaller than a whole tone, esp a semitone in the Pythagorean scale

DIESTER *n* synthetic lubricant

DIET *n* food that a person or animal regularly eats ▷ *vb* follow a special diet so as to

lose weight ▷ *adj* (of food)
suitable for a weight-
reduction diet

DIETARY *adj* of or relating to
a diet ▷ *n* regulated diet

DIETED ▸ **diet**

DIETER ▸ **diet**

DIETERS ▸ **diet**

DIETHER *n* chemical
compound

DIETHYL *adj as in* **diethyl
ether** ether

DIETINE *n* low-ranking diet

DIETING ▸ **diet**

DIETIST *another word for*
> **dietitian**

DIETS ▸ **diet**

DIF *same as* ▸ **diff**

DIFF *n* (slang) difference

DIFFER *vb* be unlike

DIFFERS ▸ **differ**

DIFFORM *adj* irregular in
form

DIFFS ▸ **diff**

DIFFUSE *vb* spread over a
wide area ▷ *adj* widely
spread

DIFS ▸ **dif**

DIG *vb* cut into, break up,
and turn over or remove
(earth), esp with a spade
▷ *n* digging

DIGAMMA *n* letter of the
Greek alphabet that
became obsolete before the
classical period of the
language.

DIGAMY *n* second marriage
contracted after the
termination of the first by
death or divorce

DIGEST *vb* subject to a
process of digestion ▷ *n*
shortened version of a
book, report, or article

DIGESTS ▸ **digest**

DIGGED *a past tense of* ▸ **dig**

DIGGER *n* machine used for
digging

DIGGERS ▸ **digger**

DIGGING ▸ **dig**

DIGHT *vb* adorn or equip, as
for battle

DIGHTED ▸ **dight**

DIGHTS ▸ **dight**

DIGICAM *n* digital camera

DIGIT *n* finger or toe

DIGITAL *adj* displaying
information as numbers
rather than with hands and
a dial ▷ *n* one of the keys on
the manuals of an organ or
on a piano, harpsichord, etc

DIGITS ▸ **digit**

DIGLOT *n* bilingual book

DIGLOTS ▸ **diglot**

DIGLYPH *n* ornament in
Doric frieze with two
grooves

DIGNIFY *vb* add distinction to

DIGNITY *n* serious, calm,
and controlled behaviour or
manner

DIGONAL *adj* of or relating
to a symmetry operation in
which the original figure is
reconstructed after a 180°
turn about an axis

DIGOXIN *n* glycoside
extracted from the leaves of
the woolly foxglove

DIGRAPH *n* two letters used
to represent a single sound,
such as *gh* in *tough*

DIGRESS *vb* depart from the
main subject in speech or
writing

DIGS ▸ **dig**

DIHEDRA > **dihedron**

DIKA *n* wild mango

DIKAS ▸ **dika**

DIKAST *same as* ▸ **dicast**

DIKASTS ▸ **dikast**

DIKDIK *n* small African
antelope

DIKDIKS ▸ **dikdik**

DIKE *same as* ▸ **dyke**

DIKED ▸ **dike**

DIKER *n* builder of dikes

DIKERS ▸ **diker**

DIKES ▸ **dike**

DIKING ▸ **dike**

DIKKOP *n* type of brownish
shore bird with a large head
and eyes

DIKKOPS ▸ **dikkop**

DIKTAT *n* dictatorial decree

DIKTATS ▸ **diktat**

DILATE *vb* make or become
wider or larger

DILATED ▸ **dilate**

DILATER *same as* ▸ **dilator**

DILATES ▸ **dilate**

DILATOR *n* something that
dilates an object, esp a
surgical instrument for
dilating a bodily cavity

DILDO *n* object used as a
substitute for an erect penis

DILDOE *same as* ▸ **dildo**

DILDOES ▸ **dildoe**

DILDOS ▸ **dildo**

DILEMMA *n* situation
offering a choice between
two equally undesirable
alternatives

DILL *vb* flavour with dill ▷ *n*
sweet-smelling herb

DILLED ▸ **dill**

DILLI *n* dilly bag; small bag,
esp one made of plaited
grass and used for carrying
food

DILLIER ▸ **dilly**

DILLIES ▸ **dilly**

DILLING ▸ **dill**

DILLIS ▸ **dilli**

DILLS ▸ **dill**

DILLY *adj* foolish ▷ *n* person
or thing that is remarkable

DILUENT *adj* causing
dilution or serving to dilute
▷ *n* substance used for or
causing dilution

DILUTE *vb* make (a liquid)
less concentrated, esp by
adding water ▷ *adj* (of a
liquid) thin and watery

DILUTED ▸ **dilute**

DILUTEE ▸ **dilute**

DILUTER ▸ **dilute**

DILUTES ▸ **dilute**

DILUTOR *n* thing intended
to have a diluting effect

DILUVIA > **diluvium**

DIM *adj* badly lit ▷ *vb* make
or become dim

DIMBLE *n* wooded hollow;
dingle

DIMBLES ▸ **dimble**

DIME *n* coin of the US and
Canada, worth ten cents

DIMER *n* molecule made up
of two identical molecules
bonded together

DIMERIC *adj* of a dimer

DIMERS ▸ **dimer**

DIMES ▸ **dime**

DIMETER *n* line of verse
consisting of two metrical
feet or a verse written in
this metre

DIMITY *n* light strong
cotton fabric with woven
stripes or squares

DIMLY ▸ **dim**

DIMMED ▸ **dim**

DIMMER ▸ **dim**

DIMMERS ▸ **dim**

DIMMEST ▸ **dim**

DIMMING *n as in* **global
dimming** decrease in the
amount of sunlight
reaching the earth

DIMMISH ▸ **dim**

DIMNESS ▸ **dim**

DIMORPH *n* either of two
forms of a substance that
exhibits dimorphism

DIMOUT *n* reduction of lighting

DIMOUTS ▸ **dimout**

DIMP *n* in Northern English dialect, a cigarette butt

DIMPLE *n* small natural dent, esp in the cheeks or chin ▸ *vb* produce dimples by smiling

DIMPLED ▸ **dimple**

DIMPLES ▸ **dimple**

DIMPLY ▸ **dimple**

DIMPS ▸ **dimp**

DIMPSY *n* twilight

DIMS ▸ **dim**

DIMWIT *n* stupid person

DIMWITS ▸ **dimwit**

DIN *n* loud unpleasant confused noise ▸ *vb* instil (something) into someone by constant repetition

DINAR *n* monetary unit of various Balkan, Middle Eastern, and North African countries

DINARS ▸ **dinar**

DINDLE *another word for* ▸ **dinnle**

DINDLED ▸ **dindle**

DINDLES ▸ **dindle**

DINE *vb* eat dinner

DINED ▸ **dine**

DINER *n* person eating a meal

DINERIC *adj* of or concerned with the interface between immiscible liquids

DINERO *n* money

DINEROS ▸ **dinero**

DINERS ▸ **diner**

DINES ▸ **dine**

DINETTE *n* alcove or small area for use as a dining room

DINFUL *adj* noisy

DING *n* small dent in a vehicle ▸ *vb* ring or cause to ring, esp with tedious repetition

DINGBAT *n* any unnamed object, esp one used as a missile

DINGE *n* dent ▸ *vb* make a dent in (something)

DINGED ▸ **dinge**

DINGER *n* (in baseball) home run

DINGERS ▸ **dinger**

DINGES *n* jocular word for something whose name is unknown or forgotten

DINGEY *same as* ▸ **dinghy**

DINGEYS ▸ **dingey**

DINGHY *n* small boat, powered by sails, oars, or a motor ▸ *vb* ignore or avoid a person or event

DINGIED ▸ **dingey**

DINGIER ▸ **dingy**

DINGIES ▸ **dingy**

DINGILY ▸ **dingy**

DINGING ▸ **dinge**

DINGLE *n* small wooded hollow or valley

DINGLES ▸ **dingle**

DINGO *n* Australian wild dog ▸ *vb* act in a cowardly manner

DINGOED ▸ **dingo**

DINGOES ▸ **dingo**

DINGS ▸ **ding**

DINGUS *same as* ▸ **dinges**

DINGY *adj* lacking light ▸ *vb* ignore or avoid a person or event

DINIC *n* remedy for vertigo

DINICS ▸ **dinic**

DINING ▸ **dine**

DINITRO *adj* containing two nitro groups

DINK *adj* neat or neatly dressed ▸ *vb* carry (a second person) on a horse, bicycle, etc ▸ *n* ball struck delicately

DINKED ▸ **dink**

DINKER ▸ **dink**

DINKEST ▸ **dink**

DINKEY *n* small locomotive

DINKEYS ▸ **dinkey**

DINKIE *n* affluent married childless person ▸ *adj* designed for or appealing to dinkies

DINKIER ▸ **dinky**

DINKIES ▸ **dinkie**

DINKING ▸ **dink**

DINKLY *adj* neat

DINKS ▸ **dink**

DINKUM *n* truth or genuineness

DINKUMS ▸ **dinkum**

DINKY *adj* small and neat

DINMONT *n* neutered sheep

DINNA *vb* a Scots word for do not

DINNAE *vb* (Scots) do not

DINNED ▸ **din**

DINNER *vb* dine ▸ *n* main meal of the day, eaten either in the evening or at midday

DINNERS ▸ **dinner**

DINNING ▸ **din**

DINNLE *vb* shake

DINNLED ▸ **dinnle**

DINNLES ▸ **dinnle**

DINO *n* dinosaur

DINOS ▸ **dino**

DINS ▸ **din**

DINT *same as* ▸ **dent**

DINTED ▸ **dint**

DINTING ▸ **dint**

DINTS ▸ **dint**

DIOBOL *n* ancient Greek coin

DIOBOLS ▸ **diobol**

DIOCESE *n* district over which a bishop has control

DIODE *n* semiconductor device for converting alternating current to direct current

DIODES ▸ **diode**

DIOECY *n* state of being dioecious

DIOL *n* any of a class of alcohols that have two hydroxyl groups in each molecule

DIOLS ▸ **diol**

DIOPTER *same as* ▸ **dioptre**

DIOPTRE *n* unit for measuring the refractive power of a lens

DIORAMA *n* miniature three-dimensional scene, in which models of figures are seen against a three-dimensional background

DIORISM *n* definition; clarity

DIORITE *n* dark coarse-grained igneous plutonic rock consisting of plagioclase feldspar and ferromagnesian minerals such as hornblende

DIOTA *n* type of ancient vase

DIOTAS ▸ **diota**

DIOXAN *n* colourless insoluble toxic liquid made by heating ethanediol with sulphuric acid

DIOXANE *same as* ▸ **dioxan**

DIOXANS ▸ **dioxan**

DIOXID *same as* ▸ **dioxide**

DIOXIDE *n* oxide containing two oxygen atoms per molecule

DIOXIDS ▸ **dioxid**

DIOXIN *n* any of a number of mostly poisonous chemical by-products of certain weedkillers

DIOXINS ▸ **dioxin**

DIP vb plunge quickly or briefly into a liquid ▷ n dipping

DIPHASE adj of, having, or concerned with two phases

DIPHONE n combination of two speech sounds

DIPLEX adj (in telecommunications) permitting the transmission of simultaneous signals in both directions

DIPLOE n spongy bone separating the two layers of compact bone of the skull

DIPLOES ▸ diploe

DIPLOIC adj relating to diploe

DIPLOID adj denoting a cell or organism with pairs of homologous chromosomes ▷ n diploid cell or organism

DIPLOMA vb bestow diploma on ▷ n qualification awarded by a college on successful completion of a course

DIPLON another name for > deuteron

DIPLONS ▸ diplon

DIPLONT n animal or plant that has the diploid number of chromosomes in its somatic cells

DIPNET vb fish using fishing net on pole

DIPNETS ▸ dipnet

DIPNOAN n lungfish

DIPODIC ▸ dipody

DIPODY n metrical unit consisting of two feet

DIPOLAR ▸ dipole

DIPOLE n two equal but opposite electric charges or magnetic poles separated by a small distance

DIPOLES ▸ dipole

DIPPED ▸ dip

DIPPER n ladle used for dipping

DIPPERS ▸ dipper

DIPPIER ▸ dippy

DIPPING ▸ dip

DIPPY adj odd, eccentric, or crazy

DIPS ▸ dip

DIPSAS n type of snake

DIPSHIT n stupid person

DIPSO n (slang) dipsomaniac or alcoholic

DIPSOS ▸ dipso

DIPT ▸ dip

DIPTERA n order of insects with two wings

DIPTYCA same as ▸ diptych

DIPTYCH n painting on two hinged panels

DIQUARK n low-energy configuration of two quarks attracted to one another by virtue of having antisymmetric colours and spins

DIQUAT n type of herbicide

DIQUATS ▸ diquat

DIRAM n money unit of Tajikistan

DIRAMS ▸ diram

DIRDAM same as ▸ dirdum

DIRDAMS ▸ dirdum

DIRDUM n tumult

DIRDUMS ▸ dirdum

DIRE adj disastrous, urgent, or terrible

DIRECT adj (of a route) shortest, straight ▷ adv in a direct manner ▷ vb lead and organize

DIRECTS ▸ direct

DIREFUL same as ▸ dire

DIRELY ▸ dire

DIREMPT vb separate with force

DIRER ▸ dire

DIREST ▸ dire

DIRGE n slow sad song of mourning

DIRGES ▸ dirge

DIRHAM n standard monetary unit of Morocco, divided into 100 centimes

DIRHAMS ▸ dirham

DIRHEM same as ▸ dirham

DIRHEMS ▸ dirhem

DIRIGE n dirge

DIRIGES ▸ dirige

DIRK n dagger, formerly worn by Scottish Highlanders ▷ vb stab with a dirk

DIRKE same as ▸ dirk

DIRKED ▸ dirk

DIRKES ▸ dirke

DIRKING ▸ dirk

DIRKS ▸ dirk

DIRL vb tingle; vibrate

DIRLED ▸ dirl

DIRLING ▸ dirl

DIRLS ▸ dirl

DIRNDL n full gathered skirt originating from Tyrolean peasant wear

DIRNDLS ▸ dirndl

DIRT vb soil ▷ n unclean substance, filth

DIRTBAG n filthy person

DIRTED ▸ dirt

DIRTIED ▸ dirty

DIRTIER ▸ dirty

DIRTIES ▸ dirty

DIRTILY ▸ dirty

DIRTING ▸ dirt

DIRTS ▸ dirt

DIRTY adj covered or marked with dirt ▷ vb make dirty

DIS same as ▸ diss

DISA n type of orchid

DISABLE vb make ineffective, unfit, or incapable

DISALLY vb separate

DISARM vb deprive of weapons

DISARMS ▸ disarm

DISAS ▸ disa

DISAVOW vb deny connection with or responsibility for

DISBAND vb (cause to) cease to function as a group

DISBAR vb deprive (a barrister) of the right to practise

DISBARK same as > disembark

DISBARS ▸ disbar

DISBUD vb remove superfluous buds, flowers, or shoots from (a plant, esp a fruit tree)

DISBUDS ▸ disbud

DISC n flat circular object ▷ vb work (land) with a disc harrow

DISCAGE vb release from cage

DISCAL adj relating to or resembling a disc

DISCANT same as ▸ descant

DISCARD vb get rid of (something or someone) as useless or undesirable ▷ n person or thing that has been cast aside

DISCASE vb remove case from

DISCED ▸ disc

DISCEPT vb discuss

DISCERN vb see or be aware of (something) clearly

DISCERP vb divide

DISCI ▸ discus

DISCIDE vb split

DISCING ▸ disc

DISCO vb go to a disco ▷ n nightclub where people dance to amplified pop records

D

D

DISCOED ▸ disco
DISCOER ▸ disco
DISCOID adj like a disc ▷ n disclike object
DISCORD n lack of agreement or harmony between people ▷ vb disagree
DISCOS ▸ disco
DISCS ▸ disc
DISCURE old form of > discover
DISCUS n heavy disc-shaped object thrown in sports competitions
DISCUSS vb consider (something) by talking it over
DISDAIN n feeling of superiority and dislike ▷ vb refuse with disdain
DISEASE vb make uneasy ▷ n illness, sickness
DISEDGE vb render blunt
DISEUR same as ▸ diseuse
DISEURS ▸ diseur
DISEUSE n (esp formerly) an actress who presents dramatic recitals, usually sung accompanied by music
DISFAME n discredit
DISFORM vb change form of
DISGEST vb digest
DISGOWN vb remove gown from
DISGUST n great loathing or distaste ▷ vb sicken, fill with loathing
DISH n shallow container used for holding or serving food ▷ vb put into a dish
DISHED adj shaped like a dish
DISHELM vb remove helmet from
DISHES ▸ dish
DISHFUL n the amount that a dish is able to hold
DISHIER ▸ dishy
DISHING ▸ dish
DISHOME vb deprive of home
DISHORN vb remove horns from
DISHPAN n large pan for washing dishes, pots, etc
DISHRAG n dishcloth
DISHY adj good-looking
DISJECT vb break apart
DISJOIN vb disconnect or become disconnected

DISJUNE n breakfast
DISK same as ▸ disc
DISKED ▸ disk
DISKING ▸ disk
DISKS ▸ disk
DISLEAF vb remove leaf or leaves from
DISLEAL archaic form of > disloyal
DISLIKE vb consider unpleasant or disagreeable ▷ n feeling of not liking something or someone
DISLIMB vb remove limbs from
DISLIMN vb efface
DISLINK vb disunite
DISLOAD vb unload
DISMAL adj gloomy and depressing
DISMALS pl n gloomy state of mind
DISMAN vb remove men from
DISMANS ▸ disman
DISMASK vb remove mask from
DISMAST vb break off the mast or masts of (a sailing vessel)
DISMAY vb fill with alarm or depression ▷ n alarm mixed with sadness
DISMAYD ▸ dismay
DISMAYL vb remove a coat of mail from
DISMAYS ▸ dismay
DISME old form of ▸ dime
DISMES ▸ disme
DISMISS vb remove (an employee) from a job ▷ sentence substitute order to end an activity or give permission to disperse
DISNEST vb remove from nest
DISOBEY vb neglect or refuse to obey
DISOMIC adj having an extra chromosome in the haploid state that is homologous to an existing chromosome in this set
DISOMY ▸ disomic
DISOWN vb deny any connection with (someone)
DISOWNS ▸ disown
DISPACE vb move or travel about
DISPARK vb release
DISPART vb separate
DISPEL vb destroy or remove

DISPELS ▸ dispel
DISPEND vb spend
DISPLAY vb make visible or noticeable ▷ n displaying
DISPLE vb punish
DISPLED ▸ disple
DISPLES ▸ disple
DISPONE vb transfer ownership
DISPORT vb indulge (oneself) in pleasure ▷ n amusement
DISPOSE vb place in a certain order
DISPOST vb remove from post
DISPRAD old form of > dispread
DISPRED old spelling of > dispread
DISPUTE n disagreement, argument ▷ vb argue about (something)
DISRANK vb demote
DISRATE vb punish (an officer) by lowering in rank
DISROBE vb undress
DISROOT vb uproot
DISRUPT vb interrupt the progress of
DISS vb treat (a person) with contempt
DISSAVE vb spend savings
DISSEAT vb unseat
DISSECT vb cut open (a corpse) to examine it
DISSED ▸ diss
DISSENT vb disagree ▷ n disagreement
DISSERT n give or make a dissertation; dissertate
DISSES ▸ diss
DISSING ▸ diss
DISTAFF n rod on which wool etc is wound for spinning
DISTAIN vb stain; tarnish
DISTAL adj (of a muscle, bone, limb, etc) situated farthest from the centre, median line, or point of attachment or origin
DISTANT adj far apart
DISTEND vb (of part of the body) swell
DISTENT adj bloated; swollen
DISTICH n unit of two verse lines
DISTIL vb subject to or obtain by distillation
DISTILL same as ▸ distil
DISTILS ▸ distil

DISTOME n parasitic flatworm

DISTORT vb misrepresent (the truth or facts)

DISTRIX n splitting of the ends of hairs

DISTUNE vb cause to be out of tune

DISTURB vb intrude on

DISTYLE n temple with two columns

DISUSE vb stop using ▷ n state of being no longer used

DISUSED adj no longer used

DISUSES ▸ disuse

DISYOKE vb unyoke

DIT vb stop something happening ▷ n short sound used, in combination with the long sound in the spoken representation of Morse and other telegraphic codes

DITA n tropical African and Asian shrub with large shiny whorled leaves and medicinal bark

DITAL n key for raising pitch of lute string

DITALS ▸ dital

DITAS ▸ dita

DITCH n narrow channel dug in the earth for drainage or irrigation ▷ vb abandon

DITCHED ▸ ditch

DITCHER ▸ ditch

DITCHES ▸ ditch

DITE vb set down in writing

DITED ▸ dite

DITES ▸ dite

DITHER vb be uncertain or indecisive ▷ n state of indecision or agitation

DITHERS ▸ dither

DITHERY ▸ dither

DITHIOL n chemical compound

DITING ▸ dite

DITONE n interval of two tones

DITONES ▸ ditone

DITS ▸ dit

DITSIER ▸ ditsy

DITSY same as ▸ ditzy

DITT same as ▸ dit

DITTANY n aromatic Cretan plant with pink drooping flowers, formerly credited with great medicinal properties

DITTAY n accusation; charge

DITTAYS ▸ dittay

DITTED ▸ dit

DITTIED ▸ ditty

DITTIES ▸ ditty

DITTING ▸ dit

DITTIT ▸ dit

DITTO n same ▷ adv in the same way ▷ sentence substitute used to avoid repeating or to confirm agreement with an immediately preceding sentence ▷ vb copy

DITTOED ▸ ditto

DITTOS ▸ ditto

DITTS ▸ ditt

DITTY vb set to music ▷ n short simple poem or song

DITZ n silly scatterbrained person

DITZES ▸ ditz

DITZIER ▸ ditzy

DITZY adj silly and scatterbrained

DIURNAL adj happening during the day or daily ▷ n service book containing all the canonical hours except matins

DIURON n type of herbicide

DIURONS ▸ diuron

DIV n stupid or foolish person

DIVA n distinguished female singer

DIVAN n low backless bed

DIVANS ▸ divan

DIVAS ▸ diva

DIVE vb plunge headfirst into water ▷ n diving

DIVED ▸ dive

DIVER n person who works or explores underwater

DIVERGE vb separate and go in different directions

DIVERS adj various ▷ determiner various

DIVERSE vb turn away ▷ adj having variety, assorted

DIVERT vb change the direction of

DIVERTS ▸ divert

DIVES ▸ dive

DIVEST vb strip (of clothes)

DIVESTS ▸ divest

DIVI alternative spelling of ▸ divvy

DIVIDE vb separate into parts ▷ n division, split

DIVIDED adj split

DIVIDER n screen used to divide a room into separate areas

DIVIDES ▸ divide

DIVIED ▸ divvied

DIVINE adj of God or a god ▷ vb discover (something) by intuition or guessing ▷ n priest who is learned in theology

DIVINED ▸ divine

DIVINER ▸ divine

DIVINES ▸ divine

DIVING ▸ dive

DIVINGS ▸ dive

DIVIS ▸ divi

DIVISIM adv separately

DIVISOR n number to be divided into another number

DIVNA vb do not

DIVO n male diva

DIVORCE n legal ending of a marriage ▷ vb legally end one's marriage (to)

DIVOS ▸ divo

DIVOT n small piece of turf

DIVOTS ▸ divot

DIVS ▸ div

DIVULGE vb make known, disclose

DIVULSE vb tear apart

DIVVIED ▸ divvy

DIVVIER ▸ divvy adj

DIVVIES ▸ divvy

DIVVY vb divide and share ▷ adj stupid ▷ n stupid person

DIVVYING ▸ divvying

DIWAN same as ▸ dewan

DIWANS ▸ diwan

DIXI interj I have spoken

DIXIE n large metal pot for cooking, brewing tea, etc

DIXIES ▸ dixie

DIXIT n statement

DIXITS ▸ dixit

DIXY same as ▸ dixie

DIYA n small oil lamp, usu made from clay

DIYAS ▸ diya

DIZAIN n ten-line poem

DIZAINS ▸ dizain

DIZEN archaic word for ▸ bedizen

DIZENED ▸ dizen

DIZENS ▸ dizen

DIZZARD n dunce

DIZZIED ▸ dizzy

DIZZIER ▸ dizzy

DIZZIES ▸ dizzy

DIZZILY ▸ dizzy

DIZZY adj having or causing a whirling sensation ▷ vb make dizzy

DJEBEL a variant spelling of ▸ jebel

DJEBELS ▸ djebel

DJEMBE n W African drum played by beating with the hand

DJEMBES ▸ djembe

DJIBBAH same as ▸ jubbah

DJIN same as ▸ jinn

DJINN ▸ djinni

DJINNI same as ▸ jinni

DJINNS ▸ djinn

DJINNY same as ▸ jinni

DJINS ▸ djin

DO vb perform or complete (a deed or action) ▷ n party, celebration

DOAB n alluvial land between two converging rivers, esp the area between the Ganges and Jumna in N India

DOABLE adj capable of being done

DOABS ▸ doab

DOAT same as ▸ dote

DOATED ▸ doat

DOATER ▸ doat

DOATERS ▸ doat

DOATING ▸ doat

DOATS ▸ doat

DOB vb as in dob in inform against or report

DOBBED ▸ dob

DOBBER n informant or traitor

DOBBERS ▸ dobber

DOBBIE same as ▸ dobby

DOBBIES ▸ dobby

DOBBIN n name for a horse, esp a workhorse, often used in children's tales, etc

DOBBING ▸ dob

DOBBINS ▸ dobbin

DOBBY n attachment to a loom, used in weaving small figures

DOBHASH n interpreter

DOBIE n cannabis

DOBIES ▸ dobie

DOBLA n medieval Spanish gold coin, probably worth 20 maravedis

DOBLAS ▸ dobla

DOBLON a variant spelling of ▸ doubloon

DOBLONS ▸ doblon

DOBRA n standard monetary unit of São Tomé e Principe, divided into 100 cêntimos

DOBRAS ▸ dobra

DOBRO n tradename for a type of acoustic guitar having a metal resonator

built into the body

DOBROS ▸ dobro

DOBS ▸ dob

DOBSON n larva of dobsonfly

DOBSONS ▸ dobson

DOBY same as ▸ dobie

DOC same as ▸ doctor

DOCENT n voluntary worker who acts as a guide in a museum, art gallery, etc

DOCENTS ▸ docent

DOCETIC adj believer in docetism: a heresy that the humanity of Christ was apparent rather than real

DOCHMII > dochmius

DOCHT ▸ dow

DOCIBLE adj easily tamed

DOCILE adj (of a person or animal) easily controlled

DOCILER ▸ docile

DOCK n enclosed area of water where ships are loaded, unloaded, or repaired ▷ vb bring or be brought into dock

DOCKAGE n charge levied upon a vessel for using a dock

DOCKED ▸ dock

DOCKEN n something of no value or importance

DOCKENS ▸ docken

DOCKER n person employed to load and unload ships

DOCKERS ▸ docker

DOCKET n label on a package or other delivery, stating contents, delivery instructions, etc ▷ vb fix a docket to (a package or other delivery)

DOCKETS ▸ docket

DOCKING ▸ dock

DOCKISE same as ▸ dockize

DOCKIZE vb convert into docks

DOCKS ▸ dock

DOCO n (slang) documentary

DOCOS ▸ doco

DOCQUET same as ▸ docket

DOCS ▸ doc

DOCTOR n person licensed to practise medicine ▷ vb alter in order to deceive

DOCTORS ▸ doctor

DOD vb clip

DODDARD adj archaic word for missing branches; rotten

DODDED ▸ dod

DODDER vb move unsteadily ▷ n type of rootless parasitic plant whose twining stems have suckers for drawing nourishment from the host plant

DODDERS ▸ dodder

DODDERY ▸ dodder

DODDIER ▸ doddy

DODDIES ▸ doddy

DODDING ▸ dod

DODDLE n something easily accomplished

DODDLES ▸ doddle

DODDY n bad mood ▷ adj sulky

DODGE vb avoid (a blow, being seen, etc) by moving suddenly ▷ n cunning or deceitful trick

DODGED ▸ dodge

DODGEM n bumper car

DODGEMS ▸ dodgem

DODGER n person who evades a responsibility or duty

DODGERS ▸ dodger

DODGERY n deception

DODGES ▸ dodge

DODGIER ▸ dodgy

DODGING ▸ dodge

DODGY adj dangerous, risky

DODKIN n coin of little value

DODKINS ▸ dodkin

DODMAN n snail

DODMANS ▸ dodman

DODO n large flightless extinct bird

DODOES ▸ dodo

DODOISM ▸ dodo

DODOS ▸ dodo

DODS ▸ dod

DOE n female deer, hare, or rabbit

DOEK n square of cloth worn on the head by women

DOEKS ▸ doek

DOEN ▸ do

DOER n active or energetic person

DOERS ▸ doer

DOES ▸ do

DOESKIN n skin of a deer, lamb, or sheep

DOEST ▸ do

DOETH ▸ do

DOF informal South African word for ▸ stupid

DOFF vb take off or lift (one's

hat) in polite greeting

DOFFED ▷ **doff**

DOFFER ▷ **doff**

DOFFERS ▷ **doff**

DOFFING ▷ **doff**

DOFFS ▷ **doff**

DOG n domesticated four-legged mammal of many different breeds ▷ vb follow (someone) closely

DOGATE n office of doge

DOGATES ▷ **dogate**

DOGBANE n N American plant with bell-shaped white or pink flowers, thought to be poisonous to dogs

DOGBOLT n bolt on cannon

DOGCART n light horse-drawn two-wheeled cart

DOGDOM n world of dogs

DOGDOMS ▷ **dogdom**

DOGE n (formerly) chief magistrate of Venice or Genoa

DOGEAR vb fold down the corner of (a page) ▷ n folded-down corner of a page

DOGEARS ▷ **dogear**

DOGEATE n office of doge

DOGEDOM n domain of doge

DOGES ▷ **doge**

DOGEY same as ▷ **dogie**

DOGEYS ▷ **dogey**

DOGFACE n WW2 US soldier

DOGFISH n small shark

DOGFOX n male fox

DOGGED ▷ **dog**

DOGGER n Dutch fishing vessel with two masts

DOGGERS ▷ **dogger**

DOGGERY n surly behaviour

DOGGESS n female dog

DOGGIE same as ▷ **doggy**

DOGGIER ▷ **doggy**

DOGGIES ▷ **doggy**

DOGGING ▷ **dog**

DOGGISH adj of or like a dog

DOGGO adv in hiding and keeping quiet

DOGGONE interj exclamation of annoyance, disappointment, etc ▷ vb damn ▷ adj damnedest

DOGGREL same as > **doggerel**

DOGGY n child's word for a dog ▷ adj of or like a dog

DOGHOLE n squalid dwelling place

DOGIE n motherless calf

DOGIES ▷ **dogy**

DOGLEG n sharp bend ▷ vb go off at an angle ▷ adj of or with the shape of a dogleg

DOGLEGS ▷ **dogleg**

DOGLIKE ▷ **dog**

DOGMA n doctrine or system of doctrines proclaimed by authority as true

DOGMAN n person who directs the operation of a crane whilst riding on an object being lifted by it

DOGMAS ▷ **dogma**

DOGMATA ▷ **dogma**

DOGMEN ▷ **dogman**

DOGNAP vb carry off and hold (a dog), usually for ransom

DOGNAPS ▷ **dognap**

DOGS ▷ **dog**

DOGSHIP n condition of being a dog

DOGSKIN n leather from dog's skin

DOGSLED n sleigh drawn by dogs

DOGTOWN n community of prairie dogs

DOGTROT n gently paced trot

DOGVANE n light windvane consisting of a feather or a piece of cloth or yarn mounted on the side of a vessel

DOGWOOD n type of tree or shrub, esp a European species with clusters of small white flowers and black berries

DOGY same as ▷ **dogie**

DOH n in tonic sol-fa, first degree of any major scale ▷ interj exclamation of annoyance when something goes wrong

> This is one of the very useful short words denoting a note of the musical scale.

DOHS ▷ **doh**

DOHYO n sumo wrestling ring

DOHYOS ▷ **dohyo**

DOILED same as ▷ **doilt**

DOILIES ▷ **doily**

DOILT adj foolish

DOILTER ▷ **doilt**

DOILY n decorative lacy paper mat, laid on a plate

DOING ▷ **do**

DOINGS pl n deeds or actions

DOIT n former small copper coin of the Netherlands

DOITED adj foolish or childish, as from senility

DOITIT same as ▷ **doited**

DOITKIN same as ▷ **doit**

DOITS ▷ **doit**

DOJO n room or hall for the practice of martial arts

DOJOS ▷ **dojo**

DOL n unit of pain intensity, as measured by dolorimetry

DOLCE n dessert ▷ adv (to be performed) gently and sweetly

DOLCES ▷ **dolce**

DOLCI ▷ **dolce**

DOLE n money received from the state while unemployed ▷ vb distribute in small quantities

DOLED ▷ **dole**

DOLEFUL adj dreary, unhappy

DOLENT adj sad

DOLENTE adv (to be performed) in a sorrowful manner

DOLES ▷ **dole**

DOLIA ▷ **dolium**

DOLINA same as ▷ **doline**

DOLINAS ▷ **dolina**

DOLINE n shallow usually funnel-shaped depression of the ground surface formed by solution in limestone regions

DOLINES ▷ **doline**

DOLING ▷ **dole**

DOLIUM n genus of molluscs

DOLL n small model of a human being, used as a toy ▷ vb as in **doll up** dress up

DOLLAR n standard monetary unit of many countries

DOLLARS ▷ **dollar**

DOLLDOM ▷ **doll**

DOLLED ▷ **doll**

DOLLIED ▷ **dolly**

DOLLIER n person who operates a dolly

DOLLIES ▷ **dolly**

DOLLING ▷ **doll**

DOLLISH ▷ **doll**

DOLLOP n lump (of food) ▷ vb serve out (food)

DOLLOPS ▷ **dollop**

DOLLS ▷ **doll**

D

DOLLY adj attractive and unintelligent ▷ n wheeled support on which a camera may be mounted; shaped block of lead used to hammer dents out of sheet metal ▷ vb wheel (a camera) backwards or forwards on a dolly

DOLMA n vine leaf stuffed with a filling of meat and rice

DOLMAN n long Turkish outer robe

DOLMANS ▶ dolman

DOLMAS ▶ dolma

DOLMEN n prehistoric monument consisting of a horizontal stone supported by vertical stones

DOLMENS ▶ dolmen

DOLOR same as ▶ dolour

DOLORS ▶ dolor

DOLOS n knucklebone of a sheep, buck, etc, used esp by diviners

DOLOSSE ▶ dolos

DOLOUR n grief or sorrow

DOLOURS ▶ dolour

DOLPHIN n sea mammal of the whale family, with a beaklike snout

DOLS ▶ dol

DOLT n stupid person

DOLTISH ▶ dolt

DOLTS ▶ dolt

DOM n title given to Benedictine, Carthusian, and Cistercian monks and to certain of the canons regular

DOMAIN n field of knowledge or activity

DOMAINE n French estate where wine is made

DOMAINS ▶ domain

DOMAL adj of a house

DOMATIA ▶ domatium

DOME n rounded roof built on a circular base ▷ vb cover with or as if with a dome

DOMED ▶ dome

DOMES ▶ dome

DOMETT n wool and cotton cloth

DOMETTS ▶ domett

DOMIC adj dome-shaped

DOMICAL ▶ dome

DOMICIL same as ▶ domicile

DOMIER ▶ domy

DOMIEST ▶ domy

DOMINE n clergyman

DOMINEE n minister of the Dutch Reformed Church

DOMINES ▶ domine

DOMING ▶ dome

DOMINIE n minister or clergyman: also used as a term of address

DOMINO n small rectangular block marked with dots, used in dominoes

DOMINOS ▶ domino

DOMOIC adj as in domoic acid kind of amino acid

DOMS ▶ dom

DOMY adj having a dome or domes

DON vb put on (clothing) ▷ n member of the teaching staff at a university or college

DONA n Spanish lady

DONAH n woman

DONAHS ▶ donah

DONARY n thing given for holy use

DONAS ▶ dona

DONATE vb give, esp to a charity or organization

DONATED ▶ donate

DONATES ▶ donate

DONATOR ▶ donate

DONDER vb beat (someone) up ▷ n wretch

DONDERS ▶ donder

DONE ▶ do

DONEE n person who receives a gift

DONEES ▶ donee

DONER n as in doner kebab grilled meat and salad served in pitta bread with chilli sauce

DONG n deep reverberating sound of a large bell ▷ vb (of a bell) to make a deep reverberating sound

DONGA n steep-sided gully created by soil erosion

DONGAS ▶ donga

DONGED ▶ dong

DONGING ▶ dong

DONGLE n electronic device that accompanies a software item to prevent the unauthorized copying of programs

DONGLES ▶ dongle

DONGOLA n leather tanned using a particular method

DONGS ▶ dong

DONING n act of giving blood

DONINGS ▶ doning

DONJON n heavily fortified central tower of a castle

DONJONS ▶ donjon

DONKEY n long-eared member of the horse family

DONKEYS ▶ donkey

DONKO n tearoom or cafeteria in a factory, wharf area, etc

DONKOS ▶ donko

DONNA n Italian lady

DONNARD same as ▶ donnert

DONNART same as ▶ donnert

DONNAS ▶ donna

DONNAT n lazy person

DONNATS ▶ donnat

DONNE same as ▶ donnee

DONNED ▶ don

DONNEE n subject or theme

DONNEES ▶ donnee

DONNERD adj stupid

DONNERT adj stunned

DONNES ▶ donne

DONNIES ▶ donny

DONNING ▶ don

DONNISH adj serious and academic

DONNISM n loftiness

DONNOT n lazy person

DONNOTS ▶ donnot

DONNY same as ▶ danny

DONOR n person who gives blood or organs for use in the treatment of another person

DONORS ▶ donor

DONS ▶ don

DONSHIP n state or condition of being a don

DONSIE adj rather unwell

DONSIER ▶ donsie

DONSY same as ▶ donsie

DONUT same as ▶ doughnut

DONUTS ▶ donut

DONZEL n man of high birth

DONZELS ▶ donzel

DOO a Scots word for ▶ dove

DOOB n cannabis cigarette

DOOBIE same as ▶ doob

DOOBIES ▶ doobie

DOOBREY n thingumabob

DOOBRIE ▶ doobrey

DOOBS ▶ doob

DOOCE vb dismiss (an employee) because of comments they have posted on the Internet

DOOCED ▶ dooce

DOOCES ▶ dooce

DOOCING ▶ dooce

DOOCOT n dovecote
DOOCOTS ▸ doocot
DOODAD same as ▸ **doodah**
DOODADS ▸ doodad
DOODAH n unnamed thing, esp an object the name of which is unknown or uncertain
DOODAHS ▸ doodah
DOODIES ▸ doody
DOODLE vb scribble or draw aimlessly ▷ n shape or picture drawn aimlessly
DOODLED ▸ doodle
DOODLER ▸ doodle
DOODLES ▸ doodle
DOODOO n excrement
DOODOOS ▸ doodoo
DOODY same as ▸ **doodoo**
DOOFER n thingamajig
DOOFERS ▸ doofer
DOOFUS n slow-witted or stupid person
DOOK n wooden plug driven into a wall to hold a nail, screw, etc ▷ vb dip or plunge
DOOKED ▸ dook
DOOKET n dovecote
DOOKETS ▸ dooket
DOOKING ▸ dook
DOOKS ▸ dook
DOOL n boundary marker
DOOLAN n Roman Catholic
DOOLANS ▸ doolan
DOOLE same as ▸ **dool**
DOOLEE same as ▸ **doolie**
DOOLEES ▸ doolee
DOOLES ▸ doole
DOOLIE n enclosed couch on poles for carrying passengers
DOOLIES ▸ doolie
DOOLS ▸ dool
DOOLY same as ▸ **doolie**
DOOM n death or a terrible fate ▷ vb destine or condemn to death or a terrible fate
DOOMED ▸ doom
DOOMFUL ▸ doom
DOOMIER ▸ doomy
DOOMILY ▸ doomy
DOOMING ▸ doom
DOOMS ▸ doom
DOOMY adj despondent or pessimistic
DOON same as ▸ **down**
DOONA n large quilt used as a bed cover in place of the top sheet and blankets
DOONAS ▸ doona
DOOR n hinged or sliding

panel for closing the entrance to a building, room, etc
DOORMAN n man employed to be on duty at the entrance to a large public building
DOORMAT n mat for wiping dirt from shoes before going indoors
DOORMEN ▸ doorman
DOORN n thorn
DOORNS ▸ doorn
DOORS ▸ door
DOORWAY n opening into a building or room
DOOS ▸ doo
DOOSRA n in cricket, a delivery, bowled by an off-spinner, that turns the opposite way from an off-break
DOOSRAS ▸ doosra
DOOWOP n style of singing in harmony
DOOWOPS ▸ doowop
DOOZER same as ▸ **doozy**
DOOZERS ▸ doozer
DOOZIE same as ▸ **doozy**
DOOZIES ▸ doozie
DOOZY n something excellent
DOP vb curtsy ▷ n tot or small drink, usually alcoholic ▷ vb fail to reach the required standard in (an examination, course, etc)
DOPA n precursor to dopamine
DOPANT n element or compound used to dope a semiconductor
DOPANTS ▸ dopant
DOPAS ▸ dopa
DOPATTA n headscarf
DOPE n illegal drug, usu cannabis ▷ vb give a drug to, esp in order to improve performance in a race ▷ adj excellent
DOPED ▸ dope
DOPER n person who administers dope
DOPERS ▸ doper
DOPES ▸ dope
DOPEY adj half-asleep, drowsy
DOPIAZA n Indian meat or fish dish cooked in onion sauce
DOPIER ▸ dopy
DOPIEST ▸ dopy
DOPILY ▸ dopey

DOPING ▸ dope
DOPINGS ▸ dope
DOPPED ▸ dop
DOPPER n member of an Afrikaner church that practises a stict Calvinism
DOPPERS ▸ dopper
DOPPIE n cartridge case
DOPPIES ▸ doppie
DOPPING ▸ dop
DOPPIO n double measure, esp of espresso coffee
DOPPIOS ▸ doppio
DOPS ▸ dop
DOPY same as ▸ **dopey**
DOR n European dung beetle that makes a droning sound when it flies
DORAD n South American river fish
DORADO n large marine percoid fish
DORADOS ▸ dorado
DORADS ▸ dorad
DORB same as ▸ **dorba**
DORBA n stupid, inept, or clumsy person
DORBAS ▸ dorba
DORBS ▸ dorb
DORBUG n type of beetle
DORBUGS ▸ dorbug
DORE n walleye fish
DOREE n type of fish
DOREES ▸ doree
DORES ▸ dore
DORHAWK n nightjar
DORIC adj rustic
DORIES ▸ dory
DORIS n woman
DORISE same as ▸ **dorize**
DORISED ▸ dorise
DORISES ▸ dorise
DORIZE vb become Doric
DORIZED ▸ dorize
DORIZES ▸ dorize
DORK n stupid person
DORKIER ▸ dork
DORKISH adj stupid or contemptible
DORKS ▸ dork
DORKY ▸ dork
DORLACH n quiver of arrows
DORM same as > **dormitory**
DORMANT n supporting beam ▷ adj temporarily quiet, inactive, or not being used
DORMER n window that sticks out from a sloping roof
DORMERS ▸ dormer
DORMICE > dormouse

DORMIE adj (of a player or side) as many holes ahead of an opponent as there are still to play

DORMIN n hormone found in plants

DORMINS ▸ dormin

DORMS ▸ dorm

DORMY same as ▸ dormie

DORNECK same as ▸ dornick

DORNICK n heavy damask cloth, formerly used for vestments, curtains, etc

DORNOCK n type of coarse fabric

DORP n small town

DORPER n breed of sheep

DORPERS ▸ dorper

DORPS ▸ dorp

DORR same as ▸ dor

DORRED ▸ dor

DORRING ▸ dor

DORRS ▸ dorr

DORS ▸ dor

DORSA ▸ dorsum

DORSAD adj towards the back or dorsal aspect

DORSAL adj of or on the back ▹ n dorsal fin

DORSALS ▸ dorsal

DORSE n type of small fish

DORSEL another word for ▸ dossal

DORSELS ▸ dorsel

DORSER n hanging tapestry

DORSERS ▸ dorser

DORSES ▸ dorse

DORSUM n the back

DORT vb sulk

DORTED ▸ dort

DORTER n dormitory

DORTERS ▸ dorter

DORTIER ▸ dorty

DORTING ▸ dort

DORTOUR same as ▸ dorter

DORTS ▸ dort

DORTY adj haughty, or sullen

DORY n spiny-finned edible sea fish

DOS ▸ do

DOSAGE same as ▸ dose

DOSAGES ▸ dosage

DOSE n specific quantity of a medicine taken at one time ▹ vb give a dose to

DOSED ▸ dose

DOSEH n former Egyptian religious ceremony

DOSEHS ▸ doseh

DOSER ▸ dose

DOSERS ▸ dose

DOSES ▸ dose

DOSH n money

DOSHES ▸ dosh

DOSING ▸ dose

DOSS vb sleep, esp in a dosshouse ▹ n bed, esp in a dosshouse

DOSSAL n ornamental hanging, placed at the back of an altar or at the sides of a chancel

DOSSALS ▸ dossal

DOSSED ▸ doss

DOSSEL same as ▸ dossal

DOSSELS ▸ dossel

DOSSER n bag or basket for carrying objects on the back

DOSSERS ▸ dosser

DOSSES ▸ doss

DOSSIER n collection of documents about a subject or person

DOSSIL n lint for dressing wound

DOSSILS ▸ dossil

DOSSING ▸ doss

DOST a singular form of the present tense (indicative mood) of ▸ do

DOT n small round mark ▹ vb mark with a dot

DOTAGE n weakness as a result of old age

DOTAGES ▸ dotage

DOTAL ▸ dot

DOTANT another word for ▸ dotard

DOTANTS ▸ dotant

DOTARD n person who is feeble-minded through old age

DOTARDS ▸ dotard

DOTCOM n company that does most of its business on the Internet

DOTCOMS ▸ dotcom

DOTE vb love to an excessive or foolish degree

DOTED ▸ dote

DOTER ▸ dote

DOTERS ▸ dote

DOTES ▸ dote

DOTH a singular form of the present tense of ▸ do

DOTIER ▸ doty

DOTIEST ▸ doty

DOTING ▸ dote

DOTINGS ▸ dote

DOTISH adj foolish

DOTS ▸ dot

DOTTED ▸ dot

DOTTEL same as ▸ dottle

DOTTELS ▸ dottel

DOTTER ▸ dot

DOTTERS ▸ dot

DOTTIER ▸ dotty

DOTTILY ▸ dotty

DOTTING ▸ dot

DOTTLE n tobacco left in a pipe after smoking ▹ adj relating to dottle

DOTTLED adj foolish

DOTTLER ▸ dottle

DOTTLES ▸ dottle

DOTTREL same as > dotterel

DOTTY adj rather eccentric

DOTY adj (of wood) rotten

DOUANE n customs house

DOUANES ▸ douane

DOUAR same as ▸ duar

DOUARS ▸ douar

DOUBLE adj as much again in number, amount, size, etc ▹ adv twice over ▹ n twice the number, amount, size, etc ▹ vb make or become twice as much or as many

DOUBLED ▸ double

DOUBLER ▸ double

DOUBLES n game between two pairs of players

DOUBLET n man's close-fitting jacket, with or without sleeves

DOUBLY adv in a greater degree, quantity, or measure

DOUBT n uncertainty about the truth, facts, or existence of something ▹ vb question the truth of

DOUBTED ▸ doubt

DOUBTER ▸ doubt

DOUBTS ▸ doubt

DOUC n Old World monkey of SE Asia with a bright yellow face surrounded by reddish-brown fur, a white tail, and white hindquarters

DOUCE adj quiet

DOUCELY ▸ douce

DOUCER ▸ douce

DOUCEST ▸ douce

DOUCET n former flute-like instrument

DOUCETS ▸ doucet

DOUCEUR n gratuity, tip, or bribe

DOUCHE n (instrument for applying) a stream of water directed onto or into the body for cleansing or

medical purposes ▷ *vb* cleanse or treat by means of a douche
DOUCHED ▸ **douche**
DOUCHES ▸ **douche**
DOUCINE *n* type of moulding for cornice
DOUCS ▸ **douc**
DOUGH *n* thick mixture of flour and water or milk, used for making bread etc
DOUGHS ▸ **dough**
DOUGHT ▸ **dow**
DOUGHTY *adj* brave and determined
DOUGHY *adj* resembling dough in consistency, colour, etc
DOUK *same as* ▸ **dook**
DOUKED ▸ **douk**
DOUKING ▸ **douk**
DOUKS ▸ **douk**
DOULA *n* woman who is trained to provide support to women and their families during pregnancy, childbirth, and the period of time following the birth
DOULAS ▸ **doula**
DOULEIA *same as* ▸ **dulia**
> This word refers to the inferior veneration accorded to saints and angels, as distinct from **latria**, the veneration accorded to God alone, and is another of the few seven-letter words that use all five vowels. It's surprising how often you want to do this!
DOUM *n* *as in* **doum palm** variety of palm tree
DOUMA *same as* ▸ **duma**
DOUMAS ▸ **douma**
DOUMS ▸ **doum**
DOUN *same as* ▸ **down**
DOUP *n* bottom
DOUPS ▸ **doup**
DOUR *adj* sullen and unfriendly
DOURA *same as* ▸ **durra**
DOURAH *same as* ▸ **durra**
DOURAHS ▸ **dourah**
DOURAS ▸ **doura**
DOURER ▸ **dour**
DOUREST ▸ **dour**
DOURINE *n* infectious venereal disease of horses
DOURLY ▸ **dour**
DOUSE *vb* drench with water or other liquid ▷ *n* immersion

DOUSED ▸ **douse**
DOUSER ▸ **douse**
DOUSERS ▸ **douse**
DOUSES ▸ **douse**
DOUSING ▸ **douse**
DOUT *vb* extinguish
DOUTED ▸ **dout**
DOUTER ▸ **dout**
DOUTERS ▸ **dout**
DOUTING ▸ **dout**
DOUTS ▸ **dout**
DOUX *adj* sweet
DOVE *vb* be semi-conscious ▷ *n* bird with a heavy body, small head, and short legs
DOVECOT *same as* > **dovecote**
DOVED ▸ **dove**
DOVEISH *adj* dovelike
DOVEKEY *same as* ▸ **dovekie**
DOVEKIE *n* small short-billed auk
DOVELET *n* small dove
DOVEN *vb* pray
DOVENED ▸ **doven**
DOVENS ▸ **doven**
DOVER *vb* doze ▷ *n* doze
DOVERED ▸ **dover**
DOVERS ▸ **dover**
DOVES ▸ **dove**
DOVIE *Scots word for* ▸ **stupid**
DOVIER ▸ **dovie**
DOVIEST ▸ **dovie**
DOVING ▸ **dove**
DOVISH ▸ **dove**
DOW *vb* archaic word meaning be of worth
DOWABLE *adj* capable of being endowed
DOWAGER *n* widow possessing property or a title obtained from her husband
DOWAR *same as* ▸ **duar**
DOWARS ▸ **dowar**
DOWD *n* woman who wears unfashionable clothes
DOWDIER ▸ **dowdy**
DOWDIES ▸ **dowdy**
DOWDILY ▸ **dowdy**
DOWDS ▸ **dowd**
DOWDY *adj* dull and old-fashioned ▷ *n* dowdy woman
DOWED ▸ **dow**
DOWEL *n* wooden or metal peg that fits into two corresponding holes to join two adjacent parts ▷ *vb* join pieces of wood using dowels

DOWELED ▸ **dowel**
DOWELS ▸ **dowel**
DOWER *n* life interest in a part of her husband's estate allotted to a widow by law ▷ *vb* endow
DOWERED ▸ **dower**
DOWERS ▸ **dower**
DOWERY *same as* ▸ **dowry**
DOWF *adj* dull; listless
DOWIE *adj* dull and dreary
DOWIER ▸ **dowie**
DOWIEST ▸ **dowie**
DOWING ▸ **dow**
DOWL *n* fluff
DOWLAS *n* coarse fabric
DOWLE *same as* ▸ **dowl**
DOWLES ▸ **dowle**
DOWLIER ▸ **dowly**
DOWLNE *obsolete form of* ▸ **down**
DOWLNES ▸ **dowlne**
DOWLNEY ▸ **dowlne**
DOWLS ▸ **dowl**
DOWLY *adj* dull
DOWN *adv* indicating movement to or position in a lower place ▷ *adj* depressed, unhappy ▷ *vb* drink quickly ▷ *n* soft fine feathers
DOWNA *obsolete Scots form of* ▸ **cannot**
DOWNBOW *n* (in music) a downward stroke of the bow across the strings
DOWNED ▸ **down**
DOWNER *n* barbiturate, tranquillizer, or narcotic
DOWNERS ▸ **downer**
DOWNIER ▸ **downy**
DOWNING ▸ **down**
DOWNS *pl n* low grassy hills, esp in S England
DOWNY *adj* covered with soft fine hair or feathers
DOWP *same as* ▸ **doup**
DOWPS ▸ **dowp**
DOWRIES ▸ **dowry**
DOWRY *n* property brought by a woman to her husband at marriage
DOWS ▸ **dow**
DOWSE *same as* ▸ **douse**
DOWSED ▸ **dowse**
DOWSER ▸ **dowse**
DOWSERS ▸ **dowse**
DOWSES ▸ **dowse**
DOWSET *same as* ▸ **doucet**
DOWSETS ▸ **dowset**
DOWSING ▸ **dowse**
DOWT *n* cigarette butt
DOWTS ▸ **dowt**

D

DOXIE same as ▸ **doxy**

DOXIES ▸ **doxy**

DOXY n opinion or doctrine, esp concerning religious matters

DOY n beloved person: used esp as an endearment

DOYEN n senior member of a group, profession, or society

DOYENNE ▸ **doyen**

DOYENS ▸ **doyen**

DOYLEY same as ▸ **doily**

DOYLEYS ▸ **doyley**

DOYLIES ▸ **doyly**

DOYLY same as ▸ **doily**

DOYS ▸ **doy**

DOZE vb sleep lightly or briefly ▷ n short sleep

DOZED adj (of timber or rubber) rotten or decayed

DOZEN vb stun

DOZENED ▸ **dozen**

DOZENS ▸ **dozen**

DOZENTH ▸ **dozen**

DOZER ▸ **doze**

DOZERS ▸ **doze**

DOZES ▸ **doze**

DOZIER ▸ **dozy**

DOZIEST ▸ **dozy**

DOZILY ▸ **dozy**

DOZING ▸ **doze**

DOZINGS ▸ **doze**

DOZY adj feeling sleepy

DRAB adj dull and dreary ▷ n light olive-brown colour ▷ vb consort with prostitutes

DRABBED ▸ **drab**

DRABBER n one who frequents low women

DRABBET n yellowish-brown fabric of coarse linen

DRABBLE vb make or become wet or dirty

DRABBY adj promiscuous

DRABLER same as ▸ **drabble**

DRABLY ▸ **drab**

DRABS ▸ **drab**

DRAC same as ▸ **drack**

DRACENA same as > **dracaena**

DRACHM same as ▸ **dram**

DRACHMA n former monetary unit of Greece

DRACHMS ▸ **drachm**

DRACK adj (esp of a woman) unattractive

DRACO n as in **draco lizard** flying lizard

DRACONE n large flexible cylindrical container towed by a ship, used for transporting liquids

DRAD ▸ **dread**

DRAFF n residue of husks after fermentation of the grain used in brewing, used as a food for cattle

DRAFFS ▸ **draff**

DRAFFY ▸ **draff**

DRAFT same as ▸ **draught**

DRAFTED ▸ **draft**

DRAFTEE n conscript

DRAFTER ▸ **draft**

DRAFTS ▸ **draft**

DRAFTY same as > **draughty**

DRAG vb pull with force, esp along the ground ▷ n person or thing that slows up progress

DRAGEE n sweet made of a nut, fruit, etc, coated with a hard sugar icing

DRAGEES ▸ **dragee**

DRAGGED ▸ **drag**

DRAGGER ▸ **drag**

DRAGGLE vb make or become wet or dirty by trailing on the ground

DRAGGY adj slow or boring

DRAGNET n net used to scour the bottom of a pond or river to search for something

DRAGON n mythical fire-breathing monster like a huge lizard

DRAGONS ▸ **dragon**

DRAGOON n heavily armed cavalryman ▷ vb coerce, force

DRAGS ▸ **drag**

DRAIL n weighted hook used in trolling ▷ vb fish with a drail

DRAILED ▸ **drail**

DRAILS ▸ **drail**

DRAIN n pipe or channel that carries off water or sewage ▷ vb draw off or remove liquid from

DRAINED ▸ **drain**

DRAINER n person or thing that drains

DRAINS ▸ **drain**

DRAKE n male duck

DRAKES ▸ **drake**

DRAM n small amount of a strong alcoholic drink, esp whisky ▷ vb drink a dram

DRAMA n serious play for theatre, television, or radio

DRAMADY same as ▸ **dramedy**

DRAMAS ▸ **drama**

DRAMEDY n television or film drama in which there are important elements of comedy

DRAMMED ▸ **dram**

DRAMS ▸ **dram**

DRANK ▸ **drink**

DRANT vb drone

DRANTED ▸ **drant**

DRANTS ▸ **drant**

DRAP a Scots word for ▸ **drop**

DRAPE vb cover with material, usu in folds ▷ n piece of cloth hung at a window or opening as a screen

DRAPED ▸ **drape**

DRAPER n person who sells fabrics and sewing materials

DRAPERS ▸ **draper**

DRAPERY n fabric or clothing arranged and draped

DRAPES pl n material hung at an opening or window to shut out light or to provide privacy

DRAPET n cloth

DRAPETS ▸ **drapet**

DRAPEY adj hanging in loose folds

DRAPIER n draper

DRAPING ▸ **drape**

DRAPPED ▸ **drap**

DRAPPIE n little drop, esp a small amount of spirits

DRAPPY n drop (of liquid)

DRAPS ▸ **drap**

DRASTIC n strong purgative ▷ adj strong and severe

DRAT interj exclamation of annoyance ▷ vb curse

DRATS ▸ **drat**

DRATTED adj wretched

DRAUGHT vb make preliminary plan ▷ n current of cold air, esp in an enclosed space ▷ adj (of an animal) used for pulling heavy loads

DRAUNT same as ▸ **drant**

DRAUNTS ▸ **draunt**

DRAVE archaic past of ▸ **drive**

DRAW vb sketch (a figure, picture, etc) with a pencil or pen ▷ n raffle or lottery

DRAWBAR n strong metal bar on a tractor, locomotive, etc, bearing a hook or link and pin to attach a trailer, wagon, etc

DRAWEE *n* person or organization on which a cheque or other order for payment is drawn

DRAWEES ▸ **drawee**

DRAWER *n* sliding box-shaped part of a piece of furniture, used for storage

DRAWERS *pl n* undergarment worn on the lower part of the body

DRAWING ▸ **draw**

DRAWL *vb* speak slowly, with long vowel sounds ▷ *n* drawling manner of speech

DRAWLED ▸ **drawl**

DRAWLER ▸ **drawl**

DRAWLS ▸ **drawl**

DRAWLY ▸ **drawl**

DRAWN ▸ **draw**

DRAWS ▸ **draw**

DRAY *vb* pull using cart ▷ *n* low cart used for carrying heavy loads

DRAYAGE *n* act of transporting something a short distance by lorry or other vehicle

DRAYED ▸ **dray**

DRAYING ▸ **dray**

DRAYMAN *n* driver of a dray

DRAYMEN ▸ **drayman**

DRAYS ▸ **dray**

DRAZEL *n* low woman

DRAZELS ▸ **drazel**

DREAD *vb* anticipate with apprehension or fear ▷ *n* great fear ▷ *adj* awesome

DREADED ▸ **dread**

DREADER ▸ **dread**

DREADLY ▸ **dread**

DREADS ▸ **dread**

DREAM *n* imagined series of events experienced in the mind while asleep ▷ *vb* see imaginary pictures in the mind while asleep ▷ *adj* ideal

DREAMED ▸ **dream**

DREAMER *n* person who dreams habitually

DREAMS ▸ **dream**

DREAMT ▸ **dream**

DREAMY *adj* vague or impractical

DREAR *same as* ▸ **dreary**

DREARE *obsolete form of* ▸ **drear**

DREARER ▸ **drear**

DREARES ▸ **dreare**

DREARS ▸ **drear**

DREARY *adj* dull, boring ▷ *n* a dreary thing or person

DRECK *n* rubbish

DRECKS ▸ **dreck**

DRECKY ▸ **dreck**

DREDGE *vb* clear or search (a river bed or harbour) by removing silt or mud ▷ *n* machine used to scoop or suck up silt or mud from a river bed or harbour

DREDGED ▸ **dredge**

DREDGER *same as* ▸ **dredge**

DREDGES ▸ **dredge**

DREE *vb* endure

DREED ▸ **dree**

DREEING ▸ **dree**

DREES ▸ **dree**

DREG *n* small quantity

DREGGY *adj* like or full of dregs

DREGS *pl n* solid particles that settle at the bottom of some liquids

DREICH *adj* dreary

DREIDEL *n* spinning top

DREIDL *same as* ▸ **dreidel**

DREIDLS ▸ **dreidl**

DREIGH *same as* ▸ **dreich**

DREK *same as* ▸ **dreck**

DREKS ▸ **drek**

DRENCH *vb* make completely wet ▷ *n* act or an instance of drenching

DRENT ▸ **drench**

DRERE *obsolete form of* ▸ **drear**

DRERES ▸ **drere**

DRESS *n* one-piece garment for a woman or girl, consisting of a skirt and bodice and sometimes sleeves ▷ *vb* put clothes on ▷ *adj* suitable for a formal occasion

DRESSED ▸ **dress**

DRESSER *n* piece of furniture with shelves and with cupboards, for storing or displaying dishes

DRESSES ▸ **dress**

DRESSY *adj* (of clothes) elegant

DREST ▸ **dress**

DREVILL *n* offensive person

DREW ▸ **draw**

DREY *n* squirrel's nest

DREYS ▸ **drey**

DRIB *vb* flow in drops

DRIBBED ▸ **drib**

DRIBBER ▸ **drib**

DRIBBLE *vb* (allow to) flow in drops ▷ *n* small quantity

of liquid falling in drops

DRIBBLY ▸ **dribble**

DRIBLET *n* small amount

DRIBS ▸ **drib**

DRICE *n* pellets of frozen carbon dioxide

DRICES ▸ **drice**

DRIED ▸ **dry**

DRIEGH *adj* tedious

DRIER ▸ **dry**

DRIERS ▸ **dry**

DRIES ▸ **dry**

DRIEST ▸ **dry**

DRIFT *vb* be carried along by currents of air or water ▷ *n* something piled up by the wind or current, such as a snowdrift

DRIFTED ▸ **drift**

DRIFTER *n* person who moves aimlessly from place to place or job to job

DRIFTS ▸ **drift**

DRIFTY ▸ **drift**

DRILL *n* tool or machine for boring holes ▷ *vb* bore a hole in (something) with or as if with a drill

DRILLED ▸ **drill**

DRILLER ▸ **drill**

DRILLS ▸ **drill**

DRILY *adv* in a dry manner

DRINK *vb* swallow (a liquid) ▷ *n* (portion of) a liquid suitable for drinking

DRINKER *n* person who drinks, esp a person who drinks alcohol habitually

DRINKS ▸ **drink**

DRIP *vb* (let) fall in drops ▷ *n* falling of drops of liquid

DRIPPED ▸ **drip**

DRIPPER ▸ **drip**

DRIPPY *adj* mawkish, insipid, or inane

DRIPS ▸ **drip**

DRIPT ▸ **drip**

DRIVE *vb* guide the movement of (a vehicle) ▷ *n* journey by car, van, etc

DRIVEL *n* foolish talk ▷ *vb* speak foolishly

DRIVELS ▸ **drivel**

DRIVEN ▸ **drive**

DRIVER *n* person who drives a vehicle

DRIVERS ▸ **driver**

DRIVES ▸ **drive**

DRIVING ▸ **drive**

DRIZZLE *n* very light rain ▷ *vb* rain lightly

DRIZZLY ▸ **drizzle**

DROGER *n* W Indian boat

DROGERS ▸ droger

DROGHER same as ▸ **droger**

DROGUE n any funnel-like device, esp one of canvas, used as a sea anchor

DROGUES ▸ drogue

DROGUET n woollen fabric

DROICH n dwarf

DROICHS ▸ droich

DROICHY adj dwarfish

DROID same as ▸ **android**

DROIDS ▸ droid

DROIL vb carry out boring menial work

DROILED ▸ droil

DROILS ▸ droil

DROIT n legal or moral right or claim

DROITS ▸ droit

DROLE adj amusing ▷ n scoundrel

DROLER ▸ drole

DROLES ▸ drole

DROLEST ▸ drole

DROLL vb speak wittily ▷ adj quaintly amusing

DROLLED ▸ droll

DROLLER ▸ droll

DROLLS ▸ droll

DROLLY ▸ droll

DROME > aerodrome

DROMES ▸ drome

DROMIC adj relating to running track

DROMOI ▸ dromos

DROMON same as ▸ **dromond**

DROMOND n large swift sailing vessel of the 12th to 15th centuries

DROMONS ▸ dromon

DROMOS n Greek passageway

DRONE n male bee ▷ vb make a monotonous low dull sound

DRONED ▸ drone

DRONER ▸ drone

DRONERS ▸ drone

DRONES ▸ drone

DRONGO n tropical songbird with a glossy black plumage, a forked tail, and a stout bill

DRONGOS ▸ drongo

DRONIER ▸ drony

DRONING ▸ drone

DRONISH ▸ drone

DRONY adj monotonous

DROOB n pathetic person

DROOBS ▸ droob

DROOG n ruffian

DROOGS ▸ droog

DROOK same as ▸ **drouk**

DROOKED ▸ drook

DROOKIT same as ▸ **droukit**

DROOKS ▸ drook

DROOL vb show excessive enthusiasm (for)

DROOLED ▸ drool

DROOLS ▸ drool

DROOLY adj tending to drool

DROOME obsolete form of ▸ **drum**

DROOMES ▸ drum

DROOP vb hang downwards loosely ▷ n act or state of drooping

DROOPED ▸ droop

DROOPS ▸ droop

DROOPY adj hanging or sagging downwards

DROP vb (allow to) fall vertically ▷ n small quantity of liquid forming a round shape

DROPFLY n (angling) artificial fly

DROPLET n very small drop of liquid

DROPOUT n person who rejects conventional society ▷ vb abandon or withdraw (from an institution or group)

DROPPED ▸ drop

DROPPER n small tube with a rubber part at one end for drawing up and dispensing drops of liquid

DROPPLE n trickle

DROPS ▸ drop

DROPSY n illness in which watery fluid collects in the body

DROPT ▸ drop

DROSERA n insectivorous plant

DROSHKY n open four-wheeled horse-drawn passenger carriage, formerly used in Russia

DROSKY same as ▸ **droshky**

DROSS n scum formed on the surfaces of molten metals

DROSSES ▸ dross

DROSSY ▸ dross

DROSTDY n office of landdrost

DROUGHT n prolonged shortage of rainfall

DROUK vb drench

DROUKED ▸ drouk

DROUKIT adj drenched

DROUKS ▸ drouk

DROUTH same as ▸ **drought**

DROUTHS ▸ drouth

DROUTHY adj thirsty or dry

DROVE ▸ drive

DROVED ▸ drive

DROVER n person who drives sheep or cattle

DROVERS ▸ drover

DROVES ▸ drive

DROVING ▸ drive

DROW n sea fog

DROWN vb die or kill by immersion in liquid

DROWND dialect form of ▸ **drown**

DROWNDS ▸ drownd

DROWNED ▸ drown

DROWNER ▸ drown

DROWNS ▸ drown

DROWS ▸ drow

DROWSE vb be sleepy, dull, or sluggish ▷ n state of being drowsy

DROWSED ▸ drowse

DROWSES ▸ drowse

DROWSY adj feeling sleepy

DRUB vb beat as with a stick ▷ n blow, as from a stick

DRUBBED ▸ drub

DRUBBER ▸ drub

DRUBS ▸ drub

DRUCKEN adj drunken

DRUDGE n person who works hard at uninteresting tasks ▷ vb work at such tasks

DRUDGED ▸ drudge

DRUDGER ▸ drudge

DRUDGES ▸ drudge

DRUG n substance used in the treatment or prevention of disease ▷ vb give a drug to (a person or animal) to cause sleepiness or unconsciousness

DRUGGED ▸ drug

DRUGGER n druggist

DRUGGET n coarse fabric used as a protective floor-covering, etc

DRUGGIE n drug addict

DRUGGY ▸ drug

DRUGS ▸ drug

DRUID n member of an ancient order of priests in Gaul, Britain, and Ireland in the pre-Christian era

DRUIDIC ▸ druid

DRUIDRY ▸ druid

DRUIDS ▸ druid

DRUM n percussion instrument sounded by

striking a membrane stretched across the opening of a hollow cylinder ▷ *vb* play (music) on a drum

DRUMBLE *vb* be inactive

DRUMLIN *n* streamlined mound of glacial drift, rounded or elongated in the direction of the original flow of ice

DRUMLY *adj* dismal; dreary

DRUMMED ▸ **drum**

DRUMMER *n* person who plays a drum or drums

DRUMMY *n* (in South Africa) drum majorette

DRUMS ▸ **drum**

DRUNK ▸ **drink**

DRUNKEN *adj* drunk or frequently drunk

DRUNKER ▸ **drink**

DRUNKS ▸ **drink**

DRUPE *n* fleshy fruit with a stone, such as the peach or cherry

DRUPEL *same as* > **drupelet**

DRUPELS ▸ **drupel**

DRUPES ▸ **drupe**

DRUSE *n* aggregate of small crystals within a cavity, esp those lining a cavity in a rock or mineral

DRUSEN *pl n* small deposits of material on the retina

DRUSES ▸ **druse**

DRUSIER ▸ **drusy**

DRUSY *adj* made of tiny crystals

DRUXIER ▸ **druxy**

DRUXY *adj* (of wood) having decayed white spots

DRY *adj* lacking moisture ▷ *vb* make or become dry

DRYABLE ▸ **dry**

DRYAD *n* wood nymph

DRYADES ▸ **dryad**

DRYADIC ▸ **dryad**

DRYADS ▸ **dryad**

DRYBEAT *vb* beat severely

DRYER ▸ **dry**

DRYERS ▸ **dry**

DRYEST ▸ **dry**

DRYING ▸ **dry**

DRYINGS ▸ **dry**

DRYISH *adj* fairly dry

DRYLAND *adj* of an arid area

DRYLOT *n* livestock enclosure

DRYLOTS ▸ **drylot**

DRYLY *same as* ▸ **drily**

DRYNESS ▸ **dry**

DRYS ▸ **dry**

DRYSUIT *n* waterproof rubber suit for wearing in esp cold water

DRYWALL *n* wall built without mortar ▷ *vb* build a wall without mortar

DRYWELL *n* type of sewage disposal system

DSO *same as* ▸ **zho**

> A **dso** is a kind of Himalayan ox; the other forms are **dzo, zho, dzho** and **zo** and it's worth remembering all of them.

DSOBO *same as* ▸ **zobo**

DSOBOS ▸ **dsobo**

DSOMO *same as* ▸ **zhomo**

DSOMOS ▸ **dsomo**

DSOS ▸ **dso**

DUAD *a rare word for* ▸ **pair**

DUADS ▸ **duad**

DUAL *adj* having two parts, functions, or aspects ▷ *n* dual number ▷ *vb* make (a road) into a dual carriageway

DUALIN *n* explosive substance

DUALINS ▸ **dualin**

DUALISE *same as* ▸ **dualize**

DUALISM *n* state of having or being believed to have two distinct parts or aspects

DUALIST ▸ **dualism**

DUALITY *n* state or quality of being two or in two parts

DUALIZE *vb* cause to have two parts

DUALLED ▸ **dual**

DUALLY ▸ **dual**

DUALS ▸ **dual**

DUAN *n* poem

DUANS ▸ **duan**

DUAR *n* Arab camp

DUARCHY *same as* ▸ **diarchy**

DUARS ▸ **duar**

DUB *vb* give (a person or place) a name or nickname ▷ *n* style of reggae record production involving exaggeration of instrumental parts, echo, etc

DUBBED ▸ **dub**

DUBBER ▸ **dub**

DUBBERS ▸ **dub**

DUBBIN *n* thick grease applied to leather to soften and waterproof it

DUBBING ▸ **dub**

DUBBINS ▸ **dubbin**

DUBBO *adj* stupid ▷ *n* stupid person

DUBBOS ▸ **dubbo**

DUBIETY *n* state of being doubtful

DUBIOUS *adj* feeling or causing doubt

DUBNIUM *n* element produced in minute quantities by bombarding plutonium with high-energy neon ions

DUBS ▸ **dub**

DUBSTEP *n* genre of electronic music

DUCAL *adj* of a duke

DUCALLY ▸ **ducal**

DUCAT *n* former European gold or silver coin

DUCATS ▸ **ducat**

DUCDAME *interj* Shakespearean nonsense word

DUCE *n* leader

DUCES ▸ **duce**

DUCHESS *n* woman who holds the rank of duke ▷ *vb* overwhelm with flattering attention

DUCHIES ▸ **duchy**

DUCHY *n* territory of a duke or duchess

DUCI ▸ **duce**

DUCK *n* water bird with short legs, webbed feet, and a broad blunt bill ▷ *vb* move (the head or body) quickly downwards, to avoid being seen or to dodge a blow

DUCKED ▸ **duck**

DUCKER ▸ **duck**

DUCKERS ▸ **duck**

DUCKIE *same as* ▸ **ducky**

DUCKIER ▸ **ducky**

DUCKIES ▸ **ducky**

DUCKING ▸ **duck**

DUCKPIN *n* short bowling pin

DUCKS ▸ **duck**

DUCKY *n* darling or dear: used as a term of endearment among women, but now often used in imitation of the supposed usage of homosexual men ▷ *adj* delightful

DUCT *vb* convey via a duct ▷ *n* tube, pipe, or channel through which liquid or gas is conveyed

D

DUCTAL ▷ duct
DUCTED ▷ duct
DUCTILE adj (of a metal) able to be shaped into sheets or wires
DUCTING ▷ duct
DUCTS ▷ duct
DUCTULE n small duct
DUD n ineffectual person or thing ▷ adj bad or useless
DUDDER n door-to-door salesman
DUDDERS ▷ dudder
DUDDERY n place where old clothes are sold
DUDDIE adj ragged
DUDDIER ▷ duddie
DUDDY same as ▷ duddie
DUDE vb dress fashionably ▷ n man
DUDED ▷ dude
DUDEEN n clay pipe with a short stem
DUDEENS ▷ dudeen
DUDES ▷ dude
DUDGEON n anger or resentment
DUDHEEN n type of pipe
DUDING ▷ dude
DUDISH ▷ dude
DUDISM n being a dude
DUDISMS ▷ dudism
DUDS ▷ dud
DUE vb supply with ▷ adj expected or scheduled to be present or arrive ▷ n something that is owed or required ▷ adv directly or exactly
DUED ▷ due
DUEFUL adj proper
DUEL n formal fight with deadly weapons between two people, to settle a quarrel ▷ vb fight in a duel
DUELED ▷ duel
DUELER ▷ duel
DUELERS ▷ duel
DUELING ▷ duel
DUELIST ▷ duel
DUELLED ▷ duel
DUELLER ▷ duel
DUELLI ▷ duello
DUELLO n art of duelling
DUELLOS ▷ duello
DUELS ▷ duel
DUENDE n Spanish goblin
DUENDES ▷ duende
DUENESS ▷ due
DUENNA n (esp in Spain) elderly woman acting as chaperone to a young woman

DUENNAS ▷ duenna
DUES pl n membership fees paid to a club or organization
DUET n piece of music for two performers ▷ vb perform a duet
DUETED ▷ duet
DUETING ▷ duet
DUETS ▷ duet
DUETT same as ▷ duet
DUETTED ▷ duet
DUETTI ▷ duetto
DUETTO same as ▷ duet
DUETTOS ▷ duetto
DUETTS ▷ duett
DUFF adj broken or useless ▷ vb change the appearance of or give a false appearance to (old or stolen goods) ▷ n rump or buttocks
DUFFED ▷ duff
DUFFEL n heavy woollen cloth with a thick nap
DUFFELS ▷ duffel
DUFFER n dull or incompetent person
DUFFERS ▷ duffer
DUFFEST ▷ duff
DUFFING ▷ duff
DUFFLE same as ▷ duffel
DUFFLES ▷ duffle
DUFFS ▷ duff
DUFUS same as ▷ doofus
DUFUSES ▷ dufus
DUG ▷ dig
DUGITE n medium-sized Australian venomous snake
DUGITES ▷ dugite
DUGONG n whalelike mammal of tropical waters
DUGONGS ▷ dugong
DUGOUT n (at a sports ground) covered bench where managers and substitutes sit
DUGOUTS ▷ dugout
DUGS ▷ dig
DUH interj ironic response to a question or statement, implying that the speaker is stupid or that the reply is obvious
┃ This word provides a useful front hook to **uh**.
DUHKHA same as ▷ dukkha
DUHKHAS ▷ duhkha
DUI ▷ duo
DUIKER n small African antelope
DUIKERS ▷ duiker
DUING ▷ due

DUIT n former Dutch coin
DUITS ▷ duit
DUKA n shop
DUKAS ▷ duka
DUKE vb fight with fists ▷ n nobleman of the highest rank
DUKED ▷ duke
DUKEDOM n title, rank, or position of a duke
DUKERY n duke's domain
DUKES pl n fists
DUKING ▷ duke
DUKKA n mix of ground roast nuts and spices, originating in Egypt, and used for sprinkling on meat or as a dip
DUKKAH same as ▷ dukka
DUKKAHS ▷ dukkah
DUKKAS ▷ dukka
DUKKHA n (in Theravada Buddhism) the belief that all things are suffering, due to the desire to seek permanence or recognise the self when neither exist: one of the three basic characteristics of existence
DUKKHAS ▷ dukkha
DULCET adj (of a sound) soothing or pleasant ▷ n soft organ stop
DULCETS ▷ dulcet
DULCIAN n precursor to the bassoon
DULCIFY vb make pleasant or agreeable
DULCITE n sweet substance
DULCOSE another word for ▷ dulcite
DULE n suffering; misery
DULES ▷ dule
DULIA n veneration accorded to saints in the Roman Catholic and Eastern Churches, as contrasted with hyperdulia and latria
DULIAS ▷ dulia
DULL adj not interesting ▷ vb make or become dull
DULLARD n dull or stupid person
DULLED ▷ dull
DULLER ▷ dull
DULLEST ▷ dull
DULLIER ▷ dull
DULLING ▷ dull
DULLISH ▷ dull
DULLS ▷ dull
DULLY ▷ dull
DULNESS ▷ dull

DULOSES ▸ dulosis
DULOSIS *n* practice of some ants, in which one species forces members of a different species to do the work of the colony
DULOTIC ▸ dulosis
DULSE *n* seaweed with large red edible fronds
DULSES ▸ dulse
DULY *adv* in a proper manner
DUMA *n* elective legislative assembly established by Tsar Nicholas II in 1905: overthrown by the Bolsheviks in 1917
DUMAIST *n* member of duma
DUMAS ▸ duma
DUMB *vb* silence ▷ *adj* lacking the power to speak
DUMBED ▸ dumb
DUMBER ▸ dumb
DUMBEST ▸ dumb
DUMBING ▸ dumb
DUMBLY ▸ dumb
DUMBO *n* slow-witted unintelligent person
DUMBOS ▸ dumbo
DUMBS ▸ dumb
DUMDUM *n* soft-nosed bullet that expands on impact and causes serious wounds
DUMDUMS ▸ dumdum
DUMELA *sentence substitute* hello
DUMKA *n* Slavonic lyrical song
DUMKY ▸ dumka
DUMMIED ▸ dummy
DUMMIER ▸ dummy
DUMMIES ▸ dummy
DUMMY *adj* sham ▷ *n* figure representing the human form, used for displaying clothes etc ▷ *adj* imitation, substitute ▷ *vb* prepare a dummy of (a proposed book, page, etc)
DUMOSE *adj* bushlike
DUMOUS *same as* ▸ dumose
DUMP *vb* drop or let fall in a careless manner ▷ *n* place where waste materials are left
DUMPBIN *n* free-standing unit in a bookshop in which a particular publisher's books are displayed
DUMPED ▸ dump

DUMPEE *n* person dumped from a relationship
DUMPEES ▸ dumpee
DUMPER ▸ dump
DUMPERS ▸ dump
DUMPIER ▸ dumpy
DUMPIES ▸ dumpy
DUMPILY ▸ dumpy
DUMPING ▸ dump
DUMPISH *same as* ▸ dumpy
DUMPLE *vb* form into dumpling shape
DUMPLED ▸ dumple
DUMPLES ▸ dumple
DUMPS *pl n* state of melancholy or depression
DUMPY *n* dumpy person ▷ *adj* short and plump
DUN *adj* brownish-grey ▷ *vb* demand payment from (a debtor) ▷ *n* demand for payment
DUNAM *n* unit of area measurement
DUNAMS ▸ dunam
DUNCE *n* person who is stupid or slow to learn
DUNCERY *n* duncelike behaviour
DUNCES ▸ dunce
DUNCH *vb* push against gently
DUNCHED ▸ dunch
DUNCHES ▸ dunch
DUNCISH *adj* duncelike
DUNDER *n* cane juice lees
DUNDERS ▸ dunder
DUNE *n* mound or ridge of drifted sand
DUNES ▸ dune
DUNG *n* faeces from animals such as cattle ▷ *vb* cover (ground) with manure
DUNGED ▸ dung
DUNGEON *vb* hold captive in dungeon ▷ *n* underground prison cell
DUNGER *n* old decrepit car
DUNGERS ▸ dunger
DUNGIER ▸ dung
DUNGING ▸ dung
DUNGS ▸ dung
DUNGY ▸ dung
DUNITE *n* ultrabasic igneous rock consisting mainly of olivine
DUNITES ▸ dunite
DUNITIC ▸ dunite
DUNK *vb* dip (a biscuit or bread) in a drink or soup before eating it
DUNKED ▸ dunk
DUNKER ▸ dunk

DUNKERS ▸ dunk
DUNKING ▸ dunk
DUNKS ▸ dunk
DUNLIN *n* small sandpiper with a brown back found in northern regions
DUNLINS ▸ dunlin
DUNNAGE *n* loose material used for packing cargo
DUNNART *n* type of mouselike insectivorous marsupial of Australia and New Guinea
DUNNED ▸ dun
DUNNER ▸ dun
DUNNESS ▸ dun
DUNNEST ▸ dun
DUNNIER ▸ dunny
DUNNIES ▸ dunny
DUNNING ▸ dun
DUNNISH ▸ dun
DUNNITE *n* explosive containing ammonium picrate
DUNNO *vb* slang for don't know
DUNNOCK *n* hedge sparrow
DUNNY *n* in Australia, toilet ▷ *adj* relating to dunny
DUNS ▸ dun
DUNSH *same as* ▸ dunch
DUNSHED ▸ dunsh
DUNSHES ▸ dunsh
DUNT *n* blow ▷ *vb* strike or hit
DUNTED ▸ dunt
DUNTING ▸ dunt
DUNTS ▸ dunt
DUO *same as* ▸ duet
DUODENA > duodenum
DUOLOG *same as* > duologue
DUOLOGS ▸ duolog
DUOMI ▸ duomo
DUOMO *n* cathedral in Italy
DUOMOS ▸ duomo
DUOPOLY *n* situation in which control of a commodity or service in a particular market is vested in just two producers or suppliers
DUOS ▸ duo
DUOTONE *n* process for producing halftone illustrations using two shades of a single colour or black and a colour
DUP *vb* open
DUPABLE ▸ dupe
DUPATTA *n* scarf worn in India

DUPE vb deceive or cheat ▷ n person who is easily deceived

DUPED ▶ dupe

DUPER ▶ dupe

DUPERS ▶ dupe

DUPERY ▶ dupe

DUPES ▶ dupe

DUPING ▶ dupe

DUPION n silk fabric made from the threads of double cocoons

DUPIONS ▶ dupion

DUPLE adj having two beats in a bar

DUPLET n pair of electrons shared between two atoms in a covalent bond

DUPLETS ▶ duplet

DUPLEX vb duplicate ▷ n apartment on two floors ▷ adj having two parts

DUPLIED ▶ duply

DUPLIES ▶ duply

DUPLY vb give a second reply

DUPPED ▶ dup

DUPPIES ▶ duppy

DUPPING ▶ dup

DUPPY n spirit or ghost

DUPS ▶ dup

DURA same as ▶ durra

DURABLE adj long-lasting

DURABLY ▶ durable

DURAL n alloy of aluminium and copper

DURALS ▶ dural

DURAMEN another name for > heartwood

DURANCE n imprisonment

DURANT n tough, leathery cloth

DURANTS ▶ durant

DURAS ▶ dura

DURBAR n (formerly) the court of a native ruler or a governor in India

DURBARS ▶ durbar

DURDUM same as ▶ dirdum

DURDUMS ▶ durdum

DURE vb endure

DURED ▶ dure

DUREFUL adj lasting

DURES ▶ dure

DURESS n compulsion by use of force or threats

DURESSE same as ▶ duress

DURGAH same as ▶ dargah

DURGAHS ▶ durgah

DURGAN n dwarf

DURGANS ▶ durgan

DURGIER ▶ durgy

DURGY adj dwarflike

DURIAN n SE Asian tree whose very large oval fruits have a hard spiny rind and an evil smell

DURIANS ▶ durian

DURING prep throughout or within the limit of (a period of time)

DURION same as ▶ durian

DURIONS ▶ durion

DURMAST n large Eurasian oak tree with lobed leaves

DURN ▶ darn

DURNED ▶ durn

DURNING ▶ durn

DURNS ▶ durn

DURO n silver peso of Spain or Spanish America

DUROC n breed of pig

DUROCS ▶ duroc

DUROS ▶ duro

DUROY n coarse woollen fabric

DUROYS ▶ duroy

DURR same as ▶ durra

DURRA n Old World variety of sorghum with hairy flower spikes and round seeds, cultivated for grain and fodder

DURRAS ▶ durra

DURRIE n cotton carpet made in India, often in rectangular pieces fringed at the ends: sometimes used as a sofa cover, wall hanging, etc

DURRIES ▶ durry

DURRS ▶ durr

DURRY n cigarette

DURST a past tense of ▶ dare

DURUM n variety of wheat cultivated mainly in the Mediterranean region, used chiefly to make pastas

DURUMS ▶ durum

DURZI n Indian tailor

DURZIS ▶ durzi

DUSH vb strike hard

DUSHED ▶ dush

DUSHES ▶ dush

DUSHING ▶ dush

DUSK n time just before nightfall, when it is almost dark ▷ adj shady ▷ vb make or become dark

DUSKED ▶ dusk

DUSKEN vb grow dark

DUSKENS ▶ dusken

DUSKER ▶ dusk

DUSKEST ▶ dusk

DUSKIER ▶ dusky

DUSKILY ▶ dusky

DUSKING ▶ dusk

DUSKISH ▶ dusk

DUSKLY ▶ dusk

DUSKS ▶ dusk

DUSKY adj dark in colour

DUST n small dry particles of earth, sand, or dirt ▷ vb remove dust from (furniture) by wiping

DUSTBIN n large container for household rubbish

DUSTED ▶ dust

DUSTER n cloth used for dusting

DUSTERS ▶ duster

DUSTIER ▶ dusty

DUSTILY ▶ dusty

DUSTING ▶ dust

DUSTMAN n man whose job is to collect household rubbish

DUSTMEN ▶ dustman

DUSTOFF n casualty evacuation helicopter

DUSTPAN n short-handled shovel into which dust is swept from floors

DUSTRAG n cloth for dusting

DUSTS ▶ dust

DUSTUP n quarrel, fight, or argument

DUSTUPS ▶ dustup

DUSTY adj covered with dust

DUTCH n wife

DUTCHES ▶ dutch

DUTEOUS adj dutiful or obedient

DUTIED adj liable for duty

DUTIES ▶ duty

DUTIFUL adj doing what is expected

DUTY n work or a task performed as part of one's job

DUUMVIR n one of two coequal magistrates or officers

DUVET same as ▶ doona

DUVETS ▶ duvet

DUVETYN n soft napped velvety fabric of cotton, silk, wool, or rayon

DUX n (in Scottish and certain other schools) the top pupil in a class or school

▌A **dux** is a leader, and is often useful for disposing of the X.

DUXES ▶ dux

DUYKER same as ▶ duiker

DUYKERS ▶ duyker

DVANDVA *n* class of compound words consisting of two elements having a coordinate relationship as if connected by *and*

DVORNIK *n* Russian doorkeeper

DWAAL *n* state of absent-mindedness

DWAALS ▸ dwaal

DWALE *n* deadly nightshade

DWALES ▸ dwale

DWALM *vb* faint

DWALMED ▸ dwalm

DWALMS ▸ dwalm

DWAM *n* stupor or daydream ▷ *vb* faint or fall ill

DWAMMED ▸ dwam

DWAMS ▸ dwam

DWANG *n* short piece of wood inserted in a timber-framed wall

DWANGS ▸ dwang

DWARF *adj* undersized ▷ *n* person who is smaller than average ▷ *adj* (of an animal or plant) much smaller than the usual size for the species ▷ *vb* cause (someone or something) to seem small by being much larger

DWARFED ▸ dwarf

DWARFER ▸ dwarf

DWARFS ▸ dwarf

DWARVES ▸ dwarf

DWAUM *same as* ▸ dwam

DWAUMED ▸ dwaum

DWAUMS ▸ dwaum

DWEEB *n* stupid or uninteresting person

DWEEBS ▸ dweeb

DWEEBY *adj* like or typical of a dweeb

DWELL *vb* live, reside ▷ *n* regular pause in the operation of a machine

DWELLED ▸ dwell

DWELLER ▸ dwell

DWELLS ▸ dwell

DWELT ▸ dwell

DWILE *n* floor cloth

DWILES ▸ dwile

DWINDLE *vb* grow less in size, strength, or number

DWINE *vb* languish

DWINED ▸ dwine

DWINES ▸ dwine

DWINING ▸ dwine

DYABLE ▸ dye

DYAD *n* operator that is the unspecified product of two vectors. It can operate on a vector to produce either a scalar or vector product

DYADIC *adj* of or relating to a dyad ▷ *n* sum of a particular number of dyads

DYADICS ▸ dyadic

DYADS ▸ dyad

DYARCHY *same as* ▸ diarchy

DYBBUK *n* (in the folklore of the cabala) the soul of a dead sinner that has transmigrated into the body of a living person

DYBBUKS ▸ dybbuk

DYE *n* colouring substance ▷ *vb* colour (hair or fabric) by applying a dye

DYEABLE ▸ dye

DYED ▸ dye

DYEING ▸ dye

DYEINGS ▸ dye

DYELINE *same as* ▸ diazo

DYER ▸ dye

DYERS ▸ dye

DYES ▸ dye

DYESTER *n* dyer

DYEWEED *n* plant that produces dye

DYEWOOD *n* any wood, such as brazil, from which dyes and pigments can be obtained

DYING ▸ die

DYINGLY ▸ die

DYINGS ▸ die

DYKE *n* wall built to prevent flooding ▷ *vb* embankment or wall built to confine a river to a particular course

DYKED ▸ dyke

DYKES ▸ dyke

DYKING ▸ dyke

DYKON *n* celebrity admired by lesbians

DYKONS ▸ dykon

DYNAMIC *adj* full of energy, ambition, and new ideas ▷ *n* energetic or driving force

DYNAMO *n* device for converting mechanical energy into electrical energy

DYNAMOS ▸ dynamo

DYNAST *n* hereditary ruler

DYNASTS ▸ dynast

DYNASTY *n* sequence of hereditary rulers

DYNE *n* cgs unit of force

DYNEIN *n* class of proteins

DYNEINS ▸ dynein

DYNEL *n* trade name for synthetic fibre

DYNELS ▸ dynel

DYNES ▸ dyne

DYNODE *n* electrode onto which a beam of electrons can fall, causing the emission of a greater number of electrons by secondary emission. They are used in photomultipliers to amplify the signal

DYNODES ▸ dynode

DYSLOGY *n* uncomplimentary remarks

DYSODIL *n* yellow or green mineral

DYSPNEA *same as* > dyspnoea

DYSURIA *n* difficult or painful urination

DYSURIC ▸ dysuria

DYSURY *same as* ▸ dysuria

DYVOUR *n* debtor

DYVOURS ▸ dyvour

DYVOURY *n* bankruptcy

DZEREN *n* Chinese yellow antelope

DZERENS ▸ dzeren

DZHO *same as* ▸ zho

DZHOS ▸ dzho

DZO *a variant spelling of* ▸ zo

DZOS ▸ zo

Ee

E is the most common tile in the game and, while it is only worth one point, as the most frequent letter in English it is extremely useful, especially when it comes to forming bonus words scoring an extra 50 points. Many words contain two or more **E**s, so, unlike many tiles, it does no harm to have two **E**s on your rack and even three can be manageable. Keep in mind three-letter words formed by an **E** on either side of a consonant, like **eye, ewe** and **eve** (6 points each), and **eke** (7). **E** can also be handy for getting rid of double consonants: think of words like **egg** or **ebb** (each 5 points). **E** also combines well with **K**: as well as **eke**, we have **elk** and **eek** (both 7), and **ewk** (10). If you have an **X** on your rack, **E** offers you all kinds of options: just think of all the words that begin with **ex-**, like **exhaust** (17), which will give you a 50-point bonus if you use all of your tiles to form it. And don't forget **ex** itself, a nice little word that earns you 9 points, and also the very useful **exo** for 10 points. Just as important are **jee** for 10 points, **zee** for 12 points and **zed** for 13 points.

EA n river
EACH pron every (one) taken separately ▷ determiner every (one) of two or more considered individually ▷ adv for, to, or from each one
EADISH n aftermath
EAGER adj showing or feeling great desire, keen ▷ n eagre
EAGERER ▶ eager
EAGERLY ▶ eager
EAGERS ▶ eager
EAGLE n bird of prey ▷ vb in golf, score two strokes under par for a hole
EAGLED ▶ eagle
EAGLES ▶ eagle
EAGLET n young eagle
EAGLETS ▶ eaglet
EAGLING ▶ eagle
EAGRE n tidal bore, esp of the Humber or Severn estuaries
EAGRES ▶ eagre
EALE n beast in Roman legend
EALES ▶ eale
EAN vb give birth
EANED ▶ ean
EANING ▶ ean
EANLING n newborn lamb
EANS ▶ ean

EAR n organ of hearing, esp the external part of it ▷ vb (of cereal plants) to develop such parts
EARACHE n pain in the ear
EARBALL n (in acupressure) a small ball kept in position in the ear and pressed when needed to relieve stress
EARBASH vb talk incessantly
EARBOB n earring
EARBOBS ▶ earbob
EARBUD n small earphone
EARBUDS ▶ earbud
EARCON n sound representing object or event
EARCONS ▶ earcon
EARD vb bury
EARDED ▶ eard
EARDING ▶ eard
EARDROP n pendant earring
EARDRUM n thin piece of skin inside the ear which enables one to hear sounds
EARDS ▶ eard
EARED adj having an ear or ears
EARFLAP n either of two pieces of fabric or fur attached to a cap, which can be let down to keep the ears warm

EARFUL n scolding or telling-off
EARFULS ▶ earful
EARING n line fastened to a corner of a sail for reefing
EARINGS ▶ earing
EARL n British nobleman ranking next below a marquess
EARLAP same as ▶ earflap
EARLAPS ▶ earlap
EARLDOM n rank, title, or dignity of an earl or countess
EARLESS ▶ ear
EARLIER ▶ early
EARLIES ▶ early
EARLIKE ▶ ear
EARLOBE n fleshy lower part of the outer ear
EARLOCK n curl of hair close to ear
EARLS ▶ earl
EARLY adv before the expected or usual time ▷ adj occurring or arriving before the correct or expected time ▷ n something which is early
EARMARK vb set (something) aside for a specific purpose ▷ n distinguishing mark

EARMUFF *n* one of a pair of pads of fur or cloth, joined by a headband, for keeping the ears warm

EARN *vb* obtain by work or merit

EARNED ▸ earn

EARNER ▸ earn

EARNERS ▸ earn

EARNEST *adj* serious and sincere ▷ *n* part payment given in advance, esp to confirm a contract

EARNING ▸ earn

EARNS ▸ earn

EARPICK *n* instrument for removing ear wax

EARPLUG *n* piece of soft material placed in the ear to keep out water or noise

EARRING *n* ornament for the lobe of the ear

EARS ▸ ear

EARSHOT *n* hearing range

EARST *adv* first; previously

EARTH *n* planet that we live on ▷ *vb* connect (a circuit) to earth

EARTHED ▸ earth

EARTHEN *adj* made of baked clay or earth

EARTHLY *adj* conceivable or possible ▷ *n* a chance

EARTHS ▸ earth

EARTHY *adj* coarse or crude

EARWAX *nontechnical name for* ▸ **cerumen**

EARWIG *n* small insect with a pincer-like tail ▷ *vb* eavesdrop

EARWIGS ▸ earwig

EARWORM *n* irritatingly catchy tune

EAS ▸ ea

EASE *n* freedom from difficulty, discomfort, or worry ▷ *vb* give bodily or mental ease to

EASED ▸ ease

EASEFUL *adj* characterized by or bringing ease

EASEL *n* frame to support an artist's canvas or a blackboard

EASELED *adj* mounted on easel

EASELS ▸ easel

EASER ▸ ease

EASERS ▸ ease

EASES ▸ ease

EASIED ▸ easy

EASIER ▸ easy

EASIES ▸ easy

EASIEST ▸ easy

EASILY *adv* without difficulty

EASING *n as in* **quantitative easing** increasing the supply of money to stimulate the economy

EASINGS ▸ easing

EASLE *n* hot ash

EASLES ▸ easle

EASSEL *adv* easterly

EASSIL *adv* easterly

EAST *n* (direction towards) the part of the horizon where the sun rises ▷ *adj* in the east ▷ *adv* in, to, or towards the east ▷ *vb* move or turn east

EASTED ▸ east

EASTER *n* most important festival of the Christian Church, commemorating the Resurrection of Christ

EASTERN *adj* situated in or towards the east

EASTERS ▸ easter

EASTING *n* net distance eastwards made by a vessel moving towards the east

EASTLIN *adj* easterly

EASTS ▸ east

EASY *adj* not needing much work or effort ▷ *vb* stop rowing

EASYING ▸ easy

EAT *vb* take (food) into the mouth and swallow it

EATABLE *adj* fit or suitable for eating

EATAGE *n* grazing rights

EATAGES ▸ eatage

EATCHE *n* adze

EATCHES ▸ eatche

EATEN ▸ eat

EATER ▸ eat

EATERIE *same as* ▸ **eatery**

EATERS ▸ eat

EATERY *n* restaurant or eating house

EATH *adj* easy

EATHE *same as* ▸ **eath**

EATHLY ▸ eath

EATING ▸ eat

EATINGS ▸ eat

EATS ▸ eat

EAU *same as* ▸ **ea**

EAUS ▸ eau

EAUX ▸ eau

EAVE *n* overhanging edge of a roof

EAVED *adj* having eaves

EAVES ▸ eave

EBAUCHE *n* rough sketch

EBAYER *n* any person who buys or sells using the internet auction site, eBay

EBAYERS ▸ ebayer

EBAYING *n* buying or selling using the internet auction site eBay

EBB *vb* (of tide water) flow back ▷ *n* flowing back of the tide

EBBED ▸ ebb

EBBET *n* type of newt

EBBETS ▸ ebbet

EBBING ▸ ebb

EBBLESS ▸ ebb

EBBS ▸ ebb

EBON *poetic word for* ▸ **ebony**

EBONICS *n* dialect used by African-Americans

EBONIES ▸ ebony

EBONISE *same as* ▸ **ebonize**

EBONIST *n* carver of ebony

EBONITE *another name for* ▸ **vulcanite**

EBONIZE *vb* stain or otherwise finish in imitation of ebony

EBONS ▸ ebon

EBONY *n* hard black wood ▷ *adj* deep black

EBOOK *n* book in electronic form

EBOOKS ▸ ebook

EBRIATE *adj* drunk

EBRIETY *n* drunkenness

EBRIOSE *adj* drunk

ECAD *n* organism whose form has been affected by its environment

ECADS ▸ ecad

ECARTE *n* card game for two, played with 32 cards and king high

ECARTES ▸ ecarte

ECBOLE *n* digression

ECBOLES ▸ ecbole

ECBOLIC *adj* hastening labour or abortion ▷ *n* drug or agent that hastens labour or abortion

ECCE *interj* behold

ECCO *interj* look there

ECCRINE *adj* of or denoting glands that secrete externally, esp the numerous sweat glands on the human body

ECDEMIC *adj* not indigenous or endemic

ECDYSES ▸ ecdysis

ECDYSIS *n* periodic

E

shedding of the cuticle in insects and other arthropods or the outer epidermal layer in reptiles

ECDYSON > ecdysone

ECESIC ▸ ecesis

ECESIS n establishment of a plant in a new environment

ECH same as ▸ eche

ECHAPPE n leap in ballet

ECHARD n water that is present in the soil but cannot be absorbed or otherwise utilized by plants

ECHARDS ▸ echard

ECHE vb eke out

ECHED ▸ eche

ECHELLE n ladder; scale

ECHELON n level of power or responsibility ▷ vb assemble in echelon

ECHES ▸ eche

ECHIDNA n Australian spiny egg-laying mammal

ECHING ▸ eche

ECHINI ▸ echinus

ECHINUS n ovolo moulding between the shaft and the abacus of a Doric column

ECHIUM n type of Eurasian and African plant

ECHIUMS ▸ echium

ECHO n repetition of sounds by reflection of sound waves off a surface ▷ vb repeat or be repeated as an echo

ECHOED ▸ echo

ECHOER ▸ echo

ECHOERS ▸ echo

ECHOES ▸ echo

ECHOEY adj producing echoes

ECHOIC adj characteristic of or resembling an echo

ECHOIER ▸ echoey

ECHOING ▸ echo

ECHOISE same as ▸ echoize

ECHOISM n onomatopoeia as a source of word formation

ECHOIST ▸ echoism

ECHOIZE vb repeat like echo

ECHOS ▸ echo

ECHT adj real

ECLAIR n finger-shaped pastry filled with cream and covered with chocolate

ECLAIRS ▸ eclair

ECLAT n brilliant success

ECLATS ▸ eclat

ECLIPSE n temporary obscuring of one star or planet by another ▷ vb surpass or outclass

ECLOGUE n pastoral or idyllic poem, usually in the form of a conversation or soliloquy

ECLOSE vb emerge

ECLOSED ▸ eclose

ECLOSES ▸ eclose

ECO n ecology activist

ECOCIDE n total destruction of an area of the natural environment, esp by human agency

ECOD same as ▸ egad

ECOLOGY n study of the relationships between living things and their environment

ECOMAP n diagram showing the relationships between an individual and their community

ECOMAPS ▸ ecomap

ECONOMY n system of interrelationship of money, industry, and employment in a country ▷ adj denoting a class of air travel that is cheaper than first-class

ECONUT n environmentalist

ECONUTS ▸ econut

ECORCHE n anatomical figure without the skin, so that the muscular structure is visible

ECOS ▸ eco

ECOTAGE n sabotage for ecological motives

ECOTONE n zone between two major ecological communities

ECOTOUR n holiday taking care not to damage environment

ECOTYPE n group of organisms within a species that is adapted to particular environmental conditions and therefore exhibits behavioural, structural, or physiological differences from other members of the species

ECRU adj pale creamy-brown ▷ n greyish-yellow to a light greyish colour

ECRUS ▸ ecru

ECSTASY n state of intense delight

ECTASES ▸ ectasis

ECTASIA n distension or dilation of a duct, vessel, or hollow viscus

ECTASIS same as ▸ ectasia

ECTATIC ▸ ectasia

ECTHYMA n local inflammation of the skin characterized by flat ulcerating pustules

ECTOPIA n congenital displacement or abnormal positioning of an organ or part

ECTOPIC ▸ ectopia

ECTOPY same as ▸ ectopia

ECTOZOA > ectozoon

ECTYPAL ▸ ectype

ECTYPE n copy as distinguished from a prototype

ECTYPES ▸ ectype

ECU n any of various former French gold or silver coins

ECUELLE n covered soup bowl with handles

ECURIE n team of motor-racing cars

ECURIES ▸ ecurie

ECUS ▸ ecu

ECZEMA n skin disease causing intense itching

ECZEMAS > eczema

ED n education

EDACITY ▸ edacious

EDAMAME n immature soybeans boiled in the pod

EDAPHIC adj of or relating to the physical and chemical conditions of the soil, esp in relation to the plant and animal life it supports

EDDIED ▸ eddy

EDDIES ▸ eddy

EDDISH n pasture grass

EDDO same as ▸ taro

EDDOES ▸ eddo

EDDY n circular movement of air, water, etc ▷ vb move with a circular motion

EDDYING ▸ eddy

EDEMA same as ▸ oedema

EDEMAS ▸ edema

EDEMATA ▸ edema

EDENIC adj delightful, like the Garden of Eden

EDENTAL adj having few or no teeth

EDGE n border or line where something ends or begins ▷ vb provide an edge or border for

EDGED ▸ edge

EDGER ▸ edge

E

EDGERS ▸ edge

EDGES ▸ edge

EDGIER ▸ edgy

EDGIEST ▸ edgy

EDGILY ▸ edgy

EDGING n anything placed along an edge to finish it ▷ adj relating to or used for making an edge

EDGINGS ▸ edging

EDGY adj nervous or irritable

EDH n character of the runic alphabet used to represent the voiced dental fricative

EDHS ▸ edh

EDIBLE adj fit to be eaten

EDIBLES pl n articles fit to eat

EDICT n order issued by an authority

EDICTAL ▸ edict

EDICTS ▸ edict

EDIFICE n large building

EDIFIED ▸ edify

EDIFIER ▸ edify

EDIFIES ▸ edify

EDIFY vb improve morally by instruction

EDILE variant spelling of ▸ aedile

EDILES ▸ edile

EDIT vb prepare (a book, film, etc) for publication or broadcast ▷ n act of editing

EDITED ▸ edit

EDITING ▸ edit

EDITION n number of copies of a new publication printed at one time ▷ vb produce multiple copies of (an original work of art)

EDITOR n person who edits

EDITORS ▸ editor

EDITRIX n female editor

EDITS ▸ edit

EDS ▸ ed

EDUCATE vb teach

EDUCE vb evolve or develop, esp from a latent or potential state

EDUCED ▸ educe

EDUCES ▸ educe

EDUCING ▸ educe

EDUCT n substance separated from another substance without chemical change

EDUCTOR ▸ educe

EDUCTS ▸ educe

EE Scots word for ▸ eye

EECH same as ▸ eche

EECHED ▸ eech

EECHES ▸ eech

EECHING ▸ eech

EEJIT Scots and Irish word for ▸ idiot

EEJITS ▸ eejit

EEK interj indicating shock or fright

EEL n snakelike fish

EELFARE n young eel

EELIER ▸ eel

EELIEST ▸ eel

EELLIKE adj resembling an eel

EELPOUT n marine eel-like blennioid fish

EELS ▸ eel

EELWORM n any of various nematode worms, esp the wheatworm or the vinegar eel

EELY ▸ eel

EEN ▸ ee

EERIE adj uncannily frightening or disturbing

EERIER ▸ eerie

EERIEST ▸ eerie

EERILY ▸ eerie

EERY same as ▸ eerie

EEVEN n evening

EEVENS ▸ eeven

EEVN n evening

EEVNING n evening

EEVNS ▸ eevn

EF n the letter F

EFF vb say the word 'fuck'

EFFABLE adj capable of being expressed in words

EFFACE vb remove by rubbing

EFFACED ▸ efface

EFFACER ▸ efface

EFFACES ▸ efface

EFFECT n change or result caused by someone or something ▷ vb cause to happen, accomplish

EFFECTS pl n personal belongings

EFFED ▸ eff

EFFEIR vb suit

EFFEIRS ▸ effeir

EFFENDI n (in the Ottoman Empire) a title of respect used to address men of learning or social standing

EFFERE same as ▸ effeir

EFFERED ▸ effere

EFFERES ▸ effere

EFFETE adj powerless, feeble

EFFIGY n image or likeness of a person

EFFING ▸ eff

EFFINGS ▸ eff

EFFLUX same as > **effluence**

EFFORCE vb force

EFFORT n physical or mental exertion

EFFORTS ▸ effort

EFFRAY same as ▸ **affray**

EFFRAYS ▸ effray

EFFS ▸ eff

EFFULGE vb radiate

EFFUSE vb pour or flow out ▷ adj (esp of an inflorescence) spreading out loosely

EFFUSED ▸ effuse

EFFUSES ▸ effuse

EFS ▸ ef

EFT n dialect or archaic name for a newt ▷ adv again

EFTEST adj nearest at hand

EFTS ▸ eft

EFTSOON > **eftsoons**

EGAD n mild oath or expression of surprise

EGADS ▸ egad

EGAL adj equal

EGALITE n equality

EGALITY n equality

EGALLY ▸ egal

EGENCE n need

EGENCES ▸ egence

EGENCY same as ▸ egence

EGER same as ▸ eagre

EGERS ▸ eger

EGEST vb excrete (waste material)

EGESTA pl n anything egested, as waste material from the body

EGESTED ▸ egest

EGESTS ▸ egest

EGG n oval or round object laid by the females of birds and other creatures, containing a developing embryo ▷ vb urge or incite, esp to daring or foolish acts

EGGAR same as ▸ egger

EGGARS ▸ eggar

EGGCUP n cup for holding a boiled egg

EGGCUPS ▸ eggcup

EGGED ▸ egg

EGGER n any of various widely distributed moths having brown bodies and wings

EGGERS ▸ egger

EGGERY n place where eggs are laid

EGGHEAD n intellectual person

E

EGGIER ▸ eggy
EGGIEST ▸ eggy
EGGING ▸ egg
EGGLER n egg dealer: sometimes itinerant
EGGLERS ▸ eggler
EGGLESS ▸ egg
EGGMASS n intelligentsia
EGGNOG n drink made of raw eggs, milk, sugar, spice, and brandy or rum
EGGNOGS ▸ eggnog
EGGS ▸ egg
EGGWASH n beaten egg for brushing on pastry
EGGY adj soaked in or tasting of egg
EGIS rare spelling of ▸ aegis
EGISES ▸ egis
EGMA mispronunciation of ▸ enigma
EGMAS ▸ egma
EGO n conscious mind of an individual
EGOISM n excessive concern for one's own interests
EGOISMS ▸ egoism
EGOIST n person who is preoccupied with his own interests
EGOISTS ▸ egoist
EGOITY n essence of the ego
EGOLESS adj without an ego
EGOS ▸ ego
EGOTISE same as ▸ egotize
EGOTISM n concern only for one's own interests and feelings
EGOTIST n conceited boastful person
EGOTIZE vb talk or write in self-important way
EGRESS same as ▸ emersion
EGRET n lesser white heron
EGRETS ▸ egret
EH interj exclamation of surprise or inquiry, or to seek confirmation of a statement or question ▷ vb say 'eh'
EHED ▸ eh
EHING ▸ eh
EHS ▸ eh
EIDE ▸ eidos
EIDENT adj diligent
EIDER n Arctic duck
EIDERS ▸ eider
EIDETIC adj (of visual, or sometimes auditory, images) exceptionally vivid and allowing detailed recall

of something previously perceived ▷ n person with eidetic ability
EIDOLA ▸ eidolon
EIDOLIC ▸ eidolon
EIDOLON n unsubstantial image
EIDOS n intellectual character of a culture or a social group
EIGHT n one more than seven ▷ adj amounting to eight
EIGHTH n (of) number eight in a series ▷ adj coming after the seventh and before the ninth in numbering or counting order, position, time, etc ▷ adv after the seventh person, position, event, etc
EIGHTHS ▸ eighth
EIGHTS ▸ eight
EIGHTVO another word for ▸ octavo
EIGHTY n eight times ten ▷ adj amounting to eighty ▷ determiner amounting to eighty
EIGNE adj firstborn
EIK variant form of ▸ eke
EIKED ▸ eik
EIKING ▸ eik
EIKON variant spelling of ▸ icon
EIKONES ▸ eikon
EIKONS ▸ eikon
EIKS ▸ eik
EILD n old age
EILDING n fuel
EILDS ▸ eild
EINA interj exclamation of pain
EINE pl n eyes
EINKORN n variety of wheat of Greece and SW Asia
EIRACK n young hen
EIRACKS ▸ eirack
EIRENIC variant spelling of ▸ irenic
EISEL n vinegar
EISELL same as ▸ eisel
EISELLS ▸ eisell
EISELS ▸ eisel
EISH interj South African exclamation expressive of surprise, disapproval, etc
EISWEIN n wine made from grapes frozen on the vine
EITHER pron one or the other (of two) ▷ adv

likewise ▷ determiner one or the other (of two)
EJECT vb force out, expel
EJECTA pl n matter thrown out of a crater by an erupting volcano or during a meteorite impact
EJECTED ▸ eject
EJECTOR n person or thing that ejects
EJECTS ▸ eject
EKE vb increase, enlarge, or lengthen
EKED ▸ eke
EKES ▸ eke
EKING ▸ eke
EKISTIC > ekistics
EKKA n type of one-horse carriage
EKKAS ▸ ekka
EKPWELE n former monetary unit of Equatorial Guinea
EKUELE same as ▸ ekpwele
EL n American elevated railway
ELAIN same as > triolein
ELAINS ▸ elain
ELAN n style and vigour
ELANCE vb throw a lance
ELANCED ▸ elance
ELANCES ▸ elance
ELAND n large antelope of southern Africa
ELANDS ▸ eland
ELANET n bird of prey
ELANETS ▸ elanet
ELANS ▸ elan
ELAPID n mostly tropical type of venomous snake
ELAPIDS ▸ elapid
ELAPINE adj of or like an elapid
ELAPSE vb (of time) pass by
ELAPSED ▸ elapse
ELAPSES ▸ elapse
ELASTIC adj resuming normal shape after distortion ▷ n tape or fabric containing interwoven strands of flexible rubber
ELASTIN n fibrous scleroprotein constituting the major part of elastic tissue, such as the walls of arteries
ELATE vb fill with high spirits, exhilaration, pride or optimism
ELATED adj extremely happy and excited
ELATER n elaterid beetle
ELATERS ▸ elater

ELATES ▶ **elate**

ELATING ▶ **elate**

ELATION n feeling of great happiness and excitement

ELATIVE adj (in the grammar of Finnish and other languages) denoting a case of nouns expressing a relation of motion or direction ▷ n elative case

ELBOW n joint between the upper arm and the forearm ▷ vb shove or strike with the elbow

ELBOWED ▶ **elbow**

ELBOWS ▶ **elbow**

ELCHEE n ambassador

ELCHEES ▶ **elchee**

ELCHI same as ▶ **elchee**

ELCHIS ▶ **elchi**

ELD n old age

ELDER adj older ▷ n older person

ELDERLY adj (fairly) old

ELDERS ▶ **elder**

ELDEST adj oldest

ELDIN n fuel

ELDING same as ▶ **eldin**

ELDINGS ▶ **elding**

ELDINS ▶ **eldin**

ELDRESS n woman elder

ELDRICH same as ▷ **eldritch**

ELDS ▶ **eld**

ELECT vb choose by voting ▷ adj appointed but not yet in office

ELECTED ▶ **elect**

ELECTEE n someone who is elected

ELECTOR n someone who has the right to vote in an election

ELECTRO vb (in printing) make a metallic copy of a page

ELECTS ▶ **elect**

ELEGANT adj pleasing or graceful in dress, style, or design

ELEGIAC adj mournful or plaintive ▷ n elegiac couplet or stanza

ELEGIES ▶ **elegy**

ELEGISE same as ▶ **elegize**

ELEGIST ▶ **elegize**

ELEGIT n writ delivering debtor's property to plaintiff

ELEGITS ▶ **elegit**

ELEGIZE vb compose an elegy or elegies (in memory of)

ELEGY n mournful poem,

esp a lament for the dead

ELEMENT n component part

ELEMI n fragrant resin obtained from various tropical trees, used to make varnishes, ointments, inks, etc

ELEMIS ▶ **elemi**

ELENCH n refutation in logic

ELENCHI > **elenchus**

ELENCHS ▶ **elench**

ELEVATE vb raise in rank or status

ELEVEN n one more than ten ▷ adj amounting to eleven ▷ determiner amounting to eleven

ELEVENS ▶ **eleven**

ELEVON n aircraft control surface that combines the functions of an elevator and aileron, usually fitted to tailless or delta-wing aircraft

ELEVONS ▶ **elevon**

ELF n (in folklore) small mischievous fairy ▷ vb entangle (esp hair)

ELFED ▶ **elf**

ELFHOOD ▶ **elf**

ELFIN adj small and delicate ▷ n young elf

ELFING ▶ **elf**

ELFINS ▶ **elfin**

ELFISH adj of, relating to, or like an elf or elves ▷ n supposed language of elves

ELFLAND another name for > **fairyland**

ELFLIKE ▶ **elf**

ELFLOCK n lock of hair, fancifully regarded as having been tangled by the elves

ELFS ▶ **elf**

ELHI adj informal word for or relating to elementary high school

ELIAD n glance

ELIADS ▶ **eliad**

ELICHE n pasta in the form of spirals

ELICHES ▶ **eliche**

ELICIT vb bring about (a response or reaction)

ELICITS ▶ **elicit**

ELIDE vb omit (a vowel or syllable) from a spoken word

ELIDED ▶ **elide**

ELIDES ▶ **elide**

ELIDING ▶ **elide**

ELINT n electronic intelligence

ELINTS ▶ **elint**

ELISION n omission of a syllable or vowel from a spoken word

ELITE n most powerful, rich, or gifted members of a group ▷ adj of, relating to, or suitable for an elite

ELITES ▶ **elite**

ELITISM n belief that society should be governed by a small group of superior people

ELITIST ▶ **elitism**

ELIXIR n imaginary liquid that can prolong life or turn base metals into gold

ELIXIRS ▶ **elixir**

ELK n large deer of N Europe and Asia

ELKHORN n as in **elkhorn fern** fern with a large leaf like an elk's horn

ELKS ▶ **elk**

ELL n obsolete unit of length equal to approximately 45 inches

ELLAGIC adj of an acid derived from gallnuts

ELLIPSE n oval shape

ELLOPS same as ▶ **elops**

ELLS ▶ **ell**

ELLWAND n stick for measuring lengths

ELM n tree with serrated leaves

ELMEN adj of or relating to elm trees

ELMIER ▶ **elmy**

ELMIEST ▶ **elmy**

ELMS ▶ **elm**

ELMWOOD n wood from an elm tree

ELMY adj of or relating to elm trees

ELOCUTE vb speak as if practising elocution

ELODEA n type of American plant

ELODEAS ▶ **elodea**

ELOGE same as ▶ **eulogy**

ELOGES ▶ **eloge**

ELOGIES ▶ **elogy**

ELOGIST ▶ **elogy**

ELOGIUM same as ▶ **eulogy**

ELOGY same as ▶ **eulogy**

ELOIGN vb remove (oneself, one's property, etc) to a distant place

ELOIGNS ▶ **eloign**

ELOIN same as ▶ **eloign**

E

ELOINED ▸ eloin
ELOINER ▸ eloign
ELOINS ▸ eloin
ELOPE vb (of two people) run away secretly to get married
ELOPED ▸ elope
ELOPER ▸ elope
ELOPERS ▸ elope
ELOPES ▸ elope
ELOPING ▸ elope
ELOPS n type of fish
ELOPSES ▸ elops
ELPEE n LP, long-playing record
ELPEES ▸ elpee
ELS ▸ el
ELSE adv in addition or more
ELSHIN n cobbler's awl
ELSHINS ▸ elshin
ELSIN same as ▸ elshin
ELSINS ▸ elsin
ELT n young female pig
ELTCHI same as ▸ elchee
ELTCHIS ▸ eltchi
ELTS ▸ elt
ELUANT same as ▸ eluent
ELUANTS ▸ eluant
ELUATE n solution of adsorbed material in the eluent obtained during the process of elution
ELUATES ▸ eluate
ELUDE vb escape from by cleverness or quickness
ELUDED ▸ elude
ELUDER ▸ elude
ELUDERS ▸ elude
ELUDES ▸ elude
ELUDING ▸ elude
ELUENT n solvent used for eluting
ELUENTS ▸ eluent
ELUSION ▸ elude
ELUSIVE adj difficult to catch or remember
ELUSORY adj avoiding the issue
ELUTE vb wash out (a substance) by the action of a solvent, as in chromatography
ELUTED ▸ elute
ELUTES ▸ elute
ELUTING ▸ elute
ELUTION ▸ elute
ELUTOR ▸ elute
ELUTORS ▸ elute
ELUVIA ▸ eluvium
ELUVIAL ▸ eluvium
ELUVIUM n mass of sand, silt, etc: a product of the erosion of rocks that has

remained in its place of origin
ELVAN n type of rock
ELVANS ▸ elvan
ELVER n young eel
ELVERS ▸ elver
ELVES ▸ elf
ELVISH same as ▸ elfish
ELYSIAN adj delightful, blissful
ELYTRA ▸ elytrum
ELYTRAL ▸ elytron
ELYTRON n either of the horny front wings of beetles and some other insects, which cover and protect the hind wings
ELYTRUM same as ▸ elytron
EM n square of a body of any size of type, used as a unit of measurement
EMACS n powerful computer program used for creating and editing text
EMACSEN ▸ emacs
EMAIL n electronic mail ▷ vb send a message by electronic mail
EMAILED ▸ email
EMAILER ▸ email
EMAILS ▸ email
EMANANT ▸ emanate
EMANATE vb issue, proceed from a source
EMBACE same as ▸ embase
EMBACES ▸ embace
EMBAIL vb enclose in a circle
EMBAILS ▸ embail
EMBALE vb bind
EMBALED ▸ embale
EMBALES ▸ embale
EMBALL vb enclose in a circle
EMBALLS ▸ emball
EMBALM vb preserve (a corpse) from decay by the use of chemicals etc
EMBALMS ▸ embalm
EMBANK vb protect, enclose, or confine (a waterway, road, etc) with an embankment
EMBANKS ▸ embank
EMBAR vb close in with bars
EMBARGO n order by a government prohibiting trade with a country ▷ vb put an embargo on
EMBARK vb board a ship or aircraft
EMBARKS ▸ embark
EMBARS ▸ embar

EMBASE vb degrade or debase
EMBASED ▸ embase
EMBASES ▸ embase
EMBASSY n offices or official residence of an ambassador
EMBASTE ▸ embase
EMBATHE vb bathe with water
EMBAY vb form into a bay
EMBAYED ▸ embay
EMBAYLD ▸ embail
EMBAYS ▸ embay
EMBED vb fix firmly in something solid ▷ n journalist accompanying an active military unit
EMBEDS ▸ embed
EMBER n glowing piece of wood or coal in a dying fire
EMBERS ▸ ember
EMBLAZE vb cause to light up
EMBLEM n object or design that symbolizes a quality, type, or group ▷ vb represent or signify
EMBLEMA n mosaic decoration
EMBLEMS ▸ emblem
EMBLIC n type of Indian tree
EMBLICS ▸ emblic
EMBLOOM vb adorn with blooms
EMBODY vb be an example or expression of
EMBOG vb sink down into a bog
EMBOGS ▸ embog
EMBOGUE vb go out through a narrow channel or passage
EMBOIL vb enrage or be enraged
EMBOILS ▸ emboil
EMBOLI ▸ embolus
EMBOLIC adj of or relating to an embolus or embolism
EMBOLUS n material, such as a blood clot, that blocks a blood vessel
EMBOLY n infolding of the outer layer of cells of an organism or part of an organism so as to form a pocket in the surface
EMBOSK vb hide or cover
EMBOSKS ▸ embosk
EMBOSOM vb enclose or envelop, esp protectively
EMBOSS vb mould or carve a decoration on (a surface)

so that it stands out from the surface

EMBOST ▶ emboss

EMBOUND vb surround or encircle

EMBOW vb design or create (a structure) in the form of an arch or vault

EMBOWED ▶ embow

EMBOWEL vb bury or embed deeply

EMBOWER vb enclose in or as in a bower

EMBOWS ▶ embow

EMBOX vb put in a box

EMBOXED ▶ embox

EMBOXES ▶ embox

EMBRACE vb clasp in the arms, hug ▷ n act of embracing

EMBRAID vb braid or interweave

EMBRAVE vb adorn or decorate

EMBREAD vb braid

EMBROIL vb involve (a person) in problems

EMBROWN vb make or become brown

EMBRUE variant spelling of ▶ imbrue

EMBRUED ▶ embrue

EMBRUES ▶ embrue

EMBRUTE same as ▶ imbrute

EMBRYO n unborn creature in the early stages of development

EMBRYON same as ▶ embryo

EMBRYOS ▶ embryo

EMBUS vb cause (troops) to board or (of troops) to board a transport vehicle

EMBUSED ▶ embus

EMBUSES ▶ embus

EMBUSY vb keep occupied

EMCEE n master of ceremonies ▷ vb act as master of ceremonies (for or at)

EMCEED ▶ emcee

EMCEES ▶ emcee

EMDASH n long dash in punctuation

EME n uncle

EMEER same as ▶ emir

EMEERS ▶ emeer

EMEND vb remove errors from

EMENDED ▶ emend

EMENDER ▶ emend

EMENDS ▶ emend

EMERALD n bright green precious stone ▷ adj bright green

EMERGE vb come into view

EMERGED ▶ emerge

EMERGES ▶ emerge

EMERIED ▶ emery

EMERIES ▶ emery

EMERITA adj retired, but retaining an honorary title ▷ n woman who is retired, but retains an honorary title

EMERITI > emeritus

EMEROD n haemorrhoid

EMERODS ▶ emerod

EMEROID same as ▶ emerod

EMERSE ▶ emersed

EMERSED adj (of the leaves or stems of aquatic plants) protruding above the surface of the water

EMERY n hard mineral used for smoothing and polishing ▷ vb apply emery to

EMES ▶ eme

EMESES ▶ emesis

EMESIS technical name for > **vomiting**

EMETIC n substance that causes vomiting ▷ adj causing vomiting

EMETICS ▶ emetic

EMETIN same as ▶ **emetine**

EMETINE n white bitter poisonous alkaloid

EMETINS ▶ emetin

EMEU same as ▶ emu

EMEUS ▶ emeu

EMEUTE n uprising or rebellion

EMEUTES ▶ emeute

EMIC adj of or relating to a significant linguistic unit

EMICANT ▶ emicate

EMICATE vb twinkle

EMIGRE n someone who has left his native country for political reasons

EMIGRES ▶ emigre

EMINENT adj distinguished, well-known

EMIR n Muslim ruler

EMIRATE n emir's country

EMIRS ▶ emir

EMIT vb give out

EMITS ▶ emit

EMITTED ▶ emit

EMITTER n person or thing that emits

EMLETS pl n as in **blood-drop emlets**

Chilean plant with red-spotted yellow flowers

EMMA n former communications code for the letter A

EMMAS ▶ emma

EMMER n variety of wheat grown in mountainous parts of Europe

EMMERS ▶ emmer

EMMESH same as ▶ **enmesh**

EMMET n tourist or holiday-maker

EMMETS ▶ emmet

EMMEW vb restrict

EMMEWED ▶ emmew

EMMEWS ▶ emmew

EMMOVE vb cause emotion in

EMMOVED ▶ emmove

EMMOVES ▶ emmove

EMMY n (in the US) one of the gold-plated statuettes awarded annually for outstanding television performances and productions

EMMYS ▶ emmy

EMO n type of music combining hard rock with emotional lyrics

EMODIN n type of chemical compound

EMODINS ▶ emodin

EMONG same as ▶ among

EMONGES same as ▶ among

EMONGST same as ▶ amongst

EMOS ▶ emo

EMOTE vb display exaggerated emotion, as if acting

EMOTED ▶ emote

EMOTER ▶ emote

EMOTERS ▶ emote

EMOTES ▶ emote

EMOTING ▶ emote

EMOTION n strong feeling

EMOTIVE adj tending to arouse emotion

EMOVE vb cause to feel emotion

EMOVED ▶ emove

EMOVES ▶ emove

EMOVING ▶ emove

EMPAIRE same as ▶ impair

EMPALE less common spelling of ▶ impale

EMPALED ▶ empale

EMPALER ▶ empale

EMPALES ▶ empale

EMPANEL vb enter on a list (names of persons to be

summoned for jury service)
EMPARE *same as* ▸ **impair**
EMPARED ▸ **empare**
EMPARES ▸ **empare**
EMPARL *same as* ▸ **imparl**
EMPARLS ▸ **emparl**
EMPART *same as* ▸ **impart**
EMPARTS ▸ **empart**
EMPATHY *n* ability to understand someone else's feelings as if they were one's own
EMPAYRE *same as* ▸ **impair**
EMPEACH *same as* ▸ **impeach**
EMPERCE *same as* > **empierce**
EMPEROR *n* ruler of an empire
EMPERY *n* dominion or power
EMPIGHT *adj* attached or positioned
EMPIRE *n* group of territories under the rule of one state or person
EMPIRES ▸ **empire**
EMPIRIC *n* person who relies on empirical methods
EMPLACE *vb* put in place or position
EMPLANE *vb* board or put on board an aeroplane
EMPLOY *vb* engage or make use of the services of (a person) in return for money ▷ *n* state of being employed
EMPLOYE *same as* > **employee**
EMPLOYS ▸ **employ**
EMPLUME *vb* put a plume on
EMPORIA > **emporium**
EMPOWER *vb* enable, authorize
EMPRESS *n* woman who rules an empire
EMPRISE *n* chivalrous or daring enterprise
EMPRIZE *same as* ▸ **emprise**
EMPT *vb* empty
EMPTED ▸ **empt**
EMPTIED ▸ **empty**
EMPTIER ▸ **empty**
EMPTIES ▸ **empty**
EMPTILY ▸ **empty**
EMPTING ▸ **empt**
EMPTINS *pl n* liquid leavening agent made from potatoes
EMPTION *n* process of buying something
EMPTS ▸ **empt**

EMPTY *adj* containing nothing ▷ *vb* make or become empty ▷ *n* empty container, esp a bottle
EMPUSA *n* goblin in Greek mythology
EMPUSAS ▸ **empusa**
EMPUSE *same as* ▸ **empusa**
EMPUSES ▸ **empuse**
EMPYEMA *n* collection of pus in a body cavity, esp in the chest
EMS ▸ **em**
EMU *n* large Australian flightless bird with long legs
EMULATE *vb* attempt to equal or surpass by imitating
EMULE *same as* ▸ **emulate**
EMULED ▸ **emule**
EMULES ▸ **emule**
EMULGE *vb* remove liquid from
EMULGED ▸ **emulge**
EMULGES ▸ **emulge**
EMULING ▸ **emule**
EMULOUS *adj* desiring or aiming to equal or surpass another
EMULSIN *n* enzyme that is found in almonds
EMULSOR *n* device that emulsifies
EMUNGE *vb* clean or clear out
EMUNGED ▸ **emunge**
EMUNGES ▸ **emunge**
EMURE *same as* ▸ **immure**
EMURED ▸ **emure**
EMURES ▸ **emure**
EMURING ▸ **emure**
EMUS ▸ **emu**
EMYD *n* freshwater tortoise or terrapin
EMYDE *same as* ▸ **emyd**
EMYDES ▸ **emyde**
EMYDS ▸ **emyd**
EMYS *n* freshwater tortoise or terrapin
EN *n* unit of measurement, half the width of an em
ENABLE *vb* provide (a person) with the means, opportunity, or authority (to do something)
ENABLED ▸ **enable**
ENABLER ▸ **enable**
ENABLES ▸ **enable**
ENACT *vb* establish by law
ENACTED ▸ **enact**
ENACTOR ▸ **enact**
ENACTS ▸ **enact**
ENAMEL *n* glasslike coating

applied to metal etc to preserve the surface ▷ *vb* cover with enamel
ENAMELS ▸ **enamel**
ENAMINE *n* type of unsaturated compound
ENAMOR *same as* ▸ **enamour**
ENAMORS ▸ **enamor**
ENAMOUR *vb* inspire with love
ENARCH *same as* ▸ **inarch**
ENARM *vb* provide with arms
ENARMED ▸ **enarm**
ENARMS ▸ **enarm**
ENATE *adj* growing out or outwards ▷ *n* relative on the mother's side
ENATES ▸ **enate**
ENATIC *adj* related on one's mother's side
ENATION ▸ **enate**
ENCAGE *vb* confine in or as in a cage
ENCAGED ▸ **encage**
ENCAGES ▸ **encage**
ENCALM *vb* becalm, settle
ENCALMS ▸ **encalm**
ENCAMP *vb* set up in a camp
ENCAMPS ▸ **encamp**
ENCASE *vb* enclose or cover completely
ENCASED ▸ **encase**
ENCASES ▸ **encase**
ENCASH *vb* exchange (a cheque) for cash
ENCAVE *same as* ▸ **incave**
ENCAVED ▸ **encave**
ENCAVES ▸ **encave**
ENCHAFE *vb* heat up
ENCHAIN *vb* bind with chains
ENCHANT *vb* delight and fascinate
ENCHARM *vb* enchant
ENCHASE *less common word for* ▸ **chase**
ENCHEER *vb* cheer up
ENCINA *n* type of oak
ENCINAL ▸ **encina**
ENCINAS ▸ **encina**
ENCLASP *vb* clasp
ENCLAVE *n* part of a country entirely surrounded by foreign territory ▷ *vb* hold in an enclave
ENCLOSE *vb* surround completely
ENCLOUD *vb* hide with clouds
ENCODE *vb* convert (a

message) into code
ENCODED ▸ encode
ENCODER ▸ encode
ENCODES ▸ encode
ENCOMIA ▸ encomium
ENCORE interj again, once
more ▷ n extra
performance due to
enthusiastic demand ▷ vb
demand an extra or
repeated performance of (a
work, piece of music, etc)
by (a performer)
ENCORED ▸ encore
ENCORES ▸ encore
ENCRATY n control of one's
desires, actions, etc
ENCRUST vb cover with a
layer of something
ENCRYPT vb put (a
message) into code
ENCYST vb enclose or
become enclosed by a cyst,
thick membrane, or shell
ENCYSTS ▸ encyst
END n furthest point or part
▷ vb bring or come to a
finish
ENDARCH adj (of a xylem
strand) having the
first-formed xylem internal
to that formed later
ENDART same as ▸ indart
ENDARTS ▸ endart
ENDASH n short dash in
punctuation
ENDEAR vb cause to be
liked
ENDEARS ▸ endear
ENDED ▸ end
ENDEMIC adj present
within a localized area or
peculiar to a particular
group of people ▷ n
endemic disease or plant
ENDER ▸ end
ENDERON same as
▸ andiron
ENDERS ▸ end
ENDEW same as ▸ endue
ENDEWED ▸ endew
ENDEWS ▸ endew
ENDGAME n closing stage
of a game of chess, in which
only a few pieces are left on
the board
ENDGATE n tailboard of a
vehicle
ENDING n last part or
conclusion of something
ENDINGS ▸ ending
ENDIRON same as
▸ andiron

ENDITE same as ▸ indict
ENDITED ▸ endite
ENDITES ▸ endite
ENDIVE n curly-leaved plant
used in salads
ENDIVES ▸ endive
ENDLANG same as
▸ endlong
ENDLEAF n endpaper in a
book
ENDLESS adj having no end
ENDLONG adv lengthways
or on end
ENDMOST adj nearest the
end
ENDNOTE n note at the end
of a section of writing
ENDOGEN n plant that
increases in size by internal
growth
ENDOPOD n inner branch
of a two-branched
crustacean
ENDORSE vb give approval
to
ENDOSS vb endorse
ENDOW vb provide
permanent income for
ENDOWED ▸ endow
ENDOWER ▸ endow
ENDOWS ▸ endow
ENDOZOA > endozoon
ENDPLAY n way of playing
the last few tricks in a hand
so that an opponent is
forced to make a particular
lead ▷ vb force (an
opponent) to make a
particular lead near the end
of a hand
ENDRIN n type of
insecticide
ENDRINS ▸ endrin
ENDS ▸ end
ENDSHIP n small village
ENDUE vb invest or provide,
as with some quality or
trait
ENDUED ▸ endue
ENDUES ▸ endue
ENDUING ▸ endue
ENDURE vb bear (hardship)
patiently
ENDURED ▸ endure
ENDURER ▸ endure
ENDURES ▸ endure
ENDURO n long-distance
race for vehicles, intended
to test endurance
ENDUROS ▸ enduro
ENDWAYS adv having the
end forwards or upwards
▷ adj vertical or upright

ENDWISE same as
▸ endways
ENDYSES ▸ endysis
ENDYSIS n formation of
new layers of integument
after ecdysis
ENDZONE n (in American
football) area at either end
of the playing field
ENE same as ▸ even
ENEMA n medicine injected
into the rectum to empty
the bowels
ENEMAS ▸ enema
ENEMATA ▸ enema
ENEMIES ▸ enemy
ENEMY n hostile person or
nation, opponent ▷ adj of
or belonging to an enemy
ENERGIC ▸ energy
ENERGID n nucleus and the
cytoplasm associated with
it in a syncytium
ENERGY n capacity for
intense activity
ENERVE vb enervate
ENERVED ▸ enerve
ENERVES ▸ enerve
ENES ▸ ene
ENEW vb force a bird into
water
ENEWED ▸ enew
ENEWING ▸ enew
ENEWS ▸ enew
ENFACE vb write, print, or
stamp (something) on the
face of (a document)
ENFACED ▸ enface
ENFACES ▸ enface
ENFANT n French child
ENFANTS ▸ enfant
ENFELON vb infuriate
ENFEOFF vb invest (a
person) with possession of
a freehold estate in land
ENFEVER vb make feverish
ENFILED adj passed
through
ENFIRE vb set alight
ENFIRED ▸ enfire
ENFIRES ▸ enfire
ENFIX same as ▸ infix
ENFIXED ▸ enfix
ENFIXES ▸ enfix
ENFLAME same as ▸ inflame
ENFLESH vb make flesh
ENFOLD vb cover by
wrapping something
around
ENFOLDS ▸ enfold
ENFORCE vb impose
obedience (to a law etc)
ENFORM same as ▸ inform

E

ENFORMS ▸ enform
ENFRAME vb put inside a frame
ENFREE vb release, make free
ENFREED ▸ enfree
ENFREES ▸ enfree
ENFROZE > enfreeze
ENG another name for ▸ **agma**
ENGAGE vb take part, participate ▷ adj (of a writer or artist, esp a man) morally or politically committed to some ideology
ENGAGED adj pledged to be married
ENGAGEE adj (of a female writer or artist) morally or politically committed to some ideology
ENGAGER ▸ engage
ENGAGES ▸ engage
ENGAOL vb put into gaol
ENGAOLS ▸ engaol
ENGILD vb cover with or as if with gold
ENGILDS ▸ engild
ENGILT ▸ engild
ENGINE n any machine which converts energy into mechanical work ▷ vb put an engine in
ENGINED ▸ engine
ENGINER ▸ engine
ENGINES ▸ engine
ENGIRD vb surround
ENGIRDS ▸ engird
ENGIRT ▸ engird
ENGLISH vb put a spinning movement on a billiard ball
ENGLOBE vb surround as if in a globe
ENGLOOM vb make dull or dismal
ENGLUT vb devour ravenously
ENGLUTS ▸ englut
ENGOBE n liquid put on pottery before glazing
ENGOBES ▸ engobe
ENGORE vb pierce or wound
ENGORED ▸ engore
ENGORES ▸ engore
ENGORGE vb clog with blood
ENGRACE vb give grace to
ENGRAFF same as ▸ **engraft**
ENGRAFT vb graft (a shoot, bud, etc) onto a stock
ENGRAIL vb decorate or mark (the edge of) (a coin)

with small carved notches
ENGRAIN variant spelling of ▸ **ingrain**
ENGRAM n physical basis of an individual memory in the brain
ENGRAMS ▸ engram
ENGRASP vb grasp or seize
ENGRAVE vb carve (a design) onto a hard surface
ENGROSS vb occupy the attention of (a person) completely
ENGS ▸ eng
ENGUARD vb protect or defend
ENGULF vb cover or surround completely
ENGULFS ▸ engulf
ENGULPH same as ▸ **engulf**
ENHALO vb surround with or as if with a halo
ENHALOS ▸ enhalo
ENHANCE vb increase in quality, value, or attractiveness
ENIAC n early type of computer built in the 1940s
ENIACS ▸ eniac
ENIGMA n puzzling thing or person
ENIGMAS ▸ enigma
ENISLE vb put on or make into an island
ENISLED ▸ enisle
ENISLES ▸ enisle
ENJAMB vb (of a line of verse) run over into the next line
ENJAMBS ▸ enjamb
ENJOIN vb order (someone) to do something
ENJOINS ▸ enjoin
ENJOY vb take joy in
ENJOYED ▸ enjoy
ENJOYER ▸ enjoy
ENJOYS ▸ enjoy
ENLACE vb bind or encircle with or as with laces
ENLACED ▸ enlace
ENLACES ▸ enlace
ENLARD vb put lard on
ENLARDS ▸ enlard
ENLARGE vb make or grow larger
ENLEVE adj having been abducted
ENLIGHT vb light up
ENLINK vb link together
ENLINKS ▸ enlink
ENLIST vb enter the armed forces
ENLISTS ▸ enlist

ENLIT ▸ enlight
ENLIVEN vb make lively or cheerful
ENLOCK vb lock or secure
ENLOCKS ▸ enlock
ENMESH vb catch or involve in or as if in a net or snare
ENMEW same as ▸ **emmew**
ENMEWED ▸ enmew
ENMEWS ▸ enmew
ENMITY n ill will, hatred
ENMOVE same as ▸ **emmove**
ENMOVED ▸ enmove
ENMOVES ▸ enmove
ENNAGE n total number of ens in a piece of matter to be set in type
ENNAGES ▸ ennage
ENNEAD n group or series of nine
ENNEADS ▸ ennead
ENNOBLE vb make noble, elevate
ENNOG n back alley
ENNOGS ▸ ennog
ENNUI n boredom, dissatisfaction ▷ vb bore
ENNUIED ▸ ennui
ENNUIS ▸ ennui
ENNUYE adj bored
ENNUYED ▸ ennui
ENNUYEE same as ▸ **ennuye**
ENODAL adj having no nodes
ENOKI same as > **enokitake**
ENOKIS ▸ enoki
ENOL n any organic compound containing the group -CH:CO-, often existing in chemical equilibrium with the corresponding keto form
ENOLASE n type of enzyme
ENOLIC ▸ enol
ENOLOGY usual US spelling of > **oenology**
ENOLS ▸ enol
ENOMOTY n division of the Spartan army in ancient Greece
ENORM same as > **enormous**
ENOSES ▸ enosis
ENOSIS n union of Greece and Cyprus
ENOUGH adj as much or as many as necessary ▷ n sufficient quantity ▷ adv sufficiently
ENOUGHS ▸ enough
ENOUNCE vb enunciate
ENOW archaic word for ▸ **enough**

ENOWS ▸ enow

ENPLANE vb board an aircraft

ENPRINT n standard photographic print produced from a negative

ENQUEUE vb add (an item) to a queue of computing tasks

ENQUIRE same as ▸ **inquire**

ENQUIRY ▸ enquire

ENRACE vb bring in a race of people

ENRACED ▸ enrace

ENRACES ▸ enrace

ENRAGE vb make extremely angry

ENRAGED ▸ enrage

ENRAGES ▸ enrage

ENRANGE vb arrange, organize

ENRANK vb put in a row

ENRANKS ▸ enrank

ENRAPT > enrapture

ENRHEUM vb pass a cold on to

ENRICH vb improve in quality

ENRING vb put a ring round

ENRINGS ▸ enring

ENRIVEN adj ripped

ENROBE vb dress in or as if in a robe

ENROBED ▸ enrobe

ENROBER ▸ enrobe

ENROBES ▸ enrobe

ENROL vb (cause to) become a member

ENROLL same as ▸ **enrol**

ENROLLS ▸ enroll

ENROLS ▸ enrol

ENROOT vb establish (plants) by fixing their roots in the earth

ENROOTS ▸ enroot

ENROUGH vb roughen

ENROUND vb encircle

ENS n being or existence in the most general abstract sense

ENSATE adj shaped like a sword

ENSEAL vb seal up

ENSEALS ▸ enseal

ENSEAM vb put a seam on

ENSEAMS ▸ enseam

ENSEAR vb dry

ENSEARS ▸ ensear

ENSERF vb enslave

ENSERFS ▸ enserf

ENSEW same as ▸ **ensue**

ENSEWED ▸ ensew

ENSEWS ▸ ensew

ENSHELL same as ▸ **inshell**

ENSIGN n naval flag ▷ vb mark with a sign

ENSIGNS ▸ ensign

ENSILE vb store and preserve (green fodder) in an enclosed pit or silo

ENSILED ▸ ensile

ENSILES ▸ ensile

ENSKIED ▸ ensky

ENSKIES ▸ ensky

ENSKY vb put in the sky

ENSKYED ▸ ensky

ENSLAVE vb make a slave of (someone)

ENSNARE vb catch in or as if in a snare

ENSNARL vb become tangled in

ENSOUL vb endow with a soul

ENSOULS ▸ ensoul

ENSTAMP vb imprint with a stamp

ENSTEEP vb soak in water

ENSTYLE vb give a name to

ENSUE vb come next, result

ENSUED ▸ ensue

ENSUES ▸ ensue

ENSUING adj following subsequently or in order

ENSURE vb make certain or sure

ENSURED ▸ ensure

ENSURER ▸ ensure

ENSURES ▸ ensure

ENSWEEP vb sweep across

ENSWEPT ▸ ensweep

ENTAIL vb bring about or impose inevitably ▷ n restriction imposed by entailing an estate

ENTAILS ▸ entail

ENTAME vb make tame

ENTAMED ▸ entame

ENTAMES ▸ entame

ENTASES ▸ entasis

ENTASIA same as ▸ **entasis**

ENTASIS n slightly convex curve given to the shaft of a column, pier, or similar structure, to correct the illusion of concavity produced by a straight shaft

ENTAYLE same as ▸ **entail**

ENTENTE n friendly understanding between nations

ENTER vb come or go in

ENTERA ▸ enteron

ENTERAL same as ▸ **enteric**

ENTERED ▸ enter

ENTERER ▸ enter

ENTERIC adj intestinal ▷ n infectious disease of the intestines

ENTERON n alimentary canal, esp of an embryo or a coelenterate

ENTERS ▸ enter

ENTETE adj obsessed

ENTETEE same as ▸ **entete**

ENTHRAL vb hold the attention of

ENTHUSE vb (cause to) show enthusiasm

ENTIA ▸ ens

> This means entities, and because of the common letters it uses is one of the most frequently played five-letter words, at least towards the end of the game.

ENTICE vb attract by exciting hope or desire, tempt

ENTICED ▸ entice

ENTICER ▸ entice

ENTICES ▸ entice

ENTIRE adj including every detail, part, or aspect of something ▷ n state of being entire

ENTIRES ▸ entire

ENTITLE vb give a right to

ENTITY n separate distinct thing

ENTOIL archaic word for ▸ **ensnare**

ENTOILS ▸ entoil

ENTOMB vb place (a corpse) in a tomb

ENTOMBS ▸ entomb

ENTOMIC adj denoting or relating to insects

ENTOPIC adj situated in its normal place or position

ENTOTIC adj of or relating to the inner ear

ENTOZOA ▸ entozoon

ENTRAIL vb twist or entangle

ENTRAIN vb board or put aboard a train

ENTRALL same as > **entrails**

ENTRANT n person who enters a university, contest, etc

ENTRAP vb trick into difficulty etc

ENTRAPS ▸ entrap

ENTREAT vb ask earnestly

ENTREE n dish served before a main course

E

ENTREES ▸ entree
ENTREZ *interj* enter
ENTRIES ▸ entry
ENTRISM *same as* **> entryism**
ENTRIST > entryism
ENTROLD *adj* surrounded
ENTROPY *n* lack of organization
ENTRUST *vb* put into the care or protection of
ENTRY *n* entrance ▷ *adj* necessary in order to enter something
ENTWINE *vb* twist together or around
ENTWIST *vb* twist together or around
ENUF *common intentional literary misspelling of* **▸ enough**
ENURE *variant spelling of* **▸ inure**
ENURED ▸ enure
ENURES ▸ enure
ENURING ▸ enure
ENURN ▸ inurn
ENURNED ▸ inurned
ENURNS ▸ inurns
ENVAULT *vb* enclose in a vault; entomb
ENVELOP *vb* wrap up, enclose
ENVENOM *vb* fill or impregnate with venom
ENVIED ▸ envy
ENVIER ▸ envy
ENVIERS ▸ envy
ENVIES ▸ envy
ENVIOUS *adj* full of envy
ENVIRO *n* environmentalist
ENVIRON *vb* encircle or surround
ENVIROS ▸ enviro
ENVOI *same as* **▸ envoy**
ENVOIS ▸ envoi
ENVOY *n* messenger
ENVOYS ▸ envoy
ENVY *n* feeling of discontent aroused by another's good fortune ▷ *vb* grudge (another's good fortune, success, or qualities)
ENVYING ▸ envy
ENWALL *vb* wall in
ENWALLS ▸ enwall
ENWHEEL *archaic word for* **> encircle**
ENWIND *vb* wind or coil around
ENWINDS ▸ enwind
ENWOMB *vb* enclose in or as if in a womb

ENWOMBS ▸ enwomb
ENWOUND ▸ enwind
ENWRAP *vb* wrap or cover up
ENWRAPS ▸ enwrap
ENZIAN *n* gentian violet
ENZIANS ▸ enzian
ENZONE *vb* enclose in a zone
ENZONED ▸ enzone
ENZONES ▸ enzone
ENZYM *same as* **▸ enzyme**
ENZYME *n* any of a group of complex proteins that act as catalysts in specific biochemical reactions
ENZYMES ▸ enzyme
ENZYMIC ▸ enzyme
ENZYMS ▸ enzym
EOAN *adj* of or relating to the dawn
EOBIONT *n* hypothetical chemical precursor of a living cell
EOCENE *adj* of, denoting, or formed in the second epoch of the Tertiary period
EOLIAN *adj* of or relating to the wind

> 6-letter words tend to be among the least known and least used, because they leave you at the mercy of the tile bag without scoring that extra 50 points you would get for using all 7 letters. This word, meaning related to the wind, often comes in useful for dumping a surplus of vowels. And its alternative spelling **aeolian** is even better for this and what's more will get you a bonus!

EOLITH *n* stone, usually crudely broken, used as a primitive tool in Eolithic times
EOLITHS ▸ eolith
EON *n* longest division of geological time, comprising two or more eras
EONIAN *adj* of or relating to an eon
EONISM *n* adoption of female dress and behaviour by a male
EONISMS ▸ eonism
EONS ▸ eon
EORL *n* Anglo-Saxon nobleman

EORLS ▸ eorl
EOSIN *n* red crystalline water-insoluble derivative of fluorescein
EOSINE *same as* **▸ eosin**
EOSINES ▸ eosine
EOSINIC ▸ eosin
EOSINS ▸ eosin
EOTHEN *adv* from the East
EPACRID *n* type of heath-like plant
EPACRIS *n* genus of the epacrids
EPACT *n* difference in time, about 11 days, between the solar year and the lunar year
EPACTS ▸ epact
EPAGOGE *n* inductive reasoning
EPARCH *n* bishop or metropolitan in charge of an eparchy
EPARCHS ▸ eparch
EPARCHY *n* diocese of the Eastern Christian Church
EPATANT *adj* startling or shocking, esp through being unconventional
EPAULE *n* shoulder of a fortification
EPAULES ▸ epaule
EPAULET *same as* **> epaulette**
EPAXIAL *adj* above the axis
EPAZOTE *n* type of herb
EPEE *n* straight-bladed sword used in fencing
EPEEIST *n* one who uses or specializes in using an epee
EPEES ▸ epee
EPEIRA *same as* **▸ epeirid**
EPEIRAS ▸ epeira
EPEIRIC *adj* in, of, or relating to a continent
EPEIRID *n* type of spider
EPERDU *adj* distracted
EPERDUE *adj* distracted
EPERGNE *n* ornamental centrepiece of a table: a stand with holders for sweetmeats, fruit, flowers, etc
EPHA *same as* **▸ ephah**
EPHAH *n* Hebrew unit of dry measure equal to approximately one bushel or about 33 litres
EPHAHS ▸ ephah
EPHAS ▸ epha
EPHEBE *n* (in ancient Greece) youth about to enter full citizenship, esp

one undergoing military
training

EPHEBES ▸ ephebe

EPHEBI ▸ ephebe

EPHEBIC ▸ ephebe

EPHEBOI ▸ ephebos

EPHEBOS same as ▸ **ephebe**

EPHEBUS same as ▸ **ephebe**

EPHEDRA n gymnosperm
shrub of warm regions of
America and Eurasia

EPHELIS n freckle

EPHOD n embroidered
vestment believed to
resemble an apron with
shoulder straps, worn by
priests in ancient Israel

EPHODS ▸ ephod

EPHOR n (in ancient Greece)
one of a board of senior
magistrates in any of
several Dorian states, esp
the five Spartan ephors,
who were elected by the
vote of all full citizens and
who wielded effective
power

EPHORAL ▸ ephor

EPHORI ▸ ephor

EPHORS ▸ ephor

EPIBLEM n outermost cell
layer of a root

EPIBOLY n process that
occurs during gastrulation
in vertebrates, in which
cells on one side of the
blastula grow over and
surround the remaining
cells and yolk and
eventually form the
ectoderm

EPIC n long poem, book, or
film about heroic events or
actions ▷ adj very
impressive or ambitious

EPICAL ▸ epic

EPICARP n outermost layer
of the pericarp of fruits:
forms the skin of a peach or
grape

EPICEDE same as
> **epicedium**

EPICENE adj having the
characteristics of both
sexes; hermaphroditic ▷ n
epicene person or creature

EPICIER n grocer

EPICISM n style or trope
characteristic of epics

EPICIST n writer of epics

EPICS ▸ epic

EPICURE n person who
enjoys good food and drink

EPIDERM same as
> **epidermis**

EPIDOTE n green mineral
consisting of hydrated
calcium iron aluminium
silicate in monoclinic
crystalline form: common
in metamorphic rocks

EPIGEAL adj of or relating to
seed germination in which
the cotyledons appear
above the ground because
of the growth of the
hypocotyl

EPIGEAN same as ▸ **epigeal**

EPIGEIC same as ▸ **epigeal**

EPIGENE adj formed or
taking place at or near the
surface of the earth

EPIGON same as ▸ **epigone**

EPIGONE n inferior follower
or imitator

EPIGONI ▸ epigone

EPIGONS ▸ epigon

EPIGRAM n short witty
remark or poem

EPIGYNY > epigynous

EPILATE vb remove hair
from

EPILOG same as > **epilogue**

EPILOGS ▸ epilog

EPIMER n isomer

EPIMERE n dorsal part of
the mesoderm of a
vertebrate embryo,
consisting of a series of
segments

EPIMERS ▸ epimer

EPINAOI ▸ epinaos

EPINAOS n rear vestibule

EPISCIA n creeping plant

EPISODE n incident in a
series of incidents

EPISOME n unit of genetic
material (DNA) in bacteria,
such as a plasmid, that can
either replicate
independently or can be
integrated into the host
chromosome

EPISTLE n letter, esp of an
apostle ▷ vb preface

EPITAPH n commemorative
inscription on a tomb ▷ vb
compose an epitaph

EPITAXY n growth of a thin
layer on the surface of a
crystal so that the layer has
the same structure as the
underlying crystal

EPITHEM n external topical
application

EPITHET n descriptive word

or name ▷ vb name

EPITOME n typical example

EPITOPE n site on an
antigen at which a specific
antibody becomes
attached

EPIZOA ▸ epizoon

EPIZOAN same as ▸ **epizoon**

EPIZOIC adj (of an animal or
plant) growing or living on
the exterior of a living
animal

EPIZOON n animal, such as
a parasite, that lives on the
body of another animal

EPOCH n period of notable
events

EPOCHA same as ▸ **epoch**

EPOCHAL ▸ epoch

EPOCHAS ▸ epocha

EPOCHS ▸ epoch

EPODE n part of a lyric ode
that follows the strophe
and the antistrophe

EPODES ▸ epode

EPODIC ▸ epode

EPONYM n name, esp a
place name, derived from
the name of a real or
mythical person

EPONYMS ▸ eponym

EPONYMY n derivation of
names of places, etc, from
those of persons

EPOPEE n epic poem

EPOPEES ▸ epopee

EPOPT n one initiated into
mysteries

EPOPTS ▸ epopt

EPOS n body of poetry in
which the tradition of a
people is conveyed, esp a
group of poems concerned
with a common epic theme

EPOSES ▸ epos

EPOXIDE n compound
containing an oxygen atom
joined to two different
groups that are themselves
joined to other groups

EPOXIED ▸ epoxy

EPOXIES ▸ epoxy

EPOXY adj of or containing
an oxygen atom joined to
two different groups that
are themselves joined to
other groups ▷ n epoxy
resin ▷ vb glue with epoxy
resin

EPOXYED ▸ epoxy

EPRIS adj enamoured

EPRISE feminine form of
▸ **epris**

EPSILON *n* fifth letter of the Greek alphabet, a short vowel, transliterated as *e*

EPUISE *adj* exhausted

EPUISEE *feminine form of* ▸ **epuise**

EPULARY *adj* of or relating to feasting

EPULIS *n* swelling of the gum, usually as a result of fibrous hyperplasia

EPURATE *vb* purify

EPYLLIA > **epyllion**

EQUABLE *adj* even-tempered

EQUABLY ▸ **equable**

EQUAL *adj* identical in size, quantity, degree, etc ▷ *n* person or thing equal to another ▷ *vb* be equal to

EQUALED ▸ **equal**

EQUALI *pl n* pieces for a group of instruments of the same kind

EQUALLY ▸ **equal**

EQUALS ▸ **equal**

EQUANT *n* circle in which a planet was formerly believed to move

EQUANTS ▸ **equant**

EQUATE *vb* make or regard as equivalent

EQUATED ▸ **equate**

EQUATES ▸ **equate**

EQUATOR *n* imaginary circle round the earth, equidistant from the poles

EQUERRY *n* officer who acts as an attendant to a member of a royal family

EQUID *n* any animal of the horse family

EQUIDS ▸ **equid**

EQUINAL *same as* ▸ **equine**

EQUINE *adj* of or like a horse ▷ *n* any animal of the horse family

EQUINES ▸ **equine**

EQUINIA *n* glanders

EQUINOX *n* time of year when day and night are of equal length

EQUIP *vb* provide with supplies, components, etc

EQUIPE *n* (esp in motor racing) team

EQUIPES ▸ **equipe**

EQUIPS ▸ **equip**

EQUITES *pl n* cavalry

EQUITY *n* fairness

ER *interj* sound made when hesitating in speech

ERA *n* period of time

considered as distinctive

ERAS ▸ **era**

ERASE *vb* destroy all traces of

ERASED ▸ **erase**

ERASER *n* object for erasing something written

ERASERS ▸ **eraser**

ERASES ▸ **erase**

ERASING ▸ **erase**

ERASION *n* act of erasing

> This means the state of being erased: not an exciting word, but its combination of common letters makes it one of the most frequently played of 7-letter bonus words.

ERASURE *n* erasing

ERATHEM *n* stratum of rocks representing a specific geological era

ERBIA *n* oxide of erbium

ERBIAS ▸ **erbia**

ERBIUM *n* metallic element of the lanthanide series

ERBIUMS ▸ **erbium**

ERE *prep* before ▷ *vb* plough

ERECT *vb* build ▷ *adj* upright

ERECTED ▸ **erect**

ERECTER *same as* ▸ **erector**

ERECTLY ▸ **erect**

ERECTOR *n* any muscle that raises a part or makes it erect

ERECTS ▸ **erect**

ERED ▸ **ere**

ERELONG *adv* before long

EREMIC *adj* of or relating to deserts

EREMITE *n* Christian hermit

EREMURI > **eremurus**

ERENOW *adv* long before the present

EREPSIN *n* mixture of proteolytic enzymes secreted by the small intestine

ERES ▸ **ere**

ERETHIC > **erethism**

EREV *n* day before

EREVS ▸ **erev**

ERF *n* plot of land, usually urban, marked off for building purposes

ERG *same as* > **ergometer**

ERGATE *n* worker ant

ERGATES ▸ **ergate**

ERGO *same as* > **ergometer**

ERGODIC *adj* of or relating to the probability that any state will recur

ERGON *n* work

ERGONS ▸ **ergon**

ERGOS ▸ **ergo**

ERGOT *n* fungal disease of cereal

ERGOTIC ▸ **ergot**

ERGOTS ▸ **ergot**

ERGS ▸ **erg**

ERHU *n* Chinese two-stringed violin

ERHUS ▸ **erhu**

ERIACH *same as* ▸ **eric**

ERIACHS ▸ **eriach**

ERIC *n* (in old Irish law) fine paid by a murderer to the family of his victim

ERICA *n* genus of plants including heathers

ERICAS ▸ **erica**

ERICK *same as* ▸ **eric**

ERICKS ▸ **erick**

ERICOID *adj* (of leaves) small and tough, resembling those of heather

ERICS ▸ **eric**

ERING ▸ **ere**

ERINGO *same as* ▸ **eryngo**

ERINGOS ▸ **eringo**

ERINITE *n* arsenate of copper

ERINUS *n* type of plant

ERISTIC *adj* of, relating, or given to controversy or logical disputation, esp for its own sake ▷ *n* person who engages in logical disputes

ERK *n* aircraftman or naval rating

ERKS ▸ **erk**

ERLANG *n* unit of traffic intensity in a telephone system equal to the intensity for a specific period when the average number of simultaneous calls is unity

ERLANGS ▸ **erlang**

ERLKING *n* malevolent spirit who carries off children

ERM *interj* expression of hesitation

ERMELIN *n* ermine

ERMINE *n* stoat in northern regions, where it has a white winter coat with a black-tipped tail

ERMINED *adj* clad in the fur of the ermine

ERMINES ▸ **ermine**

ERN *archaic variant of* ▸ **earn**

ERNE *n* fish-eating (European) sea eagle
ERNED ▸ **ern**
ERNES ▸ **erne**
ERNING ▸ **ern**
ERNS ▸ **ern**
ERODE *vb* wear away
ERODED ▸ **erode**
ERODENT ▸ **erode**
ERODES ▸ **erode**
ERODING ▸ **erode**
ERODIUM *n* type of geranium
EROS *n* lust
EROSE *adj* jagged or uneven, as though gnawed or bitten
EROSELY ▸ **erose**
EROSES ▸ **eros**
EROSION *n* wearing away of rocks or soil by the action of water, ice, or wind
EROSIVE ▸ **erosion**
EROTEMA *n* rhetorical question
EROTEME *same as* ▸ **erotema**
EROTIC *adj* relating to sexual pleasure or desire ▷ *n* person who has strong sexual desires or is especially responsive to sexual stimulation
EROTICA *n* sexual literature or art
EROTICS ▸ **erotic**
EROTISE *same as* ▸ **erotize**
EROTISM *same as* > **eroticism**
EROTIZE *vb* make erotic
ERR *vb* make a mistake
ERRABLE *adj* capable of making a mistake
ERRANCY *n* state or an instance of erring or a tendency to err
ERRAND *n* short trip to do something for someone
ERRANDS ▸ **errand**
ERRANT *adj* behaving in a manner considered to be unacceptable ▷ *n* knight-errant
ERRANTS ▸ **errant**
ERRATA ▸ **erratum**
ERRATAS *informal variant of* ▸ **errata**
ERRATIC *adj* irregular or unpredictable ▷ *n* rock that has been transported by glacial action
ERRATUM *n* error in writing or printing

ERRED ▸ **err**
ERRHINE *adj* causing nasal secretion ▷ *n* errhine drug or agent
ERRING ▸ **err**
ERRINGS ▸ **err**
ERROR *n* mistake, inaccuracy, or misjudgment
ERRORS ▸ **error**
ERRS ▸ **err**
ERS *same as* ▸ **ervil**
ERSATZ *adj* made in imitation ▷ *n* ersatz substance or article
ERSES ▸ **ers**
ERST *adv* long ago
ERUCIC *adj* *as in* **erucic acid** crystalline fatty acid derived from rapeseed, mustard seed and wallflower seed
ERUCT *vb* belch
ERUCTED ▸ **eruct**
ERUCTS ▸ **eruct**
ERUDITE *adj* having great academic knowledge ▷ *n* erudite person
ERUGO *n* verdigris
ERUGOS ▸ **erugo**
ERUPT *vb* eject (steam, water, or volcanic material) violently
ERUPTED ▸ **erupt**
ERUPTS ▸ **erupt**
ERUV *n* area, circumscribed by a symbolic line, within which certain activities forbidden to Orthodox Jews on the Sabbath are permitted
ERUVIM ▸ **eruv**
ERUVIN ▸ **eruv**
ERUVS ▸ **eruv**
ERVEN ▸ **erf**
ERVIL *n* type of vetch
ERVILS ▸ **ervil**
ERYNGO *n* type of plant with toothed or lobed leaves, such as the sea holly
ERYNGOS ▸ **eryngo**
ES *n* letter S
ESCALOP *another word for* ▸ **scallop**
ESCAPE *vb* get free (of) ▷ *n* act of escaping
ESCAPED ▸ **escape**
ESCAPEE *n* person who has escaped
ESCAPER ▸ **escape**
ESCAPES ▸ **escape**
ESCAR *same as* ▸ **esker**
ESCARP *n* inner side of the ditch separating besiegers

and besieged ▷ *vb* make into a slope
ESCARPS ▸ **escarp**
ESCARS ▸ **escar**
ESCHAR *n* dry scab or slough, esp one following a burn or cauterization of the skin
ESCHARS ▸ **eschar**
ESCHEAT *n* private possessions that become state property in the absence of an heir ▷ *vb* attain such property
ESCHEW *vb* abstain from, avoid
ESCHEWS ▸ **eschew**
ESCOLAR *n* slender spiny-finned fish
ESCORT *n* people or vehicles accompanying another person for protection or as an honour ▷ *vb* act as an escort to
ESCORTS ▸ **escort**
ESCOT *vb* maintain
ESCOTED ▸ **escot**
ESCOTS ▸ **escot**
ESCRIBE *vb* draw (a circle) so that it is tangential to one side of a triangle and to the other two sides produced
ESCROC *n* conman
ESCROCS ▸ **escroc**
ESCROL *same as* ▸ **escroll**
ESCROLL *n* scroll
ESCROLS ▸ **escroll**
ESCROW *n* money, goods, or a written document, such as a contract bond, delivered to a third party and held by him pending fulfilment of some condition ▷ *vb* place (money, a document, etc) in escrow
ESCROWS ▸ **escrow**
ESCUAGE *(in medieval Europe) another word for* ▸ **scutage**
ESCUDO *n* former monetary unit of Portugal
ESCUDOS ▸ **escudo**
ESERINE *n* crystalline alkaloid
ESES ▸ **es**
ESILE *n* vinegar
ESILES ▸ **esile**
ESKAR *same as* ▸ **esker**
ESKARS ▸ **eskar**
ESKER *n* long winding ridge of gravel, sand, etc,

E

originally deposited by a
meltwater stream running
under a glacier

ESKERS ▶ esker

ESKIES ▶ esky

ESKY n portable insulated
container for keeping food
and drink cool

ESLOIN same as ▶ **eloign**

ESLOINS ▶ esloin

ESLOYNE same as ▶ **eloign**

ESNE n household slave

ESNECY n right of the eldest
daughter to make the first
choice when dividing
inheritance

ESNES ▶ esne

ESOTERY > **esoteric**

ESPADA n sword

ESPADAS ▶ espada

ESPANOL n Spanish person

ESPARTO n grass of S
Europe and N Africa used
for making rope etc

ESPIAL n act or fact of being
seen or discovered

ESPIALS ▶ espial

ESPIED ▶ espy

ESPIER ▶ espy

ESPIERS ▶ espy

ESPIES ▶ espy

ESPOUSE vb adopt or give
support to (a cause etc)

ESPRIT n spirit, liveliness, or
wit

ESPRITS ▶ esprit

ESPY vb catch sight of

ESPYING ▶ espy

ESQUIRE n courtesy title
placed after a man's name
▷ vb escort

ESS n letter S

ESSAY n short literary
composition ▷ vb attempt

ESSAYED ▶ essay

ESSAYER ▶ essay

ESSAYS ▶ essay

ESSE n existence

ESSENCE n most important
feature of a thing which
determines its identity

ESSES ▶ ess

ESSIVE n grammatical case

ESSIVES ▶ essive

ESSOIN n excuse

ESSOINS ▶ essoin

ESSOYNE same as ▶ **essoin**

EST n treatment intended to
help people towards
psychological growth, in
which they spend many
hours in large groups,
deprived of food and water

and hectored by stewards

ESTATE n landed property
▷ vb provide with an estate

ESTATED ▶ estate

ESTATES ▶ estate

ESTEEM n high regard ▷ vb
think highly of

ESTEEMS ▶ esteem

ESTER n compound
produced by the reaction
between an acid and an
alcohol

ESTERS ▶ ester

ESTHETE US spelling of
> **aesthete**

ESTIVAL usual US spelling of
> **aestival**

ESTOC n short stabbing
sword

ESTOCS ▶ estoc

ESTOILE n heraldic star with
wavy points

ESTOP vb preclude by
estoppel

ESTOPS ▶ estop

ESTOVER same as
> **estovers**

ESTRADE n dais or raised
platform

ESTRAL US spelling of
▶ **oestral**

ESTRAY n stray domestic
animal of unknown
ownership ▷ vb stray

ESTRAYS ▶ estray

ESTREAT n true copy of or
extract from a court record
▷ vb enforce (a
recognizance that has been
forfeited) by sending an
extract of the court record
to the proper authority

ESTREPE vb lay waste

ESTRICH n ostrich

ESTRIN US spelling of
▶ **oestrin**

ESTRINS ▶ estrin

ESTRIOL usual US spelling of
> **oestriol**

ESTRO n poetic inspiration

ESTRONE usual US spelling of
> **oestrone**

ESTROS ▶ estro

ESTROUS ▶ estrus

ESTRUAL ▶ estrus

ESTRUM usual US spelling of
▶ **oestrum**

ESTRUMS ▶ estrum

ESTRUS usual US spelling of
▶ **oestrus**

ESTS ▶ est

ESTUARY n mouth of a river

ET dialect past tense of ▶ **eat**

ETA n seventh letter in the
Greek alphabet, a long
vowel sound

ETACISM n pronunciation of
eta as a long vowel sound

ETAERIO n aggregate fruit,
as one consisting of drupes
(raspberry) or achenes
(traveller's joy)

This strange-looking
word is a botanical term
for a type of fruit, and
because it uses the
commonest letters is,
along with **otarine**, the
most frequently played
of all bonus words.

ETAGE n floor in a
multi-storey building

ETAGERE n stand with open
shelves for displaying
ornaments, etc

ETAGES ▶ etage

ETALAGE n display

ETALON n device used in
spectroscopy to measure
wavelengths by
interference effects
produced by multiple
reflections between parallel
half-silvered glass or quartz
plates

ETALONS ▶ etalon

ETAMIN same as ▶ **etamine**

ETAMINE n cotton or
worsted fabric of loose
weave, used for clothing,
curtains, etc

ETAMINS ▶ etamin

ETAPE n public storehouse

ETAPES ▶ etape

ETAS ▶ eta

ETAT n state

ETATISM same as
> **etatisme**

ETATIST > **etatisme**

ETATS ▶ etat

ETCH vb wear away or cut
the surface of (metal, glass,
etc) with acid

ETCHANT n any acid or
corrosive used for etching

ETCHED ▶ etch

ETCHER ▶ etch

ETCHERS ▶ etch

ETCHES ▶ etch

ETCHING n picture printed
from an etched metal plate

ETEN n giant

ETENS ▶ eten

ETERNAL adj without
beginning or end ▷ n
eternal thing

ETERNE *archaic or poetic word for* ▸ **eternal**

ETESIAN *adj* (of NW winds) recurring annually in the summer in the E Mediterranean ▷ *n* etesian wind

ETH *same as* ▸ **edh**

ETHAL *n* cetyl alcohol

ETHALS ▸ **ethal**

ETHANAL *n* colourless volatile pungent liquid

ETHANE *n* odourless flammable gas obtained from natural gas and petroleum

ETHANES ▸ **ethane**

ETHANOL *same as* ▸ **alcohol**

ETHE *adj* easy

ETHENE *same as* > **ethylene**

ETHENES ▸ **ethene**

ETHER *n* colourless sweet-smelling liquid used as an anaesthetic

ETHERIC ▸ **ether**

ETHERS ▸ **ether**

ETHIC *n* moral principle

ETHICAL *adj* of or based on a system of moral beliefs about right and wrong ▷ *n* drug available only by prescription

ETHICS *n* code of behaviour

ETHINYL *same as* ▸ **ethynyl**

ETHION *n* type of pesticide

ETHIONS ▸ **ethion**

ETHIOPS *n* dark-coloured chemical compound

ETHMOID *adj* denoting or relating to a bone of the skull that forms part of the eye socket and the nasal cavity ▷ *n* ethmoid bone

ETHNIC *adj* relating to a people or group that shares a culture, religion, or language ▷ *n* member of an ethnic group, esp a minority group

ETHNICS ▸ **ethnic**

ETHNOS *n* ethnic group

ETHOS *n* distinctive spirit and attitudes of a people, culture, etc

ETHOSES ▸ **ethos**

ETHOXY ▸ **ethoxyl**

ETHOXYL *n* univalent radical

ETHS ▸ **eth**

ETHYL *adj* type of chemical hydrocarbon group

ETHYLIC ▸ **ethyl**

ETHYLS ▸ **ethyl**

ETHYNE *another name for* > **acetylene**

ETHYNES ▸ **ethyne**

ETHYNYL *n* univalent radical

ETIC *adj* (in linguistics) of or relating to items analyzed without consideration of their structural function

ETIOLIN *n* yellow pigment

ETNA *n* container used to heat liquids

ETNAS ▸ **etna**

ETOILE *n* star

ETOILES ▸ **etoile**

ETOURDI *adj* foolish

ETRENNE *n* New Year's gift

ETRIER *n* short portable ladder or set of webbing loops that can be attached to a karabiner or fifi hook

ETRIERS ▸ **etrier**

ETTIN *n* giant

ETTINS ▸ **ettin**

ETTLE *vb* intend

ETTLED ▸ **ettle**

ETTLES ▸ **ettle**

ETTLING ▸ **ettle**

ETUDE *n* short musical composition for a solo instrument, esp intended as a technical exercise

ETUDES ▸ **etude**

ETUI *n* small usually ornamented case for holding needles, cosmetics, or other small articles

ETUIS ▸ **etui**

ETWEE *same as* ▸ **etui**

> E is a very desirable letter, but sometimes you can have too much of even this good thing. This word for a needle-case, a variant of **etui**, can help you dispose of a few of them.

ETWEES ▸ **etui**

ETYMA ▸ **etymon**

ETYMIC ▸ **etymon**

ETYMON *n* earliest form of a word or morpheme, or a reconstructed form, from which another word or morpheme is derived

ETYMONS ▸ **etymon**

ETYPIC *n* unable to conform to type

EUCAIN *same as* ▸ **eucaine**

EUCAINE *n* crystalline optically active substance formerly used as a local anaesthetic

EUCAINS ▸ **eucain**

EUCHRE *n* US and Canadian card game similar to écarté for two to four players, using a poker pack with joker ▷ *vb* prevent (a player) from making his contracted tricks

EUCHRED ▸ **euchre**

EUCHRES ▸ **euchre**

EUCLASE *n* brittle green gem

EUCRITE *n* type of stony meteorite

EUDEMON *n* benevolent spirit or demon

EUGARIE *another name for* ▸ **pipi**

EUGE *interj* well done!

EUGENIA *n* plant of the clove family

EUGENIC > **eugenics**

EUGENOL *n* colourless or pale yellow oily liquid substance with a spicy taste and an odour of cloves, used in perfumery

EUGH *archaic form of* ▸ **yew**

EUGHEN *archaic form of* ▸ **yew**

EUGHS ▸ **eugh**

EUGLENA *n* type of freshwater unicellular organism

EUK *vb* itch

EUKED ▸ **euk**

EUKING ▸ **euk**

EUKS ▸ **euk**

EULOGIA *n* blessed bread distributed to members of the congregation after the liturgy, esp to those who have not communed

> This means blessed bread and is one of the few 7-letter words that use all the vowels. What's more, it can take a plural in E as well as S, giving **eulogiae**, which can be even better for getting you out of vowel trouble.

EULOGY *n* speech or writing in praise of a person

EUMONG *same as* ▸ **eumung**

EUMONGS ▸ **eumong**

EUMUNG *n* any of various Australian acacias

EUMUNGS ▸ **eumung**

EUNUCH *n* castrated man, esp (formerly) a guard in a harem

E

EUNUCHS ▸ eunuch

EUOI n cry of Bacchic frenzy

> This is a cry expressing Bacchic frenzy, and is forever coming in useful to dispose of a surplus of vowels. It has the less commonly played but still useful variants **evoe, evhoe** and **evohe**.

EUOUAE n a mnemonic used to recall the sequence of tones in a particular passage of the Gloria

> This word is remarkable in containing no consonants. You will be surprised at how often you will be glad to play it!

EUOUAES ▸ euouae

EUPAD n antiseptic powder

EUPADS ▸ eupad

EUPEPSY same as > eupepsia

EUPHON n glass harmonica

EUPHONS ▸ euphon

EUPHONY n pleasing sound

EUPHORY same as > euphoria

EUPHROE n wooden block with holes through which the lines of a crowfoot are rove

EUPLOID adj having chromosomes present in an exact multiple of the haploid number ▷ n euploid cell or individual

EUPNEA same as ▸ eupnoea

EUPNEAS ▸ eupnea

EUPNEIC ▸ eupnoea

EUPNOEA n normal relaxed breathing

EUREKA n exclamation of triumph at finding something

EUREKAS ▸ eureka

EURIPI ▸ euripus

EURIPUS n strait or channel with a strong current or tide

EURO n unit of the single currency of the European Union

EUROKY n ability of an organism to live under different conditions

EUROPOP n type of pop music by European artists

EUROS ▸ euro

EURYOKY same as ▸ euroky

EUSOL n solution of eupad in water

EUSOLS ▸ eusol

EUSTACY > eustatic

EUSTASY > eustatic

EUSTELE n central cylinder of a seed plant

EUSTYLE n building with columns optimally spaced

EUTAXIA n condition of being easily melted

EUTAXY n good order

EUTEXIA same as ▸ eutaxia

EUTROPY n regular variation of the crystalline structure of a series of compounds according to atomic number

EVACUEE n person evacuated from a place of danger, esp in wartime

EVADE vb get away from or avoid

EVADED ▸ evade

EVADER ▸ evade

EVADERS ▸ evade

EVADES ▸ evade

EVADING ▸ evade

EVANGEL n gospel of Christianity

EVANISH poetic word for ▸ vanish

EVASION n act of evading something, esp a duty or responsibility, by cunning or illegal means

EVASIVE adj not straightforward

EVE n evening or day before some special event

EVEJAR n nightjar

EVEJARS ▸ evejar

EVEN adj flat or smooth ▷ adv equally ▷ vb make even ▷ n eve

EVENED ▸ even

EVENER ▸ even

EVENERS ▸ even

EVENEST ▸ even

EVENING n end of the day or early part of the night ▷ adj of or in the evening

EVENLY ▸ even

EVENS adv (of a bet) winning the same as the amount staked if successful

EVENT n anything that takes place ▷ vb take part or ride (a horse) in eventing

EVENTED ▸ event

EVENTER > eventing

EVENTS ▸ event

EVER adv at any time

EVERNET n hypothetical form of internet that is

continuously accessible using a wide variety of devices

EVERT vb turn (an eyelid, the intestines, or some other bodily part) outwards or inside out

EVERTED ▸ evert

EVERTOR n any muscle that turns a part outwards

EVERTS ▸ evert

EVERY adj each without exception

EVES ▸ eve

EVET n eft

EVETS ▸ evet

EVHOE interj cry of Bacchic frenzy

EVICT vb legally expel (someone) from his or her home

EVICTED ▸ evict

EVICTEE ▸ evict

EVICTOR ▸ evict

EVICTS ▸ evict

EVIDENT adj easily seen or understood ▷ n item of evidence

EVIL n wickedness ▷ adj harmful ▷ adv in an evil manner

EVILER ▸ evil

EVILEST ▸ evil

EVILLER ▸ evil

EVILLY ▸ evil

EVILS ▸ evil

EVINCE vb make evident

EVINCED ▸ evince

EVINCES ▸ evince

EVIRATE vb castrate

EVITATE archaic word for ▸ avoid

EVITE archaic word for ▸ avoid

EVITED ▸ evite

EVITES ▸ evite

EVITING ▸ evite

EVO informal word for ▸ evening

EVOCATE vb evoke

EVOE interj cry of Bacchic frenzy

EVOHE interj cry of Bacchic frenzy

EVOKE vb call or summon up (a memory, feeling, etc)

EVOKED ▸ evoke

EVOKER ▸ evoke

EVOKERS ▸ evoke

EVOKES ▸ evoke

EVOKING ▸ evoke

EVOLUE n (in the African former colonies of Belgium

and France) African person educated according to European principles

EVOLUES ▸ evolue

EVOLUTE n geometric curve that describes the locus of the centres of curvature of another curve ▷ adj having the margins rolled outwards ▷ vb evolve

EVOLVE vb develop gradually

EVOLVED ▸ evolve

EVOLVER ▸ evolve

EVOLVES ▸ evolve

EVOS ▸ evo

EVOVAE n a mnemonic used to recall the sequence of tones in a particular passage of the Gloria Patri

EVOVAES ▸ evovae

EVULSE vb extract by force

EVULSED ▸ evulse

EVULSES ▸ evulse

EVZONE n soldier in an elite Greek infantry regiment

EVZONES ▸ evzone

EWE n female sheep

EWER n large jug with a wide mouth

EWERS ▸ ewer

EWES ▸ ewe

EWEST Scots word for ▸ **near**

EWFTES Spenserian plural of ▸ **eft**

EWGHEN archaic form of ▸ **yew**

EWHOW interj expression of pity or regret

EWK vb itch

> **Ewk** is a dialect word for **itch**. It's a handy little word and a good one to remember in case you end up with both K and W, and remember that it's a verb so you can have **ewks, ewked** and **ewking**. It's also worth knowing its variants **euk, yeuk, youk, yuck** and **yuke**!

EWKED ▸ ewk

EWKING ▸ ewk

EWKS ▸ ewk

EWT archaic form of ▸ **newt**

EWTS ▸ ewt

EX prep not including ▷ n a former husband, wife etc ▷ vb cross out or delete

EXABYTE n very large unit of computer memory

EXACT adj correct and complete in every detail ▷ vb demand (payment or obedience)

EXACTA n horse-racing bet in which the first and second horses must be named in the correct order

EXACTAS ▸ exacta

EXACTED ▸ exact

EXACTER ▸ exact

EXACTLY adv precisely, in every respect ▷ interj just so! precisely!

EXACTOR ▸ exact

EXACTS ▸ exact

EXACUM n type of tropical plant often grown as a greenhouse plant for its bluish-purple platter-shaped flowers

EXACUMS ▸ exacum

EXALT vb praise highly

EXALTED adj high or elevated in rank, position, dignity, etc

EXALTER ▸ exalt

EXALTS ▸ exalt

EXAM n examination

EXAMEN n examination of conscience, usually made daily by Jesuits and others

EXAMENS ▸ examen

EXAMINE vb look at closely

EXAMPLE n specimen typical of its group

EXAMS ▸ exam

EXAPTED adj biologically adapted

EXARATE adj (of the pupa of such insects as ants and bees) having legs, wings, antennae, etc, free and movable

EXARCH n head of certain autonomous Orthodox Christian Churches, such as that of Bulgaria and Cyprus ▷ adj (of a xylem strand) having the first-formed xylem external to that formed later

EXARCHS ▸ exarch

EXARCHY same as > **exarchate**

EXCAMB vb exchange

EXCAMBS ▸ excamb

EXCEED vb be greater than

EXCEEDS ▸ exceed

EXCEL vb be superior to

EXCELS ▸ excel

EXCEPT prep other than, not including ▷ vb leave out; omit; exclude

EXCEPTS ▸ except

EXCERPT n passage taken from a book, speech, etc ▷ vb take a passage from a book, speech, etc

EXCESS n state or act of exceeding the permitted limits ▷ vb make (a position) redundant

EXCHEAT same as ▸ **escheat**

EXCIDE vb cut out

EXCIDED ▸ excide

EXCIDES ▸ excide

EXCIMER n excited dimer formed by the association of excited and unexcited molecules, which would remain dissociated in the ground state

EXCIPLE n part of a lichen

EXCISE n tax on goods produced for the home market ▷ vb cut out or away

EXCISED ▸ excise

EXCISES ▸ excise

EXCITE vb arouse to strong emotion

EXCITED adj emotionally aroused, esp to pleasure or agitation

EXCITER n person or thing that excites

EXCITES ▸ excite

EXCITON n mobile neutral entity in a crystalline solid consisting of an excited electron bound to the hole produced by its excitation

EXCITOR n nerve that, when stimulated, causes increased activity in the organ or part it supplies

EXCLAIM vb speak suddenly, cry out

EXCLAVE n part of a country entirely surrounded by foreign territory: viewed from the position of the home country

EXCLUDE vb keep out, leave out

EXCRETA n excrement

EXCRETE vb discharge (waste matter) from the body

EXCUDIT sentence substitute (named person) made this

EXCURSE vb wander

EXCUSAL ▸ excuse

EXCUSE n explanation offered to justify (a fault etc) ▷ vb put forward a reason or justification for (a fault etc)

EXCUSED ▸ excuse

EXCUSER ▸ excuse

EXCUSES ▸ excuse

EXEAT n leave of absence from school or some other institution

EXEATS ▸ exeat

EXEC n executive

EXECS ▸ exec

EXECUTE vb put (a condemned person) to death

EXED ▸ ex

EXEDRA n building, room, portico, or apse containing a continuous bench, used in ancient Greece and Rome for holding discussions

EXEDRAE ▸ exedra

EXEEM same as ▸ exeme

EXEEMED ▸ exeem

EXEEMS ▸ exeem

EXEGETE n person who practises exegesis

EXEME vb set free

EXEMED ▸ exeme

EXEMES ▸ exeme

EXEMING ▸ exeme

EXEMPLA > exemplum

EXEMPLE same as ▸ example

EXEMPT adj not subject to an obligation etc ▷ vb release from an obligation etc ▷ n person who is exempt from an obligation, tax, etc

EXEMPTS ▸ exempt

EXEQUY n funeral rite

> Meaning a funeral rite, this word combines X and Q. Even better is its plural **exequies**, which would earn an extra 50 points for using all your tiles.

EXERGUE n space on the reverse of a coin or medal below the central design, often containing the date, place of minting, etc

EXERGY n maximum amount of useful work obtainable from a system

EXERT vb use (influence, authority, etc) forcefully or effectively

EXERTED ▸ exert

EXERTS ▸ exert

EXES ▸ ex

EXEUNT vb (they) go out

EXHALE vb breathe out

EXHALED ▸ exhale

EXHALES ▸ exhale

EXHAUST vb tire out ▷ n gases ejected from an engine as waste products

EXHEDRA same as ▸ exedra

EXHIBIT vb display to the public ▷ n object exhibited to the public

EXHORT vb urge earnestly

EXHORTS ▸ exhort

EXHUME vb dig up (something buried, esp a corpse)

EXHUMED ▸ exhume

EXHUMER ▸ exhume

EXHUMES ▸ exhume

EXIES n hysterics

EXIGENT adj urgent ▷ n emergency

EXILE n prolonged, usu enforced, absence from one's country ▷ vb expel from one's country

EXILED ▸ exile

EXILER ▸ exile

EXILERS ▸ exile

EXILES ▸ exile

EXILIAN ▸ exile

EXILIC ▸ exile

EXILING ▸ exile

EXILITY n poverty or meagreness

EXINE n outermost coat of a pollen grain or a spore

EXINES ▸ exine

EXING ▸ ex

EXIST vb have being or reality

EXISTED ▸ exist

EXISTS ▸ exist

EXIT n way out ▷ vb go out

EXITED ▸ exit

EXITING ▸ exit

EXITS ▸ exit

EXO informal word for > excellent

> Exo is an informal Australian way of saying excellent. This is a great little word as it allows you to combine X with two of the most common tiles in the game, E and O.

EXOCARP same as ▸ epicarp

EXODE n exodus

EXODERM same as > ectoderm

EXODES ▸ exode

EXODIC ▸ exode

EXODIST ▸ exodus

EXODOI ▸ exodos

EXODOS n processional song performed at the end of a play

EXODUS n departure of a large number of people

EXOGAMY n custom or an act of marrying a person belonging to another tribe, clan, or similar social unit

EXOGEN n plant with a stem that develops through the growth of new layers on its outside

EXOGENS ▸ exogen

EXOMION same as ▸ exomis

EXOMIS n sleeveless jacket

EXON n one of the four officers who command the Yeomen of the Guard

EXONIC ▸ exon

EXONS ▸ exon

EXONYM n name given to a place by foreigners

EXONYMS ▸ exonym

EXOPOD same as > exopodite

EXOPODS ▸ exopod

EXORDIA > exordium

EXOSMIC > exosmosis

EXOTIC adj having a strange allure or beauty ▷ n non-native plant

EXOTICA pl n (collection of) exotic objects

EXOTICS ▸ exotic

EXOTISM ▸ exotic

EXPAND vb make or become larger

EXPANDS ▸ expand

EXPANSE n uninterrupted wide area

EXPAT n short for

EXPATS ▸ expat

EXPECT vb regard as probable

EXPECTS ▸ expect

EXPEL vb drive out with force

EXPELS ▸ expel

EXPEND vb spend, use up

EXPENDS ▸ expend

EXPENSE n cost

EXPERT n person with extensive skill or knowledge in a particular field ▷ adj skilful or knowledgeable ▷ vb experience

EXPERTS ▸ expert

EXPIATE vb make amends for

EXPIRE vb finish or run out

EXPIRED ▸ expire

EXPIRER ▸ expire
EXPIRES ▸ expire
EXPIRY n end, esp of a contract period
EXPLAIN vb make clear and intelligible
EXPLANT vb transfer (living tissue) from its natural site to a new site or to a culture medium ▷ n piece of tissue treated in this way
EXPLODE vb burst with great violence, blow up
EXPLOIT vb take advantage of for one's own purposes ▷ n notable feat or deed
EXPLORE vb investigate
EXPO n exposition, large public exhibition
EXPORT n selling or shipping of goods to a foreign country ▷ vb sell or ship (goods) to a foreign country
EXPORTS ▸ export
EXPOS ▸ expo
EXPOSAL ▸ expose
EXPOSE vb uncover or reveal ▷ n bringing of a crime, scandal, etc to public notice
EXPOSED adj not concealed
EXPOSER ▸ expose
EXPOSES ▸ expose
EXPOSIT vb state
EXPOUND vb explain in detail
EXPRESS vb put into words ▷ adj explicitly stated ▷ n fast train or bus stopping at only a few stations ▷ adv by express delivery
EXPUGN vb storm
EXPUGNS ▸ expugn
EXPULSE vb expel
EXPUNCT vb expunge
EXPUNGE vb delete, erase, blot out
EXPURGE vb purge
EXSCIND vb cut off or out
EXSECT vb cut out
EXSECTS ▸ exsect
EXSERT vb thrust out ▷ adj protruded, stretched out, or (esp of stamens) projecting beyond the corolla of a flower
EXSERTS ▸ exsert
EXTANT adj still existing
EXTASY same as ▸ ecstasy
EXTATIC same as > ecstatic
EXTEND vb draw out or be drawn out, stretch

EXTENDS ▸ extend
EXTENSE adj extensive
EXTENT n range over which something extends, area
EXTENTS ▸ extent
EXTERN n person, such as a physician at a hospital, who has an official connection with an institution but does not reside in it
EXTERNE same as ▸ extern
EXTERNS ▸ extern
EXTINCT adj having died out ▷ vb extinguish
EXTINE same as ▸ exine
EXTINES ▸ extine
EXTIRP vb extirpate
EXTIRPS ▸ extirp
EXTOL vb praise highly
EXTOLD archaic past participle of ▸ extol
EXTOLL same as ▸ extol
EXTOLLS ▸ extoll
EXTOLS ▸ extol
EXTORT vb get (something) by force or threats
EXTORTS ▸ extort
EXTRA adj more than is usual, expected or needed ▷ n additional person or thing ▷ adv unusually or exceptionally
EXTRACT vb pull out by force ▷ n something extracted, such as a passage from a book etc
EXTRAIT n extracts
EXTRAS ▸ extra
EXTREAT n extraction
EXTREMA > extremum
EXTREME adj of a high or the highest degree or intensity ▷ n either of the two limits of a scale or range
EXTRUDE vb squeeze or force out
EXUDATE same as > exudation
EXUDE vb (of a liquid or smell) seep or flow out slowly and steadily
EXUDED ▸ exude
EXUDES ▸ exude
EXUDING ▸ exude
EXUL n exile
EXULS ▸ exul
EXULT vb be joyful or jubilant
EXULTED ▸ exult
EXULTS ▸ exult
EXURB n residential area beyond suburbs

EXURBAN ▸ exurbia
EXURBIA n region outside the suburbs of a city, consisting of residential areas that are occupied predominantly by rich commuters
EXURBS ▸ exurb
EXUVIA n cast-off exoskeleton of animal
EXUVIAE ▸ exuvia
EXUVIAL ▸ exuvia
EXUVIUM n cast-off exoskeleton of animal
EYALET n province of Ottoman Empire
EYALETS ▸ eyalet
EYAS n nestling hawk or falcon, esp one reared for training in falconry
EYASES ▸ eyas
EYASS same as ▸ eyas
EYASSES ▸ eyass
EYE n organ of sight ▷ vb look at carefully or warily
EYEABLE adj pleasant to look at
EYEBALL n ball-shaped part of the eye ▷ vb eye
EYEBANK n place in which corneas are stored for use in corneal grafts
EYEBAR n bar with flattened ends with holes for connecting pins
EYEBARS ▸ eyebar
EYEBATH same as ▸ eyecup
EYEBEAM n glance
EYEBOLT n threaded bolt, the head of which is formed into a ring or eye for lifting, pulling, or securing
EYEBROW n line of hair on the bony ridge above the eye ▷ vb equip with artificial eyebrows
EYECUP same as ▸ eyebath
EYECUPS ▸ eyecup
EYED ▸ eye
EYEFOLD n fold of skin above eye
EYEFUL n view
EYEFULS ▸ eyeful
EYEHOLE n hole through which something, such as a rope, hook, or bar, is passed
EYEHOOK n hook attached to a ring at the extremity of a rope or chain
EYEING ▸ eye
EYELASH n short hair that grows out from the eyelid
EYELESS ▸ eye

E

EYELET n small hole for a lace or cord to be passed through ▷ vb supply with an eyelet or eyelets

EYELETS ▸ **eyelet**

EYELIAD same as > **oeillade**

EYELID n fold of skin that covers the eye when it is closed

EYELIDS ▸ **eyelid**

EYELIFT n cosmetic surgery for eyes

EYELIKE ▸ **eye**

EYEN pl n eyes

EYER n someone who eyes

EYERS ▸ **eyer**

EYES ▸ **eye**

EYESHOT n range of vision

EYESOME adj attractive

EYESORE n ugly object

EYESPOT n small area of light-sensitive pigment in some protozoans, algae, and other simple organisms

EYEWASH n nonsense

EYEWEAR n spectacles; glasses

EYEWINK n wink of the eye; instant

EYING ▸ **eye**

EYLIAD same as > **oeillade**

EYLIADS ▸ **eyliad**

EYNE poetic plural of ▸ **eye**

EYOT n island

EYOTS ▸ **eyot**

EYRA n reddish-brown variety of the jaguarondi

EYRAS ▸ **eyra**

EYRE n any of the circuit courts held in each shire from 1176 until the late 13th century

EYRES ▸ **eyre**

EYRIE n nest of an eagle

EYRIES ▸ **eyrie**

EYRIR n Icelandic monetary unit worth one hundredth of a krona

EYRY same as ▸ **eyrie**

Ff

F is a useful letter in Scrabble: it begins three two-letter words (**fa**, **fe** and **fy**). There are also quite a few words that combine **F** with **X** or **Z**, allowing high scores, particularly if you can hit a bonus square with them. **Fax**, **fix** and **fox** are good examples (13 points each), and don't forget **fez** and **fiz** (15 points each). **Fay**, **fey**, **fly**, **foy** and **fry** can also be useful (9 each).

FA same as ▸ **fah**
FAA Scots word for ▸ **fall**
FAAING ▸ **faa**
FAAN ▸ **faa**
FAAS ▸ **faa**
FAB adj excellent ▷ n fabrication
FABBER ▸ **fab**
FABBEST ▸ **fab**
FABBIER ▸ **fabby**
FABBY same as ▸ **fab** adj
FABLE n story with a moral ▷ vb relate or tell (fables)
FABLED adj made famous in legend
FABLER ▸ **fable**
FABLERS ▸ **fable**
FABLES ▸ **fable**
FABLIAU n comic usually ribald verse tale, of a kind popular in France in the 12th and 13th centuries
FABLING ▸ **fable**
FABRIC n knitted or woven cloth ▷ vb to build
FABRICS ▸ **fabric**
FABS ▸ **fab**
FABULAR adj relating to fables
FACADE n front of a building
FACADES ▸ **facade**
FACE n front of the head ▷ vb look or turn towards
FACEBAR n wrestling hold in which a wrestler stretches the skin on his opponent's face backwards
FACED ▸ **face**
FACEMAN n miner who works at the coalface
FACEMEN ▸ **faceman**
FACER n difficulty or problem
FACERS ▸ **facer**

FACES ▸ **face**
FACET n aspect ▷ vb cut facets in (a gemstone)
FACETE adj witty and humorous
FACETED ▸ **facet**
FACETS ▸ **facet**
FACEUP adj with the face or surface exposed
FACIA same as ▸ **fascia**
FACIAE ▸ **facia**
FACIAL adj of or relating to the face ▷ n beauty treatment for the face
FACIALS ▸ **facial**
FACIAS ▸ **facia**
FACIEND n multiplicand
FACIES n general form and appearance of an individual or a group of plants or animals
FACILE adj (of a remark, argument, etc) superficial and showing lack of real thought
FACING n lining or covering for decoration or reinforcement
FACINGS ▸ **facing**
FACONNE adj denoting a fabric with the design woven in ▷ n such a fabric
FACT n event or thing known to have happened or existed
FACTFUL ▸ **fact**
FACTICE n soft rubbery material made by reacting sulphur or sulphur chloride with vegetable oil
FACTION n (dissenting) minority group within a larger body
FACTIS same as ▸ **factice**

FACTIVE adj (of a linguistic context) giving rise to the presupposition that a sentence occurring in that context is true, as John regrets that Mary did not attend
FACTOID n piece of unreliable information believed to be true because of the way it is presented or repeated in print
FACTOR n element contributing to a result ▷ vb engage in the business of a factor
FACTORS ▸ **factor**
FACTORY n building where goods are manufactured
FACTS ▸ **fact**
FACTUAL adj concerning facts rather than opinions or theories
FACTUM n something done, deed
FACTUMS ▸ **factum**
FACTURE n construction
FACULA n any of the bright areas on the sun's surface, usually appearing just before a sunspot and subject to the same 11-year cycle
FACULAE ▸ **facula**
FACULAR ▸ **facula**
FACULTY n physical or mental ability
FAD n short-lived fashion
FADABLE ▸ **fade**
FADAISE n silly remark
FADDIER ▸ **faddy**
FADDISH ▸ **fad**
FADDISM ▸ **fad**
FADDIST ▸ **fad**

FADDLE vb mess around, toy with

FADDLED ▸ **faddle**

FADDLES ▸ **faddle**

FADDY adj unreasonably fussy, particularly about food

FADE vb (cause to) lose brightness, colour, or strength ▷ n act or an instance of fading

FADED ▸ **fade**

FADEDLY ▸ **fade**

FADEIN n gradual appearance of image on film

FADEINS ▸ **fadein**

FADEOUT n gradual disappearance of image on film

FADER ▸ **fade**

FADERS ▸ **fade**

FADES ▸ **fade**

FADEUR n blandness, insipidness

FADEURS ▸ **fadeur**

FADGE vb agree ▷ n package of wool in a wool-bale that weighs less than 100 kilograms

FADGED ▸ **fadge**

FADGES ▸ **fadge**

FADGING ▸ **fadge**

FADIER ▸ **fady**

FADIEST ▸ **fady**

FADING n variation in the strength of received radio signals due to variations in the conditions of the transmission medium

FADINGS ▸ **fading**

FADLIKE ▸ **fad**

FADO n type of melancholy Portuguese folk song

FADOS ▸ **fado**

FADS ▸ **fad**

FADY adj faded

FAE Scots word for ▸ **from**

FAECAL adj of, relating to, or consisting of faeces

FAECES pl n waste matter discharged from the anus

FAENA n matador's final series of passes with sword and cape before the kill

FAENAS ▸ **faena**

FAERIE n land of fairies

FAERIES ▸ **faery**

FAERY same as ▸ **faerie**

FAFF vb dither or fuss

FAFFED ▸ **faff**

FAFFING ▸ **faff**

FAFFS ▸ **faff**

FAG same as ▸ **faggot**

FAGGED ▸ **fag**

FAGGING ▸ **fag**

FAGGOT n ball of chopped liver, herbs, and bread ▷ vb collect into a bundle or bundles

FAGGOTS ▸ **faggot**

FAGIN n criminal

FAGINS ▸ **fagin**

FAGOT same as ▸ **faggot**

FAGOTED ▸ **fagot**

FAGOTER ▸ **fagot**

FAGOTS ▸ **fagot**

FAGOTTI ▸ **fagotto**

FAGOTTO n bassoon

FAGS ▸ **fag**

FAH n (in tonic sol-fa) fourth degree of any major scale

FAHLERZ n copper ore

FAHLORE n copper ore

FAHS ▸ **fah**

FAIBLE same as ▸ **foible**

FAIBLES ▸ **faible**

FAIENCE n tin-glazed earthenware

FAIK vb grasp

FAIKED ▸ **faik**

FAIKES ▸ **faik**

FAIKING ▸ **faik**

FAIKS ▸ **faik**

FAIL vb be unsuccessful ▷ n instance of not passing an exam or test

FAILED ▸ **fail**

FAILING n weak point ▷ prep in the absence of

FAILLE n soft light ribbed fabric of silk, rayon, or taffeta

FAILLES ▸ **faille**

FAILS ▸ **fail**

FAILURE n act or instance of failing

FAIN adv gladly ▷ adj willing or eager

FAINE same as ▸ **fain**

FAINED ▸ **fain**

FAINER ▸ **fain**

FAINES ▸ **faine**

FAINEST ▸ **fain**

FAINING ▸ **fain**

FAINLY ▸ **fain**

FAINNE n small ring-shaped metal badge worn by advocates of the Irish language

FAINNES ▸ **fainne**

FAINS same as ▸ **fainites**

FAINT adj lacking clarity, brightness, or volume ▷ vb lose consciousness temporarily ▷ n temporary loss of consciousness

FAINTED ▸ **faint**

FAINTER ▸ **faint**

FAINTLY ▸ **faint**

FAINTS ▸ **faint**

FAINTY ▸ **faint**

FAIR adj unbiased and reasonable ▷ adv fairly ▷ n travelling entertainment with sideshows, rides, and amusements ▷ vb join together so as to form a smooth or regular shape or surface

FAIRED ▸ **fair**

FAIRER ▸ **fair**

FAIREST ▸ **fair**

FAIRIES ▸ **fairy**

FAIRILY ▸ **fairy**

FAIRING n curved metal structure fitted round part of a car, aircraft, etc to reduce drag

FAIRISH adj moderately good, well, etc

FAIRLY adv moderately

FAIRS ▸ **fair**

FAIRWAY n smooth area between the tee and the green

FAIRY n imaginary small creature with magic powers

FAITH n strong belief, esp without proof

FAITHED adj having faith or a faith

FAITHER Scots word for ▸ **father**

FAITHS ▸ **faith**

FAITOR n traitor, impostor

FAITORS ▸ **faitor**

FAITOUR n impostor

FAIX interj have faith

FAJITA ▸ **fajitas**

FAJITAS pl n Mexican dish of soft tortillas wrapped around fried strips of meat or vegetables

FAKE vb cause something not genuine to appear real or more valuable by fraud ▷ n person, thing, or act that is not genuine ▷ adj not genuine

FAKED ▸ **fake**

FAKEER same as ▸ **fakir**

FAKEERS ▸ **fakeer**

FAKER ▸ **fake**

FAKERS ▸ **fake**

FAKERY ▸ **fake**

FAKES ▸ **fake**

FAKEY *adj, adv* (of a skateboarding or snowboarding manoeuvre) performed with the board facing backwards

FAKIE ▸ fakey

FAKIER ▸ fakey

FAKIES ▸ fakie

FAKIEST ▸ fakey

FAKING ▸ fake

FAKIR *n* Muslim who spurns worldly possessions

FAKIRS ▸ fakir

FALAFEL *n* ball or cake of ground spiced chickpeas, deep-fried and often served with pitta bread

FALAJ *n* kind of irrigation channel in ancient Oman

FALBALA *n* gathered flounce, frill, or ruffle

FALCADE *n* movement of a horse

FALCATE *adj* shaped like a sickle

FALCES ▸ falx

FALCON *n* small bird of prey

FALCONS ▸ falcon

FALCULA *n* sharp curved claw, esp of a bird

FALDAGE *n* feudal right

FALL *vb* drop from a higher to a lower place through the force of gravity ▷ *n* falling

FALLACY *n* false belief

FALLAL *n* showy ornament, trinket, or article of dress

FALLALS ▸ fallal

FALLEN ▸ fall

FALLER *n* any device that falls or operates machinery by falling, as in a spinning machine

FALLERS ▸ faller

FALLING ▸ fall

FALLOFF *n* decline or drop

FALLOUT *n* radioactive particles spread as a result of a nuclear explosion ▷ *vb* disagree and quarrel ▷ *sentence substitute* order to leave a parade or disciplinary formation

FALLOW *adj* (of land) ploughed but left unseeded to regain fertility ▷ *n* land treated in this way ▷ *vb* leave (land) unseeded after ploughing and harrowing it

FALLOWS ▸ fallow

FALLS ▸ fall

FALSE *adj* not true or correct

▷ *adv* in a false or dishonest manner ▷ *vb* falsify

FALSED ▸ false

FALSELY ▸ false

FALSER ▸ false

FALSERS *n* colloquial term for false teeth

FALSES ▸ false

FALSEST ▸ false

FALSIE *n* pad used to enlarge breast shape

FALSIES ▸ falsie

FALSIFY *vb* alter fraudulently

FALSING ▸ false

FALSISH ▸ false

FALSISM ▸ false

FALSITY *n* state of being false

FALTER *vb* be hesitant, weak, or unsure ▷ *n* uncertainty or hesitancy in speech or action

FALTERS ▸ falter

FALX *n* sickle-shaped anatomical structure

FAME *n* state of being widely known or recognized ▷ *vb* make known or famous

FAMED ▸ fame

FAMES ▸ fame

FAMILLE *n* type of Chinese porcelain

FAMILY *n* group of parents and their children ▷ *adj* suitable for parents and children together

FAMINE *n* severe shortage of food

FAMINES ▸ famine

FAMING ▸ fame

FAMISH *vb* be or make very hungry or weak

FAMOUS *adj* very well-known ▷ *vb* make famous

FAMULI ▸ famulus

FAMULUS *n* (formerly) the attendant of a sorcerer or scholar

FAN *n* hand-held or mechanical object used to create a current of air for ventilation or cooling ▷ *vb* blow or cool with a fan

FANAL *n* lighthouse

FANALS ▸ fanal

FANATIC *n* person who is excessively enthusiastic about something ▷ *adj* excessively enthusiastic

FANBASE *n* body of

admirers of a particular pop singer, sports team, etc

FANBOY *n* obsessive fan of a subject or hobby

FANBOYS ▸ fanboy

FANCIED *adj* imaginary

FANCIER *n* person who is interested in and often breeds plants or animals

FANCIES ▸ fancy

FANCIFY *vb* make more beautiful

FANCILY ▸ fancy

FANCY *adj* elaborate, not plain ▷ *n* sudden irrational liking or desire ▷ *vb* be sexually attracted to

FAND *vb* try

FANDED ▸ fand

FANDING ▸ fand

FANDOM *n* collectively, the fans of a sport, pastime or person

FANDOMS ▸ fandom

FANDS ▸ fand

FANE *n* temple or shrine

FANEGA *n* Spanish unit of measurement

FANEGAS ▸ fanega

FANES ▸ fane

FANFARE *n* short loud tune played on brass instruments ▷ *vb* perform a fanfare

FANFIC *n* fiction written around previously established characters invented by other authors

FANFICS ▸ fanfic

FANFOLD *vb* fold (paper) like a fan

FANG *n* snake's tooth which injects poison ▷ *vb* seize

FANGA *same as ▸* **fanega**

FANGAS ▸ fanga

FANGED ▸ fang

FANGING ▸ fang

FANGLE *vb* fashion

FANGLED ▸ fangle

FANGLES ▸ fangle

FANGO *n* mud from thermal springs in Italy, used in the treatment of rheumatic disease

FANGOS ▸ fango

FANGS ▸ fang

FANION *n* small flag used by surveyors to mark stations

FANIONS ▸ fanion

FANJET *same as ▸* **turbofan**

FANJETS ▸ fanjet

FANK *n* sheep pen

FANKLE *vb* entangle ▷ *n* tangle

F

FANKLED ▸ fankle
FANKLES ▸ fankle
FANKS ▸ fank
FANLIKE ▸ fan
FANNED ▸ fan
FANNEL n ecclesiastical vestment
FANNELL same as ▸ fannel
FANNELS ▸ fannel
FANNER ▸ fan
FANNERS ▸ fan
FANNING ▸ fan
FANO same as ▸ fanon
FANON n collar-shaped vestment worn by the pope when celebrating mass
FANONS ▸ fanon
FANOS ▸ fano
FANS ▸ fan
FANSITE n website aimed at fans of a celebrity, film, etc
FANSUB n fan-produced subtitling of films
FANSUBS ▸ fansub
FANTAD n nervous, agitated state
FANTADS ▸ fantad
FANTAIL n small New Zealand bird with a tail like a fan
FANTASM archaic spelling of ▸ phantasm
FANTAST n dreamer or visionary
FANTASY n far-fetched notion ▹ adj of a competition in which a participant selects players for an imaginary, ideal team and points are awarded according to the actual performances of the chosen players ▹ vb fantasize
FANTEEG n nervous, agitated state
FANTOD n crotchety or faddish behaviour
FANTODS ▸ fantod
FANTOM archaic spelling of ▸ phantom
FANTOMS ▸ fantom
FANUM n temple
FANUMS ▸ fanum
FANWISE adj like a fan
FANWORT n aquatic plant
FANZINE n magazine produced by fans of a specific interest, soccer club, etc, for fellow fans
FAP adj drunk
FAQIR same as ▸ fakir

Meaning a Hindu ascetic; this is one of those invaluable words allowing you to play the Q without a U. It can also be spelt **fakeer, fakir** and **faquir**.

FAQIRS ▸ faqir
FAQUIR same as ▸ faqir
FAQUIRS ▸ faquir
FAR adv at, to, or from a great distance ▹ adj remote in space or time ▹ vb go far
FARAD n unit of electrical capacitance
FARADAY n quantity of electricity, used in electrochemical calculations
FARADIC adj of or concerned with an intermittent asymmetric alternating current such as that induced in the secondary winding of an induction coil
FARADS ▸ farad
FARAND adj pleasant or attractive in manner or appearance
FARAWAY adj very distant
FARCE n boisterous comedy ▹ vb enliven (a speech, etc) with jokes
FARCED ▸ farce
FARCER same as ▸ farceur
FARCERS ▸ farcer
FARCES ▸ farce
FARCEUR n writer of or performer in farces
FARCI adj (of food) stuffed
FARCIE same as ▸ farci
FARCIED adj afflicted with farcy
FARCIES ▸ farcy
FARCIFY vb turn into a farce
FARCIN n equine disease
FARCING ▸ farce
FARCINS ▸ farcin
FARCY n form of glanders, a bacterial disease of horses
FARD n paint for the face, esp white paint ▹ vb paint (the face) with fard
FARDAGE n material laid beneath or between cargo
FARDED ▸ fard
FARDEL n bundle or burden
FARDELS ▸ fardel
FARDEN n farthing
FARDENS ▸ farden
FARDING ▸ fard
FARDS ▸ fard

FARE n charge for a passenger's journey ▹ vb get on (as specified)
FAREBOX n box where money for bus fares is placed
FARED ▸ fare
FARER ▸ fare
FARERS ▸ fare
FARES ▸ fare
FARFAL same as ▸ felafel
FARFALS ▸ farfal
FARFEL same as ▸ felafel
FARFELS ▸ farfel
FARFET adj far-fetched
FARINA n flour or meal made from any kind of cereal grain
FARINAS ▸ farina
FARING ▸ fare
FARINHA n cassava meal
FARL n thin cake of oatmeal, often triangular in shape
FARLE same as ▸ farl
FARLES ▸ farle
FARLS ▸ farl
FARM n area of land for growing crops or rearing livestock ▹ vb cultivate (land)
FARMED adj (of fish or game) reared on a farm rather than caught in the wild
FARMER n person who owns or runs a farm
FARMERS ▸ farmer
FARMERY n farm buildings
FARMING n business or skill of agriculture
FARMOST ▸ far
FARMS ▸ farm
FARNESS ▸ far
FARO n gambling game in which players bet against the dealer on what cards he will turn up
FAROS ▸ faro
FARRAGO n jumbled mixture of things
FARRAND same as ▸ farand
FARRANT same as ▸ farand
FARRED ▸ far
FARREN n allotted ground
FARRENS ▸ farren
FARRIER n person who shoes horses
FARRING ▸ far
FARROW n litter of piglets ▹ vb (of a sow) give birth ▹ adj (of a cow) not calving in a given year

FARROWS ▶ farrow
FARRUCA n flamenco dance performed by men
FARS ▶ far
FARSE vb insert into
FARSED ▶ farse
FARSES ▶ farse
FARSIDE n part of the Moon facing away from the Earth
FARSING ▶ farse
FARTHEL same as ▶ **farl**
FARTHER ▶ far
FARTLEK n in sport, another name for interval training
FAS ▶ fa
FASCES pl n (in ancient Rome) a bundle of rods containing an axe with its blade pointing out
FASCI ▶ fascio
FASCIA n outer surface of a dashboard
FASCIAE ▶ fascia
FASCIAL ▶ fascia
FASCIAS ▶ fascia
FASCINE n bundle of long sticks used for filling in ditches and in the construction of embankments, roads, fortifications, etc
FASCIO n political group
FASCIS ▶ fasces
FASCISM n right wing totalitarian political system characterized by state control and extreme nationalism
FASCIST n adherent or practitioner of fascism ▷ adj characteristic of or relating to fascism
FASH n worry ▷ vb trouble
FASHED ▶ fash
FASHERY n difficulty, trouble
FASHES ▶ fash
FASHING ▶ fash
FASHION n style in clothes, hairstyle, etc, popular at a particular time ▷ vb form or make into a particular shape
FAST adj (capable of) acting or moving quickly ▷ adv quickly ▷ vb go without food, esp for religious reasons ▷ n period of fasting
FASTED ▶ fast
FASTEN vb make or become firmly fixed or joined

FASTENS ▶ fasten
FASTER ▶ fast
FASTERS ▶ fast
FASTEST ▶ fast
FASTI pl n in ancient Rome, days when business could legally be carried out
FASTIE n deceitful act
FASTIES ▶ fastie
FASTING ▶ fast
FASTISH ▶ fast
FASTLY ▶ fast
FASTS ▶ fast
FAT adj having excess flesh on the body ▷ n extra flesh on the body
FATAL adj causing death or ruin
FATALLY adv resulting in death or disaster
FATBACK n fat, usually salted, from the upper part of a side of pork
FATBIRD n nocturnal bird
FATE n power supposed to predetermine events ▷ vb predetermine
FATED adj destined
FATEFUL adj having important, usu disastrous, consequences
FATES ▶ fate
FATHEAD n stupid person
FATHER n male parent ▷ vb be the father of (offspring)
FATHERS ▶ father
FATHOM n unit of length, used in navigation, equal to six feet (1.83 metres) ▷ vb understand
FATHOMS ▶ fathom
FATIDIC adj prophetic
FATIGUE n extreme physical or mental tiredness ▷ vb tire out
FATING ▶ fate
FATLESS ▶ fat
FATLIKE ▶ fat
FATLING n young farm animal fattened for killing
FATLY ▶ fat
FATNESS ▶ fat
FATS ▶ fat
FATSIA n type of shrub with large deeply palmate leaves and umbels of white flowers
FATSIAS ▶ fatsia
FATTED ▶ fat
FATTEN vb (cause to) become fat
FATTENS ▶ fatten
FATTER ▶ fat

FATTEST ▶ fat
FATTIER ▶ fatty
FATTIES ▶ fatty
FATTILY ▶ fatty
FATTING ▶ fat
FATTISH ▶ fat
FATTISM n discrimination on the basis of weight, esp prejudice against those considered to be overweight
FATTIST ▶ fattism
FATTY adj containing fat ▷ n fat person
FATUITY n foolish thoughtlessness
FATUOUS adj foolish
FATWA n religious decree issued by a Muslim leader ▷ vb issue a fatwa
FATWAH same as ▶ **fatwa**
FATWAHS ▶ fatwah
FATWAS ▶ fatwa
FATWOOD n wood used for kindling
FAUCAL adj of or relating to the fauces
FAUCALS ▶ faucal
FAUCES n area between the cavity of the mouth and the pharynx, including the surrounding tissues
FAUCET n tap
FAUCETS ▶ faucet
FAUCHON same as > **fauchion**
FAUCIAL same as ▶ **faucal**
FAUGH interj exclamation of disgust, scorn, etc
FAULD n piece of armour
FAULDS ▶ fauld
FAULT n responsibility for something wrong ▷ vb criticize or blame
FAULTED ▶ fault
FAULTS ▶ fault
FAULTY adj badly designed or not working properly
FAUN n (in Roman legend) creature with a human face and torso and a goat's horns and legs
FAUNA n animals of a given place or time
FAUNAE ▶ fauna
FAUNAL ▶ fauna
FAUNAS ▶ fauna
FAUNIST ▶ fauna
FAUNS ▶ faun
FAUNULA n fauna of a small single environment
FAUNULE same as ▶ **faunula**
FAUR Scots word for ▶ **far**

F

FAURD *adj* favoured
FAURER ▸ faur
FAUREST ▸ faur
FAUT *Scots word for* ▸ **fault**
FAUTED ▸ faut
FAUTING ▸ faut
FAUTOR *n* patron
FAUTORS ▸ fautor
FAUTS ▸ faut
FAUVE *adj* of the style of the Fauve art movement ▷ *n* member of the Fauve art movement
FAUVES ▸ fauve
FAUVISM ▸ fauve
FAUVIST *n* artist following the Fauve style of painting
FAUX *adj* false
FAVA *n* type of bean
FAVAS ▸ fava
FAVE *short for* ▸ **favourite**
FAVEL *adj* (of a horse) dun-coloured
FAVELA *n* (in Brazil) a shanty or shantytown
FAVELAS ▸ favela
FAVELL *same as* ▸ **favel**
FAVELLA *n* group of spores
FAVER ▸ fave
FAVES ▸ fave
FAVEST ▸ fave
FAVICON *n* icon displayed before a website's URL
FAVISM *n* type of anaemia
FAVISMS ▸ favism
FAVOR *same as* ▸ **favour**
FAVORED ▸ favor
FAVORER ▸ favour
FAVORS *same as* ▸ **favours**
FAVOSE *same as* ▸ **faveolate**
FAVOUR *n* approving attitude ▷ *vb* prefer
FAVOURS *pl n* sexual intimacy, as when consented to by a woman
FAVOUS *adj* resembling honeycomb
FAVRILE *n* type of iridescent glass
FAVUS *n* infectious fungal skin disease of man and some domestic animals, characterized by formation of a honeycomb-like mass of roundish dry cup-shaped crusts
FAVUSES ▸ favus
FAW *n* gypsy

> A **faw** is a gypsy, a good word for taking advantage of a nearby bonus square.

FAWN *n* young deer ▷ *adj*

light yellowish-brown ▷ *vb* seek attention from (someone) by insincere flattery
FAWNED ▸ fawn
FAWNER ▸ fawn
FAWNERS ▸ fawn
FAWNIER ▸ fawny
FAWNING ▸ fawn
FAWNS ▸ fawn
FAWNY *adj* of a fawn colour
FAWS ▸ faw
FAX *n* electronic system for sending facsimiles of documents by telephone ▷ *vb* send (a document) by this system
FAXED ▸ fax
FAXES ▸ fax
FAXING ▸ fax
FAY *n* fairy or sprite ▷ *adj* of or resembling a fay ▷ *vb* fit or be fitted closely or tightly

> A **fay** is a fairy but it can also be a verb, meaning to fit closely. It has a variant **fey**. Both are useful high-scoring short words.

FAYED ▸ fay
FAYENCE *same as* ▸ **faience**
FAYER ▸ fay
FAYEST ▸ fay
FAYING ▸ fay
FAYNE *vb* pretend
FAYNED ▸ fayne
FAYNES ▸ fayne
FAYNING ▸ fayne
FAYRE *pseudo-archaic spelling of* ▸ **fair**
FAYRES ▸ fayre
FAYS ▸ fay
FAZE *vb* disconcert or fluster
FAZED *adj* worried or disconcerted
FAZENDA *n* large estate or ranch
FAZES ▸ faze
FAZING ▸ faze
FE *n* variant of Hebrew letter *pe*, transliterated as *f*
FEAGUE *vb* whip or beat
FEAGUED ▸ feague
FEAGUES ▸ feague
FEAL *vb* conceal
FEALED ▸ feal
FEALING ▸ feal
FEALS ▸ feal
FEALTY *n* (in feudal society) subordinate's loyalty to his ruler or lord
FEAR *n* distress or alarm caused by impending

danger or pain ▷ *vb* be afraid of (something or someone)
FEARE *n* companion, spouse
FEARED ▸ fear
FEARER ▸ fear
FEARERS ▸ fear
FEARES ▸ feare
FEARFUL *adj* feeling fear
FEARING ▸ fear
FEARS ▸ fear
FEART *adj* (Scots) afraid
FEASE *vb* perform an act
FEASED ▸ fease
FEASES ▸ fease
FEASING ▸ fease
FEAST *n* lavish meal ▷ *vb* eat a feast
FEASTED ▸ feast
FEASTER ▸ feast
FEASTS ▸ feast
FEAT *n* remarkable, skilful, or daring action
FEATED ▸ feat
FEATER ▸ feat
FEATEST ▸ feat
FEATHER *n* one of the barbed shafts forming the plumage of birds ▷ *vb* fit or cover with feathers
FEATING ▸ feat
FEATLY ▸ feat
FEATOUS *same as* > **feateous**
FEATS ▸ feat
FEATURE *n* part of the face, such as the eyes ▷ *vb* have as a feature or be a feature in
FEAZE *same as* ▸ **feeze**
FEAZED ▸ feaze
FEAZES ▸ feaze
FEAZING ▸ feaze
FEBRILE *adj* very active and nervous
FECAL *same as* ▸ **faecal**
FECES *same as* ▸ **faeces**
FECHT *Scots word for* ▸ **fight**
FECHTER ▸ fecht
FECHTS ▸ fecht
FECIAL *adj* heraldic
FECIALS ▸ fecial
FECIT *vb* (he or she) made it: used formerly on works of art next to the artist's name
FECULA *n* starch obtained by washing the crushed parts of plants, such as the potato
FECULAE ▸ fecula
FECULAS ▸ fecula
FECUND *adj* fertile

FED _n_ FBI agent
FEDARIE _n_ accomplice
FEDAYEE _n_ (in Arab states) a commando, esp one fighting against Israel
FEDERAL _adj_ of a system in which power is divided between one central government and several regional governments ▷ _n_ supporter of federal union or federation
FEDEX _vb_ send by FedEx
FEDEXED ▸ **fedex**
FEDEXES ▸ **fedex**
FEDORA _n_ man's soft hat with a brim
FEDORAS ▸ **fedora**
FEDS ▸ **fed**
FEE _n_ charge paid to be allowed to do something ▷ _vb_ pay a fee to
FEEB _n_ contemptible person
FEEBLE _adj_ lacking physical or mental power ▷ _vb_ make feeble
FEEBLED ▸ **feeble**
FEEBLER ▸ **feeble**
FEEBLES ▸ **feeble**
FEEBLY ▸ **feeble**
FEEBS ▸ **feeb**
FEED _vb_ give food to ▷ _n_ act of feeding
FEEDBAG _n_ any bag in which feed for livestock is sacked
FEEDBOX _n_ trough, manger
FEEDER _n_ baby's bib
FEEDERS ▸ **feeder**
FEEDING ▸ **feed**
FEEDLOT _n_ area or building where livestock are fattened rapidly for market
FEEDS ▸ **feed**
FEEING ▸ **fee**
FEEL _vb_ have a physical or emotional sensation of ▷ _n_ act of feeling
FEELBAD _n_ something inducing depression
FEELER _n_ organ of touch in some animals
FEELERS ▸ **feeler**
FEELESS ▸ **fee**
FEELING ▸ **feel**
FEELS ▸ **feel**
FEEN _n_ in Irish dialect, an informal word for 'man'
FEENS ▸ **feen**
FEER _vb_ make a furrow
FEERED ▸ **feer**
FEERIE _n_ fairyland
FEERIES ▸ **feerie**

FEERIN _n_ furrow
FEERING ▸ **feer**
FEERINS ▸ **feerin**
FEERS ▸ **feer**
FEES ▸ **fee**
FEESE _vb_ perturb
FEESED ▸ **feese**
FEESES ▸ **feese**
FEESING ▸ **feese**
FEET ▸ **foot**
FEEZE _vb_ beat ▷ _n_ rush
FEEZED ▸ **feeze**
FEEZES ▸ **feeze**
FEEZING ▸ **feeze**
FEG _same as_ ▸ **fig**
FEGARY _same as_ ▸ **vagary**
FEGS ▸ **feg**
FEH ▸ **fe**
FEHM _n_ medieval German court
FEHME ▸ **fehm**
FEHMIC ▸ **fehm**
FEHS ▸ **feh**
FEIGN _vb_ pretend
FEIGNED ▸ **feign**
FEIGNER ▸ **feign**
FEIGNS ▸ **feign**
FEIJOA _n_ evergreen myrtaceous shrub of S America
FEIJOAS ▸ **feijoa**
FEINT _n_ sham attack or blow meant to distract an opponent ▷ _vb_ make a feint ▷ _adj_ printing term meaning ruled with faint lines
FEINTED ▸ **feint**
FEINTER ▸ **feint**
FEINTS _pl n_ leavings of the second distillation of Scotch malt whisky
FEIRIE _adj_ nimble
FEIRIER ▸ **feirie**
FEIS _n_ Irish music and dance festival
FEIST _n_ small aggressive dog
FEISTS ▸ **feist**
FEISTY _adj_ showing courage or spirit
FELAFEL _same as_ ▸ **falafel**
FELICIA _n_ type of African herb
FELID _n_ any animal belonging to the cat family
FELIDS ▸ **felid**
FELINE _adj_ of cats ▷ _n_ member of the cat family
FELINES ▸ **feline**
FELL _vb_ cut or knock down ▷ _adj_ cruel or deadly
FELLA _nonstandard variant of_ ▸ **fellow**

FELLAH _n_ peasant in Arab countries
FELLAHS ▸ **fellah**
FELLAS ▸ **fella**
FELLATE _vb_ perform fellatio on (a person)
FELLED ▸ **fell**
FELLER _n_ person or thing that fells
FELLERS ▸ **feller**
FELLEST ▸ **fell**
FELLIES ▸ **felly**
FELLING ▸ **fell**
FELLOE _n_ (segment of) the rim of a wheel
FELLOES ▸ **felloe**
FELLOW _n_ man or boy ▷ _adj_ in the same group or condition
FELLOWS ▸ **fellow**
FELLS ▸ **fell**
FELLY _same as_ ▸ **felloe**
FELON _n_ (formerly) person guilty of a felony ▷ _adj_ evil
FELONRY _n_ felons collectively
FELONS ▸ **felon**
FELONY _n_ serious crime
FELSIC _adj_ relating to igneous rock
FELSITE _n_ any fine-grained igneous rock consisting essentially of quartz and feldspar
FELSPAR _same as_ ▸ **feldspar**
FELT _n_ matted fabric ▷ _vb_ become matted
FELTED ▸ **felt**
FELTER _vb_ mat together
FELTERS ▸ **felter**
FELTIER ▸ **felt**
FELTING _n_ felted material
FELTS ▸ **felt**
FELTY ▸ **felt**
FELUCCA _n_ narrow lateen-rigged vessel of the Mediterranean
FELWORT _n_ type of plant of Europe and SW China with purple flowers and rosettes of leaves
FEM _n_ passive homosexual
FEMAL _adj_ effeminate ▷ _n_ effeminate person
FEMALE _adj_ of the sex which bears offspring ▷ _n_ female person or animal
FEMALES ▸ **female**
FEMALS ▸ **femal**
FEME _n_ woman or wife
FEMES ▸ **feme**
FEMINAL _adj_ feminine, female

FEMINIE n women collectively

FEMITER same as > **fumitory**

FEMME n woman or wife

FEMMES ▶ **femme**

FEMMIER ▶ **femmy**

FEMMY adj markedly or exaggeratedly feminine in appearance, manner, etc

FEMORA ▶ **femur**

FEMORAL adj of the thigh

FEMS ▶ **fem**

FEMUR n thighbone

FEMURS ▶ **femur**

FEN n low-lying flat marshy land

FENAGLE same as ▶ **finagle**

FENCE n barrier of posts linked by wire or wood, enclosing an area ▷ vb enclose with or as if with a fence

FENCED ▶ **fence**

FENCER n person who fights with a sword, esp one who practises the art of fencing

FENCERS ▶ **fencer**

FENCES ▶ **fence**

FENCING n sport of fighting with swords

FEND vb give support (to someone, esp oneself) ▷ n shift or effort

FENDED ▶ **fend**

FENDER n low metal frame in front of a fireplace

FENDERS ▶ **fender**

FENDIER ▶ **fendy**

FENDING ▶ **fend**

FENDS ▶ **fend**

FENDY adj thrifty

FENI n Goan alcoholic drink

FENIS ▶ **feni**

FENITAR same as > **fumitory**

FENKS n whale blubber

FENLAND ▶ **fen**

FENMAN ▶ **fen**

FENMEN ▶ **fen**

FENNEC n type of very small nocturnal desert fox of N Africa and Arabia, with pale fur and enormous ears

FENNECS ▶ **fennec**

FENNEL n fragrant plant whose seeds, leaves, and root are used in cookery

FENNELS ▶ **fennel**

FENNIER ▶ **fenny**

FENNIES ▶ **fenny**

FENNISH ▶ **fen**

FENNY adj boggy or marshy ▷ n feni

FENS ▶ **fen**

FENT n piece of waste fabric

FENTS ▶ **fent**

FENURON n type of herbicide

FEOD same as ▶ **feud**

FEODAL ▶ **feod**

FEODARY ▶ **feod**

FEODS ▶ **feod**

FEOFF same as ▶ **fief**

FEOFFED ▶ **feoff**

FEOFFEE n (in feudal society) a vassal granted a fief by his lord

FEOFFER ▶ **feoff**

FEOFFOR ▶ **feoff**

FEOFFS ▶ **feoff**

FER same as ▶ **far**

FERAL adj wild ▷ n person who displays such tendencies and appearance

FERALS ▶ **feral**

FERBAM n black slightly water-soluble fluffy powder used as a fungicide

FERBAMS ▶ **ferbam**

FERE n companion ▷ adj fierce

FERER ▶ **fere**

FERES ▶ **fere**

FEREST ▶ **fere**

FERIA n weekday, other than Saturday, on which no feast occurs

FERIAE ▶ **feria**

FERIAL adj of or relating to a feria

FERIAS ▶ **feria**

FERINE same as ▶ **feral**

FERITY ▶ **feral**

FERLIE same as ▶ **ferly**

FERLIED ▶ **ferly**

FERLIER ▶ **ferly**

FERLIES ▶ **ferly**

FERLY adj wonderful ▷ n wonder ▷ vb wonder

FERM same as ▶ **farm**

FERMATA another word for ▶ **pause**

FERMATE ▶ **fermata**

FERMENT n any agent that causes fermentation ▷ vb (cause to) undergo fermentation

FERMI n unit of length used in nuclear physics equal to 10^{-15} metre

FERMION n any of a group of elementary particles, such as a nucleon, that has half-integral spin and obeys Fermi-Dirac statistics

FERMIS ▶ **fermi**

FERMIUM n element artificially produced by neutron bombardment of plutonium

FERMS ▶ **ferm**

FERN n flowerless plant with fine fronds

FERNERY n place where ferns are grown

FERNIER ▶ **fern**

FERNING n production of a fern-like pattern

FERNS ▶ **fern**

FERNY ▶ **fern**

FERRATE n type of salt

FERREL same as ▶ **ferrule**

FERRELS ▶ **ferrel**

FERRET n tamed polecat used to catch rabbits or rats ▷ vb hunt with ferrets

FERRETS ▶ **ferret**

FERRETY ▶ **ferret**

FERRIC adj of or containing iron

FERRIED ▶ **ferry**

FERRIES ▶ **ferry**

FERRITE n any of a group of ferromagnetic highly resistive ceramic compounds

FERROUS adj of or containing iron in the divalent state

FERRUGO n disease affecting plants

FERRULE n metal cap to strengthen the end of a stick ▷ vb equip (a stick, etc) with a ferrule

FERRUM Latin word for ▶ **iron**

FERRUMS ▶ **ferrum**

FERRY n boat for transporting people and vehicles ▷ vb carry by ferry

FERTILE adj capable of producing young, crops, or vegetation

FERULA n large Mediterranean plant with thick stems and dissected leaves, cultivated for its strongly-scented gum resin

FERULAE ▶ **ferula**

FERULAS ▶ **ferula**

FERULE same as ▶ **ferrule**

FERULED ▶ **ferule**

FERULES ▶ **ferule**

FERVENT adj intensely passionate and sincere

FERVID same as ▶ **fervent**

FERVOR same as ▸ **fervour**

FERVORS ▸ **fervor**

FERVOUR n intensity of feeling

FES ▸ **fe**

FESCUE n pasture and lawn grass with stiff narrow leaves

FESCUES ▸ **fescue**

FESS same as ▸ **fesse**

FESSE n ordinary consisting of a horizontal band across a shield, conventionally occupying a third of its length and being wider than a bar

FESSED ▸ **fess**

FESSES ▸ **fesse**

FESSING ▸ **fess**

FEST n event at which the emphasis is on a particular activity

FESTA n festival

FESTAL adj festive ▷ n festivity

FESTALS ▸ **festal**

FESTAS ▸ **festa**

FESTER vb grow worse and increasingly hostile ▷ n small ulcer or sore containing pus

FESTERS ▸ **fester**

FESTIER ▸ **festy**

FESTIVE adj of or like a celebration

FESTOON vb hang decorations in loops ▷ n decorative chain of flowers or ribbons suspended in loops

FESTS ▸ **fest**

FESTY adj dirty

FET vb fetch

FETA n white salty Greek cheese

FETAL adj of, relating to, or resembling a fetus

FETAS ▸ **feta**

FETCH vb go after and bring back ▷ n ghost or apparition of a living person

FETCHED ▸ **fetch**

FETCHER n person or animal that fetches

FETCHES ▸ **fetch**

FETE n gala, bazaar, etc, usu held outdoors ▷ vb honour or entertain regally

FETED ▸ **fete**

FETES ▸ **fete**

FETIAL n (in ancient Rome) any of the 20 priestly heralds involved in declarations of war and in peace negotiations ▷ adj of or relating to the fetiales

FETIALS ▸ **fetial**

FETICH same as ▸ **fetish**

FETICHE same as ▸ **fetish**

FETID adj stinking

FETIDER ▸ **fetid**

FETIDLY ▸ **fetid**

FETING ▸ **fete**

FETISH n form of behaviour in which sexual pleasure is derived from looking at or handling an inanimate object

FETLOCK n projection behind and above a horse's hoof

FETOR n offensive stale or putrid odour

FETORS ▸ **fetor**

FETS ▸ **fet**

FETT same as ▸ **fet**

FETTA same as ▸ **feta**

FETTAS ▸ **fetta**

FETTED ▸ **fet**

FETTER n chain or shackle for the foot ▷ vb restrict

FETTERS ▸ **fetter**

FETTING ▸ **fet**

FETTLE same as > **fettling**

FETTLED ▸ **fettle**

FETTLER n person employed to maintain railway tracks

FETTLES ▸ **fettle**

FETTS ▸ **fett**

FETUS n embryo of a mammal in the later stages of development

FETUSES ▸ **fetus**

FETWA same as ▸ **fatwa**

FETWAS ▸ **fetwa**

FEU n (in Scotland) right of use of land in return for a fixed annual payment

FEUAR n tenant of a feu

FEUARS ▸ **feuar**

FEUD n long bitter hostility between two people or groups ▷ vb carry on a feud

FEUDAL adj of or like feudalism

FEUDARY n holder of land through feudal right

FEUDED ▸ **feud**

FEUDING ▸ **feud**

FEUDIST n person who takes part in a feud or quarrel

FEUDS ▸ **feud**

FEUED ▸ **feu**

FEUING ▸ **feu**

FEUS ▸ **feu**

FEUTRE vb place in a resting position

FEUTRED ▸ **feutre**

FEUTRES ▸ **feutre**

FEVER n (illness causing) high body temperature ▷ vb affect with or as if with fever

FEVERED ▸ **fever**

FEVERS ▸ **fever**

FEW adj not many as in **the few** small number of people considered as a class

FEWER ▸ **few**

FEWEST ▸ **few**

FEWMET same as ▸ **fumet**

FEWMETS ▸ **fewmet**

FEWNESS ▸ **few**

FEWS ▸ **few**

FEWTER same as ▸ **feutre**

FEWTERS ▸ **feutre**

FEY adj whimsically strange ▷ vb clean out

FEYED ▸ **fey**

FEYER ▸ **fey**

FEYEST ▸ **fey**

FEYING ▸ **fey**

FEYLY ▸ **fey**

FEYNESS ▸ **fey**

FEYS ▸ **fey**

FEZ n brimless tasselled cap, orig. from Turkey

FEZES ▸ **fez**

FEZZED adj wearing a fez

FEZZES ▸ **fez**

FEZZY ▸ **fez**

FIACRE n small four-wheeled horse-drawn carriage, usually with a folding roof

FIACRES ▸ **fiacre**

FIANCE n man engaged to be married

FIANCEE n woman who is engaged to be married

FIANCES ▸ **fiance**

FIAR n property owner

FIARS n legally fixed price of corn

FIASCHI ▸ **fiasco**

FIASCO n ridiculous or humiliating failure

FIASCOS ▸ **fiasco**

FIAT n arbitrary order ▷ vb issue a fiat

FIATED ▸ **fiat**

FIATING ▸ **fiat**

FIATS ▸ **fiat**

FIAUNT n fiat

FIAUNTS ▸ **fiaunt**

FIB n trivial lie ▷ vb tell a lie

FIBBED ▸ **fib**

FIBBER ▸ **fib**

FIBBERS ▸ fib
FIBBERY ▸ fib
FIBBING ▸ fib
FIBER same as ▸ **fibre**
FIBERED ▸ fibre
FIBERS ▸ fiber
FIBRATE n drug used to lower fat levels in the body
FIBRE n thread that can be spun into yarn
FIBRED ▸ fibre
FIBRES ▸ fibre
FIBRIL n small fibre
FIBRILS ▸ fibril
FIBRIN n white insoluble elastic protein formed when blood clots
FIBRINS ▸ fibrin
FIBRO n mixture of cement and asbestos fibre, used in sheets for building
FIBROID adj (of structures or tissues) containing or resembling fibres ▷ n benign tumour composed of fibrous connective tissue
FIBROIN n tough elastic protein that is the principal component of spiders' webs and raw silk
FIBROMA n benign tumour derived from fibrous connective tissue
FIBROS ▸ fibro
FIBROSE vb become fibrous
FIBROUS adj consisting of, containing, or resembling fibres
FIBS ▸ fib
FIBSTER n fibber
FIBULA n slender outer bone of the lower leg
FIBULAE ▸ fibula
FIBULAR ▸ fibula
FIBULAS ▸ fibula
FICE n small aggressive dog
FICES ▸ fice
FICHE n sheet of film for storing publications in miniaturized form
FICHES ▸ fiche
FICHU n woman's shawl or scarf of some light material, worn esp in the 18th century
FICHUS ▸ fichu
FICIN n enzyme
FICINS ▸ ficin
FICKLE adj changeable, inconstant ▷ vb puzzle
FICKLED ▸ fickle
FICKLER ▸ fickle
FICKLES ▸ fickle

FICKLY ▸ fickle
FICO n worthless trifle
FICOES ▸ fico
FICOS ▸ fico
FICTILE adj moulded or capable of being moulded from clay
FICTION n literary works of the imagination, such as novels
FICTIVE adj of, relating to, or able to create fiction
FICTOR n sculptor
FICTORS ▸ fictor
FICUS n type of plant such as the edible fig, often grown as a greenhouse or house plant
FICUSES ▸ ficus
FID n spike for separating strands of rope in splicing
FIDDLE n violin ▷ vb play the violin
FIDDLED ▸ fiddle
FIDDLER n person who plays the fiddle
FIDDLES ▸ fiddle
FIDDLEY n vertical space above a vessel's engine room extending into its stack
FIDDLY adj awkward to do or use
FIDEISM n theological doctrine that religious truth is a matter of faith and cannot be established by reason
FIDEIST ▸ fideism
FIDES n faith or trust
FIDGE obsolete word for ▸ **fidget**
FIDGED ▸ fidge
FIDGES ▸ fidge
FIDGET vb move about restlessly ▷ n person who fidgets
FIDGETS ▸ fidget
FIDGETY ▸ fidget
FIDGING ▸ fidge
FIDIBUS n spill for lighting a candle or pipe
FIDO n generic term for a dog
FIDOS ▸ fido
FIDS ▸ fid
FIE ▸ fey
FIEF n land granted by a lord in return for war service
FIEFDOM n (in Feudal Europe) the property owned by a lord
FIEFS ▸ fief

FIELD n piece of land, usu enclosed with a fence or hedge, and used for pasture or growing crops ▷ vb stop, catch, or return (the ball) as a fielder
FIELDED ▸ field
FIELDER n (in certain sports) player whose task is to field the ball
FIELDS ▸ field
FIEND n evil spirit
FIENDS ▸ fiend
FIENT n fiend
FIENTS ▸ fient
FIER same as ▸ **fere**
FIERCE adj wild or aggressive
FIERCER ▸ fierce
FIERE ▸ fere
FIERES ▸ fere
FIERIER ▸ fiery
FIERILY ▸ fiery
FIERS ▸ fier
FIERY adj consisting of or like fire
FIEST ▸ fie
FIESTA n religious festival, carnival
FIESTAS ▸ fiesta
FIFE n small high-pitched flute ▷ vb play (music) on a fife
FIFED ▸ fife
FIFER ▸ fife
FIFERS ▸ fife
FIFES ▸ fife
FIFING ▸ fife
FIFTEEN n five and ten ▷ adj amounting to fifteen ▷ determiner amounting to fifteen
FIFTH n (of) number five in a series ▷ adj of or being number five in a series ▷ adv after the fourth person, position, event, etc
FIFTHLY same as ▸ **fifth**
FIFTHS ▸ fifth
FIFTIES ▸ fifty
FIFTY n five times ten ▷ adj amounting to fifty ▷ determiner amounting to fifty
FIG n soft pear-shaped fruit ▷ vb dress (up) or rig (out)
FIGGED ▸ fig
FIGGERY n adornment, ornament
FIGGING ▸ fig
FIGHT vb struggle (against) in battle or physical combat ▷ n aggressive conflict

between two (groups of) people

FIGHTER *n* boxer

FIGHTS ▸ fight

FIGJAM *n* very conceited person

FIGJAMS ▸ figjam

FIGMENT *n* fantastic notion, invention, or fabrication

FIGO *same as* ▸ **fico**

FIGOS ▸ figo

FIGS ▸ fig

FIGURAL *adj* composed of or relating to human or animal figures

FIGURE *n* numerical symbol ▷ *vb* calculate (sums or amounts)

FIGURED *adj* decorated with a design

FIGURER ▸ figure

FIGURES ▸ figure

FIGWORT *n* N temperate plant with square stems and small brown or greenish flowers

FIKE *vb* fidget

FIKED ▸ fike

FIKERY *n* fuss

FIKES ▸ fike

FIKIER ▸ fiky

FIKIEST ▸ fiky

FIKING ▸ fike

FIKISH *adj* fussy

FIKY *adj* fussy

FIL *same as* ▸ **fils**

FILA ▸ filum

FILABEG *same as* ▸ **filibeg**

FILACER *n* formerly, English legal officer

FILAR *adj* of thread

FILAREE *n* type of storksbill, a weed

FILARIA *n* type of parasitic nematode worm transmitted to vertebrates by insects, the cause of filariasis

FILASSE *n* vegetable fibre such as jute

FILAZER *same as* ▸ **filacer**

FILBERD *same as* ▸ **filbert**

FILBERT *n* hazelnut

FILCH *vb* steal (small amounts)

FILCHED ▸ filch

FILCHER ▸ filch

FILCHES ▸ filch

FILE *n* box or folder used to keep documents in order ▷ *vb* place (a document) in a file

FILED ▸ file

FILEMOT *n* type of brown colour

FILER ▸ file

FILERS ▸ file

FILES ▸ file

FILET *same as* ▸ **fillet**

FILETED ▸ filet

FILETS ▸ filet

FILFOT *same as* ▸ **fylfot**

FILFOTS ▸ filfot

FILIAL *adj* of or befitting a son or daughter

FILIATE *vb* fix judicially the paternity of (a child, esp one born out of wedlock)

FILIBEG *n* kilt worn by Scottish Highlanders

FILII ▸ filius

> This plural of **filius**, a Latin word for son, is the only 5-letter word that lets you get rid of three Is!

FILING ▸ file

FILINGS *pl n* shavings removed by a file

FILIUS *n* son

FILL *vb* make or become full

FILLE *n* girl

FILLED ▸ fill

FILLER *n* substance that fills a gap or increases bulk

FILLERS ▸ filler

FILLES ▸ fille

FILLET *n* boneless piece of meat or fish ▷ *vb* remove the bones from

FILLETS ▸ fillet

FILLIES ▸ filly

FILLING *n* substance that fills a gap or cavity, esp in a tooth ▷ *adj* (of food) substantial and satisfying

FILLIP *n* something that adds stimulation or enjoyment ▷ *vb* stimulate or excite

FILLIPS ▸ fillip

FILLO *same as* ▸ **filo**

FILLOS ▸ fillo

FILLS ▸ fill

FILLY *n* young female horse

FILM *n* sequence of images projected on a screen, creating the illusion of movement ▷ *vb* photograph with a movie or video camera ▷ *adj* connected with films or the cinema

FILMDOM *n* cinema industry

FILMED ▸ film

FILMER *n* film-maker

FILMERS ▸ filmer

FILMI *adj* in Indian English, of or relating to the Indian film industry or Indian films

FILMIC *adj* of or suggestive of films or the cinema

FILMIER ▸ filmy

FILMILY ▸ filmy

FILMING ▸ film

FILMIS ▸ filmi

FILMISH ▸ film

FILMS ▸ film

FILMSET *vb* set (type matter) by filmsetting

FILMY *adj* very thin, delicate

FILO *n* type of flaky Greek pastry in very thin sheets

FILOS ▸ filo

FILOSE *adj* resembling or possessing a thread or threadlike process

FILS *n* fractional monetary unit of Bahrain, Iraq, Jordan, and Kuwait, worth one thousandth of a dinar

FILTER *n* material or device permitting fluid to pass but retaining solid particles ▷ *vb* remove impurities from (a substance) with a filter

FILTERS ▸ filter

FILTH *n* disgusting dirt

FILTHS ▸ filth

FILTHY *adj* characterized by or full of filth ▷ *adv* extremely

FILTRE *adj as in* **cafe filtre** a strong black filtered coffee

FILUM *n* any threadlike structure or part

FIMBLE *n* male plant of the hemp, which matures before the female plant

FIMBLES ▸ fimble

FIMBRIA *n* fringe or fringelike margin or border, esp at the opening of the Fallopian tubes

FIN *n* any of the firm appendages that are the organs of locomotion and balance in fishes and some other aquatic mammals ▷ *vb* provide with fins

FINABLE *adj* liable to a fine

FINAGLE *vb* get or achieve by craftiness or trickery

FINAL *adj* at the end ▷ *n* deciding contest between winners of previous rounds

F

in a competition

FINALE n concluding part of a dramatic performance or musical work

FINALES ▸ **finale**

FINALIS n musical finishing note

FINALLY adv after a long delay

FINALS pl n deciding part of a competition

FINANCE vb provide or obtain funds for ▹ n system of money, credit, and investment

FINBACK another name for ▸ **rorqual**

FINCA n Spanish villa

FINCAS ▸ **finca**

FINCH n small songbird with a short strong beak

FINCHED adj with streaks or spots on the back

FINCHES ▸ **finch**

FIND vb discover by chance ▹ n person or thing found, esp when valuable

FINDER n small telescope fitted to a larger one

FINDERS ▸ **finder**

FINDING ▸ **find**

FINDRAM same as ▸ **finnan**

FINDS ▸ **find**

FINE adj very good ▹ n payment imposed as a penalty ▹ vb impose a fine on

FINED ▸ **fine**

FINEER same as ▸ **veneer**

FINEERS ▸ **fineer**

FINEISH ▸ **fine**

FINELY adv into small pieces

FINER ▸ **fine**

FINERS ▸ **fine**

FINERY n showy clothing

FINES ▸ **fine**

FINESSE n delicate skill ▹ vb bring about with finesse

FINEST ▸ **fine**

FINFISH n fish with fins, as opposed to shellfish

FINFOOT n type of tropical and subtropical aquatic bird with broadly lobed toes, a long slender head and neck, and pale brown plumage

FINGAN same as ▸ **finjan**

FINGANS ▸ **fingan**

FINGER n one of the four long jointed parts of the hand ▹ vb touch or handle with the fingers

FINGERS ▸ **finger**

FINI n end; finish

FINIAL n ornament at the apex of a gable or spire

FINIALS ▸ **finial**

FINICAL another word for ▸ **finicky**

FINICKY adj excessively particular, fussy

FINIKIN same as ▸ **finicky**

FINING n process of removing undissolved gas bubbles from molten glass

FININGS ▸ **fining**

FINIS n end; finish

FINISES ▸ **finis**

FINISH vb bring to an end, stop ▹ n end, last part

FINITE adj having limits in space, time, or size ▹ n a verb limited by person, number, tense or mood

FINITES ▸ **finite**

FINITO adj finished

FINJAN n small, handleless coffee cup

FINJANS ▸ **finjan**

FINK n strikebreaker ▹ vb inform (on someone), as to the police

FINKED ▸ **fink**

FINKING ▸ **fink**

FINKS ▸ **fink**

FINLESS ▸ **fin**

FINLIKE ▸ **fin**

FINMARK n monetary unit of Finland

FINNAC same as ▸ **finnock**

FINNACK same as ▸ **finnock**

FINNACS ▸ **finnac**

FINNAN n smoked haddock

FINNANS ▸ **finnan**

FINNED ▸ **fin**

FINNER another name for ▸ **rorqual**

FINNERS ▸ **finner**

FINNIER ▸ **finny**

FINNING ▸ **fin**

FINNOCK n young sea trout on its first return to fresh water

FINNSKO same as > **finnesko**

FINNY adj relating to or containing many fishes

FINO n very dry sherry

FINOS ▸ **fino**

FINS ▸ **fin**

FINSKO same as > **finnesko**

FIORD same as ▸ **fjord**

FIORDS ▸ **fiord**

FIORIN n type of temperate perennial grass

FIORINS ▸ **fiorin**

FIPPLE n wooden plug forming a flue in the end of a pipe, as the mouthpiece of a recorder

FIPPLES ▸ **fipple**

FIQH n Islamic jurisprudence

FIQHS ▸ **fiqh**

FIQUE n hemp

FIQUES ▸ **fique**

FIR n pyramid-shaped tree with needle-like leaves and erect cones

FIRE n state of combustion producing heat, flames, and smoke ▹ vb operate (a weapon) so that a bullet or missile is released

FIREARM n rifle, pistol, or shotgun

FIREBOX n furnace chamber of a boiler in a steam locomotive

FIREBUG n person who deliberately sets fire to property

FIRED ▸ **fire**

FIREDOG n either of a pair of decorative metal stands used to support logs in an open fire

FIREFLY n beetle that glows in the dark

FIRELIT adj lit by firelight

FIREMAN n man whose job is to put out fires and rescue people endangered by them

FIREMEN ▸ **fireman**

FIREPAN n metal container for a fire in a room

FIREPOT n Chinese fondue-like cooking pot

FIRER ▸ **fire**

FIRERS ▸ **fire**

FIRES ▸ **fire**

FIRIE n in Australian English, informal word for a firefighter

FIRIES ▸ **firie**

FIRING n discharge of a firearm

FIRINGS ▸ **firing**

FIRK vb beat

FIRKED ▸ **firk**

FIRKIN n small wooden barrel or similar container

FIRKING ▸ **firk**

FIRKINS ▸ **firkin**

FIRKS ▸ **firk**

FIRLOT n unit of measurement for grain

FIRLOTS ▸ firlot

FIRM adj not soft or yielding ▷ adv in an unyielding manner ▷ vb make or become firm ▷ n business company

FIRMAN n edict of an Oriental sovereign

FIRMANS ▸ firman

FIRMED ▸ firm

FIRMER ▸ firm

FIRMERS ▸ firm

FIRMEST ▸ firm

FIRMING ▸ firm

FIRMLY ▸ firm

FIRMS ▸ firm

FIRN another name for ▸ **neve**

FIRNS ▸ firn

FIRRIER ▸ firry

FIRRING n wooden battens used in building construction

FIRRY adj of, relating to, or made from fir trees

FIRS ▸ fir

FIRST adj earliest in time or order ▷ n person or thing coming before all others ▷ adv before anything else

FIRSTLY adv coming before other points, questions, etc

FIRSTS pl n saleable goods of the highest quality

FIRTH n narrow inlet of the sea, esp in Scotland

FIRTHS ▸ firth

FIRWOOD n wood of the fir tree

FISC n state or royal treasury

FISCAL adj of government finances, esp taxes ▷ n (in some countries) a public prosecutor

FISCALS ▸ fiscal

FISCS ▸ fisc

FISGIG same as ▸ **fishgig**

FISGIGS ▸ fisgig

FISH n cold-blooded vertebrate with gills, that lives in water ▷ vb try to catch fish

FISHED ▸ fish

FISHER n fisherman

FISHERS ▸ fisher

FISHERY n area of the sea used for fishing

FISHES ▸ fish

FISHEYE n in photography, a lens of small focal length, having a highly curved protruding front element, that covers an angle of view

of almost 180°

FISHFUL adj teeming with fish

FISHGIG n pole with barbed prongs for impaling fish

FISHIER ▸ fishy

FISHIFY vb change into fish

FISHILY ▸ fishy

FISHING n job or pastime of catching fish

FISHNET n open mesh fabric resembling netting

FISHWAY n fish ladder

FISHY adj of or like fish

FISK vb frisk

FISKED ▸ fisk

FISKING ▸ fisk

FISKS ▸ fisk

FISSATE ▸ fissile

FISSILE adj capable of undergoing nuclear fission

FISSION n splitting

FISSIVE ▸ fissile

FISSLE vb rustle

FISSLED ▸ fissle

FISSLES ▸ fissle

FISSURE n long narrow cleft or crack ▷ vb crack or split apart

FIST n clenched hand ▷ vb hit with the fist

FISTED ▸ fist

FISTFUL n quantity that can be held in a fist or hand

FISTIC adj of or relating to fisticuffs or boxing

FISTIER ▸ fist

FISTING ▸ fist

FISTS ▸ fist

FISTULA n long narrow ulcer

FISTY ▸ fist

FIT vb be appropriate or suitable for ▷ adj appropriate ▷ n way in which something fits

FITCH n fur of the polecat or ferret

FITCHE adj pointed

FITCHEE same as ▸ **fitche**

FITCHES ▸ fitch

FITCHET same as ▸ **fitch**

FITCHEW archaic name for ▸ **polecat**

FITCHY same as ▸ **fitche**

FITFUL adj occurring in irregular spells

FITLIER ▸ fitly

FITLY adv in a proper manner or place or at a proper time

FITMENT n accessory attached to a machine

FITNA n state of trouble or chaos

FITNAS ▸ fitna

FITNESS n state of being fit

FITS ▸ fit

FITT n song

FITTE same as ▸ **fitt**

FITTED ▸ fit

FITTER ▸ fit

FITTERS ▸ fit

FITTES ▸ fitte

FITTEST ▸ fit

FITTING ▸ fit

FITTS ▸ fitt

FIVE n one more than four ▷ adj amounting to five ▷ determiner amounting to five

FIVEPIN > fivepins

FIVER n five-pound note

FIVERS ▸ fiver

FIVES n ball game resembling squash but played with bats or the hands

FIX vb make or become firm, stable, or secure ▷ n difficult situation

FIXABLE ▸ fix

FIXATE vb become or cause to become fixed

FIXATED ▸ fixate

FIXATES ▸ fixate

FIXATIF same as ▸ **fixative**

FIXED adj attached or placed so as to be immovable

FIXEDLY ▸ fixed

FIXER n solution used to make a photographic image permanent

FIXERS ▸ fixer

FIXES ▸ fix

FIXING n means of attaching one thing to another, as a pipe to a wall, slate to a roof, etc

FIXINGS pl n apparatus or equipment

FIXIT n solution to a complex problem

FIXITY n state or quality of a person's gaze, attitude, or concentration not changing or weakening

FIXIVE ▸ fix

FIXT adj fixed

FIXTURE n permanently fitted piece of household equipment

FIXURE n firmness

FIXURES ▸ fixure

FIZ same as ▸ **fizz**

F

F

FIZGIG *vb* inform on someone to the police
FIZGIGS ▸ fizgig
FIZZ *vb* make a hissing or bubbling noise ▷ *n* hissing or bubbling noise
FIZZED ▸ fizz
FIZZEN *same as* ▸ foison
FIZZENS ▸ fizzen
FIZZER *n* anything that fizzes
FIZZERS ▸ fizzer
FIZZES ▸ fizz
FIZZGIG *same as* ▸ fishgig
FIZZIER ▸ fizz
FIZZING ▸ fizz
FIZZLE *vb* make a weak hissing or bubbling sound ▷ *n* hissing or bubbling sound
FIZZLED ▸ fizzle
FIZZLES ▸ fizzle
FIZZY ▸ fizz
FJELD *n* high rocky plateau with little vegetation in Scandinavian countries
FJELDS ▸ fjeld
FJORD *n* long narrow inlet of the sea between cliffs, esp in Norway
FJORDIC ▸ fjord
FJORDS ▸ fjord
FLAB *n* unsightly body fat
FLABBY *adj* having flabby flesh
FLABS ▸ flab
FLACCID *adj* soft and limp
FLACK *vb* flutter
FLACKED ▸ flack
FLACKER *vb* flutter like a bird
FLACKET *n* flagon
FLACKS ▸ flack
FLACON *n* small stoppered bottle or flask, such as one used for perfume
FLACONS ▸ flacon
FLAFF *vb* flap
FLAFFED ▸ flaff
FLAFFER *vb* flutter
FLAFFS ▸ flaff
FLAG *n* piece of cloth attached to a pole as an emblem or signal ▷ *vb* mark with a flag or sticker
FLAGGED ▸ flag
FLAGGER ▸ flag
FLAGGY *adj* drooping
FLAGMAN *n* person who has charge of, carries, or signals with a flag, esp a railway employee
FLAGMEN ▸ flagman

FLAGON *n* wide bottle for wine or cider
FLAGONS ▸ flagon
FLAGS ▸ flag
FLAIL *vb* wave about wildly ▷ *n* tool formerly used for threshing grain by hand
FLAILED ▸ flail
FLAILS ▸ flail
FLAIR *n* natural ability
FLAIRS ▸ flair
FLAK *n* anti-aircraft fire
FLAKE *n* small thin piece, esp chipped off something ▷ *vb* peel off in flakes
FLAKED ▸ flake
FLAKER ▸ flake
FLAKERS ▸ flake
FLAKES ▸ flake
FLAKEY *same as* ▸ flaky
FLAKIER ▸ flaky
FLAKIES *n* dandruff
FLAKILY ▸ flaky
FLAKING ▸ flake
FLAKS ▸ flak
FLAKY *adj* like or made of flakes
FLAM *n* falsehood, deception, or sham ▷ *vb* cheat or deceive
FLAMBE *vb* cook or serve (food) in flaming brandy ▷ *adj* (of food, such as steak or pancakes) served in flaming brandy
FLAMBEE *same as* ▸ flambe
FLAMBES ▸ flambe
FLAME *n* luminous burning gas coming from burning material ▷ *vb* burn brightly
FLAMED ▸ flame
FLAMEN *n* (in ancient Rome) any of 15 priests who each served a particular deity
FLAMENS ▸ flamen
FLAMER ▸ flame
FLAMERS ▸ flame
FLAMES ▸ flame
FLAMFEW *n* fantastic trifle
FLAMIER ▸ flame
FLAMING *adj* burning with flames ▷ *adv* extremely
FLAMM *same as* ▸ flam
FLAMMED ▸ flam
FLAMMS ▸ flamm
FLAMS ▸ flam
FLAMY ▸ flame
FLAN *n* open sweet or savoury tart
FLANCH *same as* ▸ flaunch
FLANES *n* arrows
FLANEUR *n* idler or loafer
FLANGE *n* projecting rim or

collar ▷ *vb* attach or provide (a component) with a flange
FLANGED ▸ flange
FLANGER ▸ flange
FLANGES ▸ flange
FLANK *n* part of the side between the hips and ribs ▷ *vb* be at or move along the side of
FLANKED ▸ flank
FLANKEN *n* cut of beef
FLANKER *n* one of a detachment of soldiers detailed to guard the flanks, esp of a formation
FLANKS ▸ flank
FLANNEL *n* small piece of cloth for washing the face ▷ *vb* talk evasively
FLANNEN *adj* made of flannel
FLANNIE ▸ flanny
FLANNY *n* a shirt made of flannel
FLANS ▸ flan
FLAP *vb* move back and forwards or up and down ▷ *n* action or sound of flapping
FLAPPED ▸ flap
FLAPPER *n* (in the 1920s) a lively young woman who dressed and behaved unconventionally
FLAPPY *adj* loose
FLAPS ▸ flap
FLARE *vb* blaze with a sudden unsteady flame ▷ *n* sudden unsteady flame
FLARED ▸ flare
FLARES *pl n* trousers with legs that widen below the knee
FLAREUP *n* outbreak of something
FLARIER ▸ flare
FLARING ▸ flare
FLARY ▸ flare
FLASER *n* type of sedimentary structure in rock
FLASERS ▸ flaser
FLASH *n* sudden burst of light or flame ▷ *adj* vulgarly showy ▷ *vb* (cause to) burst into flame
FLASHED ▸ flash
FLASHER *n* man who exposes himself indecently
FLASHES ▸ flash
FLASHY *adj* showy in a vulgar way

FLASK *n* flat bottle for carrying alcoholic drink in the pocket

FLASKET *n* long shallow basket

FLASKS ▸ flask

FLAT *adj* level and horizontal ▷ *adv* in or into a flat position ▷ *n* flat surface ▷ *vb* live in a flat

FLATBED *n* printing machine on which the type forme is carried on a flat bed under a revolving paper-bearing cylinder

FLATCAP *n* Elizabethan man's hat with a narrow down-turned brim

FLATCAR *n* flatbed

FLATLET *n* small flat

FLATLY ▸ flat

FLATS ▸ flat

FLATTED ▸ flat

FLATTEN *vb* make or become flat or flatter

FLATTER *vb* praise insincerely

FLATTIE *n* flat tyre

FLATTOP *n* informal name for an aircraft carrier

FLATTY *n* flat shoe

FLATUS *n* gas generated in the alimentary canal

FLAUGHT *vb* flutter

FLAUNCH *n* cement or mortar slope around a chimney top, manhole, etc, to throw off water ▷ *vb* cause to slope in this manner

FLAUNE *same as* ▸ **flam**

FLAUNES ▸ flaune

FLAUNT *vb* display (oneself or one's possessions) arrogantly ▷ *n* act of flaunting

FLAUNTS ▸ flaunt

FLAUNTY *adj* characterized by or inclined to ostentatious display or flaunting

FLAUTA *n* tortilla rolled around a filling

FLAUTAS ▸ flauta

FLAVA *n* individual style

FLAVAS ▸ flava

FLAVIN *n* heterocyclic ketone

FLAVINE *same as* ▸ **flavin**

FLAVINS ▸ flavin

FLAVONE *n* crystalline compound occurring in plants

FLAVOR *same as* ▸ **flavour**

FLAVORS ▸ flavor

FLAVORY *adj* flavoursome

FLAVOUR *n* distinctive taste ▷ *vb* give flavour to

FLAW *n* imperfection or blemish ▷ *vb* make or become blemished, defective, or imperfect

FLAWED ▸ flaw

FLAWIER ▸ flaw

FLAWING ▸ flaw

FLAWN *same as* ▸ **flam**

FLAWNS ▸ flawn

FLAWS ▸ flaw

FLAWY ▸ flaw

FLAX *n* plant grown for its stem fibres and seeds

FLAXEN *adj* (of hair) pale yellow

FLAXES ▸ flax

FLAXIER ▸ flaxy

FLAXY *same as* ▸ **flaxen**

FLAY *same as* ▸ **fley**

FLAYED ▸ flay

FLAYER ▸ flay

FLAYERS ▸ flay

FLAYING ▸ flay

FLAYS ▸ flay

FLEA *n* small wingless jumping bloodsucking insect

FLEABAG *n* dirty or unkempt person, esp a woman

FLEADH *n* festival of Irish music, dancing, and culture

FLEADHS ▸ fleadh

FLEAM *n* lancet used for letting blood

FLEAMS ▸ fleam

FLEAPIT *n* shabby cinema or theatre

FLEAS ▸ flea

FLECHE *n* slender spire, esp over the intersection of the nave and transept ridges of a church roof

FLECHES ▸ fleche

FLECK *n* small mark, streak, or speck ▷ *vb* speckle

FLECKED ▸ fleck

FLECKER *same as* ▸ **fleck**

FLECKS ▸ fleck

FLECKY ▸ fleck

FLED ▸ flee

FLEDGE *vb* feed and care for (a young bird) until it is able to fly

FLEDGED ▸ fledge

FLEDGES ▸ fledge

FLEDGY *adj* feathery or feathered

FLEE *vb* run away (from)

FLEECE *n* sheep's coat of wool ▷ *vb* defraud or overcharge

FLEECED ▸ fleece

FLEECER ▸ fleece

FLEECES ▸ fleece

FLEECH *vb* flatter

FLEECIE *n* person who collects fleeces after shearing and prepares them for baling

FLEECY *adj* made of or like fleece ▷ *n* person who collects fleeces after shearing and prepares them for baling

FLEEING ▸ flee

FLEER *vb* grin or laugh at ▷ *n* derisory glance or grin

FLEERED ▸ fleer

FLEERER ▸ fleer

FLEERS ▸ fleer

FLEES ▸ flee

FLEET *n* number of warships organized as a unit ▷ *adj* swift in movement ▷ *vb* move rapidly

FLEETED ▸ fleet

FLEETER ▸ fleet

FLEETLY ▸ fleet

FLEETS ▸ fleet

FLEG *vb* scare

FLEGGED ▸ fleg

FLEGS ▸ fleg

FLEHMEN *vb* (of mammal) grimace

FLEME *vb* drive out

FLEMES ▸ fleme

FLEMING *n* native or inhabitant of Flanders or a Flemish-speaking Belgian

FLEMISH *vb* stow (a rope) in a Flemish coil

FLEMIT ▸ fleme

FLENCH *same as* ▸ **flense**

FLENSE *vb* strip (a whale, seal, etc) of (its blubber or skin)

FLENSED ▸ flense

FLENSER ▸ flense

FLENSES ▸ flense

FLESH *n* soft part of a human or animal body

FLESHED ▸ flesh

FLESHER *n* person or machine that fleshes hides or skins

FLESHES ▸ flesh

FLESHLY *adj* carnal

FLESHY *adj* plump

FLETCH *same as* ▸ **fledge**

FLETTON *n* type of brick

FLEURET *same as*
> **fleurette**
FLEURON *n* decorative
piece of pastry
FLEURY *same as* ▸ **flory**
FLEW ▸ **fly**
FLEWED *adj* having large
flews
FLEWS *pl n* fleshy hanging
upper lip of a bloodhound
or similar dog
FLEX *n* flexible insulated
electric cable ▷ *vb* bend
FLEXED ▸ **flex**
FLEXES ▸ **flex**
FLEXILE *same as* > **flexible**
FLEXING ▸ **flex**
FLEXION *n* act of bending a
joint or limb
FLEXO *n, adj, adv*
flexography
FLEXOR *n* any muscle
whose contraction serves
to bend a joint or limb
FLEXORS ▸ **flexor**
FLEXOS ▸ **flexo**
FLEXURE *n* act of flexing or
the state of being flexed
FLEY *vb* be afraid or cause to
be afraid
FLEYED ▸ **fley**
FLEYING ▸ **fley**
FLEYS ▸ **fley**
FLIC *n* French police officer
FLICK *vb* touch or move
with the finger or hand in a
quick movement ▷ *n* tap or
quick stroke
FLICKED ▸ **flick**
FLICKER *vb* shine unsteadily
or intermittently ▷ *n*
unsteady brief light
FLICKS ▸ **flick**
FLICS ▸ **flic**
FLIED ▸ **fly**
FLIER ▸ **fly**
FLIERS ▸ **fly**
FLIES ▸ **fly**
FLIEST ▸ **fly**
FLIGHT *n* journey by air ▷ *vb*
cause (a ball, dart, etc) to
float slowly or deceptively
towards its target
FLIGHTS ▸ **flight**
FLIGHTY *adj* frivolous and
fickle
FLIM *n* five-pound note
FLIMP *vb* steal
FLIMPED ▸ **flimp**
FLIMPS ▸ **flimp**
FLIMS ▸ **flim**
FLIMSY *adj* not strong or
substantial ▷ *n* thin paper

used for making carbon
copies of a letter, etc
FLINCH *same as* ▸ **flense**
FLINDER *n* fragment
FLING *vb* throw, send, or
move forcefully or hurriedly
▷ *n* spell of self-indulgent
enjoyment
FLINGER ▸ **fling**
FLINGS ▸ **fling**
FLINT *n* hard grey stone
▷ *vb* fit or provide with a
flint
FLINTED ▸ **flint**
FLINTS ▸ **flint**
FLINTY *adj* cruel
FLIP *vb* throw (something
small or light) carelessly ▷ *n*
snap or tap ▷ *adj* flippant
FLIPPED ▸ **flip**
FLIPPER *n* limb of a sea
animal adapted for
swimming
FLIPPY *adj* (of clothes)
tending to move to and fro
as the wearer walks
FLIPS ▸ **flip**
FLIR *n* forward looking
infrared radar
FLIRS ▸ **flir**
FLIRT *vb* behave as if
sexually attracted to
someone ▷ *n* person who
flirts
FLIRTED ▸ **flirt**
FLIRTER ▸ **flirt**
FLIRTS ▸ **flirt**
FLIRTY ▸ **flirt**
FLISK *vb* skip
FLISKED ▸ **flisk**
FLISKS ▸ **flisk**
FLISKY ▸ **flisk**
FLIT *vb* move lightly and
rapidly ▷ *n* act of flitting
FLITCH *n* side of pork salted
and cured ▷ *vb* cut (a tree
trunk) into flitches
FLITE *vb* scold or rail at ▷ *n*
dispute or scolding
FLITED ▸ **flite**
FLITES ▸ **flite**
FLITING ▸ **flite**
FLITS ▸ **flit**
FLITT *adj* fleet
FLITTED ▸ **flit**
FLITTER ▸ **flit**
FLIVVER *n* old, cheap, or
battered car
FLIX *n* fur ▷ *vb* have fur
FLIXED ▸ **flix**
FLIXES ▸ **flix**
FLIXING ▸ **flix**
FLOAT *vb* rest on the surface

of a liquid ▷ *n* light object
used to help someone or
something float
FLOATED ▸ **float**
FLOATEL *same as* ▸ **flotel**
FLOATER *n* person or thing
that floats
FLOATS *pl n* footlights
FLOATY *adj* filmy and light
FLOB *vb* spit
FLOBBED ▸ **flob**
FLOBS ▸ **flob**
FLOC *same as* ▸ **flock**
FLOCCED ▸ **floc**
FLOCCI ▸ **floccus**
FLOCCUS *n* downy or
woolly covering, as on the
young of certain birds ▷ *adj*
(of a cloud) having the
appearance of woolly tufts
at odd intervals in its
structure
FLOCK *n* number of animals
of one kind together ▷ *vb*
gather in a crowd ▷ *adj* (of
wallpaper) with a velvety
raised pattern
FLOCKED ▸ **flock**
FLOCKS ▸ **flock**
FLOCKY ▸ **flock**
FLOCS ▸ **floc**
FLOE *n* sheet of floating ice
FLOES ▸ **floe**
FLOG *vb* beat with a whip or
stick
FLOGGED ▸ **flog**
FLOGGER ▸ **flog**
FLOGS ▸ **flog**
FLOKATI *n* Greek
hand-woven shaggy
woollen rug
FLONG *n* material, usually
pulped paper or cardboard,
used for making moulds in
stereotyping
FLONGS ▸ **flong**
FLOOD *n* overflow of water
onto a normally dry area
▷ *vb* cover or become
covered with water
FLOODED ▸ **flood**
FLOODER ▸ **flood**
FLOODS ▸ **flood**
FLOOEY *adj* awry
FLOOIE *same as* ▸ **flooey**
FLOOR *n* lower surface of a
room ▷ *vb* knock down
FLOORED ▸ **floor**
FLOORER *n* coup de grâce
FLOORS ▸ **floor**
FLOOSIE *same as* ▸ **floozy**
FLOOSY *same as* ▸ **floosie**
FLOOZIE *same as* ▸ **floozy**

FLOOZY n disreputable woman

FLOP vb bend, fall, or collapse loosely or carelessly ▷ n failure

FLOPPED ▸ **flop**

FLOPPER ▸ **flop**

FLOPPY adj hanging downwards, loose ▷ n floppy disk

FLOPS ▸ **flop**

FLOR n yeast formed on the surface of sherry after fermentation

FLORA n plants of a given place or time

FLORAE ▸ **flora**

FLORAL adj consisting of or decorated with flowers ▷ n class of perfume

FLORALS ▸ **floral**

FLORAS ▸ **flora**

FLOREAT vb may (a person, institution, etc) flourish

FLORET n small flower forming part of a composite flower head

FLORETS ▸ **floret**

FLORID adj with a red or flushed complexion

FLORIER ▸ **flory**

FLORIN n former British and Australian coin

FLORINS ▸ **florin**

FLORIST n seller of flowers

FLORS ▸ **flor**

FLORUIT prep (he or she) flourished: used to indicate the period when a historical figure, whose birth and death dates are unknown, was most active ▷ n such a period in a person's life

FLORULA n flora of a small single environment

FLORULE same as ▸ **florula**

FLORY adj containing a fleur-de-lys

FLOSH n hopper-shaped box

FLOSHES ▸ **flosh**

FLOSS n fine silky fibres ▷ vb clean (between the teeth) with dental floss

FLOSSED ▸ **floss**

FLOSSER ▸ **floss**

FLOSSES ▸ **floss**

FLOSSIE same as ▸ **flossy**

FLOSSY adj consisting of or resembling floss ▷ n floozy

FLOTA n formerly, Spanish commercial fleet

FLOTAGE n act or state of floating

FLOTANT adj in heraldry, flying in the air

FLOTAS ▸ **flota**

FLOTE n aquatic perennial grass

FLOTEL n (in the oil industry) an oil rig or boat used as accommodation for workers in off-shore oil fields

FLOTELS ▸ **flotel**

FLOTES ▸ **flote**

FLOTSAM n floating wreckage

FLOUNCE vb go with emphatic movements ▷ n flouncing movement

FLOUNCY ▸ **flounce**

FLOUR n powder made by grinding grain, esp wheat ▷ vb sprinkle with flour

FLOURED ▸ **flour**

FLOURS ▸ **flour**

FLOURY ▸ **flour**

FLOUSE vb splash

FLOUSED ▸ **flouse**

FLOUSES ▸ **flouse**

FLOUSH same as ▸ **flouse**

FLOUT vb deliberately disobey (a rule, law, etc)

FLOUTED ▸ **flout**

FLOUTER ▸ **flout**

FLOUTS ▸ **flout**

FLOW vb (of liquid) move in a stream ▷ n act, rate, or manner of flowing

FLOWAGE n act of flowing or overflowing or the state of having overflowed

FLOWED ▸ **flow**

FLOWER n part of a plant that produces seeds ▷ vb produce flowers, bloom

FLOWERS ▸ **flower**

FLOWERY adj decorated with a floral design

FLOWING ▸ **flow**

FLOWN ▸ **fly**

FLOWS ▸ **flow**

FLOX adj as in **flox silk** type of silk

FLU n any of various viral infections, esp a respiratory or intestinal infection

FLUATE n fluoride

FLUATES ▸ **fluate**

FLUB vb bungle

FLUBBED ▸ **flub**

FLUBBER ▸ **flub**

FLUBDUB n bunkum

FLUBS ▸ **flub**

FLUE n passage or pipe for smoke or hot air

FLUED adj having a flue

FLUENCE ▸ **fluency**

FLUENCY n quality of being fluent, esp facility in speech or writing

FLUENT adj able to speak or write with ease ▷ n variable quantity in fluxions

FLUENTS ▸ **fluent**

FLUERIC adj of or relating to fluidics

FLUES ▸ **flue**

FLUEY adj involved in, caused by, or like influenza

FLUFF n soft fibres ▷ vb make or become soft and puffy

FLUFFED ▸ **fluff**

FLUFFER n person employed on a pornographic film set to ensure that male actors are kept aroused

FLUFFS ▸ **fluff**

FLUFFY adj of, resembling, or covered with fluff

FLUGEL n grand piano or harpsichord

FLUGELS ▸ **flugel**

FLUID n substance able to flow and change its shape ▷ adj able to flow or change shape easily

FLUIDAL ▸ **fluid**

FLUIDIC ▸ **fluidics**

FLUIDLY ▸ **fluid**

FLUIDS ▸ **fluid**

FLUIER ▸ **fluey**

FLUIEST ▸ **fluey**

FLUISH ▸ **flu**

FLUKE n accidental stroke of luck ▷ vb gain, make, or hit by a fluke

FLUKED ▸ **fluke**

FLUKES ▸ **fluke**

FLUKEY same as ▸ **fluky**

FLUKIER ▸ **fluky**

FLUKILY ▸ **fluky**

FLUKING ▸ **fluke**

FLUKY adj done or gained by an accident, esp a lucky one

FLUME n narrow sloping channel for water ▷ vb transport (logs) in a flume

FLUMED ▸ **flume**

FLUMES ▸ **flume**

FLUMING ▸ **flume**

FLUMMOX vb puzzle or confuse

FLUMP vb move or fall heavily

FLUMPED ▸ **flump**

F

FLUMPS ▸ flump
FLUNG ▸ fling
FLUNK vb fail ▷ n low grade below the pass standard
FLUNKED ▸ flunk
FLUNKER ▸ flunk
FLUNKEY same as ▸ **flunky**
FLUNKIE same as ▸ **flunky**
FLUNKS ▸ flunk
FLUNKY n servile person
FLUOR ▸ fluorspar
FLUORIC adj of, concerned with, or produced from fluorine or fluorspar
FLUORID same as ▸ **fluoride**
FLUORIN same as ▸ **fluorine**
FLUORS ▸ fluor
FLURR vb scatter
FLURRED ▸ flurr
FLURRS ▸ flurr
FLURRY n sudden commotion ▷ vb confuse
FLUS ▸ flu
FLUSH vb blush or cause to blush ▷ n blush ▷ adj level with the surrounding surface ▷ adv so as to be level
FLUSHED ▸ flush
FLUSHER ▸ flush
FLUSHES ▸ flush
FLUSHY adj ruddy
FLUSTER vb make nervous or upset ▷ n nervous or upset state
FLUTE n wind instrument consisting of a tube with sound holes and a mouth hole in the side ▷ vb utter in a high-pitched tone
FLUTED adj having decorative grooves
FLUTER n craftsman who makes flutes or fluting
FLUTERS ▸ fluter
FLUTES ▸ flute
FLUTEY ▸ flute
FLUTIER ▸ flute
FLUTINA n type of accordion
FLUTING n design of decorative grooves
FLUTIST same as ▸ **flautist**
FLUTTER vb wave rapidly ▷ n flapping movement
FLUTY ▸ flute
FLUVIAL adj of rivers
FLUX n constant change or instability ▷ vb make or become fluid
FLUXED ▸ flux
FLUXES ▸ flux
FLUXING ▸ flux

FLUXION n rate of change of a function, especially the instantaneous velocity of a moving body
FLUXIVE ▸ flux
FLUYT n Dutch sailing ship
FLUYTS ▸ fluyt
FLY vb move through the air on wings or in an aircraft ▷ n fastening at the front of trousers ▷ adj sharp and cunning
FLYABLE ▸ fly
FLYAWAY adj (of hair) very fine and soft ▷ n person who is frivolous or flighty
FLYBACK n fast return of the spot on a cathode-ray tube after completion of each trace
FLYBANE n type of campion
FLYBELT n strip of tsetse-infested land
FLYBLEW ▸ flyblow
FLYBLOW vb contaminate, esp with the eggs or larvae of the blowfly ▷ n egg or young larva of a blowfly, deposited on meat, paper, etc
FLYBOAT n any small swift boat
FLYBOOK n small case or wallet used by anglers for storing artificial flies
FLYBOY n air force pilot
FLYBOYS ▸ flyboy
FLYBY n flight past a particular position or target, esp the close approach of a spacecraft to a planet or satellite for investigation of conditions
FLYBYS ▸ flyby
FLYER ▸ fly
FLYERS ▸ fly
FLYEST ▸ fly
FLYHAND n device for transferring printed sheets from the press to a flat pile
FLYING ▸ fly
FLYINGS ▸ fly
FLYLEAF n blank leaf at the beginning or end of a book
FLYLESS ▸ fly
FLYMAN n stagehand who operates the scenery, curtains, etc, in the flies
FLYMEN ▸ flyman
FLYOFF n total volume of water transferred from the earth to the atmosphere
FLYOFFS ▸ flyoff

FLYOVER n road passing over another by a bridge
FLYPAST n ceremonial flight of aircraft over a given area
FLYPE vb fold back
FLYPED ▸ flype
FLYPES ▸ flype
FLYPING ▸ flype
FLYSCH n marine sedimentary facies consisting of a sequence of sandstones, conglomerates, marls, shales, and clays that were formed by erosion during a period of mountain building and subsequently deformed as the mountain building continued
FLYTE same as ▸ **flite**
FLYTED ▸ flyte
FLYTES ▸ flyte
FLYTIER n person who makes his own fishing flies
FLYTING ▸ flyte
FLYTRAP n any of various insectivorous plants, esp Venus's flytrap
FLYWAY n usual route used by birds when migrating
FLYWAYS ▸ flyway
FOAL n young of a horse or related animal ▷ vb give birth to a foal
FOALED ▸ foal
FOALING ▸ foal
FOALS ▸ foal
FOAM n mass of small bubbles on a liquid ▷ vb produce foam
FOAMED ▸ foam
FOAMER n (possibly obsessive) enthusiast
FOAMERS ▸ foamer
FOAMIER ▸ foamy
FOAMILY ▸ foamy
FOAMING ▸ foam
FOAMS ▸ foam
FOAMY adj of, resembling, consisting of, or covered with foam
FOB n short watch chain ▷ vb cheat
FOBBED ▸ fob
FOBBING ▸ fob
FOBS ▸ fob
FOCAL adj of or at a focus
FOCALLY ▸ focal
FOCI ▸ focus
FOCUS n point at which light or sound waves converge ▷ vb bring or come into focus

FOCUSED ▸ focus
FOCUSER ▸ focus
FOCUSES ▸ focus
FODDER n feed for livestock ▷ vb supply (livestock) with fodder
FODDERS ▸ fodder
FODGEL adj buxom
FOE n enemy, opponent
FOEHN same as ▸ **fohn**
FOEHNS ▸ foehn
FOEMAN n enemy in war
FOEMEN ▸ foeman
FOEN ▸ foe
FOES ▸ foe
FOETAL same as ▸ **fetal**
FOETID same as ▸ **fetid**
FOETOR same as ▸ **fetor**
FOETORS ▸ foetor
FOETUS same as ▸ **fetus**
FOG n mass of condensed water vapour in the lower air, often greatly reducing visibility ▷ vb cover with steam
FOGASH n type of Hungarian pike perch
FOGBOW n faint arc of light sometimes seen in a fog bank
FOGBOWS ▸ fogbow
FOGDOG n whitish spot sometimes seen in fog near the horizon
FOGDOGS ▸ fogdog
FOGEY n old-fashioned person
FOGEYS ▸ fogey
FOGGAGE n grass grown for winter grazing
FOGGED ▸ fog
FOGGER n device that generates a fog
FOGGERS ▸ togger
FOGGIER ▸ fog
FOGGILY ▸ fog
FOGGING ▸ fog
FOGGY ▸ fog
FOGHORN n large horn sounded to warn ships in fog
FOGIE same as ▸ **fogey**
FOGIES ▸ fogie
FOGLE n silk handkerchief
FOGLES ▸ fogle
FOGLESS ▸ fog
FOGMAN n person in charge of railway fog-signals
FOGMEN ▸ fogman
FOGOU n man-made subterranean passage or chamber found in Cornwall

FOGOUS ▸ fogou
FOGRAM n fogey
FOGRAMS ▸ fogram
FOGS ▸ fog
FOGY same as ▸ **fogey**
FOGYDOM ▸ fogy
FOGYISH ▸ fogy
FOGYISM ▸ fogy
FOH interj expression of disgust
FOHN n warm dry wind blowing down the northern slopes of the Alps
FOHNS ▸ fohn
FOIBLE n minor weakness or slight peculiarity
FOIBLES ▸ foible
FOID n rock-forming mineral similar to feldspar
FOIDS ▸ foid
FOIL vb ruin (someone's plan) ▷ n metal in a thin sheet, esp for wrapping food
FOILED ▸ foil
FOILING ▸ foil
FOILS ▸ foil
FOIN n thrust or lunge with a weapon ▷ vb thrust with a weapon
FOINED ▸ foin
FOINING ▸ foin
FOINS ▸ foin
FOISON n plentiful supply or yield
FOISONS ▸ foison
FOIST vb force or impose on
FOISTED ▸ foist
FOISTER ▸ foist
FOISTS ▸ foist
FOLACIN n folic acid
FOLATE n folic acid
FOLATES ▸ folic
FOLD vb bend so that one part covers another ▷ n folded piece or part
FOLDED ▸ fold
FOLDER n piece of folded cardboard for holding loose papers
FOLDERS ▸ folder
FOLDING ▸ fold
FOLDOUT another name for > **gatefold**
FOLDS ▸ fold
FOLDUP n something that folds up
FOLDUPS ▸ foldup
FOLEY n footsteps editor
FOLEYS ▸ foley
FOLIA ▸ folium
FOLIAGE n leaves
FOLIAR adj of or relating to

a leaf or leaves
FOLIATE adj relating to, possessing, or resembling leaves ▷ vb ornament with foliage or with leaf forms such as foils
FOLIC adj as in **folic acid** any of a group of vitamins of the B complex, including pteroylglutamic acid and its derivatives: used in the treatment of megaloblastic anaemia
FOLIE n madness
FOLIES ▸ folie
FOLIO n sheet of paper folded in half to make two leaves of a book ▷ adj of or made in the largest book size, common esp in early centuries of European printing ▷ vb number the leaves of (a book) consecutively
FOLIOED ▸ folio
FOLIOLE n part of a compound leaf
FOLIOS ▸ folio
FOLIOSE adj (of a tree) leaf-bearing
FOLIOUS adj foliose
FOLIUM n plane geometrical curve consisting of a loop whose two ends, intersecting at a node, are asymptotic to the same line
FOLIUMS ▸ folium
FOLK n people in general ▷ adj originating from or traditional to the common people of a country
FOLKIE n devotee of folk music ▷ adj of or relating to folk music
FOLKIER ▸ folkie
FOLKIES ▸ folkie
FOLKISH ▸ folk
FOLKMOT same as > **folkmoot**
FOLKS ▸ folk
FOLKSY adj simple and unpretentious
FOLKWAY singular form of > **folkways**
FOLKY same as ▸ **folkie**
FOLLES ▸ follis
FOLLIED ▸ folly
FOLLIES ▸ folly
FOLLIS n Roman coin
FOLLOW vb go or come after
FOLLOWS ▸ follow

F

FOLLY n foolishness ▷ vb behave foolishly

FOMENT vb encourage or stir up (trouble)

FOMENTS ▸ foment

FOMES n any material, such as bedding or clothing, that may harbour pathogens and therefore convey disease

FOMITE ▸ fomes

FOMITES ▸ fomes

FON vb compel

FOND adj tender, loving ▷ n background of a design, as in lace ▷ vb dote

FONDA n Spanish hotel

FONDANT n (sweet made from) flavoured paste of sugar and water ▷ adj (of a colour) soft

FONDAS ▸ fonda

FONDED ▸ fond

FONDER ▸ fond

FONDEST ▸ fond

FONDING ▸ fond

FONDLE vb caress

FONDLED ▸ fondle

FONDLER ▸ fondle

FONDLES ▸ fondle

FONDLY ▸ fond

FONDS ▸ fond

FONDU n ballet movement, lowering the body by bending the leg(s)

FONDUE n Swiss dish of a hot melted cheese sauce into which pieces of bread are dipped ▷ vb cook and serve (food) as a fondue

FONDUED ▸ fondue

FONDUES ▸ fondue

FONDUS ▸ fondu

FONE same as ▸ foe

FONLY adv foolishly

FONNED ▸ fon

FONNING ▸ fon

FONS ▸ fon

FONT n bowl in a church for baptismal water

FONTAL ▸ font

FONTINA n semihard, pale yellow, mild Italian cheese made from cow's milk

FONTLET ▸ font

FONTS ▸ font

FOOBAR same as ▸ fubar

FOOD n what one eats; solid nourishment

FOODFUL adj supplying abundant food

FOODIE n gourmet

FOODIES ▸ foodie

FOODISM n enthusiasm for and interest in the preparation and consumption of good food

FOODS ▸ food

FOODY same as ▸ foodie

FOOL n person lacking sense or judgment ▷ vb deceive (someone)

FOOLED ▸ fool

FOOLERY n foolish behaviour

FOOLING ▸ fool

FOOLISH adj unwise, silly, or absurd

FOOLS ▸ fool

FOOT n part of the leg below the ankle ▷ vb kick

FOOTAGE n amount of film used

FOOTBAG n sport of keeping small round object off the ground by kicking it

FOOTBAR n any bar designed as a footrest or to be operated by the foot

FOOTBOY n boy servant

FOOTED ▸ foot

FOOTER n person who goes on foot ▷ vb potter

FOOTERS ▸ footer

FOOTIE same as ▸ footy

FOOTIER ▸ footy

FOOTIES ▸ footie

FOOTING n basis or foundation

FOOTLE vb loiter aimlessly ▷ n foolishness

FOOTLED ▸ footle

FOOTLER ▸ footle

FOOTLES ▸ footle

FOOTMAN n male servant in uniform

FOOTMEN ▸ footman

FOOTPAD n highwayman, on foot rather than horseback

FOOTRA same as ▸ foutra

FOOTRAS ▸ footra

FOOTS pl n sediment that accumulates at the bottom of a vessel containing any of certain liquids, such as vegetable oil or varnish

FOOTSIE n flirtation involving the touching together of feet

FOOTSY same as ▸ footsie

FOOTWAY n way or path for pedestrians, such as a raised walk along the edge of a bridge

FOOTY n football ▷ adj mean

FOOZLE vb bungle (a shot) ▷ n bungled shot

FOOZLED ▸ foozle

FOOZLER ▸ foozle

FOOZLES ▸ foozle

FOP n man excessively concerned with fashion ▷ vb act like a fop

FOPLING n vain affected dandy

FOPPED ▸ fop

FOPPERY n clothes, affectations, obsessions, etc, of or befitting a fop

FOPPING ▸ fop

FOPPISH ▸ fop

FOPS ▸ fop

FOR prep indicating a person intended to benefit from or receive something, span of time or distance, person or thing represented by someone, etc

FORA ▸ forum

FORAGE vb search about (for) ▷ n food for cattle or horses

FORAGED ▸ forage

FORAGER ▸ forage

FORAGES ▸ forage

FORAM n a marine protozoan

FORAMEN n natural hole, esp one in a bone through which nerves pass

FORAMS ▸ foram

FORANE adj as in vicar forane in the Roman Catholic church, vicar or priest appointed to act in a certain area of the diocese

FORAY n brief raid or attack ▷ vb raid or ravage (a town, district, etc)

FORAYED ▸ foray

FORAYER ▸ foray

FORAYS ▸ foray

FORB n any herbaceous plant that is not a grass

FORBAD ▸ forbid

FORBADE ▸ forbid

FORBARE ▸ forbear

FORBEAR vb cease or refrain (from doing something)

FORBID vb prohibit, refuse to allow

FORBIDS ▸ forbid

FORBODE vb obsolete word meaning forbid ▷ n obsolete word meaning forbidding

FORBORE past tense of

▶ **forbear**

FORBS ▶ **forb**

FORBY adv besides

FORBYE same as ▶ **forby**

FORCAT n convict or galley slave

FORCATS ▶ **forcat**

FORCE n strength or power ▷ vb compel, make (someone) do something

FORCED adj compulsory

FORCEPS pl n surgical pincers

FORCER ▶ **force**

FORCERS ▶ **force**

FORCES ▶ **force**

FORCING ▶ **force**

FORD n shallow place where a river may be crossed ▷ vb cross (a river) at a ford

FORDED ▶ **ford**

FORDID ▶ **fordo**

FORDING ▶ **ford**

FORDO vb destroy

FORDOES ▶ **fordo**

FORDONE ▶ **fordo**

FORDS ▶ **ford**

FORE adj in, at, or towards the front ▷ n front part ▷ interj golfer's shouted warning to a person in the path of a ball

FOREARM n arm from the wrist to the elbow ▷ vb prepare beforehand

FOREBAY n reservoir or canal

FOREBY same as ▶ **forby**

FOREBYE same as ▶ **forby**

FORECAR n three-wheeled passenger vehicle attached to a motorcycle

FOREDID ▶ **foredo**

FOREDO same as ▶ **fordo**

FOREGO same as ▶ **forgo**

FOREGUT n anterior part of the digestive tract of vertebrates, between the buccal cavity and the bile duct

FOREIGN adj not of, or in, one's own country

FOREL n type of parchment

FORELAY archaic word for ▶ **ambush**

FORELEG n either of the front legs of an animal

FORELIE vb lie in front of

FORELS ▶ **forel**

FOREMAN n person in charge of a group of workers

FOREMEN ▶ **foreman**

FOREPAW n either of the front feet of a land mammal that does not have hooves

FORERAN ▶ **forerun**

FORERUN vb serve as a herald for

FORES ▶ **fore**

FORESAW ▶ **foresee**

FORESAY vb foretell

FORESEE vb see or know beforehand

FOREST n large area with a thick growth of trees ▷ vb create a forest (in)

FORESTS ▶ **forest**

FORETOP n platform at the top of the foremast

FOREVER adv without end

FOREX n foreign exchange

FOREXES ▶ **forex**

FORFAIR vb perish

FORFEIT n thing lost or given up as a penalty for a fault or mistake ▷ vb lose as a forfeit ▷ adj lost as a forfeit

FORFEND vb protect or secure

FORFEX n pair of pincers, esp the paired terminal appendages of an earwig

FORGAT past tense of ▶ **forget**

FORGAVE ▶ **forgive**

FORGE n place where metal is worked, smithy ▷ vb make a fraudulent imitation of (something)

FORGED ▶ **forge**

FORGER ▶ **forge**

FORGERS ▶ **forge**

FORGERY n illegal copy of something

FORGES ▶ **forge**

FORGET vb fail to remember

FORGETS ▶ **forget**

FORGING n process of producing a metal component by hammering

FORGIVE vb cease to blame or hold resentment against, pardon

FORGO vb do without or give up

FORGOER ▶ **forgo**

FORGOES ▶ **forgo**

FORGONE ▶ **forgo**

FORGOT past tense of ▶ **forget**

FORHENT same as ▶ **forehent**

FORHOO vb forsake

FORHOOS ▶ **forhoo**

FORHOW same as ▶ **forhoo**

FORHOWS ▶ **forhow**

FORINT n standard monetary unit of Hungary, divided into 100 fillér

FORINTS ▶ **forint**

FORK n tool for eating food, with prongs and a handle ▷ vb pick up, dig, etc with a fork

FORKED adj having a fork or forklike parts

FORKER ▶ **fork**

FORKERS ▶ **fork**

FORKFUL ▶ **fork**

FORKIER ▶ **forky**

FORKING ▶ **fork**

FORKS ▶ **fork**

FORKY adj forked

FORLANA n Venetian dance

FORLEND same as ▶ **forelend**

FORLENT ▶ **forlend**

FORLORN adj lonely and unhappy ▷ n forsaken person

FORM n shape or appearance ▷ vb give a (particular) shape to or take a (particular) shape

FORMAL adj of or characterized by established conventions of ceremony and behaviour

FORMALS ▶ **formal**

FORMANT n any of several frequency ranges within which the partials of a sound, esp a vowel sound, are at their strongest, thus imparting to the sound its own special quality, tone colour, or timbre

FORMAT n size and shape of a publication ▷ vb arrange in a format

FORMATE n any salt or ester of formic acid containing the ion $HCOO^-$ or the group $HCOO-$ ▷ vb fly aircraft in formation

FORMATS ▶ **format**

FORME n type matter, blocks, etc, assembled in a chase and ready for printing

FORMED ▶ **form**

FORMEE n type of heraldic cross

FORMER adj of an earlier time, previous ▷ n person or thing that forms or shapes

F

FORMERS ▸ former
FORMES ▸ forme
FORMFUL *adj* imaginative
FORMIC *adj* of, relating to, or derived from ants
FORMICA *n* tradename for any of various laminated plastic sheets, containing melamine, used esp for heat-resistant surfaces that can be easily cleaned
FORMING ▸ form
FORMOL *same as* ▸ **formalin**
FORMOLS ▸ formol
FORMS ▸ form
FORMULA *n* group of numbers, letters, or symbols expressing a scientific or mathematical rule
FORMYL *n* of, consisting of, or containing the monovalent group HCO-
FORMYLS ▸ formyl
FORNENT *same as* ▸ **fornenst**
FORNIX *n* any archlike structure, esp the arched band of white fibres at the base of the brain
FORPET *n* quarter of a peck (measure)
FORPETS ▸ forpet
FORPINE *vb* waste away
FORPIT *same as* ▸ **forpet**
FORPITS ▸ forpit
FORRAD *adv* forward
FORRAY *archaic variant of* ▸ **foray**
FORRAYS ▸ forray
FORREN *adj* foreign
FORRIT *adv* forward(s)
FORSAID ▸ forsay
FORSAKE *vb* withdraw support or friendship from
FORSAY *vb* renounce
FORSAYS ▸ forsay
FORSLOE *same as* ▸ **forslow**
FORSLOW *vb* hinder
FORSOOK *past tense of* ▸ **forsake**
FORT *n* fortified building or place ▷ *vb* fortify
FORTE *n* thing at which a person excels ▷ *adv* loudly
FORTED ▸ fort
FORTES ▸ fortis
FORTH *adv* forwards, out, or away ▷ *prep* out of
FORTHY *adv* therefore
FORTIES ▸ forty
FORTIFY *vb* make (a place)

defensible, as by building walls
FORTING ▸ fort
FORTIS *adj* (of a consonant) articulated with considerable muscular tension of the speech organs or with a great deal of breath pressure or plosion ▷ *n* consonant, such as English p or f, pronounced with considerable muscular force or breath pressure
FORTLET ▸ fort
FORTS ▸ fort
FORTUNE *n* luck, esp when favourable ▷ *vb* befall
FORTY *n* four times ten ▷ *adj* amounting to forty ▷ *determiner* amounting to forty
FORUM *n* meeting or medium for open discussion or debate
FORUMS ▸ forum
FORWARD *same as* ▸ **forwards**
FORWARN *archaic word for* ▸ **forbid**
FORWENT *past tense of* ▸ **forgo**
FORWHY *adv* for what reason
FORWORN *adj* weary
FORZA *n* force
FORZATI ▸ forzato
FORZATO *same as* ▸ **forzando**
FORZE ▸ forza
FOSS *same as* ▸ **fosse**
FOSSA *n* anatomical depression, trench, or hollow area
FOSSAE ▸ fossa
FOSSAS ▸ fossa
FOSSATE *adj* having cavities or depressions
FOSSE *n* ditch or moat, esp one dug as a fortification
FOSSED *adj* having a ditch or moat
FOSSES ▸ fosse
FOSSICK *vb* search, esp for gold or precious stones
FOSSIL *n* hardened remains of a prehistoric animal or plant preserved in rock ▷ *adj* of, like, or being a fossil
FOSSILS ▸ fossil
FOSSOR *n* grave digger
FOSSORS ▸ fossor

FOSSULA *n* small fossa
FOSTER *vb* promote the growth or development of ▷ *adj* of or involved in fostering a child
FOSTERS ▸ foster
FOTHER *vb* stop a leak in a ship's hull
FOTHERS ▸ fother
FOU *adj* full ▷ *n* bushel
FOUAT *n* succulent pink-flowered plant
FOUATS ▸ fouat
FOUD *n* sheriff in Orkney and Shetland
FOUDRIE *n* foud's district or office
FOUDS ▸ foud
FOUER ▸ fou
FOUEST ▸ fou
FOUET *n* archaic word for a whip
FOUETS ▸ fouet
FOUETTE *n* step in ballet in which the dancer stands on one foot and makes a whiplike movement with the other
FOUGADE *n* booby-trapped pit or type of mine
FOUGHT ▸ fight
FOUGHTY *adj* musty
FOUL *adj* loathsome or offensive ▷ *n* violation of the rules ▷ *vb* make dirty or polluted
FOULARD *n* soft light fabric of plain-weave or twill-weave silk or rayon, usually with a printed design
FOULDER *vb* flash like lightning
FOULE *n* type of woollen cloth
FOULED ▸ foul
FOULER ▸ foul
FOULES ▸ foule
FOULEST ▸ foul
FOULIE *n* bad mood
FOULIES ▸ foulie
FOULING ▸ foul
FOULLY ▸ foul
FOULS ▸ foul
FOUMART *former name for the* ▸ **polecat**
FOUND *vb* set up or establish (an institution, etc)
FOUNDED ▸ found
FOUNDER *vb* break down or fail ▷ *n* person who establishes an institution,

company, society, etc
FOUNDRY n place where metal is melted and cast
FOUNDS ▸ found
FOUNT same as ▸ **font**
FOUNTS ▸ fount
FOUR n one more than three ▹ adj amounting to four ▹ determiner amounting to four
FOURGON n long covered wagon, used mainly for carrying baggage, supplies, etc
FOURS ▸ four
FOURSES n snack eaten at four o'clock
FOURTH n (of) number four in a series ▹ adj of or being number four in a series ▹ adv after the third person, position, event, etc
FOURTHS ▸ fourth
FOUS ▸ fou
FOUSSA n Madagascan civet-like animal
FOUSSAS ▸ foussa
FOUSTY archaic variant of ▸ **fusty**
FOUTER same as ▸ **footer**
FOUTERS ▸ fouter
FOUTH n abundance
FOUTHS ▸ fouth
FOUTRA n fig; expression of contempt
FOUTRAS ▸ foutra
FOUTRE vb footer
FOUTRED ▸ foutre
FOUTRES ▸ foutre
FOVEA n any small pit or depression in the surface of a bodily organ or part
FOVEAE ▸ fovea
FOVEAL ▸ fovea
FOVEAS ▸ fovea
FOVEATE ▸ fovea
FOVEOLA n small fovea
FOVEOLE same as ▸ **foveola**
FOWL n domestic cock or hen ▹ vb hunt or snare wild birds
FOWLED ▸ fowl
FOWLER ▸ fowling
FOWLERS ▸ fowling
FOWLING n shooting or trapping of birds for sport or as a livelihood
FOWLPOX n viral infection of poultry and other birds
FOWLS ▸ fowl
FOWTH same as ▸ **fouth**
FOWTHS ▸ fowth
FOX n reddish-brown

bushy-tailed animal of the dog family ▹ vb perplex or deceive
FOXED ▸ fox
FOXES ▸ fox
FOXFIRE n luminescent glow emitted by certain fungi on rotting wood
FOXFISH n type of shark
FOXHOLE n small pit dug for protection
FOXHUNT n hunting of foxes with hounds ▹ vb hunt foxes with hounds
FOXIE n fox terrier
FOXIER ▸ foxy
FOXIES ▸ foxie
FOXIEST ▸ foxy
FOXILY ▸ foxy
FOXING n piece of leather used to reinforce or trim part of the upper of a shoe
FOXINGS ▸ foxing
FOXLIKE ▸ fox
FOXSHIP n cunning
FOXSKIN adj made from the skin of a fox ▹ n skin of a fox
FOXTAIL n European, Asian, and S American grass with soft cylindrical spikes of flowers, cultivated as a pasture grass
FOXTROT n ballroom dance with slow and quick steps ▹ vb perform this dance
FOXY adj of or like a fox, esp in craftiness
FOY n loyalty

▌This unusual word for loyalty can be a good scorer.

FOYBOAT n small rowing boat
FOYER n entrance hall in a theatre, cinema, or hotel
FOYERS ▸ foyer
FOYLE same as ▸ **foil**
FOYLED ▸ foyle
FOYLES ▸ foyle
FOYLING ▸ foyle
FOYNE same as ▸ **foin**
FOYNED ▸ foyne
FOYNES ▸ foyne
FOYNING ▸ foyne
FOYS ▸ foy
FOZIER ▸ fozy
FOZIEST ▸ fozy
FOZY adj spongy
FRA n brother: a title given to an Italian monk or friar
FRAB vb nag
FRABBED ▸ frab
FRABBIT adj peevish

FRABS ▸ frab
FRACAS n noisy quarrel
FRACK adj bold
FRACT vb break
FRACTAL n figure or surface generated by successive subdivisions of a simpler polygon or polyhedron, according to some iterative process ▹ adj of, relating to, or involving such a process
FRACTED ▸ fract
FRACTI ▸ fractus
FRACTS ▸ fract
FRACTUR same as ▸ **fraktur**
FRACTUS n ragged-shaped cloud formation
FRAE Scots word for ▸ **from**
FRAENA ▸ fraenum
FRAENUM n fold of membrane or skin, such as the fold beneath the tongue, that supports an organ
FRAG vb kill or wound (a fellow soldier or superior officer) deliberately with an explosive device
FRAGGED ▸ frag
FRAGILE adj easily broken or damaged
FRAGOR n sudden sound
FRAGORS ▸ fragor
FRAGS ▸ frag
FRAIL adj physically weak ▹ n rush basket for figs or raisins
FRAILER ▸ frail
FRAILLY ▸ frail
FRAILS ▸ frail
FRAILTY n physical or moral weakness
FRAIM n stranger
FRAIMS ▸ fraim
FRAISE n neck ruff worn during the 16th century ▹ vb provide a rampart with a palisade
FRAISED ▸ fraise
FRAISES ▸ fraise
FRAKTUR n style of typeface, formerly used in German typesetting for many printed works
FRAME n structure giving shape or support ▹ vb put together, construct
FRAMED ▸ frame
FRAMER ▸ frame
FRAMERS ▸ frame
FRAMES ▸ frame
FRAMING n frame, framework, or system of frames

F

FRAMPAL same as
> **frampold**
FRANC n monetary unit of
Switzerland, various
African countries, and
formerly of France and
Belgium
FRANCO adj post-free
FRANCS ▸ **franc**
FRANGER n condom
FRANION n lover, paramour
FRANK adj honest and
straightforward in speech
or attitude ▸ n official mark
on a letter permitting
delivery ▸ vb put such a
mark on (a letter)
FRANKED ▸ **frank**
FRANKER ▸ **frank**
FRANKLY adv in truth
FRANKS ▸ **frank**
FRANTIC adj distracted
with rage, grief, joy, etc
FRANZY adj irritable
FRAP vb lash down or
together
FRAPE adj tightly bound
FRAPPE adj (of drinks)
chilled ▸ n drink consisting
of a liqueur, etc, poured
over crushed ice
FRAPPED ▸ **frap**
FRAPPEE ▸ **frappe**
FRAPPES ▸ **frappe**
FRAPS ▸ **frap**
FRAS ▸ **fra**
FRASS n excrement or other
refuse left by insects and
insect larvae
FRASSES ▸ **frass**
FRAT n member of a
fraternity
FRATCH n quarrel
FRATCHY adj quarrelsome
FRATE n friar
FRATER n mendicant friar
or a lay brother in a
monastery or priory
FRATERS ▸ **frater**
FRATERY ▸ **frater**
FRATI ▸ **frate**
FRATRY ▸ **frater**
FRATS ▸ **frat**
FRAU n married German
woman
FRAUD n (criminal)
deception, swindle
FRAUDS ▸ **fraud**
FRAUGHT adj tense or
anxious ▸ vb archaic word
for load ▸ n archaic word
for freight
FRAUS ▸ **frau**

FRAWZEY n celebration
FRAY n noisy quarrel or
conflict ▸ vb make or
become ragged at the edge
FRAYED ▸ **fray**
FRAYING ▸ **fray**
FRAYS ▸ **fray**
FRAZIL n small pieces of ice
that form in water moving
turbulently enough to
prevent the formation of a
sheet of ice
FRAZILS ▸ **frazil**
FRAZZLE n exhausted state
▸ vb tire out
FREAK n abnormal person
or thing ▸ adj abnormal
▸ vb streak with colour
FREAKED ▸ **freak**
FREAKS ▸ **freak**
FREAKY adj weird, peculiar
FRECKLE n small brown
spot on the skin ▸ vb mark
or become marked with
freckles
FRECKLY ▸ **freckle**
FREE adj able to act at will,
not compelled or restrained
▸ vb release, liberate
FREEBEE same as ▸ **freebie**
FREEBIE n something
provided without charge
▸ adj without charge
FREED ▸ **free**
FREEDOM n being free
FREEGAN n person who
avoids buying consumer
goods, recycling discarded
goods instead
FREEING ▸ **free**
FREELY ▸ **free**
FREEMAN n person who
has been given the freedom
of a city
FREEMEN ▸ **freeman**
FREER n liberator
FREERS ▸ **freer**
FREES ▸ **free**
FREESIA n plant with
fragrant tubular flowers
FREEST ▸ **free**
FREET n omen or
superstition
FREETS ▸ **freet**
FREETY adj superstitious
FREEWAY n motorway
FREEZE vb change from a
liquid to a solid by the
reduction of temperature,
as water to ice ▸ n period of
very cold weather
FREEZER n insulated
cabinet for cold-storage of

perishable foods
FREEZES ▸ **freeze**
FREIGHT n commercial
transport of goods ▸ vb
send by freight
FREIT same as ▸ **freet**
FREITS ▸ **freit**
FREITY adj superstitious
FREMD adj, n alien or
strange (person or thing)
FREMDS ▸ **fremd**
FREMIT same as ▸ **fremd**
FREMITS ▸ **fremit**
FRENA ▸ **frenum**
FRENCH vb (of food) cut
into thin strips
FRENNE same as ▸ **fremd**
FRENNES ▸ **frenne**
FRENULA > **frenulum**
FRENUM same as
▸ **fraenum**
FRENUMS ▸ **frenum**
FRENZY n violent mental
derangement ▸ vb make
frantic
FRERE n friar
FRERES ▸ **frere**
FRESCO n watercolour
painting done on wet
plaster on a wall ▸ vb paint
a fresco
FRESCOS ▸ **fresco**
FRESH adj newly made,
acquired, etc ▸ adv recently
▸ vb freshen
FRESHED ▸ **fresh**
FRESHEN vb make or
become fresh or fresher
FRESHER n first-year
student
FRESHES ▸ **fresh**
FRESHET n sudden
overflowing of a river
FRESHIE n in Indian English,
new immigrant to the UK
from the Asian
subcontinent
FRESHLY ▸ **fresh**
FRESNEL n unit of
frequency equivalent to 10^{12}
hertz
FRET vb be worried ▸ n
worried state
FRETFUL adj irritable
FRETS ▸ **fret**
FRETSAW n fine saw with a
narrow blade, used for
fretwork
FRETTED ▸ **fret**
FRETTER ▸ **fret**
FRETTY adj decorated with
frets
FRIABLE adj easily crumbled

FRIAND n small almond cake

FRIANDE same as ▸ **friand**

FRIANDS ▸ **friand**

FRIAR n member of a male Roman Catholic religious order

FRIARLY ▸ **friar**

FRIARS ▸ **friar**

FRIARY n house of friars

FRIB n short heavy-conditioned piece of wool removed from a fleece during classing

FRIBBLE vb fritter away ▸ n wasteful or frivolous person or action ▸ adj frivolous

FRIBS ▸ **frib**

FRICHT vb frighten

FRICHTS ▸ **fricht**

FRIDGE n apparatus in which food and drinks are kept cool ▸ vb archaic word for chafe

FRIDGED ▸ **fridge**

FRIDGES ▸ **fridge**

FRIED ▸ **fry**

FRIEND n person whom one knows well and likes ▸ vb befriend

FRIENDS ▸ **friend**

FRIER same as ▸ **fryer**

FRIERS ▸ **frier**

FRIES ▸ **fry**

FRIEZE n ornamental band on a wall ▸ vb give a nap to (cloth)

FRIEZED ▸ **frieze**

FRIEZES ▸ **frieze**

FRIGATE n medium-sized fast warship

FRIGHT n sudden fear or alarm

FRIGHTS ▸ **fright**

FRIGID adj (of a woman) sexually unresponsive

FRIGOT same as ▸ **frigate**

FRIGOTS ▸ **frigot**

FRIJOL n variety of bean, esp of the French bean, extensively cultivated for food in Mexico

FRIJOLE same as ▸ **frijol**

FRILL n gathered strip of fabric attached at one edge ▸ vb adorn or fit with a frill or frills

FRILLED ▸ **frill**

FRILLER ▸ **frill**

FRILLS ▸ **frill**

FRILLY adj with a frill or frills

FRINGE n hair cut short and hanging over the forehead

▸ vb decorate with a fringe ▸ adj (of theatre) unofficial or unconventional

FRINGED ▸ **fringe**

FRINGES ▸ **fringe**

FRINGY adj having a fringe

FRIPON n rogue

FRIPONS ▸ **fripon**

FRIPPER n dealer in old clothes

FRIPPET n frivolous or flamboyant young woman

FRIS ▸ **friska**

FRISBEE n tradename of a light plastic disc, thrown with a spinning motion for recreation or in competition

FRISE n fabric with a long normally uncut nap used for upholstery and rugs

FRISEE n endive

FRISEES ▸ **frisee**

FRISES ▸ **fris**

FRISEUR n hairdresser

FRISK vb move or leap playfully ▸ n playful movement

FRISKA n (in Hungarian music) the fast movement of a piece

FRISKAS ▸ **friska**

FRISKED ▸ **frisk**

FRISKER ▸ **frisk**

FRISKET n light rectangular frame, attached to the tympan of a hand printing press, that carries a parchment sheet to protect the nonprinting areas

FRISKS ▸ **frisk**

FRISKY adj lively or high-spirited

FRISSON n shiver of fear or excitement

FRIST archaic word for > **postpone**

FRISTED ▸ **frist**

FRISTS ▸ **frist**

FRISURE n styling the hair into curls

FRIT n basic materials, partially or wholly fused, for making glass, glazes for pottery, enamel, etc ▸ vb fuse (materials) in making frit

FRITES pl n chipped potatoes

FRITFLY n type of small black fly whose larvae are destructive to grain crops

FRITH same as ▸ **firth**

FRITHS ▸ **frith**

FRITS ▸ **frit**

FRITT same as ▸ **frit**

FRITTED ▸ **frit**

FRITTER n piece of food fried in batter ▸ vb waste or squander

FRITTS ▸ **fritt**

FRITURE archaic word for ▸ **fritter**

FRITZ n as in **on the fritz** state of disrepair

FRIVOL vb behave frivolously

FRIVOLS ▸ **frivol**

FRIZ same as ▸ **frizz**

FRIZE n coarse woollen fabric ▸ vb freeze

FRIZED ▸ **frize**

FRIZER n person who gives nap to cloth

FRIZERS ▸ **frizer**

FRIZES ▸ **frize**

FRIZING ▸ **frize**

FRIZZ vb form (hair) into stiff wiry curls ▸ n hair that has been frizzed

FRIZZED ▸ **frizz**

FRIZZER ▸ **frizz**

FRIZZES ▸ **frizz**

FRIZZLE vb cook or heat until crisp and shrivelled ▸ n tight curl

FRIZZLY ▸ **frizzle**

FRIZZY adj (of the hair) in tight crisp wiry curls

FRO adv away ▸ n afro

FROCK n dress ▸ vb invest (a person) with the office or status of a cleric

FROCKED ▸ **frock**

FROCKS ▸ **frock**

FROE n cutting tool with handle and blade at right angles, used for stripping young trees, etc

FROES ▸ **froe**

FROG n smooth-skinned tailless amphibian with long back legs used for jumping

FROGBIT n floating aquatic Eurasian plant

FROGEYE n plant disease

FROGGED adj decorated with frogging

FROGGY adj like a frog

FROGLET n young frog

FROGMAN n swimmer with a rubber suit and breathing equipment for working underwater

FROGMEN ▸ **frogman**

FROGS ▸ frog

FROING *n as in* **toing and froing** going back and forth

FROINGS ▸ froing

FROISE *n* kind of pancake

FROISES ▸ froise

FROLIC *vb* run and play in a lively way ▷ *n* lively and merry behaviour ▷ *adj* full of merriment or fun

FROLICS ▸ frolic

FROM *prep* indicating the point of departure, source, distance, cause, change of state, etc

FROMAGE *n as in* **fromage frais** low-fat soft cheese

FROND *n* long leaf or leaflike part of a fern, palm, or seaweed

FRONDED *adj* having fronds

FRONDS ▸ frond

FRONS *n* anterior cuticular plate on the head of some insects, in front of the clypeus

FRONT *n* fore part ▷ *adj* of or at the front ▷ *vb* face (onto)

FRONTAL *adj* of, at, or in the front ▷ *n* decorative hanging for the front of an altar

FRONTED ▸ front

FRONTER ▸ front

FRONTES ▸ frons

FRONTON *n* wall against which pelota or jai alai is played

FRONTS ▸ front

FRORE *adj* very cold or frosty

FROREN *same as* ▸ **frore**

FRORN *same as* ▸ **frore**

FRORNE *same as* ▸ **frore**

FRORY *adj* frozen

FROS ▸ fro

FROSH *n* freshman

FROSHES ▸ frosh

FROST *n* white frozen dew or mist ▷ *vb* become covered with frost

FROSTED *adj* (of glass) having a rough surface to make it opaque ▷ *n* type of ice cream dish

FROSTS ▸ frost

FROSTY *adj* characterized or covered by frost

FROTH *n* mass of small bubbles ▷ *vb* foam

FROTHED ▸ froth

FROTHER ▸ froth

FROTHS ▸ froth

FROTHY ▸ froth

FROUGHY *adj* rancid

FROUNCE *vb* wrinkle

FROUZY *same as* ▸ **frowzy**

FROW *same as* ▸ **froe**

FROWARD *adj* obstinate

FROWIE *same as* ▸ **froughy**

FROWIER ▸ frowie

FROWN *vb* wrinkle one's brows in worry, anger, or thought ▷ *n* frowning expression

FROWNED ▸ frown

FROWNER ▸ frown

FROWNS ▸ frown

FROWS ▸ frow

FROWST *n* hot and stale atmosphere ▷ *vb* abandon oneself to such an atmosphere

FROWSTS ▸ frowst

FROWSTY *adj* stale or musty

FROWSY *same as* ▸ **frowzy**

FROWY *same as* ▸ **froughy**

FROWZY *adj* dirty or unkempt

FROZE ▸ freeze

FROZEN ▸ freeze

FRUCTAN *n* type of polymer of fructose, present in certain fruits

FRUCTED *adj* fruit-bearing

FRUG *vb* perform the frug, a 1960s dance

FRUGAL *adj* thrifty, sparing

FRUGGED ▸ frug

FRUGS ▸ frug

FRUICT *obsolete variant of* ▸ **fruit**

FRUICTS ▸ fruict

FRUIT *n* part of a plant containing seeds, esp if edible ▷ *vb* bear fruit

FRUITED ▸ fruit

FRUITER *n* fruit grower

FRUITS ▸ fruit

FRUITY *adj* of or like fruit

FRUMP *n* dowdy woman ▷ *vb* mock or taunt

FRUMPED ▸ frump

FRUMPLE *vb* wrinkle or crumple

FRUMPS ▸ frump

FRUMPY *adj* (of a woman, clothes, etc) dowdy, drab, or unattractive

FRUSH *vb* break into pieces

FRUSHED ▸ frush

FRUSHES ▸ frush

FRUST *n* fragment

FRUSTA ▸ frustum

FRUSTS ▸ frust

FRUSTUM *n* part of a cone or pyramid contained between the base and a plane parallel to the base that intersects the solid

FRUTEX *n* shrub

FRUTIFY *vb* malapropism for notify; used for comic effect by Shakespeare

FRY *vb* cook or be cooked in fat or oil ▷ *n* dish of fried food

FRYABLE ▸ fry

FRYER *n* person or thing that fries

FRYERS ▸ fryer

FRYING ▸ fry

FRYINGS ▸ fry

FRYPAN *n* long-handled shallow pan used for frying

FRYPANS ▸ frypan

FUB *vb* cheat

FUBAR *adj* irreparably damaged or bungled

FUBBED ▸ fub

FUBBERY *n* cheating

FUBBIER ▸ fubby

FUBBING ▸ fub

FUBBY *adj* chubby

FUBS ▸ fub

FUBSIER ▸ fubsy

FUBSY *adj* short and stout

FUCHSIA *n* ornamental shrub with hanging flowers

FUCHSIN *n* greenish crystalline substance

FUCI ▸ fucus

FUCOID *n* type of seaweed

FUCOIDS ▸ fucoid

FUCOSE *n* aldose

FUCOSES ▸ fucose

FUCOUS *same as* ▸ **fucoidal**

FUCUS *n* type of seaweed typically with greenish-brown slimy fronds

FUCUSED *adj* archaic word meaning made up with cosmetics

FUCUSES ▸ fucus

FUD *n* rabbit's tail

FUDDIES ▸ fuddy

FUDDLE *vb* cause to be intoxicated or confused ▷ *n* confused state

FUDDLED ▸ fuddle

FUDDLER ▸ fuddle

FUDDLES ▸ fuddle

FUDDY *n* old-fashioned person

FUDGE *n* soft caramel-like sweet ▷ *vb* make (an issue) less clear deliberately

▷ *interj* mild exclamation of annoyance

FUDGED ▸ **fudge**
FUDGES ▸ **fudge**
FUDGING ▸ **fudge**
FUDS ▸ **fud**
FUEHRER *n* leader: applied esp to Adolf Hitler
FUEL *n* substance burned or treated to produce heat or power ▷ *vb* provide with fuel
FUELED ▸ **fuel**
FUELER ▸ **fuel**
FUELERS ▸ **fuel**
FUELING ▸ **fuel**
FUELLED ▸ **fuel**
FUELLER ▸ **fuel**
FUELS ▸ **fuel**
FUERO *n* Spanish code of laws
FUEROS ▸ **fuero**
FUFF *vb* puff
FUFFED ▸ **fuff**
FUFFIER ▸ **fuffy**
FUFFING ▸ **fuff**
FUFFS ▸ **fuff**
FUFFY *adj* puffy
FUG *n* hot stale atmosphere ▷ *vb* sit in a fug
FUGAL *adj* of, relating to, or in the style of a fugue
FUGALLY ▸ **fugal**
FUGATO *adj* in the manner or style of a fugue ▷ *n* movement, section, or piece in this style
FUGATOS ▸ **fugato**
FUGGED ▸ **fug**
FUGGIER ▸ **fug**
FUGGILY ▸ **fug**
FUGGING ▸ **fug**
FUGGY ▸ **fug**
FUGIE *n* runaway
FUGIES ▸ **fugie**
FUGIO *n* former US copper coin worth one dollar, the first authorized by Congress (1787)
FUGIOS ▸ **fugio**
FUGLE *vb* act as a fugleman
FUGLED ▸ **fugle**
FUGLES ▸ **fugle**
FUGLING ▸ **fugle**
FUGS ▸ **fug**
FUGU *n* puffer fish
U is not normally a desirable letter to have on your rack unless you happen to have the Q, and two Us can be trouble. This Japanese fish can help you out.

FUGUE *n* musical composition in which a theme is repeated in different parts ▷ *vb* be in a dreamlike, altered state of consciousness
FUGUED ▸ **fugue**
FUGUES ▸ **fugue**
FUGUING ▸ **fugue**
FUGUIST *n* composer of fugues
FUGUS ▸ **fugu**
FUHRER *same as* ▸ **fuehrer**
FUHRERS ▸ **fuhrer**
FUJI *n* type of African music
FUJIS ▸ **fuji**
FULCRA ▸ **fulcrum**
FULCRUM *n* pivot about which a lever turns
FULFIL *vb* bring about the achievement of (a desire or promise)
FULFILL *same as* ▸ **fulfil**
FULFILS ▸ **fulfil**
FULGENT *adj* shining brilliantly
FULGID *same as* ▸ **fulgent**
FULGOR *n* brilliance
FULGORS ▸ **fulgor**
FULGOUR *same as* ▸ **fulgor**
FULHAM *n* loaded die
FULHAMS ▸ **fulham**
FULL *adj* containing as much or as many as possible ▷ *adv* completely ▷ *vb* clean, shrink, and press cloth
FULLAGE *n* price charged for fulling cloth
FULLAM *same as* ▸ **fulham**
FULLAMS ▸ **fullam**
FULLAN *same as* ▸ **fulham**
FULLANS ▸ **fullan**
FULLED ▸ **full**
FULLER *n* person who fulls cloth for his living ▷ *vb* forge (a groove) or caulk (a riveted joint) with a fuller
FULLERS ▸ **fuller**
FULLERY *n* place where fulling is carried out
FULLEST ▸ **full**
FULLING ▸ **full**
FULLISH ▸ **full**
FULLS ▸ **full**
FULLY *adv* greatest degree or extent
FULMAR *n* Arctic sea bird
FULMARS ▸ **fulmar**
FULMINE *vb* fulminate
FULNESS ▸ **full**
FULSOME *adj* distastefully excessive or insincere

FULVID *same as* ▸ **fulvous**
FULVOUS *adj* of a dull brownish-yellow colour
FUM *n* phoenix, in Chinese mythology
FUMADO *n* salted, smoked fish
FUMADOS ▸ **fumado**
FUMAGE *n* hearth money
FUMAGES ▸ **fumage**
FUMARIC *adj* as in **fumaric acid** colourless crystalline acid with a fruity taste, found in some plants and manufactured from benzene
FUMBLE *vb* handle awkwardly ▷ *n* act of fumbling
FUMBLED ▸ **fumble**
FUMBLER ▸ **fumble**
FUMBLES ▸ **fumble**
FUME *vb* be very angry ▷ *pl n* pungent smoke or vapour
FUMED *adj* (of wood, esp oak) having a dark colour and distinctive grain from exposure to ammonia fumes
FUMER ▸ **fume**
FUMERS ▸ **fume**
FUMES ▸ **fume**
FUMET *n* strong-flavoured liquor from cooking fish, meat, or game: used to flavour sauces
FUMETS ▸ **fumet**
FUMETTE *same as* ▸ **fumet**
FUMETTI ▸ **fumetto**
FUMETTO *n* speech balloon in a comic or cartoon
FUMIER ▸ **fume**
FUMIEST ▸ **fume**
FUMING ▸ **fume**
FUMOUS ▸ **fume**
FUMS ▸ **fum**
FUMULI ▸ **fumulus**
FUMULUS *n* smokelike cloud
FUMY ▸ **fume**
FUN *n* enjoyment or amusement ▷ *vb* trick
FUNCKIA *n* type of plant resembling the lily
FUNCTOR *n* performer of a function
FUND *n* stock of money for a special purpose ▷ *vb* provide money to
FUNDED ▸ **fund**
FUNDER ▸ **fund**
FUNDERS ▸ **fund**
FUNDI *n* expert or boffin

FUNDIC ▸ **fundus**
FUNDIE n fundamentalist Christian
FUNDIES ▸ **fundie**
FUNDING ▸ **fund**
FUNDIS ▸ **fundi**
FUNDS pl n money that is readily available
FUNDUS n base of an organ or the part farthest away from its opening
FUNDY n fundamentalist
FUNEBRE adj funereal or mournful
FUNERAL n ceremony of burying or cremating a dead person
FUNEST adj lamentable
FUNFAIR n entertainment with machines to ride on and stalls
FUNFEST n enjoyable time
FUNG same as ▸ **funk**
FUNGAL adj of, derived from, or caused by a fungus or fungi ▸ n fungus or fungal infection
FUNGALS ▸ **fungal**
FUNGI ▸ **fungus**
FUNGIC ▸ **fungus**
FUNGO n in baseball, act of tossing and hitting the ball ▸ vb toss and hit a ball
FUNGOES ▸ **fungo**
FUNGOID adj resembling a fungus
FUNGOUS adj appearing suddenly and spreading quickly like a fungus
FUNGS ▸ **fung**
FUNGUS n plant without leaves, flowers, or roots, such as a mushroom or mould
FUNICLE n stalk that attaches an ovule or seed to the wall of the ovary
FUNK n style of dance music with a strong beat ▸ vb avoid (doing something) through fear
FUNKED ▸ **funk**
FUNKER ▸ **funk**
FUNKERS ▸ **funk**
FUNKIA n hosta
FUNKIAS ▸ **funkia**
FUNKIER ▸ **funky**
FUNKILY ▸ **funky**
FUNKING ▸ **funk**
FUNKS ▸ **funk**
FUNKY adj (of music) having a strong beat
FUNNED ▸ **fun**

FUNNEL n cone-shaped tube for pouring liquids into a narrow opening ▸ vb (cause to) move through or as if through a funnel
FUNNELS ▸ **funnel**
FUNNER ▸ **fun**
FUNNEST ▸ **fun**
FUNNIER ▸ **funny**
FUNNIES pl n comic strips in a newspaper
FUNNILY ▸ **funny**
FUNNING ▸ **fun**
FUNNY adj comical, humorous ▸ n joke or witticism
FUNPLEX n large amusement centre
FUNS ▸ **fun**
FUNSTER n funnyman
FUR n soft hair of a mammal ▸ vb cover or become covered with fur
FURAL n furfural
FURALS ▸ **fural**
FURAN n colourless flammable toxic liquid heterocyclic compound
FURANE same as ▸ **furan**
FURANES ▸ **furane**
FURANS ▸ **furan**
FURBISH vb smarten up
FURCA n any forklike structure, esp in insects
FURCAE ▸ **furca**
FURCAL ▸ **furca**
FURCATE vb divide into two parts ▸ adj forked, branching
FURCULA n any forklike part or organ, esp the fused clavicles (wishbone) of birds
FURDER same as ▸ **further**
FUREUR n rage or anger
FUREURS ▸ **fureur**
FURFAIR same as ▸ **furfur**
FURFUR n scurf or scaling of the skin
FURFURS ▸ **furfur**
FURIES ▸ **fury**
FURIOSO adv in a frantically rushing manner ▸ n passage or piece to be performed in this way
FURIOUS adj very angry
FURKID n companion animal
FURKIDS ▸ **furkid**
FURL vb roll up and fasten (a sail, umbrella, or flag) ▸ n act or an instance of furling
FURLANA same as ▸ **forlana**

FURLED ▸ **furl**
FURLER ▸ **furl**
FURLERS ▸ **furl**
FURLESS ▸ **fur**
FURLING ▸ **furl**
FURLONG n unit of length equal to 220 yards (201.168 metres)
FURLS ▸ **furl**
FURMETY same as ▸ **frumenty**
FURMITY same as ▸ **frumenty**
FURNACE n enclosed chamber containing a very hot fire ▸ vb burn in a furnace
FURNISH vb provide (a house or room) with furniture
FUROL same as ▸ **furfural**
FUROLE same as ▸ **furfural**
FUROLES ▸ **furole**
FUROLS ▸ **furol**
FUROR same as ▸ **furore**
FURORE n very excited or angry reaction
FURORES ▸ **furore**
FURORS ▸ **furor**
FURPHY n rumour or fictitious story
FURR vb furrow
FURRED same as ▸ **furry**
FURRIER n dealer in furs
FURRIES ▸ **furry**
FURRILY ▸ **furry**
FURRING ▸ **fur**
FURROW n trench made by a plough ▸ vb make or become wrinkled
FURROWS ▸ **furrow**
FURROWY ▸ **furrow**
FURRS ▸ **furr**
FURRY adj like or covered with fur or something furlike ▸ n child's fur-covered toy animal
FURS ▸ **fur**
FURTH adv out
FURTHER adv in addition ▸ adj more distant ▸ vb promote
FURTIVE adj sly and secretive
FURY n wild anger
FURZE n gorse
FURZES ▸ **furze**
FURZIER ▸ **furze**
FURZY ▸ **furze**
FUSAIN n fine charcoal pencil or stick made from the spindle tree
FUSAINS ▸ **fusain**

FUSARIA > **fusarium**
FUSAROL *same as*
> **fusarole**
FUSBALL > **foosball**
FUSC *adj* dark or
dark-brown
FUSCOUS *adj* of a brownish-
grey colour
FUSE *n* cord containing an
explosive for detonating a
bomb ▷ *vb* (cause) to fail as
a result of a blown fuse
FUSED ▸ **fuse**
FUSEE *n* (in early clocks and
watches) a spirally grooved
spindle, functioning as an
equalizing force on the
unwinding of the
mainspring
FUSEES ▸ **fusee**
FUSEL *n* mixture of amyl
alcohols, propanol, and
butanol: a by-product in
the distillation of
fermented liquors used as a
source of amyl alcohols
FUSELS ▸ **fusel**
FUSES ▸ **fuse**
FUSHION *n* spirit
FUSIBLE *adj* capable of
being melted
FUSIBLY ▸ **fusible**
FUSIDIC *adj as in* **fusidic
acid** kind of acid
FUSIL *n* light flintlock
musket
FUSILE *adj* easily melted
FUSILLI *n* spiral-shaped
pasta
FUSILS ▸ **fusil**
FUSING ▸ **fuse**
FUSION *n* melting ▷ *adj* of a
style of cooking that
combines traditional
Western techniques and
ingredients with those used
in Eastern cuisine
FUSIONS ▸ **fusion**
FUSS *n* needless activity or
worry ▷ *vb* make a fuss
FUSSED ▸ **fuss**
FUSSER ▸ **fuss**
FUSSERS ▸ **fuss**
FUSSES ▸ **fuss**
FUSSIER ▸ **fussy**
FUSSILY ▸ **fussy**

FUSSING ▸ **fuss**
FUSSPOT *n* person who is
difficult to please and
complains often
FUSSY *adj* inclined to fuss
FUST *vb* become mouldy
FUSTED ▸ **fust**
FUSTET *n* wood of the
Venetian sumach shrub
FUSTETS ▸ **fustet**
FUSTIAN *n* (formerly) a
hard-wearing fabric of
cotton mixed with flax or
wool ▷ *adj* cheap
FUSTIC *n* large tropical
American tree
FUSTICS ▸ **fustic**
FUSTIER ▸ **fusty**
FUSTILY ▸ **fusty**
FUSTING ▸ **fust**
FUSTOC *same as* ▸ **fustic**
FUSTOCS ▸ **fustoc**
FUSTS ▸ **fust**
FUSTY *adj* stale-smelling
FUSUMA *n* Japanese sliding
door
FUTCHEL *n* timber support
in a carriage
FUTHARC *same as* ▸ **futhark**
FUTHARK *n* phonetic
alphabet consisting of
runes
FUTHORC *same as*
▸ **futhark**
FUTHORK *same as*
▸ **futhark**
FUTILE *adj* unsuccessful or
useless
FUTILER ▸ **futile**
FUTON *n* Japanese-style
bed
FUTONS ▸ **futon**
FUTSAL *n* form of
association football, played
indoors with five players on
each side
FUTSALS ▸ **futsal**
FUTTOCK *n* one of the ribs
in the frame of a wooden
vessel
FUTURAL *adj* relating to the
future
FUTURE *n* time to come
▷ *adj* yet to come or be
FUTURES *pl n* commodities
bought or sold at an agreed

price for delivery at a
specified future date
FUTZ *vb* fritter time away
FUTZED ▸ **futz**
FUTZES ▸ **futz**
FUTZING ▸ **futz**
FUZE *same as* ▸ **fuse**
FUZED ▸ **fuze**
FUZEE *same as* ▸ **fusee**
FUZEES ▸ **fuzee**
FUZES ▸ **fuze**
FUZIL *same as* ▸ **fusil**
FUZILS ▸ **fuzil**
FUZING ▸ **fuze**
FUZZ *n* mass of fine or curly
hairs or fibres ▷ *vb* make or
become fuzzy
FUZZBOX *n* device that
distorts the sound of eg an
electric guitar
FUZZED ▸ **fuzz**
FUZZES ▸ **fuzz**
FUZZIER ▸ **fuzzy**
FUZZILY ▸ **fuzzy**
FUZZING ▸ **fuzz**
FUZZLE *vb* make drunk
FUZZLED ▸ **fuzzle**
FUZZLES ▸ **fuzzle**
FUZZY *adj* of, like, or
covered with fuzz
FY *same as* ▸ **fie**
FYCE *same as* ▸ **fice**
FYCES ▸ **fyce**
FYKE *n* fish trap consisting
of a net suspended over a
series of hoops, laid
horizontally in the water
▷ *vb* catch fish in this
manner
FYKED ▸ **fyke**
FYKES ▸ **fyke**
FYKING ▸ **fyke**
FYLE *same as* ▸ **file**
FYLES ▸ **fyle**
FYLFOT *rare word for*
> **swastika**
FYLFOTS ▸ **fylfot**
FYNBOS *n* area of
low-growing, evergreen
vegetation
FYRD *n* local militia of an
Anglo-Saxon shire, in which
all freemen had to serve
FYRDS ▸ **fyrd**
FYTTE *n* song
FYTTES ▸ **fytte**

F

Gg

Only three two-letter words begin with **G** (**gi**, **go** and **gu**). Knowing these will save you worrying about other possibilities. There are quite a few short words beginning with **G** that use **Y**, which can prove very useful. These include **gay, gey, goy** and **guy** (7 points each), as well as **gym** and **gyp** (9 points each). And don't forget the very useful **gox** for 11 points.

GAB *vb* talk or chatter ▷ *n* hook or open notch in a rod or lever that drops over the spindle of a valve to form a temporary connection for operating the valve

GABBA *n* type of electronic dance music

GABBARD *same as* ▶ **gabbart**

GABBART *n* Scottish sailing barge

GABBAS ▶ **gabba**

GABBED ▶ **gab**

GABBER ▶ **gab**

GABBERS ▶ **gab**

GABBIER ▶ **gabby**

GABBING ▶ **gab**

GABBLE *vb* speak rapidly and indistinctly ▷ *n* rapid indistinct speech

GABBLED ▶ **gabble**

GABBLER ▶ **gabble**

GABBLES ▶ **gabble**

GABBRO *n* dark coarse-grained basic plutonic igneous rock consisting of plagioclase feldspar, pyroxene, and often olivine

GABBROS ▶ **gabbro**

GABBY *adj* talkative

GABELLE *n* salt tax levied until 1790

GABFEST *n* prolonged gossiping or conversation

GABIES ▶ **gaby**

GABION *n* cylindrical metal container filled with stones, used in the construction of underwater foundations

GABIONS ▶ **gabion**

GABLE *n* triangular upper

part of a wall between sloping roofs

GABLED ▶ **gable**

GABLES ▶ **gable**

GABLET *n* small gable

GABLETS ▶ **gablet**

GABLING ▶ **gable**

GABNASH *n* chatter

GABOON *n* dark wood from a western and central African tree, used in plywood, for furniture, and as a veneer

GABOONS ▶ **gaboon**

GABS ▶ **gab**

GABY *n* simpleton

GAD *vb* go about in search of pleasure ▷ *n* carefree adventure

GADDED ▶ **gad**

GADDER ▶ **gad**

GADDERS ▶ **gad**

GADDI *n* cushion on an Indian prince's throne

GADDING ▶ **gad**

GADDIS ▶ **gaddi**

GADE *same as* ▶ **gad**

GADES ▶ **gade**

GADFLY *n* fly that bites cattle

GADGE *n* man

GADGES ▶ **gadge**

GADGET *n* small mechanical device or appliance

GADGETS ▶ **gadget**

GADGETY ▶ **gadget**

GADGIE *n* fellow

GADGIES ▶ **gadgie**

GADI *n* Indian throne

GADID *n* type of marine fish of the family which includes the cod, haddock, whiting, and pollack

GADIDS ▶ **gadid**

GADIS ▶ **gadi**

GADJE *same as* ▶ **gadgie**

GADJES ▶ **gadje**

GADJO ▶ **gorgio**

GADLING *n* vagabond

GADOID *adj* of the cod family of marine fishes ▷ *n* gadoid fish

GADOIDS ▶ **gadoid**

GADROON *n* moulding composed of a series of convex flutes and curves joined to form a decorative pattern, used esp as an edge to silver articles

GADS ▶ **gad**

GADSMAN *n* person who uses a gad when driving animals

GADSMEN ▶ **gadsman**

GADSO *n* archaic expression of surprise

GADWALL *n* type of duck related to the mallard

GAE *Scots word for* ▶ **go**

GAED ▶ **gae**

GAEING ▶ **gae**

GAEN ▶ **gae**

GAES ▶ **gae**

GAFF *n* stick with an iron hook for landing large fish ▷ *vb* hook or land (a fish) with a gaff

GAFFE *n* social blunder

GAFFED ▶ **gaff**

GAFFER *n* foreman or boss

GAFFERS ▶ **gaffer**

GAFFES ▶ **gaffe**

GAFFING ▶ **gaff**

GAFFS ▶ **gaff**

GAG *vb* choke or retch ▷ *n* cloth etc put into or tied across the mouth

GAGA *adj* senile

GAGAKU *n* type of traditional Japanese music

GAGAKUS ▸ **gagaku**

GAGE *vb* gauge ▸ *n* (formerly) a glove or other object thrown down to indicate a challenge to fight

GAGED ▸ **gage**

GAGER *same as* ▸ **gauger**

GAGERS ▸ **gager**

GAGES ▸ **gage**

GAGGED ▸ **gag**

GAGGER *n* person or thing that gags

GAGGERS ▸ **gagger**

GAGGERY *n* practice of telling jokes

GAGGING ▸ **gag**

GAGGLE *n* disorderly crowd ▸ *vb* (of geese) to cackle

GAGGLED ▸ **gaggle**

GAGGLES ▸ **gaggle**

GAGING ▸ **gage**

GAGMAN *n* person who writes gags for a comedian

GAGMEN ▸ **gagman**

GAGS ▸ **gag**

GAGSTER *n* standup comedian

GAHNITE *n* dark green mineral of the spinel group consisting of zinc aluminium oxide

GAID *same as* ▸ **gad**

GAIDS ▸ **gaid**

GAIETY *n* cheerfulness

GAIJIN *n* (in Japan) a foreigner

GAILY *adv* merrily

GAIN *vb* acquire or obtain ▸ *n* profit or advantage ▸ *adj* straight or near

GAINED ▸ **gain**

GAINER *n* person or thing that gains

GAINERS ▸ **gainer**

GAINEST ▸ **gain**

GAINFUL *adj* useful or profitable

GAINING ▸ **gain**

GAINLY *adj* graceful or well-formed ▸ *adv* conveniently or suitably

GAINS *pl n* profits or winnings

GAINSAY *vb* deny or contradict

GAINST *short for* ▸ **against**

GAIR *n* strip of green grass on a hillside

GAIRS ▸ **gair**

GAIT *n* manner of walking

▷ *vb* teach (a horse) a particular gait

GAITA *n* type of bagpipe played in Spain and Portugal

GAITAS ▸ **gaita**

GAITED ▸ **gait**

GAITER *n* cloth or leather covering for the lower leg

GAITERS ▸ **gaiter**

GAITING ▸ **gait**

GAITS ▸ **gait**

GAITT *Scots word for* ▸ **gate**

GAITTS ▸ **gaitt**

GAJO *same as* ▸ **gorgio**

GAJOS ▸ **gajo**

GAK *n* (slang) cocaine

GAKS ▸ **gak**

GAL *n* girl

GALA *n* festival

GALABEA *same as* > **djellaba**

GALABIA *same as* > **djellaba**

GALAGE *same as* ▸ **galosh**

GALAGES ▸ **galage**

GALAGO *another name for* > **bushbaby**

GALAGOS ▸ **galago**

GALAH *n* Australian cockatoo with grey wings, back, and crest and a pink body

GALAHS ▸ **galah**

GALANGA *same as* > **galingale**

GALANT *n* 18th-century style of music characterized by homophony and elaborate ornamentation

GALANTY *n as in* **galanty show** pantomime shadow play, esp one in miniature using figures cut from paper

GALAS ▸ **gala**

GALATEA *n* strong twill-weave cotton fabric, striped or plain, for clothing

GALAX *n* coltsfoot

GALAXES ▸ **galax**

GALAXY *n* system of stars

GALE *n* strong wind

GALEA *n* part or organ shaped like a helmet or hood, such as the petals of certain flowers

GALEAE ▸ **galea**

GALEAS ▸ **galea**

GALEATE ▸ **galea**

GALENA *n* soft bluish-grey mineral consisting of lead sulphide: the chief source of lead

GALENAS ▸ **galena**

GALENIC ▸ **galena**

GALERE *n* group of people having a common interest, esp a coterie of undesirable people

GALERES ▸ **galere**

GALES ▸ **gale**

GALETTE *n* type of savoury pancake

GALILEE *n* porch or chapel at the entrance to some medieval churches and cathedrals in England

GALIOT *n* small swift galley formerly sailed on the Mediterranean

GALIOTS ▸ **galiot**

GALIPOT *n* resin obtained from several species of pine

GALL *n* impudence ▸ *vb* annoy

GALLANT *adj* brave and noble ▸ *n* young man who tried to impress women with his fashionable clothes or daring acts ▸ *vb* court or flirt (with)

GALLATE *n* salt of gallic acid

GALLED ▸ **gall**

GALLEIN *n* type of dyestuff

GALLEON *n* large three-masted sailing ship of the 15th–17th centuries

GALLERY *n* room or building for displaying works of art ▸ *vb* tunnel; form an underground gallery

GALLET *vb* (in roofing) use small pieces of slate mixed with mortar to support an upper slate

GALLETA *n* low-growing, coarse grass

GALLETS ▸ **gallet**

GALLEY *n* kitchen of a ship or aircraft

GALLEYS ▸ **galley**

GALLFLY *n* any of several small insects that produce galls in plant tissues, such as the gall wasp and gall midge

GALLIC *adj* of or containing gallium in the trivalent state

GALLICA *n* variety of rose

GALLIED ▸ **gally**

GALLIES ▸ **gally**

GALLING *adj* annoying or bitterly humiliating

GALLIOT *same as* ▸ **galiot**

GALLISE *vb* add water and sugar to unfermented

grape juice to increase the quantity of wine produced

GALLIUM n soft grey metallic element used in semiconductors

GALLIZE same as ▸ **gallise**

GALLNUT n type of plant gall that resembles a nut

GALLOCK adj left-handed

GALLON n liquid measure of eight pints, equal to 4.55 litres

GALLONS ▸ **gallon**

GALLOON n narrow band of cord, embroidery, silver or gold braid, etc, used on clothes and furniture

GALLOOT same as ▸ **galoot**

GALLOP n horse's fastest pace ▷ vb go or ride at a gallop

GALLOPS ▸ **gallop**

GALLOUS adj of or containing gallium in the divalent state

GALLOW vb frighten

GALLOWS n wooden structure used for hanging criminals

GALLS ▸ **gall**

GALLUS adj bold ▷ n suspender for trousers

GALLY vb frighten

GALOCHE same as ▸ **galosh**

GALOOT n clumsy or uncouth person

GALOOTS ▸ **galoot**

GALOP n 19th-century dance in quick duple time ▷ vb dance a galop

GALOPED ▸ **galop**

GALOPIN n boy who ran errands for a cook

GALOPS ▸ **galop**

GALORE adv in abundance ▷ adj in abundance ▷ n abundance

GALORES ▸ **galore**

GALOSH n waterproof overshoe ▷ vb cover with galoshes

GALOSHE same as ▸ **galosh**

GALS ▸ **gal**

GALUMPH vb leap or move about clumsily

GALUT same as ▸ **galuth**

GALUTH n exile of Jews from Palestine

GALUTHS ▸ **galuth**

GALUTS ▸ **galut**

GALVO n instrument for measuring electric current

GALVOS ▸ **galvo**

GALYAC same as ▸ **galyak**

GALYACS ▸ **galyac**

GALYAK n smooth glossy fur obtained from the skins of newborn or premature lambs and kids

GALYAKS ▸ **galyak**

GAM n school of whales ▷ vb (of whales) form a school

GAMA n tall perennial grass

GAMAS ▸ **gama**

GAMASH n type of gaiter

GAMAY n red grape variety, or the wine made from it

GAMAYS ▸ **gamay**

GAMB n in heraldry, the whole foreleg of a beast

GAMBA n second-largest member of the viol family

GAMBADE same as ▸ **gambado**

GAMBADO n leap or gambol; caper ▷ vb perform a gambado

GAMBAS ▸ **gamba**

GAMBE same as ▸ **gamb**

GAMBES ▸ **gambe**

GAMBET n tattler

GAMBETS ▸ **gambet**

GAMBIA same as ▸ **gambier**

GAMBIAS ▸ **gambia**

GAMBIER n astringent resinous substance obtained from a tropical Asian climbing plant

GAMBIR same as ▸ **gambier**

GAMBIRS ▸ **gambir**

GAMBIST n person who plays the (viola da) gamba

GAMBIT n opening line or move intended to secure an advantage ▷ vb sacrifice a chess piece, in opening, to gain a better position

GAMBITS ▸ **gambit**

GAMBLE vb play games of chance to win money ▷ n risky undertaking

GAMBLED ▸ **gamble**

GAMBLER ▸ **gamble**

GAMBLES ▸ **gamble**

GAMBO n farm cart

GAMBOES ▸ **gambo**

GAMBOGE n gum resin used as a yellow pigment and purgative

GAMBOL vb jump about playfully, frolic ▷ n frolic

GAMBOLS ▸ **gambol**

GAMBREL n hock of a horse or similar animal

GAMBS ▸ **gamb**

GAME n amusement or

pastime ▷ vb gamble ▷ adj brave

GAMED ▸ **game**

GAMELAN n type of percussion orchestra common in the East Indies

GAMELY adv in a brave or sporting manner

GAMER n person who plays computer games

GAMERS ▸ **gamer**

GAMES ▸ **game**

GAMEST ▸ **game**

GAMESY adj sporty

GAMETAL ▸ **gamete**

GAMETE n reproductive cell

GAMETES ▸ **gamete**

GAMETIC ▸ **gamete**

GAMEY adj having the smell or flavour of game

GAMGEE n as in **gamgee tissue** type of wound-dressing

GAMIC adj (esp of reproduction) requiring the fusion of gametes

GAMIER ▸ **gamey**

GAMIEST ▸ **gamey**

GAMILY ▸ **gamey**

GAMIN n street urchin

GAMINE n slim boyish young woman

GAMINES ▸ **gamine**

GAMING n gambling

GAMINGS ▸ **gaming**

GAMINS ▸ **gamin**

GAMMA n third letter of the Greek alphabet

GAMMAS ▸ **gamma**

GAMME n musical scale

GAMMED ▸ **gam**

GAMMES ▸ **gamme**

GAMMING ▸ **gam**

GAMMOCK vb clown around

GAMMON n cured or smoked ham ▷ vb score a double victory in backgammon over

GAMMONS ▸ **gammon**

GAMONE n any chemical substance secreted by a gamete that attracts another gamete during sexual reproduction

GAMONES ▸ **gamone**

GAMP n umbrella

GAMPISH adj bulging

GAMPS ▸ **gamp**

GAMS ▸ **gam**

GAMUT n whole range or scale (of music, emotions, etc)

GAMUTS ▸ gamut
GAMY same as ▸ gamey
GAN vb go
GANACHE n rich icing or filling made of chocolate and cream
GANCH vb impale
GANCHED ▸ ganch
GANCHES ▸ ganch
GANDER n male goose ▷ vb look
GANDERS ▸ gander
GANDY adj as in **gandy dancer** railway track maintenance worker
GANE ▸ gangue
GANEF n unscrupulous opportunist who stoops to sharp practice
GANEFS ▸ ganef
GANEV same as ▸ ganef
GANEVS ▸ ganev
GANG n (criminal) group ▷ vb become or act as a gang
GANGED ▸ gang
GANGER n foreman of a gang of labourers
GANGERS ▸ ganger
GANGING ▸ gang
GANGLIA > ganglion
GANGLY same as > gangling
GANGREL n wandering beggar
GANGS ▸ gang
GANGSTA n member of a street gang
GANGUE n valueless material in an ore
GANGUES ▸ gangue
GANGWAY same as > gangplank
GANJA n highly potent form of cannabis, usually used for smoking
GANJAH same as ▸ ganja
GANJAHS ▸ ganjah
GANJAS ▸ ganja
GANNED ▸ gan
GANNET n large sea bird
GANNETS ▸ gannet
GANNING ▸ gan
GANOF same as ▸ ganef
GANOFS ▸ ganof
GANOID adj (of the scales of certain fishes) consisting of an inner bony layer covered with an enamel-like substance ▷ n ganoid fish
GANOIDS ▸ ganoid
GANOIN n substance of which the outer layer of fish scales is composed

GANOINE same as ▸ ganoin
GANOINS ▸ ganoin
GANS ▸ gan
GANSEY n jersey or pullover
GANSEYS ▸ gansey
GANT vb yawn
GANTED ▸ gant
GANTING ▸ gant
GANTLET n section of a railway where two tracks overlap ▷ vb make railway tracks form a gantlet
GANTRY n structure supporting something such as a crane or rocket
GANTS ▸ gant
GAOL same as ▸ jail
GAOLED ▸ gaol
GAOLER ▸ gaol
GAOLERS ▸ gaol
GAOLING ▸ gaol
GAOLS ▸ gaol
GAP n break or opening
GAPE vb stare in wonder ▷ n act of gaping
GAPED ▸ gape
GAPER n person or thing that gapes
GAPERS ▸ gaper
GAPES n disease of young domestic fowl, characterized by gaping or gasping for breath and caused by gapeworms
GAPIER ▸ gapes
GAPIEST ▸ gapes
GAPING adj wide open ▷ n state of having a gaping mouth
GAPINGS ▸ gaping
GAPLESS ▸ gap
GAPO n forest near a river, regularly flooded in the rainy season
GAPOS ▸ gapo
GAPOSIS n gap between closed fastenings on a garment
GAPPED ▸ gap
GAPPER n in British English, person taking a year out between school and further education
GAPPERS ▸ gapper
GAPPIER ▸ gap
GAPPING n the act of taking a gap year
GAPPY ▸ gap
GAPS ▸ gap
GAPY ▸ gapes
GAR same as ▸ garpike
GARAGE n building used to house cars ▷ vb put or keep

a car in a garage
GARAGED ▸ garage
GARAGES ▸ garage
GARAGEY adj (of music) in a garage style
GARB n clothes ▷ vb clothe
GARBAGE n rubbish
GARBAGY ▸ garbage
GARBE n in heraldry, a wheat-sheaf
GARBED ▸ garb
GARBES ▸ garb
GARBING ▸ garb
GARBLE vb jumble (a story, quotation, etc), esp unintentionally ▷ n act of garbling
GARBLED adj (of a story etc) jumbled and confused
GARBLER ▸ garble
GARBLES ▸ garble
GARBO n dustman
GARBOIL n confusion or disturbance
GARBOS ▸ garbo
GARBS ▸ garb
GARBURE n thick soup from Bearn in France
GARCON n waiter
GARCONS ▸ garcon
GARDA n member of the police force of the Republic of Ireland
GARDAI ▸ garda
GARDANT same as > guardant
GARDEN n piece of land for growing flowers, fruit, or vegetables ▷ vb cultivate a garden
GARDENS ▸ garden
GARE n filth
GARFISH same as ▸ garpike
GARGET n inflammation of the mammary gland of domestic animals, esp cattle
GARGETS ▸ garget
GARGETY ▸ garget
GARGLE vb wash the throat with (a liquid) by breathing out slowly through the liquid ▷ n liquid used for gargling
GARGLED ▸ gargle
GARGLER ▸ gargle
GARGLES ▸ gargle
GARI n thinly sliced pickled ginger, often served with sushi
GARIAL same as ▸ gavial
GARIALS ▸ garial
GARIGUE n open shrubby

vegetation of dry Mediterranean regions, consisting of spiny or aromatic dwarf shrubs interspersed with colourful ephemeral species

GARIS ▸ **gari**

GARISH adj crudely bright or colourful ▷ vb heal

GARJAN same as ▸ **gurjun**

GARJANS ▸ **garjan**

GARLAND n wreath of flowers worn or hung as a decoration ▷ vb decorate with garlands

GARLIC n pungent bulb of a plant of the onion family, used in cooking

GARLICS ▸ **garlic**

GARMENT n article of clothing ▷ vb cover or clothe

GARNER vb collect or store ▷ n place for storage or safekeeping

GARNERS ▸ **garner**

GARNET n red semiprecious stone

GARNETS ▸ **garnet**

GARNI adj garnished

GARNISH vb decorate (food) ▷ n decoration for food

GAROTE same as > **garrotte**

GAROTED ▸ **garote**

GAROTES ▸ **garote**

GAROTTE same as > **garrotte**

GAROUPA in Chinese and SE Asian cookery, another name for ▸ **groper**

GARPIKE n primitive N and Central American freshwater bony fish with very long toothed jaws and thick scales

GARRAN same as ▸ **garron**

GARRANS ▸ **garran**

GARRE vb compel

GARRED ▸ **gar**

GARRES ▸ **garre**

GARRET n attic in a house

GARRETS ▸ **garret**

GARRING ▸ **gar**

GARRON n small sturdy pony bred and used chiefly in Scotland and Ireland

GARRONS ▸ **garron**

GARROT n goldeneye duck

GARROTE same as > **garrotte**

GARROTS ▸ **garrot**

GARRYA n N American ornamental catkin-bearing evergreen shrub

GARRYAS ▸ **garrya**

GARS ▸ **gar**

GART vb compel

GARTER n band worn round the leg to hold up a sock or stocking ▷ vb secure with a garter

GARTERS ▸ **garter**

GARTH n courtyard surrounded by a cloister

GARTHS ▸ **garth**

GARUDA n Hindu god

GARUDAS ▸ **garuda**

GARUM n fermented fish sauce

GARUMS ▸ **garum**

GARVEY n small flat-bottomed yacht

GARVEYS ▸ **garvey**

GARVIE n sprat

GARVIES ▸ **garvie**

GARVOCK n sprat

GAS n airlike substance that is not liquid or solid ▷ vb poison or render unconscious with gas

GASAHOL n mixture of petrol and alcohol used as fuel

GASBAG n person who talks too much ▷ vb talk in a voluble way, esp about unimportant matters

GASBAGS ▸ **gasbag**

GASCON n boaster

GASCONS ▸ **gascon**

GASEITY n state of being gaseous

GASEOUS adj of or like gas

GASES ▸ **gas**

GASH vb make a long deep cut in ▷ n long deep cut ▷ adj surplus to requirements ▷ adj witty

GASHED ▸ **gash**

GASHER ▸ **gash**

GASHES ▸ **gash**

GASHEST ▸ **gash**

GASHFUL adj full of gashes

GASHING ▸ **gash**

GASHLY adv wittily

GASIFY vb change into a gas

GASKET n piece of rubber etc placed between the faces of a metal joint to act as a seal

GASKETS ▸ **gasket**

GASKIN n lower part of a horse's thigh, between the hock and the stifle

GASKING same as ▸ **gasket**

GASKINS ▸ **gaskin**

GASLESS ▸ **gas**

GASLIT adj lit by gas

GASMAN n man employed to read household gas meters and install or repair gas fittings, etc

GASMEN ▸ **gasman**

GASOHOL n mixture of 80% or 90% petrol with 20% or 10% ethyl alcohol, for use as a fuel in internal-combustion engines

GASP vb draw in breath sharply or with difficulty ▷ n convulsive intake of breath

GASPED ▸ **gasp**

GASPER n person who gasps

GASPERS ▸ **gasper**

GASPIER ▸ **gasp**

GASPING ▸ **gasp**

GASPS ▸ **gasp**

GASPY ▸ **gasp**

GASSED ▸ **gas**

GASSER n drilling or well that yields natural gas

GASSERS ▸ **gasser**

GASSES ▸ **gas**

GASSIER ▸ **gassy**

GASSILY ▸ **gassy**

GASSING ▸ **gas**

GASSY adj filled with gas

GAST vb frighten

GASTED ▸ **gast**

GASTER ▸ **gast**

GASTERS ▸ **gast**

GASTING ▸ **gast**

GASTRAL adj relating to the stomach

GASTREA same as > **gastraea**

GASTRIC adj of the stomach

GASTRIN n polypeptide hormone secreted by the stomach: stimulates secretion of gastric juice

GASTS ▸ **gast**

GAT n pistol or revolver

GATE n movable barrier, usu hinged, in a wall or fence ▷ vb provide with a gate or gates

GATEAU n rich elaborate cake

GATEAUS ▸ **gateau**

GATEAUX ▸ **gateau**

GATED ▸ **gate**

GATELEG adj (of a table) with one or two drop leaves that are supported when in use by a hinged leg swung out from the frame

GATEMAN n gatekeeper
GATEMEN ▸ gateman
GATER same as ▸ gator
GATERS ▸ gater
GATES ▸ gate
GATEWAY n entrance with a gate
GATH n (in Indian music) second section of a raga
GATHER vb assemble ▷ n act of gathering
GATHERS ▸ gather
GATHS ▸ gath
GATING ▸ gate
GATINGS ▸ gate
GATLING n as in **gatling gun** kind of machinegun
GATOR shortened form of > **alligator**
GATORS ▸ gator
GATS ▸ gat
GATVOL adj in South African English, fed up
GAU n district set up by the Nazi Party during the Third Reich
GAUCHE adj socially awkward
GAUCHER ▸ gauche
GAUCHO n S American cowboy
GAUCHOS ▸ gaucho
GAUCIE same as ▸ gaucy
GAUCIER ▸ gaucy
GAUCY adj plump or jolly
GAUD n article of cheap finery ▷ vb decorate gaudily
GAUDED ▸ gaud
GAUDERY n cheap finery or display
GAUDGIE same as ▸ gadgie
GAUDIER ▸ gaudy
GAUDIES ▸ gaudy
GAUDILY ▸ gaudy
GAUDING ▸ gaud
GAUDS ▸ gaud
GAUDY adj vulgarly bright or colourful ▷ n celebratory festival or feast held at some schools and colleges
GAUFER n wafer
GAUFERS ▸ gaufer
GAUFFER same as ▸ goffer
GAUFRE same as ▸ gaufer
GAUFRES ▸ gaufre
GAUGE vb estimate or judge ▷ n measuring instrument ▷ adj (of a pressure measurement) measured on a pressure gauge that registers zero at atmospheric pressure

GAUGED ▸ gauge
GAUGER n person or thing that gauges
GAUGERS ▸ gauger
GAUGES ▸ gauge
GAUGING ▸ gauge
GAUJE same as ▸ gadgie
GAUJES ▸ gauje
GAULT n stiff compact clay or thick heavy clayey soil
GAULTER n person who digs gault
GAULTS ▸ gault
GAUM vb understand
GAUMED ▸ gaum
GAUMIER ▸ gaumy
GAUMING ▸ gaum
GAUMS ▸ gaum
GAUMY adj clogged
GAUN ▸ go
GAUNCH same as ▸ ganch
GAUNT adj lean and haggard ▷ vb yawn
GAUNTED ▸ gaunt
GAUNTER ▸ gaunt
GAUNTLY ▸ gaunt
GAUNTRY same as ▸ gantry
GAUNTS ▸ gaunt
GAUP same as ▸ gawp
GAUPED ▸ gaup
GAUPER ▸ gaup
GAUPERS ▸ gaup
GAUPING ▸ gaup
GAUPS ▸ gaup
GAUPUS same as ▸ gawpus
GAUR n large wild member of the cattle tribe, inhabiting mountainous regions of S Asia
GAURS ▸ gaur
GAUS ▸ gau
GAUSS n cgs unit of magnetic flux density
GAUSSES ▸ gauss
GAUZE n transparent loosely-woven fabric, often used for surgical dressings
GAUZES ▸ gauze
GAUZIER ▸ gauzy
GAUZILY ▸ gauzy
GAUZY adj resembling gauze
GAVAGE n forced feeding by means of a tube inserted into the stomach through the mouth
GAVAGES ▸ gavage
GAVE ▸ give
GAVEL n small hammer banged on a table by a judge, auctioneer, or chairman to call for attention ▷ vb use a gavel

to restore order
GAVELED ▸ gavel
GAVELS ▸ gavel
GAVIAL n as in **false gavial** small crocodile
GAVIALS ▸ gavial
GAVOT same as ▸ gavotte
GAVOTS ▸ gavot
GAVOTTE n old formal dance ▷ vb dance a gavotte
GAW n as in **weather gaw** partial rainbow
GAWCIER ▸ gawcy
GAWCY same as ▸ gaucy
GAWD same as ▸ gaud
GAWDS ▸ gawd
GAWK vb stare stupidly ▷ n clumsy awkward person
GAWKED ▸ gawk
GAWKER ▸ gawk
GAWKERS ▸ gawk
GAWKIER ▸ gawky
GAWKIES ▸ gawky
GAWKILY ▸ gawky
GAWKING ▸ gawk
GAWKISH same as ▸ gawky
GAWKS ▸ gawk
GAWKY adj clumsy or awkward ▷ n simpleton
GAWP vb stare stupidly
GAWPED ▸ gawp
GAWPER ▸ gawp
GAWPERS ▸ gawp
GAWPING ▸ gawp
GAWPS ▸ gawp
GAWPUS n silly person
GAWS ▸ gaw
GAWSIE same as ▸ gaucy
GAWSIER ▸ gawsie
GAWSY same as ▸ gaucy
GAY adj homosexual ▷ n homosexual
GAYAL n type of ox of India and Myanmar, black or brown with white stockings
GAYALS ▸ gayal
GAYDAR n supposed ability of a homosexual person to determine whether or not another person is homosexual
GAYDARS ▸ gaydar
GAYER ▸ gay
GAYEST ▸ gay
GAYETY same as ▸ gaiety
GAYLY ▸ gay
GAYNESS ▸ gay
GAYS ▸ gay
GAYSOME adj full of merriment
GAZABO n fellow or companion

G

G

GAZABOS ▸ gazabo
GAZAL same as ▸ ghazal
GAZALS ▸ gazal
GAZANIA n S African plant grown for its variegated flowers
GAZAR n type of silk cloth
GAZARS ▸ gazar
GAZE vb look fixedly ▷ n fixed look
GAZEBO n summerhouse with a good view
GAZEBOS ▸ gazebo
GAZED ▸ gaze
GAZEFUL adj gazing
GAZELLE n small graceful antelope
GAZER ▸ gaze
GAZERS ▸ gaze
GAZES ▸ gaze
GAZETTE n official publication containing announcements ▷ vb announce or report (facts or an event) in a gazette
GAZIER ▸ gazy
GAZIEST ▸ gazy
GAZING ▸ gaze
GAZINGS ▸ gaze
GAZON n sod used to cover a parapet in a fortification
GAZONS ▸ gazon
GAZOO n kazoo
GAZOOKA same as ▸ gazoo
GAZOON same as ▸ gazon
GAZOONS ▸ gazoon
GAZOOS ▸ gazoo
GAZUMP vb raise the price of a property after verbally agreeing with it with (a prospective buyer) ▷ n act or an instance of gazumping
GAZUMPS ▸ gazump
GAZY adj prone to gazing
GEAL vb congeal
GEALED ▸ geal
GEALING ▸ geal
GEALOUS Spenserian spelling of ▸ jealous
GEALS ▸ geal
GEAN n white-flowered tree of Europe, W Asia, and N Africa, the ancestor of cultivated sweet cherries
GEANS ▸ gean
GEAR n set of toothed wheels connecting with another or with a rack to change the direction or speed of transmitted motion ▷ vb prepare or organize for something

GEARBOX n case enclosing a set of gears in a motor vehicle
GEARE Spenserian spelling of ▸ jeer
GEARED ▸ gear
GEARES ▸ geare
GEARING n system of gears designed to transmit motion
GEARS ▸ gear
GEASON adj wonderful
GEAT n in casting, the channel through which molten metal runs into a mould
GEATS ▸ geat
GEBUR n tenant farmer
GEBURS ▸ gebur
GECK vb beguile
GECKED ▸ geck
GECKING ▸ geck
GECKO n small tropical lizard
GECKOES ▸ gecko
GECKOS ▸ gecko
GECKS ▸ geck
GED Scots word for ▸ pike
GEDACT n flutelike stopped metal diapason organ pipe
GEDACTS ▸ gedact
GEDDIT interj exclamation meaning do you understand it?
GEDECKT same as ▸ gedact
GEDS ▸ ged
GEE interj mild exclamation of surprise, admiration, etc ▷ vb move (an animal, esp a horse) ahead
GEEBUNG n Australian tree or shrub with an edible but tasteless fruit
GEECHEE n Black person from the southern states of the US
GEED ▸ gee
GEEGAW same as ▸ gewgaw
GEEGAWS ▸ geegaw
GEEING ▸ gee
GEEK n boring, unattractive person
GEEKDOM ▸ geek
GEEKED adj highly excited
GEEKIER ▸ geek
GEEKS ▸ geek
GEEKY ▸ geek
GEELBEK n edible marine fish
GEEP n cross between a goat and a sheep
GEEPS ▸ geep
GEES ▸ gee

GEESE ▸ goose
GEEST n area of sandy heathland in N Germany and adjacent areas
GEESTS ▸ geest
GEEZ interj expression of surprise
GEEZAH variant spelling of ▸ geezer
GEEZAHS ▸ geezah
GEEZER n man
GEEZERS ▸ geezer
GEFILTE adj as in gefilte fish dish of fish stuffed with various ingredients
GEGGIE Scottish, esp Glaswegian, slang word for the ▸ mouth
GEGGIES ▸ geggie
GEISHA n (in Japan) professional female companion for men
GEISHAS ▸ geisha
GEIST n spirit
GEISTS ▸ geist
GEIT n border on clothing
GEITS ▸ geit
GEL n jelly-like substance, esp one used to secure a hairstyle ▷ vb form a gel
GELABLE adj capable of forming a gel
GELADA n NE African baboon with a dark brown mane over the shoulders, a bare red chest, and a ridge muzzle
GELADAS ▸ gelada
GELANDE adj as in gelande jump jump made in downhill skiing
GELANT same as ▸ gellant
GELANTS ▸ gelant
GELATE vb form a gel
GELATED ▸ gelate
GELATES ▸ gelate
GELATI n layered dessert of frozen custard and ice cream
GELATIN same as > gelatine
GELATIS ▸ gelati
GELATO n Italian frozen dessert, similar to ice cream
GELATOS ▸ gelato
GELCAP n dose of medicine enclosed in a soluble case of gelatine
GELCAPS ▸ gelcap
GELD vb castrate ▷ n tax on land levied in late Anglo-Saxon and Norman England
GELDED ▸ geld

GELDER ▸ geld
GELDERS ▸ geld
GELDING ▸ geld
GELDS ▸ geld
GELEE *n* jelly
GELEES ▸ gelee
GELID *adj* very cold, icy, or frosty
GELIDER ▸ gelid
GELIDLY ▸ gelid
GELLANT *n* compound that forms a solid structure
GELLED ▸ gel
GELLIES ▸ gelly
GELLING ▸ gel
GELLY *same as* > **gelignite**
GELOSY *Spenserian spelling of* > **jealousy**
GELS ▸ gel
GELT ▸ geld
GELTS ▸ geld
GEM *n* precious stone or jewel ▷ *vb* set or ornament with gems
GEMCLIP *n* paperclip
GEMEL *n* in heraldry, parallel bars
GEMELS ▸ gemel
GEMFISH *n* Australian food fish with a delicate flavour
GEMINAL *adj* occurring in pairs
GEMINI *n* expression of surprise
GEMINY *n* pair
GEMLIKE ▸ gem
GEMMA *n* small asexual reproductive structure in liverworts, mosses, etc, that becomes detached from the parent and develops into a new individual
GEMMAE ▸ gemma
GEMMAN *dialect form of* > **gentleman**
GEMMATE *adj* (of some plants and animals) having or reproducing by gemmae ▷ *vb* produce or reproduce by gemmae
GEMMED ▸ gem
GEMMEN ▸ gemman
GEMMERY *n* gems collectively
GEMMIER ▸ gem
GEMMILY ▸ gem
GEMMING ▸ gem
GEMMULE *n* cell or mass of cells produced asexually by sponges and developing into a new individual
GEMMY ▸ gem

GEMONY *same as* ▸ **jiminy**
GEMOT *n* (in Anglo-Saxon England) a legal or administrative assembly of a community, such as a shire or hundred
GEMOTE *same as* ▸ **gemot**
GEMOTES ▸ gemote
GEMOTS ▸ gemot
GEMS ▸ gem
GEMSBOK *same as* ▸ **oryx**
GEN *n* information ▷ *vb* gain information
GENA *n* cheek
GENAL ▸ gena
GENAPPE *n* smooth worsted yarn used for braid, etc
GENAS ▸ gena
GENDER *n* state of being male or female ▷ *vb* have sex
GENDERS ▸ gender
GENE *n* part of a cell which determines inherited characteristics
GENERA ▸ genus
GENERAL *adj* common or widespread ▷ *n* very senior army officer ▷ *vb* act as a general
GENERIC *adj* of a class, group, or genus ▷ *n* drug, food product, etc that does not have a trademark
GENES ▸ gene
GENESES ▸ genesis
GENESIS *n* beginning or origin
GENET *n* type of agile catlike mammal of Africa and S Europe, with an elongated head, thick spotted fur, and a very long tail
GENETIC *adj* of genes or genetics
GENETS ▸ genet
GENETTE *same as* ▸ **genet**
GENEVA *n* gin
GENEVAS ▸ geneva
GENIAL *adj* cheerful and friendly
GENIC *adj* of or relating to a gene or genes
GENIE *n* (in fairy tales) servant who appears by magic and grants wishes
GENIES ▸ genie
GENII ▸ genius
GENIP *same as* ▸ **genipap**
GENIPAP *n* evergreen Caribbean tree with reddish-brown edible

orange-like fruits
GENIPS ▸ genip
GENISTA *n* any member of the broom family
GENITAL *adj* of the sexual organs or reproduction
GENITOR *n* biological father as distinguished from the pater or legal father
GENIUS *n* (person with) exceptional ability in a particular field
GENIZAH *n* repository (usually in a synagogue) for books and other sacred objects which can no longer be used but which may not be destroyed
GENIZOT ▸ genizah
GENLOCK *n* generator locking device
GENNED ▸ gen
GENNEL *same as* ▸ **ginnel**
GENNELS ▸ gennel
GENNET *n* female donkey or ass
GENNETS ▸ gennet
GENNIES ▸ genny
GENNING ▸ gen
GENNY *same as* ▸ **genoa**
GENOA *n* large triangular jib sail, often with a foot that extends as far aft as the clew of the mainsail
GENOAS ▸ genoa
GENOISE *n* rich sponge cake
GENOM *same as* ▸ **genome**
GENOME *n* full complement of genetic material within an organism
GENOMES ▸ genome
GENOMIC ▸ genome
GENOMS ▸ genom
GENRE *n* style of literary, musical, or artistic work
GENRES ▸ genre
GENRO *n* group of highly respected elder statesmen in late 19th- and early 20th-century Japan
GENROS ▸ genro
GENS *n* (in ancient Rome) any of a group of aristocratic families, having a common name and claiming descent from a common ancestor in the male line
GENSENG *same as* ▸ **ginseng**
GENT *n* gentleman
GENTEEL *adj* affectedly proper and polite

GENTES ▸ gens
GENTIAN n mountain plant with deep blue flowers
GENTIER ▸ genty
GENTIL adj gentle
GENTILE n non-Jewish (person) ▷ adj denoting an adjective or proper noun used to designate a place or the inhabitants of a place
GENTLE adj mild or kindly ▷ vb tame or subdue (a horse) ▷ n maggot, esp when used as bait in fishing
GENTLED ▸ gentle
GENTLER ▸ gentle
GENTLES ▸ gentle
GENTLY ▸ gentle
GENTOO n grey-backed penguin
GENTOOS ▸ gentoo
GENTRY n informal, often derogatory term for people just below the nobility in social rank
GENTS n men's public toilet
GENTY adj neat
GENU n any knee-like bend in a structure or part
GENUA ▸ genu
GENUINE adj not fake, authentic
GENUS n group into which a family of animals or plants is divided
GENUSES ▸ genus
GEO n (esp in Shetland) a small fjord or gully
GEODE n cavity, usually lined with crystals, within a rock mass or nodule
GEODES ▸ geode
GEODESY n study of the shape and size of the earth
GEODIC ▸ geode
GEODUCK n king clam
GEOFACT n rock shaped by natural forces, as opposed to a manmade artefact
GEOGENY same as ▸ geogony
GEOGONY n science of the earth's formation
GEOID n hypothetical surface that corresponds to mean sea level and extends at the same level under the continents
GEOIDAL ▸ geoid
GEOIDS ▸ geoid
GEOLOGY n study of the earth's origin, structure, and composition

GEOMANT n geomancer
GEORGIC adj agricultural ▷ n poem about rural or agricultural life
GEOS ▸ geo
GER n portable Mongolian dwelling
GERAH n ancient Hebrew unit of weight
GERAHS ▸ gerah
GERBE same as ▸ garbe
GERBERA n type of plant grown, usually as a greenhouse plant, for its large brightly coloured daisy-like flowers
GERBES ▸ garbe
GERBIL n burrowing desert rodent of Asia and Africa
GERBILS ▸ gerbil
GERE Spenserian spelling of ▸ gear
GERENT n person who rules or manages
GERENTS ▸ gerent
GERENUK n slender E African antelope with a long thin neck and backward-curving horns
GERES ▸ gear
GERLE Spenserian spelling of ▸ girl
GERLES ▸ gerle
GERM n microbe, esp one causing disease ▷ vb sprout
GERMAIN same as ▸ germen
GERMAN n dance consisting of complicated figures and changes of partners ▷ adj having the same parents as oneself
GERMANE adj relevant
GERMANS ▸ german
GERMED ▸ germ
GERMEN n mass of undifferentiated cells that gives rise to the germ cells
GERMENS ▸ germen
GERMIER ▸ germy
GERMIN same as ▸ germen
GERMINA ▸ germen
GERMING ▸ germ
GERMINS ▸ germin
GERMS ▸ germ
GERMY adj full of germs
GERNE vb grin
GERNED ▸ gerne
GERNES ▸ gerne
GERNING ▸ gerne
GERS ▸ ger
GERT adv in dialect, great or very big

GERTCHA interj get out of here!
GERUND n noun formed from a verb
GERUNDS ▸ gerund
GESSE Spenserian spelling of ▸ guess
GESSED ▸ gesse
GESSES ▸ gesse
GESSING ▸ gesse
GESSO n plaster used for painting or in sculpture ▷ vb apply gesso to
GESSOED ▸ gesso
GESSOES ▸ gesso
GEST n notable deed or exploit
GESTALT n perceptual pattern or structure possessing qualities as a whole that cannot be described merely as a sum of its parts
GESTANT adj laden
GESTAPO n any secret state police organization
GESTATE vb carry (developing young) in the uterus during pregnancy
GESTE same as ▸ gest
GESTES ▸ geste
GESTIC adj consisting of gestures
GESTS ▸ gest
GESTURE n movement to convey meaning ▷ vb gesticulate
GET vb obtain or receive
GETA n type of Japanese wooden sandal
GETABLE ▸ get
GETAS ▸ geta
GETAWAY n used in escape
GETS ▸ get
GETTER n person or thing that gets ▷ vb remove (a gas) by the action of a getter
GETTERS ▸ getter
GETTING ▸ get
GETUP n outfit
GETUPS ▸ getup
GEUM n type of herbaceous plant with compound leaves and red, orange, or white flowers
GEUMS ▸ geum
GEWGAW n showy but valueless trinket ▷ adj showy and valueless
GEWGAWS ▸ gewgaw
GEY adv extremely ▷ adj gallant

GEYAN adv somewhat
GEYER ▸ gey
GEYEST ▸ gey
GEYSER n spring that discharges steam and hot water
GEYSERS ▸ geyser
GHARIAL same as ▸ **gavial**
GHARRI same as ▸ **gharry**
GHARRIS ▸ gharri
GHARRY n (in India) horse-drawn vehicle available for hire
GHAST vb terrify
GHASTED ▸ ghast
GHASTLY adj unpleasant ▷ adv unhealthily
GHASTS ▸ ghast
GHAT n (in India) steps leading down to a river
GHATS ▸ ghat
GHAUT n small cleft in a hill through which a rivulet runs down to the sea
GHAUTS ▸ ghaut
GHAZAL n Arabic love poem
GHAZALS ▸ ghazal
GHAZEL same as ▸ **ghazal**
GHAZELS ▸ ghazel
GHAZI n Muslim fighter against infidels
GHAZIES ▸ ghazi
GHAZIS ▸ ghazi
GHEE n (in Indian cookery) clarified butter
GHEES ▸ ghee
GHERAO n form of industrial action in India in which workers imprison their employers on the premises until their demands are met ▷ vb trap an employer in his office, to indicate the workforce's discontent
GHERAOS ▸ gherao
GHERKIN n small pickled cucumber
GHESSE Spenserian spelling of ▸ **guess**
GHESSED ▸ ghesse
GHESSES ▸ ghesse
GHEST ▸ ghesse
GHETTO n slum area inhabited by a deprived minority ▷ vb ghettoize
GHETTOS ▸ ghetto
GHI same as ▸ **ghee**
GHIBLI n fiercely hot wind of North Africa
GHIBLIS ▸ ghibli
GHILGAI same as ▸ **gilgai**
GHILLIE n type of

tongueless shoe with lacing up the instep, originally worn by the Scots ▷ vb act as a g(h)illie
GHIS ▸ ghi
GHOST n disembodied spirit of a dead person ▷ vb ghostwrite
GHOSTED ▸ ghost
GHOSTLY adj frightening in appearance or effect
GHOSTS ▸ ghost
GHOSTY adj pertaining to ghosts
GHOUL n person with morbid interests
GHOULIE n goblin
GHOULS ▸ ghoul
GHRELIN n hormone that stimulates appetite
GHUBAR adj as in **ghubar numeral** type of numeral
GHYLL same as ▸ **gill**
GHYLLS ▸ ghyll
GI n loose-fitting white suit worn in judo, karate, and other martial arts
GIANT n mythical being of superhuman size ▷ adj huge
GIANTLY adj giantlike
GIANTRY n collective term for giants
GIANTS ▸ giant
GIARDIA n species of parasite
GIB n metal wedge, pad, or thrust bearing, esp a brass plate let into a steam engine crosshead ▷ vb fasten or supply with a gib
GIBBED ▸ gib
GIBBER vb speak or utter rapidly and unintelligibly ▷ n boulder
GIBBERS ▸ gibber
GIBBET n gallows for displaying executed criminals ▷ vb put to death by hanging on a gibbet
GIBBETS ▸ gibbet
GIBBING ▸ gib
GIBBON n agile tree-dwelling ape of S Asia
GIBBONS ▸ gibbon
GIBBOSE same as ▸ **gibbous**
GIBBOUS adj (of the moon) more than half but less than fully illuminated
GIBE vb make jeering or scoffing remarks (at) ▷ n derisive or provoking remark

GIBED ▸ gibe
GIBEL n Prussian carp
GIBELS ▸ gibel
GIBER ▸ gibe
GIBERS ▸ gibe
GIBES ▸ gibe
GIBING ▸ gibe
GIBLET ▸ giblets
GIBLETS pl n gizzard, liver, heart, and neck of a fowl
GIBLI same as ▸ **ghibli**
GIBLIS ▸ gibli
GIBS ▸ gib
GIBSON n martini garnished with onion
GIBSONS ▸ gibson
GIBUS n collapsible top hat operated by a spring
GIBUSES ▸ gibus
GID n disease of sheep characterized by an unsteady gait and staggering
GIDDAP interj exclamation used to make a horse go faster
GIDDAY interj expression of greeting
GIDDIED ▸ giddy
GIDDIER ▸ giddy
GIDDIES ▸ giddy
GIDDILY ▸ giddy
GIDDUP same as ▸ **giddyup**
GIDDY adj having or causing a feeling of dizziness ▷ vb make giddy
GIDDYAP same as ▸ **giddyup**
GIDDYUP interj exclamation used to make a horse go faster
GIDGEE n small acacia tree, which at times emits an unpleasant smell
GIDGEES ▸ gidgee
GIDJEE same as ▸ **gidgee**
GIDJEES ▸ gidjee
GIDS ▸ gid
GIE Scots word for ▸ **give**
GIED ▸ give
GIEING ▸ give
GIEN ▸ give
GIES ▸ give
GIF obsolete word for ▸ **if**
GIFT n present ▷ vb make a present of
GIFTED adj talented
GIFTEE n person given a gift
GIFTEES ▸ giftee
GIFTING ▸ gift
GIFTS ▸ gift
GIG n single performance by pop or jazz musicians ▷ vb play a gig or gigs

GIGA same as ▸ **gigue**
GIGABIT n unit of information in computing
GIGAS ▸ **giga**
GIGATON n unit of explosive force
GIGGED ▸ **gig**
GIGGING ▸ **gig**
GIGGIT vb move quickly
GIGGITS ▸ **giggit**
GIGGLE vb laugh nervously or foolishly ▷ n such a laugh
GIGGLED ▸ **giggle**
GIGGLER ▸ **giggle**
GIGGLES ▸ **giggle**
GIGGLY ▸ **giggle**
GIGHE ▸ **giga**
GIGLET n flighty girl
GIGLETS ▸ **giglet**
GIGLOT same as ▸ **giglet**
GIGLOTS ▸ **giglot**
GIGMAN n one who places great importance on respectability
GIGMEN ▸ **gigman**
GIGOLO n man paid by an older woman to be her escort or lover
GIGOLOS ▸ **gigolo**
GIGOT n leg of lamb or mutton
GIGOTS ▸ **gigot**
GIGS ▸ **gig**
GIGUE n piece of music, usually in six-eight time and often fugal, incorporated into the classical suite
GIGUES ▸ **gigue**
GILA n large venomous brightly coloured lizard
GILAS ▸ **gila**
GILBERT n unit of magnetomotive force
GILCUP same as ▸ **giltcup**
GILCUPS ▸ **gilcup**
GILD vb put a thin layer of gold on
GILDED ▸ **gild**
GILDEN adj gilded
GILDER ▸ **gild**
GILDERS ▸ **gild**
GILDING ▸ **gild**
GILDS ▸ **gild**
GILET n waist- or hip-length garment, usually sleeveless, fastening up the front
GILETS ▸ **gilet**
GILGAI n natural water hole
GILGAIS ▸ **gilgai**
GILGIE n type of freshwater crayfish
GILGIES ▸ **gilgie**

GILL n radiating structure beneath the cap of a mushroom ▷ vb catch (fish) or (of fish) to be caught in a gill net
GILLED ▸ **gill**
GILLER ▸ **gill**
GILLERS ▸ **gill**
GILLET n mare
GILLETS ▸ **gillet**
GILLIE n (in Scotland) attendant for hunting or fishing ▷ vb act as a gillie
GILLIED ▸ **gillie**
GILLIES ▸ **gilly**
GILLING ▸ **gill**
GILLION n (no longer in technical use) one thousand million
GILLNET n net designed to catch fish by the gills ▷ vb fish using a gillnet
GILLS pl n breathing organs in fish and other water creatures
GILLY vb act as a gillie
GILPEY n mischievous, frolicsome boy or girl
GILPEYS ▸ **gilpey**
GILPIES ▸ **gilpey**
GILPY same as ▸ **gilpey**
GILT ▸ **gild**
GILTCUP n buttercup
GILTS ▸ **gild**
GIMBAL vb support on gimbals
GIMBALS pl n set of pivoted rings which allow nautical instruments to remain horizontal at sea
GIMEL n third letter of the Hebrew alphabet
GIMELS ▸ **gimel**
GIMLET n small tool with a screwlike tip for boring holes in wood ▷ adj penetrating or piercing ▷ vb make holes in (wood) using a gimlet
GIMLETS ▸ **gimlet**
GIMMAL n ring composed of interlocking rings ▷ vb provide with gimmals
GIMMALS ▸ **gimmal**
GIMME interj give me! ▷ n short putt that one is excused from playing because it is considered too easy to miss
GIMMER n year-old ewe
GIMMERS ▸ **gimmer**
GIMMES ▸ **gimme**
GIMMICK n something

designed to attract attention or publicity ▷ vb make gimmicky
GIMMIE n in golf, an easy putt conceded to one's opponent
GIMMIES ▸ **gimmie**
GIMMOR n mechanical device
GIMMORS ▸ **gimmor**
GIN n spirit flavoured with juniper berries ▷ vb free (cotton) of seeds with an engine; begin
GING n child's catapult
GINGAL n type of musket mounted on a swivel
GINGALL same as ▸ **gingal**
GINGALS ▸ **gingal**
GINGE n person with ginger hair
GINGELI same as ▸ **gingili**
GINGELY same as ▸ **gingili**
GINGER n root of a tropical plant, used as a spice ▷ adj light reddish-brown ▷ vb add the spice ginger to (a dish)
GINGERS ▸ **ginger**
GINGERY adj like or tasting of ginger
GINGES ▸ **ginge**
GINGHAM n cotton cloth, usu checked or striped
GINGILI n oil obtained from sesame seeds
GINGIVA same as ▸ **gum**
GINGKO same as ▸ **ginkgo**
GINGKOS ▸ **gingko**
GINGLE same as ▸ **jingle**
GINGLES ▸ **gingle**
GINGS ▸ **ging**
GINK n man or boy, esp one considered to be odd
GINKGO n ornamental Chinese tree
GINKGOS ▸ **ginkgo**
GINKS ▸ **gink**
GINN same as ▸ **jinn**
GINNED ▸ **gin**
GINNEL n narrow passageway between buildings
GINNELS ▸ **ginnel**
GINNER ▸ **gin**
GINNERS ▸ **gin**
GINNERY another word for > **ginhouse**
GINNIER ▸ **ginny**
GINNING ▸ **gin**
GINNY adj relating to the spirit gin
GINS ▸ **gin**

GINSENG n (root of) a plant believed to have tonic and energy-giving properties

GINSHOP n tavern

GIO same as ▸ **geo**

GIOCOSO adv (of music) to be expressed joyfully or playfully

GIOS ▸ **gio**

GIP same as ▸ **gyp**

GIPON another word for ▸ **jupon**

GIPONS ▸ **gipon**

GIPPED ▸ **gip**

GIPPER ▸ **gip**

GIPPERS ▸ **gip**

GIPPIES ▸ **gippy**

GIPPING ▸ **gip**

GIPPO same as ▸ **gippy**

GIPPOES ▸ **gippo**

GIPPOS ▸ **gippo**

GIPPY n starling

GIPS ▸ **gip**

GIPSEN obsolete word for ▸ **gypsy**

GIPSENS ▸ **gipsen**

GIPSIED ▸ **gipsy**

GIPSIES ▸ **gipsy**

GIPSY n member of a nomadic people scattered throughout Europe and North America ▷ vb live like a gypsy

GIRAFFE n African ruminant mammal with a spotted yellow skin and long neck and legs

GIRASOL n type of opal that has a red or pink glow in bright light

GIRD vb put a belt round ▷ n blow or stroke

GIRDED ▸ **gird**

GIRDER n large metal beam

GIRDERS ▸ **girder**

GIRDING ▸ **gird**

GIRDLE n woman's elastic corset ▷ vb surround or encircle

GIRDLED ▸ **girdle**

GIRDLER n person or thing that girdles

GIRDLES ▸ **girdle**

GIRDS ▸ **gird**

GIRKIN same as ▸ **gherkin**

GIRKINS ▸ **girkin**

GIRL n female child

GIRLIE adj (of a magazine, calendar, etc) featuring pictures of naked or scantily clad women ▷ n little girl

GIRLIER ▸ **girly**

GIRLIES ▸ **girlie**

GIRLISH adj of or like a girl in looks, behaviour, innocence, etc

GIRLOND obsolete word for ▸ **garland**

GIRLS ▸ **girl**

GIRLY same as ▸ **girlie**

GIRN vb snarl

GIRNED ▸ **girn**

GIRNEL n large chest for storing meal

GIRNELS ▸ **girnel**

GIRNER ▸ **girn**

GIRNERS ▸ **girn**

GIRNIE adj peevish

GIRNIER ▸ **girnie**

GIRNING ▸ **girn**

GIRNS ▸ **girn**

GIRO n (in some countries) system of transferring money within a post office or bank directly from one account to another

GIROLLE n chanterelle mushroom

GIRON n charge consisting of the lower half of a diagonally divided quarter, usually in the top left corner of the shield

GIRONIC ▸ **giron**

GIRONNY adj divided into segments from the fesse point

GIRONS ▸ **giron**

GIROS ▸ **giro**

GIROSOL same as ▸ **girasol**

GIRR same as ▸ **gird**

GIRRS ▸ **girr**

GIRSH n currency unit of Saudi Arabia

GIRSHES ▸ **girsh**

GIRT vb gird; bind

GIRTED ▸ **gird**

GIRTH n measurement round something ▷ vb fasten a girth on (a horse)

GIRTHED ▸ **girth**

GIRTHS ▸ **girth**

GIRTING ▸ **gird**

GIRTS ▸ **girt**

GIS ▸ **gi**

GISARME n long-shafted battle-axe with a sharp point on the back of the axe head

GISMO same as ▸ **gizmo**

GISMOS ▸ **gismo**

GIST n substance or main point of a matter

GISTS ▸ **gist**

GIT n contemptible person ▷ vb dialect version of get

GITANA n female gypsy

GITANAS ▸ **gitana**

GITANO n male gypsy

GITANOS ▸ **gitano**

GITE n self-catering holiday cottage for let in France

GITES ▸ **gite**

GITS ▸ **git**

GITTED ▸ **git**

GITTERN n obsolete medieval stringed instrument resembling the guitar ▷ vb play the gittern

GITTIN n Jewish divorce

GITTING ▸ **git**

GIUST same as ▸ **joust**

GIUSTED ▸ **giust**

GIUSTO adv observed strictly

GIUSTS ▸ **giust**

GIVABLE ▸ **give**

GIVE vb present (something) to another person ▷ n resilience or elasticity

GIVED same as ▸ **gyved**

GIVEN n assumed fact

GIVENS ▸ **given**

GIVER ▸ **give**

GIVERS ▸ **give**

GIVES ▸ **give**

GIVING ▸ **give**

GIVINGS ▸ **give**

GIZMO n device

GIZMOS ▸ **gizmo**

GIZZ n wig

GIZZARD n part of a bird's stomach

GIZZEN vb (of wood) to warp

GIZZENS ▸ **gizzen**

GIZZES ▸ **gizz**

GJETOST n type of Norwegian cheese

GJU n type of violin used in Shetland

This unusual word for a Shetland fiddle is great for disposing of awkward letters for a good score.

GJUS ▸ **gju**

GLACE adj preserved in a thick sugary syrup ▷ vb ice or candy (cakes, fruits, etc)

GLACEED ▸ **glace**

GLACES ▸ **glace**

GLACIAL adj of ice or glaciers ▷ n ice age

GLACIER n slow-moving mass of ice formed by accumulated snow

GLACIS n slight incline

GLAD adj pleased and happy

▷ *vb* become glad ▷ *n* gladiolus
GLADDED ▸ **glad**
GLADDEN *vb* make glad
GLADDER ▸ **glad**
GLADDIE *same as* ▸ **glad**
GLADDON *n* stinking iris
GLADE *n* open space in a forest
GLADES ▸ **glade**
GLADFUL *adj* full of gladness
GLADIER ▸ **glade**
GLADIUS *n* short sword used by Roman legionaries
GLADLY ▸ **glad**
GLADS ▸ **glad**
GLADY ▸ **glade**
GLAIK *n* prank
GLAIKET *same as* ▸ **glaikit**
GLAIKIT *adj* foolish
GLAIKS ▸ **glaik**
GLAIR *n* white of egg, esp when used as a size, glaze, or adhesive, usually in bookbinding ▷ *vb* apply glair to (something)
GLAIRE *same as* ▸ **glair**
GLAIRED ▸ **glair**
GLAIRES ▸ **glaire**
GLAIRIN *n* viscous deposit found in some mineral waters
GLAIRS ▸ **glair**
GLAIRY ▸ **glair**
GLAIVE *archaic word for* ▸ **sword**
GLAIVED *adj* armed with a sword
GLAIVES ▸ **glaive**
GLAM *n* magical illusion ▷ *vb* make oneself look glamorous
GLAMMED ▸ **glam** *vb*
GLAMMY *adj* glamorous
GLAMOR *same as* ▸ **glamour**
GLAMORS ▸ **glamor**
GLAMOUR *n* alluring charm or fascination ▷ *vb* bewitch
GLAMS ▸ **glam**
GLANCE *vb* look rapidly or briefly ▷ *n* brief look
GLANCED ▸ **glance**
GLANCER *n* log or pole used to protect standing trees from damage
GLANCES ▸ **glance**
GLAND *n* organ that produces and secretes substances in the body
GLANDES ▸ **glans**
GLANDS ▸ **gland**

GLANS *n* any small rounded body or glandlike mass, such as the head of the penis
GLARE *vb* stare angrily ▷ *n* angry stare ▷ *adj* smooth and glassy
GLAREAL *adj* (of a plant) growing in cultivated land
GLARED ▸ **glare**
GLARES ▸ **glare**
GLARIER ▸ **glare**
GLARING *adj* conspicuous
GLARY ▸ **glare**
GLASS *n* hard brittle, usu transparent substance consisting of metal silicates or similar compounds ▷ *vb* cover with, enclose in, or fit with glass
GLASSED ▸ **glass**
GLASSEN *adj* glassy
GLASSES *pl n* pair of lenses for correcting faulty vision, in a frame that rests on the nose and hooks behind the ears
GLASSIE *same as* ▸ **glassy**
GLASSY *adj* like glass ▷ *n* glass marble
GLAUM *vb* snatch
GLAUMED ▸ **glaum**
GLAUMS ▸ **glaum**
GLAUR *n* mud or mire
GLAURS ▸ **glaur**
GLAURY ▸ **glaur**
GLAZE *vb* fit or cover with glass ▷ *n* transparent coating
GLAZED ▸ **glaze**
GLAZEN *adj* glazed
GLAZER ▸ **glaze**
GLAZERS ▸ **glaze**
GLAZES ▸ **glaze**
GLAZIER *n* person who fits windows with glass
GLAZILY ▸ **glaze**
GLAZING *n* surface of a glazed object
GLAZY ▸ **glaze**
GLEAM *n* small beam or glow of light ▷ *vb* emit a gleam
GLEAMED ▸ **gleam**
GLEAMER *n* mirror used to cheat in card games
GLEAMS ▸ **gleam**
GLEAMY ▸ **gleam**
GLEAN *vb* gather (facts etc) bit by bit
GLEANED ▸ **glean**
GLEANER ▸ **glean**
GLEANS ▸ **glean**

GLEAVE *same as* ▸ **sword**
GLEAVES ▸ **gleave**
GLEBA *n* mass of spores
GLEBAE ▸ **gleba**
GLEBE *n* land granted to a member of the clergy as part of his or her benefice
GLEBES ▸ **glebe**
GLEBIER ▸ **gleby**
GLEBOUS *adj* gleby
GLEBY *adj* relating to a glebe
GLED *n* kite
GLEDE *same as* ▸ **gled**
GLEDES ▸ **glede**
GLEDGE *vb* glance sideways
GLEDGED ▸ **gledge**
GLEDGES ▸ **gledge**
GLEDS ▸ **gled**
GLEE *n* triumph and delight ▷ *vb* be full of glee
GLEED *n* burning ember or hot coal
GLEEDS ▸ **gleed**
GLEEFUL *adj* merry or joyful, esp over someone else's mistake or misfortune
GLEEING ▸ **glee**
GLEEK *vb* jeer
GLEEKED ▸ **gleek**
GLEEKS ▸ **gleek**
GLEEMAN *n* minstrel
GLEEMEN ▸ **gleeman**
GLEENIE *n* guinea fowl
GLEES ▸ **glee**
GLEET *n* inflammation of the urethra with a slight discharge of thin pus and mucus: a stage of chronic gonorrhoea ▷ *vb* discharge gleet
GLEETED ▸ **gleet**
GLEETS ▸ **gleet**
GLEETY ▸ **gleet**
GLEG *adj* quick
GLEGGER ▸ **gleg**
GLEGLY ▸ **gleg**
GLEI *same as* ▸ **gley**
GLEIS ▸ **glei**
GLEN *n* deep narrow valley, esp in Scotland
GLENOID *adj* resembling or having a shallow cavity ▷ *n* shallow cavity
GLENS ▸ **glen**
GLENT *same as* ▸ **glint**
GLENTED ▸ **glent**
GLENTS ▸ **glent**
GLEY *n* bluish-grey compact sticky soil occurring in certain humid regions ▷ *vb* squint
GLEYED ▸ **gley**

GLEYING ▸ **gley**
GLEYS ▸ **gley**
GLIA *n* delicate web of connective tissue that surrounds and supports nerve cells
GLIADIN *n* protein of cereals, esp wheat, with a high proline content: forms a sticky mass with water that binds flour into dough
GLIAL ▸ **glia**
GLIAS ▸ **glia**
GLIB *adj* fluent but insincere or superficial ▸ *vb* castrate
GLIBBED ▸ **glib**
GLIBBER ▸ **glib**
GLIBLY ▸ **glib**
GLIBS ▸ **glib**
GLID *adj* moving smoothly and easily
GLIDDER ▸ **glid**
GLIDE *vb* move easily and smoothly ▸ *n* smooth easy movement
GLIDED ▸ **glide**
GLIDER *n* flying phalanger
GLIDERS ▸ **glider**
GLIDES ▸ **glide**
GLIDING *n* sport of flying gliders
GLIFF *n* slap
GLIFFS ▸ **gliff**
GLIFT *n* moment
GLIFTS ▸ **glift**
GLIKE *same as* ▸ **gleek**
GLIKES ▸ **glike**
GLIM *n* light or lamp
GLIME *vb* glance sideways
GLIMED ▸ **glime**
GLIMES ▸ **glime**
GLIMING ▸ **glime**
GLIMMER *vb* shine faintly, flicker ▸ *n* faint gleam
GLIMPSE *n* brief or incomplete view ▸ *vb* catch a glimpse of
GLIMS ▸ **glim**
GLINT *vb* gleam brightly ▸ *n* bright gleam
GLINTED ▸ **glint**
GLINTS ▸ **glint**
GLINTY ▸ **glint**
GLIOMA *n* tumour of the brain and spinal cord, composed of neuroglia cells and fibres
GLIOMAS ▸ **glioma**
GLIOSES ▸ **gliosis**
GLIOSIS *n* process leading to scarring in the central nervous system
GLISK *n* glimpse

GLISKS ▸ **glisk**
GLISTEN *vb* gleam by reflecting light ▸ *n* gleam or gloss
GLISTER *archaic word for* ▸ **glitter**
GLIT *n* slimy matter
GLITCH *n* small problem that stops something from working properly
GLITCHY ▸ **glitch**
GLITS ▸ **glit**
GLITTER *vb* shine with bright flashes ▸ *n* sparkle or brilliance
GLITZ *n* ostentatious showiness ▸ *vb* make something more attractive
GLITZED ▸ **glitz**
GLITZES ▸ **glitz**
GLITZY *adj* showily attractive
GLOAM *n* dusk
GLOAMS ▸ **gloam**
GLOAT *vb* regard one's own good fortune or the misfortune of others with smug or malicious pleasure ▸ *n* act of gloating
GLOATED ▸ **gloat**
GLOATER ▸ **gloat**
GLOATS ▸ **gloat**
GLOB *n* rounded mass of thick fluid
GLOBAL *adj* worldwide
GLOBATE *adj* shaped like a globe
GLOBBY *adj* thick and lumpy
GLOBE *n* sphere with a map of the earth on it ▸ *vb* form or cause to form into a globe
GLOBED ▸ **globe**
GLOBES ▸ **globe**
GLOBI ▸ **globus**
GLOBIN *n* protein component of the pigments myoglobin and haemoglobin
GLOBING ▸ **globe**
GLOBINS ▸ **globin**
GLOBOID *adj* shaped approximately like a globe ▸ *n* globoid body, such as any of those occurring in certain plant granules
GLOBOSE *adj* spherical or approximately spherical ▸ *n* globose object
GLOBOUS *same as* ▸ **globose**
GLOBS ▸ **glob**
GLOBULE *n* small round drop

GLOBUS *n* any spherelike structure
GLOBY *adj* round
GLOCHID *n* barbed spine on a plant
GLODE ▸ **glide**
GLOGG *n* hot alcoholic mixed drink, originally from Sweden, consisting of sweetened brandy, red wine, bitters or other flavourings, and blanched almonds
GLOGGS ▸ **glogg**
GLOIRE *n* glory
GLOIRES ▸ **gloire**
GLOM *vb* attach oneself to or associate oneself with
GLOMERA ▸ **glomus**
GLOMMED ▸ **glom**
GLOMS ▸ **glom**
GLOMUS *n* small anastomosis in an artery or vein
GLONOIN *n* nitroglycerin
GLOOM *n* melancholy or depression ▸ *vb* look sullen or depressed
GLOOMED ▸ **gloom**
GLOOMS ▸ **gloom**
GLOOMY *adj* despairing or sad
GLOOP *vb* cover with a viscous substance
GLOOPED ▸ **gloop**
GLOOPS ▸ **gloop**
GLOOPY ▸ **gloop**
GLOP *vb* cover with a viscous substance
GLOPPED ▸ **glop**
GLOPPY ▸ **glop**
GLOPS ▸ **glop**
GLORIA *n* silk, wool, cotton, or nylon fabric used esp for umbrellas
GLORIAS ▸ **gloria**
GLORIED ▸ **glory**
GLORIES ▸ **glory**
GLORIFY *vb* make (something) seem more worthy than it is
GLORY *n* praise or honour ▸ *vb* triumph or exalt
GLOSS *n* surface shine or lustre ▸ *vb* make glossy
GLOSSA *n* paired tonguelike lobe in the labium of an insect
GLOSSAE ▸ **glossa**
GLOSSAL ▸ **glossa**
GLOSSAS ▸ **glossa**
GLOSSED ▸ **gloss**
GLOSSER ▸ **gloss**

G

GLOSSES ▸ gloss

GLOSSY *adj* smooth and shiny ▸ *n* expensively produced magazine

GLOST *n* lead glaze used for pottery

GLOSTS ▸ glost

GLOTTAL *adj* of the glottis

GLOTTIC *adj* of or relating to the tongue or the glottis

GLOTTIS *n* vocal cords and the space between them

GLOUT *vb* look sullen

GLOUTED ▸ glout

GLOUTS ▸ glout

GLOVE *n* covering for the hand with individual sheaths for each finger and the thumb

GLOVED ▸ glove

GLOVER *n* person who makes or sells gloves

GLOVERS ▸ glover

GLOVES ▸ glove

GLOVING ▸ glove

GLOW *vb* emit light and heat without flames ▸ *n* glowing light

GLOWED ▸ glow

GLOWER *n* scowl ▸ *vb* stare angrily

GLOWERS ▸ glower

GLOWFLY *n* firefly

GLOWING *adj* full of praise

GLOWS ▸ glow

GLOZE *vb* explain away ▸ *n* flattery or deceit

GLOZED ▸ gloze

GLOZES ▸ gloze

GLOZING ▸ gloze

GLUCAN *n* any polysaccharide consisting of a polymer of glucose, such as cellulose or starch

GLUCANS ▸ glucan

GLUCINA *n* oxide of glucinium

GLUCOSE *n* kind of sugar found in fruit

GLUE *n* natural or synthetic sticky substance used as an adhesive ▸ *vb* fasten with glue

GLUED ▸ glue

GLUEING ▸ glue

GLUEPOT *n* container for holding glue

GLUER ▸ glue

GLUERS ▸ glue

GLUES ▸ glue

GLUEY ▸ glue

GLUG *n* word representing a gurgling sound, as of liquid being poured from a bottle or swallowed ▸ *vb* drink noisily, taking big gulps

GLUGGED ▸ glug

GLUGS ▸ glug

GLUIER ▸ glue

GLUIEST ▸ glue

GLUILY ▸ glue

GLUING ▸ glue

GLUISH ▸ glue

GLUM *adj* sullen or gloomy

GLUME *n* one of a pair of dry membranous bracts at the base of the spikelet of grasses

GLUMES ▸ glume

GLUMLY ▸ glum

GLUMMER ▸ glum

GLUMPS *n* state of sulking

GLUMPY *adj* sullen

GLUMS *n* gloomy feelings

GLUNCH *vb* look sullen

GLUON *n* hypothetical particle believed to be exchanged between quarks in order to bind them together to form particles

GLUONS ▸ gluon

GLURGE *n* stories, often sent by email, that are supposed to be true and uplifting, but which are often fabricated and sentimental

GLURGES ▸ glurge

GLUT *n* excessive supply ▸ *vb* oversupply

GLUTAEI ▸ glutaeus

GLUTE *n* same as ▸ **gluteus**

GLUTEAL ▸ gluteus

GLUTEI ▸ gluteus

GLUTEN *n* protein found in cereal grain

GLUTENS ▸ gluten

GLUTES ▸ glute

GLUTEUS *n* any of the three muscles of the buttock

GLUTS ▸ glut

GLUTTED ▸ glut

GLUTTON *n* greedy person

GLYCAN *n* polysaccharide

GLYCANS ▸ glycan

GLYCIN same as ▸ **glycine**

GLYCINE *n* nonessential amino acid occurring in most proteins

GLYCINS ▸ glycin

GLYCOL *n* another name (not in technical usage) for or a diol

GLYCOLS ▸ glycol

GLYCOSE *n* any of various monosaccharides

GLYCYL *n* radical of glycine

GLYCYLS ▸ glycyl

GLYPH *n* carved channel or groove, esp a vertical one as used on a Doric frieze

GLYPHIC ▸ glyph

GLYPHS ▸ glyph

GLYPTAL *n* alkyd resin obtained from polyhydric alcohols and polybasic organic acids or their anhydrides

GLYPTIC *adj* of or relating to engraving or carving, esp on precious stones

GNAMMA same as ▸ **namma**

GNAR same as ▸ **gnarl**

GNARL *n* any knotty protuberance or swelling on a tree ▸ *vb* knot or cause to knot

GNARLED *adj* rough, twisted, and knobbly

GNARLS ▸ gnarl

GNARLY *adj* good

GNARR same as ▸ **gnarl**

GNARRED ▸ gnar

GNARRS ▸ gnarr

GNARS ▸ gnar

GNASH *vb* grind (the teeth) together in anger or pain ▸ *n* act of gnashing the teeth

GNASHED ▸ gnash

GNASHER *n* tooth

GNASHES ▸ gnash

GNAT *n* small biting two-winged fly

GNATHAL same as ▸ **gnathic**

GNATHIC *adj* of or relating to the jaw

GNATS ▸ gnat

GNATTY *adj* infested with gnats

GNAW *vb* bite or chew steadily ▸ *n* act or an instance of gnawing

GNAWED ▸ gnaw

GNAWER ▸ gnaw

GNAWERS ▸ gnaw

GNAWING ▸ gnaw

GNAWN ▸ gnaw

GNAWS ▸ gnaw

GNEISS *n* coarse-grained metamorphic rock

GNOCCHI *n* dumplings made of pieces of semolina pasta, or sometimes potato, used to garnish soup or served alone with sauce

GNOMAE ▸ **gnome**
GNOME n imaginary creature like a little old man
GNOMES ▸ **gnome**
GNOMIC adj of pithy sayings
GNOMISH ▸ **gnome**
GNOMIST n writer of pithy sayings
GNOMON n stationary arm that projects the shadow on a sundial
GNOMONS ▸ **gnomon**
GNOSES ▸ **gnosis**
GNOSIS n supposedly revealed knowledge of various spiritual truths, esp that said to have been possessed by ancient Gnostics
GNOSTIC adj of, relating to, or possessing knowledge, esp esoteric spiritual knowledge ▸ n one who knows
GNOW n Australian wild bird
GNOWS ▸ **gnow**
GNU n ox-like S African antelope
GNUS ▸ **gnu**
GO vb move to or from a place ▸ n attempt
GOA n Tibetan gazelle with a brownish-grey coat and backward-curving horns
GOAD vb provoke (someone) to take some kind of action, usu in anger ▸ n spur or provocation
GOADED ▸ **goad**
GOADING ▸ **goad**
GOADS ▸ **goad**
GOAF n waste left in old mine workings
GOAFS ▸ **goaf**
GOAL n posts through which the ball or puck has to be propelled to score ▸ vb in rugby, to convert a try into a goal
GOALED ▸ **goal**
GOALIE n goalkeeper
GOALIES ▸ **goalie**
GOALING ▸ **goal**
GOALS ▸ **goal**
GOANNA n large Australian lizard
GOANNAS ▸ **goanna**
GOARY variant spelling of ▸ **gory**
GOAS ▸ **goa**
GOAT n sure-footed ruminant animal with horns

GOATEE n pointed tuft-like beard
GOATEED ▸ **goatee**
GOATEES ▸ **goatee**
GOATIER ▸ **goat**

| This means more like a goat: it may seem a silly sort of word but because it uses such common letters the chance to play it as a bonus comes up very frequently.

GOATISH adj of, like, or relating to a goat
GOATS ▸ **goat**
GOATY ▸ **goat**
GOB n lump of a soft substance ▸ vb spit
GOBAN n board on which go is played
GOBANG n Japanese board-game
GOBANGS ▸ **gobang**
GOBANS ▸ **goban**
GOBAR adj as in **gobar numeral** kind of numeral
GOBBED ▸ **gob**
GOBBET n lump, esp of food
GOBBETS ▸ **gobbet**
GOBBI ▸ **gobbo**
GOBBIER ▸ **gobby**
GOBBING ▸ **gob**
GOBBLE vb eat hastily and greedily ▸ n rapid gurgling cry of the male turkey ▸ interj imitation of this sound
GOBBLED ▸ **gobble**
GOBBLER n turkey
GOBBLES ▸ **gobble**
GOBBO n hunchback
GOBBY adj loudmouthed and offensive
GOBI n (in Indian cookery) cauliflower
GOBIES ▸ **goby**
GOBIID n member of the genus Gobius
GOBIIDS ▸ **gobiid**
GOBIOID n type of spiny-finned fish of the suborder which includes the goby and mudskipper
GOBIS ▸ **gobi**
GOBLET n drinking cup without handles
GOBLETS ▸ **goblet**
GOBLIN n (in folklore) small malevolent creature
GOBLINS ▸ **goblin**
GOBO n shield placed around a microphone to exclude unwanted sounds

GOBOES ▸ **gobo**
GOBONEE same as ▸ **gobony**
GOBONY adj in heraldry, composed of a row of small, alternately-coloured, squares
GOBOS ▸ **gobo**
GOBS ▸ **gob**
GOBURRA n kookaburra
GOBY n small spiny-finned fish
GOD n spirit or being worshipped as having supernatural power ▸ vb deify
GODDAM vb damn
GODDAMN interj oath expressing anger, surprise, etc ▸ adj extremely ▸ vb damn
GODDAMS ▸ **goddam**
GODDED ▸ **god**
GODDEN n evening greeting
GODDENS ▸ **godden**
GODDESS n female divinity
GODDING ▸ **god**
GODET n triangular piece of material inserted into a garment, such as into a skirt to create a flare
GODETIA n plant with showy flowers
GODETS ▸ **godet**
GODHEAD n essential nature and condition of being a god
GODHOOD n state of being divine
GODLESS adj wicked or unprincipled
GODLIER ▸ **godly**
GODLIKE adj resembling or befitting a god or God
GODLILY ▸ **godly**
GODLING n little god
GODLY adj devout or pious
GODOWN n (in East Asia and India) warehouse
GODOWNS ▸ **godown**
GODROON same as ▸ **gadroon**
GODS ▸ **god**
GODSEND n something unexpected but welcome
GODSHIP n divinity
GODSLOT n time in a television or radio schedule traditionally reserved for religious broadcasts
GODSO same as ▸ **gadso**
GODSON n male godchild

G

GODSONS ▸ **godson**
GODWARD adv towards God
GODWIT n shore bird with long legs and an upturned bill
GODWITS ▸ **godwit**
GOE same as ▸ **go**
GOEL n in Jewish law, blood-avenger
GOELS ▸ **goel**
GOER n person who attends something regularly
GOERS ▸ **goer**
GOES ▸ **go**
GOEST vb archaic 2nd person sing present of go
GOETH vb archaic 3rd person sing present of go
GOETIC ▸ **goety**
GOETIES ▸ **goety**
GOETY n witchcraft
GOEY adj go-ahead
GOFER n employee or assistant whose tasks include menial tasks such as running errands
GOFERS ▸ **gofer**
GOFF obsolete variant of ▸ **golf**
GOFFED ▸ **goff**
GOFFER vb press pleats into (a frill) ▹ n ornamental frill made by pressing pleats
GOFFERS ▸ **goffer**
GOFFING ▸ **goff**
GOFFS ▸ **goff**
GOGGA n any small insect
GOGGAS ▸ **gogga**
GOGGLE vb (of the eyes) bulge ▹ n fixed or bulging stare
GOGGLED ▸ **goggle**
GOGGLER n big-eyed scad
GOGGLES ▸ **goggle**
GOGGLY ▸ **goggle**
GOGLET n long-necked water-cooling vessel of porous earthenware, used esp in India
GOGLETS ▸ **goglet**
GOGO n disco
GOGOS ▸ **gogo**
GOIER ▸ **goey**
GOIEST ▸ **goey**
GOING ▸ **go**
GOINGS ▸ **go**
GOITER same as ▸ **goitre**
GOITERS ▸ **goiter**
GOITRE n swelling of the thyroid gland in the neck
GOITRED ▸ **goitre**
GOITRES ▸ **goitre**
GOJI > **wolfberry**

GOJIS ▸ **goji**
GOLD n yellow precious metal ▹ adj made of gold
GOLDARN euphemistic variant of ▸ **goddamn**
GOLDBUG n American beetle with a bright metallic lustre
GOLDEN adj made of gold ▹ vb gild
GOLDENS ▸ **golden**
GOLDER ▸ **gold**
GOLDEST ▸ **gold**
GOLDEYE n N American fish with yellowish eyes, silvery sides, and a dark blue back
GOLDIER ▸ **goldy**
GOLDISH ▸ **gold**
GOLDS ▸ **gold**
GOLDURN same as ▸ **goddamn**
GOLDY adj gold-like
GOLE obsolete spelling of ▸ **goal**
GOLEM n (in Jewish legend) artificially created human being brought to life by supernatural means
GOLEMS ▸ **golem**
GOLES ▸ **gole**
GOLF n outdoor game in which a ball is struck with clubs into a series of holes ▹ vb play golf
GOLFED ▸ **golf**
GOLFER n person who plays golf
GOLFERS ▸ **golfer**
GOLFING ▸ **golf**
GOLFS ▸ **golf**
GOLIARD n one of a number of wandering scholars in 12th- and 13th-century Europe famed for their riotous behaviour, intemperance, and composition of satirical and ribald Latin verse
GOLIAS vb behave outrageously
GOLIATH n giant
GOLLAN n yellow flower
GOLLAND same as ▸ **gollan**
GOLLANS ▸ **gollan**
GOLLAR same as ▸ **goller**
GOLLARS ▸ **gollar**
GOLLER vb roar
GOLLERS ▸ **goller**
GOLLIED ▸ **golly**
GOLLIES ▸ **golly**
GOLLOP vb eat or drink (something) quickly or greedily

GOLLOPS ▸ **gollop**
GOLLY interj exclamation of mild surprise ▹ n short for golliwog: used chiefly by children ▹ vb spit
GOLOSH same as ▸ **galosh**
GOLOSHE same as ▸ **galosh**
GOLP same as ▸ **golpe**
GOLPE n in heraldry, a purple circle
GOLPES ▸ **golpe**
GOLPS ▸ **golp**
GOMBEEN n usury
GOMBO same as ▸ **gumbo**
GOMBOS ▸ **gombo**
GOMBRO same as ▸ **gumbo**
GOMBROS ▸ **gombro**
GOMER n unwanted hospital patient
GOMERAL same as ▸ **gomeril**
GOMEREL same as ▸ **gomeril**
GOMERIL n slow-witted or stupid person
GOMERS ▸ **gomer**
GOMOKU another word for ▸ **gobang**
GOMOKUS ▸ **gomoku**
GOMPA n Tibetan monastery
GOMPAS ▸ **gompa**
GOMUTI n E Indian feather palm whose sweet sap is a source of sugar
GOMUTIS ▸ **gomuti**
GOMUTO same as ▸ **gomuti**
GOMUTOS ▸ **gomuto**
GON n geometrical grade
GONAD n organ producing reproductive cells, such as a testicle or ovary
GONADAL ▸ **gonad**
GONADIC ▸ **gonad**
GONADS ▸ **gonad**
GONDOLA n long narrow boat used in Venice
GONE ▸ **go**
GONEF same as ▸ **ganef**
GONEFS ▸ **gonef**
GONER n person or thing beyond help or recovery
GONERS ▸ **goner**
GONG n rimmed metal disc that produces a note when struck ▹ vb sound a gong
GONGED ▸ **gong**
GONGING ▸ **gong**
GONGS ▸ **gong**
GONGYO n (in Nichiren Buddhism) ceremony, performed twice a day, involving reciting parts of

the Lotus Sutra and chanting the Daimoku to the Gohonzon

GONGYOS ▸ gongyo

GONIA ▸ gonion

GONIDIA > gonidium

GONIDIC > gonidium

GONIF *same as* ▸ **ganef**

GONIFF *same as* ▸ **ganef**

GONIFFS ▸ goniff

GONIFS ▸ gonif

GONION *n* point or apex of the angle of the lower jaw

GONIUM *n* immature reproductive cell

GONK *n* stuffed toy, often used as a mascot

GONKS ▸ gonk

GONNA *vb* going to

GONOF *same as* ▸ **ganef**

GONOFS ▸ ganof

GONOPH *same as* ▸ **ganef**

GONOPHS ▸ gonoph

GONOPOD *n* either member of a pair of appendages that are the external reproductive organs of insects and some other arthropods

GONS ▸ gon

GONYS *n* lower outline of a bird's bill

GONYSES ▸ gonys

GONZO *adj* wild or crazy

GOO *n* sticky substance

GOOBER *another name for* ▸ **peanut**

GOOBERS ▸ goober

GOOBIES ▸ gooby

GOOBY *n* spittle

GOOD *adj* giving pleasure ▷ *n* benefit

GOODBY *same as* ▸ **goodbye**

GOODBYE *n* expression used on parting ▷ *interj* expression used on parting ▷ *sentence substitute* farewell: a conventional expression used at leave-taking or parting with people and at the loss or rejection of things or ideas

GOODBYS ▸ goodby

GOODIE *same as* ▸ **goody**

GOODIER ▸ goody

GOODIES ▸ goody

GOODISH ▸ good

GOODLY *adj* considerable

GOODMAN *n* husband

GOODMEN ▸ goodman

GOODS ▸ good

GOODY *n* hero in a book or film ▷ *interj* child's exclamation of pleasure ▷ *adj* smug and sanctimonious

GOOEY *adj* sticky and soft

GOOF *n* mistake ▷ *vb* make a mistake

GOOFED ▸ goof

GOOFIER ▸ goofy

GOOFILY ▸ goofy

GOOFING ▸ goof

GOOFS ▸ goof

GOOFY *adj* silly or ridiculous

GOOG *n* egg

GOOGLE *vb* search for (something) on the internet using a search engine

GOOGLED ▸ google

GOOGLES ▸ google

GOOGLY *n* ball that spins unexpectedly from off to leg on the bounce

GOOGOL *n* number represented as one followed by 100 zeros (10^{100})

GOOGOLS ▸ googol

GOOGS ▸ goog

GOOIER ▸ gooey

GOOIEST ▸ gooey

GOOILY ▸ gooey

GOOKY *adj* sticky and messy

GOOL *n* corn marigold

GOOLD *Scots word for* ▸ **gold**

GOOLDS ▸ goold

GOOLS ▸ gool

GOOMBAH *n* patron or mentor

GOOMBAY *n* Bahamian soft drink

GOON *n* stupid person

GOONDA *n* (in India) habitual criminal

GOONDAS ▸ goonda

GOONEY *n* albatross

GOONEYS ▸ gooney

GOONIE *Scots word for a* ▸ **gown**

GOONIER ▸ goon

GOONIES ▸ goonie

GOONS ▸ goon

GOONY ▸ goon

GOOP *n* rude or ill-mannered person

GOOPED *adj as in* **gooped up** sticky with goop

GOOPIER ▸ goopy

GOOPS ▸ goop

GOOPY ▸ goop

GOOR *same as* ▸ **gur**

GOORAL *same as* ▸ **goral**

GOORALS ▸ gooral

GOORIE ▸ kuri

GOORIES ▸ goorie

GOOROO *same as* ▸ **guru**

GOOROOS ▸ gooroo

GOORS ▸ goor

GOORY ▸ kuri

GOOS ▸ goo

GOOSE *n* web-footed bird like a large duck ▷ *vb* prod (someone) playfully in the bottom

GOOSED ▸ goose

GOOSERY *n* place for keeping geese

GOOSES ▸ goose

GOOSEY *same as* ▸ **goosy**

GOOSEYS ▸ goosey

GOOSIER ▸ goosy

GOOSIES ▸ goosy

GOOSING ▸ goose

GOOSY *adj* of or like a goose

GOPAK *n* spectacular high-leaping Russian peasant dance for men

GOPAKS ▸ gopak

GOPHER *n* American burrowing rodent ▷ *vb* burrow

GOPHERS ▸ gopher

GOPIK *n* money unit of Azerbaijan

GOPIKS ▸ gopik

GOPURA *n* gateway tower of an Indian temple

GOPURAM *same as* ▸ **gopura**

GOPURAS ▸ gopura

GOR *interj* God!

GORA *n* (in informal Indian English) White or fair-skinned male

GORAL *n* small S Asian goat antelope with a yellowish-grey and black coat and small conical horns

GORALS ▸ goral

GORAMY ▸ gourami

GORAS ▸ gora

GORCOCK *n* male of the red grouse

GORCROW *n* carrion crow

GORDITA *n* small thick tortilla

GORE *n* blood from a wound ▷ *vb* pierce with horns

GORED ▸ gore

GORES ▸ gore

GORGE *n* deep narrow valley ▷ *vb* eat greedily

GORGED ▸ gorge

GORGER ▸ gorge

GORGERS ▸ gorge

GORGES ▸ gorge
GORGET n collar-like piece of armour worn to protect the throat
GORGETS ▸ gorget
GORGIA n improvised sung passage
GORGIAS ▸ gorgia
GORGING ▸ gorge
GORGIO n word used by gypsies for a non-gypsy
GORGIOS ▸ gorgio
GORGON n terrifying or repulsive woman
GORGONS ▸ gorgon
GORHEN n female red grouse
GORHENS ▸ gorhen
GORI n in informal Indian English, a White or fair-skinned female
GORIER ▸ gory
GORIEST ▸ gory
GORILLA n largest of the apes, found in Africa
GORILY ▸ gory
GORING ▸ gore
GORINGS ▸ gore
GORIS ▸ gori
GORM n foolish person ▷ vb understand
GORMAND same as > **gourmand**
GORMED ▸ gorm
GORMIER ▸ gormy
GORMING ▸ gorm
GORMS ▸ gorm
GORMY adj gormless
GORP same as ▸ **gawp**
GORPED ▸ gawp
GORPING ▸ gawp
GORPS ▸ gawp
GORSE n prickly yellow-flowered shrub
GORSEDD n meeting of bards and druids held daily before an eisteddfod
GORSES ▸ gorse
GORSIER ▸ gorse
GORSOON n young boy
GORSY ▸ gorse
GORY adj horrific or bloodthirsty
GOS ▸ go
GOSH interj exclamation of mild surprise or wonder
GOSHAWK n large hawk
GOSHT n Indian meat dish
GOSHTS ▸ gosht
GOSLET n pygmy goose
GOSLETS ▸ goslet
GOSLING n young goose
GOSPEL n any of the first

four books of the New Testament ▷ adj denoting a kind of religious music originating in the churches of the Black people in the Southern US ▷ vb teach the gospel
GOSPELS ▸ gospel
GOSPODA > gospodin
GOSPORT n aeroplane communication device
GOSS vb spit
GOSSAN n oxidised portion of a mineral vein in rock
GOSSANS ▸ gossan
GOSSE same as ▸ **gorse**
GOSSED ▸ goss
GOSSES ▸ gosse
GOSSIB n gossip
GOSSIBS ▸ gossib
GOSSING ▸ goss
GOSSIP n idle talk, esp about other people ▷ vb engage in gossip
GOSSIPS ▸ gossip
GOSSIPY ▸ gossip
GOSSOON n boy, esp a servant boy
GOSTER vb laugh uncontrollably
GOSTERS ▸ goster
GOT ▸ get
GOTCHA adj as in **gotcha lizard** Australian name for a crocodile
GOTCHAS ▸ gotcha
GOTH n aficionado of Goth music and fashion
GOTHIC adj of or relating to a literary style characterized by gloom, the grotesque, and the supernatural ▷ n family of heavy script typefaces
GOTHICS ▸ gothic
GOTHITE same as > **goethite**
GOTHS ▸ goth
GOTTA vb got to
GOTTEN past participle of ▸ **get**
GOUACHE n (painting using) watercolours mixed with glue
GOUCH vb become drowsy or lethargic under the influence of narcotics
GOUCHED ▸ gouch
GOUCHES ▸ gouch
GOUGE vb scoop or force out ▷ n hole or groove
GOUGED ▸ gouge
GOUGER n person or tool that gouges

GOUGERE n choux pastry flavoured with cheese
GOUGERS ▸ gouger
GOUGES ▸ gouge
GOUGING ▸ gouge
GOUJON n small strip of fish or chicken, coated in breadcrumbs and deep-fried
GOUJONS ▸ goujon
GOUK same as ▸ **gowk**
GOUKS ▸ gouk
GOULASH n rich stew seasoned with paprika
GOURA n large, crested ground pigeon found in New Guinea
GOURAMI n large SE Asian labyrinth fish used for food and (when young) as an aquarium fish
GOURAS ▸ goura
GOURD n fleshy fruit of a climbing plant
GOURDE n standard monetary unit of Haiti, divided into 100 centimes
GOURDES ▸ gourde
GOURDS ▸ gourd
GOURDY adj (of horses) swollen-legged
GOURMET n connoisseur of food and drink
GOUSTY adj dismal
GOUT n disease causing inflammation of the joints
GOUTFLY n fly whose larvae infect crops
GOUTIER ▸ gout
GOUTILY ▸ gout
GOUTS ▸ gout
GOUTTE n in heraldry, charge shaped like a drop of liquid
GOUTTES ▸ goutte
GOUTY ▸ gout
GOV n boss
GOVERN vb rule, direct, or control ▷ n ability to be governed
GOVERNS ▸ govern
GOVS ▸ gov
GOWAN n any of various yellow or white flowers growing in fields, esp the common daisy
GOWANED ▸ gowan
GOWANS ▸ gowan
GOWANY ▸ gowan
GOWD Scots word for ▸ **gold**
GOWDER ▸ gowd
GOWDEST ▸ gowd
GOWDS ▸ gowd

GOWF *vb* strike
GOWFED ▸ gowf
GOWFER ▸ gowf
GOWFERS ▸ gowf
GOWFING ▸ gowf
GOWFS ▸ gowf
GOWK *n* stupid person
GOWKS ▸ gowk
GOWL *n* substance often found in the corner of the eyes after sleep ▷ *vb* howl
GOWLAN *same as* ▸ **gollan**
GOWLAND *same as* ▸ **gollan**
GOWLANS ▸ gowlan
GOWLED ▸ gowl
GOWLING ▸ gowl
GOWLS ▸ gowl
GOWN *n* woman's long formal dress ▷ *vb* supply with or dress in a gown
GOWNBOY *n* foundationer schoolboy who wears a gown
GOWNED ▸ gown
GOWNING ▸ gown
GOWNMAN *n* professional person, such as a lawyer, who wears a gown
GOWNMEN ▸ gownman
GOWNS ▸ gown
GOWPEN *n* pair of cupped hands
GOWPENS ▸ gowpen
GOX *n* gaseous oxygen

> **Gox** is gaseous oxygen, especially useful if you can use it to hit a bonus square.

GOXES ▸ gox
GOYLE *n* ravine
GOYLES ▸ goyle
GOZZAN *same as* ▸ **gossan**
GOZZANS ▸ gozzan
GRAAL *n* holy grail
GRAALS ▸ graal
GRAB *vb* grasp suddenly, snatch ▷ *n* sudden snatch
GRABBED ▸ grab
GRABBER ▸ grab
GRABBLE *vb* scratch or feel about with the hands
GRABBY *adj* greedy or selfish
GRABEN *n* elongated trough of land produced by subsidence of the earth's crust between two faults
GRABENS ▸ graben
GRABS ▸ grab
GRACE *n* beauty and elegance ▷ *vb* honour
GRACED ▸ grace
GRACES ▸ grace

GRACILE *adj* gracefully thin or slender
GRACING ▸ grace
GRACKLE *n* American songbird with a dark iridescent plumage
GRAD *n* graduate
GRADATE *vb* change or cause to change imperceptibly, as from one colour, tone, or degree to another
GRADDAN *vb* dress corn
GRADE *n* place on a scale of quality, rank, or size ▷ *vb* arrange in grades
GRADED ▸ grade
GRADELY *adj* fine
GRADER *n* person or thing that grades
GRADERS ▸ grader
GRADES ▸ grade
GRADIN *n* ledge above or behind an altar on which candles, a cross, or other ornaments stand
GRADINE *same as* ▸ **gradin**
GRADING ▸ grade
GRADINI ▸ gradino
GRADINO *n* step above an altar
GRADINS ▸ gradin
GRADS ▸ grad
GRADUAL *adj* occurring, developing, or moving in small stages ▷ *n* antiphon or group of several antiphons, usually from the Psalms, sung or recited immediately after the epistle at Mass
GRADUS *n* book of études or other musical exercises arranged in order of increasing difficulty
GRAFF *same as* ▸ **graft**
GRAFFED ▸ graff
GRAFFS ▸ graff
GRAFT *n* surgical transplant of skin or tissue ▷ *vb* transplant (living tissue) surgically
GRAFTED ▸ graft
GRAFTER ▸ graft
GRAFTS ▸ graft
GRAHAM *n* made of graham flour
GRAHAMS ▸ graham
GRAIL *n* any desired ambition or goal
GRAILE *same as* ▸ **grail**
GRAILES ▸ graile
GRAILS ▸ grail

GRAIN *n* seedlike fruit of a cereal plant ▷ *vb* paint in imitation of the grain of wood or leather
GRAINE *n* eggs of the silkworm
GRAINED ▸ grain
GRAINER ▸ grain
GRAINES ▸ graine
GRAINS ▸ grain
GRAINY *adj* resembling, full of, or composed of grain
GRAIP *n* long-handled gardening fork
GRAIPS ▸ graip
GRAITH *vb* clothe
GRAITHS ▸ graith
GRAKLE *same as* ▸ **grackle**
GRAKLES ▸ grakle
GRAM *n* metric unit of mass equal to one thousandth of a kilogram
GRAMA *n* type of grass of W North America and S America, often used as a pasture grass
GRAMARY *same as* > **gramarye**
GRAMAS ▸ grama
GRAMASH *n* type of gaiter
GRAME *n* sorrow
GRAMES ▸ grame
GRAMMA *n* pasture grass of the South American plains
GRAMMAR *n* branch of linguistics dealing with the form, function, and order of words
GRAMMAS ▸ gramma
GRAMME *same as* ▸ **grame**
GRAMMES ▸ gram
GRAMP *n* grandfather
GRAMPA *same as* ▸ **grandpa**
GRAMPAS ▸ grampa
GRAMPS ▸ gramp
GRAMPUS *n* dolphin-like mammal
GRAMS ▸ gram
GRAN *n* grandmother
GRANA ▸ granum
GRANARY *n* storehouse for grain
GRAND *adj* large or impressive, imposing ▷ *n* thousand pounds or dollars
GRANDAD *n* grandfather
GRANDAM *n* archaic word for grandmother
GRANDE *feminine form of* ▸ **grand**
GRANDEE *n* Spanish nobleman of the highest rank**

GRANDER ▸ grand
GRANDLY ▸ grand
GRANDMA n grandmother
GRANDPA n grandfather
GRANDS ▸ grand
GRANFER n grandfather
GRANGE n country house with farm buildings
GRANGER n keeper or member of a grange
GRANGES ▸ grange
GRANITA n Italian iced drink
GRANITE n very hard igneous rock often used in building
GRANNAM n old woman
GRANNIE vb defeat (in a game or contest) so that one's opponent does not score a single point
GRANNOM n type of caddis fly esteemed as a bait by anglers
GRANNY n grandmother ▷ vb defeat (in a game or contest) so that one's opponent does not score a single point
GRANOLA n muesli-like breakfast cereal
GRANS ▸ gran
GRANT vb consent to fulfil (a request) ▷ n sum of money provided by a government for a specific purpose, such as education
GRANTED ▸ grant
GRANTEE n person to whom a grant is made
GRANTER ▸ grant
GRANTOR n person who makes a grant
GRANTS ▸ grant
GRANULE n small grain
GRANUM n membrane layers in a chloroplast
GRAPE n small juicy green or purple berry, eaten raw or used to produce wine, raisins, currants, or sultanas ▷ vb grope
GRAPED ▸ grape
GRAPERY n building where grapes are grown
GRAPES n abnormal growth, resembling a bunch of grapes, on the fetlock of a horse
GRAPEY ▸ grape
GRAPH n drawing showing the relation of different numbers or quantities

plotted against a set of axes ▷ vb draw or represent in a graph
GRAPHED ▸ graph
GRAPHIC adj vividly descriptive
GRAPHS ▸ graph
GRAPIER ▸ grape
GRAPING ▸ grape
GRAPLE same as ▸ grapple
GRAPLES ▸ graple
GRAPLIN same as ▸ grapnel
GRAPNEL n device with several hooks, used to grasp or secure things
GRAPPA n spirit distilled from the fermented remains of grapes after pressing
GRAPPAS ▸ grappa
GRAPPLE vb try to cope with (something difficult) ▷ n grapnel
GRAPY ▸ grape
GRASP vb grip something firmly ▷ n grip or clasp
GRASPED ▸ grasp
GRASPER ▸ grasp
GRASPS ▸ grasp
GRASS n common type of plant with jointed stems and long narrow leaves, including cereals and bamboo ▷ vb cover with grass
GRASSED ▸ grass
GRASSER n police informant
GRASSES ▸ grass
GRASSUM n in Scots law, lump sum paid when taking up a lease
GRASSY adj covered with, containing, or resembling grass
GRASTE archaic past participle of ▸ grace
GRAT ▸ greet
GRATE vb rub into small bits on a rough surface ▷ n framework of metal bars for holding fuel in a fireplace
GRATED ▸ grate
GRATER n tool with a sharp surface for grating food
GRATERS ▸ grater
GRATES ▸ grate
GRATIFY vb satisfy or please ▷ adj giving one satisfaction or pleasure
GRATIN n crust of browned breadcrumbs

GRATINE adj cooked au gratin
GRATING adj harsh or rasping ▷ n framework of metal bars covering an opening
GRATINS ▸ gratin
GRATIS adj free, for nothing
GRAUNCH vb crush or destroy
GRAUPEL n soft hail or snow pellets
GRAV n unit of acceleration equal to the standard acceleration of free fall
GRAVE n hole for burying a corpse ▷ adj causing concern ▷ vb cut, carve, sculpt, or engrave ▷ adv to be performed in a solemn manner
GRAVED ▸ grave
GRAVEL n mixture of small stones and coarse sand ▷ vb cover with gravel
GRAVELS ▸ gravel
GRAVELY ▸ grave
GRAVEN ▸ grave
GRAVER n any of various engraving, chasing, or sculpting tools, such as a burin
GRAVERS ▸ graver
GRAVES ▸ grave
GRAVEST ▸ grave
GRAVID adj pregnant
GRAVIDA n pregnant woman
GRAVIES ▸ gravy
GRAVING ▸ grave
GRAVIS adj as in myasthenia gravis chronic muscle-weakening disease
GRAVITY n force of attraction of one object for another, esp of objects to the earth
GRAVLAX n dry-cured salmon, marinated in salt, sugar, and spices, as served in Scandinavia
GRAVS ▸ grav
GRAVURE n method of intaglio printing using a plate with many small etched recesses
GRAVY n juices from meat in cooking
GRAY same as ▸ grey
GRAYED ▸ gray
GRAYER ▸ gray
GRAYEST ▸ gray

GRAYFLY n trumpet fly

GRAYING ▸ gray

GRAYISH ▸ gray

GRAYLAG same as ▸ greylag

GRAYLE n holy grail

GRAYLES ▸ grayle

GRAYLY ▸ gray

GRAYOUT n in aeronautics, impairment of vision due to lack of oxygen

GRAYS ▸ gray

GRAZE vb feed on grass ▷ n slight scratch or scrape

GRAZED ▸ graze

GRAZER ▸ graze

GRAZERS ▸ graze

GRAZES ▸ graze

GRAZIER n person who feeds cattle for market

GRAZING n land on which grass for livestock is grown

GREASE n soft melted animal fat ▷ vb apply grease to

GREASED ▸ grease

GREASER n mechanic, esp of motor vehicles

GREASES ▸ grease

GREASY adj covered with or containing grease ▷ n shearer

GREAT adj large in size or number ▷ n distinguished person

GREATEN vb make or become great

GREATER ▸ great

GREATLY ▸ great

GREATS ▸ great

GREAVE n piece of armour for the shin ▷ vb grieve

GREAVED ▸ greave

GREAVES pl n residue left after the rendering of tallow

GREBE n diving water bird

GREBES ▸ grebe

GREBO ▸ greebo

GREBOS ▸ greebo

GRECE n flight of steps

GRECES ▸ grece

GRECIAN same as ▸ grece

GRECISE same as ▸ graecize

GRECIZE same as ▸ graecize

GRECQUE n ornament of Greek origin

GREE n superiority or victory ▷ vb come or cause to come to agreement or harmony

GREEBO n unkempt or dirty-looking young man

GREECE same as ▸ grece

GREECES ▸ greece

GREED n excessive desire for food, wealth, etc

GREEDS ▸ greed

GREEDY adj having an excessive desire for something, such as food or money

GREEING ▸ gree

GREEK vb represent text as grey lines on a computer screen

GREEKED ▸ greek

GREEN adj of a colour between blue and yellow ▷ n colour between blue and yellow ▷ vb make or become green

GREENED ▸ green

GREENER n recent immigrant

GREENIE n conservationist

GREENLY ▸ green

GREENS ▸ green

GREENTH n greenness

GREENY ▸ green

GREES ▸ gree

GREESE same as ▸ grece

GREESES ▸ greese

GREET vb meet with expressions of welcome ▷ n weeping

GREETE same as ▸ greet

GREETED ▸ greet

GREETER n person who greets people at the entrance of a shop, restaurant, casino, etc

GREETES ▸ greete

GREETS ▸ greet

GREGALE n northeasterly wind occurring in the Mediterranean

GREGE vb make heavy

GREGO n short, thick jacket

GREGOS ▸ grego

GREIGE adj (of a fabric or material) not yet dyed ▷ n unbleached or undyed cloth or yarn

GREIGES ▸ greige

GREIN vb desire fervently

GREINED ▸ grein

GREINS ▸ grein

GREISEN n light-coloured metamorphic rock consisting mainly of quartz, white mica, and topaz formed by the pneumatolysis of granite

GREISLY same as ▸ grisly

GREMIAL n cloth spread upon the lap of a bishop when seated during Mass

GREMLIN n imaginary being blamed for mechanical malfunctions

GREMMIE n young surfer

GREMMY same as ▸ gremmie

GREN same as ▸ grin

GRENADE n small bomb thrown by hand or fired from a rifle

GRENNED ▸ gren

GRENS ▸ gren

GRESE same as ▸ grece

GRESES ▸ grese

GREVE same as ▸ greave

GREVES ▸ greve

GREW vb shudder

GREWED ▸ grow

GREWING ▸ grow

GREWS ▸ grow

GREX n group of plants that has arisen from the same hybrid parent group

GREXES ▸ grex

GREY adj of a colour between black and white ▷ n grey colour ▷ vb become or make grey

GREYED ▸ grey

GREYER ▸ grey

GREYEST ▸ grey

GREYHEN n female of the black grouse

GREYING ▸ grey

GREYISH ▸ grey

GREYLAG n large grey goose

GREYLY ▸ grey

GREYS ▸ grey

GRIBBLE n type of small marine crustacean which bores into and damages submerged wooden structures such as wharves

GRICE vb (of a railway enthusiast) to collect objects or visit places connected with trains and railways ▷ n object collected or place visited by a railway enthusiast

GRICED ▸ grice

GRICER ▸ grice

GRICERS ▸ grice

GRICES ▸ grice

GRICING ▸ grice

GRID n network of horizontal and vertical lines, bars, etc

GRIDDED ▸ grid

GRIDDER n American football player

GRIDDLE n flat iron plate for cooking ▷ vb cook (food) on a griddle

GRIDE vb grate or scrape harshly ▷ n harsh or piercing sound

GRIDED ▸ gride

GRIDES ▸ gride

GRIDING ▸ gride

GRIDS ▸ grid

GRIECE same as ▸ grece

GRIECED ▸ griece

GRIECES ▸ griece

GRIEF n deep sadness

GRIEFER n online game player who intentionally spoils the game for other players

GRIEFS ▸ grief

GRIESIE same as ▸ grisy

GRIESLY same as ▸ grisy

GRIESY same as ▸ grisy

GRIEVE vb (cause to) feel grief ▷ n farm manager or overseer

GRIEVED ▸ grieve

GRIEVER ▸ grieve

GRIEVES ▸ grieve

GRIFF n information

GRIFFE n carved ornament at the base of a column, often in the form of a claw

GRIFFES ▸ griffe

GRIFFIN n mythical monster with an eagle's head and wings and a lion's body

GRIFFON same as ▸ griffin

GRIFFS ▸ griff

GRIFT vb swindle

GRIFTED ▸ grift

GRIFTER ▸ grift

GRIFTS ▸ grift

GRIG n lively person ▷ vb fish for grigs

GRIGGED ▸ grig

GRIGRI n African talisman, amulet, or charm

GRIGRIS ▸ grigri

GRIGS ▸ grig

GRIKE n solution fissure, a vertical crack about 0.5 m wide formed by the dissolving of limestone by water, that divides an exposed limestone surface into sections or clints

GRIKES ▸ grike

GRILL n device on a cooker that radiates heat downwards ▷ vb cook under a grill

GRILLE n grating over an opening

GRILLED adj cooked on a grill or gridiron

GRILLER ▸ grill

GRILLES ▸ grille

GRILLS ▸ grill

GRILSE n salmon on its first return from the sea to fresh water

GRILSES ▸ grilse

GRIM adj stern

GRIMACE n ugly or distorted facial expression of pain, disgust, etc ▷ vb make a grimace

GRIME n ingrained dirt ▷ vb make very dirty

GRIMED ▸ grime

GRIMES ▸ grime

GRIMIER ▸ grime

GRIMILY ▸ grime

GRIMING ▸ grime

GRIMLY ▸ grim

GRIMMER ▸ grim

GRIMY ▸ grime

GRIN vb smile broadly, showing the teeth ▷ n broad smile

GRINCH n person whose lack of enthusiasm or bad temper has a depressing effect on others

GRIND vb crush or rub to a powder ▷ n hard work

GRINDED obsolete past participle of ▸ grind

GRINDER n device for grinding substances

GRINDS ▸ grind

GRINNED ▸ grin

GRINNER ▸ grin

GRINS ▸ grin

GRIOT n (in Western Africa) member of a caste responsible for maintaining an oral record of tribal history in the form of music, poetry, and storytelling

GRIOTS ▸ griot

GRIP n firm hold or grasp ▷ vb grasp or hold tightly

GRIPE vb complain persistently ▷ n complaint

GRIPED ▸ gripe

GRIPER ▸ gripe

GRIPERS ▸ gripe

GRIPES ▸ gripe

GRIPEY adj causing gripes

GRIPIER ▸ gripey

GRIPING ▸ gripe

GRIPLE same as ▸ gripple

GRIPMAN n cable-car operator

GRIPMEN ▸ gripman

GRIPPE former name for > influenza

GRIPPED ▸ grip

GRIPPER ▸ grip

GRIPPES ▸ grippe

GRIPPLE adj greedy ▷ n hook

GRIPPY adj having grip

GRIPS ▸ grip

GRIPT archaic variant of ▸ gripped

GRIPY same as ▸ gripey

GRIS same as ▸ grece

GRISE vb shudder

GRISED ▸ grise

GRISELY same as ▸ grisly

GRISES ▸ grise

GRISING ▸ grise

GRISKIN n lean part of a loin of pork

GRISLED another word for > grizzled

GRISLY adj horrifying or ghastly ▷ n large American bear

GRISON n type of mammal of Central and S America with a greyish back and black face and underparts

GRISONS ▸ grison

GRIST n grain for grinding

GRISTER n device for grinding grain

GRISTLE n tough stringy animal tissue found in meat

GRISTLY ▸ gristle

GRISTS ▸ grist

GRISY adj grim

GRIT n rough particles of sand ▷ vb spread grit on (an icy road etc) ▷ adj great

GRITH n security, peace, or protection, guaranteed either in a certain place, such as a church, or for a period of time

GRITHS ▸ grith

GRITS ▸ grit

GRITTED ▸ grit

GRITTER n vehicle that spreads grit on the roads in icy weather

GRITTY adj courageous and tough

GRIVET n E African monkey with long white tufts of hair on either side of the face

GRIVETS ▸ grivet

GRIZE same as ▸ grece

GRIZES ▸ grize

GRIZZLE vb whine or complain ▷ n grey colour

GRIZZLY n large American bear ▷ adj somewhat grey

GROAN n deep sound of grief or pain ▷ vb utter a groan

GROANED ▸ **groan**

GROANER n person or thing that groans

GROANS ▸ **groan**

GROAT n fourpenny piece

GROATS pl n hulled and crushed grain of various cereals

GROCER n shopkeeper selling foodstuffs

GROCERS ▸ **grocer**

GROCERY n business or premises of a grocer

GROCKED ▸ **grokked**

GROCKLE n tourist, esp one from the Midlands or the North of England

GRODIER ▸ **grody**

GRODY adj unpleasant

GROG n spirit, usu rum, and water ▷ vb drink grog

GROGGED ▸ **grog**

GROGGY adj faint, shaky, or dizzy

GROGRAM n coarse fabric of silk, wool, or silk mixed with wool or mohair, often stiffened with gum, formerly used for clothing

GROGS ▸ **grog**

GROIN n place where the legs join the abdomen ▷ vb provide or construct with groins

GROINED ▸ **groin**

GROINS ▸ **groin**

GROK vb understand completely and intuitively

GROKED ▸ **grokked**

GROKING > **grokking**

GROKKED ▸ **grok**

GROKS ▸ **grok**

GROMA n Roman surveying instrument

GROMAS ▸ **groma**

GROMET same as ▸ **grommet**

GROMETS ▸ **gromet**

GROMMET n ring or eyelet

GRONE obsolete word for ▸ **groan**

GRONED ▸ **grone**

GRONES ▸ **grone**

GRONING ▸ **grone**

GROOF n face, or front of the body

GROOFS ▸ **groof**

GROOLY adj gruesome

GROOM n person who looks after horses ▷ vb make or keep one's clothes and appearance neat and tidy

GROOMED ▸ **groom**

GROOMER ▸ **groom**

GROOMS ▸ **groom**

GROOVE n long narrow channel in a surface

GROOVED ▸ **groove**

GROOVER n device that makes grooves

GROOVES ▸ **groove**

GROOVY adj attractive or exciting

GROPE vb feel about or search uncertainly ▷ n instance of groping

GROPED ▸ **grope**

GROPER n type of large fish of warm and tropical seas

GROPERS ▸ **groper**

GROPES ▸ **grope**

GROPING ▸ **grope**

GROSER n gooseberry

GROSERS ▸ **groser**

GROSERT another word for ▸ **groser**

GROSET another word for ▸ **groser**

GROSETS ▸ **groset**

GROSS adj flagrant ▷ n twelve dozen ▷ vb make as total revenue before deductions ▷ interj exclamation indicating disgust

GROSSED ▸ **gross**

GROSSER ▸ **gross**

GROSSES ▸ **gross**

GROSSLY ▸ **gross**

GROSZ n Polish monetary unit worth one hundredth of a zloty

GROSZE ▸ **grosz**

GROSZY ▸ **grosz**

GROT n rubbish

GROTS ▸ **grot**

GROTTO n small picturesque cave

GROTTOS ▸ **grotto**

GROTTY adj nasty or in bad condition

GROUCH vb grumble or complain ▷ n person who is always complaining

GROUCHY adj bad-tempered

GROUF same as ▸ **groof**

GROUFS ▸ **grouf**

GROUGH n natural channel or fissure in a peat moor

GROUGHS ▸ **grough**

GROUND n surface of the earth ▷ adj on or of the ground ▷ vb base or establish

GROUNDS ▸ **ground**

GROUP n number of people or things regarded as a unit ▷ vb place or form into a group

GROUPED ▸ **group**

GROUPER n large edible sea fish

GROUPIE n ardent fan of a celebrity or of a sport or activity

GROUPS ▸ **group**

GROUPY same as ▸ **groupie**

GROUSE n stocky game bird ▷ vb grumble or complain ▷ adj fine or excellent ▷ adj excellent

GROUSED ▸ **grouse**

GROUSER ▸ **grouse**

GROUSES ▸ **grouse**

GROUT n thin mortar ▷ vb fill up with grout

GROUTED ▸ **grout**

GROUTER ▸ **grout**

GROUTS pl n sediment or grounds, as from making coffee

GROUTY adj sullen or surly

GROVE n small group of trees

GROVED ▸ **grove**

GROVEL vb behave humbly in order to win a superior's favour

GROVELS ▸ **grovel**

GROVES ▸ **grove**

GROVET n wrestling hold in which a wrestler in a kneeling position grips the head of his kneeling opponent with one arm and forces his shoulders down with the other

GROVETS ▸ **grovet**

GROW vb develop physically

GROWER n person who grows plants

GROWERS ▸ **grower**

GROWING ▸ **grow**

GROWL vb make a low rumbling sound ▷ n growling sound

GROWLED ▸ **growl**

GROWLER n person, animal, or thing that growls

GROWLS ▸ **growl**

GROWLY ▸ **growl**

GROWN ▸ **grow**

G

GROWNUP n adult

GROWS ▸ grow

GROWTH n growing ▷ adj of or relating to growth

GROWTHS ▸ growth

GROWTHY adj rapid-growing

GROYNE n wall built out from the shore to control erosion

GROYNES ▸ groyne

GROZING adj as in **grozing iron** iron for smoothing joints between lead pipes

GRRL n as in **riot grrl** young woman who plays or enjoys an aggressively feminist style of punk rock music

| This slang term for a girl who likes loud rock music can come in useful when you are short of vowels. And it can also be spelt **grrrl**.

GRRLS ▸ grrl

GRRRL n as in **riot grrrl** young woman who plays or enjoys an aggressively feminist style of punk rock music

GRRRLS ▸ grrrl

GRUB n legless insect larva ▷ vb search carefully for something by digging or by moving things about

GRUBBED ▸ grub

GRUBBER n person who grubs

GRUBBLE same as ▸ **grabble**

GRUBBY adj dirty

GRUBS ▸ grub

GRUDGE vb be unwilling to give or allow ▷ n resentment ▷ adj planned or carried out in order to settle a grudge

GRUDGED ▸ grudge

GRUDGER ▸ grudge

GRUDGES ▸ grudge

GRUE n shiver or shudder ▷ vb shiver or shudder

GRUED ▸ grue

GRUEING ▸ grue

GRUEL n thin porridge ▷ vb subject to exhausting experiences

GRUELED ▸ gruel

GRUELER ▸ gruel

GRUELS ▸ gruel

GRUES ▸ grue

GRUFE same as ▸ **groof**

GRUFES ▸ grufe

GRUFF adj rough or surly in manner or voice ▷ vb talk gruffly

GRUFFED ▸ gruff

GRUFFER ▸ gruff

GRUFFLY ▸ gruff

GRUFFS ▸ gruff

GRUFFY adj gruff

GRUFTED adj dirty

GRUGRU n tropical American palm with a spiny trunk and leaves and edible nuts

GRUGRUS ▸ grugru

GRUING ▸ grue

GRUM adj surly

GRUMBLE vb complain ▷ n complaint

GRUMBLY ▸ grumble

GRUME n clot

GRUMES ▸ grume

GRUMLY ▸ grum

GRUMMER ▸ grum

GRUMMET same as ▸ **grommet**

GRUMOSE same as ▸ **grumous**

GRUMOUS adj (esp of plant parts) consisting of granular tissue

GRUMP n surly or bad-tempered person ▷ vb complain or grumble

GRUMPED ▸ grump

GRUMPH vb grunt

GRUMPHS ▸ grumph

GRUMPHY same as ▸ **grumphie**

GRUMPS ▸ grump

GRUMPY adj bad-tempered

GRUND n as in **grund mail** payment for right of burial

GRUNGE n style of rock music with a fuzzy guitar sound

GRUNGER n fan of grunge music

GRUNGES ▸ grunge

GRUNGEY adj messy or dirty

GRUNGY adj squalid or seedy

GRUNION n Californian marine fish that spawns on beaches

GRUNT vb make a low short gruff sound, like a pig ▷ n pig's sound

GRUNTED ▸ grunt

GRUNTER n person or animal that grunts, esp a pig

GRUNTLE vb grunt or groan

GRUNTS ▸ grunt

GRUSHIE adj healthy and strong

GRUTCH vb grudge

GRUTTEN ▸ greet

GRUYERE n hard flat whole-milk cheese with holes

GRYCE same as ▸ **grice**

GRYCES ▸ gryce

GRYDE same as ▸ **gride**

GRYDED ▸ gryde

GRYDES ▸ gryde

GRYDING ▸ gryde

GRYESY adj grey

GRYFON same as ▸ **griffin**

GRYFONS ▸ gryfon

GRYKE same as ▸ **grike**

GRYKES ▸ gryke

GRYPE same as ▸ **gripe**

GRYPES ▸ gripe

GRYPHON same as ▸ **griffin**

GRYPT archaic form of ▸ **gripped**

GRYSBOK n small antelope of central and S Africa with small straight horns

GRYSELY same as ▸ **grisly**

GRYSIE same as ▸ **grisy**

GU same as ▸ **gju**

GUACO n any of several tropical American plants whose leaves are used as an antidote to snakebite

GUACOS ▸ guaco

GUAIAC same as > **guaiacum**

GUAIACS > **guaiacum**

GUAN n type of bird of Central and S America

GUANA another word for ▸ **iguana**

GUANACO n S American animal related to the llama

GUANAS ▸ guana

GUANASE n enzyme that converts guanine to xanthine by removal of an amino group

GUANAY n type of cormorant

GUANAYS ▸ guanay

GUANGO n rain tree

GUANGOS ▸ guango

GUANIN same as ▸ **guanine**

GUANINE n white almost insoluble compound: one of the purine bases in nucleic acids

GUANINS ▸ guanine

GUANO n dried sea-bird manure, used as fertilizer

GUANOS ▸ guano

GUANS ▸ guan

GUANXI n Chinese social concept based on the exchange of favours

GUANXIS ▶ **guanxi**

GUAR n Indian plant grown as a fodder crop and for the gum obtained from its seeds

GUARANA n type of shrub native to Venezuela

GUARANI n standard monetary unit of Paraguay, divided into 100 céntimos

GUARD vb watch over to protect or to prevent escape ▷ n person or group that guards

GUARDED adj cautious or noncommittal

GUARDEE n guardsman, esp considered as representing smartness and dash

GUARDER ▶ **guard**

GUARDS ▶ **guard**

GUARISH vb heal

GUARS ▶ **guar**

GUAVA n yellow-skinned tropical American fruit

GUAVAS ▶ **guava**

GUAYULE n bushy shrub of the southwestern US

GUB n white man ▷ vb hit or defeat

GUBBAH same as ▶ **gub**

GUBBAHS ▶ **gubbah**

GUBBED ▶ **gub**

GUBBING ▶ **gub**

GUBBINS n object of little or no value

GUBS ▶ **gub**

GUCK n slimy matter

GUCKIER ▶ **gucky**

GUCKS ▶ **guck**

GUCKY adj slimy and mucky

GUDDLE vb catch (fish) by groping with the hands under the banks or stones of a stream ▷ n muddle

GUDDLED ▶ **guddle**

GUDDLES ▶ **guddle**

GUDE Scots word for ▶ **good**

GUDEMAN n male householder

GUDEMEN ▶ **gudeman**

GUDES n goods

GUDGEON n small freshwater fish ▷ vb trick or cheat

GUE same as ▶ **gju**

GUELDER adj as in **guelder rose** kind of shrub

GUENON n slender Old World monkey of Africa with long hind limbs and tail and long hair surrounding the face

GUENONS ▶ **guenon**

GUERDON n reward or payment ▷ vb give a guerdon to

GUEREZA n handsome colobus monkey of the mountain forests of Ethiopsa

GUERITE n turret used by a sentry

GUES ▶ **gue**

GUESS vb estimate or draw a conclusion without proper knowledge ▷ n estimate or conclusion reached by guessing

GUESSED ▶ **guess**

GUESSER ▶ **guess**

GUESSES ▶ **guess**

GUEST n person entertained at another's house or at another's expense ▷ vb appear as a visiting player or performer

GUESTED ▶ **guest**

GUESTEN vb stay as a guest in someone's house

GUESTS ▶ **guest**

GUFF n nonsense

GUFFAW n crude noisy laugh ▷ vb laugh in this way

GUFFAWS ▶ **guffaw**

GUFFIE Scots word for ▶ **pig**

GUFFIES ▶ **guffie**

GUFFS ▶ **guff**

GUGA n gannet chick

GUGAS ▶ **guga**

GUGGLE vb drink making a gurgling sound

GUGGLED ▶ **guggle**

GUGGLES ▶ **guggle**

GUGLET same as ▶ **goglet**

GUGLETS ▶ **guglet**

GUICHET n grating, hatch, or small opening in a wall, esp a ticket-office window

GUID Scots word for ▶ **good**

GUIDAGE n guidance

GUIDE n person who conducts tour expeditions ▷ vb act as a guide for

GUIDED ▶ **guide**

GUIDER ▶ **guide**

GUIDERS ▶ **guide**

GUIDES ▶ **guide**

GUIDING ▶ **guide**

GUIDON n small pennant, used as a marker or standard, esp by cavalry regiments

GUIDONS ▶ **guidon**

GUIDS n possessions

GUILD n organization or club

GUILDER n former monetary unit of the Netherlands

GUILDRY n in Scotland, corporation of merchants in a burgh

GUILDS ▶ **guild**

GUILE n cunning or deceit ▷ vb deceive

GUILED ▶ **guile**

GUILER n deceiver

GUILERS ▶ **guiler**

GUILES ▶ **guile**

GUILING ▶ **guile**

GUILT n fact or state of having done wrong

GUILTS ▶ **guilt**

GUILTY adj responsible for an offence or misdeed

GUIMP same as ▶ **guimpe**

GUIMPE n short blouse with sleeves worn under a pinafore dress ▷ vb make with gimp

GUIMPED ▶ **guimpe**

GUIMPES ▶ **guimpe**

GUIMPS ▶ **guimp**

GUINEA n former British monetary unit worth 21 shillings (1.05 pounds)

GUINEAS ▶ **guinea**

GUIPURE n heavy lace that has its pattern connected by threads, rather than supported on a net mesh

GUIRO n percussion instrument made from a hollow gourd

GUIROS ▶ **guiro**

GUISARD n guiser

GUISE n false appearance ▷ vb disguise or be disguised in fancy dress

GUISED ▶ **guise**

GUISER n mummer, esp at Christmas or Halloween revels

GUISERS ▶ **guiser**

GUISES ▶ **guise**

GUISING ▶ **guise**

GUITAR n stringed instrument with a flat back and a long neck, played by plucking or strumming

GUITARS ▶ **guitar**

GUIZER same as ▶ **guiser**

GUIZERS ▶ **guizer**

G

G

GUL n design used in oriental carpets

GULA n gluttony

GULAG n forced-labour camp

GULAGS ▸ gulag

GULAR adj of, relating to, or situated in the throat or oesophagus

GULAS ▸ gula

GULCH n deep narrow valley ▷ vb swallow fast

GULCHED ▸ gulch

GULCHES ▸ gulch

GULDEN same as ▸ guilder

GULDENS ▸ gulden

GULE Scots word for > marigold

GULES n red in heraldry

GULET n wooden Turkish sailing boat

GULETS ▸ gulet

GULF n large deep bay ▷ vb swallow up

GULFED ▸ gulf

GULFIER ▸ gulf

GULFING ▸ gulf

GULFS ▸ gulf

GULFY ▸ gulf

GULL n long-winged sea bird ▷ vb cheat or deceive

GULLED ▸ gull

GULLER n deceiver

GULLERS ▸ guller

GULLERY n breeding-place for gulls

GULLET n muscular tube through which food passes from the mouth to the stomach

GULLETS ▸ gullet

GULLEY same as ▸ gully

GULLEYS ▸ gulley

GULLIED ▸ gully

GULLIES ▸ gully

GULLING ▸ gull

GULLISH adj stupid

GULLS ▸ gull

GULLY n channel cut by running water ▷ vb make (channels) in (the ground, sand, etc)

GULP vb swallow hastily ▷ n gulping

GULPED ▸ gulp

GULPER ▸ gulp

GULPERS ▸ gulp

GULPH archaic word for ▸ gulf

GULPHS ▸ gulph

GULPIER ▸ gulp

GULPING ▸ gulp

GULPS ▸ gulp

GULPY ▸ gulp

GULS ▸ gul

GULY adj relating to gules

GUM n firm flesh in which the teeth are set ▷ vb stick with gum

GUMBALL n round piece of chewing gum

GUMBO n mucilaginous pods of okra

GUMBOIL n abscess on the gum

GUMBOOT n rubber boot

GUMBOS ▸ gumbo

GUMDROP n hard jelly-like sweet

GUMLESS ▸ gum

GUMLIKE ▸ gum

GUMLINE n line where gums meet teeth

GUMMA n rubbery tumour characteristic of advanced syphilis, occurring esp on the skin, liver, brain or heart

GUMMAS ▸ gumma

GUMMATA ▸ gumma

GUMMED ▸ gum

GUMMER n punch-cutting tool

GUMMERS ▸ gummer

GUMMIER ▸ gummy

GUMMIES ▸ gummy

GUMMILY ▸ gummy

GUMMING ▸ gum

GUMMITE n orange or yellowish amorphous secondary mineral consisting of hydrated uranium oxides

GUMMOSE same as ▸ gummous

GUMMOUS adj resembling or consisting of gum

GUMMY adj toothless ▷ n type of small crustacean-eating shark whose mouth has bony ridges resembling gums

GUMNUT n hardened seed container of the gumtree

GUMNUTS ▸ gumnut

GUMP vb guddle

GUMPED ▸ gump

GUMPING ▸ gump

GUMPS ▸ gump

GUMS ▸ gum

GUMSHOE n waterproof overshoe ▷ vb act stealthily

GUMTREE n any of various trees that yield gum, such as the eucalyptus, sweet gum, and sour gum

GUMWEED n any of several American yellow-flowered plants that have sticky flower heads

GUMWOOD same as ▸ gumtree

GUN n weapon with a metal tube from which missiles are fired by explosion ▷ vb cause (an engine) to run at high speed

GUNBOAT n small warship

GUNDIES ▸ gundy

GUNDOG n dog trained to work with a hunter or gamekeeper

GUNDOGS ▸ gundog

GUNDY n toffee

GUNFIRE n repeated firing of guns

GUNG adj as in gung ho extremely or excessively enthusiastic about something

GUNGE n sticky unpleasant substance ▷ vb block or encrust with gunge

GUNGED ▸ gunge

GUNGES ▸ gunge

GUNGIER ▸ gunge

GUNGING ▸ gunge

GUNGY ▸ gunge

GUNITE n cement-sand mortar that is sprayed onto formwork, walls, or rock by a compressed air ejector giving a very dense strong concrete layer: used to repair reinforced concrete, to line tunnel walls or mine airways, etc

GUNITES ▸ gunite

GUNK n slimy or filthy substance

GUNKIER ▸ gunk

GUNKS ▸ gunk

GUNKY ▸ gunk

GUNLESS ▸ gun

GUNLOCK n mechanism in some firearms that causes the charge to be exploded

GUNMAN n armed criminal

GUNMEN ▸ gunman

GUNNAGE n number of guns carried by a warship

GUNNED ▸ gun

GUNNEL same as ▸ gunwale

GUNNELS ▸ gunnel

GUNNEN ▸ gun

GUNNER n artillery soldier

GUNNERA n type of herbaceous plant found throughout the S hemisphere and cultivated

for its large leaves
GUNNERS ▸ gunner
GUNNERY n use or science of large guns
GUNNIES ▸ gunny
GUNNING ▸ gun
GUNNY n strong coarse fabric used for sacks
GUNPLAY n use of firearms, as by criminals
GUNPORT n porthole, or other, opening for a gun
GUNROOM n (esp in the Royal Navy) the mess allocated to subordinate or junior officers
GUNS ▸ gun
GUNSEL n catamite
GUNSELS ▸ gunsel
GUNSHIP n ship or helicopter armed with heavy guns
GUNSHOT n shot or range of a gun
GUNTER n type of gaffing in which the gaff is hoisted parallel to the mast
GUNTERS ▸ gunter
GUNWALE n top of a ship's side
GUNYAH n hut or shelter in the bush
GUNYAHS ▸ gunyah
GUP n gossip
GUPPIES ▸ guppy
GUPPY n small colourful aquarium fish
GUPS ▸ gup
GUQIN n type of Chinese zither
GUQINS ▸ guqin
GUR n unrefined cane sugar
GURAMI same as ▸ **gourami**
GURAMIS ▸ gurami
GURGE vb swallow up
GURGED ▸ gurge
GURGES ▸ gurge
GURGING ▸ gurge
GURGLE n bubbling noise ▷ vb (of water) to make low bubbling noises when flowing
GURGLED ▸ gurgle
GURGLES ▸ gurgle
GURGLET same as ▸ **goglet**
GURJUN n S or SE Asian tree that yields a resin
GURJUNS ▸ gurjun
GURL vb snarl
GURLED ▸ gurl
GURLET n type of pickaxe
GURLETS ▸ gurlet
GURLIER ▸ gurly

GURLING ▸ gurl
GURLS ▸ gurl
GURLY adj stormy
GURN variant spelling of ▸ **girn**
GURNARD n spiny armour-headed sea fish
GURNED ▸ gurn
GURNET same as ▸ **gurnard**
GURNETS ▸ gurnard
GURNEY n wheeled stretcher for transporting hospital patients
GURNEYS ▸ gurney
GURNING ▸ gurn
GURNS ▸ gurn
GURRAH n type of coarse muslin
GURRAHS ▸ gurrah
GURRIER n low-class tough ill-mannered person
GURRIES ▸ gurry
GURRY n dog-fight
GURS ▸ gur
GURSH n unit of currency in Saudi Arabia
GURSHES ▸ gursh
GURU n Hindu or Sikh religious teacher or leader
GURUDOM n state of being a guru
GURUISM ▸ guru
GURUS ▸ guru
GUS ▸ gu
GUSH vb flow out suddenly and profusely ▷ n sudden copious flow
GUSHED ▸ gush
GUSHER n spurting oil well
GUSHERS ▸ gusher
GUSHES ▸ gush
GUSHIER ▸ gushy
GUSHILY ▸ gushy
GUSHING ▸ gush
GUSHY adj displaying excessive admiration or sentimentality
GUSLA n Balkan single-stringed musical instrument
GUSLAR n player of the gusla
GUSLARS ▸ guslar
GUSLAS ▸ gusla
GUSLE same as ▸ **gusla**
GUSLES ▸ gusle
GUSLI n Russian harp-like musical instrument
GUSLIS ▸ gusli
GUSSET n piece of material sewn into a garment to strengthen it ▷ vb put a gusset in (a garment)

GUSSETS ▸ gusset
GUSSIE n young pig
GUSSIED ▸ gussy
GUSSIES ▸ gussy
GUSSY vb dress elaborately
GUST n sudden blast of wind ▷ vb blow in gusts
GUSTED ▸ gust
GUSTFUL adj tasty
GUSTIE adj tasty
GUSTIER ▸ gusty
GUSTILY ▸ gusty
GUSTING ▸ gust
GUSTO n enjoyment or zest
GUSTOES ▸ gusto
GUSTOS ▸ gusto
GUSTS ▸ gust
GUSTY adj blowing or occurring in gusts or characterized by blustery weather
GUT n intestine ▷ vb remove the guts from ▷ adj basic or instinctive
GUTCHER n grandfather
GUTFUL n bellyful
GUTFULS ▸ gutful
GUTLESS adj cowardly
GUTLIKE ▸ gut
GUTROT n diarrhoea
GUTROTS ▸ gutrot
GUTS vb devour greedily
GUTSED ▸ guts
GUTSER n as in come a gutser fall heavily to the ground
GUTSERS ▸ gutser
GUTSES ▸ guts
GUTSFUL n bellyful
GUTSIER ▸ gutsy
GUTSILY ▸ gutsy
GUTSING ▸ guts
GUTSY adj courageous
GUTTA n one of a set of small drop-like ornaments, esp as used on the architrave of a Doric entablature ▷ n rubber substance obtained from the coagulated latex of the guttapercha tree
GUTTAE ▸ gutta
GUTTAS ▸ gutta
GUTTATE adj (esp of plants) covered with small drops or drop-like markings, esp oil glands ▷ vb exude droplets of liquid
GUTTED ▸ gut
GUTTER n shallow channel for carrying away water from a roof or roadside ▷ vb (of a candle) burn

unsteadily, with wax running down the sides

GUTTERS ▸ **gutter**

GUTTERY ▸ **gutter**

GUTTIER ▸ **gutty**

GUTTIES ▸ **gutty**

GUTTING ▸ **gut**

GUTTLE *vb* eat greedily

GUTTLED ▸ **guttle**

GUTTLER ▸ **guttle**

GUTTLES ▸ **guttle**

GUTTY *n* urchin or delinquent ▷ *adj* courageous

GUTZER *n* bad fall

GUTZERS ▸ **gutzer**

GUV *informal name for* > **governor**

GUVS ▸ **guv**

GUY *n* man or boy ▷ *vb* make fun of

GUYED ▸ **guy**

GUYING ▸ **guy**

GUYLE *same as* ▸ **guile**

GUYLED ▸ **guyle**

GUYLER ▸ **guyle**

GUYLERS ▸ **guyle**

GUYLES ▸ **guyle**

GUYLINE *n* guy rope

GUYLING ▸ **guyle**

GUYOT *n* flat-topped submarine mountain, common in the Pacific Ocean, usually an extinct volcano whose summit did not reach above the sea surface

GUYOTS ▸ **guyot**

GUYS ▸ **guy**

GUYSE *same as* ▸ **guise**

GUYSES ▸ **guyse**

GUZZLE *vb* eat or drink greedily

GUZZLED ▸ **guzzle**

GUZZLER *n* person or thing that guzzles

GUZZLES ▸ **guzzle**

GWEDUC *same as* ▸ **geoduck**

GWEDUCK *same as* ▸ **geoduck**

GWEDUCS ▸ **gweduck**

GWINE *dialect form of* ▸ **going**

GWINIAD *n* powan

GWYNIAD *n* type of freshwater white fish occurring in Lake Bala in Wales

GYAL *same as* ▸ **gayal**

GYALS ▸ **gyal**

GYBE *vb* (of a fore-and-aft sail) swing suddenly from one side to the other ▷ *n* instance of gybing

GYBED ▸ **gybe**

GYBES ▸ **gybe**

GYBING ▸ **gybe**

GYELD *n* guild

GYELDS ▸ **gyeld**

GYLDEN *adj* golden

GYM *n* gymnasium

GYMBAL *same as* ▸ **gimbal**

GYMBALS ▸ **gymbal**

GYMMAL *same as* ▸ **gimmal**

GYMMALS ▸ **gymmal**

GYMNAST *n* expert in gymnastics

GYMNIC *adj* gymnastic

GYMPIE *n* tall tree with stinging hairs on its leaves

GYMPIES ▸ **gympie**

GYMS ▸ **gym**

GYMSLIP *n* tunic or pinafore formerly worn by schoolgirls

GYNAE *adj* gynaecological ▷ *n* gynaecology

GYNAES ▸ **gynae**

GYNECIA > **gynecium**

GYNECIC *adj* relating to the female sex

GYNIE *n* gynaecology

GYNIES ▸ **gynie**

GYNNEY *n* guinea hen

GYNNEYS ▸ **gynney**

GYNNIES ▸ **gynny**

GYNNY *same as* ▸ **gynney**

GYNY *n* gynaecology

GYOZA *n* Japanese fried dumpling

GYOZAS ▸ **gyoza**

GYP *vb* swindle, cheat, or defraud ▷ *n* act of cheating

| This little word, meaning to swindle, can be useful when you are short of vowels.

GYPLURE *n* synthetic version of the gypsy moth sex pheromone

GYPPED ▸ **gyp**

GYPPER ▸ **gyp**

GYPPERS ▸ **gyp**

GYPPIE *same as* ▸ **gippy**

GYPPIES ▸ **gyppy**

GYPPING ▸ **gyp**

GYPPY *same as* ▸ **gippy**

GYPS ▸ **gyp**

GYPSIED ▸ **gypsy**

GYPSIES ▸ **gypsy**

GYPSTER *n* swindler

GYPSUM *n* chalklike mineral used to make plaster of Paris

GYPSUMS ▸ **gypsum**

GYPSY *n* member of a nomadic people scattered throughout Europe and North America ▷ *vb* live like a gypsy

GYRAL *adj* having a circular, spiral, or rotating motion

GYRALLY ▸ **gyral**

GYRANT *adj* gyrating

GYRASE *n* topoisomerase enzyme

GYRASES ▸ **gyrase**

GYRATE *vb* rotate or spiral about a point or axis ▷ *adj* curved or coiled into a circle

GYRATED ▸ **gyrate**

GYRATES ▸ **gyrate**

GYRATOR *n* electronic circuit that inverts the impedance

GYRE *n* circular or spiral movement or path ▷ *vb* whirl

GYRED ▸ **gyre**

GYRENE *n* nickname for a member of the US Marine Corps

GYRENES ▸ **gyrene**

GYRES ▸ **gyre**

GYRI ▸ **gyrus**

GYRING ▸ **gyre**

GYRO *n* gyrocompass: nonmagmetic compass that uses a motor-driven gyroscope to indicate true north

GYROCAR *n* two-wheeled car

GYRON *same as* ▸ **giron**

GYRONIC ▸ **gyron**

GYRONNY *same as* ▸ **gironny**

GYRONS ▸ **gyron**

GYROS ▸ **gyro**

GYROSE *adj* marked with sinuous lines

GYROUS *adj* gyrose

GYRUS *n* convolution

GYRUSES ▸ **gyrus**

GYTE *n* spoilt child

GYTES ▸ **gyte**

GYTRASH *n* spirit that haunts lonely roads

GYTTJA *n* sediment on lake bottom

GYTTJAS ▸ **gyttja**

GYVE *vb* shackle or fetter ▷ *n* fetters

GYVED ▸ **gyve**

GYVES ▸ **gyve**

GYVING ▸ **gyve**

G

Hh

H forms a two-letter word in front of every vowel except **U** (and you can make **uh** with **U**), making it a versatile tile when you want to form words in more than one direction. It also goes with **M** to make **hm**. As **H** is worth 4 points on its own, you can earn some very high scores by doing this: even **ha**, **he**, **hi** and **ho** will give 5 points each. There are lots of good short words beginning with **H**, like **haw, hew, how, hay, hey** and **hoy** (9 each), while **hyp** can be useful if you are short of vowels. More high-scoring words with **H** include **haj, hex** and **hox** for 13 points each, and never forget the invaluable **zho** for 15 points.

H

HA *interj* exclamation expressing triumph, surprise, or scorn
HAAF *n* deep-sea fishing ground off the Shetland and Orkney Islands
HAAFS ▸ **haaf**
HAAR *n* cold sea mist or fog off the North Sea
HAARS ▸ **haar**
HABDABS *n* highly nervous state
HABILE *adj* skilful
HABIT *n* established way of behaving ▷ *vb* clothe
HABITAN *same as* ▸ **habitant**
HABITAT *n* natural home of an animal or plant
HABITED *adj* dressed in a habit
HABITS ▸ **habit**
HABITUE *n* frequent visitor to a place
HABITUS *n* general physical state, esp with regard to susceptibility to disease
HABLE *old form of* ▸ **able**
HABOOB *n* sandstorm
HABOOBS ▸ **haboob**
HABU *n* large venomous snake
HABUS ▸ **habu**
HACEK *n* pronunciation symbol in Slavonic language
HACEKS ▸ **hacek**
HACHIS *n* hash
HACHURE *n* shading of

short lines drawn on a map to indicate the degree of steepness of a hill ▷ *vb* mark or show by hachures
HACK *vb* cut or chop violently ▷ *n* (inferior) writer or journalist ▷ *adj* unoriginal or of a low standard
HACKBUT *another word for* ▸ **arquebus**
HACKED ▸ **hack**
HACKEE *n* chipmunk
HACKEES ▸ **hackee**
HACKER *n* computer enthusiast, esp one who breaks into the computer system of a company or government
HACKERS ▸ **hacker**
HACKERY *n* journalism
HACKIE *n* US word meaning cab driver
HACKIES ▸ **hackie**
HACKING ▸ **hack**
HACKLE *same as* ▸ **heckle**
HACKLED ▸ **hackle**
HACKLER ▸ **hackle**
HACKLES *pl n* hairs on the back of the neck and the back of a dog, cat, etc, which rise when the animal is angry or afraid
HACKLET *n* kittiwake
HACKLY *adj* rough or jagged
HACKMAN *n* taxi driver
HACKMEN ▸ **hackman**
HACKNEY *n* taxi ▷ *vb* make commonplace and banal by

too frequent use
HACKS ▸ **hack**
HACKSAW *n* small saw for cutting metal ▷ *vb* cut with a hacksaw
HAD *vb* Scots form of hold
HADAL *adj* of, relating to, or constituting very deep zones of the oceans
HADARIM ▸ **heder**
HADAWAY *sentence substitute* exclamation urging the hearer to refrain from delay in the execution of a task
HADDEN ▸ **have**
HADDEST *same as* ▸ **hadst**
HADDIE *n* finnan haddock
HADDIES ▸ **haddie**
HADDING ▸ **have**
HADDOCK *n* edible sea fish of N Atlantic
HADE *n* angle made to the vertical by the plane of a fault or vein ▷ *vb* incline from the vertical
HADED ▸ **hade**
HADEDAH *n* large grey-green S African ibis
HADES ▸ **hade**
HADING ▸ **hade**
HADITH *n* body of tradition and legend about Mohammed and his followers, used as a basis of Islamic law
HADITHS ▸ **hadith**
HADJ *same as* ▸ **hajj**
HADJEE *same as* ▸ **hadji**
HADJEES ▸ **hadjee**

HADJES ▸ hadj
HADJI *same as* ▸ **hajji**
HADJIS ▸ hadji
HADROME *n* part of xylem
HADRON *n* any elementary particle capable of taking part in a strong nuclear interaction and therefore excluding leptons and photons
HADRONS ▸ hadron
HADS ▸ have
HADST *singular form of the past tense (indicative mood) of* ▸ **have**
HAE *Scots variant of* ▸ **have**
HAED ▸ hae
HAEING ▸ hae
HAEM *n* complex red organic pigment containing ferrous iron, present in haemoglobin
HAEMAL *adj* of the blood
HAEMIC *same as* > **haematic**
HAEMIN *n* haematin chloride
HAEMINS ▸ haemin
HAEMOID *same as* > **haematoid**
HAEMONY *n* plant mentioned in Milton's poetry
HAEMS ▸ haem
HAEN ▸ hae
HAERES *same as* ▸ **heres**
HAES ▸ hae
HAET *n* whit
HAETS ▸ haet
HAFF *n* lagoon
HAFFET *n* side of head
HAFFETS ▸ haffet
HAFFIT *same as* ▸ **haffet**
HAFFITS ▸ haffit
HAFFLIN *same as* > **halfling**
HAFFS ▸ haff
HAFIZ *n* title for a person who knows the Koran by heart
HAFIZES ▸ hafiz
HAFNIUM *n* metallic element found in zirconium ores
HAFT *n* handle of an axe, knife, or dagger ▷ *vb* provide with a haft
HAFTARA *same as* > **haftarah**
HAFTED ▸ haft
HAFTER ▸ haft
HAFTERS ▸ haft
HAFTING ▸ haft
HAFTS ▸ haft

HAG *n* ugly old woman ▷ *vb* hack
HAGADIC > haggadic
HAGBOLT *same as* > **hackbolt**
HAGBORN *adj* born of a witch
HAGBUSH *same as* > **arquebus**
HAGBUT > arquebus
HAGBUTS ▸ hagbut
HAGDEN *same as* > **hackbolt**
HAGDENS ▸ hagden
HAGDON *same as* > **hackbolt**
HAGDONS ▸ hagdon
HAGDOWN *same as* > **hackbolt**
HAGFISH *n* any of various primitive eel-like marine vertebrates
HAGG *n* boggy place
HAGGADA *same as* > **haggadah**
HAGGARD *adj* looking tired and ill ▷ *n* hawk that has reached maturity before being caught
HAGGED ▸ hag
HAGGING ▸ hag
HAGGIS *n* Scottish dish made from sheep's offal, oatmeal, suet, and seasonings, boiled in a bag made from the sheep's stomach
HAGGISH ▸ hag
HAGGLE *vb* bargain or wrangle over a price
HAGGLED ▸ haggle
HAGGLER ▸ haggle
HAGGLES ▸ haggle
HAGGS ▸ hagg
HAGLET *same as* ▸ **hacklet**
HAGLETS ▸ haglet
HAGLIKE ▸ hag
HAGRIDE *vb* torment or obsess
HAGRODE ▸ hagride
HAGS ▸ hag
HAH *same as* ▸ **ha**
HAHA *n* wall or other boundary marker that is set in a ditch so as not to interrupt the landscape
HAHAS ▸ haha
HAHNIUM *n* transuranic element artificially produced from californium
HAHS ▸ hah
HAICK *same as* ▸ **haik**
HAICKS ▸ haick

HAIDUK *n* rural brigand
HAIDUKS ▸ haiduk
HAIK *n* Arab's outer garment of cotton, wool, or silk, for the head and body
HAIKA ▸ haik
HAIKAI *same as* ▸ **haiku**
HAIKS ▸ haik
HAIKU *n* Japanese verse form in 17 syllables
HAIKUS ▸ haiku
HAIL *n* (shower of) small pellets of ice ▷ *vb* fall as or like hail ▷ *sentence substitute* exclamation of greeting
HAILED ▸ hail
HAILER ▸ hail
HAILERS ▸ hail
HAILIER ▸ hail
HAILING ▸ hail
HAILS ▸ hail
HAILY ▸ hail
HAIMISH *same as* ▸ **heimish**
HAIN *vb* Scots word meaning save
HAINCH *Scots form of* ▸ **haunch**
HAINED ▸ hain
HAINING ▸ hain
HAINS ▸ hain
HAINT *same as* ▸ **haunt**
HAINTS ▸ haint
HAIQUE *same as* ▸ **haik**
HAIQUES ▸ haik
HAIR *n* threadlike growth on the skin ▷ *vb* provide with hair
HAIRCAP *n* type of moss
HAIRCUT *n* act or an instance of cutting the hair
HAIRDO *n* hairstyle
HAIRDOS ▸ hairdo
HAIRED *adj* with hair
HAIRIER ▸ hairy
HAIRIF *another name for* > **cleavers**
HAIRIFS ▸ hairif
HAIRING ▸ hair
HAIRNET *n* any of several kinds of light netting worn over the hair to keep it in place
HAIRPIN *n* U-shaped wire used to hold the hair in place
HAIRS ▸ hair
HAIRST *Scots form of* ▸ **harvest**
HAIRSTS ▸ hairst
HAIRY *adj* covered with hair
HAITH *interj* Scots oath
HAJ *same as* ▸ **hadj**

A **haj** is a Muslim pilgrimage to Mecca, and one of the key words to remember for using the J. It can also be spelt **hadj** or **hajj**, and one who makes a haj is called a **hadjee, hadji, haji** or **hajji**.

HAJES ▸ haj

HAJI same as ▸ **hajji**

HAJIS ▸ haji

HAJJ n pilgrimage a Muslim makes to Mecca

HAJJAH n Muslim woman who has made a pilgrimage to Mecca

HAJJAHS ▸ hajjah

HAJJES ▸ hajj

HAJJI n Muslim who has made a pilgrimage to Mecca

HAJJIS ▸ hajji

HAKA n ceremonial Maori dance with chanting

HAKAM n text written by a rabbi

HAKAMS ▸ hakam

HAKARI n Maori ritual feast

HAKARIS ▸ hakari

HAKAS ▸ haka

HAKE n edible sea fish of N hemisphere

HAKEA n Australian tree or shrub with hard woody fruit

HAKEAS ▸ hakea

HAKEEM same as ▸ **hakim**

HAKEEMS ▸ hakeem

HAKES ▸ hake

HAKIM n Muslim judge, ruler, or administrator

HAKIMS ▸ hakim

HAKU in New Zealand English, same as ▸ **kingfish**

HAKUS ▸ haku

HALACHA n Jewish religious law

HALAKAH same as ▸ **halacha**

HALAKHA same as ▸ **halacha**

HALAKIC ▸ halakha

HALAL n meat from animals slaughtered according to Muslim law ▷ adj of or relating to such meat ▷ vb kill (animals) in this way

HALALA n money unit in Saudi Arabia

HALALAH same as ▸ **halala**

HALALAS ▸ halala

HALALS ▸ halal

HALAVAH same as ▸ **halvah**

HALBERD n spear with an axe blade

HALBERT same as ▸ **halberd**

HALCYON adj peaceful and happy ▷ n (in Greek mythology) fabulous bird associated with the winter solstice

HALE adj healthy, robust ▷ vb pull or drag

HALED ▸ hale

HALER same as ▸ **heller**

HALERS ▸ haler

HALERU ▸ haler

HALES ▸ hale

HALEST ▸ hale

HALF n either of two equal parts ▷ adj denoting one of two equal parts ▷ adv to the extent of half

HALFA n African grass

HALFAS ▸ halfa

HALFEN ▸ half

HALFLIN same as ▸ **halfling**

HALFS ▸ half

HALFWAY adj at or to half the distance

HALFWIT n foolish or stupid person

HALIBUT n large edible flatfish of N Atlantic

HALID same as ▸ **halide**

HALIDE n binary compound containing a halogen atom or ion in combination with a more electropositive element

HALIDES ▸ halide

HALIDOM n holy place or thing

HALIDS ▸ halid

HALIMOT n court held by lord

HALING ▸ hale

HALITE n colourless or white mineral sometimes tinted by impurities, found in beds as an evaporite

HALITES ▸ halite

HALITUS n vapour

HALL n entrance passage

HALLAH variant spelling of ▸ **challah**

HALLAHS ▸ hallah

HALLAL same as ▸ **halal**

HALLALI n bugle call

HALLALS ▸ hallal

HALLAN n partition in cottage

HALLANS ▸ hallan

HALLEL n (in Judaism) section of the liturgy

consisting of Psalms 113–18, read during the morning service on festivals, Chanukah, and Rosh Chodesh

HALLELS ▸ hallel

HALLIAN same as ▸ **hallion**

HALLING n Norwegian country dance

HALLION n lout

HALLO same as ▸ **halloo**

HALLOA same as ▸ **halloo**

HALLOAS ▸ halloa

HALLOED ▸ hallo

HALLOES ▸ hallo

HALLOO interj shout used to call hounds at a hunt ▷ sentence substitute shout to attract attention, esp to call hounds at a hunt ▷ n shout of "halloo" ▷ vb shout (something) to (someone)

HALLOOS ▸ halloo

HALLOS ▸ hallo

HALLOT ▸ hallah

HALLOTH same as ▸ **challah**

HALLOW vb consecrate or set apart as being holy

HALLOWS ▸ hallow

HALLS ▸ hall

HALLUX n first digit on the hind foot of a mammal, bird, reptile, or amphibian

HALLWAY n entrance area

HALLYON same as ▸ **hallion**

HALM same as ▸ **haulm**

HALMA n board game in which players attempt to transfer their pieces from their own to their opponents' bases

HALMAS ▸ halma

HALMS ▸ halm

HALO n ring of light round the head of a sacred figure ▷ vb surround with a halo

HALOED ▸ halo

HALOES ▸ halo

HALOGEN n any of a group of nonmetallic elements including chlorine and iodine

HALOID adj resembling or derived from a halogen ▷ n compound containing halogen atoms in its molecules

HALOIDS ▸ haloid

HALOING ▸ halo

HALON n any of a class of chemical compounds derived from hydrocarbons by replacing one or more

H

hydrogen atoms by bromine atoms and other hydrogen atoms by other halogen atoms (chlorine, fluorine, or iodine). Halons are stable compounds that are used in fire extinguishers, although they may contribute to depletion of the ozone layer

HALONS ▸ **halon**

HALOS ▸ **halo**

HALOUMI same as ▸ **halloumi**

HALSE vb embrace

HALSED ▸ **halse**

HALSER ▸ **halse**

HALSERS ▸ **halse**

HALSES ▸ **halse**

HALSING ▸ **halse**

HALT vb come or bring to a stop ▹ n temporary stop ▹ adj lame

HALTED ▸ **halt**

HALTER n strap round a horse's head with a rope to lead it with ▹ vb put a halter on (a horse)

HALTERE n one of a pair of short projections in dipterous insects that are modified hind wings, used for maintaining equilibrium during flight

HALTERS ▸ **halter**

HALTING ▸ **halt**

HALTS ▸ **halt**

HALUTZ variant spelling of ▸ **chalutz**

HALVA same as ▸ **halvah**

HALVAH n Eastern Mediterranean, Middle Eastern, or Indian sweetmeat made of honey and containing sesame seeds, nuts, rose water, saffron, etc

HALVAHS ▸ **halvah**

HALVAS ▸ **halva**

HALVE vb divide in half

HALVED ▸ **halve**

HALVER ▸ **halve**

HALVERS ▸ **halve**

HALVES ▸ **halve**

HALVING ▸ **halve**

HALYARD n rope for raising a ship's sail or flag

HAM n smoked or salted meat from a pig's thigh ▹ vb overact

HAMADA n rocky plateau in desert

HAMADAS ▸ **hamada**

HAMAL n (in Middle Eastern countries) a porter, bearer, or servant

HAMALS ▸ **hamal**

HAMATE adj hook-shaped ▹ n small bone in the wrist

HAMATES ▸ **hamate**

HAMAUL same as ▸ **hamal**

HAMAULS ▸ **hamaul**

HAMBLE vb mutilate

HAMBLED ▸ **hamble**

HAMBLES ▸ **hamble**

HAMBONE vb strike body to provide percussion

HAMBURG same as ▸ **hamburger**

HAME n either of the two curved bars holding the traces of the harness, attached to the collar of a draught animal

HAMED ▸ **hame**

HAMES ▸ **hame**

HAMING ▸ **hame**

HAMLET n small village

HAMLETS ▸ **hamlet**

HAMMADA same as ▸ **hamada**

HAMMAL same as ▸ **hamal**

HAMMALS ▸ **hammal**

HAMMAM n bathing establishment, such as a Turkish bath

HAMMAMS ▸ **hammam**

HAMMED ▸ **ham**

HAMMER n tool with a heavy metal head and a wooden handle, used to drive in nails etc ▹ vb hit (as if) with a hammer

HAMMERS ▸ **hammer**

HAMMIER ▸ **hammy**

HAMMILY ▸ **hammy**

HAMMING ▸ **ham**

HAMMOCK same as ▸ **hummock**

HAMMY adj (of an actor) overacting or tending to overact

HAMOSE adj shaped like a hook

HAMOUS same as ▸ **hamose**

HAMPER vb make it difficult for (someone or something) to move or progress ▹ n large basket with a lid

HAMPERS ▸ **hamper**

HAMS ▸ **ham**

HAMSTER n small rodent with a short tail and cheek pouches

HAMULAR ▸ **hamulus**

HAMULI ▸ **hamulus**

HAMULUS n hook or hooklike process at the end of some bones or between the fore and hind wings of a bee or similar insect

HAMZA n sign used in Arabic to represent the glottal stop

HAMZAH same as ▸ **hamza**

HAMZAHS ▸ **hamzah**

HAMZAS ▸ **hamza**

HAN archaic inflected form of ▸ **have**

HANAP n medieval drinking cup

HANAPER n small wickerwork basket, often used to hold official papers

HANAPS ▸ **hanap**

HANCE same as ▸ **haunch**

HANCES ▸ **hance**

HANCH vb try to bite

HANCHED ▸ **hanch**

HANCHES ▸ **hanch**

HAND n part of the body at the end of the arm, consisting of a palm, four fingers, and a thumb ▹ vb pass, give

HANDAX n small axe held in one hand

HANDBAG n woman's small bag for carrying personal articles in

HANDCAR n small railway vehicle propelled by hand-pumped mechanism

HANDED ▸ **hand**

HANDER ▸ **hand**

HANDERS ▸ **hand**

HANDFED > **handfeed**

HANDFUL n amount that can be held in the hand

HANDGUN n firearm that can be held, carried, and fired with one hand, such as a pistol

HANDIER ▸ **handy**

HANDILY adv in a handy way or manner

HANDING ▸ **hand**

HANDISM n discrimination against people on the grounds of whether they are left-handed or right-handed

HANDJAR n Persian dagger

HANDLE n part of an object that is held so that it can be used ▹ vb hold, feel, or move with the hands

HANDLED ▸ **handle**

HANDLER *n* person who controls an animal

HANDLES ▸ **handle**

HANDOFF *n* (in rugby) act of warding off an opposing player with the open hand

HANDOUT *n* clothing, food, or money given to a needy person

HANDS ▸ **hand**

HANDSAW *n* any saw for use in one hand only

HANDSEL *n* gift for good luck at the beginning of a new year, new venture, etc ▷ *vb* give a handsel to (a person)

HANDSET *n* telephone mouthpiece and earpiece in a single unit

HANDY *adj* convenient, useful

HANG *vb* attach or be attached at the top with the lower part free

HANGAR *n* large shed for storing aircraft ▷ *vb* put in a hangar

HANGARS ▸ **hangar**

HANGDOG *adj* guilty, ashamed ▷ *n* furtive or sneaky person

HANGED ▸ **hang**

HANGER *n* curved piece of wood, wire, or plastic, with a hook, for hanging up clothes

HANGERS ▸ **hanger**

HANGI *n* Maori oven consisting of a hole in the ground filled with hot stones

HANGING ▸ **hang**

HANGIS ▸ **hangi**

HANGMAN *n* man who executes people by hanging

HANGMEN ▸ **hangman**

HANGOUT *n* place where one lives or that one frequently visits

HANGS ▸ **hang**

HANGTAG *n* attached label

HANGUL *n* Korean language

HANGUP *n* emotional or psychological preoccupation or problem

HANGUPS ▸ **hangup**

HANIWA *n* Japanese funeral offering

HANJAR *same as* ▸ **handjar**

HANJARS ▸ **hanjar**

HANK *n* coil, esp of yarn ▷ *vb*

attach (a sail) to a stay by hanks

HANKED ▸ **hank**

HANKER *vb* desire intensely

HANKERS ▸ **hanker**

HANKIE *same as* ▸ **hanky**

HANKIES ▸ **hanky**

HANKING ▸ **hank**

HANKS ▸ **hank**

HANKY *n* handkerchief

HANSA *same as* ▸ **hanse**

HANSAS ▸ **hansa**

HANSE *n* medieval guild of merchants

HANSEL *same as* ▸ **handsel**

HANSELS ▸ **hansel**

HANSES ▸ **hanse**

HANSOM *n* formerly, a two-wheeled one-horse carriage with a fixed hood

HANSOMS ▸ **hansom**

HANT *same as* ▸ **haunt**

HANTED ▸ **hant**

HANTING ▸ **hant**

HANTLE *n* good deal

HANTLES ▸ **hantle**

HANTS ▸ **hant**

HANUMAN *n* type of monkey

HAO *n* monetary unit of Vietnam, worth one tenth of a đồng

HAOMA *n* type of ritual drink

HAOMAS ▸ **haoma**

HAOS ▸ **hao**

HAP *n* luck ▷ *vb* cover up

HAPAX *n* word that only appears once in a work of literature, or in a body of work by a particular author

HAPAXES ▸ **hapax**

HAPKIDO *n* Korean martial art

HAPLESS *adj* unlucky

HAPLITE *same as* ▸ **aplite**

HAPLOID *adj* denoting a cell or organism with unpaired chromosomes ▷ *n* haploid cell or organism

HAPLONT *n* organism, esp a plant, that has the haploid number of chromosomes in its somatic cells

HAPLY *archaic word for* ▸ **perhaps**

HAPPED ▸ **hap**

HAPPEN *vb* take place, occur

HAPPENS ▸ **happen**

HAPPIED ▸ **happy**

HAPPIER ▸ **happy**

HAPPIES ▸ **happy**

HAPPILY ▸ **happy**

HAPPING ▸ **hap**

HAPPY *adj* feeling or causing joy ▷ *vb* make happy

HAPS ▸ **hap**

HAPTEN *n* incomplete antigen that can stimulate antibody production only when it is chemically combined with a particular protein

HAPTENE *same as* ▸ **hapten**

HAPTENS ▸ **hapten**

HAPTIC *adj* relating to or based on the sense of touch

HAPTICS *n* science of sense of touch

HAPU *n* subtribe

HAPUKA *another name for* ▸ **groper**

HAPUKAS ▸ **hapuka**

HAPUKU *same as* ▸ **hapuka**

HAPUKUS ▸ **hapuku**

HAPUS ▸ **hapu**

HARAM *n* anything that is forbidden by Islamic law

HARAMS ▸ **haram**

HARASS *vb* annoy or trouble constantly

HARBOR *same as* ▸ **harbour**

HARBORS ▸ **harbor**

HARBOUR *n* sheltered port ▷ *vb* maintain secretly in the mind

HARD *adj* firm, solid, or rigid ▷ *adv* with great energy or effort

HARDASS *n* tough person

HARDEN *vb* make or become hard ▷ *n* rough fabric made from hards

HARDENS ▸ **harden**

HARDER ▸ **hard**

HARDEST ▸ **hard**

HARDHAT *n* hat made of a hard material for protection, worn esp by construction workers, equestrians, etc ▷ *adj* (in US English) characteristic of the presumed conservative attitudes and prejudices typified by construction workers

HARDIER ▸ **hardy**

HARDIES ▸ **hardy**

HARDILY *adv* in a hardy manner

HARDISH ▸ **hard**

HARDLY *adv* scarcely or not at all

HARDMAN *n* tough,

H

ruthless, or violent man

HARDMEN ▸ **hardman**

HARDOKE n burdock

HARDPAN n hard impervious layer of clay below the soil, resistant to drainage and root growth

HARDS pl n coarse fibres and other refuse from flax and hemp

HARDSET adj in difficulties

HARDTOP n car equipped with a metal or plastic roof that is sometimes detachable

HARDY adj able to stand difficult conditions ▷ n any blacksmith's tool made with a square shank so that it can be lodged in a square hole in an anvil

HARE n animal like a large rabbit, with longer ears and legs ▷ vb run (away) quickly

HARED ▸ **hare**

HAREEM same as ▸ **harem**

HAREEMS ▸ **hareem**

HARELD n long-tailed duck

HARELDS ▸ **hareld**

HARELIP n slight split in the upper lip

HAREM n (apartments of) a Muslim man's wives and concubines

HAREMS ▸ **harem**

HARES ▸ **hare**

HARIANA n Indian breed of cattle

HARICOT n variety of French bean with light-coloured edible seeds, which can be dried and stored

HARIJAN n member of an Indian caste once considered untouchable

HARIM same as ▸ **harem**

HARIMS ▸ **harim**

HARING ▸ **hare**

HARIRA n Moroccan soup made from a variety of vegetables with lentils, chickpeas, and coriander

HARIRAS ▸ **harira**

HARISH adj like hare

HARISSA n hot paste made from chilli peppers, tomatoes, spices, and olive oil

HARK vb listen

HARKED ▸ **hark**

HARKEN same as ▸ **hearken**

HARKENS ▸ **harken**

HARKING ▸ **hark**

HARKS ▸ **hark**

HARL same as ▸ **herl**

HARLED ▸ **harl**

HARLING ▸ **harl**

HARLOT n prostitute ▷ adj of or like a harlot

HARLOTS ▸ **harlot**

HARLS ▸ **harl**

HARM vb injure physically, mentally, or morally ▷ n physical, mental, or moral injury

HARMALA n African plant

HARMAN n constable

HARMANS ▸ **harman**

HARMED ▸ **harm**

HARMEL same as ▸ **harmala**

HARMELS ▸ **harmel**

HARMER ▸ **harm**

HARMERS ▸ **harm**

HARMFUL adj causing or tending to cause harm, esp to a person's health

HARMIN same as > **harmalin**

HARMINE same as > **harmalin**

HARMING ▸ **harm**

HARMINS ▸ **harmin**

HARMONY n peaceful agreement and cooperation

HARMOST n Spartan governor

HARMS ▸ **harm**

HARN n coarse linen

HARNESS n arrangement of straps for attaching a horse to a cart or plough ▷ vb put a harness on

HARNS ▸ **harn**

HARO interj cry meaning alas

HAROS ▸ **haro**

HAROSET n Jewish dish eaten at Passover

HARP n large triangular stringed instrument played with the fingers ▷ vb play the harp

HARPED ▸ **harp**

HARPER ▸ **harp**

HARPERS ▸ **harp**

HARPIES ▸ **harpy**

HARPIN n type of protein

HARPING ▸ **harp**

HARPINS same as > **harpings**

HARPIST ▸ **harp**

HARPOON n barbed spear attached to a rope used for hunting whales ▷ vb spear with a harpoon

HARPS ▸ **harp**

HARPY n nasty or bad-tempered woman

HARRIED ▸ **harry**

HARRIER n cross-country runner

HARRIES ▸ **harry**

HARROW n implement used to break up lumps of soil ▷ vb draw a harrow over

HARROWS ▸ **harrow**

HARRY vb keep asking (someone) to do something, pester

HARSH adj severe and difficult to cope with ▷ vb ruin or end a state of elation

HARSHED ▸ **harsh**

HARSHEN vb make harsh

HARSHER ▸ **harsh**

HARSHES ▸ **harsh**

HARSHLY ▸ **harsh**

HARSLET same as ▸ **haslet**

HART n adult male deer

HARTAL n (in India) the act of closing shops or suspending work, esp in political protest

HARTALS ▸ **hartal**

HARTELY archaic spelling of > **heartily**

HARTEN same as ▸ **hearten**

HARTENS ▸ **harten**

HARTS ▸ **hart**

HARUMPH same as > **harrumph**

HARVEST n (season for) the gathering of crops ▷ vb gather (a ripened crop)

HAS ▸ **have**

HASBIAN n former lesbian who has become heterosexual or bisexual

HASH n dish of diced cooked meat and vegetables reheated ▷ vb chop into small pieces

HASHED ▸ **hash**

HASHES ▸ **hash**

HASHIER ▸ **hash**

HASHING ▸ **hash**

HASHISH n drug made from the cannabis plant, smoked for its intoxicating effects

HASHY ▸ **hash**

HASK n archaic name for a basket for transporting fish

HASKS ▸ **hask**

HASLET n loaf of cooked minced pig's offal, eaten cold

HASLETS ▸ haslet

HASP n clasp that fits over a staple and is secured by a bolt or padlock, used as a fastening ▷ vb secure (a door, window, etc) with a hasp

HASPED ▸ hasp

HASPING ▸ hasp

HASPS ▸ hasp

HASS n as in **white hass** oatmeal pudding made with sheep's gullet

HASSAR n South American catfish

HASSARS ▸ hassar

HASSEL same as ▸ **hassle**

HASSELS ▸ hassel

HASSES ▸ hass

HASSIUM n element synthetically produced in small quantities by high-energy ion bombardment

HASSLE n trouble, bother ▷ vb bother or annoy

HASSLED ▸ hassle

HASSLES ▸ hassle

HASSOCK n cushion for kneeling on in church

HAST singular form of the present tense (indicative mood) of ▸ **have**

HASTA Spanish for ▸ **until**

HASTATE adj (of a leaf) having a pointed tip and two outward-pointing lobes at the base

HASTE n (excessive) quickness ▷ vb hasten

HASTED ▸ haste

HASTEN vb (cause to) hurry

HASTENS ▸ hasten

HASTES ▸ haste

HASTIER ▸ hasty

HASTILY ▸ hasty

HASTING ▸ haste

HASTY adj (too) quick

HAT n covering for the head, often with a brim ▷ vb supply (a person) with a hat or put a hat on (someone)

HATABLE ▸ hate

HATBAND n band or ribbon around the base of the crown of a hat

HATBOX n box or case for a hat or hats

HATCH vb (cause to) emerge from an egg ▷ n hinged door covering an opening in a floor or wall

HATCHED ▸ hatch

HATCHEL same as ▸ **heckle**

HATCHER ▸ hatch

HATCHES ▸ hatch

HATCHET n small axe

HATE vb dislike intensely ▷ n intense dislike

HATED ▸ hate

HATEFUL adj causing or deserving hate

HATER ▸ hate

HATERS ▸ hate

HATES ▸ hate

HATFUL n amount a hat will hold

HATFULS ▸ hatful

HATH form of the present tense (indicative mood) of ▸ **have**

HATHA n as in **hatha yoga** form of yoga

HATING ▸ hate

HATLESS ▸ hat

HATLIKE ▸ hat

HATPEG n peg to hang hat on

HATPEGS ▸ hatpeg

HATPIN n sturdy pin used to secure a woman's hat to her hair, often having a decorative head

HATPINS ▸ hatpin

HATRACK n rack for hanging hats on

HATRED n intense dislike

HATREDS ▸ hatred

HATS ▸ hat

HATSFUL ▸ hatful

HATTED ▸ hat

HATTER n person who makes and sells hats ▷ vb annoy

HATTERS ▸ hatter

HATTING ▸ hat

HATTOCK n small hat

HAUBERK n long sleeveless coat of mail

HAUBOIS same as ▸ **hautboy**

HAUD Scots word for ▸ **hold**

HAUDING ▸ haud

HAUDS ▸ haud

HAUF Scots word for ▸ **half**

HAUFS ▸ hauf

HAUGH n low-lying often alluvial riverside meadow

HAUGHS ▸ haugh

HAUGHT same as ▸ **haughty**

HAUGHTY adj proud, arrogant

HAUL vb pull or drag with effort ▷ n hauling

HAULAGE n (charge for) transporting goods

HAULD Scots word for ▸ **hold**

HAULDS ▸ hauld

HAULED ▸ haul

HAULER same as ▸ **haulier**

HAULERS ▸ hauler

HAULIER n firm or person that transports goods by road

HAULING ▸ haul

HAULM n stalks of beans, peas, or potatoes collectively

HAULMS ▸ haulm

HAULMY adj having haulms

HAULS ▸ haul

HAULST same as ▸ **halse**

HAULT same as ▸ **haughty**

HAUNCH n human hip or fleshy hindquarter of an animal ▷ vb in archaic usage, cause (an animal) to come down on its haunches

HAUNT vb visit in the form of a ghost ▷ n place visited frequently

HAUNTED adj frequented by ghosts

HAUNTER ▸ haunt

HAUNTS ▸ haunt

HAUSE same as ▸ **halse**

HAUSED ▸ hause

HAUSEN n variety of sturgeon

HAUSENS ▸ hausen

HAUSES ▸ hause

HAUSING ▸ hause

HAUT same as ▸ **haughty**

HAUTBOY n type of strawberry

HAUTE adj French word meaning high

HAUTEUR n haughtiness

HAUYNE n blue mineral containing calcium

HAUYNES ▸ hauyne

HAVARTI n Danish cheese

HAVE vb possess, hold

HAVEN n place of safety ▷ vb secure or shelter in or as if in a haven

HAVENED ▸ haven

HAVENS ▸ haven

HAVEOUR same as ▸ **havior**

HAVER vb talk nonsense ▷ n nonsense

HAVERED ▸ haver

HAVEREL n fool

HAVERS ▸ haver

HAVES ▸ have

HAVING ▸ have

HAVINGS ▸ have

HAVIOR same as ▸ **haviour**

HAVIORS ▸ havior

HAVIOUR n possession
HAVOC n disorder and confusion ▷ vb lay waste
HAVOCS ▸ havoc
HAW n hawthorn berry ▷ vb make an inarticulate utterance
HAWALA n Middle Eastern system of money transfer
HAWALAS ▸ hawala
HAWBUCK n bumpkin
HAWED ▸ haw
HAWING ▸ haw
HAWK n bird of prey with a short hooked bill and very good eyesight ▷ vb offer (goods) for sale in the street or door-to-door
HAWKBIT n any of three perennial plants with yellow dandelion-like flowers
HAWKED ▸ hawk
HAWKER n person who travels from place to place selling goods
HAWKERS ▸ hawker
HAWKEY same as ▸ **hockey**
HAWKEYS ▸ hawkey
HAWKIE n cow with white stripe on face
HAWKIES ▸ hawkie
HAWKING another name for > **falconry**
HAWKISH adj favouring the use or display of force rather than diplomacy to achieve foreign policy goals
HAWKIT adj having a white streak
HAWKS ▸ hawk
HAWM vb be idle and relaxed
HAWMED ▸ hawm
HAWMING ▸ hawm
HAWMS ▸ hawm
HAWS ▸ haw
HAWSE vb of boats, pitch violently when at anchor
HAWSED ▸ hawse
HAWSER n large rope used on a ship
HAWSERS ▸ hawser
HAWSES ▸ hawse
HAWSING ▸ hawse
HAY n grass cut and dried as fodder ▷ vb cut, dry, and store (grass, clover, etc) as fodder
HAYBAND n rope made by twisting hay together
HAYBOX n airtight box full of hay or other insulating

material used to keep partially cooked food warm and allow cooking by retained heat
HAYCOCK n small cone-shaped pile of hay left in the field until dry enough to carry to the rick or barn
HAYED ▸ hay
HAYER n person who makes hay
HAYERS ▸ hayer
HAYEY ▸ hay
HAYFORK n long-handled fork with two long curved prongs, used for moving or turning hay
HAYIER ▸ hayey
HAYIEST ▸ hayey
HAYING ▸ hay
HAYINGS ▸ hay
HAYLAGE n type of hay for animal fodder
HAYLE n welfare
HAYLES ▸ hayle
HAYLOFT n loft for storing hay
HAYMOW n part of a barn where hay is stored
HAYMOWS ▸ haymow
HAYRACK n rack for holding hay for feeding to animals
HAYRAKE n large rake used to collect hay
HAYRICK same as > **haystack**
HAYRIDE n pleasure trip in hay wagon
HAYS ▸ hay
HAYSEED n seeds or fragments of grass or straw
HAYSEL n season for making hay
HAYSELS ▸ haysel
HAYWARD n parish officer in charge of enclosures and fences
HAYWIRE adj (of things) not functioning properly ▷ n wire for binding hay
HAZAN same as ▸ **cantor**
HAZANIM ▸ hazan
HAZANS ▸ hazan
HAZARD n something that could be dangerous ▷ vb put in danger
HAZARDS ▸ hazard
HAZE n mist, often caused by heat ▷ vb make or become hazy
HAZED ▸ haze
HAZEL n small tree producing edible nuts ▷ adj

(of eyes) greenish-brown
HAZELLY ▸ hazel
HAZELS ▸ hazel
HAZER ▸ haze
HAZERS ▸ haze
HAZES ▸ haze
HAZIER ▸ hazy
HAZIEST ▸ hazy
HAZILY ▸ hazy
HAZING ▸ haze
HAZINGS ▸ haze
HAZMAT n hazardous material
HAZMATS ▸ hazmat
HAZY adj not clear, misty
HAZZAN same as ▸ **cantor**
HAZZANS ▸ hazzan
HE pron male person or animal ▷ n male person or animal ▷ interj expression of amusement or derision
HEAD n upper or front part of the body, containing the sense organs and the brain ▷ adj chief, principal ▷ vb be at the top or front of
HEADAGE n payment to farmer based on number of animals kept
HEADED adj having a head or heads
HEADEND n facility from which cable television is transmitted
HEADER n striking a ball with the head
HEADERS ▸ header
HEADFUL n amount head will hold
HEADIER ▸ heady
HEADILY ▸ heady
HEADING same as ▸ **head**
HEADMAN n chief or leader
HEADMEN ▸ headman
HEADPIN another word for ▸ **kingpin**
HEADRIG n edge of ploughed field
HEADS adv with the side of a coin which has a portrait of a head on it uppermost
HEADSET n pair of headphones, esp with a microphone attached
HEADWAY same as > **headroom**
HEADY adj intoxicating or exciting
HEAL vb make or become well
HEALD same as ▸ **heddle**
HEALDED ▸ heald
HEALDS ▸ heald

HEALED ▸ **heal**
HEALEE n person who is being healed
HEALEES ▸ **healee**
HEALER ▸ **heal**
HEALERS ▸ **heal**
HEALING ▸ **heal**
HEALS ▸ **heal**
HEALTH n normal (good) condition of someone's body ▷ interj exclamation wishing someone good health as part of a toast
HEALTHS ▸ **health**
HEALTHY adj having good health
HEAME old form of ▸ **home**
HEAP n pile of things one on top of another ▷ vb gather into a pile
HEAPED ▸ **heap**
HEAPER ▸ **heap**
HEAPERS ▸ **heap**
HEAPIER ▸ **heapy**
HEAPING adj (of a spoonful) heaped
HEAPS ▸ **heap**
HEAPY adj having many heaps
HEAR vb perceive (a sound) by ear
HEARD same as ▸ **herd**
HEARDS ▸ **herd**
HEARE old form of ▸ **hair**
HEARER ▸ **hear**
HEARERS ▸ **hear**
HEARES ▸ **heare**
HEARIE old form of ▸ **hairy**
HEARING ▸ **hear**
HEARKEN vb listen
HEARS ▸ **hear**
HEARSAY n gossip, rumour
HEARSE n funeral car used to carry a coffin ▷ vb put in hearse
HEARSED ▸ **hearse**
HEARSES ▸ **hearse**
HEARSY adj like a hearse
HEART n organ that pumps blood round the body ▷ vb (of vegetables) form a heart
HEARTED ▸ **heart**
HEARTEN vb encourage, make cheerful
HEARTH n floor of a fireplace
HEARTHS ▸ **hearth**
HEARTLY adv vigorously
HEARTS n card game in which players must avoid winning tricks containing hearts or the queen of spades

HEARTY adj substantial, nourishing ▷ n comrade, esp a sailor
HEAST same as ▸ **hest**
HEASTE same as ▸ **hest**
HEASTES ▸ **heaste**
HEASTS ▸ **heast**
HEAT vb make or become hot ▷ n state of being hot
HEATED adj angry and excited
HEATER n device for supplying heat
HEATERS ▸ **heater**
HEATH n area of open uncultivated land
HEATHEN n (of) a person who does not believe in an established religion ▷ adj of or relating to heathen peoples
HEATHER n low-growing plant with small purple, pinkish, or white flowers, growing on heaths and mountains ▷ adj of a heather colour
HEATHS ▸ **heath**
HEATHY ▸ **heath**
HEATING n device or system for supplying heat, esp central heating, to a building
HEATS ▸ **heat**
HEAUME n (in the 12th and 13th centuries) a large helmet reaching and supported by the shoulders
HEAUMES ▸ **heaume**
HEAVE vb lift with effort ▷ n heaving
HEAVED ▸ **heave**
HEAVEN n place believed to be the home of God, where good people go when they die
HEAVENS ▸ **heaven**
HEAVER ▸ **heave**
HEAVERS ▸ **heave**
HEAVES ▸ **heave**
HEAVIER ▸ **heavy**
HEAVIES ▸ **heavy**
HEAVILY ▸ **heavy**
HEAVING ▸ **heave**
HEAVY adj of great weight
HEBE n any of various flowering shrubs
HEBEN old form of ▸ **ebony**
HEBENON n source of poison
HEBENS ▸ **heben**
HEBES ▸ **hebe**
HEBETIC adj of or relating to puberty

HEBONA same as ▸ **hebenon**
HEBONAS ▸ **hebona**
HECH interj expression of surprise
HECHT same as ▸ **hight**
HECHTS ▸ **hecht**
HECK interj mild exclamation of surprise, irritation, etc ▷ n frame for obstructing the passage of fish in a river
HECKLE vb interrupt (a public speaker) with comments, questions, or taunts ▷ n instrument for combing flax or hemp
HECKLED ▸ **heckle**
HECKLER ▸ **heckle**
HECKLES ▸ **heckle**
HECKS ▸ **heck**
HECTARE n one hundred ares or 10 000 square metres (2.471 acres)
HECTICS ▸ **hectic**
HECTIC adj rushed or busy ▷ n hectic fever or flush
HECTICS ▸ **hectic**
HECTOR vb bully ▷ n blustering bully
HECTORS ▸ **hector**
HEDDLE n one of a set of frames of vertical wires on a loom, each wire having an eye through which a warp thread can be passed ▷ vb pass thread through heddle
HEDDLED ▸ **heddle**
HEDDLES ▸ **heddle**
HEDER variant spelling of ▸ **cheder**
HEDERA ▸ **ivy**
HEDERAL ▸ **hedera**
HEDERAS ▸ **hedera**
HEDERS ▸ **heder**
HEDGE n row of bushes forming a barrier or boundary ▷ vb be evasive or noncommittal
HEDGED ▸ **hedge**
HEDGER ▸ **hedge**
HEDGERS ▸ **hedge**
HEDGES ▸ **hedge**
HEDGIER ▸ **hedge**
HEDGING ▸ **hedge**
HEDGY ▸ **hedge**
HEDONIC > **hedonism**
HEED n careful attention ▷ vb pay careful attention to
HEEDED ▸ **heed**
HEEDER ▸ **heed**
HEEDERS ▸ **heed**
HEEDFUL ▸ **heed**

HEEDING ▸ heed
HEEDS ▸ heed
HEEDY ▸ heed
HEEHAW *interj* representation of the braying sound of a donkey ▷ *vb* make braying sound
HEEHAWS ▸ heehaw
HEEL *n* back part of the foot ▷ *vb* repair the heel of (a shoe)
HEELBAR *n* small shop or counter where shoes are repaired
HEELED ▸ heel
HEELER *n* dog that herds cattle by biting at their heels
HEELERS ▸ heeler
HEELING ▸ heel
HEELS ▸ heel
HEELTAP *n* layer of leather, etc, in the heel of a shoe
HEEZE *Scots word for* ▸ **hoist**
HEEZED ▸ heeze
HEEZES ▸ heeze
HEEZIE *n* act of lifting
HEEZIES ▸ heezie
HEEZING ▸ heeze
HEFT *vb* assess the weight of (something) by lifting ▷ *n* weight
HEFTE *same as* ▸ **heave**
HEFTED ▸ heft
HEFTER ▸ heft
HEFTERS ▸ heft
HEFTIER ▸ hefty
HEFTILY ▸ hefty
HEFTING ▸ heft
HEFTS ▸ heft
HEFTY *adj* large, heavy, or strong
HEGARI *n* African sorghum
HEGARIS ▸ hegari
HEGEMON *n* person in authority
HEGIRA *n* emigration escape or flight
HEGIRAS ▸ hegira
HEGUMEN *n* head of a monastery of the Eastern Church
HEH *interj* exclamation of surprise or inquiry
HEHS ▸ heh
HEID *Scots word for* ▸ **head**
HEIDS ▸ heid
HEIFER *n* young cow
HEIFERS ▸ heifer
HEIGH *same as* ▸ **hey**
HEIGHT *n* distance from base to top
HEIGHTH *obsolete form of*

▸ height
HEIGHTS ▸ height
HEIL *vb* give a German greeting
HEILED ▸ heil
HEILING ▸ heil
HEILS ▸ heil
HEIMISH *adj* comfortable
HEINIE *n* buttocks
HEINIES ▸ heinie
HEINOUS *adj* evil and shocking
HEIR *n* person entitled to inherit property or rank ▷ *vb* inherit
HEIRDOM *n* succession by right of blood
HEIRED ▸ heir
HEIRESS *n* woman who inherits or expects to inherit great wealth
HEIRING ▸ heir
HEIRS ▸ heir
HEISHI *n* Native American shell jewellery
HEIST *n* robbery ▷ *vb* steal or burgle
HEISTED ▸ heist
HEISTER ▸ heist
HEISTS ▸ heist
HEITIKI *n* Maori neck ornament of greenstone
HEJAB *same as* ▸ **hijab**
HEJABS ▸ hejab
HEJIRA *same as* ▸ **hegira**
HEJIRAS ▸ hejira
HEJRA *same as* ▸ **hegira**
HEJRAS ▸ hejra
HEKTARE *same as* ▸ **hectare**
HELCOID *adj* having ulcers
HELD ▸ hold
HELE *vb* as in **hele in** dialect expression meaning insert (cuttings, shoots, etc) into soil before planting to keep them moist
HELED ▸ hele
HELES ▸ hele
HELIAC *same as* > **heliacal**
HELIAST *n* ancient Greek juror
HELIBUS *n* helicopter carrying passengers
HELICAL *adj* spiral
HELICES ▸ helix
HELICON *n* bass tuba made to coil over the shoulder of a band musician
HELIMAN *n* helicopter pilot
HELIMEN ▸ heliman
HELING ▸ hele
HELIO *n* instrument for sending messages in Morse

code by reflecting the sun's rays
HELIOS ▸ helio
HELIPAD *n* place for helicopters to land and take off
HELIUM *n* very light colourless odourless gas
HELIUMS ▸ helium
HELIX *n* spiral
HELIXES ▸ helix
HELL *n* place believed to be where wicked people go when they die ▷ *vb* act wildly
HELLBOX *n* (in printing) container for broken type
HELLCAT *n* spiteful fierce-tempered woman
HELLED ▸ hell
HELLER *n* monetary unit of the Czech Republic and Slovakia
HELLERI *n* Central American fish
HELLERS ▸ heller
HELLERY *n* wild or mischievous behaviour
HELLIER *n* slater
HELLING ▸ hell
HELLION *n* rough or rowdy person, esp a child
HELLISH *adj* very unpleasant ▷ *adv* (intensifier)
HELLO *interj* expression of greeting or surprise ▷ *n* act of saying 'hello' ▷ *sentence substitute* expression of greeting used on meeting a person or at the start of a telephone call ▷ *vb* say hello
HELLOED ▸ hello
HELLOES ▸ hello
HELLOS ▸ hello
HELLOVA *same as* ▸ **helluva**
HELLS ▸ hell
HELLUVA *adj* (intensifier)
HELM *n* tiller or wheel for steering a ship ▷ *vb* direct or steer
HELMED ▸ helm
HELMER *n* film director
HELMERS ▸ helmer
HELMET *n* hard hat worn for protection
HELMETS ▸ helmet
HELMING ▸ helm
HELMS ▸ helm
HELO *n* helicopter
HELOS ▸ helo
HELOT *n* serf or slave

HELOTRY n serfdom or slavery

HELOTS ▶ helot

HELP vb make something easier, better, or quicker for (someone) ▷ n assistance or support

HELPED ▶ help

HELPER ▶ help

HELPERS ▶ help

HELPFUL adj giving help

HELPING n single portion of food

HELPS ▶ help

HELVE n handle of a hand tool such as an axe or pick ▷ vb fit a helve to (a tool)

HELVED ▶ helve

HELVES ▶ helve

HELVING ▶ helve

HEM n bottom edge of a garment, folded under and stitched down ▷ vb provide with a hem

HEMAGOG same as > hemagogue

HEMAL same as ▶ haemal

HEMATAL same as ▶ hemal

HEMATIC same as > haematic

HEMATIN same as > haematin

HEME same as ▶ haem

HEMES ▶ heme

HEMIC > haematic

HEMIN same as ▶ haemin

HEMINA n old liquid measure

HEMINAS ▶ hemina

HEMINS ▶ hemin

HEMIOLA n rhythmic device involving the superimposition of, for example, two notes in the time of three

HEMIONE same as > hemionus

HEMIPOD same as > hemipode

HEMLINE n level to which the hem of a skirt hangs

HEMLOCK n poison made from a plant with spotted stems and small white flowers

HEMMED ▶ hem

HEMMER n attachment on a sewing machine for hemming

HEMMERS ▶ hemmer

HEMMING ▶ hem

HEMOID same as > haematoid

HEMP n Asian plant with tough fibres

HEMPEN ▶ hemp

HEMPIE same as ▶ hempy

HEMPIER ▶ hempy

HEMPIES ▶ hempy

HEMPS ▶ hemp

HEMPY adj of or like hemp ▷ n rogue

HEMS ▶ hem

HEN n female domestic fowl ▷ vb lose one's courage

HENBANE n poisonous plant with sticky hairy leaves

HENBIT n European plant with small dark red flowers

HENBITS ▶ henbit

HENCE adv from this time ▷ interj begone! away!

HENCOOP n cage for poultry

HEND vb seize

HENDED ▶ hend

HENDING ▶ hend

HENDS ▶ hend

HENGE n circular monument, often containing a circle of stones, dating from the Neolithic and Bronze Ages

HENGES ▶ henge

HENLEY n type of sweater

HENLEYS ▶ henley

HENLIKE ▶ hen

HENNA n reddish dye made from a shrub or tree ▷ vb dye (the hair) with henna

HENNAED ▶ henna

HENNAS ▶ henna

HENNED ▶ hen

HENNER n challenge

HENNERS ▶ henner

HENNERY n place or farm for keeping poultry

HENNIER ▶ henny

HENNIES ▶ henny

HENNIN n former women's hat

HENNING ▶ hen

HENNINS ▶ hennin

HENNISH ▶ hen

HENNY adj like hen ▷ n cock that looks like hen

HENOTIC adj acting to reconcile

HENPECK vb (of a woman) to harass or torment (a man, esp her husband) by persistent nagging

HENRIES ▶ henry

HENRY n unit of electrical inductance

HENRYS ▶ henry

HENS ▶ hen

HENT vb seize ▷ n anything that has been grasped, esp by the mind

HENTED ▶ hent

HENTING ▶ hent

HENTS ▶ hent

HEP same as ▶ hip

HEPAR n compound containing sulphur

HEPARIN n polysaccharide, containing sulphate groups, present in most body tissues: an anticoagulant used in the treatment of thrombosis

HEPARS ▶ hepar

HEPATIC adj of the liver ▷ n any of various drugs for use in treating diseases of the liver

HEPCAT n person who is hep, esp a player or admirer of jazz and swing in the 1940s

HEPCATS ▶ hepcat

HEPPER ▶ hep

HEPPEST ▶ hep

HEPS ▶ hep

HEPSTER same as ▶ hipster

HEPT archaic spelling of ▶ heaped

HEPTAD n group or series of seven

HEPTADS ▶ heptad

HEPTANE n alkane found in petroleum and used as an anaesthetic

HEPTOSE n any monosaccharide that has seven carbon atoms per molecule

HER pron refers to a female person or animal or anything personified as feminine when the object of a sentence or clause ▷ adj belonging to her ▷ determiner of, belonging to, or associated with her

HERALD n person who announces important news ▷ vb signal the approach of

HERALDS ▶ herald

HERB n plant used for flavouring in cookery, and in medicine

HERBAGE n herbaceous plants collectively, esp those on which animals graze

H

HERBAL adj of or relating to herbs, usually culinary or medicinal herbs ▷ n book describing and listing the properties of plants
HERBALS ▸ herbal
HERBAR same as ▸ herbary
HERBARS ▸ herbar
HERBARY n herb garden
HERBED adj flavoured with herbs
HERBIER ▸ herby
HERBIST same as > herbalist
HERBLET n little herb
HERBOSE same as ▸ herbous
HERBOUS adj with abundance of herbs
HERBS ▸ herb
HERBY adj abounding in herbs
HERD n group of animals feeding and living together ▷ vb collect into a herd
HERDBOY n boy who looks after herd
HERDED ▸ herd
HERDEN n type of coarse cloth
HERDENS ▸ herden
HERDER same as > herdsman
HERDERS ▸ herder
HERDESS n female herder
HERDIC n small horse-drawn carriage with a rear entrance and side seats
HERDICS ▸ herdic
HERDING ▸ herd
HERDMAN same as > herdsman
HERDMEN ▸ herdman
HERDS ▸ herd
HERE adv in, at, or to this place or point ▷ n this place
HEREAT adv because of this
HEREBY adv by means of or as a result of this
HEREDES ▸ heres
HEREIN adv in this place, matter, or document
HEREOF adv of or concerning this
HEREON archaic word for > hereupon
HERES ▸ here
HERESY n opinion contrary to accepted opinion or belief
HERETIC n person who holds unorthodox opinions
HERETO adv this place,

matter, or document
HERIED ▸ hery
HERIES ▸ hery
HERIOT n (in medieval England) a death duty paid by villeins and free tenants to their lord, often consisting of the dead man's best beast or chattel
HERIOTS ▸ heriot
HERISSE adj with bristles
HERITOR n person who inherits
HERL n barb or barbs of a feather, used to dress fishing flies
HERLING n Scots word for a type of fish
HERLS ▸ herl
HERM n (in ancient Greece) a stone head of Hermes surmounting a square stone pillar
HERMA same as ▸ herm
HERMAE ▸ herma
HERMAI ▸ herma
HERMIT n person living in solitude, esp for religious reasons
HERMITS ▸ hermit
HERMS ▸ herm
HERN archaic or dialect word for ▸ heron
HERNIA n protrusion of an organ or part through the lining of the surrounding body cavity
HERNIAE ▸ hernia
HERNIAL ▸ hernia
HERNIAS ▸ hernia
HERNS ▸ hern
HERO n principal character in a film, book, etc
HEROES ▸ hero
HEROIC adj courageous
HEROICS pl n extravagant behaviour
HEROIN n highly addictive drug derived from morphine
HEROINE n principal female character in a novel, play, etc
HEROINS ▸ heroin
HEROISE same as ▸ heroize
HEROISM n great courage and bravery
HEROIZE vb make into hero
HERON n long-legged wading bird
HERONRY n colony of breeding herons
HERONS ▸ heron

HEROON n temple or monument dedicated to hero
HEROONS ▸ heroon
HEROS ▸ hero
HERPES n any of several inflammatory skin diseases, including shingles and cold sores
HERRIED ▸ herry
HERRIES ▸ herry
HERRING n important food fish of northern seas
HERRY vb harry
HERS pron something belonging to her
HERSALL n rehearsal
HERSE n harrow
HERSED adj arranged like a harrow
HERSELF pron feminine singular reflexive form
HERSES ▸ herse
HERSHIP n act of plundering
HERTZ n unit of frequency
HERTZES ▸ hertz
HERY vb praise
HERYE same as ▸ hery
HERYED ▸ herye
HERYES ▸ herye
HERYING ▸ hery
HES ▸ he
HESP same as ▸ hasp
HESPED ▸ hesp
HESPING ▸ hesp
HESPS ▸ hesp
HESSIAN n coarse jute fabric
HESSITE n black or grey metallic mineral consisting of silver telluride in cubic crystalline form
HEST archaic word for ▸ behest
HESTS ▸ hest
HET n short for heterosexual ▷ adj Scots word for hot
HETAERA n (esp in ancient Greece) a female prostitute, esp an educated courtesan
HETAIRA same as ▸ hetaera
HETE same as ▸ hight
HETERO n short for heterosexual
HETEROS ▸ hetero
HETES ▸ hete
HETH n eighth letter of the Hebrew alphabet
HETHER same as ▸ hither
HETHS ▸ heth
HETING ▸ hete
HETMAN another word for

▶ ataman

HETMANS ▶ hetman

HETS ▶ het

HETTIE *n* slang term for a heterosexual

HETTIES ▶ hettie

HEUCH *Scots word for* ▶ **crag**

HEUCHS ▶ heuch

HEUGH *same as* ▶ **heuch**

HEUGHS ▶ heugh

HEUREKA *same as* ▶ **eureka**

HEURISM *n* use of logic

HEVEA *n* rubber-producing South American tree

HEVEAS ▶ hevea

HEW *vb* cut with an axe

HEWABLE ▶ hew

HEWED ▶ hew

HEWER ▶ hew

HEWERS ▶ hew

HEWGH *interj* sound made to imitate the flight of an arrow

HEWING ▶ hew

HEWINGS ▶ hew

HEWN ▶ hew

HEWS ▶ hew

HEX *adj* of or relating to hexadecimal notation ▷ *n* evil spell ▷ *vb* bewitch

⬛ This word, meaning to bewitch, is a really useful one for using the X.

HEXACT *n* part of a sponge with six rays

HEXACTS ▶ hexact

HEXAD *n* group or series of six

HEXADE *same as* ▶ **hexad**

HEXADES ▶ hexade

HEXADIC ▶ hexad

HEXADS ▶ hexad

HEXAGON *n* geometrical figure with six sides

HEXANE *n* liquid alkane existing in five isomeric forms that are found in petroleum and used as solvents

HEXANES ▶ hexane

HEXAPLA *n* edition of the Old Testament compiled by Origen, containing six versions of the text

HEXAPOD *n* six-footed arthropod

HEXARCH *adj* (of plant) with six veins

HEXED ▶ hex

HEXENE *same as* ▶ **hexylene**

HEXENES ▶ hexene

HEXER ▶ hex

HEXEREI *n* witchcraft

HEXERS ▶ hex

HEXES ▶ hex

HEXING ▶ hex

HEXINGS ▶ hex

HEXONE *n* colourless insoluble liquid ketone used as a solvent for organic compounds

HEXONES ▶ hexone

HEXOSAN *n* any of a group of polysaccharides that yield hexose on hydrolysis

HEXOSE *n* monosaccharide, such as glucose, that contains six carbon atoms per molecule

HEXOSES ▶ hexose

HEXYL *adj* of, consisting of, or containing the group of atoms C_6H_{13}, esp the isomeric form of this group, $CH_3(CH_2)_4CH_2-$

HEXYLIC ▶ hexyl

HEXYLS ▶ hexyl

HEY *interj* expression of surprise or for catching attention ▷ *vb* perform a country dance

HEYDAY *n* time of greatest success, prime

HEYDAYS ▶ heyday

HEYDEY *same as* ▶ **heyday**

HEYDEYS ▶ heydey

HEYDUCK *same as* ▶ **haiduk**

HEYED ▶ hey

HEYING ▶ hey

HEYS ▶ hey

HI *interj* hello

HIANT *adj* gaping

HIATAL ▶ hiatus

HIATUS *n* pause or interruption in continuity

HIBACHI *n* portable brazier for heating and cooking food

HIC *interj* representation of the sound of a hiccup

HICATEE *same as* ▶ **hiccatee**

HICCUP *n* spasm of the breathing organs with a sharp coughlike sound ▷ *vb* make a hiccup

HICCUPS ▶ hiccup

HICCUPY ▶ hiccup

HICK *n* unsophisticated country person

HICKEY *n* object or gadget: used as a name when the correct name is forgotten, etc

HICKEYS ▶ hickey

HICKIE *same as* ▶ **hickey**

HICKIES ▶ hickie

HICKISH ▶ hick

HICKORY *n* N American nut-bearing tree

HICKS ▶ hick

HID ▶ hide

HIDABLE ▶ hide

HIDAGE *n* former tax on land

HIDAGES ▶ hidage

HIDALGA *n* Spanish noblewoman

HIDALGO *n* member of the lower nobility in Spain

HIDDEN ▶ hide

HIDDER *n* young ram

HIDDERS ▶ hidder

HIDE *vb* put (oneself or an object) somewhere difficult to see or find ▷ *n* place of concealment, esp for a bird-watcher

HIDED ▶ hide

HIDEOUS *adj* ugly, revolting

HIDEOUT *n* hiding place, esp a remote place used by outlaws, etc; hideaway

HIDER ▶ hide

HIDERS ▶ hide

HIDES ▶ hide

HIDING ▶ hide

HIDINGS ▶ hide

HIDLING *n* hiding place

HIDLINS *same as* ▶ **hidlings**

HIE *vb* hurry

HIED ▶ hie

HIEING ▶ hie

HIELAND *adj* characteristic of Highlanders, esp alluding to their supposed gullibility or foolishness in towns or cities

HIEMAL *less common word for* ▶ **hibernal**

HIEMS *n* winter

HIES ▶ hie

HIGGLE *less common word for* ▶ **haggle**

HIGGLED ▶ higgle

HIGGLER ▶ higgle

HIGGLES ▶ higgle

HIGH *adj* being a relatively great distance from top to bottom; tall ▷ *adv* at or to a height ▷ *n* a high place or level ▷ *vb* hie

HIGHBOY *n* tall chest of drawers in two sections, the lower section being a lowboy

HIGHED ▶ high

HIGHER *n* advanced level of the Scottish Certificate of Education ▷ *vb* raise up

HIGHERS ▸ higher
HIGHEST ▸ high
HIGHING ▸ high
HIGHISH ▸ high
HIGHLY adv extremely
HIGHMAN n dice weighted to make it fall in particular way
HIGHMEN ▸ highman
HIGHS ▸ high
HIGHT vb archaic word for name or call
HIGHTED ▸ hight
HIGHTH old form of ▸ **height**
HIGHTHS ▸ highth
HIGHTOP n top of ship's mast
HIGHTS ▸ hight
HIGHWAY n main road
HIJAB n covering for the head and face, worn by Muslim women
HIJABS ▸ hijab
HIJACK vb seize control of (an aircraft or other vehicle) while travelling ▷ n instance of hijacking
HIJACKS ▸ hijack
HIJINKS n lively enjoyment
HIJRA same as ▸ **hijrah**
HIJRAH same as ▸ **hegira**
HIJRAHS ▸ hijrah
HIJRAS ▸ hijra
HIKE n long walk in the country, esp for pleasure ▷ vb go for a long walk
HIKED ▸ hike
HIKER ▸ hike
HIKERS ▸ hike
HIKES ▸ hike
HIKING ▸ hike
HIKOI n walk or march, esp a Maori protest march ▷ vb take part in such a march
HIKOIED ▸ hikoi
HIKOIS ▸ hikoi
HILA ▸ hilum
HILAR ▸ hilus
HILCH vb hobble
HILCHED ▸ hilch
HILCHES ▸ hilch
HILD same as ▸ **hold**
HILDING n coward
HILI ▸ hilus
HILL n raised part of the earth's surface, less high than a mountain ▷ vb form into a hill or mound
HILLED ▸ hill
HILLER ▸ hill
HILLERS ▸ hill
HILLIER ▸ hill
HILLING ▸ hill

HILLMEN same as > **hillfolk**
HILLO same as ▸ **hello**
HILLOA same as ▸ **halloa**
HILLOAS ▸ hilloa
HILLOCK n small hill
HILLOED ▸ hillo
HILLOES ▸ hillo
HILLOS ▸ hillo
HILLS ▸ hill
HILLTOP n top of hill
HILLY ▸ hill
HILT n handle of a sword or knife ▷ vb supply with a hilt
HILTED ▸ hilt
HILTING ▸ hilt
HILTS ▸ hilt
HILUM n scar on a seed marking its point of attachment to the seed vessel
HILUS rare word for ▸ **hilum**
HIM pron refers to a male person or animal when the object of a sentence or clause ▷ n male person
HIMATIA > **himation**
HIMS ▸ him
HIMSELF pron masculine singular reflexive form
HIN n Hebrew unit of capacity equal to about 12 pints or 3.5 litres
HINAU n New Zealand tree
HINAUS ▸ hinau
HIND adj situated at the back ▷ n female deer
HINDER vb get in the way of ▷ adj situated at the back
HINDERS ▸ hinder
HINDGUT n part of the vertebrate digestive tract comprising the colon and rectum
HINDLEG n back leg
HINDS ▸ hind
HING n asafoetida
HINGE n device for holding together two parts so that one can swing freely ▷ vb depend (on)
HINGED ▸ hinge
HINGER n tool for making hinges
HINGERS ▸ hinger
HINGES ▸ hinge
HINGING ▸ hinge
HINGS ▸ hing
HINKIER ▸ hinky
HINKY adj strange
HINNIED ▸ hinny
HINNIES ▸ hinny
HINNY n offspring of a male horse and a female donkey

▷ vb whinny
HINS ▸ hin
HINT n indirect suggestion ▷ vb suggest indirectly
HINTED ▸ hint
HINTER ▸ hint
HINTERS ▸ hint
HINTING ▸ hint
HINTS ▸ hint
HIOI n New Zealand plant of the mint family
HIOIS ▸ hioi
HIP n either side of the body between the pelvis and the thigh ▷ adj aware of or following the latest trends ▷ interj exclamation used to introduce cheers
HIPBONE n either of the two bones that form the sides of the pelvis
HIPLESS ▸ hip
HIPLIKE ▸ hip
HIPLINE n widest part of a person's hips
HIPLY ▸ hip
HIPNESS ▸ hip
HIPPED adj having a hip or hips
HIPPEN n baby's nappy
HIPPENS ▸ hippen
HIPPER ▸ hip
HIPPEST ▸ hip
HIPPIC adj of horses
HIPPIE same as ▸ **hippy**
HIPPIER ▸ hippy
HIPPIES ▸ hippy
HIPPIN same as ▸ **hippen**
HIPPING same as ▸ **hippen**
HIPPINS ▸ hippin
HIPPISH adj in low spirits
HIPPO n hippopotamus
HIPPOS ▸ hippo
HIPPUS n spasm of eye
HIPPY n (esp in the 1960s) person whose behaviour and dress imply a rejection of conventional values ▷ adj having large hips
HIPS ▸ hip
HIPSHOT adj having a dislocated hip
HIPSTER n enthusiast of modern jazz
HIPT ▸ hip
HIRABLE ▸ hire
HIRAGE n fee for hiring
HIRAGES ▸ hirage
HIRCINE adj of or like a goat, esp in smell
HIRE vb pay to have temporary use of ▷ n hiring
HIREAGE same as ▸ **hirage**

HIRED ▸ hire
HIREE n hired person
HIREES ▸ hiree
HIRER ▸ hire
HIRERS ▸ hire
HIRES ▸ hire
HIRING ▸ hire
HIRINGS ▸ hire
HIRLING n Scots word for a type of fish
HIRPLE vb limp ▷ n limping gait
HIRPLED ▸ hirple
HIRPLES ▸ hirple
HIRSEL vb sort into groups
HIRSELS ▸ hirsel
HIRSLE vb wriggle or fidget
HIRSLED ▸ hirsle
HIRSLES ▸ hirsle
HIRSTIE adj dry
HIRSUTE adj hairy
HIRUDIN n anticoagulant extracted from the mouth glands of leeches
HIS adj belonging to him
HISH same as ▸ **hiss**
HISHED ▸ hish
HISHES ▸ hish
HISHING ▸ hish
HISN dialect form of ▸ **his**
HISPID adj covered with stiff hairs or bristles
HISS n sound like that of a long s (as an expression of contempt) ▷ vb utter a hiss ▷ interj exclamation of derision or disapproval
HISSED ▸ hiss
HISSELF dialect form of ▸ **himself**
HISSER ▸ hiss
HISSERS ▸ hiss
HISSES ▸ hiss
HISSIER ▸ hissy
HISSIES ▸ hissy
HISSING ▸ hiss
HISSY n temper tantrum ▷ adj sound similar to a hiss
HIST interj exclamation used to attract attention or as a warning to be silent ▷ vb make hist sound
HISTED ▸ hist
HISTIE same as ▸ **hirstie**
HISTING ▸ hist
HISTOID adj (esp of a tumour)
HISTONE n any of a group of basic proteins present in cell nuclei and implicated in the spatial organization of DNA
HISTORY n (record or

account of) past events and developments
HISTRIO n actor
HISTS ▸ hist
HIT vb strike, touch forcefully ▷ n hitting
HITCH n minor problem ▷ vb obtain (a lift) by hitchhiking
HITCHED ▸ hitch
HITCHER ▸ hitch
HITCHES ▸ hitch
HITCHY ▸ hitch
HITHE n small harbour
HITHER adv or towards this place ▷ vb come
HITHERS ▸ hither
HITHES ▸ hithe
HITLESS ▸ hit
HITMAN n professional killer
HITMEN ▸ hitman
HITS ▸ hit
HITTER n boxer who has a hard punch rather than skill or finesse
HITTERS ▸ hitter
HITTING ▸ hit
HIVE n structure in which social bees live and rear their young ▷ vb cause (bees) to collect or (of bees) to collect inside a hive
HIVED ▸ hive
HIVER n person who keeps beehives
HIVERS ▸ hiver
HIVES n allergic reaction in which itchy red or whitish patches appear on the skin
HIVING ▸ hive
HIYA sentence substitute informal term of greeting
HIZEN n type of Japanese porcelain
HIZENS ▸ hizen
HIZZ same as ▸ **hiss**
HIZZED ▸ hizz
HIZZES ▸ hizz
HIZZING ▸ hizz
HM interj sound made to express hesitation or doubt
HMM same as ▸ **hm**

| This variant of **hm**, like its shorter form, can be useful when you have a shortage of vowels.

HOAGIE n sandwich made with long bread roll
HOAGIES ▸ hoagie
HOAGY same as ▸ **hoagie**
HOAR adj covered with hoarfrost ▷ vb make hoary
HOARD n store hidden

away for future use ▷ vb save or store
HOARDED ▸ hoard
HOARDER ▸ hoard
HOARDS ▸ hoard
HOARED ▸ hoar
HOARIER ▸ hoary
HOARILY ▸ hoary
HOARING ▸ hoar
HOARS ▸ hoar
HOARSE adj (of a voice) rough and unclear
HOARSEN vb make or become hoarse
HOARSER ▸ hoarse
HOARY adj grey or white(-haired)
HOAST n cough ▷ vb cough
HOASTED ▸ hoast
HOASTS ▸ hoast
HOATZIN n South American bird with a brownish plumage and very small crested head
HOAX n deception or trick ▷ vb deceive or play a trick upon
HOAXED ▸ hoax
HOAXER ▸ hoax
HOAXERS ▸ hoax
HOAXES ▸ hoax
HOAXING ▸ hoax
HOB n flat top part of a cooker, or a separate flat surface, containing gas or electric rings for cooking on ▷ vb cut or form with a hob
HOBBED ▸ hob
HOBBER n machine used in making gears
HOBBERS ▸ hobber
HOBBIES ▸ hobby
HOBBING ▸ hob
HOBBISH adj like a clown
HOBBIT n one of an imaginary race of half-size people living in holes
HOBBITS ▸ hobbit
HOBBLE vb walk lamely ▷ n strap, rope, etc, used to hobble a horse
HOBBLED ▸ hobble
HOBBLER ▸ hobble
HOBBLES ▸ hobble
HOBBY n activity pursued in one's spare time
HOBDAY vb alleviate (a breathing problem in certain horses) by the surgical operation of removing soft tissue ventricles to pull back the vocal fold

H

HOBDAYS ▸ hobday
HOBJOB *vb* do odd jobs
HOBJOBS ▸ hobjob
HOBLIKE ▸ hob
HOBNAIL *n* short nail with a large head for protecting the soles of heavy footwear ▷ *vb* provide with hobnails
HOBNOB *vb* be on friendly terms (with)
HOBNOBS ▸ hobnob
HOBO *n* tramp or vagrant ▷ *vb* live as hobo
HOBODOM ▸ hobo
HOBOED ▸ hobo
HOBOES ▸ hobo
HOBOING ▸ hobo
HOBOISM ▸ hobo
HOBOS ▸ hobo
HOBS ▸ hob
HOC *adj* Latin for this
HOCK *n* joint in the back leg of an animal such as a horse that corresponds to the human ankle ▷ *vb* pawn
HOCKED ▸ hock
HOCKER ▸ hock
HOCKERS ▸ hock
HOCKEY *n* team game played on a field with a ball and curved sticks
HOCKEYS ▸ hockey
HOCKING ▸ hock
HOCKLE *vb* spit
HOCKLED ▸ hockle
HOCKLES ▸ hockle
HOCKS ▸ hock
HOCUS *vb* take in
HOCUSED ▸ hocus
HOCUSES ▸ hocus
HOD *n* open wooden box attached to a pole, for carrying bricks or mortar ▷ *vb* bob up and down
HODAD *n* person who pretends to be a surfer
HODADDY *same as* ▸ **hodad**
HODADS ▸ hodad
HODDED ▸ hod
HODDEN *n* coarse homespun cloth produced in Scotland: hodden grey is made by mixing black and white wools
HODDENS ▸ hodden
HODDIN *same as* ▸ **hodden**
HODDING ▸ hod
HODDINS ▸ hoddin
HODDLE *vb* waddle
HODDLED ▸ hoddle
HODDLES ▸ hoddle
HODJA *n* respectful Turkish form of address

HODJAS ▸ hodja
HODMAN *n* hod carrier
HODMEN ▸ hodman
HODS ▸ hod
HOE *n* long-handled tool used for loosening soil or weeding ▷ *vb* scrape or weed with a hoe
HOECAKE *n* maize cake
HOED ▸ hoe
HOEDOWN *n* boisterous square dance
HOEING ▸ hoe
HOELIKE ▸ hoe
HOER ▸ hoe
HOERS ▸ hoe
HOES ▸ hoe
HOG *n* castrated male pig ▷ *vb* take more than one's share of
HOGAN *n* wooden dwelling covered with earth, typical of the Navaho Indians of N America
HOGANS ▸ hogan
HOGBACK *n* narrow ridge that consists of steeply inclined rock strata
HOGEN *n* strong alcoholic drink
HOGENS ▸ hogen
HOGFISH *n* type of fish
HOGG *same as* ▸ **hog**
HOGGED ▸ hog
HOGGER ▸ hog
HOGGERS ▸ hog
HOGGERY *n* hogs collectively
HOGGET *n* sheep up to the age of one year that has yet to be sheared
HOGGETS ▸ hogget
HOGGIN *n* finely sifted gravel containing enough clay binder for it to be used in its natural form for making paths or roads
HOGGING *same as* ▸ **hoggin**
HOGGINS ▸ hoggin
HOGGISH *adj* selfish, gluttonous, or dirty
HOGGS ▸ hogg
HOGH *n* ridge of land
HOGHOOD *n* condition of being hog
HOGHS ▸ hogh
HOGLIKE ▸ hog
HOGMANE *n* short stiff mane
HOGNOSE *n as in* **hognose snake** puff adder
HOGNUT *another name for* ▸ **pignut**

HOGNUTS ▸ hognut
HOGS ▸ hog
HOGTIE *vb* tie together the legs or the arms and legs of
HOGTIED ▸ hogtie
HOGTIES ▸ hogtie
HOGWARD *n* person looking after hogs
HOGWASH *n* nonsense
HOGWEED *n* any of several coarse weedy umbelliferous plants, esp cow parsnip
HOHA *adj* bored or annoyed
HOI *same as* ▸ **hoy**
HOICK *vb* raise abruptly and sharply
HOICKED ▸ hoick
HOICKS *interj* cry used to encourage hounds to hunt ▷ *vb* shout hoicks
HOIDEN *same as* ▸ **hoyden**
HOIDENS ▸ hoiden
HOIK *same as* ▸ **hoick**
HOIKED ▸ hoik
HOIKING ▸ hoik
HOIKS ▸ hoik
HOISE *same as* ▸ **hoist**
HOISED ▸ hoise
HOISES ▸ hoise
HOISIN *n* Chinese sweet spicy reddish-brown sauce made from soya beans, sugar, vinegar, and garlic
HOISING ▸ hoise
HOISINS ▸ hoisin
HOIST *vb* raise or lift up ▷ *n* device for lifting things
HOISTED ▸ hoist
HOISTER ▸ hoist
HOISTS ▸ hoist
HOKA *n* red cod
HOKAS ▸ hoka
HOKE *vb* overplay (a part, etc)
HOKED ▸ hoke
HOKES ▸ hoke
HOKEY *adj* corny
HOKI *n* fish of New Zealand waters
HOKIER ▸ hokey
HOKIEST ▸ hokey
HOKILY ▸ hokey
HOKING ▸ hoke
HOKIS ▸ hoki
HOKKU *same as* ▸ **haiku**
HOKONUI *n* illicit whisky
HOKUM *n* rubbish, nonsense
HOKUMS ▸ hokum
HOLARD *n* amount of water contained in soil
HOLARDS ▸ holard
HOLD *vb* keep or support in

or with the hands or arms ▷ *n* act or way of holding
HOLDALL *n* large strong travelling bag
HOLDEN *past participle of* ▸ **hold**
HOLDER *n* person or thing that holds
HOLDERS ▸ **holder**
HOLDING ▸ **hold**
HOLDOUT *n* (in US English) person, country, organization, etc, that continues to resist or refuses to change
HOLDS ▸ **hold**
HOLDUP *n* robbery, esp an armed one
HOLDUPS ▸ **holdup**
HOLE *n* area hollowed out in a solid ▷ *vb* make holes in
HOLED ▸ **hole**
HOLES ▸ **hole**
HOLESOM *same as* > **holesome**
HOLEY *adj* full of holes
HOLEYER ▸ **holey**
HOLIBUT *same as* ▸ **halibut**
HOLIDAY *n* time spent away from home for rest or recreation ▷ *vb* spend a holiday
HOLIER ▸ **holy**
HOLIES ▸ **holy**
HOLIEST ▸ **holy**
HOLILY *adv* in a holy, devout, or sacred manner
HOLING ▸ **hole**
HOLINGS ▸ **hole**
HOLISM *n* view that a whole is greater than the sum of its parts
HOLISMS ▸ **holism**
HOLIST ▸ **holism**
HOLISTS ▸ **holism**
HOLK *vb* dig
HOLKED ▸ **holk**
HOLKING ▸ **holk**
HOLKS ▸ **holk**
HOLLA *same as* ▸ **hollo**
HOLLAED ▸ **holla**
HOLLAND *n* coarse linen cloth, used esp for furnishing
HOLLAS ▸ **holla**
HOLLER *n* shout, yell ▷ *vb* shout or yell
HOLLERS ▸ **holler**
HOLLIES ▸ **holly**
HOLLO *interj* cry for attention, or of encouragement ▷ *vb* shout
HOLLOA *same as* ▸ **hollo**

HOLLOAS ▸ **holloa**
HOLLOED ▸ **hollo**
HOLLOES ▸ **hollo**
HOLLOO *same as* ▸ **halloo**
HOLLOOS ▸ **holloo**
HOLLOS ▸ **hollo**
HOLLOW *adj* having a hole or space inside ▷ *n* cavity or space ▷ *vb* form a hollow in
HOLLOWS ▸ **hollow**
HOLLY *n* evergreen tree with prickly leaves and red berries
HOLM *n* island in a river, lake, or estuary
HOLMIA *n* oxide of holmium
HOLMIAS ▸ **holmia**
HOLMIC *adj* of or containing holmium
HOLMIUM *n* silver-white metallic element, the compounds of which are highly magnetic
HOLMS ▸ **holm**
HOLON *n* autonomous self-reliant unit, esp in manufacturing
HOLONIC ▸ **holon**
HOLONS ▸ **holon**
HOLP *past tense of* ▸ **help**
HOLPEN *past participle of* ▸ **help**
HOLS *pl n* holidays
HOLSTER *n* leather case for a pistol, hung from a belt ▷ *vb* return (a pistol) to its holster
HOLT *n* otter's lair
HOLTS ▸ **holt**
HOLY *adj* of God or a god
HOLYDAM *same as* ▸ **halidom**
HOLYDAY *n* day on which a religious festival is observed
HOM *n* sacred plant of the Parsees and ancient Persians
HOMA *same as* ▸ **hom**
HOMAGE *n* show of respect or honour towards someone or something ▷ *vb* render homage to
HOMAGED ▸ **homage**
HOMAGER ▸ **homage**
HOMAGES ▸ **homage**
HOMAS ▸ **homa**
HOMBRE *slang word for* ▸ **man**
HOMBRES ▸ **hombre**
HOMBURG *n* man's soft felt hat with a dented crown and a stiff upturned brim
HOME *n* place where one

lives ▷ *adj* of one's home, birthplace, or native country ▷ *adv* to or at home ▷ *vb* direct towards (a point or target)
HOMEBOY *n* close friend
HOMED ▸ **home**
HOMELY *adj* simple, ordinary, and comfortable
HOMELYN *n* species of ray
HOMER *n* homing pigeon ▷ *vb* score a home run in baseball
HOMERED ▸ **homer**
HOMERIC *adj* grand or heroic
HOMERS ▸ **homer**
HOMES ▸ **home**
HOMEY *same as* ▸ **homy**
HOMEYS ▸ **homey**
HOMIE *short for* ▸ **homeboy**
HOMIER ▸ **homy**
HOMIES ▸ **homie**
HOMIEST ▸ **homy**
HOMILY *n* speech telling people how they should behave
HOMINES ▸ **homo**
HOMING *adj* denoting the ability to return home after travelling great distances ▷ *n* relating to the ability to return home after travelling great distances
HOMINGS ▸ **homing**
HOMINID *n* man or any extinct forerunner of man ▷ *adj* of or belonging to this family
HOMININ *n* member of zoological family that includes humans and direct ancestors
HOMINY *n* coarsely ground maize prepared as a food by boiling in milk or water
HOMME *French word for* ▸ **man**
HOMMES ▸ **homme**
HOMMOCK *same as* ▸ **hummock**
HOMMOS *same as* ▸ **hummus**
HOMO *n* homogenized milk
HOMOLOG *same as* > **homologue**
HOMONYM *n* word spelt or pronounced the same as another, but with a different meaning
HOMOS ▸ **homo**
HOMOSEX *n* sexual activity between homosexuals

HOMS ▸ hom
HOMY *adj* like a home
HON *short for* ▸ **honey**
HONAN *n* silk fabric of rough weave
HONANS ▸ honan
HONCHO *n* person in charge ▷ *vb* supervise or be in charge of
HONCHOS ▸ honcho
HOND *old form of* ▸ **hand**
HONDA *n* loop through which rope is threaded to make a lasso
HONDAS ▸ honda
HONDLE *vb* negotiate on price
HONDLED ▸ hondle
HONDLES ▸ hondle
HONDS ▸ hond
HONE *vb* sharpen ▷ *n* fine whetstone used for sharpening edged tools and knives
HONED ▸ hone
HONER ▸ hone
HONERS ▸ hone
HONES ▸ hone
HONEST *adj* truthful and moral
HONESTY *n* quality of being honest
HONEY *n* sweet edible sticky substance made by bees from nectar; term of endearment ▷ *vb* sweeten with or as if with honey
HONEYED ▸ honey
HONEYS ▸ honey
HONG *n* (in China) a factory, warehouse, etc ▷ *vb* archaic form of hang
HONGI *n* Maori greeting in which people touch noses ▷ *vb* touch noses
HONGIED ▸ hongi
HONGIES ▸ hongi
HONGING ▸ hong
HONGIS ▸ hongi
HONGS ▸ hong
HONIED ▸ honey
HONING ▸ hone
HONK *n* sound made by a car horn ▷ *vb* (cause to) make this sound
HONKED ▸ honk
HONKER *n* person or thing that honks
HONKERS ▸ honker
HONKING ▸ honk
HONKS ▸ honk
HONOR *same as* ▸ **honour**
HONORED ▸ honor

HONOREE *same as* > **honorand**
HONORER ▸ honour
HONORS *same as* ▸ **honours**
HONOUR *n* sense of honesty and fairness ▷ *vb* give praise and attention to
HONOURS ▸ honour
HONS ▸ hon
HOO *interj* expression of joy, excitement, etc
HOOCH *n* alcoholic drink, esp illicitly distilled spirits
HOOCHES ▸ hooch
HOOCHIE *n* immoral woman
HOOD *n* head covering, often attached to a coat or jacket ▷ *vb* cover with or as if with a hood
HOODED *adj* (of a garment) having a hood
HOODIA *n* any of several southern African succulent plants whose sap has appetite-suppressing properties
HOODIAS ▸ hoodia
HOODIE *n* hooded sweatshirt
HOODIER ▸ hood
HOODIES ▸ hoodie
HOODING ▸ hood
HOODLUM *n* violent criminal, gangster
HOODMAN *n* blindfolded person in blindman's buff
HOODMEN ▸ hoodman
HOODOO *n* (cause of) bad luck ▷ *vb* bring bad luck to
HOODOOS ▸ hoodoo
HOODS ▸ hood
HOODY ▸ hood
HOOEY *n* nonsense ▷ *interj* nonsense
HOOEYS ▸ hooey
HOOF *n* horny covering of the foot of a horse, deer, etc ▷ *vb* kick or trample with the hooves
HOOFED *adj* having a hoof or hoofs
HOOFER *n* professional dancer
HOOFERS ▸ hoofer
HOOFING ▸ hoof
HOOFROT *n* disease of hoof
HOOFS ▸ hoof
HOOK *n* curved piece of metal, plastic, etc, used to hang, hold, or pull something ▷ *vb* fasten or

catch (as if) with a hook
HOOKA *same as* ▸ **hookah**
HOOKAH *n* oriental pipe in which smoke is drawn through water and a long tube
HOOKAHS ▸ hookah
HOOKAS ▸ hooka
HOOKED *adj* bent like a hook
HOOKER *n* prostitute
HOOKERS ▸ hooker
HOOKEY *same as* ▸ **hooky**
HOOKEYS ▸ hookey
HOOKIER ▸ hooky
HOOKIES ▸ hooky
HOOKING ▸ hook
HOOKLET *n* little hook
HOOKS ▸ hook
HOOKUP *n* contact of an aircraft in flight with the refuelling hose of a tanker aircraft
HOOKUPS ▸ hookup
HOOKY *n* truancy, usually from school (esp in the phrase play hooky) ▷ *adj* hooklike
HOOLEY *n* lively party
HOOLEYS ▸ hooley
HOOLIE *same as* ▸ **hooley**
HOOLIER ▸ hooly
HOOLIES ▸ hoolie
HOOLOCK *n* Indian gibbon
HOOLY *adj* careful or gentle
HOON *n* loutish youth who drives irresponsibly ▷ *vb* drive irresponsibly
HOONED ▸ hoon *vb*
HOONING ▸ hoon *vb*
HOONS ▸ hoon
HOOP *n* rigid circular band, used esp as a child's toy or for animals to jump through in the circus ▷ *vb* surround with or as if with a hoop
HOOPED ▸ hoop
HOOPER *rare word for* ▸ **cooper**
HOOPERS ▸ hooper
HOOPING ▸ hoop
HOOPLA *n* fairground game in which hoops are thrown over objects in an attempt to win them
HOOPLAS ▸ hoopla
HOOPOE *n* bird with a pinkish-brown plumage and a fanlike crest
HOOPOES ▸ hoopoe
HOOPOO *same as* ▸ **hoopoe**
HOOPOOS ▸ hoopoo

HOOPS ▸ hoop
HOOR *n* unpleasant or difficult thing
HOORAH *same as* ▸ **hurrah**
HOORAHS ▸ **hoorah**
HOORAY *same as* ▸ **hurrah**
HOORAYS ▸ **hooray**
HOORD *same as* ▸ **hoard**
HOORDS ▸ **hoord**
HOOROO *same as* ▸ **hurrah**
HOORS ▸ **hoor**
HOOSGOW ▸ **jail**
HOOSH *vb* shoo away
HOOSHED ▸ **hoosh**
HOOSHES ▸ **hoosh**
HOOT *n* sound of a car horn ▷ *vb* sound (a car horn) ▷ *interj* exclamation of impatience or dissatisfaction: a supposed Scotticism
HOOTCH *same as* ▸ **hooch**
HOOTED ▸ **hoot**
HOOTER *n* device that hoots
HOOTERS ▸ **hooter**
HOOTIER ▸ **hoot**
HOOTING ▸ **hoot**
HOOTS *same as* ▸ **hoot**
HOOTY ▸ **hoot**
HOOVE *same as* ▸ **heave**
HOOVED ▸ **hoove**
HOOVEN ▸ **hoove**
HOOVER *vb* vacuum-clean (a carpet, furniture, etc)
HOOVERS ▸ **hoover**
HOOVES ▸ **hoof**
HOOVING ▸ **hoove**
HOP *vb* jump on one foot ▷ *n* instance of hopping
HOPBIND *n* stalk of the hop
HOPBINE *same as* ▸ **hopbind**
HOPDOG *n* species of caterpillar
HOPDOGS ▸ **hopdog**
HOPE *vb* want (something) to happen or be true ▷ *n* expectation of something desired
HOPED ▸ **hope**
HOPEFUL *adj* having, expressing, or inspiring hope ▷ *n* person considered to be on the brink of success
HOPER ▸ **hope**
HOPERS ▸ **hope**
HOPES ▸ **hope**
HOPHEAD *n* heroin or opium addict
HOPING ▸ **hope**
HOPLITE *n* (in ancient Greece) a heavily armed infantryman

HOPPED ▸ **hop**
HOPPER *n* container for storing substances such as grain or sand
HOPPERS ▸ **hopper**
HOPPIER ▸ **hoppy**
HOPPING ▸ **hop**
HOPPLE *same as* ▸ **hobble**
HOPPLED ▸ **hopple**
HOPPLER ▸ **hopple**
HOPPLES ▸ **hopple**
HOPPUS *adj as in* **hoppus foot** unit of volume for round timber
HOPPY *adj* tasting of hops
HOPS ▸ **hop**
HOPSACK *n* roughly woven fabric of wool, cotton, etc, used for clothing
HOPTOAD *n* toad
HORA *n* traditional Israeli or Romanian circle dance
HORAH *same as* ▸ **hora**
HORAHS ▸ **horah**
HORAL *less common word for* ▸ **hourly**
HORARY *adj* relating to the hours
HORAS ▸ **hora**
HORDE *n* large crowd ▷ *vb* form, move in, or live in a horde
HORDED ▸ **horde**
HORDEIN *n* simple protein, rich in proline, that occurs in barley
HORDES ▸ **horde**
HORDING ▸ **horde**
HORDOCK *same as* ▸ **hardoke**
HORE *same as* ▸ **hoar**
HORIZON *n* apparent line that divides the earth and the sky
HORKEY *same as* ▸ **hockey**
HORKEYS ▸ **horkey**
HORME *n* (in the psychology of C. G. Jung) fundamental vital energy
HORMES ▸ **horme**
HORMIC ▸ **horme**
HORMONE *n* substance secreted by certain glands which stimulates certain organs of the body
HORN *n* one of a pair of bony growths sticking out of the heads of cattle, sheep, etc ▷ *vb* provide with a horn or horns
HORNBUG *n* stag beetle
HORNED *adj* having a horn, horns, or hornlike parts

HORNER *n* dealer in horn
HORNERS ▸ **horner**
HORNET *n* large wasp with a severe sting
HORNETS ▸ **hornet**
HORNFUL *n* amount a horn will hold
HORNIER ▸ **horny**
HORNILY ▸ **horny**
HORNING ▸ **horn**
HORNISH *adj* like horn
HORNIST *n* horn player
HORNITO *n* small vent in volcano
HORNLET *n* small horn
HORNS ▸ **horn**
HORNY *adj* of or like horn
HOROEKA *n* New Zealand tree
HORRENT *adj* bristling
HORRID *adj* disagreeable, unpleasant
HORRIFY *vb* cause to feel horror or shock
HORROR *n* (thing or person causing) terror or hatred ▷ *adj* having a frightening subject, usually concerned with the supernatural
HORRORS *pl n* fit of depression or anxiety ▷ *interj* expression of dismay, sometimes facetious
HORS *adv as in* **hors d'oeuvre** appetizer
HORSE *n* large animal with hooves, a mane, and a tail, used for riding and pulling carts etc ▷ *vb* provide with a horse
HORSED ▸ **horse**
HORSES ▸ **horse**
HORSEY *adj* very keen on horses
HORSIER ▸ **horsy**
HORSILY ▸ **horsy**
HORSING ▸ **horse**
HORSON *same as* > **whoreson**
HORSONS ▸ **horson**
HORST *n* ridge of land that has been forced upwards between two parallel faults
HORSTE *same as* ▸ **horst**
HORSTES ▸ **horste**
HORSTS ▸ **horst**
HORSY *same as* ▸ **horsey**
HOSANNA *interj* exclamation of praise to God ▷ *n* act of crying "hosanna" ▷ *vb* cry hosanna
HOSE *n* flexible pipe for

conveying liquid ▷ vb water with a hose

HOSED ▸ hose

HOSEL n socket in head of golf club

HOSELS ▸ hosel

HOSEMAN n fireman in charge of hose

HOSEMEN ▸ hoseman

HOSEN ▸ hose

HOSER n person who swindles or deceives others

HOSERS ▸ hoser

HOSES ▸ hose

HOSEY vb claim possession

HOSEYED ▸ hosey

HOSEYS ▸ hosey

HOSIER n person who sells stockings, etc

HOSIERS ▸ hosier

HOSIERY n stockings, socks, and tights collectively

HOSING ▸ hose

HOSPICE n nursing home for the terminally ill

HOSS n horse

HOSSES ▸ hoss

HOST n person who entertains guests, esp in his own home ▷ vb be the host of

HOSTA n ornamental plant

HOSTAGE n person who is illegally held prisoner until certain demands are met by other people

HOSTAS ▸ hosta

HOSTED ▸ host

HOSTEL n building providing accommodation at a low cost for a specific group of people such as students, travellers, homeless people, etc ▷ vb stay in hostels

HOSTELS ▸ hostel

HOSTESS n woman who receives and entertains guests, esp in her own house ▷ vb act as hostess

HOSTIE n informal Australian word for an air hostess

HOSTIES ▸ hostie

HOSTILE adj unfriendly ▷ n hostile person

HOSTING ▸ host

HOSTLER another name (esp Brit) for ▸ **ostler**

HOSTLY ▸ host

HOSTRY n lodging

HOSTS ▸ host

HOT adj having a high temperature

HOTBED n any place encouraging a particular activity

HOTBEDS ▸ hotbed

HOTBOX n closed room where marijuana is smoked

HOTCAKE n pancake

HOTCH vb jog

HOTCHED ▸ hotch

HOTCHES ▸ hotch

HOTDOG vb perform a series of manoeuvres in skiing, surfing, etc, esp in a showy manner

HOTDOGS ▸ hotdog

HOTE ▸ hight

HOTEL n commercial establishment providing lodging and meals

HOTELS ▸ hotel

HOTEN ▸ hight

HOTFOOT adv quickly and eagerly ▷ vb move quickly

HOTHEAD n excitable or fiery person

HOTLINE n direct telephone link for emergency use

HOTLINK n area on website connecting to another site

HOTLY ▸ hot

HOTNESS ▸ hot

HOTPOT n casserole of meat and vegetables, topped with potatoes

HOTPOTS ▸ hotpot

HOTROD n car with an engine that has been radically modified to produce increased power

HOTRODS ▸ hotrod

HOTS pl n as in **the hots** feeling of lust

HOTSHOT n important person or expert, esp when showy

HOTSPOT n place where wireless broadband services are provided through a wireless local area network

HOTSPUR n impetuous or fiery person

HOTTED ▸ hot

HOTTER vb simmer

HOTTERS ▸ hotter

HOTTEST ▸ hot

HOTTIE n sexually attractive person

HOTTIES ▸ hottie

HOTTING n practice of stealing fast cars and

putting on a show of skilful but dangerous driving

HOTTISH adj fairly hot

HOTTY same as ▸ **hottie**

HOUDAH same as ▸ **howdah**

HOUDAHS ▸ houdah

HOUDAN n breed of light domestic fowl originally from France, with a distinctive full crest

HOUDANS ▸ houdan

HOUF same as ▸ **howf**

HOUFED ▸ houf

HOUFF same as ▸ **howf**

HOUFFED ▸ houff

HOUFFS ▸ houff

HOUFING ▸ houf

HOUFS ▸ houf

HOUGH n in Scotland, a cut of meat corresponding to shin ▷ vb hamstring (cattle, horses, etc)

HOUGHED ▸ hough

HOUGHS ▸ hough

HOUHERE n small evergreen New Zealand tree

HOUMMOS same as ▸ **hummus**

HOUMOUS ▸ hummus

HOUMUS same as ▸ **hummus**

HOUND n hunting dog ▷ vb pursue relentlessly

HOUNDED ▸ hound

HOUNDER ▸ hound

HOUNDS ▸ hound

HOUNGAN n voodoo priest

HOUR n twenty-fourth part of a day, sixty minutes

HOURI n any of the nymphs of paradise

HOURIS ▸ houri

HOURLY adv (happening) every hour ▷ adj of, occurring, or done once every hour ▷ n something that is done by the hour; someone who is paid by the hour

HOURS pl n indefinite time

HOUSE n building used as a home ▷ vb give accommodation to ▷ adj (of wine) sold in a restaurant at a lower price than wines on the wine list

HOUSED ▸ house

HOUSEL vb give the Eucharist to (someone)

HOUSELS ▸ housel

HOUSER ▸ house

HOUSERS ▸ house
HOUSES ▸ house
HOUSEY adj of or like house music
HOUSIER ▸ housey
HOUSING n (providing of) houses
HOUT same as ▸ hoot
HOUTED ▸ hout
HOUTING n type of fish that lives in salt water but spawns in freshwater lakes and is valued for its edible flesh
HOUTS ▸ hout
HOVE ▸ heave
HOVEA n Australian plant with purple flowers
HOVEAS ▸ hovea
HOVED ▸ heave
HOVEL n small dirty house or hut ▷ vb shelter or be sheltered in a hovel
HOVELED ▸ hovel
HOVELS ▸ hovel
HOVEN ▸ heave
HOVER vb (of a bird etc) remain suspended in one place in the air ▷ n act of hovering
HOVERED ▸ hover
HOVERER ▸ hover
HOVERS ▸ hover
HOVES ▸ heave
HOVING ▸ heave
HOW adv in what way, by what means ▷ n the way a thing is done ▷ sentence substitute greeting supposed to be or have been used by American Indians and often used humorously
HOWBE same as ▸ howbeit
HOWBEIT adv in archaic usage, however
HOWDAH n canopied seat on an elephant's back
HOWDAHS ▸ howdah
HOWDIE n midwife
HOWDIED ▸ howdy
HOWDIES ▸ howdy
HOWDY vb greet someone
HOWE n depression in the earth's surface, such as a basin or valley
HOWES ▸ howe
HOWEVER adv nevertheless
HOWF n haunt, esp a public house ▷ vb visit place frequently
HOWFED ▸ howf
HOWFF vb visit place frequently

HOWFFED ▸ howff
HOWFFS ▸ howff
HOWFING ▸ howf
HOWFS ▸ howf
HOWK vb dig (out or up)
HOWKED ▸ howk
HOWKER ▸ howk
HOWKERS ▸ howk
HOWKING ▸ howk
HOWKS ▸ howk
HOWL n loud wailing cry ▷ vb utter a howl
HOWLED ▸ howl
HOWLER n stupid mistake
HOWLERS ▸ howler
HOWLET another word for ▸ owl
HOWLETS ▸ howlet
HOWLING adj great
HOWLS ▸ howl
HOWRE same as ▸ hour
HOWRES ▸ howre
HOWS ▸ how
HOWSO same as > howsoever
HOWZAT ▸ how
HOWZIT informal word for ▸ hello
HOX vb hamstring
This is a word found in Shakespeare's plays, and means to cut a horse's hamstring; it's one of the many short words with X that can get you a high score.
HOXED ▸ hox
HOXES ▸ hox
HOXING ▸ hox
HOY interj cry used to attract someone's attention ▷ n freight barge ▷ vb drive animal with cry
HOYA n any of various E Asian or Australian plants
HOYAS ▸ hoya
HOYDEN n wild or boisterous girl ▷ vb behave like a hoyden
HOYDENS ▸ hoyden
HOYED ▸ hoy
HOYING ▸ hoy
HOYLE n archer's mark used as a target
HOYLES ▸ hoyle
HOYS ▸ hoy
HRYVNA n standard monetary unit of Ukraine, divided into 100 kopiykas
HRYVNAS ▸ hryvna
HRYVNIA n money unit of Ukraine
HRYVNYA same as ▸ hryvna

HUANACO same as ▸ guanaco
HUB n centre of a wheel, through which the axle passes
HUBBIES ▸ hubby
HUBBLY adj having an irregular surface
HUBBUB n confused noise of many voices
HUBBUBS ▸ hubbub
HUBBY n husband
HUBCAP n metal disc that fits on to and protects the hub of a wheel, esp on a car
HUBCAPS ▸ hubcap
HUBRIS n pride, arrogance
HUBS ▸ hub
HUCK same as ▸ huckle
HUCKED ▸ huck
HUCKERY adj ugly
HUCKING ▸ huck
HUCKLE n hip or haunch ▷ vb force out or arrest roughly
HUCKLED ▸ huckle vb
HUCKLES ▸ huckle
HUCKS ▸ huck
HUDDEN ▸ haud
HUDDLE vb hunch (oneself) through cold or fear ▷ n small group
HUDDLED ▸ huddle
HUDDLER ▸ huddle
HUDDLES ▸ huddle
HUDDUP interj get up
HUDNA n truce or ceasefire for a fixed duration
HUDNAS ▸ hudna
HUDUD n set of laws and punishments specified by Allah in the Koran
HUDUDS ▸ hudud
HUE n colour, shade
HUED adj having a hue or colour as specified
HUELESS ▸ hue
HUER n pilchard fisherman
HUERS ▸ huer
HUES ▸ hue
HUFF n passing mood of anger or resentment ▷ vb blow or puff heavily
HUFFED ▸ huff
HUFFER ▸ huffing
HUFFERS ▸ huffing
HUFFIER ▸ huff
HUFFILY ▸ huff
HUFFING n practice of inhaling toxic fumes from glue and other household products for their intoxicating effects

HUFFISH ▸ **huff**
HUFFKIN n type of muffin
HUFFS ▸ **huff**
HUFFY ▸ **huff**
HUG vb clasp tightly in the arms, usu with affection ▷ n tight or fond embrace
HUGE adj very big
HUGELY adv very much
HUGEOUS same as ▸ **huge**
HUGER ▸ **huge**
HUGEST ▸ **huge**
HUGGED ▸ **hug**
HUGGER ▸ **hug**
HUGGERS ▸ **hug**
HUGGIER ▸ **huggy**
HUGGING ▸ **hug**
HUGGY adj sensitive and caring
HUGS ▸ **hug**
HUGY same as ▸ **huge**
HUH interj exclamation of derision, bewilderment, or inquiry
HUHU n type of hairy New Zealand beetle
HUHUS ▸ **huhu**
HUI n meeting of Maori people
HUIA n extinct bird of New Zealand, prized by early Maoris for its distinctive tail feathers
HUIAS ▸ **huia**
HUIC interj in hunting, a call to hounds
HUIPIL n Mayan woman's blouse
HUIPILS ▸ **huipil**
HUIS ▸ **hui**
HUITAIN n verse of eighteen lines
HULA n swaying Hawaiian dance
HULAS ▸ **hula**
HULE same as ▸ **ule**
HULES ▸ **hule**
HULK n body of an abandoned ship ▷ vb move clumsily
HULKED ▸ **hulk**
HULKIER ▸ **hulky**
HULKING adj bulky, unwieldy
HULKS ▸ **hulk**
HULKY same as ▸ **hulking**
HULL n main body of a boat ▷ vb remove the hulls from
HULLED ▸ **hull**
HULLER ▸ **hull**
HULLERS ▸ **hull**
HULLIER ▸ **hully**
HULLING ▸ **hull**

HULLO same as ▸ **hello**
HULLOA same as ▸ **halloa**
HULLOAS ▸ **hulloa**
HULLOED ▸ **hullo**
HULLOES ▸ **hullo**
HULLOO same as ▸ **halloo**
HULLOOS ▸ **hulloo**
HULLOS ▸ **hullo**
HULLS ▸ **hull**
HULLY adj having husks
HUM vb make a low continuous vibrating sound ▷ n humming sound
HUMA n mythical bird
HUMAN adj of or typical of people ▷ n human being
HUMANE adj kind or merciful
HUMANER ▸ **humane**
HUMANLY adv by human powers or means
HUMANS ▸ **human**
HUMAS ▸ **huma**
HUMATE n decomposed plants used as fertilizer
HUMATES ▸ **humate**
HUMBLE adj conscious of one's failings ▷ vb cause to feel humble, humiliate
HUMBLED ▸ **humble**
HUMBLER ▸ **humble**
HUMBLES ▸ **humble**
HUMBLY ▸ **humble**
HUMBUG n hard striped peppermint sweet ▷ vb cheat or deceive (someone)
HUMBUGS ▸ **humbug**
HUMBUZZ n type of beetle
HUMDRUM adj ordinary, dull ▷ n monotonous routine, task, or person
HUMECT vb make moist
HUMECTS ▸ **humect**
HUMEFY same as ▸ **humify**
HUMERAL adj of or relating to the humerus ▷ n silk shawl worn by a priest at High Mass; humeral veil
HUMERI ▸ **humerus**
HUMERUS n bone from the shoulder to the elbow
HUMF same as ▸ **humph**
HUMFED ▸ **humf**
HUMFING ▸ **humf**
HUMFS ▸ **humf**
HUMHUM n Indian cotton cloth
HUMHUMS ▸ **humhum**
HUMIC adj of, relating to, derived from, or resembling humus
HUMID adj damp and hot
HUMIDER ▸ **humid**

HUMIDEX n system of measuring discomfort showing the combined effect of humidity and temperature
HUMIDLY ▸ **humid**
HUMIDOR n humid place or container for storing cigars, tobacco, etc
HUMIFY vb convert or be converted into humus
HUMINT n human intelligence
HUMINTS ▸ **humint**
HUMITE n mineral containing magnesium
HUMITES ▸ **humite**
HUMLIE n hornless cow
HUMLIES ▸ **humlie**
HUMMAUM same as ▸ **hammam**
HUMMED ▸ **hum**
HUMMEL adj (of cattle) hornless ▷ vb remove horns from
HUMMELS ▸ **hummel**
HUMMER ▸ **hum**
HUMMERS ▸ **hum**
HUMMING ▸ **hum**
HUMMLE adj as in **hummle bonnet** type of Scottish cap
HUMMOCK n very small hill ▷ vb form into a hummock or hummocks
HUMMUM same as ▸ **hammam**
HUMMUMS ▸ **hummum**
HUMMUS n creamy dip originating in the Middle East, made from puréed chickpeas
HUMOGEN n type of fertilizer
HUMOR same as ▸ **humour**
HUMORAL adj denoting or relating to a type of immunity caused by free antibodies circulating in the blood
HUMORED ▸ **humor**
HUMORS ▸ **humor**
HUMOUR n ability to say or perceive things that are amusing ▷ vb be kind and indulgent to
HUMOURS ▸ **humour**
HUMOUS same as ▸ **humus**
HUMP n raised piece of ground ▷ vb carry or heave
HUMPED ▸ **hump**
HUMPEN n old German drinking glass
HUMPENS ▸ **humpen**

HUMPER ▸ hump
HUMPERS ▸ hump
HUMPH *interj* exclamation of annoyance or scepticism ▷ *vb* exclaim humph
HUMPHED ▸ humph
HUMPHS ▸ humph
HUMPIER ▸ humpy
HUMPIES ▸ humpy
HUMPING ▸ hump
HUMPS ▸ hump
HUMPTY *n* low padded seat
HUMPY *adj* full of humps ▷ *n* primitive hut
HUMS ▸ hum
HUMUS *n* decomposing vegetable and animal mould in the soil
HUMUSES ▸ humus
HUMUSY ▸ humus
HUMVEE *n* military vehicle
HUMVEES ▸ humvee
HUN *n* member of any of several Asiatic nomadic peoples speaking Mongoloid or Turkic languages
HUNCH *n* feeling or suspicion not based on facts ▷ *vb* draw (one's shoulders) up or together
HUNCHED ▸ hunch
HUNCHES ▸ hunch
HUNDRED *n* ten times ten ▷ *adj* amounting to a hundred
HUNG ▸ hang
HUNGAN *same as* ▸ **houngan**
HUNGANS ▸ hungan
HUNGER *n* discomfort or weakness from lack of food ▷ *vb* want very much
HUNGERS ▸ hunger
HUNGRY *adj* desiring food
HUNH *same as* ▸ **huh**
HUNK *n* large piece
HUNKER *vb* squat
HUNKERS *pl n* haunches
HUNKIER ▸ hunky
HUNKS *n* crotchety old person
HUNKSES ▸ hunks
HUNKY *adj* excellent
HUNNISH ▸ hun
HUNS ▸ hun
HUNT *vb* seek out and kill (wild animals) for food or sport ▷ *n* hunting
HUNTED *adj* harassed and worn
HUNTER *n* person or animal that hunts wild animals for

food or sport
HUNTERS ▸ hunter
HUNTING *n* pursuit and killing or capture of game and wild animals, regarded as a sport
HUNTS ▸ hunt
HUP *vb* cry hup to get a horse to move
HUPIRO *in New Zealand English, same as* ▸ **stinkwood**
HUPIROS ▸ hupiro
HUPPAH *variant spelling of* ▸ **chuppah**
HUPPAHS ▸ huppah
HUPPED ▸ hup
HUPPING ▸ hup
HUPPOT ▸ huppah
HUPPOTH ▸ huppot
HUPS ▸ hup
HURDEN *same as* ▸ **harden**
HURDENS ▸ hurden
HURDIES *pl n* buttocks or haunches
HURDLE *n* light barrier for jumping over in some races ▷ *vb* jump over (something)
HURDLED ▸ hurdle
HURDLER ▸ hurdle
HURDLES ▸ hurdle
HURDS *same as* ▸ **hards**
HURL *vb* throw or utter forcefully ▷ *n* act or an instance of hurling
HURLBAT *same as* ▸ **whirlbat**
HURLED ▸ hurl
HURLER ▸ hurl
HURLERS ▸ hurl
HURLEY *n* another word for the game of hurling
HURLEYS ▸ hurley
HURLIES ▸ hurly
HURLING *n* Irish game like hockey
HURLS ▸ hurl
HURLY *n* wheeled barrow
HURRA *same as* ▸ **hurrah**
HURRAED ▸ hurra
HURRAH *interj* exclamation of joy or applause ▷ *n* cheer of joy or victory ▷ *vb* shout "hurrah"
HURRAHS ▸ hurrah
HURRAS ▸ hurra
HURRAY *same as* ▸ **hurrah**
HURRAYS ▸ hurray
HURRIED *adj* done quickly or too quickly
HURRIER ▸ hurry
HURRIES ▸ hurry
HURRY *vb* (cause to) move

or act very quickly ▷ *n* doing something quickly or the need to do something quickly
HURST *n* wood
HURSTS ▸ hurst
HURT *vb* cause physical or mental pain to ▷ *n* physical or mental pain ▷ *adj* injured or pained
HURTER ▸ hurt
HURTERS ▸ hurt
HURTFUL *adj* unkind
HURTING ▸ hurt
HURTLE *vb* move quickly or violently
HURTLED ▸ hurtle
HURTLES ▸ hurtle
HURTS ▸ hurt
HUSBAND *n* woman's partner in marriage ▷ *vb* use economically
HUSH *vb* make or be silent ▷ *n* stillness or silence ▷ *interj* plea or demand for silence
HUSHABY *interj* used in quietening a baby or child to sleep ▷ *n* lullaby ▷ *vb* quieten to sleep
HUSHED ▸ hush
HUSHER *same as* ▸ **usher**
HUSHERS ▸ husher
HUSHES ▸ hush
HUSHFUL *adj* quiet
HUSHIER ▸ hushy
HUSHING ▸ hush
HUSHY *adj* secret
HUSK *n* outer covering of certain seeds and fruits ▷ *vb* remove the husk from
HUSKED ▸ husk
HUSKER ▸ husk
HUSKERS ▸ husk
HUSKIER ▸ husky
HUSKIES ▸ husky
HUSKILY ▸ husky
HUSKING ▸ husk
HUSKS ▸ husk
HUSKY *adj* slightly hoarse ▷ *n* Arctic sledge dog with thick hair and a curled tail
HUSO *n* sturgeon
HUSOS ▸ huso
HUSS *n* flesh of the European dogfish, when used as food
HUSSAR *n* lightly armed cavalry soldier
HUSSARS ▸ hussar
HUSSES ▸ huss
HUSSIES ▸ hussy
HUSSIF *n* sewing kit**

H

HUSSIFS ▸ hussif
HUSSY *n* immodest or promiscuous woman
HUSTLE *vb* push about, jostle ▷ *n* lively activity or bustle
HUSTLED ▸ hustle
HUSTLER ▸ hustle
HUSTLES ▸ hustle
HUSWIFE *same as* ▸ **housewife**
HUT *n* small house, shelter, or shed
HUTCH *n* cage for pet rabbits etc ▷ *vb* store or keep in or as if in a hutch
HUTCHED ▸ hutch
HUTCHES ▸ hutch
HUTCHIE *n* groundsheet draped over an upright stick, used as a temporary shelter
HUTIA *n* rodent of West Indies
HUTIAS ▸ hutia
HUTLIKE ▸ hut
HUTMENT *n* number or group of huts
HUTS ▸ hut
HUTTED ▸ hut
HUTTING ▸ hut
HUTZPA *same as* ▸ **hutzpah**
HUTZPAH *variant spelling of* ▸ **chutzpah**
HUTZPAS ▸ hutzpa
HUZOOR *n* person of rank in India
HUZOORS ▸ huzoor
HUZZA *same as* ▸ **huzzah**
HUZZAED ▸ huzza
HUZZAH *archaic word for* ▸ **hurrah**
HUZZAHS ▸ huzzah
HUZZAS ▸ huzza
HUZZIES ▸ huzzy
HUZZY *same as* ▸ **hussy**
HWAN *another name for* ▸ **won**
HWYL *n* emotional fervour, as in the recitation of poetry

> This Welsh word can come in very useful for dealing with a consonant-heavy rack.

HWYLS ▸ hwyl
HYACINE *same as* > **hyacinth**
HYAENA *same as* ▸ **hyena**
HYAENAS ▸ hyaena
HYAENIC ▸ hyaena
HYALIN *n* glassy translucent substance,

such as occurs in certain degenerative skin conditions or in hyaline cartilage
HYALINE *adj* clear and translucent, with no fibres or granules ▷ *n* glassy transparent surface
HYALINS ▸ hyalin
HYALITE *n* clear and colourless variety of opal in globular form
HYALOID *adj* clear and transparent ▷ *n* delicate transparent membrane enclosing the vitreous humour of the eye
HYBRID *n* offspring of two plants or animals of different species ▷ *adj* of mixed origin
HYBRIDS ▸ hybrid
HYBRIS *same as* ▸ **hubris**
HYDATID *n* cyst containing tapeworm larvae
HYDRA *n* mythical many-headed water serpent
HYDRAE ▸ hydra
HYDRANT *n* outlet from a water main with a nozzle for a hose
HYDRAS ▸ hydra
HYDRASE *n* enzyme that removes water
HYDRATE *n* chemical compound of water with another substance ▷ *vb* treat or impregnate with water
HYDRIA *n* (in ancient Greece and Rome) a large water jar
HYDRIAE ▸ hydria
HYDRIC *adj* of or containing hydrogen
HYDRID *same as* ▸ **hydroid**
HYDRIDE *n* compound of hydrogen with another element
HYDRIDS ▸ hydrid
HYDRO *n* hotel offering facilities for hydropathy ▷ *adj* electricity as supplied to a residence, business, etc
HYDROID *adj* of or relating to an order of colonial hydrozoan coelenterates that have the polyp phase dominant ▷ *n* hydroid colony or individual
HYDROMA *same as* ▸ **hygroma**

HYDROPS *n* anaemia in a fetus
HYDROS ▸ hydro
HYDROUS *adj* containing water
HYDROXY *adj* (of a chemical compound) containing one or more hydroxyl groups
HYDYNE *n* type of rocket fuel
HYDYNES ▸ hydyne
HYE *same as* ▸ **hie**
HYED ▸ hye
HYEING ▸ hye
HYEN *same as* ▸ **hyena**
HYENA *n* scavenging doglike mammal of Africa and S Asia
HYENAS ▸ hyena
HYENIC ▸ hyena
HYENINE *adj* of hyenas
HYENOID *adj* of or like hyenas
HYENS ▸ hyen
HYES ▸ hye
HYETAL *adj* of or relating to rain, rainfall, or rainy regions
HYGEIST *same as* > **hygienist**
HYGIENE *n* principles and practice of health and cleanliness
HYGROMA *n* swelling in the soft tissue that occurs over a joint, usually caused by repeated injury
HYING ▸ hie
HYKE *same as* ▸ **haik**
HYKES ▸ hyke
HYLA *n* type of tropical American tree frog
HYLAS ▸ hyla
HYLDING *same as* ▸ **hilding**
HYLE *n* wood
HYLEG *n* dominant planet when someone is born
HYLEGS ▸ hyleg
HYLES ▸ hyle
HYLIC *adj* solid
HYLISM *same as* > **hylicism**
HYLISMS ▸ hylism
HYLIST ▸ hylism
HYLISTS ▸ hylism
HYLOIST *n* materialist
HYMEN *n* membrane partly covering the opening of a girl's vagina, which breaks before puberty or at the first occurrence of sexual intercourse
HYMENAL ▸ hymen

HYMENIA > **hymenium**
HYMENS ▸ **hymen**
HYMN n Christian song of praise sung to God or a saint ▷ vb express (praises, thanks, etc) by singing hymns
HYMNAL n book of hymns ▷ adj of, relating to, or characteristic of hymns
HYMNALS ▸ **hymnal**
HYMNARY same as ▸ **hymnal**
HYMNED ▸ **hymn**
HYMNIC ▸ **hymn**
HYMNING ▸ **hymn**
HYMNIST n person who composes hymns
HYMNODY n composition or singing of hymns
HYMNS ▸ **hymn**
HYNDE same as ▸ **hind**
HYNDES ▸ **hynde**
HYOID adj of or relating to the hyoid bone ▷ n horseshoe-shaped bone that lies at the base of the tongue and above the thyroid cartilage
HYOIDAL adj of or relating to the hyoid bone
HYOIDS ▸ **hyoid**
HYP n short for hypotenuse
HYPATE n string of lyre
HYPATES ▸ **hypate**
HYPE n intensive or exaggerated publicity or

sales promotion ▷ vb promote (a product) using intensive or exaggerated publicity
HYPED ▸ **hype**
HYPER ▸ **hype**
HYPERON n any baryon that is not a nucleon
HYPERS ▸ **hype**
HYPES ▸ **hype**
HYPHA n any of the filaments that constitute the body (mycelium) of a fungus
HYPHAE ▸ **hypha**
HYPHAL ▸ **hypha**
HYPHEN n punctuation mark (-) indicating that two words or syllables are connected ▷ vb hyphenate
HYPHENS ▸ **hyphen**
HYPHIES ▸ **hyphy**
HYPHY n type of hip-hop music
HYPING ▸ **hype**
HYPINGS ▸ **hype**
HYPNIC n sleeping drug
HYPNICS ▸ **hypnic**
HYPNOID adj of or relating to a state resembling sleep or hypnosis
HYPNONE n sleeping drug
HYPNUM n species of moss
HYPNUMS ▸ **hypnum**
HYPO vb inject with a hypodermic syringe
HYPOED ▸ **hypo**

HYPOGEA > **hypogeum**
HYPOID adj as in **hypoid gear** gear having a tooth form generated by a hypocycloidal curve; used extensively in motor vehicle transmissions to withstand a high surface loading
HYPOING ▸ **hypo**
HYPONEA same as > **hypopnea**
HYPONYM n word whose meaning is included in that of another word
HYPOS ▸ **hypo**
HYPOXIA n deficiency in the amount of oxygen delivered to the body tissues
HYPOXIC ▸ **hypoxia**
HYPPED ▸ **hyp**
HYPPING ▸ **hyp**
HYPS ▸ **hyp**
HYPURAL adj below the tail
HYRACES ▸ **hyrax**
HYRAX n type of hoofed rodent-like animal of Africa and Asia
HYRAXES ▸ **hyrax**
HYSON n Chinese green tea
HYSONS ▸ **hyson**
HYSSOP n sweet-smelling herb used in folk medicine
HYSSOPS ▸ **hyssop**
HYTE adj insane
HYTHE same as ▸ **hithe**
HYTHES ▸ **hythe**

H

I i

The letter **I** can prove a difficult tile to use effectively in Scrabble. It's one of the most common tiles in the game, so you often end up with two or more on your rack, but it can be hard to get rid of. Where **I** does come in very useful, though, is in the number of everyday short words that can be formed from it, which are very helpful when you need to form short words in addition to the main word that you want to play. These words include **in**, **is**, **it** (2 points each), **id** (3) and **if** (5). Other handy words are **icy** (8), **ivy** (9) and **imp** (7). Don't forget the three-letter words that use **K**: **ilk**, **ink** and **irk** (7 each), while **iwi** for 6 points can be very useful in getting rid of a surplus of **I**s.

IAMB *n* metrical foot of two syllables, a short one followed by a long one
IAMBI ▸ **iambus**
IAMBIC *adj* written in metrical units of one short and one long syllable ▷ *n* iambic foot, line, or stanza
IAMBICS ▸ **iambic**
IAMBIST *n* one who writes iambs
IAMBS ▸ **iamb**
IAMBUS *same as* ▸ **iamb**
IATRIC *adj* relating to medicine or physicians
IBADAH *n* following of Islamic beliefs and practices
IBADAT ▸ **ibadah**
IBERIS *n* plant with white or purple flowers
IBEX *n* wild goat with large backward-curving horns
IBEXES ▸ **ibex**
IBICES ▸ **ibex**
IBIDEM *adv* in the same place
IBIS *n* large wading bird with long legs
IBISES ▸ **ibis**
IBRIK ▸ **cezve**
IBRIKS ▸ **ibrik**
ICE *n* water in the solid state, formed by freezing liquid water ▷ *vb* form or cause to form ice
ICEBALL *n* ball of ice
ICEBERG *n* large floating mass of ice
ICEBOAT *n* boat that breaks up bodies of ice in water
ICEBOX *n* refrigerator
ICECAP *n* mass of ice permanently covering an area
ICECAPS ▸ **icecap**
ICED *adj* covered with icing
ICEFALL *n* very steep part of a glacier that has deep crevasses and resembles a frozen waterfall
ICELESS ▸ **ice**
ICELIKE ▸ **ice**
ICEMAN *n* person who sells or delivers ice
ICEMEN ▸ **iceman**
ICEPACK *n* bag or folded cloth containing ice, applied to a part of the body, esp the head, to cool, reduce swelling, etc
ICER *n* person who ices cakes
ICERS ▸ **icer**
ICES ▸ **ice**
ICEWINE *n* dessert wine made from grapes that have frozen before being harvested
ICH *archaic form of* ▸ **eke**
　A Shakespearean spelling of **eke**, this is a useful little word worth remembering because of its unusual combination of letters and relatively high score.
ICHABOD *interj* the glory has departed
ICHED ▸ **ich**
ICHES ▸ **ich**
ICHING ▸ **ich**
ICHNITE *n* trace fossil
ICHOR *n* fluid said to flow in the veins of the gods
ICHORS ▸ **ichor**
ICHS ▸ **ich**
ICHTHIC *same as* > **ichthyic**
ICHTHYS *n* early Christian emblem
ICICLE *n* tapering spike of ice hanging where water has dripped
ICICLED *adj* covered with icicles
ICICLES ▸ **icicle**
ICIER ▸ **icy**
ICIEST ▸ **icy**
ICILY *adv* in an icy or reserved manner
ICINESS *n* condition of being icy or very cold
ICING *n* mixture of sugar and water etc, used to cover and decorate cakes
ICINGS ▸ **icing**
ICK *interj* expression of disgust
　An interjection expressing disgust, this is one of the highest-scoring three-letter words beginning with I. It does not take an S, but it does take a Y to make **icky**.
ICKER *n* ear of corn
ICKERS ▸ **icker**

ICKIER ▸ icky
ICKIEST ▸ icky
ICKILY ▸ icky
ICKLE *ironically childish word for* ▸ **little**
ICKLER ▸ ickle
ICKLEST ▸ ickle
ICKY *adj* sticky
ICON *n* picture of Christ or another religious figure, regarded as holy in the Orthodox Church
ICONES ▸ icon
ICONIC *adj* relating to, resembling, or having the character of an icon
ICONIFY *vb* render as an icon
ICONISE *same as* ▸ **iconize**
ICONIZE *vb* render as an icon
ICONS ▸ icon
ICTAL ▸ ictus
ICTERIC ▸ icterus
ICTERID *n* bird of the oriole family
ICTERUS *n* yellowing of plant leaves, caused by excessive cold or moisture
ICTIC ▸ ictus
ICTUS *n* metrical or rhythmic stress in verse feet, as contrasted with the stress accent on words
ICTUSES ▸ ictus
ICY *adj* very cold
ID *n* mind's instinctive unconscious energies
IDANT *n* chromosome
IDANTS ▸ idant
IDE *n* silver orfe fish
IDEA *n* plan or thought formed in the mind ▷ *vb* have or form an idea
IDEAED ▸ idea
IDEAL *adj* most suitable ▷ *n* conception of something that is perfect
IDEALLY ▸ ideal
IDEALS ▸ ideal
IDEAS ▸ idea
IDEATA ▸ ideatum
IDEATE *vb* form or have an idea of
IDEATED ▸ ideate
IDEATES ▸ ideate
IDEATUM *n* objective reality with which human ideas are supposed to correspond
IDEE *n* idea
IDEES ▸ idee
IDEM *adj* same: used to refer to an article, chapter, or book already quoted
IDENT *n* short visual image employed between television programmes that works as a logo to locate the viewer to the channel
IDENTIC *adj* (esp of opinions expressed by two or more governments) having the same wording or intention regarding another power
IDENTS ▸ ident
IDES *n* (in the Ancient Roman calendar) the 15th of March, May, July, or October, or the 13th of other months
IDIOCY *n* utter stupidity
IDIOM *n* group of words which when used together have a different meaning from the words individually
IDIOMS ▸ idiom
IDIOT *n* foolish or stupid person
IDIOTCY *same as* ▸ **idiocy**
IDIOTIC *adj* of or resembling an idiot
IDIOTS ▸ idiot
IDLE *adj* not doing anything ▷ *vb* spend (time) doing very little
IDLED ▸ idle
IDLER *n* person who idles
IDLERS ▸ idler
IDLES ▸ idle
IDLESSE ▸ idle
IDLEST ▸ idle
IDLING ▸ idle
IDLY ▸ idle
IDOL *n* object of excessive devotion
IDOLA ▸ idolum
IDOLISE *same as* ▸ **idolize**
IDOLISM ▸ idolize
IDOLIST ▸ idolize
IDOLIZE *vb* love or admire excessively
IDOLON *n* mental image
IDOLS ▸ idol
IDOLUM *n* mental picture
IDS ▸ id
IDYL *same as* ▸ **idyll**
IDYLIST *same as* > **idyllist**
IDYLL *n* scene or time of great peace and happiness
IDYLLIC *adj* of or relating to an idyll
IDYLLS ▸ idyll
IDYLS ▸ idyl
IF *n* uncertainty or doubt
IFF *conj* in logic, a shortened form of if and only if
This word is one of the highest-scoring three-letter words beginning with I, and of course provides a useful extension to **if**.
IFFIER ▸ iffy
IFFIEST ▸ iffy
IFFY *adj* doubtful, uncertain
IFS ▸ if
IFTAR *n* meal eaten by Muslims to break their fast after sunset every day during Ramadan
IFTARS ▸ iftar
IGAD *same as* ▸ **egad**
IGAPO *n* flooded forest
IGAPOS ▸ igapo
IGARAPE *n* canoe route
IGG *vb* antagonize
IGGED ▸ igg
IGGING ▸ igg
IGGS ▸ igg
IGLOO *n* dome-shaped Inuit house made of snow and ice
IGLOOS ▸ igloo
IGLU *same as* ▸ **igloo**
IGLUS ▸ iglu
IGNARO *n* ignoramus
IGNAROS ▸ ignaro
IGNATIA *n* dried seed
IGNEOUS *adj* (of rock) formed as molten rock cools and hardens
IGNIFY *vb* turn into fire
IGNITE *vb* catch fire or set fire to
IGNITED ▸ ignite
IGNITER *n* person or thing that ignites
IGNITES ▸ ignite
IGNITOR *same as* ▸ **igniter**
IGNOBLE *adj* dishonourable
IGNOBLY ▸ ignoble
IGNOMY *Shakespearean variant of* > **ignominy**
IGNORE *vb* refuse to notice, disregard deliberately ▷ *n* disregard
IGNORED ▸ ignore
IGNORER ▸ ignore
IGNORES ▸ ignore
IGUANA *n* large tropical American lizard
IGUANAS ▸ iguana
IGUANID *same as* ▸ **iguana**
IHRAM *n* customary white robes worn by Muslim pilgrims to Mecca, symbolizing a sacred or consecrated state

IHRAMS ▸ **ihram**

IJTIHAD n effort of a Muslim scholar to derive a legal ruling from the Koran

IKAN n (in Malaysia) fish used esp in names of cooked dishes

IKANS ▸ **ikan**

IKAT n method of creating patterns in fabric by tie-dyeing the yarn before weaving

IKATS ▸ **ikat**

IKEBANA n Japanese art of flower arrangement

IKON same as ▸ **icon**

IKONS ▸ **ikon**

ILEA ▸ **ileum**

This is the plural of **ileum**, part of the small intestine, and is often useful as a rack-balancing play when you have too many vowels.

ILEAC adj of or relating to the ileum

ILEAL same as ▸ **ileac**

ILEITIS n inflammation of the ileum

ILEUM n lowest part of the small intestine

ILEUS n obstruction of the intestine, esp the ileum, by mechanical occlusion or as the result of distension of the bowel following loss of muscular action

ILEUSES ▸ **ileus**

ILEX n any of a genus of trees or shrubs that includes holly

ILEXES ▸ **ilex**

ILIA ▸ **ilium**

ILIAC adj of or relating to the ilium

ILIACUS n iliac

ILIAD n epic poem

ILIADS ▸ **iliad**

ILIAL ▸ **ilium**

ILICES ▸ **ilex**

ILIUM n uppermost and widest of the three sections of the hipbone

ILK n type ▷ determiner each

ILKA same as ▸ **ilk**

ILKADAY n every day

ILKS ▸ **ilk**

ILL adj not in good health ▷ n evil, harm ▷ adv badly

ILLAPSE vb slide in

ILLEGAL adj against the law ▷ n person who has entered or attempted to enter a country illegally

ILLER ▸ **ill**

ILLEST ▸ **ill**

ILLIAD n wink

ILLIADS ▸ **illiad**

ILLICIT adj illegal

ILLIPE n Asian tree

ILLIPES ▸ **illipe**

ILLITE n clay mineral of the mica group, found in shales and mudstones

ILLITES ▸ **illite**

ILLITIC ▸ **illite**

ILLNESS n disease or indisposition

ILLOGIC n reasoning characterized by lack of logic

ILLS ▸ **ill**

ILLTH n condition of poverty or misery

ILLTHS ▸ **illth**

ILLUDE vb trick or deceive

ILLUDED ▸ **illude**

ILLUDES ▸ **illude**

ILLUME vb illuminate

ILLUMED ▸ **illume**

ILLUMES ▸ **illume**

ILLUPI same as ▸ **illipe**

ILLUPIS ▸ **illupi**

ILLUVIA ▸ **illuvium**

ILLY adv badly

IMAGE n mental picture of someone or something ▷ vb picture in the mind

IMAGED ▸ **image**

IMAGER n device that produces images

IMAGERS ▸ **imager**

IMAGERY n images collectively, esp in the arts

IMAGES ▸ **image**

IMAGINE vb form a mental image of ▷ sentence substitute exclamation of surprise

IMAGING ▸ **image**

IMAGISM n poetic movement in England and America between 1912 and 1917

IMAGIST ▸ **imagism**

IMAGO n sexually mature adult insect

IMAGOES ▸ **imago**

IMAGOS ▸ **imago**

IMAM n leader of prayers in a mosque

IMAMATE n region or territory governed by an imam

IMAMS ▸ **imam**

IMARET n (in Turkey) a hospice for pilgrims or travellers

IMARETS ▸ **imaret**

IMARI n Japanese porcelain

IMARIS ▸ **imari**

IMAUM same as ▸ **imam**

IMAUMS ▸ **imaum**

IMBALM same as ▸ **embalm**

IMBALMS ▸ **imbalm**

IMBAR vb bar in

IMBARK vb cover in bark

IMBARKS ▸ **imbark**

IMBARS ▸ **imbar**

IMBASE vb degrade

IMBASED ▸ **imbase**

IMBASES ▸ **imbase**

IMBATHE vb bathe

IMBED same as ▸ **embed**

IMBEDS ▸ **imbed**

IMBIBE vb drink (alcoholic drinks)

IMBIBED ▸ **imbibe**

IMBIBER ▸ **imbibe**

IMBIBES ▸ **imbibe**

IMBIZO n meeting, esp a gathering of the Zulu people called by the king or a traditional leader

IMBIZOS ▸ **imbizo**

IMBLAZE vb depict heraldically

IMBODY same as ▸ **embody**

IMBOSK vb conceal

IMBOSKS ▸ **imbosk**

IMBOSOM vb hold in one's heart

IMBOSS same as ▸ **emboss**

IMBOWER vb enclose in a bower

IMBRAST Spenserian past participle of ▸ **embrace**

IMBREX n curved tile

IMBROWN vb make brown

IMBRUE vb stain, esp with blood

IMBRUED ▸ **imbrue**

IMBRUES ▸ **imbrue**

IMBRUTE vb reduce to a bestial state

IMBUE vb fill or inspire with (ideals or principles)

IMBUED ▸ **imbue**

IMBUES ▸ **imbue**

IMBUING ▸ **imbue**

IMBURSE vb pay

IMID n immunomodulatory drug

IMIDE n any of a class of organic compounds

IMIDES ▸ **imide**

IMIDIC ▸ **imide**

IMIDO ▸ **imide**

IMIDS ▸ **imid**

IMINE *n* any of a class of organic compounds

IMINES ▸ imine

IMINO ▸ imine

IMITANT *same as* ▸ **imitation**

IMITATE *vb* take as a model

IMMANE *adj* monstrous

IMMASK *vb* disguise

IMMASKS ▸ immask

IMMENSE *adj* extremely large

IMMERGE *archaic word for* ▸ **immerse**

IMMERSE *vb* involve deeply, engross

IMMESH *same as* ▸ **enmesh**

IMMEW *vb* confine

IMMEWED ▸ immew

IMMEWS ▸ immew

IMMIES ▸ immy

IMMIT *vb* insert

IMMITS ▸ immit

IMMIX *vb* mix in

IMMIXED ▸ immix

IMMIXES ▸ immix

IMMORAL *adj* morally wrong, corrupt

IMMUNE *adj* protected against a specific disease ▷ *n* immune person or animal

IMMUNES ▸ immune

IMMURE *vb* imprison

IMMURED ▸ immure

IMMURES ▸ immure

IMMY *n* image-orthicon camera

IMP *n* (in folklore) mischievous small creature with magical powers ▷ *vb* insert (new feathers) into the stumps of broken feathers in order to repair the wing of a hawk or falcon

IMPACT *n* strong effect ▷ *vb* have a strong effect on

IMPACTS ▸ impact

IMPAINT *vb* paint

IMPAIR *vb* weaken or damage

IMPAIRS ▸ impair

IMPALA *n* southern African antelope

IMPALAS ▸ impala

IMPALE *vb* pierce with a sharp object

IMPALED ▸ impale

IMPALER ▸ impale

IMPALES ▸ impale

IMPANEL *variant spelling (esp US) of* ▸ **empanel**

IMPARK *vb* make into a park

IMPARKS ▸ impark

IMPARL *vb* parley

IMPARLS ▸ imparl

IMPART *vb* communicate (information)

IMPARTS ▸ impart

IMPASSE *n* situation in which progress is impossible

IMPASTE *vb* apply paint thickly to

IMPASTO *n* technique of applying paint thickly, so that brush marks are evident ▷ *vb* apply impasto

IMPAVE *vb* set in a pavement

IMPAVED ▸ impave

IMPAVES ▸ impave

IMPAVID *adj* fearless

IMPAWN *vb* pawn

IMPAWNS ▸ impawn

IMPEACH *vb* charge with a serious crime against the state

IMPEARL *vb* adorn with pearls

IMPED ▸ imp

IMPEDE *vb* hinder in action or progress

IMPEDED ▸ impede

IMPEDER ▸ impede

IMPEDES ▸ impede

IMPEDOR *n* component, such as an inductor or resistor, that offers impedance

IMPEL *vb* push or force (someone) to do something

IMPELS ▸ impel

IMPEND *vb* (esp of something threatening) to be about to happen

IMPENDS ▸ impend

IMPERIA ▸ imperium

IMPERIL *vb* put in danger

IMPETUS *n* incentive, impulse

IMPHEE *n* African sugar cane

IMPHEES ▸ imphee

IMPI *n* group of Zulu warriors

IMPIES ▸ impi

IMPIETY *n* lack of respect or religious reverence

IMPING ▸ imp

IMPINGE *vb* affect or restrict

IMPINGS ▸ imp

IMPIOUS *adj* showing a lack of respect or reverence

IMPIS ▸ impi

IMPISH *adj* mischievous

IMPLANT *n* something put into someone's body, usu by surgical operation ▷ *vb* put (something) into someone's body, usu by surgical operation

IMPLATE *vb* sheathe

IMPLEAD *vb* sue or prosecute

IMPLED ▸ implead

IMPLETE *vb* fill

IMPLEX *n* part of an arthropod

IMPLIED *adj* hinted at or suggested

IMPLIES ▸ imply

IMPLODE *vb* collapse inwards

IMPLORE *vb* beg earnestly

IMPLY *vb* indicate by hinting, suggest

IMPONE *vb* impose

IMPONED ▸ impone

IMPONES ▸ impone

IMPORT *vb* bring in (goods) from another country ▷ *n* something imported

IMPORTS ▸ import

IMPOSE *vb* force the acceptance of

IMPOSED ▸ impose

IMPOSER ▸ impose

IMPOSES ▸ impose

IMPOSEX *n* imposition of male sexual characteristics on female gastropods, caused by pollutants

IMPOST *n* tax, esp a customs duty ▷ *vb* classify (imported goods) according to the duty payable on them

IMPOSTS ▸ impost

IMPOT *n* slang term for the act of imposing

IMPOTS ▸ impot

IMPOUND *vb* take legal possession of, confiscate

IMPOWER *less common spelling of* ▸ **empower**

IMPREGN *vb* impregnate

IMPRESA *n* heraldic device

IMPRESE *same as* ▸ **impresa**

IMPRESS *vb* affect strongly, usu favourably ▷ *n* impressing

IMPREST *n* fund of cash from which a department or other unit pays incidental expenses, topped up periodically from central funds

IMPRINT n mark made by printing or stamping ▷ vb produce (a mark) by printing or stamping

IMPROV n improvisational comedy

IMPROVE vb make or become better

IMPROVS ▸ improv

IMPS ▸ imp

IMPUGN vb challenge the truth or validity of

IMPUGNS ▸ impugn

IMPULSE vb give an impulse to ▷ n sudden urge to do something

IMPURE adj having dirty or unwanted substances mixed in

IMPURER ▸ impure

IMPUTE vb attribute responsibility to

IMPUTED ▸ impute

IMPUTER ▸ impute

IMPUTES ▸ impute

IMSHI interj go away!

IMSHY same as ▸ imshi

IN prep indicating position inside, state or situation, etc ▷ adv indicating position inside, entry into, etc ▷ adj fashionable ▷ n way of approaching or befriending a person ▷ vb to take in

INANE adj senseless, silly ▷ n something that is inane

INANELY ▸ inane

INANER ▸ inane

INANES ▸ inane

INANEST ▸ inane

INANGA n common type of New Zealand grass tree

INANGAS ▸ inanga

INANITY n lack of intelligence or imagination

INAPT adj not apt or fitting

INAPTLY ▸ inapt

INARCH vb graft (a plant) by uniting stock and scion while both are still growing independently

INARM vb embrace

INARMED ▸ inarm

INARMS ▸ inarm

INBEING n existence in something else

INBENT adj bent inwards

INBOARD adj (of a boat's engine) inside the hull ▷ adv within the sides of or towards the centre of a vessel or aircraft

INBORN adj existing from birth, natural

INBOUND vb pass into the playing area from outside it ▷ adj coming in

INBOX n folder which stores in-coming email messages

INBOXES ▸ inbox

INBREAK n breaking in

INBRED n inbred person or animal ▷ adj produced as a result of inbreeding

INBREDS ▸ inbred

INBREED vb breed from closely related individuals

INBRING vb bring in

INBUILT adj present from the start

INBURST n irruption

INBY adv into the house or an inner room ▷ adj located near or nearest to the house

INBYE adv near the house

INCAGE vb confine in or as in a cage

INCAGED ▸ incage

INCAGES ▸ incage

INCANT vb chant (a spell)

INCANTS ▸ incant

INCASE variant spelling of ▸ encase

INCASED ▸ incase

INCASES ▸ incase

INCAVE vb hide

INCAVED ▸ incave

INCAVES ▸ incave

INCAVI ▸ incavo

INCAVO n incised part of a carving

INCEDE vb advance

INCEDED ▸ incede

INCEDES ▸ incede

INCENSE vb make very angry ▷ n substance that gives off a sweet perfume when burned

INCENT vb provide incentive

INCENTS ▸ incent

INCEPT vb (of organisms) to ingest (food) ▷ n rudimentary organ

INCEPTS ▸ incept

INCEST n sexual intercourse between two people too closely related to marry

INCESTS ▸ incest

INCH n unit of length equal to one twelfth of a foot or 2.54 centimetres ▷ vb move slowly and gradually

INCHASE same as ▸ enchase

INCHED ▸ inch

INCHER n something measuring given amount of inches

INCHERS ▸ incher

INCHES ▸ inch

INCHING ▸ inch

INCHPIN n cervine sweetbread

INCIPIT n Latin introductory phrase

INCISAL adj relating to the cutting edge of incisors and cuspids

INCISE vb cut into with a sharp tool

INCISED ▸ incise

INCISES ▸ incise

INCISOR n front tooth, used for biting into food

INCITE vb stir up, provoke

INCITED ▸ incite

INCITER ▸ incite

INCITES ▸ incite

INCIVIL archaic form of ▸ uncivil

INCLASP vb clasp

INCLE same as ▸ inkle

INCLES ▸ incle

INCLINE vb lean, slope ▷ n slope

INCLIP vb embrace

INCLIPS ▸ inclip

INCLOSE less common spelling of ▸ enclose

INCLUDE vb have as part of the whole

INCOG n incognito

INCOGS ▸ incog

INCOME n amount of money earned from work, investments, etc

INCOMER n person who comes to live in a place in which he or she was not born

INCOMES ▸ income

INCONIE adj fine or delicate

INCONNU n whitefish of Arctic waters

INCONY adj fine or delicate

INCROSS n plant or animal produced by continued inbreeding ▷ vb inbreed or produce by inbreeding

INCRUST same as ▸ encrust

INCUBI ▸ incubus

INCUBUS n (in folklore) demon believed to have sex with sleeping women

INCUDAL ▸ incus

INCUDES ▸ incus

INCULT adj (of land) uncultivated

INCUR vb cause (something unpleasant) to happen
INCURS ▸ **incur**
INCURVE vb curve or cause to curve inwards
INCUS n central of the three small bones in the middle ear of mammals
INCUSE n design stamped or hammered onto a coin ▷ vb impress (a design) in a coin or to impress (a coin) with a design by hammering or stamping ▷ adj stamped or hammered onto a coin
INCUSED ▸ **incuse**
INCUSES ▸ **incuse**
INCUT adj cut or etched in
INDABA n (among native peoples of southern Africa) a meeting to discuss a serious topic
INDABAS ▸ **indaba**
INDAMIN same as
▷ **indamine**
INDART vb dart in
INDARTS ▸ **indart**
INDEED adv really, certainly ▷ interj expression of indignation or surprise
INDENE n colourless liquid hydrocarbon extracted from petroleum and coal tar and used in making synthetic resins
INDENES ▸ **indene**
INDENT vb make a dent in
INDENTS ▸ **indent**
INDEW same as ▸ **indue**
INDEWED ▸ **indew**
INDEWS ▸ **indew**
INDEX n alphabetical list of names or subjects dealt with in a book ▷ vb provide (a book) with an index
INDEXAL ▸ **index**
INDEXED ▸ **index**
INDEXER ▸ **index**
INDEXES ▸ **index**
INDIA n code word for the letter I
INDIAS ▸ **india**
INDICAN n compound secreted in the urine, usually in the form of its potassium salt
INDICES plural of ▸ **index**
INDICIA > **indicium**
INDICT vb formally charge with a crime
INDICTS ▸ **indict**
INDIE adj (of rock music)

released by an independent record company ▷ n independent record company
INDIES ▸ **indie**
INDIGEN same as > **indigene**
INDIGN adj undeserving
INDIGO adj deep violet-blue ▷ n dye of this colour
INDIGOS ▸ **indigo**
INDITE vb write
INDITED ▸ **indite**
INDITER ▸ **indite**
INDITES ▸ **indite**
INDIUM n soft silvery-white metallic element
INDIUMS ▸ **indium**
INDOL same as ▸ **indole**
INDOLE n white or yellowish crystalline heterocyclic compound extracted from coal tar and used in perfumery, medicine, and as a flavouring agent
INDOLES ▸ **indole**
INDOLS ▸ **indol**
INDOOR adj inside a building
INDOORS adj inside or into a building
INDORSE variant spelling of ▸ **endorse**
INDOW archaic variant of ▸ **endow**
INDOWED ▸ **indow**
INDOWS ▸ **indow**
INDOXYL n yellow water-soluble crystalline compound occurring in woad as its glucoside and in urine as its ester
INDRAFT same as > **indraught**
INDRAWN adj drawn or pulled in
INDRI same as ▸ **indris**
INDRIS n large Madagascan arboreal lemuroid primate
INDUCE vb persuade or influence
INDUCED ▸ **induce**
INDUCER ▸ **induce**
INDUCES ▸ **induce**
INDUCT vb formally install (someone, esp a clergyman) in office
INDUCTS ▸ **induct**
INDUE variant spelling of ▸ **endue**
INDUED ▸ **indue**
INDUES ▸ **indue**
INDUING ▸ **indue**

INDULGE vb allow oneself pleasure
INDULIN same as > **induline**
INDULT n faculty granted by the Holy See allowing a specific deviation from the Church's common law
INDULTS ▸ **indult**
INDUNA n (in South Africa) a Black African overseer in a factory, mine, etc
INDUNAS ▸ **induna**
INDUSIA > **indusium**
INDWELL vb (of a spirit, principle, etc) to inhabit
INDWELT ▸ **indwell**
INEARTH poetic word for ▸ **bury**
INEDITA pl n unpublished writings
INEPT adj clumsy, lacking skill
INEPTER ▸ **inept**
INEPTLY ▸ **inept**
INERM adj without thorns
INERT n inert thing ▷ adj without the power of motion or resistance
INERTER ▸ **inert**
INERTIA n feeling of unwillingness to do anything

This is not the easiest of words to see, but its combination of common letters makes it one of the most frequently played of 7-letter bonuses, while its plurals, which can be **inertiae** or **inertias**, are among the 8-letter bonus words that come up most often.

INERTLY ▸ **inert**
INERTS ▸ **inert**
INEXACT adj not exact or accurate
INFALL vb move towards a black hole, etc, under the influence of gravity
INFALLS ▸ **infall**
INFAME vb defame
INFAMED ▸ **infame**
INFAMES ▸ **infame**
INFAMY n state of being infamous
INFANCY n early childhood
INFANT n very young child ▷ adj of, relating to, or designed for young children
INFANTA n (formerly)

daughter of a king of Spain or Portugal

INFANTE *n* (formerly) any son of a king of Spain or Portugal, except the heir to the throne

INFANTS ▸ infant

INFARCT *n* localized area of dead tissue (necrosis) resulting from obstruction of the blood supply to that part, esp by an embolus ▷ *vb* obstruct the blood supply to part of a body

INFARE *vb* enter

INFARES ▸ infare

INFAUNA *n* animals that live in ocean and river beds

INFAUST *adj* unlucky

INFECT *vb* affect with a disease ▷ *adj* contaminated or polluted with or as if with a disease

INFECTS ▸ infect

INFEFT *vb* give possession of heritable property

INFEFTS ▸ infeft

INFELT *adj* heartfelt

INFEOFF *same as* ▸ enfeoff

INFER *vb* work out from evidence

INFERE *adv* together

INFERNO *n* intense raging fire

INFERS ▸ infer

INFEST *vb* inhabit or overrun in unpleasantly large numbers

INFESTS ▸ infest

INFIDEL *n* person with no religion ▷ *adj* of unbelievers or unbelief

INFIELD *n* area of the field near the pitch

INFIGHT *vb* box at close quarters

INFILL *vb* fill in ▷ *n* act of filling or closing gaps, etc, in something, such as a row of buildings

INFILLS ▸ infill

INFIMA ▸ infimum

INFIMUM *n* greatest lower bound

INFIRM *vb* make infirm ▷ *adj* physically or mentally weak

INFIRMS ▸ infirm

INFIX *vb* fix firmly in ▷ *n* affix inserted into the middle of a word

INFIXED ▸ infix

INFIXES ▸ infix

INFLAME *vb* make angry or excited

INFLATE *vb* expand by filling with air or gas

INFLECT *vb* change (the voice) in tone or pitch

INFLICT *vb* impose (something unpleasant) on

INFLOW *n* something, such as liquid or gas, that flows in ▷ *vb* flow in

INFLOWS ▸ inflow

INFLUX *n* arrival or entry of many people or things

INFO *n* information

INFOLD *variant spelling of* ▸ enfold

INFOLDS ▸ infold

INFORCE *same as* ▸ enforce

INFORM *vb* tell ▷ *adj* without shape

INFORMS ▸ inform

INFOS ▸ info

INFRA *adv* (esp in textual annotation) below

INFRACT *vb* violate or break (a law, an agreement, etc)

INFULA *same as* ▸ infulae

INFULAE *pl n* two ribbons hanging from the back of a bishop's mitre

INFUSE *vb* fill (with an emotion or quality)

INFUSED ▸ infuse

INFUSER *n* any device used to make an infusion, esp a tea maker

INFUSES ▸ infuse

ING *n* meadow near a river

INGAN *Scots word for* ▸ onion

INGANS ▸ ingan

INGATE *n* entrance

INGATES ▸ ingate

INGENER *Shakespearean form of* ▸ engineer

INGENU *n* artless or inexperienced boy or young man

INGENUE *n* artless or inexperienced girl or young woman

INGENUS ▸ ingenu

INGEST *vb* take (food or liquid) into the body

INGESTA *pl n* nourishment taken into the body through the mouth

INGESTS ▸ ingest

INGINE *n* genius

INGINES ▸ ingine

INGLE *n* fire in a room or a fireplace

INGLES ▸ ingle

INGLOBE *vb* shape as a sphere

INGO *n* a reveal

INGOES ▸ ingo

INGOING *same as* ▸ ingo

INGOT *n* oblong block of cast metal ▷ *vb* shape (metal) into ingots

INGOTED ▸ ingot

INGOTS ▸ ingot

INGRAFT *variant spelling of* ▸ engraft

INGRAIN *vb* impress deeply on the mind or nature ▷ *adj* (of carpets) made of dyed yarn or of fibre that is dyed before being spun into yarn ▷ *n* carpet made from ingrained yarn

INGRAM *adj* ignorant

INGRATE *n* ungrateful person ▷ *adj* ungrateful

INGRESS *n* entrance

INGROSS *archaic form of* ▸ engross

INGROUP *n* highly cohesive and relatively closed social group

INGROWN *adj* (esp of a toenail) grown abnormally into the flesh

INGRUM *adj* ignorant

INGS ▸ ing

INGULF *variant spelling of* ▸ engulf

INGULFS ▸ ingulf

INGULPH *archaic form of* ▸ engulf

INHABIT *vb* live in

INHALE *vb* breathe in (air, smoke, etc)

INHALED ▸ inhale

INHALER *n* container for an inhalant

INHALES ▸ inhale

INHAUL *n* line for hauling in a sail

INHAULS ▸ inhaul

INHAUST *vb* drink in

INHERCE *same as* ▸ inhearse

INHERE *vb* be an inseparable part (of)

INHERED ▸ inhere

INHERES ▸ inhere

INHERIT *vb* receive (money etc) from someone who has died

INHIBIN *n* peptide hormone

INHIBIT *vb* restrain (an impulse or desire)

INHOOP *vb* confine

INHOOPS ▸ inhoop
INHUMAN *adj* cruel or brutal
INHUME *vb* inter
INHUMED ▸ inhume
INHUMER ▸ inhume
INHUMES ▸ inhume
INIA ▸ inion
INION *n* most prominent point at the back of the head, used as a point of measurement in craniometry
INIONS ▸ inion
INISLE *vb* put on or make into an island
INISLED ▸ inisle
INISLES ▸ inisle
INITIAL *adj* first, at the beginning ▷ *n* first letter, esp of a person's name ▷ *vb* sign with one's initials
INJECT *vb* put (a fluid) into the body with a syringe
INJECTS ▸ inject
INJELLY *vb* place in jelly
INJERA *n* white Ethiopian flatbread, similar to a crepe
INJERAS ▸ injera
INJOINT *vb* join
INJUNCT *vb* issue a legal injunction against (a person)
INJURE *vb* hurt physically or mentally
INJURED ▸ injure
INJURER ▸ injure
INJURES ▸ injure
INJURY *n* physical hurt
INK *n* coloured liquid used for writing or printing ▷ *vb* mark in ink (something already marked in pencil)
INKBLOT *n* abstract patch of ink, one of ten commonly used in the Rorschach test
INKED ▸ ink
INKER ▸ ink
INKERS ▸ ink
INKHORN *n* (formerly) a small portable container for ink, usually made from horn
INKHOSI *n* Zulu clan chief
INKIER ▸ inky
INKIEST ▸ inky
INKING ▸ ink
INKJET *adj* of a method of printing streams of electrically charged ink
INKLE *n* kind of linen tape used for trimmings ▷ *vb* to hint

INKLED ▸ inkle
INKLES ▸ inkle
INKLESS ▸ ink
INKLIKE ▸ ink
INKLING *n* slight idea or suspicion
INKOSI ▸ inkhosi
INKOSIS ▸ inkosi
INKPAD *n* ink-soaked pad used for rubber-stamping or fingerprinting
INKPADS ▸ inkpad
INKPOT *n* ink-bottle
INKPOTS ▸ inkpot
INKS ▸ ink
INKSPOT *n* ink stain
INKWELL *n* small container for ink, often fitted into the surface of a desk
INKWOOD *n* type of tree
INKY *adj* dark or black
INLACE *variant spelling of* ▸ **enlace**
INLACED ▸ inlace
INLACES ▸ inlace
INLAID ▸ inlay
INLAND *adv* in or towards the interior of a country, away from the sea ▷ *adj* of or in the interior of a country or region, away from a sea or border ▷ *n* interior of a country or region
INLANDS ▸ inland
INLAY *n* inlaid substance or pattern ▷ *vb* decorate (an article, esp of furniture) by inserting pieces of wood, ivory, or metal so that the surfaces are smooth and flat
INLAYER ▸ inlay
INLAYS ▸ inlay
INLET *n* narrow strip of water extending from the sea into the land ▷ *vb* insert or inlay
INLETS ▸ inlet
INLIER *n* outcrop of rocks that is entirely surrounded by younger rocks
INLIERS ▸ inlier
INLOCK *vb* lock up
INLOCKS ▸ inlock
INLY *adv* inwardly
INLYING *adj* situated within or inside
INMATE *n* person living in an institution such as a prison
INMATES ▸ inmate
INMESH *variant spelling of*

▸ **enmesh**
INMOST *adj* innermost
INN *n* pub or small hotel, esp in the country ▷ *vb* stay at an inn
INNAGE *n* measurement from bottom of container to surface of liquid
INNAGES ▸ innage
INNARDS *pl n* internal organs
INNATE *adj* being part of someone's nature, inborn
INNED ▸ inn
INNER *adj* happening or located inside ▷ *n* red innermost ring on a target
INNERLY ▸ inner
INNERS ▸ inner
INNERVE *vb* supply with nervous energy
INNING *n* division of cricket consisting of a turn at batting and a turn in the field for each side
INNINGS ▸ inning
INNIT *interj* isn't it
INNLESS *adj* without inns
INNS ▸ inn
INNYARD *n* courtyard of an inn
INOCULA > inoculum
INORB *vb* enclose in or as if in an orb
INORBED ▸ inorb
INORBS ▸ inorb
INOSINE *n* type of molecule making up cell
INOSITE *same as* > **inositol**
INPHASE *adj* in the same phase
INPOUR *vb* pour in
INPOURS ▸ inpour
INPUT *n* resources put into a project etc ▷ *vb* enter (data) in a computer
INPUTS ▸ input
INQILAB *n* (in India, Pakistan, etc) revolution
INQUERE *Spenserian form of* ▸ **inquire**
INQUEST *n* official inquiry into a sudden death
INQUIET *vb* disturb
INQUIRE *vb* seek information or ask (about)
INQUIRY *n* question
INRO *n* Japanese seal-box
INROAD *n* invasion or hostile attack
INROADS ▸ inroad
INRUN *n* slope down which ski jumpers ski**

INRUNS ▸ inrun
INRUSH n sudden and overwhelming inward flow
INS ▸ in
INSANE adj mentally ill
INSANER ▸ insane
INSANIE n insanity
INSCAPE n essential inner nature of a person, an object, etc
INSCULP vb engrave
INSEAM vb contain
INSEAMS ▸ inseam
INSECT n small animal with six legs and usu wings, such as an ant or fly
INSECTS ▸ insect
INSEEM vb cover with grease
INSEEMS ▸ inseem
INSERT vb put inside or include ▷ n something inserted
INSERTS ▸ insert
INSET n small picture inserted within a larger one ▷ vb place in or within ▷ adj decorated with something inserted
INSETS ▸ inset
INSHELL vb retreat, as into a shell
INSHIP vb travel or send by ship
INSHIPS ▸ inship
INSHORE adj close to the shore ▷ adv towards the shore
INSIDE prep in or to the interior of ▷ adj on or of the inside ▷ adv on, in, or to the inside, indoors ▷ n inner side, surface, or part
INSIDER n member of a group who has privileged knowledge about it
INSIDES ▸ inside
INSIGHT n deep understanding
INSIGNE same as ▸ insignia
INSINEW vb connect or strengthen, as with sinews
INSIPID adj lacking interest, spirit, or flavour
INSIST vb demand or state firmly
INSISTS ▸ insist
INSNARE less common spelling of ▸ ensnare
INSOFAR adv to the extent
INSOLE n inner sole of a shoe or boot
INSOLES ▸ insole

INSOOTH adv indeed
INSOUL same as ▸ ensoul
INSOULS ▸ insoul
INSPAN vb harness (animals) to (a vehicle)
INSPANS ▸ inspan
INSPECT vb check closely or officially
INSPIRE vb fill with enthusiasm, stimulate
INSTAL same as ▸ install
INSTALL vb put in and prepare (equipment) for use
INSTALS ▸ instal
INSTANT n very brief time ▷ adj happening at once
INSTAR vb decorate with stars ▷ n stage in the development of an insect between any two moults
INSTARS ▸ instar
INSTATE vb place in a position or office
INSTEAD adv as a replacement or substitute
INSTEP n part of the foot forming the arch between the ankle and toes
INSTEPS ▸ instep
INSTIL vb introduce (an idea etc) gradually into someone's mind
INSTILL same as ▸ instil
INSTILS ▸ instil
INSULA n pyramid-shaped area of the brain within each cerebral hemisphere beneath parts of the frontal and temporal lobes
INSULAE ▸ insula
INSULAR adj not open to new ideas, narrow-minded ▷ n islander
INSULIN n hormone produced in the pancreas that controls the amount of sugar in the blood
INSULSE adj stupid
INSULT vb behave rudely to, offend ▷ n insulting remark or action
INSULTS ▸ insult
INSURE vb protect by insurance
INSURED adj covered by insurance ▷ n person, persons, or organization covered by an insurance policy
INSURER n person or company that sells insurance

INSURES ▸ insure
INSWEPT adj narrowed towards the front
INSWING n movement of a bowled ball from off to leg through the air
INTACT adj not changed or damaged in any way
INTAGLI > intaglio
INTAKE n amount or number taken in
INTAKES ▸ intake
INTEGER n positive or negative whole number or zero
INTEL n US military intelligence
INTELS ▸ intel
INTEND vb propose or plan (to do something)
INTENDS ▸ intend
INTENSE adj of great strength or degree
INTENT n intention ▷ adj paying close attention
INTENTS ▸ intent
INTER vb bury (a corpse)
INTERIM adj temporary, provisional, or intervening ▷ n intervening time ▷ adv meantime
INTERN vb imprison, esp during a war ▷ n trainee doctor in a hospital
INTERNE same as ▸ intern
INTERNS ▸ intern
INTERS ▸ inter
INTHRAL archaic form of ▸ enthral
INTI n former monetary unit of Peru
INTIL Scots form of ▸ into
INTIMA n innermost layer of an organ or part, esp a blood vessel
INTIMAE ▸ intima
INTIMAL ▸ intima
INTIMAS ▸ intima
INTIME adj intimate
INTINE n inner wall of a pollen grain or a spore
INTINES ▸ intine
INTIRE archaic form of ▸ entire
INTIS ▸ inti
INTITLE archaic form of ▸ entitle
INTO prep indicating motion towards the centre, result of a change, division, etc
INTOED adj having inward-turning toes
INTOMB same as ▸ entomb

INTOMBS ▸ intomb

INTONE vb speak or recite in an unvarying tone of voice

INTONED ▸ intone

INTONER ▸ intone

INTONES ▸ intone

INTORT vb twist inward

INTORTS ▸ intort

INTOWN adj infield

INTRA prep within

INTRADA n prelude

INTRANT n one who enters

INTREAT archaic spelling of ▸ entreat

INTRO n introduction

INTROFY vb increase the wetting properties

INTROIT n short prayer said or sung as the celebrant is entering the sanctuary to celebrate Mass

INTROLD same as ▸ entrold

INTRON n stretch of DNA that interrupts a gene and does not contribute to the specification of a protein

INTRONS ▸ intron

INTROS ▸ intro

INTRUDE vb come in or join in without being invited

INTRUST same as ▸ entrust

INTUIT vb know or discover by intuition

INTUITS ▸ intuit

INTURN n inward turn

INTURNS ▸ inturn

INTUSE n contusion

INTUSES ▸ intuse

INTWINE less common spelling of ▸ entwine

INTWIST vb twist together

INULA n plant of the elecampane genus

INULAS ▸ lnula

INULASE n enzyme that hydrolyses inulin to fructose

INULIN n fructose polysaccharide present in the tubers and rhizomes of some plants

INULINS ▸ inulin

INURE vb cause to accept or become hardened to

INURED ▸ inure

INURES ▸ inure

INURING ▸ inure

INURN vb place (esp cremated ashes) in an urn

INURNED ▸ inurn

INURNS ▸ inurn

INUST adj burnt in

INUTILE adj useless

INVADE vb enter (a country) by military force

INVADED ▸ invade

INVADER ▸ invade

INVADES ▸ invade

INVALID n disabled or chronically ill person ▷ vb dismiss from active service because of illness or injury ▷ adj having no legal force

INVAR n alloy made from iron and nickel

INVARS ▸ invar

INVEIGH vb criticize strongly

INVENIT sentence substitute (he or she) designed it: used formerly on objects such as pocket watches next to the designer's name

INVENT vb think up or create (something new)

INVENTS ▸ invent

INVERSE vb make something opposite or contrary in effect ▷ adj reversed in effect, sequence, direction, etc ▷ n exact opposite

INVERT vb turn upside down or inside out ▷ n homosexual

INVERTS ▸ invert

INVEST vb spend (money, time, etc) on something with the expectation of profit

INVESTS ▸ invest

INVEXED adj concave

INVIOUS adj without paths or roads

INVITAL adj not vital

INVITE vb request the company of ▷ n invitation

INVITED ▸ invite

INVITEE n one who is invited

INVITER ▸ invite

INVITES ▸ invite

INVOICE n (present with) a bill for goods or services supplied ▷ vb present (a customer) with an invoice

INVOKE vb put (a law or penalty) into operation

INVOKED ▸ invoke

INVOKER ▸ invoke

INVOKES ▸ invoke

INVOLVE vb include as a necessary part

INWALL vb surround with a wall

INWALLS ▸ inwall

INWARD adj directed towards the middle ▷ adv towards the inside or middle ▷ n inward part

INWARDS adv towards the inside or middle of something

INWEAVE vb weave together into or as if into a design, fabric, etc

INWICK vb perform a curling stroke in which the stone bounces off another stone

INWICKS ▸ inwick

INWIND vb wind or coil around

INWINDS ▸ inwind

INWIT n conscience

INWITH adv within

INWITS ▸ inwit

INWORK vb work in

INWORKS ▸ inwork

INWORN adj worn in

INWOUND ▸ inwind

INWOVE ▸ inweave

INWOVEN ▸ inweave

INWRAP less common spelling of ▸ enwrap

INWRAPS ▸ inwrap

INYALA n antelope

INYALAS ▸ inyala

IO interj an exclamation expressing joy, triumph, grief etc ▷ n a cry of "io"

IODATE same as ▸ iodize

IODATED ▸ iodate

IODATES ▸ iodate

IODIC adj of or containing iodine

IODID same as ▸ iodide

IODIDE n compound containing an iodine atom, such as methyl iodide

IODIDES ▸ iodide

IODIDS ▸ iodid

IODIN same as ▸ iodine

IODINE n bluish-black element used in medicine and photography

IODINES ▸ iodine

IODINS ▸ iodin

IODISE same as ▸ iodize

IODISED ▸ iodise

IODISER ▸ iodise

IODISES ▸ iodise

IODISM n poisoning induced by ingestion of iodine or its compounds

IODISMS ▸ iodism

IODIZE vb treat with iodine

IODIZED ▸ iodize

IODIZER ▸ iodize

IODIZES ▸ iodize
IODOUS adj of or containing iodine, esp in the trivalent state
IODURET n iodide
IOLITE n grey or violet-blue dichroic mineral
IOLITES ▸ iolite
ION n electrically charged atom
IONIC adj of or in the form of ions
IONICS pl n study of ions
IONISE same as ▸ **ionize**
IONISED ▸ ionise
IONISER same as ▸ **ionizer**
IONISES ▸ ionise
IONIUM n naturally occurring radioisotope of thorium
IONIUMS ▸ ionium
IONIZE vb change into ions
IONIZED ▸ ionize
IONIZER n person or thing that ionizes, esp an electrical device used within a room to refresh its atmosphere by restoring negative ions
IONIZES ▸ ionize
IONOGEN n compound that exists as ions when dissolved
IONOMER n thermoplastic with ionic bonding between polymer chains
IONONE n yellowish liquid mixture of two isomers with an odour of violets
IONONES ▸ ionone
IONS ▸ ion
IOS ▸ io
IOTA n ninth letter in the Greek alphabet

> This word for a Greek letter is another of those that often come in handy when you are trying to rid your rack of too many vowels.

IOTAS ▸ iota
IPECAC n type of S American shrub
IPECACS ▸ ipecac
IPOMOEA n tropical or subtropical convolvulaceous plant
IPPON n winning point awarded in a judo or karate competition
IPPONS ▸ ippon
IRACUND adj easily angered

IRADE n written edict of a Muslim ruler
IRADES ▸ irade
IRATE adj very angry
IRATELY ▸ irate
IRATER ▸ irate
IRATEST ▸ irate
IRE vb anger ▷ n anger
IRED ▸ ire
IREFUL ▸ ire
IRELESS ▸ ire
IRENIC adj tending to conciliate or promote peace
IRENICS n that branch of theology that is concerned with unity between Christian sects and denominations
IRES ▸ ire
IRID n type of iris
IRIDAL ▸ irid
IRIDEAL ▸ irid
IRIDES ▸ iris
IRIDIAL ▸ irid
IRIDIAN ▸ irid
IRIDIC adj of or containing iridium, esp in the tetravalent state
IRIDISE vb make iridescent
IRIDIUM n very hard corrosion-resistant metal
IRIDIZE vb make iridescent
IRIDS ▸ irid
IRING ▸ ire
IRIS n coloured circular membrane of the eye containing the pupil ▷ vb display iridescence
IRISATE vb make iridescent
IRISED ▸ iris
IRISES ▸ iris
IRISING ▸ iris
IRITIC ▸ iritis
IRITIS n inflammation of the iris of the eye

> Since a plague of Is tends to afflict every Scrabble player's rack at regular intervals, it is well worth knowing words like this one, meaning inflammation of the iris, which use several of the wretched letter!

IRK vb irritate, annoy
IRKED ▸ irk
IRKING ▸ irk
IRKS ▸ irk
IRKSOME adj irritating, annoying
IROKO n tropical African hardwood tree

IROKOS ▸ iroko
IRON n strong silvery-white metallic element, widely used for structural and engineering purposes ▷ adj made of iron ▷ vb smooth (clothes or fabric) with an iron
IRONE n fragrant liquid

> You may surprise your opponent by adding an E to **iron** if you know this word for a kind of aromatic oil.

IRONED ▸ iron
IRONER ▸ iron
IRONERS ▸ iron
IRONES ▸ irone
IRONIC adj using irony
IRONIER ▸ irony
IRONIES ▸ irony
IRONING n clothes to be ironed
IRONISE same as ▸ **ironize**
IRONIST ▸ ironize
IRONIZE vb use or indulge in irony
IRONMAN n very strong man
IRONMEN ▸ ironman
IRONS ▸ iron
IRONY n mildly sarcastic use of words to imply the opposite of what is said ▷ adj of, resembling, or containing iron
IRREAL adj unreal
IRRUPT vb enter forcibly or suddenly
IRRUPTS ▸ irrupt
IS third person singular present tense of ▸ **be**
ISABEL n brown yellow colour
ISABELS ▸ isabel
ISAGOGE n academic introduction to a specialized subject field or area of research
ISATIN n yellowish-red crystalline compound soluble in hot water, used for the preparation of vat dyes
ISATINE same as ▸ **isatin**
ISATINS ▸ isatin
ISBA n log hut
ISBAS ▸ isba
ISCHIA ▸ ischium
ISCHIAL ▸ ischium
ISCHIUM n one of the three sections of the hipbone, situated below the ilium

ISH *n* issue

An **ish** is a word for an issue in Scots law. If you have I, S and H on your rack, remember that as well as adding **ish** to the end of many words, you can also play those letters as a word in its own right.

ISHES ▸ ish
ISIT *sentence substitute* expression used to seek confirmation of something or show one is listening
ISLAND *n* piece of land surrounded by water ▷ *vb* cause to become an island
ISLANDS ▸ island
ISLE *vb* make an isle of ▷ *n* island
ISLED ▸ isle
ISLEMAN *n* islander
ISLEMEN ▸ isleman
ISLES ▸ isle
ISLET *n* small island
ISLETED *adj* having islets
ISLETS ▸ islet
ISLING ▸ isle
ISM *n* doctrine, system, or practice

While **ism** can be added to the ends of many words as a suffix, it's worth remembering as a word in its own right.

ISMATIC *adj* following fashionable doctrines
ISMS ▸ ism
ISNA *vb* is not
ISNAE *same as ▸* **isna**
ISO *n* short segment of film that can be replayed easily
ISOAMYL *n as in* **isoamyl acetate** colourless volatile compound used as a solvent for cellulose lacquers and as a flavouring
ISOBAR *n* line on a map connecting places of equal atmospheric pressure
ISOBARE *same as ▸* **isobar**
ISOBARS ▸ isobar
ISOBASE *n* line connecting points of equal land upheaval
ISOBATH *n* line on a map connecting points of equal underwater depth
ISOCHOR *n* line on a graph showing the variation of the temperature of a fluid with its pressure, when the volume is kept constant
ISODICA ▸ isodicon
ISODOMA ▸ isodomon
ISODONT *n* animal in which the teeth are of similar size
ISODOSE *n* dose of radiation applied to a part of the body in radiotherapy that is equal to the dose applied to a different part
ISOETES *n* quillwort
ISOFORM *n* protein similar in function but not form to another
ISOGAMY *n* (in some algae and fungi) sexual fusion of gametes of similar size and form
ISOGENY ▸ isogenous
ISOGON *n* equiangular polygon
ISOGONE *same as ▸* **isogonic**
ISOGONS ▸ isogon
ISOGONY ▸ isogonic
ISOGRAM *same as ▸* **isopleth**
ISOGRIV *n* line connecting points of equal angular difference between magnetic north and grid north
ISOHEL *n* line on a map connecting places with an equal period of sunshine
ISOHELS ▸ isohel
ISOHYET *n* line on a map connecting places having equal rainfall
ISOKONT *same as ▸* **isokontan**
ISOLATE *vb* place apart or alone ▷ *n* isolated person or group
ISOLEAD *n* line on a ballistic graph
ISOLEX *n* isogloss marking off the area in which a particular item of vocabulary is found
ISOLINE *same as ▸* **isopleth**
ISOLOG ▸ isologous
ISOLOGS ▸ isologous
ISOMER *n* substance whose molecules contain the same atoms as another but in a different arrangement
ISOMERE *same as ▸* **isomer**
ISOMERS ▸ isomer
ISONOME *n* line on a chart connecting points of equal abundance values of a plant species sampled in different sections of an area
ISONOMY *n* equality before the law of the citizens of a state
ISOPACH *n* line on a map connecting points below which a particular rock stratum has the same thickness
ISOPOD *n* type of crustacean including woodlice and pill bugs ▷ *adj* of this type of crustacean
ISOPODS ▸ isopod
ISOS ▸ iso
ISOSPIN *n* internal quantum number used in the classification of elementary particles
ISOTACH *n* line on a map connecting points of equal wind speed
ISOTONE *n* one of two or more atoms of different atomic number that contain the same number of neutrons
ISOTOPE *n* one of two or more atoms with the same number of protons in the nucleus but a different number of neutrons
ISOTOPY ▸ isotope
ISOTRON *n* device for separating small quantities of isotopes by ionizing them and separating the ions by a mass spectrometer
ISOTYPE *n* presentation of statistical information in a row of diagrams
ISOZYME *n* any of a set of structural variants of an enzyme occurring in different tissues in a single species
ISSEI *n* first-generation Japanese immigrant
ISSEIS ▸ issei
ISSUANT *adj* emerging or issuing
ISSUE *n* topic of interest or discussion ▷ *vb* make (a statement etc) publicly
ISSUED ▸ issue
ISSUER ▸ issue
ISSUERS ▸ issue
ISSUES ▸ issue
ISSUING ▸ issue
ISTANA *n* (in Malaysia) a royal palace
ISTANAS ▸ istana

ISTHMI ▸ isthmus
ISTHMIC ▸ isthmus
ISTHMUS *n* narrow strip of land connecting two areas of land
ISTLE *n* fibre obtained from various tropical American agave and yucca trees used in making carpets, cord, etc
ISTLES ▸ istle
IT *pron* refers to a nonhuman, animal, plant, or inanimate object ▷ *n* player whose turn it is to catch the others in children's games
ITA *n* type of palm
ITACISM *n* pronunciation of the Greek letter eta as in Modern Greek
ITALIC *adj* (of printing type) sloping to the right ▷ *n* style of printing type modelled on this, chiefly used to indicate emphasis, a foreign word, etc
ITALICS ▸ italic
ITAS ▸ ita
ITCH *n* skin irritation causing a desire to scratch ▷ *vb* have an itch
ITCHED ▸ itch

ITCHES ▸ itch
ITCHIER ▸ itch
ITCHILY ▸ itch
ITCHING ▸ itch
ITCHY ▸ itch
ITEM *n* single thing in a list or collection ▷ *adv* likewise ▷ *vb* itemize
ITEMED ▸ item
ITEMING ▸ item
ITEMISE *same as* ▸ **itemize**
ITEMIZE *vb* make a list of
ITEMS ▸ item
ITERANT ▸ iterate
ITERATE *vb* repeat
ITERUM *adv* again
ITHER *Scots word for* ▸ **other**
ITS *pron* belonging to it ▷ *adj* of or belonging to it
ITSELF *pron* reflexive form of it
IURE *adv* by law
IVIED *adj* covered with ivy
IVIES ▸ ivy
IVORIED ▸ ivory
IVORIES *pl n* keys of a piano
IVORIST *n* worker in ivory
IVORY *n* hard white bony substance forming the tusks of elephants ▷ *adj* yellowish-white
IVRESSE *n* drunkenness

IVY *n* evergreen climbing plant
IVYLIKE ▸ ivy
IWI *n* Maori tribe

This Maori word for a tribe is a great one for getting rid of an awkward combination of letters.

IWIS *archaic word for* ▸ **certainly**
IXIA *n* southern African plant of the iris family with showy ornamental funnel-shaped flowers
IXIAS ▸ ixia
IXODID *n* hard-bodied tick
IXODIDS ▸ ixodid
IXORA *n* flowering shrub
IXORAS ▸ ixora
IXTLE *same as* ▸ **istle**
IXTLES ▸ ixtle
IZAR *n* long garment worn by Muslim women
IZARD *n* type of goat-antelope
IZARDS ▸ izard
IZARS ▸ izar
IZZARD *n* letter Z
IZZARDS ▸ izzard
IZZAT *n* honour or prestige
IZZATS ▸ izzat

Jj

J, being worth 8 points on its own, is a good tile for scoring well with, especially as it combines well with **Z** to make **jiz** and with **X** to make great words like **jeux**, **jinx** and **jynx**. However, **J** is a difficult letter when it comes to making bonus words scoring that extra 50 points, so you will normally want to play it off fairly quickly. There are two two-letter words that begin with **J**: **ja** and **jo**. As **J** has such a high value, look out for double- and triple-letter squares when playing these. There are plenty of good three-letter words starting with **J**: **jab** (12 points), **jak** (14), **jam** (12), **jar** (10), **jaw** (13), **jay** (13), **jet** (10), **jib** (12), **jig** (11), **job** (12), **jog** (11), **jot** (10), **joy** (13), **jug** (11) and **jut** (10).

JA *interj* yes ▷ *sentence substitute* yes
JAB *vb* poke sharply ▷ *n* quick punch or poke
JABBED ▸ **jab**
JABBER *vb* talk rapidly or incoherently ▷ *n* rapid or incoherent talk
JABBERS ▸ **jabber**
JABBING ▸ **jab**
JABBLE *vb* ripple
JABBLED ▸ **jabble**
JABBLES ▸ **jabble**
JABERS *interj* Irish exclamation
JABIRU *n* large white-and-black Australian stork
JABIRUS ▸ **jabiru**
JABOT *n* frill or ruffle on the front of a blouse or shirt
JABOTS ▸ **jabot**
JABS ▸ **jab**
JACAL *n* Mexican daub hut
JACALES ▸ **jacal**
JACALS ▸ **jacal**
JACAMAR *n* tropical American bird with an iridescent plumage
JACANA *n* long-legged long-toed bird of tropical and subtropical marshy regions
JACANAS ▸ **jacana**
JACARE *another name for* ▸ **cayman**
JACARES ▸ **jacare**
JACCHUS *n* small monkey
JACENT *adj* lying
JACINTH *another name for*

> **hyacinth**
JACK *n* device for raising a motor vehicle or other heavy object ▷ *vb* lift or push (an object) with a jack
JACKAL *n* doglike wild animal of Africa and Asia ▷ *vb* behave like a jackal
JACKALS ▸ **jackal**
JACKASS *n* fool
JACKDAW *n* black-and-grey Eurasian bird of the crow family
JACKED ▸ **jack**
JACKEEN *n* slick self-assertive lower-class Dubliner
JACKER *n* labourer
JACKERS ▸ **jacker**
JACKET *n* short coat ▷ *vb* put a jacket on (someone or something)
JACKETS ▸ **jacket**
JACKING ▸ **jack**
JACKLEG *n* unskilled worker
JACKMAN *n* retainer
JACKMEN ▸ **jackman**
JACKPOT *n* largest prize that may be won in a game
JACKS *n* game in which metal, bone, or plastic pieces are thrown and then picked up between throws of a small ball
JACOBIN *n* variety of fancy pigeon with a hood of feathers swept up over and around the head
JACOBUS *n* English gold

coin minted in the reign of James I
JACONET *n* light cotton fabric used for clothing, bandages, etc
JACUZZI *n* bath or pool equipped with a system of underwater jets
JADE *n* ornamental semiprecious stone, usu dark green ▷ *adj* bluish-green ▷ *vb* exhaust or make exhausted from work or use
JADED *adj* tired and unenthusiastic
JADEDLY ▸ **jaded**
JADEITE *n* usually green or white mineral, found in igneous and metamorphic rocks
JADERY *n* shrewishness
JADES ▸ **jade**
JADING ▸ **jade**
JADISH ▸ **jade**
JADITIC ▸ **jade**
JAEGER *n* marksman in certain units of the German or Austrian armies
JAEGERS ▸ **jaeger**
JAFFA *n* (in cricket) well-bowled ball that is practically unplayable
JAFFAS ▸ **jaffa**
JAG *n* period of uncontrolled indulgence in an activity ▷ *vb* cut unevenly
JAGA *n* guard ▷ *vb* guard or watch

JAGAED ▸ jaga
JAGAING ▸ jaga
JAGAS ▸ jaga
JAGER same as ▸ **jaeger**
JAGERS ▸ jager
JAGG same as ▸ **jag**
JAGGARY same as
  ▸ **jaggery**
JAGGED ▸ jag
JAGGER n pedlar
JAGGERS ▸ jagger
JAGGERY n coarse brown
  sugar made in the East
  Indies from the sap of the
  date palm
JAGGIER ▸ jaggy
JAGGIES ▸ jaggy
JAGGING ▸ jag
JAGGS ▸ jagg
JAGGY adj prickly ▷ n jagged
  computer image
JAGHIR n Indian regional
  governance
JAGHIRE n Indian regional
  governance
JAGHIRS ▸ jaghir
JAGIR n Indian regional
  governance
JAGIRS ▸ jagir
JAGLESS ▸ jag
JAGRA n Hindu festival
JAGRAS ▸ jagra
JAGS ▸ jag
JAGUAR n large S American
  spotted cat
JAGUARS ▸ jaguar
JAI interj victory (to)
JAIL n prison ▷ vb send to
  prison
JAILED ▸ jail
JAILER n person in charge of
  a jail
JAILERS ▸ jailer
JAILING ▸ jail
JAILOR same as ▸ **jailer**
JAILORS ▸ jailor
JAILS ▸ jail
JAK ▸ jack
JAKE adj slang word
  meaning all right
JAKES n human excrement
JAKESES ▸ jakes
JAKS ▸ jack
JALABIB ▸ jilbab
JALAP n Mexican
  convolvulaceous plant
JALAPIC ▸ jalap
JALAPIN n purgative resin
JALAPS ▸ jalap
JALOP same as ▸ **jalap**
JALOPPY same as ▸ **jalopy**
JALOPS ▸ jalop
JALOPY n old car

JALOUSE vb suspect
JAM vb pack tightly into a
  place ▷ n fruit preserve or
  hold-up of traffic
JAMAAT n Islamic council
JAMAATS ▸ jamaat
JAMADAR n Indian army
  officer
JAMB n side post of a door or
  window frame ▷ vb climb
  up a crack in rock
JAMBART same as ▸ **greave**
JAMBE same as ▸ **jamb**
JAMBEAU another word for
  ▸ **greave**
JAMBED ▸ jamb
JAMBEE n light cane
JAMBEES ▸ jambee
JAMBER same as ▸ **greave**
JAMBERS ▸ jamber
JAMBES ▸ jambe
JAMBEUX ▸ jambeau
JAMBIER n greave
JAMBING ▸ jamb
JAMBIYA n curved dagger
JAMBO sentence substitute E
  African salutation
JAMBOK same as ▸ **sjambok**
JAMBOKS ▸ jambok
JAMBONE n type of play in
  the card game euchre
JAMBOOL same as
  ▸ **jambolan**
JAMBS ▸ jamb
JAMBU same as ▸ **jambolan**
JAMBUL same as
  ▸ **jambolan**
JAMBULS ▸ jambul
JAMBUS ▸ jambu
JAMDANI n patterned
  muslin
JAMES n jemmy
JAMESES ▸ james
JAMJAR n container for
  preserves
JAMJARS ▸ jamjar
JAMLIKE ▸ jam
JAMMED ▸ jam
JAMMER ▸ jam
JAMMERS ▸ jam
JAMMIER ▸ jammy
JAMMIES informal word for
  ▸ **pyjamas**
JAMMING ▸ jam
JAMMY adj lucky
JAMON n as in **jamon
  serrano** cured ham from
  Spain
JAMPAN n type of sedan
  chair used in India
JAMPANI same as
  ▸ **jampanee**
JAMPANS ▸ jampan

JAMPOT n container for
  preserves
JAMPOTS ▸ jampot
JAMS ▸ jam
JANE n girl or woman
JANES ▸ jane
JANGLE vb (cause to) make a
  harsh ringing noise ▷ n
  harsh ringing noise
JANGLED ▸ jangle
JANGLER ▸ jangle
JANGLES ▸ jangle
JANGLY adj making a
  jangling sound
JANITOR n caretaker of a
  school or other building
JANIZAR n > **Turkish soldier**
  This is an old word for a
  Turkish soldier,
  combining J and Z. If your
  opponent plays it,
  remember that you can
  add not only an S to it to
  form the plural, but also
  a Y, making the variant
  spelling **janizary**.
JANKER n device for
  transporting logs
JANKERS ▸ janker
JANN n lesser jinn
JANNIES ▸ janny
JANNOCK same as
  ▸ **jonnock**
JANNS ▸ jann
JANNY n janitor
JANSKY n unit of flux
  density used
  predominantly in radio and
  infrared astronomy
JANSKYS ▸ jansky
JANTEE archaic version of
  ▸ **jaunty**
JANTIER ▸ janty
JANTIES ▸ janty
JANTY n petty officer ▷ adj
  (in archaic usage) jaunty
JAP vb splash
JAPAN n very hard varnish,
  usu black ▷ vb cover with
  this varnish ▷ adj relating
  to or varnished with japan
JAPANS ▸ japan
JAPE n joke or prank ▷ vb
  joke or jest (about)
JAPED ▸ jape
JAPER ▸ jape
JAPERS ▸ jape
JAPERY ▸ jape
JAPES ▸ jape
JAPING ▸ jape
JAPINGS ▸ jape
JAPPED ▸ jap
JAPPING ▸ jap

JAPS ▸ **jap**
JAR n wide-mouthed container, usu round and made of glass ▷ vb have a disturbing or unpleasant effect
JARFUL same as ▸ **jar**
JARFULS ▸ **jarful**
JARGON n specialized technical language of a particular subject ▷ vb use or speak in jargon
JARGONS ▸ **jargon**
JARGONY ▸ **jargon**
JARGOON same as ▸ **jargon**
JARHEAD n US Marine
JARINA n South American palm tree
JARINAS ▸ **jarina**
JARK n seal or pass
JARKMAN n forger of passes or licences
JARKMEN ▸ **jarkman**
JARKS ▸ **jark**
JARL n Scandinavian chieftain or noble
JARLDOM ▸ **jarl**
JARLS ▸ **jarl**
JAROOL n Indian tree
JAROOLS ▸ **jarool**
JARP vb strike or smash, esp to break the shell of (an egg) at Easter
JARPED ▸ **jarp**
JARPING ▸ **jarp**
JARPS ▸ **jarp**
JARRAH n Australian eucalypt yielding valuable timber
JARRAHS ▸ **jarrah**
JARRED ▸ **jar**
JARRING ▸ **jar**
JARS ▸ **jar**
JARSFUL ▸ **jarful**
JARTA n heart
JARTAS ▸ **jarta**
JARUL same as ▸ **jarool**
JARULS ▸ **jarul**
JARVEY n hackney coachman
JARVEYS ▸ **jarvey**
JARVIE same as ▸ **jarvey**
JARVIES ▸ **jarvie**
JASEY n wig
JASEYS ▸ **jasey**
JASIES ▸ **jasey**
JASMIN same as ▸ **jasmine**
JASMINE n shrub with sweet-smelling yellow or white flowers
JASMINS ▸ **jasmin**
JASP another word for ▸ **jasper**

JASPE adj resembling jasper ▷ n subtly striped woven fabric
JASPER n red, yellow, dark green, or brown variety of quartz
JASPERS ▸ **jasper**
JASPERY ▸ **jasper**
JASPES ▸ **jaspe**
JASPIS archaic word for ▸ **jasper**
JASPS ▸ **jasp**
JASS obsolete variant of ▸ **jazz**
JASSES ▸ **jass**
JASSID n leafhopper
JASSIDS ▸ **jassid**
JASY n wig
JATAKA n text describing the birth of Buddha
JATAKAS ▸ **jataka**
JATO n jet-assisted takeoff
JATOS ▸ **jato**
JAUK vb dawdle
JAUKED ▸ **jauk**
JAUKING ▸ **jauk**
JAUKS ▸ **jauk**
JAUNCE vb prance
JAUNCED ▸ **jaunce**
JAUNCES ▸ **jaunce**
JAUNSE same as ▸ **jaunce**
JAUNSED ▸ **jaunse**
JAUNSES ▸ **jaunse**
JAUNT n short journey for pleasure ▷ vb make such a journey
JAUNTED ▸ **jaunt**
JAUNTEE old spelling of ▸ **jaunty**
JAUNTIE old spelling of ▸ **jaunty**
JAUNTS ▸ **jaunt**
JAUNTY adj sprightly and cheerful ▷ n master-at-arms on a naval ship
JAUP same as ▸ **jarp**
JAUPED ▸ **jaup**
JAUPING ▸ **jaup**
JAUPS ▸ **jaup**
JAVA n coffee or a variety of it
JAVAS ▸ **java**
JAVEL adj as in **javel water** aqueous solution containing sodium hypochlorite and some sodium chloride, used as a bleach and disinfectant
JAVELIN n light spear thrown in sports competitions ▷ vb spear with a javelin
JAVELS ▸ **javel**
JAW n one of the bones in

which the teeth are set ▷ vb talk lengthily
JAWAN n (in India) a soldier
JAWANS ▸ **jawan**
JAWARI n variety of sorghum
JAWARIS ▸ **jawari**
JAWBONE n lower jaw of a person or animal ▷ vb try to persuade or bring pressure to bear (on) by virtue of one's high office or position, esp in urging compliance with official policy
JAWBOX n metal sink

> This Scots word for a sink combines the J and X, and of course its plural **jawboxes**, earning an extra 50 points, would be even better.

JAWED ▸ **jaw**
JAWFALL n depression
JAWHOLE n cesspit
JAWING ▸ **jaw**
JAWINGS ▸ **jaw**
JAWLESS ▸ **jaw**
JAWLIKE ▸ **jaw**
JAWLINE n outline of the jaw
JAWS ▸ **jaw**
JAY n bird with a pinkish body and blue-and-black wings
JAYBIRD n jay
JAYCEE n member of a Junior Chamber of Commerce
JAYCEES ▸ **jaycee**
JAYGEE n lieutenant junior grade in the US army
JAYGEES ▸ **jaygee**
JAYS ▸ **jay**
JAYVEE n junior varsity sports team
JAYVEES ▸ **jayvee**
JAYWALK vb cross or walk in a street recklessly or illegally
JAZIES ▸ **jazy**
JAZY n wig

> This means a wig and is a wonderfully useful little word, combining J and Z for a high score.

JAZZ n kind of music with an exciting rhythm, usu involving improvisation ▷ vb play or dance to jazz music
JAZZBO n jazz musician or fan
JAZZBOS ▸ **jazzbo**

JAZZED ▸ jazz
JAZZER ▸ jazz
JAZZERS ▸ jazz
JAZZES ▸ jazz
JAZZIER ▸ jazzy
JAZZILY ▸ jazzy
JAZZING ▸ jazz
JAZZMAN ▸ jazz
JAZZMEN ▸ jazz
JAZZY *adj* flashy or showy
JEALOUS *adj* fearful of losing a partner or possession to a rival
JEAN *n* tough twill-weave cotton fabric used for hard-wearing trousers, overalls, etc
JEANED *adj* wearing jeans
JEANS *pl n* casual denim trousers
JEAT *n* jet
JEATS ▸ jeat
JEBEL *n* hill or mountain in an Arab country
JEBELS ▸ jebel
JEDI *n* person claiming to live according to a philosophy based on that of the fictional Jedi, from the *Star Wars* films
JEDIS ▸ jedi
JEE *same as* **▸ gee**
JEED ▸ jee
JEEING ▸ jee
JEEL *vb* make into jelly
JEELED ▸ jeel
JEELIE *same as* **▸ jeely**
JEELIED ▸ jeely
JEELIES ▸ jeely
JEELING ▸ jeel
JEELS ▸ jeel
JEELY *n* jelly ▷ *vb* make into jelly
JEEP *n* small military four-wheel drive road vehicle ▷ *vb* travel in a jeep
JEEPED ▸ jeep
JEEPERS *interj* mild exclamation of surprise
JEEPING ▸ jeep
JEEPNEY *n* Filipino bus converted from a jeep
JEEPS ▸ jeep
JEER *vb* scoff or deride ▷ *n* cry of derision
JEERED ▸ jeer
JEERER ▸ jeer
JEERERS ▸ jeer
JEERING ▸ jeer
JEERS ▸ jeer
JEES ▸ jee
JEEZ *interj* expression of surprise or irritation

JEFE *n* (in Spanish-speaking countries) a military or political leader
JEFES ▸ jefe
JEFF *vb* downsize or close down (an organization)
JEFFED ▸ jeff
JEFFING ▸ jeff
JEFFS ▸ jeff
JEHAD *same as* **▸ jihad**
JEHADI *same as* **▸ jihadi**
JEHADIS ▸ jehadi
JEHADS ▸ jehad
JEHU *n* fast driver
JEHUS ▸ jehu
JEJUNA ▸ jejunum
JEJUNAL ▸ jejunum
JEJUNE *adj* simple or naive
JEJUNUM *n* part of the small intestine between the duodenum and the ileum
JELAB *same as* **▸ jellaba**
JELABS ▸ jelab
JELL *vb* form into a jelly-like substance
JELLABA *n* loose robe with a hood, worn by some Arab men
JELLED ▸ jell
JELLIED ▸ jelly
JELLIES ▸ jelly
JELLIFY *vb* make into or become jelly
JELLING ▸ jell
JELLO *n* (in US English) fruit-flavoured clear dessert set with gelatine
JELLOS ▸ jello
JELLS ▸ jell
JELLY *n* fruit-flavoured clear dessert set with gelatine ▷ *vb* jellify
JEMADAR *n* native junior officer belonging to a locally raised regiment serving as mercenaries in India, esp with the British Army (until 1947)
JEMBE *n* hoe
JEMBES ▸ jembe
JEMIDAR *same as* **▸ jemadar**
JEMIMA *n* boot with elastic sides
JEMIMAS ▸ jemima
JEMMIED ▸ jemmy
JEMMIER ▸ jemmy
JEMMIES ▸ jemmy
JEMMY *n* short steel crowbar used by burglars ▷ *vb* prise (something) open with a jemmy ▷ *adj* neat

JENNET *n* female donkey or ass
JENNETS ▸ jennet
JENNIES ▸ jenny
JENNY *same as* **▸ jennet**
JEOFAIL *n* oversight in legal pleading
JEON *n* Korean pancake
JEOPARD *vb* put in jeopardy
JERBIL *variant spelling of* **▸ gerbil**
JERBILS ▸ jerbil
JERBOA *n* small mouselike rodent with long hind legs
JERBOAS ▸ jerboa
JEREED *same as* **▸ jerid**
JEREEDS ▸ jereed
JERID *n* wooden javelin used in Muslim countries in military displays on horseback
JERIDS ▸ jerid
JERK *vb* move or throw abruptly ▷ *n* sharp or abruptly stopped movement
JERKED ▸ jerk
JERKER ▸ jerk
JERKERS ▸ jerk
JERKIER ▸ jerky
JERKIES ▸ jerky
JERKILY ▸ jerky
JERKIN *n* sleeveless jacket
JERKING ▸ jerk
JERKINS ▸ jerkin
JERKS ▸ jerk
JERKY *adj* characterized by jerks ▷ *n* type of cured meat
JERQUE *vb* search for contraband

> To **jerque** is to search a vessel for stolen goods, and if you have the right additional letters to make **jerqued, jerquer, jerques** or **jerquing**, using all your letters, you would get a really great score.

JERQUED ▸ jerque
JERQUER ▸ jerque
JERQUES ▸ jerque
JERREED *variant spelling of* **▸ jerid**
JERRID *n* blunt javelin
JERRIDS ▸ jerrid
JERRIES ▸ jerry
JERRY *short for* **> jeroboam**
JERSEY *n* knitted jumper
JERSEYS ▸ jersey
JESS *n* short leather strap, one end of which is permanently attached to

the leg of a hawk or falcon
while the other can be
attached to a leash ▷ *vb*
put jesses on (a hawk or
falcon)
JESSAMY *n* fop
JESSANT *adj* emerging
JESSE *same as* ▶ **jess**
JESSED ▶ **jess**
JESSES ▶ **jess**
JESSIE *n* effeminate, weak,
or cowardly boy or man
JESSIES ▶ **jessie**
JESSING ▶ **jess**
JEST *vb* joke ▷ *n* something
done or said for
amusement
JESTED ▶ **jest**
JESTEE *n* person about
whom a joke is made
JESTEES ▶ **jestee**
JESTER *n* professional clown
at court
JESTERS ▶ **jester**
JESTFUL ▶ **jest**
JESTING ▶ **jest**
JESTS ▶ **jest**
JESUS *n* French paper size
JET *n* aircraft driven by jet
propulsion ▷ *vb* fly by jet
aircraft
JETBEAD *n* ornamental
shrub
JETE *n* step in which the
dancer springs from one leg
and lands on the other
JETES ▶ **jete**
JETFOIL *n* type of hydrofoil
that is propelled by water
jets
JETLAG *n* tiredness caused
by crossing timezones in jet
flight
JETLAGS ▶ **jetlag**
JETLIKE ▶ **jet**
JETON *n* gambling chip
JETONS ▶ **jeton**
JETPORT *n* airport for jet
planes
JETS ▶ **jet**
JETSAM *n* goods thrown
overboard to lighten a ship
JETSAMS ▶ **jetsam**
JETSOM *same as* ▶ **jetsam**
JETSOMS ▶ **jetsom**
JETSON *archaic form of*
▶ **jetsam**
JETSONS ▶ **jetson**
JETTED ▶ **jet**
JETTIED ▶ **jetty**
JETTIER ▶ **jetty**
JETTIES ▶ **jetty**
JETTING ▶ **jet**

JETTON *n* counter or token,
esp a chip used in such
gambling games as
roulette
JETTONS ▶ **jetton**
JETTY *n* small pier ▷ *adj* of or
resembling jet, esp in
colour or polish ▷ *vb* equip
with a cantilevered floor
JETWAY *n* tradename of a
mobile elevated gangway
connecting an aircraft to a
departure gate, allowing
passengers to board and
disembark
JETWAYS ▶ **jetway**
JEU *n* game

> *Jeu* is the French word
> for game or play. The
> plural form, **jeux**, is a
> great little word, using
> both J and X, particularly
> if you can play it on a
> double- or triple-word
> square.

JEUNE *adj* young
JEUX ▶ **jeu**
JEWEL *n* precious or
semiprecious stone ▷ *vb* fit
or decorate with a jewel or
jewels
JEWELED ▶ **jewel**
JEWELER *same as* > **jeweller**
JEWELRY *same as*
> **jewellery**
JEWELS ▶ **jewel**
JEWFISH *n* freshwater
catfish
JEWIE *n* jewfish
JEWIES ▶ **jewie**
JEZAIL *n* Afghan musket

> A *jezail* is a kind of
> Afghan musket, and if
> you have an S to go with
> it, earning the extra 50
> points, so much the
> better.

JEZAILS ▶ **jezail**
JEZEBEL *n* shameless or
scheming woman
JHALA *n* Indian musical
style
JHALAS ▶ **jhala**
JHATKA *n* slaughter of
animals for food according
to Sikh law
JHATKAS ▶ **jhatka**
JIAO *n* Chinese currency unit
JIAOS ▶ **jiao**
JIB *same as* ▶ **jibe**
JIBB *same as* ▶ **jibe**
JIBBA *n* long, loose coat
worn by Muslim men

JIBBAH *same as* ▶ **jubbah**
JIBBAHS ▶ **jibbah**
JIBBAS ▶ **jibba**
JIBBED ▶ **jibb**
JIBBER *same as* ▶ **gibber**
JIBBERS ▶ **jibber**
JIBBING ▶ **jibb**
JIBBONS *pl n* spring onions
JIBBOOM *n* spar forming an
extension of the bowsprit
JIBBS ▶ **jibb**
JIBE *vb* taunt or jeer ▷ *n*
insulting or taunting
remark
JIBED ▶ **jibe**
JIBER ▶ **jibe**
JIBERS ▶ **jibe**
JIBES ▶ **jibe**
JIBING ▶ **jibe**
JIBS ▶ **jib**
JICAMA *n* pale brown turnip
with crisp sweet flesh,
originating in Mexico
JICAMAS ▶ **jicama**
JIFF *same as* ▶ **jiffy**
JIFFIES ▶ **jiffy**
JIFFS ▶ **jiff**
JIFFY *n* very short period of
time
JIG *n* type of lively dance ▷ *vb*
dance a jig
JIGAJIG *vb* engage in sexual
intercourse
JIGAJOG *same as* ▶ **jigajig**
JIGGED ▶ **jig**
JIGGER *n* small whisky glass
▷ *vb* interfere or alter
JIGGERS ▶ **jigger**
JIGGIER ▶ **jiggy**
JIGGING ▶ **jig**
JIGGISH ▶ **jig**
JIGGLE *vb* move up and
down with short jerky
movements ▷ *n* short jerky
motion
JIGGLED ▶ **jiggle**
JIGGLES ▶ **jiggle**
JIGGLY ▶ **jiggle**
JIGGY *adj* resembling a jig
JIGJIG *same as* ▶ **jigajig**
JIGJIGS ▶ **jigjig**
JIGLIKE ▶ **jig**
JIGOT *same as* ▶ **gigot**
JIGOTS ▶ **jigot**
JIGS ▶ **jig**
JIGSAW *n* picture cut into
interlocking pieces, which
the user tries to fit together
again ▷ *vb* cut with a
jigsaw
JIGSAWN ▶ **jigsaw**
JIGSAWS ▶ **jigsaw**
JIHAD *n* Islamic holy war**

J

against unbelievers

JIHADI *n* person who takes part in a jihad

JIHADIS ▸ **jihadi**

JIHADS ▸ **jihad**

JILBAB *n* long robe worn by Muslim women

JILBABS ▸ **jilbab**

JILGIE *n* freshwater crayfish

JILGIES ▸ **jilgie**

JILL *variant spelling of* ▸ **gill**

JILLET *n* wanton woman

JILLETS ▸ **jillet**

JILLION *n* extremely large number or amount

JILLS ▸ **jill**

JILT *vb* leave or reject (one's lover) ▹ *n* woman who jilts a lover

JILTED ▸ **jilt**

JILTER ▸ **jilt**

JILTERS ▸ **jilt**

JILTING ▸ **jilt**

JILTS ▸ **jilt**

JIMINY *interj* expression of surprise

JIMJAM ▸ **jimjams**

JIMJAMS *pl n* state of nervous tension, excitement, or anxiety

JIMMIE *same as* ▸ **jimmy**

JIMMIED ▸ **jimmy**

JIMMIES ▸ **jimmy**

JIMMINY *interj* expression of surprise

JIMMY *same as* ▸ **jemmy**

JIMP *adj* handsome

JIMPER ▸ **jimp**

JIMPEST ▸ **jimp**

JIMPIER ▸ **jimpy**

JIMPLY *adv* neatly

JIMPSON ▸ **jimson**

JIMPY *adj* neat and tidy

JIMSON *n as in* **jimson weed** type of poisonous plant with white flowers and shiny fruits

JIN *n* Chinese unit of weight

JINGAL *n* swivel-mounted gun

JINGALL *same as* ▸ **jingal**

JINGALS ▸ **jingal**

JINGKO *same as* ▸ **gingko**

JINGLE *n* catchy verse or song used in a radio or television advert ▹ *vb* (cause to) make a gentle ringing sound

JINGLED ▸ **jingle**

JINGLER ▸ **jingle**

JINGLES ▸ **jingle**

JINGLET *n* sleigh-bell clapper

JINGLY ▸ **jingle**

JINGO *n* loud and bellicose patriot; chauvinism

JINGOES ▸ **jingo**

JINJILI *n* type of sesame

JINK *vb* move quickly or jerkily in order to dodge someone ▹ *n* jinking movement

JINKED ▸ **jink**

JINKER *n* vehicle for transporting timber, consisting of a tractor and two sets of wheels for supporting the logs ▹ *vb* carry or transport in a jinker

JINKERS ▸ **jinker**

JINKING ▸ **jink**

JINKS ▸ **jink**

JINN ▸ **jinni**

JINNE *interj* South African exclamation expressing surprise, admiration, shock, etc

JINNEE *same as* ▸ **jinni**

JINNI *n* spirit in Muslim mythology

JINNIS ▸ **jinni**

JINNS ▸ **jinni**

JINS ▸ **jin**

JINX *n* person or thing bringing bad luck ▹ *vb* be or put a jinx on

JINXED ▸ **jinx**

JINXES ▸ **jinx**

JINXING ▸ **jinx**

JIPYAPA *same as* > **jipijapa**

JIRBLE *vb* pour carelessly

JIRBLED ▸ **jirble**

JIRBLES ▸ **jirble**

JIRD *n* gerbil

JIRDS ▸ **jird**

JIRGA *n* Afghan council

JIRGAS ▸ **jirga**

JIRRE *same as* ▸ **jinne**

JITNEY *n* small bus that carries passengers for a low price, originally five cents

JITNEYS ▸ **jitney**

JITTER *vb* be anxious or nervous

JITTERS ▸ **jitter**

JITTERY *adj* nervous

JIVE *n* lively dance of the 1940s and '50s ▹ *vb* dance the jive

JIVEASS *adj* misleading or phoney

JIVED ▸ **jive**

JIVER ▸ **jive**

JIVERS ▸ **jive**

JIVES ▸ **jive**

JIVEY ▸ **jive**

JIVIER ▸ **jive**

JIVIEST ▸ **jive**

JIVING ▸ **jive**

JIVY ▸ **jive**

JIZ *n* wig

> When you find yourself with J and Z but nothing else that looks promising, there may well be an I on the board around which you can form **jiz**, which means a wig.

JIZZ *n* term for the total combination of characteristics that serve to identify a particular species of bird or plant

JIZZES ▸ **jizz**

JNANA *n* type of yoga

JNANAS ▸ **jnana**

JO *n* Scots word for sweetheart

JOANNA *n* piano

JOANNAS ▸ **joanna**

JOANNES *same as* > **johannes**

JOB *n* occupation or paid employment ▹ *vb* work at casual jobs

JOBBED ▸ **job**

JOBBER *n* person who jobs

JOBBERS ▸ **jobber**

JOBBERY *n* practice of making private profit out of a public office

JOBBIE *n* piece of excrement

JOBBIES ▸ **jobbie**

JOBBING *adj* doing individual jobs for payment ▹ *n* act of seeking work

JOBE *vb* scold

JOBED ▸ **jobe**

JOBES ▸ **jobe**

JOBING ▸ **jobe**

JOBLESS *pl n* unemployed people ▹ *adj* unemployed

JOBNAME *n* title of position

JOBS ▸ **job**

JOCK *n* athlete

JOCKEY *n* person who rides horses in races, esp as a profession or for hire ▹ *vb* ride (a horse) in a race

JOCKEYS ▸ **jockey**

JOCKISH *adj* macho

JOCKO *n* chimpanzee

JOCKOS ▸ **jocko**

JOCKS ▸ **jock**

JOCO *adj* relaxed

JOCOSE *adj* playful or humorous

JOCULAR *adj* fond of joking

JOCUND adj merry or cheerful

JODEL same as ▶ **yodel**

JODELS ▶ **jodel**

JODHPUR n as in **jodhpur boots** ankle-length leather riding boots

JOE same as ▶ **jo**

JOES ▶ **joe**

JOEY n young kangaroo

JOEYS ▶ **joey**

JOG vb run at a gentle pace, esp for exercise ▷ n slow run

JOGGED ▶ **jog**

JOGGER n person who runs at a jog trot over some distance for exercise, usually regularly

JOGGERS ▶ **jogger**

JOGGING ▶ **jog**

JOGGLE vb shake or move jerkily ▷ n act of joggling

JOGGLED ▶ **joggle**

JOGGLER ▶ **joggle**

JOGGLES ▶ **joggle**

JOGS ▶ **jog**

JOGTROT n easy bouncy gait, esp of a horse, midway between a walk and a trot

JOHN n toilet

JOHNNIE same as ▶ **johnny**

JOHNNY n chap

JOHNS ▶ **john**

JOIN vb become a member (of) ▷ n place where two things are joined

JOINDER n act of joining, esp in legal contexts

JOINED ▶ **join**

JOINER n maker of finished woodwork

JOINERS ▶ **joiner**

JOINERY n joiner's work

JOINING ▶ **join**

JOINS ▶ **join**

JOINT adj shared by two or more ▷ n place where bones meet but can move ▷ vb divide meat into joints

JOINTED adj having a joint or joints

JOINTER n tool for pointing mortar joints, as in brickwork

JOINTLY ▶ **joint**

JOINTS ▶ **joint**

JOIST n horizontal beam that helps support a floor or ceiling ▷ vb construct (a floor, roof, etc) with joists

JOISTED ▶ **joist**

JOISTS ▶ **joist**

JOJOBA n shrub of SW North America whose seeds yield oil used in cosmetics

JOJOBAS ▶ **jojoba**

JOKE n thing said or done to cause laughter ▷ vb make jokes

JOKED ▶ **joke**

JOKER n person who jokes

JOKERS ▶ **joker**

JOKES ▶ **joke**

JOKEY adj intended as a joke

JOKIER ▶ **jokey**

JOKIEST ▶ **jokey**

JOKILY ▶ **joke**

JOKING ▶ **joke**

JOKOL Shetland word for ▶ **yes**

JOKY same as ▶ **jokey**

JOL n party ▷ vb have a good time

JOLE vb knock

JOLED ▶ **jole**

JOLES ▶ **jole**

JOLING ▶ **jole**

JOLL same as ▶ **jole**

JOLLED ▶ **jol**

JOLLER n person who has a good time

JOLLERS ▶ **joller**

JOLLEY same as ▶ **jolly**

JOLLEYS ▶ **jolley**

JOLLIED ▶ **jolly**

JOLLIER n joker

JOLLIES ▶ **jolly**

JOLLIFY vb be or cause to be jolly

JOLLILY ▶ **jolly**

JOLLING ▶ **jol**

JOLLITY n condition of being jolly

JOLLOP n cream or unguent

JOLLOPS ▶ **jollop**

JOLLS ▶ **joll**

JOLLY adj full of good humour ▷ adv extremely ▷ vb try to make or keep (someone) cheerful ▷ n festivity or celebration

JOLLYER ▶ **jolly**

JOLS ▶ **jol**

JOLT n unpleasant surprise or shock ▷ vb surprise or shock

JOLTED ▶ **jolt**

JOLTER ▶ **jolt**

JOLTERS ▶ **jolt**

JOLTIER ▶ **jolt**

JOLTILY ▶ **jolt**

JOLTING ▶ **jolt**

JOLTS ▶ **jolt**

JOLTY ▶ **jolt**

JOMO same as ▶ **zo**

JOMON n particular era in Japanese history

JOMOS ▶ **jomo**

JONES vb desire

JONESED ▶ **jones**

JONESES ▶ **jones**

JONG n friend, often used in direct address

JONGS ▶ **jong**

JONNOCK adj genuine ▷ adv honestly

JONQUIL n fragrant narcissus

JONTIES ▶ **jonty**

JONTY n petty officer

JOOK vb poke or puncture (the skin) ▷ n jab or the resulting wound

JOOKED ▶ **jook**

JOOKERY n mischief

JOOKING ▶ **jook**

JOOKS ▶ **jook**

JOR n movement in Indian music

JORAM same as ▶ **jorum**

JORAMS ▶ **joram**

JORDAN n chamber pot

JORDANS ▶ **jordan**

JORS ▶ **jor**

JORUM n large drinking bowl or vessel or its contents

JORUMS ▶ **jorum**

JOSEPH n woman's floor-length riding coat with a small cape, worn esp in the 18th century

JOSEPHS ▶ **joseph**

JOSH vb tease ▷ n teasing or bantering joke

JOSHED ▶ **josh**

JOSHER ▶ **josh**

JOSHERS ▶ **josh**

JOSHES ▶ **josh**

JOSHING ▶ **josh**

JOSKIN n bumpkin

JOSKINS ▶ **joskin**

JOSS n Chinese deity worshipped in the form of an idol

JOSSER n simpleton

JOSSERS ▶ **josser**

JOSSES ▶ **joss**

JOSTLE vb knock or push against ▷ n act of jostling

JOSTLED ▶ **jostle**

JOSTLER ▶ **jostle**

JOSTLES ▶ **jostle**

JOT vb write briefly ▷ n very small amount

JOTA n Spanish dance with castanets in fast triple time, usually to a guitar and voice

J

accompaniment
JOTAS ▸ jota
JOTS ▸ jot
JOTTED ▸ jot
JOTTER n notebook
JOTTERS ▸ jotter
JOTTIER ▸ jotty
JOTTING ▸ jot
JOTTY ▸ jot
JOTUN n giant
JOTUNN same as ▸ **jotun**
JOTUNNS ▸ jotunn
JOTUNS ▸ jotun
JOUAL n nonstandard variety of Canadian French
JOUALS ▸ joual
JOUGS pl n iron ring, fastened by a chain to a wall, post, or tree, in which an offender was held by the neck
JOUK vb duck or dodge ▷ n sudden evasive movement
JOUKED ▸ jouk
JOUKERY same as ▸ **jookery**
JOUKING ▸ jouk
JOUKS ▸ jouk
JOULE n unit of work or energy ▷ vb knock
JOULED ▸ joule
JOULES ▸ joule
JOULING ▸ joule
JOUNCE vb shake or jolt or cause to shake or jolt ▷ n jolting movement
JOUNCED ▸ jounce
JOUNCES ▸ jounce
JOUNCY ▸ jounce
JOUR n day
JOURNAL n daily newspaper or magazine ▷ vb record in a journal
JOURNEY n act or process of travelling from one place to another ▷ vb travel
JOURNO n journalist
JOURNOS ▸ journo
JOURS ▸ jour
JOUST n combat with lances between two mounted knights ▷ vb fight on horseback using lances
JOUSTED ▸ joust
JOUSTER ▸ joust
JOUSTS ▸ joust
JOVIAL adj happy and cheerful
JOW vb ring (a bell)
JOWAR n variety of sorghum
JOWARI same as ▸ **jowar**
JOWARIS ▸ jowar
JOWARS ▸ jowar

JOWED ▸ jow
JOWING ▸ jow
JOWL n lower jaw ▷ vb knock
JOWLED ▸ jowl
JOWLER n dog with prominent jowls
JOWLERS ▸ jowler
JOWLIER ▸ jowl
JOWLING ▸ jowl
JOWLS ▸ jowl
JOWLY ▸ jowl
JOWS ▸ jow
JOY n feeling of great delight or pleasure ▷ vb feel joy
JOYANCE n joyous feeling or festivity
JOYED ▸ joy
JOYFUL adj feeling or bringing great joy
JOYING ▸ joy
JOYLESS adj feeling or bringing no joy
JOYOUS adj extremely happy and enthusiastic
JOYPAD n computer games console consisting of buttons on a pad
JOYPADS ▸ joypad
JOYPOP vb take addictive drugs occasionally without becoming addicted
JOYPOPS ▸ joypop
JOYRIDE n drive in a car one has stolen ▷ vb take such a ride
JOYRODE ▸ joyride
JOYS ▸ joy
JUBA n lively African-American dance developed in the southern US
JUBAS ▸ juba
JUBATE adj possessing a mane
JUBBAH n long loose outer garment with wide sleeves, worn by Muslim men and women, esp in India
JUBBAHS ▸ jubbah
JUBE n gallery or loft over the rood screen in a church or cathedral
JUBES ▸ jube
JUBHAH same as ▸ **jubbah**
JUBHAHS ▸ jubhah
JUBILE same as ▸ **jubilee**
JUBILEE n special anniversary, esp 25th or 50th
JUBILES ▸ jubile
JUCO n junior college in America
JUCOS ▸ juco

JUD n large block of coal
JUDAS n peephole or a very small window in a door
JUDASES ▸ judas
JUDDER vb vibrate violently ▷ n violent vibration
JUDDERS ▸ judder
JUDDERY adj shaky
JUDGE n public official who tries cases and passes sentence in a court of law ▷ vb act as a judge
JUDGED ▸ judge
JUDGER ▸ judge
JUDGERS ▸ judge
JUDGES ▸ judge
JUDGING ▸ judge
JUDIES ▸ judy
JUDO n sport in which two opponents try to throw each other to the ground
JUDOGI n white two-piece cotton costume worn during judo contests
JUDOGIS ▸ judogi
JUDOIST ▸ judo
JUDOKA n competitor or expert in judo
JUDOKAS ▸ judoka
JUDOS ▸ judo
JUDS ▸ jud
JUDY n woman
JUG n container for liquids, with a handle and small spout ▷ vb stew or boil (meat, esp hare) in an earthenware container
JUGA ▸ jugum
JUGAL adj of or relating to the zygomatic bone ▷ n cheekbone
JUGALS ▸ jugal
JUGATE adj (esp of compound leaves) having parts arranged in pairs
JUGFUL same as ▸ **jug**
JUGFULS ▸ jugful
JUGGED ▸ jug
JUGGING ▸ jug
JUGGINS n silly person
JUGGLE vb throw and catch (several objects) so that most are in the air at the same time ▷ n act of juggling
JUGGLED ▸ juggle
JUGGLER n person who juggles, esp a professional entertainer
JUGGLES ▸ juggle
JUGHEAD n clumsy person
JUGLET n small jug
JUGLETS ▸ juglet

JUGS ▸ jug
JUGSFUL ▸ jugful
JUGULA ▸ jugulum
JUGULAR *n* one of three large veins of the neck that return blood from the head to the heart
JUGULUM *n* lower throat
JUGUM *n* small process at the base of each forewing in certain insects by which the forewings are united to the hindwings during flight
JUGUMS ▸ jugum
JUICE *n* liquid part of vegetables, fruit, or meat ▷ *vb* extract juice from fruits and vegetables
JUICED ▸ juice
JUICER *n* kitchen appliance, usually operated by electricity, for extracting juice from fruits and vegetables
JUICERS ▸ juicer
JUICES ▸ juice
JUICIER ▸ juicy
JUICILY ▸ juicy
JUICING ▸ juice
JUICY *adj* full of juice
JUJITSU *n* Japanese art of wrestling and self-defence
JUJU *n* W African magic charm or fetish
JUJUBE *n* chewy sweet made of flavoured gelatine
JUJUBES ▸ jujube
JUJUISM ▸ juju
JUJUIST ▸ juju
JUJUS ▸ juju
JUJUTSU *same as* ▸ jujitsu
JUKE *vb* dance or play dance music
JUKEBOX *n* coin-operated machine on which records, CDs, or videos can be played
JUKED ▸ juke
JUKES ▸ juke
JUKING ▸ juke
JUKSKEI *n* game in which a peg is thrown over a fixed distance at a stake fixed into the ground
JUKU *n* Japanese martial art
JUKUS ▸ juku
JULEP *n* sweet alcoholic drink
JULEPS ▸ julep
JULIET *n* code word for the letter J
JULIETS ▸ juliet
JUMAR *n* clamp with a handle that can move freely

up a rope on which it is clipped but locks when downward pressure is applied ▷ *vb* climb (up a fixed rope) using jumars
JUMARED ▸ jumar
JUMARS ▸ jumar
JUMART *n* mythical offspring of a bull and a mare
JUMARTS ▸ jumart
JUMBAL *same as* ▸ jumble
JUMBALS ▸ jumbal
JUMBIE *n* Caribbean ghost
JUMBIES ▸ jumbie
JUMBLE *n* confused heap or state ▷ *vb* mix in a disordered way
JUMBLED ▸ jumble
JUMBLER ▸ jumble
JUMBLES ▸ jumble
JUMBLY ▸ jumble
JUMBO *adj* very large ▷ *n* large jet airliner
JUMBOS ▸ jumbo
JUMBUCK *n* sheep
JUMBY *n* Caribbean ghost
JUMELLE *n* paired objects
JUMP *vb* leap or spring into the air using the leg muscles ▷ *n* act of jumping
JUMPED ▸ jump
JUMPER *n* sweater or pullover
JUMPERS ▸ jumper
JUMPIER ▸ jumpy
JUMPILY ▸ jumpy
JUMPING ▸ jump
JUMPOFF *n* extra round in a showjumping contest when two or more horses are equal first, the fastest round deciding the winner
JUMPS ▸ jump
JUMPY *adj* nervous
JUN *same as* ▸ chon
JUNCATE *same as* ▸ junket
JUNCO *n* North American bunting
JUNCOES ▸ junco
JUNCOS ▸ junco
JUNCUS *n* type of rush
JUNGLE *n* tropical forest of dense tangled vegetation
JUNGLED *adj* covered with jungle
JUNGLES ▸ jungle
JUNGLI *n* uncultured person
JUNGLIS ▸ jungli
JUNGLY ▸ jungle
JUNIOR *adj* of lower standing ▷ *n* junior person
JUNIORS ▸ junior

JUNIPER *n* evergreen shrub with purple berries
JUNK *n* discarded or useless objects ▷ *vb* discard as junk
JUNKED ▸ junk
JUNKER *n* (formerly) young German nobleman
JUNKERS ▸ junker
JUNKET *n* excursion by public officials paid for from public funds ▷ *vb* (of a public official, committee, etc) to go on a junket
JUNKETS ▸ junket
JUNKIE *n* drug addict
JUNKIER ▸ junky
JUNKIES ▸ junky
JUNKING ▸ junk
JUNKMAN *n* man who buys and sells discarded clothing, furniture, etc
JUNKMEN ▸ junkman
JUNKS ▸ junk
JUNKY *n* drug addict ▷ *adj* of low quality
JUNTA *n* group of military officers holding power in a country, esp after a coup
JUNTAS ▸ junta
JUNTO *same as* ▸ junta
JUNTOS ▸ junto
JUPATI *n* type of palm tree
JUPATIS ▸ jupati
JUPE *n* sleeveless jacket
JUPES ▸ jupe
JUPON *n* short close-fitting sleeveless padded garment, used in the late 14th and early 15th centuries with armour
JUPONS ▸ jupon
JURA ▸ jus
JURAL *adj* of or relating to law or to the administration of justice
JURALLY ▸ jural
JURANT *n* person taking oath
JURANTS ▸ jurant
JURAT *n* statement at the foot of an affidavit, naming the parties, stating when, where, and before whom it was sworn, etc
JURATS ▸ jurat
JURE *adv* by legal right
JUREL *n* edible fish found in warm American Atlantic waters
JURELS ▸ jurel
JURIDIC *same as* > juridical
JURIED ▸ jury
JURIES ▸ jury

JURIST *n* expert in law
JURISTS ▸ jurist
JUROR *n* member of a jury
JURORS ▸ juror
JURY *n* group of people sworn to deliver a verdict in a court of law ▷ *adj* makeshift ▷ *vb* evaluate by jury
JURYING ▸ jury
JURYMAN *n* member of a jury, esp a man
JURYMEN ▸ juryman
JUS *n* right, power, or authority
JUSSIVE *n* mood of verbs used for giving orders; imperative
JUST *adv* very recently ▷ *adj* fair or impartial in action or judgment ▷ *vb* joust

JUSTED ▸ just
JUSTER ▸ just
JUSTERS ▸ just
JUSTEST ▸ just
JUSTICE *n* quality of being just
JUSTIFY *vb* prove right or reasonable
JUSTING ▸ joust
JUSTLE *less common word for* ▸ jostle
JUSTLED ▸ justle
JUSTLES ▸ justle
JUSTLY ▸ just
JUSTS *same as* ▸ joust
JUT *vb* project or stick out ▷ *n* something that juts out
JUTE *n* plant fibre, used for rope, canvas, etc
JUTES ▸ jute
JUTS ▸ jut

JUTTED ▸ jut
JUTTIED ▸ jutty
JUTTIES ▸ jutty
JUTTING ▸ jut
JUTTY *vb* project beyond
JUVE *same as* ▸ juvenile
JUVENAL *variant spelling (esp US) of* ▸ **juvenile**
JUVES ▸ juve
JUVIE *n* juvenile detention centre
JUVIES ▸ juvie
JYMOLD *adj* having a hinge
JYNX *n* wryneck

> This unusual word, another name for the bird known as a wryneck, is unique in combining J, Y and X without using any vowels.

JYNXES ▸ jynx

J

Kk

Worth 5 points, **K** is a valuable tile to have in your rack. However, it's not the most useful tile for forming bonus words scoring that extra 50 points, so, as with the **J**, you will normally want to play it off fairly quickly. There are four two-letter words beginning with **K**: **ka, ki, ko** and **ky**. When it comes to three-letter words, remember **keg** (8 points), **ken** (7), **key** (10), **kex** (14), **kid** (8), **kin** (7), **kip** (9) and **kit** (7). Other three-letter words with **K** well worth remembering are **jak** (14) and **zek** (16).

KA n (in ancient Egypt) attendant spirit supposedly dwelling as a vital force in a man or statue ▷ vb (in archaic usage) help
KAAL adj naked
KAAMA n large African antelope with lyre-shaped horns
KAAMAS ▸ kaama
KAAS n Dutch cabinet or wardrobe
KAB variant spelling of ▸ cab
KABAB same as ▸ kebab
KABABS ▸ kabab
KABADDI n game in which players try to touch opposing players but avoid being captured by them
KABAKA n any of the former rulers of the Baganda people of S Uganda
KABAKAS ▸ kabaka
KABALA same as > kabbalah
KABALAS ▸ kabala
KABAR archaic form of ▸ caber
KABARS ▸ kabar
KABAYA n tunic
KABAYAS ▸ kabaya
KABBALA same as > kabbalah
KABELE same as ▸ kebele
KABELES ▸ kabele
KABIKI n fruit tree found in India
KABIKIS ▸ kabiki
KABOB same as ▸ kebab
KABOBS ▸ kabob
KABS ▸ kab
KABUKI n form of Japanese drama based on popular

legends and characterized by elaborate costumes, stylized acting, and the use of male actors for all roles
KABUKIS ▸ kabuki
KACCHA n trousers worn traditionally by Sikhs
KACCHAS ▸ kaccha
KACHA adj crude
KACHCHA same as ▸ kacha
KACHERI same as > kachahri
KACHINA n any of the supernatural beings believed by the Hopi Indians to be the ancestors of living humans
KADDISH n ancient Jewish liturgical prayer
KADE same as ▸ ked
KADES ▸ kade
KADI variant spelling of ▸ cadi
KADIS ▸ kadi
KAE n dialect word for jackdaw or jay ▷ vb (in archaic usage) help
KAED ▸ kae
KAEING ▸ kae
KAES ▸ kae
KAF n letter of the Hebrew alphabet
KAFFIR n Southern African variety of sorghum, cultivated in dry regions for its grain and as fodder
KAFFIRS ▸ kaffir
KAFILA n caravan
KAFILAS ▸ kafila
KAFIR same as ▸ kaffir
KAFIRS ▸ kafir
KAFS ▸ kaf
KAFTAN n long loose

Eastern garment
KAFTANS ▸ kaftan
KAGO n Japanese sedan chair
KAGOOL variant spelling of ▸ cagoule
KAGOOLS ▸ kagool
KAGOS ▸ kago
KAGOUL variant spelling of ▸ cagoule
KAGOULE same as ▸ kagoul
KAGOULS ▸ kagoul
KAGU n crested nocturnal bird of New Caledonia with a red bill and greyish plumage
KAGUS ▸ kagu
KAHAL n Jewish community
KAHALS ▸ kahal
KAHAWAI n food and game fish of New Zealand
KAHUNA n Hawaiian priest, shaman, or expert
KAHUNAS ▸ kahuna
KAI n food
KAIAK same as ▸ kayak
KAIAKED ▸ kaiak
KAIAKS ▸ kaiak
KAID n North African chieftan or leader
KAIDS ▸ kaid
KAIE archaic form of ▸ key
KAIES ▸ kaie
KAIF same as ▸ kif
KAIFS ▸ kaif
KAIK same as ▸ kainga
KAIKA same as ▸ kainga
KAIKAI n food
KAIKAIS ▸ kaikai
KAIKAS ▸ kaika
KAIKS ▸ kaik
KAIL same as ▸ kale
KAILS ▸ kail

KAIM *same as* ▸ **kame**
KAIMS ▸ **kaim**
KAIN *variant spelling of* ▸ **cain**
KAING ▸ **ka**
KAINGA *n* (in New Zealand) a Maori village or small settlement
KAINGAS ▸ **kainga**
KAINIT *same as* ▸ **kainite**
KAINITE *n* white mineral consisting of potassium chloride and magnesium sulphate: a fertilizer and source of potassium salts
KAINITS ▸ **kainit**
KAINS ▸ **kain**
KAIS ▸ **kai**
KAISER *n* German or Austro-Hungarian emperor
KAISERS ▸ **kaiser**
KAIZEN *n* philosophy of continuous improvement of working practices that underlies total quality management and just-in-time business techniques
KAIZENS ▸ **kaizen**
KAJAWAH *n* type of seat or panier used on a camel
KAJEPUT *n* variety of Australian melaleuca
KAKA *n* parrot of New Zealand
KAKAPO *n* ground-living nocturnal New Zealand parrot that resembles an owl
KAKAPOS ▸ **kakapo**
KAKAS ▸ **kaka**
KAKI *n* Asian persimmon tree
KAKIS ▸ **kaki**
KAKODYL *variant spelling of* ▸ **cacodyl**
KAKURO *n* crossword-style puzzle with numbers
KAKUROS ▸ **kakuro**
KALAM *n* discussion and debate, especially relating to Islamic theology
KALAMS ▸ **kalam**
KALE *n* cabbage with crinkled leaves
KALENDS *same as* ▸ **calends**
KALES ▸ **kale**
KALI *another name for* > **saltwort**
KALIAN *another name for* ▸ **hookah**
KALIANS ▸ **kalian**

KALIF *variant spelling of* ▸ **caliph**
KALIFS ▸ **kalif**
KALIMBA *n* musical instrument
KALIPH *variant spelling of* ▸ **caliph**
KALIPHS ▸ **kaliph**
KALIS ▸ **kali**
KALIUM *n* Latin for potassium
KALIUMS ▸ **kalium**
KALMIA *n* N American evergreen ericaceous shrub with showy clusters of white or pink flowers
KALMIAS ▸ **kalmia**
KALONG *n* fruit bat
KALONGS ▸ **kalong**
KALOOKI *n* version of contract rummy popular in Jamaica
KALPA *n* (in Hindu cosmology) period in which the universe experiences a cycle of creation and destruction
KALPAC *same as* ▸ **calpac**
KALPACS ▸ **kalpac**
KALPAK *variant spelling of* ▸ **calpac**
KALPAKS ▸ **kalpak**
KALPAS ▸ **kalpa**
KALPIS *n* Greek water jar
KALUKI ▸ **kalooki**
KALUKIS ▸ **kaluki**
KAM *Shakespearean word for* ▸ **crooked**
KAMA *n* large African antelope with lyre-shaped horns
KAMAHI *n* tall New Zealand hardwood tree with pinkish flowers
KAMAHIS ▸ **kamahi**
KAMALA *n* East Indian tree
KAMALAS ▸ **kamala**
KAMAS ▸ **kama**
KAME *n* irregular mound or ridge of gravel, sand, etc, deposited by water derived from melting glaciers
KAMEES ▸ **kameez**
KAMEEZ *n* long tunic worn in the Indian subcontinent, often with shalwar
KAMELA *same as* ▸ **kamala**
KAMELAS ▸ **kamela**
KAMERAD *interj* shout of surrender ▷ *vb* surrender
KAMES ▸ **kame**
KAMI *n* divine being or spiritual force in Shinto

KAMICHI *n* South American bird
KAMIK *n* traditional Inuit boot made of caribou hide or sealskin
KAMIKS ▸ **kamik**
KAMILA *same as* ▸ **kamala**
KAMILAS ▸ **kamila**
KAMIS *same as* ▸ **kameez**
KAMISES ▸ **kamis**
KAMME *same as* ▸ **kam**
KAMPONG *n* (in Malaysia) village
KAMSEEN *same as* ▸ **khamsin**
KAMSIN *same as* ▸ **kamseen**
KAMSINS ▸ **kamsin**
KANA *n* Japanese syllabary, which consists of two written varieties
KANAE *n* grey mullet
KANAES ▸ **kanae**
KANAKA *n* Australian word for any native of the South Pacific islands, esp (formerly) one abducted to work in Australia
KANAKAS ▸ **kanaka**
KANAS ▸ **kana**
KANBAN *n* just-in-time manufacturing process in which the movements of materials through a process are recorded on specially designed cards
KANBANS ▸ **kanban**
KANDIES ▸ **kandy**
KANDY *same as* ▸ **candie**
KANE *n* Hawaiian man or boy
KANEH *n* 6-cubit Hebrew measure
KANEHS ▸ **kaneh**
KANES ▸ **kane**
KANG *n* Chinese heatable platform used for sleeping and sitting on
KANGA *n* piece of gaily decorated thin cotton cloth used as a garment by women in E Africa
KANGAS ▸ **kanga**
KANGHA *n* comb traditionally worn by Sikhs as a symbol of their religious and cultural loyalty
KANGHAS ▸ **kangha**
KANGS ▸ **kang**
KANJI *n* Japanese writing system using characters mainly derived from Chinese ideograms

KANJIS ▶ kanji

KANS n Indian wild sugar cane

KANSES ▶ kans

KANT archaic spelling of ▶ **cant**

KANTAR n unit of weight used in E Mediterranean countries, equivalent to 100 pounds or 45 kilograms but varying from place to place

KANTARS ▶ kantar

KANTED ▶ kant

KANTELA same as ▶ **kantele**

KANTELE n Finnish stringed instrument

KANTEN same as ▶ **agar**

KANTENS ▶ kanten

KANTHA n Bengali embroidered quilt

KANTHAS ▶ kantha

KANTING ▶ kant

KANTS ▶ kant

KANUKA n New Zealand myrtaceous tree

KANUKAS ▶ kanuka

KANZU n long garment, usually white, with long sleeves, worn by E African men

KANZUS ▶ kanzu

KAOLIN n fine white clay used to make porcelain and in some medicines

KAOLINE same as ▶ **kaolin**

KAOLINS ▶ kaolin

KAON n meson that has a positive or negative charge and a rest mass of about 966 electron masses, or no charge and a rest mass of 974 electron masses

KAONIC ▶ kaon

KAONS ▶ kaon

KAPA n Hawaiian cloth made from beaten mulberry bark

KAPAS ▶ kapa

KAPH n 11th letter of the Hebrew alphabet

KAPHS ▶ kaph

KAPOK n fluffy fibre from a tropical tree, used to stuff cushions etc

KAPOKS ▶ kapok

KAPPA n tenth letter in the Greek alphabet

KAPPAS ▶ kappa

KAPUKA same as > **broadleaf**

KAPUKAS ▶ kapuka

KAPUT adj ruined or broken

KAPUTT same as ▶ **kaput**

KARA n steel bangle traditionally worn by Sikhs as a symbol of their religious and cultural loyalty

KARAISM n beliefs and doctrines of a Jewish sect rejecting Rabbinism

KARAIT same as ▶ **krait**

KARAITS ▶ krait

KARAKA n New Zealand tree

KARAKAS ▶ karaka

KARAKIA n prayer

KARAKUL n sheep of central Asia, the lambs of which have soft curled dark hair

KARAMU n small New Zealand tree with glossy leaves and orange fruit

KARAMUS ▶ karamu

KARANGA n call or chant of welcome, sung by a female elder ▷ vb perform a karanga

KARAOKE n form of entertainment in which people sing over a prerecorded backing tape

KARAS ▶ kara

KARAT n measure of the proportion of gold in an alloy, expressed as the number of parts of gold in 24 parts of the alloy

KARATE n Japanese system of unarmed combat using blows with the feet, hands, elbows, and legs

KARATES ▶ karate

KARATS ▶ karat

KARENGO n edible type of Pacific seaweed

KARITE n shea tree

KARITES ▶ karite

KARK variant spelling of ▶ **cark**

KARKED ▶ kark

KARKING ▶ kark

KARKS ▶ kark

KARMA n person's actions affecting his or her fate in the next reincarnation

KARMAS ▶ karma

KARMIC ▶ karma

KARN old word for ▶ **cairn**

KARNS ▶ karn

KARO n small New Zealand tree or shrub with sweet-smelling brown flowers

KAROO n high arid plateau

KAROOS ▶ karoo

KARORO n large seagull with black feathers on its back

KAROROS ▶ karoro

KAROS ▶ karo

KAROSHI n (in Japan) death caused by overwork

KAROSS n blanket made of animal skins sewn together

KARRI n Australian eucalypt

KARRIS ▶ karri

KARROO same as ▶ **karoo**

KARROOS ▶ karroo

KARSEY variant spelling of ▶ **khazi**

KARSEYS ▶ karsey

KARSIES ▶ karsy

KARST n denoting the characteristic scenery of a limestone region, including underground streams, gorges, etc

KARSTIC ▶ karst

KARSTS ▶ karst

KARSY variant spelling of ▶ **khazi**

KART n light low framed vehicle with small wheels and engine used for recreational racing

KARTER ▶ kart

KARTERS ▶ kart

KARTING ▶ kart

KARTS ▶ kart

KARYON n nucleus of a cell

KARYONS ▶ karyon

KARZIES ▶ karzy

KARZY variant spelling of ▶ **khazi**

KAS ▶ ka

KASBAH n citadel of any of various North African cities

KASBAHS ▶ kasbah

KASHA n dish originating in Eastern Europe, consisting of boiled or baked buckwheat

KASHAS ▶ kasha

KASHER vb make fit for use

KASHERS ▶ kasher

KASHMIR variant spelling of > **cashmere**

KASHRUS same as > **kashruth**

KASHRUT same as > **kashruth**

KASME interj (in Indian English) I swear

KAT same as ▶ **khat**

KATA n exercise consisting of a sequence of the specific

KATAL n SI unit of catalytic activity

KATALS ▸ katal

KATANA n Japanese samurai sword

KATANAS ▸ katana

KATAS ▸ kata

KATCINA variant spelling of ▸ kachina

KATHAK n form of N Indian classical dancing that tells a story

KATHAKS ▸ kathak

KATHODE variant spelling of ▸ cathode

KATI variant spelling of ▸ catty

KATION variant spelling of ▸ cation

KATIONS ▸ kation

KATIPO n small poisonous New Zealand spider

KATIPOS ▸ katipo

KATIS ▸ kati

KATORGA n labour camp in Imperial Russia or the Soviet Union

KATS ▸ kat

KATSURA n Asian tree

KATTI variant spelling of ▸ catty

KATTIS ▸ katti

KATYDID n large green grasshopper of N America

KAUGH same as ▸ kiaugh

KAUGHS ▸ kaugh

KAUPAPA n strategy, policy, or cause

KAURI n large NZ conifer that yields valuable timber and resin

KAURIES ▸ kaury

KAURIS ▸ kauri

KAURU n edible stem of the cabbage tree

KAURUS ▸ kauru

KAURY variant spelling of ▸ kauri

KAVA n Polynesian shrub

KAVAL n type of flute played in the Balkans

KAVALS ▸ kaval

KAVAS ▸ kava

KAVASS n armed Turkish constable

KAW variant spelling of ▸ caw

KAWA n protocol or etiquette, particularly in a Maori tribal meeting place

KAWAS ▸ kawa

KAWAU n New Zealand name for black shag

KAWAUS ▸ kawau

KAWED ▸ kaw

KAWING ▸ kaw

KAWS ▸ kaw

KAY n name of the letter K

KAYAK n Inuit canoe made of sealskins stretched over a frame ▷ vb travel by kayak

KAYAKED ▸ kayak

KAYAKER ▸ kayak

KAYAKS ▸ kayak

KAYLE n one of a set of ninepins

KAYLES pl n ninepins

KAYLIED adj (in British slang) intoxicated or drunk

KAYO another term for > knockout

KAYOED ▸ kayo

KAYOES ▸ kayo

KAYOING ▸ kayo

KAYOS ▸ kayo

KAYS ▸ kay

KAZI variant spelling of ▸ khazi

KAZIS ▸ kazi

KAZOO n cigar-shaped metal musical instrument that produces a buzzing sound when the player hums into it

KAZOOS ▸ kazoo

KBAR n kilobar

KBARS ▸ kbar

KEA n large brownish-green parrot of NZ

KEAS ▸ kea

KEASAR archaic variant of ▸ kaiser

KEASARS ▸ keasar

KEAVIE n archaic or dialect word for a type of crab

KEAVIES ▸ keavie

KEB vb Scots word meaning miscarry or reject a lamb

KEBAB n dish of small pieces of meat grilled on skewers ▷ vb skewer

KEBABS ▸ kebab

KEBAR n Scots word for beam or rafter

KEBARS ▸ kebar

KEBBED ▸ keb

KEBBIE n Scots word for shepherd's crook

KEBBIES ▸ kebbie

KEBBING ▸ keb

KEBBOCK n Scots word for a cheese

KEBBUCK same as ▸ kebbock

KEBELE n Ethiopian local council

KEBELES ▸ kebele

KEBLAH same as ▸ kiblah

KEBLAHS ▸ keblah

KEBOB same as ▸ kebab

KEBOBS ▸ kebob

KEBS ▸ keb

KECK vb retch or feel nausea

KECKED ▸ keck

KECKING ▸ keck

KECKLE Scots variant of ▸ cackle

KECKLED ▸ keckle

KECKLES ▸ keckle

KECKS pl n trousers

KECKSES ▸ kecks

KECKSY n dialect word meaning hollow plant stalk

KED n as in **sheep ked** sheep tick

KEDDAH same as ▸ kheda

KEDDAHS ▸ keddah

KEDGE vb move (a ship) along by hauling in on the cable of a light anchor ▷ n light anchor used for kedging

KEDGED ▸ kedge

KEDGER n small anchor

KEDGERS ▸ kedger

KEDGES ▸ kedge

KEDGIER ▸ kedgy

KEDGING ▸ kedge

KEDGY adj dialect word for happy or lively

KEDS ▸ ked

KEECH n old word for lump of fat

KEECHES ▸ keech

KEEF same as ▸ kif

KEEFS ▸ keef

KEEK Scots word for ▸ peep

KEEKED ▸ keek

KEEKER ▸ keek

KEEKERS ▸ keek

KEEKING ▸ keek

KEEKS ▸ keek

KEEL n main lengthways timber or steel support along the base of a ship ▷ vb mark with this stain

KEELAGE n fee charged by certain ports to allow a ship to dock

KEELED ▸ keel

KEELER n bargeman

KEELERS ▸ keeler

KEELIE n kestrel

KEELIES ▸ keelie

KEELING ▸ keel

KEELMAN n bargeman

KEELMEN ▸ keelman

KEELS ▸ keel

KEELSON n lengthways beam fastened to the keel of a ship for strength

KEEMA n (in Indian cookery) minced meat

KEEMAS ▸ keema

KEEN adj eager or enthusiastic ▹ vb wail over the dead ▹ n lament for the dead

KEENED ▸ keen

KEENER ▸ keen

KEENERS ▸ keen

KEENEST ▸ keen

KEENING ▸ keen

KEENLY ▸ keen

KEENO same as ▸ keno

KEENOS ▸ keeno

KEENS ▸ keen

KEEP vb have or retain possession of ▹ n cost of food and everyday expenses

KEEPER n person who looks after animals in a zoo

KEEPERS ▸ keeper

KEEPING ▸ keep

KEEPNET n cylindrical net strung on wire hoops and sealed at one end, suspended in water by anglers to keep alive the fish they have caught

KEEPS ▸ keep

KEESTER same as ▸ keister

KEET short for ▸ parakeet

KEETS ▸ keet

KEEVE n tub or vat

KEEVES ▸ keeve

KEF same as ▸ kif

KEFFEL dialect word for ▸ horse

KEFFELS ▸ keffel

KEFIR n effervescent drink of the Caucasus made from fermented milk

KEFIRS ▸ kefir

KEFS ▸ kef

KEG n small metal beer barrel ▹ vb put in kegs

KEGELER same as ▸ kegler

KEGGED ▸ keg

KEGGER ▸ keg

KEGGERS ▸ keg

KEGGING ▸ keg

KEGLER n participant in a game of tenpin bowling

KEGLERS ▸ kegler

KEGLING n bowling

KEGS ▸ keg

KEHUA n ghost or spirit

KEHUAS ▸ kehua

KEIGHT ▸ ketch

KEIR same as ▸ kier

KEIREN n type of track cycling event

KEIRENS ▸ keiren

KEIRIN n cycling race originating in Japan

KEIRINS ▸ keirin

KEIRS ▸ keir

KEISTER n rump

KEITLOA n southern African black two-horned rhinoceros

KEKENO n New Zealand fur seal

KEKENOS ▸ kekeno

KEKS same as ▸ kecks

KEKSYE same as ▸ kex

KEKSYES ▸ keksye

KELEP n large ant found in Central and South America

KELEPS ▸ kelep

KELIM same as ▸ kilim

KELIMS ▸ kelim

KELL dialect word for ▸ hairnet

KELLAUT same as ▸ khilat

KELLIES ▸ kelly

KELLS ▸ kell

KELLY n part of a drill system

KELOID n hard smooth pinkish raised growth of scar tissue at the site of an injury, tending to occur more frequently in dark-skinned races

KELOIDS ▸ keloid

KELP n large brown seaweed ▹ vb burn seaweed to make a type of ash used as a source for iodine and potash

KELPED ▸ kelp

KELPER n Falkland Islander

KELPERS ▸ kelper

KELPIE n Australian sheepdog with a smooth coat and upright ears

KELPIES ▸ kelpy

KELPING ▸ kelp

KELPS ▸ kelp

KELPY same as ▸ kelpie

KELSON same as ▸ keelson

KELSONS ▸ kelson

KELT n salmon that has recently spawned

KELTER same as ▸ kilter

KELTERS ▸ kelter

KELTIE variant spelling of ▸ kelty

KELTIES ▸ kelty

KELTS ▸ kelt

KELTY n old Scots word for an extra drink imposed on someone not thought to be drinking enough

KELVIN n SI unit of temperature

KELVINS ▸ kelvin

KEMB old word for ▸ comb

KEMBED ▸ kemb

KEMBING ▸ kemb

KEMBLA n small change

KEMBLAS ▸ kembla

KEMBO same as ▸ kimbo

KEMBOED ▸ kembo

KEMBOS ▸ kembo

KEMBS ▸ kemb

KEMP n coarse hair or strand of hair, esp one in a fleece that resists dyeing ▹ vb dialect word meaning to compete or try to come first

KEMPED ▸ kemp

KEMPER ▸ kemp

KEMPERS ▸ kemp

KEMPIER ▸ kempy

KEMPING ▸ kemp

KEMPLE n variable Scottish measure for hay or straw

KEMPLES ▸ kemple

KEMPS ▸ kemp

KEMPT adj (of hair) tidy

KEMPY ▸ kemp

KEN vb know ▹ n range of knowledge or perception

KENAF another name for ▸ ambary

KENAFS ▸ kenaf

KENCH n bin for salting and preserving fish

KENCHES ▸ kench

KENDO n Japanese sport of fencing using wooden staves

KENDOS ▸ kendo

KENNED ▸ ken

KENNEL n hutlike shelter for a dog ▹ vb put or go into a kennel

KENNELS ▸ kennel

KENNER ▸ ken

KENNERS ▸ ken

KENNET n old word for a small hunting dog

KENNETS ▸ kennet

KENNETT vb spoil or destroy ruthlessly

KENNING ▸ ken

KENO n game of chance similar to bingo

KENOS ▸ keno

KENOSES ▸ kenosis

KENOSIS n Christ's

K

voluntary renunciation of certain divine attributes, in order to identify himself with mankind

KENOTIC ▸ kenosis

KENS ▸ ken

KENT *dialect word for* ▸ **punt**

KENTE *n* brightly coloured handwoven cloth of Ghana, usually with some gold thread

KENTED ▸ kent

KENTES ▸ kente

KENTIA *n* plant name formerly used to include palms now allotted to several different genera

KENTIAS ▸ kentia

KENTING ▸ kent

KENTS ▸ kent

KEP *vb* catch

KEPHIR *same as* ▸ **kefir**

KEPHIRS ▸ kephir

KEPI *n* French military cap with a flat top and a horizontal peak

KEPIS ▸ kepi

KEPPED ▸ kep

KEPPEN ▸ kep

KEPPING ▸ kep

KEPPIT ▸ kep

KEPS ▸ kep

KEPT ▸ keep

KERAMIC *rare variant of* ▸ **ceramic**

KERATIN *n* fibrous protein found in the hair and nails

KERB *n* edging to a footpath ▷ *vb* provide with or enclose with a kerb

KERBAYA *n* blouse worn by Malay women

KERBED ▸ kerb

KERBING *n* material used for a kerb

KERBS ▸ kerb

KERCHOO *interj* atishoo

KEREL *n* chap or fellow

KERELS ▸ kerel

KERERU *n* New Zealand pigeon

KERERUS ▸ kereru

KERF *n* cut made by a saw, an axe, etc ▷ *vb* cut

KERFED ▸ kerf

KERFING ▸ kerf

KERFS ▸ kerf

KERKIER ▸ kerky

KERKY *adj* stupid

KERMA *n* quotient of the sum of the initial kinetic energies of all the charged particles liberated by

indirectly ionizing radiation in a volume element of a material divided by the mass of the volume element

KERMAS ▸ kerma

KERMES *n* dried bodies of female scale insects, used as a red dyestuff

KERMESS *same as* ▸ **kermis**

KERMIS *n* (formerly, esp in Holland and Northern Germany) annual country festival or carnival

KERN *n* part of the character on a piece of printer's type that projects beyond the body ▷ *vb* furnish (a typeface) with a kern

KERNE *same as* ▸ **kern**

KERNED ▸ kerne

KERNEL *n* seed of a nut, cereal, or fruit stone ▷ *vb* form kernels

KERNELS ▸ kernel

KERNES ▸ kerne

KERNING *n* adjustment of space between the letters of words to improve the appearance of text matter

KERNISH *adj* of, belonging to, or resembling an armed foot soldier or peasant

KERNITE *n* light soft colourless or white mineral consisting of a hydrated sodium borate in monoclinic crystalline form: an important source of borax and other boron compounds

KERNS ▸ kern

KERO *short for* ▸ **kerosene**

KEROGEN *n* solid organic material found in some rocks, such as oil shales, that produces hydrocarbons similar to petroleum when heated

KEROS ▸ kero

KERRIA *n* type of shrub with yellow flowers

KERRIAS ▸ kerria

KERRIES ▸ kerry

KERRY *n* breed of dairy cattle

KERSEY *n* smooth woollen cloth used for overcoats, etc

KERSEYS ▸ kersey

KERVE *dialect word for* ▸ **carve**

KERVED ▸ kerve

KERVES ▸ kerve

KERVING ▸ kerve

KERYGMA *n* essential news of Jesus, as preached by the early Christians to elicit faith rather than to educate or instruct

KESAR *old variant of* ▸ **kaiser**

KESARS ▸ kesar

KESH *n* beard and uncut hair, covered by the turban, traditionally worn by Sikhs as a symbol of their religious and cultural loyalty

KESHES ▸ kesh

KEST *old form of* ▸ **cast**

KESTING ▸ kest

KESTREL *n* type of small falcon

KESTS ▸ kest

KET *n* dialect word for carrion

KETA *n* type of salmon

KETAS ▸ keta

KETCH *n* two-masted sailing vessel ▷ *vb* (in archaic usage) catch

KETCHES ▸ ketch

KETCHUP *n* thick cold sauce, usu made of tomatoes

KETE *n* basket woven from flax

KETENE *n* colourless irritating toxic gas used as an acetylating agent in organic synthesis

KETENES ▸ ketene

KETES ▸ kete

KETMIA *n as in* **bladder ketmia** plant with pale yellow flowers and a bladder-like calyx

KETMIAS ▸ ketmia

KETO *adj as in* **keto form** form of tautomeric compounds when they are ketones rather than enol

KETOL *n* nitrogenous substance

KETOLS ▸ ketol

KETONE *n* type of organic solvent

KETONES ▸ ketone

KETONIC ▸ ketone

KETOSE *n* any monosaccharide that contains a ketone group

KETOSES ▸ ketosis

KETOSIS *n* high concentration of ketone

bodies in the blood

KETOTIC ▸ ketosis

KETS ▸ ket

KETTLE n container with a spout and handle used for boiling water

KETTLES ▸ kettle

KETUBAH n contract that states the obligations within Jewish marriage

KETUBOT ▸ ketubah

KEVEL n strong bitt or bollard for securing heavy hawsers

KEVELS ▸ kevel

KEVIL old variant of ▸ kevel

KEVILS ▸ kevil

KEWL nonstandard variant spelling of ▸ cool

KEWLER ▸ kewl

KEWLEST ▸ kewl

KEWPIE n type of brightly coloured doll, commonly given as a prize at a carnival

KEWPIES ▸ kewpie

KEX n any of several large hollow-stemmed umbelliferous plants, such as cow parsnip and chervil
> This is another of the great high-scoring three-letter words that use X.

KEXES ▸ kex

KEY n device for operating a lock by moving a bolt ▷ adj of great importance ▷ vb enter (text) using a keyboard

KEYCARD n card with an electronic strip or code on it that allows it to open a corresponding keycard-operated door

KEYED ▸ key

KEYHOLE n opening for inserting a key into a lock

KEYING ▸ key

KEYINGS ▸ key

KEYLESS ▸ key

KEYLINE n outline image of something on artwork or plans to show where it is to be placed

KEYNOTE adj central or dominating ▷ n dominant idea of a speech etc ▷ vb deliver a keynote address to (a political convention, etc)

KEYPAD n small panel with a set of buttons for operating a Teletext system, electronic calculator, etc

KEYPADS ▸ keypad

KEYPAL n person with whom one regularly exchanges emails for fun

KEYPALS ▸ keypal

KEYRING adj of a type of computer drive

KEYS interj children's cry for truce or respite from the rules of a game

KEYSET n set of computer keys used for a particular purpose

KEYSETS ▸ keyset

KEYSTER same as ▸ keister

KEYWAY n longitudinal slot cut into a component to accept a key that engages with a similar slot on a mating component to prevent relative motion of the two components

KEYWAYS ▸ keyway

KEYWORD n word or phrase that a computer will search for in order to locate the information or file that the computer user has requested

KGOTLA n (in South African English) meeting place for village assemblies, court cases, and meetings of village leaders

KGOTLAS ▸ kgotla

KHADDAR n cotton cloth of plain weave, produced in India

KHADI same as ▸ khaddar

KHADIS ▸ khadi

KHAF n letter of the Hebrew alphabet

KHAFS ▸ khaf

KHAKI adj dull yellowish-brown ▷ n hard-wearing fabric of this colour used for military uniforms

KHAKIS ▸ khaki

KHALAT same as ▸ khilat

KHALATS ▸ khalat

KHALIF variant spelling of ▸ caliph

KHALIFA same as ▸ caliph

KHALIFS ▸ khalif

KHAMSIN n hot southerly wind blowing from about March to May, esp in Egypt

KHAN n title of respect in Afghanistan and central Asia

KHANATE n territory ruled by a khan

KHANDA n double-edged

sword that appears as the emblem on the Sikh flag and is used in the Amrit ceremony to stir the amrit

KHANDAS ▸ khanda

KHANGA same as ▸ kanga

KHANGAS ▸ khanga

KHANJAR n type of dagger

KHANS ▸ khan

KHANUM feminine form of ▸ khan

KHANUMS ▸ khanum

KHAPH n letter of the Hebrew alphabet

KHAPHS ▸ khaph

KHARIF n (in Pakistan, India, etc) crop that is harvested at the beginning of winter

KHARIFS ▸ kharif

KHAT n white-flowered evergreen shrub of Africa and Arabia whose leaves have narcotic properties

KHATS ▸ khat

KHAYA n type of African tree

KHAYAL n kind of Indian classical vocal music

KHAYALS ▸ khayal

KHAYAS ▸ khaya

KHAZEN same as ▸ chazan

KHAZENS ▸ khazen

KHAZI n lavatory

KHAZIS ▸ khazi

KHEDA n (in India, Myanmar, etc) enclosure into which wild elephants are driven to be captured

KHEDAH same as ▸ kheda

KHEDAHS ▸ khedah

KHEDAS ▸ kheda

KHEDIVA n khedive's wife

KHEDIVE n viceroy of Egypt under Ottoman suzerainty

KHET n Thai district

KHETH same as ▸ heth

KHETHS ▸ kheth

KHETS ▸ khet

KHI n letter of the Greek alphabet
> This is a letter of the Greek alphabet, also spelt chi. It is worth remembering as one of the higher-scoring three-letter words starting with K.

KHILAT n (in the Middle East) robe or other gift given to someone by a superior as a mark of honour

KHILATS ▸ khilat

KHILIM same as ▸ **kilim**

KHILIMS ▸ **khilim**

KHIMAR n type of headscarf worn by Muslim women

KHIMARS ▸ **khimar**

KHIRKAH n dervish's woollen or cotton outer garment

KHIS ▸ **khi**

KHODJA same as ▸ **khoja**

KHODJAS ▸ **khodja**

KHOJA n teacher in a Muslim school

KHOJAS ▸ **khoja**

KHOR n watercourse

KHORS ▸ **khor**

KHOTBAH same as ▸ **khutbah**

KHOTBEH same as ▸ **khutbah**

KHOUM n Mauritanian monetary unit

KHOUMS ▸ **khoum**

KHUD n Indian ravine

KHUDS ▸ **khud**

KHURTA same as ▸ **kurta**

KHURTAS ▸ **khurta**

KHUTBAH n sermon in a Mosque, especially on a Friday

KI n vital energy

KIAAT n tropical African leguminous tree

KIAATS ▸ **kiaat**

KIANG n variety of wild ass that occurs in Tibet and surrounding regions

KIANGS ▸ **kiang**

KIAUGH n (in Scots) anxiety

KIAUGHS ▸ **kiaugh**

KIBBE n Middle Eastern dish made with minced meat and bulgur

KIBBEH same as ▸ **kibbe**

KIBBEHS ▸ **kibbeh**

KIBBES ▸ **kibbe**

KIBBI same as ▸ **kibbe**

KIBBIS ▸ **kibbi**

KIBBITZ same as ▸ **kibitz**

KIBBLE n bucket used in wells or in mining for hoisting ▷ vb grind into small pieces

KIBBLED ▸ **kibble**

KIBBLES ▸ **kibble**

KIBBUTZ n communal farm or factory in Israel

KIBE n chilblain, esp an ulcerated one on the heel

KIBEI n someone of Japanese ancestry born in the US and educated in Japan

KIBEIS ▸ **kibei**

KIBES ▸ **kibe**

KIBITKA n (in Russia) covered sledge or wagon

KIBITZ vb interfere or offer unwanted advice, esp as a spectator at a card game

KIBLA same as ▸ **kiblah**

KIBLAH n direction of Mecca, to which Muslims turn in prayer, indicated in mosques by a niche (mihrab) in the wall

KIBLAHS ▸ **kiblah**

KIBLAS ▸ **kibla**

KIBOSH vb put a stop to

KICK vb drive, push, or strike with the foot ▷ n thrust or blow with the foot

KICKBOX vb box with hands and feet

KICKED ▸ **kick**

KICKER n person or thing that kicks

KICKERS ▸ **kicker**

KICKIER ▸ **kicky**

KICKING ▸ **kick**

KICKOFF n kick from the centre of the field that starts a game of football

KICKOUT n (in basketball) instance of kicking the ball

KICKS ▸ **kick**

KICKUP n fuss

KICKUPS ▸ **kickup**

KICKY adj excitingly unusual and different

KID n child ▷ vb tease or deceive (someone) ▷ adj younger

KIDDED ▸ **kid**

KIDDER ▸ **kid**

KIDDERS ▸ **kid**

KIDDIE same as ▸ **kiddy**

KIDDIED ▸ **kiddy**

KIDDIER n old word for a market trader

KIDDIES ▸ **kiddy**

KIDDING ▸ **kid**

KIDDISH ▸ **kid**

KIDDLE n device, esp a barrier constructed of nets and stakes, for catching fish in a river or in the sea

KIDDLES ▸ **kiddle**

KIDDO n very informal term of address for a young person

KIDDOES ▸ **kiddo**

KIDDOS ▸ **kiddo**

KIDDUSH n (in Judaism) special blessing said before a meal on sabbaths and festivals

KIDDY n affectionate word for a child ▷ vb tease or deceive

KIDEL same as ▸ **kiddle**

KIDELS ▸ **kidel**

KIDGE dialect word for ▸ **lively**

KIDGIE adj dialect word for friendly and welcoming

KIDGIER ▸ **kidgie**

KIDLET n humorous word for small child

KIDLETS ▸ **kidlet**

KIDLIKE ▸ **kid**

KIDLING n young kid

KIDNAP vb seize and hold (a person) to ransom

KIDNAPS ▸ **kidnap**

KIDNEY n either of the pair of organs that filter waste products from the blood to produce urine

KIDNEYS ▸ **kidney**

KIDS ▸ **kid**

KIDSKIN n soft smooth leather made from the hide of a young goat

KIDULT n adult who is interested in forms of entertainment such as computer games, television programmes, etc that are intended for children ▷ adj aimed at or suitable for kidults, or both children and adults

KIDULTS ▸ **kidult**

KIDVID n informal word for children's video or television

KIDVIDS ▸ **kidvid**

KIEF same as ▸ **kif**

KIEFS ▸ **kief**

KIEKIE n climbing bush plant of New Zealand

KIEKIES ▸ **kiekie**

KIER n vat in which cloth is bleached

KIERIE n South African cudgel

KIERIES ▸ **kierie**

KIERS ▸ **kier**

KIESTER same as ▸ **keister**

KIEV n chicken breast filled with garlic butter and coated in breadcrumbs

KIEVE same as ▸ **keeve**

KIEVES ▸ **kieve**

KIEVS ▸ **kiev**

KIF n any drug or agent that when smoked is capable of producing a euphoric condition

KIFF *adj* South African slang for excellent

KIFS ► **kif**

KIGHT *n* archaic spelling of kite, the bird of prey

KIGHTS ► **kight**

KIKOI *n* piece of cotton cloth with coloured bands, worn wrapped around the body

KIKOIS ► **kikoi**

KIKUMON *n* chrysanthemum emblem of the imperial family of Japan

KIKUYU *n* type of grass

KIKUYUS ► **kikuyu**

KILD *old spelling of* ► **killed**

KILERG *n* 1000 ergs

KILERGS ► **kilerg**

KILEY *same as* ► **kylie**

KILEYS ► **kiley**

KILIM *n* pileless woven rug of intricate design made in the Middle East

KILIMS ► **kilim**

KILL *vb* cause the death of ▷ *n* act of killing

KILLAS *n* Cornish clay slate

KILLCOW *n* important person

KILLDEE *same as* > **killdeer**

KILLED ► **kill**

KILLER *n* person or animal that kills, esp habitually

KILLERS ► **killer**

KILLICK *n* small anchor, esp one made of a heavy stone

KILLIE *same as* ► **killifish**

KILLIES ► **killie**

KILLING *adj* very tiring ▷ *n* sudden financial success

KILLJOY *n* person who spoils others' pleasure

KILLOCK *same as* ► **killick**

KILLS ► **kill**

KILLUT *same as* ► **khilat**

KILLUTS ► **killut**

KILN *n* oven for baking, drying, or processing pottery, bricks, etc ▷ *vb* fire or process in a kiln

KILNED ► **kiln**

KILNING ► **kiln**

KILNS ► **kiln**

KILO *n* code word for the letter k

KILOBAR *n* 1000 bars

KILOBIT *n* 1024 bits

KILORAD *n* 1000 rads

KILOS ► **kilo**

KILOTON *n* one thousand tons

KILP *dialect form of* ► **kelp**

KILPS ► **kilp**

KILT *n* knee-length pleated tartan skirt-like garment worn orig. by Scottish Highlanders ▷ *vb* put pleats in (cloth)

KILTED ► **kilt**

KILTER *n* working order or alignment

KILTERS ► **kilter**

KILTIE *n* someone wearing a kilt

KILTIES ► **kiltie**

KILTING ► **kilt**

KILTS ► **kilt**

KILTY *same as* ► **kiltie**

KIMBO *vb* place akimbo

KIMBOED ► **kimbo**

KIMBOS ► **kimbo**

KIMCHEE *same as* ► **kimchi**

KIMCHI *n* Korean dish made from fermented cabbage or other vegetables, garlic, and chillies

KIMCHIS ► **kimchi**

KIMMER *same as* ► **cummer**

KIMMERS ► **kimmer**

KIMONO *n* loose wide-sleeved Japanese robe, fastened with a sash

KIMONOS ► **kimono**

KIN *n* person's relatives collectively ▷ *adj* related by blood

KINA *n* standard monetary unit of Papua New Guinea, divided into 100 toea

KINARA *n* African candle holder

KINARAS ► **kinara**

KINAS ► **kina**

KINASE *n* any enzyme that can convert an inactive zymogen to the corresponding enzyme

KINASES ► **kinase**

KINCHIN *old slang word for* ► **child**

KINCOB *n* fine silk fabric embroidered with threads of gold or silver, of a kind made in India

KINCOBS ► **kincob**

KIND *adj* considerate, friendly, and helpful ▷ *n* class or group with common characteristics ▷ *vb* old word for beget or father

KINDA *adv* very informal shortening of kind of

KINDED ► **kind**

KINDER *adj* more kind ▷ *n* kindergarten or nursery school

KINDERS ► **kind**

KINDEST ► **kind**

KINDIE *same as* ► **kindy**

KINDIES ► **kindy**

KINDING ► **kind**

KINDLE *vb* set (a fire) alight

KINDLED ► **kindle**

KINDLER ► **kindle**

KINDLES ► **kindle**

KINDLY *adj* having a warm-hearted nature ▷ *adv* in a considerate way

KINDRED *adj* having similar qualities ▷ *n* blood relationship

KINDS ► **kind**

KINDY *n* kindergarten

KINE *pl n* cows or cattle ▷ *n* Japanese pestle

KINEMA *same as* ► **cinema**

KINEMAS ► **kinema**

KINES *n* ► **kine**

KINESES ► **kinesis**

KINESIC *adj* of or relating to kinesics

KINESIS *n* nondirectional movement of an organism or cell in response to a stimulus, the rate of movement being dependent on the strength of the stimulus

KINETIC *adj* relating to or caused by motion

KINETIN *n* plant hormone

KINFOLK *another word for* > **kinsfolk**

KING *n* male ruler of a monarchy ▷ *vb* make king

KINGCUP *n* yellow-flowered plant

KINGDOM *n* state ruled by a king or queen

KINGED ► **king**

KINGING ► **king**

KINGLE *n* Scots word for a type of hard rock

KINGLES ► **kingle**

KINGLET *n* king of a small or insignificant territory

KINGLY *adj* appropriate to a king ▷ *adv* in a manner appropriate to a king

KINGPIN *n* most important person in an organization

KINGS ► **king**

KININ *n* any of a group of polypeptides in the blood that cause dilation of the blood vessels and make

K

smooth muscles contract
KININS ▸ **kinin**
KINK n twist or bend in
rope, wire, hair, etc ▸ vb
form or cause to form a kink
KINKED ▸ **kink**
KINKIER ▸ **kinky**
KINKILY ▸ **kinky**
KINKING ▸ **kink**
KINKLE n little kink
KINKLES ▸ **kinkle**
KINKS ▸ **kink**
KINKY adj given to unusual
sexual practices
KINLESS adj without any
relatives
KINO same as ▸ **keno**
KINONE n benzoquinone, a
yellow crystalline
water-soluble ketone used
in the production of
dyestuffs
KINONES ▸ **kinone**
KINOS ▸ **kino**
KINRED old form of
▸ **kindred**
KINREDS ▸ **kinred**
KINS ▸ **kin**
KINSHIP n blood
relationship
KINSMAN n relative
KINSMEN ▸ **kinsman**
KIORE n small brown rat
native to New Zealand
KIORES ▸ **kiore**
KIOSK n small booth selling
drinks, cigarettes,
newspapers, etc
KIOSKS ▸ **kiosk**
KIP vb sleep ▸ n sleep or
slumber
KIPE n dialect word for a
basket for catching fish
KIPES ▸ **kipe**
KIPP uncommon variant of
▸ **kip**
KIPPA n skullcap worn by
orthodox male Jews at all
times and by others for
prayer, esp a crocheted one
worn by those with a
specifically religious Zionist
affiliation
KIPPAGE n Scots word for a
state of anger or
excitement
KIPPAS ▸ **kippa**
KIPPED ▸ **kip**
KIPPEN ▸ **kep**
KIPPER n cleaned, salted,
and smoked herring ▸ vb
cure (a herring) by salting
and smoking it

KIPPERS ▸ **kipper**
KIPPING ▸ **kip**
KIPPS ▸ **kipp**
KIPS ▸ **kip**
KIPSKIN same as ▸ **kip**
KIPUNJI n Tanzanian species
of monkey
KIR n drink made from dry
white wine and cassis
KIRANA n small
family-owned shop in India
KIRANAS ▸ **kirana**
KIRBEH n leather bottle
KIRBEHS ▸ **kirbeh**
KIRBY n as in **kirby grip**
hairgrip consisting of a
piece of wire bent back on
itself and partly bent into
ridges
KIRIMON n Japanese
imperial crest
KIRK Scots word for ▸ **church**
KIRKED ▸ **kirk**
KIRKING ▸ **kirk**
KIRKMAN n member or
strong upholder of the Kirk
KIRKMEN ▸ **kirkman**
KIRKS ▸ **kirk**
KIRKTON n village or town
with a parish church
KIRMESS same as ▸ **kermis**
KIRN dialect word for ▸ **churn**
KIRNED ▸ **kirn**
KIRNING ▸ **kirn**
KIRNS ▸ **kirn**
KIRPAN n short sword
traditionally carried by
Sikhs as a symbol of their
religious and cultural
loyalty
KIRPANS ▸ **kirpan**
KIRRI n Hottentot stick
KIRRIS ▸ **kirri**
KIRS ▸ **kir**
KIRSCH n cherry brandy
KIRTAN n devotional
singing, usually
accompanied by musical
instruments
KIRTANS ▸ **kirtan**
KIRTLE n woman's skirt or
dress ▸ vb dress with a
kirtle
KIRTLED ▸ **kirtle**
KIRTLES ▸ **kirtle**
KIS ▸ **ki**
KISAN n peasant or farmer
KISANS ▸ **kisan**
KISH n graphite formed on
the surface of molten iron
that contains a large
amount of carbon
KISHES ▸ **kish**

KISHKA same as ▸ **kishke**
KISHKAS ▸ **kishka**
KISHKE n beef or fowl
intestine or skin stuffed
with flour, onion, etc, and
boiled and roasted
KISHKES ▸ **kishke**
KISMAT same as ▸ **kismet**
KISMATS ▸ **kismat**
KISMET n fate or destiny
KISMETS ▸ **kismet**
KISS vb touch with the lips
in affection or greeting ▸ n
touch with the lips
KISSED ▸ **kiss**
KISSEL n Russian dessert of
sweetened fruit purée
thickened with arrowroot
KISSELS ▸ **kissel**
KISSER n mouth or face
KISSERS ▸ **kisser**
KISSES ▸ **kiss**
KISSIER ▸ **kissy**
KISSING ▸ **kiss**
KISSY adj showing
exaggerated affection, esp
by frequent touching or
kissing
KIST n large wooden chest
▸ vb place in a coffin
KISTED ▸ **kist**
KISTFUL ▸ **kist**
KISTING ▸ **kist**
KISTS ▸ **kist**
KIT n outfit or equipment
for a specific purpose ▸ vb
fit or provide
KITBAG n bag for a soldier's
or traveller's belongings
KITBAGS ▸ **kitbag**
KITCHEN n room used for
cooking ▸ vb (in archaic
usage) provide with food
KITE n light frame covered
with a thin material flown
on a string in the wind ▸ vb
soar and glide
KITED ▸ **kite**
KITENGE n thick cotton
cloth
KITER ▸ **kite**
KITERS ▸ **kite**
KITES ▸ **kite**
KITH n one's friends and
acquaintances
KITHARA same as ▸ **cithara**
KITHE same as ▸ **kythe**
KITHED ▸ **kithe**
KITHES ▸ **kithe**
KITHING ▸ **kithe**
KITHS ▸ **kith**
KITING ▸ **kite**
KITINGS ▸ **kite**

KITLING *dialect word for* ► **kitten**

KITS ► **kit**

KITSCH *n* art or literature with popular sentimental appeal ▷ *n* object or art that is tawdry, vulgarized, oversentimental or pretentious

KITSCHY ► **kitsch**

KITSET *n* New Zealand word for a piece of furniture supplied in pieces for the purchaser to assemble

KITSETS ► **kitset**

KITTED ► **kit**

KITTEL *n* white garment worn for certain Jewish rituals or burial

KITTELS ► **kittel**

KITTEN *n* young cat ▷ *vb* (of cats) give birth

KITTENS ► **kitten**

KITTENY ► **kitten**

KITTIES ► **kitty**

KITTING ► **kit**

KITTLE *adj* capricious and unpredictable ▷ *vb* be troublesome or puzzling to (someone)

KITTLED ► **kittle**

KITTLER ► **kittle**

KITTLES ► **kittle**

KITTLY *Scots word for* ► **ticklish**

KITTUL *n* type of palm from which jaggery sugar comes

KITTULS ► **kittul**

KITTY *n* communal fund

KITUL ► **kittul**

KITULS ► **kitul**

KIVA *n* large underground or partly underground room in a Pueblo Indian village, used chiefly for religious ceremonies

KIVAS ► **kiva**

KIWI *n* New Zealand flightless bird with a long beak and no tail

KIWIS ► **kiwi**

KLANG *n* (in music) kind of tone

KLANGS ► **klang**

KLAP *vb* slap or spank

KLAPPED ► **klap**

KLAPS ► **klap**

KLATCH *n* gathering, especially over coffee

KLATSCH *same as* ► **klatch**

KLAVERN *n* local Ku Klux Klan group

KLAVIER *same as* ► **clavier**

KLAXON *n* loud horn used on emergency vehicles as a warning signal ▷ *vb* hoot with a klaxon

KLAXONS ► **klaxon**

KLEAGLE *n* person with a particular rank in the Ku Klux Klan

KLEENEX *n* tradename for a kind of soft paper tissue, used esp as a handkerchief

KLEPHT *n* any of the Greeks who fled to the mountains after the 15th-century Turkish conquest of Greece and whose descendants survived as brigands into the 19th century

KLEPHTS ► **klepht**

KLEPTO *n* compulsive thief

KLEPTOS ► **klepto**

KLETT *n* lightweight climbing boot

KLETTS ► **klett**

KLEZMER *n* Jewish folk musician, usually a member of a small band

KLICK *n* kilometre

KLICKS ► **klick**

KLIEG *n as in* **klieg light** intense carbon-arc light used for illumination in producing films

KLIK *US military slang word for* ► **kilometre**

KLIKS ► **klik**

KLINKER *n* type of brick used in paving

KLIPDAS *n* rock hyrax

KLISTER *n* type of ski dressing for improving grip on snow

KLONG *n* type of canal in Thailand

KLONGS ► **klong**

KLOOCH *same as* ► **kloochman**

KLOOF *n* mountain pass or gorge

KLOOFS ► **kloof**

KLOOTCH *same as* ► **kloochman**

KLUDGE *n* untidy solution involving a variety of cobbled-together elements ▷ *vb* cobble something together

KLUDGED ► **kludge**

KLUDGES ► **kludge**

KLUDGEY ► **kludge**

KLUDGY ► **kludge**

KLUGE *same as* ► **kludge**

KLUGED ► **kluge**

KLUGES ► **kluge**

KLUGING ► **kluge**

KLUTZ *n* clumsy or stupid person

KLUTZES ► **klutz**

KLUTZY ► **klutz**

KNACK *n* skilful way of doing something ▷ *vb* dialect word for crack or snap

KNACKED *adj* broken or worn out

KNACKER *n* buyer of old horses for killing ▷ *vb* exhaust

KNACKS ► **knack**

KNACKY *adj* old or dialect word for cunning or artful

KNAG *n* knot in wood

KNAGGY *adj* knotty

KNAGS ► **knag**

KNAIDEL *same as* ► **kneidel**

KNAP *n* crest of a hill ▷ *vb* hit, hammer, or chip

KNAPPED ► **knap**

KNAPPER ► **knap**

KNAPPLE *old word for* ► **nibble**

KNAPS ► **knap**

KNAR *old spelling of* ► **gnar**

KNARL *old spelling of* ► **gnarl**

KNARLS ► **knarl**

KNARLY *same as* ► **gnarly**

KNARRED ► **knar**

KNARRY ► **knar**

KNARS ► **knar**

KNAUR *variant form of* ► **knur**

KNAURS ► **knaur**

KNAVE *n* jack at cards

KNAVERY *n* dishonest behaviour

KNAVES ► **knave**

KNAVISH ► **knave**

KNAWE *same as* ► **knawel**

KNAWEL *n* type of Old World plant with heads of minute petal-less flowers

KNAWELS ► **knawel**

KNAWES ► **knawe**

KNEAD *vb* work (dough) into a smooth mixture with the hands

KNEADED ► **knead**

KNEADER ► **knead**

KNEADS ► **knead**

KNEE *n* joint between thigh and lower leg ▷ *vb* strike or push with the knee

KNEECAP *nontechnical name for* ► **patella**

KNEED ► **knee**

KNEEING ► **knee**

K

KNEEL *vb* fall or rest on one's knees ▷ *n* act or position of kneeling

KNEELED ▸ **kneel**

KNEELER ▸ **kneel**

KNEELS ▸ **kneel**

KNEEPAD *n* any of several types of protective covering for the knees

KNEEPAN *another word for* ▸ **patella**

KNEES ▸ **knee**

KNEIDEL *n* (in Jewish cookery) small dumpling, usually served in chicken soup

KNELL *n* sound of a bell, esp at a funeral or death ▷ *vb* ring a knell

KNELLED ▸ **knell**

KNELLS ▸ **knell**

KNELT ▸ **kneel**

KNESSET *n* parliament or assembly

KNEVELL *vb* old Scots word meaning beat

KNEW ▸ **know**

KNICKER *n* woman's or girl's undergarment covering the lower trunk and having legs or legholes

KNICKS *pl n* knickers

KNIFE *n* cutting tool or weapon consisting of a sharp-edged blade with a handle ▷ *vb* cut or stab with a knife

KNIFED ▸ **knife**

KNIFER ▸ **knife**

KNIFERS ▸ **knife**

KNIFES ▸ **knife**

KNIFING ▸ **knife**

KNIGHT *n* man who has been given a knighthood ▷ *vb* award a knighthood to

KNIGHTS ▸ **knight**

KNISH *n* piece of dough stuffed with potato, meat, or some other filling and baked or fried

KNISHES ▸ **knish**

KNIT *vb* make (a garment) by interlocking a series of loops in wool or other yarn ▷ *n* fabric made by knitting

KNITCH *dialect word for* ▸ **bundle**

KNITS ▸ **knit**

KNITTED ▸ **knit**

KNITTER ▸ **knit**

KNITTLE *n* old word for string or cord

KNIVE *rare variant of* ▸ **knife**

KNIVED ▸ **knive**

KNIVES ▸ **knife**

KNIVING ▸ **knive**

KNOB *n* rounded projection, such as a switch on a radio ▷ *vb* supply with knobs

KNOBBED ▸ **knob**

KNOBBER *n* two-year-old male deer

KNOBBLE *n* small knob ▷ *vb* dialect word meaning strike

KNOBBLY *adj* covered with small bumps

KNOBBY ▸ **knob**

KNOBS ▸ **knob**

KNOCK *vb* give a blow or push to ▷ *n* blow or rap

KNOCKED ▸ **knock**

KNOCKER *n* metal fitting for knocking on a door

KNOCKS ▸ **knock**

KNOLL *n* small rounded hill ▷ *vb* (in archaic or dialect usage) knell

KNOLLED ▸ **knoll**

KNOLLER ▸ **knoll**

KNOLLS ▸ **knoll**

KNOLLY ▸ **knoll**

KNOP *n* knob, esp an ornamental one

KNOPPED ▸ **knop**

KNOPS ▸ **knop**

KNOSP *n* budlike architectural feature

KNOSPS ▸ **knosp**

KNOT *n* fastening made by looping and pulling tight strands of string, cord, or rope ▷ *vb* tie with or into a knot

KNOTS ▸ **knot**

KNOTTED ▸ **knot**

KNOTTER ▸ **knot**

KNOTTY *adj* full of knots

KNOUT *n* stout whip used formerly in Russia as an instrument of punishment ▷ *vb* whip

KNOUTED ▸ **knout**

KNOUTS ▸ **knout**

KNOW *vb* be or feel certain of the truth of (information etc)

KNOWE *same as* ▸ **knoll**

KNOWER ▸ **know**

KNOWERS ▸ **know**

KNOWES ▸ **knowe**

KNOWHOW *n* ingenuity, knack, or skill

KNOWING ▸ **know**

KNOWN ▸ **know**

KNOWNS ▸ **know**

KNOWS ▸ **know**

KNUB *dialect word for* ▸ **knob**

KNUBBLE *vb* dialect word for beat or pound using one's fists

KNUBBLY *adj* having small lumps or protuberances

KNUBBY *adj* knub

KNUBS ▸ **knub**

KNUCKLE *n* bone at the finger joint

KNUCKLY ▸ **knuckle**

KNUR *n* knot or protuberance in a tree trunk or in wood

KNURL *n* small ridge, often one of a series ▷ *vb* impress with a series of fine ridges or serrations

KNURLED ▸ **knurl**

KNURLS ▸ **knurl**

KNURLY *rare word for* ▸ **gnarled**

KNURR *same as* ▸ **knur**

KNURRS ▸ **knurr**

KNURS ▸ **knur**

KNUT *n* dandy

KNUTS ▸ **knut**

KO *n* (in New Zealand) traditional digging tool

KOA *n* Hawaiian leguminous tree

KOALA *n* tree-dwelling Australian marsupial with dense grey fur

KOALAS ▸ **koala**

KOAN *n* (in Zen Buddhism) problem or riddle that admits no logical solution

KOANS ▸ **koan**

KOAS ▸ **koa**

KOB *n* any of several waterbuck-like species of African antelope

KOBAN *n* old oval-shaped Japanese gold coin

KOBANG *same as* ▸ **koban**

KOBANGS ▸ **kobang**

KOBANS ▸ **koban**

KOBO *n* Nigerian monetary unit, worth one hundredth of a naira

KOBOLD *n* mischievous household sprite

KOBOLDS ▸ **kobold**

KOBOS ▸ **kobo**

KOBS ▸ **kob**

KOCHIA *n* any of several plants whose foliage turns dark red in late summer

KOCHIAS ▸ **kochia**

KOEKOEA *n* long-tailed cuckoo of New Zealand

KOEL *n* any of several parasitic cuckoos of S and SE Asia and Australia

KOELS ▸ koel

KOFF *n* Dutch masted merchant vessel

KOFFS ▸ koff

KOFTA *n* Indian dish of seasoned minced meat shaped into small balls and cooked

KOFTAS ▸ kofta

KOFTGAR *n* (in India) person skilled in the art of inlaying steel with gold

KOGAL *n* (in Japan) teenage girl noted for her busy social life and trendy purchases

KOGALS ▸ kogal

KOHA *n* gift or donation, esp of cash

KOHANIM ▸ kohen

KOHAS ▸ koha

KOHEN *n* member of the Jewish priestly caste

KOHL *n* cosmetic powder used to darken the edges of the eyelids

KOHLS ▸ kohl

KOI *n* any of various ornamental forms of the common carp

KOINE *n* common language among speakers of different languages

KOINES ▸ koine

KOIS ▸ koi

KOJI *n* Japanese steamed rice

KOJIS ▸ koji

KOKA *n* former type of score in judo

KOKAKO *n* dark grey long-tailed wattled crow of New Zealand

KOKAKOS ▸ kokako

KOKANEE *n* freshwater salmon of lakes and rivers in W North America

KOKAS ▸ koka

KOKER *n* Guyanese sluice

KOKERS ▸ koker

KOKIRI *n* type of rough-skinned New Zealand triggerfish

KOKIRIS ▸ kokiri

KOKOBEH *adj* (of certain fruit) having a rough skin

KOKOPU *n* any of several small freshwater fish of New Zealand

KOKOPUS ▸ kokopu

KOKOWAI *n* type of clay

used in decoration because of its red colour

KOKRA *n* type of wood

KOKRAS ▸ kokra

KOKUM *n* tropical tree

KOKUMS ▸ kokum

KOLA *n* *as in* **kola nut** caffeine-containing seed used in medicine and soft drinks

KOLACKY *n* sweet bun with a fruit, jam, or nut filling

KOLAS ▸ kola

KOLBASI *same as* ▸ **kolbassi**

KOLHOZ *same as* ▸ **kolkhoz**

KOLHOZY *same as* ▸ **kolkhoz**

KOLKHOS *same as* ▸ **kolkhoz**

KOLKHOZ *n* (formerly) collective farm in the Soviet Union

KOLKOZ *same as* ▸ **kolkhoz**

KOLKOZY ▸ **kolkoz**

KOLO *n* Serbian folk dance in which a circle of people dance slowly around one or more dancers in the centre

KOLOS ▸ kolo

KOMATIK *n* sledge with wooden runners and crossbars bound with animal hides

KOMBU *n* dark brown seaweed, the leaves of which are dried and used esp in Japanese cookery

KOMBUS ▸ kombu

KON *old word for* ▸ **know**

KONAKI *same as* ▸ **koneke**

KONAKIS ▸ konaki

KONBU *same as* ▸ **kombu**

KONBUS ▸ konbu

KOND ▸ kon

KONDO *n* (in Uganda) thief or armed robber

KONDOS ▸ kondo

KONEKE *n* farm vehicle with runners in front and wheels at the rear

KONEKES ▸ koneke

KONFYT *n* South African fruit preserve

KONFYTS ▸ konfyt

KONGONI *n* E African hartebeest

KONINI *n* edible dark purple berry of the kotukutuku or tree fuchsia

KONINIS ▸ konini

KONK *same as* ▸ **conk**

KONKED ▸ konk

KONKING ▸ konk

KONKS ▸ konk

KONNING ▸ kon

KONS ▸ kon

KOODOO *same as* ▸ **kudu**

KOODOOS ▸ koodoo

KOOK *n* eccentric person ▷ *vb* dialect word for vanish

KOOKED ▸ kook

KOOKIE *same as* ▸ **kooky**

KOOKIER ▸ kooky

KOOKILY ▸ kooky

KOOKING ▸ kook

KOOKS ▸ kook

KOOKY *adj* crazy, eccentric, or foolish

KOOLAH *old form of* ▸ **koala**

KOOLAHS ▸ koolah

KOORI *n* Australian Aborigine

KOORIES ▸ koori

KOORIS ▸ koori

KOP *n* prominent isolated hill or mountain in southern Africa

KOPECK *n* former Russian monetary unit, one hundredth of a rouble

KOPECKS ▸ kopeck

KOPEK *same as* ▸ **kopeck**

KOPEKS ▸ kopek

KOPH *n* 19th letter in the Hebrew alphabet

KOPHS ▸ koph

KOPIYKA *n* monetary unit of Ukraine, worth one hundredth of a hryvna

KOPIYOK ▸ kopiyka

KOPJE *n* small hill

KOPJES ▸ kopje

KOPPA *n* consonantal letter in the Greek alphabet pronounced like kappa (K) with the point of articulation further back in the throat

KOPPAS ▸ koppa

KOPPIE *same as* ▸ **kopje**

KOPPIES ▸ koppie

KOPS ▸ kop

KOR *n* ancient Hebrew unit of capacity

KORA *n* West African instrument with twenty-one strings, combining features of the harp and the lute

KORAI ▸ kore

KORARI *n* native New Zealand flax plant

KORARIS ▸ korari

KORAS ▸ kora

KORAT *n* *as in* **korat cat** rare blue-grey breed of cat

K

with brilliant green eyes

KORATS ▸ **korat**

KORE n ancient Greek statue of a young woman wearing clothes

KORERO n talk or discussion ▷ vb speak or converse

KOREROS ▸ **korero**

KORES ▸ **kore**

KORKIR n variety of lichen used in dyeing

KORKIRS ▸ **korkir**

KORMA n type of mild Indian dish consisting of meat or vegetables cooked in water, yoghurt, or cream

KORMAS ▸ **korma**

KORO n elderly Maori man

KORORA n small New Zealand penguin

KORORAS ▸ **korora**

KOROS ▸ **koro**

KOROWAI n decorative woven cloak worn by a Maori chief

KORS ▸ **kor**

KORU n stylized curved pattern used esp in carving

KORUN ▸ **koruna**

KORUNA n standard monetary unit of the Czech Republic and Slovakia, divided into 100 hellers

KORUNAS ▸ **koruna**

KORUNY ▸ **koruna**

KORUS ▸ **koru**

KOS n Indian unit of distance having different values in different localities

KOSES ▸ **kos**

KOSHER adj conforming to Jewish religious law, esp (of food) to Jewish dietary law ▷ n kosher food ▷ vb prepare in accordance with Jewish dietary rules

KOSHERS ▸ **kosher**

KOSMOS variant form of ▸ **cosmos**

KOSS same as ▸ **kos**

KOSSES ▸ **koss**

KOTARE n small greenish-blue kingfisher found in New Zealand, Australia, and some Pacific islands to the north

KOTARES ▸ **kotare**

KOTO n Japanese stringed instrument, consisting of a rectangular wooden body over which are stretched silk strings, which are

plucked with plectrums or a nail-like device

KOTOS ▸ **koto**

KOTOW same as ▸ **kowtow**

KOTOWED ▸ **kotow**

KOTOWER ▸ **kotow**

KOTOWS ▸ **kotow**

KOTUKU n white heron with brilliant white plumage, black legs and yellow eyes and bill

KOTUKUS ▸ **kotuku**

KOTWAL n senior police officer or magistrate in an Indian town

KOTWALS ▸ **kotwal**

KOULAN same as ▸ **kulan**

KOULANS ▸ **koulan**

KOUMIS same as ▸ **kumiss**

KOUMISS same as ▸ **kumiss**

KOUMYS same as ▸ **kumiss**

KOUMYSS same as ▸ **kumiss**

KOUPREY n large wild SE Asian ox

KOURA n New Zealand freshwater crayfish

KOURAS ▸ **koura**

KOUROI ▸ **kouros**

KOUROS n ancient Greek statue of a young man

KOUSSO n Abyssinian tree whose flowers have useful antiparasitic properties

KOUSSOS ▸ **kousso**

KOW old variant of ▸ **cow**

> This dialect variant of **cow** scores well for a three-letter word, and can be a good one to form when playing in more than one direction.

KOWHAI n New Zealand tree with clusters of yellow flowers

KOWHAIS ▸ **kowhai**

KOWS ▸ **kow**

KOWTOW vb be servile (towards) ▷ n act of kowtowing

KOWTOWS ▸ **kowtow**

KRAAL n S African village surrounded by a strong fence ▷ adj denoting or relating to the tribal aspects of the Black African way of life ▷ vb enclose (livestock) in a kraal

KRAALED ▸ **kraal**

KRAALS ▸ **kraal**

KRAB same as > **karabiner**

KRABS ▸ **krab**

KRAFT n strong wrapping paper, made from pulp

processed with a sulphate solution

KRAFTS ▸ **kraft**

KRAIT n brightly coloured venomous snake of S and SE Asia

KRAITS ▸ **krait**

KRAKEN n legendary sea monster

KRAKENS ▸ **kraken**

KRANG n dead whale from which the blubber has been removed

KRANGS ▸ **krang**

KRANS n sheer rock face

KRANSES ▸ **krans**

KRANTZ same as ▸ **krans**

KRANZ same as ▸ **krans**

KRANZES ▸ **krans**

KRATER same as ▸ **crater**

KRATERS ▸ **krater**

KRAUT n sauerkraut

KRAUTS ▸ **kraut**

KREEP n lunar substance that is high in potassium, rare earth elements, and phosphorus

KREEPS ▸ **kreep**

KREESE same as ▸ **kris**

KREESED ▸ **kreese**

KREESES ▸ **kreese**

KREMLIN n citadel of any Russian city

KRENG same as ▸ **krang**

KRENGS ▸ **kreng**

KREUZER same as > **kreutzer**

KREWE n club taking part in New Orleans carnival parade

KREWES ▸ **krewe**

KRILL n small shrimplike sea creature

KRILLS ▸ **krill**

KRIMMER n tightly curled light grey fur obtained from the skins of lambs from the Crimean region

KRIS n Malayan and Indonesian stabbing or slashing knife with a scalloped edge ▷ vb stab or slash with a kris

KRISED ▸ **kris**

KRISES ▸ **kris**

KRISING ▸ **kris**

KRONA n standard monetary unit of Sweden

KRONE n standard monetary unit of Norway and Denmark

KRONEN ▸ **krone**

KRONER ▸ **krone**

KRONOR ▶ krona
KRONUR ▶ krona
KROON *n* standard monetary unit of Estonia, divided into 100 senti
KROONI ▶ kroon
KROONS ▶ kroon
KRUBI *n* aroid plant with an unpleasant smell
KRUBIS ▶ krubi
KRUBUT *same as* ▶ **krubi**
KRUBUTS ▶ krubut
KRULLER *variant spelling of* ▶ **cruller**
KRUMPER > krumping
KRUNK *n* style of hip-hop music
KRUNKED ▶ crunked
KRUNKS ▶ krunk
KRYPSES ▶ krypsis
KRYPSIS *n* idea that Christ made secret use of his divine attributes
KRYPTON *n* colourless gas present in the atmosphere and used in fluorescent lights
KRYTRON *n* type of fast electronic gas-discharge switch, used as a trigger in nuclear weapons
KSAR *old form of* ▶ **tsar**
KSARS ▶ ksar
KUCCHA ▶ kaccha
KUCCHAS ▶ kuccha
KUCHCHA *same as* ▶ **kacha**
KUCHEN *n* breadlike cake containing apple, nuts, and sugar, originating from Germany
KUCHENS ▶ kuchen
KUDLIK *n* Inuit soapstone seal-oil lamp
KUDLIKS ▶ kudlik
KUDO *same as* ▶ **kudos**
KUDOS *n* fame or credit
KUDOSES ▶ kudos
KUDU *n* African antelope with spiral horns
KUDUS ▶ kudu
KUDZU *n* hairy leguminous climbing plant of China and Japan, with trifoliate leaves and purple fragrant flowers
KUDZUS ▶ kudzu
KUE *n* name of the letter Q
KUEH *n* (in Malaysia) any cake of Malay, Chinese, or Indian origin
KUES ▶ kue
KUFI *n* cap for Muslim man
KUFIS ▶ kufi
KUFIYAH *same as* > **keffiyeh**

KUGEL *n* baked pudding in traditional Jewish cooking
KUGELS ▶ kugel
KUIA *n* Maori female elder or elderly woman
KUIAS ▶ kuia
KUKRI *n* heavy, curved knife used by Gurkhas
KUKRIS ▶ kukri
KUKU *n* mussel
KUKUS ▶ kuku
KULA *n* ceremonial gift exchange practised among a group of islanders in the W Pacific, used to establish relations between islands
KULAK *n* (formerly) property-owning Russian peasant
KULAKI ▶ kulak
KULAKS ▶ kulak
KULAN *n* Asiatic wild ass of the Russian steppes, probably a variety of kiang or onager
KULANS ▶ kulan
KULAS ▶ kula
KULBASA > kielbasa
KULFI *n* Indian dessert made by freezing milk which has been concentrated by boiling away some of the water in it, and flavoured with nuts and cardamom seeds
KULFIS ▶ kulfi
KULTUR *n* German civilization
KULTURS ▶ kultur
KUMARA *n* tropical root vegetable with yellow flesh
KUMARAS ▶ kumara
KUMARI *n* (in Indian English) maiden
KUMARIS ▶ kumari
KUMERA *same as* ▶ **kumara**
KUMERAS ▶ kumera
KUMISS *n* drink made from fermented mare's or other milk, drunk by certain Asian tribes, esp in Russia or used for dietetic and medicinal purposes
KUMITE *n* freestyle sparring or fighting
KUMITES ▶ kumite
KUMMEL *n* German liqueur flavoured with aniseed and cumin
KUMMELS ▶ kummel
KUMQUAT *n* citrus fruit resembling a tiny orange
KUMYS *same as* ▶ **kumiss**

KUMYSES ▶ kumys
KUNA *n* standard monetary unit of Croatia, divided into 100 lipa
KUNE ▶ kuna
KUNJOOS *adj* (in Indian English) mean or stingy
KUNKAR *n* type of limestone
KUNKARS ▶ kunkar
KUNKUR *same as* ▶ **kunkar**
KUNKURS ▶ kunkar
KUNZITE *n* pink-coloured transparent variety of the mineral spodumene: a gemstone
KURBASH *vb* whip with a hide whip
KURGAN *n* Russian burial mound
KURGANS ▶ kurgan
KURI *n* mongrel dog
KURIS ▶ kuri
KURRE *old variant of* ▶ **cur**
KURRES ▶ kurre
KURSAAL *n* public room at a health resort
KURTA *n* long loose garment like a shirt without a collar worn in India
KURTAS ▶ kurta
KURU *n* degenerative disease of the nervous system, restricted to certain tribes in New Guinea, marked by loss of muscular control and thought to be caused by a slow virus

> This word for a kind of sickness found in New Guinea can give you something to laugh about when you have two Us to dispose of.

KURUS ▶ kuru
KURVEY *vb* (in old South African English) transport goods by ox cart
KURVEYS ▶ kurvey
KUSSO *variant spelling of* ▶ **kousso**
KUSSOS ▶ kusso
KUTA *n* (in Indian English) male dog
KUTAS ▶ kuta
KUTCH *same as* ▶ **catechu**
KUTCHA *adj* makeshift or not solid
KUTCHES ▶ kutch
KUTI *n* (in Indian English) female dog or bitch

KUTIS ▸ kuti
KUTU *n* body louse
KUTUS ▸ kutu
KUVASZ *n* breed of dog from Hungary
KUZU *same as* ▸ **kudzu**

A Japanese climbing plant. This can be a great word for getting a high score out of a difficult rack.

KUZUS ▸ kuzu
KVAS *same as* ▸ **kvass**
KVASES ▸ kvas
KVASS *n* alcoholic drink of low strength made in Russia and E Europe from cereals and stale bread
KVASSES ▸ kvass
KVELL *vb* US word meaning be happy
KVELLED ▸ kvell
KVELLS ▸ kvell
KVETCH *vb* complain or grumble
KVETCHY *adj* tending to grumble or complain
KWACHA *n* standard monetary unit of Zambia, divided into 100 ngwee
KWACHAS ▸ kwacha
KWAITO *n* type of South African pop music with lyrics spoken over an instrumental backing usually consisting of slowed-down house music layered with African percussion and melodies
KWAITOS ▸ kwaito
KWANZA *n* standard monetary unit of Angola, divided into 100 lwei
KWANZAS ▸ kwanza
KWELA *n* type of pop music

popular among the Black communities of South Africa
KWELAS ▸ kwela
KY *pl n* Scots word for cows
KYACK *n* type of panier
KYACKS ▸ kyack
KYAK *same as* ▸ **kayak**
KYAKS ▸ kyak
KYANG *same as* ▸ **kiang**
KYANGS ▸ kyang
KYANISE *same as* ▸ **kyanize**
KYANITE *n* grey, green, or blue mineral consisting of aluminium silicate in triclinic crystalline form
KYANIZE *vb* treat (timber) with corrosive sublimate to make it resistant to decay
KYAR *same as* ▸ **coir**
KYARS ▸ kyar
KYAT *n* standard monetary unit of Myanmar, divided into 100 pyas
KYATS ▸ kyat
KYBO *n* temporary lavatory constructed for use when camping
KYBOS ▸ kybo
KYBOSH *same as* ▸ **kibosh**
KYDST ▸ kythe
KYE *n* Korean fundraising meeting
KYES ▸ kye
KYLE *n* narrow strait or channel
KYLES ▸ kyle
KYLICES ▸ kylix
KYLIE *n* boomerang that is flat on one side and convex on the other
KYLIES ▸ kylie
KYLIKES ▸ kylix
KYLIN *n* (in Chinese art) mythical animal of

composite form
KYLINS ▸ kylin
KYLIX *n* shallow two-handled drinking vessel used in ancient Greece
KYLOE *n* breed of small long-horned long-haired beef cattle from NW Scotland
KYLOES ▸ kyloe
KYND *old variant of* ▸ **kind**
KYNDE *old variant of* ▸ **kind**
KYNDED ▸ kynd
KYNDES ▸ kynde
KYNDING ▸ kynd
KYNDS ▸ kynd
KYNE *pl n* archaic word for cows
KYOGEN *n* type of Japanese drama
KYOGENS ▸ kyogen
KYPE *n* hook on the lower jaw of a mature male salmon
KYPES ▸ kype
KYRIE *n* type of prayer
KYRIES ▸ kyrie
KYTE *n* belly
KYTES ▸ kyte
KYTHE *vb* appear
KYTHED ▸ kythe
KYTHES ▸ kythe
KYTHING ▸ kythe
KYU *n* (in judo) one of the five student grades for inexperienced competitors

This means a novice grade in judo, and its unusual combination of letters makes it a useful word to remember when you have an unpromising set of letters on your rack.

KYUS ▸ kyu

L

L can be a difficult letter to use well, especially when you need to play short words. Just three two-letter words begin with **L**: **la**, **li** and **lo**. Knowing this will save you valuable time in a game, especially when you are trying to fit words into a crowded board. There aren't very many three-letter words either, but don't forget common words like **lab** (5 points), **law** (6), **lay** (6), **low** (6) and **lye** (6). Try to remember the three-letter words that combine **L** with **X**: **lax**, **lex**, **lox** and **lux** (10 points each). These are particularly useful towards the end of a game if you have an **X** but little opportunity to play it. There is also the very useful **luz** for 12 points.

LA *n* exclamation of surprise or emphasis ▷ *n* the sixth note of the musical scale

LAAGER *n* (in Africa) a camp defended by a circular formation of wagons ▷ *vb* form (wagons) into a laager

LAAGERS ▸ **laager**

LAARI *same as* ▸ **lari**

LAARIS ▸ **laari**

LAB *n* laboratory

LABARA ▸ **labarum**

LABARUM *n* standard or banner carried in Christian religious processions

LABDA *same as* ▸ **lambda**

LABDAS ▸ **labda**

LABEL *n* piece of card or other material fixed to an object to show its ownership, destination, etc ▷ *vb* give a label to

LABELED ▸ **label**

LABELER ▸ **label**

LABELLA > **labellum**

LABELS ▸ **label**

LABIA ▸ **labium**

LABIAL *adj* of the lips ▷ *n* speech sound that involves the lips

LABIALS ▸ **labial**

LABIATE *n* any of a family of plants with square stems, aromatic leaves, and a two-lipped flower, such as mint or thyme ▷ *adj* of this family

LABILE *adj* (of a compound) prone to chemical change

LABIS *n* cochlear

LABISES ▸ **labis**

LABIUM *n* lip or liplike structure

LABLAB *n* twining leguminous plant

LABLABS ▸ **lablab**

LABOR *same as* ▸ **labour**

LABORED *same as* > **laboured**

LABORER *same as* > **labourer**

LABORS ▸ **labor**

LABOUR *n* physical work or exertion ▷ *vb* work hard

LABOURS ▸ **labour**

LABRA ▸ **labrum**

LABRAL *adj* of or like a lip

LABRET *n* piece of bone, shell, etc

LABRETS ▸ **labret**

LABRID *same as* ▸ **labroid**

LABRIDS ▸ **labrid**

LABROID *n* type of fish ▷ *adj* of or relating to such fish

LABROSE *adj* thick-lipped

LABRUM *n* lip or liplike part

LABRUMS ▸ **labrum**

LABRYS *n* type of axe

LABS ▸ **lab**

LAC *same as* ▸ **lakh**

LACE *n* delicate loosely woven decorative fabric ▷ *vb* fasten with shoelaces, cords, etc

LACED ▸ **lace**

LACER ▸ **lace**

LACERS ▸ **lace**

LACES ▸ **lace**

LACET *n* braidwork

LACETS ▸ **lacet**

LACEY *same as* ▸ **lacy**

LACHES *n* negligence or unreasonable delay in pursuing a legal remedy

LACIER ▸ **lacy**

LACIEST ▸ **lacy**

LACILY ▸ **lacy**

LACING ▸ **lace**

LACINGS ▸ **lace**

LACINIA *n* narrow fringe on petal

LACK *n* shortage or absence of something needed or wanted ▷ *vb* need or be short of (something)

LACKED ▸ **lack**

LACKER *variant spelling of* ▸ **lacquer**

LACKERS ▸ **lacker**

LACKEY *n* servile follower ▷ *vb* act as a lackey (to)

LACKEYS ▸ **lackey**

LACKING ▸ **lack**

LACKS ▸ **lack**

LACMUS *n* old form of litmus

LACONIC *adj* using only a few words, terse

LACQUER *n* hard varnish for wood or metal ▷ *vb* apply lacquer to

LACQUEY *same as* ▸ **lackey**

LACS ▸ **lac**

LACTAM *n* any of a group of inner amides

LACTAMS ▸ **lactam**

LACTARY *adj* relating to milk

LACTASE *n* any of a group of enzymes that hydrolyse lactose to glucose and galactose

LACTATE *vb* (of mammals)

to secrete milk ▷ *n* ester or salt of lactic acid

LACTEAL *adj* of or like milk ▷ *n* any of the lymphatic vessels that convey chyle from the small intestine to the blood

LACTEAN *another word for* > **lacteous**

LACTIC *adj* of or derived from milk

LACTONE *n* any of a class of organic compounds

LACTOSE *n* white crystalline sugar found in milk

LACUNA *n* gap or missing part, esp in a document or series

LACUNAE ▸ **lacuna**

LACUNAL ▸ **lacuna**

LACUNAR *n* ceiling, soffit, or vault having coffers ▷ *adj* of, relating to, or containing a lacuna or lacunas

LACUNAS ▸ **lacuna**

LACUNE *n* hiatus

LACUNES ▸ **lacune**

LACY *adj* fine, like lace

LAD *n* boy or young man

LADANUM *same as* > **labdanum**

LADDER *n* frame of two poles connected by horizontal steps used for climbing ▷ *vb* have or cause to have such a line of undone stitches

LADDERS ▸ **ladder**

LADDERY ▸ **ladder**

LADDIE *n* familiar term for a male, esp a young man

LADDIES ▸ **laddie**

LADDISH *adj* informal word for behaving in a macho or immature manner

LADDISM *n* laddish attitudes and behaviour

LADE *vb* put cargo on board (a ship) or (of a ship) to take on cargo ▷ *n* watercourse, esp a millstream

LADED ▸ **lade**

LADEN *adj* loaded ▷ *vb* load with cargo

LADENED ▸ **laden**

LADENS ▸ **laden**

LADER ▸ **lade**

LADERS ▸ **lade**

LADES ▸ **lade**

LADETTE *n* young woman whose social behaviour is

similar to that of male adolescents or young men

LADHOOD ▸ **lad**

LADIES *n* women's public toilet

LADIFY *same as* ▸ **ladyfy**

LADING ▸ **lade**

LADINGS ▸ **lade**

LADINO *n* Italian variety of white clover

LADINOS ▸ **ladino**

LADLE *n* spoon with a long handle and a large bowl, used for serving soup etc ▷ *vb* serve out

LADLED ▸ **ladle**

LADLER *n* person who serves with a ladle

LADLERS ▸ **ladler**

LADLES ▸ **ladle**

LADLING ▸ **ladle**

LADRON *same as* ▸ **ladrone**

LADRONE *n* thief

LADRONS ▸ **ladron**

LADS ▸ **lad**

LADY *n* woman regarded as having characteristics of good breeding or high rank ▷ *adj* female

LADYBOY *n* transvestite or transsexual, esp one from the Far East

LADYBUG *same as* > **ladybird**

LADYCOW *another word for* > **ladybird**

LADYFLY *another word for* > **ladybird**

LADYFY *vb* make a lady of (someone)

LADYISH ▸ **lady**

LADYISM ▸ **lady**

LADYKIN *n* endearing form of lady

LAER *another word for* ▸ **laager**

LAERED ▸ **laer**

LAERING ▸ **laer**

LAERS ▸ **laer**

LAESIE *old form of* ▸ **lazy**

LAETARE *n* fourth Sunday of Lent

LAEVO *adj* on the left

LAG *vb* go too slowly, fall behind ▷ *n* delay between events

LAGAN *n* goods or wreckage on the sea bed, sometimes attached to a buoy to permit recovery

LAGANS ▸ **lagan**

LAGENA *n* bottle with a narrow neck

LAGENAS ▸ **lagena**

LAGEND *same as* ▸ **lagan**

LAGENDS ▸ **lagend**

LAGER *n* light-bodied beer ▷ *vb* ferment into lager

LAGERED ▸ **lager**

LAGERS ▸ **lager**

LAGGARD *n* person who lags behind ▷ *adj* sluggish, slow, or dawdling

LAGGED ▸ **lag**

LAGGEN *n* spar of a barrel

LAGGENS ▸ **laggen**

LAGGER *n* person who lags pipes

LAGGERS ▸ **lagger**

LAGGIN *same as* ▸ **laggen**

LAGGING ▸ **lag**

LAGGINS ▸ **laggin**

LAGOON *n* body of water cut off from the open sea by coral reefs or sand bars

LAGOONS ▸ **lagoon**

LAGS ▸ **lag**

LAGUNA *n* lagoon

LAGUNAS ▸ **laguna**

LAGUNE *same as* ▸ **lagoon**

LAGUNES ▸ **lagune**

LAH *n* (in tonic sol-fa) sixth degree of any major scale

LAHAR *n* landslide of volcanic debris and water

LAHARS ▸ **lahar**

LAHS ▸ **lah**

LAIC *adj* laical ▷ *n* layman

LAICAL *adj* secular

LAICH *n* low-lying piece of land

LAICHS ▸ **laich**

LAICISE *same as* ▸ **laicize**

LAICISM ▸ **laic**

LAICITY *n* state of being laical

LAICIZE *vb* withdraw clerical or ecclesiastical character or status from (an institution, building, etc)

LAICS ▸ **laic**

LAID *Scots form of* ▸ **load**

LAIDED ▸ **laid**

LAIDING ▸ **laid**

LAIDLY *adj* very ugly

LAIDS ▸ **laid**

LAIGH *adj* low-lying ▷ *n* area of low-lying ground

LAIGHER ▸ **laigh**

LAIGHS ▸ **laigh**

LAIK *vb* play (a game, etc)

LAIKA *n* type of small dog

LAIKAS ▸ **laika**

LAIKED ▸ **laik**

LAIKER ▸ **laik**

LAIKERS ▸ laik
LAIKING ▸ laik
LAIKS ▸ laik
LAIN ▸ lie
LAIPSE vb beat soundly
LAIPSED ▸ laipse
LAIPSES ▸ laipse
LAIR n resting place of an animal ▷ vb (esp of a wild animal) to retreat to or rest in a lair
LAIRAGE n accommodation for farm animals, esp at docks or markets
LAIRD n Scottish landowner
LAIRDLY adj pertaining to laird or lairds
LAIRDS ▸ laird
LAIRED ▸ lair
LAIRIER ▸ lairy
LAIRING ▸ lair
LAIRISE same as ▸ lairize
LAIRIZE vb show off
LAIRS ▸ lair
LAIRY adj gaudy or flashy
LAISSE n type of rhyme scheme
LAISSES ▸ laisse
LAITH Scots form of ▸ loath
LAITHLY same as ▸ laidly
LAITIES ▸ laity
LAITY n people who are not members of the clergy
LAKE n expanse of water entirely surrounded by land ▷ vb take time away from work
LAKEBED n bed of lake
LAKED ▸ lake
LAKELET n small lake
LAKER n cargo vessel used on lakes
LAKERS ▸ laker
LAKES ▸ lake
LAKH n (in India) 100 000, esp referring to this sum of rupees
LAKHS ▸ lakh
LAKIER ▸ laky
LAKIEST ▸ laky
LAKIN short form of ▸ ladykin
LAKING ▸ lake
LAKINGS ▸ lake
LAKINS ▸ lakin
LAKISH adj similar to poetry of Lake poets
LAKSA n (in Malaysia) a dish of Chinese origin consisting of rice noodles served in curry or hot soup
LAKSAS ▸ laksa
LAKY adj of the reddish

colour of the pigment lake
LALANG n coarse weedy Malaysian grass
LALANGS ▸ lalang
LALDIE n great gusto
LALDIES ▸ laldie
LALDY same as ▸ laldie
LALIQUE n type of ornamental glass
LALL vb make imperfect 'l' or 'r' sounds
LALLAN n literary version of the English spoken in Lowland Scotland
LALLAND same as ▸ lallan
LALLANS ▸ lallan
LALLED ▸ lall
LALLING ▸ lall
LALLS ▸ lall
LAM vb attack vigorously
LAMA n Buddhist priest in Tibet or Mongolia
LAMAS ▸ lama
LAMB n young sheep ▷ vb (of sheep) give birth to a lamb or lambs
LAMBADA n erotic Brazilian dance
LAMBAST vb beat or thrash
LAMBDA n 11th letter of the Greek alphabet
LAMBDAS ▸ lambda
LAMBED ▸ lamb
LAMBENT adj (of a flame) flickering softly
LAMBER n person that attends to lambing ewes
LAMBERS ▸ lamber
LAMBERT n cgs unit of illumination, equal to 1 lumen per square centimetre
LAMBIE same as ▸ lambkin
LAMBIER ▸ lamby
LAMBIES ▸ lambie
LAMBING n birth of lambs at the end of winter
LAMBKIN n small or young lamb
LAMBOYS n skirt-like piece of armour made from metal strips
LAMBS ▸ lamb
LAMBY adj lamb-like
LAME adj having an injured or disabled leg or foot ▷ vb make lame ▷ n fabric interwoven with gold or silver threads
LAMED n 12th letter in the Hebrew alphabet
LAMEDH same as ▸ lamed
LAMEDHS ▸ lamedh

LAMEDS ▸ lamed
LAMELLA n thin layer, plate, or membrane, esp any of the calcified layers of which bone is formed
LAMELY ▸ lame
LAMENT vb feel or express sorrow (for) ▷ n passionate expression of grief
LAMENTS ▸ lament
LAMER ▸ lame
LAMES ▸ lame
LAMEST ▸ lame
LAMETER Scots form of ▸ lamiger
LAMIA n one of a class of female monsters depicted with a snake's body and a woman's head and breasts
LAMIAE ▸ lamia
LAMIAS ▸ lamia
LAMIGER n disabled person
LAMINA n thin plate, esp of bone or mineral
LAMINAE ▸ lamina
LAMINAL n consonant articulated with blade of tongue
LAMINAR ▸ lamina
LAMINAS ▸ lamina
LAMING ▸ lame
LAMININ n type of protein
LAMISH adj rather lame
LAMITER same as ▸ lameter
LAMMED ▸ lam
LAMMER Scots word for ▸ amber
LAMMERS ▸ lammer
LAMMIE same as ▸ lammy
LAMMIES ▸ lammy
LAMMING ▸ lam
LAMMY n thick woollen jumper
LAMP n device which produces light from electricity, oil, or gas ▷ vb go quickly with long steps
LAMPAD n candlestick
LAMPADS ▸ lampad
LAMPAS n swelling of the mucous membrane of the hard palate of horses
LAMPED ▸ lamp
LAMPER n lamprey
LAMPERN n migratory European lamprey
LAMPERS ▸ lamper
LAMPING ▸ lamp
LAMPION n oil-burning lamp
LAMPLIT adj lit by lamps
LAMPOON n humorous satire ridiculing someone

L

▷ *vb* satirize or ridicule
LAMPREY *n* eel-like fish with a round sucking mouth
LAMPS ▸ lamp
LAMPUKA *same as* ▸ **lampuki**
LAMPUKI *n* type of fish
LAMS ▸ lam
LAMSTER *n* fugitive
LANA *n* wood from genipap tree
LANAI *Hawaiian word for* ▸ **veranda**
LANAIS ▸ lanai
LANAS ▸ lana
LANATE *adj* having or consisting of a woolly covering of hairs
LANATED *same as* ▸ **lanate**
LANCE *n* long spear used by a mounted soldier ▷ *vb* pierce (a boil or abscess) with a lancet
LANCED ▸ lance
LANCER *n* formerly, cavalry soldier armed with a lance
LANCERS *n* quadrille for eight or sixteen couples
LANCES ▸ lance
LANCET *n* pointed two-edged surgical knife
LANCETS ▸ lancet
LANCH *obsolete form of* ▸ **launch**
LANCHED ▸ lanch
LANCHES ▸ lanch
LANCING ▸ lance
LAND *n* solid part of the earth's surface ▷ *vb* come or bring to earth after a flight, jump, or fall
LANDAU *n* four-wheeled carriage with two folding hoods
LANDAUS ▸ landau
LANDE *n* type of moorland in SW France
LANDED *adj* possessing or consisting of lands
LANDER *n* spacecraft designed to land on a planet or other body
LANDERS ▸ lander
LANDES ▸ lande
LANDING *n* floor area at the top of a flight of stairs
LANDLER *n* Austrian country dance in which couples spin and clap
LANDMAN *n* person who lives and works on land
LANDMEN ▸ landman

LANDS *pl n* holdings in land
LANE *n* narrow road
LANELY *Scots form of* ▸ **lonely**
LANES ▸ lane
LANEWAY *n* lane
LANG *Scots word for* ▸ **long**
LANGAHA *n* type of Madagascan snake
LANGAR *n* dining hall in a gurdwara
LANGARS ▸ langar
LANGEST ▸ lang
LANGLEY *n* unit of solar radiation
LANGREL *same as* > **langrage**
LANGUE *n* language considered as an abstract system or a social institution
LANGUED *adj* having a tongue
LANGUES ▸ langue
LANGUET *n* anything resembling a tongue in shape or function
LANGUID *adj* lacking energy or enthusiasm
LANGUOR *n* state of dreamy relaxation
LANGUR *n* type of arboreal Old World monkey
LANGURS ▸ langur
LANIARD *same as* ▸ **lanyard**
LANIARY *adj* (esp of canine teeth) adapted for tearing ▷ *n* tooth adapted for tearing
LANITAL *n* fibre used in production of synthetic wool
LANK *adj* (of hair) straight and limp ▷ *vb* become or cause to become lank
LANKED ▸ lank
LANKER ▸ lank
LANKEST ▸ lank
LANKIER ▸ lanky
LANKILY ▸ lanky
LANKING ▸ lank
LANKLY ▸ lank
LANKS ▸ lank
LANKY *adj* ungracefully tall and thin
LANNER *n* large falcon of Mediterranean regions, N Africa, and S Asia
LANNERS ▸ lanner
LANOLIN *n* grease from sheep's wool used in ointments etc
LANOSE *same as* ▸ **lanate**

LANT *n* stale urine
LANTANA *n* shrub with orange or yellow flowers, considered a weed in Australia
LANTERN *n* light in a transparent protective case ▷ *vb* supply with lantern
LANTS ▸ lant
LANUGO *n* layer of fine hairs, esp the covering of the human fetus before birth
LANUGOS ▸ lanugo
LANX *n* dish; plate
LANYARD *n* cord worn round the neck to hold a knife or whistle
LAOGAI *n* forced labour camp in China
LAOGAIS ▸ laogai
LAP *n* part between the waist and knees of a person when sitting ▷ *vb* overtake an opponent so as to be one or more circuits ahead
LAPDOG *n* small pet dog
LAPDOGS ▸ lapdog
LAPEL *n* part of the front of a coat or jacket folded back towards the shoulders
LAPELED ▸ lapel
LAPELS ▸ lapel
LAPFUL *same as* ▸ **lap**
LAPFULS ▸ lapful
LAPHELD *adj* (esp of a personal computer) small enough to be used on one's lap
LAPIDES ▸ lapis
LAPILLI > **lapillus**
LAPIN *n* castrated rabbit
LAPINS ▸ lapin
LAPIS *n as in* **lapis lazuli** brilliant blue mineral used as a gemstone
LAPISES ▸ lapis
LAPJE *same as* ▸ **lappie**
LAPJES ▸ lapje
LAPPED ▸ lap
LAPPEL *same as* ▸ **lapel**
LAPPELS ▸ lappel
LAPPER *n* one that laps ▷ *vb* curdle
LAPPERS ▸ lapper
LAPPET *n* small hanging flap or piece of lace
LAPPETS ▸ lappet
LAPPIE *n* rag
LAPPIES ▸ lappie
LAPPING ▸ lap
LAPS ▸ lap
LAPSANG *n* smoky-tasting

Chinese tea

LAPSE n temporary drop in a standard, esp through forgetfulness or carelessness ▷ vb drop in standard

LAPSED ▶ lapse

LAPSER ▶ lapse

LAPSERS ▶ lapse

LAPSES ▶ lapse

LAPSING ▶ lapse

LAPSUS n lapse or error

LAPTOP adj small enough to fit on a user's lap ▷ n computer small enough to fit on a user's lap

LAPTOPS ▶ laptop

LAPTRAY n tray with a cushioned underside, designed to rest in a person's lap while supporting reading material, etc

LAPWING n plover with a tuft of feathers on the head

LAPWORK n work with lapping edges

LAR n boy or young man

LARCENY n theft

LARCH n deciduous coniferous tree

LARCHEN adj of larch

LARCHES ▶ larch

LARD n soft white fat obtained from a pig ▷ vb insert strips of bacon in (meat) before cooking

LARDED ▶ lard

LARDER n storeroom for food

LARDERS ▶ larder

LARDIER ▶ lardy

LARDING ▶ lard

LARDON n strip or cube of fat or bacon used in larding meat

LARDONS ▶ lardon

LARDOON same as ▶ lardon

LARDS ▶ lard

LARDY adj fat

LARE another word for ▶ lore

LAREE n Asian fish-hook formerly used as currency

LAREES ▶ laree

LARES ▶ lare

LARGE adj great in size, number, or extent ▷ n formerly, musical note of particular length

LARGELY adv principally

LARGEN another word for ▶ enlarge

LARGENS ▶ largen

LARGER ▶ large

LARGES ▶ large

LARGESS same as > largesse

LARGEST ▶ large

LARGISH adj fairly large

LARGO adv in a slow and dignified manner ▷ n piece or passage to be performed in a slow and stately manner

LARGOS ▶ largo

LARI n standard monetary unit of Georgia, divided into 100 tetri

LARIAT n lasso ▷ vb tether with lariat

LARIATS ▶ lariat

LARINE adj of, relating to, or resembling a gull

LARIS ▶ lari

LARK n small brown songbird, skylark ▷ vb have a good time by frolicking

LARKED ▶ lark

LARKER ▶ lark

LARKERS ▶ lark

LARKIER ▶ larky

LARKING ▶ lark

LARKISH ▶ lark

LARKS ▶ lark

LARKY adj frolicsome or mischievous

LARMIER n pouch under lower eyelid of deer

LARN vb learn

LARNAX n coffin made of terracotta

LARNED ▶ larn

LARNEY n white person ▷ adj (of clothes) smart

LARNEYS ▶ larney

LARNIER ▶ larney

LARNING ▶ larn

LARNS ▶ larn

LAROID adj relating to Larus genus of gull family

LARRUP vb beat or flog

LARRUPS ▶ larrup

LARS ▶ lar

LARUM archaic word for ▶ alarm

LARUMS ▶ larum

LARVA n insect in an immature stage, often resembling a worm

LARVAE ▶ larva

LARVAL ▶ larva

LARVAS ▶ larva

LARVATE adj masked; concealed

LARYNX n part of the throat containing the vocal cords

LAS ▶ la

LASAGNA same as ▶ lasagne

LASAGNE n pasta in wide flat sheets

LASCAR n East Indian seaman

LASCARS ▶ lascar

LASE vb (of a substance, such as carbon dioxide or ruby) to be capable of acting as a laser

LASED ▶ lase

LASER n device that produces a very narrow intense beam of light, used for cutting very hard materials and in surgery etc

LASERS ▶ laser

LASES ▶ lase

LASH n eyelash ▷ vb hit with a whip

LASHED ▶ lash

LASHER ▶ lash

LASHERS ▶ lash

LASHES ▶ lash

LASHING ▶ lash

LASHINS same as > lashings

LASHKAR n troop of Indian men with weapons

LASING ▶ lase

LASINGS ▶ lase

LASKET n loop at the foot of a sail onto which an extra sail may be fastened

LASKETS ▶ lasket

LASQUE n flat-cut diamond

LASQUES ▶ lasque

LASS n girl

LASSES ▶ lass

LASSI n cold drink made with yoghurt or buttermilk and flavoured with sugar, salt, or a mild spice

LASSIE n little lass

LASSIES ▶ lassie

LASSIS ▶ lassi

LASSO n rope with a noose for catching cattle and horses ▷ vb catch with a lasso

LASSOCK another word for ▶ lass

LASSOED ▶ lasso

LASSOER ▶ lasso

LASSOES ▶ lasso

LASSOS ▶ lasso

LASSU n slow part of csárdás folk dance

LASSUS ▶ lassu

LAST adv coming at the end or after all others ▷ adj only remaining ▷ n last person or thing ▷ vb continue

LASTAGE n space for storing goods in ship

LASTED ▸ **last**

LASTER ▸ **last**

LASTERS ▸ **last**

LASTING adj existing or remaining effective for a long time ▷ n strong durable closely woven fabric used for shoe uppers, etc

LASTLY adv at the end or at the last point

LASTS ▸ **last**

LAT n former coin of Latvia

LATAH n psychological condition in which a traumatized individual becomes anxious and suggestible

LATAHS ▸ **latah**

LATAKIA n type of Turkish tobacco

LATCH n fastening for a door with a bar and lever ▷ vb fasten with a latch

LATCHED ▸ **latch**

LATCHES ▸ **latch**

LATCHET n shoe fastening, such as a thong or lace

LATE adj after the normal or expected time ▷ adv after the normal or expected time

LATED archaic word for ▸ **belated**

LATEEN adj denoting a rig with a triangular sail bent to a yard hoisted to the head of a low mast

LATEENS ▸ **lateen**

LATELY adv in recent times

LATEN vb become or cause to become late

LATENCE ▸ **latent**

LATENCY ▸ **latent**

LATENED ▸ **laten**

LATENS ▸ **laten**

LATENT adj hidden and not yet developed ▷ n fingerprint that is not visible to the eye

LATENTS ▸ **latent**

LATER adv afterwards

LATERAD adv towards the side

LATERAL adj of or relating to the side or sides ▷ n lateral object, part, passage, or movement ▷ vb pass laterally

LATEST n the most recent news, fashion, etc

LATESTS ▸ **latest**

LATEX n milky fluid found in some plants, esp the rubber tree, used in making rubber

LATEXES ▸ **latex**

LATH n thin strip of wood used to support plaster, tiles, etc ▷ vb attach laths to (a ceiling, roof, floor, etc)

LATHE n machine for turning wood or metal while it is being shaped ▷ vb shape, bore, or cut a screw thread in or on (a workpiece) on a lathe

LATHED ▸ **lathe**

LATHEE same as ▸ **lathi**

LATHEES ▸ **lathee**

LATHEN adj covered with laths

LATHER n froth of soap and water ▷ vb make frothy

LATHERS ▸ **lather**

LATHERY ▸ **lather**

LATHES ▸ **lathe**

LATHI n long heavy wooden stick used as a weapon in India, esp by the police

LATHIER ▸ **lathy**

LATHING ▸ **lathe**

LATHIS ▸ **lathi**

LATHS ▸ **lath**

LATHY adj resembling a lath, esp in being tall and thin

LATI ▸ **lat**

LATICES ▸ **latex**

LATIGO n strap on horse's saddle

LATIGOS ▸ **latigo**

LATILLA n stick making up part of ceiling

LATINA n female inhabitant of the US who is of Latin American origin

LATINAS ▸ **latina**

LATINO n male inhabitant of the US who is of Latin American origin

LATINOS ▸ **latino**

LATISH adv rather late ▷ adj rather late

LATITAT n writ presuming that person accused was hiding

LATKE n crispy Jewish pancake

LATKES ▸ **latke**

LATOSOL n type of deep, well-drained soil

LATRANT adj barking

LATRIA n adoration that may be offered to God alone

LATRIAS ▸ **latria**

LATRINE n toilet in a barracks or camp

LATRON n bandit

LATRONS ▸ **latron**

LATS ▸ **lat**

LATTE n coffee made with hot milk

LATTEN n metal or alloy, esp brass, made in thin sheets

LATTENS ▸ **latten**

LATTER adj second of two

LATTES ▸ **latte**

LATTICE n framework of intersecting strips of wood, metal, etc ▷ vb make, adorn, or supply with a lattice

LATTIN n brass alloy beaten into a thin sheet

LATTINS ▸ **lattin**

LATU ▸ **lat**

LAUAN n type of wood used in furniture-making

LAUANS ▸ **lauan**

LAUCH Scots form of ▸ **laugh**

LAUCHS ▸ **lauch**

LAUD vb praise or glorify ▷ n praise or glorification

LAUDED ▸ **laud**

LAUDER ▸ **laud**

LAUDERS ▸ **laud**

LAUDING ▸ **laud**

LAUDS n traditional morning prayer of the Western Church, constituting with matins the first of the seven canonical hours

LAUF n run in bobsleighing

LAUFS ▸ **lauf**

LAUGH vb make inarticulate sounds with the voice expressing amusement, merriment, or scorn ▷ n act or instance of laughing

LAUGHED ▸ **laugh**

LAUGHER ▸ **laugh**

LAUGHS ▸ **laugh**

LAUGHY adj tending to laugh a lot

LAUNCE old form of ▸ **lance**

LAUNCED ▸ **launce**

LAUNCES ▸ **launce**

LAUNCH vb put (a ship or boat) into the water, esp for the first time ▷ n launching

LAUND n open grassy space

LAUNDER vb wash and iron (clothes and linen) ▷ n water trough, esp one used for washing ore in mining

LAUNDRY n clothes etc for washing or which have recently been washed

LAUNDS ▸ laund

LAURA n group of monastic cells

LAURAE ▸ laura

LAURAS ▸ laura

LAUREL n glossy-leaved shrub, bay tree ▷ vb crown with laurel

LAURELS ▸ laurel

LAURIC adj as in lauric acid dodecanoic acid

LAURYL n as in lauryl alcohol crystalline solid used to make detergents

LAURYLS ▸ lauryl

LAUWINE n avalanche

LAV short for > lavatory

LAVA n molten rock thrown out by volcanoes, which hardens as it cools

LAVABO n ritual washing of the celebrant's hands after the offertory at Mass

LAVABOS ▸ lavabo

LAVAGE n washing out of a hollow organ by flushing with water

LAVAGES ▸ lavage

LAVAS ▸ lava

LAVASH n Armenian flat bread

LAVE archaic word for ▸ wash

LAVED ▸ lave

LAVEER vb (in sailing) tack

LAVEERS ▸ laveer

LAVER n large basin of water used by priests for ritual ablutions

LAVERS ▸ laver

LAVES ▸ lave

LAVING ▸ lave

LAVISH adj great in quantity or richness ▷ vb give or spend generously

LAVOLT same as ▸ lavolta

LAVOLTA n Italian dance of the 16th and 17th centuries ▷ vb dance the lavolta

LAVOLTS ▸ lavolt

LAVRA same as ▸ laura

LAVRAS ▸ lavra

LAVROCK same as > laverock

LAVS ▸ lav

LAVVIES ▸ lavvy

LAVVY n lavatory

LAW n rule binding on a community ▷ vb prosecute ▷ adj (in archaic usage) low

LAWBOOK n book on subject of law

LAWED ▸ law

LAWER ▸ law

LAWEST ▸ law

LAWFARE n use of the law by a country against its enemies

LAWFUL adj allowed by law

LAWIN n bill or reckoning

LAWINE n avalanche

LAWINES ▸ lawine

LAWING same as ▸ lawin

LAWINGS ▸ lawing

LAWINS ▸ lawin

LAWK interj used to show surprise

LAWKS same as ▸ lawk

LAWLAND same as ▸ lowland

LAWLESS adj breaking the law, esp in a violent way

LAWLIKE ▸ law

LAWMAN n officer of the law, such as a policeman or sheriff

LAWMEN ▸ lawman

LAWN n area of tended and mown grass

LAWNED adj having a lawn

LAWNIER ▸ lawn

LAWNS ▸ lawn

LAWNY ▸ lawn

LAWS ▸ law

LAWSUIT n court case brought by one person or group against another

LAWYER n professionally qualified legal expert ▷ vb act as lawyer

LAWYERS ▸ lawyer

LAX adj not strict ▷ n laxative

LAXATOR n muscle that loosens body part

LAXER ▸ lax

LAXES ▸ lax

LAXEST ▸ lax

LAXISM ▸ laxist

LAXISMS ▸ laxist

LAXIST n lenient or tolerant person

LAXISTS ▸ laxist

LAXITY ▸ lax

LAXLY ▸ lax

LAXNESS ▸ lax

LAY ▸ lie

LAYAWAY n merchandise reserved for future delivery

LAYBACK n technique for climbing cracks by pulling on one side of the crack with the hands and pressing on the other with the feet ▷ vb in climbing, use layback technique

LAYDEEZ pl n jocular spelling of ladies, as pronounced in a mid-Atlantic accent

LAYED ▸ lay

LAYER n single thickness of some substance, as a cover or coating on a surface ▷ vb form a layer

LAYERED ▸ layer

LAYERS ▸ layer

LAYETTE n clothes for a newborn baby

LAYIN n basketball score made by dropping ball into basket

LAYING ▸ lay

LAYINGS ▸ lay

LAYINS ▸ layin

LAYLOCK old form of ▸ lilac

LAYMAN n person who is not a member of the clergy

LAYMEN ▸ layman

LAYOFF n act of suspending employees

LAYOFFS ▸ layoff

LAYOUT n arrangement, esp of matter for printing or of a building

LAYOUTS ▸ layout

LAYOVER n break in a journey

LAYS ▸ lie

LAYTIME n time allowed for loading cargo

LAYUP n period of incapacity through illness

LAYUPS ▸ layup

LAZAR archaic word for ▸ leper

LAZARET same as > lazaretto

LAZARS ▸ lazar

LAZE vb be idle or lazy ▷ n time spent lazing

LAZED ▸ laze

LAZES ▸ laze

LAZIED ▸ lazy

LAZIER ▸ lazy

LAZIES ▸ lazy

LAZIEST ▸ lazy

LAZILY ▸ lazy

LAZING ▸ laze

LAZO another word for ▸ lasso

LAZOED ▸ lazo

LAZOES ▸ lazo

LAZOING ▸ lazo

LAZOS ▸ lazo

LAZULI n lapis lazuli

LAZULIS ▸ lazuli

LAZY vb laze ▷ adj not

inclined to work or exert oneself
LAZYING ▸ lazy
LAZYISH ▸ lazy
LAZZI ▸ lazzo
LAZZO n comic routine in the commedia dell'arte
LEA n meadow
LEACH vb remove or be removed from a substance by a liquid passing through it ▷ n act or process of leaching
LEACHED ▸ leach
LEACHER ▸ leach
LEACHES ▸ leach
LEACHY adj porous
LEAD vb guide or conduct ▷ n first or most prominent place ▷ adj acting as a leader or lead
LEADED adj (of windows) made from many small panes of glass held together by lead strips
LEADEN adj heavy or sluggish ▷ vb become or cause to become leaden
LEADENS ▸ leaden
LEADER n person who leads
LEADERS ▸ leader
LEADIER ▸ leady
LEADING ▸ lead
LEADMAN n man who leads
LEADMEN ▸ leadman
LEADOFF n initial move or action
LEADS ▸ lead
LEADY adj like lead
LEAF n flat usu green blade attached to the stem of a plant ▷ vb turn (pages) cursorily
LEAFAGE n leaves of plants
LEAFBUD n bud producing leaves rather than flowers
LEAFED ▸ leaf
LEAFERY n foliage
LEAFIER ▸ leafy
LEAFING ▸ leaf
LEAFLET n sheet of printed matter for distribution ▷ vb distribute leaflets (to)
LEAFS ▸ leaf
LEAFY adj covered with leaves
LEAGUE n association promoting the interests of its members
LEAGUED ▸ league
LEAGUER vb harass; beset ▷ n encampment, esp of besiegers

LEAGUES ▸ league
LEAK n hole or defect that allows the escape or entrance of liquid, gas, radiation, etc ▷ vb let liquid etc in or out
LEAKAGE n act or instance of leaking
LEAKED ▸ leak
LEAKER ▸ leak
LEAKERS ▸ leak
LEAKIER ▸ leaky
LEAKILY ▸ leaky
LEAKING ▸ leak
LEAKS ▸ leak
LEAKY adj leaking or tending to leak
LEAL adj loyal
LEALER ▸ leal
LEALEST ▸ leal
LEALLY ▸ leal
LEALTY ▸ leal
LEAM vb shine
LEAMED ▸ leam
LEAMING ▸ leam
LEAMS ▸ leam
LEAN vb rest (against) ▷ adj thin but healthy-looking ▷ n lean part of meat
LEANED ▸ lean
LEANER ▸ lean
LEANERS ▸ lean
LEANEST ▸ lean
LEANING ▸ lean
LEANLY ▸ lean
LEANS ▸ lean
LEANT ▸ lean
LEANY old form of ▸ lean
LEAP vb make a sudden powerful jump ▷ n sudden powerful jump
LEAPED ▸ leap
LEAPER ▸ leap
LEAPERS ▸ leap
LEAPING ▸ leap
LEAPS ▸ leap
LEAPT ▸ leap
LEAR vb instruct
LEARE same as ▸ lear
LEARED ▸ lear
LEARES ▸ leare
LEARIER ▸ leary
LEARING ▸ lear
LEARN vb gain skill or knowledge by study, practice, or teaching
LEARNED ▸ learn
LEARNER n someone who is learning something
LEARNS ▸ learn
LEARNT ▸ learn
LEARS ▸ lear
LEARY same as ▸ leery

LEAS ▸ lea
LEASE n contract by which land or property is rented for a stated time by the owner to a tenant ▷ vb let or rent by lease
LEASED ▸ lease
LEASER ▸ lease
LEASERS ▸ lease
LEASES ▸ lease
LEASH n lead for a dog ▷ vb control by a leash
LEASHED ▸ leash
LEASHES ▸ leash
LEASING ▸ lease
LEASOW vb pasture
LEASOWE same as ▸ leasow
LEASOWS ▸ leasow
LEAST n smallest amount ▷ adj smallest ▷ n smallest one ▷ adv in the smallest degree
LEASTS ▸ least
LEASURE old form of ▸ leisure
LEAT n trench or ditch that conveys water to a mill wheel
LEATHER n material made from specially treated animal skins ▷ adj made of leather ▷ vb beat or thrash
LEATS ▸ leat
LEAVE vb go away from ▷ n permission to be absent from work or duty
LEAVED adj with leaves
LEAVEN n substance that causes dough to rise ▷ vb raise with leaven
LEAVENS ▸ leaven
LEAVER ▸ leave
LEAVERS ▸ leave
LEAVES ▸ leaf
LEAVIER ▸ leavy
LEAVING ▸ leave
LEAVY same as ▸ leafy
LEAZE same as ▸ lease
LEAZES ▸ leaze
LEBBEK n type of timber tree
LEBBEKS ▸ lebbek
LEBEN n semiliquid food made from curdled milk in N Africa and the Levant
LEBENS ▸ leben
LECCIES ▸ leccy
LECCY n electricity
LECH vb behave lecherously (towards) ▷ n lecherous act or indulgence
LECHAIM interj drinking toast ▷ n small drink with

which to toast something or someone

LECHED ▸ **lech**

LECHER *n* man who has or shows excessive sexual desire ▷ *vb* behave lecherously

LECHERS ▸ **lecher**

LECHERY *n* unrestrained and promiscuous sexuality

LECHES ▸ **lech**

LECHING ▸ **lech**

LECHWE *n* African antelope

LECHWES ▸ **lechwe**

LECTERN *n* sloping reading desk, esp in a church

LECTIN *n* type of protein possessing high affinity for a specific sugar

LECTINS ▸ **lectin**

LECTION *n* variant reading of a passage in a particular copy or edition of a text

LECTOR *n* lecturer or reader in certain universities

LECTORS ▸ **lector**

LECTURE *n* informative talk to an audience on a subject ▷ *vb* give a talk

LECTURN *old form of* ▸ **lectern**

LECYTHI > **lecythus**

LED ▸ **lead**

LEDDEN *n* language; speech

LEDDENS ▸ **ledden**

LEDGE *n* narrow shelf sticking out from a wall

LEDGED ▸ **ledge**

LEDGER *n* book of debit and credit accounts of a firm ▷ *vb* fish using a wire trace that allows the bait to float freely while the weight sinks

LEDGERS ▸ **ledger**

LEDGES ▸ **ledge**

LEDGIER ▸ **ledge**

LEDGY ▸ **ledge**

LEDUM *n* evergreen shrub

LEDUMS ▸ **ledum**

LEE *n* sheltered side ▷ *vb* Scots for lie

LEEAR *Scots form of* ▸ **liar**

LEEARS ▸ **leear**

LEECH *n* species of bloodsucking worm ▷ *vb* use leeches to suck the blood of

LEECHED ▸ **leech**

LEECHEE *same as* ▸ **litchi**

LEECHES ▸ **leech**

LEED ▸ **lee**

LEEING ▸ **lee**

LEEK *n* vegetable of the onion family with a long bulb and thick stem

LEEKS ▸ **leek**

LEEP *vb* boil; scald

LEEPED ▸ **leep**

LEEPING ▸ **leep**

LEEPS ▸ **leep**

LEER *vb* look or grin at in a sneering or suggestive manner ▷ *n* sneering or suggestive look or grin

LEERED ▸ **leer**

LEERIER ▸ **leery**

LEERILY ▸ **leery**

LEERING ▸ **leer**

LEERS ▸ **leer**

LEERY *adj* suspicious or wary (of)

LEES *pl n* sediment of wine

LEESE *old form of* ▸ **loose**

LEESES ▸ **leese**

LEESING ▸ **leese**

LEET *n* list of candidates for an office

LEETLE *form of* ▸ **little**

LEETS ▸ **leet**

LEEWARD *n* lee side ▷ *adv* towards this side ▷ *adj* of, in, or moving in the direction towards which the wind blows

LEEWAY *n* room for free movement within limits

LEEWAYS ▸ **leeway**

LEEZE *adj as in* **leeze me** Scots for lief is me, an expression of affection

LEFT *adj* on the opposite side from right ▷ *n* left side

LEFTE *old past tense of* ▸ **lift**

LEFTER ▸ **left**

LEFTEST ▸ **left**

LEFTIE *same as* ▸ **lefty**

LEFTIES ▸ **lefty**

LEFTISH ▸ **left**

LEFTISM ▸ **leftist**

LEFTIST *adj* (person) of the political left ▷ *n* person who supports the political left

LEFTS ▸ **left**

LEFTY *n* left-winger

LEG *n* one of the limbs on which a person or animal walks, runs, or stands

LEGACY *n* thing left in a will

LEGAL *adj* established or permitted by law ▷ *n* legal expert

LEGALLY ▸ **legal**

LEGALS ▸ **legal**

LEGATE *n* messenger or

representative, esp from the Pope ▷ *vb* leave as legacy

LEGATED ▸ **legate**

LEGATEE *n* recipient of a legacy

LEGATES ▸ **legate**

LEGATO *adv* (piece to be played) smoothly ▷ *n* style of playing with no gaps between notes

LEGATOR *n* person who gives a legacy or makes a bequest

LEGATOS ▸ **legato**

LEGEND *n* traditional story or myth

LEGENDS ▸ **legend**

LEGER *same as* ▸ **ledger**

LEGERS ▸ **leger**

LEGES ▸ **lex**

LEGGE *vb* lighten or lessen

LEGGED ▸ **leg**

LEGGER *n* man who moves barge through tunnel using legs

LEGGERS ▸ **legger**

LEGGES ▸ **legge**

LEGGIE *n* (in cricket) leg spin bowler

LEGGIER ▸ **leggy**

LEGGIES ▸ **leggie**

LEGGIN *same as* ▸ **legging**

LEGGING *n* extra outer covering for the lower leg

LEGGINS ▸ **leggin**

LEGGISM *n* blacklegging

LEGGY *adj* having long legs

LEGHORN *n* type of Italian wheat straw that is woven into hats

LEGIBLE *adj* easily read

LEGIBLY ▸ **legible**

LEGION *n* large military force ▷ *adj* very large or numerous

LEGIONS ▸ **legion**

LEGIST *n* person versed in the law

LEGISTS ▸ **legist**

LEGIT *n* legitimate or professionally respectable drama ▷ *adj* legitimate

LEGITIM *n* amount of inheritance due to children from father

LEGITS ▸ **legit**

LEGLAN *same as* ▸ **leglin**

LEGLANS ▸ **leglan**

LEGLEN *same as* ▸ **leglin**

LEGLENS ▸ **leglen**

LEGLESS *adj* without legs

LEGLET *n* jewellery worn

L

around the leg
LEGLETS ▸ **leglet**
LEGLIKE ▸ **leg**
LEGLIN *n* milk-pail
LEGLINS ▸ **leglin**
LEGMAN *n* newsman who reports on news stories from the scene of action or original source
LEGMEN ▸ **legman**
LEGONG *n* Indonesian dance
LEGONGS ▸ **legong**
LEGROOM *n* space to move one's legs comfortably, as in a car
LEGS ▸ **leg**
LEGSIDE *n* part of a cricket field to the left of a right-handed batsman as he faces the bowler
LEGUAAN *n* large S African lizard
LEGUAN ▸ **leguaan**
LEGUANS ▸ **leguan**
LEGUME *n* pod of a plant of the pea or bean family
LEGUMES ▸ **legume**
LEGUMIN *n* protein obtained mainly from the seeds of leguminous plants
LEGWEAR *n* clothing worn on the legs
LEGWORK *n* work that involves travelling on foot or as if on foot
LEHAIM *same as* ▸ **lechaim**
LEHAIMS ▸ **lehaim**
LEHAYIM *same as* ▸ **lehaim**
LEHR *n* long tunnel-shaped oven used for annealing glass
LEHRS ▸ **lehr**
LEHUA *n* flower of Hawaii
LEHUAS ▸ **lehua**
LEI ▸ **leu**
LEIDGER *same as* ▸ **ledger**
LEIGER *same as* ▸ **ledger**
LEIGERS ▸ **leiger**
LEIPOA *n* Australian bird
LEIPOAS ▸ **leipoa**
LEIR *same as* ▸ **lear**
LEIRED ▸ **leir**
LEIRING ▸ **leir**
LEIRS ▸ **leir**
LEIS ▸ **leu**
LEISH *adj* agile
LEISHER ▸ **leish**
LEISLER *n* small bat
LEISTER *n* spear with three or more prongs for spearing fish, esp salmon ▷ *vb* spear (a fish) with a leister

LEISURE *n* time for relaxation or hobbies ▷ *vb* have leisure
LEK *n* area where birds gather for sexual display and courtship ▷ *vb* (of birds) gather at lek
LEKE *old form of* ▸ **leak**
LEKKED ▸ **lek**
LEKKER *adj* attractive or nice
LEKKING ▸ **lek**
LEKS ▸ **lek**
LEKU ▸ **lek**
LEKVAR *n* prune or apricot pie filling
LEKVARS ▸ **lekvar**
LEKYTHI > **lekythos**
LEMAN *n* beloved
LEMANS ▸ **leman**
LEME *same as* ▸ **leam**
LEMED ▸ **leme**
LEMEL *n* metal filings
LEMELS ▸ **lemel**
LEMES ▸ **leme**
LEMING ▸ **leme**
LEMMA *n* subsidiary proposition, proved for use in the proof of another proposition
LEMMAS ▸ **lemma**
LEMMATA ▸ **lemma**
LEMMING *n* rodent of arctic regions, reputed to run into the sea and drown during mass migrations
LEMON *n* yellow oval fruit that grows on trees ▷ *adj* pale-yellow ▷ *vb* flavour with lemon
LEMONED ▸ **lemon**
LEMONS ▸ **lemon**
LEMONY *adj* having or resembling the taste or colour of a lemon
LEMPIRA *n* standard monetary unit of Honduras, divided into 100 centavos
LEMUR *n* nocturnal animal like a small monkey, found in Madagascar
LEMURES *pl n* spirits of the dead
LEMURS ▸ **lemur**
LEND *vb* give the temporary use of
LENDER ▸ **lend**
LENDERS ▸ **lend**
LENDING ▸ **lend**
LENDS ▸ **lend**
LENES ▸ **lenis**
LENG *vb* linger ▷ *adj* long

LENGED ▸ **leng**
LENGER ▸ **leng**
LENGEST ▸ **leng**
LENGING ▸ **leng**
LENGS ▸ **leng**
LENGTH *n* extent or measurement from end to end
LENGTHS ▸ **length**
LENGTHY *adj* very long or tiresome
LENIENT *adj* tolerant, not strict or severe ▷ *n* lenient person
LENIFY *vb* make lenient
LENIS *adj* (of a consonant) pronounced with little muscular tension ▷ *n* consonant pronounced like this
LENITE *vb* undergo lenition
LENITED ▸ **lenite**
LENITES ▸ **lenite**
LENITY *n* mercy or clemency
LENO *n* (in textiles) a weave in which the warp yarns are twisted together in pairs between the weft or filling yarns
LENOS ▸ **leno**
LENS *n* piece of glass or similar material with one or both sides curved, used to bring together or spread light rays in cameras, spectacles, telescopes, etc
LENSE *same as* ▸ **lens**
LENSED *adj* incorporating a lens
LENSES ▸ **lens**
LENSING *n* materials which colour and diffuse light
LENSMAN *n* camera operator
LENSMEN ▸ **lensman**
LENT ▸ **lend**
LENTEN *adj* of or relating to Lent
LENTI ▸ **lento**
LENTIC *adj* of, relating to, or inhabiting still water
LENTIGO *technical name for a* ▸ **freckle**
LENTIL *n* edible seed of a leguminous Asian plant
LENTILS ▸ **lentil**
LENTISC ▸ **lentisk**
LENTISK *n* mastic tree
LENTO *adv* slowly ▷ *n* movement or passage performed slowly
LENTOID *adj* lentiform ▷ *n* lentiform object

LENTOR *n* lethargy
LENTORS ▸ lentor
LENTOS ▸ lento
LENTOUS *adj* lethargic
LENVOY *another word for* ▸ **envoy**
LENVOYS ▸ lenvoy
LEONE *n* standard monetary unit of Sierra Leone, divided into 100 cents
LEONES ▸ leone
LEONINE *adj* like a lion
LEOPARD *n* large spotted carnivorous animal of the cat family
LEOTARD *n* tight-fitting garment covering the upper body, worn for dancing or exercise
LEP *dialect word for* ▸ **leap**
LEPER *n* person suffering from leprosy
LEPERS ▸ leper
LEPID *adj* amusing
LEPORID *adj* of, relating to, or belonging to the family of mammals that includes rabbits and hares ▷ *n* any animal belonging to this family
LEPPED ▸ lep
LEPPING ▸ lep
LEPRA *n* leprosy
LEPRAS ▸ lepra
LEPROSE *adj* having or denoting a whitish scurfy surface
LEPROSY *n* disease attacking the nerves and skin, resulting in loss of feeling in the affected parts
LEPROUS *adj* having leprosy
LEPS ▸ lep
LEPT ▸ leap
LEPTA ▸ lepton
LEPTIN *n* protein, produced by fat cells in the body, that acts on the brain to regulate the amount of additional fat laid down in the body
LEPTINS ▸ leptin
LEPTOME *n* tissue of plant conducting food
LEPTON *n* any of a group of elementary particles with weak interactions
LEPTONS ▸ lepton
LEQUEAR *same as* ▸ **lacunar**
LERE *same as* ▸ **lear**
LERED ▸ lere
LERES ▸ lere

LERING ▸ lere
LERP *n* crystallized honeydew
LERPS ▸ lerp
LESBIAN *n* homosexual woman ▷ *adj* of homosexual women
LESBIC *adj* relating to lesbians
LESION *n* structural change in an organ of the body caused by illness or injury ▷ *vb* cause lesions
LESIONS ▸ lesion
LESS *n* smaller amount ▷ *adj* smaller in extent, degree, or duration ▷ *pron* smaller part or quantity ▷ *adv* smaller extent or degree ▷ *prep* after deducting, minus
LESSEE *n* person to whom a lease is granted
LESSEES ▸ lessee
LESSEN *vb* make or become smaller or not as much
LESSENS ▸ lessen
LESSER *adj* not as great in quantity, size, or worth
LESSES ▸ less
LESSON *n* class or single period of instruction in a subject ▷ *vb* censure or punish
LESSONS ▸ lesson
LESSOR *n* person who grants a lease of property
LESSORS ▸ lessor
LEST *conj* so as to prevent any possibility that ▷ *vb* listen
LESTED ▸ lest
LESTING ▸ lest
LESTS ▸ lest
LET *n* act of letting property ▷ *vb* obstruct
LETCH *same as* ▸ **lech**
LETCHED ▸ letch
LETCHES ▸ letch
LETDOWN *n* disappointment
LETHAL *adj* deadly ▷ *n* weapon, etc capable of causing death
LETHALS ▸ lethal
LETHE *n* forgetfulness
LETHEAN ▸ lethe
LETHEE *n* life-blood
LETHEES ▸ lethee
LETHES ▸ lethe
LETHIED *adj* forgetful
LETS ▸ let
LETTED ▸ let

LETTER *n* written message, usu sent by post ▷ *vb* inscribe letters on
LETTERN *another word for* ▸ **lectern**
LETTERS *pl n* literary knowledge or ability
LETTING ▸ let
LETTRE *n* letter
LETTRES ▸ lettre
LETTUCE *n* plant with large green leaves used in salads
LETUP *n* lessening or abatement
LETUPS ▸ letup
LEU *n* standard monetary unit of Romania and Moldova, divided into 100 bani
LEUCH ▸ lauch
LEUCHEN ▸ lauch
LEUCIN *same as* ▸ **leucine**
LEUCINE *n* essential amino acid found in many proteins
LEUCINS ▸ leucin
LEUCITE *n* grey or white mineral consisting of potassium aluminium silicate
LEUCO *n as in* **leuco base** colourless compound formed by reducing a dye
LEUCOMA *n* white opaque scar of the cornea
LEUD *Scots word for* ▸ **breadth**
LEUDES ▸ leud
LEUDS ▸ leud
LEUGH ▸ lauch
LEUGHEN ▸ lauch
LEUKOMA *same as* ▸ **leucoma**
LEUKON *n* white blood cell count
LEUKONS ▸ leukon
LEV *n* standard monetary unit of Bulgaria, divided into 100 stotinki
LEVA ▸ lev
LEVANT *n* type of leather made from the skins of goats, sheep, or seals ▷ *vb* bolt or abscond, esp to avoid paying debts
LEVANTS ▸ levant
LEVATOR *n* any of various muscles that raise a part of the body
LEVE *adj* darling ▷ *adv* gladly
LEVEE *n* natural or artificial river embankment ▷ *vb* go to the reception of

LEVEED ▸ levee
LEVEES ▸ levee
LEVEL *adj* horizontal ▷ *vb* make even or horizontal ▷ *n* horizontal line or surface
LEVELED ▸ level
LEVELER *same as* ▸ **leveller**
LEVELLY ▸ level
LEVELS ▸ level
LEVER *n* handle used to operate machinery ▷ *vb* prise or move with a lever
LEVERED ▸ lever
LEVERET *n* young hare
LEVERS ▸ lever
LEVES ▸ leve
LEVIED ▸ levy
LEVIER ▸ levy
LEVIERS ▸ levy
LEVIES ▸ levy
LEVIN *archaic word for* ▸ **lightning**
LEVINS ▸ levin
LEVIS *n* jeans
LEVITE *n* Christian clergyman
LEVITES ▸ levite
LEVITIC ▸ levite
LEVITY *n* inclination to make a joke of serious matters
LEVO *adj* anticlockwise
LEVULIN *n* substance obtained from certain bulbs
LEVY *vb* impose and collect (a tax) ▷ *n* imposition or collection of taxes
LEVYING ▸ levy
LEW *adj* tepid
LEWD *adj* lustful or indecent
LEWDER ▸ lewd
LEWDEST ▸ lewd
LEWDLY ▸ lewd
LEWDSBY *another word for* ▸ **lewdster**
LEWIS *n* lifting device for heavy stone or concrete blocks
LEWISES ▸ lewis
LEWISIA *n* type of herb
LEX *n* system or body of laws
LEXEME *n* minimal meaningful unit of language, the meaning of which cannot be understood from that of its component morphemes
LEXEMES ▸ lexeme
LEXEMIC ▸ lexeme
LEXES ▸ lex
LEXICA ▸ lexicon
LEXICAL *adj* relating to the vocabulary of a language
LEXICON *n* dictionary
LEXIS *n* totality of vocabulary items in a language, including all forms having lexical meaning or grammatical function
LEXISES ▸ lexis
LEY *n* land temporarily under grass
LEYS ▸ ley
LI *n* Chinese measurement of distance
LIABLE *adj* legally obliged or responsible
LIAISE *vb* establish and maintain communication (with)
LIAISED ▸ liaise
LIAISES ▸ liaise
LIAISON *n* communication and contact between groups
LIANA *n* climbing plant in tropical forests
LIANAS ▸ liana
LIANE *same as* ▸ **liana**
LIANES ▸ liane
LIANG *n* Chinese unit of weight
LIANGS ▸ liang
LIANOID ▸ liana
LIAR *n* person who tells lies
LIARD *adj* grey ▷ *n* former small coin of various European countries
LIARDS ▸ liard
LIARS ▸ liar
LIART *Scots form of* ▸ **liard**
LIAS *n* lowest series of rocks of the Jurassic system
LIASES ▸ lias
LIATRIS *n* type of North American plant with small white flowers
LIB *n* informal, sometimes derogatory word for liberation ▷ *vb* geld
LIBANT *adj* touching lightly
LIBATE *vb* offer as gift to the gods
LIBATED ▸ libate
LIBATES ▸ libate
LIBBARD *another word for* ▸ **leopard**
LIBBED ▸ lib
LIBBING ▸ lib
LIBEL *n* published statement falsely damaging a person's reputation ▷ *vb* falsely damage the reputation of (someone)

LIBELED ▸ libel
LIBELEE *same as* ▸ **libellee**
LIBELER ▸ libel
LIBELS ▸ libel
LIBER *n* tome or book
LIBERAL *adj* having social and political views that favour progress and reform ▷ *n* person who has liberal ideas or opinions
LIBERO *another name for* ▸ **sweeper**
LIBEROS ▸ libero
LIBERS ▸ liber
LIBERTY *n* freedom
LIBIDO *n* psychic energy
LIBIDOS ▸ libido
LIBKEN *n* lodging
LIBKENS ▸ libken
LIBLAB *n* 19th century British liberal
LIBLABS ▸ liblab
LIBRA *n* ancient Roman unit of weight corresponding to 1 pound, but equal to about 12 ounces
LIBRAE ▸ libra
LIBRARY *n* room or building where books are kept
LIBRAS ▸ libra
LIBRATE *vb* oscillate or waver
LIBRI ▸ liber
LIBS ▸ lib
LICE ▸ louse
LICENCE *n* document giving official permission to do something ▷ *vb* (in the US) give permission to
LICENSE *vb* grant or give a licence for
LICENTE *adj* permitted; allowed
LICH *n* dead body
LICHEE *same as* ▸ **litchi**
LICHEES ▸ lichee
LICHEN *n* small flowerless plant forming a crust on rocks, trees, etc ▷ *vb* cover with lichen
LICHENS ▸ lichen
LICHES ▸ lich
LICHI *same as* ▸ **litchi**
LICHIS ▸ lichi
LICHT *Scots word for* ▸ **light**
LICHTED ▸ licht
LICHTER ▸ licht
LICHTLY *vb* treat discourteously
LICHTS ▸ licht
LICHWAY *n* path used to carry coffin into church

LICIT adj lawful, permitted
LICITLY ▸ licit
LICK vb pass the tongue over ▹ n licking
LICKED ▸ lick
LICKER ▸ lick
LICKERS ▸ lick
LICKING n beating
LICKS ▸ lick
LICTOR n one of a group of ancient Roman officials
LICTORS ▸ lictor
LID n movable cover
LIDAR n radar-type instrument
LIDARS ▸ lidar
LIDDED ▸ lid
LIDDING n lids
LIDGER variant form of ▸ ledger
LIDGERS ▸ ledger
LIDLESS adj having no lid or top
LIDO n open-air centre for swimming and water sports
LIDOS ▸ lido
LIDS ▸ lid
LIE vb make a deliberately false statement ▹ n deliberate falsehood
LIED n setting for solo voice and piano of a poem
LIEDER ▸ lied
LIEF adv gladly ▹ adj ready ▹ n beloved person
LIEFER ▸ lief
LIEFEST ▸ lief
LIEFLY ▸ lief
LIEFS ▸ lief
LIEGE adj bound to give or receive feudal service ▹ n lord
LIEGER same as ▸ ledger
LIEGERS ▸ lieger
LIEGES ▸ liege
LIEN n right to hold another's property until a debt is paid
LIENAL adj of or relating to the spleen
LIENS ▸ lien
LIER n person who lies down
LIERNE n short secondary rib that connects the intersections of the primary ribs, esp as used in Gothic vaulting
LIERNES ▸ lierne
LIERS ▸ lier
LIES ▸ lie
LIEU n stead
LIEUS ▸ lieu

LIEVE same as ▸ leve
LIEVER ▸ lieve
LIEVES ▸ lieve
LIEVEST ▸ lieve
LIFE n state of living beings, characterized by growth, reproduction, and response to stimuli
LIFEFUL adj full of life
LIFER n prisoner sentenced to imprisonment for life
LIFERS ▸ lifer
LIFES pl n as in **still lifes** paintings or drawings of inanimate objects
LIFEWAY n way of life
LIFT vb move upwards in position, status, volume, etc ▹ n cage raised and lowered in a vertical shaft to transport people or goods
LIFTBOY n person who operates a lift, esp in large public or commercial buildings and hotels
LIFTED ▸ lift
LIFTER ▸ lift
LIFTERS ▸ lift
LIFTING ▸ lift
LIFTMAN same as ▸ liftboy
LIFTMEN ▸ liftman
LIFTOFF n moment a rocket leaves the ground ▹ vb (of a rocket) to leave its launch pad
LIFTS ▸ lift
LIFULL obsolete form of ▸ lifeful
LIG n (esp in the media) a function with free entertainment and refreshments ▹ vb attend such a function
LIGAN same as ▸ lagan
LIGAND n atom, molecule, radical, or ion forming a complex with a central atom
LIGANDS ▸ ligand
LIGANS ▸ ligan
LIGASE n any of a class of enzymes
LIGASES ▸ ligase
LIGATE vb tie up or constrict (something) with a ligature
LIGATED ▸ ligate
LIGATES ▸ ligate
LIGER n hybrid offspring of a female tiger and a male lion
LIGERS ▸ liger
LIGGE obsolete form of ▸ lie
LIGGED ▸ lig

LIGGER ▸ lig
LIGGERS ▸ lig
LIGGES ▸ ligge
LIGGING ▸ lig
LIGHT n electromagnetic radiation by which things are visible ▹ adj bright ▹ vb ignite ▹ adv with little equipment or luggage
LIGHTED ▸ light
LIGHTEN vb make less dark
LIGHTER n device for lighting cigarettes etc ▹ vb convey in a type of flat-bottomed barge
LIGHTLY adv in a light way ▹ vb belittle
LIGHTS ▸ light
LIGNAGE another word for ▸ lineage
LIGNAN n beneficial substance found in plants
LIGNANS ▸ lignan
LIGNE n unit of measurement
LIGNES ▸ ligne
LIGNIFY vb make or become woody as a result of the deposition of lignin in the cell walls
LIGNIN n complex polymer occurring in certain plant cell walls making the plant rigid
LIGNINS ▸ lignin
LIGNITE n woody textured rock used as fuel
LIGNOSE n explosive compound
LIGNUM n wood
LIGNUMS ▸ lignum
LIGROIN n volatile fraction of petroleum that is used as a solvent
LIGS ▸ lig
LIGULA same as ▸ ligule
LIGULAE ▸ ligula
LIGULAR ▸ ligula
LIGULAS ▸ ligula
LIGULE n membranous outgrowth at the junction between the leaf blade and sheath in many grasses and sedges
LIGULES ▸ ligule
LIGURE n any of the 12 precious stones used in the breastplates of high priests
LIGURES ▸ ligure
LIKABLE adj easy to like
LIKABLY ▸ likable
LIKE adj similar ▹ vb find enjoyable ▹ n favourable

L

feeling, desire, or
preference
LIKED ▸ **like**
LIKELY adj tending or
inclined ▹ adv probably
LIKEN vb compare
LIKENED ▸ **liken**
LIKENS ▸ **liken**
LIKER ▸ **like**
LIKERS ▸ **like**
LIKES ▸ **like**
LIKEST ▸ **like**
LIKIN n historically, Chinese
tax
LIKING n fondness
LIKINGS ▸ **liking**
LIKINS ▸ **likin**
LIKUTA n (formerly) a coin
used in Zaïre
LILAC n shrub with pale
mauve or white flowers
▹ adj light-purple
LILACS ▸ **lilac**
LILIED adj decorated with
lilies
LILIES ▸ **lily**
LILL obsolete form of ▸ **loll**
LILLED ▸ **lill**
LILLING ▸ **lill**
LILLS ▸ **lill**
LILO n trademark for a type
of inflatable plastic
mattress
LILOS ▸ **lilo**
LILT n pleasing musical
quality in speaking ▹ vb
speak with a lilt
LILTED ▸ **lilt**
LILTING ▸ **lilt**
LILTS ▸ **lilt**
LILY n plant which grows
from a bulb and has large,
often white, flowers
LIMA n type of edible bean
LIMACEL n small shell inside
some kinds of slug
LIMACES ▸ **limax**
LIMACON n heart-shaped
curve
LIMAIL same as ▸ **lemel**
LIMAILS ▸ **limail**
LIMAN n lagoon
LIMANS ▸ **liman**
LIMAS ▸ **lima**
LIMAX n slug
LIMB n arm, leg, or wing
▹ vb dismember
LIMBA n type of African tree
LIMBAS ▸ **limba**
LIMBATE adj having an edge
or border of a different
colour from the rest
LIMBEC obsolete form of

▸ **alembic**
LIMBECK obsolete form of
▸ **alembic**
LIMBECS ▸ **limbec**
LIMBED ▸ **limb**
LIMBER vb loosen stiff
muscles by exercising ▹ adj
pliant or supple ▹ n part of
a gun carriage, consisting
of an axle, pole, and two
wheels
LIMBERS ▸ **limber**
LIMBI ▸ **limbus**
LIMBIC ▸ **limbus**
LIMBIER ▸ **limby**
LIMBING ▸ **limb**
LIMBO n supposed region
intermediate between
Heaven and Hell for the
unbaptized
LIMBOS ▸ **limbo**
LIMBOUS adj with
overlapping edges
LIMBS ▸ **limb**
LIMBUS n border
LIMBY adj with long legs,
stem, branches, etc
LIME n calcium compound
used as a fertilizer or in
making cement ▹ vb spread
a calcium compound upon
(land) ▹ adj having the
flavour of lime fruit
LIMEADE n drink made
from sweetened lime juice
and plain or carbonated
water
LIMED ▸ **lime**
LIMELIT > **limelight**
LIMEN another term for
> **threshold**
LIMENS ▸ **limen**
LIMEPIT n pit containing
lime in which hides are
placed to remove the hair
LIMES n fortified boundary
of the Roman Empire
LIMEY n British person ▹ adj
British
LIMEYS ▸ **limey**
LIMIER ▸ **limy**
LIMIEST ▸ **limy**
LIMINA ▸ **limen**
LIMINAL adj relating to the
point (or threshold) beyond
which a sensation becomes
too faint to be experienced
LIMING ▸ **lime**
LIMINGS ▸ **lime**
LIMIT n ultimate extent,
degree, or amount of
something ▹ vb restrict or
confine

LIMITED adj having a limit
▹ n limited train, bus, etc
LIMITER n electronic circuit
that produces an output
signal whose positive or
negative amplitude, or
both, is limited to some
predetermined value above
which the peaks become
flattened
LIMITES ▸ **limes**
LIMITS ▸ **limit**
LIMMA n semitone
LIMMAS ▸ **limma**
LIMMER n scoundrel
LIMMERS ▸ **limmer**
LIMN vb represent in
drawing or painting
LIMNED ▸ **limn**
LIMNER ▸ **limn**
LIMNERS ▸ **limn**
LIMNIC adj relating to lakes
LIMNING ▸ **limn**
LIMNS ▸ **limn**
LIMO short for > **limousine**
LIMOS ▸ **limo**
LIMOSES ▸ **limosis**
LIMOSIS n excessive hunger
LIMOUS adj muddy
LIMP vb walk with an
uneven step ▹ n limping
walk ▹ adj without
firmness or stiffness
LIMPA n type of rye bread
LIMPAS ▸ **limpa**
LIMPED ▸ **limp**
LIMPER ▸ **limp**
LIMPERS ▸ **limp**
LIMPEST ▸ **limp**
LIMPET n shellfish which
sticks tightly to rocks ▹ adj
denoting certain weapons
that are magnetically
attached to their targets
and resist removal
LIMPETS ▸ **limpet**
LIMPID adj clear or
transparent
LIMPING ▸ **limp**
LIMPKIN n rail-like wading
bird
LIMPLY ▸ **limp**
LIMPS ▸ **limp**
LIMPSEY same as ▸ **limpsy**
LIMPSY adj limp
LIMULI ▸ **limulus**
LIMULUS n type of
horseshoe crab
LIMY adj of, like, or smeared
with birdlime
LIN vb cease
LINABLE ▸ **line**
LINAC n linear accelerator

LINACS ▸ linac
LINAGE n number of lines in written or printed matter
LINAGES ▸ linage
LINALOL same as ▸ linalool
LINCH n ledge
LINCHES ▸ linch
LINCHET another word for ▸ linch
LINCTUS n syrupy cough medicine
LIND same as ▸ linden
LINDANE n white poisonous crystalline powder
LINDEN n large tree with heart-shaped leaves and fragrant yellowish flowers
LINDENS ▸ linden
LINDIES ▸ lindy
LINDS ▸ lind
LINDY n lively dance
LINE n long narrow mark ▷ vb mark with lines
LINEAGE n descent from an ancestor
LINEAL adj in direct line of descent
LINEAR adj of or in lines
LINEATE adj marked with lines
LINECUT n method of relief printing
LINED ▸ line
LINEMAN same as ▸ linesman
LINEMEN ▸ lineman
LINEN n cloth or thread made from flax
LINENS ▸ linen
LINENY ▸ linen
LINER n large passenger ship or aircraft
LINERS ▸ liner
LINES ▸ line
LINEUP n row or arrangement of people or things
LINEUPS ▸ lineup
LINEY ▸ line
LING n slender food fish
LINGA same as ▸ lingam
LINGAM n (in Sanskrit grammar) the masculine gender
LINGAMS ▸ lingam
LINGAS ▸ linga
LINGCOD n type of food fish
LINGEL n strong shoemaker's thread
LINGELS ▸ lingel
LINGER vb delay or prolong departure

LINGERS ▸ linger
LINGIER ▸ lingy
LINGLE same as ▸ lingel
LINGLES ▸ lingle
LINGO n foreign or unfamiliar language or jargon
LINGOES ▸ lingo
LINGOT n ingot
LINGOTS ▸ lingot
LINGS ▸ ling
LINGUA n any tongue-like structure
LINGUAE ▸ lingua
LINGUAL adj of the tongue ▷ n lingual consonant, such as Scots (r)
LINGUAS ▸ lingua
LINGULA n small tongue
LINGY adj heather-covered
LINHAY n farm building with an open front
LINHAYS ▸ linhay
LINIER ▸ line
LINIEST ▸ line
LININ n network of viscous material in the nucleus of a cell that connects the chromatin granules
LINING n layer of cloth attached to the inside of a garment etc
LININGS ▸ lining
LININS ▸ linin
LINISH vb polish metal
LINK n any of the rings forming a chain ▷ vb connect with or as if with links
LINKAGE n act of linking or the state of being linked
LINKBOY n (formerly) a boy who carried a torch for pedestrians in dark streets
LINKED ▸ link
LINKER n person or thing that links
LINKERS ▸ linker
LINKIER ▸ linky
LINKING ▸ link
LINKMAN same as ▸ linkboy
LINKMEN ▸ linkman
LINKROT n state or condition of having expired hyperlinks on a website
LINKS ▸ link
LINKUP n establishing of a connection or union between objects, groups, organizations, etc
LINKUPS ▸ linkup
LINKY adj (of countryside) consisting of links

LINN n waterfall or a pool at the foot of it
LINNED ▸ lin
LINNET n songbird of the finch family
LINNETS ▸ linnet
LINNEY same as ▸ linhay
LINNEYS ▸ linney
LINNIES ▸ linny
LINNING ▸ lin
LINNS ▸ linn
LINNY same as ▸ linhay
LINO same as ▸ linoleum
LINOCUT n design cut in relief in linoleum mounted on a block of wood
LINOS ▸ lino
LINS ▸ lin
LINSANG n any of several forest-dwelling viverrine mammals
LINSEED n seed of the flax plant
LINSEY n type of cloth
LINSEYS ▸ linsey
LINT n shreds of fibre, etc ▷ vb shed or remove lint
LINTED adj having lint
LINTEL n horizontal beam at the top of a door or window
LINTELS ▸ lintel
LINTER n machine for stripping the short fibres of ginned cotton seeds
LINTERS ▸ linter
LINTIE Scots word for ▸ linnet
LINTIER ▸ lint
LINTIES ▸ lintie
LINTING ▸ lint vb
LINTOL same as ▸ lintel
LINTOLS ▸ lintel
LINTS ▸ lint
LINTY ▸ lint
LINUM n type of plant of temperate regions
LINUMS ▸ linum
LINURON n type of herbicide
LINUX n nonproprietary computer operating system suitable for use on personal computers
LINUXES ▸ linux
LINY ▸ line
LION n large animal of the cat family, the male of which has a shaggy mane
LIONCEL n (in heraldry) small lion
LIONEL same as ▸ lioncel
LIONELS ▸ lionel
LIONESS n female lion

LIONET n young lion

LIONETS ▸ lionet

LIONISE same as ▸ lionize

LIONISM n lion-like appearance of leprosy

LIONIZE vb treat as a celebrity

LIONLY ▸ lion

LIONS ▸ lion

LIP n either of the fleshy edges of the mouth ▷ vb touch with the lips

LIPA n monetary unit of Croatia worth one hundredth of a kuna

LIPAS ▸ lipa

LIPASE n any of a group of enzymes that digest fat

LIPASES ▸ lipase

LIPE ▸ lipa

LIPEMIA same as ▸ lipaemia

LIPID n any of a group of organic compounds including fats, oils, waxes, and sterols

LIPIDE same as ▸ lipid

LIPIDES ▸ lipide

LIPIDIC ◂ lipid

LIPIDS ▸ lipid

LIPIN n family of nuclear proteins

LIPINS ▸ lipin

LIPLESS ▸ lip

LIPLIKE ▸ lip

LIPO n liposuction

LIPOIC adj as in **lipoic acid** sulphur-containing fatty acid

LIPOID n fatlike substance, such as wax

LIPOIDS ▸ lipoid

LIPOMA n benign tumour composed of fatty tissue

LIPOMAS ▸ lipoma

LIPOS ▸ lipo

LIPPED ▸ lip

LIPPEN vb trust

LIPPENS ▸ lippen

LIPPER Scots word for ▸ ripple

LIPPERS ▸ lipper

LIPPIE same as ▸ lippy

LIPPIER ▸ lippy

LIPPIES ▸ lippie

LIPPING ▸ lip

LIPPY adj insolent or cheeky ▷ n lipstick

LIPREAD vb follow what someone says by watching their lips

LIPS ▸ lip

LIPURIA n presence of fat in the urine

LIQUATE vb separate one component of (an alloy, impure metal, or ore) by heating so that the more fusible part melts

LIQUEFY vb make or become liquid

LIQUEUR n flavoured and sweetened alcoholic spirit ▷ vb flavour with liqueur

LIQUID n substance in a physical state which can change shape but not size ▷ adj of or being a liquid

LIQUIDS ▸ liquid

LIQUIFY same as ▸ liquefy

LIQUOR n alcoholic drink, esp spirits ▷ vb steep (malt) in warm water to form wort in brewing

LIQUORS ▸ liquor

LIRA n monetary unit of Turkey, Malta, and formerly of Italy

LIRAS ▸ lira

LIRE ▸ lira

LIRI ▸ lira

LIRIOPE n grasslike plant

LIRK vb wrinkle

LIRKED ▸ lirk

LIRKING ▸ lirk

LIRKS ▸ lirk

LIROT ▸ lira

LIROTH ▸ lira

LIS n fleur-de-lis

LISENTE ▸ sente

LISK Yorkshire dialect for ▸ groin

LISKS ▸ lisk

LISLE n strong fine cotton thread or fabric

LISLES ▸ lisle

LISP n speech defect in which s and z are pronounced th ▷ vb speak or utter with a lisp

LISPED ▸ lisp

LISPER ▸ lisp

LISPERS ▸ lisp

LISPING ▸ lisp

LISPS ▸ lisp

LISPUND same as ▸ lispound

LISSES ▸ lis

LISSOM adj supple, agile

LISSOME same as ▸ lissom

LIST n item-by-item record of names or things, usu written one below another ▷ vb make a list of

LISTED ▸ list

LISTEE n person on list

LISTEES ▸ listee

LISTEL another name for ▸ fillet

LISTELS ▸ listel

LISTEN vb concentrate on hearing something

LISTENS ▸ listen

LISTER n plough with a double mouldboard designed to throw soil to either side of a central furrow

LISTERS ▸ lister

LISTETH ▸ list

LISTFUL adj paying attention

LISTING n list or an entry in a list

LISTS pl n field of combat in a tournament

LIT n archaic word for dye or colouring

LITAI ▸ litas

LITANY n prayer with responses from the congregation

LITAS n standard monetary unit of Lithuania, divided into 100 centai

LITCHI n Chinese sapindaceous tree cultivated for its round edible fruits

LITCHIS ▸ litchi

LITE same as ▸ light

LITED ▸ light

LITER same as ▸ litre

LITERAL adj according to the explicit meaning of a word or text, not figurative ▷ n misprint or misspelling in a text

LITERS ▸ liter

LITES ▸ lite

LITH n limb or joint

LITHATE n salt of uric acid

LITHE adj flexible or supple, pliant ▷ vb listen

LITHED ▸ lithe

LITHELY ▸ lithe

LITHER ▸ lithe

LITHES ▸ lithe

LITHEST ▸ lithe

LITHIA n lithium present in mineral waters as lithium salts

LITHIAS ▸ lithia

LITHIC adj of, relating to, or composed of stone

LITHIFY vb turn into rock

LITHING ▸ lithe

LITHITE n part of cell with sensory element

LITHIUM n chemical element, the lightest

known metal

LITHO n lithography ▷ vb print using lithography

LITHOED ▸ **litho**

LITHOID adj resembling stone or rock

LITHOPS n fleshy-leaved plant

LITHOS ▸ **litho**

LITHS ▸ **lith**

LITING ▸ **lite**

LITMUS n blue dye turned red by acids and restored to blue by alkalis

LITORAL same as > **littoral**

LITOTES n ironical understatement used for effect

LITOTIC ▸ **litotes**

LITRE n unit of liquid measure equal to 1000 cubic centimetres or 1.76 pints

LITRES ▸ **litre**

LITS ▸ **lit**

LITTEN adj lighted

LITTER n untidy rubbish dropped in public places ▷ vb strew with litter

LITTERS ▸ **litter**

LITTERY adj covered in litter

LITTLE adj small or smaller than average ▷ adv not a lot ▷ n small amount, extent, or duration

LITTLER ▸ **little**

LITTLES ▸ **little**

LITTLIE n young child

LITTLIN same as > **littling**

LITU ▸ **litas**

LITURGY n prescribed form of public worship

LITUUS n type of curved trumpet

LIVABLE adj tolerable or pleasant to live (with)

LIVE vb be alive ▷ adj living, alive ▷ adv in the form of a live performance

LIVED ▸ **live**

LIVEDO n reddish discoloured patch on the skin

LIVEDOS ▸ **livedo**

LIVELOD n livelihood

LIVELY adj full of life or vigour

LIVEN vb make or become lively

LIVENED ▸ **liven**

LIVENER ▸ **liven**

LIVENS ▸ **liven**

LIVER n person who lives in

a specified way

LIVERED adj having liver

LIVERS ▸ **liver**

LIVERY n distinctive dress, esp a servant or servants ▷ adj of or resembling liver

LIVES ▸ **life**

LIVEST ▸ **live**

LIVEYER n (in Newfoundland) a full-time resident

LIVID adj angry or furious

LIVIDER ▸ **livid**

LIVIDLY ▸ **livid**

LIVIER same as ▸ **liveyer**

LIVIERS ▸ **livier**

LIVING adj possessing life, not dead or inanimate ▷ n condition of being alive

LIVINGS ▸ **living**

LIVOR another word for > **lividity**

LIVORS ▸ **livor**

LIVRE n former French unit of money of account, equal to 1 pound of silver

LIVRES ▸ **livre**

LIVYER same as ▸ **liveyer**

LIVYERS ▸ **livyer**

LIXIVIA > **lixivium**

LIZARD n four-footed reptile with a long body and tail

LIZARDS ▸ **lizard**

LIZZIE n as in tin lizzie an old or decrepit car

LIZZIES ▸ **lizzie**

LLAMA n woolly animal of the camel family used as a beast of burden in S America

LLAMAS ▸ **llama**

LLANERO n native of llanos

LLANO n extensive grassy treeless plain, esp in South America

LLANOS ▸ **llano**

LO interj look!

LOACH n carplike freshwater fish

LOACHES ▸ **loach**

LOAD n burden or weight ▷ vb put a load on or into

LOADED adj (of a question) containing a hidden trap or implication

LOADEN vb load

LOADENS ▸ **loaden**

LOADER n person who loads a gun or other firearm

LOADERS ▸ **loader**

LOADING n load or burden

LOADS pl n lots or a lot

LOAF n shaped mass of baked bread ▷ vb idle, loiter

LOAFED ▸ **loaf**

LOAFER n person who avoids work

LOAFERS ▸ **loafer**

LOAFING ▸ **loaf**

LOAFS ▸ **loaf**

LOAM n fertile soil ▷ vb cover, treat, or fill with loam

LOAMED ▸ **loam**

LOAMIER ▸ **loam**

LOAMING ▸ **loam**

LOAMS ▸ **loam**

LOAMY ▸ **loam**

LOAN n money lent at interest ▷ vb lend

LOANED ▸ **loan**

LOANEE n sportsperson who is loaned from one organization to another

LOANEES ▸ **loanee**

LOANER ▸ **loan**

LOANERS ▸ **loan**

LOANING ▸ **loan**

LOANS ▸ **loan**

LOAST ▸ **lose**

LOATH adj unwilling or reluctant (to)

LOATHE vb hate, be disgusted by

LOATHED ▸ **loathe**

LOATHER ▸ **loathe**

LOATHES ▸ **loathe**

LOATHLY adv with reluctance

LOATHY obsolete form of > **loathsome**

LOAVE vb make into the form of a loaf

LOAVED ▸ **loave**

LOAVES ▸ **loaf**

LOAVING ▸ **loave**

LOB n ball struck or thrown in a high arc ▷ vb strike or throw (a ball) in a high arc

LOBAR adj of or affecting a lobe

LOBATE adj with or like lobes

LOBATED same as ▸ **lobate**

LOBBED ▸ **lob**

LOBBER n one who lobs

LOBBERS ▸ **lobber**

LOBBIED ▸ **lobby**

LOBBIES ▸ **lobby**

LOBBING ▸ **lob**

LOBBY n corridor into which rooms open ▷ vb try to influence (legislators) in the formulation of policy

LOBBYER ▸ **lobby**

L

LOBE n rounded projection

LOBED ▸ **lobe**

LOBEFIN n type of fish

LOBELET n small lobe

LOBELIA n garden plant with blue, red, or white flowers

LOBES ▸ **lobe**

LOBI ▸ **lobus**

LOBING n formation of lobes

LOBINGS ▸ **lobing**

LOBIPED adj with lobed toes

LOBO n timber wolf

LOBOLA n (in African custom) price paid by a bridegroom's family to his bride's family

LOBOLAS ▸ **lobola**

LOBOLO same as ▸ **lobola**

LOBOLOS ▸ **lobolo**

LOBOS ▸ **lobo**

LOBOSE another word for ▸ **lobate**

LOBS ▸ **lob**

LOBSTER n shellfish with a long tail and claws, which turns red when boiled ▷ vb fish for lobsters

LOBULAR ▸ **lobule**

LOBULE n small lobe or a subdivision of a lobe

LOBULES ▸ **lobule**

LOBULI ▸ **lobulus**

LOBULUS n small lobe

LOBUS n lobe

LOBWORM same as ▸ **lugworm**

LOCA ▸ **locus**

LOCAL adj of or existing in a particular place ▷ n person belonging to a particular district

LOCALE n scene of an event

LOCALES ▸ **locale**

LOCALLY adv within a particular area or place

LOCALS ▸ **local**

LOCATE vb discover the whereabouts of

LOCATED ▸ **locate**

LOCATER ▸ **locate**

LOCATES ▸ **locate**

LOCATOR n part of index that indicates where to look for information

LOCH n lake

LOCHAN n small inland loch

LOCHANS ▸ **lochan**

LOCHIA n vaginal discharge of cellular debris, mucus, and blood following childbirth

LOCHIAL ▸ **lochia**

LOCHS ▸ **loch**

LOCI ▸ **locus**

LOCK n appliance for fastening a door, case, etc ▷ vb fasten or become fastened securely

LOCKAGE n system of locks in a canal

LOCKBOX n system of collecting funds from companies by banks

LOCKED ▸ **lock**

LOCKER n small cupboard with a lock

LOCKERS ▸ **locker**

LOCKET n small hinged pendant for a portrait etc

LOCKETS ▸ **locket**

LOCKFUL n sufficient to fill a canal lock

LOCKING ▸ **lock**

LOCKJAW n tetanus

LOCKMAN n lock-keeper

LOCKMEN ▸ **lockman**

LOCKNUT n supplementary nut screwed down upon a primary nut to prevent it from shaking loose

LOCKOUT n closing of a workplace by an employer to force workers to accept terms

LOCKRAM n type of linen cloth

LOCKS ▸ **lock**

LOCKSET n hardware used to lock door

LOCKUP n prison

LOCKUPS ▸ **lockup**

LOCO n locomotive ▷ adj insane ▷ vb poison with locoweed

LOCOED ▸ **loco**

LOCOES ▸ **loco**

LOCOING ▸ **loco**

LOCOISM n disease of cattle, sheep, and horses caused by eating locoweed

LOCOMAN n railwayman, esp an engine-driver

LOCOMEN ▸ **locoman**

LOCOS ▸ **loco**

LOCULAR adj divided into compartments by septa

LOCULE n any of the chambers of an ovary or anther

LOCULED adj having locules

LOCULES ▸ **locule**

LOCULI ▸ **loculus**

LOCULUS same as ▸ **locule**

LOCUM n temporary

stand-in for a doctor or clergyman

LOCUMS ▸ **locum**

LOCUS n area or place where something happens

LOCUST n destructive insect that flies in swarms and eats crops ▷ vb ravage, as locusts

LOCUSTA n flower cluster unit in grasses

LOCUSTS ▸ **locust**

LOD n type of logarithm

LODE n vein of ore

LODEN n thick heavy waterproof woollen cloth with a short pile, used to make garments, esp coats

LODENS ▸ **loden**

LODES ▸ **lode**

LODGE n gatekeeper's house ▷ vb live in another's house at a fixed charge

LODGED ▸ **lodge**

LODGER n person who pays rent in return for accommodation in someone else's home

LODGERS ▸ **lodger**

LODGES ▸ **lodge**

LODGING n temporary residence

LODS ▸ **lod**

LOERIE same as ▸ **lourie**

LOERIES ▸ **loerie**

LOESS n fine-grained soil, found mainly in river valleys, originally deposited by the wind

LOESSAL ▸ **loess**

LOESSES ▸ **loess**

LOESSIC adj relating to or consisting of loess

LOFT n space between the top storey and roof of a building ▷ vb strike, throw, or kick (a ball) high into the air

LOFTED ▸ **loft**

LOFTER n type of golf club

LOFTERS ▸ **lofter**

LOFTIER ▸ **lofty**

LOFTILY ▸ **lofty**

LOFTING ▸ **loft**

LOFTS ▸ **loft**

LOFTY adj of great height

LOG n portion of a felled tree stripped of branches ▷ vb saw logs from a tree

LOGAN another name for ▸ **bogan**

LOGANIA n type of Australian plant

LOGANS ▸ **logan**
LOGBOOK n book recording the details about a car or a ship's journeys
LOGE n small enclosure or box in a theatre or opera house
LOGES ▸ **loge**
LOGGAT n small piece of wood
LOGGATS ▸ **loggat**
LOGGED ▸ **log**
LOGGER n tractor or crane for handling logs
LOGGERS ▸ **logger**
LOGGETS n old-fashioned game played with sticks
LOGGIA n covered gallery at the side of a building
LOGGIAS ▸ **loggia**
LOGGIE ▸ **loggia**
LOGGIER ▸ **loggy**
LOGGING ▸ **log**
LOGGISH ▸ **log**
LOGGY adj slow, sluggish, or listless
LOGIA ▸ **logion**
LOGIC n philosophy of reasoning
LOGICAL adj of logic
LOGICS ▸ **logic**
LOGIE n fire-place of a kiln
LOGIER ▸ **logy**
LOGIES ▸ **logie**
LOGIEST ▸ **logy**
LOGILY ▸ **logy**
LOGIN n process by which a computer user logs on
LOGINS ▸ **login**
LOGION n saying of Christ regarded as authentic
LOGIONS ▸ **logion**
LOGJAM n blockage caused by the crowding together of a number of logs floating in a river ▷ vb cause a logjam
LOGJAMS ▸ **logjam**
LOGLINE n synopsis of screenplay
LOGLOG n logarithm of a logarithm (in equations, etc)
LOGLOGS ▸ **loglog**
LOGO same as ▸ **logotype**
LOGOFF n process by which a computer user logs out
LOGOFFS ▸ **logoff**
LOGOI ▸ **logos**
LOGON same as ▸ **login**
LOGONS ▸ **logon**
LOGOS n reason or the rational principle expressed in words and things,

argument, or justification
LOGOUT same as ▸ **logoff**
LOGOUTS ▸ **logout**
LOGROLL vb use logrolling in order to procure the passage of (legislation)
LOGS ▸ **log**
LOGWAY another name for ▸ **gangway**
LOGWAYS ▸ **logway**
LOGWOOD n leguminous tree of the Caribbean and Central America
LOGY adj dull or listless
LOHAN another word for ▸ **arhat**
LOHANS ▸ **lohan**
LOID vb open (a lock) using a celluloid strip
LOIDED ▸ **loid**
LOIDING ▸ **loid**
LOIDS ▸ **loid**
LOIN n part of the body between the ribs and the hips
LOINS pl n hips and the inner surface of the legs where they join the body
LOIPE n cross-country skiing track
LOIPEN ▸ **loipe**
LOIR n large dormouse
LOIRS ▸ **loir**
LOITER vb stand or wait aimlessly or idly
LOITERS ▸ **loiter**
LOKE n track
LOKES ▸ **loke**
LOKSHEN pl n noodles
LOLIGO n type of squid
LOLIGOS ▸ **loligo**
LOLIUM n type of grass
LOLIUMS ▸ **lolium**
LOLL vb lounge lazily ▷ n act or instance of lolling
LOLLED ▸ **loll**
LOLLER ▸ **loll**
LOLLERS ▸ **loll**
LOLLIES ▸ **lolly**
LOLLING ▸ **loll**
LOLLOP vb move clumsily
LOLLOPS ▸ **lollop**
LOLLOPY ▸ **lollop**
LOLLS ▸ **loll**
LOLLY n lollipop or ice lolly
LOLOG same as ▸ **loglog**
LOLOGS ▸ **lolog**
LOMA n lobe
LOMAS ▸ **loma**
LOMATA ▸ **loma**
LOME vb cover with lome
LOMED ▸ **lome**
LOMEIN n Chinese dish

LOMEINS ▸ **lomein**
LOMENT n pod of certain leguminous plants
LOMENTA > **lomentum**
LOMENTS ▸ **loment**
LOMES ▸ **lome**
LOMING ▸ **lome**
LOMPISH another word for ▸ **lumpish**
LONE adj solitary
LONELY adj sad because alone
LONER n person who prefers to be alone
LONERS ▸ **loner**
LONG adj having length, esp great length, in space or time ▷ adv for a certain time ▷ vb have a strong desire (for)
LONGA n long note
LONGAN n sapindaceous tree of tropical and subtropical Asia
LONGANS ▸ **longan**
LONGAS ▸ **longa**
LONGBOW n large powerful bow
LONGE n rope used in training a horse ▷ vb train using a longe
LONGED ▸ **long**
LONGER n line of barrels on a ship
LONGERS ▸ **longer**
LONGES ▸ **longe**
LONGEST ▸ **long**
LONGIES n long johns
LONGING n yearning ▷ adj having or showing desire
LONGISH adj rather long
LONGLY ▸ **long**
LONGS pl n full-length trousers
LOO n informal word meaning lavatory ▷ vb Scots word meaning love
LOOBIER ▸ **looby**
LOOBIES ▸ **looby**
LOOBILY ▸ **looby**
LOOBY adj foolish ▷ n foolish or stupid person
LOOED ▸ **loo**
LOOEY n lieutenant
LOOEYS ▸ **looey**
LOOF n part of ship's side
LOOFA same as ▸ **loofah**
LOOFAH n sponge made from the dried pod of a gourd
LOOFAHS ▸ **loofah**
LOOFAS ▸ **loofa**
LOOFFUL n handful

L

LOOFS ▸ loof
LOOIE *same as* ▸ **looey**
LOOIES ▸ looie
LOOING ▸ loo
LOOK *vb* direct the eyes or attention (towards) ▷ *n* instance of looking
LOOKED ▸ look
LOOKER *n* person who looks
LOOKERS ▸ looker
LOOKING ▸ look
LOOKISM *n* discrimination against a person on the grounds of physical appearance
LOOKIST ▸ lookism
LOOKOUT *n* act of watching for danger or for an opportunity ▷ *vb* be careful
LOOKS ▸ look
LOOKUP *n* act of looking up information, esp on the internet
LOOKUPS ▸ lookup
LOOM *n* machine for weaving cloth ▷ *vb* appear dimly
LOOMED ▸ loom
LOOMING ▸ loom
LOOMS ▸ loom
LOON *n* diving bird
LOONEY *same as* ▸ **loony**
LOONEYS ▸ loony
LOONIE *n* Canadian dollar coin with a loon bird on one of its faces
LOONIER ▸ loony
LOONIES ▸ loony
LOONILY ▸ loony
LOONING *n* cry of the loon
LOONS ▸ loon
LOONY *adj* foolish or insane ▷ *n* foolish or insane person
LOOP *n* rounded shape made by a curved line or rope crossing itself ▷ *vb* form or fasten with a loop
LOOPED ▸ loop
LOOPER *n* person or thing that loops or makes loops
LOOPERS ▸ looper
LOOPIER ▸ loopy
LOOPILY ▸ loopy
LOOPING ▸ loop
LOOPS ▸ loop
LOOPY *adj* slightly mad or crazy
LOOR ▸ lief
LOORD *obsolete word for* ▸ **lout**
LOORDS ▸ loord

LOOS ▸ loo
LOOSE *adj* not tight, fastened, fixed, or tense ▷ *adv* in a loose manner ▷ *vb* free
LOOSED ▸ loose
LOOSELY ▸ loose
LOOSEN *vb* make loose
LOOSENS ▸ loosen
LOOSER ▸ loose
LOOSES ▸ loose
LOOSEST ▸ loose
LOOSIE *n* informal word for loose forward
LOOSIES *pl n* cigarettes sold individually
LOOSING *n* celebration of one's 21st birthday
LOOT *vb* pillage ▷ *n* goods stolen during pillaging
LOOTED ▸ loot
LOOTEN *Scots past form of* ▸ **let**
LOOTER ▸ loot
LOOTERS ▸ loot
LOOTING ▸ loot
LOOTS ▸ loot
LOOVES ▸ loof
LOP *vb* cut away (twigs and branches) ▷ *n* part or parts lopped off, as from a tree
LOPE *vb* run with long easy strides ▷ *n* loping stride
LOPED ▸ lope
LOPER ▸ lope
LOPERS ▸ lope
LOPES ▸ lope
LOPING ▸ lope
LOPPED ▸ lop
LOPPER *n* tool for lopping ▷ *vb* curdle
LOPPERS ▸ lopper
LOPPIER ▸ loppy
LOPPIES ▸ loppy
LOPPING ▸ lop
LOPPY *adj* floppy ▷ *n* man employed to do maintenance tasks on a ranch
LOPS ▸ lop
LOQUAT *n* ornamental evergreen rosaceous tree
LOQUATS ▸ loquat
LOR *interj* exclamation of surprise or dismay
LORAL *adj* of part of side of bird's head
LORAN *n* radio navigation system operating over long distances
LORANS ▸ loran
LORATE *adj* like a strap
LORCHA *n* junk-rigged vessel

LORCHAS ▸ lorcha
LORD *n* person with power over others, such as a monarch or master ▷ *vb* act in a superior manner
LORDED ▸ lord
LORDING *n* gentleman
LORDKIN *n* little lord
LORDLY *adj* imperious, proud ▷ *adv* in the manner of a lord
LORDOMA *same as* > **lordosis**
LORDS ▸ lord
LORDY *interj* exclamation of surprise or dismay
LORE *n* body of traditions on a subject
LOREAL *adj* concerning or relating to lore
LOREL *another word for* ▸ **losel**
LORELS ▸ lorel
LORES ▸ lore
LORETTE *n* concubine
LORGNON *n* monocle or pair of spectacles
LORIC ▸ lorica
LORICA *n* hard outer covering of rotifers, ciliate protozoans, and similar organisms
LORICAE ▸ lorica
LORICS ▸ lorica
LORIES ▸ lory
LORIMER *n* (formerly) a person who made bits, spurs, and other small metal objects
LORINER *same as* ▸ **lorimer**
LORING *n* teaching
LORINGS ▸ loring
LORIOT *n* golden oriole (bird)
LORIOTS ▸ loriot
LORIS *n* any of several omnivorous nocturnal slow-moving prosimian primates
LORISES ▸ loris
LORN *adj* forsaken or wretched
LORRELL *obsolete word for* ▸ **losel**
LORRIES ▸ lorry
LORRY *n* large vehicle for transporting loads by road
LORY *n* any of various small brightly coloured parrots of Australia and Indonesia
LOS *n* approval
LOSABLE ▸ loose
LOSE *vb* part with or come

to be without

LOSED ▸ lose

LOSEL n worthless person ▹ adj (of a person) worthless, useless, or wasteful

LOSELS ▸ losel

LOSEN ▸ loose

LOSER n person or thing that loses

LOSERS ▸ loser

LOSES ▸ loose

LOSH interj lord

LOSING ▸ lose

LOSINGS pl n losses, esp money lost in gambling

LOSS n losing

LOSSES ▸ loss

LOSSIER ▸ lossy

LOSSY adj (of a dielectric material, transmission line, etc) designed to have a high attenuation

LOST adj missing

LOT pron great number ▹ n collection of people or things ▹ vb draw lots for

LOTA n globular water container, usually of brass, used in India, Myanmar, etc

LOTAH same as ▸ lota

LOTAHS ▸ lotah

LOTAS ▸ lota

LOTE another word for ▸ lotus

LOTES ▸ lote

LOTH same as ▸ loath

LOTHER ▸ loth

LOTHEST ▸ loth

LOTI n standard monetary unit of Lesotho, divided into 100 lisente

LOTIC adj of, relating to, or designating natural communities living in rapidly flowing water

LOTION n medical or cosmetic liquid for use on the skin

LOTIONS ▸ lotion

LOTO same as ▸ lotto

LOTOS same as ▸ lotus

LOTOSES ▸ lotos

LOTS ▸ lot

LOTTE n type of fish

LOTTED ▸ lot

LOTTER n someone who works an allotment

LOTTERS ▸ lotter

LOTTERY n method of raising money by selling tickets that win prizes by chance

LOTTES ▸ lotte

LOTTING ▸ lot

LOTTO n game of chance like bingo

LOTTOS ▸ lotto

LOTUS n legendary plant whose fruit induces forgetfulness

LOTUSES ▸ lotus

LOU Scots word for ▸ love

LOUCHE adj shifty or disreputable

LOUCHER ▸ louche

LOUD adj relatively great in volume

LOUDEN vb make or become louder

LOUDENS ▸ louden

LOUDER ▸ loud

LOUDEST ▸ loud

LOUDISH adj fairly loud

LOUDLY ▸ loud

LOUED ▸ lou

LOUGH n loch

LOUGHS ▸ lough

LOUIE same as ▸ looey

LOUIES ▸ louie

LOUING ▸ lou

LOUIS n former French gold coin

LOUMA n weekly market in rural areas of developing countries

LOUMAS ▸ louma

LOUN same as ▸ lown

LOUND same as ▸ loun

LOUNDED ▸ lound

LOUNDER vb beat severely

LOUNDS ▸ lound

LOUNED ▸ loun

LOUNGE n living room in a private house ▹ vb sit, lie, or stand in a relaxed manner

LOUNGED ▸ lounge

LOUNGER n comfortable sometimes adjustable couch or extending chair designed for someone to relax on

LOUNGES ▸ lounge

LOUNGEY n suggestive of a lounge bar or easy-listening music

LOUNGY adj casual; relaxed

LOUNING ▸ loun

LOUNS ▸ loun

LOUP Scots word for ▸ leap

LOUPE n magnifying glass used by jewellers, horologists, etc

LOUPED ▸ loup

LOUPEN ▸ loup

LOUPES ▸ loupe

LOUPING ▸ loup

LOUPIT ▸ loup

LOUPS ▸ loup

LOUR vb (esp of the sky, weather, etc) to be overcast, dark, and menacing ▹ n menacing scowl or appearance

LOURE n slow, former French dance

LOURED ▸ lour

LOURES ▸ loure

LOURIE n type of African bird with either crimson or grey plumage

LOURIER ▸ loury

LOURIES ▸ lourie

LOURING ▸ lour

LOURS ▸ lour

LOURY adj sombre

LOUS ▸ lou

LOUSE n wingless parasitic insect ▹ vb ruin or spoil

LOUSED ▸ louse

LOUSER n mean nasty person

LOUSERS ▸ louser

LOUSES ▸ louse

LOUSIER ▸ lousy

LOUSILY ▸ lousy

LOUSING ▸ louse

LOUSY adj mean or unpleasant

LOUT n crude, oafish, or aggressive person ▹ vb bow or stoop

LOUTED ▸ lout

LOUTING ▸ lout

LOUTISH adj characteristic of a lout

LOUTS ▸ lout

LOUVAR n large silvery whalelike scombroid fish

LOUVARS ▸ louvar

LOUVER same as ▸ louvre

LOUVERS ▸ louver

LOUVRE n one of a set of parallel slats slanted to admit air but not rain

LOUVRED adj (of a window, door, etc) having louvres

LOUVRES ▸ louvre

LOVABLE adj attracting or deserving affection

LOVABLY ▸ lovable

LOVAGE n European plant used for flavouring food

LOVAGES ▸ lovage

LOVAT n yellowish-green or bluish-green mixture, esp in tweeds or woollens

LOVATS ▸ lovat

LOVE vb have a great

L

affection for ▷ *n* great
affection
LOVEBUG *n* small US flying
insect
LOVED ▸ **love**
LOVELY *adj* very attractive
▷ *n* attractive woman
LOVER *n* person having a
sexual relationship outside
marriage
LOVERED *adj* having a lover
LOVERLY *adj* loverlike
LOVERS ▸ **lover**
LOVES ▸ **love**
LOVEY *another word for*
▸ **love**
LOVEYS ▸ **lovey**
LOVING *adj* affectionate,
tender
LOVINGS ▸ **loving**
LOW *adj* not tall, high, or
elevated ▷ *adv* in or to a low
position, level, or degree
▷ *n* low position, level, or
degree ▷ *vb* moo
LOWAN *n* type of Australian
bird
LOWANS ▸ **lowan**
LOWBALL *vb* deliberately
under-charge
LOWBORN *adj* of ignoble or
common parentage
LOWBOY *n* table fitted with
drawers
LOWBOYS ▸ **lowboy**
LOWBRED *same as*
▸ **lowborn**
LOWBROW *adj* with
nonintellectual tastes and
interests ▷ *n* person with
uncultivated or
nonintellectual tastes
LOWDOWN *n* inside
information
LOWE *same as* ▸ **low**
LOWED ▸ **low**
LOWER *adj* below one or
more other things ▷ *vb*
cause or allow to move
down
LOWERED ▸ **lower**
LOWERS ▸ **lower**
LOWERY *adj* sombre
LOWES ▸ **lowe**
LOWEST ▸ **low**
LOWING ▸ **low**
LOWINGS ▸ **low**
LOWISH ▸ **low**
LOWLAND *n* low-lying
country ▷ *adj* of a lowland
or lowlands
LOWLIER ▸ **lowly**
LOWLIFE *n* member or

members of the
underworld
LOWLILY ▸ **lowly**
LOWLY *adj* modest, humble
▷ *adv* in a low or lowly
manner
LOWN *vb* calm
LOWND *same as* ▸ **lown**
LOWNDED ▸ **lownd**
LOWNDS ▸ **lownd**
LOWNE *same as* ▸ **loon**
LOWNED ▸ **lown**
LOWNES ▸ **lowne**
LOWNESS ▸ **low**
LOWNING ▸ **lown**
LOWNS ▸ **lown**
LOWP *same as* ▸ **loup**
LOWPED ▸ **lowp**
LOWPING ▸ **lowp**
LOWPS ▸ **lowp**
LOWRIE *another name for*
▸ **lory**
LOWRIES ▸ **lowry**
LOWRY *another name for*
▸ **lory**
LOWS ▸ **low**
LOWSE *vb* release or loose
▷ *adj* loose
LOWSED ▸ **lowse**
LOWSER ▸ **lowse**
LOWSES ▸ **lowse**
LOWSEST ▸ **lowse**
LOWSING ▸ **lowse**
LOWSIT ▸ **lowse**
LOWT *same as* ▸ **lout**
LOWTED ▸ **lowt**
LOWTING ▸ **lowt**
LOWTS ▸ **lowt**
LOWVELD *n* low ground in S
Africa
LOX *vb* load fuel tanks of
spacecraft with liquid
oxygen ▷ *n* kind of smoked
salmon

This is another good
word when you have an X
to dispose of.

LOXED ▸ **lox**
LOXES ▸ **lox**
LOXING ▸ **lox**
LOXYGEN *n* liquid oxygen
LOY *n* narrow spade with a
single footrest
LOYAL *adj* faithful to one's
friends, country, or
government
LOYALER ▸ **loyal**
LOYALLY ▸ **loyal**
LOYALTY *n* quality of being
loyal
LOYS ▸ **loy**
LOZELL *obsolete form of*
▸ **losel**

LOZELLS ▸ **lozell**
LOZEN *n* window pane
LOZENGE *n* medicated
tablet held in the mouth
until it dissolves
LOZENGY *adj* divided by
diagonal lines to form a
lattice
LOZENS ▸ **lozen**
LUACH *n* calendar that
shows the dates of festivals
and, usually, the times of
start and finish of the
Sabbath
LUAU *n* feast of Hawaiian
food
LUAUS ▸ **luau**
LUBBARD *same as* ▸ **lubber**
LUBBER *n* big, awkward, or
stupid person
LUBBERS ▸ **lubber**
LUBE *n* lubricating oil ▷ *vb*
lubricate with oil
LUBED ▸ **lube**
LUBES ▸ **lube**
LUBFISH *n* type of fish
LUBING ▸ **lube**
LUBRA *n* Aboriginal woman
LUBRAS ▸ **lubra**
LUBRIC *adj* slippery
LUCARNE *n* type of dormer
window
LUCE *another name for* ▸ **pike**
LUCENCE ▸ **lucent**
LUCENCY ▸ **lucent**
LUCENT *adj* brilliant,
shining, or translucent
LUCERN *same as* ▸ **lucerne**
LUCERNE *n* alfalfa
LUCERNS ▸ **lucern**
LUCES ▸ **luce**
LUCHOT ▸ **luach**
LUCHOTH ▸ **luach**
LUCID *adj* clear and easily
understood
LUCIDER ▸ **lucid**
LUCIDLY ▸ **lucid**
LUCIFER *n* friction match
LUCIGEN *n* lamp burning oil
mixed with hot air
LUCITE *n* brand name of a
type of transparent
acrylic-based plastic
LUCITES ▸ **lucite**
LUCK *n* fortune, good or bad
▷ *vb* have good fortune
LUCKED ▸ **luck**
LUCKEN *adj* shut
LUCKIE *same as* ▸ **lucky**
LUCKIER ▸ **lucky**
LUCKIES ▸ **luckie**
LUCKILY ▸ **lucky**
LUCKING ▸ **luck**

LUCKS ▸ luck
LUCKY adj having or bringing good luck ▷ n old woman
LUCRE n money or wealth
LUCRES ▸ lucre
LUCUMA n type of S American tree
LUCUMAS ▸ lucuma
LUCUMO n Etruscan king
LUCUMOS ▸ lucumo
LUD n lord ▷ interj exclamation of dismay or surprise
LUDE n slang word for drug for relieving anxiety
LUDES ▸ lude
LUDIC adj playful
LUDO n game played with dice and counters on a board
LUDOS ▸ ludo
LUDS ▸ lud
LUDSHIP ▸ lud
LUES n any venereal disease
LUETIC ▸ lues
LUETICS ▸ lues
LUFF vb sail (a ship) towards the wind ▷ n leading edge of a fore-and-aft sail
LUFFA same as ▸ loofah
LUFFAS ▸ luffa
LUFFED ▸ luff
LUFFING ▸ luff
LUFFS ▸ luff
LUG vb carry or drag with great effort ▷ n projection serving as a handle
LUGE n racing toboggan on which riders lie on their backs, descending feet first ▷ vb ride on a luge
LUGED ▸ luge
LUGEING ▸ luge
LUGER n tradename for a type of German automatic pistol
LUGERS ▸ luger
LUGES ▸ luge
LUGGAGE n suitcases, bags, etc
LUGGED ▸ lug
LUGGER n small working boat with an oblong sail
LUGGERS ▸ lugger
LUGGIE n wooden bowl with handles
LUGGIES ▸ luggie
LUGGING ▸ lug
LUGHOLE informal word for ▸ ear
LUGING ▸ luge
LUGINGS ▸ luge

LUGS ▸ lug
LUGSAIL n four-sided sail bent and hoisted on a yard
LUGWORM n large worm used as bait
LUIT Scots past form of ▸ let
LUITEN ▸ let
LUKE same as ▸ lukewarm
LULIBUB obsolete form of ▸ lollipop
LULL vb soothe (someone) by soft sounds or motions ▷ n brief time of quiet in a storm etc
LULLABY n quiet song to send a child to sleep ▷ vb quiet or soothe with or as if with a lullaby
LULLED ▸ lull
LULLER ▸ lull
LULLERS ▸ lull
LULLING ▸ lull
LULLS ▸ lull
LULU n person or thing considered to be outstanding in size, appearance, etc
LULUS ▸ lulu
LUM n chimney
LUMA n a monetary unit of Armenia worth one hundredth of a dram
LUMAS ▸ luma
LUMBAGO n pain in the lower back
LUMBANG n type of tree
LUMBAR adj of the part of the body between the lowest ribs and the hipbones ▷ n old-fashioned kind of ship
LUMBARS ▸ lumbar
LUMBER n unwanted disused household articles ▷ vb burden with something unpleasant
LUMBERS ▸ lumber
LUMEN n derived SI unit of luminous flux
LUMENAL ▸ lumen
LUMENS ▸ lumen
LUMINA ▸ lumen
LUMINAL ▸ lumen
LUMINE vb illuminate
LUMINED ▸ lumine
LUMINES ▸ lumine
LUMME interj exclamation of surprise or dismay
LUMMIER ▸ lummy
LUMMOX n clumsy or stupid person
LUMMY interj exclamation of surprise ▷ adj excellent

LUMP n shapeless piece or mass ▷ vb consider as a single group
LUMPED ▸ lump
LUMPEN adj stupid or unthinking ▷ n member of underclass
LUMPENS ▸ lumpen
LUMPER n stevedore
LUMPERS ▸ lumper
LUMPIER ▸ lumpy
LUMPILY ▸ lumpy
LUMPING ▸ lump
LUMPISH adj stupid or clumsy
LUMPKIN n lout
LUMPS ▸ lump
LUMPY adj full of or having lumps
LUMS ▸ lum
LUNA n type of large American moth
LUNACY n foolishness
LUNAR adj relating to the moon ▷ n lunar distance
LUNARS ▸ lunar
LUNARY n moonwort herb
LUNAS ▸ luna
LUNATE adj shaped like a crescent ▷ n crescent-shaped bone forming part of the wrist
LUNATED same as ▸ lunate
LUNATES ▸ lunate
LUNATIC adj foolish and irresponsible ▷ n foolish or annoying person
LUNCH n meal taken in the middle of the day ▷ vb eat lunch
LUNCHED ▸ lunch
LUNCHER ▸ lunch
LUNCHES ▸ lunch
LUNE same as ▸ lunette
LUNES ▸ lune
LUNET n small moon or satellite
LUNETS ▸ lunet
LUNETTE n anything that is shaped like a crescent
LUNG n organ that allows an animal or bird to breathe air
LUNGAN same as ▸ longan
LUNGANS ▸ lungan
LUNGE n sudden forward motion ▷ vb move with or make a lunge
LUNGED ▸ lunge
LUNGEE same as ▸ lungi
LUNGEES ▸ lungee
LUNGER ▸ lunge
LUNGERS ▸ lunge

L

LUNGES ▸ lunge
LUNGFUL ▸ lung
LUNGI *n* long piece of cotton cloth worn as a loincloth, sash, or turban by Indian men or as a skirt
LUNGIE *n* guillemot
LUNGIES ▸ lungie
LUNGING ▸ lunge
LUNGIS ▸ lungi
LUNGS ▸ lung
LUNGYI *same as* ▸ **lungi**
LUNGYIS ▸ lungyi
LUNIER ▸ luny
LUNIES ▸ luny
LUNIEST ▸ luny
LUNK *n* awkward, heavy, or stupid person
LUNKER *n* very large fish, esp bass
LUNKERS ▸ lunker
LUNKS ▸ lunk
LUNT *vb* produce smoke
LUNTED ▸ lunt
LUNTING ▸ lunt
LUNTS ▸ lunt
LUNULA *n* white crescent-shaped area at the base of the human fingernail
LUNULAE ▸ lunula
LUNULAR *same as* ▸ **lunulate**
LUNULE *same as* ▸ **lunula**
LUNULES ▸ lunule
LUNY *same as* ▸ **loony**
LUNYIE *same as* ▸ **lungie**
LUNYIES ▸ lunyie
LUPANAR *n* brothel
LUPIN *n* garden plant with tall spikes of flowers
LUPINE *adj* like a wolf ▷ *n* lupin
LUPINES ▸ lupine
LUPINS ▸ lupin
LUPOID *adj* suffering from lupus
LUPOUS *adj* relating to lupus
LUPPEN *Scots past form of* ▸ **leap**
LUPULIN *n* resinous powder extracted from the female flowers of the hop plant
LUPUS *n* ulcerous skin disease
LUPUSES ▸ lupus
LUR *n* large bronze musical horn found in Danish peat bogs
LURCH *vb* tilt or lean suddenly to one side ▷ *n* lurching movement

LURCHED ▸ lurch
LURCHER *n* crossbred dog trained to hunt silently
LURCHES ▸ lurch
LURDAN *n* stupid or dull person ▷ *adj* dull or stupid
LURDANE *same as* ▸ **lurdan**
LURDANS ▸ lurdan
LURDEN *same as* ▸ **lurdan**
LURDENS ▸ lurden
LURE *vb* tempt or attract by the promise of reward ▷ *n* person or thing that lures
LURED ▸ lure
LURER ▸ lure
LURERS ▸ lure
LURES ▸ lure
LUREX *n* thin glittery thread
LUREXES ▸ lurex
LURGI *same as* ▸ **lurgy**
LURGIES ▸ lurgy
LURGIS ▸ lurgi
LURGY *n* any undetermined illness
LURID *adj* vivid in shocking detail, sensational
LURIDER ▸ lurid
LURIDLY ▸ lurid
LURING ▸ lure
LURINGS ▸ luring
LURK *vb* lie hidden or move stealthily, esp for sinister purposes
LURKED ▸ lurk
LURKER ▸ lurk
LURKERS ▸ lurk
LURKING *adj* lingering but almost unacknowledged
LURKS ▸ lurk
LURRIES ▸ lurry
LURRY *n* confused jumble
LURS ▸ lur
LURVE *n* love
LURVES ▸ lurve
LUSER *n* user of a computer system, as considered by a systems administator or other member of a technical support team
LUSERS ▸ luser
LUSH *adj* (of grass etc) growing thickly and healthily ▷ *n* alcoholic ▷ *vb* drink (alcohol) to excess
LUSHED ▸ lush
LUSHER *adj* more lush ▷ *n* drunkard
LUSHERS ▸ lusher
LUSHES ▸ lush
LUSHEST ▸ lush
LUSHIER ▸ lushy
LUSHING ▸ lush
LUSHLY ▸ lush

LUSHY *adj* slightly intoxicated
LUSK *vb* lounge around
LUSKED ▸ lusk
LUSKING ▸ lusk
LUSKISH *adj* lazy
LUSKS ▸ lusk
LUST *n* strong sexual desire ▷ *vb* have passionate desire (for)
LUSTED ▸ lust
LUSTER *same as* ▸ **lustre**
LUSTERS ▸ luster
LUSTFUL *adj* driven by lust
LUSTICK *obsolete word for* ▸ **lusty**
LUSTIER ▸ lusty
LUSTILY ▸ lusty
LUSTING ▸ lust
LUSTRA ▸ lustrum
LUSTRAL *adj* of or relating to a ceremony of purification
LUSTRE *n* gloss, sheen ▷ *vb* make, be, or become lustrous
LUSTRED ▸ lustre
LUSTRES ▸ lustre
LUSTRUM *n* period of five years
LUSTS ▸ lust
LUSTY *adj* vigorous, healthy
LUSUS *n* freak, mutant, or monster
LUSUSES ▸ lusus
LUTE *n* ancient guitar-like musical instrument with a body shaped like a half pear ▷ *vb* seal (a joint or surface) with a mixture of cement and clay
LUTEA *adj* yellow
LUTEAL *adj* relating to or characterized by the development of the corpus luteum
LUTED ▸ lute
LUTEIN *n* xanthophyll pigment that has a light-absorbing function in photosynthesis
LUTEINS ▸ lutein
LUTEOUS *adj* of a light to moderate greenish-yellow colour
LUTER *n* lute player
LUTERS ▸ luter
LUTES ▸ lute
LUTEUM *adj* yellow
LUTFISK *same as* ▸ **lutefisk**
LUTHERN *another name for* ▸ **dormer**
LUTHIER *n* lute-maker

LUTING n mixture of cement and clay

LUTINGS ▸ **luting**

LUTIST same as > **lutenist**

LUTISTS ▸ **lutist**

LUTITE another name for ▸ **pelite**

LUTITES ▸ **lutite**

LUTTEN ▸ **loot**

LUTZ n jump in which the skater takes off from the back outside edge of one skate, makes one, two, or three turns in the air, and lands on the back outside edge of the other skate

LUTZES ▸ **lutz**

LUV n love

LUVS ▸ **love**

LUVVIE n person who is involved in acting or the theatre

LUVVIES ▸ **luvvy**

LUVVY same as ▸ **luvvie**

LUX n unit of illumination

A **lux** is a unit of illumination, and is another of the key words using X.

LUXATE vb put (a shoulder, knee, etc) out of joint

LUXATED ▸ **luxate**

LUXATES ▸ **luxate**

LUXE n as in **de luxe** rich, elegant, or sumptuous

LUXES ▸ **luxe**

LUXURY n enjoyment of rich, very comfortable living ▷ adj of or providing luxury

LUZ n supposedly indestructible bone of the human body

This very unusual word, meaning a supposedly indestructible bone in the human body, is very useful for playing the Z.

LUZERN n alfalfa

LUZERNS ▸ **luzern**

LUZZES ▸ **luz**

LWEI n Angolan monetary unit

LWEIS ▸ **lwei**

LYAM n leash

LYAMS ▸ **lyam**

LYARD same as ▸ **liard**

LYART same as ▸ **liard**

LYASE n any enzyme that catalyses the separation of two parts of a molecule

LYASES ▸ **lyase**

LYCEA ▸ **lyceum**

LYCEE n secondary school

LYCEES ▸ **lycee**

LYCEUM n public building for events such as concerts and lectures

LYCEUMS ▸ **lyceum**

LYCH same as ▸ **lich**

LYCHEE same as ▸ **litchi**

LYCHEES ▸ **lychee**

LYCHES ▸ **lych**

LYCHNIS n type of plant with red, pink, or white five-petalled flowers

LYCOPOD n type of moss

LYCRA n tradename for a type of synthetic elastic fabric and fibre used for tight-fitting garments, such as swimming costumes

LYCRAS ▸ **lycra**

LYDDITE n explosive consisting chiefly of fused picric acid

LYE n caustic solution obtained by leaching wood ash

LYES ▸ **lye**

LYFULL obsolete form of ▸ **lifeful**

LYING ▸ **lie**

LYINGLY ▸ **lie**

LYINGS ▸ **lie**

LYM obsolete form of ▸ **lyam**

LYME n as in **lyme grass** type of perennial dune grass

LYMES ▸ **lyme**

LYMITER same as ▸ **limiter**

LYMPH n colourless bodily fluid consisting mainly of white blood cells

LYMPHAD n ancient rowing boat

LYMPHS n lymph

LYMS ▸ **lym**

LYNAGE obsolete form of ▸ **lineage**

LYNAGES ▸ **lynage**

LYNCEAN adj of or resembling a lynx

LYNCH vb put to death without a trial

LYNCHED ▸ **lynch**

LYNCHER ▸ **lynch**

LYNCHES ▸ **lynch**

LYNCHET n terrace or ridge formed in prehistoric or medieval times by ploughing a hillside

LYNE n flax

LYNES ▸ **lyne**

LYNX n animal of the cat family with tufted ears and a short tail

LYNXES ▸ **lynx**

LYOPHIL same as > **lyophilic**

LYRA n as in **lyra viol** lutelike musical instrument of the 16th and 17th centuries

LYRATE adj shaped like a lyre

LYRATED same as ▸ **lyrate**

LYRE n ancient musical instrument like a U-shaped harp

LYRES ▸ **lyre**

LYRIC adj (of poetry) expressing personal emotion in songlike style ▷ n short poem in a songlike style

LYRICAL same as ▸ **lyric**

LYRICON n wind synthesizer

LYRICS ▸ **lyric**

LYRISM n art or technique of playing the lyre

LYRISMS ▸ **lyrism**

LYRIST same as > **lyricist**

LYRISTS ▸ **lyrist**

LYSATE n material formed by lysis

LYSATES ▸ **lysate**

LYSE vb undergo or cause to undergo lysis

LYSED ▸ **lyse**

LYSES ▸ **lysis**

LYSIN n any of a group of antibodies that cause dissolution of cells against which they are directed

LYSINE n essential amino acid that occurs in proteins

LYSINES ▸ **lysine**

LYSING ▸ **lyse**

LYSINS ▸ **lysin**

LYSIS n destruction or dissolution of cells by the action of a particular lysin

LYSOGEN n lysis-inducing agent

LYSOL n tradename for a solution used as an antiseptic and disinfectant

LYSOLS ▸ **lysol**

LYSSA less common word for ▸ **rabies**

LYSSAS ▸ **lyssa**

LYTE vb dismount

LYTED ▸ **lyte**

LYTES ▸ **lyte**

LYTHE *n* type of fish
LYTHES ▶ lythe
LYTIC *adj* relating to, causing, or resulting from lysis

LYTING ▶ lyte
LYTTA *n* rodlike mass of cartilage beneath the tongue in the dog and other carnivores

LYTTAE ▶ lytta
LYTTAS ▶ lytta

L

Mm

M is a very useful letter when you need to form short words as it starts a two-letter word with every vowel, as well as with **Y** and with another **M**. Remembering this allows you to use **M** effectively when you're forming a word parallel to, and in contact with, a word that is already on the board. **M** also combines well with **X** and **Z**, so there is a lot of potential for high-scoring words. Keep **max, mix** and **mux** (12 points each) in mind, as well as **miz** and **muz** (14 each). It's also worth remembering the three-letter words ending in **W**: **maw, mew** and **mow** (8 points each). **Myc** is another useful word to remember when you are short of vowels.

MA *n* mother
MAA *vb* (of goats) bleat
MAAED ▶ maa
MAAING ▶ maa
MAAR *n* coneless volcanic crater that has been formed by a single explosion
MAARE ▶ maar
MAARS ▶ maar
MAAS *n* thick soured milk
MAASES ▶ maas
MAATJES *n* pickled herring
MABE *n* type of pearl
MABELA *n* ground kaffir corn used for making porridge
MABELAS ▶ mabela
MABES ▶ mabe
MAC *n* macintosh
MACABER *same as* ▶ macabre
MACABRE *adj* strange and horrible, gruesome
MACACO *n* type of lemur
MACACOS ▶ macaco
MACADAM *n* road surface of pressed layers of small broken stones
MACAQUE *n* monkey of Asia and Africa with cheek pouches and either a short tail or no tail
MACAW *n* large tropical American parrot
MACAWS ▶ macaw
MACCHIA *n* thicket in Italy
MACCHIE ▶ macchia
MACE *n* club, usually having a spiked metal head, used esp in the Middle Ages ▷ *vb* use a mace

MACED ▶ mace
MACER *n* macebearer, esp (in Scotland) an official who acts as usher in a court of law
MACERAL *n* any of the organic units that constitute coal: equivalent to any of the mineral constituents of a rock
MACERS ▶ macer
MACES ▶ mace
MACH *n* ratio of the speed of a body in a particular medium to the speed of sound in that medium
MACHAIR *n* (in the western Highlands of Scotland) a strip of sandy, grassy, often lime-rich land just above the high-water mark at a sandy shore: used as grazing or arable land
MACHAN *n* (in India) a raised platform used in tiger hunting
MACHANS ▶ machan
MACHE *n* papier-mâché
MACHER *n* important or influential person: often used ironically
MACHERS ▶ macher
MACHES ▶ mache
MACHETE *n* broad heavy knife used for cutting or as a weapon
MACHI *n as in* **machi chips** in Indian English, fish and chips
MACHINE *n* apparatus, usu powered by electricity,

designed to perform a particular task ▷ *vb* make or produce by machine
MACHO *adj* strongly or exaggeratedly masculine ▷ *n* strong or exaggerated masculinity
MACHOS ▶ macho
MACHREE *n* Irish form of address meaning my dear
MACHS ▶ mach
MACHZOR *n* Jewish prayer book containing prescribed holiday rituals
MACING ▶ mace
MACK *same as* ▶ mac
MACKLE *n* double or blurred impression caused by shifting paper or type ▷ *vb* mend hurriedly or in a makeshift way
MACKLED ▶ mackle
MACKLES ▶ mackle
MACKS ▶ mack
MACLE *n* crystal consisting of two parts
MACLED ▶ macle
MACLES ▶ macle
MACON *n* red or white wine from the Mâcon area, heavier than the other burgundies
MACONS ▶ macon
MACOYA *n* South American tree
MACOYAS ▶ macoya
MACRAME *n* ornamental work of knotted cord
MACRAMI *same as* ▶ macrame
MACRO *n* close-up lens

MACRON n mark placed over a letter to represent a long vowel

MACRONS ▸ macron

MACROS ▸ macro

MACS ▸ mac

MACULA n small spot or area of distinct colour, such as a freckle

MACULAE ▸ macula

MACULAR ▸ macula

MACULAS ▸ macula

MACULE same as ▸ **mackle**

MACULED ▸ macule

MACULES ▸ macule

MACUMBA n religious cult in Brazil that combines Christian and voodoo elements

MAD adj mentally deranged, insane ▷ vb make mad

MADAFU n coconut milk

MADAFUS ▸ madafu

MADAM n polite term of address for a woman ▷ vb call someone madam

MADAME n French title equivalent to Mrs

MADAMED ▸ madam

MADAMES ▸ madame

MADAMS ▸ madam

MADCAP adj foolish or reckless ▷ n impulsive or reckless person

MADCAPS ▸ madcap

MADDED ▸ mad

MADDEN vb infuriate or irritate

MADDENS ▸ madden

MADDER n type of rose

MADDERS ▸ madder

MADDEST ▸ mad

MADDING ▸ mad

MADDISH ▸ mad

MADDOCK same as ▸ **mattock**

MADE ▸ make

MADEFY vb make moist

MADEIRA n kind of rich sponge cake

MADGE n type of hammer

MADGES ▸ madge

MADID adj wet

MADISON n type of cycle relay race

MADLING n insane person

MADLY adv with great speed and energy

MADMAN n person who is insane

MADMEN ▸ madman

MADNESS n insanity

MADONNA n picture or statue of the Virgin Mary

MADOQUA n Ethiopian antelope

MADRAS n medium-hot curry

MADRASA same as ▸ **madrasah**

MADRE Spanish word for ▸ **mother**

MADRES ▸ madre

MADRONA n N American evergreen tree or shrub with white flowers and red berry-like fruits

MADRONE same as ▸ **madrona**

MADRONO same as ▸ **madrona**

MADS ▸ mad

MADTOM n species of catfish

MADTOMS ▸ madtom

MADURO adj (of cigars) dark and strong ▷ n cigar of this type

MADUROS ▸ maduro

MADWORT n low-growing Eurasian plant with small blue flowers

MADZOON same as ▸ **matzoon**

MAE adj more

MAELID n mythical spirit of apple

MAELIDS ▸ maelid

MAENAD n female disciple of Dionysus, the Greek god of wine

MAENADS ▸ maenad

MAERL n type of red coralline algae

MAERLS ▸ maerl

MAES ▸ mae

MAESTRI ▸ maestro

MAESTRO n outstanding musician or conductor

MAFFIA same as ▸ **mafia**

MAFFIAS ▸ maffia

MAFFICK vb celebrate extravagantly and publicly

MAFFLED adj baffled

MAFFLIN n half-witted person

MAFIA n international secret organization founded in Sicily, probably in opposition to tyranny. It developed into a criminal organization and in the late 19th century was carried to the US by Italian immigrants

MAFIAS ▸ mafia

MAFIC n collective term for minerals present in igneous rock

MAFICS ▸ mafic

MAFIOSI ▸ mafioso

MAFIOSO n member of the Mafia

MAFTED adj suffering under oppressive heat

MAFTIR n final section of the weekly Torah reading

MAFTIRS ▸ maftir

MAG vb talk ▷ n talk

MAGALOG same as ▸ **magalogue**

MAGE archaic word for ▸ **magician**

MAGENTA adj deep purplish-red ▷ n deep purplish red that is the complementary colour of green and, with yellow and cyan, forms a set of primary colours

MAGES ▸ mage

MAGG same as ▸ **mag**

MAGGED ▸ mag

MAGGIE n magpie

MAGGIES ▸ maggie

MAGGING ▸ mag

MAGGOT n larva of an insect

MAGGOTS ▸ maggot

MAGGOTY adj relating to, resembling, or ridden with maggots

MAGGS ▸ magg

MAGI ▸ magus

MAGIAN ▸ magus

MAGIANS ▸ magus

MAGIC n supposed art of invoking supernatural powers to influence events ▷ vb to transform or produce by or as if by magic ▷ adj of, using, or like magic

MAGICAL ▸ magic

MAGICS ▸ magic

MAGILP same as ▸ **megilp**

MAGILPS ▸ magilp

MAGISM ▸ magus

MAGISMS ▸ magus

MAGLEV n type of high-speed train that runs on magnets supported by a magnetic field generated around the track

MAGLEVS ▸ maglev

MAGMA n molten rock inside the earth's crust

MAGMAS ▸ magma

MAGMATA ▸ magma

MAGNATE n influential or wealthy person, esp in industry

MAGNES n magnetic iron ore

MAGNET n piece of iron or steel capable of attracting iron and pointing north when suspended

MAGNETO n apparatus for ignition in an internal-combustion engine

MAGNETS ▶ magnet

MAGNIFY vb increase in apparent size, as with a lens

MAGNON n short for Cro-Magnon

MAGNONS ▶ magnon

MAGNOX n alloy composed mainly of magnesium, used in fuel elements of some nuclear reactors

MAGNUM n large wine bottle holding about 1.5 litres

MAGNUMS ▶ magnum

MAGNUS adj as in **magnus hitch** knot similar to a clove hitch but having one more turn

MAGOT n Chinese or Japanese figurine in a crouching position, usually grotesque

MAGOTS ▶ magot

MAGPIE n black-and-white bird

MAGPIES ▶ magpie

MAGS ▶ mag

MAGSMAN n raconteur

MAGSMEN ▶ magsman

MAGUEY n tropical American agave plant

MAGUEYS ▶ maguey

MAGUS n Zoroastrian priest of the ancient Medes and Persians

MAGYAR adj of or relating to a style of sleeve cut in one piece with the bodice

MAHA n as in **maha yoga** form of yoga

MAHATMA n person revered for holiness and wisdom

MAHEWU n (in South Africa) fermented liquid mealie-meal porridge, used as a stimulant, esp by Black Africans

MAHEWUS ▶ mahewu

MAHJONG n game of Chinese origin, usually

played by four people, in which tiles bearing various designs are drawn and discarded until one player has an entire hand of winning combinations

MAHMAL n litter used in Muslim ceremony

MAHMALS ▶ mahmal

MAHOE n New Zealand tree

MAHOES ▶ mahoe

MAHONIA n Asian and American evergreen shrub cultivated for its ornamental spiny leaves and clusters of small yellow flowers

MAHOUT n (in India and the East Indies) elephant driver or keeper

MAHOUTS ▶ mahout

MAHSEER n large freshwater Indian fish

MAHSIR same as **▶ mahseer**

MAHSIRS ▶ mahsir

MAHUA n Indian tree

MAHUANG n herbal medicine from shrub

MAHUAS ▶ mahua

MAHWA same as **▶ mahua**

MAHWAS ▶ mahwa

MAHZOR same as **▶ machzor**

MAHZORS ▶ mahzor

MAID n female servant ▷ vb work as maid

MAIDAN n (in Pakistan, India, etc) an open space used for meetings, sports, etc

MAIDANS ▶ maidan

MAIDED ▶ maid

MAIDEN n young unmarried woman ▷ adj unmarried

MAIDENS ▶ maiden

MAIDING ▶ maid

MAIDISH ▶ maid

MAIDISM n pellagra

MAIDS ▶ maid

MAIGRE adj not containing flesh, and so permissible as food on days of religious abstinence ▷ n species of fish

MAIGRES ▶ maigre

MAIHEM same as **▶ mayhem**

MAIHEMS ▶ maihem

MAIK n old halfpenny

MAIKO n apprentice geisha

MAIKOS ▶ maiko

MAIKS ▶ maik

MAIL n letters and packages

transported and delivered by the post office ▷ vb send by mail

MAILBAG n large bag for transporting or delivering mail

MAILBOX n box into which letters and parcels are delivered

MAILCAR same as **▶ mailcoach**

MAILE n halfpenny

MAILED ▶ mail

MAILER n person who addresses or mails letters, etc

MAILERS ▶ mailer

MAILES ▶ maile

MAILING ▶ mail

MAILL n Scots word meaning rent

MAILLOT n tights worn for ballet, gymnastics, etc

MAILLS ▶ maill

MAILMAN n postman

MAILMEN ▶ mailman

MAILS ▶ mail

MAILVAN n vehicle to transport post

MAIM vb cripple or mutilate ▷ n injury or defect

MAIMED ▶ maim

MAIMER ▶ maim

MAIMERS ▶ maim

MAIMING ▶ maim

MAIMS ▶ malm

MAIN adj chief or principal ▷ n principal pipe or line carrying water, gas, or electricity ▷ vb lower sails

MAINED ▶ main

MAINER ▶ main

MAINEST ▶ main

MAINING ▶ main

MAINLY adv for the most part, chiefly

MAINOR n act of doing something

MAINORS ▶ mainor

MAINOUR same as **▶ mainor**

MAINS ▶ main

MAINTOP n top or platform at the head of the mainmast

MAIR Scots form of **▶ more**

MAIRE n New Zealand tree

MAIRES ▶ maire

MAIRS ▶ mair

MAISE n measure of herring

MAISES ▶ maise

MAIST Scots word for **▶ most**

MAISTER Scots word for **▶ master**

M

MAISTRY ▶ **maister**
MAISTS ▶ **maist**
MAIZE *n* type of corn with spikes of yellow grains
MAIZES ▶ **maize**
MAJAGUA *same as* ▶ **mahoe**
MAJESTY *n* stateliness or grandeur
MAJLIS *n* (in various N African and Middle Eastern countries) an assembly; council
MAJOR *adj* greater in number, quality, or extent ▷ *n* middle-ranking army officer ▷ *vb* do one's principal study in (a particular subject)
MAJORAT *n* estate, the right to which is that of the first born child of a family
MAJORED ▶ **major**
MAJORLY *adv* very
MAJORS ▶ **major**
MAK *Scots word for* ▶ **make**
MAKABLE ▶ **make**
MAKAR *same as* ▶ **maker**
MAKARS ▶ **makar**
MAKE *vb* create, construct, or establish ▷ *n* brand, type, or style
MAKER *n* person or company that makes something
MAKERS ▶ **maker**
MAKES ▶ **make**
MAKEUP *n* cosmetics, such as powder, lipstick, etc, applied to the face to improve its appearance ▷ *vb* devise, construct, or compose, sometimes with the intent to deceive
MAKEUPS ▶ **makeup**
MAKI *n* in Japanese cuisine, rice and other ingredients wrapped in a short seaweed roll
MAKING ▶ **make**
MAKINGS *pl n* potentials, qualities, or materials
MAKIS ▶ **maki**
MAKO *n* powerful shark of the Atlantic and Pacific Oceans
MAKOS ▶ **mako**
MAKS ▶ **mak**
MAKUTA *plural of* ▶ **likuta**
MAKUTU *n* Polynesian witchcraft ▷ *vb* cast a spell on
MAKUTUS ▶ **makutu**
MAL *n* illness

MALA *n* string of beads or knots, used in praying and meditating
MALACCA *n* stem of the rattan palm
MALACIA *n* pathological softening of an organ or tissue, such as bone
MALADY *n* disease or illness
MALAISE *n* something wrong which affects a section of society or area of activity
MALAM *same as* ▶ **mallam**
MALAMS ▶ **malam**
MALANGA *same as* ▶ **cocoyam**
MALAR *n* cheekbone ▷ *adj* of or relating to the cheek or cheekbone
MALARIA *n* infectious disease caused by the bite of some mosquitoes
MALARKY *same as* > **malarkey**
MALARS ▶ **malar**
MALAS ▶ **mala**
MALATE *n* any salt or ester of malic acid
MALATES ▶ **malate**
MALAX *vb* soften
MALAXED ▶ **malax**
MALAXES ▶ **malax**
MALE *adj* of the sex which can fertilize female reproductive cells ▷ *n* male person or animal
MALEATE *n* any salt or ester of maleic acid
MALEFIC *adj* causing evil
MALEIC *adj as in* **maleic acid** colourless soluble crystalline substance used to synthesize other compounds
MALES ▶ **male**
MALFED *adj* having malfunctioned
MALGRE *same as* ▶ **maugre**
MALGRED ▶ **malgre**
MALGRES ▶ **malgre**
MALI *n* member of an Indian caste
MALIBU *n as in* **malibu board** lightweight surfboard
MALIC *adj as in* **malic acid** colourless crystalline compound occurring in apples and other fruit
MALICE *n* desire to cause harm to others ▷ *vb* wish harm to

MALICED ▶ **malice**
MALICES ▶ **malice**
MALICHO *n* mischief
MALIGN *vb* slander or defame ▷ *adj* evil in influence or effect
MALIGNS ▶ **malign**
MALIK *n* person of authority in India
MALIKS ▶ **malik**
MALINE *n* stiff net
MALINES ▶ **maline**
MALIS ▶ **mali**
MALISM *n* belief that evil dominates world
MALISMS ▶ **malism**
MALISON *archaic or poetic word for* ▶ **curse**
MALIST ▶ **malism**
MALKIN *archaic or dialect name for a* ▶ **cat**
MALKINS ▶ **malkin**
MALL *n* street or shopping area closed to vehicles ▷ *vb* maul
MALLAM *n* (in Islamic W Africa) a man learned in Koranic studies
MALLAMS ▶ **mallam**
MALLARD *n* wild duck
MALLED ▶ **mall**
MALLEE *n* low-growing eucalypt in dry regions
MALLEES ▶ **mallee**
MALLEI ▶ **malleus**
MALLET *n* (wooden) hammer
MALLETS ▶ **mallet**
MALLEUS *n* outermost and largest of the three small bones in the middle ear of mammals
MALLING ▶ **mall**
MALLOW *n* plant with pink or purple flowers
MALLOWS ▶ **mallow**
MALLS ▶ **mall**
MALM *n* soft greyish limestone that crumbles easily
MALMAG *n* Asian monkey
MALMAGS ▶ **malmag**
MALMIER ▶ **malmy**
MALMS ▶ **malm**
MALMSEY *n* sweet Madeira wine
MALMY *adj* looking like malm
MALODOR *same as* > **malodour**
MALONIC *adj as in* **malonic acid** colourless crystalline compound occurring in sugar beet

MALOTI plural of ▶ **loti**

MALS ▶ **mal**

MALT n grain, such as barley, prepared for use in making beer or whisky ▷ vb make into or make with malt

MALTASE n enzyme that hydrolyses maltose and similar glucosides to glucose

MALTED ▶ **malt**

MALTEDS ▶ **malt**

MALTESE adj as in **maltese cross** cross-shaped part of a film projector

MALTHA n any of various naturally occurring mixtures of hydrocarbons, such as ozocerite

MALTHAS ▶ **maltha**

MALTIER ▶ **malty**

MALTING n building in which malt is made or stored

MALTMAN same as ▶ **maltster**

MALTMEN ▶ **maltman**

MALTOL n food additive

MALTOLS ▶ **maltol**

MALTOSE n sugar formed by the action of enzymes on starch

MALTS ▶ **malt**

MALTY adj of, like, or containing malt

MALVA n mallow plant

MALVAS ▶ **malva**

MALWA n Ugandan drink brewed from millet

MALWARE n computer program designed to cause damage or disruption to a system

MALWAS ▶ **malwa**

MAM same as ▶ **mother**

MAMA n mother

MAMAGUY vb deceive or tease, either in jest or by deceitful flattery ▷ n instance of such deception or flattery

MAMAKAU same as ▶ **mamaku**

MAMAKO same as ▶ **mamaku**

MAMAKOS ▶ **mamako**

MAMAKU n tall edible New Zealand tree fern

MAMAKUS ▶ **mamaku**

MAMAS ▶ **mama**

MAMBA n deadly S African snake

MAMBAS ▶ **mamba**

MAMBO n Latin American dance resembling the rumba ▷ vb perform this dance

MAMBOED ▶ **mambo**

MAMBOES ▶ **mambo**

MAMBOS ▶ **mambo**

MAMEE same as ▶ **mamey**

MAMEES ▶ **mamee**

MAMELON n small rounded hillock

MAMEY n tropical tree

MAMEYES ▶ **mamey**

MAMEYS ▶ **mamey**

MAMIE n tropical tree

MAMIES ▶ **mamie**

MAMILLA n nipple or teat

MAMLUK same as > **mameluke**

MAMLUKS ▶ **mamluk**

MAMMA n buxom and voluptuous woman

MAMMAE ▶ **mamma**

MAMMAL n animal of the type that suckles its young

MAMMALS ▶ **mammal**

MAMMARY adj of the breasts or milk-producing glands

MAMMAS ▶ **mamma**

MAMMATE adj having breasts

MAMMATI > **mammatus**

MAMMEE same as ▶ **mamey**

MAMMEES ▶ **mammee**

MAMMER vb hesitate

MAMMERS ▶ **mammer**

MAMMET same as ▶ **maumet**

MAMMETS ▶ **mammet**

MAMMEY same as ▶ **mamey**

MAMMEYS ▶ **mammey**

MAMMIE same as ▶ **mammy**

MAMMIES ▶ **mammy**

MAMMOCK n fragment ▷ vb tear or shred

MAMMON n wealth regarded as a source of evil

MAMMONS ▶ **mammon**

MAMMOTH n extinct elephant-like mammal ▷ adj colossal

MAMMY n Black woman employed as a nurse or servant to a White family

MAMPARA n foolish person, idiot

MAMPOER n home-distilled brandy made from peaches, prickly pears, etc

MAMS ▶ **mam**

MAMZER n child of an incestuous or adulterous union

MAMZERS ▶ **mamzer**

MAN n adult male ▷ vb supply with sufficient people for operation or defence

MANA n authority, influence

MANACLE vb handcuff or fetter ▷ n metal ring or chain put round the wrists or ankles, used to restrict the movements of a prisoner or convict

MANAGE vb succeed in doing

MANAGED ▶ **manage**

MANAGER n person in charge of a business, institution, actor, sports team, etc

MANAGES ▶ **manage**

MANAIA n common figure in Māori carving consisting of a human body and a bird like head

MANAIAS ▶ **manaia**

MANAKIN same as ▶ **manikin**

MANANA n tomorrow ▷ adv tomorrow

MANANAS ▶ **manana**

MANAS ▶ **mana**

MANAT n standard monetary unit of Azerbaijan, divided into 100 gopik

MANATEE n large tropical plant-eating aquatic mammal

MANATI same as ▶ **manatee**

MANATIS ▶ **manati**

MANATS ▶ **manat**

MANATU n large flowering deciduous New Zealand tree

MANATUS ▶ **manatu**

MANAWA in New Zealand, same as > **mangrove**

MANAWAS ▶ **manawa**

MANCALA n African and Asian board game

MANCHE n long sleeve

MANCHES ▶ **manche**

MANCHET n type of bread

MANCUS n former English coin

MAND ▶ **man**

M

MANDALA n circular design symbolizing the universe

MANDATE n official or authoritative command ▷ vb give authority to

MANDI n (in India) a big market

MANDIOC same as ▶ **manioc**

MANDIR n Hindu or Jain temple

MANDIRA same as ▶ **mandir**

MANDIRS ▶ **mandir**

MANDIS ▶ **mandi**

MANDOLA n early type of mandolin

MANDOM n mankind

MANDOMS ▶ **mandom**

MANDORA n ancestor of mandolin

MANDREL n shaft on which work is held in a lathe

MANDRIL same as ▶ **mandrel**

MANE n long hair on the neck of a horse, lion, etc

MANED ▶ **mane**

MANEGE n art of training horses and riders ▷ vb train horse

MANEGED ▶ **manege**

MANEGES ▶ **manege**

MANEH same as ▶ **mina**

MANEHS ▶ **maneh**

MANENT ▶ **manet**

MANES pl n spirits of the dead, often revered as minor deities

MANET vb theatre direction, remain on stage

MANFUL adj determined and brave

MANG vb speak

MANGA n type of Japanese comic book with an adult theme

MANGABY same as > **mangabey**

MANGAL n Turkish brazier

MANGALS ▶ **mangal**

MANGAS ▶ **manga**

MANGE n skin disease of domestic animals

MANGEAO n small New Zealand tree with glossy leaves

MANGED ▶ **mang**

MANGEL n Eurasian variety of the beet plant with a large yellowish root, cultivated as a cattle food

MANGELS ▶ **mangel**

MANGER n eating trough in a stable or barn

MANGERS ▶ **manger**

MANGES ▶ **mange**

MANGEY same as ▶ **mangy**

MANGIER ▶ **mangy**

MANGILY ▶ **mangy**

MANGING ▶ **mang**

MANGLE vb destroy by crushing and twisting ▷ n machine with rollers for squeezing water from washed clothes

MANGLED ▶ **mangle**

MANGLER ▶ **mangle**

MANGLES ▶ **mangle**

MANGO n tropical fruit with sweet juicy yellow flesh

MANGOES ▶ **mango**

MANGOLD n type of root vegetable

MANGOS ▶ **mango**

MANGS ▶ **mang**

MANGY adj having mange

MANHOLE n hole with a cover, through which a person can enter a drain or sewer

MANHOOD n state or quality of being a man or being manly

MANHUNT n organized search, usu by police, for a wanted man or a fugitive

MANI n place to pray

MANIA n extreme enthusiasm

MANIAC n mad person

MANIACS ▶ **maniac**

MANIAS ▶ **mania**

MANIC adj extremely excited or energetic ▷ n person afflicted with mania

MANICS ▶ **manic**

MANIES ▶ **many**

MANIHOC variation of ▶ **manioc**

MANIHOT n tropical American plant

MANIKIN n little man or dwarf

MANILA n strong brown paper used for envelopes

MANILAS ▶ **manila**

MANILLA n early currency in W Africa in the form of a small bracelet

MANILLE n (in ombre and quadrille) the second best trump

MANIOC same as ▶ **cassava**

MANIOCA same as ▶ **manioc**

MANIOCS ▶ **manioc**

MANIPLE n (in ancient Rome) a unit of 120 to 200 foot soldiers

MANIS n pangolin

MANITO same as ▶ **manitou**

MANITOS ▶ **manito**

MANITOU n (among the Algonquian Indians) a deified spirit or force

MANITU same as ▶ **manitou**

MANITUS ▶ **manitu**

MANJACK n single individual

MANKIER ▶ **manky**

MANKIND n human beings collectively

MANKINI n a revealing man's swimming costume

MANKY adj worthless, rotten, or in bad taste

MANLESS ▶ **man**

MANLIER ▶ **manly**

MANLIKE adj resembling or befitting a man

MANLILY ▶ **manly**

MANLY adj (possessing qualities) appropriate to a man

MANMADE adj made or produced by man

MANNA n miraculous food which sustained the Israelites in the wilderness

MANNAN n drug derived from mannose

MANNANS ▶ **mannan**

MANNAS ▶ **manna**

MANNED ▶ **man**

MANNER n way a thing happens or is done

MANNERS pl n person's social conduct viewed in the light of whether it is regarded as polite or acceptable or not

MANNING ▶ **man**

MANNISH adj (of a woman) like a man

MANNITE same as > **mannitol**

MANNOSE n hexose sugar

MANO n stone for grinding grain

MANOAO n New Zealand shrub

MANOAOS ▶ **manoao**

MANOR n large country house and its lands

MANORS ▶ **manor**

MANOS ▶ **mano**

MANPACK n load carried by one person

MANQUE *adj* would-be
MANRED *n* homage
MANREDS ▸ **manred**
MANRENT *same as*
▸ **manred**
MANROPE *n* rope railing
MANS ▸ **man**
MANSARD *n* roof with two
slopes on both sides and
both ends, the lower slopes
being steeper than the upper
MANSE *n* house provided
for a minister in some
religious denominations
MANSES ▸ **manse**
MANSION *n* large house
MANTA *n* type of large ray
with very wide winglike
pectoral fins
MANTAS ▸ **manta**
MANTEAU *n* cloak or
mantle
MANTEEL *n* cloak
MANTEL *n* structure round
a fireplace ▸ *vb* construct a
mantel
MANTELS ▸ **mantel**
MANTES ▸ **mantis**
MANTIC *adj* of or relating to
divination and prophecy
MANTID *same as* ▸ **mantis**
MANTIDS ▸ **mantid**
MANTIES ▸ **manty**
MANTIS *n* carnivorous
insect like a grasshopper
MANTLE *same as* ▸ **mantel**
MANTLED ▸ **mantle**
MANTLES ▸ **mantle**
MANTLET *same as*
> **mantelet**
MANTO *same as* ▸ **manteau**
MANTOES ▸ **manto**
MANTOS ▸ **manto**
MANTRA *n* any sacred word
or syllable used as an object
of concentration
MANTRAM *same as*
▸ **mantra**
MANTRAP *n* snare for
catching people, esp
trespassers
MANTRAS ▸ **mantra**
MANTRIC ▸ **mantra**
MANTUA *n* loose gown of
the 17th and 18th centuries,
worn open in front to show
the underskirt
MANTUAS ▸ **mantua**
MANTY *Scots variant of*
▸ **mantua**
MANUAL *adj* of or done
with the hands ▸ *n*
handbook

MANUALS ▸ **manual**
MANUARY *same as*
▸ **manual**
MANUKA *n* New Zealand
tree with strong elastic
wood and aromatic leaves
MANUKAS ▸ **manuka**
MANUL *n* Asian wildcat
MANULS ▸ **manul**
MANUMEA *n* pigeon of
Samoa
MANUMIT *vb* free from
slavery
MANURE *n* animal
excrement used as a
fertilizer ▸ *vb* fertilize
(land) with this
MANURED ▸ **manure**
MANURER ▸ **manure**
MANURES ▸ **manure**
MANUS *n* wrist and hand
MANWARD *adv* towards
humankind
MANWISE *adv* in human
way
MANY *adj* numerous ▸ *n*
large number
MANYATA *same as*
> **manyatta**
MAOMAO *n* fish of New
Zealand seas
MAOMAOS ▸ **maomao**
MAORMOR *same as*
▸ **mormaor**
MAP *n* representation of the
earth's surface or some part
of it, showing geographical
features ▸ *vb* make a map of
MAPAU *n* small New
Zealand tree with reddish
bark, aromatic leaves, and
dark berries
MAPAUS ▸ **mapau**
MAPLE *n* tree with broad
leaves, a variety of which
yields sugar
MAPLES ▸ **maple**
MAPLESS ▸ **map**
MAPLIKE ▸ **map**
MAPPED ▸ **map**
MAPPER ▸ **map**
MAPPERS ▸ **map**
MAPPERY *n* making of
maps
MAPPING ▸ **map**
MAPPIST ▸ **map**
MAPS ▸ **map**
MAPWISE *adv* like map
MAQUI *n* Chilean shrub
MAQUILA *n* US-owned
factory in Mexico
MAQUIS *n* French
underground movement

that fought against the
German occupying forces in
World War II
MAR *vb* spoil or impair ▸ *n*
disfiguring mark
MARA *n* harelike S American
rodent inhabiting the
pampas of Argentina
MARABI *n* kind of music
popular in S African
townships in the 1930s
MARABIS ▸ **marabi**
MARABOU *n* large
black-and-white African
stork
MARACA *n* shaken
percussion instrument
made from a gourd
containing dried seeds etc
MARACAS ▸ **maraca**
MARAE *n* enclosed space in
front of a Māori meeting
house
MARAES ▸ **marae**
MARAH *n* bitterness
MARAHS ▸ **marah**
MARANTA *n* tropical
American plant, some
species of which are grown
as pot plants for their
showy variegated leaves
MARARI *n* eel-like blennoid
food fish
MARARIS ▸ **marari**
MARAS ▸ **mara**
MARASCA *n* European
cherry tree with red
acid-tasting fruit from
which maraschino is made
MARAUD *vb* wander or raid
in search of plunder
MARAUDS ▸ **maraud**
MARBLE *n* kind of limestone
with a mottled appearance,
which can be highly
polished ▸ *vb* mottle with
variegated streaks in
imitation of marble
MARBLED ▸ **marble**
MARBLER ▸ **marble**
MARBLES *n* game in which
marble balls are rolled at
one another
MARBLY ▸ **marble**
MARC *n* remains of grapes
or other fruit that have
been pressed for
wine-making
MARCATO *adj* (of notes)
heavily accented ▸ *adv*
with each note heavily
accented ▸ *n* a heavily
accented note

M

MARCEL n hairstyle characterized by repeated regular waves, popular in the 1920s ▷ vb make such waves in (the hair) with special hot irons
MARCELS ▶ marcel
MARCH vb walk with a military step ▷ n action of marching
MARCHED ▶ march
MARCHEN n German story
MARCHER n person who marches
MARCHES ▶ march
MARCONI vb communicate by wireless
MARCS ▶ marc
MARD ▶ mar
MARDIED ▶ mardy
MARDIER ▶ mardy
MARDIES ▶ mardy
MARDY adj (of a child) spoilt ▷ vb behave in mardy way
MARE n female horse or zebra
MAREMMA n marshy unhealthy region near the shore, esp in Italy
MAREMME ▶ maremma
MARENGO adj browned in oil and cooked with tomatoes, mushrooms, garlic, wine, etc
MARERO n member of a C American organized criminal gang
MAREROS ▶ marero
MARES ▶ mare
MARG short for > margarine
MARGAY n feline mammal of Central and S America with a dark-striped coat
MARGAYS ▶ margay
MARGE n margarine
MARGENT same as ▶ margin
MARGES ▶ marge
MARGIN n edge or border ▷ vb provide with a margin
MARGINS ▶ margin
MARGOSA n Indian tree
MARGS ▶ marg
MARIA ▶ mare
MARID n spirit in Muslim mythology
MARIDS ▶ marid
MARIES ▶ mary
MARIMBA n Latin American percussion instrument resembling a xylophone
MARINA n harbour for yachts and other pleasure boats

MARINAS ▶ marina
MARINE adj of the sea or shipping ▷ n (esp in Britain and the US) soldier trained for land and sea combat
MARINER n sailor
MARINES ▶ marine
MARISH n marsh
MARITAL adj relating to marriage
MARK n line, dot, scar, etc visible on a surface ▷ vb make a mark on
MARKA n unit of currency introduced as an interim currency in Bosnia-Herzegovina
MARKAS ▶ marka
MARKED adj noticeable
MARKER n object used to show the position of something
MARKERS ▶ marker
MARKET n assembly or place for buying and selling ▷ vb offer or produce for sale
MARKETS ▶ market
MARKHOR n large wild Himalayan goat with a reddish-brown coat and large spiralled horns
MARKING n arrangement of colours on an animal or plant
MARKKA n former standard monetary unit of Finland, divided into 100 penniä
MARKKAA ▶ markka
MARKKAS ▶ markka
MARKMAN n person owning land
MARKMEN ▶ markman
MARKS ▶ mark
MARKUP n percentage or amount added to the cost of a commodity to provide the seller with a profit and to cover overheads, costs, etc
MARKUPS ▶ markup
MARL n soil formed of clay and lime, used as fertilizer ▷ vb fertilize (land) with marl
MARLE same as ▶ marvel
MARLED ▶ marl
MARLES ▶ marle
MARLIER ▶ marly
MARLIN same as ▶ marline
MARLINE n light rope, usually tarred, made of two strands laid left-handed

MARLING same as ▶ marline
MARLINS ▶ marlin
MARLITE n type of marl that contains clay and calcium carbonate and is resistant to the decomposing action of air
MARLS ▶ marl
MARLY adj marl-like
MARM same as ▶ madam
MARMEM n as in marmem alloy type of alloy
MARMITE n large cooking pot
MARMOSE n South American opossum
MARMOT n burrowing rodent
MARMOTS ▶ marmot
MARMS ▶ marm
MARON n freshwater crustacean
MARONS ▶ maron
MAROON adj reddish-purple ▷ vb abandon ashore, esp on an island ▷ n exploding firework or flare used as a warning signal
MAROONS ▶ maroon
MAROR n Jewish ceremonial dish of bitter herbs
MARORS ▶ maror
MARPLOT n person interfering with plot
MARQUE n brand of product, esp of a car
MARQUEE n large tent used for a party or exhibition
MARQUES ▶ marque
MARQUIS n (in some European countries) nobleman of the rank above a count
MARRAM n as in marram grass any of several grasses of the genus that grow on sandy shores and can withstand drying
MARRAMS ▶ marram
MARRANO n Spanish or Portuguese Jew of the late Middle Ages who was converted to Christianity, esp one forcibly converted but secretly adhering to Judaism
MARRED ▶ mar
MARRELS same as ▶ merils
MARRER ▶ mar
MARRERS ▶ mar
MARRI n W Australian

eucalyptus widely cultivated for its coloured flowers

MARRIED ▶ marry

MARRIER ▶ marry

MARRIES ▶ marry

MARRING ▶ mar

MARRIS ▶ marri

MARRON n large edible sweet chestnut

MARRONS ▶ marron

MARROW n fatty substance inside bones ▷ vb be mate to

MARROWS ▶ marrow

MARROWY ▶ marrow

MARRUM same as ▶ marram

MARRUMS ▶ marrum

MARRY vb take as a husband or wife ▷ interj exclamation of surprise or anger

MARS ▶ mar

MARSALA n dark sweet dessert wine made in Sicily

MARSE same as ▶ master

MARSES ▶ marse

MARSH n low-lying wet land

MARSHAL n officer of the highest rank ▷ vb arrange in order

MARSHES ▶ marsh

MARSHY adj of, involving, or like a marsh

MART n market ▷ vb sell or trade

MARTED ▶ mart

MARTEL n hammer-shaped weapon ▷ vb use such a weapon

MARTELS ▶ martel

MARTEN n weasel-like animal

MARTENS ▶ marten

MARTEXT n preacher who makes many mistakes

MARTIAL adj of war, warlike

MARTIAN n inhabitant of Mars

MARTIN n bird with a slightly forked tail

MARTING ▶ mart

MARTINI n cocktail of vermouth and gin

MARTINS ▶ martin

MARTLET n footless bird often found in coats of arms, standing for either a martin or a swallow

MARTS ▶ mart

MARTYR n person who dies

or suffers for his or her beliefs ▷ vb make a martyr of

MARTYRS ▶ martyr

MARTYRY n shrine or chapel erected in honour of a martyr

MARVEL vb be filled with wonder ▷ n wonderful thing

MARVELS ▶ marvel

MARVER vb roll molten glass on slab

MARVERS ▶ marver

MARVIER ▶ marvy

MARVY shortened form of > marvelous

MARY n woman

MARYBUD n bud of marigold

MAS ▶ ma

MASA n Mexican maize dough

MASALA n mixture of spices ground into a paste ▷ adj spicy

MASALAS ▶ masala

MASAS ▶ masa

MASCARA n cosmetic for darkening the eyelashes

MASCLE n charge consisting of a lozenge with a lozenge-shaped hole in the middle

MASCLED ▶ mascle

MASCLES ▶ mascle

MASCON n any of several lunar regions of high gravity

MASCONS ▶ mascon

MASCOT n person, animal, or thing supposed to bring good luck

MASCOTS ▶ mascot

MASCULY ▶ mascle

MASE vb function as maser

MASED ▶ mase

MASER n device for amplifying microwaves

MASERS ▶ maser

MASES ▶ mase

MASH n soft pulpy mass ▷ vb crush into a soft mass

MASHED ▶ mash

MASHER ▶ mash

MASHERS ▶ mash

MASHES ▶ mash

MASHIE n (formerly) a club, corresponding to the modern No. 5 or No. 6 iron, used for approach shots

MASHIER ▶ mashy

MASHIES ▶ mashie

MASHING ▶ mash

MASHLAM same as ▶ maslin

MASHLIM same as ▶ maslin

MASHLIN same as ▶ maslin

MASHLUM same as ▶ maslin

MASHMAN n brewery worker

MASHMEN ▶ mashman

MASHUA n South American plant

MASHUAS ▶ mashua

MASHUP n piece of recorded or live music in which a producer or DJ blends together two or more tracks, often of contrasting genres

MASHUPS ▶ mashup

MASHY adj like mash

MASING ▶ mase

MASJID same as ▶ mosque

MASJIDS ▶ masjid

MASK n covering for the face, as a disguise or protection ▷ vb cover with a mask

MASKED adj disguised or covered by or as if by a mask

MASKEG n North American bog

MASKEGS ▶ maskeg

MASKER n person who wears a mask or takes part in a masque

MASKERS ▶ masker

MASKING n act or practice of masking

MASKS ▶ mask

MASLIN n mixture of wheat, rye or other grain

MASLINS ▶ maslin

MASON n person who works with stone ▷ vb construct or strengthen with masonry

MASONED ▶ mason

MASONIC adj of, characteristic of, or relating to Freemasons or Freemasonry

MASONRY n stonework

MASONS ▶ mason

MASQUE n 16th–17th-century form of dramatic entertainment

MASQUER same as ▶ masker

MASQUES ▶ masque

MASS n coherent body of matter ▷ adj large-scale ▷ vb form into a mass

M

MASSA *old fashioned variant of* ▶ **master**

MASSAGE *n* rubbing and kneading of parts of the body to reduce pain or stiffness ▷ *vb* give a massage to

MASSAS ▶ **massa**

MASSE *n* stroke made by hitting the cue ball off centre with the cue held nearly vertically, esp so as to make the ball move in a curve around another ball before hitting the object ball

MASSED ▶ **mass**

MASSES *pl n* body of common people

MASSEUR *n* person who gives massages

MASSIER ▶ **massy**

MASSIF *n* connected group of mountains

MASSIFS ▶ **massif**

MASSING ▶ **mass**

MASSIVE *adj* large and heavy ▷ *n* group of friends or associates

MASSY *literary word for* ▶ **massive**

MAST *n* tall pole for supporting something, esp a ship's sails

MASTABA *n* mud-brick superstructure above tombs in ancient Egypt

MASTED ▶ **mast**

MASTER *n* person in control, such as an employer or an owner of slaves or animals ▷ *vb* acquire knowledge of or skill in

MASTERS ▶ **master**

MASTERY *n* expertise

MASTFUL ▶ **mast**

MASTIC *n* gum obtained from certain trees

MASTICH *same as* ▶ **mastic**

MASTICS ▶ **mastic**

MASTIER ▶ **mast**

MASTIFF *n* large dog

MASTING ▶ **mast**

MASTIX *n* type of gum

MASTOID *n* projection of the bone behind the ear ▷ *adj* shaped like a nipple or breast

MASTS ▶ **mast**

MASTY ▶ **mast**

MASU *n* Japanese salmon

MASULA *same as*

> **masoolah**

MASULAS ▶ **masula**

MASUS ▶ **masu**

MAT *n* piece of fabric used as a floor covering or to protect a surface ▷ *vb* tangle or become tangled into a dense mass ▷ *adj* having a dull, lustreless, or roughened surface

MATADOR *n* man who kills the bull in bullfights

MATAI *n* New Zealand tree, the wood of which is used for timber for building

MATAIS ▶ **matai**

MATATA *same as* > **fernbird**

MATATAS ▶ **matata**

MATATU *n* type of shared taxi used in Kenya

MATATUS ▶ **matatu**

MATCH *n* contest in a game or sport ▷ *vb* be exactly like, equal to, or in harmony with

MATCHED ▶ **match**

MATCHER ▶ **match**

MATCHES ▶ **match**

MATCHET *same as* ▶ **machete**

MATCHUP *n* sports match

MATE *n* friend ▷ *vb* pair (animals) or (of animals) be paired for reproduction

MATED ▶ **mate**

MATELOT *n* sailor

MATER *n* mother: often used facetiously

MATERS ▶ **mater**

MATES ▶ **mate**

MATEY *adj* friendly or intimate ▷ *n* friend or fellow: usually used in direct address

MATEYS ▶ **matey**

MATH *same as* ▶ **maths**

MATHS *same as* ▶ **math**

MATICO *n* Peruvian shrub

MATICOS ▶ **matico**

MATIER ▶ **maty**

MATIES ▶ **maty**

MATIEST ▶ **maty**

MATILDA *n* bushman's swag

MATILY ▶ **maty**

MATIN *adj* of or relating to matins

MATINAL *same as* ▶ **matin**

MATINEE *n* afternoon performance in a theatre or cinema

MATING ▶ **mate**

MATINGS ▶ **mate**

MATINS *pl n* early morning service in various Christian Churches

MATIPO *n* New Zealand shrub

MATIPOS ▶ **matipo**

MATJES *same as* ▶ **maatjes**

MATLESS ▶ **mat**

MATLO *same as* ▶ **matelot**

MATLOS ▶ **matlo**

MATLOW *same as* ▶ **matelot**

MATLOWS ▶ **matlow**

MATOKE *n* (in Uganda) the flesh of bananas, boiled and mashed as a food

MATOKES ▶ **matoke**

MATOOKE *same as* ▶ **matoke**

MATRASS *n* long-necked glass flask, used for distilling, dissolving substances, etc

MATRES ▶ **mater**

MATRIC *n* matriculation

MATRICE *same as* ▶ **matrix**

MATRICS ▶ **matric**

MATRIX *n* substance or situation in which something takes form, or is enclosed

MATRON *n* staid or dignified married woman

MATRONS ▶ **matron**

MATROSS *n* gunner's assistant

MATS ▶ **mat**

MATSAH *same as* ▶ **matzo**

MATSAHS ▶ **matsah**

MATSURI *n* Japanese religious ceremony

MATT *adj* dull, not shiny

MATTE *same as* ▶ **matt**

MATTED ▶ **mat**

MATTER *n* substance of which something is made ▷ *vb* be of importance

MATTERS ▶ **matter**

MATTERY *adj* discharging pus

MATTES ▶ **matte**

MATTIE *n* young herring

MATTIES ▶ **mattie**

MATTIFY *vb* make (the skin of the face) less oily or shiny using cosmetics

MATTIN *same as* ▶ **matin**

MATTING ▶ **mat**

MATTINS *same as* ▶ **matins**

MATTOCK *n* large pick with one of its blade ends flattened for loosening soil

MATTOID *n* person

displaying eccentric behaviour and mental characteristics that approach the psychotic

MATTS ▶ matt

MATURE adj fully developed or grown-up ▷ vb make or become mature

MATURED ▶ mature

MATURER ▶ mature

MATURES ▶ mature

MATWEED n grass found on moors

MATY same as ▶ matey

MATZA same as ▶ matzo

MATZAH same as ▶ matzo

MATZAHS ▶ matzah

MATZAS ▶ matza

MATZO n large very thin biscuit of unleavened bread, traditionally eaten by Jews during Passover

MATZOH same as ▶ matzo

MATZOHS ▶ matzoh

MATZOON n fermented milk product similar to yogurt

MATZOS ▶ matzo

MATZOT ▶ matzo

MATZOTH ▶ matzo

MAUBIES ▶ mauby

MAUBY n (in the E Caribbean) a bittersweet drink made from the bark of a rhamnaceous tree

MAUD n shawl or rug of grey wool plaid formerly worn in Scotland

MAUDLIN adj foolishly or tearfully sentimental

MAUDS ▶ maud

MAUGER same as ▶ maugre

MAUGRE prep in spite of ▷ vb behave spitefully towards

MAUGRED ▶ maugre

MAUGRES ▶ maugre

MAUL vb handle roughly ▷ n loose scrum

MAULED ▶ maul

MAULER ▶ maul

MAULERS pl n hands

MAULGRE same as ▶ maugre

MAULING ▶ maul

MAULS ▶ maul

MAULVI n expert in Islamic law

MAULVIS ▶ maulvi

MAUMET n false god

MAUMETS ▶ maumet

MAUN dialect word for ▶ must

MAUND n unit of weight used in Asia, esp India, having different values in different localities. A common value in India is 82 pounds or 37 kilograms ▷ vb beg

MAUNDED ▶ maund

MAUNDER vb talk or act aimlessly or idly

MAUNDS ▶ maund

MAUNDY n ceremonial washing of the feet of poor persons in commemoration of Jesus' washing of his disciples' feet (John 13:4–34) re-enacted in some churches on Maundy Thursday

MAUNGY adj (esp of a child) sulky, bad-tempered, or peevish

MAUNNA vb Scots term meaning must not

MAURI n soul

MAURIS ▶ mauri

MAUT same as ▶ mahout

MAUTHER n girl

MAUTS ▶ maut

MAUVAIS adj bad

MAUVE adj pale purple ▷ n any of various pale to moderate pinkish-purple or bluish-purple colours

MAUVEIN same as ▷ mauveine

MAUVER ▶ mauve

MAUVES ▶ mauve

MAUVEST ▶ mauve

MAUVIN same as ▷ mauveine

MAUVINE same as ▷ mauveine

MAUVINS ▶ mauvin

MAVEN n expert or connoisseur

MAVENS ▶ maven

MAVIE n type of thrush

MAVIES ▶ mavie

MAVIN same as ▶ maven

MAVINS ▶ mavin

MAVIS n song thrush

MAVISES ▶ mavis

MAW n animal's mouth, throat, or stomach ▷ vb eat or bite

MAWED ▶ maw

MAWGER adj (of persons or animals) thin or lean

MAWING ▶ maw

MAWK n maggot

MAWKIER ▶ mawk

MAWKIN n slovenly woman

MAWKINS ▶ mawkin

MAWKISH adj foolishly sentimental

MAWKS ▶ mawk

MAWKY ▶ mawk

MAWMET same as ▶ maumet

MAWMETS ▶ mawmet

MAWN ▶ maw

MAWPUS same as ▶ mopus

MAWR same as ▶ mauther

MAWRS ▶ mawr

MAWS ▶ maw

MAWSEED n poppy seed

MAWTHER same as ▶ mauther

MAX vb reach the full extent

> Max is a short form of **maximum**, and can also be a verb giving **maxed, maxes** and **maxing**. Another of the key words using X, and it can be extended to **maxi**.

MAXED ▶ max

MAXES ▶ max

MAXI adj (of a garment) very long ▷ n type of large racing yacht

MAXILLA n upper jawbone of a vertebrate

MAXIM n general truth or principle

MAXIMA ▶ maximum

MAXIMAL adj maximum ▷ n maximum

MAXIMIN n highest of a set of minimum values

MAXIMS ▶ maxim

MAXIMUM n greatest possible (amount or number) ▷ adj of, being, or showing a maximum or maximums

MAXIMUS n method rung on twelve bells

MAXING ▶ max

MAXIS ▶ maxi

MAXIXE n Brazilian dance in duple time, a precursor of the tango

MAXIXES ▶ maxixe

MAXWELL n cgs unit of magnetic flux

MAY vb used as an auxiliary to express possibility, permission, opportunity, etc ▷ vb gather may

MAYA n illusion, esp the material world of the senses regarded as illusory

MAYAN ▶ maya

MAYAS ▶ maya

M

MAYBE adv perhaps, possibly ▷ sentence substitute possibly

MAYBES ▶ maybe

MAYBIRD n American songbird

MAYBUSH n flowering shrub

MAYDAY n international radiotelephone distress signal

MAYDAYS ▶ mayday

MAYED ▶ may

MAYEST same as ▶ mayst

MAYFLY n short-lived aquatic insect

MAYHAP archaic word for ▶ perhaps

MAYHEM n violent destruction or confusion

MAYHEMS ▶ mayhem

MAYING ▶ may

MAYINGS ▶ maying

MAYO n mayonnaise

MAYOR n head of a municipality

MAYORAL ▶ mayor

MAYORS ▶ mayor

MAYOS ▶ mayo

MAYPOLE n pole set up for dancing round on the first day of May to celebrate spring

MAYPOP n American wild flower

MAYPOPS ▶ maypop

MAYS ▶ may

MAYST singular form of the present tense of ▶ may

MAYSTER same as ▶ master

MAYVIN same as ▶ maven

MAYVINS ▶ mayvin

MAYWEED n widespread Eurasian weedy plant, having evil-smelling leaves and daisy-like flower heads

MAZARD same as ▶ mazer

MAZARDS ▶ mazard

MAZE n complex network of paths or lines designed to puzzle

MAZED ▶ maze

MAZEDLY adv in a bewildered way

MAZEFUL ▶ maze

MAZER n large hardwood drinking bowl

MAZERS ▶ mazer

MAZES ▶ maze

MAZEY adj dizzy

MAZHBI n low-caste Sikh

MAZHBIS ▶ mazhbi

MAZIER ▶ mazy

MAZIEST ▶ mazy

MAZILY ▶ mazy

MAZING ▶ maze

MAZOUT same as ▶ mazut

MAZOUTS ▶ mazout

MAZUMA n money

MAZUMAS ▶ mazuma

MAZURKA n lively Polish dance

MAZUT n residue left after distillation of petrol

MAZUTS ▶ mazut

MAZY adj of or like a maze

MAZZARD same as ▶ mazard

MBIRA n African musical instrument consisting of tuned metal strips attached to a resonating box, which are plucked with the thumbs

MBIRAS ▶ mbira

ME n (in tonic sol-fa) third degree of any major scale ▷ pron refers to the speaker or writer

MEACOCK n timid person

MEAD n alcoholic drink made from honey

MEADOW n piece of grassland

MEADOWS ▶ meadow

MEADOWY ▶ meadow

MEADS ▶ mead

MEAGER same as ▶ meagre

MEAGRE adj scanty or insufficient ▷ n Mediterranean fish

MEAGRER ▶ meagre

MEAGRES ▶ meagre

MEAL n occasion when food is served and eaten ▷ vb cover with meal

MEALED ▶ meal

MEALER n person eating but not lodging at boarding house

MEALERS ▶ mealer

MEALIE n maize

MEALIER ▶ mealy

MEALIES South African word for ▶ maize

MEALING ▶ meal

MEALS ▶ meal

MEALY adj resembling meal

MEAN vb intend to convey or express ▷ adj miserly, ungenerous, or petty ▷ n middle point between two extremes

MEANDER vb follow a winding course ▷ n winding course

MEANE vb moan

MEANED ▶ meane

MEANER ▶ mean

MEANERS ▶ mean

MEANES ▶ meane

MEANEST ▶ mean

MEANIE n unkind or miserly person

MEANIES ▶ meany

MEANING n what something means

MEANLY ▶ mean

MEANS ▶ mean

MEANT ▶ mean

MEANY same as ▶ meanie

MEARE same as ▶ mere

MEARES ▶ meare

MEARING adj forming boundary

MEASE vb assuage

MEASED ▶ mease

MEASES ▶ mease

MEASING ▶ mease

MEASLE vb infect with measles

MEASLED adj (of cattle, sheep, or pigs) infested with tapeworm larvae

MEASLES n infectious disease producing red spots

MEASLY adj meagre

MEASURE n size or quantity ▷ vb determine the size or quantity of

MEAT n animal flesh as food

MEATAL ▶ meatus

MEATAXE n meat cleaver

MEATED adj fattened

MEATH same as ▶ mead

MEATHE same as ▶ mead

MEATHES ▶ meathe

MEATHS ▶ meath

MEATIER ▶ meaty

MEATILY ▶ meaty

MEATMAN n meat seller

MEATMEN ▶ meatman

MEATS ▶ meat

MEATUS n natural opening or channel, such as the canal leading from the outer ear to the eardrum

MEATY adj (tasting) of or like meat

MEAWES same as ▶ mews

MEAZEL same as ▶ mesel

MEAZELS ▶ meazel

MEBOS n South African dish of dried apricots

MEBOSES ▶ mebos

MECCA n place that attracts many visitors

MECCAS ▶ mecca

MECK same as ▶ maik

MECKS ▸ meck
MECONIC adj derived from poppies
MECONIN n substance found in opium
MED n doctor
MEDACCA n Japanese freshwater fish
MEDAKA same as ▸ medacca
MEDAKAS ▸ medaka
MEDAL n piece of metal with an inscription etc, given as a reward or memento ▷ vb honour with a medal
MEDALED ▸ medal
MEDALET n small medal
MEDALS ▸ medal
MEDDLE vb interfere annoyingly
MEDDLED ▸ meddle
MEDDLER ▸ meddle
MEDDLES ▸ meddle
MEDEVAC n evacuation of casualties from forward areas to the nearest hospital or base ▷ vb transport (a wounded or sick person) to hospital by medevac
MEDFLY n Mediterranean fruit fly
MEDIA n a medium of cultivation, conveyance, or expression
MEDIACY n quality or state of being mediate
MEDIAD adj situated near the median line or plane of an organism
MEDIAE ▸ medium
MEDIAL adj of or in the middle ▷ n speech sound between being fortis and lenis
MEDIALS ▸ medial
MEDIAN n middle (point or line) ▷ adj of, relating to, situated in, or directed towards the middle
MEDIANS ▸ median
MEDIANT n third degree of a major or minor scale
MEDIAS ▸ media
MEDIATE vb intervene in a dispute to bring about agreement ▷ adj occurring as a result of or dependent upon mediation
MEDIC n doctor or medical student
MEDICAL adj of the science

of medicine ▷ n medical examination
MEDICK n type of small leguminous plant with yellow or purple flowers and trifoliate leaves
MEDICKS ▸ medick
MEDICO n doctor or medical student
MEDICOS ▸ medico
MEDICS ▸ medic
MEDIGAP n private health insurance
MEDII ▸ medius
MEDINA n ancient quarter of any of various North African cities
MEDINAS ▸ medina
MEDIUM adj midway between extremes, average ▷ n middle state, degree, or condition
MEDIUMS pl n medium-dated gilt-edged securities
MEDIUS n middle finger
MEDIVAC variant spelling of ▸ medevac
MEDLAR n apple-like fruit of a small tree, eaten when it begins to decay
MEDLARS ▸ medlar
MEDLE same as ▸ meddle
MEDLED ▸ medle
MEDLES ▸ medle
MEDLEY n miscellaneous mixture ▷ adj of, being, or relating to a mixture or variety
MEDLEYS ▸ medley
MEDLING ▸ medle
MEDRESA > madrasah
MEDRESE same as > madrasah
MEDS ▸ med
MEDULLA n marrow, pith, or inner tissue
MEDUSA n jellyfish
MEDUSAE ▸ medusa
MEDUSAL ▸ medusa
MEDUSAN ▸ medusa
MEDUSAS ▸ medusa
MEE n Malaysian noodle dish
MEED n recompense
MEEDS ▸ meed
MEEK adj submissive or humble
MEEKEN vb make meek
MEEKENS ▸ meeken
MEEKER ▸ meek
MEEKEST ▸ meek
MEEKLY ▸ meek
MEEMIE n hysterical person

MEEMIES ▸ meemie
MEER same as ▸ mere
MEERCAT same as ▸ meerkat
MEERED ▸ meer
MEERING ▸ meer
MEERKAT n S African mongoose
MEERS ▸ meer
MEES ▸ mee
MEET vb come together (with) ▷ n meeting, esp a sports meeting ▷ adj fit or suitable
MEETER ▸ meet
MEETERS ▸ meet
MEETEST ▸ meet
MEETING ▸ meet
MEETLY ▸ meet
MEETS ▸ meet
MEFF dialect word for ▸ tramp
MEFFS ▸ meff
MEG short for > megabyte
MEGA adj extremely good, great, or successful
MEGABAR n unit of million bars
MEGABIT n one million bits
MEGAFOG n amplified fog signal
MEGAHIT n great success
MEGAPOD same as > megapode
MEGARA ▸ megaron
MEGARAD n unit of million rads
MEGARON n tripartite rectangular room containing a central hearth surrounded by four pillars, found in Bronze Age Greece and Asia Minor
MEGASS another name for ▸ bagasse
MEGASSE same as ▸ megass
MEGATON n explosive power equal to that of one million tons of TNT
MEGILLA same as > megillah
MEGILP n oil-painting medium of linseed oil mixed with mastic varnish or turpentine
MEGILPH same as ▸ megilp
MEGILPS ▸ megilp
MEGOHM n one million ohms
MEGOHMS ▸ megohm
MEGRIM n caprice
MEGRIMS n fit of depression

M

MEGS ▸ meg
MEH *interj* expression of indifference or boredom
MEHNDI *n* (esp in India) the practice of painting designs on the hands, feet, etc using henna
MEHNDIS ▸ mehndi
MEIKLE *adj* Scots word meaning large
MEIN Scots word for ▸ moan
MEINED ▸ mein
MEINEY same as ▸ meiny
MEINEYS ▸ meiney
MEINIE same as ▸ meiny
MEINIES ▸ meiny
MEINING ▸ mein
MEINS ▸ mein
MEINT same as ▸ ming
MEINY *n* retinue or household
MEIOSES ▸ meiosis
MEIOSIS *n* type of cell division in which reproductive cells are produced, each containing half the chromosome number of the parent nucleus
MEIOTIC ▸ meiosis
MEISHI *n* business card in Japan
MEISHIS ▸ meishi
MEISTER *n* person who excels at a particular activity
MEITH *n* landmark
MEITHS ▸ meith
MEJLIS same as ▸ majlis
MEKKA same as ▸ mecca
MEKKAS ▸ mekka
MEL *n* pure form of honey formerly used in pharmaceutical products
MELA *n* Asian cultural or religious fair or festival
MELAMED *n* Hebrew teacher
MELANGE *n* mixture
MELANIC *adj* relating to melanism or melanosis ▷ *n* darker form of creature
MELANIN *n* dark pigment found in the hair, skin, and eyes of humans and animals
MELANO *n* person with abnormally dark skin
MELANOS ▸ melano
MELAS ▸ mela
MELBA *adj* relating to a type of dessert sauce or toast
MELD *vb* merge or blend ▷ *n* act of melding

MELDED ▸ meld
MELDER ▸ meld
MELDERS ▸ meld
MELDING ▸ meld
MELDS ▸ meld
MELEE *n* noisy confused fight or crowd
MELEES ▸ melee
MELENA *n* excrement or vomit stained by blood
MELENAS ▸ melena
MELIC *adj* (of poetry, esp ancient Greek lyric poems) intended to be sung ▷ *n* type of grass
MELICK *n* either of two pale green perennial grasses
MELICKS ▸ melick
MELICS ▸ melic
MELIK same as ▸ malik
MELIKS ▸ melik
MELILOT *n* Old World leguminous plant with narrow clusters of small white or yellow fragrant flowers
MELISMA *n* expressive vocal phrase or passage consisting of several notes sung to one syllable
MELL *vb* mix
MELLAY same as ▸ melee
MELLAYS ▸ mellay
MELLED ▸ mell
MELLING ▸ mell
MELLITE *n* soft yellow mineral
MELLOW *adj* soft, not harsh ▷ *vb* make or become mellow
MELLOWS ▸ mellow
MELLOWY same as ▸ mellow
MELLS ▸ mell
MELODIA same as > melodica
MELODIC *adj* of melody
MELODY *n* series of musical notes which make a tune
MELOID *n* type of long-legged beetle of the family which includes the blister beetles and oil beetles
MELOIDS ▸ meloid
MELON *n* large round juicy fruit with a hard rind
MELONS ▸ melon
MELS ▸ mel
MELT *vb* (cause to) become liquid by heat ▷ *n* act or process of melting
MELTAGE *n* process or result

of melting or the amount melted
MELTED ▸ melt
MELTEMI *n* northerly wind in the northeast Mediterranean
MELTER ▸ melt
MELTERS ▸ melt
MELTIER ▸ melty
MELTING ▸ melt
MELTITH *n* meal
MELTON *n* heavy smooth woollen fabric with a short nap, used esp for overcoats
MELTONS ▸ melton
MELTS ▸ melt
MELTY *adj* tending to melt
MEM *n* 13th letter in the Hebrew alphabet, transliterated as *m*
MEMBER *n* individual making up a body or society ▷ *adj* (of a (country or group) belonging to an organization or alliance
MEMBERS ▸ member
MEMBRAL *adj* of limbs
MEME *n* idea or element of social behaviour (passed on through generations in a culture, esp by imitation
MEMENTO *n* thing serving to remind, souvenir
MEMES ▸ meme
MEMETIC *adj* of or relating to a meme
MEMO *n* memorandum
MEMOIR *n* biography or historical account based on personal knowledge
MEMOIRS *pl n* collection of reminiscences about a period or series of events, written from personal experience
MEMORY *n* ability to remember
MEMOS ▸ memo
MEMS ▸ mem
MEN ▸ man
MENACE *n* threat ▷ *vb* threaten, endanger
MENACED ▸ menace
MENACER ▸ menace
MENACES ▸ menace
MENAD same as ▸ maenad
MENADS ▸ menad
MENAGE old form of ▸ manage
MENAGED ▸ menage
MENAGES ▸ menage
MENAZON *n* type of insecticide

MEND vb repair or patch ▷ n mended area

MENDED ▶ mend

MENDER ▶ mend

MENDERS ▶ mend

MENDIGO n Spanish beggar or vagrant

MENDING n something to be mended, esp clothes

MENDS ▶ mend

MENE Scots form of ▶ moan

MENED ▶ mene

MENEER n S African title of address

MENEERS ▶ meneer

MENES ▶ mene

MENFOLK pl n men collectively, esp the men of a particular family

MENG vb mix

MENGE same as ▶ meng

MENGED ▶ meng

MENGES ▶ menge

MENGING ▶ meng

MENGS ▶ meng

MENHIR n single upright prehistoric stone

MENHIRS ▶ menhir

MENIAL adj involving boring work of low status ▷ n person with a menial job

MENIALS ▶ menial

MENING ▶ mene

MENINX n one of three membranes that envelop the brain and spinal cord

MENISCI > meniscus

MENO adv (esp preceding a dynamic or tempo marking) to be played less quickly, less softly, etc

MENORAH n seven-branched candelabrum used as an emblem of Judaism

MENSA n faint constellation in the S hemisphere lying between Hydrus and Volans and containing part of the Large Magellanic Cloud

MENSAE n star of the mensa constellation

MENSAL adj monthly

MENSAS ▶ mensa

MENSCH n decent person

MENSCHY ▶ mensch

MENSE vb grace

MENSED ▶ mense

MENSES n menstruation

MENSH vb mention

MENSHED ▶ mensh

MENSHEN n Chinese door god

MENSHES ▶ mensh

MENSING ▶ mense

MENSUAL same as ▶ mensal

MENT same as ▶ ming

MENTA ▶ mentum

MENTAL adj of, in, or done by the mind

MENTEE n person trained by mentor

MENTEES ▶ mentee

MENTHOL n organic compound found in peppermint, used medicinally

MENTION vb refer to briefly ▷ n brief reference to a person or thing

MENTO n Jamaican song

MENTOR n adviser or guide ▷ vb act as a mentor to (someone) ▷ vb act as mentor for

MENTORS ▶ mentor

MENTOS ▶ mento

MENTUM n chin

MENU n list of dishes to be served, or from which to order

MENUDO n Mexican soup

MENUDOS ▶ menudo

MENUS ▶ menu

MENYIE same as ▶ meinie

MENYIES ▶ menyie

MEOU same as ▶ meow

MEOUED ▶ meou

MEOUING ▶ meou

MEOUS ▶ meou

MEOW vb (of a cat) to make a characteristic crying sound ▷ interj imitation of this sound

MEOWED ▶ meow

MEOWING ▶ meow

MEOWS ▶ meow

MERANTI n wood from any of several Malaysian trees

MERC n mercenary

MERCAT Scots word for ▶ market

MERCATS ▶ mercat

MERCER n dealer in textile fabrics and fine cloth

MERCERS ▶ mercer

MERCERY ▶ mercer

MERCES ▶ merc

MERCH n merchandise

MERCHES ▶ merch

MERCHET n (in feudal England) a fine paid by a tenant, esp a villein, to his lord for allowing the marriage of his daughter

MERCIES ▶ mercy

MERCIFY vb show mercy to

MERCS ▶ merc

MERCURY n silvery liquid metal

MERCY n compassionate treatment of an offender or enemy who is in one's power

MERDE French word for > excrement

MERDES ▶ merde

MERE adj nothing more than ▷ n lake ▷ vb old form of survey

MERED adj forming a boundary

MEREL same as ▶ meril

MERELL same as ▶ meril

MERELLS same as ▶ merils

MERELS ▶ merils

MERELY adv only

MERER ▶ mere

MERES ▶ mere

MEREST ▶ mere

MERFOLK n mermaids and mermen

MERGE vb combine or blend

MERGED ▶ merge

MERGEE n business taken over by merger

MERGEES ▶ mergee

MERGER n combination of business firms into one

MERGERS ▶ merger

MERGES ▶ merge

MERGING ▶ merge

MERI n Māori war club

MERIL n counter used in merils

MERILS n old board game

MERING ▶ mere

MERINGS ▶ mering

MERINO n breed of sheep with fine soft wool

MERINOS ▶ merino

MERIS ▶ meri

MERISES ▶ merisis

MERISIS n growth by division of cells

MERISM n duplication of biological parts

MERISMS ▶ merism

MERIT n excellence or worth ▷ vb deserve

MERITED ▶ merit

MERITS ▶ merit

MERK n old Scots coin

MERKIN n artificial hairpiece for the pudendum

MERKINS ▶ merkin

MERKS ▶ merk

MERL same as ▶ merle

M

MERLE adj (of a dog, esp a collie) having a bluish-grey coat with speckles or streaks of black
MERLES ▸ merle
MERLIN n small falcon
MERLING n whiting
MERLINS ▸ merlin
MERLON n solid upright section in a crenellated battlement
MERLONS ▸ merlon
MERLOT n black grape grown in France and now throughout the wine-producing world, used, often in a blend, for making wine
MERLOTS ▸ merlot
MERLS ▸ merl
MERMAID n imaginary sea creature with the upper part of a woman and the lower part of a fish
MERMAN n male counterpart of the mermaid
MERMEN ▸ merman
MEROME same as ▸ merosome
MEROMES ▸ merome
MERONYM n part of something used to refer to the whole
MEROPIA n partial blindness
MEROPIC ▸ meropia
MERRIER ▸ merry
MERRIES ▸ merry
MERRILY ▸ merry
MERRY adj cheerful or jolly ▸ n gean
MERSE n low level ground by a river or shore, often alluvial and fertile
MERSES ▸ merse
MERSION n dipping in water
MES ▸ me
MESA n flat-topped hill found in arid regions
MESAIL n visor
MESAILS ▸ mesail
MESAL same as ▸ mesial
MESALLY ▸ mesal
MESARCH adj (of a xylem strand) having the first-formed xylem surrounded by that formed later, as in fern stems
MESAS ▸ mesa
MESCAL n spineless globe-shaped cactus of

Mexico and the SW of the USA
MESCALS ▸ mescal
MESCLUM same as ▸ mesclun
MESCLUN n type of green salad
MESE n middle string on lyre
MESEEMS vb it seems to me
MESEL n leper
MESELED adj afflicted by leprosy
MESELS ▸ mesel
MESES ▸ mese
MESETA n plateau in Spain
MESETAS ▸ meseta
MESH n network or net ▸ vb (of gear teeth) engage ▸ adj made from mesh
MESHED ▸ mesh
MESHES ▸ mesh
MESHIER ▸ mesh
MESHING ▸ mesh
MESHUGA adj crazy
MESHY ▸ mesh
MESIAD adj relating to or situated at the middle or centre
MESIAL another word for ▸ medial
MESIAN same as ▸ mesial
MESIC ▸ meson
MESNE adj in Law, intermediate or intervening: used esp of any assignment of property before the last
MESNES ▸ mesne
MESON n elementary atomic particle
MESONIC ▸ meson
MESONS ▸ meson
MESQUIN adj mean
MESQUIT same as ▸ mesquite
MESS n untidy or dirty confusion ▸ vb muddle or dirty
MESSAGE n communication sent ▸ vb send as a message
MESSAN Scots word for ▸ dog
MESSANS ▸ messan
MESSED ▸ mess
MESSES ▸ mess
MESSIAH n exceptional or hoped for liberator of a country or people
MESSIAS same as ▸ messiah
MESSIER ▸ messy
MESSILY ▸ messy
MESSING ▸ mess
MESSMAN n sailor working

in ship's mess
MESSMEN ▸ messman
MESSY adj dirty, confused, or untidy
MESTEE same as ▸ mustee
MESTEES ▸ mestee
MESTER n master: used as a term of address for a man who is the head of a house
MESTERS ▸ mester
MESTESO n Spanish music genre
MESTINO n person of mixed race
MESTIZA ▸ mestizo
MESTIZO n person of mixed parentage, esp the offspring of a Spanish American and an American Indian
MESTO adj sad
MESTOM same as ▸ mestome
MESTOME n conducting tissue associated with parenchyma
MESTOMS ▸ mestom
MET n meteorology
META adj in a self-parodying style
METAGE n official measuring of weight or contents
METAGES ▸ metage
METAL n chemical element, such as iron or copper, that is malleable and capable of conducting heat and electricity ▸ adj made of metal ▸ vb fit or cover with metal
METALED ▸ metal
METALLY adj like metal
METALS ▸ metal
METAMER n any of two or more isomeric compounds exhibiting metamerism
METATAG n element of HTML describing the contents of a web page and used by search engines to index pages by subject
METATE n stone for grinding grain on
METATES ▸ metate
METAYER n farmer who pays rent in kind
METAZOA > metazoan
METCAST n weather forecast
METE vb deal out as punishment ▸ n (to) measure

METED ▶ mete

METEOR *n* small fast-moving heavenly body, visible as a streak of incandescence if it enters the earth's atmosphere

METEORS ▶ meteor

METEPA *n* type of pesticide

METEPAS ▶ metepa

METER *same as* ▶ metre

METERED ▶ meter

METERS ▶ meter

METES ▶ mete

METH *n* variety of amphetamine

METHANE *n* colourless inflammable gas

METHINK *same as* > methinks

METHO *n* methylated spirits

METHOD *n* way or manner

METHODS ▶ method

METHOS ▶ metho

METHOXY *n* steroid drug

METHS *n* methylated spirits

METHYL *n* compound containing a saturated hydrocarbon group of atoms

METHYLS ▶ methyl

METIC *n* (in ancient Greece) an alien having some rights of citizenship in the city in which he lives

METICAL *n* money unit in Mozambique

METICS ▶ metic

METIER *n* profession or trade

METIERS ▶ metier

METIF *n* person of mixed race

METIFS ▶ metif

METING ▶ mete

METIS *n* person of mixed parentage

METISSE ▶ metis

METOL *n* colourless soluble organic substance used, (in the form of its sulphate, as a photographic developer

METOLS ▶ metol

METONYM *n* word used in a metonymy

METOPAE ▶ metope

METOPE *n* square space between two triglyphs in a Doric frieze

METOPES ▶ metope

METOPIC *adj* of or relating to the forehead

METOPON *n* painkilling drug

METRE *n* basic unit of length equal to about 1.094 yards (100 centimetres) ▷ *vb* express in poetry

METRED ▶ metre

METRES ▶ metre

METRIC *adj* of the decimal system of weights and measures based on the metre

METRICS *n* art of using poetic metre

METRIFY *vb* render into poetic metre

METRING ▶ metre

METRIST *n* person skilled in the use of poetic metre

METRO *n* underground railway system, esp in Paris

METROS ▶ metro

METS ▶ met

METTLE *n* courage or spirit

METTLED *adj* spirited, courageous, or valiant

METTLES ▶ mettle

METUMP *n* band for carrying a load or burden

METUMPS ▶ metump

MEU *another name for* ▶ spignel

MEUS ▶ meu

MEUSE *n* gap (in fence, wall etc) through which an animal passed ▷ *vb* go through this gap

MEUSED ▶ meuse

MEUSES ▶ meuse

MEUSING ▶ meuse

MEVE *same as* ▶ move

MEVED ▶ meve

MEVES ▶ meve

MEVING ▶ meve

MEVROU *n* S African title of address

MEVROUS ▶ mevrou

MEW *n* cry of a cat ▷ *vb* utter this cry

MEWED ▶ mew

MEWING ▶ mew

MEWL *vb* (esp of a baby) to cry weakly ▷ *n* weak or whimpering cry

MEWLED ▶ mewl

MEWLER ▶ mewl

MEWLERS ▶ mewl

MEWLING ▶ mewl

MEWLS ▶ mewl

MEWS *same as* ▶ meuse

MEWSED ▶ mews

MEWSES ▶ mews

MEWSING ▶ mews

MEYNT ▶ ming

MEZAIL *same as* ▶ mesail

MEZAILS ▶ mezail

MEZCAL *variant spelling of* ▶ mescal

MEZCALS ▶ mezcal

MEZE *n* type of hors d'oeuvre eaten esp with an apéritif or other drink in Greece and the Near East

MEZES ▶ meze

MEZQUIT *same as* > mesquite

> A **mezquit** is a kind of American tree, and makes a great bonus to play. Remember also that it takes an E to form the variant spelling **mezquite**.

MEZUZA *same as* ▶ mezuzah

MEZUZAH *n* piece of parchment inscribed with biblical passages and fixed to the doorpost of the rooms of a Jewish house

MEZUZAS ▶ mezuza

MEZUZOT ▶ mezuzah

MEZZ *same as* > mezzanine

MEZZE *same as* ▶ meze

MEZZES ▶ mezze

MEZZO *adv* moderately

MEZZOS ▶ mezzo

MGANGA *n* witch doctor

MGANGAS ▶ mganga

MHO *former name for* ▶ siemens

MHORR *n* African gazelle

MHORRS ▶ mhorr

MHOS ▶ mho

MI *n* (in tonic sol-fa) the third degree of any major scale

MIAOU *same as* ▶ meow

MIAOUED ▶ miaou

> These 7-letter words using all of the vowels are not easy to see on your rack, but they come in useful so often that it's well worth paying them special attention.

MIAOUS ▶ miaou

MIAOW *same as* ▶ meow

MIAOWED ▶ miaow

MIAOWS ▶ miaow

MIASM *same as* ▶ miasma

MIASMA *n* unwholesome or foreboding atmosphere

MIASMAL ▶ miasma

MIASMAS ▶ miasma

MIASMIC ▶ miasma

MIASMS ▶ miasm

MIAUL *same as* ▶ meow

M

MIAULED ▸ miaul

MIAULS ▸ miaul

MIB n marble used in games

MIBS ▸ mib

MIBUNA n type of Japanese leafy vegetable

MIBUNAS ▸ mibuna

MIC n microphone

MICA n glasslike mineral used as an electrical insulator

MICAS ▸ mica

MICATE vb add mica to

MICATED ▸ micate

MICATES ▸ micate

MICE ▸ mouse

MICELL same as ▸ **micelle**

MICELLA same as ▸ **micelle**

MICELLE n charged aggregate of molecules of colloidal size in a solution

MICELLS ▸ micell

MICH same as ▸ **mitch**

MICHAEL n as in **take the michael** teasing

MICHE same as ▸ **mich**

MICHED ▸ mich

MICHER ▸ mich

MICHERS ▸ mich

MICHES ▸ mich

MICHING ▸ mich

MICHT n Scots word for might

MICHTS ▸ micht

MICKERY n waterhole, esp in a dry riverbed

MICKEY n young bull, esp one that is wild and unbranded ▸ vb drug person's drink

MICKEYS ▸ mickey

MICKIES ▸ micky

MICKLE adj large or abundant ▸ adv much ▸ n great amount

MICKLER ▸ mickle

MICKLES ▸ mickle

MICKY same as ▸ **mickey**

MICO n marmoset

MICOS ▸ mico

MICRA ▸ micron

MICRIFY vb make very small

MICRO n small computer

MICROBE n minute organism, esp one causing disease

MICROHM n millionth of ohm

MICRON n unit of length equal to 10^{-6} metre

MICRONS ▸ micron

MICROS ▸ micro

MICS ▸ mic

MICTION n urination

MID adj intermediate, middle ▸ n middle ▸ prep amid

MIDAIR n some point above ground level, in the air

MIDAIRS ▸ midair

MIDBAND adj (of telecommunication transmissions) using a range of frequencies between narrowband and broadband

MIDCAP adj (of investments) involving medium-sized amounts of capital

MIDCULT n middlebrow culture

MIDDAY n noon

MIDDAYS ▸ midday

MIDDEN n dunghill or rubbish heap

MIDDENS ▸ midden

MIDDEST adj in middle

MIDDIE n glass or bottle containing 285ml of beer

MIDDIES ▸ middy

MIDDLE adj equidistant from two extremes ▸ n middle point or part ▸ vb place in the middle

MIDDLED ▸ middle

MIDDLER n pupil in middle years at school

MIDDLES ▸ middle

MIDDY n middle-sized glass of beer

MIDGE n small mosquito-like insect

MIDGES ▸ midge

MIDGET n very small person or thing ▸ adj much smaller than normal

MIDGETS ▸ midget

MIDGIE n informal word for a small winged biting insect such as the midge or sandfly

MIDGIER ▸ midge

MIDGIES ▸ midgie

MIDGUT n middle part of the digestive tract of vertebrates, including the small intestine

MIDGUTS ▸ midgut

MIDGY ▸ midge

MIDI adj (of a skirt, coat, etc) reaching to below the knee or midcalf ▸ n a skirt, coat, etc reaching to below the knee or midcalf

MIDIRON n club, usually a

No. 5, 6, or 7 iron, used for medium-length approach shots

MIDIS ▸ midi

MIDLAND n middle part of a country

MIDLEG n middle of leg

MIDLEGS ▸ midleg

MIDLIFE n middle age

MIDLINE n line at middle of something

MIDLIST n books in publisher's range that sell reasonably well

MIDMOST adv in the middle or midst ▸ n the middle or midst

MIDNOON n noon

MIDRASH n homily on a scriptural passage derived by traditional Jewish exegetical methods and consisting usually of embellishment of the scriptural narrative

MIDRIB n main vein of a leaf, running down the centre of the blade

MIDRIBS ▸ midrib

MIDRIFF n middle part of the body

MIDS ▸ mid

MIDSHIP adj in, of, or relating to the middle of a vessel ▸ n middle of a vessel

MIDSIZE adj medium-sized

MIDSOLE n layer between the inner and the outer sole of a shoe, contoured for absorbing shock

MIDST See ▸ **amid**

MIDSTS ▸ midst

MIDTERM n middle of a term in a school, university, etc

MIDTOWN n centre of a town

MIDWAY adv halfway ▸ adj in or at the middle of the distance ▸ n place in a fair, carnival, etc, where sideshows are located

MIDWAYS ▸ midway

MIDWEEK n middle of the week

MIDWIFE n trained person who assists at childbirth ▸ vb act as midwife

MIDWIVE vb act as midwife

MIDYEAR n middle of the year

MIELIE same as ▸ **mealie**

MIELIES ▸ mielie

MIEN n person's bearing, demeanour, or appearance
MIENS ▸ mien
MIEVE same as ▸ move
MIEVED ▸ mieve
MIEVES ▸ mieve
MIEVING ▸ mieve
MIFF vb take offence or offend ▸ n petulant mood
MIFFED ▸ miff
MIFFIER ▸ miffy
MIFFILY ▸ miffy
MIFFING ▸ miff
MIFFS ▸ miff
MIFFY adj easily upset
MIFTY same as ▸ miffy
MIG n marble used in games
MIGG same as ▸ mig
MIGGLE n US word for playing marble
MIGGLES ▸ miggle
MIGGS ▸ migg
MIGHT ▸ may
MIGHTS ▸ may
MIGHTST ▸ may
MIGHTY adj powerful ▸ adv very
MIGNON adj small and pretty ▸ n tender boneless cut of meat
MIGNONS ▸ mignon
MIGRANT n person or animal that moves from one place to another ▸ adj moving from one place to another
MIGRATE vb move from one place to settle in another
MIGS ▸ mig
MIHA n young fern frond which has not yet opened
MIHAS ▸ miha
MIHI n Māori ceremonial greeting ▸ vb greet
MIHIED ▸ mihi
MIHIING ▸ mihi
MIHIS ▸ mihi
MIHRAB n niche in a mosque showing the direction of Mecca
MIHRABS ▸ mihrab
MIKADO n Japanese emperor
MIKADOS ▸ mikado
MIKE n microphone
MIKED ▸ mike
MIKES ▸ mike
MIKING ▸ mike
MIKRA ▸ mikron
MIKRON same as ▸ micron
MIKRONS ▸ mikron
MIKVAH n pool used esp by women for ritual

purification after their monthly period
MIKVAHS ▸ mikvah
MIKVEH same as ▸ mikvah
MIKVEHS ▸ mikveh
MIKVOS ▸ mikveh
MIKVOT ▸ mikveh
MIKVOTH ▸ mikvah
MIL n unit of length equal to one thousandth of an inch
MILADI same as ▸ milady
MILADIS ▸ miladi
MILADY n (formerly) a continental title for an English gentlewoman
MILAGE same as ▸ mileage
MILAGES ▸ milage
MILCH adj (of a cow) giving milk
MILCHIG same as ▸ milchik
MILCHIK adj containing or used in the preparation of milk products and so not to be used with meat products
MILD adj not strongly flavoured ▸ n dark beer flavoured with fewer hops than bitter ▸ vb become gentle
MILDED ▸ mild
MILDEN vb make or become mild or milder
MILDENS ▸ milden
MILDER ▸ mild
MILDEST ▸ mild
MILDEW same as ▸ mould
MILDEWS ▸ mildew
MILDEWY ▸ mildew
MILDING ▸ mild
MILDLY ▸ mild
MILDS ▸ mild
MILE n unit of length equal to 1760 yards or 1.609 kilometres
MILEAGE n distance travelled in miles
MILER n athlete, horse, etc, that specializes in races of one mile
MILERS ▸ miler
MILES ▸ mile
MILFOIL same as ▸ yarrow
MILIA ▸ milium
MILIARY adj resembling or relating to millet seeds
MILIEU n environment or surroundings
MILIEUS ▸ milieu
MILIEUX ▸ milieu
MILITAR same as ▸ military
MILITIA n military force of trained citizens for use in emergency only

MILIUM n pimple
MILK n white fluid produced by female mammals to feed their young ▸ vb draw milk from
MILKED ▸ milk
MILKEN adj of or like milk
MILKER n cow, goat, etc, that yields milk, esp of a specified quality or amount
MILKERS ▸ milker
MILKIER ▸ milky
MILKILY ▸ milky
MILKING ▸ milk
MILKMAN n man who delivers milk to people's houses
MILKMEN ▸ milkman
MILKO informal name for ▸ milkman
MILKOS ▸ milko
MILKS ▸ milk
MILKSOP n feeble man
MILKY adj of or like milk
MILL n factory ▸ vb grind, press, or process in or as if in a mill
MILLAGE adj American tax rate calculated in thousandths per dollar
MILLDAM n dam built in a stream to raise the water level sufficiently for it to turn a millwheel
MILLE French word for ▸ thousand
MILLED adj crushed or ground in a mill
MILLER n person who works in a mill
MILLERS ▸ miller
MILLES ▸ mille
MILLET n type of cereal grass
MILLETS ▸ millet
MILLIER n metric weight of million grams
MILLIME same as ▸ millieme
MILLINE n measurement of advertising space
MILLING n act or process of grinding, cutting, pressing, or crushing in a mill
MILLION n one thousand thousands
MILLRUN same as ▸ millrace
MILLS ▸ mill
MILNEB n type of pesticide
MILNEBS ▸ milneb
MILO n any of various early-growing cultivated varieties of sorghum with heads of yellow or pinkish

M

seeds resembling millet

MILOR same as ▸ **milord**

MILORD n (formerly) a continental title used for an English gentleman

MILORDS ▸ **milord**

MILORS ▸ **milor**

MILOS ▸ **milo**

MILPA n form of subsistence agriculture in Mexico

MILPAS ▸ **milpa**

MILREIS n former monetary unit of Portugal and Brazil, divided into 1000 reis

MILS ▸ **mil**

MILSEY n milk strainer

MILSEYS ▸ **milsey**

MILT n sperm of fish ▸ vb fertilize (the roe of a female fish) with milt, esp artificially

MILTED ▸ **milt**

MILTER n male fish that is mature and ready to breed

MILTERS ▸ **milter**

MILTIER ▸ **milty**

MILTING ▸ **milt**

MILTS ▸ **milt**

MILTY adj full of milt

MILTZ same as ▸ **milt**

MILTZES ▸ **miltz**

MILVINE adj of kites and related birds

MIM adj prim, modest, or demure

MIMBAR n pulpit in mosque

MIMBARS ▸ **mimbar**

MIME n acting without the use of words ▸ vb act in mime

MIMED ▸ **mime**

MIMEO vb mimeograph

MIMEOED ▸ **mimeo**

MIMEOS ▸ **mimeo**

MIMER ▸ **mime**

MIMERS ▸ **mime**

MIMES ▸ **mime**

MIMESES ▸ **mimesis**

MIMESIS n imitative representation of nature or human behaviour

MIMETIC adj imitating or representing something

MIMIC vb imitate (a person or manner), esp for satirical effect ▸ n person or animal that is good at mimicking ▸ adj of, relating to, or using mimicry

MIMICAL ▸ **mimic**

MIMICRY n act or art of copying or imitating closely

MIMICS ▸ **mimic**

MIMING ▸ **mime**

MIMMER ▸ **mim**

MIMMEST ▸ **mim**

MIMMICK same as ▸ **minnick**

MIMOSA n shrub with fluffy yellow flowers and sensitive leaves

MIMOSAE ▸ **mimosa**

MIMOSAS ▸ **mimosa**

MIMSEY same as ▸ **mimsy**

MIMSIER ▸ **mimsy**

MIMSY adj prim, underwhelming, and ineffectual

MIMULUS n plants cultivated for their yellow or red flowers

MINA n ancient unit of weight and money, used in Asia Minor, equal to one sixtieth of a talent

MINABLE ▸ **mine**

MINAE ▸ **mina**

MINAR n tower

MINARET n tall slender tower of a mosque

MINARS ▸ **minar**

MINAS ▸ **mina**

MINBAR same as ▸ **mimbar**

MINBARS ▸ **minbar**

MINCE vb cut or grind into very small pieces ▸ n minced meat

MINCED ▸ **mince**

MINCER n machine for mincing meat

MINCERS ▸ **mincer**

MINCES ▸ **mince**

MINCEUR adj (of food) low-fat

MINCIER ▸ **mincy**

MINCING adj affected in manner

MINCY adj effeminate

MIND n thinking faculties ▸ vb take offence at

MINDED adj having an inclination as specified

MINDER n aide or bodyguard

MINDERS ▸ **minder**

MINDFUL adj heedful

MINDING ▸ **mind**

MINDS ▸ **mind**

MINDSET n ideas and attitudes with which a person approaches a situation, esp when these are seen as being difficult to alter

MINE pron belonging to me ▸ n deep hole for digging

out coal, ores, etc ▸ vb dig for minerals

MINED ▸ **mine**

MINEOLA same as > **minneola**

MINER n person who works in a mine

MINERAL n naturally occurring inorganic substance, such as metal ▸ adj of, containing, or like minerals

MINERS ▸ **miner**

MINES ▸ **mine**

MINETTE n type of rock

MINEVER same as ▸ **miniver**

MING vb mix

MINGED ▸ **ming**

MINGIER ▸ **mingy**

MINGING adj unattractive or unpleasant

MINGLE vb mix or blend

MINGLED ▸ **mingle**

MINGLER ▸ **mingle**

MINGLES ▸ **mingle**

MINGS ▸ **ming**

MINGY adj miserly

MINI same as > **minidress**

MINIATE vb paint with minium

MINIBAR n selection of drinks and confectionery provided in a hotel room

MINIBUS n small bus

MINICAB n ordinary car used as a taxi

MINICAM n portable television camera

MINICAR n small car

MINICOM n device used by deaf and hard-of-hearing people, allowing typed telephone messages to be sent and received

MINIER ▸ **miny**

MINIEST ▸ **miny**

MINIFY vb minimize or lessen the size or importance of (something)

MINIKIN n small, dainty, or affected person or thing ▸ adj dainty, prim, or affected

MINILAB n equipment for processing photographic film

MINIM n note half the length of a semibreve ▸ adj very small

MINIMA ▸ **minimum**

MINIMAL adj minimum ▸ n small surfboard

MINIMAX n lowest of a set of maximum values ▷ vb make maximum as low as possible

MINIMS ▶ minim

MINIMUM n least possible (amount or number) ▷ adj of, being, or showing a minimum or minimums

MINIMUS adj youngest: sometimes used after the surname of a schoolboy having elder brothers at the same school

MINING n act, process, or industry of extracting coal or ores from the earth

MININGS ▶ mining

MINION n servile assistant ▷ adj dainty, pretty, or elegant

MINIONS ▶ minion

MINIS ▶ mini

MINISH vb diminish

MINISKI n short ski

MINIUM n bright red poisonous insoluble oxide of lead usually obtained as a powder by heating litharge in air

MINIUMS ▶ minium

MINIVAN n small van, esp one with seats in the back for carrying passengers

MINIVER n white fur, used in ceremonial costumes

MINIVET n brightly coloured tropical Asian cuckoo shrike

MINK n stoatlike animal

MINKE n as in minke whale type of small whalebone whale or rorqual

MINKES ▶ minke

MINKS ▶ mink

MINNICK vb behave in fussy way

MINNIE n mother

MINNIES ▶ minnie

MINNOCK same as ▶ minnick

MINNOW n small freshwater fish

MINNOWS ▶ minnow

MINNY same as ▶ minnie

MINO same as ▶ mynah

MINOR adj lesser ▷ n person regarded legally as a child ▷ vb take a minor

MINORCA n breed of light domestic fowl with glossy white, black, or blue plumage

MINORED ▶ minor

MINORS ▶ minor

MINOS ▶ mino

MINSTER n cathedral or large church

MINT n plant with aromatic leaves used for seasoning and flavouring ▷ vb make (coins)

MINTAGE n process of minting

MINTED ▶ mint

MINTER ▶ mint

MINTERS ▶ mint

MINTIER ▶ mint

MINTING ▶ mint

MINTS ▶ mint

MINTY ▶ mint

MINUEND n number from which another number is to be subtracted

MINUET n stately dance

MINUETS ▶ minuet

MINUS adj indicating subtraction ▷ n sign (-) denoting subtraction or a number less than zero ▷ prep reduced by the subtraction of

MINUSES ▶ minus

MINUTE n 60th part of an hour or degree ▷ vb record in the minutes ▷ adj very small

MINUTED ▶ minute

MINUTER ▶ minute

MINUTES pl n official record of the proceedings of a meeting or conference

MINUTIA singular noun of > minutiae

MINX n bold or flirtatious girl

MINXES ▶ minx

MINXISH ▶ minx

MINY adj of or like mines

MINYAN n number of persons required by Jewish law to be present for a religious service, namely, at least ten males over thirteen years of age

MINYANS ▶ minyan

MIOCENE adj of, denoting, or formed in the fourth epoch of the Tertiary period, between the Oligocene and Pliocene epochs, which lasted for 19 million years

MIOMBO n (in E Africa) a dry wooded area with sparse deciduous growth

MIOMBOS ▶ miombo

MIOSES ▶ miosis

MIOSIS n excessive contraction of the pupil of the eye, as in response to drugs

MIOTIC ▶ miosis

MIOTICS ▶ miosis

MIPS n million instructions per second: a unit used to express the speed of a computer's central processing unit

MIR n peasant commune in prerevolutionary Russia

MIRABLE adj wonderful

MIRACLE n wonderful supernatural event

MIRADOR n window, balcony, or turret

MIRAGE n optical illusion, esp one caused by hot air

MIRAGES ▶ mirage

MIRBANE n substance used in perfumes

MIRCHI Indian English word for ▶ hot

MIRE n swampy ground ▷ vb sink or be stuck in a mire

MIRED ▶ mire

MIRES ▶ mire

MIREX n type of insecticide

MIREXES ▶ mirex

MIRI ▶ mir

MIRIER ▶ mire

MIRIEST ▶ mire

MIRIFIC adj achieving wonderful things

MIRIN n Japanese rice wine

MIRING ▶ mire

MIRINS ▶ mirin

MIRITI n South American palm

MIRITIS ▶ miriti

MIRK same as ▶ murk

MIRKER ▶ mirk

MIRKEST ▶ mirk

MIRKIER ▶ mirk

MIRKILY ▶ mirk

MIRKS ▶ mirk

MIRKY ▶ mirk

MIRLIER ▶ mirly

MIRLY same as ▶ marly

MIRO n tall New Zealand tree

MIROS ▶ miro

MIRROR n coated glass surface for reflecting images ▷ vb reflect in or as if in a mirror

MIRRORS ▶ mirror

MIRS ▶ mir

M

MIRTH n laughter, merriment, or gaiety

MIRTHS ▸ **mirth**

MIRV n missile that has several warheads, each one being directed to different enemy targets ▷ vb arm with mirvs

MIRVED ▸ **mirv**

MIRVING ▸ **mirv**

MIRVS ▸ **mirv**

MIRY ▸ **mire**

MIRZA n title of respect placed before the surname of an official, scholar, or other distinguished man

MIRZAS ▸ **mirza**

MIS ▸ **mi**

MISACT vb act wrongly

MISACTS ▸ **misact**

MISADD vb add badly

MISADDS ▸ **misadd**

MISAIM vb aim badly

MISAIMS ▸ **misaim**

MISALLY vb form unsuitable alliance

MISATE ▸ **miseat**

MISAVER vb claim wrongly

MISBIAS vb prejudice wrongly

MISBILL vb present inaccurate bill

MISBIND vb bind wrongly

MISBORN adj abortive

MISCALL vb call by the wrong name

MISCAST vb cast (a role or actor) in (a play or film) inappropriately

MISCH adj as in **misch metal** alloy of cerium and other rare earth metals, used esp as a flint in cigarette lighters

MISCITE vb cite wrongly

MISCODE vb code wrongly

MISCOIN vb coin wrongly

MISCOOK vb cook badly

MISCOPY vb copy badly

MISCUE n faulty stroke in which the cue tip slips off the cue ball or misses it altogether ▷ vb make a miscue

MISCUED ▸ **miscue**

MISCUES ▸ **miscue**

MISCUT n cut wrongly

MISCUTS ▸ **miscut**

MISDATE vb date (a letter, event, etc) wrongly

MISDEAL vb deal out cards incorrectly ▷ n faulty deal

MISDEED n wrongful act

MISDEEM vb form bad opinion of

MISDIAL vb dial telephone number incorrectly

MISDID ▸ **misdo**

MISDIET n wrong diet

MISDO vb do badly or wrongly

MISDOER ▸ **misdo**

MISDOES ▸ **misdo**

MISDONE adj done badly

MISDRAW vb draw poorly

MISDREW ▸ **misdraw**

MISE n issue in the obsolete writ of right

MISEASE n unease

MISEAT vb eat unhealthy food

MISEATS ▸ **miseat**

MISEDIT vb edit badly

MISER n person who hoards money and hates spending it

MISERE n call in solo whist and other card games declaring a hand that will win no tricks

MISERES ▸ **misere**

MISERLY adj of or resembling a miser

MISERS ▸ **miser**

MISERY n great unhappiness

MISES ▸ **mise**

MISFALL vb happen as piece of bad luck

MISFARE vb get on badly

MISFED ▸ **misfeed**

MISFEED vb feed wrongly

MISFELL ▸ **misfall**

MISFILE vb file (papers, records, etc) wrongly

MISFIRE vb (of a firearm or engine) fail to fire correctly ▷ n act or an instance of misfiring

MISFIT n person not suited to his or her social environment ▷ vb fail to fit or be fitted

MISFITS ▸ **misfit**

MISFORM vb form badly

MISGAVE ▸ **misgive**

MISGIVE vb make or be apprehensive or suspicious

MISGO vb go wrong way

MISGOES ▸ **misgo**

MISGONE ▸ **misgo**

MISGREW ▸ **misgrow**

MISGROW vb grow in unsuitable way

MISHAP n minor accident ▷ vb happen as bad luck

MISHAPS ▸ **mishap**

MISHAPT same as ▸ **misshapen**

MISHEAR vb hear (what someone says) wrongly

MISHIT n faulty shot, kick, or stroke ▷ vb hit or kick a ball with a faulty stroke

MISHITS ▸ **mishit**

MISHMEE n root of Asian plant

MISHMI n evergreen perennial plant

MISHMIS ▸ **mishmi**

MISJOIN vb join badly

MISKAL n unit of weight in Iran

MISKALS ▸ **miskal**

MISKEEP vb keep wrongly

MISKEN vb be unaware of

MISKENS ▸ **misken**

MISKENT ▸ **misken**

MISKEPT ▸ **miskeep**

MISKEY vb key wrongly

MISKEYS ▸ **miskey**

MISKICK vb fail to kick properly

MISKNEW vb ▸ **misknow**

MISKNOW vb have wrong idea about

MISLAID ▸ **mislay**

MISLAIN ▸ **mislay**

MISLAY vb lose (something) temporarily

MISLAYS ▸ **mislay**

MISLEAD vb give false or confusing information to

MISLED ▸ **mislead**

MISLIE vb lie wrongly

MISLIES ▸ **mislie**

MISLIKE vb dislike ▷ n dislike or aversion

MISLIT ▸ **mislight**

MISLIVE vb live wickedly

MISLUCK vb have bad luck

MISMADE ▸ **mismake**

MISMAKE vb make badly

MISMARK vb mark wrongly

MISMATE vb mate wrongly

MISMEET vb fail to meet

MISMET ▸ **mismeet**

MISMOVE vb move badly

MISNAME vb name badly

MISO n thick brown salty paste made from soya beans, used to flavour savoury dishes, esp soups

MISOS ▸ **miso**

MISPAGE vb page wrongly

MISPART vb part wrongly

MISPEN vb write wrongly

MISPENS ▸ **mispen**

MISPLAN vb plan badly or wrongly

MISPLAY vb play badly or wrongly in games or sports ▷ n wrong or unskilful play

MISPLED > misplead

MISRATE vb rate wrongly

MISREAD vb misinterpret (a situation etc)

MISRELY vb rely wrongly

MISRULE vb govern inefficiently or unjustly ▷ n inefficient or unjust government

MISS vb fail to notice, hear, hit, reach, find, or catch ▷ n fact or instance of missing

MISSA n Roman Catholic mass

MISSAE ▶ missa

MISSAID ▶ missay

MISSAL n book containing the prayers and rites of the Mass

MISSALS ▶ missal

MISSAW ▶ missee

MISSAY vb say wrongly

MISSAYS ▶ missay

MISSEAT vb seat wrongly

MISSED ▶ miss

MISSEE vb see wrongly

MISSEEM vb be unsuitable for

MISSEEN ▶ missee

MISSEES ▶ missee

MISSEL adj as in missel thrush large European thrush with a brown back and spotted breast, noted for feeding on mistletoe berries

MISSELL vb sell (a product, esp a financial one) misleadingly

MISSELS ▶ missel

MISSEND vb send wrongly

MISSENT ▶ missend

MISSES ▶ miss

MISSET vb set wrongly

MISSETS ▶ misset

MISSHOD adj badly shod

MISSIER ▶ missy

MISSIES ▶ missy

MISSILE n rocket with an exploding warhead, used as a weapon

MISSING adj lost or absent

MISSION n specific task or duty ▷ vb direct a mission to or establish a mission in (a given region)

MISSIS same as ▶ missus

MISSISH adj like a schoolgirl

MISSIVE n letter ▷ adj sent or intended to be sent

MISSOLD ▶ missell

MISSORT vb sort wrongly

MISSOUT n someone who has been overlooked

MISSTEP n false step ▷ vb take a false step

MISSTOP vb stop wrongly

MISSUIT vb be unsuitable for

MISSUS n one's wife or the wife of the person addressed or referred to

MISSY n affectionate or disparaging form of address to a girl ▷ adj missish

MIST n thin fog ▷ vb cover or be covered with mist

MISTAKE n error or blunder ▷ vb misunderstand

MISTAL n cow shed

MISTALS ▶ mistal

MISTBOW same as ▶ fogbow

MISTED ▶ mist

MISTELL vb tell wrongly

MISTEND vb tend wrongly

MISTER n informal form of address for a man ▷ vb call (someone) mister

MISTERM vb term badly

MISTERS ▶ mister

MISTERY same as ▶ mystery

MISTEUK Scots variant of ▶ mistook

MISTFUL ▶ mist

MISTICO n small Mediterranean sailing ship

MISTIER ▶ misty

MISTILY ▶ misty

MISTIME vb do (something) at the wrong time

MISTING n application of a fake suntan by spray

MISTLE same as ▶ mizzle

MISTLED ▶ mistle

MISTLES ▶ mistle

MISTOLD ▶ mistell

MISTOOK past tense of ▶ mistake

MISTRAL n strong dry northerly wind of S France

MISTS ▶ mist

MISTUNE vb fail to tune properly

MISTY adj full of mist

MISTYPE vb type badly

MISUSE n incorrect, improper, or careless use ▷ vb use wrongly

MISUSED ▶ misuse

MISUSER n abuse of some right, privilege, office, etc, such as one that may lead to its forfeiture

MISUSES ▶ misuse

MISUST ▶ misuse

MISWEEN vb assess wrongly

MISWEND vb become lost

MISWENT ▶ miswend

MISWORD vb word badly

MISWRIT > miswrite

MISYOKE vb join wrongly

MITCH vb play truant from school

MITCHED ▶ mitch

MITCHES ▶ mitch

MITE n very small spider-like animal

MITER same as ▶ mitre

MITERED ▶ miter

MITERER ▶ miter

MITERS ▶ miter

MITES ▶ mite

MITHER vb fuss over or moan about something

MITHERS ▶ mither

MITIER ▶ mity

MITIEST ▶ mity

MITIS n malleable iron, fluid enough for casting, made by adding a small amount of aluminium to wrought iron

MITISES ▶ mitis

MITOGEN n any agent that induces mitosis

MITOSES ▶ mitosis

MITOSIS n type of cell division in which the nucleus divides into two nuclei which each contain the same number of chromosomes as the original nucleus

MITOTIC ▶ mitosis

MITRAL adj of or like a mitre

MITRE n bishop's pointed headdress ▷ vb join with a mitre joint

MITRED ▶ mitre

MITRES ▶ mitre

MITRING ▶ mitre

MITSVAH same as ▶ mitzvah

MITT same as ▶ mitten

MITTEN n glove with one section for the thumb and one for the four fingers together

MITTENS ▶ mitten

MITTS ▶ mitt

MITUMBA n used clothes imported for sale in African countries

M

MITY adj having mites

MITZVAH n commandment or precept, esp one found in the Bible

MIURUS n type of rhythm in poetry

MIX vb combine or blend into one mass ▷ n mixture

MIXABLE ▶ mix

MIXDOWN n (in sound recording) the transfer of a multitrack master mix to two-track stereo tape

MIXED adj formed or blended together by mixing

MIXEDLY ▶ mixed

MIXEN n dunghill

MIXENS ▶ mixen

MIXER n kitchen appliance used for mixing foods

MIXERS ▶ mixer

MIXES ▶ mix

MIXIBLE ▶ mix

MIXIER ▶ mix

MIXIEST ▶ mix

MIXING ▶ mix

MIXT ▶ mix

MIXTE adj of or denoting a type of bicycle frame, usually for women, in which angled twin lateral tubes run back to the rear axle

MIXTION n amber-based mixture used in making gold leaf

MIXTURE n something mixed

MIXUP n something that is mixed up

MIXUPS ▶ mixup

MIXY adj mixed

MIZ shortened form of ▶ misery

> Miz is an informal short form of **misery**, very useful as a Z word. But you'll need a blank tile for the second Z if you want to form the plural **mizzes**.

MIZEN same as ▶ mizzen

MIZENS ▶ mizen

MIZMAZE n maze

MIZUNA n Japanese variety of lettuce having crisp green leaves

MIZUNAS ▶ mizuna

MIZZ same as ▶ miz

MIZZEN n sail set on a mizzenmast ▷ adj of or relating to any kind of gear used with a mizzenmast

MIZZENS ▶ mizzen

MIZZES ▶ miz

MIZZLE vb decamp

MIZZLED ▶ mizzle

MIZZLES ▶ mizzle

MIZZLY ▶ mizzle

MIZZY adj as in **mizzy maze** dialect expression meaning state of confusion

MM interj expression of enjoyment of taste or smell

MNA same as ▶ mina

MNAS ▶ mna

MNEME n ability to retain memory

MNEMES ▶ mneme

MNEMIC ▶ mneme

MNEMON n unit of memory

MNEMONS ▶ mnemon

MO n moment

MOA n large extinct flightless New Zealand bird

MOAI n any of the gigantic carved stone figures found on Easter Island (Rapa Nui)

MOAN n low cry of pain ▷ vb make or utter with a moan

MOANED ▶ moan

MOANER ▶ moan

MOANERS ▶ moan

MOANFUL ▶ moan

MOANING ▶ moan

MOANS ▶ moan

MOAS ▶ moa

MOAT n deep wide ditch, esp round a castle ▷ vb surround with or as if with a moat

MOATED ▶ moat

MOATING ▶ moat

MOATS ▶ moat

MOB n disorderly crowd ▷ vb surround in a mob to acclaim or attack

MOBBED ▶ mob

MOBBER ▶ mob

MOBBERS ▶ mob

MOBBIE same as ▶ mobby

MOBBIES ▶ mobby

MOBBING ▶ mob

MOBBISH ▶ mob

MOBBISM n behaviour as mob

MOBBLE same as ▶ moble

MOBBLED ▶ mobble

MOBBLES ▶ mobble

MOBBY n West Indian drink

MOBCAP n woman's 18th-century cotton cap with a pouched crown

MOBCAPS ▶ mobcap

MOBCAST vb create and upload a podcast directly from a mobile phone

MOBE n mobile phone

MOBES ▶ mobe

MOBEY ▶ moby

MOBEYS ▶ mobey

MOBIE n mobile phone

MOBIES ▶ moby

MOBILE adj able to move ▷ n hanging structure designed to move in air currents

MOBILES ▶ mobile

MOBLE vb muffle

MOBLED ▶ moble

MOBLES ▶ moble

MOBLING ▶ moble

MOBLOG n chronicle, which may be shared with others, of someone's thoughts and experiences recorded in the form of mobile phone calls, text messages, and photographs

MOBLOGS ▶ moblog

MOBS ▶ mob

MOBSMAN n person in mob

MOBSMEN ▶ mobsman

MOBSTER n member of a criminal organization

MOBY n mobile phone

MOC shortening of > moccasin

MOCCIES pl n informal Australian word for moccasins

MOCH n spell of humid weather

MOCHA n kind of strong dark coffee

MOCHAS ▶ mocha

MOCHELL same as ▶ much

MOCHIE adj damp or humid

MOCHIER ▶ mochie

MOCHILA n South American shoulder bag

MOCHS ▶ moch

MOCHY same as ▶ mochie

MOCK vb make fun of ▷ adj sham or imitation ▷ n act of mocking

MOCKADO n imitation velvet

MOCKAGE same as ▶ mockery

MOCKED ▶ mock

MOCKER vb dress up

MOCKERS ▶ mocker

MOCKERY n derision

MOCKING ▶ mock

MOCKNEY n person who affects a cockney accent ▷ adj denoting an affected cockney accent or a person

who has one
MOCKS ▶ mock
MOCKUP *n* working full-scale model of a machine, apparatus, etc, for testing, research, etc
MOCKUPS ▶ mockup
MOCOCK *n* Native American birchbark container
MOCOCKS ▶ mocock
MOCS ▶ moc
MOCUCK *same as* ▶ **mocock**
MOCUCKS ▶ mocuck
MOD *n* member of a group of young people, orig. in the mid-1960s, who were very clothes-conscious and rode motor scooters ▷ *vb* modify (a piece of software or hardware)
MODAL *adj* of or relating to mode or manner ▷ *n* modal word
MODALLY ▶ modal
MODALS ▶ modal
MODDED ▶ mod *vb*
MODDER *n* person who modifies a piece of hardware or software
MODDERS ▶ modder
MODDING *n* practice of modifying a car to alter its appearance or performance
MODE *n* method or manner
MODEL *n* (miniature) representation ▷ *adj* excellent or perfect ▷ *vb* make a model of
MODELED ▶ model
MODELER ▶ model
MODELLI ▶ modello
MODELLO *n* artist's preliminary sketch or model
MODELS ▶ model
MODEM *n* device for connecting two computers by a telephone line ▷ *vb* send or receive by modem
MODEMED ▶ modem
MODEMS ▶ modem
MODENA *n* popular variety of domestic fancy pigeon originating in Modena
MODENAS ▶ modena
MODER *n* intermediate layer in humus
MODERN *adj* of present or recent times ▷ *n* contemporary person
MODERNE *n* the style of architecture and design,

prevalent in Europe and the US in the late 1920s and 1930s, typified by the use of straight lines, tubular chromed steel frames, contrasting inlaid woods, etc ▷ *adj* of or relating to this style of architecture and design
MODERNS ▶ modern
MODERS ▶ moder
MODES ▶ mode
MODEST *adj* not vain or boastful
MODESTY *n* quality or condition of being modest
MODGE *vb* do shoddily
MODGED ▶ modge
MODGES ▶ modge
MODGING ▶ modge
MODI ▶ modus
MODICA ▶ modicum
MODICUM *n* small quantity
MODIFY *vb* change slightly
MODII ▶ modius
MODIOLI > modiolus
MODISH *adj* in fashion
MODIST *n* follower of fashion
MODISTE *n* fashionable dressmaker or milliner
MODISTS ▶ modist
MODIUS *n* ancient Roman quantity measure
MODS ▶ mod
MODULAR *adj* of, consisting of, or resembling a module or modulus ▷ *n* thing comprised of modules
MODULE *n* self-contained unit, section, or component with a specific function
MODULES ▶ module
MODULI ▶ modulus
MODULO *adv* with reference to modulus
MODULUS *n* coefficient expressing a specified property, for instance elasticity, of a specified substance
MODUS *n* way of doing something
MOE *adv* more ▷ *n* a wry face
MOELLON *n* rubble
MOER *n* in South Africa, slang word for the womb ▷ *vb* in South Africa, attack (someone or something) violently
MOERED ▶ moer

MOERING ▶ moer
MOERS ▶ moer
MOES ▶ moe
MOFETTE *n* opening in a region of nearly extinct volcanic activity, through which carbon dioxide, nitrogen, and other gases pass
MOFFIE *n* homosexual ▷ *adj* homosexual
MOFFIES ▶ moffie
MOG *vb* go away
MOGGAN *n* stocking without foot
MOGGANS ▶ moggan
MOGGED ▶ mog
MOGGIE *same as* ▶ **moggy**
MOGGIES ▶ moggy
MOGGING ▶ mog
MOGGY *n* cat
MOGHUL *same as* ▶ **mogul**
MOGHULS ▶ moghul
MOGS ▶ mog
MOGUL *n* important or powerful person
MOGULED *adj* having moguls
MOGULS ▶ mogul
MOHAIR *n* fine hair of the Angora goat
MOHAIRS ▶ mohair
MOHALIM *same as* ▶ **mohelim**
MOHAWK *n* half turn from either edge of either skate to the corresponding edge of the other skate
MOHAWKS ▶ mohawk
MOHEL *n* man qualified to conduct circumcisions
MOHELIM ▶ mohel
MOHELS ▶ mohel
MOHICAN *n* punk hairstyle
MOHR *same as* ▶ **mhorr**
MOHRS ▶ mohr
MOHUA *n* small New Zealand bird with a yellow head and breast
MOHUAS ▶ mohua
MOHUR *n* former Indian gold coin worth 15 rupees
MOHURS ▶ mohur
MOI ▶ me
MOIDER *same as* ▶ **moither**
MOIDERS ▶ moider
MOIDORE *n* former Portuguese gold coin
MOIETY *n* half
MOIL *vb* moisten or soil or become moist, soiled, etc ▷ *n* toil
MOILED ▶ moil

M

MOILER ▸ moil
MOILERS ▸ moil
MOILING ▸ moil
MOILS ▸ moil
MOINEAU n small fortification

> Meaning part of a fortification, this is another of those very useful 7-letter vowel dumps.

MOIRA n fate
MOIRAI ▸ moira
MOIRE adj having a watered or wavelike pattern ▷ n any fabric that has such a pattern
MOIRES ▸ moire
MOISER n informer
MOISERS ▸ moiser
MOIST adj slightly wet ▷ vb moisten
MOISTED ▸ moist
MOISTEN vb make or become moist
MOISTER ▸ moist
MOISTLY ▸ moist
MOISTS ▸ moist
MOIT same as ▸ mote
MOITHER vb bother or bewilder
MOITS ▸ moit
MOJARRA n tropical American sea fish
MOJITO n cocktail consisting of rum, lime, mint, and soda water
MOJITOS ▸ mojito
MOJO n charm or magic spell
MOJOES ▸ mojo
MOJOS ▸ mojo
MOKE n donkey
MOKES ▸ moke
MOKI n edible sea fish of New Zealand
MOKIHI n Māori raft
MOKIHIS ▸ mokihi
MOKIS ▸ moki
MOKO n Māori tattoo or tattoo pattern
MOKORO n (in Botswana) the traditional dugout canoe of the people of the Okavango Delta
MOKOROS ▸ mokoro
MOKOS ▸ moko
MOKSHA n freedom from the endless cycle of transmigration into a state of bliss
MOKSHAS ▸ moksha
MOL n the SI unit mole

MOLA another name for ▸ sunfish
MOLAL adj of or consisting of a solution containing one mole of solute per thousand grams of solvent
MOLAR n large back tooth used for grinding ▷ adj of any of these teeth
MOLARS ▸ molar
MOLAS ▸ mola
MOLASSE n soft sediment produced by the erosion of mountain ranges after the final phase of mountain building
MOLD same as ▸ mould
MOLDED ▸ mold
MOLDER same as ▸ moulder
MOLDERS ▸ molder
MOLDIER ▸ moldy
MOLDING same as > moulding
MOLDS ▸ mold
MOLDY same as ▸ mouldy
MOLE n small dark raised spot on the skin
MOLES ▸ mole
MOLEST vb interfere with sexually
MOLESTS ▸ molest
MOLIES ▸ moly
MOLIMEN n effort needed to perform bodily function
MOLINE adj (of a cross) having arms of equal length, forked and curved back at the ends ▷ n moline cross
MOLINES ▸ moline
MOLINET n stick for whipping chocolate
MOLL n gangster's female accomplice
MOLLA same as ▸ mollah
MOLLAH same as ▸ mullah
MOLLAHS ▸ mollah
MOLLAS ▸ molla
MOLLIE same as ▸ molly
MOLLIES ▸ molly
MOLLIFY vb pacify or soothe
MOLLS ▸ moll
MOLLUSC n soft-bodied, usu hard-shelled, animal, such as a snail or oyster
MOLLUSK same as ▸ mollusc
MOLLY n brightly coloured tropical or subtropical American freshwater fish
MOLOCH n spiny Australian

desert-living lizard that feeds on ants
MOLOCHS ▸ moloch
MOLOSSI > molossus
MOLS ▸ mol
MOLT same as ▸ moult
MOLTED ▸ molt
MOLTEN ▸ melt
MOLTER ▸ molt
MOLTERS ▸ molt
MOLTING ▸ molt
MOLTO adv very
MOLTS ▸ molt
MOLY n magic herb given by Hermes to Odysseus to nullify the spells of Circe
MOM same as ▸ mother
MOME n fool
MOMENT n short space of time
MOMENTA > momentum
MOMENTO same as ▸ memento
MOMENTS ▸ moment
MOMES ▸ mome
MOMI same as ▸ mom
MOMISM n excessive domination of a child by his or her mother
MOMISMS ▸ momism
MOMMA same as ▸ mamma
MOMMAS ▸ momma
MOMMET same as ▸ mammet
MOMMETS ▸ mommet
MOMMIES ▸ mommy
MOMMY same as ▸ mom
MOMS ▸ mom
MOMSER same as ▸ momzer
MOMSERS ▸ momser
MOMUS n person who ridicules
MOMUSES ▸ momus
MOMZER same as ▸ mamzer
MOMZERS ▸ momzer
MON dialect variant of ▸ man
MONA n W African guenon monkey with dark fur on the back and white or yellow underparts
MONACID same as > monoacid
MONACT adj (of sponge) with single-spiked structures in skeleton
MONAD n any fundamental singular metaphysical entity
MONADAL ▸ monad
MONADES ▸ monas

MONADIC *adj* being or relating to a monad

MONADS ▶ **monad**

MONAL *n* S Asian pheasant, the male of which has a brilliantly coloured plumage

MONALS ▶ **monal**

MONARCH *n* sovereign ruler of a state

MONARDA *n* mintlike N American plant

MONAS *same as* ▶ **monad**

MONASES ▶ **monas**

MONAUL *same as* ▶ **monal**

MONAULS ▶ **monaul**

MONAXON *n* type of sponge

MONDAIN *n* man who moves in fashionable society ▷ *adj* characteristic of fashionable society

MONDE *n* French word meaning world or society

MONDES ▶ **monde**

MONDIAL *adj* of or involving the whole world

MONDO *n* Buddhist questioning technique

MONDOS ▶ **mondo**

MONEME *less common word for* > **morpheme**

MONEMES ▶ **moneme**

MONER *n* hypothetical simple organism

MONERA ▶ **moner**

MONERAN *n* type of bacterium

MONERON *same as* ▶ **moner**

MONETH *same as* ▶ **month**

MONETHS ▶ **moneth**

MONEY *n* medium of exchange, coins or banknotes

MONEYED *adj* rich

MONEYER *n* person who coins money

MONEYS ▶ **money**

MONGED *adj* under the influence of drugs

MONGER *n* trader or dealer ▷ *vb* deal in

MONGERS ▶ **monger**

MONGERY ▶ **monger**

MONGO *same as* ▶ **mungo**

MONGOE *same as* ▶ **mongo**

MONGOES ▶ **mongoe**

MONGOS ▶ **mongo**

MONGREL *n* animal, esp a dog, of mixed breed ▷ *adj* of mixed breed or origin

MONGST *short for*

▶ **amongst**

MONIAL *n* mullion

MONIALS ▶ **monial**

MONIE *Scots word for* ▶ **many**

MONIED *same as* ▶ **moneyed**

MONIES ▶ **money**

MONIKER *n* person's name or nickname

MONILIA *n* type of fungus

MONISH *same as* > **admonish**

MONISM *n* doctrine that reality consists of only one basic substance or element, such as mind or matter

MONISMS ▶ **monism**

MONIST ▶ **monism**

MONISTS ▶ **monism**

MONITOR *n* person or device that checks, controls, warns, or keeps a record of something ▷ *vb* watch and check on

MONK *n* member of an all-male religious community bound by vows

MONKEY *n* long-tailed primate ▷ *vb* meddle or fool

MONKEYS ▶ **monkey**

MONKISH *adj* of, relating to, or resembling a monk or monks

MONKS ▶ **monk**

MONO *n* monophonic sound

MONOAO *n* New Zealand plant with rigid leaves

MONOAOS ▶ **monoao**

MONOCLE *n* eyeglass for one eye only

MONOCOT *n* type of flowering plant with a single embryonic seed leaf, such as grasses, lilies, palms, and orchids

MONODIC ▶ **monody**

MONODY *n* (in Greek tragedy) an ode sung by a single actor

MONOECY *same as* > **monoecism**

MONOFIL *n* synthetic thread or yarn composed of a single strand rather than twisted fibres

MONOLOG *same as* > **monologue**

MONOMER *n* compound whose molecules can join together to form a polymer

MONONYM *n* person who

is famous enough to be known only by one name, usually the first name

MONOPOD *same as* > **monopode**

MONOS ▶ **mono**

MONOSES ▶ **monosis**

MONOSIS *n* abnormal separation

MONOSKI *n* wide ski on which the skier stands with both feet ▷ *vb* ski on a monoski

MONOSY *same as* ▶ **monosis**

MONS ▶ **mon**

MONSOON *n* seasonal wind of SE Asia

MONSTER *n* imaginary, usu frightening, beast ▷ *adj* huge ▷ *vb* criticize (a person or group) severely

MONTAGE *n* (making of) a picture composed from pieces of others ▷ *vb* make as a montage

MONTAN *adj* as in **montan wax** hard wax obtained from lignite and peat used in polishes and candles

MONTANE *n* area of mountain dominated by vegetation ▷ *adj* of or inhabiting mountainous regions

MONTANT *n* vertical part in woodwork

MONTE *n* gambling card game of Spanish origin

MONTEM *n* former money-raising practice at Eton school

MONTEMS ▶ **montem**

MONTERO *n* round cap with a flap at the back worn by hunters, esp in Spain in the 17th and 18th centuries

MONTES ▶ **monte**

MONTH *n* one of the twelve divisions of the calendar year

MONTHLY *adj* happening or payable once a month ▷ *adv* once a month ▷ *n* monthly magazine

MONTHS ▶ **month**

MONTIES ▶ **monty**

MONTRE *n* pipes of organ

MONTRES ▶ **montre**

MONTURE *n* mount or frame

MONTY *n* complete form of something

M

MONURON n type of weedkiller

MONY Scots word for ▶ **many**

MOO n long deep cry of a cow ▷ vb make this noise ▷ interj instance or imitation of this sound

MOOBS pl n overdeveloped breasts on a man, caused by excess weight or lack of exercise

MOOCH vb loiter about aimlessly

MOOCHED ▶ mooch

MOOCHER ▶ mooch

MOOCHES ▶ mooch

MOOD n temporary (gloomy) state of mind

MOODIED ▶ moody

MOODIER ▶ moody

MOODIES ▶ moody

MOODILY ▶ moody

MOODS ▶ mood

MOODY adj sullen or gloomy ▷ vb flatter

MOOED ▶ moo

MOOI adj pleasing or nice

MOOING ▶ moo

MOOKTAR same as ▶ mukhtar

MOOL same as ▶ mould

MOOLA same as ▶ moolah

MOOLAH slang word for ▶ money

MOOLAHS ▶ moolah

MOOLAS ▶ moola

MOOLED ▶ mool

MOOLEY same as ▶ mooly

MOOLEYS ▶ mooley

MOOLI n type of large white radish

MOOLIES ▶ mooly

MOOLING ▶ mool

MOOLIS ▶ mooli

MOOLOO n person from the Waikato

MOOLOOS ▶ mooloo

MOOLS ▶ mool

MOOLVI same as ▶ moolvie

MOOLVIE n (esp in India) a Muslim doctor of the law, teacher, or learned man also used as a title of respect

MOOLVIS ▶ moolvi

MOOLY same as ▶ muley

MOON n natural satellite of the earth ▷ vb be idle in a listless or dreamy way

MOONBOW n rainbow made by moonlight

MOONED adj decorated with a moon

MOONER ▶ moon

MOONERS ▶ moon

MOONEYE n N American large-eyed freshwater fish

MOONG n as in moong bean kind of bean

MOONIER ▶ moony

MOONIES ▶ moony

MOONILY ▶ moony

MOONING ▶ moon

MOONISH ▶ moon

MOONLET n small moon

MOONLIT adj illuminated by the moon

MOONS ▶ moon

MOONSET n moment when the moon disappears below the horizon

MOONY adj dreamy or listless ▷ n crazy or foolish person

MOOP same as ▶ moup

MOOPED ▶ moop

MOOPING ▶ moop

MOOPS ▶ moop

MOOR n tract of open uncultivated ground covered with grass and heather ▷ vb secure (a ship) with ropes etc

MOORAGE n place for mooring a vessel

MOORED ▶ moor

MOORHEN n small black water bird

MOORIER ▶ moor

MOORILL n disease of cattle on moors

MOORING n place for mooring a ship

MOORISH adj of or relating to the Moor people of North Africa

MOORLOG n rotted wood below the surface of a moor

MOORMAN n person living on a moor

MOORMEN ▶ moorman

MOORS ▶ moor

MOORVA same as ▶ murva

MOORVAS ▶ moorva

MOORY ▶ moor

MOOS ▶ moo

MOOSE n large N American deer

MOOT adj debatable ▷ vb bring up for discussion ▷ n (in Anglo-Saxon England) a local administrative assembly

MOOTED ▶ moot

MOOTER ▶ moot

MOOTERS ▶ moot

MOOTEST ▶ moot

MOOTING ▶ moot

MOOTMAN n person taking part in a moot

MOOTMEN ▶ mootman

MOOTS ▶ moot

MOOVE same as ▶ move

MOOVED ▶ moove

MOOVES ▶ moove

MOOVING ▶ moove

MOP n long stick with twists of cotton or a sponge on the end, used for cleaning ▷ vb clean or soak up with or as if with a mop

MOPANE same as ▶ mopani

MOPANES ▶ mopane

MOPANI n S African tree that is highly resistant to drought and produces very hard wood

MOPANIS ▶ mopani

MOPE vb be gloomy and apathetic ▷ n gloomy person

MOPED n light motorized cycle

MOPEDS ▶ moped

MOPER ▶ mope

MOPERS ▶ mope

MOPERY n gloominess

MOPES ▶ mope

MOPEY ▶ mope

MOPHEAD n person with shaggy hair

MOPIER ▶ mope

MOPIEST ▶ mope

MOPILY ▶ mopy

MOPING ▶ mope

MOPISH ▶ mope

MOPOKE n species of owl

MOPOKES ▶ mopoke

MOPPED ▶ mop

MOPPER ▶ mop

MOPPERS ▶ mop

MOPPET same as ▶ poppet

MOPPETS ▶ moppet

MOPPIER ▶ moppy

MOPPING ▶ mop

MOPPY adj drunk

MOPS ▶ mop

MOPSIES ▶ mopsy

MOPSY n untidy or dowdy person

MOPUS n person who mopes

MOPUSES ▶ mopus

MOPY ▶ mope

MOR n layer of acidic humus formed in cool moist areas where decomposition is slow

MORA n quantity of a short syllable in verse

MORAE ▶ **mora**

MORAINE n accumulated mass of debris deposited by a glacier

MORAL adj concerned with right and wrong conduct ▷ n lesson to be obtained from a story or event ▷ vb moralize

MORALE n degree of confidence or hope of a person or group

MORALES ▶ **morale**

MORALL same as ▶ **mural**

MORALLS ▶ **morall**

MORALLY ▶ **moral**

MORALS ▶ **moral**

MORAS ▶ **mora**

MORASS n marsh

MORASSY ▶ **morass**

MORAT n drink containing mulberry juice

MORATS ▶ **morat**

MORAY n large voracious eel

MORAYS ▶ **moray**

MORBID adj unduly interested in death or unpleasant events

MORBUS n disease

MORCEAU n fragment or morsel

MORCHA n (in India) a hostile demonstration against the government

MORCHAS ▶ **morcha**

MORDANT adj sarcastic or scathing ▷ n substance used to fix dyes ▷ vb treat (a fabric, yarn, etc) with a mordant

MORDENT n melodic ornament consisting of the rapid alternation of a note with a note one degree lower than it

MORE adj greater in amount or degree ▷ adv greater extent ▷ pron greater or additional amount or number

MOREEN n heavy, usually watered, fabric of wool or wool and cotton, used esp in furnishing

MOREENS ▶ **moreen**

MOREISH adj (of food) causing a desire for more

MOREL n edible mushroom with a pitted cap

MORELLE n nightshade

MORELLO n variety of small very dark sour cherry

MORELS ▶ **morel**

MORENDO adv (in music) dying away

MORES pl n customs and conventions embodying the fundamental values of a community

MORGAN n American breed of small compact saddle horse

MORGANS ▶ **morgan**

MORGAY n small dogfish

MORGAYS ▶ **morgay**

MORGEN n South African unit of area, equal to about two acres or 0.8 hectare

MORGENS ▶ **morgen**

MORGUE same as ▷ **mortuary**

MORGUES ▶ **morgue**

MORIA n folly

MORIAS ▶ **moria**

MORICHE same as ▶ **miriti**

MORION n 16th-century helmet with a brim and wide comb

MORIONS ▶ **morion**

MORISCO n a morris dance

MORISH same as ▶ **moreish**

MORKIN n animal dying in accident

MORKINS ▶ **morkin**

MORLING n sheep killed by disease

MORMAOR n former high-ranking Scottish nobleman

MORN n morning

MORNAY adj served with a cheese sauce

MORNAYS ▶ **mornay**

MORNE same as ▶ **mourn**

MORNED ▶ **morne**

MORNES ▶ **morne**

MORNING n part of the day before noon

MORNS ▶ **morn**

MOROCCO n goatskin leather

MORON n foolish or stupid person

MORONIC ▶ **moron**

MORONS ▶ **moron**

MOROSE adj sullen or moody

MOROSER ▶ **morose**

MORPH n phonological representation of a morpheme ▷ vb undergo or cause to undergo morphing

MORPHED ▶ **morph**

MORPHEW n blemish on skin

MORPHIA same as ▷ **morphine**

MORPHIC adj as in **morphic resonance** idea that, through a telepathic effect or sympathetic vibration, an event or act can lead to similar events or acts in the future or an idea conceived in one mind can then arise in another

MORPHIN variant form of ▷ **morphine**

MORPHO n type of butterfly

MORPHOS ▶ **morpho**

MORPHS ▶ **morph**

MORRA same as ▶ **mora**

MORRAS ▶ **morra**

MORRELL n tall SW Australian eucalyptus with pointed buds

MORRHUA n cod

MORRICE same as ▶ **morris**

MORRION same as ▶ **morion**

MORRIS vb perform morris dance

MORRO n rounded hill or promontory

MORROS ▶ **morro**

MORROW n next day

MORROWS ▶ **morrow**

MORS ▶ **mor**

MORSAL ▶ **morsure**

MORSE n clasp or fastening on a cope

MORSEL n small piece, esp of food ▷ vb divide into morsels

MORSELS ▶ **morsel**

MORSES ▶ **morse**

MORSURE ▶ **morsal**

MORT n call blown on a hunting horn to signify the death of the animal hunted

MORTAL adj subject to death ▷ n human being

MORTALS ▶ **mortal**

MORTAR n small cannon with a short range ▷ vb fire on with mortars

MORTARS ▶ **mortar**

MORTARY adj of or like mortar

MORTICE same as ▶ **mortise**

MORTIFY vb humiliate

MORTISE n slot or recess, usually rectangular, cut into a piece of wood, stone,

M

M

etc, to receive a matching projection (tenon) of another piece, or a mortise lock ▷ *vb* cut a slot or recess in (a piece of wood, stone, etc)

MORTS ▶ **mort**

MORULA *n* solid ball of cells resulting from cleavage of a fertilized ovum

MORULAE ▶ **morula**

MORULAR ▶ **morula**

MORULAS ▶ **morula**

MORWONG *n* food fish of Australasian coastal waters

MORYAH *interj* exclamation of annoyance, disbelief, etc

MOS ▶ **mo**

MOSAIC *n* design or decoration using small pieces of coloured stone or glass

MOSAICS ▶ **mosaic**

MOSE *vb* have glanders

MOSED ▶ **mose**

MOSELLE *n* German white wine from the Moselle valley

MOSES ▶ **mose**

MOSEY *vb* walk in a leisurely manner

MOSEYED ▶ **mosey**

MOSEYS ▶ **mosey**

MOSH *n* type of dance, performed to loud rock music, in which people throw themselves about in a frantic and violent manner ▷ *vb* dance in this manner

MOSHAV *n* cooperative settlement in Israel, consisting of a number of small farms

MOSHED ▶ **mosh**

MOSHER ▶ **mosh**

MOSHERS ▶ **mosh**

MOSHES ▶ **mosh**

MOSHING ▶ **mosh**

MOSING ▶ **mose**

MOSK *same as* ▶ **mosque**

MOSKS ▶ **mosk**

MOSQUE *n* Muslim temple

MOSQUES ▶ **mosque**

MOSS *n* small flowerless plant growing in masses on moist surfaces ▷ *vb* gather moss

MOSSED ▶ **moss**

MOSSER ▶ **moss**

MOSSERS ▶ **moss**

MOSSES ▶ **moss**

MOSSIE *n* common sparrow

MOSSIER ▶ **moss**

MOSSIES ▶ **mossie**

MOSSING ▶ **moss**

MOSSO *adv* to be performed with rapidity

MOSSY ▶ **moss**

MOST *n* greatest number or degree ▷ *adj* greatest in number or degree ▷ *adv* in the greatest degree

MOSTE ▶ **mote**

MOSTEST ▶ **most**

MOSTLY *adv* for the most part, generally

MOSTS ▶ **most**

MOT *n* girl or young woman, esp one's girlfriend

MOTE *n* tiny speck ▷ *vb* may or might

MOTED *adj* containing motes

MOTEL *n* roadside hotel for motorists

MOTELS ▶ **motel**

MOTEN ▶ **mote**

MOTES ▶ **mote**

MOTET *n* short sacred choral song

MOTETS ▶ **motet**

MOTETT *same as* ▶ **motet**

MOTETTS ▶ **motet**

MOTEY *adj* containing motes

MOTH *n* nocturnal insect like a butterfly

MOTHED *adj* damaged by moths

MOTHER *n* female parent ▷ *adj* native or inborn ▷ *vb* look after as a mother

MOTHERS ▶ **mother**

MOTHERY ▶ **mother**

MOTHIER ▶ **mothy**

MOTHS ▶ **moth**

MOTHY *adj* ragged

MOTIER ▶ **motey**

MOTIEST ▶ **motey**

MOTIF *n* (recurring) theme or design

MOTIFIC *adj* causing motion

MOTIFS ▶ **motif**

MOTILE *adj* capable of independent movement ▷ *n* person whose mental imagery strongly reflects movement, esp his own

MOTILES ▶ **motile**

MOTION *n* process, action, or way of moving ▷ *vb* direct (someone) by gesture

MOTIONS ▶ **motion**

MOTIVE *n* reason for a

course of action ▷ *adj* causing motion ▷ *vb* motivate

MOTIVED ▶ **motive**

MOTIVES ▶ **motive**

MOTIVIC *adj* of musical motif

MOTLEY *adj* miscellaneous ▷ *n* costume of a jester

MOTLEYS ▶ **motley**

MOTLIER ▶ **motley**

MOTMOT *n* tropical American bird with a long tail and blue and brownish-green plumage

MOTMOTS ▶ **motmot**

MOTOR *n* engine, esp of a vehicle ▷ *vb* travel by car ▷ *adj* of or relating to cars and other vehicles powered by petrol or diesel engines

MOTORED ▶ **motor**

MOTORIC ▶ **motor**

MOTORS ▶ **motor**

MOTORY ▶ **motor**

MOTS ▶ **mot**

MOTSER *n* large sum of money, esp a gambling win

MOTSERS ▶ **motser**

MOTT *n* clump of trees

MOTTE *n* mound on which a castle was built

MOTTES ▶ **motte**

MOTTIER ▶ **motty**

MOTTIES ▶ **motty**

MOTTLE *vb* colour with streaks or blotches of different shades ▷ *n* mottled appearance, as of the surface of marble

MOTTLED ▶ **mottle**

MOTTLER *n* paintbrush for mottled effects

MOTTLES ▶ **mottle**

MOTTO *n* saying expressing an ideal or rule of conduct

MOTTOED *adj* having motto

MOTTOES ▶ **motto**

MOTTOS ▶ **motto**

MOTTS ▶ **mott**

MOTTY *n* target at which coins are aimed in pitch-and-toss ▷ *adj* containing motes

MOTUCA *n* Brazilian fly

MOTUCAS ▶ **motuca**

MOTZA *same as* ▶ **motser**

MOTZAS ▶ **motza**

MOU *Scots word for* ▶ **mouth**

MOUCH *same as* ▶ **mooch**

MOUCHED ▶ **mouch**

MOUCHER ▶ **mouch**

MOUCHES ▶ **mouch**

MOUE n disdainful or pouting look

MOUES ▶ moue

MOUFLON n wild short-fleeced mountain sheep of Corsica and Sardinia

MOUGHT ▶ mote

MOUILLE adj palatalized, as in the sounds represented by Spanish ll or ñ

MOUJIK same as ▶ **muzhik**

MOUJIKS ▶ moujik

MOULAGE n mould making

MOULD n hollow container in which metal etc is cast ▷ vb shape

MOULDED ▶ mould

MOULDER vb decay into dust ▷ n person who moulds or makes moulds

MOULDS ▶ mould

MOULDY adj stale or musty

MOULIN n vertical shaft in a glacier, maintained by a constant descending stream of water and debris

MOULINS ▶ moulin

MOULS Scots word for ▶ **mould**

MOULT vb shed feathers, hair, or skin to make way for new growth ▷ n process of moulting

MOULTED ▶ moult

MOULTEN adj having moulted

MOULTER ▶ moult

MOULTS ▶ moult

MOUND n heap, esp of earth or stones ▷ vb gather into a mound

MOUNDED ▶ mound

MOUNDS ▶ mound

MOUNT vb climb or ascend ▷ n backing or support on which something is fixed

MOUNTED adj riding horses

MOUNTER ▶ mount

MOUNTS ▶ mount

MOUP n nibble

MOUPED ▶ moup

MOUPING ▶ moup

MOUPS ▶ moup

MOURN vb feel or express sorrow for (a dead person or lost thing)

MOURNED ▶ mourn

MOURNER n person attending a funeral

MOURNS ▶ mourn

MOUS ▶ mou

MOUSAKA same as

▶ **moussaka**

MOUSE n small long-tailed rodent ▷ vb stalk and catch mice

MOUSED ▶ mouse

MOUSER n cat used to catch mice

MOUSERS ▶ mouser

MOUSERY n place infested with mice

MOUSES ▶ mouse

MOUSEY same as ▶ **mousy**

MOUSIE n little mouse

MOUSIER ▶ mousy

MOUSIES ▶ mousie

MOUSILY ▶ mousy

MOUSING n lashing, shackle, etc, for closing off a hook to prevent a load from slipping off

MOUSLE vb handle roughly

MOUSLED ▶ mousle

MOUSLES ▶ mousle

MOUSME n Japanese girl

MOUSMEE same as

▶ **mousme**

MOUSMES ▶ mousme

MOUSSE n dish of flavoured cream whipped and set ▷ vb apply mousse to

MOUSSED ▶ mousse

MOUSSES ▶ mousse

MOUST same as ▶ **must**

MOUSTED ▶ moust

MOUSTS ▶ moust

MOUSY adj like a mouse, esp in hair colour

MOUTAN n variety of peony

MOUTANS ▶ moutan

MOUTER same as ▶ **multure**

MOUTERS ▶ mouter

MOUTH n opening in the head for eating and issuing sounds ▷ vb form (words) with the lips without speaking

MOUTHED ▶ mouth

MOUTHER ▶ mouth

MOUTHS ▶ mouth

MOUTHY adj bombastic

MOUTON n sheepskin processed to resemble the fur of another animal, esp beaver or seal

MOUTONS ▶ mouton

MOVABLE adj able to be moved or rearranged ▷ n movable article, esp a piece of furniture

MOVABLY ▶ movable

MOVE vb change in place or position ▷ n moving

MOVED ▶ move

MOVER n person or animal that moves in a particular way

MOVERS ▶ mover

MOVES ▶ move

MOVIE n cinema film

MOVIES ▶ movie

MOVING adj arousing or touching the emotions

MOVIOLA n viewing machine used in cutting and editing film

MOW vb cut (grass or crops) ▷ n part of a barn where hay, straw, etc, is stored

MOWA same as ▶ **mahua**

MOWAS ▶ mowa

MOWBURN vb heat up in mow

MOWDIE Scots words for ▶ **mole**

MOWDIES ▶ mowdie

MOWED ▶ mow

MOWER ▶ mow

MOWERS ▶ mow

MOWING ▶ mow

MOWINGS ▶ mow

MOWN ▶ mow

MOWRA same as ▶ **mahua**

MOWRAS ▶ mowra

MOWS ▶ mow

MOXA n downy material obtained from various plants and used in Oriental medicine by being burned on the skin as a cauterizing agent or counterirritant for the skin

MOXAS ▶ moxa

MOXIE n courage, nerve, or vigour

MOXIES ▶ moxie

MOY n coin

MOYA n mud emitted from a volcano

MOYAS ▶ moya

MOYITY same as ▶ **moiety**

MOYL same as ▶ **moyle**

MOYLE vb toil

MOYLED ▶ moyle

MOYLES ▶ moyle

MOYLING ▶ moyle

MOYLS ▶ moyl

MOYS ▶ moy

MOZ n hex

This unusual word, Australian slang for bad luck, is another of the very useful short words that use the Z, and it can be extended to **moze** or **mozo**.

MOZE vb give nap to

M

MOZED ▶ moze
MOZES ▶ moze
MOZETTA *same as* > **mozzetta**
MOZETTE ▶ mozetta
MOZING ▶ moze
MOZO *n* porter in southwest USA
MOZOS ▶ mozo
MOZZ *same as* ▶ **moz**
MOZZES ▶ mozz
MOZZIE *same as* ▶ **mossie**
MOZZIES ▶ mozzie
MOZZLE *n* luck
MOZZLES ▶ mozzle
MPRET *n* former Albanian ruler
MPRETS ▶ mpret
MRIDANG *n* drum used in Indian music
MU *n* 12th letter in the Greek alphabet, a consonant, transliterated as *m*
MUCATE *n* salt of mucic acid
MUCATES ▶ mucate
MUCH *adj* large amount or degree of ▷ *n* large amount or degree ▷ *adv* great degree
MUCHEL *same as* ▶ **much**
MUCHELL *same as* ▶ **much**
MUCHELS ▶ muchel
MUCHES ▶ much
MUCHLY ▶ much
MUCHO *adv* Spanish for very
MUCIC *adj* as in **mucic acid** colourless crystalline solid carboxylic acid found in milk sugar and used in the manufacture of pyrrole
MUCID *adj* mouldy, musty, or slimy
MUCIGEN *n* substance present in mucous cells that is converted into mucin
MUCIN *n* any of a group of nitrogenous mucoproteins occurring in saliva, skin, tendon, etc, that produce a very viscous solution in water
MUCINS ▶ mucin
MUCK *n* dirt, filth
MUCKED ▶ muck
MUCKER *n* person who shifts broken rock or waste ▷ *vb* hoard
MUCKERS ▶ mucker
MUCKIER ▶ mucky
MUCKILY ▶ mucky
MUCKING ▶ muck

MUCKLE *same as* ▶ **mickle**
MUCKLES ▶ muckle
MUCKS ▶ muck
MUCKY *adj* dirty or muddy
MUCLUC *same as* ▶ **mukluk**
MUCLUCS ▶ mucluc
MUCOID *adj* of the nature of or resembling mucin ▷ *n* substance like mucin
MUCOIDS ▶ mucoid
MUCOR *n* type of fungus which comprises many common moulds
MUCORS ▶ mucor
MUCOSA *n* mucous membrane: mucus-secreting membrane that lines body cavities or passages that are open to the external environment
MUCOSAE ▶ mucosa
MUCOSAL ▶ mucosa
MUCOSAS ▶ mucosa
MUCOSE *same as* ▶ **mucous**
MUCOUS *adj* of, resembling, or secreting mucus
MUCRO *n* short pointed projection from certain parts or organs, as from the tip of a leaf
MUCROS ▶ mucro
MUCUS *n* slimy secretion of the mucous membranes
MUCUSES ▶ mucus
MUD *n* wet soft earth ▷ *vb* cover in mud
MUDBATH *n* medicinal bath in heated mud
MUDBUG *n* crayfish
MUDBUGS ▶ mudbug
MUDCAP *vb* use explosive charge in blasting
MUDCAPS ▶ mudcap
MUDCAT *n* any of several large North American catfish living in muddy rivers, esp in the Mississippi valley
MUDCATS ▶ mudcat
MUDDED ▶ mud
MUDDER *n* horse that runs well in mud
MUDDERS ▶ mudder
MUDDIED ▶ muddy
MUDDIER ▶ muddy
MUDDIES ▶ muddy
MUDDILY ▶ muddy
MUDDING ▶ mud
MUDDLE *vb* confuse ▷ *n* state of confusion
MUDDLED ▶ muddle
MUDDLER *n* person who

muddles or muddles through
MUDDLES ▶ muddle
MUDDLY ▶ muddle
MUDDY *adj* covered or filled with mud ▷ *vb* make muddy
MUDEJAR *n* Spanish Moor, esp one permitted to stay in Spain after the Christian reconquest ▷ *adj* of or relating to a style of architecture originated by Mudéjares
MUDEYE *n* larva of the dragonfly, commonly used as a fishing bait
MUDEYES ▶ mudeye
MUDFISH *n* any of various fishes, such as the bowfin and cichlids, that live at or frequent the muddy bottoms of rivers, lakes, etc
MUDFLAP *n* flap above wheel to deflect mud
MUDFLAT *n* tract of low muddy land, esp near an estuary, that is covered at high tide and exposed at low tide
MUDFLOW *n* flow of soil or fine-grained sediment mixed with water down a steep unstable slope
MUDGE *vb* speak vaguely
MUDGED ▶ mudge
MUDGER ▶ mudge
MUDGERS ▶ mudge
MUDGES ▶ mudge
MUDGING ▶ mudge
MUDHEN *n* water bird living in muddy place
MUDHENS ▶ mudhen
MUDHOLE *n* hole with mud at bottom
MUDHOOK *n* anchor
MUDIR *n* local governor
MUDIRIA *n* province of mudir
MUDIRS ▶ mudir
MUDLARK *n* street urchin ▷ *vb* play in mud
MUDPACK *n* cosmetic paste applied to the face to improve the complexion
MUDRA *n* any of various ritual hand movements in Hindu religious dancing
MUDRAS ▶ mudra
MUDROCK *n* type of sedimentary rock
MUDROOM *n* room where muddy shoes may be left

MUDS ▸ mud
MUDSCOW n boat for travelling over mudflats
MUDSILL n support for building at or below ground
MUDWORT n plant growing in mud
MUEDDIN same as ▸ muezzin
MUESLI n mixture of grain, nuts, and dried fruit, eaten with milk
MUESLIS ▸ muesli
MUEZZIN n official who summons Muslims to prayer
MUFF n tube-shaped covering to keep the hands warm ▷ vb bungle (an action)
MUFFED ▸ muff
MUFFIN n light round flat yeast cake
MUFFING ▸ muff
MUFFINS ▸ muffin
MUFFISH ▸ muff
MUFFLE vb wrap up for warmth or to deaden sound ▷ n something that muffles
MUFFLED ▸ muffle
MUFFLER n scarf
MUFFLES ▸ muffle
MUFFS ▸ muff
MUFLON same as > moufflon
MUFLONS ▸ muflon
MUFTI n civilian clothes worn by a person who usually wears a uniform
MUFTIS ▸ mufti
MUG n large drinking cup ▷ vb attack in order to rob
MUGFUL same as ▸ mug
MUGFULS ▸ mugful
MUGG same as ▸ mug
MUGGA n Australian eucalyptus tree with dark bark and pink flowers
MUGGAR same as ▸ mugger
MUGGARS ▸ muggar
MUGGAS ▸ mugga
MUGGED ▸ mug
MUGGEE n mugged person
MUGGEES ▸ muggee
MUGGER n person who commits robbery with violence, esp in the street
MUGGERS ▸ mugger
MUGGIER ▸ muggy
MUGGILY ▸ muggy
MUGGING ▸ mug
MUGGINS n stupid or gullible person

MUGGISH same as ▸ muggy
MUGGS ▸ mug
MUGGUR same as ▸ mugger
MUGGURS ▸ muggur
MUGGY adj (of weather) damp and stifling
MUGHAL same as ▸ mogul
MUGHALS ▸ mughal
MUGS ▸ mug
MUGSHOT n police photograph of person's face
MUGWORT n N American herbaceous plant with aromatic leaves and clusters of small greenish-white flowers
MUGWUMP n neutral or independent person, esp in politics
MUHLIES ▸ muhly
MUHLY n American grass
MUID n former French measure of capacity
MUIDS ▸ muid
MUIL same as ▸ mule
MUILS ▸ muil
MUIR same as ▸ moor
MUIRS ▸ muir
MUIST same as ▸ must
MUISTED ▸ muist
MUISTS ▸ muist
MUJIK same as ▸ muzhik
MUJIKS ▸ mujik
MUKHTAR n lawyer in India
MUKLUK n soft boot, usually of sealskin, worn in the American Arctic
MUKLUKS ▸ mukluk
MUKTUK n thin outer skin of the beluga, used as food
MUKTUKS ▸ muktuk
MULATTA n female mulatto
MULATTO n child of one Black and one White parent ▷ adj of a light brown colour
MULCH n mixture of wet straw, leaves, etc, used to protect the roots of plants ▷ vb cover (land) with mulch
MULCHED ▸ mulch
MULCHES ▸ mulch
MULCT vb cheat or defraud ▷ n fine or penalty
MULCTED ▸ mulct
MULCTS ▸ mulct
MULE n offspring of a horse and a donkey ▷ vb strike coin with different die on each side
MULED ▸ mule
MULES vb surgically remove folds of skin from a sheep

MULESED ▸ mules
MULESES ▸ mules
MULETA n small cape attached to a stick used by the matador during the final stages of a bullfight
MULETAS ▸ muleta
MULEY adj (of cattle) having no horns ▷ n any hornless cow
MULEYS ▸ muley
MULGA n Australian acacia shrub growing in desert regions
MULGAS ▸ mulga
MULING ▸ mule
MULISH adj obstinate
MULL vb think (over) or ponder ▷ n promontory or headland
MULLA same as ▸ mullah
MULLAH n Muslim scholar, teacher, or religious leader
MULLAHS ▸ mullah
MULLAS ▸ mulla
MULLED ▸ mull
MULLEIN n type of European plant
MULLEN same as ▸ mullein
MULLENS ▸ mullen
MULLER n flat heavy implement of stone or iron used to grind material against a slab of stone ▷ vb beat up or defeat thoroughly
MULLERS ▸ muller
MULLET n edible sea fish
MULLETS ▸ mullet
MULLEY same as ▸ muley
MULLEYS ▸ mulley
MULLING ▸ mull
MULLION n vertical dividing bar in a window ▷ vb furnish (a window, screen, etc) with mullions
MULLITE n colourless mineral
MULLOCK n waste material from a mine
MULLS ▸ mull
MULMUL n muslin
MULMULL same as ▸ mulmul
MULMULS ▸ mulmul
MULSE n drink containing honey
MULSES ▸ mulse
MULSH same as ▸ mulch
MULSHED ▸ mulsh
MULSHES ▸ mulsh
MULTUM n substance used in brewing
MULTUMS ▸ multum

M

MULTURE n fee formerly paid to a miller for grinding grain ▷ vb take multure

MUM n mother ▷ vb act in a mummer's play

MUMBLE vb speak indistinctly, mutter ▷ n indistinct utterance

MUMBLED ▶ mumble

MUMBLER ▶ mumble

MUMBLES ▶ mumble

MUMBLY ▶ mumble

MUMM same as ▶ mum

MUMMED ▶ mum

MUMMER n actor in a traditional English folk play or mime

MUMMERS ▶ mummer

MUMMERY n performance by mummers

MUMMIA n mummified flesh used as medicine

MUMMIAS ▶ mummia

MUMMIED ▶ mummy

MUMMIES ▶ mummy

MUMMIFY vb preserve the body of (a human or animal) as a mummy

MUMMING ▶ mum

MUMMOCK same as ▶ mammock

MUMMS ▶ mumm

MUMMY n body embalmed and wrapped for burial in ancient Egypt ▷ vb mummify

MUMP vb be silent

MUMPED ▶ mump

MUMPER ▶ mump

MUMPERS ▶ mump

MUMPING ▶ mump

MUMPISH ▶ mumps

MUMPS n infectious disease with swelling in the glands of the neck

MUMS ▶ mum

MUMSIER ▶ mumsy

MUMSY adj out of fashion

MUMU n oven in Papua New Guinea

MUMUS ▶ mumu

MUN same as ▶ maun

MUNCH vb chew noisily and steadily

MUNCHED ▶ munch

MUNCHER ▶ munch

MUNCHES ▶ munch

MUNDANE adj everyday

MUNDIC n iron pyrites

MUNDICS ▶ mundic

MUNDIFY vb cleanse

MUNG vb process (computer data)

MUNGA n army canteen

MUNGAS ▶ munga

MUNGE vb modify a password into an unguessable state

MUNGED ▶ mung

MUNGES ▶ mung

MUNGING ▶ mung

MUNGO n cheap felted fabric made from waste wool

MUNGOES ▶ mungo

MUNGOS ▶ mungo

MUNGS ▶ mung

MUNI n municipal radio broadcast

MUNIFY vb fortify

MUNIS ▶ muni

MUNITE vb strengthen

MUNITED ▶ munite

MUNITES ▶ munite

MUNNION archaic word for ▶ mullion

MUNS ▶ mun

MUNSHI n secretary in India

MUNSHIS ▶ munshi

MUNSTER same as > muenster

MUNTIN n supporting or strengthening bar for a glass window, door, etc

MUNTING same as ▶ muntin

MUNTINS ▶ muntin

MUNTJAC n small Asian deer of the genus typically with a chestnut-brown coat, small antlers, and a barklike cry

MUNTJAK same as ▶ muntjac

MUNTRIE n Australian shrub with green-red edible berries

MUON n positive or negative elementary particle with a mass 207 times that of an electron

MUONIC ▶ muon

MUONIUM n form of hydrogen

MUONS ▶ muon

MUPPET n stupid person

MUPPETS ▶ muppet

MURA n group of people living together in Japanese countryside

MURAENA n moray eel

MURAGE n tax levied for the construction or maintenance of town walls

MURAGES ▶ murage

MURAL n painting on a wall ▷ adj of or relating to a wall

MURALED same as > muralled

MURALS ▶ mural

MURAS ▶ mura

MURDER n unlawful intentional killing of a human being ▷ vb kill in this way

MURDERS ▶ murder

MURE archaic or literary word for ▶ immure

MURED ▶ mure

MUREIN n polymer found in cells

MUREINS ▶ murein

MURENA same as ▶ muraena

MURENAS ▶ murena

MURES ▶ mure

MUREX n type of spiny-shelled marine gastropod formerly used as a source of the dye Tyrian purple

MUREXES ▶ murex

MURGEON vb grimace at

MURIATE obsolete name for a > chloride

MURICES ▶ murex

MURID n animal of mouse family

MURIDS ▶ murid

MURINE n type of animal belonging to the Old World family of rodents that includes rats and mice

MURINES ▶ murine

MURING ▶ mure

MURK n thick darkness ▷ adj dark or gloomy

MURKER ▶ murk

MURKEST ▶ murk

MURKIER ▶ murky

MURKILY ▶ murky

MURKISH ▶ murk

MURKLY ▶ murk

MURKS ▶ murk

MURKY adj dark or gloomy

MURL vb crumble

MURLAIN n type of basket

MURLAN same as ▶ murlain

MURLANS ▶ murlan

MURLED ▶ murl

MURLIER ▶ murl

MURLIN same as ▶ murlain

MURLING ▶ murl

MURLINS ▶ murlin

MURLS ▶ murl

MURLY ▶ murl

MURMUR vb speak or say in a quiet indistinct way ▷ n continuous low indistinct sound

MURMURS ▶ murmur

MURPHY *dialect or informal word for* ▶ **potato**

MURR *n* former name for a cold

MURRA *same as* ▶ **murrhine**

MURRAGH *n* type of large caddis fly

MURRAIN *n* cattle plague

MURRAM *n* type of gravel

MURRAMS ▶ **murram**

MURRAS ▶ **murra**

MURRAY *n* large Australian freshwater fish

MURRAYS ▶ **murray**

MURRE *n* type of guillemot

MURREE *n* native Australian

MURREES ▶ **murree**

MURREN *same as* ▶ **murrain**

MURRENS ▶ **murren**

MURRES ▶ **murre**

MURREY *adj* mulberry colour

MURREYS ▶ **murrey**

MURRHA *same as* ▶ **murra**

MURRHAS ▶ **murrha**

MURRI *same as* ▶ **murree**

MURRIES ▶ **murry**

MURRIN *same as* ▶ **murrain**

MURRINE *same as* > **murrhine**

MURRINS ▶ **murrin**

MURRION *same as* ▶ **murrain**

MURRIS ▶ **murri**

MURRS ▶ **murr**

MURRY *same as* ▶ **moray**

MURTHER *same as* ▶ **murder**

MURTI *n* image of a deity, which itself is considered divine once consecrated

MURTIS ▶ **murti**

MURVA *n* type of hemp

MURVAS ▶ **murva**

MUS ▶ **mu**

MUSANG *n* catlike animal of Malaysia

MUSANGS ▶ **musang**

MUSAR *n* rabbinic literature concerned with ethics, right conduct, etc

MUSARS ▶ **musar**

MUSCA *n* small constellation in the S hemisphere lying between the Southern Cross and Chamaeleon

MUSCAE ▶ **musca**

MUSCAT *same as* > **muscatel**

MUSCATS ▶ **muscat**

MUSCID *n* type of fly of the family which includes the housefly and tsetse fly

MUSCIDS ▶ **muscid**

MUSCLE *n* tissue in the body which produces movement by contracting ▷ *vb* force one's way (in)

MUSCLED ▶ **muscle**

MUSCLES ▶ **muscle**

MUSCLY ▶ **muscle**

MUSCOID *adj* of family of plants

MUSCONE *same as* ▶ **muskone**

MUSCOSE *adj* like moss

MUSCOVY *adj as in* **muscovy duck** a kind of duck

MUSE *vb* ponder quietly ▷ *n* state of abstraction

MUSED ▶ **muse**

MUSEFUL ▶ **muse**

MUSER ▶ **muse**

MUSERS ▶ **muse**

MUSES ▶ **muse**

MUSET *same as* ▶ **musit**

MUSETS ▶ **muset**

MUSETTE *n* type of bagpipe with a bellows popular in France during the 17th and 18th centuries

MUSEUM *n* building where natural, artistic, historical, or scientific objects are exhibited and preserved

MUSEUMS ▶ **museum**

MUSH *n* soft pulpy mass ▷ *interj* order to dogs in a sled team to start up or go faster ▷ *vb* travel by or drive a dogsled

MUSHA *interj* Irish exclamation of surprise

MUSHED ▶ **mush**

MUSHER ▶ **mush**

MUSHERS ▶ **mush**

MUSHES ▶ **mush**

MUSHIER ▶ **mushy**

MUSHILY ▶ **mushy**

MUSHING ▶ **mush**

MUSHY *adj* soft and pulpy

MUSIC *n* art form using a melodious and harmonious combination of notes ▷ *vb* play music

MUSICAL *adj* of or like music ▷ *n* play or film with songs and dancing

MUSICK *same as* ▶ **music**

MUSICKS ▶ **musick**

MUSICS ▶ **music**

MUSIMON *same as* > **moufflon**

MUSING ▶ **muse**

MUSINGS ▶ **muse**

MUSIT *n* gap in fence

MUSITS ▶ **musit**

MUSIVE *adj* mosaic

MUSJID *same as* ▶ **masjid**

MUSJIDS ▶ **musjid**

MUSK *n* scent obtained from a gland of the musk deer or produced synthetically ▷ *vb* perfume with musk

MUSKED ▶ **musk**

MUSKEG *n* area of undrained boggy land

MUSKEGS ▶ **muskeg**

MUSKET *n* long-barrelled gun

MUSKETS ▶ **musket**

MUSKIE *n* large North American freshwater game fish

MUSKIER ▶ **muskie**

MUSKIES ▶ **muskie**

MUSKILY ▶ **musky**

MUSKING ▶ **musk**

MUSKIT *same as* > **mesquite**

MUSKITS ▶ **muskit**

MUSKLE *same as* ▶ **mussel**

MUSKLES ▶ **muskle**

MUSKONE *n* substance in musk

MUSKOX *n* large Canadian mammal

MUSKRAT *n* N American beaver-like rodent

MUSKS ▶ **musk**

MUSKY *same as* ▶ **muskie**

MUSLIN *n* fine cotton fabric

MUSLINS ▶ **muslin**

MUSMON *same as* ▶ **musimon**

MUSMONS ▶ **musmon**

MUSO *n* musician, esp a pop musician, regarded as being overconcerned with technique rather than musical content or expression

MUSOS ▶ **muso**

MUSPIKE *n* Canadian freshwater fish

MUSROL *n* part of bridle

MUSROLS ▶ **musrol**

MUSS *vb* make untidy ▷ *n* state of disorder

MUSSE *same as* ▶ **muss**

MUSSED ▶ **muss**

MUSSEL *n* edible shellfish with a dark hinged shell

MUSSELS ▶ **mussel**

MUSSES ▶ **muss**

MUSSIER ▶ **mussy**

MUSSILY ▶ **mussy**

M

MUSSING ▸ muss
MUSSY *adj* untidy or disordered
MUST *vb* used as an auxiliary to express obligation, certainty, or resolution ▸ *n* essential or necessary thing
MUSTANG *n* wild horse of SW USA
MUSTARD *n* paste made from the powdered seeds of a plant, used as a condiment ▸ *adj* brownish-yellow
MUSTED ▸ must
MUSTEE *n* offspring of a White and a quadroon
MUSTEES ▸ mustee
MUSTER *vb* summon up (strength, energy, or support) ▸ *n* assembly of military personnel
MUSTERS ▸ muster
MUSTH *n* state of frenzied sexual excitement in the males of certain large mammals, esp elephants, associated with discharge from a gland between the ear and eye
MUSTHS ▸ musth
MUSTIER ▸ musty
MUSTILY ▸ musty
MUSTING ▸ must
MUSTS ▸ must
MUSTY *adj* smelling mouldy and stale
MUT *another word for* ▸ **em**
MUTABLE *adj* liable to change
MUTABLY ▸ mutable
MUTAGEN *n* any substance that can induce genetic mutation
MUTANDA > **mutandum**
MUTANT *n* mutated animal, plant, etc ▸ *adj* of or resulting from mutation
MUTANTS ▸ mutant
MUTASE *n* type of enzyme
MUTASES ▸ mutase
MUTATE *vb* (cause to) undergo mutation
MUTATED ▸ mutate
MUTATES ▸ mutate
MUTCH *n* close-fitting linen cap formerly worn by women and children in Scotland ▸ *vb* cadge
MUTCHED ▸ mutch
MUTCHES ▸ mutch
MUTE *adj* silent ▸ *n* person

who is unable to speak ▸ *vb* reduce the volume or soften the tone of a musical instrument by means of a mute or soft pedal
MUTED *adj* (of sound or colour) softened
MUTEDLY ▸ muted
MUTELY ▸ mute
MUTER ▸ mute
MUTES ▸ mute
MUTEST ▸ mute
MUTI *n* medicine, esp herbal medicine
MUTINE *vb* mutiny
MUTINED ▸ mutine
MUTINES ▸ mutine
MUTING ▸ mute
MUTINY *n* rebellion against authority, esp by soldiers or sailors ▸ *vb* commit mutiny
MUTIS ▸ muti
MUTISM *n* state of being mute
MUTISMS ▸ mutism
MUTON *n* part of gene
MUTONS ▸ muton
MUTS ▸ mut
MUTT *n* mongrel dog
MUTTER *vb* utter or speak indistinctly ▸ *n* muttered sound or grumble
MUTTERS ▸ mutter
MUTTON *n* flesh of sheep, used as food
MUTTONS ▸ mutton
MUTTONY ▸ mutton
MUTTS ▸ mutt
MUTUAL *adj* felt or expressed by each of two people about the other ▸ *n* mutual company
MUTUALS ▸ mutual
MUTUCA *same as* ▸ **motuca**
MUTUCAS ▸ mutuca
MUTUEL *n* system of betting in which those who have bet on the winners of a race share in the total amount wagered less a percentage for the management
MUTUELS ▸ mutuel
MUTULAR ▸ mutule
MUTULE *n* one of a set of flat blocks below the corona of a Doric cornice
MUTULES ▸ mutule
MUTUUM *n* contract for loan of goods
MUTUUMS ▸ mutuum
MUUMUU *n* loose brightly-coloured dress

worn by women in Hawaii
MUUMUUS ▸ muumuu
MUX *vb* spoil
> This word meaning to spoil or botch is very useful not only because it contains an X, but because its verb forms can enable you to clear your rack of unpromising letters.
MUXED ▸ mux
MUXES ▸ mux
MUXING ▸ mux
MUZAKY *adj* having a bland sound
MUZHIK *n* Russian peasant, esp under the tsars
MUZHIKS ▸ muzhik
MUZJIK *same as* ▸ **muzhik**
> Meaning a Russian peasant, this is a wonderful high-scoring word, combining Z, J and K, and if you can play the plural using all of your tiles, you'll get a bonus of 50 points.
MUZJIKS ▸ muzjik
MUZZ *vb* make (something) muzzy
MUZZED ▸ muzz
MUZZES ▸ muzz
MUZZIER ▸ muzzy
MUZZILY ▸ muzzy
MUZZING ▸ muzz
MUZZLE *n* animal's mouth and nose ▸ *vb* prevent from being heard or noticed
MUZZLED ▸ muzzle
MUZZLER ▸ muzzle
MUZZLES ▸ muzzle
MUZZY *adj* confused or muddled
MVULE *n* tropical African tree
MVULES ▸ mvule
MWAH *interj* representation of the sound of a kiss
MWALIMU *n* teacher
MY *adj* belonging to me ▸ *interj* exclamation of surprise or awe
MYAL ▸ myalism
MYALGIA *n* pain in a muscle or a group of muscles
MYALGIC ▸ myalgia
MYALISM *n* kind of witchcraft, similar to obi, practised esp in the Caribbean
MYALIST ▸ myalism
MYALL *n* Australian acacia

with hard scented wood
MYALLS ▶ myall
MYASES ▶ myasis
MYASIS same as ▶ myiasis
MYC n oncogene that aids the growth of tumorous cells
MYCELE n microscopic spike-like structure in mucus
MYCELES ▶ mycele
MYCELIA > mycelium
MYCELLA n blue-veined Danish cream cheese, less strongly flavoured than Danish blue
MYCETES n fungus
MYCOSES ▶ mycosis
MYCOSIS n any infection or disease caused by fungus
MYCOTIC ▶ mycosis
MYCS ▶ myc
MYELIN n white tissue forming an insulating sheath around certain nerve fibres
MYELINE same as ▶ myelin
MYELINS ▶ myelin
MYELOID adj of or relating to the spinal cord or the bone marrow
MYELOMA n tumour of the bone marrow
MYELON n spinal cord
MYELONS ▶ myelon
MYGALE n large American spider
MYGALES ▶ mygale
MYIASES ▶ myiasis
MYIASIS n infestation of the body by the larvae of flies
MYLAR n tradename for a kind of strong polyester film
MYLARS ▶ mylar
MYLODON n prehistoric giant sloth
MYNA same as ▶ mynah
MYNAH n tropical Asian starling which can mimic human speech
MYNAHS ▶ mynah
MYNAS ▶ myna
MYNHEER n Dutch title of address
MYOGEN n albumin found in muscle
MYOGENS ▶ myogen
MYOGRAM n tracings of muscular contractions
MYOID adj like muscle

MYOLOGY n branch of medical science concerned with the structure and diseases of muscles
MYOMA n benign tumour composed of muscle tissue
MYOMAS ▶ myoma
MYOMATA ▶ myoma
MYOPE n any person afflicted with myopia
MYOPES ▶ myope
MYOPIA n short-sightedness
MYOPIAS ▶ myopia
MYOPIC n shortsighted person
MYOPICS ▶ myopic
MYOPIES ▶ myopy
MYOPS same as ▶ myope
MYOPSES ▶ myops
MYOPY same as ▶ myopia
MYOSES ▶ myosis
MYOSIN n chief protein of muscle that interacts with actin to form actomyosin during muscle contraction
MYOSINS ▶ myosin
MYOSIS same as ▶ miosis
MYOSOTE same as > myosotis
MYOTIC ▶ miosis
MYOTICS ▶ miosis
MYOTOME n any segment of embryonic mesoderm that develops into skeletal muscle in the adult
MYOTUBE n cylindrical cell in muscle
MYRBANE same as ▶ mirbane
MYRIAD adj innumerable ▷ n large indefinite number
MYRIADS ▶ myriad
MYRICA n dried root bark of the wax myrtle, used as a tonic and to treat diarrhoea
MYRICAS ▶ myrica
MYRINGA n eardrum
MYRRH n aromatic gum used in perfume, incense, and medicine
MYRRHIC ▶ myrrh
MYRRHOL n oil of myrrh
MYRRHS ▶ myrrh
MYRTLE n flowering evergreen shrub
MYRTLES ▶ myrtle
MYSELF pron reflexive form of I or me
MYSID n small shrimplike

crustacean
MYSIDS ▶ mysid
MYSOST n Norwegian cheese
MYSOSTS ▶ mysost
MYSPACE vb search for (someone) on the MySpace website
MYSTERY n strange or inexplicable event or phenomenon
MYSTIC n person who seeks spiritual knowledge ▷ adj mystical
MYSTICS ▶ mystic
MYSTIFY vb bewilder or puzzle
MYTH n tale with supernatural characters, usu of how the world and mankind began
MYTHI ▶ mythus
MYTHIC same as > mythical
MYTHIER ▶ mythy
MYTHISE same as ▶ mythize
MYTHISM same as > mythicism
MYTHIST ▶ mythism
MYTHIZE same as > mythicize
MYTHOI ▶ mythos
MYTHOS n complex of beliefs, values, attitudes, etc, characteristic of a specific group or society
MYTHS ▶ myth
MYTHUS same as ▶ mythos
MYTHY adj of or like myth
MYXO n infectious and usually fatal viral disease of rabbits characterized by swelling of the mucous membranes and formation of skin tumours
MYXOID adj containing mucus
MYXOMA n tumour composed of mucous connective tissue, usually situated in subcutaneous tissue
MYXOMAS ▶ myxoma
MYXOS ▶ myxo
MZEE n old person ▷ adj advanced in years
MZEES ▶ mzee
MZUNGU n White person
MZUNGUS ▶ mzungu

M

Nn

Along with **R** and **T**, **N** is one of the most common consonants in Scrabble. As you'll often have it on your rack, it's well worth learning what **N** can do in different situations. **N** is useful when you need short words, as it begins two-letter words with every vowel except **I**, and with **Y** as well. There are plenty of three-letter words starting with **N**, but there aren't many high-scoring ones apart from **nix** and **nox** for 10 points each and **nek** for 7 points. Remember words like **nab** (5 points), **nag** (4), **nap** (5), **nay** (6), **new** (6), **nib** (5), **nob** (5), **nod** (4) and **now** (6).

NA *same as* ▶ **nae**
NAAM *same as* ▶ **nam**
NAAMS ▶ **naam**
NAAN *n* slightly leavened flat Indian bread
NAANS ▶ **naan**
NAARTJE *same as* > **naartjie**
NAB *vb* arrest (someone)
NABBED ▶ **nab**
NABBER *n* thief
NABBERS ▶ **nabber**
NABBING ▶ **nab**
NABE *n* Japanese hotpot
NABES ▶ **nabe**
NABIS *n* Parisian art movement
NABK *n* edible berry
NABKS ▶ **nabk**
NABLA *another name for* ▶ **del**
NABLAS ▶ **nabla**
NABOB *same as* ▶ **nawab**
NABOBS ▶ **nabob**
NABS ▶ **nab**
NACARAT *n* red-orange colour
NACELLE *n* streamlined enclosure on an aircraft, esp one housing an engine
NACH *n* Indian dance
NACHAS *n* pleasure
NACHE *n* rump
NACHO *n* snack of a piece of tortilla topped with cheese, peppers, etc
NACHOS ▶ **nacho**
NACKET *n* light lunch, snack
NACKETS ▶ **nacket**
NACRE *n* mother of pearl
NACRED ▶ **nacre**
NACRES ▶ **nacre**

NACRITE *n* mineral
NACROUS ▶ **nacre**
NADA *n* nothing
NADAS ▶ **nada**
NADIR *n* point in the sky opposite the zenith
NADIRAL ▶ **nadir**
NADIRS ▶ **nadir**
NADORS *n* thirst brought on by excessive consumption of alcohol
NAE *Scots word for* ▶ **no**
NAEBODY *Scots variant of* ▶ **nobody**
NAEVE *n* birthmark
NAEVES ▶ **naevus**
NAEVI ▶ **naevus**
NAEVOID ▶ **naevus**
NAEVUS *n* birthmark or mole
NAFF *adj* lacking quality or taste ▷ *vb* go away
NAFFED ▶ **naff**
NAFFER ▶ **naff**
NAFFEST ▶ **naff**
NAFFING ▶ **naff**
NAFFLY ▶ **naff**
NAFFS ▶ **naff**
NAG *vb* scold or find fault constantly ▷ *n* person who nags
NAGA *n* cobra
NAGANA *n* disease of all domesticated animals of central and southern Africa
NAGANAS ▶ **nagana**
NAGAPIE *n* bushbaby
NAGARI *n* set of scripts used as the writing systems for several languages of India
NAGARIS ▶ **nagari**
NAGAS ▶ **naga**

NAGGED ▶ **nag**
NAGGER ▶ **nag**
NAGGERS ▶ **nag**
NAGGIER ▶ **nag**
NAGGING ▶ **nag**
NAGGY ▶ **nag**
NAGMAAL *n* Communion
NAGOR *another name for* > **reedbuck**
NAGORS ▶ **nagor**
NAGS ▶ **nag**
NAH *same as* ▶ **no**
NAHAL *n* agricultural settlement run by an Israeli military youth organization
NAHALS ▶ **nahal**
NAIAD *n* nymph living in a lake or river
NAIADES ▶ **naiad**
NAIADS ▶ **naiad**
NAIANT *adj* swimming
NAIF *less common word for* ▶ **naive**
NAIFER ▶ **naif**
NAIFEST ▶ **naif**
NAIFLY ▶ **naive**
NAIFS ▶ **naif**
NAIK *n* chief
NAIKS ▶ **naik**
NAIL *n* pointed piece of metal with a head, hit with a hammer to join two objects together ▷ *vb* attach (something) with nails
NAILED ▶ **nail**
NAILER ▶ **nail**
NAILERS ▶ **nail**
NAILERY *n* nail factory
NAILING ▶ **nail**
NAILS ▶ **nail**
NAILSET *n* punch for driving the head of a nail below the

surrounding surface

NAIN adj own

NAIRA n standard monetary unit of Nigeria, divided into 100 kobo

NAIRAS ▶ naira

NAIRU n Non-Accelerating Inflation Rate of Unemployment

NAIRUS ▶ nairu

NAIVE adj innocent and gullible ▷ n person who is naive, esp in artistic style

NAIVELY ▶ naive

NAIVER ▶ naive

NAIVES ▶ naive

NAIVEST ▶ naive

NAIVETE same as ▶ naivety

NAIVETY n state or quality of being naive

NAIVIST ▶ naive

NAKED adj without clothes

NAKEDER ▶ naked

NAKEDLY ▶ naked

NAKER n one of a pair of small kettledrums used in medieval music

NAKERS ▶ naker

NAKFA n standard currency unit of Eritrea

NAKFAS ▶ nakfa

NALA n ravine

NALAS ▶ nala

NALED n type of insecticide

NALEDS ▶ naled

NALLA n ravine

NALLAH same as ▶ nalla

NALLAHS ▶ nallah

NALLAS ▶ nalla

NAM n distraint

NAMABLE ▶ name

NAMASTE n Indian greeting

NAME n word by which a person or thing is known ▷ vb give a name to

NAMED ▶ name

NAMELY adv that is to say

NAMER ▶ name

NAMERS ▶ name

NAMES ▶ name

NAMETAG n identification badge

NAMING ▶ name

NAMINGS ▶ name

NAMMA adj as in **namma hole** Australian word for a natural well in rock

NAMS ▶ nam

NAMU n black New Zealand sandfly

NAMUS ▶ namu

NAN n grandmother

NANA same as ▶ nan

NANAS ▶ nana

NANDIN n type of shrub

NANDINA n type of shrub

NANDINE n African palm civet

NANDINS ▶ nandin

NANDOO ▶ nandu

NANDOOS ▶ nandoo

NANDU n type of ostrich

NANDUS ▶ nandu

NANE Scots word for ▶ none

NANG adj excellent; cool

NANISM n dwarfism

NANISMS ▶ nanism

NANITE n microscopically small machine or robot

NANITES ▶ nanite

NANKEEN n hard-wearing buff-coloured cotton fabric

NANKIN same as ▶ nankeen

NANKINS ▶ nankin

NANNA same as ▶ nan

NANNAS ▶ nanna

NANNIE same as ▶ nanny

NANNIED ▶ nanny

NANNIES ▶ nanny

NANNY n woman whose job is looking after young children ▷ vb be too protective towards

NANOBE n microbe that is smaller than the smallest known bacterium

NANOBES ▶ nanobe

NANOBOT n microscopically small robot

NANODOT n microscopic cluster of several hundred nickel atoms used to store large amounts of data in a computer chip

NANOOK n polar bear

NANOOKS ▶ nanook

NANS ▶ nan

NANUA same as ▶ moki

NANUAS ▶ nanua

NAOI ▶ naos

> The plural of **naos**, the inner cell of a temple. A very useful word for ridding your rack of unwanted vowels.

NAOS n ancient classical temple

NAOSES ▶ naos

NAP n short sleep ▷ vb have a short sleep

NAPA n type of leather

NAPALM n highly inflammable jellied petrol, used in bombs ▷ vb attack (people or places) with napalm

NAPALMS ▶ napalm

NAPAS ▶ napa

NAPE n back of the neck ▷ vb attack with napalm

NAPED ▶ nape

NAPERY n household linen, esp table linen

NAPES ▶ nape

NAPHTHA n liquid mixture distilled from coal tar or petroleum, used as a solvent and in petrol

NAPHTOL same as > naphthol

NAPING ▶ nape

NAPKIN same as ▶ nappy

NAPKINS ▶ napkin

NAPLESS adj threadbare

NAPOO vb kill

NAPOOED ▶ napoo

NAPOOS ▶ napoo

NAPPA n soft leather, used in gloves and clothes, made from sheepskin, lambskin, or kid

NAPPAS ▶ nappa

NAPPE n large sheet or mass of rock that has been thrust from its original position by earth movements

NAPPED ▶ nap

NAPPER n person or thing that raises the nap on cloth

NAPPERS ▶ napper

NAPPES ▶ nappe

NAPPIE same as ▶ nappy

NAPPIER ▶ nappy

NAPPIES ▶ nappy

NAPPING ▶ nap

NAPPY n piece of absorbent material fastened round a baby's lower torso to absorb urine and faeces ▷ adj having a nap

NAPRON same as ▶ apron

NAPRONS ▶ napron

NAPS ▶ nap

NARAS same as ▶ narras

NARASES ▶ naras

NARC n narcotics agent

NARCEEN same as > narceine

NARCEIN same as > narceine

NARCISM n exceptional admiration for oneself

NARCIST n narcissist

NARCO n officer working in the area of anti-drug operations

NARCOMA n coma caused by intake of narcotic drugs

N

NARCOS n drug smugglers

NARCOSE same as
> narcosis

NARCS ▸ narc

NARD n any of several
plants whose aromatic
roots were formerly used in
medicine ▷ vb anoint with
nard oil

NARDED ▸ nard

NARDINE ▸ nard

NARDING ▸ nard

NARDOO n any of certain
cloverlike ferns which grow
in swampy areas

NARDOOS ▸ nardoo

NARDS ▸ nard

NARE n nostril

NARES pl n nostrils

NARGILE same as > narghile

NARGILY same as > narghile

NARIAL adj of or relating to
the nares

NARIC ▸ nare

NARINE same as ▸ narial

NARIS ▸ nares

NARK vb annoy ▷ n
informer or spy

NARKED ▸ nark

NARKIER ▸ narky

NARKING ▸ nark

NARKS ▸ nark

NARKY adj irritable or
complaining

NARRAS n type of shrub

NARRATE vb tell (a story)

NARRE adj nearer

NARROW adj small in
breadth in comparison to
length ▷ vb make or
become narrow

NARROWS pl n narrow part
of a strait, river, or current

NARTHEX n portico at the
west end of a basilica or
church

NARTJIE same as > naartjie

This word for a small
sweet orange is one to
look out for when you
have the J with the good
letters of 'retain'. And it
has alternative spellings
naartje and **naartjie**.

NARWAL same as
▸ narwhal

NARWALS ▸ narwal

NARWHAL n arctic whale
with a long spiral tusk

NARY adv not

NAS vb has not

NASAL adj of the nose ▷ n
nasal speech sound, such as

English m, n, or ng

NASALLY ▸ nasal

NASALS ▸ nasal

NASARD n organ stop

NASARDS ▸ nasard

NASCENT adj starting to
grow or develop

NASHGAB n chatter

NASHI n fruit of the
Japanese pear

NASHIS ▸ nashi

NASIAL ▸ nasion

NASION n craniometric
point where the top of the
nose meets the ridge of the
forehead

NASIONS ▸ nasion

NASTIC adj (of movement of
plants) independent of the
direction of the external
stimulus

NASTIER ▸ nasty

NASTIES ▸ nasty

NASTILY ▸ nasty

NASTY adj unpleasant ▷ n
something unpleasant

NASUTE n type of termite

NASUTES ▸ nasute

NAT n supporter of
nationalism

NATAL adj of or relating to
birth

NATANT adj (of aquatic
plants) floating on the
water

NATCH sentence substitute
naturally ▷ n notch

NATCHES ▸ natch

NATES pl n buttocks

NATHEMO same as
> nathemore

NATION n people of one or
more cultures or races
organized as a single state

NATIONS ▸ nation

NATIS ▸ nates

NATIVE adj relating to a
place where a person was
born ▷ n person born in a
specified place

NATIVES ▸ native

NATRIUM obsolete name for
▸ sodium

NATRON n whitish or
yellow mineral

NATRONS ▸ natron

NATS ▸ nat

NATTER vb talk idly or
chatter ▷ n long idle chat

NATTERS ▸ natter

NATTERY adj irritable

NATTIER ▸ natty

NATTILY ▸ natty

NATTY adj smart and spruce

NATURA n nature

NATURAE ▸ natura

NATURAL adj normal or to
be expected ▷ n person
with an inborn talent or
skill

NATURE n whole system of
the existence, forces, and
events of the physical world
that are not controlled by
human beings

NATURED adj having a
certain disposition

NATURES ▸ nature

NAUCH same as ▸ nautch

NAUCHES ▸ nauch

NAUGHT n nothing ▷ adv
not at all

NAUGHTS ▸ naught

NAUGHTY adj disobedient
or mischievous ▷ n act of
sexual intercourse

NAUNT n aunt

NAUNTS ▸ naunt

NAUPLII > nauplius

NAUSEA n feeling of being
about to vomit

NAUSEAS ▸ nausea

NAUTCH n intricate
traditional Indian dance
performed by professional
dancing girls

NAUTIC same as > nautical

NAUTICS ▸ nautic

NAUTILI > nautilus

NAVAID n navigational aid

NAVAIDS ▸ navaid

NAVAL adj of or relating to a
navy or ships

NAVALLY ▸ naval

NAVAR n system of air
navigation

NAVARCH n admiral

NAVARHO n aircraft
navigation system

NAVARIN n stew of mutton
or lamb with root
vegetables

NAVARS ▸ navar

NAVE n long central part of
a church

NAVEL n hollow in the
middle of the abdomen
where the umbilical cord
was attached

NAVELS ▸ navel

NAVES ▸ nave

NAVETTE n gem cut

NAVEW another name for
▸ turnip

NAVEWS ▸ navew

NAVIES ▸ navy

NAVVIED ▸ **navvy**

NAVVIES ▸ **navvy**

NAVVY n labourer employed on a road or a building site ▷ vb work as a navvy

NAVY n branch of a country's armed services comprising warships with their crews and organization ▷ adj navy-blue

NAW same as ▸ **no**

NAWAB n (formerly) a Muslim ruler or powerful landowner in India

NAWABS ▸ **nawab**

NAY interj no ▷ n person who votes against a motion ▷ adv used for emphasis ▷ sentence substitute no

NAYS ▸ **nay**

NAYSAID ▸ **naysay**

NAYSAY vb say no

NAYSAYS ▸ **naysay**

NAYWARD n towards denial

NAYWORD n proverb

NAZE n flat marshy headland

NAZES ▸ **naze**

NAZI n person who thinks or acts in a brutal or dictatorial way

NAZIFY vb make nazi in character

NAZIR n Muslim official

NAZIRS ▸ **nazir**

NAZIS ▸ **nazi**

NE conj nor

NEAFE same as ▸ **nieve**

NEAFES ▸ **neafe**

NEAFFE same as ▸ **nieve**

NEAFFES ▸ **neaffe**

NEAL same as ▸ **anneal**

NEALED ▸ **neal**

NEALING ▸ **neal**

NEALS ▸ **neal**

NEANIC adj of or relating to the early stages in the life cycle of an organism

NEAP adj of, relating to, or constituting a neap tide ▷ vb be grounded by a neap tide

NEAPED ▸ **neap**

NEAPING ▸ **neap**

NEAPS ▸ **neap**

NEAR adj indicating a place or time not far away ▷ vb draw close (to) ▷ prep at or to a place or time not far away from ▷ adv at or to a place or time not far away ▷ n left side of a horse or vehicle

NEARBY adj not far away ▷ adv close at hand

NEARED ▸ **near**

NEARER ▸ **near**

NEAREST ▸ **near**

NEARING ▸ **near**

NEARLY adv almost

NEARS ▸ **near**

NEAT adj tidy and clean ▷ n domestic bovine animal

NEATEN vb make neat

NEATENS ▸ **neaten**

NEATER ▸ **neat**

NEATEST ▸ **neat**

NEATH short for ▸ **beneath**

NEATLY ▸ **neat**

NEATNIK n very neat and tidy person

NEATS ▸ **neat**

NEB n beak of a bird or the nose of an animal ▷ vb look around nosily

NEBBED ▸ **neb**

NEBBICH same as ▸ **nebbish**

NEBBING ▸ **neb**

NEBBISH n unfortunate simpleton

NEBBUK n type of shrub

NEBBUKS ▸ **nebbuk**

NEBECK same as ▸ **nebbuk**

NEBECKS ▸ **nebeck**

NEBEK same as ▸ **nebbuk**

NEBEKS ▸ **nebek**

NEBEL n Hebrew musical instrument

NEBELS ▸ **nebel**

NEBISH same as ▸ **nebbish**

NEBRIS n fawn-skin

NEBS ▸ **neb**

NEBULA n hazy cloud of particles and gases

NEBULAE ▸ **nebula**

NEBULAR ▸ **nebula**

NEBULAS ▸ **nebula**

NEBULE n cloud

NEBULES ▸ **nebule**

NEBULY adj wavy

NECK n part of the body joining the head to the shoulders ▷ vb kiss and cuddle

NECKED ▸ **neck**

NECKER ▸ **neck**

NECKERS ▸ **neck**

NECKING n activity of kissing and embracing passionately

NECKLET n ornament worn round the neck

NECKS ▸ **neck**

NECKTIE same as ▸ **tie**

NECROSE vb cause or undergo necrosis

NECTAR n sweet liquid collected from flowers by bees

NECTARS ▸ **nectar**

NECTARY n any of various glandular structures secreting nectar in a plant

NEDDIER ▸ **neddy**

NEDDIES ▸ **neddy**

NEDDISH ▸ **neddy**

NEDDY n donkey ▷ adj of or relating to neds

NEE prep indicating the maiden name of a married woman ▷ adj indicating the maiden name of a married woman

NEED vb require or be in want of ▷ n condition of lacking something

NEEDED ▸ **need**

NEEDER ▸ **need**

NEEDERS ▸ **need**

NEEDFUL adj necessary or required

NEEDIER ▸ **needy**

NEEDILY ▸ **needy**

NEEDING ▸ **need**

NEEDLE n thin pointed piece of metal with an eye through which thread is passed for sewing ▷ vb goad or provoke

NEEDLED ▸ **needle**

NEEDLER n needle maker

NEEDLES ▸ **needle**

NEEDLY ▸ **needle**

NEEDS adv necessarily ▷ pl n what is required

NEEDY adj poor, in need of financial support

NEELD same as ▸ **needle**

NEELDS ▸ **neeld**

NEELE same as ▸ **needle**

NEELES ▸ **neele**

NEEM n type of large Indian tree

NEEMB same as ▸ **neem**

NEEMBS ▸ **neemb**

NEEMS ▸ **neem**

NEEP dialect name for ▸ **turnip**

NEEPS ▸ **neep**

NEESE same as ▸ **neeze**

NEESED ▸ **neese**

NEESES ▸ **neese**

NEESING ▸ **neese**

NEEZE vb sneeze

NEEZED ▸ **neeze**

NEEZES ▸ **neeze**

NEEZING ▸ **neeze**

N

NEF *n* church nave
NEFAST *adj* wicked
NEFS ▸ **nef**
NEG *n* photographic negative
NEGATE *vb* invalidate
NEGATED ▸ **negate**
NEGATER ▸ **negate**
NEGATES ▸ **negate**
NEGATON *same as* > **negatron**
NEGATOR ▸ **negate**
NEGLECT *vb* take no care of ▷ *n* neglecting or being neglected
NEGLIGE *same as* > **negligee**
NEGRONI *n* type of cocktail
NEGS ▸ **neg**
NEGUS *n* hot drink of port and lemon juice, usually spiced and sweetened
NEGUSES ▸ **negus**
NEIF *same as* ▸ **nieve**
NEIFS ▸ **neif**
NEIGH *n* loud high-pitched sound made by a horse ▷ *vb* make this sound
NEIGHED ▸ **neigh**
NEIGHS ▸ **neigh**
NEINEI *n* type of plant
NEINEIS ▸ **neinei**
NEIST *Scots variant of* ▸ **next**
NEITHER *pron* not one nor the other ▷ *adj* not one nor the other (of two)
NEIVE *same as* ▸ **nieve**
NEIVES ▸ **neive**
NEK *n* mountain pass
NEKS ▸ **nek**
NEKTON *n* population of free-swimming animals that inhabits the middle depths of a sea or lake
NEKTONS ▸ **nekton**
NELIES *same as* ▸ **nelis**
NELIS *n* type of pear
NELLIE *n* effeminate man
NELLIES ▸ **nellie**
NELLY *n as in* **not on your nelly** not under any circumstances
NELSON *n* type of wrestling hold
NELSONS ▸ **nelson**
NELUMBO *n* type of aquatic plant
NEMA *n* filament
NEMAS ▸ **nema**
NEMATIC *adj* (of a substance) existing in or having a mesomorphic state in which a linear orientation of the

molecules causes anisotropic properties
NEMESES ▸ **nemesis**
NEMESIA *n* type of southern African plant
NEMESIS *n* retribution or vengeance
NEMN *vb* name
NEMNED ▸ **nemn**
NEMNING ▸ **nemn**
NEMNS ▸ **nemn**
NEMORAL *adj* of a wood
NEMPT *adj* named
NENE *n* rare black-and-grey short-winged Hawaiian goose
NENES ▸ **nene**
NEOCON *n* supporter of conservative politics
NEOCONS ▸ **neocon**
NEOGENE *adj* of, denoting, or formed during the Miocene and Pliocene epochs
NEOLITH *n* Neolithic stone implement
NEOLOGY *same as* > **neologism**
NEON *n* colourless odourless gaseous element used in illuminated signs and lights ▷ *adj* of or illuminated by neon
NEONATE *n* newborn child, esp in the first week of life and up to four weeks old
NEONED *adj* lit with neon
NEONS ▸ **neon**
NEOSOUL *n* type of popular music combining soul with other genres
NEOTENY *n* persistence of larval or fetal features in the adult form of an animal
NEOTYPE *n* specimen selected to replace a type specimen that has been lost or destroyed
NEP *n* catmint
NEPER *n* unit expressing the ratio of two quantities
NEPERS ▸ **neper**
NEPETA *same as* ▸ **catmint**
NEPETAS ▸ **nepeta**
NEPHEW *n* son of one's sister or brother
NEPHEWS ▸ **nephew**
NEPHRIC *adj* renal
NEPHRON *n* minute urine-secreting tubule in the kidney
NEPIT *n* a unit of information equal to 1.44 bits

NEPITS ▸ **nepit**
NEPOTIC > **nepotism**
NEPS ▸ **nep**
NERAL *n* isomer of citral
NERALS ▸ **neral**
NERD *n* boring person obsessed with a particular subject
NERDIC > **geekspeak**
NERDICS ▸ **nerdic**
NERDIER ▸ **nerd**
NERDISH ▸ **nerd**
NERDS ▸ **nerd**
NERDY ▸ **nerd**
NEREID *n* sea nymph in Greek mythology
NEREIDS ▸ **nereid**
NEREIS *n* type of marine worm
NERINE *n* type of S African plant related to the amaryllis
NERINES ▸ **nerine**
NERITE *n* type of sea snail
NERITES ▸ **nerite**
NERITIC *adj* of or formed in the region of shallow seas near a coastline
NERK *n* fool
NERKA *n* type of salmon
NERKAS ▸ **nerka**
NERKS ▸ **nerk**
NEROL *n* scented liquid
NEROLI *n* brown oil used in perfumery
NEROLIS ▸ **neroli**
NEROLS ▸ **nerol**
NERTS *interj* nuts
NERTZ *same as* ▸ **nerts**
NERVAL ▸ **nerve**
NERVATE *adj* (of leaves) with veins
NERVE *n* cordlike bundle of fibres that conducts impulses between the brain and other parts of the body ▷ *vb* give courage to oneself
NERVED ▸ **nerve**
NERVER ▸ **nerve**
NERVERS ▸ **nerve**
NERVES ▸ **nerve**
NERVIER ▸ **nervy**
NERVILY ▸ **nervy**
NERVINE *adj* having a soothing or calming effect upon the nerves ▷ *n* nervine drug or agent
NERVING ▸ **nerve**
NERVOUS *adj* apprehensive or worried
NERVULE *n* small vein
NERVURE *n* any of the stiff rods that form the

supporting framework of an insect's wing

NERVY adj excitable or nervous

NESH adj sensitive to the cold

NESHER ▸ nesh

NESHEST ▸ nesh

NESS n headland, cape

NESSES ▸ ness

NEST n place or structure in which birds or certain animals lay eggs or give birth to young ▷ vb make or inhabit a nest

NESTED ▸ nest

NESTER ▸ nest

NESTERS ▸ nest

NESTFUL ▸ nest

NESTING ▸ nest

NESTLE vb snuggle

NESTLED ▸ nestle

NESTLER ▸ nestle

NESTLES ▸ nestle

NESTOR n wise old man

NESTORS ▸ nestor

NESTS ▸ nest

NET n fabric of meshes of string, thread, or wire with many openings ▷ vb catch (a fish or animal) in a net ▷ adj left after all deductions

NETBALL n team game in which a ball has to be thrown through a net hanging from a ring at the top of a pole

NETE n lyre string

NETES ▸ nete

NETFUL ▸ net

NETFULS ▸ net

NETHEAD n person who is enthusiastic about or an expert on the internet

NETHER adj lower

NETIZEN n person who regularly uses the internet

NETLESS ▸ net

NETLIKE ▸ net

NETOP n friend

NETOPS ▸ netop

NETROOT n political activist who promotes a cause via the internet

NETS ▸ net

NETSUKE n (in Japan) a carved toggle worn dangling from the waist

NETT same as ▸ net

NETTED ▸ net

NETTER n person that makes nets

NETTERS ▸ netter

NETTIE n habitual and enthusiastic user of the internet

NETTIER ▸ net

NETTIES ▸ netty

NETTING ▸ net

NETTLE n plant with stinging hairs on the leaves ▷ vb bother or irritate

NETTLED ▸ nettle

NETTLER ▸ nettle

NETTLES ▸ nettle

NETTLY ▸ nettle

NETTS ▸ nett

NETTY n lavatory, originally an earth closet

NETWORK n system of intersecting lines, roads, etc ▷ vb broadcast (a programme) over a network

NEUK Scots word for ▸ nook

NEUKS ▸ neuk

NEUM same as ▸ neume

NEUME n one of a series of notational symbols used before the 14th century

NEUMES ▸ neume

NEUMIC ▸ neume

NEUMS ▸ neum

NEURAL adj of a nerve or the nervous system

NEURINE n poisonous alkaloid

NEURISM n nerve force

NEURITE n biological cell component

NEUROID adj nervelike

NEUROMA n any tumour composed of nerve tissue

NEURON same as ▸ neurone

NEURONE n cell specialized to conduct nerve impulses

NEURONS ▸ neuron

NEURULA n stage of embryonic development

NEUSTIC ▸ neuston

NEUSTON n organisms, similar to plankton, that float on the surface film of open water

NEUTER adj belonging to a particular class of grammatical inflections in some languages ▷ vb castrate (an animal) ▷ n neuter gender

NEUTERS ▸ neuter

NEUTRAL adj taking neither side in a war or dispute ▷ n neutral person or nation

NEUTRON n electrically neutral elementary particle of about the same mass as a proton

NEVE n mass of porous ice, formed from snow, that has not yet become frozen into glacier ice

NEVEL vb beat with the fists

NEVELS ▸ nevel

NEVER adv at no time ▷ sentence substitute at no time ▷ interj surely not!

NEVES ▸ neve

NEVI ▸ nevus

NEVOID ▸ naevus

NEVUS same as ▸ naevus

NEW adj not existing before ▷ adv recently ▷ vb make new

NEWBIE n person new to a job, club, etc

NEWBIES ▸ newbie

NEWBORN adj recently or just born ▷ n newborn baby

NEWCOME > newcomer

NEWED ▸ new

NEWEL n post at the top or bottom of a flight of stairs that supports the handrail

NEWELL n new thing

NEWELLS ▸ newell

NEWELS ▸ newel

NEWER ▸ new

NEWEST ▸ new

NEWIE n fresh idea or thing

NEWIES ▸ newie

NEWING ▸ new

NEWISH adj fairly new

NEWLY adv recently

NEWMOWN adj freshly cut

NEWNESS ▸ new

NEWS n important or interesting new happenings ▷ vb report

NEWSBOY n boy who sells or delivers newspapers

NEWSED ▸ news

NEWSES ▸ news

NEWSIE same as ▸ newsy

NEWSIER ▸ newsy

NEWSIES ▸ newsie

NEWSING ▸ news

NEWSMAN n male newsreader or reporter

NEWSMEN ▸ newsman

NEWSY adj full of news ▷ n newsagent

NEWT n small amphibious creature with a long slender body and tail

NEWTON n unit of force

NEWTONS ▸ newton

N

NEWTS ► newt
NEXT adv immediately following ▷ n next person or thing
NEXTLY ► next
NEXTS ► next
NEXUS n connection or link
NEXUSES ► nexus
NGAI n clan or tribe
NGAIO n small New Zealand tree
NGAIOS ► ngaio
NGANA same as ► **nagana**
NGANAS ► ngana
NGARARA n lizard found in New Zealand
NGATI n (occurring as part of the tribe name) a tribe or clan
NGATIS ► ngati
NGOMA n type of drum
NGOMAS ► ngoma
NGWEE n Zambian monetary unit worth one hundredth of a kwacha
NHANDU n type of spider
NHANDUS ► nhandu
NIACIN n vitamin of the B complex that occurs in milk, liver, and yeast
NIACINS ► niacin
NIB n writing point of a pen ▷ vb provide with a nib
NIBBED ► nib
NIBBING ► nib
NIBBLE vb take little bites (of) ▷ n little bite
NIBBLED ► nibble
NIBBLER n person, animal, or thing that nibbles
NIBBLES ► nibble
NIBLICK n (formerly) a club, a No. 9 iron, giving a great deal of lift
NIBLIKE ► nib
NIBS ► nib
NICAD n rechargeable dry-cell battery
NICADS ► nicad
NICE adj pleasant
NICEISH ► nice
NICELY ► nice
NICER ► nice
NICEST ► nice
NICETY n subtle point
NICHE n hollow area in a wall ▷ adj of or aimed at a specialist group or market ▷ vb place (a statue) in a niche
NICHED ► niche
NICHER vb snigger
NICHERS ► nicher

NICHES ► niche
NICHING ► niche
NICHT Scots word for ► **night**
NICHTS ► nicht
NICISH ► nice
NICK vb make a small cut in ▷ n small cut
NICKAR n hard seed
NICKARS ► nickar
NICKED ► nick
NICKEL n silvery-white metal often used in alloys ▷ vb plate with nickel
NICKELS ► nickel
NICKER n pound sterling ▷ vb (of a horse) to neigh softly
NICKERS ► nicker
NICKING ► nick
NICKLE same as ► **nickel**
NICKLED ► nickle
NICKLES ► nickle
NICKS ► nick
NICKUM n mischievous person
NICKUMS ► nickum
NICOISE adj prepared with tomatoes, black olives, garlic and anchovies
NICOL n device for producing plane-polarized light
NICOLS ► nicol
NICOTIN same as > **nicotine**
NICTATE same as > **nictitate**
NID same as ► **nide**
NIDAL ► nidus
NIDATE vb undergo nidation
NIDATED ► nidate
NIDATES ► nidate
NIDDICK n nape of the neck
NIDE vb nest
NIDED ► nide
NIDES ► nide
NIDGET n fool
NIDGETS ► nidget
NIDI ► nidus
NIDIFY vb (of a bird) to make or build a nest
NIDING n coward
NIDINGS ► niding
NIDOR n cooking smell
NIDORS ► nidor
NIDS ► nid
NIDUS n nest in which insects or spiders deposit their eggs
NIDUSES ► nidus
NIE archaic spelling of ► **nigh**
NIECE n daughter of one's sister or brother
NIECES ► niece

NIED ► nie
NIEF same as ► **nieve**
NIEFS ► nief
NIELLI ► niello
NIELLO n black compound of sulphur and silver, lead, or copper ▷ vb decorate or treat with niello
NIELLOS ► niello
NIES ► nie
NIEVE n closed hand
NIEVES ► nieve
NIFE n earth's core, thought to be composed of nickel and iron
NIFES ► nife
NIFF n stink ▷ vb stink
NIFFED ► niff
NIFFER vb barter
NIFFERS ► niffer
NIFFIER ► niff
NIFFING ► niff
NIFFS ► niff
NIFFY ► niff
NIFTIER ► nifty
NIFTIES ► nifty
NIFTILY ► nifty
NIFTY adj neat or smart ▷ n nifty thing
NIGELLA n type of plant the Mediterranean and W Asia
NIGGARD n stingy person ▷ adj miserly ▷ vb act in a niggardly way
NIGGLE vb worry slightly ▷ n small worry or doubt
NIGGLED ► niggle
NIGGLER ► niggle
NIGGLES ► niggle
NIGGLY ► niggle
NIGH prep near ▷ adv nearly ▷ adj near ▷ vb approach
NIGHED ► nigh
NIGHER ► nigh
NIGHEST ► nigh
NIGHING ► nigh
NIGHLY ► nigh
NIGHS ► nigh
NIGHT n time of darkness between sunset and sunrise ▷ adj of, occurring, or working at night
NIGHTED adj darkened
NIGHTIE same as > **nightgown**
NIGHTLY adv (happening) each night ▷ adj happening each night
NIGHTS adv at night or on most nights
NIGHTY same as ► **nightie**
NIGIRI n small oval block of cold rice, wasabi and fish,

sometimes held together by a seaweed band

NIGIRIS ▸ nigiri

NIGRIFY vb blacken

NIHIL n nil

NIHILS ▸ nihil

NIHONGA n Japanese form of painting

NIKAB ▸ niqab

NIKABS ▸ nikab

NIKAH n Islamic marriage contract

NIKAHS ▸ nikah

NIKAU n palm tree native to New Zealand

NIKAUS ▸ nikau

NIL n nothing, zero

NILGAI n large Indian antelope

NILGAIS ▸ nilgai

NILGAU same as ▸ **nilghau**

NILGAUS ▸ nilgau

NILGHAI same as ▸ **nilgai**

NILGHAU same as ▸ **nilgai**

NILL vb be unwilling

NILLED ▸ nill

NILLING ▸ nill

NILLS ▸ nill

NILS ▸ nil

NIM n game in which two players alternately remove one or more small items from one of several rows or piles ▷ vb steal

NIMB n halo

NIMBED ▸ nimb

NIMBI ▸ nimbus

NIMBLE adj agile and quick

NIMBLER ▸ nimble

NIMBLY ▸ nimble

NIMBS ▸ nimb

NIMBUS n dark grey rain cloud

NIMIETY rare word for ▸ **excess**

NIMIOUS ▸ nimiety

NIMMED ▸ nim

NIMMER ▸ nim

NIMMERS ▸ nim

NIMMING ▸ nim

NIMONIC adj as in **nimonic alloy** type of nickel-based alloy used at high temperature

NIMPS adj easy

NIMROD n hunter

NIMRODS ▸ nimrod

NIMS ▸ nim

NINCOM same as ▸ nicompoop

NINCOMS ▸ nincom

NINCUM same as ▸ nicompoop

NINCUMS ▸ nincum

NINE n one more than eight

NINEPIN n skittle used in ninepins

NINES ▸ nine

NINETY n ten times nine ▷ determiner amounting to ninety

NINJA n person skilled in ninjutsu

NINJAS ▸ ninja

NINNIES ▸ ninny

NINNY n stupid person

NINON n fine strong silky fabric

NINONS ▸ ninon

NINTH n (of) number nine in a series ▷ adj coming after the eighth in counting order, position, time, etc ▷ adv after the eighth person, position, event, etc

NINTHLY same as ▸ **ninth**

NINTHS ▸ ninth

NIOBATE n type of salt crystal

NIOBIC adj of or containing niobium in the pentavalent state

NIOBITE another name for ▸ columbite

NIOBIUM n white superconductive metallic element

NIOBOUS adj of or containing niobium in the trivalent state

NIP vb hurry ▷ n pinch or light bite

NIPA n palm tree of S and SE Asia

NIPAS ▸ nipa

NIPPED ▸ nip

NIPPER n small child ▷ vb secure with rope

NIPPERS pl n instrument or tool for snipping, pinching, or squeezing

NIPPIER ▸ nippy

NIPPILY ▸ nippy

NIPPING ▸ nip

NIPPLE n projection in the centre of a breast ▷ vb provide with a nipple

NIPPLED ▸ nipple

NIPPLES ▸ nipple

NIPPY adj frosty or chilly

NIPS ▸ nip

NIPTER n type of religious ceremony

NIPTERS ▸ nipter

NIQAB n type of veil worn by some Muslim women

One of those invaluable words allowing you to play the Q without a U. It can also be spelt **nikab**.

NIQABS ▸ niqab

NIRL vb shrivel

NIRLED ▸ nirl

NIRLIE same as ▸ **nirly**

NIRLIER ▸ nirly

NIRLING ▸ nirl

NIRLIT ▸ nirl

NIRLS ▸ nirl

NIRLY adj shrivelled

NIRVANA n absolute spiritual enlightenment and bliss

NIS n friendly goblin

NISEI n native-born citizen of the US or Canada whose parents were Japanese immigrants

NISEIS ▸ nisei

NISGUL n smallest and weakest bird in a brood of chickens

NISGULS ▸ nisgul

NISH n nothing

NISHES ▸ nish

NISI adj (of a court order) coming into effect on a specified date

NISSE same as ▸ **nis**

NISSES ▸ nisse

NISUS n impulse towards or striving after a goal

NIT n egg or larva of a louse

NITE same as ▸ **night**

NITER same as ▸ **nitre**

NITERIE n nightclub

NITERS ▸ niter

NITERY ▸ niter

NITES ▸ nite

NITHER vb shiver

NITHERS ▸ nither

NITHING n coward

NITID adj bright

NITINOL n metal alloy

NITON less common name for ▸ radon

NITONS ▸ niton

NITPICK vb criticize unnecessarily

NITRATE n compound of nitric acid, used as a fertilizer ▷ vb treat with nitric acid or a nitrate

NITRE n potassium nitrate

NITRES ▸ nitre

NITRIC adj of or containing nitrogen

NITRID same as ▸ **nitride**

NITRIDE n compound of nitrogen with a more electropositive element ▷ vb make into a nitride

NITRIDS ▶ nitrid

NITRIFY vb treat (a substance) or cause (a substance) to react with nitrogen

NITRIL same as ▶ nitrile

NITRILE n any one of a particular class of organic compounds

NITRILS ▶ nitril

NITRITE n salt or ester of nitrous acid

NITRO n nitroglycerine

NITROS ▶ nitro

NITROSO adj of a particular monovalent group

NITROUS adj derived from or containing nitrogen in a low valency state

NITROX n mixture of nitrogen and oxygen used in diving instead of air

NITRY adj nitrous

NITRYL n chemical compound

NITRYLS ▶ nitryl

NITS ▶ nit

NITTIER ▶ nitty

NITTY adj infested with nits

NITWIT n stupid person

NITWITS ▶ nitwit

NIVAL adj of or growing in or under snow

NIVEOUS adj resembling snow, esp in colour

NIX sentence substitute be careful! watch out! ▷ n rejection or refusal ▷ vb veto, deny, reject, or forbid (plans, suggestions, etc)

This is a handy little word, combining X with two of the most common tiles in the game.

NIXE n water sprite

NIXED ▶ nix

NIXER n spare-time job

NIXERS ▶ nixer

NIXES ▶ nix

NIXIE n female water sprite, usually unfriendly to humans

NIXIES ▶ nixie

NIXING ▶ nix

NIXY same as ▶ nixie

NIZAM n (formerly) a Turkish regular soldier

NIZAMS ▶ nizam

NKOSI n term of address to a superior

NKOSIS ▶ nkosi

NO interj expresses denial, disagreement, or refusal ▷ adj not any, not a ▷ adv not at all ▷ n answer or vote of 'no'

NOAH n shark

NOAHS ▶ noah

NOB n person of wealth or social distinction

NOBBIER ▶ nob

NOBBILY ▶ nob

NOBBLE vb attract the attention of (someone) in order to talk to him or her

NOBBLED ▶ nobble

NOBBLER ▶ nobble

NOBBLES ▶ nobble

NOBBUT adv nothing but

NOBBY ▶ nob

NOBLE adj showing or having high moral qualities ▷ n member of the nobility

NOBLER ▶ noble

NOBLES ▶ noble

NOBLEST ▶ noble

NOBLY ▶ noble

NOBODY pron no person ▷ n person of no importance

NOBS ▶ nob

NOCAKE n Indian meal made from dried corn

NOCAKES ▶ nocake

NOCENT n guilty person

NOCENTS ▶ nocent

NOCHEL ▶ notchel

NOCHELS ▶ nochel

NOCK n notch on an arrow or a bow for the bowstring ▷ vb fit (an arrow) on a bowstring

NOCKED ▶ nock

NOCKET same as ▶ nacket

NOCKETS ▶ nocket

NOCKING ▶ nock

NOCKS ▶ nock

NOCTUA n type of moth

NOCTUAS ▶ noctua

NOCTUID n type of nocturnal moth ▷ adj of or relating to this type of moth

NOCTULE n any of several large Old World insectivorous bats

NOCTURN n any of the main sections of the office of matins

NOCUOUS adj harmful

NOD vb lower and raise (one's head) briefly in

agreement or greeting ▷ n act of nodding

NODAL adj of or like a node

NODALLY ▶ nodal

NODATED adj knotted

NODDED ▶ nod

NODDER ▶ nod

NODDERS ▶ nod

NODDIER ▶ noddy

NODDIES ▶ noddy

NODDING ▶ nod

NODDLE n head ▷ vb nod (the head), as through drowsiness

NODDLED ▶ noddle

NODDLES ▶ noddle

NODDY n tropical tern with a dark plumage ▷ adj very easy to use or understand

NODE n point on a plant stem from which leaves grow

NODES ▶ node

NODI ▶ nodus

NODICAL adj of or relating to the nodes of a celestial body, esp of the moon

NODOSE adj having nodes or knotlike swellings

NODOUS same as ▶ nodose

NODS ▶ nod

NODULAR ▶ nodule

NODULE n small knot or lump

NODULED ▶ nodule

NODULES ▶ nodule

NODUS n problematic idea, situation, etc

NOEL n Christmas

NOELS ▶ noel

NOES ▶ no

NOESES ▶ noesis

NOESIS n exercise of reason, esp in the apprehension of universal forms

NOETIC adj of or relating to the mind, esp to its rational and intellectual faculties

NOG same as ▶ nogging

NOGAKU n Japanese style of drama

NOGG same as ▶ nog

NOGGED adj built with timber and brick

NOGGIN n head

NOGGING n short horizontal timber member used between the studs of a framed partition

NOGGINS ▶ noggin

NOGGS ▶ nogg

NOGS ▶ nog

NOH *n* stylized classic drama of Japan

NOHOW *adv* under any conditions

NOIL *n* short or knotted fibres that are separated from the long fibres by combing

NOILIER ▶ noily

NOILS ▶ noil

NOILY ▶ noil

NOINT *vb* anoint

NOINTED ▶ noint

NOINTER *n* mischievous child

NOINTS ▶ noint

NOIR *adj* (of a film) showing characteristics of a *film noir*, in plot or style ▷ *n* film noir

NOIRISH ▶ noir

NOIRS ▶ noir

NOISE *n* sound, usu a loud or disturbing one

NOISED ▶ noise

NOISES ▶ noise

NOISIER ▶ noisy

NOISILY ▶ noisy

NOISING ▶ noise

NOISOME *adj* (of smells) offensive

NOISY *adj* making a lot of noise

NOLE *same as* ▶ noll

NOLES ▶ nole

NOLL *n* head

NOLLS ▶ noll

NOLO *vb as in* nolo contendere plea indicating that the defendant does not wish to contest the case

NOLOS ▶ nolo

NOM *n* name

NOMA *n* gangrenous inflammation of the mouth, esp one affecting malnourished children

NOMAD *n* member of a tribe with no fixed dwelling place, wanderer

NOMADE *same as* ▶ nomad

NOMADES ▶ nomade

NOMADIC *adj* relating to or characteristic of nomads or their way of life

NOMADS ▶ nomad

NOMADY *n* practice of living like nomads

NOMARCH *n* head of an ancient Egyptian nome

NOMAS ▶ noma

NOMBLES *variant spelling of*

▶ numbles

NOMBRIL *n* point on a shield between the fesse point and the lowest point

NOME *n* any of the former provinces of modern Greece

NOMEN *n* ancient Roman's second name, designating his gens or clan

NOMES ▶ nome

NOMIC *adj* normal or habitual

NOMINA ▶ nomen

NOMINAL *adj* in name only ▷ *n* nominal element

NOMINEE *n* candidate

NOMISM *n* adherence to a law or laws as a primary exercise of religion

NOMISMS ▶ nomism

NOMOI ▶ nomos

NOMOS *n* convention

NOMS ▶ nom

NON *adv* not

NONA *n* sleeping sickness

NONACID *adj* not acid ▷ *n* nonacid substance

NONAGE *n* state of being under full legal age for various actions

NONAGED ▶ nonage

NONAGES ▶ nonage

NONAGON *n* geometric figure with nine sides

NONANE *n* type of chemical compound

NONANES ▶ nonane

NONART *n* something that does not constitute art

NONARTS ▶ nonart

NONARY *adj* based on the number nine

NONAS ▶ nones

NONBANK *n* business or institution that is not a bank but provides similar services

NONBODY *n* nonphysical nature of a person

NONBOOK *n* book with little substance

NONCASH *adj* other than cash

NONCE *n* present time or occasion

NONCES ▶ nonce

NONCOLA *n* soft drink other than cola

NONCOM *n* person not involved in combat

NONCOMS ▶ noncom

NONCORE *adj* not central or essential

NONDRIP *adj* (of paint) specially formulated to minimize dripping during application

NONDRUG *adj* not involving the use of drugs

NONE *pron* not any

NONEGO *n* everything that is outside one's conscious self, such as one's environment

NONEGOS ▶ nonego

NONES *n* (in the Roman calendar) the ninth day before the ides of each month

NONET *n* piece of music composed for a group of nine instruments

NONETS ▶ nonet

NONETTE *same as* ▶ nonet

NONETTI *same as* ▶ nonet

NONETTO *same as* ▶ nonet

NONFACT *n* event or thing not provable

NONFAN *n* person who is not a fan

NONFANS ▶ nonfan

NONFARM *adj* not connected with a farm

NONFAT *adj* fat free

NONFOOD *n* item that is not food

NONFUEL *adj* not relating to fuel

NONG *n* stupid or incompetent person

NONGAME *adj* not pursued for competitive sport purposes

NONGAY *n* person who is not gay

NONGAYS ▶ nongay

NONGS ▶ nong

NONHEME *adj* of dietary iron, obtained from vegetable foods

NONHERO *n* person who is not a hero

NONHOME *adj* not of the home

NONI *n* type of tree of SE Asia and the Pacific islands whose fruit provides a possibly health-promoting juice

NONIRON *adj* not requiring ironing

NONIS ▶ noni

NONJURY *n* trial without a jury

NONLIFE *n* matter which is not living**

NONMAN *n* being that is not a man

NONMEAT *n* not containing meat

NONMEN ▸ **nonman**

NONNEWS *adj* not concerned with news

NONNIES ▸ **nonny**

NONNY *n* meaningless word

NONOILY *adj* not oily

NONORAL *adj* not oral

NONPAID *adj* without payment

NONPAR *adj* nonparticipating

NONPAST *n* grammatical term

NONPEAK *n* period of low demand

NONPLAY *n* social behaviour that is not classed as play

NONPLUS *vb* put at a loss ▸ *n* state of utter perplexity prohibiting action or speech

NONPOOR *adj* not poor

NONPROS *vb* enter a judgment of non prosequitur against a plaintiff

NONSELF *n* foreign molecule in the body

NONSKED *n* non-scheduled aeroplane

NONSKID *adj* designed to reduce skidding

NONSLIP *adj* designed to prevent slipping

NONSTOP *adv* without a stop ▸ *adj* without a stop ▸ *n* nonstop flight

NONSUCH *same as* > **nonesuch**

NONSUIT *n* order of a judge dismissing a suit when the plaintiff fails to show a good cause of action or to produce any evidence ▸ *vb* order the dismissal of the suit of (a person)

NONTAX *n* tax that has little real effect

NONUPLE *adj* ninefold ▸ *n* ninefold number

NONUSE *n* failure to use

NONUSER ▸ **nonuse**

NONUSES ▸ **nonuse**

NONWAGE *adj* not part of wages

NONWAR *n* state of nonviolence

NONWARS ▸ **nonwar**

NONWOOL *adj* not wool

NONWORD *n* series of letters not recognised as a word

NONWORK *adj* not involving work

NONYL *n* type of chemical

NONYLS ▸ **nonyl**

NONZERO *adj* not equal to zero

NOO *n* type of Japanese musical drama

NOOB ▸ **newbie**

NOOBS ▸ **noob**

NOODGE *vb* annoy persistently

NOODGED ▸ **noodge**

NOODGES ▸ **noodge**

NOODLE *n* simpleton ▸ *vb* improvise aimlessly on a musical instrument

NOODLED ▸ **noodle**

NOODLES ▸ **noodle**

NOOGIE *n* act of inflicting pain by rubbing someone's head hard

NOOGIES ▸ **noogie**

NOOIT *interj* South African exclamation of pleased or shocked surprise

NOOK *n* corner or recess

NOOKS ▸ **nook**

NOOLOGY *n* study of intuition

NOON *n* twelve o'clock midday ▸ *vb* take a rest at noon

NOONDAY *adj* happening at noon ▸ *n* middle of the day

NOONED ▸ **noon**

NOONER *n* sexual encounter during a lunch hour

NOONERS ▸ **nooner**

NOONING *n* midday break for rest or food

NOONS ▸ **noon**

NOOP *n* point of the elbow

NOOPS ▸ **noop**

NOOSE *n* loop in the end of a rope, tied with a slipknot

NOOSED ▸ **noose**

NOOSER *n* person who uses a noose

NOOSERS ▸ **nooser**

NOOSES ▸ **noose**

NOOSING ▸ **noose**

NOPAL *n* type of cactus

NOPALES ▸ **nopal**

NOPALS ▸ **nopal**

NOPE *interj* no

NOPLACE *same as* ▸ **nowhere**

NOR *prep* and not

NORDIC *adj* of competitions in cross-country racing and ski-jumping

NORI *n* edible seaweed often used in Japanese cookery, esp for wrapping sushi or rice balls

NORIA *n* water wheel with buckets attached to its rim for raising water from a stream into irrigation canals

NORIAS ▸ **noria**

NORIMON *n* Japanese passenger vehicle

NORIS ▸ **nori**

NORITE *n* variety of gabbro composed mainly of hypersthene and labradorite feldspar

NORITES ▸ **norite**

NORITIC ▸ **norite**

NORK *n* female breast

NORKS ▸ **nork**

NORLAND *n* north part of a country or the earth

NORM *n* standard that is regarded as normal

NORMA *n* norm or standard

NORMAL *adj* usual, regular, or typical ▸ *n* usual or regular state, degree or form

NORMALS ▸ **normal**

NORMAN *n* post used for winding on a ship

NORMANS ▸ **norman**

NORMAS ▸ **norma**

NORMED *n* mathematical term

NORMS ▸ **norm**

NORSEL *vb* fit with short lines for fastening hooks

NORSELS ▸ **norsel**

NORTENA *same as* ▸ **norteno**

NORTENO *n* type of Mexican music

NORTH *n* direction towards the North Pole, opposite south ▸ *adj* or in the north ▸ *adv* in, to, or towards the north ▸ *vb* move north

NORTHED ▸ **north**

NORTHER *n* wind or storm from the north ▸ *vb* move north

NORTHS ▸ **north**

NORWARD *same as* > **northward**

NOS ▷ **no**

NOSE n organ of smell, used also in breathing ▷ vb move forward slowly and carefully

NOSEAN n type of mineral

NOSEANS ▷ **nosean**

NOSEBAG n bag containing feed fastened round a horse's head

NOSED ▷ **nose**

NOSEGAY n small bunch of flowers

NOSER n strong headwind

NOSERS ▷ **noser**

NOSES ▷ **nose**

NOSEY adj prying or inquisitive ▷ n nosey person

NOSEYS ▷ **nosey**

NOSH n food ▷ vb eat

NOSHED ▷ **nosh**

NOSHER ▷ **nosh**

NOSHERS ▷ **nosh**

NOSHERY n restaurant or other place where food is served

NOSHES ▷ **nosh**

NOSHING ▷ **nosh**

NOSIER ▷ **nosy**

NOSIES ▷ **nosy**

NOSIEST ▷ **nosy**

NOSILY ▷ **nosy**

NOSING n edge of a step or stair tread that projects beyond the riser

NOSINGS ▷ **nosing**

NOSODE n homeopathic remedy

NOSODES ▷ **nosode**

NOSTOC n type of bacterium occurring in moist places

NOSTOCS ▷ **nostoc**

NOSTOI ▷ **nostos**

NOSTOS n story of a return home

NOSTRIL n one of the two openings at the end of the nose

NOSTRO adj as in **nostro account** bank account conducted by a British bank with a foreign bank

NOSTRUM n quack medicine

NOSY adj prying or inquisitive

NOT adv expressing negation, refusal, or denial

NOTA ▷ **notum**

NOTABLE adj worthy of being noted, remarkable ▷ n person of distinction

NOTABLY adv particularly or especially

NOTAEUM n back of a bird's body

NOTAIRE n (in France) notary

NOTAL ▷ **notum**

NOTANDA > **notandum**

NOTARY n person authorized to witness the signing of legal documents

NOTATE vb write (esp music) in notation

NOTATED ▷ **notate**

NOTATES ▷ **notate**

NOTCH n V-shaped cut ▷ vb make a notch in

NOTCHED ▷ **notch**

NOTCHEL vb refuse to pay another person's debts

NOTCHER n person who cuts notches

NOTCHES ▷ **notch**

NOTCHY adj (of a motor vehicle gear mechanism) requiring careful gear-changing

NOTE n short letter ▷ vb notice, pay attention to

NOTED adj well-known

NOTEDLY ▷ **noted**

NOTELET n small folded card with a design on the front, used for writing informal letters

NOTEPAD n number of sheets of paper fastened together along one edge

NOTER n person who takes notes

NOTERS ▷ **noter**

NOTES pl n short descriptive or summarized jottings taken down for future reference

NOTHER same as ▷ **other**

NOTHING pron not anything ▷ adv not at all ▷ n person or thing of no importance

NOTICE n observation or attention ▷ vb observe, become aware of

NOTICED ▷ **notice**

NOTICER n person who takes notice

NOTICES ▷ **notice**

NOTIFY vb inform

NOTING ▷ **note**

NOTION n idea or opinion

NOTIONS pl n pins, cotton, ribbon, and similar wares used for sewing

NOTITIA n register or list, esp of ecclesiastical districts

NOTOUR adj notorious

NOTT same as ▷ **not**

NOTUM n cuticular plate covering the dorsal surface of a thoracic segment of an insect

NOUGAT n chewy sweet containing nuts and fruit

NOUGATS ▷ **nougat**

NOUGHT n figure o

NOUGHTS ▷ **nought**

NOUL same as ▷ **noll**

NOULD vb would not

NOULDE same as ▷ **nould**

NOULE same as ▷ **noll**

NOULES ▷ **noule**

NOULS ▷ **noul**

NOUMENA > **noumenon**

NOUN n word that refers to a person, place, or thing

NOUNAL ▷ **noun**

NOUNIER ▷ **nouny**

NOUNS ▷ **noun**

NOUNY adj nounlike

NOUP n steep headland

NOUPS ▷ **noup**

NOURICE n nurse

NOURISH vb feed

NOURSLE vb nurse

NOUS n common sense

NOUSELL vb foster

NOUSES ▷ **nous**

NOUSLE vb nuzzle

NOUSLED ▷ **nousle**

NOUSLES ▷ **nousle**

NOUT same as ▷ **nought**

NOUVEAU adj having recently become the thing specified

NOVA n star that suddenly becomes brighter and then gradually decreases to its original brightness

NOVAE ▷ **nova**

NOVALIA n newly reclaimed land

NOVAS ▷ **nova**

NOVATE vb substitute one thing (esp a legal contract) in place of another

NOVATED adj as in **novated lease** Australian system of employer-aided car purchase

NOVATES ▷ **novate**

NOVEL n long fictitious story in book form ▷ adj fresh, new, or original

NOVELLA n short novel

NOVELLE ▷ **novella**

NOVELLY ▷ **novel**

N

NOVELS ▶ novel
NOVELTY n newness
NOVENA n set of prayers or services on nine consecutive days
NOVENAE ▶ novena
NOVENAS ▶ novena
NOVICE n beginner
NOVICES ▶ novice
NOVITY n novelty
NOVUM n game played with dice
NOVUMS ▶ novum
NOW adv at or for the present time
NOWAY adv in no manner ▷ sentence substitute used to make an emphatic refusal, denial etc
NOWAYS same as ▶ noway
NOWED adj knotted
NOWHERE adv not anywhere ▷ n nonexistent or insignicant place
NOWISE another word for ▶ noway
NOWL n crown of the head
NOWLS ▶ nowl
NOWN same as ▶ own
NOWNESS ▶ nown
NOWS ▶ now
NOWT n nothing
NOWTIER ▶ nowty
NOWTS ▶ nowt
NOWTY adj bad-tempered
NOWY adj having a small projection at the centre (of a cross)
NOX n nitrogen oxide

| Meaning nitrogen oxide, this is another of those very useful short words containing X.

NOXAL adj relating to damage done by something belonging to another
NOXES ▶ nox
NOXIOUS adj poisonous or harmful
NOY vb harrass
NOYADE n execution by drowning
NOYADES ▶ noyade
NOYANCE n nuisance
NOYAU n liqueur made from brandy flavoured with nut kernels
NOYAUS ▶ noyau
NOYED ▶ noy
NOYES archaic form of ▶ noise
NOYESES ▶ noyes
NOYING ▶ noy

NOYOUS ▶ noy
NOYS ▶ noy
NOYSOME ▶ noy
NOZZER n new recruit (in the Navy)
NOZZERS ▶ nozzer
NOZZLE n projecting spout through which fluid is discharged
NOZZLES ▶ nozzle
NTH adj of an unspecified number

| A good word to remember for awkward situations on the board, as it's one of very few three-letter words that doesn't contain a vowel.

NU n 13th letter in the Greek alphabet
NUANCE n subtle difference in colour, meaning, or tone ▷ vb give subtle differences to
NUANCED ▶ nuance
NUANCES ▶ nuance
NUB n point or gist (of a story etc) ▷ vb hang from the gallows
NUBBED ▶ nub
NUBBIER ▶ nubby
NUBBIN n something small or undeveloped, esp a fruit or ear of corn
NUBBING ▶ nub
NUBBINS ▶ nubbin
NUBBLE n small lump
NUBBLED ▶ nubble
NUBBLES ▶ nubble
NUBBLY ▶ nubble
NUBBY adj having small lumps or protuberances
NUBIA n fleecy scarf for the head, worn by women
NUBIAS ▶ nubia
NUBILE adj sexually attractive
NUBS ▶ nub
NUBUCK n type of leather with a velvety finish
NUBUCKS ▶ nubuck
NUCELLI > nucellus
NUCHA n back or nape of the neck
NUCHAE ▶ nucha
NUCHAL n scale on a reptile's neck
NUCHALS ▶ nuchal
NUCLEAL ▶ nucleus
NUCLEAR adj of nuclear weapons or energy
NUCLEI ▶ nucleus
NUCLEIC adj as in nucleic

acid type of complex compound that is a vital constituent of living cells
NUCLEIN n any of a group of proteins that occur in the nuclei of living cells
NUCLEON n proton or neutron
NUCLEUS n centre, esp of an atom or cell
NUCLIDE n species of atom characterized by its atomic number and its mass number
NUCULE n small seed
NUCULES ▶ nucule
NUDDIES ▶ nuddy
NUDDY n as in in the nuddy in the nude
NUDE adj naked ▷ n naked figure in painting, sculpture, or photography
NUDELY ▶ nude
NUDER ▶ nude
NUDES ▶ nude
NUDEST ▶ nude
NUDGE vb push gently, esp with the elbow ▷ n gentle push or touch
NUDGED ▶ nudge
NUDGER ▶ nudge
NUDGERS ▶ nudge
NUDGES ▶ nudge
NUDGING ▶ nudge
NUDIE n film, show, or magazine depicting nudity
NUDIES ▶ nudie
NUDISM n practice of not wearing clothes
NUDISMS ▶ nudism
NUDIST ▶ nudism
NUDISTS ▶ nudism
NUDITY n state or fact of being nude
NUDNICK same as ▶ nudnik
NUDNIK n boring person
NUDNIKS ▶ nudnik
NUDZH same as ▶ nudge
NUDZHED ▶ nudzh
NUDZHES ▶ nudzh
NUFF slang form of ▶ enough
NUFFIN slang form of ▶ nothing
NUFFINS ▶ nuffin
NUFFS ▶ nuff
NUGAE n jests
NUGGAR n sailing boat used to carry cargo on the Nile
NUGGARS ▶ nuggar
NUGGET n small lump of gold in its natural state ▷ vb

polish footwear
NUGGETS ▷ nugget
NUGGETY *adj* of or resembling a nugget
NUKE *vb* attack with nuclear weapons ▷ *n* nuclear weapon
NUKED ▷ nuke
NUKES ▷ nuke
NUKING ▷ nuke
NULL *adj* without legal force ▷ *vb* make negative
NULLA *same as* ▷ **nullah**
NULLAH *n* stream or drain
NULLAHS ▷ nullah
NULLAS ▷ nulla
NULLED ▷ null
NULLIFY *vb* make ineffective
NULLING *n* knurling
NULLITY *n* state of being null
NULLS ▷ null
NUMB *adj* without feeling, as through cold, shock, or fear ▷ *vb* make numb
NUMBAT *n* small Australian marsupial with a long snout and tongue
NUMBATS ▷ numbat
NUMBED ▷ numb
NUMBER *n* sum or quantity ▷ *vb* count
NUMBERS ▷ number
NUMBEST ▷ numb
NUMBING ▷ numb
NUMBLES *pl n* heart, lungs, liver, etc, of a deer or other animal, cooked for food
NUMBLY ▷ numb
NUMBS ▷ numb
NUMDAH *n* coarse felt made esp in India
NUMDAHS ▷ numdah
NUMEN *n* (esp in ancient Roman religion) a deity or spirit presiding over a thing or place
NUMERAL *n* word or symbol used to express a sum or quantity ▷ *adj* of, consisting of, or denoting a number
NUMERIC *n* number or numeral
NUMINA *plural of* ▷ **numen**
NUMMARY *adj* of or relating to coins
NUMNAH *same as* ▷ **numdah**
NUMNAHS ▷ numnah
NUMPTY *n* stupid person
NUN *n* female member of a

religious order
NUNATAK *n* isolated mountain peak projecting through the surface of surrounding glacial ice
NUNCIO *n* pope's ambassador
NUNCIOS ▷ nuncio
NUNCLE *archaic or dialect word for* ▷ **uncle**
NUNCLES ▷ nuncle
NUNDINE *n* market day
NUNHOOD *n* condition, practice, or character of a nun
NUNLIKE ▷ nun
NUNNERY *n* convent
NUNNISH ▷ nun
NUNNY *n as in* **nunny bag** small sealskin haversack used in Canada
NUNS ▷ nun
NUNSHIP ▷ nun
NUPTIAL *adj* relating to marriage
NUR *n* wooden ball
NURAGHE *n* Sardinian round tower
NURAGHI ▷ nuraghe
NURD *same as* ▷ **nerd**
NURDIER ▷ nerd
NURDISH ▷ nerd
NURDLE *vb* score runs in cricket by deflecting the ball rather than striking it hard
NURDLED ▷ nurdle
NURDLES ▷ nurdle
NURDS ▷ nurd
NURDY ▷ nurd
NURHAG *n* Sardinian round tower
NURHAGS ▷ nurhag
NURL *same as* ▷ **knurl**
NURLED ▷ nurl
NURLING ▷ nurl
NURLS ▷ nurl
NURR *n* wooden ball
NURRS ▷ nurr
NURS ▷ nur
NURSE *n* person employed to look after sick people, usu in a hospital ▷ *vb* look after (a sick person)
NURSED ▷ nurse
NURSER *n* person who treats something carefully
NURSERS ▷ nurser
NURSERY *n* room where children sleep or play
NURSES ▷ nurse
NURSING *n* practice or profession of caring for the

sick and injured
NURSLE *vb* nuzzle
NURSLED ▷ nursle
NURSLES ▷ nursle
NURTURE *n* act or process of promoting the development of a child or young plant ▷ *vb* promote or encourage the development of
NUS ▷ nu
NUT *n* fruit consisting of a hard shell and a kernel ▷ *vb* to gather nuts
NUTANT *adj* having the apex hanging down
NUTATE *vb* nod
NUTATED ▷ nutate
NUTATES ▷ nutate
NUTGALL *n* nut-shaped gall caused by gall wasps on the oak and other trees
NUTJOB *n* crazy person
NUTJOBS ▷ nutjob
NUTLET *n* any of the one-seeded portions of a fruit that fragments when mature
NUTLETS ▷ nutlet
NUTLIKE ▷ nut
NUTMEAL *n* type of grain
NUTMEAT *n* kernel of a nut
NUTMEG *n* spice made from the seed of a tropical tree ▷ *vb* kick or hit the ball between the legs of (an opposing player)
NUTMEGS ▷ nutmeg
NUTPICK *n* tool used to dig the meat from nuts
NUTRIA *n* fur of the coypu
NUTRIAS ▷ nutria
NUTS ▷ nut
NUTTED ▷ nut
NUTTERY *n* place where nut trees grow
NUTTIER ▷ nutty
NUTTILY ▷ nutty
NUTTING *n* act of gathering nuts
NUTTY *adj* containing or resembling nuts
NUTWOOD *n* any of various nut-bearing trees, such as walnut
NUZZER *n* present given to a superior in India
NUZZERS ▷ nuzzer
NUZZLE *vb* push or rub gently with the nose or snout
NUZZLED ▷ nuzzle
NUZZLER *n* person or thing

that nuzzles
NUZZLES ▶ nuzzle
NY *same as* ▶ **nigh**
NYAFF *n* small or
contemptible person ▷ *vb*
yelp like a small dog
NYAFFED ▶ nyaff
NYAFFS ▶ nyaff
NYALA *n* spiral-horned
southern African antelope
NYALAS ▶ nyala
NYANZA *n* (in E Africa) a
lake
NYANZAS ▶ nyanza
NYAS *n* young hawk
NYASES ▶ nyas

NYBBLE *n* small byte
NYBBLES ▶ nybble
NYE *n* flock of pheasants
▷ *vb* near
NYED ▶ nye
NYES ▶ nye
NYING ▶ nye
NYLGHAI *same as* ▶ **nilgai**
NYLGHAU *same as* ▶ **nilgai**
NYLON *n* synthetic material
used for clothing etc
NYLONS *pl n* stockings
made of nylon
NYMPH *n* mythical spirit of
nature, represented as a
beautiful young woman

NYMPHA *n* either one of the
labia minora
NYMPHAE ▶ nympha
NYMPHAL ▶ nymph
NYMPHET *n* sexually
precocious young girl
NYMPHIC ▶ nymph
NYMPHLY ▶ nymph
NYMPHO *n* nymphomaniac
NYMPHOS ▶ nympho
NYMPHS ▶ nymph
NYS ▶ ny
NYSSA *n* type of tree
NYSSAS ▶ nyssa

N

Oo

With eight **O**s in the bag, you're likely to have at least one on your rack during a game. There are plenty of good two-letter words starting with **O**. It's worth knowing that **O** will form a two-letter word in front of every other vowel except **A**, as well as in front of **Y**. **O** also combines well with **X**, with **ox** (9 points) as the obvious starting point, and several words that refer to **oxygen** (17), including **oxo** (10) and **oxy** (13). Don't forget the short everyday words that begin with **O**. While **on** and **or** (2 each) won't earn you many points, they can be very helpful when you are trying to score in more than one direction at a time. **Of** and **oh** (5 each) can also prove very useful.

OAF *n* stupid or clumsy person
OAFISH ▶ **oaf**
OAFS ▶ **oaf**
OAK *n* deciduous forest tree
OAKED *adj* relating to wine that is stored for a time in oak barrels prior to bottling
OAKEN *adj* made of the wood of the oak
OAKER *same as* ▶ **ochre**
OAKERS ▶ **oaker**
OAKIER ▶ **oaky**
OAKIES ▶ **oaky**
OAKIEST ▶ **oaky**
OAKLIKE ▶ **oak**
OAKLING *n* young oak
OAKMOSS *n* type of lichen
OAKS ▶ **oak**
OAKUM *n* fibre obtained by unravelling old rope
OAKUMS ▶ **oakum**
OAKY *adj* hard like the wood of an oak ▷ *n* ice cream
OAR *n* pole with a broad blade, used for rowing a boat ▷ *vb* propel with oars
OARAGE *n* use or number of oars
OARAGES ▶ **oarage**
OARED *adj* equipped with oars
OARFISH *n* very long ribbonfish with long slender ventral fins
OARIER ▶ **oary**
OARIEST ▶ **oary**
OARING ▶ **oar**
OARLESS ▶ **oar**
OARLIKE ▶ **oar**
OARLOCK *n* swivelling

device attached to the gunwale of a boat that holds an oar in place
OARS ▶ **oar**
OARSMAN *n* person who rows
OARSMEN ▶ **oarsman**
OARWEED *n* type of brown seaweed
OARY *adj* of or like an oar
OASES ▶ **oasis**
OASIS *n* fertile area in a desert
OAST *n* oven for drying hops
OASTS ▶ **oast**
OAT *n* hard cereal grown as food
OATCAKE *n* thin flat biscuit of oatmeal
OATEN *adj* made of oats or oat straw
OATER *n* film about the American Wild West
OATERS ▶ **oater**
OATH *n* solemn promise, esp to be truthful in court
OATHS ▶ **oath**
OATIER ▶ **oaty**
OATIEST ▶ **oaty**
OATLIKE ▶ **oat**
OATMEAL *n* coarse flour made from oats ▷ *adj* pale brownish-cream
OATS ▶ **oat**
OATY *adj* of, like, or containing oats
OAVES ▶ **oaf**
OB *n* expression of opposition
OBA *n* (in W Africa) a Yoruba chief or ruler

OBANG *n* former Japanese coin
OBANGS ▶ **obang**
OBAS ▶ **oba**
OBCONIC *adj* (of a fruit or similar part) shaped like a cone and attached at the pointed end
OBDURE *vb* make obdurate
OBDURED ▶ **obdure**
OBDURES ▶ **obdure**
OBE *n* ancient Laconian village
OBEAH *vb* cast spell on
OBEAHED ▶ **obeah**
OBEAHS ▶ **obeah**
OBECHE *n* African tree
OBECHES ▶ **obeche**
OBEISM *n* belief in obeah
OBEISMS ▶ **obeism**
OBELI ▶ **obelus**
OBELIA *n* type of jellyfish
OBELIAS ▶ **obelia**
OBELION *n* area of skull
OBELISE *same as* ▶ **obelize**
OBELISK *n* four-sided stone column tapering to a pyramid at the top
OBELISM *n* practice of marking passages in text
OBELIZE *vb* mark (a word or passage) with an obelus
OBELUS *n* mark used in editions of ancient documents to indicate spurious words or passages
OBENTO *n* Japanese lunch box
OBENTOS ▶ **obento**
OBES ▶ **obe**
OBESE *adj* very fat

OBESELY ▶ obese
OBESER ▶ obese
OBESEST ▶ obese
OBESITY ▶ obese
OBEY vb carry out instructions or orders
OBEYED ▶ obey
OBEYER ▶ obey
OBEYERS ▶ obey
OBEYING ▶ obey
OBEYS ▶ obey
OBI n broad sash tied in a large flat bow at the back, worn by Japanese women and children ▷ vb bewitch
OBIA same as ▶ obeah
OBIAS ▶ obia
OBIED ▶ obi
OBIING ▶ obi
OBIISM ▶ obi
OBIISMS ▶ obi
OBIIT vb died
OBIS ▶ obi
OBIT n memorial service
OBITAL adj of obits
OBITER adv by the way
OBITS ▶ obit
OBITUAL adj of obits
OBJECT n physical thing ▷ vb express disapproval
OBJECTS ▶ object
OBJET n object
OBJETS ▶ objet
OBJURE vb put on oath
OBJURED ▶ objure
OBJURES ▶ objure
OBLAST n administrative division of the constituent republics of Russia
OBLASTI ▶ oblast
OBLASTS ▶ oblast
OBLATE adj (of a sphere) flattened at the poles ▷ n person dedicated to a monastic or religious life
OBLATES ▶ oblate
OBLIGE vb compel (someone) morally or by law to do something
OBLIGED ▶ oblige
OBLIGEE n person in whose favour an obligation, contract, or bond is created
OBLIGER ▶ oblige
OBLIGES ▶ oblige
OBLIGOR n person who binds himself by contract to perform some obligation
OBLIQUE adj slanting ▷ n symbol (/) ▷ vb take or have an oblique direction
OBLONG adj having two long sides, two short sides,

and four right angles ▷ n oblong figure
OBLONGS ▶ oblong
OBLOQUY n verbal abuse
OBO n ship carrying oil and ore
OBOE n double-reeded woodwind instrument
OBOES ▶ oboe
OBOIST ▶ oboe
OBOISTS ▶ oboe
OBOL same as ▶ obolus
OBOLARY adj very poor
OBOLE n former weight unit in pharmacy
OBOLES ▶ obole
OBOLI ▶ obolus
OBOLS ▶ obol
OBOLUS n modern Greek unit of weight equal to one tenth of a gram
OBOS ▶ obo
OBOVATE adj (of a leaf) shaped like the longitudinal section of an egg with the narrower end at the base
OBOVOID adj (of a fruit) egg-shaped with the narrower end at the base
OBS ▶ ob
OBSCENE adj portraying sex offensively
OBSCURE adj not well known ▷ vb make (something) obscure
OBSEQUY singular of > obsequies
OBSERVE vb see or notice
OBSESS vb preoccupy (someone) compulsively
OBSIGN vb confirm
OBSIGNS ▶ obsign
OBTAIN vb acquire intentionally
OBTAINS ▶ obtain
OBTECT adj (of a pupa) encased in a hardened secretion
OBTEND vb put forward
OBTENDS ▶ obtend
OBTEST vb beg (someone) earnestly
OBTESTS ▶ obtest
OBTRUDE vb push oneself or one's ideas on others
OBTUND vb deaden or dull
OBTUNDS ▶ obtund
OBTUSE adj mentally slow
OBTUSER ▶ obtuse
OBVERSE n opposite way of looking at an idea ▷ adj facing or turned towards the observer

OBVERT vb deduce the obverse of (a proposition)
OBVERTS ▶ obvert
OBVIATE vb make unnecessary
OBVIOUS adj easy to see or understand, evident
OCA n any of various South American herbaceous plants
OCARINA n small oval wind instrument
OCAS ▶ oca
OCCAM n computer programming language
OCCAMS ▶ occam
OCCAMY n type of alloy
OCCIES ▶ occy
OCCIPUT n back of the head
OCCLUDE vb obstruct
OCCULT adj relating to the supernatural ▷ vb (of a celestial body) to hide (another celestial body) from view
OCCULTS ▶ occult
OCCUPY vb live or work in (a building)
OCCUR vb happen
OCCURS ▶ occur
OCCY n as in all over the occy dialect expression meaning in every direction
OCEAN n vast area of sea between continents
OCEANIC adj of or relating to the ocean
OCEANID n ocean nymph in Greek mythology
OCEANS ▶ ocean
OCELLAR ▶ ocellus
OCELLI ▶ ocellus
OCELLUS n simple eye of insects and some other invertebrates
OCELOID adj of or like an ocelot
OCELOT n American wild cat with a spotted coat
OCELOTS ▶ ocelot
OCH interj expression of surprise, annoyance, or disagreement
OCHE n (in darts) mark on the floor behind which a player must stand
OCHER same as ▶ ochre
OCHERED ▶ ocher
OCHERS ▶ ocher
OCHERY ▶ ocher
OCHES ▶ oche
OCHONE interj expression of sorrow or regret

OCHRE n brownish-yellow earth ▷ adj moderate yellow-orange to orange ▷ vb colour with ochre

OCHREA n cup-shaped structure that sheathes the stems of certain plants

OCHREAE ▶ ochrea

OCHRED ▶ ochre

OCHRES ▶ ochre

OCHREY ▶ ochre

OCHRING ▶ ochre

OCHROID ▶ ocker

OCHROUS ▶ ochre

OCHRY ▶ ochre

OCICAT n breed of large short-haired cat with a spotted coat

OCICATS ▶ ocicat

OCKER n uncultivated or boorish Australian

OCKERS ▶ ocker

OCREA same as ▶ ochrea

OCREAE ▶ ocrea

OCREATE adj possessing an ocrea

OCTA same as ▶ okta

OCTAD n group or series of eight

OCTADIC ▶ octad

OCTADS ▶ octad

OCTAGON n geometric figure with eight sides

OCTAL n number system with a base 8

OCTALS ▶ octal

OCTAN n illness that occurs weekly

OCTANE n hydrocarbon found in petrol

OCTANES ▶ octane

OCTANOL n alcohol containing eight carbon atoms

OCTANS ▶ octan

OCTANT n any of the eight parts into which the three planes containing the Cartesian coordinate axes divide space

OCTANTS ▶ octant

OCTAPLA n book with eight texts

OCTAS ▶ octa

OCTAVAL ▶ octave

OCTAVE n (interval between the first and) eighth note of a scale ▷ adj consisting of eight parts

OCTAVES ▶ octave

OCTAVO n book size in which the sheets are folded into eight leaves

OCTAVOS ▶ octavo

OCTET n group of eight performers

OCTETS ▶ octet

OCTETT same as ▶ octet

OCTETTE same as ▶ octet

OCTETTS ▶ octett

OCTOFID adj divided into eight

OCTOPI ▶ octopus

OCTOPOD n type of mollusc ▷ adj of these molluscs

OCTOPUS n sea creature with a soft body and eight tentacles

OCTROI n duty on various goods brought into certain European towns

OCTROIS ▶ octroi

OCTUOR n octet

OCTUORS ▶ octuor

OCTUPLE n quantity or number eight times as great as another ▷ adj eight times as much or as many ▷ vb multiply by eight

OCTUPLY adv by eight times

OCTYL n group of atoms

OCTYLS ▶ octyl

OCULAR adj relating to the eyes or sight ▷ n lens in an optical instrument

OCULARS ▶ ocular

OCULATE adj possessing eyes

OCULI ▶ oculus

OCULIST n ophthalmologist

OCULUS n round window

OD n hypothetical force formerly thought to be responsible for many natural phenomena

ODA n room in a harem

ODAH same as ▶ oda

ODAHS ▶ odah

ODAL same as ▶ udal

ODALISK same as ▶ odalisque

ODALLER ▶ odal

ODALS ▶ odal

ODAS ▶ oda

ODD adj unusual

ODDBALL n eccentric person ▷ adj strange or peculiar

ODDER ▶ odd

ODDEST ▶ odd

ODDISH ▶ odd

ODDITY n odd person or thing

ODDLY ▶ odd

ODDMENT n odd piece or thing

ODDNESS ▶ odd

ODDS pl n (ratio showing) the probability of something happening

ODDSMAN n umpire

ODDSMEN ▶ oddsman

ODE n lyric poem, usu addressed to a particular subject

ODEA ▶ odeum

ODEON same as ▶ odeum

ODEONS ▶ odeon

ODES ▶ ode

ODEUM n (esp in ancient Greece and Rome) a building for musical performances

ODEUMS ▶ odeum

ODIC ▶ od

ODIOUS adj offensive

ODISM ▶ od

ODISMS ▶ od

ODIST ▶ od

ODISTS ▶ od

ODIUM n widespread dislike

ODIUMS ▶ odium

ODONATE n dragonfly or related insect

ODONTIC adj of teeth

ODOR same as ▶ odour

ODORANT n something with a strong smell

ODORATE adj having a strong smell

ODORED same as ▶ odoured

ODORFUL same as ▶ odourful

ODORISE same as ▶ odorize

ODORIZE vb give an odour to

ODOROUS adj having or emitting a characteristic smell or odour

ODORS ▶ odor

ODOUR n particular smell

ODOURED adj having odour

ODOURS ▶ odour

ODS ▶ od

ODSO n cry of suprise

ODYL same as ▶ od

ODYLE same as ▶ od

ODYLES ▶ odyle

ODYLISM ▶ odyl

ODYLS ▶ odyl

ODYSSEY n long eventful journey

ODZOOKS interj cry of surprise

OE n grandchild

OECIST n colony founder

OECISTS ▶ oecist

O

OEDEMA n abnormal swelling

OEDEMAS ▶ oedema

OEDIPAL adj relating to an Oedipus complex, whereby a male child wants to replace his father

OENOMEL n drink made of wine and honey

OERSTED n cgs unit of magnetic field strength

OES ▶ oe

OESTRAL ▶ oestrus

OESTRIN obsolete term for > oestrogen

OESTRUM same as ▶ oestrus

OESTRUS n regularly occurring period of fertility and sexual receptivity in most female mammals

OEUVRE n work of art, literature, music, etc

OEUVRES ▶ oeuvre

OF prep belonging to

OFF prep away from ▷ adv away ▷ adj not operating ▷ n side of the field to which the batsman's feet point ▷ vb kill

OFFAL n edible organs of an animal, such as liver or kidneys

OFFALS ▶ offal

OFFBEAT adj unusual or eccentric ▷ n any of the normally unaccented beats in a bar

OFFCAST n cast-off

OFFCUT n piece remaining after the required parts have been cut out

OFFCUTS ▶ offcut

OFFED ▶ off

OFFENCE n (cause of) hurt feelings or annoyance

OFFEND vb hurt the feelings of, insult

OFFENDS ▶ offend

OFFENSE same as ▶ offence

OFFER vb present (something) for acceptance or rejection ▷ n something offered

OFFERED ▶ offer

OFFEREE n person to whom an offer is made

OFFERER ▶ offer

OFFEROR ▶ offer

OFFERS ▶ offer

OFFHAND adj casual, curt ▷ adv without preparation

OFFICE n room or building where people work at desks

OFFICER n person in authority in the armed services ▷ vb furnish with officers

OFFICES ▶ office

OFFIE n off-licence

OFFIES ▶ offie

OFFING n area of the sea visible from the shore

OFFINGS ▶ offing

OFFISH adj aloof or distant in manner

OFFKEY adj out of tune

OFFLINE adj disconnected from a computer or the internet

OFFLOAD vb pass responsibilty for (something unpleasant) to someone else

OFFPEAK adj relating to times outside periods of intensive use

OFFPUT n act of putting off

OFFPUTS ▶ offput

OFFRAMP n road allowing traffic to leave a motorway

OFFS ▶ off

OFFSCUM n scum

OFFSET vb cancel out, compensate for ▷ n printing method in which the impression is made onto a surface which transfers it to the paper

OFFSETS ▶ offset

OFFSIDE adv (positioned) illegally ahead of the ball ▷ n side of a vehicle nearest the centre of the road

OFFTAKE n act of taking off

OFFY ▶ offie

OFLAG n German prisoner-of-war camp for officers in World War II

OFLAGS ▶ oflag

OFT adv often

OFTEN adv frequently, much of the time

OFTENER ▶ often

OFTER ▶ oft

OFTEST ▶ oft

OGAM same as ▶ ogham

OGAMIC ▶ ogam

OGAMS ▶ ogam

OGDOAD n group of eight

OGDOADS ▶ ogdoad

OGEE n moulding having a cross section in the form of a letter S

OGEED adj (of an arch or moulding) having an ogee

OGEES ▶ ogee

OGGIN n sea

OGGINS ▶ oggin

OGHAM n ancient alphabetical writing system used by the Celts in Britain and Ireland

OGHAMIC ▶ ogham

OGHAMS ▶ ogham

OGIVAL ▶ ogive

OGIVE n diagonal rib or groin of a Gothic vault

OGIVES ▶ ogive

OGLE vb stare at (someone) lustfully ▷ n flirtatious or lewd look

OGLED ▶ ogle

OGLER ▶ ogle

OGLERS ▶ ogle

OGLES ▶ ogle

OGLING ▶ ogle

OGLINGS ▶ ogle

OGMIC ▶ ogam

OGRE n giant that eats human flesh

OGREISH ▶ ogre

OGREISM ▶ ogre

OGRES ▶ ogre

OGRESS ▶ ogre

OGRISH ▶ ogre

OGRISM ▶ ogre

OGRISMS ▶ ogre

OH interj exclamation of surprise, pain, etc ▷ vb say oh

OHED ▶ oh

OHIA n Hawaiian plant

OHIAS ▶ ohia

OHING ▶ oh

OHM n unit of electrical resistance

OHMAGE n electrical resistance in ohms

OHMAGES ▶ ohmage

OHMIC adj of or relating to a circuit element

OHMS ▶ ohm

OHO n exclamation expressing surprise, exultation, or derision

OHONE same as ▶ ochone

OHS ▶ oh

OI interj shout to attract attention ▷ n grey-faced petrel

OIDIA ▶ oidium

OIDIOID ▶ oidium

OIDIUM n type of fungal spore

OIKIST same as ▶ oecist

OIKISTS ▶ oikist

OIL n viscous liquid, insoluble in water and usu

flammable ▷ *vb* lubricate (a machine) with oil

OILBIRD *n* type of nocturnal gregarious cave-dwelling bird

OILCAMP *n* camp for oilworkers

OILCAN *n* container with a long nozzle for applying oil to machinery

OILCANS ▶ **oilcan**

OILCUP *n* cup-shaped oil reservoir in a machine providing continuous lubrication for a bearing

OILCUPS ▶ **oilcup**

OILED ▶ **oil**

OILER *n* person, device, etc, that lubricates or supplies oil

OILERS ▶ **oiler**

OILERY *n* oil business

OILGAS *n* gaseous mixture of hydrocarbons used as a fuel

OILHOLE *n* hole for oil

OILIER ▶ **oily**

OILIEST ▶ **oily**

OILILY ▶ **oily**

OILING ▶ **oil**

OILLET *same as* ▶ **eyelet**

OILLETS ▶ **oillet**

OILMAN *n* person who owns or operates oil wells

OILMEN ▶ **oilman**

OILNUT *n* nut from which oil is extracted

OILNUTS ▶ **oilnut**

OILS ▶ **oil**

OILSEED *n* seed from which oil is extracted

OILSKIN *n* (garment made from) waterproof material

OILWAY *n* channel for oil

OILWAYS ▶ **oilway**

OILY *adj* soaked or covered with oil

OINK *n* grunt of a pig or an imitation of this ▷ *interj* imitation or representation of the grunt of a pig ▷ *vb* make noise of pig

OINKED ▶ **oink**

OINKING ▶ **oink**

OINKS ▶ **oink**

OINOMEL *same as* ▶ **oenomel**

OINT *vb* anoint

OINTED ▶ **oint**

OINTING ▶ **oint**

OINTS ▶ **oint**

OIS ▶ **oi**

OJIME *n* Japanese bead used

to secure cords

OJIMES ▶ **ojime**

OKA *n* unit of weight used in Turkey

OKAPI *n* African animal related to the giraffe but with a shorter neck

OKAPIS ▶ **okapi**

OKAS ▶ **oka**

OKAY *adj* satisfactory ▷ *vb* approve or endorse ▷ *n* approval or agreement ▷ *interj* expression of approval

OKAYED ▶ **okay**

OKAYING ▶ **okay**

OKAYS ▶ **okay**

OKE *same as* ▶ **oka**

OKEH *same as* ▶ **okay**

OKEHS ▶ **okeh**

OKES ▶ **oke**

OKIMONO *n* Japanese ornamental item

OKRA *n* tropical plant with edible green pods

OKRAS ▶ **okra**

OKTA *n* unit used in meteorology to measure cloud cover

OKTAS ▶ **okta**

OLD *adj* having lived or existed for a long time ▷ *n* earlier or past time

OLDE *adj* old-world or quaint, used facetiously

OLDEN *adj* old ▷ *vb* grow old

OLDENED ▶ **olden**

OLDENS ▶ **olden**

OLDER *adj* having lived or existed longer

OLDEST ▶ **old**

OLDIE *n* old but popular song or film

OLDIES ▶ **oldie**

OLDISH ▶ **old**

OLDNESS ▶ **old**

OLDS ▶ **old**

OLDSTER *n* older person

OLDWIFE *n* any of various fishes, esp the menhaden or the alewife

OLDY *same as* ▶ **oldie**

OLE *interj* exclamation of approval or encouragement customary at bullfights ▷ *n* cry of olé

OLEA ▶ **oleum**

OLEARIA *n* daisy bush

OLEATE *n* any salt or ester of oleic acid

OLEATES ▶ **oleate**

OLEFIN *same as* ▶ **olefine**

OLEFINE *another name for* ▶ **alkene**

OLEFINS ▶ **olefin**

OLEIC *adj as in* **oleic acid** colourless oily liquid used in making soap

OLEIN *another name for* ▶ **triolein**

OLEINE *same as* ▶ **olein**

OLEINES ▶ **oleine**

OLEINS ▶ **olein**

OLENT *adj* having smell

OLEO *n as in* **oleo oil** oil extracted from beef fat

OLEOS ▶ **oleo**

OLES ▶ **ole**

OLESTRA *n* trademark term for an artificial fat

OLEUM *n* type of sulphuric acid

OLEUMS ▶ **oleum**

OLFACT *vb* smell something

OLFACTS ▶ **olfact**

OLICOOK *n* doughnut

OLID *adj* foul-smelling

OLIGIST *n* type of iron ore

OLINGO *n* South American mammal

OLINGOS ▶ **olingo**

OLIO *n* dish of many different ingredients

OLIOS ▶ **olio**

OLITORY *n* kitchen garden

OLIVARY *adj* shaped like an olive

OLIVE *n* small green or black fruit used as food or pressed for its oil ▷ *adj* greyish-green

OLIVER *n as in* **Bath oliver** type of unsweetened biscuit

OLIVERS ▶ **oliver**

OLIVES ▶ **olive**

OLIVET *n* button shaped like olive

OLIVETS ▶ **olivet**

OLIVINE *n* olive-green mineral of the olivine group

OLLA *n* cooking pot

OLLAMH *n* old Irish term for a wise man

OLLAMHS ▶ **ollamh**

OLLAS ▶ **olla**

OLLAV *same as* ▶ **ollamh**

OLLAVS ▶ **ollav**

OLLER *n* waste ground

OLLERS ▶ **oller**

OLLIE *n* (in skateboarding and snowboarding) a jump into the air executed by stamping on the tail of the board

OLLIES ▶ ollie
OLM n pale blind eel-like salamander
OLMS ▶ olm
OLOGIES ▶ ology
OLOGIST n scientist
OLOGOAN vb complain loudly without reason
OLOGY n science or other branch of knowledge
OLOROSO n golden-coloured sweet sherry
OLPAE ▶ olpe
OLPE n ancient Greek jug
OLPES ▶ olpe
OLYCOOK same as ▶ olykoek
OLYKOEK n American type of doughnut
OM n sacred syllable in Hinduism
OMASA ▶ omasum
OMASAL ▶ omasum
OMASUM n compartment in the stomach of a ruminant animal
OMBER same as ▶ ombre
OMBERS ▶ ombre
OMBRE n 18th-century card game
OMBRES ▶ ombre
OMBU n South American tree
OMBUS ▶ ombu
OMEGA n last letter in the Greek alphabet
OMEGAS ▶ omega
OMELET same as > **omelette**
OMELETS ▶ omelet
OMEN n happening or object thought to foretell success or misfortune ▷ vb portend
OMENED ▶ omen
OMENING ▶ omen
OMENS ▶ omen
OMENTA ▶ omentum
OMENTAL ▶ omentum
OMENTUM n double fold of the peritoneum connecting the stomach with other abdominal organs
OMER n ancient Hebrew unit of dry measure equal to one tenth of an ephah
OMERS ▶ omer
OMERTA n conspiracy of silence
OMERTAS ▶ omerta
OMICRON n 15th letter in the Greek alphabet
OMIGOD interj exclamation of surprise, pleasure,

dismay, etc
OMIKRON same as ▶ omicron
OMINOUS adj worrying, seeming to foretell misfortune
OMIT vb leave out
OMITS ▶ omit
OMITTED ▶ omit
OMITTER ▶ omit
OMLAH n staff team in India
OMLAHS ▶ omlah
OMMATEA > ommateum
OMMATEUM n state of being all
OMNIANA n miscellaneous collection
OMNIBUS n several books or TV or radio programmes made into one ▷ adj consisting of or dealing with several different things at once
OMNIETY same as ▶ omneity
OMNIFIC adj creating all things
OMNIFY vb make something universal
OMNIUM n total value
OMNIUMS ▶ omnium
OMOV n one member one vote: a voting system in which each voter has one vote to cast
OMOVS ▶ omov
OMPHALI > omphalos
OMRAH n Muslim noble
OMRAHS ▶ omrah
OMS ▶ om
ON prep indicating position above, attachment, closeness, etc ▷ adv in operation ▷ adj operating ▷ n side of the field on which the batsman stands ▷ vb go on
ONAGER n wild ass of Persia
ONAGERS ▶ onager
ONAGRI ▶ onager
ONANISM n withdrawal in sexual intercourse before ejaculation
ONANIST ▶ onanism
ONBEAT n first and third beats in a bar of four-four time
ONBEATS ▶ onbeat
ONBOARD adj on a ship or other craft
ONCE adv on one occasion ▷ n one occasion
ONCER n (formerly) a

one-pound note
ONCERS ▶ oncer
ONCES ▶ once
ONCET dialect form of ▶ once
ONCOGEN n substance causing tumours to form
ONCOME n act of coming on
ONCOMES ▶ oncome
ONCOST same as > **overheads**
ONCOSTS ▶ oncost
ONCUS same as ▶ onkus
ONDATRA same as > **musquash**
ONDINE same as ▶ undine
ONDINES ▶ ondine
ONDING Scots word for ▶ onset
ONDINGS ▶ onding
ONE adj single, lone ▷ n number or figure 1 ▷ pron any person
ONEFOLD adj simple
ONEIRIC adj of or relating to dreams
ONELY same as ▶ only
ONENESS n unity
ONER n single continuous action
ONERIER ▶ onery
ONEROUS adj (of a task) difficult to carry out
ONERS ▶ oner
ONERY same as ▶ ornery
ONES ▶ one
ONESELF pron reflexive form of one
ONETIME adj at some time in the past
ONEYER old form of ▶ one
ONEYERS ▶ oneyer
ONEYRE same as ▶ oneyer
ONEYRES ▶ oneyre
ONFALL n attack or onset
ONFALLS ▶ onfall
ONFLOW n flowing on
ONFLOWS ▶ onflow
ONGOING adj in progress, continuing
ONIE variant spelling of ▶ ony
ONION n strongly flavoured edible bulb ▷ vb add onion to
ONIONED ▶ onion
ONIONS ▶ onion
ONIONY ▶ onion
ONIRIC same as ▶ oneiric
ONIUM n as in onium compound type of chemical salt
ONIUMS ▶ onium
ONKUS adj bad

ONLAY n artificial veneer for a tooth

ONLAYS ▶ onlay

ONLIEST same as ▶ only

ONLINE adj connected to a computer or the internet

ONLINER n person who uses the internet regularly

ONLOAD vb load files on to a computer

ONLOADS ▶ onload

ONLY adj alone of its kind ▷ adv exclusively

ONNED ▶ on

ONNING ▶ on

ONO n Hawaiian fish

ONOS ▶ ono

ONRUSH n forceful forward rush or flow

ONS ▶ on

ONSET n beginning

ONSETS ▶ onset

ONSHORE adv towards the land

ONSIDE adv (of a player in various sports) in a legal position ▷ adj taking one's part or side ▷ n part of cricket field where a batsman stands

ONSIDES ▶ onside

ONST same as ▶ once

ONSTAGE adj visible by audience

ONSTEAD Scots word for > farmstead

ONTIC adj having real existence

ONTO prep a position on

ONUS n responsibility or burden

ONUSES ▶ onus

ONWARD same as ▶ onwards

ONWARDS adv at or towards a point or position ahead, in advance, etc

ONY Scots word for ▶ any

ONYCHA n part of mollusc

ONYCHAS ▶ onycha

ONYCHIA n inflammation of the nails or claws of animals

ONYMOUS adj (of a book) bearing its author's name

ONYX n type of quartz with coloured layers

ONYXES ▶ onyx

OO Scots word for ▶ wool

OOBIT n hairy caterpillar

OOBITS ▶ oobit

OOCYST n type of zygote

OOCYSTS ▶ oocyst

OOCYTE n immature female germ cell that gives rise to an ovum

OOCYTES ▶ oocyte

OODLES pl n great quantities

OODLINS same as ▶ oodles

OOF n money

OOFIER ▶ oof

OOFIEST ▶ oof

OOFS ▶ oof

OOFTISH n money

OOFY ▶ oof

OOGAMY n sexual reproduction involving a small motile male gamete and a large much less motile female gamete

OOGENY same as > oogenesis

OOGONIA > oogonium

OOH interj exclamation of surprise, pleasure, pain, etc ▷ vb say ooh

OOHED ▶ ooh

OOHING ▶ ooh

OOHS ▶ ooh

OOIDAL adj shaped like egg

OOLAKAN same as > eulachon

OOLITE n limestone made up of tiny grains of calcium carbonate

OOLITES ▶ oolite

OOLITH n any of the tiny spherical grains of sedimentary rock of which oolite is composed

OOLITHS ▶ oolith

OOLITIC ▶ oolite

OOLOGIC ▶ oology

OOLOGY n branch of ornithology concerned with the study of birds' eggs

OOLONG n kind of dark tea that is partly fermented before being dried

OOLONGS ▶ oolong

OOM n title of respect used to refer to an elderly man

OOMIAC same as ▶ umiak

OOMIACK same as ▶ umiak

OOMIACS ▶ oomiac

OOMIAK same as ▶ umiak

OOMIAKS ▶ oomiak

OOMPAH n representation of the sound made by a deep brass instrument ▷ vb make the noise of a brass instrument

OOMPAHS ▶ oompah

OOMPH n enthusiasm, vigour, or energy

OOMPHS ▶ oomph

OOMS ▶ oom

OON Scots word for ▶ oven

OONS ▶ oon

OONT n camel

OONTS ▶ oont

OOP vb Scots word meaning to bind

OOPED ▶ oop

OOPHYTE n gametophyte in mosses, liverworts, and ferns

OOPING ▶ oop

OOPS interj exclamation of surprise or apology

OOR Scots form of ▶ our

OORALI n member of Indian people

OORALIS ▶ oorali

OORIAL n Himalayan sheep

OORIALS ▶ oorial

OORIE adj Scots word meaning shabby

This Scots word is one of the classic 5-letter vowel dumps. It has almost equally useful variants **ourie** and **owrie**.

OORIER ▶ oorie

OORIEST ▶ oorie

OOS ▶ oo

OOSE n dust

OOSES ▶ oose

OOSIER ▶ oose

OOSIEST ▶ oose

OOSPERM n fertilized ovum

OOSPORE n thick-walled sexual spore that develops from a fertilized oosphere

OOSY ▶ oose

OOT Scots word for ▶ out

OOTHECA n capsule containing eggs that is produced by some insects and molluscs

OOTID n immature female gamete that develops into an ovum

OOTIDS ▶ ootid

OOTS ▶ oot

OOZE vb flow slowly ▷ n sluggish flow

OOZED ▶ ooze

OOZES ▶ ooze

OOZIER ▶ oozy

OOZIEST ▶ oozy

OOZILY ▶ oozy

OOZING ▶ ooze

OOZY adj moist or dripping

OP n operation

OPACIFY vb become or make opaque

OPACITY n state or quality

of being opaque

OPACOUS same as
▶ **opaque**

OPAH n large soft-finned
deep-sea fish

OPAHS ▶ **opah**

OPAL n iridescent precious
stone

OPALED adj made like opal

OPALINE adj opalescent ▷ n
opaque or semiopaque
whitish glass

OPALS ▶ **opal**

OPAQUE adj not able to be
seen through, not
transparent ▷ n opaque
pigment used to block out
particular areas on a
negative ▷ vb make opaque

OPAQUED ▶ **opaque**

OPAQUER ▶ **opaque**

OPAQUES ▶ **opaque**

OPCODE n computer code
containing operating
instructions

OPCODES ▶ **opcode**

OPE archaic or poetic word for
▶ **open**

OPED ▶ **ope**

OPEN adj not closed ▷ vb
(cause to) become open ▷ n
competition which all may
enter

OPENED ▶ **open**

OPENER n tool for opening
cans and bottles

OPENERS ▶ **opener**

OPENEST ▶ **open**

OPENING n beginning ▷ adj
first

OPENLY ▶ **open**

OPENS ▶ **open**

OPEPE n African tree

OPEPES ▶ **opepe**

OPERA n drama in which
the text is sung to an
orchestral accompaniment

OPERAND n quantity,
variable, or function upon
which an operation is
performed

OPERANT adj producing
effects ▷ n person or thing
that operates

OPERAS ▶ **opera**

OPERATE vb (cause to)
work

OPERON n group of
adjacent genes in bacteria
functioning as a unit

OPERONS ▶ **operon**

OPEROSE adj laborious

OPES ▶ **ope**

OPHITE n any of several
greenish mottled rocks

OPHITES ▶ **ophite**

OPHITIC adj having small
elongated feldspar crystals
enclosed

OPHIURA n sea creature
like a starfish

OPIATE n narcotic drug
containing opium ▷ adj
containing or consisting of
opium ▷ vb treat with an
opiate

OPIATED ▶ **opiate**

OPIATES ▶ **opiate**

OPINE vb express an opinion

OPINED ▶ **opine**

OPINES ▶ **opine**

OPING ▶ **ope**

OPINING ▶ **opine**

OPINION n personal belief
or judgment

OPIOID n substance that
resembles morphine in its
physiological or
pharmacological effect

OPIOIDS ▶ **opioid**

OPIUM n addictive narcotic
drug made from poppy
seeds

OPIUMS ▶ **opium**

OPORICE n former
medicine made from fruit

OPOSSUM n small
marsupial of America or
Australasia

OPPIDAN adj of a town ▷ n
person living in a town

OPPO n counterpart in
another organization

OPPOS ▶ **oppo**

OPPOSE vb work against

OPPOSED ▶ **oppose**

OPPOSER ▶ **oppose**

OPPOSES ▶ **oppose**

OPPRESS vb control by
cruelty or force

OPPUGN vb call into
question

OPPUGNS ▶ **oppugn**

OPS ▶ **op**

OPSIN n type of protein

OPSINS ▶ **opsin**

OPSONIC ▶ **opsonin**

OPSONIN n constituent of
blood serum

OPT vb show a preference,
choose

OPTANT n person who opts

OPTANTS ▶ **optant**

OPTED ▶ **opt**

OPTER ▶ **opt**

OPTERS ▶ **opt**

OPTIC adj relating to the
eyes or sight

OPTICAL adj of or involving
light or optics

OPTICS n science of sight
and light

OPTIMA ▶ **optimum**

OPTIMAL adj best or most
favourable

OPTIME n mathematics
student at Cambridge
University

OPTIMES ▶ **optime**

OPTIMUM n best possible
conditions ▷ adj most
favourable

OPTING ▶ **opt**

OPTION n choice ▷ vb
obtain an option on

OPTIONS ▶ **option**

OPTS ▶ **opt**

OPULENT adj having or
indicating wealth

OPULUS n flowering shrub

OPUNTIA n type of cactus

OPUS n artistic creation,
esp a musical work

OPUSCLE same as
> **opuscule**

OPUSES ▶ **opus**

OQUASSA n American trout

OR prep before ▷ adj of the
metal gold ▷ n gold

ORA ▶ **os**

ORACH same as ▶ **orache**

ORACHE n type of plant

ORACHES ▶ **orache**

ORACIES ▶ **oracy**

ORACLE n shrine of an
ancient god ▷ vb utter as
an oracle

ORACLED ▶ **oracle**

ORACLES ▶ **oracle**

ORACY n capacity to
express oneself in and
understand speech

ORAD adv towards the
mouth

ORAL adj spoken ▷ n
spoken examination

ORALISM n oral method of
communicating with deaf
people

ORALIST ▶ **oralism**

ORALITY n state of being
oral

ORALLY ▶ **oral**

ORALS ▶ **oral**

ORANG n orangutan

ORANGE n reddish-yellow
citrus fruit ▷ adj
reddish-yellow

ORANGER ▶ **orange**

ORANGES ▶ orange
ORANGEY ▶ orange
ORANGS ▶ orang
ORANGY ▶ orange
ORANT *n* artistic representation of worshipper
ORANTS ▶ orant
ORARIA ▶ orarium
ORARIAN *n* person who lives on the coast
ORARION *n* garment worn by Greek clergyman
ORARIUM *n* handkerchief
ORATE *vb* make or give an oration
ORATED ▶ orate
ORATES ▶ orate
ORATING ▶ orate
ORATION *n* formal speech
ORATOR *n* skilful public speaker
ORATORS ▶ orator
ORATORY *n* art of making speeches
ORATRIX *n* female orator
ORB *n* ceremonial decorated sphere with a cross on top, carried by a monarch ▷ *vb* make or become circular or spherical
ORBED ▶ orb
ORBIER ▶ orby
ORBIEST ▶ orby
ORBING ▶ orb
ORBIT *n* curved path of a planet, satellite, or spacecraft around another body ▷ *vb* move in an orbit around
ORBITA *same as* ▶ **orbit**
ORBITAL *adj* of or denoting an orbit ▷ *n* region surrounding an atomic nucleus
ORBITAS ▶ orbita
ORBITED ▶ orbit
ORBITER *n* spacecraft or satellite designed to orbit a planet without landing on it
ORBITS ▶ orbit
ORBITY *n* bereavement
ORBLESS ▶ orb
ORBS ▶ orb
ORBY *adj* orb-shaped
ORC *n* any of various whales, such as the killer and grampus
ORCA *n* killer whale
ORCAS ▶ orca
ORCEIN *n* brown crystalline material

ORCEINS ▶ orcein
ORCHARD *n* area where fruit trees are grown
ORCHAT *same as* ▶ **orchard**
ORCHATS ▶ orchat
ORCHEL *same as* ▶ **orchil**
ORCHELS ▶ orchel
ORCHID *n* plant with flowers that have unusual lip-shaped petals
ORCHIDS ▶ orchid
ORCHIL *n* any of various lichens
ORCHILS ▶ orchil
ORCHIS *n* type of orchid
ORCIN *same as* ▶ **orcinol**
ORCINE *same as* ▶ **orcinol**
ORCINES ▶ orcine
ORCINOL *n* colourless crystalline water-soluble solid
ORCINS ▶ orcin
ORCS ▶ orc
ORD *n* pointed weapon
ORDAIN *vb* make (someone) a member of the clergy
ORDAINS ▶ ordain
ORDEAL *n* painful or difficult experience
ORDEALS ▶ ordeal
ORDER *n* instruction to be carried out ▷ *vb* give an instruction to
ORDERED ▶ order
ORDERER ▶ order
ORDERLY *adj* well-organized ▷ *n* hospital attendant ▷ *adv* according to custom or rule
ORDERS ▶ order
ORDINAL *adj* denoting a certain position in a sequence of numbers ▷ *n* book containing the forms of services for the ordination of ministers
ORDINAR *Scots word for* ▶ **ordinary**
ORDINEE *n* person being ordained
ORDINES ▶ ordo
ORDO *n* religious order
ORDOS ▶ ordo
ORDS ▶ ord
ORDURE *n* excrement
ORDURES ▶ ordure
ORE *n* (rock containing) a mineral which yields metal
OREAD *n* mountain nymph
OREADES ▶ oread
OREADS ▶ oread
ORECTIC *adj* of or relating

to the desires
OREGANO *n* sweet-smelling herb used in cooking
OREIDE *same as* ▶ **oroide**
OREIDES ▶ oreide
ORES ▶ ore
OREWEED *n* seaweed
OREXIN *n* hormone that promotes wakefulness and stimulates the appetite
OREXINS ▶ orexin
OREXIS *n* appetite
ORF *n* infectious disease of sheep and sometimes goats and cattle
ORFE *n* small slender European fish
ORFES ▶ orfe
ORFRAY *same as* ▶ **orphrey**
ORFRAYS ▶ orfray
ORFS ▶ orf
ORGAN *n* part of an animal or plant that has a particular function
ORGANA ▶ organon
ORGANDY *same as* > **organdie**
ORGANIC *adj* of or produced from animals or plants ▷ *n* substance that is derived from animal or vegetable matter
ORGANON *n* system of logical or scientific rules, esp that of Aristotle
ORGANS ▶ organ
ORGANUM *same as* ▶ **organon**
ORGANZA *n* thin stiff fabric of silk, cotton, or synthetic fibre
ORGASM *n* most intense point of sexual pleasure ▷ *vb* experience orgasm
ORGASMS ▶ orgasm
ORGEAT *n* drink made from barley or almonds, and orange flower water
ORGEATS ▶ orgeat
ORGIA *same as* ▶ **orgy**
ORGIAC ▶ orgy
ORGIAS ▶ orgia
ORGIAST *n* participant in orgy
ORGIC ▶ orgy
ORGIES ▶ orgy
ORGONE *n* substance claimed to be needed in people for sexual activity and mental health
ORGONES ▶ orgone
ORGUE *n* number of stakes

O

lashed together

ORGUES ▶ orgue

ORGY n party involving promiscuous sexual activity

ORIBI n small African antelope

ORIBIS ▶ oribi

ORIEL n type of bay window

ORIELS ▶ oriel

ORIENCY n state of being orient

ORIENT vb position (oneself) according to one's surroundings ▷ n eastern sky or the dawn ▷ adj eastern

ORIENTS ▶ orient

ORIFEX same as ▶ orifice

ORIFICE n opening or hole

ORIGAMI n Japanese decorative art of paper folding

ORIGAN another name for ▶ marjoram

ORIGANE same as ▶ origan

ORIGANS ▶ origan

ORIGIN n point from which something develops

ORIGINS ▶ origin

ORIHOU n small New Zealand tree

ORIHOUS ▶ orihou

ORIOLE n tropical or American songbird

ORIOLES ▶ oriole

ORISHA n any of the minor gods or spirits of traditional Yoruba religion

ORISHAS ▶ orisha

ORISON another word for ▶ prayer

ORISONS ▶ orison

ORIXA same as ▶ orisha

ORIXAS ▶ orixa

ORLE n border around a shield

ORLEANS n type of fabric

ORLES ▶ orle

ORLON n tradename for a crease-resistant acrylic fibre or fabric used for clothing, furnishings, etc

ORLONS ▶ orlon

ORLOP n (in a vessel with four or more decks) the lowest deck

ORLOPS ▶ orlop

ORMER n edible marine mollusc

ORMERS ▶ ormer

ORMOLU n gold-coloured alloy used for decoration

ORMOLUS ▶ ormolu

ORNATE adj highly decorated, elaborate

ORNATER ▶ ornate

ORNERY adj stubborn or vile-tempered

ORNIS less common word for ▶ avifauna

ORNISES ▶ ornis

OROGEN n part of earth subject to orogeny

OROGENS ▶ orogen

OROGENY n formation of mountain ranges by intense upward displacement of the earth's crust

OROIDE n alloy containing copper, tin, and other metals, used as imitation gold

OROIDES ▶ oroide

OROLOGY same as ▶ orography

OROPESA n float used in minesweeping

OROTUND adj (of the voice) resonant and booming

ORPHAN n child whose parents are dead ▷ vb deprive of parents

ORPHANS ▶ orphan

ORPHIC adj mystical or occult

ORPHISM n style of abstract art

ORPHREY n richly embroidered band or border

ORPIN same as ▶ orpine

ORPINE n type of plant

ORPINES ▶ orpine

ORPINS ▶ orpin

ORRA adj odd or unmatched

ORRAMAN n man who does odd jobs

ORRAMEN ▶ orraman

ORRERY n mechanical model of the solar system

ORRICE same as ▶ orris

ORRICES ▶ orrice

ORRIS n kind of iris

ORRISES ▶ orris

ORS ▶ or

ORT n fragment

ORTHIAN adj having high pitch

ORTHO n type of photographic plate

ORTHOS ▶ ortho

ORTHROS n canonical hour in the Greek Church

ORTOLAN n small European

songbird eaten as a delicacy

ORTS pl n scraps or leavings

ORVAL n plant of sage family

ORVALS ▶ orval

ORYX n large African antelope

ORYXES ▶ oryx

ORZO n pasta in small grain shapes

ORZOS ▶ orzo

OS n mouth or mouthlike part or opening

OSAR ▶ os

OSCAR n cash

OSCARS ▶ oscar

OSCHEAL adj of scrotum

OSCINE n songbird ▷ adj of songbirds

OSCINES ▶ oscine

OSCULA ▶ osculum

OSCULAR adj of or relating to an osculum

OSCULE n small mouth or opening

OSCULES ▶ oscule

OSCULUM n mouthlike aperture

OSE same as ▶ esker

OSES ▶ ose

OSETRA n type of caviar

OSETRAS ▶ osetra

OSHAC n plant smelling of ammonia

OSHACS ▶ oshac

OSIER n willow tree

OSIERED adj covered with osiers

OSIERS ▶ osier

OSIERY n work done with osiers

OSMATE n salt of osmic acid

OSMATES ▶ osmate

OSMATIC adj relying on sense of smell

OSMIATE same as ▶ osmate

OSMIC adj of or containing osmium in a high valence state

OSMICS n science of smell

OSMIOUS same as ▶ osmous

OSMIUM n heaviest known metallic element

OSMIUMS ▶ osmium

OSMOL same as ▶ osmole

OSMOLAL ▶ osmole

OSMOLAR adj containing one osmole per litre

OSMOLE n unit of osmotic pressure

OSMOLES ▶ osmole

OSMOLS ▶ osmol

OSMOSE vb undergo or cause to undergo osmosis

OSMOSED ▸ osmose

OSMOSES ▸ osmose

OSMOSIS n movement of a liquid through a membrane from a lower to a higher concentration

OSMOTIC ▸ osmosis

OSMOUS adj of or containing osmium in a low valence state

OSMUND same as ▸ osmunda

OSMUNDA n type of fern

OSMUNDS ▸ osmund

OSPREY n large fish-eating bird of prey

OSPREYS ▸ osprey

OSSA ▸ os

OSSEIN n protein that forms the organic matrix of bone

OSSEINS ▸ ossein

OSSELET n growth on knee of horse

OSSEOUS adj consisting of or like bone

OSSETER n sturgeon

OSSETRA same as ▸ osetra

OSSIA conj (in music) or

OSSICLE n small bone, esp one of those in the middle ear

OSSIFIC adj making something turn to bone

OSSIFY vb (cause to) become bone, harden

OSSUARY n any container for the burial of human bones, such as an urn or vault

OSTEAL adj of or relating to bone or to the skeleton

OSTENT n appearance

OSTENTS ▸ ostent

OSTEOID adj of or resembling bone ▹n bony deposit

OSTEOMA n benign tumour composed of bone or bonelike tissue

OSTIA ▸ ostium

OSTIAL ▸ ostium

OSTIARY another word for ▸ porter

OSTIATE adj having ostium

OSTIOLE n pore in the reproductive bodies of certain algae and fungi through which spores pass

OSTIUM n any of the pores in sponges through which water enters the body

OSTLER n stableman at an inn

OSTLERS ▸ ostler

OSTMARK n currency of the former East Germany

OSTOMY n surgically made opening connecting organ to surface of body

OSTOSES ▸ ostosis

OSTOSIS n formation of bone

OSTRACA > ostracon

OSTRAKA > ostrakon

OSTRICH n large African bird that runs fast but cannot fly

OTAKU n Japanese computer geeks

OTALGIA technical name for ▸ earache

OTALGIC ▸ otalgia

OTALGY same as ▸ otalgia

OTARIES ▸ otary

OTARINE ▸ otary

> This means like an otary or eared seal, and is perhaps the most commonly played of all 7-letter bonus words, so well worth learning for that extra 50 points it can give you.

OTARY n seal with ears

OTHER adj remaining in a group of which one or some have been specified ▹n other person or thing

OTHERS ▸ other

OTIC adj of or relating to the ear

OTIOSE adj not useful

OTITIC ▸ otitis

OTITIS n inflammation of the ear

OTOCYST n embryonic structure in vertebrates that develops into the inner ear in the adult

OTOLITH n granule of calcium carbonate in the inner ear of vertebrates

OTOLOGY n branch of medicine concerned with the ear

OTTAR same as ▸ attar

OTTARS ▸ ottar

OTTAVA n interval of an octave

OTTAVAS ▸ ottava

OTTER n small brown freshwater mammal that eats fish ▹vb fish using an otter board

OTTERED ▸ otter

OTTERS ▸ otter

OTTO another name for ▸ attar

OTTOMAN n storage chest with a padded lid for use as a seat

OTTOS ▸ otto

OU interj expressing concession ▹n man, bloke, or chap

OUABAIN n poisonous white crystalline glycoside

OUAKARI n South American monkey

OUBAAS n man in authority

OUBIT n hairy caterpillar

OUBITS ▸ oubit

OUCH interj exclamation of sudden pain ▹n brooch or clasp set with gems ▹vb say ouch

OUCHED ▸ ouch

OUCHES ▸ ouch

OUCHING ▸ ouch

OUCHT Scots word for > anything

OUCHTS ▸ oucht

OUD n Arabic stringed musical instrument resembling a lute or mandolin

OUDS ▸ oud

OUENS ▸ ou

OUGHLY same as ▸ ugly

OUGHT vb have an obligation ▹n zero

OUGHTED ▸ ought

OUGHTS ▸ ought

OUGLIE same as ▸ ugly

OUGLIED ▸ ouglie

OUGLIES ▸ ouglie

OUGUIYA n standard monetary unit of Mauritania

OUIJA n tradename for a board through which spirits supposedly answer questions

OUIJAS ▸ ouija

OUK Scots word for ▸ week

OUKS ▸ ouk

OULAKAN same as > eulachon

OULD Scots or Irish form of ▸ old

OULDER ▸ ould

OULDEST ▸ ould

OULK Scots form of ▸ week

OULKS ▸ oulk

OULONG same as ▸ oolong

OULONGS ▸ oulong

OUMA n grandmother,

often as a title with a
surname

OUMAS ▶ **ouma**

OUNCE n unit of weight
equal to one sixteenth of a
pound

OUNCES ▶ **ounce**

OUNDY adj wavy

OUP same as ▶ **oop**

OUPA n grandfather, often
as a title with a surname

OUPAS ▶ **oupa**

OUPED ▶ **oup**

OUPH same as ▶ **oaf**

OUPHE same as ▶ **oaf**

OUPHES ▶ **ouphe**

OUPHS ▶ **ouph**

OUPING ▶ **oup**

OUPS ▶ **oup**

OUR adj belonging to us
▷ determiner of, belonging
to, or associated in some
way with us

OURALI n plant from which
curare comes

OURALIS ▶ **ourali**

OURANG same as ▶ **orang**

OURANGS ▶ **ourang**

OURARI same as ▶ **ourali**

OURARIS ▶ **ourari**

OUREBI same as ▶ **oribi**

OUREBIS ▶ **ourebi**

OURIE same as ▶ **oorie**

OURIER ▶ **ourie**

OURIEST ▶ **ourie**

OURN dialect form of
▶ **our**

OURS pron thing(s)
belonging to us

OURSELF pron formal word
for myself used by monarchs

OUS ▶ **ou**

OUSEL same as ▶ **ouzel**

OUSELS ▶ **ousel**

OUST vb force (someone)
out, expel

OUSTED ▶ **oust**

OUSTER n act or instance of
forcing someone out of a
position

OUSTERS ▶ **ouster**

OUSTING ▶ **oust**

OUSTITI n device for
opening locked door

OUSTS ▶ **oust**

OUT adj denoting
movement or distance
away from ▶ vb name
(a public figure) as being
homosexual

OUTACT vb surpass in
acting

OUTACTS ▶ **outact**

OUTADD vb beat or surpass
at adding

OUTADDS ▶ **outadd**

OUTAGE n period of power
failure

OUTAGES ▶ **outage**

OUTASK vb declare
wedding banns

OUTASKS ▶ **outask**

OUTATE ▶ **outeat**

OUTBACK n remote bush
country of Australia

OUTBAKE vb bake more or
better than

OUTBAR vb keep out

OUTBARK vb bark more or
louder than

OUTBARS ▶ **outbar**

OUTBAWL vb bawl more or
louder than

OUTBEAM vb beam more or
brighter than

OUTBEG vb beg more or
better than

OUTBEGS ▶ **outbeg**

OUTBID vb offer a higher
price than

OUTBIDS ▶ **outbid**

OUTBOX vb surpass in
boxing

OUTBRAG vb brag more or
better than

OUTBRED > **outbreed**

OUTBULK vb exceed in bulk

OUTBURN vb burn longer
or brighter than

OUTBUY vb buy more than

OUTBUYS ▶ **outbuy**

OUTBY adv outside

OUTBYE same as ▶ **outby**

OUTCALL n visit to
customer's home by
professional

OUTCAST n person rejected
by a particular group ▷ adj
rejected, abandoned, or
discarded

OUTCHID > **outchide**

OUTCITY n anywhere
outside a city's confines

OUTCOME n result

OUTCOOK vb cook more or
better than

OUTCROP n part of a rock
formation that sticks out of
the earth ▷ vb (of rock
strata) to protrude through
the surface of the earth

OUTCROW vb exceed in
crowing

OUTCRY n vehement or
widespread protest ▷ vb
cry louder or make more

noise than (someone or
something)

OUTDARE vb be more brave
than

OUTDATE vb make or
become old-fashioned or
obsolete

OUTDID ▶ **outdo**

OUTDO vb surpass in
performance

OUTDOER ▶ **outdo**

OUTDOES ▶ **outdo**

OUTDONE ▶ **outdo**

OUTDOOR adj taking place,
existing, or intended for use
in the open air

OUTDRAG vb beat in drag
race

OUTDRAW vb draw (a gun)
faster than

OUTDREW ▶ **outdraw**

OUTDROP same as
▶ **outcrop**

OUTDUEL vb defeat in duel

OUTDURE vb last longer
than

OUTEARN vb earn more
than

OUTEAT vb eat more than

OUTEATS ▶ **outeat**

OUTECHO vb echo more
than

OUTED ▶ **out**

OUTEDGE n furthest limit

OUTER adj on the outside
▷ n white outermost ring
on a target

OUTERS ▶ **outer**

OUTFACE vb subdue or
disconcert (someone) by
staring

OUTFALL n mouth of a river
or drain

OUTFAST vb fast longer
than

OUTFAWN vb exceed in
fawning

OUTFEEL vb exceed in
feeling

OUTFELT ▶ **outfeel**

OUTFIND vb exceed in
finding

OUTFIRE vb exceed in firing

OUTFISH vb catch more fish
than

OUTFIT n matching set of
clothes ▷ vb furnish or be
furnished with an outfit,
equipment, etc

OUTFITS ▶ **outfit**

OUTFLEW ▶ **outfly**

OUTFLOW n anything that
flows out, such as liquid or

money ▷ vb flow faster than

OUTFLY vb fly better or faster than

OUTFOOL vb be more foolish than

OUTFOOT vb (of a boat) to go faster than (another boat)

OUTFOX vb defeat or foil (someone) by being more cunning

OUTGAIN vb gain more than

OUTGAS vb undergo the removal of adsorbed or absorbed gas from solids

OUTGATE n way out

OUTGAVE ▶ outgive

OUTGAZE vb gaze beyond

OUTGIVE vb exceed in giving

OUTGLOW vb glow more than

OUTGNAW vb exceed in gnawing

OUTGO vb exceed or outstrip ▷ n cost

OUTGOER ▶ outgo

OUTGOES ▶ outgo

OUTGONE ▶ outgo

OUTGREW ▶ outgrow

OUTGRIN vb exceed in grinning

OUTGROW vb become too large or too old for

OUTGUN vb surpass in fire power

OUTGUNS ▶ outgun

OUTGUSH vb gush out

OUTHAUL n line or cable for tightening the foot of a sail

OUTHEAR vb exceed in hearing

OUTHER same as ▶ other

OUTHIRE vb hire out

OUTHIT vb hit something further than (someone else)

OUTHITS ▶ outhit

OUTHOWL vb exceed in howling

OUTHUNT vb exceed in hunting

OUTHYRE same as ▶ outhire

OUTING n leisure trip

OUTINGS ▶ outing

OUTJEST vb exceed in jesting

OUTJET n projecting part

OUTJETS ▶ outjet

OUTJINX vb exceed in jinxing

If someone else plays **jinx**, you can outjinx them by adding O, U and T! And if you can form the whole word using all of your letters, you'll get a 50-point bonus.

OUTJUMP vb jump higher or farther than

OUTJUT vb jut out ▷ n projecting part

OUTJUTS ▶ outjut

OUTKEEP vb beat or surpass at keeping

OUTKEPT ▶ outkeep

OUTKICK vb exceed in kicking

OUTKILL vb exceed in killing

OUTKISS vb exceed in kissing

OUTLAID ▶ outlay

OUTLAIN ▶ outlay

OUTLAND adj outlying or distant ▷ n outlying areas of a country or region

OUTLASH n sudden attack

OUTLAST vb last longer than

OUTLAW n criminal deprived of legal protection, bandit ▷ vb make illegal

OUTLAWS ▶ outlaw

OUTLAY n expenditure ▷ vb spend (money)

OUTLAYS ▶ outlay

OUTLEAD vb be better leader than

OUTLEAP vb leap higher or farther than

OUTLED ▶ outlead

OUTLER n farm animal kept out of doors

OUTLERS ▶ outler

OUTLET n means of expressing emotion

OUTLETS ▶ outlet

OUTLIE vb lie outside a particular place

OUTLIED ▶ outlie

OUTLIER n outcrop of rocks that is entirely surrounded by older rocks

OUTLIES ▶ outlie

OUTLINE n short general explanation ▷ vb summarize

OUTLIVE vb live longer than

OUTLOOK n attitude ▷ vb look out

OUTLOVE vb exceed in loving

OUTMAN vb surpass in manpower

OUTMANS ▶ outman

OUTMODE vb make unfashionable

OUTMOST another word for ▷ outermost

OUTMOVE vb move faster or better than

OUTNAME vb be more notorious than

OUTNESS n state or quality of being external

OUTPACE vb go faster than (someone)

OUTPART n remote region

OUTPASS vb exceed in passing

OUTPEEP vb peep out

OUTPEER vb surpass

OUTPITY vb exceed in pitying

OUTPLAN vb exceed in planning

OUTPLAY vb perform better than one's opponent in a sport or game

OUTPLOD vb exceed in plodding

OUTPLOT vb exceed in plotting

OUTPOLL vb win more votes than

OUTPORT n isolated fishing village, esp in Newfoundland

OUTPOST n outlying settlement

OUTPOUR n act of flowing or pouring out ▷ vb pour or cause to pour out freely or rapidly

OUTPRAY vb exceed in praying

OUTPULL vb exceed in pulling

OUTPUSH vb exceed in pushing

OUTPUT n amount produced ▷ vb produce (data) at the end of a process

OUTPUTS ▶ output

OUTRACE vb surpass in racing

OUTRAGE n great moral indignation ▷ vb offend morally

OUTRAN ▶ outrun

OUTRANG ▶ outring

OUTRANK vb be of higher

O

rank than (someone)

OUTRATE vb offer better rate than

OUTRAVE vb outdo in raving

OUTRE adj shockingly eccentric

OUTREAD vb outdo in reading

OUTRED vb be redder than

OUTREDS ▸ outred

OUTRIDE vb outdo by riding faster, farther, or better than ▷ n extra unstressed syllable within a metrical foot

OUTRIG vb supply with outfit

OUTRIGS ▸ outrig

OUTRING vb exceed in ringing

OUTRO n instrumental passage that concludes a piece of music

OUTROAR vb roar louder than

OUTROCK vb outdo in rocking

OUTRODE ▸ outride

OUTROLL vb exceed in rolling

OUTROOP n auction

OUTROOT vb root out

OUTROPE same as ▸ **outroop**

OUTROS ▸ outro

OUTROW vb outdo in rowing

OUTROWS ▸ outrow

OUTRUN vb run faster than

OUTRUNG ▸ outring

OUTRUNS ▸ outrun

OUTRUSH n flowing or rushing out ▷ vb rush out

OUTS ▸ out

OUTSAID ▸ outsay

OUTSAIL vb sail better than

OUTSANG ▸ outsing

OUTSAT ▸ outsit

OUTSAW ▸ outsee

OUTSAY vb say something out loud

OUTSAYS ▸ outsay

OUTSEE vb exceed in seeing

OUTSEEN ▸ outsee

OUTSEES ▸ outsee

OUTSELL vb be sold in greater quantities than

OUTSERT another word for > **wraparound**

OUTSET n beginning

OUTSETS ▸ outset

OUTSHOT n projecting part

OUTSIDE adv indicating movement to or position on the exterior ▷ adj unlikely ▷ n external area or surface

OUTSIN vb sin more than

OUTSING vb sing better or louder than

OUTSINS ▸ outsin

OUTSIT vb sit longer than

OUTSITS ▸ outsit

OUTSIZE adj larger than normal ▷ n outsize garment

OUTSOAR vb fly higher than

OUTSOLD ▸ outsell

OUTSOLE n outermost sole of a shoe

OUTSPAN vb relax

OUTSPED > outspeed

OUTSTAY vb overstay

OUTSTEP vb step farther than

OUTSULK vb outdo in sulking

OUTSUM vb add up to more than

OUTSUMS ▸ outsum

OUTSUNG ▸ outsing

OUTSWAM ▸ outswim

OUTSWIM vb outdo in swimming

OUTSWUM ▸ outswim

OUTTAKE n unreleased take from a recording session, film, or TV programme ▷ vb take out

OUTTALK vb talk more, longer, or louder than (someone)

OUTTASK vb assign task to staff outside organization

OUTTELL vb make known

OUTTOLD ▸ outtell

OUTTOOK ▸ outtake

OUTTOP vb rise higher than

OUTTOPS ▸ outtop

OUTTROT vb exceed at trotting

OUTTURN same as ▸ **output**

OUTVIE vb outdo in competition

OUTVIED ▸ outvie

OUTVIES ▸ outvie

OUTVOTE vb defeat by getting more votes than

OUTWAIT vb wait longer than

OUTWALK vb walk farther or longer than

OUTWAR vb surpass or

exceed in warfare

OUTWARD same as > **outwards**

OUTWARS ▸ outwar

OUTWASH n mass of gravel carried and deposited by the water derived from melting glaciers

OUTWEAR vb use up or destroy by wearing

OUTWEED vb root out

OUTWEEP vb outdo in weeping

OUTWELL vb pour out

OUTWENT ▸ outgo

OUTWEPT ▸ outweep

OUTWICK vb move one curling stone by striking with another

OUTWILE vb surpass in cunning

OUTWILL vb demonstrate stronger will than

OUTWIN vb get out of

OUTWIND vb unwind

OUTWING vb surpass in flying

OUTWINS ▸ outwin

OUTWISH vb surpass in wishing

OUTWIT vb get the better of (someone) by cunning

OUTWITH prep outside

OUTWITS ▸ outwit

OUTWON ▸ outwin

OUTWORE ▸ outwear

OUTWORK n defences which lie outside main defensive works ▷ vb work better, harder, etc, than

OUTWORN adj no longer in use

OUTWRIT > outwrite

OUTYELL vb outdo in yelling

OUTYELP vb outdo in yelping

OUVERT adj open

OUVERTE feminine form of ▸ **ouvert**

OUVRAGE n work

OUVRIER n worker

OUZEL n type of bird

OUZELS ▸ ouzel

OUZO n strong aniseed-flavoured spirit from Greece

OUZOS ▸ ouzo

OVA ▸ ovum

OVAL adj egg-shaped ▷ n anything that is oval in shape

OVALITY ▸ oval

OVALLY ▸ oval

OVALS ▸ oval

OVARIAL ▸ ovary
OVARIAN ▸ ovary
OVARIES ▸ ovary
OVARY n female egg-producing organ
OVATE adj shaped like an egg ▷ vb give ovation
OVATED ▸ ovate
OVATELY ▸ ovate
OVATES ▸ ovate
OVATING ▸ ovate
OVATION n enthusiastic round of applause
OVATOR ▸ ovate
OVATORS ▸ ovate
OVEL n mourner, esp during the first seven days after a death
OVELS ▸ ovel
OVEN n heated compartment or container for cooking or for drying or firing ceramics ▷ vb cook in an oven
OVENED ▸ oven
OVENING ▸ oven
OVENS ▸ oven
OVER adv indicating position on the top of, amount greater than, etc ▷ adj finished ▷ n (in cricket) series of six balls bowled from one end ▷ vb jump over
OVERACT vb act in an exaggerated way
OVERAGE adj beyond a specified age ▷ n amount beyond given limit
OVERALL adv in total ▷ n coat-shaped protective garment ▷ adj from one end to the other
OVERAPT adj tending excessively
OVERARM adv with the arm above the shoulder ▷ adj bowled, thrown, or performed with the arm raised above the shoulder ▷ vb throw (a ball) overarm
OVERATE ▸ overeat
OVERAWE vb affect (someone) with an overpowering sense of awe
OVERBED adj fitting over bed
OVERBET vb bet too much
OVERBID vb bid for more tricks than one can expect to win ▷ n bid higher than someone else's bid
OVERBIG adj too big

OVERBUY vb buy too much or too many
OVERBY adv Scots expression meaning over the road or across the way
OVERCOY adj too modest
OVERCUT vb cut too much
OVERDID ▸ overdo
OVERDO vb do to excess
OVERDOG n person or side in an advantageous position
OVERDRY vb dry too much
OVERDUB vb add (new sounds) to a tape so that the old and the new sounds can be heard ▷ n sound or series of sounds added by this method
OVERDUE adj still due after the time allowed
OVERDYE vb dye (a fabric, yarn, etc) excessively
OVEREAT vb eat more than is necessary or healthy
OVERED ▸ over
OVEREGG vb exaggerate absurdly
OVEREYE vb survey
OVERFAR adv too far
OVERFAT adj too fat
OVERFED > overfeed
OVERFIT adj too fit
OVERFLY vb fly over (a territory) or past (a point)
OVERGET vb overtake
OVERGO vb go beyond
OVERGOT ▸ overget
OVERHIT vb hit too strongly
OVERHOT adj too hot
OVERING ▸ over
OVERJOY vb give great delight to
OVERLAP vb share part of the same space or period of time (as) ▷ n area overlapping
OVERLAX adj too lax
OVERLAY vb cover with a thin layer ▷ n something that is laid over something else
OVERLET vb let to too many
OVERLIE vb lie on or cover (something or someone)
OVERLIT > overlight
OVERLY adv excessively
OVERMAN vb provide with too many staff ▷ n man who oversees others
OVERMEN ▸ overman
OVERMIX vb mix too much
OVERNET vb cover with net

OVERNEW adj too new
OVERPAY vb pay (someone) at too high a rate
OVERPLY vb ply too much
OVERRAN ▸ overrun
OVERRED vb paint over in red
OVERREN same as ▸ overrun
OVERRUN vb conquer rapidly ▷ n act or an instance of overrunning
OVERS ▸ over
OVERSAD adj too sad
OVERSAW ▸ oversee
OVERSEA same as > overseas
OVERSEE vb watch over from a position of authority
OVERSET vb disturb or upset
OVERSEW vb sew (two edges) with stitches that pass over them both
OVERSOW vb sow again after first sowing
OVERSUP vb sup too much
OVERT adj open, not hidden
OVERTAX vb put too great a strain on
OVERTIP vb give too much money as a tip
OVERTLY ▸ overt
OVERTOP vb exceed in height
OVERUSE vb use excessively ▷ n excessive use
OVERWET vb make too wet
OVIBOS n type of ox
OVICIDE n killing of sheep
OVIDUCT n tube through which eggs are conveyed from the ovary
OVIFORM adj shaped like an egg
OVINE adj of or like a sheep ▷ n member of sheep family
OVINES ▸ ovine
OVIPARA n all oviparous animals
OVISAC n capsule or sac, such as an ootheca, in which egg cells are produced
OVISACS ▸ ovisac
OVIST n person believing ovum contains all subsequent generations
OVISTS ▸ ovist
OVOID adj egg-shaped ▷ n something that is ovoid
OVOIDAL adj ovoid ▷ n something that is ovoid

O

OVOIDS ▶ ovoid

OVOLI ▶ ovolo

OVOLO n convex moulding having a cross section in the form of a quarter of a circle or ellipse

> Two Os on your rack can normally be dealt with; three can get a bit much, but this word for a kind of architectural moulding can handle them. Note that the plural can be **ovolos** or **ovoli**.

OVOLOS ▶ ovolo

OVONIC adj using particular electronic storage batteries

OVONICS n science of ovonic equipment

OVULAR ▶ ovule

OVULARY ▶ ovule

OVULATE vb produce or release an egg cell from an ovary

OVULE n plant part that contains the egg cell and becomes the seed after fertilization

OVULES ▶ ovule

OVUM n unfertilized egg cell

OW interj exclamation of pain

OWCHE same as ▶ ouch

OWCHES ▶ owche

OWE vb be obliged to pay (a sum of money) to (a person)

OWED ▶ owe

OWELTY n equality, esp in financial transactions

OWER Scots word for ▶ over

OWERBY adv over there

OWES ▶ owe

OWING ▶ owe

OWL n night bird of prey ▷ vb act like an owl

OWLED ▶ owl

OWLER vb smuggler

OWLERS ▶ owler

OWLERY n place where owls live

OWLET n young or nestling owl

OWLETS ▶ owlet

OWLIER ▶ owly

OWLIEST ▶ owly

OWLING ▶ owl

OWLISH adj like an owl

OWLLIKE ▶ owl

OWLS ▶ owl

OWLY same as ▶ owlish

OWN adj used to emphasize possession ▷ pron thing(s)

belonging to a particular person ▷ vb possess

OWNABLE adj able to be owned

OWNED ▶ own

OWNER n person who owns

OWNERS ▶ owner

OWNING ▶ own

OWNS ▶ own

OWRE same as ▶ ower

OWRELAY Scots form of ▶ overlay

OWRES ▶ owre

OWRIE same as ▶ oorie

OWRIER ▶ owrie

OWRIEST ▶ owrie

OWSE Scots form of ▶ ox

OWSEN Scots word for ▶ oxen

OWT dialect word for > anything

OWTS ▶ owt

OX n castrated bull

OXALATE n salt or ester of oxalic acid ▷ vb treat with oxalate

OXALIC adj as in **oxalic acid** poisonous acid found in many plants

OXALIS n type of plant

OXAZINE n type of chemical compound

OXBLOOD n dark reddish-brown colour ▷ adj of this colour

OXBOW n U-shaped piece of wood fitted around the neck of a harnessed ox and attached to the yoke

OXBOWS ▶ oxbow

OXCART n cart pulled by ox

OXCARTS ▶ oxcart

OXEN ▶ ox

OXER n high fence

OXERS ▶ oxer

OXES ▶ ox

OXEYE n daisy-like flower

OXEYES ▶ oxeye

OXFORD n type of stout laced shoe with a low heel

OXFORDS ▶ oxford

OXGANG n old measure of farmland

OXGANGS ▶ oxgang

OXGATE same as ▶ oxgang

OXGATES ▶ oxgate

OXHEAD n head of an ox

OXHEADS ▶ oxhead

OXHEART n heart-shaped cherry

OXHIDE n leather made from the hide of an ox

OXHIDES ▶ oxhide

OXID same as ▶ oxide

OXIDANT n substance that acts or is used as an oxidizing agent

OXIDASE n any of a group of enzymes that bring about biological oxidation

OXIDATE another word for ▶ oxidize

OXIDE n compound of oxygen and one other element

OXIDES ▶ oxide

OXIDIC ▶ oxide

OXIDISE same as ▶ oxidize

OXIDIZE vb combine chemically with oxygen, as in burning or rusting

OXIDS ▶ oxid

OXIES ▶ oxy

OXIM same as ▶ oxime

OXIME n type of chemical compound

OXIMES ▶ oxime

OXIMS ▶ oxim

OXLAND same as ▶ oxgang

OXLANDS ▶ oxland

OXLIKE ▶ ox

OXLIP n type of woodland plant with small drooping pale yellow flowers

OXLIPS ▶ oxlip

OXO n as in **oxo acid** acid that contains oxygen

OXONIUM n as in **oxonium compound** type of salt derived from an organic ether

OXSLIP same as ▶ oxlip

OXSLIPS ▶ oxslip

OXTAIL n tail of an ox, used in soups and stews

OXTAILS ▶ oxtail

OXTER n armpit ▷ vb grip under arm

OXTERED ▶ oxter

OXTERS ▶ oxter

OXY ▶ oxo

OXYACID n any acid that contains oxygen

OXYGEN n gaseous element essential to life and combustion

OXYGENS ▶ oxygen

OXYMEL n mixture of vinegar and honey

OXYMELS ▶ oxymel

OXYMORA > oxymoron

OXYNTIC adj of or denoting stomach cells that secrete acid

OXYPHIL n type of cell found in glands

OXYSALT *n* any salt of an oxyacid

OXYSOME *n* group of molecules

OXYTONE *adj* having an accent on the final syllable ▷ *n* oxytone word

OY *n* grandchild

OYE *same as* ▶ **oy**

OYER *n* (in the 13th century) an assize

OYERS ▶ **oyer**

OYES *same as* ▶ **oyez**

OYESES ▶ **oyes**

OYESSES ▶ **oyes**

OYEZ *interj* shouted three times by a public crier calling for attention before a proclamation ▷ *n* such a cry

OYEZES ▶ **oyez**

OYS ▶ **oy**

OYSTER *n* edible shellfish ▷ *vb* dredge for, gather, or raise oysters

OYSTERS ▶ **oyster**

OZAENA *n* inflammation of nasal mucous membrane

OZAENAS ▶ **ozaena**

OZALID *n* method of duplicating writing or illustrations

OZALIDS ▶ **ozalid**

OZEKI *n* sumo wrestling champion

OZEKIS ▶ **ozeki**

OZONATE *vb* add ozone to

OZONE *n* strong-smelling form of oxygen

OZONES ▶ **ozone**

OZONIC ▶ **ozone**

OZONIDE *n* type of unstable explosive compound

OZONISE *same as* ▶ **ozonize**

OZONIZE *vb* convert (oxygen) into ozone

OZONOUS ▶ **ozone**

OZZIE *n* hospital

OZZIES ▶ **ozzie**

O

Pp

P forms a two-letter word in front of every vowel except **U**, which makes it very useful for joining a new word to one already on the board. It also forms several three-letter words with **X**: pax, pix, pox (12 points each) and **pyx** (15). Other three-letter words with **P** well worth remembering are **zap, zep** and **zip** for 14 points each and **jap** for 12 points.

PA n (formerly) fortified Māori settlement

PAAL n stake driven into the ground

PAALS ▶ paal

PAAN n leaf of the betel tree

PAANS ▶ paan

PABLUM same as ▶ pabulum

PABLUMS ▶ pablum

PABULAR ▶ pabulum

PABULUM n food

PAC n soft shoe

PACA n large burrowing hystricomorph rodent of Central and South America

PACABLE adj easily appeased

PACAS ▶ paca

PACE n single step in walking ▷ vb walk up and down, esp in anxiety ▷ prep with due respect to: used to express polite disagreement

PACED ▶ pace

PACEMAN n (in cricket) fast bowler

PACEMEN ▶ paceman

PACER n horse trained to move at a special gait, esp for racing

PACERS ▶ pacer

PACES ▶ pace

PACEWAY n racecourse for trotting and pacing

PACEY adj fast-moving, quick, lively

PACHA same as ▶ pasha

PACHAK n fragrant roots of Asian plant

PACHAKS ▶ pachak

PACHAS ▶ pacha

PACHISI n Indian game somewhat resembling backgammon, played on a cruciform board using six cowries as dice

PACHUCO n young Mexican living in the US, esp one of low social status who belongs to a street gang

PACIER ▶ pacy

PACIEST ▶ pacy

PACIFIC adj tending to bring peace

PACIFY vb soothe, calm

PACING ▶ pace

PACK vb put (clothes etc) together in a suitcase or bag ▷ n bag carried on a person's or animal's back

PACKAGE same as ▶ packet

PACKED adj completely filled

PACKER n person or company whose business is to pack goods, esp food

PACKERS ▶ packer

PACKET n small container (and contents) ▷ vb wrap up in a packet or as a packet

PACKETS ▶ packet

PACKING n material, such as paper or plastic, used to protect packed goods

PACKLY ▶ pack

PACKMAN n person carrying pack

PACKMEN ▶ packman

PACKS ▶ pack

PACKWAX n neck ligament

PACKWAY n path for pack animals

PACO n S American mammal

PACOS ▶ paco

PACS ▶ pac

PACT n formal agreement

PACTA ▶ pactum

PACTION vb concur with

PACTS ▶ pact

PACTUM n pact

PACY same as ▶ pacey

PAD n piece of soft material used for protection, support, absorption of liquid, etc ▷ vb protect or fill with soft material

PADANG n (in Malaysia) playing field

PADANGS ▶ padang

PADAUK n tropical African or Asian leguminous tree with reddish wood

PADAUKS ▶ padauk

PADDED ▶ pad

PADDER n highwayman who robs on foot

PADDERS ▶ padder

PADDIES ▶ paddy

PADDING ▶ pad

PADDLE n short oar with a broad blade at one or each end ▷ vb move (a canoe etc) with a paddle

PADDLED ▶ paddle

PADDLER ▶ paddle

PADDLES ▶ paddle

PADDOCK n small field or enclosure for horses ▷ vb place (a horse) in a paddock

PADDY n fit of temper

PADELLA n type of candle

PADI same as ▶ paddy

PADIS ▶ padi

PADKOS n snacks and provisions for a journey

PADLE another name for > lumpfish

PADLES ▶ padle

PADLOCK n detachable lock with a hinged hoop fastened over a ring on the object to be secured ▷ vb fasten (something) with a padlock

PADMA n type of lotus

PADMAS ▶ padma
PADNAG n ambling horse
PADNAGS ▶ padnag
PADOUK same as ▶ padauk
PADOUKS ▶ padouk
PADRE n chaplain to the armed forces
PADRES ▶ padre
PADRI ▶ padre
PADRONE n owner or proprietor of an inn, esp in Italy
PADRONI ▶ padrone
PADS ▶ pad
PADSAW n small narrow saw used for cutting curves
PADSAWS ▶ padsaw
PADSHAH same as ▶ padishah
PAEAN n song of triumph or thanksgiving
PAEANS ▶ paean
PAEDO n paedophile
PAEDOS ▶ paedo
PAELLA n Spanish dish of rice, chicken, shellfish, and vegetables
PAELLAS ▶ paella
PAENULA n ancient Roman cloak
PAEON n metrical foot of four syllables, with one long one and three short ones in any order
PAEONIC ▶ paeon
PAEONS ▶ paeon
PAEONY same as ▶ peony
PAESAN n fellow countryman
PAESANI ▶ paesano
PAESANO n Italian-American man
PAESANS ▶ paesan
PAGAN adj not belonging to one of the world's main religions ▷ n pagan person
PAGANS ▶ pagan
PAGE n (one side of) sheet of paper forming a book etc ▷ vb summon (someone) by bleeper or loudspeaker, in order to pass on a message
PAGEANT n parade or display of people in costume, usu illustrating a scene from history
PAGEBOY n hairstyle in which the hair is smooth and the same medium length with the ends curled under
PAGED ▶ page
PAGEFUL n amount (of text,

etc) that a page will hold
PAGER n small electronic device, capable of receiving short messages
PAGERS ▶ pager
PAGES ▶ page
PAGINAL adj page-for-page
PAGING ▶ page
PAGINGS ▶ page
PAGLE same as ▶ paigle
PAGLES ▶ pagle
PAGOD n oriental idol
PAGODA n pyramid-shaped Asian temple or tower
PAGODAS ▶ pagoda
PAGODS ▶ pagod
PAGRI n type of turban
PAGRIS ▶ pagri
PAGURID same as ▶ pagurian
PAH same as ▶ pa
PAHLAVI n Iranian coin
PAHS ▶ pah
PAID ▶ pay
PAIDLE Scots variant of paddle n
PAIDLES ▶ paidle
PAIGLE n cowslip
PAIGLES ▶ paigle
PAIK vb thump or whack
PAIKED ▶ paik
PAIKING ▶ paik
PAIKS ▶ paik
PAIL n bucket
PAILFUL same as ▶ pail
PAILLON n thin leaf of metal
PAILS ▶ pail
PAIN n physical or mental suffering ▷ vb cause (someone) mental or physical suffering
PAINCH Scots variant of ▶ paunch
PAINED adj having or suggesting pain or distress
PAINFUL adj causing pain or distress
PAINIM n heathen or pagan
PAINIMS ▶ painim
PAINING ▶ pain
PAINS pl n care or trouble
PAINT n coloured substance, spread on a surface with a brush or roller ▷ vb colour or coat with paint
PAINTED ▶ paint
PAINTER n rope at the front of a boat, for tying it up
PAINTS ▶ paint
PAINTY ▶ paint
PAIOCK obsolete word for ▶ peacock

PAIOCKE obsolete word for ▶ peacock
PAIOCKS ▶ paiock
PAIR n set of two things matched for use together ▷ vb group or be grouped in twos
PAIRE obsolete spelling of ▶ pair
PAIRED ▶ pair
PAIRER ▶ pair
PAIRES ▶ paire
PAIREST ▶ pair
PAIRIAL same as ▶ prial
PAIRING ▶ pair
PAIRS ▶ pair
PAIS n country
PAISA n monetary unit of Bangladesh, Bhutan, India, Nepal, and Pakistan worth one hundredth of a rupee
PAISAN n fellow countryman
PAISANA n female peasant
PAISANO n friend
PAISANS ▶ paisan
PAISAS ▶ paisa
PAISE ▶ paisa
PAISLEY n pattern of small curving shapes with intricate detailing, usually printed in bright colours
PAJAMA same as ▶ pyjama
PAJAMAS ▶ pajama
PAJOCK obsolete word for ▶ peacock
PAJOCKE obsolete word for ▶ peacock
PAJOCKS ▶ pajock
PAKAHI n acid land that is unsuitable for cultivation
PAKAHIS ▶ pakahi
PAKAPOO n Chinese lottery with betting slips marked with Chinese characters
PAKEHA n person of European descent, as distinct from a Māori
PAKEHAS ▶ pakeha
PAKFONG same as ▶ packfong
PAKIHI n area of swampy infertile land
PAKIHIS ▶ pakihi
PAKKA same as ▶ pukka
PAKOKO n small freshwater fish
PAKOKOS ▶ pakoko
PAKORA n Indian dish consisting of pieces of vegetable, chicken, etc, dipped in a spiced batter and deep-fried

P

PAKORAS ▶ pakora
PAKTONG same as
> **pakthong**
PAL n friend ▷ vb associate
as friends
PALABRA n word
PALACE n residence of a
king, bishop, etc
PALACED adj having palaces
PALACES ▶ palace
PALADIN n knight who did
battle for a monarch
PALAGI n (in Samoa)
European
PALAGIS ▶ palagi
PALAIS n dance hall
PALAMA n webbing on
bird's feet
PALAMAE ▶ palama
PALAPA n open-sided
tropical building
PALAPAS ▶ palapa
PALAS n East Indian tree
PALASES ▶ palas
PALATAL adj of or relating to
the palate ▷ n bony plate
that forms the palate
PALATE n roof of the mouth
▷ vb perceive by taste
PALATED ▶ palate
PALATES ▶ palate
PALAVER n time-wasting
fuss ▷ vb (often used
humorously) have a
conference
PALAY n type of rubber
PALAYS ▶ palay
PALAZZI ▶ palazzo
PALAZZO n Italian palace
PALE adj light, whitish ▷ vb
become pale ▷ n wooden
or metal post used in fences
PALEA n inner of two bracts
surrounding each floret in a
grass spikelet
PALEAE ▶ palea
PALEAL ▶ palea
PALEATE adj having scales
PALED ▶ pale
PALELY ▶ pale
PALER ▶ pale
PALES ▶ pale
PALEST ▶ pale
PALET n perpendicular band
on escutcheon
PALETOT n loose outer
garment
PALETS ▶ palet
PALETTE n artist's flat board
for mixing colours on
PALFREY n light saddle
horse, esp ridden by
women

PALIER ▶ paly
PALIEST ▶ paly
PALIKAR n Greek soldier in
the war of independence
against Turkey
PALING n wooden or metal
post used in fences
PALINGS ▶ paling
PALINKA n type of apricot
brandy, originating in
Central and Eastern Europe
PALISH adj rather pale
PALKEE n covered Oriental
litter
PALKEES ▶ palkee
PALKI same as ▶ **palkee**
PALKIS ▶ palki
PALL n cloth spread over a
coffin ▷ vb become boring
PALLA n ancient Roman
cloak
PALLAE ▶ palla
PALLAH n S African
antelope
PALLAHS ▶ pallah
PALLED ▶ pall
PALLET same as ▶ **palette**
PALLETS ▶ pallet
PALLIA ▶ pallium
PALLIAL adj relating to
cerebral cortex
PALLID adj pale, esp
because ill or weak
PALLIED ▶ pally
PALLIER ▶ pally
PALLIES ▶ pally
PALLING ▶ pall
PALLIUM n garment worn
by men in ancient Greece or
Rome, made by draping a
large rectangular cloth
about the body
PALLONE n Italian ball
game
PALLOR n paleness of
complexion, usually
because of illness, shock, or
fear
PALLORS ▶ pallor
PALLS ▶ pall
PALLY adj on friendly terms
▷ vb as in **pally up** to
become friends with
PALM n inner surface of the
hand ▷ vb conceal in or
about the hand, as in
sleight-of-hand tricks
PALMAR adj of or relating to
the palm of the hand
PALMARY adj worthy of
praise
PALMATE adj shaped like an
open hand

PALMED ▶ palm
PALMER n (in Medieval
Europe) pilgrim bearing a
palm branch as a sign of his
visit to the Holy Land
PALMERS ▶ palmer
PALMFUL n amount that
can be held in the palm of a
hand
PALMIE n palmtop
computer
PALMIER ▶ palmy
PALMIES ▶ palmie
PALMIET n South African
rush
PALMING ▶ palm
PALMIST > palmistry
PALMS ▶ palm
PALMTOP adj small enough
to be held in the hand ▷ n
computer small enough to
be held in the hand
PALMY adj successful,
prosperous and happy
PALMYRA n tall tropical
Asian palm
PALOLO n polychaete worm
of the S Pacific Ocean
PALOLOS ▶ palolo
PALOOKA n stupid or
clumsy boxer or other
person
PALP n either of a pair of
sensory appendages that
arise from the mouthparts
of crustaceans and insects
▷ vb feel
PALPAL ▶ palp
PALPATE vb examine (an
area of the body) by
touching ▷ adj of, relating
to, or possessing a palp or
palps
PALPED ▶ palp
PALPI ▶ palpus
PALPING ▶ palp
PALPS ▶ palp
PALPUS same as ▶ **palp**
PALS ▶ pal
PALSHIP n state of being
pals
PALSIED ▶ palsy
PALSIER ▶ palsy
PALSIES ▶ palsy
PALSY n paralysis ▷ vb
paralyse ▷ adj friendly
PALTER vb act or talk
insincerely
PALTERS ▶ palter
PALTRY adj insignificant
PALUDAL adj of, relating to,
or produced by marshes
PALUDIC adj of malaria

PALY *adj* vertically striped

PAM *n* knave of clubs

PAMPA *n* grassland area

PAMPAS *pl n* vast grassy plains in S America

PAMPEAN ▷ **pampas**

PAMPER *vb* treat (someone) with great indulgence, spoil

PAMPERO *n* dry cold wind in South America blowing across the pampas from the south or southwest

PAMPERS ▷ **pamper**

PAMPOEN *n* pumpkin

PAMS ▷ **pam**

PAN *n* wide long-handled metal container used in cooking ▷ *vb* sift gravel from (a river) in a pan to search for gold

PANACEA *n* remedy for all diseases or problems

PANACHE *n* confident elegant style

PANADA *n* mixture of flour, water, etc, or of breadcrumbs soaked in milk, used as a thickening

PANADAS ▷ **panada**

PANAMA *n* hat made of the plaited leaves of the jipijapa plant

PANAMAS ▷ **panama**

PANARY *n* storehouse for bread

PANAX *n* genus of perennial herbs

PANAXES ▷ **panax**

PANCAKE *n* thin flat circle of fried batter ▷ *vb* cause (an aircraft) to make a pancake landing or (of an aircraft) to make a pancake landing

PANCE *n* pansy

PANCES ▷ **pance**

PANCHAX *n* brightly coloured tropical Asian cyprinodont fish

PAND *n* valance

PANDA *n* large black-and-white bearlike mammal from China

PANDANI *n* tropical tree

PANDAR *vb* act as a pimp

PANDARS ▷ **pandar**

PANDAS ▷ **panda**

PANDECT *n* treatise covering all aspects of a particular subject

PANDER *vb* indulge (a person his or her desires) ▷ *n* person who procures a sexual partner for someone

PANDERS ▷ **pander**

PANDIED ▷ **pandy**

PANDIES ▷ **pandy**

PANDIT *same as* ▷ **pundit**

PANDITS ▷ **pandit**

PANDOOR *same as* ▷ **pandour**

PANDORA *n* handsome red sea bream

PANDORE *another word for* ▷ **bandore**

PANDOUR *n* one of an 18th-century force of Croatian soldiers in the Austrian service, notorious for their brutality

PANDS ▷ **pand**

PANDURA *n* ancient stringed instrument

PANDY *n* (in schools) stroke on the hand with a strap as a punishment ▷ *vb* punish with such strokes

PANE *n* sheet of glass in a window or door ▷ *adj* (of fish, meat, etc) dipped or rolled in breadcrumbs before cooking

PANED ▷ **pane**

PANEER *n* soft white cheese, used in Indian cookery

PANEERS ▷ **paneer**

PANEITY *n* state of being bread

PANEL *n* flat distinct section of a larger surface, for example in a door ▷ *vb* cover or decorate with panels ▷ *adj* of a group acting as a panel

PANELED ▷ **panel**

PANELS ▷ **panel**

PANES ▷ **pane**

PANFISH *n* small food fish

PANFRY *vb* fry in a pan

PANFUL ▷ **pan**

PANFULS ▷ **pan**

PANG *n* sudden sharp feeling of pain or sadness ▷ *vb* cause pain

PANGA *n* broad heavy knife of E Africa, used as a tool or weapon

PANGAMY *n* unrestricted mating

PANGAS ▷ **panga**

PANGED ▷ **pang**

PANGEN *same as* ▷ **pangene**

PANGENE *n* hypothetical particle of protoplasm

PANGENS ▷ **pangen**

PANGING ▷ **pang**

PANGRAM *n* sentence incorporating all the letters of the alphabet

PANGS ▷ **pang**

PANIC *n* sudden overwhelming fear, often affecting a whole group of people ▷ *vb* feel or cause to feel panic ▷ *adj* of or resulting from such terror

PANICK *old word for* ▷ **panic**

PANICKS ▷ **panick**

PANICKY ▷ **panic**

PANICLE *n* loose, irregularly branched cluster of flowers

PANICS ▷ **panic**

PANICUM *n* type of grass

PANIER *same as* ▷ **pannier**

PANIERS ▷ **panier**

PANIM *n* heathen or pagan

PANIMS ▷ **panim**

PANING ▷ **pane**

PANINI ▷ **panino**

PANINIS ▷ **panini**

PANINO *n* Italian sandwich

PANISC *n* faun; attendant of Pan

PANISCS ▷ **panisc**

PANISK *same as* ▷ **panisc**

PANISKS ▷ **panisk**

PANKO *n* flaky breadcrumbs used as a coating in Japanese cookery

PANKOS ▷ **panko**

PANNAGE *n* pasturage for pigs, esp in a forest

PANNE *n* lightweight velvet fabric

PANNED ▷ **pan**

PANNER ▷ **pan**

PANNERS ▷ **pan**

PANNES ▷ **panne**

PANNICK *old spelling of the noun* ▷ **panic**

PANNIER *n* bag fixed on the back of a cycle

PANNING ▷ **pan**

PANNOSE *adj* like felt

PANNUS *n* inflammatory fleshy lesion on the surface of the eye

PANOCHA *n* coarse grade of sugar made in Mexico

PANOCHE *n* type of dark sugar

PANOPLY *n* magnificent array

PANPIPE *n* wind instrument

PANS ▷ **pan**

PANSIED *adj* covered with pansies

PANSIES ▷ **pansy**

PANSY *n* small garden

flower with velvety purple, yellow, or white petals

PANT vb breathe quickly and noisily during or after exertion ▷ n act of panting

PANTED ▸ **pant**

PANTER n person who pants

PANTERS ▸ **panter**

PANTHER n leopard, esp a black one

PANTIE same as ▸ **panty**

PANTIES pl n women's underpants

PANTILE n roofing tile with an S-shaped cross section ▷ vb tile roof with pantiles

PANTINE n pasteboard puppet

PANTING ▸ **pant**

PANTLER n pantry servant

PANTO same as > **pantomime**

PANTON n type of horseshoe

PANTONS ▸ **panton**

PANTOS ▸ **panto**

PANTOUM n verse form

PANTRY n small room or cupboard for storing food

PANTS pl n undergarment for the lower part of the body

PANTUN n Malayan poetry

PANTUNS ▸ **pantun**

PANTY n woman's undergarment

PANZER n German tank

PANZERS ▸ **panzer**

PAOLI ▸ **paolo**

PAOLO n Italian silver coin

PAP n soft food for babies or invalids ▷ vb (of the paparazzi) to follow and photograph (a famous person) ▷ vb feed with pap

PAPA n father

PAPABLE adj suitable for papacy

PAPACY n position or term of office of a pope

PAPADAM same as > **poppadom**

PAPADOM same as > **poppadom**

PAPADUM same as > **poppadom**

PAPAIN n proteolytic enzyme occurring in the unripe fruit of the papaya tree

PAPAINS ▸ **papain**

PAPAL adj of the pope

PAPALLY ▸ **papal**

PAPAS ▸ **papa**

PAPAUMA n New Zealand word for broadleaf

PAPAW same as ▸ **papaya**

PAPAWS ▸ **papaw**

PAPAYA n large sweet West Indian fruit

PAPAYAN ▸ **papaya**

PAPAYAS ▸ **papaya**

PAPE n spiritual father

PAPER n material made in sheets from wood pulp or other fibres ▷ vb cover (walls) with wallpaper

PAPERED ▸ **paper**

PAPERER ▸ **paper**

PAPERS ▸ **paper**

PAPERY adj like paper, esp in thinness, flimsiness, or dryness

PAPES ▸ **pape**

PAPHIAN n prostitute

PAPILIO n butterfly

PAPILLA n small projection of tissue at the base of a hair, tooth, or feather

PAPOOSE n Native American child

PAPPED ▸ **pap**

PAPPI ▸ **pappus**

PAPPIER ▸ **pappy**

PAPPIES ▸ **pappy**

PAPPING ▸ **pap**

PAPPOSE ▸ **pappus**

PAPPOUS ▸ **pappus**

PAPPUS n ring of fine feathery hairs surrounding the fruit in composite plants, such as the thistle

PAPPY adj resembling pap

PAPRICA same as ▸ **paprika**

PAPRIKA n mild powdered seasoning made from red peppers

PAPS ▸ **pap**

PAPULA same as ▸ **papule**

PAPULAE ▸ **papula**

PAPULAR ▸ **papule**

PAPULE n small solid usually round elevation of the skin

PAPULES ▸ **papule**

PAPYRAL ▸ **papyrus**

PAPYRI ▸ **papyrus**

PAPYRUS n tall water plant

PAR n usual or average condition ▷ vb play (a golf hole) in par

PARA n paratrooper

PARABEN n carcinogenic ester

PARABLE n story that illustrates a religious

teaching ▷ vb write parable

PARACME n phase where fever lessens

PARADE n procession or march ▷ vb display or flaunt

PARADED ▸ **parade**

PARADER ▸ **parade**

PARADES ▸ **parade**

PARADOR n state-run hotel in Spain

PARADOS n bank behind a trench or other fortification, giving protection from being fired on from the rear

PARADOX n person or thing made up of contradictory elements

PARAE n type of fish

PARAFLE same as > **paraffle**

PARAGE n type of feudal land tenure

PARAGES ▸ **parage**

PARAGON n model of perfection ▷ vb equal or surpass

PARAMO n high plateau in the Andes between the tree line and the permanent snow line

PARAMOS ▸ **paramo**

PARANG n short stout straight-edged knife used by the Dyaks of Borneo

PARANGS ▸ **parang**

PARANYM n euphemism

PARAPET n low wall or railing along the edge of a balcony or roof ▷ vb provide with a parapet

PARAPH n flourish after a signature, originally to prevent forgery ▷ vb embellish signature

PARAPHS ▸ **paraph**

PARAS ▸ **para**

PARASOL n umbrella-like sunshade

PARATHA n (in Indian cookery) flat unleavened bread, resembling a small nan bread, that is fried on a griddle

PARAZOA > **parazoan**

PARBAKE vb partially bake

PARBOIL vb boil until partly cooked

PARCEL n something wrapped up, package ▷ vb wrap up

PARCELS ▸ **parcel**

PARCH vb make very hot and dry

PARCHED ▶ **parch**

PARCHES ▶ **parch**

PARD n leopard or panther

PARDAH same as ▶ **purdah**

PARDAHS ▶ **pardah**

PARDAL variant spelling of ▶ **pardale**

PARDALE n leopard

PARDALS ▶ **pardal**

PARDED adj having spots

PARDEE adv certainly

PARDI same as ▶ **pardee**

PARDIE same as ▶ **pardee**

PARDINE adj spotted

PARDNER n friend or partner: used as a term of address

PARDON vb forgive, excuse ▷ n forgiveness ▷ interj sorry ▷ sentence substitute sorry

PARDONS ▶ **pardon**

PARDS ▶ **pard**

PARDY same as ▶ **pardee**

PARE vb cut off the skin or top layer of

PARED ▶ **pare**

PAREIRA n root of a South American menispermaceous climbing plant

PARELLA n type of lichen

PARELLE same as ▶ **parella**

PARENT n father or mother ▷ vb raise offspring

PARENTS ▶ **parent**

PAREO same as ▶ **pareu**

PAREOS ▶ **pareu**

PARER ▶ **pare**

PARERA n New Zealand duck with grey-edged brown feathers

PARERAS ▶ **parera**

PARERGA ▶ **parergon**

PARERS ▶ **pare**

PARES ▶ **pare**

PARESES ▶ **paresis**

PARESIS n incomplete or slight paralysis of motor functions

PARETIC ▶ **paresis**

PAREU n rectangle of fabric worn by Polynesians as a skirt or loincloth

PAREUS ▶ **pareu**

PAREV adj containing neither meat nor milk products and so fit for use with either meat or milk dishes

PAREVE same as ▶ **parev**

PARFAIT n dessert consisting of layers of ice cream, fruit, and sauce, topped with whipped cream, and served in a tall glass

PARGANA n Indian sub-district

PARGE vb coat with plaster

PARGED ▶ **parge**

PARGES ▶ **parge**

PARGET n plaster, mortar, etc, used to line chimney flues or cover walls ▷ vb cover or decorate with parget

PARGETS ▶ **parget**

PARGING ▶ **parge**

PARGO n sea bream

PARGOS ▶ **pargo**

PARIAH n social outcast

PARIAHS ▶ **pariah**

PARIAL n pair royal of playing cards

PARIALS ▶ **parial**

PARIAN n type of marble or porcelain

PARIANS ▶ **parian**

PARIES n wall of an organ or bodily cavity

PARING n piece pared off

PARINGS ▶ **paring**

PARIS n type of herb

PARISES ▶ **paris**

PARISH n area that has its own church and a priest or pastor

PARISON n unshaped mass of glass before it is moulded into its final form

PARITOR n official who summons witnesses

PARITY n equality or equivalence

PARK n area of open land for recreational use by the public ▷ vb stop and leave (a vehicle) temporarily

PARKA n large waterproof jacket with a hood

PARKADE n building used as a car park

PARKAS ▶ **parka**

PARKED ▶ **park**

PARKEE n Eskimo outer garment

PARKEES ▶ **parkee**

PARKER ▶ **park**

PARKERS ▶ **park**

PARKI same as ▶ **parka**

PARKIE n park keeper

PARKIER ▶ **parky**

PARKIES ▶ **parkie**

PARKIN n moist spicy ginger cake usually containing oatmeal

PARKING ▶ **park**

PARKINS ▶ **parkin**

PARKIS ▶ **parki**

PARKISH adj like a park

PARKLY adj having many parks or resembling a park

PARKOUR n sport of running in urban areas performing gymnastics on manmade obstacles

PARKS ▶ **park**

PARKWAY n (in the US and Canada) wide road planted with trees, turf, etc

PARKY adj (of the weather) chilly

PARLAY vb stake (winnings from one bet) on a subsequent wager ▷ n bet in which winnings from one wager are staked on another, or a series of such bets

PARLAYS ▶ **parlay**

PARLE vb speak

PARLED ▶ **parle**

PARLES ▶ **parle**

PARLEY n meeting between leaders or representatives of opposing forces to discuss terms ▷ vb have a parley

PARLEYS ▶ **parley**

PARLIES pl n small Scottish biscuits

PARLING ▶ **parle**

PARLOR same as ▶ **parlour**

PARLORS ▶ **parlor**

PARLOUR n living room for receiving visitors

PARLOUS adj dire ▷ adv extremely

PARLY n short form of parliament

PARODIC ▶ **parody**

PARODOI n path leading to Greek theatre

PARODOS n ode sung by Greek chorus

PARODY n exaggerated and amusing imitation of someone else's style ▷ vb make a parody of

PAROL n (formerly) pleadings in an action when presented by word of mouth ▷ adj (of a contract, lease, etc) made orally or in writing but not under seal

PAROLE n early freeing of a

prisoner on condition that
he or she behaves well ▷ *vb*
put on parole

PAROLED ▶ **parole**

PAROLEE ▶ **parole**

PAROLES ▶ **parole**

PAROLS ▶ **parol**

PARONYM *n* cognate word

PARORE *n* type of fish found
around Australia and New
Zealand

PARORES ▶ **parore**

PAROTIC *adj* situated near
the ear

PAROTID *adj* relating to or
situated near the parotid
gland ▷ *n* parotid gland

PAROTIS *n* parotid gland

PAROUS *adj* having given
birth

PARP *vb* make a honking
sound

PARPANE *n* parapet on
bridge

PARPED ▶ **parp**

PARPEN *same as* ▶ **parpend**

PARPEND *same as*
▶ **perpend**

PARPENS ▶ **parpen**

PARPENT *n* parapet on
bridge

PARPING ▶ **parp**

PARPS ▶ **parp**

PARQUET *n* floor covering
made of wooden blocks
arranged in a geometric
pattern ▷ *vb* cover with
parquet

PARR *n* salmon up to two
years of age

PARRA *n* tourist or
non-resident on a beach

PARRAL *same as* ▶ **parrel**

PARRALS ▶ **parral**

PARRAS ▶ **parra**

PARRED ▶ **par**

PARREL *n* ring that holds
the jaws of a boom to the
mast but lets it slide up and
down

PARRELS ▶ **parrel**

PARRIED ▶ **parry**

PARRIER ▶ **parry**

PARRIES ▶ **parry**

PARRING ▶ **par**

PARROCK *vb* put (an
animal) in a small field

PARROT *n* tropical bird with
a short hooked beak and an
ability to imitate human
speech ▷ *vb* repeat
(someone else's words)
without thinking

PARROTS ▶ **parrot**

PARROTY *adj* like a parrot;
chattering

PARRS ▶ **parr**

PARRY *vb* ward off (an
attack) ▷ *n* parrying

PARS ▶ **par**

PARSE *vb* analyse (a
sentence) in terms of
grammar

PARSEC *n* unit of
astronomical distance

PARSECS ▶ **parsec**

PARSED ▶ **parse**

PARSER *n* program or part
of a program that
interprets input to a
computer by recognizing
key words or analysing
sentence structure

PARSERS ▶ **parser**

PARSES ▶ **parse**

PARSING ▶ **parse**

PARSLEY *n* herb used for
seasoning and decorating
food ▷ *vb* garnish with
parsley

PARSNEP *same as*
▶ **parsnip**

PARSNIP *n* long tapering
cream-coloured root
vegetable

PARSON *n* Anglican parish
priest

PARSONS ▶ **parson**

PART *n* one of the pieces
that make up a whole ▷ *vb*
divide or separate

PARTAKE *vb* take (food or
drink)

PARTAN *Scottish word for*
▶ **crab**

PARTANS ▶ **partan**

PARTED *adj* divided almost
to the base

PARTER *n* thing that parts

PARTERS ▶ **parter**

PARTI *n* concept of
architectural design

PARTIAL *adj* not complete
▷ *n* any of the component
tones of a single musical
sound, including both
those that belong to the
harmonic series of the
sound and those that do
not ▷ *vb* remove (a factor)
from a set of statistics

PARTIED ▶ **party**

PARTIER *n* person who
parties

PARTIES ▶ **party**

PARTIM *adv* in part

PARTING *same as* ▶ **part**

PARTIS ▶ **parti**

PARTITA *n* type of suite

PARTITE *adj* composed of or
divided into a specified
number of parts

PARTLET *n* woman's
garment covering the neck
and shoulders

PARTLY *adv* not completely

PARTNER *n* either member
of a couple in a relationship
or activity ▷ *vb* be the
partner of

PARTON *n* hypothetical
elementary particle
postulated as a constituent
of neutrons and protons

PARTONS ▶ **parton**

PARTOOK ▶ **partake**

PARTS *pl n* abilities or
talents

PARTURE *n* departure

PARTWAY *adv* some of the
way

PARTY *n* social gathering
for pleasure ▷ *vb* celebrate,
have fun ▷ *adj* (of a shield)
divided vertically into two
colours, metals, or furs

PARTYER *n* person who
parties

PARULIS *another name for*
▶ **gumboil**

PARURA *same as* ▶ **parure**

PARURAS ▶ **parura**

PARURE *n* set of jewels or
other ornaments

PARURES ▶ **parure**

PARVE *same as* ▶ **parev**

PARVENU *n* person newly
risen to a position of power
or wealth ▷ *adj* of or
characteristic of a parvenu

PARVIS *n* court or portico in
front of a building, esp a
church

PARVISE *same as* ▶ **parvis**

PARVO *n* disease of cattle
and dogs

PARVOS ▶ **parvo**

PAS *n* dance step or
movement, esp in ballet

PASCAL *n* unit of pressure

PASCALS ▶ **pascal**

PASCHAL *adj* of the
Passover or Easter ▷ *n*
Passover or Easter

PASCUAL *adj* relating to
pasture

PASE *n* movement of the
cape or muleta by a
matador to attract the

bull's attention and guide its attack

PASEAR vb go for a rambling walk

PASEARS ▶ pasear

PASELA same as ▶ bonsela

PASELAS ▶ pasela

PASEO n bullfighters' procession

PASEOS ▶ paseo

PASES ▶ pase

PASH n infatuation ▷ vb throw or be thrown and break or be broken to bits

PASHA n high official of the Ottoman Empire

PASHAS ▶ pasha

PASHED ▶ pash

PASHES ▶ pash

PASHIM same as ▶ pashm

PASHIMS ▶ pashm

PASHING ▶ pash

PASHKA n rich Russian dessert made of cottage cheese, cream, almonds, currants, etc

PASHKAS ▶ pashka

PASHM n underfur of various Tibetan animals, esp goats, used for cashmere shawls

PASHMS ▶ pashm

PASPIES ▶ paspy

PASPY n piece of music in triple time

PASQUIL n abusive lampoon or satire ▷ vb ridicule with pasquil

PASS vb go by, past, or through ▷ n successful result in a test or examination

PASSADE n act of moving back and forth in the same place

PASSADO n forward thrust with sword

PASSAGE n channel or opening providing a way through ▷ vb move or cause to move at a passage

PASSANT adj (of a beast) walking, with the right foreleg raised

PASSATA n sauce made from sieved tomatoes, often used in Italian cookery

PASSE adj out-of-date

PASSED ▶ pass

PASSEE adj out of fashion

PASSEL n group or quantity of no fixed number

PASSELS ▶ passel

PASSER n person or thing that passes

PASSERS ▶ passer

PASSES ▶ pass

PASSIM adv everywhere, throughout

PASSING adj brief or transitory ▷ n death

PASSION n intense sexual love ▷ vb give passionate character to

PASSIVE adj not playing an active part ▷ n passive form of a verb

PASSKEY n private key

PASSMAN n student who passes without honours

PASSMEN ▶ passman

PASSOUT n (in ice hockey) pass by an attacking player from behind the opposition goal line

PASSUS n (esp in medieval literature) division or section of a poem, story, etc

PAST adj of the time before the present ▷ n period of time before the present ▷ adv ago ▷ prep beyond

PASTA n type of food, such as spaghetti, that is made in different shapes from flour and water

PASTAS ▶ pasta

PASTE n moist soft mixture, such as toothpaste ▷ vb fasten with paste

PASTED ▶ paste

PASTEL n coloured chalk crayon for drawing ▷ adj pale and delicate in colour

PASTELS ▶ pastel

PASTER n person or thing that pastes

PASTERN n part of a horse's foot between the fetlock and the hoof

PASTERS ▶ paster

PASTES ▶ paste

PASTEUP n assembly of typeset matter, illustrations, etc, pasted on a sheet of paper or board

PASTIE n decorative cover for nipple

PASTIER ▶ pasty

PASTIES ▶ pasty

PASTIL same as > **pastille**

PASTILS ▶ pastil

PASTILY ▶ pasty

PASTIME n activity that makes time pass pleasantly

PASTINA n small pieces of pasta

PASTING n heavy defeat

PASTIS n anise-flavoured alcoholic drink

PASTOR n member of the clergy in charge of a congregation ▷ vb act as a pastor

PASTORS ▶ pastor

PASTRY n baking dough made of flour, fat, and water

PASTS ▶ past

PASTURE n grassy land for farm animals to graze on ▷ vb cause (livestock) to graze or (of livestock) to graze (a pasture)

PASTY adj (of a complexion) pale and unhealthy ▷ n round of pastry folded over a savoury filling

PAT vb tap lightly ▷ n gentle tap or stroke ▷ adj quick, ready, or glib

PATACA n monetary unit of Macao

PATACAS ▶ pataca

PATAGIA > patagium

PATAKA n building on stilts, used for storing provisions

PATAKAS ▶ pataka

PATAMAR n type of boat

PATBALL n game like squash but using hands instead of rackets

PATCH n piece of material sewn on a garment ▷ vb mend with a patch

PATCHED ▶ patch

PATCHER ▶ patch

PATCHES ▶ patch

PATCHY adj of uneven quality or intensity

PATE n head

PATED ▶ pate

PATELLA n kneecap

PATEN n plate, usually made of silver or gold, used for the bread at Communion

PATENCY n condition of being obvious

PATENS ▶ paten

PATENT n document giving the exclusive right to make or sell an invention ▷ adj open to public inspection ▷ vb obtain a patent for

PATENTS ▶ patent

PATER n father

PATERA n shallow ancient Roman bowl

PATERAE ▸ patera
PATERS ▸ pater
PATES ▸ pate
PATH n surfaced walk or track ▷ vb make a path
PATHED ▸ path
PATHIC n catamite ▷ adj of or relating to a catamite
PATHICS ▸ pathic
PATHING ▸ path
PATHOS n power of arousing pity or sadness
PATHS ▸ path
PATHWAY n path
PATIBLE adj endurable
PATIENT adj enduring difficulties or delays calmly ▷ n person receiving medical treatment ▷ vb make calm
PATIKI n New Zealand sand flounder or dab
PATIKIS ▸ patiki
PATIN same as ▸ paten
PATINA n fine layer on a surface
PATINAE ▸ patina
PATINAS ▸ patina
PATINE vb cover with patina
PATINED ▸ patine
PATINES ▸ patine
PATINS ▸ patin
PATIO n paved area adjoining a house
PATIOS ▸ patio
PATKA n head covering worn by Sikh men in place of or under a turban
PATKAS ▸ patka
PATLY adv fitly
PATNESS n appropriateness
PATOIS n regional dialect, esp of French
PATONCE adj (of cross) with limbs which broaden from centre
PATRIAL n (in Britain, formerly) person with a right by statute to live in the United Kingdom, and so not subject to immigration control
PATRICK n former Irish coin
PATRICO n fraudulent priest
PATRIOT n person who loves his or her country and supports its interests
PATROL n regular circuit by a guard ▷ vb go round on guard, or reconnoitring
PATROLS ▸ patrol
PATRON n person who gives financial support to

charities, artists, etc
PATRONS ▸ patron
PATROON n Dutch land-holder in New Netherland and New York with manorial rights in the colonial era
PATS ▸ pat
PATSIES ▸ patsy
PATSY n person who is easily cheated, victimized, etc
PATTE n band keeping belt in place
PATTED ▸ pat
PATTEE adj (of a cross) having triangular arms widening outwards
PATTEN n wooden clog or sandal on a raised wooden platform or metal ring ▷ vb wear pattens
PATTENS ▸ patten
PATTER vb make repeated soft tapping sounds ▷ n quick succession of taps
PATTERN n arrangement of repeated parts or decorative designs ▷ vb model
PATTERS ▸ patter
PATTES ▸ patte
PATTIE same as ▸ patty
PATTIES ▸ patty
PATTING ▸ pat
PATTLE dialect for ▸ paddle
PATTLES ▸ pattle
PATTY n small flattened cake of minced food
PATU n short Māori club, now used ceremonially
PATULIN n toxic antibiotic
PATUS ▸ patu
PATY adj (of cross) having arms of equal length
PATZER n novice chess player
PATZERS ▸ patzer
PAUA n edible shellfish of New Zealand, which has a pearly shell used for jewellery
PAUAS ▸ paua
PAUCAL n grammatical number occurring in some languages for words in contexts where a few of their referents are described or referred to ▷ adj relating to or inflected for this number
PAUCALS ▸ paucal
PAUCITY n scarcity

PAUGHTY Scots word for ▸ haughty
PAUL same as ▸ pawl
PAULIN n tarpaulin
PAULINS ▸ paulin
PAULS ▸ paul
PAUNCE n pansy
PAUNCES ▸ paunce
PAUNCH n protruding belly ▷ vb stab in the stomach
PAUNCHY adj having a protruding belly or abdomen
PAUPER n very poor person ▷ vb reduce to beggary
PAUPERS ▸ pauper
PAUSAL ▸ pause
PAUSE vb stop for a time ▷ n stop or rest in speech or action
PAUSED ▸ pause
PAUSER ▸ pause
PAUSERS ▸ pause
PAUSES ▸ pause
PAUSING ▸ pause
PAV short for ▸ pavlova
PAVAGE n tax towards paving streets, or the right to levy such a tax
PAVAGES ▸ pavage
PAVAN same as ▸ pavane
PAVANE n slow and stately dance of the 16th and 17th centuries
PAVANES ▸ pavane
PAVANS ▸ pavan
PAVE vb form (a surface) with stone or brick ▷ n paved surface, esp an uneven one
PAVED ▸ pave
PAVEED adj (of jewels) set close together
PAVEN same as ▸ pavane
PAVENS ▸ paven
PAVER ▸ pave
PAVERS ▸ pave
PAVES ▸ pave
PAVID adj fearful
PAVIN same as ▸ pavane
PAVING n paved surface ▷ adj of or for a paved surface or pavement
PAVINGS ▸ paving
PAVINS ▸ pavin
PAVIOR same as ▸ paviour
PAVIORS ▸ pavior
PAVIOUR n person who lays paving
PAVIS n large square shield, developed in the 15th century, at first portable but later heavy and set up in

a permanent position

PAVISE same as ▶ **pavis**

PAVISER n soldier holding pavise

PAVISES ▶ **pavise**

PAVISSE same as ▶ **pavis**

PAVLOVA n meringue cake topped with whipped cream and fruit

PAVONE n peacock

PAVONES ▶ **pavone**

PAVS ▶ **pav**

PAW n animal's foot with claws and pads ▷ vb scrape with the paw or hoof

PAWA old word for ▶ **peacock**

PAWAS ▶ **pawa**

PAWAW vb recite N American incantation

PAWAWED ▶ **pawaw**

PAWAWS ▶ **pawaw**

PAWED ▶ **paw**

PAWER n person or animal that paws

PAWERS ▶ **pawer**

PAWING ▶ **paw**

PAWK Scots word for ▶ **trick**

PAWKIER ▶ **pawky**

PAWKILY ▶ **pawky**

PAWKS ▶ **pawk**

PAWKY adj having or characterized by a dry wit

PAWL n pivoted lever shaped to engage with a ratchet to prevent motion in a particular direction

PAWLS ▶ **pawl**

PAWN vb deposit (an article) as security for money borrowed ▷ n chessman of the lowest value

PAWNAGE ▶ **pawn**

PAWNCE old word for ▶ **pansy**

PAWNCES ▶ **pawnce**

PAWNED ▶ **pawn**

PAWNEE n one who accepts goods in pawn

PAWNEES ▶ **pawnee**

PAWNER n one who pawns his or her possessions

PAWNERS ▶ **pawner**

PAWNING ▶ **pawn**

PAWNOR same as ▶ **pawner**

PAWNORS ▶ **pawnor**

PAWNS ▶ **pawn**

PAWPAW same as ▶ **papaw**

PAWPAWS ▶ **pawpaw**

PAWS ▶ **paw**

PAX n peace ▷ interj call signalling a desire to end hostilities

Latin for peace, this is yet another of those very useful short words containing X.

PAXES ▶ **pax**

PAXIUBA n tropical tree

PAXWAX n strong ligament in the neck of many mammals, which supports the head

PAY vb give money etc in return for goods or services ▷ n wages or salary

PAYABLE adj due to be paid

PAYABLY ▶ **payable**

PAYBACK n return on an investment

PAYDAY n day on which wages or salaries are paid

PAYDAYS ▶ **payday**

PAYED ▶ **pay**

PAYEE n person to whom money is paid or due

PAYEES ▶ **payee**

PAYER n person who pays

PAYERS ▶ **payer**

PAYFONE US spelling of ▶ **payphone**

PAYING ▶ **pay**

PAYINGS ▶ **pay**

PAYLIST n list of people to be paid

PAYLOAD n passengers or cargo of an aircraft

PAYMENT n act of paying

PAYNIM n heathen or pagan

PAYNIMS ▶ **paynim**

PAYOFF n final settlement, esp in retribution

PAYOFFS ▶ **payoff**

PAYOLA n bribe to get special treatment, esp to promote a commercial product

PAYOLAS ▶ **payola**

PAYOR same as ▶ **payer**

PAYORS ▶ **payor**

PAYOUT n sum of money paid out

PAYOUTS ▶ **payout**

PAYROLL n list of employees who receive regular pay

PAYS ▶ **pay**

PAYSAGE n landscape

PAYSD Spenserian form of ▶ **poised**

PAYSLIP n note of payment given to employee

PAZAZZ same as ▶ **pizzazz**

PAZZAZZ same as ▶ **pizzazz**

PE n 17th letter of the Hebrew alphabet, transliterated as p

PEA n climbing plant with seeds growing in pods

PEACE n calm, quietness

PEACED ▶ **peace**

PEACES ▶ **peace**

PEACH n soft juicy fruit with a stone and a downy skin ▷ adj pinkish-orange ▷ vb inform against an accomplice

PEACHED ▶ **peach**

PEACHER ▶ **peach**

PEACHES ▶ **peach**

PEACHY adj of or like a peach, esp in colour or texture

PEACING ▶ **peace**

PEACOAT n woollen jacket

PEACOCK n large male bird with a brilliantly coloured fanlike tail ▷ vb display (oneself) proudly

PEACOD same as ▶ **peapod**

PEACODS ▶ **peacod**

PEAFOWL n peacock or peahen

PEAG n (formerly) money used by North American Indians, made of cylindrical shells strung or woven together

PEAGE same as ▶ **peag**

PEAGES ▶ **peage**

PEAGS ▶ **peag**

PEAHEN ▶ **peacock**

PEAHENS ▶ **peacock**

PEAK n pointed top, esp of a mountain ▷ vb form or reach a peak ▷ adj of or at the point of greatest demand

PEAKED adj having a peak

PEAKIER ▶ **peak**

PEAKING ▶ **peak**

PEAKISH adj sickly

PEAKS ▶ **peak**

PEAKY ▶ **peak**

PEAL n long loud echoing sound, esp of bells or thunder ▷ vb sound with a peal or peals

PEALED ▶ **peal**

PEALIKE ▶ **pea**

PEALING ▶ **peal**

PEALS ▶ **peal**

PEAN ▶ **peen** (sense 2)

PEANED ▶ **pean**

PEANING ▶ **pean**

PEANS ▶ **pean**

PEANUT n pea-shaped nut that ripens underground

PEANUTS ▶ **peanut**

P

PEAPOD n pod of the pea plant

PEAPODS ▷ peapod

PEAR n sweet juicy fruit with a narrow top and rounded base

PEARCE old spelling of ▷ **pierce**

PEARCED ▷ pearce

PEARCES ▷ pearce

PEARE obsolete spelling of ▷ **pear**

PEARES ▷ peare

PEARL same as ▷ **purl**

PEARLED ▷ pearl

PEARLER n person who dives for or trades in pearls ▷ adj excellent

PEARLIN n type of lace used to trim clothes

PEARLS ▷ pearl

PEARLY adj resembling a pearl, esp in lustre ▷ n London costermonger who wears on ceremonial occasions a traditional dress of dark clothes covered with pearl buttons

PEARS ▷ pear

PEARST archaic variant of ▷ **pierced**

PEART adj lively

PEARTER ▷ peart

PEARTLY ▷ peart

PEAS ▷ pea

PEASANT n person working on the land, esp in poorer countries or in the past

PEASCOD same as ▷ **cod**

PEASE n archaic or dialect word for pea ▷ vb appease

PEASED ▷ pease

PEASEN obsolete plural of ▷ **pease**

PEASES ▷ pease

PEASING ▷ pease

PEASON obsolete plural of ▷ **pease**

PEAT n decayed vegetable material found in bogs, used as fertilizer or fuel

PEATARY n area covered with peat

PEATERY same as ▷ **peatary**

PEATIER ▷ peat

PEATMAN n person who collects peat

PEATMEN ▷ peatman

PEATS ▷ peat

PEATY ▷ peat

PEAVEY n wooden lever with a metal pointed end

and a hinged hook, used for handling logs

PEAVEYS ▷ peavey

PEAVIES ▷ peavy

PEAVY same as ▷ **peavey**

PEAZE same as ▷ **pease**

PEAZED ▷ peaze

PEAZES ▷ peaze

PEAZING ▷ peaze

PEBA n type of armadillo

PEBAS ▷ peba

PEBBLE n small roundish stone ▷ vb cover with pebbles

PEBBLED ▷ pebble

PEBBLES ▷ pebble

PEBBLY ▷ pebble

PEBRINE n disease of silkworms

PEC n pectoral muscle

PECAN n edible nut of a N American tree

PECANS ▷ pecan

PECCANT adj guilty of an offence

PECCARY n piglike animal of American forests

PECCAVI n confession of guilt

PECH Scottish word for ▷ **pant**

PECHAN Scots word for ▷ **stomach**

PECHANS ▷ pechan

PECHED ▷ pech

PECHING ▷ pech

PECHS ▷ pech

PECK vb strike or pick up with the beak ▷ n pecking movement

PECKE n quarter of bushel

PECKED ▷ peck

PECKES ▷ pecke

PECKIER ▷ pecky

PECKING ▷ peck

PECKISH adj slightly hungry

PECKS ▷ peck

PECKY adj discoloured

PECS pl n pectoral muscles

PECTASE n enzyme occurring in certain ripening fruits

PECTATE n salt or ester of pectic acid

PECTEN n comblike structure in the eye of birds and reptiles

PECTENS ▷ pecten

PECTIC ▷ pectin

PECTIN n substance in fruit that makes jam set

PECTINS ▷ pectin

PECTISE same as ▷ **pectize**

PECTIZE vb change into a jelly

PECTOSE n insoluble carbohydrate found in the cell walls of unripe fruit that is converted to pectin by enzymic processes

PECULIA > peculium

PED n pannier

PEDAGOG same as > **pedagogue**

PEDAL n foot-operated lever used to control a vehicle or machine, or to modify the tone of a musical instrument ▷ vb propel (a bicycle) by using its pedals ▷ adj of or relating to the foot or the feet

PEDALED ▷ pedal

PEDALER ▷ pedal

PEDALO n pleasure craft driven by pedal-operated paddle wheels

PEDALOS ▷ pedalo

PEDALS ▷ pedal

PEDANT n person who is excessively concerned with details and rules, esp in academic work

PEDANTS ▷ pedant

PEDATE adj (of a plant leaf) divided into several lobes arising at a common point, the lobes often being stalked and the lateral lobes sometimes divided into smaller lobes

PEDDER old form of ▷ **pedlar**

PEDDERS ▷ pedder

PEDDLE vb sell (goods) from door to door

PEDDLED ▷ peddle

PEDDLER same as ▷ **pedlar**

PEDDLES ▷ peddle

PEDES ▷ pes

PEDESES ▷ pedesis

PEDESIS n random motion of small particles

PEDETIC adj of feet

PEDICAB n pedal-operated tricycle, available for hire, with an attached seat for one or two passengers

PEDICEL n stalk bearing a single flower of an inflorescence

PEDICLE n any small stalk

PEDLAR n person who sells goods from door to door

PEDLARS ▷ pedlar

PEDLARY same as ▷ **pedlery**

PEDLER same as ▶ **pedlar**
PEDLERS ▶ **pedler**
PEDLERY n business of pedler
PEDOCAL n type of zonal soil that is rich in lime and characteristic of relatively dry areas
PEDRAIL n device replacing wheel on rough surfaces
PEDRERO n type of cannon
PEDRO n card game
PEDROS ▶ **pedro**
PEDS ▶ **ped**
PEE vb urinate ▷ n urine
PEEBEEN n type of large evergreen
PEECE obsolete variant of ▶ **piece**
PEECES ▶ **peece**
PEEK n peep or glance ▷ vb glance quickly or secretly
PEEKABO same as > **peekaboo**
PEEKED ▶ **peek**
PEEKING ▶ **peek**
PEEKS ▶ **peek**
PEEL vb remove the skin or rind of (a vegetable or fruit) ▷ n rind or skin
PEELED ▶ **peel**
PEELER n special knife or mechanical device for peeling vegetables, fruit, etc
PEELERS ▶ **peeler**
PEELING n strip of skin, rind, bark, etc, that has been peeled off
PEELS ▶ **peel**
PEEN n end of a hammer head opposite the striking face, often rounded or wedge-shaped ▷ vb strike with the peen of a hammer or with a stream of metal shot in order to bend or shape (a sheet of metal)
PEENED ▶ **peen**
PEENGE vb complain
PEENGED ▶ **peenge**
PEENGES ▶ **peenge**
PEENING ▶ **peen**
PEENS ▶ **peen**
PEEOY n homemade firework
PEEOYS ▶ **peeoy**
PEEP vb look slyly or quickly ▷ n peeping look
PEEPE old spelling of ▶ **pip**
PEEPED ▶ **peep**
PEEPER n person who peeps
PEEPERS ▶ **peeper**

PEEPES archaic spelling of ▶ **peeps**
PEEPING ▶ **peep**
PEEPS ▶ **peep**
PEEPUL n Indian moraceous tree
PEEPULS ▶ **peepul**
PEER n (in Britain) member of the nobility ▷ vb look closely and intently
PEERAGE n whole body of peers
PEERED ▶ **peer**
PEERESS n (in Britain) woman holding the rank of a peer
PEERIE n spinning top ▷ adj small
PEERIER ▶ **peerie**
PEERIES ▶ **peerie**
PEERING ▶ **peer**
PEERS ▶ **peer**
PEERY n child's spinning top
PEES ▶ **pee**
PEEVE vb irritate or annoy ▷ n something that irritates
PEEVED ▶ **peeve**
PEEVER n hopscotch
PEEVERS ▶ **peever**
PEEVES ▶ **peeve**
PEEVING ▶ **peeve**
PEEVISH adj fretful or irritable
PEEWEE same as ▶ **pewee**
PEEWEES ▶ **peewee**
PEEWIT same as ▶ **lapwing**
PEEWITS ▶ **peewit**
PEG n pin or clip for joining, fastening, marking, etc ▷ vb fasten with pegs
PEGASUS n winged horse
PEGBOX n part of stringed instrument that holds tuning pegs
PEGGED ▶ **peg**
PEGGIES ▶ **peggy**
PEGGING ▶ **peg**
PEGGY n type of small warbler
PEGH same as ▶ **pech**
PEGHED ▶ **pegh**
PEGHING ▶ **pegh**
PEGHS ▶ **pegh**
PEGLESS ▶ **peg**
PEGLIKE ▶ **peg**
PEGS ▶ **peg**
PEH ▶ **pe**
PEHS ▶ **peh**
PEIN same as ▶ **peen**
PEINCT vb paint
PEINCTS ▶ **peinct**
PEINED ▶ **pein**
PEINING ▶ **pein**

PEINS ▶ **pein**
PEISE same as ▶ **peize**
PEISED ▶ **peise**
PEISES ▶ **peise**
PEISHWA n Indian leader
PEISING ▶ **peise**
PEIZE vb weight or poise
PEIZED ▶ **peize**
PEIZES ▶ **peize**
PEIZING ▶ **peize**
PEKAN n large North American marten
PEKANS ▶ **pekan**
PEKE n Pekingese dog
PEKEPOO same as > **pekepoo**
PEKES ▶ **peke**
PEKIN n silk fabric
PEKINS ▶ **pekin**
PEKOE n high-quality tea made from the downy tips of the young buds of the tea plant
PEKOES ▶ **pekoe**
PEL n pixel
PELA n insect living on wax
PELAGE n coat of a mammal, consisting of hair, wool, fur, etc
PELAGES ▶ **pelage**
PELAGIC adj of or relating to the open sea ▷ n any pelagic creature
PELAS ▶ **pela**
PELE Spenserian variant of ▶ **peal**
PELES ▶ **pele**
PELF n money or wealth
PELFS ▶ **pelf**
PELHAM n horse's bit for a double bridle, less severe than a curb but more severe than a snaffle
PELHAMS ▶ **pelham**
PELICAN n large water bird with a pouch beneath its bill for storing fish
PELISSE n cloak or loose coat which is usually fur-trimmed
PELITE n any argillaceous rock such as shale
PELITES ▶ **pelite**
PELITIC ▶ **pelite**
PELL n hide of an animal
PELLACH same as ▶ **pellack**
PELLACK n porpoise
PELLET n small ball of something ▷ vb strike with pellets
PELLETS ▶ **pellet**
PELLOCK n porpoise
PELLS ▶ **pell**

P

PELLUM *n* dust
PELLUMS ▶ **pellum**
PELMA *n* sole of the foot
PELMAS ▶ **pelma**
PELMET *n* ornamental drapery or board, concealing a curtain rail
PELMETS ▶ **pelmet**
PELOID *n* mud used therapeutically
PELOIDS ▶ **peloid**
PELON *adj* hairless
PELORIA *n* abnormal production of actinomorphic flowers in a plant of a species that usually produces zygomorphic flowers
PELORIC ▶ **peloria**
PELORUS *n* sighting device used in conjunction with a magnetic compass or a gyrocompass for measuring the relative bearings of observed points
PELORY *n* floral mutation
PELOTA *n* game played by two players who use a basket strapped to their wrists or a wooden racket to propel a ball against a specially marked wall
PELOTAS ▶ **pelota**
PELOTON *n* main field of riders in a road race
PELS ▶ **pel**
PELT *vb* throw missiles at ▷ *n* skin of a fur-bearing animal
PELTA *n* small ancient shield
PELTAE ▶ **pelta**
PELTAS ▶ **pelta**
PELTAST *n* (in ancient Greece) lightly armed foot soldier
PELTATE *adj* (of leaves) having the stalk attached to the centre of the lower surface
PELTED ▶ **pelt**
PELTER *vb* rain heavily
PELTERS ▶ **pelt**
PELTING ▶ **pelt**
PELTRY *n* pelts of animals collectively
PELTS ▶ **pelt**
PELVES ▶ **pelvis**
PELVIC *adj* of, near, or relating to the pelvis ▷ *n* pelvic bone
PELVICS ▶ **pelvic**
PELVIS *n* framework of bones at the base of the

spine, to which the hips are attached
PEMBINA *n* type of cranberry
PEMICAN *same as* > **pemmican**
PEMPHIX *n* type of crustacean
PEN *n* instrument for writing in ink ▷ *vb* write or compose
PENAL *adj* of or used in punishment
PENALLY ▶ **penal**
PENALTY *n* punishment for a crime or offence
PENANCE *n* voluntary self-punishment to make amends for wrongdoing ▷ *vb* (of ecclesiastical authorities) impose a penance upon (a sinner)
PENANG *same as* ▶ **pinang**
PENANGS ▶ **penang**
PENATES *pl n* household gods .
PENCE ▶ **penny**
PENCEL *n* small pennon, originally one carried by a knight's squire
PENCELS ▶ **pencel**
PENCES ▶ **penny**
PENCIL *n* thin cylindrical instrument containing graphite, for writing or drawing ▷ *vb* draw, write, or mark with a pencil
PENCILS ▶ **pencil**
PEND *vb* await judgment or settlement ▷ *n* archway or vaulted passage
PENDANT *n* ornament worn on a chain round the neck
PENDED ▶ **pend**
PENDENT *adj* hanging ▷ *n* pendant
PENDING *prep* while waiting for ▷ *adj* not yet decided or settled
PENDS ▶ **pend**
PENDU *adj* in informal Indian English, culturally backward
PENDULE *n* manoeuvre by which a climber on a rope from above swings in a pendulum-like series of movements to reach another line of ascent
PENE *same as* ▶ **peen**
PENED ▶ **pene**
PENES ▶ **penis**

PENFOLD *same as* ▶ **pinfold**
PENFUL *n* contents of pen
PENFULS ▶ **penful**
PENGO *n* standard monetary unit of Hungary, replaced by the forint in 1946
PENGOS ▶ **pengo**
PENGUIN *n* flightless black-and-white sea bird of the southern hemisphere
PENI *old spelling of* ▶ **penny**
PENIAL ▶ **penis**
PENICIL *n* small pad for wounds
PENIE *old spelling of* ▶ **penny**
PENIES ▶ **penie**
PENILE *adj* of or relating to the penis
PENILL > **penillion**
PENING ▶ **pene**
PENIS *n* organ of copulation and urination in male mammals
PENISES ▶ **penis**
PENK *n* small fish
PENKS ▶ **penk**
PENLITE *same as* > **penlight**
PENMAN *n* person skilled in handwriting
PENMEN ▶ **penman**
PENNA *n* any large feather that has a vane and forms part of the main plumage of a bird
PENNAE ▶ **penna**
PENNAL *n* first-year student of Protestant university
PENNALS ▶ **pennal**
PENNAME *n* author's pseudonym
PENNANT *same as* ▶ **pendant**
PENNATE *adj* having feathers, wings, or winglike structures
PENNE *n* pasta in the form of short tubes
PENNED ▶ **pen**
PENNER *n* person who writes
PENNERS ▶ **penner**
PENNES ▶ **penne**
PENNI *n* former Finnish monetary unit worth one hundredth of a markka
PENNIA ▶ **penni**
PENNIED *adj* having money
PENNIES ▶ **penny**
PENNILL *n* stanza in a Welsh poem
PENNINE *n* mineral found in the Pennine Alps

PENNING ▸ **pen**
PENNIS ▸ **penni**
PENNON *n* triangular or tapering flag
PENNONS ▸ **pennon**
PENNY *n* British bronze coin worth one hundredth of a pound
PENOCHE *n* type of fudge
PENS ▸ **pen**
PENSEE *n* thought put down on paper
PENSEES ▸ **pensee**
PENSEL *same as* ▸ **pencel**
PENSELS ▸ **pensel**
PENSIL *same as* ▸ **pencel**
PENSILE *adj* designating or building a hanging nest
PENSILS ▸ **pensil**
PENSION *n* regular payment to people above a certain age, retired employees, widows, etc ▸ *vb* grant a pension to
PENSIVE *adj* deeply thoughtful, often with a tinge of sadness
PENSTER *n* writer
PENSUM *n* school exercise
PENSUMS ▸ **pensum**
PENT *n* penthouse
PENTACT *n* sponge spicule with five rays
PENTAD *n* group or series of five
PENTADS ▸ **pentad**
PENTANE *n* alkane hydrocarbon with three isomers
PENTENE *n* colourless flammable liquid alkene with several straight-chained isomeric forms
PENTHIA *n* child born fifth
PENTICE *vb* accommodate in a penthouse
PENTISE *same as* ▸ **pentice**
PENTITI ▸ **pentito**
PENTITO *n* person involved in organized crime who offers information to the police in return for immunity from prosecution
PENTODE *n* electronic valve having five electrodes: a cathode, anode, and three grids
PENTOSE *n* monosaccharide containing five atoms of carbon per molecule
PENTS ▸ **pent**
PENTYL *n* one of a

particular chemical group
PENTYLS ▸ **pentyl**
PENUCHE *same as* ▸ **panocha**
PENUCHI *same as* ▸ **panocha**
PENULT *n* last syllable but one in a word
PENULTS ▸ **penult**
PENURY *n* extreme poverty
PEON *n* Spanish-American farm labourer or unskilled worker
PEONAGE *n* state of being a peon
PEONES ▸ **peon**
PEONIES ▸ **peony**
PEONISM *same as* ▸ **peonage**
PEONS ▸ **peon**
PEONY *n* garden plant with showy red, pink, or white flowers
PEOPLE *pl n* persons generally ▸ *vb* provide with inhabitants
PEOPLED ▸ **people**
PEOPLER *n* settler
PEOPLES ▸ **people**
PEP *n* high spirits, energy, or enthusiasm ▸ *vb* liven by imbuing with new vigour
PEPFUL *adj* full of vitality
PEPINO *n* purple-striped yellow fruit
PEPINOS ▸ **pepino**
PEPLA ▸ **peplum**
PEPLOS *n* (in ancient Greece) top part of a woman's attire, caught at the shoulders and hanging in folds to the waist
PEPLUM *same as* ▸ **peplos**
PEPLUMS ▸ **peplum**
PEPLUS *same as* ▸ **peplos**
PEPO *n* fruit such as the melon, squash, cucumber, or pumpkin
PEPOS ▸ **pepo**
PEPPED ▸ **pep**
PEPPER *n* sharp hot condiment made from the fruit of an East Indian climbing plant ▸ *vb* season with pepper
PEPPERS ▸ **pepper**
PEPPERY *adj* tasting of pepper
PEPPIER ▸ **peppy**
PEPPILY ▸ **peppy**
PEPPING ▸ **pep**
PEPPY *adj* full of vitality
PEPS ▸ **pep**

PEPSIN *n* enzyme produced in the stomach, which, when activated by acid, breaks down proteins
PEPSINE *same as* ▸ **pepsin**
PEPSINS ▸ **pepsin**
PEPTALK *n* talk meant to inspire ▸ *vb* give a peptalk to
PEPTIC *adj* relating to digestion or the digestive juices ▸ *n* substance that aids digestion
PEPTICS ▸ **peptic**
PEPTID *same as* ▸ **peptide**
PEPTIDE *n* compound consisting of two or more amino acids linked by chemical bonding between the amino group of one and the carboxyl group of another
PEPTIDS ▸ **peptid**
PEPTISE *same as* ▸ **peptize**
PEPTIZE *vb* disperse (a substance) into a colloidal state, usually to form a sol
PEPTONE *n* any of a group of compounds that form an intermediary group in the digestion of proteins to amino acids
PER *prep* for each
PERACID *n* acid, such as perchloric acid, in which the element forming the acid radical exhibits its highest valency
PERAEA ▸ **peraeon**
PERAEON *same as* ▸ **pereion**
PERAI *another name for* ▸ **piranha**
PERAIS ▸ **perai**
PERCALE *n* close-textured woven cotton fabric, plain or printed, used esp for sheets
PERCASE *adv* perchance
PERCE *obsolete word for* ▸ **pierce**
PERCED ▸ **perce**
PERCEN ▸ **perce**
PERCENT *n* percentage or proportion
PERCEPT *n* concept that depends on recognition by the senses, such as sight, of some external object or phenomenon
PERCES ▸ **perce**
PERCH *n* resting place for a bird ▸ *vb* alight, rest, or

place on or as if on a perch

PERCHED ▶ perch

PERCHER ▶ perch

PERCHES ▶ perch

PERCINE adj of perches

PERCING ▶ perce

PERCOCT adj well-cooked

PERCOID n type of spiny-finned teleost fish

PERCUSS vb strike sharply, rapidly, or suddenly

PERDIE adv certainly

PERDU adj (of a soldier) placed on hazardous sentry duty ▷ n soldier placed on hazardous sentry duty

PERDUE same as ▶ perdu

PERDUES ▶ perdue

PERDURE vb last for long time

PERDUS ▶ perdu

PERDY adv certainly

PERE n addition to a French surname to specify the father rather than the son of the same name

PEREA ▶ pereon

PEREGAL adj equal ▷ n equal

PEREIA ▶ pereion

PEREION n thorax of some crustaceans

PEREIRA n bark of a South American apocynaceous tree

PERENTY same as > perentie

PEREON same as ▶ pereion

PEREONS ▶ pereon

PERES ▶ pere

PERFAY interj by my faith

PERFECT adj having all the essential elements ▷ n perfect tense ▷ vb improve

PERFET obsolete variant of ▶ perfect

PERFIDY n perfidious act

PERFIN former name for ▶ spif

PERFING n practice of taking early retirement, with financial compensation, from the police force

PERFINS ▶ perfin

PERFORM vb carry out (an action)

PERFUME n liquid cosmetic worn for its pleasant smell ▷ vb give a pleasant smell to

PERFUMY adj like perfume

PERFUSE vb permeate (a liquid, colour, etc) through

or over (something)

PERGOLA n arch or framework of trellis supporting climbing plants

PERHAPS adv possibly, maybe ▷ sentence substitute it may happen, be so, etc ▷ n something that might have happened

PERI n (in Persian folklore) one of a race of beautiful supernatural beings

PERIAPT n charm or amulet

PERICON n Argentinian dance

PERIDIA > peridium

PERIDOT n pale green transparent gemstone

PERIGEE n point in the orbit of the moon or a satellite that is nearest the earth

PERIGON n angle of 360°

PERIL n great danger ▷ vb expose to danger

PERILED ▶ peril

PERILLA n type of mint

PERILS ▶ peril

PERINEA ▶ perineum

PERIOD n particular portion of time ▷ adj (of furniture, dress, a play, etc) dating from or in the style of an earlier time ▷ vb divide into periods

PERIODS ▶ period

PERIOST n thick fibrous two-layered membrane covering the surface of bones

PERIQUE n strong highly-flavoured tobacco cured in its own juices and grown in Louisiana

PERIS ▶ peri

PERISH vb be destroyed or die

PERITI ▶ peritus

PERITUS n Catholic theology consultant

PERIWIG same as ▶ peruke

PERJINK adj prim or finicky

PERJURE vb render (oneself) guilty of perjury

PERJURY n act or crime of lying while under oath in a court

PERK n incidental benefit gained from a job, such as a company car ▷ adj pert ▷ vb (of coffee) percolate

PERKED ▶ perk

PERKIER ▶ perky

PERKILY ▶ perky

PERKIN same as ▶ parkin

PERKING ▶ perk

PERKINS ▶ perkin

PERKISH adj perky

PERKS ▶ perk

PERKY adj lively or cheerful

PERLITE n variety of obsidian consisting of masses of small pearly globules

PERLOUS same as > perilous

PERM n long-lasting curly hairstyle produced by treating the hair with chemicals ▷ vb give (hair) a perm

PERMED ▶ perm

PERMIAN adj of, denoting, or formed in the last period of the Palaeozoic era

PERMIE n person, esp an office worker, employed by a firm on a permanent basis

PERMIES ▶ permie

PERMING ▶ perm

PERMIT vb give permission, allow ▷ n document giving permission to do something

PERMITS ▶ permit

PERMS ▶ perm

PERMUTE vb change the sequence of

PERN n type of buzzard

PERNIO n chilblain

PERNOD n aniseed-flavoured aperitif from France

PERNODS ▶ pernod

PERNS ▶ pern

PEROGI n type of Polish dumpling

PERONE n fibula

PERONES ▶ perone

PERORAL adj administered through mouth

PEROXID same as > peroxide

PEROXO n type of acid

PEROXY adj containing the peroxide group

PERP n informal US and Canadian word for someone who has committed a crime

PERPEND n large stone that passes through a wall from one side to the other ▷ vb ponder

PERPENT same as ▶ perpend

PERPLEX vb puzzle, bewilder

PERPS ▶ perp
PERRIER n short mortar
PERRIES ▶ perry
PERRON n external flight of steps, esp one at the front entrance of a building
PERRONS ▶ perron
PERRY n alcoholic drink made from fermented pears
PERSALT n any salt of a peracid
PERSANT adj piercing
PERSE old variant of ▶ pierce
PERSES ▶ perse
PERSICO same as > persicot
PERSING ▶ perse
PERSIST vb continue to be or happen, last
PERSON n human being
PERSONA n someone's personality as presented to others
PERSONS ▶ person
PERSPEX n tradename for any of various clear acrylic resins, used chiefly as a substitute for glass
PERST adj perished
PERSUE obsolete form of ▶ pursue
PERSUED ▶ persue
PERSUES ▶ persue
PERT adj saucy and cheeky ▷ n pert person
PERTAIN vb belong or be relevant (to)
PERTAKE obsolete form of ▶ partake
PERTER ▶ pert
PERTEST ▶ pert
PERTLY ▶ pert
PERTOOK ▶ pertake
PERTS ▶ pert
PERTURB vb disturb greatly
PERTUSE adj having holes
PERUKE n wig for men worn in the 17th and 18th centuries
PERUKED adj wearing wig
PERUKES ▶ peruke
PERUSAL ▶ peruse
PERUSE vb read in a careful or leisurely manner
PERUSED ▶ peruse
PERUSER ▶ peruse
PERUSES ▶ peruse
PERV n pervert ▷ vb give a person an erotic look
PERVADE vb spread right through (something)
PERVE same as ▶ perv
PERVED ▶ perv

PERVERT vb use or alter for a wrong purpose ▷ n person who practises sexual perversion
PERVES ▶ perv
PERVIER ▶ pervy
PERVING ▶ perv
PERVS ▶ perv
PERVY adj perverted
PES n animal part corresponding to the human foot
PESADE n position in which the horse stands on the hind legs with the forelegs in the air
PESADES ▶ pesade
PESANT obsolete spelling of ▶ peasant
PESANTE adv to be performed clumsily
PESANTS ▶ pesant
PESAUNT obsolete spelling of ▶ peasant
PESETA n former monetary unit of Spain
PESETAS ▶ peseta
PESEWA n Ghanaian monetary unit worth one hundredth of a cedi
PESEWAS ▶ pesewa
PESHWA same as ▶ peishwa
PESHWAS ▶ peshwa
PESKIER ▶ pesky
PESKILY ▶ pesky
PESKY adj troublesome
PESO n monetary unit of Argentina, Mexico, etc
PESOS ▶ peso
PESSARY n appliance worn in the vagina, either to prevent conception or to support the womb
PESSIMA n lowest point
PEST n annoying person
PESTER vb annoy or nag continually
PESTERS ▶ pester
PESTFUL adj causing annoyance
PESTIER ▶ pesty
PESTLE n club-shaped implement for grinding things to powder in a mortar ▷ vb pound (a substance or object) with or as if with a pestle
PESTLED ▶ pestle
PESTLES ▶ pestle
PESTO n sauce for pasta, consisting of basil leaves, pine nuts, garlic, oil, and Parmesan cheese, all

crushed together
PESTOS ▶ pesto
PESTS ▶ pest
PESTY adj persistently annoying
PET n animal kept for pleasure and companionship ▷ adj kept as a pet ▷ vb treat as a pet
PETAL n one of the brightly coloured outer parts of a flower
PETALED ▶ petal
PETALS ▶ petal
PETAR obsolete variant of ▶ petard
PETARA n clothes basket
PETARAS ▶ petara
PETARD n device containing explosives used to breach a wall, doors, etc
PETARDS ▶ petard
PETARS ▶ petar
PETARY n weapon for hurling stones
PETASOS same as ▶ petasus
PETASUS n broad-brimmed hat worn by the ancient Greeks
PETCOCK n small valve for checking the water level in a steam boiler or draining condensed steam from the cylinder of a steam engine
PETER vb fall (off) in volume, intensity, etc, and finally cease ▷ n act of petering
PETERED ▶ peter
PETERS ▶ peter
PETHER old variant of ▶ pedlar
PETHERS ▶ pether
PETIOLE n stalk which attaches a leaf to a plant
PETIT adj of little or lesser importance
PETITE adj (of a woman) small and dainty ▷ n clothing size for small women
PETITES ▶ petite
PETNAP vb steal pet
PETNAPS ▶ petnap
PETRALE n type of sole
PETRARY n weapon for hurling stones
PETRE same as > saltpetre
PETREL n sea bird with a hooked bill and tubular nostrils
PETRELS ▶ petrel
PETRES ▶ petre

P

PETRI n as in **petri dish** shallow glass dish used for cultures of bacteria

PETRIFY vb frighten severely

PETROL n flammable liquid obtained from petroleum, used as fuel in internal-combustion engines ▷ vb supply with petrol

PETROLS ▶ petrol

PETROUS adj denoting the dense part of the temporal bone that surrounds the inner ear

PETS ▶ pet

PETSAI n Chinese cabbage

PETSAIS ▶ petsai

PETTED ▶ pet

PETTER ▶ pet

PETTERS ▶ pet

PETTI ▶ petto

PETTIER ▶ petty

PETTIES ▶ petti

PETTILY ▶ petty

PETTING ▶ pet

PETTISH adj peevish or fretful

PETTLE vb pat animal

PETTLED ▶ pettle

PETTLES ▶ pettle

PETTO n breast of animal

PETTY adj unimportant, trivial

PETUNIA n garden plant with funnel-shaped flowers

PEW n fixed benchlike seat in a church

PEWEE n small N American flycatcher with a greenish-brown plumage

PEWEES ▶ pewee

PEWIT another name for ▶ lapwing

PEWITS ▶ pewit

PEWS ▶ pew

PEWTER n greyish metal made of tin and lead

PEWTERS ▶ pewter

PEYOTE another name for ▶ mescal

PEYOTES ▶ peyote

PEYOTL same as ▶ peyote

PEYOTLS ▶ peyotl

PEYSE vb weight or poise

PEYSED ▶ peyse

PEYSES ▶ peyse

PEYSING ▶ peyse

PEYTRAL same as ▶ peytrel

PEYTREL n breastplate of horse's armour

PEZANT obsolete spelling of ▶ peasant

PEZANTS ▶ pezant

PFENNIG n former German monetary unit worth one hundredth of a mark

PFFT interj sound indicating sudden disappearance of something

PFUI interj phooey

PHACOID adj lentil- or lens-shaped

PHAEIC adj (of animals) having dusky coloration

PHAEISM ▶ phaeic

PHAETON n light four-wheeled horse-drawn carriage with or without a top

PHAGE n virus that is parasitic in a bacterium and multiplies within its host, which is destroyed when the new viruses are released

PHAGES ▶ phage

PHALANX n closely grouped mass of people

PHALLI ▶ phallus

PHALLIC adj of or resembling a phallus

PHALLIN n poisonous substance from mushroom

PHALLUS n penis, esp as a symbol of reproductive power in primitive rites

PHANG old variant spelling of ▶ fang

PHANGED ▶ phang

PHANGS ▶ phang

PHANTOM n ghost ▷ adj deceptive or unreal

PHARAOH n ancient Egyptian king

PHARE n beacon tower

PHARES ▶ phare

PHARM vb redirect (a website user) to another, bogus website for fraudulent purposes

PHARMA n pharmaceutical companies considered together as an industry

PHARMAS ▶ pharma

PHARMED ▶ pharm

PHARMS ▶ pharm

PHAROS n lighthouse

PHARYNX n cavity forming the back part of the mouth

PHASE n any distinct or characteristic stage in a development or chain of events ▷ vb arrange or carry out in stages or to coincide with something else

PHASEAL ▶ phase

PHASED ▶ phase

PHASES ▶ phase

PHASIC ▶ phase

PHASING n tonal sweep achieved by varying the phase relationship of two similar audio signals by mechanical or electronic means

PHASIS another word for ▶ phase

PHASMID n stick insect or leaf insect

PHASOR n rotating vector representing a quantity, such as an alternating current or voltage, that varies sinusoidally

PHASORS ▶ phasor

PHAT adj terrific

PHATIC adj (of speech, esp of conversational phrases) used to establish social contact and to express sociability rather than specific meaning

PHATTER ▶ phat

PHEAZAR old variant of ▶ vizier

PHEER same as ▶ fere

PHEERE same as ▶ fere

PHEERES ▶ pheere

PHEERS ▶ pheer

PHEESE vb worry

PHEESED ▶ pheese

PHEESES ▶ pheese

PHEEZE same as ▶ pheese

PHEEZED ▶ pheeze

PHEEZES ▶ pheeze

PHELLEM technical name for ▶ cork

PHENATE n ester or salt of phenol

PHENE n genetically determined characteristic of organism

PHENES ▶ phene

PHENIC adj of phenol

PHENIX same as ▶ phoenix

PHENOL n chemical used in disinfectants and antiseptics

PHENOLS ▶ phenol

PHENOM n person or thing of outstanding abilities or qualities

PHENOMS ▶ phenom

PHENOXY modifier as in **phenoxy resin** any of a class of resins derived from polyhydroxy ethers

PHENYL n chemical substance

PHENYLS ▶ phenyl

PHEON n barbed iron head of dart

PHEONS ▶ pheon

PHESE same as ▶ **pheese**

PHESED ▶ phese

PHESES ▶ phese

PHESING ▶ phese

PHEW interj exclamation of relief, surprise, etc

PHI n 21st letter in the Greek alphabet

PHIAL n small bottle for medicine etc ▷ vb put in phial

PHIALS ▶ phial

PHILTER vb drink supposed to arouse love, desire, etc ▷ vb arouse sexual or romantic feelings by means of a philter

PHILTRA > philtrum

PHILTRE n magic drink supposed to arouse love in the person who drinks it ▷ vb mix with love potion

PHIS ▶ phi

PHIZ n face or a facial expression

PHIZES ▶ phiz

PHIZOG same as ▶ **phiz**

PHIZOGS ▶ phizog

PHIZZES ▶ phiz

PHLEGM n thick yellowish substance formed in the nose and throat during a cold

PHLEGMS ▶ phlegm

PHLEGMY ▶ phlegm

PHLOEM n plant tissue that acts as a path for the distribution of food substances to all parts of the plant

PHLOEMS ▶ phloem

PHLOMIS n plant of Phlomis genus

PHLOX n flowering garden plant

PHLOXES ▶ phlox

PHO n Vietnamese noodle soup

PHOBIA n intense and unreasoning fear or dislike

PHOBIAS ▶ phobia

PHOBIC adj of, relating to, or arising from a phobia ▷ n person suffering from a phobia

PHOBICS ▶ phobic

PHOBISM n phobia

PHOBIST ▶ phobism

PHOCA n genus of seals

PHOCAE ▶ phoca

PHOCAS ▶ phoca

PHOCINE adj of, relating to, or resembling a seal

PHOEBE n greyish-brown North American flycatcher

PHOEBES ▶ phoebe

PHOEBUS n sun

PHOENIX n legendary bird said to set fire to itself and rise anew from its ashes

PHOH same as ▶ **foh**

PHOLAS n type of bivalve mollusc

PHON n unit of loudness

PHONAL adj relating to voice

PHONATE vb articulate speech sounds, esp to cause the vocal cords to vibrate in the execution of a voiced speech sound

PHONE vb telephone ▷ n single uncomplicated speech sound

PHONED ▶ phone

PHONEME n one of the set of speech sounds in any given language that serve to distinguish one word from another

PHONER n person making a telephone call

PHONERS ▶ phoner

PHONES ▶ phone

PHONEY adj not genuine ▷ n phoney person or thing ▷ vb fake

PHONEYS ▶ phoney

PHONIC ▶ phonics

PHONICS n method of teaching people to read by training them to associate letters with their phonetic values

PHONIED ▶ phony

PHONIER ▶ phony

PHONIES ▶ phony

PHONILY ▶ phony

PHONING ▶ phone

PHONO n phonograph

PHONON n quantum of vibrational energy in the acoustic vibrations of a crystal lattice

PHONONS ▶ phonon

PHONOS ▶ phono

PHONS ▶ phon

PHONY vb fake

PHOOEY interj exclamation of scorn or contempt

PHORATE n type of insecticide

PHORESY n association in which one animal clings to another to ensure movement from place to place, as some mites use some insects

PHOS ▶ pho

PHOSSY adj as in **phossy jaw** gangrenous condition of the lower jawbone caused by prolonged exposure to phosphorus fumes

PHOT n unit of illumination equal to one lumen per square centimetre

PHOTIC adj of or concerned with light

PHOTICS n science of light

PHOTISM n sensation of light or colour caused by stimulus of another sense

PHOTO n photograph ▷ vb take a photograph of

PHOTOED ▶ photo

PHOTOG n photograph

PHOTOGS ▶ photog

PHOTON n quantum of electromagnetic radiation energy, such as light, having both particle and wave behaviour

PHOTONS ▶ photon

PHOTOS ▶ photo

PHOTS ▶ phot

PHPHT interj expressing irritation or reluctance

PHRASAL adj of, relating to, or composed of phrases

PHRASE n group of words forming a unit of meaning, esp within a sentence ▷ vb express in words

PHRASED ▶ phrase

PHRASER ▶ phrase

PHRASES ▶ phrase

PHRASY adj containing phrases

PHRATRY n group of people within a tribe who have a common ancestor

PHREAK vb hack into a telecommunications system

PHREAKS ▶ phreak

PHRENIC adj of or relating to the diaphragm ▷ n (a nerve, blood vessel, etc) located in the diaphragm

PHRENSY obsolete spelling of ▶ **frenzy**

PHT same as ▶ **phpht**

It is easy to overlook this little word, that may offer a way out when your rack seems hopelessly clogged with consonants.

PHUT vb make muffled explosive sound
PHUTS ▸ phut
PHUTTED ▸ phut
PHWOAH ▸ phwoar
PHWOAR interj expression of sexual interest or attraction
PHYLA ▸ phylum
PHYLAE ▸ phyle
PHYLAR ▸ phylum
PHYLE n tribe or clan of an ancient Greek people such as the Ionians
PHYLIC ▸ phyle
PHYLLID n leaf of a liverwort or moss
PHYLLO same as ▸ **filo**
PHYLLOS ▸ phyllo
PHYLON n tribe
PHYLUM n major taxonomic division of animals and plants that contains one or more classes
PHYSED n physical education
PHYSEDS ▸ physed
PHYSES ▸ physis
PHYSIC n medicine or drug, esp a cathartic or purge ▷ vb treat (a patient) with medicine
PHYSICS n science of the properties of matter and energy
PHYSIO n physiotherapy
PHYSIOS ▸ physio
PHYSIS n part of bone responsible for lengthening
PHYTANE n hydrocarbon found in some fossilised plant remains
PHYTIN n substance from plants used as an energy supplement
PHYTINS ▸ phytin
PHYTOID adj resembling plant
PHYTOL n alcohol used to synthesize some vitamins
PHYTOLS ▸ phytol
PHYTON n unit of plant structure, usually considered as the smallest part of the plant that is capable of growth when

detached from the parent plant
PHYTONS ▸ phyton
PI n sixteenth letter in the Greek alphabet ▷ vb spill and mix (set type) indiscriminately
PIA n innermost of the three membranes that cover the brain and the spinal cord
PIAFFE n passage done on the spot ▷ vb strut on the spot
PIAFFED ▸ piaffe
PIAFFER ▸ piaffe
PIAFFES ▸ piaffe
PIAL adj relating to pia mater
PIAN n contagious tropical skin disease
PIANI ▸ piano
PIANIC adj of piano
PIANINO n small upright piano
PIANISM n technique, skill, or artistry in playing the piano
PIANIST n person who plays the piano
PIANO n musical instrument with strings which are struck by hammers worked by a keyboard ▷ adv quietly
PIANOS ▸ piano
PIANS ▸ pian
PIARIST n member of a Roman religious order
PIAS ▸ pia
PIASABA same as > **piassava**
PIASAVA same as > **piassava**
PIASTER same as ▸ **piastre**
PIASTRE n standard monetary unit of South Vietnam, divided into 100 cents
PIAZZA n square or marketplace, esp in Italy
PIAZZAS ▸ piazza
PIAZZE ▸ piazza
PIBAL n method of measuring wind
PIBALS ▸ pibal
PIBROCH n form of bagpipe music
PIC n photograph or illustration
PICA n abnormal craving to ingest substances such as clay, dirt, and hair
PICACHO n pointed solitary mountain

PICADOR n mounted bullfighter with a lance
PICAL adj relating to pica
PICAMAR n hydrocarbon extract of beechwood tar
PICANTE adj spicy
PICARA n female adventurer
PICARAS ▸ picara
PICARO n roguish adventurer
PICAROS ▸ picaro
PICAS ▸ pica
PICCATA adj sautéed and served in a sauce containing lemon, butter, parsley and spices
PICCIES ▸ piccy
PICCOLO n small flute
PICCY n picture or photograph
PICE n former Indian coin worth one sixty-fourth of a rupee
PICENE n type of hydrocarbon
PICENES ▸ picene
PICEOUS adj of, relating to, or resembling pitch
PICINE adj relating to woodpeckers
PICK vb choose ▷ n choice
PICKAX same as ▸ **pickaxe**
PICKAXE n large pick ▷ vb use a pickaxe on (earth, rocks, etc)
PICKED ▸ pick
PICKEER vb make raid for booty
PICKER n person or thing that picks, esp that gathers fruit, crops, etc
PICKERS ▸ picker
PICKERY n petty theft
PICKET n person or group standing outside a workplace to deter would-be workers during a strike ▷ vb form a picket outside (a workplace)
PICKETS ▸ picket
PICKIER ▸ picky
PICKILY ▸ picky
PICKIN n small child
PICKING ▸ pick
PICKINS ▸ pickin
PICKLE n food preserved in vinegar or salt water ▷ vb preserve in vinegar or salt water
PICKLED adj (of food) preserved
PICKLER ▸ pickle

PICKLES ▸ pickle
PICKMAW n type of gull
PICKOFF n baseball play
PICKS ▸ pick
PICKUP n small truck with an open body and low sides
PICKUPS ▸ pickup
PICKY adj fussy
PICNIC n informal meal out of doors ▷ vb have a picnic
PICNICS ▸ picnic
PICOLIN same as ▸ **picoline**
PICONG n any teasing or satirical banter, originally a verbal duel in song
PICONGS ▸ picong
PICOT n any of pattern of small loops, as on lace ▷ vb decorate material with small loops
PICOTE adj (of material) picoted
PICOTED ▸ picot
PICOTEE n type of carnation having pale petals edged with a darker colour, usually red
PICOTS ▸ picot
PICQUET vb provide early warning of attack
PICRA n powder of aloes and canella
PICRAS ▸ picra
PICRATE n any salt or ester of picric acid, such as sodium picrate
PICRIC adj as in **picric acid** toxic sparingly soluble crystalline yellow acid
PICRITE n coarse-grained ultrabasic igneous rock consisting of olivine and augite with small amounts of plagioclase feldspar
PICS ▸ pic
PICTURE n drawing or painting ▷ vb visualize, imagine
PICUL n unit of weight, used in China, Japan, and SE Asia
PICULET n small tropical woodpecker with a short tail
PICULS ▸ picul
PIDDLE vb urinate
PIDDLED ▸ piddle
PIDDLER ▸ piddle
PIDDLES ▸ piddle
PIDDLY adj trivial
PIDDOCK n marine bivalve that bores into rock, clay, or wood
PIDGEON same as ▸ **pidgin**

PIDGIN n language, not a mother tongue, made up of elements of two or more other languages
PIDGINS ▸ pidgin
PIE n dish of meat, fruit, etc baked in pastry
PIEBALD adj (horse) with irregular black-and-white markings ▷ n black-and-white horse
PIECE n separate bit or part
PIECED ▸ piece
PIECEN vb join broken threads
PIECENS ▸ piecen
PIECER n person who mends, repairs, or joins something, esp broken threads on a loom
PIECERS ▸ piecer
PIECES ▸ piece
PIECING ▸ piece
PIED ▸ pi
PIEDISH n container for baking pies
PIEFORT same as ▸ **piedfort**
PIEHOLE n person's mouth
PIEING ▸ pie
PIEMAN n seller of pies
PIEMEN ▸ pieman
PIEND n a salient angle
PIENDS ▸ piend
PIER n platform on stilts sticking out into the sea
PIERAGE n accommodation for ships at piers
PIERCE vb make a hole in or through with a sharp instrument
PIERCED ▸ pierce
PIERCER ▸ pierce
PIERCES ▸ pierce
PIERID n type of butterfly
PIERIDS ▸ pierid
PIERIS n American or Asiatic shrub
PIEROGI n Polish dumpling
PIERROT n clown or masquerader with a whitened face, white costume, and pointed hat
PIERS ▸ pier
PIERST archaic spelling of ▸ **pierced**
PIERT n small plant with small greenish flowers
PIERTS ▸ piert
PIES ▸ pie
PIET n magpie
PIETA n sculpture, painting, or drawing of the dead Christ, supported by the

Virgin Mary
PIETAS ▸ pieta
PIETIES ▸ piety
PIETISM n exaggerated piety
PIETIST ▸ pietism
PIETS ▸ piet
PIETY n deep devotion to God and religion
PIEZO adj piezoelectric
PIFFERO n small rustic flute
PIFFLE n nonsense ▷ vb talk or behave feebly
PIFFLED ▸ piffle
PIFFLER n talker of nonsense
PIFFLES ▸ piffle
PIG n animal kept and killed for pork, ham, and bacon ▷ vb eat greedily
PIGBOAT n submarine
PIGEON n bird with a heavy body and short legs, sometimes trained to carry messages ▷ vb pigeonhole
PIGEONS ▸ pigeon
PIGFACE n creeping succulent plant with bright-coloured flowers and red fruits
PIGFEED n food for pigs
PIGFISH n grunting fish of the North American Atlantic coast
PIGGED ▸ pig
PIGGERY n place for keeping and breeding pigs
PIGGIE same as ▸ **piggy**
PIGGIER ▸ piggy
PIGGIES ▸ piggy
PIGGIN n small wooden bucket or tub
PIGGING ▸ pig
PIGGINS ▸ piggin
PIGGISH adj like a pig, esp in appetite or manners
PIGGY n child's word for a pig, esp a piglet ▷ adj like a pig, esp in appetite
PIGHT vb pierce
PIGHTED ▸ pight
PIGHTLE n small enclosure
PIGHTS ▸ pight
PIGLET n young pig
PIGLETS ▸ piglet
PIGLIKE ▸ pig
PIGLING n young pig
PIGMEAN same as ▸ **pygmaean**
PIGMEAT less common name for ▸ **pork**
PIGMENT n colouring matter, paint or dye ▷ vb

colour with pigment

PIGMIES ▶ pigmy

PIGMOID *adj* of pygmies

PIGMY *same as* ▶ **pygmy**

PIGNOLI *same as* > **pignolia**

PIGNORA ▶ pignus

PIGNUS *n* pawn or pledge

PIGNUT *n* bitter nut of any of several North American hickory trees

PIGNUTS ▶ pignut

PIGOUT *n* binge

PIGOUTS ▶ pigout

PIGPEN *same as* ▶ **pigsty**

PIGPENS ▶ pigpen

PIGS ▶ pig

PIGSKIN *n* skin of the domestic pig ▷ *adj* made of pigskin

PIGSNEY *same as* ▶ **pigsny**

PIGSNIE *same as* ▶ **pigsny**

PIGSNY *n* former pet name for girl

PIGSTY *same as* ▶ **pigpen**

PIGTAIL *n* plait of hair hanging from the back or either side of the head

PIGWASH *n* wet feed for pigs

PIGWEED *n* coarse North American amaranthaceous weed

PIING ▶ pi

PIKA *n* burrowing lagomorph mammal of mountainous regions of North America and Asia

PIKAKE *n* type of Asian vine

PIKAKES ▶ pikake

PIKAS ▶ pika

PIKAU *n* pack, knapsack, or rucksack

PIKAUS ▶ pikau

PIKE *n* large predatory freshwater fish ▷ *vb* stab or pierce using a pike ▷ *adj* (of the body position of a diver) bent at the hips but with the legs straight

PIKED ▶ pike

PIKELET *n* small thick pancake

PIKEMAN *n* (formerly) soldier armed with a pike

PIKEMEN ▶ pikeman

PIKER *n* shirker

PIKERS ▶ piker

PIKES ▶ pike

PIKI *n* bread made from blue cornmeal

PIKING ▶ pike

PIKINGS ▶ pike

PIKIS ▶ piki

PIKUL *same as* ▶ **picul**

PIKULS ▶ pikul

PILA *n* pillar-like anatomical structure

PILAF *same as* ▶ **pilau**

PILAFF *same as* ▶ **pilau**

PILAFFS ▶ pilaff

PILAFS ▶ pilaf

PILAO *same as* ▶ **pilau**

PILAOS ▶ pilao

PILAR *adj* relating to hair

PILAU *n* Middle Eastern dish of meat, fish, or poultry boiled with rice, spices, etc

PILAUS ▶ pilau

PILAW *same as* ▶ **pilau**

PILAWS ▶ pilaw

PILCH *n* outer garment, originally one made of skin

PILCHER *n* scabbard for sword

PILCHES ▶ pilch

PILCORN *n* type if oat

PILCROW *n* paragraph mark

PILE *n* number of things lying on top of each other ▷ *vb* collect into a pile

PILEA *n* artillery or gunpowder plant, which releases a cloud of pollen when shaken

PILEAS ▶ pilea

PILEATE *adj* (of birds) having a crest

PILED ▶ pile

PILEI ▶ pileus

PILEOUS *adj* hairy

PILER *n* placer of things on pile

PILERS ▶ piler

PILES *pl n* swollen veins in the rectum, haemorrhoids

PILEUM *n* top of a bird's head from the base of the bill to the occiput

PILEUP *n* multiple collision of vehicles

PILEUPS ▶ pileup

PILEUS *n* upper cap-shaped part of a mushroom or similar spore-producing body

PILFER *vb* steal in small quantities

PILFERS ▶ pilfer

PILFERY *n* theft

PILGRIM *n* person who journeys to a holy place

PILI *n* Philippine tree with edible seeds resembling almonds

PILING *n* act of driving piles

PILINGS ▶ piling

PILINUT *n* type of nut found in the Philippines

PILIS ▶ pili

PILL *n* small ball of medicine swallowed whole ▷ *vb* peel or skin (something)

PILLAGE *vb* steal property by violence in war ▷ *n* violent seizure of goods, esp in war

PILLAR *n* upright post, usu supporting a roof ▷ *vb* provide or support with pillars

PILLARS ▶ pillar

PILLAU *same as* ▶ **pilau**

PILLAUS ▶ pillau

PILLBOX *n* small box for pills

PILLED ▶ pill

PILLIE *n* pilchard

PILLIES ▶ pillie

PILLING ▶ pill

PILLION *n* seat for a passenger behind the rider of a motorcycle ▷ *adv* on a pillion ▷ *vb* ride pillion

PILLOCK *n* stupid or annoying person

PILLORY *n* frame with holes for the head and hands in which an offender was locked and exposed to public abuse ▷ *vb* ridicule publicly

PILLOW *n* stuffed cloth bag for supporting the head in bed ▷ *vb* rest as if on a pillow

PILLOWS ▶ pillow

PILLOWY ▶ pillow

PILLS ▶ pill

PILOSE *adj* covered with fine soft hairs

PILOT *n* person qualified to fly an aircraft or spacecraft ▷ *adj* experimental and preliminary ▷ *vb* act as the pilot of

PILOTED ▶ pilot

PILOTIS *pl n* posts raising a building up from the ground

PILOTS ▶ pilot

PILOUS *same as* ▶ **pilose**

PILOW *same as* ▶ **pilau**

PILOWS ▶ pilow

PILSNER *n* type of pale beer with a strong flavour of hops

PILULA *n* pill

PILULAE ▶ pilula

PILULAR ▶ pilule

PILULAS ▶ pilula
PILULE *n* small pill
PILULES ▶ pilule
PILUM *n* ancient Roman javelin
PILUS ▶ pili
PILY *adj* like wool or pile
PIMA *n* type of cotton
PIMAS ▶ pima
PIMENT *n* wine flavoured with spices
PIMENTO *same as* > **pimiento**
PIMENTS ▶ piment
PIMP *n* man who gets customers for a prostitute in return for a share of his or her earnings ▷ *vb* act as a pimp
PIMPED ▶ pimp
PIMPING ▶ pimp
PIMPLE *n* small pus-filled spot on the skin
PIMPLED ▶ pimple
PIMPLES ▶ pimple
PIMPLY ▶ pimple
PIMPS ▶ pimp
PIN *n* short thin piece of stiff wire with a point and head, for fastening things ▷ *vb* fasten with a pin
PINA *n* cone of silver amalgam
PINANG *n* areca tree
PINANGS ▶ pinang
PINAS ▶ pina
PINATA *n* papier-mâché party decoration filled with sweets, hung up during parties, and struck with a stick until it breaks open
PINATAS ▶ pinata
PINBALL *vb* ricochet
PINBONE *n* part of sirloin
PINCASE *n* case for holding pins
PINCER *vb* grip with pincers
PINCERS *pl n* tool consisting of two hinged arms, for gripping
PINCH *vb* squeeze between finger and thumb ▷ *n* act of pinching
PINCHED ▶ pinch
PINCHER ▶ pinch
PINCHES ▶ pinch
PINDAN *n* desert region of Western Australia
PINDANS ▶ pindan
PINDARI *n* former irregular Indian horseman
PINDER *n* person who impounds

PINDERS ▶ pinder
PINDOWN *n* wrestling manoeuvre
PINE *n* evergreen coniferous tree ▷ *vb* feel great longing (for)
PINEAL *adj* resembling a pine cone ▷ *n* pineal gland
PINEALS ▶ pineal
PINED ▶ pine
PINENE *n* isomeric terpene found in many essential oils
PINENES ▶ pinene
PINERY *n* place, esp a hothouse, where pineapples are grown
PINES ▶ pine
PINESAP *n* red herb of N America
PINETA ▶ pinetum
PINETUM *n* area of land where pine trees and other conifers are grown
PINEY ▶ piny
PINFALL *another name for* ▶ **fall**
PINFISH *n* small porgy of the SE North American coast of the Atlantic
PINFOLD *n* pound for stray cattle ▷ *vb* gather or confine in or as if in a pinfold
PING *n* short high-pitched sound ▷ *vb* make such a noise
PINGED ▶ ping
PINGER *n* device, esp a timer, that makes a pinging sound
PINGERS ▶ pinger
PINGING ▶ ping
PINGLE *vb* enclose small area of ground
PINGLED ▶ pingle
PINGLER ▶ pingle
PINGLES ▶ pingle
PINGO *n* mound of earth or gravel formed through pressure from a layer of water trapped between newly frozen ice and underlying permafrost in Arctic regions
PINGOES ▶ pingo
PINGOS ▶ pingo
PINGS ▶ ping
PINGUID *adj* fatty, oily, or greasy
PINGUIN *same as* ▶ **penguin**
PINHEAD *n* head of a pin
PINHOLE *n* small hole made with or as if with a pin
PINIER ▶ piny

PINIES ▶ piny
PINIEST ▶ piny
PINING ▶ pine
PINION *n* bird's wing ▷ *vb* immobilize (someone) by tying or holding his or her arms
PINIONS ▶ pinion
PINITE *n* greyish-green or brown mineral containing amorphous aluminium and potassium sulphates
PINITES ▶ pinite
PINITOL *n* compound found in pinewood
PINK *n* pale reddish colour ▷ *adj* of the colour pink ▷ *vb* (of an engine) make a metallic noise because not working properly, knock
PINKED ▶ pink
PINKEN *vb* turn pink
PINKENS ▶ pinken
PINKER *n* something that pinks
PINKERS ▶ pinker
PINKEST ▶ pink
PINKEY *n* type of ship
PINKEYE *n* acute contagious inflammation of the conjunctiva of the eye
PINKEYS ▶ pinkey
PINKIE *n* little finger
PINKIER ▶ pinky
PINKIES ▶ pinkie
PINKING ▶ pink
PINKISH ▶ pink
PINKLY ▶ pink
PINKO *n* person regarded as mildly left-wing
PINKOES ▶ pinko
PINKOS ▶ pinko
PINKS ▶ pink
PINKY *adj* of a pink colour
PINNA *n* external part of the ear
PINNACE *n* ship's boat
PINNAE ▶ pinna
PINNAL ▶ pinna
PINNAS ▶ pinna
PINNATE *adj* (of compound leaves) having leaflets growing opposite each other in pairs
PINNED ▶ pin
PINNER *n* person or thing that pins
PINNERS ▶ pinner
PINNET *n* pinnacle
PINNETS ▶ pinnet
PINNIE *same as* ▶ **pinny**
PINNIES ▶ pinnie

P

PINNING ▸ **pin**
PINNOCK n small bird
PINNOED adj held or bound by the arms
PINNULA same as ▸ **pinnule**
PINNULE n any of the lobes of a leaflet of a pinnate compound leaf, which is itself pinnately divided
PINNY informal or child's name for > **pinafore**
PINOCLE same as > **pinochle**
PINOLE n (in the southwestern United States) flour made of parched ground corn, mesquite beans, sugar, etc
PINOLES ▸ **pinole**
PINON n low-growing pine
PINONES ▸ **pinon**
PINONS ▸ **pinon**
PINOT n any of several grape varieties
PINOTS ▸ **pinot**
PINS ▸ **pin**
PINT n liquid measure, 1/8 gallon (.568 litre)
PINTA n pint of milk
PINTADA same as ▸ **pintado**
PINTADO n species of seagoing petrel
PINTAIL n greyish-brown duck with a pointed tail
PINTANO n tropical reef fish
PINTAS ▸ **pinta**
PINTLE n pin or bolt forming the pivot of a hinge
PINTLES ▸ **pintle**
PINTO adj marked with patches of white ▷ n pinto horse
PINTOES ▸ **pinto**
PINTOS ▸ **pinto**
PINTS ▸ **pint**
PINUP n picture of a sexually attractive person, esp when partially or totally undressed
PINUPS ▸ **pinup**
PINWALE n fabric with narrow ridges
PINWEED n herb with tiny flowers
PINWORK n (in needlepoint lace) fine raised stitches
PINWORM n parasitic nematode worm
PINXIT vb (he or she) painted (it): used formerly on paintings next to the artist's name
PINY same as ▸ **peony**
PINYIN n system of

romanized spelling for the Chinese language
PINYON n low-growing pine
PINYONS ▸ **pinyon**
PIOLET n type of ice axe
PIOLETS ▸ **piolet**
PION n any of three subatomic particles which are classified as mesons
PIONED adj abounding in marsh marigolds
PIONEER n explorer or early settler of a new country ▷ vb be the pioneer or leader of
PIONER obsolete spelling of ▸ **pioneer**
PIONERS ▸ **pioner**
PIONEY same as ▸ **peony**
PIONEYS ▸ **pioney**
PIONIC ▸ **pion**
PIONIES ▸ **piony**
PIONING n work of pioneers
PIONS ▸ **pion**
PIONY same as ▸ **peony**
PIOPIO n New Zealand thrush, thought to be extinct
PIOPIOS ▸ **piopio**
PIOSITY n grandiose display of piety
PIOTED adj pied
PIOUS adj deeply religious, devout
PIOUSLY ▸ **pious**
PIOY same as ▸ **peeoy**
PIOYE same as ▸ **peeoy**
PIOYES ▸ **pioye**
PIOYS ▸ **pioy**
PIP n small seed in a fruit ▷ vb chirp
PIPA n tongueless S American toad that carries its young in pits in the skin of its back
PIPAGE n pipes collectively
PIPAGES ▸ **pipage**
PIPAL same as ▸ **peepul**
PIPALS ▸ **pipal**
PIPAS ▸ **pipa**
PIPE n tube for conveying liquid or gas ▷ vb play on a pipe
PIPEAGE same as ▸ **pipage**
PIPED ▸ **pipe**
PIPEFUL ▸ **pipe**
PIPER n player on a pipe or bagpipes
PIPERIC > **piperine**
PIPERS ▸ **piper**
PIPES ▸ **pipe**
PIPET same as ▸ **pipette**
PIPETS ▸ **pipet**

PIPETTE n slender glass tube used to transfer or measure fluids ▷ vb transfer or measure out (a liquid) using a pipette
PIPI n edible mollusc often used as bait
PIPIER ▸ **pipe**
PIPIEST ▸ **pipe**
PIPING n system of pipes
PIPINGS ▸ **piping**
PIPIS ▸ **pipi**
PIPIT n small brownish songbird
PIPITS ▸ **pipit**
PIPKIN same as ▸ **piggin**
PIPKINS ▸ **pipkin**
PIPLESS ▸ **pip**
PIPPED ▸ **pip**
PIPPIER ▸ **pippy**
PIPPIN n type of eating apple
PIPPING ▸ **pip**
PIPPINS ▸ **pippin**
PIPPY adj containing many pips
PIPS ▸ **pip**
PIPUL n Indian fig tree
PIPULS ▸ **pipul**
PIPY ▸ **pipe**
PIQUANT adj having a pleasant spicy taste
PIQUE n feeling of hurt pride, baffled curiosity, or resentment ▷ vb hurt the pride of
PIQUED ▸ **pique**
PIQUES ▸ **pique**
PIQUET n card game for two ▷ vb play game of piquet
PIQUETS ▸ **piquet**
PIQUING ▸ **pique**
PIR n Sufi master
PIRACY n robbery on the seas
PIRAGUA same as ▸ **pirogue**
PIRAI n large S American fish
PIRAIS ▸ **pirai**
PIRANA same as ▸ **piranha**
PIRANAS ▸ **pirana**
PIRANHA n small fierce freshwater fish of tropical America
PIRATE n sea robber ▷ vb sell or reproduce (artistic work etc) illegally
PIRATED ▸ **pirate**
PIRATES ▸ **pirate**
PIRATIC ▸ **pirate**
PIRAYA same as ▸ **pirai**
PIRAYAS ▸ **piraya**
PIRL n ripple in water

PIRLS ▶ pirl
PIRN n reel or bobbin
PIRNIE n stripy nightcap
PIRNIES ▶ pirnie
PIRNIT adj striped
PIRNS ▶ pirn
PIROG n large pie filled with meat, vegetables, etc
PIROGEN n turnovers made from kneaded dough
PIROGHI ▶ pirog
PIROGI ▶ pirog
PIROGUE n any of various kinds of dugout canoes
PIROJKI same as > piroshki
PIROQUE same as ▶ pirogue
PIRS ▶ pir
PIS ▶ pi
PISCARY n place where fishing takes place
PISCINA n stone basin, with a drain, in a church or sacristy where water used at Mass is poured away
PISCINE n pond or pool
PISCO n S American brandy
PISCOS ▶ pisco
PISE n rammed earth or clay used to make floors or walls
PISES ▶ pise
PISH interj exclamation of impatience or contempt ▷ vb make this exclamation at (someone or something)
PISHED ▶ pish
PISHEOG > pishogue
PISHER n Yiddish term for small boy
PISHERS ▶ pisher
PISHES ▶ pish
PISHING ▶ pish
PISHOGE same as > pishogue
PISKIES ▶ pisky
PISKY n Cornish fairy
PISMIRE archaic or dialect word for ▶ ant
PISO n peso of the Philippines
PISOS ▶ piso
PISTE n ski slope
PISTES ▶ piste
PISTIL n seed-bearing part of a flower
PISTILS ▶ pistil
PISTOL n short-barrelled handgun ▷ vb shoot with a pistol
PISTOLE n any of various gold coins of varying value, formerly used in Europe
PISTOLS ▶ pistol
PISTON n cylindrical part in

an engine that slides to and fro in a cylinder
PISTONS ▶ piston
PISTOU n French sauce
PISTOUS ▶ pistou
PIT n deep hole in the ground ▷ vb mark with small dents or scars
PITA n any of several agave plants yielding a strong fibre
PITAPAT adv with quick light taps ▷ n such taps ▷ vb make quick light taps or beats
PITARA same as ▶ petara
PITARAH same as ▶ petara
PITARAS ▶ pitara
PITAS ▶ pita
PITAYA same as > pitahaya
PITAYAS ▶ pitaya
PITCH vb throw, hurl ▷ n area marked out for playing sport
PITCHED ▶ pitch
PITCHER n large jug with a narrow neck
PITCHES ▶ pitch
PITCHY adj full of or covered with pitch
PITEOUS adj arousing pity
PITFALL n hidden difficulty or danger
PITH n soft white lining of the rind of oranges etc ▷ vb destroy the brain and spinal cord of (a laboratory animal) by piercing or severing
PITHEAD n top of a mine shaft and the buildings and hoisting gear around it
PITHED ▶ pith
PITHFUL ▶ pith
PITHIER ▶ pithy
PITHILY ▶ pithy
PITHING ▶ pith
PITHOI ▶ pithos
PITHOS n large ceramic container for oil or grain
PITHS ▶ pith
PITHY adj short and full of meaning
PITIED ▶ pity
PITIER ▶ pity
PITIERS ▶ pity
PITIES ▶ pity
PITIETH vb as in it pitieth me archaic inflection of 'pity'
PITIFUL adj arousing pity
PITMAN n coal miner ▷ n connecting rod (in a machine)

PITMANS ▶ pitman
PITMEN ▶ pitman
PITON n metal spike used in climbing to secure a rope
PITONS ▶ piton
PITPROP n support beam in mine shaft
PITS ▶ pit
PITSAW n large saw formerly used for cutting logs into planks, operated by two men, one standing on top of the log and the other in a pit underneath it
PITSAWS ▶ pitsaw
PITTA n small brightly coloured ground-dwelling tropical bird
PITTAS ▶ pitta
PITTED ▶ pit
PITTEN adj having been put
PITTER vb make pattering sound
PITTERS ▶ pitter
PITTING ▶ pit
PITTITE n occupant of a theatre pit
PITUITA n thick nasal secretion
PITUITE n mucus
PITURI n Australian solanaceous shrub
PITURIS ▶ pituri
PITY n sympathy or sorrow for others' suffering ▷ vb feel pity for
PITYING ▶ pity
PIU adv more (quickly, softly, etc)
PIUM n stinging insect
PIUMS ▶ pium
PIUPIU n skirt made from the leaves of the New Zealand flax, worn by Māoris on ceremonial occasions
PIUPIUS ▶ piupiu
PIVOT n central shaft on which something turns ▷ vb provide with or turn on a pivot
PIVOTAL adj of crucial importance
PIVOTED ▶ pivot
PIVOTER ▶ pivot
PIVOTS ▶ pivot
PIX less common spelling of ▶ pyx
PIXEL n any of a number of very small picture elements that make up a picture, as on a visual display unit
PIXELS ▶ pixel

PIXES ▸ pix
PIXIE *n* (in folklore) fairy
PIXIES ▸ pixy
PIXY *same as* ▸ **pixie**
PIXYISH ▸ pixy
PIZAZZ *same as* ▸ **pizzazz**
PIZAZZY ▸ pizazz
PIZE *vb* strike (someone a blow)
PIZED ▸ pize
PIZES ▸ pize
PIZING ▸ pize
PIZZA *n* flat disc of dough covered with a wide variety of savoury toppings and baked
PIZZAS ▸ pizza
PIZZAZ *same as* ▸ **pzazz**
PIZZAZZ *n* attractive combination of energy and style
PIZZLE *n* penis of an animal, esp a bull
PIZZLES ▸ pizzle
PLAAS *n* farm
PLAASES ▸ plaas
PLACARD *n* notice that is carried or displayed in public ▷ *vb* attach placards to
PLACATE *vb* make (someone) stop feeling angry or upset
PLACCAT *same as* ▸ **placket**
PLACE *n* particular part of an area or space ▷ *vb* put in a particular place
PLACEBO *n* sugar pill etc given to an unsuspecting patient instead of an active drug
PLACED ▸ place
PLACER *n* surface sediment containing particles of gold or some other valuable mineral
PLACERS ▸ placer
PLACES ▸ place
PLACET *n* vote or expression of assent by saying the word *placet*
PLACETS ▸ placet
PLACID *adj* not easily excited or upset, calm
PLACING *n* method of issuing securities to the public using an intermediary, such as a stockbroking firm
PLACIT *n* decree or dictum
PLACITA > placitum
PLACITS ▸ placit
PLACK *n* small former Scottish coin

PLACKET *n* opening at the waist of a dress or skirt for buttons or zips or for access to a pocket
PLACKS ▸ plack
PLACOID *adj* platelike or flattened ▷ *n* fish with placoid scales
PLAFOND *n* ceiling, esp one having ornamentation
PLAGAL *adj* (of a cadence) progressing from the subdominant to the tonic chord, as in the *Amen* of a hymn
PLAGE *n* bright patch in the sun's chromosphere
PLAGES ▸ plage
PLAGIUM *n* crime of kidnapping
PLAGUE *n* fast-spreading fatal disease ▷ *vb* trouble or annoy continually
PLAGUED ▸ plague
PLAGUER ▸ plague
PLAGUES ▸ plague
PLAGUEY *same as* ▸ **plaguy**
PLAGUY *adj* disagreeable or vexing ▷ *adv* disagreeably or annoyingly
PLAICE *n* edible European flatfish
PLAICES ▸ plaice
PLAID *n* long piece of tartan cloth worn as part of Highland dress ▷ *vb* weave cloth into plaid
PLAIDED ▸ plaid
PLAIDS ▸ plaid
PLAIN *adj* easy to see or understand ▷ *n* large stretch of level country ▷ *adv* clearly or simply ▷ *vb* complain
PLAINED ▸ plain
PLAINER ▸ plain
PLAINLY ▸ plain
PLAINS *pl n* extensive tracts of level or almost level treeless countryside
PLAINT *n* complaint or lamentation
PLAINTS ▸ plaint
PLAIT *n* intertwined length of hair ▷ *vb* intertwine separate strands in a pattern
PLAITED ▸ plait
PLAITER ▸ plait
PLAITS ▸ plait
PLAN *n* way thought out to do or achieve something ▷ *vb* arrange beforehand

PLANAR *adj* of or relating to a plane
PLANATE *adj* having been flattened
PLANCH *vb* cover with planks
PLANCHE *same as* ▸ **planch**
PLANE *n* aeroplane ▷ *adj* perfectly flat or level ▷ *vb* glide or skim
PLANED ▸ plane
PLANER *n* machine with a cutting tool that makes repeated horizontal strokes across the surface of a workpiece
PLANERS ▸ planer
PLANES ▸ plane
PLANET *n* large body in space that revolves round the sun or another star
PLANETS ▸ planet
PLANING ▸ plane
PLANISH *vb* give a final finish to (metal) by hammering or rolling to produce a smooth surface
PLANK *n* long flat piece of sawn timber ▷ *vb* cover or provide (an area) with planks
PLANKED ▸ plank
PLANKS ▸ plank
PLANNED ▸ plan
PLANNER *n* person who makes plans, esp for the development of a town, building, etc
PLANS ▸ plan
PLANT *n* living organism that grows in the ground and has no power to move ▷ *vb* put in the ground to grow
PLANTA *n* sole of foot
PLANTAE ▸ planta
PLANTAR *adj* of, relating to, or occurring on the sole of the foot or a corresponding part
PLANTAS ▸ planta
PLANTED ▸ plant
PLANTER *n* owner of a plantation
PLANTS ▸ plant
PLANULA *n* ciliated free-swimming larva of hydrozoan coelenterates such as the hydra
PLANURY *another name for* > **planuria**
PLANXTY *n* Celtic melody for harp

PLAP *same as* ▶ **plop**
PLAPPED ▶ **plap**
PLAPS ▶ **plap**
PLAQUE *n* inscribed commemorative stone or metal plate
PLAQUES ▶ **plaque**
PLASH *same as* ▶ **pleach**
PLASHED ▶ **plash**
PLASHER *n* type of farm tool
PLASHES ▶ **plash**
PLASHET *n* small pond
PLASHY *adj* wet or marshy
PLASM *same as* ▶ **plasma**
PLASMA *n* clear liquid part of blood
PLASMAS ▶ **plasma**
PLASMIC ▶ **plasma**
PLASMID *n* small circle of bacterial DNA that is independent of the main bacterial chromosome
PLASMIN *n* proteolytic enzyme that causes fibrinolysis in blood clots
PLASMON *n* sum total of plasmagenes in a cell
PLASMS ▶ **plasm**
PLAST *archaic past participle of* ▶ **place**
PLASTE *archaic past participle of* ▶ **place**
PLASTER *n* mixture of lime, sand, etc for coating walls ▷ *vb* cover with plaster
PLASTIC *n* synthetic material that can be moulded when soft but sets in a hard long-lasting shape ▷ *adj* made of plastic
PLASTID *n* any of various small particles in the cytoplasm of the cells of plants and some animals
PLAT *n* small area of ground
PLATAN *n* plane tree
PLATANE *same as* ▶ **platan**
PLATANS ▶ **platan**
PLATE *n* shallow dish for holding food ▷ *vb* cover with a thin coating of gold, silver, or other metal
PLATEAU *n* area of level high land ▷ *vb* remain stable for a long period
PLATED *adj* coated with a layer of metal
PLATEN *n* roller of a typewriter, against which the paper is held
PLATENS ▶ **platen**
PLATER *n* person or thing

that plates
PLATERS ▶ **plater**
PLATES ▶ **plate**
PLATIER ▶ **platy**
PLATIES ▶ **platy**
PLATINA *n* alloy of platinum and several other metals, including palladium, osmium, and iridium
PLATING *n* coating of metal
PLATOON *n* smaller unit within a company of soldiers ▷ *vb* organise into platoons
PLATS ▶ **plat**
PLATTED ▶ **plat**
PLATTER *n* large dish
PLATY *adj* of, relating to, or designating rocks the constituents of which occur in flaky layers ▷ *n* small brightly coloured freshwater cyprinodont fish
PLATYPI > **platypus**
PLATYS ▶ **platy**
PLAUDIT *n* expression of enthusiastic approval
PLAY *vb* occupy oneself in (a game or recreation) ▷ *n* story performed on stage or broadcast
PLAYA *n* (in the US) temporary lake, or its dry often salty bed, in a desert basin
PLAYACT *vb* pretend or make believe
PLAYAS ▶ **playa**
PLAYBOY *n* rich man who lives only for pleasure
PLAYDAY *n* day given to play
PLAYED ▶ **play**
PLAYER *n* person who plays a game or sport
PLAYERS ▶ **player**
PLAYFUL *adj* lively
PLAYING > **play**
PLAYLET *n* short play
PLAYOFF *n* extra contest to decide the winner when two or more competitors are tied
PLAYPEN *n* small portable enclosure in which a young child can safely be left to play
PLAYS ▶ **play**
PLAZA *n* open space or square
PLAZAS ▶ **plaza**
PLEA *n* serious or urgent

request, entreaty ▷ *vb* entreat
PLEACH *vb* interlace the stems or boughs of (a tree or hedge)
PLEAD *vb* ask urgently or with deep feeling
PLEADED ▶ **plead**
PLEADER ▶ **plead**
PLEADS ▶ **plead**
PLEAED ▶ **plea**
PLEAING ▶ **plea**
PLEAS ▶ **plea**
PLEASE *vb* give pleasure or satisfaction to ▷ *adv* polite word of request
PLEASED ▶ **please**
PLEASER ▶ **please**
PLEASES ▶ **please**
PLEAT *n* fold made by doubling material back on itself ▷ *vb* arrange (material) in pleats
PLEATED ▶ **pleat**
PLEATER *n* attachment on a sewing machine that makes pleats
PLEATS ▶ **pleat**
PLEB *n* common vulgar person
PLEBBY *adj* common or vulgar
PLEBE *n* member of the lowest class at the US Naval Academy or Military Academy
PLEBEAN *old variant of* > **plebeian**
PLEBES ▶ **plebe**
PLEBIFY *vb* make plebeian
PLEBS *n* common people
PLECTRA > **plectrum**
PLECTRE *same as* > **plectrum**
PLED ▶ **plead**
PLEDGE *n* solemn promise ▷ *vb* promise solemnly
PLEDGED ▶ **pledge**
PLEDGEE *n* person to whom a pledge is given
PLEDGER *same as* ▶ **pledgor**
PLEDGES ▶ **pledge**
PLEDGET *n* small flattened pad of wool, cotton, etc, esp for use as a pressure bandage to be applied to wounds or sores
PLEDGOR *n* person who gives or makes a pledge
PLEIAD *n* brilliant or talented group, esp one with seven members
PLEIADS ▶ **pleiad**

P

PLENA ▸ plenum
PLENARY adj (of a meeting) attended by all members ▷ n book of the gospels or epistles and homilies read at the Eucharist
PLENCH n tool combining wrench and pliers
PLENIPO n plenipotentiary diplomat
PLENISH vb fill, stock, or resupply
PLENISM n philosophical theory
PLENIST ▸ plenism
PLENTY n large amount or number ▷ adj very many ▷ adv more than adequately
PLENUM n enclosure containing gas at a higher pressure than the surrounding environment
PLENUMS ▸ plenum
PLEON n abdomen of crustacean
PLEONAL adj of the abdomen of a crustacean
PLEONIC ▸ pleon
PLEONS ▸ pleon
PLEOPOD another name for > **swimmeret**
PLERION n filled-centre supernova remnant in which radiation is emitted by the centre as well as the shell
PLEROMA n abundance
PLEROME n central column in growing stem or root
PLESH n small pool
PLESHES ▸ plesh
PLESSOR same as ▸ **plexor**
PLEUCH same as ▸ **pleugh**
PLEUCHS ▸ pleuch
PLEUGH Scottish word for ▸ **plough**
PLEUGHS ▸ pleugh
PLEURA ▸ pleuron
PLEURAE ▸ pleuron
PLEURAL ▸ pleuron
PLEURAS ▸ pleuron
PLEURON n part of the cuticle of arthropods that covers the lateral surface of a body segment
PLEW n (formerly in Canada) beaver skin used as a standard unit of value in the fur trade
PLEWS ▸ plew
PLEX n shortening of multiplex

PLEXAL ▸ plexus
PLEXES ▸ plex
PLEXOR n small hammer with a rubber head for use in percussion of the chest and testing reflexes
PLEXORS ▸ plexor
PLEXURE n act of weaving together
PLEXUS n complex network of nerves or blood vessels
PLIABLE adj easily bent
PLIABLY ▸ pliable
PLIANCY ▸ pliant
PLIANT adj pliable
PLICA n folding over of parts, such as a fold of skin, muscle, peritoneum, etc
PLICAE ▸ plica
PLICAL ▸ plica
PLICATE adj having or arranged in parallel folds or ridges ▷ vb arrange into parallel folds
PLIE n classic ballet practice posture with back erect and knees bent
PLIED ▸ ply
PLIER n person who plies a trade
PLIERS pl n tool with hinged arms and jaws for gripping
PLIES ▸ ply
PLIGHT n difficult or dangerous situation
PLIGHTS ▸ plight
PLIM vb swell with water
PLIMMED ▸ plim
PLIMS ▸ plim
PLIMSOL same as > **plimsole**
PLING n (in computer jargon) an exclamation mark
PLINGS ▸ pling
PLINK n short sharp often metallic sound as of a string on a musical instrument being plucked or a bullet striking metal ▷ vb make such a sound
PLINKED ▸ plink
PLINKER ▸ plink
PLINKS ▸ plink
PLINKY adj (of a sound) short, sharp, and often metallic
PLINTH n slab forming the base of a statue, column, etc
PLINTHS ▸ plinth
PLISKIE n practical joke
PLISKY same as ▸ **pliskie**
PLISSE n fabric with a

wrinkled finish, achieved by treatment involving caustic soda
PLISSES ▸ plisse
PLOAT vb thrash
PLOATED ▸ ploat
PLOATS ▸ ploat
PLOD vb walk with slow heavy steps ▷ n act of plodding
PLODDED ▸ plod
PLODDER n person who plods, esp one who works in a slow and persevering but uninspired manner
PLODGE vb wade in water, esp the sea ▷ n act of wading
PLODGED ▸ plodge
PLODGES ▸ plodge
PLODS ▸ plod
PLOIDY n number of copies of set of chromosomes in cell
PLONG obsolete variant of ▸ **plunge**
PLONGD ▸ plong
PLONGE ▸ plunge vb
PLONGED ▸ plonge
PLONGES ▸ plonge
PLONGS ▸ plong
PLONK vb put (something) down heavily and carelessly ▷ n cheap inferior wine ▷ interj exclamation imitative of this sound
PLONKED ▸ plonk
PLONKER n stupid person
PLONKO n alcoholic, esp one who drinks wine
PLONKOS ▸ plonko
PLONKS ▸ plonk
PLONKY ▸ plonk
PLOOK same as ▸ **plouk**
PLOOKIE same as ▸ **plouky**
PLOOKS ▸ plook
PLOOKY ▸ plook
PLOP n sound of an object falling into water without a splash ▷ vb make this sound ▷ interj exclamation imitative of this sound
PLOPPED ▸ plop
PLOPS ▸ plop
PLOSION n sound of an abrupt break or closure, esp the audible release of a stop
PLOSIVE adj pronounced with a sudden release of breath ▷ n plosive consonant
PLOT n secret plan to do something illegal or wrong

▷ *vb* plan secretly, conspire
PLOTFUL ▶ plot
PLOTS ▶ plot
PLOTTED ▶ plot
PLOTTER *same as* **▶ plouter**
PLOTTIE *n* hot spiced drink
PLOTTY *adj* intricately
plotted
PLOTZ *vb* faint or collapse
PLOTZED ▶ plotz
PLOTZES ▶ plotz
PLOUGH *n* agricultural tool
for turning over soil ▷ *vb*
turn over (earth) with a
plough
PLOUGHS ▶ plough
PLOUK *n* pimple
PLOUKIE ▶ plouk
PLOUKS ▶ plouk
PLOUKY ▶ plouk
PLOUTER *same as*
▶ plowter
PLOVER *n* shore bird with a
straight bill and long
pointed wings
PLOVERS ▶ plover
PLOVERY ▶ plover
PLOW *same as* **▶ plough**
PLOWBOY *same as*
> **ploughboy**
PLOWED ▶ plow
PLOWER ▶ plow
PLOWERS ▶ plow
PLOWING ▶ plow
PLOWMAN *same as*
> **ploughman**
PLOWMEN ▶ plowman
PLOWS ▶ plow
PLOWTER *vb* work or play in
water or mud ▷ *n* act of
plowtering
PLOY *n* manoeuvre
designed to gain an
advantage ▷ *vb* form a
column from a line of
troops
PLOYED ▶ ploy
PLOYING ▶ ploy
PLOYS ▶ ploy
PLU *same as* **▶ plew**
PLUCK *vb* pull or pick off ▷ *n*
courage
PLUCKED ▶ pluck
PLUCKER ▶ pluck
PLUCKS ▶ pluck
PLUCKY *adj* brave
PLUE *same as* **▶ plew**
PLUES ▶ plue
PLUFF *vb* expel in puffs
PLUFFED ▶ pluff
PLUFFS ▶ pluff
PLUFFY ▶ pluff
PLUG *n* thing fitting into

and filling a hole ▷ *vb* block
or seal (a hole or gap) with a
plug
PLUGGED ▶ plug
PLUGGER ▶ plug
PLUGOLA *n* plugging of
products on television
PLUGS ▶ plug
PLUM *n* oval usu dark red
fruit with a stone in the
middle ▷ *adj* dark
purplish-red
PLUMAGE *n* bird's feathers
PLUMATE *adj* of, relating to,
or possessing one or more
feathers or plumes
PLUMB *vb* understand
(something obscure) ▷ *adv*
exactly ▷ *n* weight, usually
of lead, suspended at the
end of a line and used to
determine water depth or
verticality
PLUMBED ▶ plumb
PLUMBER *n* person who fits
and repairs pipes and
fixtures for water and
drainage systems
PLUMBIC *adj* of or
containing lead in the
tetravalent state
PLUMBS ▶ plumb
PLUMBUM *n* obsolete
name for lead (the metal)
PLUMCOT *n* hybrid of
apricot and plum
PLUME *n* feather, esp one
worn as an ornament ▷ *vb*
adorn or decorate with
feathers or plumes
PLUMED ▶ plume
PLUMERY *n* plumes
collectively
PLUMES ▶ plume
PLUMIER ▶ plumy
PLUMING ▶ plume
PLUMIST *n* person who
makes plumes
PLUMMER ▶ plum
PLUMMET *vb* plunge
downward ▷ *n* weight on a
plumb line or fishing line
PLUMMY *adj* of, full of, or
like plums
PLUMOSE *same as*
▶ plumate
PLUMOUS *adj* having
plumes or feathers
PLUMP *adj* moderately or
attractively fat ▷ *vb* sit or
fall heavily and suddenly
▷ *n* heavy abrupt fall or the
sound of this ▷ *adv*

suddenly or heavily
PLUMPED ▶ plump
PLUMPEN *vb* make or
become plump
PLUMPER *n* pad carried in
the mouth by actors to
round out the cheeks
PLUMPIE *same as* **▶ plumpy**
PLUMPLY ▶ plump
PLUMPS ▶ plump
PLUMPY *adj* plump
PLUMS ▶ plum
PLUMULA *n* down feather
PLUMULE *n* embryonic
shoot of seed-bearing
plants
PLUMY *adj* like a feather
PLUNDER *vb* take by force,
esp in time of war ▷ *n*
things plundered, spoils
PLUNGE *vb* put or throw
forcibly or suddenly (into)
▷ *n* plunging dive
PLUNGED ▶ plunge
PLUNGER *n* rubber suction
cup used to clear blocked
pipes
PLUNGES ▶ plunge
PLUNK *vb* pluck the strings
of (a banjo etc) to produce a
twanging sound ▷ *n* act or
sound of plunking ▷ *interj*
exclamation imitative of
the sound of something
plunking ▷ *adv* exactly
PLUNKED ▶ plunk
PLUNKER ▶ plunk
PLUNKS ▶ plunk
PLUNKY *adj* sounding like
plucked banjo string
PLURAL *adj* of or consisting
of more than one ▷ *n* word
indicating more than one
PLURALS ▶ plural
PLURRY *euphemism for*
▶ bloody
PLUS *vb* make or become
greater in value
PLUSAGE *same as*
> **plussage**
PLUSED ▶ plus
PLUSES ▶ plus
PLUSH *n* fabric with long
velvety pile ▷ *adj* luxurious
PLUSHER ▶ plush
PLUSHES ▶ plush
PLUSHLY ▶ plush
PLUSHY *same as* **▶ plush**
PLUSING ▶ plus
PLUSSED ▶ plus
PLUSSES ▶ plus
PLUTEAL ▶ pluteus
PLUTEI ▶ pluteus

P

PLUTEUS n larva of sea urchin

PLUTON n any mass of igneous rock that has solidified below the surface of the earth

PLUTONS ▶ pluton

PLUVIAL adj of or caused by the action of rain ▷ n of or relating to rainfall or precipitation

PLUVIAN n crocodile bird

PLUVIUS adj as in **pluvius insurance** insurance against rain

PLY vb work at (a job or trade) ▷ n thickness of wool, fabric, etc

PLYER n person who plies trade

PLYERS ▶ plyer

PLYING ▶ ply

PLYWOOD n board made of thin layers of wood glued together

PNEUMA n person's vital spirit, soul, or creative energy

PNEUMAS ▶ pneuma

PO n chamber pot

POA n type of grass

POACH vb catch (animals) illegally on someone else's land

POACHED ▶ poach

POACHER n person who catches animals illegally on someone else's land

POACHES ▶ poach

POACHY adj (of land) wet and soft

POAKA n type of stilt (bird) native to New Zealand

POAKAS ▶ poaka

POAKE n waste matter from tanning of hides

POAKES ▶ poake

POAS ▶ poa

POBLANO n variety of chilli pepper

POBOY n New Orleans sandwich

POBOYS ▶ poboy

POCHARD n European diving duck

POCHAY n post chaise: a closed horse-drawn four-wheeled coach

POCHAYS ▶ pochay

POCHOIR n print made from stencils

POCK n pus-filled blister resulting from smallpox

▷ vb mark with scars

POCKARD same as ▶ pochard

POCKED ▶ pock

POCKET n small bag sewn into clothing for carrying things ▷ vb put into one's pocket ▷ adj small

POCKETS ▶ pocket

POCKIER ▶ pock

POCKIES pl n woollen mittens

POCKILY ▶ pock

POCKING ▶ pock

POCKPIT n mark left on skin after a pock has gone

POCKS ▶ pock

POCKY ▶ pock

POCO adv little

POCOSEN same as ▶ pocosin

POCOSIN n swamp in US upland coastal region

POCOSON same as ▶ pocosin

POD n long narrow seed case of peas, beans, etc ▷ vb remove the pod from

PODAGRA n gout of the foot or big toe

PODAL adj relating to feet

PODALIC adj relating to feet

PODCAST n audio file similar to a radio broadcast, which can be downloaded and listened to on a computer or MP3 player ▷ vb make available in this format

PODDED ▶ pod

PODDIE n user of or enthusiast for the iPod, a portable digital music player

PODDIER ▶ poddy

PODDIES ▶ poddy

PODDING ▶ pod

PODDLE vb move or travel in a leisurely manner

PODDLED ▶ poddle

PODDLES ▶ poddle

PODDY n handfed calf or lamb ▷ adj fat

PODESTA n (in modern Italy) subordinate magistrate in some towns

PODEX n posterior

PODEXES ▶ podex

PODGE n short chubby person

PODGES ▶ podge

PODGIER ▶ podgy

PODGILY ▶ podgy

PODGY adj short and fat

PODIA ▶ podium

PODIAL ▶ podium

PODITE n crustacean leg

PODITES ▶ podite

PODITIC adj similar to the limb segment of an arthropod

PODIUM n small raised platform for a conductor or speaker

PODIUMS ▶ podium

PODLEY n young coalfish

PODLEYS ▶ podley

PODLIKE ▶ pod

PODS ▶ pod

PODSOL same as ▶ podzol

PODSOLS ▶ podsol

PODZOL n type of soil characteristic of coniferous forest regions having a greyish-white colour in its upper leached layers

PODZOLS ▶ podzol

POEM n imaginative piece of writing in rhythmic lines

POEMS ▶ poem

POEP n emission of gas from the anus

POEPS ▶ poep

POESIED ▶ poesy

POESIES ▶ poesy

POESY n poetry ▷ vb write poems

POET n writer of poems

POETESS n female poet

POETIC adj of or like poetry

POETICS n principles and forms of poetry or the study of these, esp as a form of literary criticism

POETISE same as ▶ poeticize

POETIZE same as ▶ poeticize

POETRY n poems

POETS ▶ poet

POFFLE n small piece of land

POFFLES ▶ poffle

POGEY n financial or other relief given to the unemployed by the government

POGEYS ▶ pogey

POGGE n European marine scorpaenoid fish

POGGES ▶ pogge

POGIES ▶ pogy

POGO vb jump up and down in one spot, as in a punk dance of the 1970s

POGOED ▶ pogo

POGOER ▶ pogo

POGOERS ▶ pogo

POGOING ▸ **pogo**

POGONIA n orchid with pink or white fragrant flowers

POGONIP n icy winter fog

POGOS ▸ **pogo**

POGROM n organized persecution and massacre ▷ vb carry out a pogrom

POGROMS ▸ **pogrom**

POGY same as ▸ **pogey**

POH interj exclamation expressing contempt or disgust

POHIRI variant spelling of ▸ **powhiri**

POHIRIS ▸ **pohiri**

POI n ball of woven flax swung rhythmically by Māori women during poi dances

POILU n infantryman in the French Army, esp one in the front lines in World War I

POILUS ▸ **poilu**

POINADO old variant of ▸ **poniard**

POIND vb take (property of a debtor) in execution or by way of distress

POINDED ▸ **poind**

POINDER ▸ **poind**

POINDS ▸ **poind**

POINT n main idea in a discussion, argument, etc ▷ vb show the direction or position of something or draw attention to it by extending a finger or other pointed object towards it

POINTE n tip of the toe

POINTED adj having a sharp end

POINTEL n engraver's tool

POINTER n helpful hint

POINTES ▸ **pointe**

POINTS ▸ **point**

POINTY adj having a sharp point or points

POIS ▸ **poi**

POISE n calm dignified manner ▷ vb be balanced or suspended

POISED adj absolutely ready

POISER n balancing organ of some insects

POISERS ▸ **poiser**

POISES ▸ **poise**

POISHA n monetary unit of Bangladesh

POISING ▸ **poise**

POISON n substance that kills or injures when swallowed or absorbed ▷ vb give poison to

POISONS ▸ **poison**

POISSON n fish

POITIN variant spelling of ▸ **poteen**

POITINS ▸ **poitin**

POITREL n breastplate of horse's armour

POKABLE ▸ **poke**

POKAL n tall drinking cup

POKALS ▸ **pokal**

POKE vb jab or prod with one's finger, a stick, etc ▷ n poking

POKED ▸ **poke**

POKEFUL n contents of small bag

POKER n metal rod for stirring a fire

POKERS ▸ **poker**

POKES ▸ **poke**

POKEY same as ▸ **pokie**

POKEYS ▸ **pokey**

POKIE n poker machine

POKIER ▸ **poky**

POKIES ▸ **poky**

POKIEST ▸ **poky**

POKILY ▸ **poky**

POKING ▸ **poke**

POKY adj small and cramped

POL n political campaigner

POLACCA same as ▸ **polacre**

POLACRE n three-masted sailing vessel used in the Mediterranean

POLAR adj of or near either of the earth's poles ▷ n type of line in geometry

POLARON n kind of electron

POLARS ▸ **polar**

POLDER n land reclaimed from the sea, esp in the Netherlands ▷ vb reclaim land from the sea

POLDERS ▸ **polder**

POLE n long rounded piece of wood etc ▷ vb strike or push with a pole

POLEAX same as ▸ **poleaxe**

POLEAXE vb hit or stun with a heavy blow ▷ n axe formerly used in battle or used by a butcher

POLECAT n small animal of the weasel family

POLED ▸ **pole**

POLEIS ▸ **polis**

POLEMIC n fierce attack on or defence of a particular opinion, belief, etc ▷ adj of or involving dispute or controversy

POLENTA n thick porridge made in Italy, usually from maize

POLER n person or thing that poles, esp a punter

POLERS ▸ **poler**

POLES ▸ **pole**

POLEY adj (of cattle) hornless or polled ▷ n animal with horns removed

POLEYN n piece of armour for protecting the knee

POLEYNS ▸ **poleyn**

POLEYS ▸ **poley**

POLICE n organized force in a state which keeps law and order ▷ vb control or watch over with police or a similar body

POLICED ▸ **police**

POLICER n computer device controlling use

POLICES ▸ **police**

POLICY n plan of action adopted by a person, group, or state

POLIES ▸ **poly**

POLING ▸ **pole**

POLINGS ▸ **pole**

POLIO n acute viral disease

POLIOS ▸ **polio**

POLIS n ancient Greek city-state

POLISES ▸ **polis**

POLISH vb make smooth and shiny by rubbing ▷ n substance used for polishing

POLITE adj showing consideration for others in one's manners, speech, etc

POLITER ▸ **polite**

POLITIC adj wise and likely to prove advantageous

POLITY n politically organized state, church, or society

POLJE n large elliptical depression in karst regions, sometimes containing a marsh or small lake

POLJES ▸ **polje**

POLK vb dance a polka

POLKA n lively 19th-century dance ▷ vb dance a polka

POLKAED ▸ **polka**

POLKAS ▸ **polka**

POLKED ▸ **polk**

POLKING ▸ **polk**

POLKS ▸ **polk**

POLL n questioning of a

random sample of people to find out general opinion ▷ vb receive (votes)

POLLACK n food fish related to the cod, found in northern seas

POLLAN n whitefish that occurs in lakes in Northern Ireland

POLLANS ▶ pollan

POLLARD n animal that has shed its horns or has had them removed ▷ vb cut off the top of (a tree) to make it grow bushy

POLLAXE ▶ poleaxe

POLLED adj (of animals, esp cattle) having the horns cut off or being naturally hornless

POLLEE ▶ poll

POLLEES ▶ poll

POLLEN n fine dust produced by flowers to fertilize other flowers ▷ vb collect pollen

POLLENS ▶ pollen

POLLENT adj strong

POLLER ▶ poll

POLLERS ▶ poll

POLLEX n first digit of the forelimb of amphibians, reptiles, birds, and mammals, such as the thumb of man and other primates

POLLICY obsolete spelling of ▶ policy

POLLIES ▶ polly

POLLING n casting or registering of votes at an election

POLLIST n one advocating the use of polls

POLLMAN n one passing a degree without honours

POLLMEN ▶ pollman

POLLOCK same as ▶ pollack

POLLS ▶ poll

POLLUTE vb contaminate with something poisonous or harmful

POLLY n politician

POLO n game like hockey played by teams of players on horseback

POLOIST n devotee of polo

POLONIE same as ▶ polony

POLONY n bologna sausage

POLOS ▶ polo

POLS ▶ pol

POLT n thump or blow ▷ vb strike

POLTED ▶ polt

POLTING ▶ polt

POLTS ▶ polt

POLY n polytechnic

POLYACT adj (of a sea creature) having many tentacles or limb-like protrusions

POLYCOT n plant that has or appears to have more than two cotyledons

POLYENE n chemical compound containing a chain of alternating single and double carbon-carbon bonds

POLYGAM n plant of the Polygamia class

POLYGON n geometrical figure with three or more angles and sides

POLYMER n chemical compound with large molecules made of simple molecules of the same kind

POLYNIA same as ▶ polynya

POLYNYA n stretch of open water surrounded by ice, esp near the mouths of large rivers, in arctic seas

POLYNYI ▶ polynya

POLYOL n type of alcohol

POLYOLS ▶ polyol

POLYOMA n type of tumour caused by virus

POLYP n small simple sea creature with a hollow cylindrical body

POLYPE same as ▶ polyp

POLYPED same as ▶ polypod

POLYPES ▶ polype

POLYPI ▶ polypus

POLYPOD adj (esp of insect larvae) having many legs or similar appendages ▷ n animal of this type

POLYPS ▶ polyp

POLYPUS same as ▶ polyp

POLYS ▶ poly

POLYZOA n small mosslike aquatic creatures

POMACE n apple pulp left after pressing for juice

POMACES ▶ pomace

POMADE n perfumed oil put on the hair to make it smooth and shiny ▷ vb put pomade on

POMADED ▶ pomade

POMADES ▶ pomade

POMATO n hybrid of tomato and potato

POMATUM same as ▶ pomade

POMBE n any alcoholic drink

POMBES ▶ pombe

POME n fleshy fruit of the apple and related plants, consisting of an enlarged receptacle enclosing the ovary and seeds

POMELO n edible yellow fruit, like a grapefruit, of a tropical tree

POMELOS ▶ pomelo

POMEROY n bullet used to down airships

POMES ▶ pome

POMFRET n small black rounded liquorice sweet

POMMEE adj (of cross) having end of each arm ending in disk

POMMEL same as ▶ pummel

POMMELE adj having a pommel

POMMELS ▶ pommel

POMO n postmodernism

POMOS ▶ pomo

POMP n stately display or ceremony

POMPANO n deep-bodied carangid food fish

POMPELO n large Asian citrus fruit

POMPEY vb mollycoddle

POMPEYS ▶ pompey

POMPIER adj slavishly conventional

POMPION n pumpkin

POMPOM n decorative ball of tufted wool, silk, etc

POMPOMS ▶ pompom

POMPON same as ▶ pompom

POMPONS ▶ pompon

POMPOON same as ▶ pompom

POMPOUS adj foolishly serious and grand, self-important

POMPS ▶ pomp

POMROY same as ▶ pomeroy

POMROYS ▶ pomroy

POMS ▶ pom

PONCEAU n scarlet red

PONCHO n loose circular cloak with a hole for the head

PONCHOS ▶ poncho

POND n small area of still water ▷ vb hold back

(flowing water)

PONDAGE n water held in reservoir

PONDED ▸ pond

PONDER vb think thoroughly or deeply (about)

PONDERS ▸ ponder

PONDING ▸ pond

PONDOK n (in southern Africa) crudely made house or shack

PONDOKS ▸ pondok

PONDS ▸ pond

PONE n bread made of maize

PONENT adj westerly

PONES ▸ pone

PONEY same as ▸ pony

PONEYS ▸ poney

PONG n strong unpleasant smell ▷ vb give off a strong unpleasant smell

PONGA n tall New Zealand tree fern with large leathery leaves

PONGAS ▸ ponga

PONGED ▸ pong

PONGEE n thin plain-weave silk fabric from China or India, left in its natural colour

PONGEES ▸ pongee

PONGID n primate of the family which includes the gibbons and the great apes

PONGIDS ▸ pongid

PONGIER ▸ pong

PONGING ▸ pong

PONGO n anthropoid ape, esp an orang-utan or (formerly) a gorilla

PONGOES ▸ pongo

PONGOS ▸ pongo

PONGS ▸ pong

PONGY ▸ pong

PONIARD n small slender dagger ▷ vb stab with a poniard

PONIED ▸ pony

PONIES ▸ pony

PONK n evil spirit ▷ vb stink

PONKED ▸ ponk

PONKING ▸ ponk

PONKS ▸ ponk

PONS n bridge of connecting tissue

PONT n (in South Africa) river ferry, esp one that is guided by a cable from one bank to the other

PONTAGE n tax paid for repairing bridge

PONTAL adj of or relating to the pons

PONTES ▸ pons

PONTIC adj of or relating to the pons

PONTIE same as ▸ ponty

PONTIES ▸ ponty

PONTIFF n Pope

PONTIFY vb speak or behave in a pompous or dogmatic manner

PONTIL same as ▸ punty

PONTILE adj relating to pons ▷ n metal bar used in glass-making

PONTILS ▸ pontil

PONTINE adj of or relating to bridges

PONTON same as ▸ pontoon

PONTONS ▸ ponton

PONTOON n floating platform supporting a temporary bridge ▷ vb cross a river using pontoons

PONTS ▸ pont

PONTY n rod used for shaping molten glass

PONY n small horse ▷ vb settle bill or debt

PONYING ▸ pony

PONZU n type of Japanese dipping sauce made from orange juice, sake, sugar, soy sauce, and red pepper

PONZUS ▸ ponzu

POO vb defecate

POOCH n slang word for dog ▷ vb bulge or protrude

POOCHED ▸ pooch

POOCHES ▸ pooch

POOD n unit of weight, used in Russia, equal to 36.1 pounds or 16.39 kilograms

POODLE n dog with curly hair often clipped fancifully

POODLES ▸ poodle

POODS ▸ pood

POOED ▸ poo

POOGYE n Hindu nose-flute

POOGYES ▸ poogye

POOH interj exclamation of disdain, contempt, or disgust ▷ vb make such an exclamation

POOHED ▸ pooh

POOHING ▸ pooh

POOHS ▸ pooh

POOING ▸ poo

POOJA same as ▸ puja

POOJAH same as ▸ puja

POOJAHS ▸ poojah

POOJAS ▸ pooja

POOK vb pluck

POOKA n malevolent Irish spirit

POOKAS ▸ pooka

POOKING ▸ pook

POOKIT ▸ pook

POOKS ▸ pook

POOL n small body of still water ▷ vb put in a common fund

POOLED ▸ pool

POOLER n person taking part in pool

POOLERS ▸ pooler

POOLING ▸ pool

POOLS pl n organized nationwide principally postal gambling pool betting on the result of football matches

POON n SE Asian tree with lightweight hard wood and shiny leathery leaves

POONAC n coconut residue

POONACS ▸ poonac

POONS ▸ poon

POOP n raised part at the back of a sailing ship ▷ vb (of a wave or sea) break over the stern of (a vessel)

POOPED ▸ poop

POOPER n as in party pooper person whose behaviour or personality spoils other people's enjoyment

POOPERS ▸ pooper

POOPING ▸ poop

POOPS ▸ poop

POOR adj having little money and few possessions

POORER ▸ poor

POOREST ▸ poor

POORI n unleavened Indian bread

POORIS ▸ poori

POORISH ▸ poor

POORLY adv in a poor manner ▷ adj not in good health

POORT n (in South Africa) steep narrow mountain pass, usually following a river or stream

POORTS ▸ poort

POOS ▸ poo

POOT vb break wind

POOTED ▸ poot

POOTER ▸ poot

POOTERS ▸ poot

POOTING ▸ poot

POOTLE vb travel or go in a relaxed or leisurely manner

P

POOTLED ▸ **pootle**
POOTLES ▸ **pootle**
POOTS ▸ **poot**
POP *vb* make or cause to make a small explosive sound ▸ *n* small explosive sound ▸ *adj* popular
POPADUM *same as* > **poppadom**
POPCORN *n* grains of maize heated until they puff up and burst
POPE *n* bishop of Rome as head of the Roman Catholic Church
POPEDOM *n* office or dignity of a pope
POPERA *n* music drawing on opera or classical music and aiming for popular appeal
POPERAS ▸ **popera**
POPERIN *n* kind of pear
POPES ▸ **pope**
POPETTE *n* young female fan or performer of pop music
POPEYED *adj* staring in astonishment
POPGUN *n* toy gun that fires a pellet or cork by means of compressed air
POPGUNS ▸ **popgun**
POPJOY *vb* amuse oneself
POPJOYS ▸ **popjoy**
POPLAR *n* tall slender tree
POPLARS ▸ **poplar**
POPLIN *n* ribbed cotton material
POPLINS ▸ **poplin**
POPOVER *n* individual Yorkshire pudding, often served with roast beef
POPPA *same as* ▸ **papa**
POPPAS ▸ **poppa**
POPPED ▸ **pop**
POPPER *n* press stud
POPPERS ▸ **popper**
POPPET *n* term of affection for a small child or sweetheart
POPPETS ▸ **poppet**
POPPIED *adj* covered with poppies
POPPIER ▸ **poppy**
POPPIES ▸ **poppy**
POPPING ▸ **pop**
POPPISH *adj* like pop music
POPPIT *n* bead used to form necklace
POPPITS ▸ **poppit**
POPPLE *vb* (of boiling water

or a choppy sea) to heave or toss
POPPLED ▸ **popple**
POPPLES ▸ **popple**
POPPLY *adj* covered in small bumps
POPPY *n* plant with a large red flower ▸ *adj* reddish-orange
POPRIN *same as* ▸ **poperin**
POPS ▸ **pop**
POPSIE *same as* ▸ **popsy**
POPSIES ▸ **popsy**
POPSOCK *n* women's knee-length nylon stocking
POPSTER *n* pop star
POPSY *n* attractive young woman
POPULAR *adj* widely liked and admired ▸ *n* cheap newspapers with mass circulation
PORAE *n* large edible sea fish of New Zealand waters
PORAES ▸ **porae**
PORAL *adj* relating to pores
PORANGI *adj* crazy
PORCH *n* covered approach to the entrance of a building
PORCHES ▸ **porch**
PORCINE *adj* of or like a pig
PORCINI ▸ **porcino**
PORCINO *n* edible woodland fungus
PORE *n* tiny opening in the skin or in the surface of a plant ▸ *vb* make a close intent examination or study (of a book, map, etc)
PORED ▸ **pore**
PORER *n* person who pores
PORERS ▸ **pore**
PORES ▸ **pore**
PORGE *vb* cleanse (slaughtered animal) ceremonially
PORGED ▸ **porge**
PORGES ▸ **porge**
PORGIE *same as* ▸ **porgy**
PORGIES ▸ **porgy**
PORGING ▸ **porge**
PORGY *n* any of various sparid fishes, many of which occur in American Atlantic waters
PORIER ▸ **pory**
PORIEST ▸ **pory**
PORIFER *n* type of invertebrate
PORINA *n* larva of a moth which causes damage to grassland

PORINAS ▸ **porina**
PORING ▸ **pore**
PORISM *n* type of mathematical proposition, the meaning of which is now obscure
PORISMS ▸ **porism**
PORK *vb* to eat ravenously ▸ *n* the flesh of pigs used as food
PORKED ▸ **pork**
PORKER *n* pig raised for food
PORKERS ▸ **porker**
PORKIER ▸ **porky**
PORKIES ▸ **porky**
PORKING ▸ **pork**
PORKPIE *n* hat with a round flat crown and a brim that can be turned up or down
PORKS ▸ **pork**
PORKY *adj* of or like pork ▸ *n* lie
PORLOCK *vb* interrupt or intrude at an awkward moment
PORN *n* pornography
PORNIER ▸ **porny**
PORNO *same as* ▸ **porn**
PORNOS ▸ **porno**
PORNS ▸ **porn**
PORNY *adj* pornographic
POROSE *adj* pierced with small pores
POROSES ▸ **porosis**
POROSIS *n* porous condition of bones
POROUS *adj* allowing liquid to pass through gradually
PORPESS *n* type of fish
PORRECT *adj* extended forwards ▸ *vb* stretch forward
PORRIGO *n* disease of the scalp
PORT *same as* > **porthole**
PORTA *n* aperture in an organ, such as the liver, esp one providing an opening for blood vessels
PORTAGE *n* (route for) transporting boats and supplies overland between navigable waterways ▸ *vb* transport (boats and supplies) in this way
PORTAL *n* large imposing doorway or gate
PORTALS ▸ **portal**
PORTAS ▸ **porta**
PORTATE *adj* diagonally athwart escutcheon
PORTED ▸ **port**

P

PORTEND vb be a sign of

PORTENT n sign of a future event

PORTER n man who carries luggage ▷ vb carry luggage

PORTERS ▶ porter

PORTESS same as > **portesse**

PORTHOS same as > **portesse**

PORTICO n porch or covered walkway with columns supporting the roof

PORTIER ▶ port

PORTING ▶ port

PORTION n part or share ▷ vb divide (something) into shares

PORTLY adj rather fat

PORTMAN n inhabitant of port

PORTMEN ▶ portman

PORTOUS same as > **portesse**

PORTRAY vb describe or represent by artistic means, as in writing or film

PORTS ▶ port

PORTY adj like port

PORY adj containing pores

POS ▶ po

POSABLE ▶ pose

POSADA n inn in a Spanish-speaking country

POSADAS ▶ posada

POSAUNE n organ chorus reed

POSE vb place in or take up a particular position to be photographed or drawn ▷ n position while posing

POSED ▶ pose

POSER n puzzling question

POSERS ▶ poser

POSES ▶ pose

POSEUR n person who behaves in an affected way to impress others

POSEURS ▶ poseur

POSEUSE n female poseur

POSEY adj (of a place) for, characteristic of, or full of posers

POSH adj smart, luxurious ▷ adv in a manner associated with the upper class ▷ vb make posh

POSHED ▶ posh

POSHER ▶ posh

POSHES ▶ posh

POSHEST ▶ posh

POSHING ▶ posh

POSHLY ▶ posh

POSHO n corn meal

POSHOS ▶ posho

POSIER ▶ posy

POSIES ▶ posy

POSIEST ▶ posy

POSING ▶ pose

POSINGS ▶ pose

POSIT vb lay down as a basis for argument ▷ n fact, idea, etc, that is posited

POSITED ▶ posit

POSITIF n (on older organs) manual controlling soft stops

POSITON n part of chromosome

POSITS ▶ posit

POSNET n small basin or dish

POSNETS ▶ posnet

POSOLE n hominy

POSOLES ▶ posole

POSS vb wash (clothes) by agitating them with a long rod, pole, etc

POSSE n group of men organized to maintain law and order

POSSED ▶ poss

POSSER n short stick used for stirring clothes in a washtub

POSSERS ▶ posser

POSSES ▶ posse

POSSESS vb have as one's property

POSSET n drink of hot milk curdled with ale, beer, etc, flavoured with spices, formerly used as a remedy for colds ▷ vb treat with a posset

POSSETS ▶ posset

POSSIE n place

POSSIES ▶ possie

POSSING ▶ poss

POSSUM vb pretend to be dead, asleep, ignorant, etc, to deceive an opponent

POSSUMS ▶ possum

POST n official system of delivering letters and parcels ▷ vb send by post

POSTAGE n charge for sending a letter or parcel by post

POSTAL adj of a Post Office or the mail-delivery service ▷ n postcard

POSTALS ▶ postal

POSTBAG n postman's bag

POSTBOX n box into which mail is put for collection by the postal service

POSTBOY n man or boy who brings the post round to offices

POSTBUS n (in Britain, esp in rural districts) vehicle carrying the mail that also carries passengers

POSTDOC n postdoctoral degree

POSTED ▶ post

POSTEEN n Afghan leather jacket

POSTER n large picture or notice stuck on a wall ▷ vb cover with posters

POSTERN n small back door or gate ▷ adj situated at the rear or the side

POSTERS ▶ poster

POSTFIX vb add or append at the end of something

POSTIE n postman

POSTIES ▶ postie

POSTIL n commentary or marginal note, as in a Bible ▷ vb annotate (a biblical passage)

POSTILS ▶ postil

POSTIN same as ▶ **posteen**

POSTING n job to which someone is assigned by his or her employer which involves moving to a particular town or country

POSTINS ▶ postin

POSTMAN n person who collects and delivers post

POSTMEN ▶ postman

POSTOP n person recovering from surgery

POSTOPS ▶ postop

POSTS ▶ post

POSTTAX adj of the period after tax is paid

POSTURE n position or way in which someone stands, walks, etc ▷ vb behave in an exaggerated way to get attention

POSTWAR adj occurring or existing after a war

POSY n small bunch of flowers

POT n round deep container ▷ vb plant in a pot

POTABLE adj drinkable ▷ n something fit to drink

POTAE n hat

POTAES ▶ potae

POTAGE n thick soup

P

POTAGER n small kitchen garden

POTAGES ▶ potage

POTALE n residue from a grain distillery, used as animal feed

POTALES ▶ potale

POTAMIC adj of or relating to rivers

POTASH n white powdery substance obtained from ashes and used as fertilizer ▷ vb treat with potash

POTASS abbreviated form of > **potassium**

POTASSA n potassium oxide

POTATO n roundish starchy vegetable that grows underground

POTBOIL vb boil in a pot

POTBOY n (esp formerly) youth or man employed at a public house to serve beer, etc

POTBOYS ▶ potboy

POTCH n inferior quality opal used in jewellery for mounting precious opals

POTCHE vb stab

POTCHED ▶ potche

POTCHER ▶ potche

POTCHES ▶ potch

POTE vb push

POTED ▶ pote

POTEEN n (in Ireland) illegally made alcoholic drink

POTEENS ▶ poteen

POTENCE same as ▶ **potency**

POTENCY n state or quality of being potent

POTENT adj having great power or influence ▷ n potentate or ruler

POTENTS ▶ potent

POTES ▶ pote

POTFUL n amount held by a pot

POTFULS ▶ potful

POTGUN n pot-shaped mortar

POTGUNS ▶ potgun

POTHEAD n habitual user of cannabis

POTHEEN rare variant of ▶ **poteen**

POTHER n fuss or commotion ▷ vb make or be troubled or upset

POTHERB n plant whose leaves, flowers, or stems are used in cooking

POTHERS ▶ pother

POTHERY adj stuffy

POTHOLE n hole in the surface of a road

POTHOOK n S-shaped hook for suspending a pot over a fire

POTHOS n climbing plant

POTICHE n tall vase or jar, as of porcelain, with a round or polygonal body that narrows towards the neck and a detached lid or cover

POTIN n bronze alloy with high tin content

POTING ▶ pote

POTINS ▶ potin

POTION n dose of medicine or poison

POTIONS ▶ potion

POTJIE n three-legged iron pot used for cooking

POTJIES ▶ potjie

POTLACH same as > **potlatch**

POTLIKE ▶ pot

POTLINE n row of electrolytic cells for reducing metals

POTLUCK n whatever food happens to be available without special preparation

POTMAN same as ▶ **potboy**

POTMEN ▶ potman

POTOO n nocturnal tropical bird

POTOOS ▶ potoo

POTOROO n Australian leaping rodent

POTPIE n meat and vegetable stew with a pie crust on top

POTPIES ▶ potpie

POTS ▶ pot

POTSHOP n public house

POTSHOT n chance shot taken casually, hastily, or without careful aim

POTSIE same as ▶ **potsy**

POTSIES ▶ potsy

POTSY n hopscotch

POTT old variant of ▶ **pot**

POTTAGE n thick soup or stew

POTTED ▶ pot

POTTEEN same as ▶ **poteen**

POTTER same as ▶ **putter**

POTTERS ▶ potter

POTTERY n articles made from baked clay

POTTIER ▶ potty

POTTIES ▶ potty

POTTING ▶ pot

POTTLE n liquid measure equal to half a gallon

POTTLES ▶ pottle

POTTO n short-tailed prosimian primate

POTTOS ▶ potto

POTTS ▶ pott

POTTY adj crazy or silly ▷ n bowl used by a small child as a toilet

POTZER same as ▶ **patzer**

POTZERS ▶ potzer

POUCH n small bag ▷ vb place in or as if in a pouch

POUCHED ▶ pouch

POUCHES ▶ pouch

POUCHY ▶ pouch

POUDER obsolete spelling of ▶ **powder**

POUDERS ▶ pouder

POUDRE old spelling of ▶ **powder**

POUDRES ▶ poudre

POUF n large solid cushion used as a seat ▷ vb pile up hair into rolled puffs

POUFED ▶ pouf

POUFF same as ▶ **pouf**

POUFFE same as ▶ **pouf**

POUFFED ▶ pouffe

POUFFES ▶ pouffe

POUFFS ▶ pouff

POUFING ▶ pouf

POUFS ▶ pouf

POUK Scots variant of ▶ **poke**

POUKE n mischievous spirit

POUKES ▶ pouke

POUKING ▶ pouk

POUKIT ▶ pouk

POUKS ▶ pouk

POULARD n hen that has been spayed for fattening

POULDER obsolete spelling of **powder** n

POULDRE archaic spelling of ▶ **powder**

POULE n fowl suitable for slow stewing

POULES ▶ poule

POULP n octopus

POULPE same as ▶ **poulp**

POULPES ▶ poulpe

POULPS ▶ poulp

POULT n young of a gallinaceous bird, esp of domestic fowl

POULTER n poultry dealer

POULTRY n domestic fowls

POULTS ▶ poult

POUNCE vb spring upon suddenly to attack or capture ▷ n pouncing

POUNCED ▶ **pounce**

POUNCER ▶ **pounce**

POUNCES ▶ **pounce**

POUNCET n box with a perforated top used for perfume

POUND n monetary unit of Britain and some other countries ▷ vb hit heavily and repeatedly

POUNDAL n fps unit of force

POUNDED ▶ **pound**

POUNDER ▶ **pound**

POUNDS ▶ **pound**

POUPE vb make sudden blowing sound

POUPED ▶ **poupe**

POUPES ▶ **poupe**

POUPING ▶ **poupe**

POUPT ▶ **poupe**

POUR vb flow or cause to flow out in a stream

POURED ▶ **pour**

POURER ▶ **pour**

POURERS ▶ **pour**

POURIE n jug

POURIES ▶ **pourie**

POURING ▶ **pour**

POURS ▶ **pour**

POURSEW obsolete spelling of ▶ **pursue**

POURSUE obsolete spelling of ▶ **pursue**

POUSADA n traditional Portuguese hotel

POUSSE same as ▶ **pease**

POUSSES ▶ **pousse**

POUSSIE old variant of ▶ **pussy**

POUSSIN n young chicken reared for eating

POUT vb thrust out one's lips, look sulky ▷ n pouting look

POUTED ▶ **pout**

POUTER n pigeon that can puff out its crop

POUTERS ▶ **pouter**

POUTFUL adj tending to pout

POUTHER Scots variant of ▶ **powder**

POUTIER ▶ **pout**

POUTINE n dish of chipped potatoes topped with curd cheese and a tomato-based sauce

POUTING ▶ **pout**

POUTS ▶ **pout**

POUTY ▶ **pout**

POVERTY n state of being without enough food or money

POW interj exclamation to indicate that a collision or explosion has taken place ▷ n head or a head of hair

POWAN n type of freshwater whitefish occurring in some Scottish lakes

POWANS ▶ **powan**

POWDER n substance in the form of tiny loose particles ▷ vb apply powder to

POWDERS ▶ **powder**

POWDERY ▶ **powder**

POWER n ability to do or act ▷ vb give or provide power to

POWERED ▶ **power**

POWERS ▶ **power**

POWHIRI n Māori ceremony of welcome, esp to a marae

POWIN n peacock

POWINS ▶ **powin**

POWN same as ▶ **powin**

POWND obsolete spelling of ▶ **pound**

POWNDED ▶ **pownd**

POWNDS ▶ **pownd**

POWNEY old Scots spelling of ▶ **pony**

POWNEYS ▶ **powney**

POWNIE old Scots spelling of ▶ **pony**

POWNIES ▶ **pownie**

POWNS ▶ **pown**

POWNY old Scots spelling of ▶ **pony**

POWRE obsolete spelling of ▶ **power**

POWRED ▶ **powre**

POWRES ▶ **powre**

POWRING ▶ **powre**

POWS ▶ **pow**

POWTER vb scrabble about

POWTERS ▶ **powter**

POWWAW interj expression of disbelief or contempt

POWWOW n talk or conference ▷ vb hold a powwow

POWWOWS ▶ **powwow**

POX n disease in which skin pustules form ▷ vb infect with pox

POXED ▶ **pox**

POXES ▶ **pox**

POXIER ▶ **poxy**

POXIEST ▶ **poxy**

POXING ▶ **pox**

POXY adj having or having had syphilis

POYNANT old variant of ▶ **poignant**

POYNT obsolete spelling of ▶ **point**

POYNTED ▶ **poynt**

POYNTS ▶ **poynt**

POYOU n type of armadillo

POYOUS ▶ **poyou**

POYSE obsolete variant of ▶ **poise**

POYSED ▶ **poyse**

POYSES ▶ **poyse**

POYSING ▶ **poyse**

POYSON obsolete spelling of ▶ **poison**

POYSONS ▶ **poyson**

POZ adj positive

> **Poz** is an old-fashioned short form of **positive**, and one of the most frequently played short Z words.

POZOLE same as ▶ **posole**

POZOLES ▶ **pozole**

POZZ adj positive

POZZIES ▶ **pozzy**

POZZY same as ▶ **possie**

PRAAM same as ▶ **pram**

PRAAMS ▶ **praam**

PRABBLE same as ▶ **brabble**

PRACTIC adj practical ▷ n practice

PRAD n horse

PRADS ▶ **prad**

PRAESES n Roman governor

PRAETOR n (in ancient Rome) senior magistrate ranking just below the consuls

PRAHU same as ▶ **proa**

PRAHUS ▶ **prahu**

PRAIRIE n large treeless area of grassland, esp in N America and Canada

PRAISE vb express approval or admiration of (someone or something) ▷ n something said or written to show approval or admiration

PRAISED ▶ **praise**

PRAISER ▶ **praise**

PRAISES ▶ **praise**

PRAJNA n wisdom or understanding considered as the goal of Buddhist contemplation

PRAJNAS ▶ **prajna**

PRALINE n sweet made of nuts and caramelized sugar

PRAM n four-wheeled

P

carriage for a baby, pushed by hand

PRAMS ▶ pram

PRANA *n* (in Oriental medicine, martial arts, etc) cosmic energy believed to come from the sun and connecting the elements of the universe

PRANAS ▶ prana

PRANCE *vb* walk with exaggerated bouncing steps ▷ *n* act of prancing

PRANCED ▶ prance

PRANCER ▶ prance

PRANCES ▶ prance

PRANCK *obsolete variant of* ▶ **prank**

PRANCKE *obsolete variant of* ▶ **prank**

PRANCKS ▶ pranck

PRANG *n* crash in a car or aircraft ▷ *vb* crash or damage (an aircraft or car)

PRANGED ▶ prang

PRANGS ▶ prang

PRANK *n* mischievous trick ▷ *vb* dress or decorate showily or gaudily

PRANKED ▶ prank

PRANKLE *obsolete variant of* ▶ **prance**

PRANKS ▶ prank

PRANKY ▶ prank

PRAO *same as* ▶ **proa**

PRAOS ▶ prao

PRASE *n* light green translucent variety of chalcedony

PRASES ▶ prase

PRAT *n* stupid person

PRATE *vb* talk idly and at length ▷ *n* chatter

PRATED ▶ prate

PRATER ▶ prate

PRATERS ▶ prate

PRATES ▶ prate

PRATIE *n* potato

PRATIES ▶ pratie

PRATING ▶ prate

PRATS ▶ prat

PRATT *n* buttocks ▷ *vb* hit on the buttocks

PRATTED ▶ pratt

PRATTLE *vb* chatter in a childish or foolish way ▷ *n* childish or foolish talk

PRATTS ▶ pratt

PRATY *obsolete variant of* ▶ **pretty**

PRAU *same as* ▶ **proa**

PRAUNCE *obsolete variant of* ▶ **prance**

PRAUS ▶ prau

PRAVITY *n* moral degeneracy

PRAWLE *n* Shakespearian phonetic spelling of "brawl" meant to indicate that the speaker is Welsh

PRAWLES ▶ prawle

PRAWLIN *same as* ▶ **praline**

PRAWN *n* edible shellfish like a large shrimp ▷ *vb* catch prawns

PRAWNED ▶ prawn

PRAWNER ▶ prawn

PRAWNS ▶ prawn

PRAXES ▶ praxis

PRAXIS *n* practice as opposed to theory

PRAY *vb* say prayers ▷ *adv* I beg you ▷ *interj* I beg you

PRAYED ▶ pray

PRAYER *n* thanks or appeal addressed to one's God

PRAYERS ▶ prayer

PRAYING ▶ pray

PRAYS ▶ pray

PRE *prep* before

PREACE *obsolete variant of* ▶ **press**

PREACED ▶ preace

PREACES ▶ preace

PREACH *vb* give a talk on a religious theme as part of a church service

PREACHY *adj* inclined to or marked by preaching

PREACT *vb* act beforehand

PREACTS ▶ preact

PREAGED *adj* treated to appear older

PREAMP *n* electronic amplifier used to improve the signal-to-noise ratio of an electronic device

PREAMPS ▶ preamp

PREANAL *adj* situated in front of anus

PREARM *vb* arm beforehand

PREARMS ▶ prearm

PREASE *vb* crowd or press

PREASED ▶ prease

PREASES ▶ prease

PREASSE *obsolete spelling of* ▶ **press**

PREAVER *vb* aver in advance

PREBADE ▶ prebid

PREBAKE *vb* bake before further cooking

PREBEND *n* allowance paid by a cathedral or collegiate church to a canon or

member of the chapter

PREBID *vb* bid beforehand

PREBIDS ▶ prebid

PREBILL *vb* issue an invoice before the service has been provided

PREBIND *vb* bind a book in a hard-wearing binding

PREBOIL *vb* boil beforehand

PREBOOK *vb* book well in advance

PREBOOM *adj* of the period before an economic boom

PREBORN *adj* unborn

PREBUY *vb* buy in advance

PREBUYS ▶ prebuy

PRECAST *adj* (esp of concrete when employed as a structural element in building) cast in a particular form before being used ▷ *vb* cast (concrete) in a particular form before use

PRECAVA *n* superior vena cava

PRECEDE *vb* go or be before

PRECENT *vb* issue a command or law

PRECEPT *n* rule of behaviour

PRECES *pl n* prayers

PRECESS *vb* undergo or cause to undergo precession

PRECIPE *n* type of legal document

PRECIS *n* short written summary of a longer piece ▷ *vb* make a precis of

PRECISE *adj* exact, accurate in every detail

PRECODE *vb* code beforehand

PRECOOK *vb* cook (food) beforehand

PRECOOL *vb* cool in advance

PRECOUP *adj* of the period before a coup

PRECURE *vb* cure in advance

PRECUT *vb* cut in advance

PRECUTS ▶ precut

PREDATE *vb* occur at an earlier date than

PREDAWN *n* period before dawn

PREDIAL *same as* ▶ **praedial**

PREDICT *vb* tell about in advance, prophesy

PREDIED ▶ predy

PREDIES ▶ predy

PREDIVE *adj* happening

before a dive

PREDOOM vb pronounce (someone or something's) doom beforehand

PREDRY vb dry beforehand

PREDUSK n period before dawn

PREDY vb prepare for action

PREE vb try or taste

PREED ▸ pree

PREEDIT vb edit beforehand

PREEING ▸ pree

PREEMIE n premature infant

PREEMPT vb acquire in advance of or to the exclusion of others

PREEN vb (of a bird) clean or trim (feathers) with the beak ▹ n pin, esp a decorative one

PREENED ▸ preen

PREENER ▸ preen

PREENS ▸ preen

PREES ▸ pree

PREEVE old form of ▸ **prove**

PREEVED ▸ preeve

PREEVES ▸ preeve

PREFAB n prefabricated house ▹ vb manufacture sections of (building) in factory

PREFABS ▸ prefab

PREFACE n introduction to a book ▹ vb serve as an introduction to (a book, speech, etc)

PREFADE vb fade beforehand

PREFARD vb old form of preferred

PREFECT n senior pupil in a school, with limited power over others

PREFER vb like better

PREFERS ▸ prefer

PREFILE vb file beforehand

PREFIRE vb fire beforehand

PREFIX n letter or group of letters put at the beginning of a word to make a new word, such as un- in unhappy ▹ vb put as an introduction or prefix (to)

PREFORM vb form beforehand

PREFUND vb pay for in advance

PREGAME adj of the period before a sports match ▹ n such a period

PREGGY informal word for > **pregnant**

PREHEAT vb heat (an oven, grill, pan, etc) beforehand

PREHEND vb take hold of

PREIF old form of ▸ **proof**

PREIFE old form of ▸ **proof**

PREIFES ▸ preife

PREIFS ▸ preif

PREJINK same as ▸ **perjink**

PRELACY n office or status of a prelate

PRELATE n bishop or other churchman of high rank

PRELATY n prelacy

PRELAW adj before taking up study of law

PRELECT vb lecture or discourse in public

PRELIFE n life lived before one's life on earth

PRELIM n event which precedes another

PRELIMS pl n pages of a book, such as the title page and contents, which come before the main text

PRELOAD vb load beforehand

PRELUDE n introductory movement in music ▹ vb act as a prelude to (something)

PRELUDI > preludio

PREM n informal word for a premature infant

PREMADE adj made in advance

PREMAN n a hominid

PREMEAL adj of the period before a meal

PREMED n premedical student

PREMEDS ▸ premed

PREMEET adj happening before a meet

PREMEN ▸ preman

PREMIA ▸ premium

PREMIE same as ▸ **preemie**

PREMIER n prime minister ▹ adj chief, leading

PREMIES ▸ premie

PREMISE n statement assumed to be true and used as the basis of reasoning ▹ vb state or assume (a premise (a proposition) as a premise in an argument, theory, etc

PREMISS same as ▸ **premise**

PREMIUM n additional sum of money, as on a wage or charge

PREMIX vb mix beforehand

PREMIXT ▸ premix

PREMOLD vb mold in advance

PREMOLT adj happening in the period before an animal molts

PREMOVE vb prompt to action

PREMS ▸ prem

PREMUNE adj having immunity to a disease as a result of latent infection

PREMY same as ▸ **preemie**

PRENAME n forename

PRENEED adj arranged in advance of eventual requirements

PRENOON adj of the period before noon

PRENT Scots variant of ▸ **print**

PRENTED ▸ prent

PRENTS ▸ prent

PRENUP n prenuptial agreement

PRENUPS ▸ prenup

PRENZIE adj Shakespearian word, possibly a mistake, supposed by some to mean "princely"

PREON n (in particle physics) hypothetical subcomponent of a quark

PREONS ▸ preon

PREOP n patient being prepared for surgery

PREOPS ▸ preop

PREORAL adj situated in front of mouth

PREP vb prepare

PREPACK vb pack in advance of sale

PREPAID ▸ prepay

PREPARE vb make or get ready

PREPAVE vb pave beforehand

PREPAY vb pay for in advance

PREPAYS ▸ prepay

PREPILL adj of the period before the contraceptive pill became available

PREPLAN vb plan beforehand

PREPONE vb bring forward to an earlier time

PREPOSE vb place before

PREPPED ▸ prep

PREPPIE same as ▸ **preppy**

PREPPY adj characteristic of or denoting a fashion style of neat, understated, and often expensive clothes ▹ n person exhibiting such style

PREPREG n material already impregnated with synthetic resin

PREPS ▶ prep

PREPUCE n foreskin

PREPUPA n insect in stage of life before pupa

PREQUEL n film or book about an earlier stage of a story or a character's life, released because the later part of it has already been successful

PRERACE adj of the period before a race

PRERIOT adj of the period before a riot

PREROCK adj of the era before rock music

PRERUPT adj abrupt

PRESA n sign or symbol used in a canon, round, etc, to indicate the entry of each part

PRESAGE vb be a sign or warning of ▷ n omen

PRESALE n practice of arranging the sale of a product before it is available

PRESE ▶ presa

PRESELL vb promote (a product, entertainment, etc) with publicity in advance of its appearance

PRESENT adj being in a specified place ▷ n present time or tense ▷ vb introduce formally or publicly

PRESES same as **▶ praeses**

PRESET vb set the timer on a piece of equipment so that it starts to work at a specific time ▷ adj (of equipment) with the controls set in advance ▷ n control, such as a variable resistor, that is not as accessible as the main controls and is used to set initial conditions

PRESETS ▶ preset

PRESHIP vb ship in advance

PRESHOW vb show in advance

PRESIDE vb be in charge, esp of a meeting

PRESIFT vb sift beforehand

PRESOAK vb soak beforehand

PRESOLD ▶ presell

PRESONG adj of the period before a song is sung

PRESORT vb sort in advance

PRESS vb apply force or weight to ▷ n printing machine

PRESSED ▶ press

PRESSER ▶ press

PRESSES ▶ press

PRESSIE informal word for **▶ present**

PRESSOR n something that produces an increase in blood pressure

PREST adj prepared for action or use ▷ n loan of money ▷ vb give as a loan

PRESTED ▶ prest

PRESTER ▶ prest

PRESTO adv very quickly ▷ n passage to be played very quickly

PRESTOS ▶ presto

PRESTS ▶ prest

PRESUME vb suppose to be the case

PRETAPE vb tape in advance

PRETAX adj before tax

PRETEEN n boy or girl approaching his or her teens

PRETELL vb predict

PRETEND vb claim or give the appearance of (something untrue) to deceive or in play ▷ adj fanciful

PRETERM n premature baby

PRETEST vb test (something) before presenting it to its intended public or client ▷ n act or instance of pretesting

PRETEXT n false reason given to hide the real one ▷ vb get personal information under false pretences

PRETOLD ▶ pretell

PRETOR same as **▶ praetor**

PRETORS ▶ pretor

PRETRIM vb trim in advance

PRETTY adj pleasing to look at ▷ adv fairly, moderately ▷ vb pretty

PRETYPE vb type in advance

PRETZEL n brittle salted biscuit

PREVAIL vb gain mastery

PREVE vb prove

PREVED ▶ preve

PREVENE vb come before

PREVENT vb keep from happening or doing

PREVERB n particle preceding root of verb

PREVES ▶ preve

PREVIEW n advance showing of a film or exhibition before it is shown to the public ▷ vb view in advance

PREVING ▶ preve

PREVISE vb predict or foresee

PREVUE same as **▶ preview**

PREVUED ▶ prevue

PREVUES ▶ prevue

PREWAR adj relating to the period before a war, esp before World War I or II

PREWARM vb warm beforehand

PREWARN vb warn in advance

PREWASH vb give a preliminary wash to (clothes), esp in a washing machine ▷ n preliminary wash, esp in a washing machine

PREWIRE vb wire beforehand

PREWORK vb work in advance

PREWORN adj (of clothes) second-hand

PREWRAP vb wrap in advance

PREWYN obsolete spelling of **▶ prune**

PREWYNS ▶ prewyn

PREX same as **▶ prexy**

PREXES ▶ prex

PREXIES ▶ prexy

PREXY n US college president

PREY n animal hunted and killed for food by another animal ▷ vb hunt or seize food by killing other animals

PREYED ▶ prey

PREYER ▶ prey

PREYERS ▶ prey

PREYFUL adj rich in prey

PREYING ▶ prey

PREYS ▶ prey

PREZ n president

PREZES ▶ prez

PREZZIE same as **▶ pressie**

PRIAL n pair royal of cards

PRIALS ▶ prial

PRIAPI ▶ priapus

PRIAPIC adj phallic

PRIAPUS n representation of the penis

PRIBBLE same as ▶ **prabble**

PRICE n amount of money for which a thing is bought or sold ▷ vb fix or ask the price of

PRICED ▶ **price**

PRICER ▶ **price**

PRICERS ▶ **price**

PRICES ▶ **price**

PRICEY adj expensive

PRICIER ▶ **pricey**

PRICILY ▶ **pricey**

PRICING ▶ **price**

PRICK vb pierce lightly with a sharp point ▷ n sudden sharp pain caused by pricking

PRICKED ▶ **prick**

PRICKER n person or thing that pricks

PRICKET n male deer in the second year of life having unbranched antlers

PRICKLE n thorn or spike on a plant ▷ vb have a tingling or pricking sensation

PRICKLY adj having prickles

PRICKS ▶ **prick**

PRICKY adj covered with pricks

PRICY same as ▶ **pricey**

PRIDE n feeling of pleasure and satisfaction when one has done well

PRIDED ▶ **pride**

PRIDES ▶ **pride**

PRIDIAN adj relating to yesterday

PRIDING ▶ **pride**

PRIED ▶ **pry**

PRIEF obsolete variant of **proof** n

PRIEFE obsolete variant of ▶ **proof**

PRIEFES ▶ **priefe**

PRIEFS ▶ **prief**

PRIER n person who pries

PRIERS ▶ **prier**

PRIES ▶ **pry**

PRIEST n (in the Christian church) person who can administer the sacraments and preach ▷ vb make a priest

PRIESTS ▶ **priest**

PRIEVE obsolete variant of ▶ **proof**

PRIEVED ▶ **prieve**

PRIEVES ▶ **prieve**

PRIG n self-righteous person who acts as if

superior to others

PRIGGED ▶ **prig**

PRIGGER n thief

PRIGS ▶ **prig**

PRILL vb convert (a material) into a granular free-flowing form ▷ n prilled material

PRILLED ▶ **prill**

PRILLS ▶ **prill**

PRIM adj formal, proper, and rather prudish ▷ vb make prim

PRIMA same as ▶ **primo**

PRIMACY n state of being first in rank, grade, etc

PRIMAGE n tax added to customs duty

PRIMAL adj of basic causes or origins

PRIMARY adj chief, most important ▷ n person or thing that is first in position, time, or importance

PRIMAS ▶ **prima**

PRIMATE n member of an order of mammals including monkeys and humans

PRIME adj main, most important ▷ n time when someone is at his or her best or most vigorous ▷ vb give (someone) information in advance to prepare them for something

PRIMED ▶ **prime**

PRIMELY ▶ **prime**

PRIMER n special paint applied to bare wood etc before the main paint

PRIMERO n 16th- and 17th-century card game

PRIMERS ▶ **primer**

PRIMES ▶ **prime**

PRIMEUR n anything (esp fruit) produced early

PRIMI ▶ **primo**

PRIMINE n integument surrounding an ovule or the outer of two such integuments

PRIMING same as ▶ **primer**

PRIMLY ▶ **prim**

PRIMMED ▶ **prim**

PRIMMER ▶ **prim**

PRIMO n upper or right-hand part in a piano duet

PRIMOS ▶ **primo**

PRIMP vb tidy (one's hair or

clothes) fussily

PRIMPED ▶ **primp**

PRIMPS ▶ **primp**

PRIMS ▶ **prim**

PRIMSIE Scots variant of ▶ **prim**

PRIMULA n type of primrose with brightly coloured flowers

PRIMUS n presiding bishop in the Synod

PRIMY adj prime

PRINCE vb act the prince

PRINCED ▶ **prince**

PRINCES ▶ **prince**

PRINCOX n pert youth

PRINK vb dress (oneself) finely

PRINKED ▶ **prink**

PRINKER ▶ **prink**

PRINKS ▶ **prink**

PRINT vb reproduce (a newspaper, book, etc) in large quantities by mechanical or electronic means ▷ n printed words etc

PRINTED ▶ **print**

PRINTER n person or company engaged in printing

PRINTS ▶ **print**

PRION n dovelike petrel with a serrated bill

PRIONS ▶ **prion**

PRIOR adj earlier ▷ n head monk in a priory

PRIORLY ▶ **prior**

PRIORS ▶ **prior**

PRIORY n place where certain orders of monks or nuns live

PRISAGE n customs duty levied until 1809 upon wine imported into England

PRISE same as ▶ **pry**

PRISED ▶ **prise**

PRISER ▶ **prise**

PRISERE n primary sere or succession from bare ground to the community climax

PRISERS ▶ **prise**

PRISES ▶ **prise**

PRISING ▶ **prise**

PRISM n transparent block usu with triangular ends and rectangular sides, used to disperse light into a spectrum or refract it in optical instruments

PRISMS ▶ **prism**

PRISMY ▶ **prism**

P

PRISON n building where criminals and accused people are held ▷ vb imprison

PRISONS ▶ prison

PRISS n prissy person ▷ vb act prissily

PRISSED ▶ priss

PRISSES ▶ priss

PRISSY adj prim, correct, and easily shocked ▷ n prissy person

PRITHEE interj pray thee

PRIVACY n condition of being private

PRIVADO n close friend

PRIVATE adj for the use of one person or group only ▷ n soldier of the lowest rank

PRIVET n bushy evergreen shrub used for hedges

PRIVETS ▶ privet

PRIVIER ▶ privy

PRIVIES ▶ privy

PRIVILY adv in a secret way

PRIVITY n legally recognized relationship existing between two parties, such as that between lessor and lessee and between the parties to a contract

PRIVY adj sharing knowledge of something secret ▷ n toilet, esp an outside one

PRIZE n reward given for success in a competition etc ▷ adj winning or likely to win a prize ▷ vb value highly

PRIZED ▶ prize

PRIZER n contender for prize

PRIZERS ▶ prizer

PRIZES ▶ prize

PRIZING ▶ prize

PRO prep in favour of ▷ n professional ▷ adv in favour of a motion etc

PROA n any of several kinds of canoe-like boats used in the South Pacific, esp one equipped with an outrigger and sails

PROAS ▶ proa

PROB n problem

PROBALL adj believable

PROBAND n first patient to be investigated in a family study, to whom all relationships are referred

PROBANG n long flexible rod, often with a small sponge at one end, for inserting into the oesophagus, as to apply medication

PROBATE n process of proving the validity of a will ▷ vb establish officially the authenticity and validity of (a will)

PROBE vb search into or examine closely ▷ n surgical instrument used to examine a wound, cavity, etc

PROBED ▶ probe

PROBER ▶ probe

PROBERS ▶ probe

PROBES ▶ probe

PROBING ▶ probe

PROBIT n statistical measurement

PROBITS ▶ probit

PROBITY n honesty, integrity

PROBLEM n something difficult to deal with or solve ▷ adj of a literary work that deals with difficult moral questions

PROBS ▶ prob

PROCARP n female reproductive organ in red algae

PROCEED vb start or continue doing

PROCESS n series of actions or changes ▷ vb handle or prepare by a special method of manufacture

PROCTAL adj relating to the rectum

PROCTOR n member of the staff of certain universities having duties including the enforcement of discipline ▷ vb invigilate (an examination)

PROCURE vb get, provide

PROD vb poke with something pointed ▷ n prodding

PRODDED ▶ prod

PRODDER ▶ prod

PRODIGY n person with some marvellous talent

PRODRUG n compound that is itself biologically inactive but is metabolized in the body to produce an active therapeutic drug

PRODS ▶ prod

PRODUCE vb bring into existence ▷ n food grown for sale

PRODUCT n something produced

PROEM n introduction or preface

PROEMS ▶ proem

PROETTE n female golfing professional

PROF short for > **professor**

PROFACE interj much good may it do you

PROFANE adj showing disrespect for religion or holy things ▷ vb treat (something sacred) irreverently, desecrate

PROFESS vb state or claim (something as true), sometimes falsely

PROFFER vb offer ▷ n act of proffering

PROFILE n outline, esp of the face, as seen from the side ▷ vb draw, write, or make a profile of

PROFIT n money gained ▷ vb gain or benefit

PROFITS ▶ profit

PROFS ▶ prof

PROFUSE adj plentiful

PROG vb prowl about for or as if for food or plunder ▷ n food obtained by begging

PROGENY n children

PROGGED ▶ prog

PROGGER n fan of progressive rock

PROGRAM same as > **programme**

PROGS ▶ prog

PROGUN adj in favour of public owning firearms

PROIGN same as ▶ **proin**

PROIGNS ▶ proign

PROIN vb trim or prune

PROINE same as ▶ **proin**

PROINED ▶ proin

PROINES ▶ proine

PROINS ▶ proin

PROJECT n planned scheme to do or examine something over a period ▷ vb make a forecast based on known data

PROJET n draft of a proposed treaty

PROJETS ▶ projet

PROKE vb thrust or poke

PROKED ▶ proke

PROKER ▶ proke

PROKERS ▶ proke

PROKES ▶ proke
PROKING ▶ proke
PROLAN n constituent of human pregnancy urine
PROLANS ▶ prolan
PROLATE adj having a polar diameter which is longer than the equatorial diameter ▷ vb pronounce or utter
PROLE old form of ▶ prowl
PROLED ▶ prole
PROLEG n any of the short paired unjointed appendages on each abdominal segment of a caterpillar and any of certain other insect larvae
PROLEGS ▶ proleg
PROLER n prowler
PROLERS ▶ proler
PROLES ▶ prole
PROLINE n nonessential amino acid that occurs in protein
PROLING ▶ prole
PROLIX adj (of speech or a piece of writing) overlong and boring
PROLL vb prowl or search
PROLLED ▶ proll
PROLLER ▶ proll
PROLLS ▶ proll
PROLOG same as ▶ prologue
PROLOGS ▶ prolog
PROLONG vb make (something) last longer
PROM n formal dance held at a high school or college
PROMINE n substance promoting cell growth
PROMISE vb say that one will definitely do or not do something ▷ n undertaking to do or not to do something
PROMMER n spectator at promenade concert
PROMO vb promote (something)
PROMOED ▶ promo
PROMOS ▶ promo
PROMOTE vb help to make (something) happen or increase
PROMPT vb cause (an action) ▷ adj done without delay ▷ adv exactly ▷ n anything that serves to remind
PROMPTS ▶ prompt
PROMS ▶ prom
PRONAOI ▶ pronaos

PRONAOS n inner area of the portico of a classical temple
PRONATE vb turn (a limb, hand, or foot) so that the palm or sole is directed downwards
PRONE n sermon
PRONELY ▶ prone
PRONER ▶ prone
PRONES ▶ prone
PRONEST ▶ prone
PRONEUR n flatterer
PRONG n one spike of a fork or similar instrument ▷ vb prick or spear with or as if with a prong
PRONGED ▶ prong
PRONGS ▶ prong
PRONK vb jump straight up
PRONKED ▶ pronk
PRONKS ▶ pronk
PRONOTA > pronotum
PRONOUN n word, such as she or it, used to replace a noun
PRONTO adv at once
PROO interj (to a horse) stop!
PROOF n evidence that shows that something is true or has happened ▷ adj able to withstand ▷ vb take a proof from (type matter)
PROOFED ▶ proof
PROOFER n reader of proofs
PROOFS ▶ proof
PROOTIC n bone in front of ear
PROP vb support (something) so that it stays upright or in place ▷ n pole, beam, etc used as a support
PROPAGE vb propagate
PROPALE vb publish (something)
PROPANE n flammable gas found in petroleum and used as a fuel
PROPEL vb cause to move forward
PROPELS ▶ propel
PROPEND vb be inclined or disposed
PROPENE n colourless gaseous alkene obtained by cracking petroleum
PROPER adj real or genuine ▷ n service or psalm regarded as appropriate to a specific day, season, etc
PROPERS ▶ proper
PROPHET n person

supposedly chosen by God to spread His word
PROPINE vb to drink a toast to
PROPJET another name for > turboprop
PROPMAN n member of the stage crew in charge of the stage props
PROPMEN ▶ propman
PROPONE vb propose or put forward, esp before a court
PROPOSE vb put forward for consideration
PROPPED ▶ prop
PROPRIA > proprium
PROPS ▶ prop
PROPYL n of, consisting of, or containing the monovalent group of atoms C_3H_7-
PROPYLA > propylon
PROPYLS ▶ propyl
PRORATE vb divide, assess, or distribute (something) proportionately
PRORE n forward part of ship
PRORES ▶ prore
PROS ▶ pro
PROSAIC adj lacking imagination, dull
PROSE n ordinary speech or writing in contrast to poetry ▷ vb speak or write in a tedious style
PROSECT vb dissect a cadaver for a public demonstration
PROSED ▶ prose
PROSER n writer of prose
PROSERS ▶ proser
PROSES ▶ prose
PROSIER ▶ prosy
PROSIFY vb write prose
PROSILY ▶ prosy
PROSING ▶ prose
PROSIT interj good health! cheers!
PROSO n millet
PROSODY n study of poetic metre and techniques
PROSOMA n head and thorax of an arachnid
PROSOS ▶ proso
PROSPER vb be successful
PROSS n prostitute
PROSSES ▶ pross
PROSSIE n prostitute
PROST same as ▶ prosit
PROSTIE n prostitute
PROSY adj dull and long-winded

PROTEA *n* African shrub with showy flowers

PROTEAN *adj* constantly changing ▷ *n* creature that can change shape

PROTEAS ▶ **protea**

PROTECT *vb* defend from trouble, harm, or loss

PROTEGE *n* person who is protected and helped by another

PROTEI ▶ **proteus**

PROTEID *n* protein

PROTEIN *n* any of a group of complex organic compounds that are essential for life

PROTEND *vb* hold out or stretch

PROTEST *n* declaration or demonstration of objection ▷ *vb* object, disagree

PROTEUS *n* aerobic bacterium

PROTHYL *same as* ▶ **protyle**

PROTIST *n* organism belonging to the kingdom which comprises protozoans, unicellular algae, and simple fungi

PROTIUM *n* most common isotope of hydrogen

PROTO *n as in* **proto team** relating to a team of people trained to deal with underground rescues, etc

PROTON *n* positively charged particle in the nucleus of an atom

PROTONS ▶ **proton**

PROTORE *n* primary mineral deposit

PROTYL *same as* ▶ **protyle**

PROTYLE *n* hypothetical primitive substance from which the chemical elements were supposed to have been formed

PROTYLS ▶ **protyl**

PROUD *adj* feeling pleasure and satisfaction

PROUDER ▶ **proud**

PROUDLY ▶ **proud**

PROUL *same as* ▶ **prowl**

PROULED ▶ **proul**

PROULER *Scots variant of* ▶ **prowler**

PROULS ▶ **proul**

PROVAND *n* food

PROVANT *adj* supplied with provisions

PROVE *vb* establish the validity of

PROVED ▶ **prove**

PROVEN ▶ **prove**

PROVEND *same as* ▶ **provand**

PROVER ▶ **prove**

PROVERB *n* short saying that expresses a truth or gives a warning ▷ *vb* utter or describe (something) in the form of a proverb

PROVERS ▶ **prove**

PROVES ▶ **prove**

PROVIDE *vb* make available

PROVINE *vb* plant branch of vine in ground for propagation

PROVING ▶ **prove**

PROVISO *n* condition, stipulation

PROVOKE *vb* deliberately anger

PROVOST *n* head of certain university colleges in Britain

PROW *n* bow of a vessel ▷ *adj* gallant

PROWAR *adj* in favour of or supporting war

PROWER ▶ **prow**

PROWESS *n* superior skill or ability

PROWEST ▶ **prow**

PROWL *vb* move stealthily around a place as if in search of prey or plunder ▷ *n* prowling

PROWLED ▶ **prowl**

PROWLER ▶ **prowl**

PROWLS ▶ **prowl**

PROWS ▶ **prow**

PROXIES ▶ **proxy**

PROXIMO *adv* in or during the next or coming month

PROXY *n* person authorized to act on behalf of someone else

PROYN *obsolete spelling of* ▶ **prune**

PROYNE *obsolete spelling of* ▶ **prune**

PROYNED ▶ **proyn**

PROYNES ▶ **proyne**

PROYNS ▶ **proyn**

PRUDE *n* person who is excessively modest, prim, or proper

PRUDENT *adj* cautious, discreet, and sensible

PRUDERY ▶ **prude**

PRUDES ▶ **prude**

PRUDISH ▶ **prude**

PRUH *same as* ▶ **proo**

PRUINA *n* woolly white covering on some lichens

PRUINAS ▶ **pruina**

PRUINE *obsolete spelling of* ▶ **prune**

PRUINES ▶ **pruine**

PRUNE *n* dried plum ▷ *vb* cut off dead parts or excessive branches from (a tree or plant)

PRUNED ▶ **prune**

PRUNER ▶ **prune**

PRUNERS ▶ **prune**

PRUNES ▶ **prune**

PRUNING ▶ **prune**

PRUNT *n* glass ornamentation

PRUNTED ▶ **prunt**

PRUNTS ▶ **prunt**

PRUNUS *n* type of ornamental tree or shrub

PRURIGO *n* chronic inflammatory disease of the skin characterized by the formation of papules and intense itching

PRUSIK *n* sliding knot that locks under pressure and can be used to form a loop in which a climber can place his or her foot in order to stand or ascend a rope ▷ *vb* climb (up a standing rope) using prusiks

PRUSIKS ▶ **prusik**

PRUSSIC *adj as in* **prussic acid** weakly acidic extremely poisonous aqueous solution of hydrogen cyanide

PRUTA *same as* ▶ **prutah**

PRUTAH *n* former Israeli coin

PRUTOT ▶ **prutah**

PRUTOTH ▶ **prutah**

PRY *vb* make an impertinent or uninvited inquiry into a private matter ▷ *n* act of prying

PRYER *same as* ▶ **prier**

PRYERS ▶ **pryer**

PRYING ▶ **pry**

PRYINGS ▶ **pry**

PRYS *old variant of* ▶ **price**

PRYSE *old variant of* ▶ **price**

PRYSED ▶ **pryse**

PRYSES ▶ **pryse**

PRYSING ▶ **pryse**

PRYTHEE *same as* ▶ **prithee**

PSALM *n* sacred song ▷ *vb* sing a psalm

PSALMED ▶ **psalm**

PSALMIC ▶ **psalm**

PSALMS ▶ **psalm**

PSALTER n devotional or liturgical book containing a version of Psalms

PSALTRY same as > **psaltery**

PSAMMON n community of microscopic life forms living between grains of sand on shores

PSCHENT n ancient Egyptian crown

PSEUD n pretentious person

PSEUDO n pretentious person

PSEUDOS ▶ **pseudo**

PSEUDS ▶ **pseud**

PSHAW n exclamation of disgust, impatience, disbelief, etc ▷ vb make this exclamation

PSHAWED ▶ **pshaw**

PSHAWS ▶ **pshaw**

PSI n 23rd letter of the Greek alphabet

PSION n type of elementary particle

PSIONIC > **psionics**

PSIONS ▶ **psion**

PSIS ▶ **psi**

PSOAE ▶ **psoas**

PSOAI ▶ **psoas**

PSOAS n either of two muscles of the loins that aid in flexing and rotating the thigh

PSOASES ▶ **psoas**

PSOATIC ▶ **psoas**

PSOCID n tiny wingless insect

PSOCIDS ▶ **psocid**

PSORA n itching skin complaint

PSORAS ▶ **psora**

PSORIC ▶ **psora**

PSST interj sound made to attract someone's attention, esp without others noticing

PST interj sound made to attract someone's attention

> You would need to be fairly desperate to use good letters to play this exclamation, but sometimes with no vowels on your rack things can be that desperate.

PSYCH vb psychoanalyse

PSYCHE same as ▶ **psych**

PSYCHED ▶ **psych**

PSYCHES ▶ **psych**

PSYCHIC adj having mental

powers which cannot be explained by natural laws ▷ n person with psychic powers

PSYCHS ▶ **psych**

PSYLLA same as ▶ **psyllid**

PSYLLAS ▶ **psylla**

PSYLLID n type of insect of the family which comprises the jumping plant lice

PSYOP n psychological operation

PSYOPS ▶ **psyop**

PSYWAR n psychological warfare

PSYWARS ▶ **psywar**

PTARMIC n material that causes sneezing

PTERIA ▶ **pterion**

PTERIN n compound such as folic acid

PTERINS ▶ **pterin**

PTERION n point on the side of the skull where a number of bones meet

PTEROIC adj as in **pteroic acid** a kind of acid found in spinach

PTERYLA n any of the tracts of skin that bear contour feathers, arranged in lines along the body of a bird

PTISAN n grape juice drained off without pressure

PTISANS ▶ **ptisan**

PTOMAIN same as > **ptomaine**

PTOOEY interj imitation of the sound of spitting

PTOSES ▶ **ptosis**

PTOSIS n prolapse or drooping of a part, esp the eyelid

PTOTIC ▶ **ptosis**

PTUI same as ▶ **ptooey**

PTYALIN n amylase secreted in the saliva of man and other animals

PTYXES ▶ **ptyxis**

PTYXIS n folding of a leaf in a bud

PUB n building with a bar licensed to sell alcoholic drinks ▷ vb visit a pub or pubs

PUBBED ▶ **pub**

PUBBING ▶ **pub**

PUBCO n company operating a chain of pubs

PUBCOS ▶ **pubco**

PUBE n pubic hair

PUBERAL adj relating to puberty

PUBERTY n beginning of sexual maturity

PUBES ▶ **pube**

PUBIC adj of the lower abdomen

PUBIS n one of the three sections of the hipbone that forms part of the pelvis

PUBISES ▶ **pubis**

PUBLIC adj of or concerning the people as a whole ▷ n community, people in general

PUBLICS ▶ **public**

PUBLISH vb produce and issue (printed matter) for sale

PUBS ▶ **pub**

PUCAN n traditional Connemara open sailing boat

PUCANS ▶ **pucan**

PUCCOON n N American plant that yields a red dye

PUCE adj purplish-brown ▷ n colour varying from deep red to dark purplish brown

PUCELLE n maid or virgin

PUCER ▶ **puce**

PUCES ▶ **puce**

PUCEST ▶ **puce**

PUCK n mischievous or evil spirit ▷ vb strike (the ball) in hurling

PUCKA same as ▶ **pukka**

PUCKED ▶ **puck**

PUCKER vb gather into wrinkles ▷ n wrinkle or crease

PUCKERS ▶ **pucker**

PUCKERY adj (of wine) high in tannins

PUCKING ▶ **puck**

PUCKISH ▶ **puck**

PUCKLE n early type of machine gun

PUCKLES ▶ **puckle**

PUCKOUT n (in hurling) free hit made by the goalkeeper

PUCKS ▶ **puck**

PUD short for ▶ **pudding**

PUDDEN dialect spelling of ▶ **pudding**

PUDDENS ▶ **pudden**

PUDDER vb make bother or fuss

PUDDERS ▶ **pudder**

PUDDIES ▶ **puddy**

PUDDING n dessert, esp a cooked one served hot

PUDDLE n small pool of water, esp of rain ▷ vb

make (clay etc) into puddle

PUDDLED ▶ puddle

PUDDLER ▶ puddle

PUDDLES ▶ puddle

PUDDLY ▶ puddle

PUDDOCK same as ▶ **paddock**

PUDDY n paw

PUDENCY n modesty, shame, or prudishness

PUDENDA > pudendum

PUDENT adj lacking in ostentation; humble

PUDGE same as ▶ **podge**

PUDGES ▶ pudge

PUDGIER ▶ pudgy

PUDGILY ▶ pudgy

PUDGY adj podgy

PUDIC > pudendum

PUDOR n sense of shame

PUDORS ▶ pudor

PUDS ▶ pud

PUDSEY same as ▶ **pudsy**

PUDSIER ▶ pudsy

PUDSY adj plump

PUDU n diminutive Andean antelope with short straight horns and reddish-brown spotted coat

PUDUS ▶ pudu

PUEBLO n communal village, built by certain Indians of the southwestern US and parts of Latin America, consisting of one or more flat-roofed stone or adobe houses

PUEBLOS ▶ pueblo

PUER vb steep hides in an alkaline substance from the dung of dogs

PUERED ▶ puer

PUERILE adj silly and childish

PUERING ▶ puer

PUERS ▶ puer

PUFF n (sound of) short blast of breath, wind, etc ▷ vb blow or breathe in short quick draughts

PUFFED ▶ puff

PUFFER n person or thing that puffs

PUFFERS ▶ puffer

PUFFERY n exaggerated praise, esp in publicity or advertising

PUFFIER ▶ puffy

PUFFILY ▶ puffy

PUFFIN n black-and-white sea bird with a brightly-coloured beak

PUFFING ▶ puff

PUFFINS ▶ puffin

PUFFS ▶ puff

PUFFY adj short of breath

PUG n small snub-nosed dog ▷ vb mix or knead (clay) with water to form a malleable mass or paste

PUGAREE same as ▶ **puggree**

PUGGED ▶ pug

PUGGERY same as ▶ **puggree**

PUGGIE n Scottish word for fruit machine

PUGGIER ▶ puggy

PUGGIES ▶ puggie

PUGGING ▶ pug

PUGGISH ▶ pug

PUGGLE vb stir up by poking

PUGGLED ▶ puggle

PUGGLES ▶ puggle

PUGGREE n scarf, usually pleated, around the crown of some hats, esp sun helmets

PUGGRY same as ▶ **puggree**

PUGGY adj sticky, claylike ▷ n term of endearment

PUGH interj exclamation of disgust

PUGIL n pinch or small handful

PUGILS ▶ pugil

PUGMARK n trail of an animal

PUGREE same as ▶ **puggree**

PUGREES ▶ pugree

PUGS ▶ pug

PUH interj exclamation expressing contempt or disgust

PUHA n sow thistle

PUHAS ▶ puha

PUIR Scottish word for ▶ **poor**

PUIRER ▶ puir

PUIREST ▶ puir

PUISNE adj (esp of a subordinate judge) of lower rank ▷ n judge of lower rank

PUISNES ▶ puisne

PUISNY adj younger or inferior

PUJA n ritual in honour of the gods, performed either at home or in the mandir (temple)

PUJAH same as ▶ **puja**

PUJAHS ▶ pujah

PUJARI n Hindu priest

PUJARIS ▶ pujari

PUJAS ▶ puja

PUKA in New Zealand English, same as > **broadleaf**

PUKAS ▶ puka

PUKATEA n aromatic New Zealand tree, valued for its high-quality timber

PUKE vb vomit ▷ n act of vomiting

PUKED ▶ puke

PUKEKO n brightly coloured New Zealand wading bird

PUKEKOS ▶ pukeko

PUKER n person who vomits

PUKERS ▶ puker

PUKES ▶ puke

PUKEY adj of or like vomit

PUKIER ▶ pukey

PUKIEST ▶ pukey

PUKING ▶ puke

PUKKA adj properly done, constructed, etc

PUKU n belly or stomach

PUKUS ▶ puku

PUKY same as ▶ **pukey**

PUL n Afghan monetary unit worth one hundredth of an afghani

PULA n standard monetary unit of Botswana, divided into 100 thebe

PULAO same as ▶ **pilau**

PULAOS ▶ pulao

PULAS ▶ pula

PULDRON same as > **pauldron**

PULE vb whine or whimper

PULED ▶ pule

PULER ▶ pule

PULERS ▶ pule

PULES ▶ pule

PULI ▶ pul

PULIER ▶ puly

PULIEST ▶ puly

PULIK ▶ pul

PULING ▶ pule

PULINGS ▶ pule

PULIS ▶ pul

PULK same as ▶ **pulka**

PULKA n reindeer-drawn sleigh

PULKAS ▶ pulka

PULKHA same as ▶ **pulka**

PULKHAS ▶ pulkha

PULKS ▶ pulk

PULL vb exert force on (an object) to move it towards the source of the force ▷ n act of pulling

PULLED ▶ pull

PULLER ▶ pull

PULLERS ▶ pull

PULLET n young hen

PULLETS ▶ pullet
PULLEY n wheel with a grooved rim in which a belt, chain, or piece of rope runs in order to lift weights by a downward pull
PULLEYS ▶ pulley
PULLI ▶ pullus
PULLING ▶ pull
PULLMAN n luxurious railway coach, esp a sleeping car
PULLOUT n removable section of a magazine, etc
PULLS ▶ pull
PULLUP n exercise in which the body is raised up by the arms pulling on a horizontal bar fixed above the head
PULLUPS ▶ pullup
PULLUS n technical term for a chick or young bird
PULMO n lung
PULP n soft wet substance made from crushed or beaten matter ▷ vb reduce to pulp
PULPAL ▶ pulp
PULPED ▶ pulp
PULPER ▶ pulp
PULPERS ▶ pulp
PULPIER ▶ pulpy
PULPIFY vb reduce to pulp
PULPILY ▶ pulpy
PULPING ▶ pulp
PULPIT n raised platform for a preacher
PULPITS ▶ pulpit
PULPOUS n soft and yielding
PULPS ▶ pulp
PULPY adj having a soft or soggy consistency
PULQUE n light alcoholic drink from Mexico made from the juice of various agave plants, esp the maguey
PULQUES ▶ pulque
PULS ▶ pul
PULSANT adj vibrant
PULSAR n small dense star which emits regular bursts of radio waves
PULSARS ▶ pulsar
PULSATE vb throb, quiver
PULSE n regular beating of blood through the arteries at each heartbeat ▷ vb beat, throb, or vibrate
PULSED ▶ pulse
PULSER n thing that pulses

PULSERS ▶ pulser
PULSES ▶ pulse
PULSING ▶ pulse
PULSION n act of driving forward
PULTAN n native Indian regiment
PULTANS ▶ pultan
PULTON same as ▶ pultan
PULTONS ▶ pulton
PULTOON same as ▶ pultan
PULTUN same as ▶ pultan
PULTUNS ▶ pultun
PULTURE n food and drink claimed by foresters as their right from anyone within the limits of a given forest
PULU n substance from Hawaiian ferns, used for stuffing cushions, etc
PULUS ▶ pulu
PULVER vb make into powder
PULVERS ▶ pulver
PULVIL vb apply perfumed powder
PULVILS ▶ pulvil
PULVINI > pulvinus
PULWAR n light Indian river boat
PULWARS ▶ pulwar
PULY adj whiny
PUMA n large American wild cat with a greyish-brown coat
PUMAS ▶ puma
PUMELO same as ▶ pomelo
PUMELOS ▶ pumelo
PUMICE n light porous stone used for scouring ▷ vb rub or polish with pumice
PUMICED ▶ pumice
PUMICER ▶ pumice
PUMICES ▶ pumice
PUMIE n small stone
PUMIES ▶ pumie
PUMMEL vb strike repeatedly with or as if with the fists
PUMMELO same as ▶ pomelo
PUMMELS ▶ pummel
PUMP n machine used to force a liquid or gas to move in a particular direction ▷ vb raise or drive with a pump
PUMPED ▶ pump
PUMPER ▶ pump
PUMPERS ▶ pump
PUMPING ▶ pump
PUMPION archaic word for

▶ pumpkin
PUMPKIN n large round fruit with an orange rind, soft flesh, and many seeds
PUMPS ▶ pump
PUMY adj large and round
PUN n use of words to exploit double meanings for humorous effect ▷ vb make puns
PUNA n high cold dry plateau, esp in the Andes
PUNALUA n marriage between the sisters of one family to the brothers of another
PUNAS ▶ puna
PUNCE n kick ▷ vb kick
PUNCED ▶ punce
PUNCES ▶ punce
PUNCH vb strike at with a clenched fist ▷ n blow with a clenched fist
PUNCHED ▶ punch
PUNCHER ▶ punch
PUNCHES ▶ punch
PUNCHY adj forceful
PUNCING ▶ punce
PUNCTA ▶ punctum
PUNCTO n tip of a fencing sword
PUNCTOS ▶ puncto
PUNCTUM n tip or small point
PUNDIT n expert who speaks publicly on a subject
PUNDITS ▶ pundit
PUNG n horse-drawn sleigh with a boxlike body on runners
PUNGA variant spelling of ▶ ponga
PUNGAS ▶ punga
PUNGENT adj having a strong sharp bitter flavour
PUNGLE vb make payment
PUNGLED ▶ pungle
PUNGLES ▶ pungle
PUNGS ▶ pung
PUNIER ▶ puny
PUNIEST ▶ puny
PUNILY ▶ puny
PUNISH vb cause (someone) to suffer or undergo a penalty for some wrongdoing
PUNJI n sharpened bamboo stick
PUNJIS ▶ punji
PUNK n anti-Establishment youth movement and style of rock music of the late 1970s ▷ adj relating to the

P

punk youth movement of the late 1970s

PUNKA n fan made of a palm leaf or leaves

PUNKAH same as ▸ **punka**

PUNKAHS ▸ **punkah**

PUNKAS ▸ **punka**

PUNKER ▸ **punk**

PUNKERS ▸ **punk**

PUNKEST ▸ **punk**

PUNKEY n small winged insect

PUNKEYS ▸ **punkey**

PUNKIE same as ▸ **punkey**

PUNKIER ▸ **punky**

PUNKIES ▸ **punkie**

PUNKIN same as ▸ **pumpkin**

PUNKINS ▸ **punkin**

PUNKISH ▸ **punk**

PUNKS ▸ **punk**

PUNKY adj of punk music

PUNNED ▸ **pun**

PUNNER ▸ **pun**

PUNNERS ▸ **pun**

PUNNET n small basket for fruit

PUNNETS ▸ **punnet**

PUNNIER ▸ **punny**

PUNNING ▸ **pun**

PUNNY adj of puns

PUNS ▸ **pun**

PUNSTER n person who is fond of making puns

PUNT n open flat-bottomed boat propelled by a pole ▷ vb travel in a punt

PUNTED ▸ **punt**

PUNTEE same as ▸ **punty**

PUNTEES ▸ **puntee**

PUNTER n person who bets

PUNTERS ▸ **punter**

PUNTIES ▸ **punty**

PUNTING ▸ **punt**

PUNTO n hit in fencing

PUNTOS ▸ **punto**

PUNTS ▸ **punt**

PUNTY n long iron rod used in the finishing process of glass-blowing

PUNY adj small and feeble

PUP n young of certain animals, such as dogs and seals ▷ vb (of dogs, seals, etc) to give birth to pups

PUPA n insect at the stage of development between a larva and an adult

PUPAE ▸ **pupa**

PUPAL ▸ **pupa**

PUPARIA > **puparium**

PUPAS ▸ **pupa**

PUPATE vb (of an insect larva) to develop into a pupa

PUPATED ▸ **pupate**

PUPATES ▸ **pupate**

PUPFISH n type of small fish

PUPIL n person who is taught by a teacher

PUPILAR ▸ **pupil**

PUPILS ▸ **pupil**

PUPPED ▸ **pup**

PUPPET n small doll or figure moved by strings or by the operator's hand

PUPPETS ▸ **puppet**

PUPPIED ▸ **puppy**

PUPPIES ▸ **puppy**

PUPPING ▸ **pup**

PUPPY n young dog ▷ vb have puppies

PUPS ▸ **pup**

PUPU n Hawaiian dish

PUPUNHA n fruit of a type of palm tree

PUPUS ▸ **pupu**

PUR same as ▸ **purr**

PURANA n any of a class of Sanskrit writings not included in the Vedas, characteristically recounting the birth and deeds of Hindu gods and the creation, destruction, or recreation of the universe

PURANAS ▸ **purana**

PURANIC ▸ **purana**

PURDA same as ▸ **purdah**

PURDAH n Muslim and Hindu custom of keeping women in seclusion, with clothing that conceals them completely when they go out

PURDAHS ▸ **purdah**

PURDAS ▸ **purda**

PURE adj unmixed, untainted ▷ vb make pure

PURED ▸ **pure**

PUREE n smooth thick pulp of cooked and sieved fruit, vegetables, meat, or fish ▷ vb make (cooked foods) into a puree

PUREED ▸ **puree**

PUREES ▸ **puree**

PURELY adv in a pure manner

PURER ▸ **pure**

PURES ▸ **pure**

PUREST ▸ **pure**

PURFLE n ruffled or curved ornamental band, as on clothing, furniture, etc ▷ vb decorate with such a band or bands

PURFLED ▸ **purfle**

PURFLER ▸ **purfle**

PURFLES ▸ **purfle**

PURFLY ▸ **purfle**

PURGE vb rid (a thing or place) of (unwanted things or people) ▷ n purging

PURGED ▸ **purge**

PURGER ▸ **purge**

PURGERS ▸ **purge**

PURGES ▸ **purge**

PURGING ▸ **purge**

PURI n unleavened flaky Indian bread, that is deep-fried in ghee and served hot

PURIFY vb make or become pure

PURIN same as ▸ **purine**

PURINE n colourless crystalline solid that can be prepared from uric acid

PURINES ▸ **purine**

PURING ▸ **pure**

PURINS ▸ **purin**

PURIRI n forest tree of New Zealand

PURIRIS ▸ **puriri**

PURIS ▸ **puri**

PURISM n strict insistence on the correct usage or style, such as in grammar or art

PURISMS ▸ **purism**

PURIST ▸ **purism**

PURISTS ▸ **purism**

PURITAN n person who follows strict moral or religious principles ▷ adj of or like a puritan

PURITY n state or quality of being pure

PURL n stitch made by knitting a plain stitch backwards ▷ vb knit in purl

PURLED ▸ **purl**

PURLER n headlong or spectacular fall

PURLERS ▸ **purler**

PURLIEU n land on the edge of a royal forest

PURLIN n horizontal beam that supports the rafters of a roof

PURLINE same as ▸ **purlin**

PURLING ▸ **purl**

PURLINS ▸ **purlin**

PURLOIN vb steal

PURLS ▸ **purl**

PURPIE old Scots word for > **purslane**

PURPIES ▸ **purpie**

PURPLE n colour between

red and blue ▷ adj of a colour between red and blue ▷ vb make purple
PURPLED ▶ purple
PURPLER ▶ purple
PURPLES ▶ purple
PURPLY ▶ purple
PURPORT vb claim (to be or do something) ▷ n apparent meaning, significance
PURPOSE n reason for which something is done or exists
PURPURA n any of several blood diseases causing purplish spots or patches on the skin due to subcutaneous bleeding
PURPURE n purple
PURPY same as ▶ **purpie**
PURR vb (of cats) make low vibrant sound, usu when pleased ▷ n this sound
PURRED ▶ purr
PURRING ▶ purr
PURRS ▶ purr
PURS ▶ pur
PURSE n small bag for money ▷ vb draw (one's lips) together into a small round shape
PURSED ▶ purse
PURSER n ship's officer who keeps the accounts
PURSERS ▶ purser
PURSES ▶ purse
PURSEW archaic spelling of ▶ **pursue**
PURSEWS ▶ pursew
PURSIER ▶ pursy
PURSILY ▶ pursy
PURSING ▶ purse
PURSUAL n act of pursuit
PURSUE vb chase
PURSUED ▶ pursue
PURSUER ▶ pursue
PURSUES ▶ pursue
PURSUIT n pursuing
PURSY adj short-winded
PURTIER ▶ purty
PURTY adj pretty
PURVEY vb supply (provisions) ▷ n food and drink laid on at a wedding reception, etc
PURVEYS ▶ purvey
PURVIEW n scope or range of activity or outlook
PUS n yellowish matter produced by infected tissue
PUSES ▶ pus
PUSH vb move or try to

move by steady force ▷ n act of pushing
PUSHED adj short of
PUSHER n person who sells illegal drugs
PUSHERS ▶ pusher
PUSHES ▶ push
PUSHFUL ▶ push
PUSHIER ▶ pushy
PUSHILY ▶ pushy
PUSHING prep almost or nearly (a certain age, speed, etc) ▷ adj aggressively ambitious ▷ adv almost or nearly (a certain age, speed, etc)
PUSHPIN n pin with a small ball-shaped head
PUSHPIT n safety rail at the stern of a boat
PUSHROD n metal rod transmitting the reciprocating motion that operates the valves of an internal-combustion engine having the camshaft in the crankcase
PUSHUP n exercise in which the body is alternately raised from and lowered to the floor by the arms only, the trunk being kept straight with the toes and hands resting on the floor
PUSHUPS ▶ pushup
PUSHY adj too assertive or ambitious
PUSLE old spelling of ▶ **puzzle**
PUSLED ▶ pusle
PUSLES ▶ pusle
PUSLEY same as > **purslane**
PUSLEYS ▶ pusley
PUSLIKE ▶ pus
PUSLING ▶ pusle
PUSS same as ▶ **pussy**
PUSSEL n slatternly woman
PUSSELS ▶ pussel
PUSSER n naval purser
PUSSERS ▶ pusser
PUSSES ▶ puss
PUSSIER ▶ pussy
PUSSIES ▶ pussy
PUSSLEY n weedy trailing herb
PUSSLY same as ▶ **pussley**
PUSSY n cat ▷ adj containing or full of pus
PUSTULE n pimple containing pus
PUT vb cause to be (in a position, state, or place) ▷ n throw in putting the shot

PUTAMEN n hard endocarp or stone of fruits such as the peach, plum, and cherry
PUTCHER n trap for catching salmon
PUTCHUK same as ▶ **pachak**
PUTDOWN n snub or insult
PUTEAL n enclosure around a well
PUTEALS ▶ puteal
PUTELI n (in India) type of boat
PUTELIS ▶ puteli
PUTID adj having an unpleasant odour
PUTLOCK same as ▶ **putlog**
PUTLOG n short horizontal beam that with others supports the floor planks of a scaffold
PUTLOGS ▶ putlog
PUTOFF n pretext or delay
PUTOFFS ▶ putoff
PUTOIS n brush to paint pottery
PUTON n hoax or piece of mockery
PUTONS ▶ puton
PUTOUT n baseball play in which the batter or runner is put out
PUTOUTS ▶ putout
PUTREFY vb rot and produce an offensive smell
PUTRID adj rotten and foul-smelling
PUTS ▶ put
PUTSCH n sudden violent attempt to remove a government from power
PUTT n stroke on the putting green to roll the ball into or near the hole ▷ vb strike (the ball) in this way
PUTTED ▶ putt
PUTTEE n (esp as part of a military uniform) strip of cloth worn wound around the leg from the ankle to the knee
PUTTEES ▶ puttee
PUTTEN old Scots past participle of ▶ **put**
PUTTER n golf club for putting ▷ vb busy oneself in a desultory though agreeable manner
PUTTERS ▶ putter
PUTTI ▶ putto
PUTTIE same as ▶ **puttee**
PUTTIED ▶ putty
PUTTIER n glazier

P

PUTTIES ▶ putty
PUTTING ▶ put
PUTTO n representation of a small boy, a cherub or cupid, esp in baroque painting or sculpture
PUTTOCK n type of bird of prey
PUTTS ▶ putt
PUTTY n stiff paste of whiting and linseed oil ▷ vb fill, fix, or coat with putty
PUTURE n claim of foresters for food for men, horses, hawks, and hounds, within the bounds of the forest
PUTURES ▶ puture
PUTZ n despicable or stupid person ▷ vb waste time
PUTZED ▶ putz
PUTZES ▶ putz
PUTZING ▶ putz
PUY n small volcanic cone
PUYS ▶ puy
PUZEL same as ▶ pucelle
PUZELS ▶ puzel
PUZZEL n prostitute
PUZZELS ▶ puzzel
PUZZLE vb perplex and confuse or be perplexed or confused ▷ n problem that cannot be easily solved
PUZZLED ▶ puzzle
PUZZLER n person or thing that puzzles
PUZZLES ▶ puzzle
PYA n monetary unit of Myanmar worth one hundredth of a kyat
PYAEMIA n blood poisoning with pus-forming microorganisms in the blood
PYAEMIC ▶ pyaemia
PYAS ▶ pya
PYAT n magpie ▷ adj pied
PYATS ▶ pyat
PYCNIC same as pyknic adj
PYCNITE n variety of topaz
PYCNON old word for > semitone
PYCNONS ▶ pycnon
PYE same as ▶ pie
PYEBALD same as ▶ piebald
PYEING ▶ pye
PYEMIA same as ▶ pyaemia
PYEMIAS ▶ pyemia
PYEMIC ▶ pyaemia
PYES ▶ pye
PYET same as ▶ pyat
PYETS ▶ pyet
PYGAL n rear part
PYGALS ▶ pygal

PYGARG n type of horned mammal
PYGARGS ▶ pygarg
PYGIDIA > pygidium
PYGMEAN ▶ pygmy
PYGMIES ▶ pygmy
PYGMOID adj of or like pygmies
PYGMY n something that is a very small example of its type ▷ adj very small
PYIC adj relating to pus
PYIN n constituent of pus
PYINS ▶ pyin
PYJAMA same as ▶ pyjamas
PYJAMAS pl n loose-fitting trousers and top worn in bed
PYKNIC adj (of a physical type) characterized by a broad squat fleshy physique with a large chest and abdomen ▷ n person with this physical type
PYKNICS ▶ pyknic
PYLON n steel tower-like structure supporting electrical cables
PYLONS ▶ pylon
PYLORI ▶ pylorus
PYLORIC ▶ pylorus
PYLORUS n small circular opening at the base of the stomach through which partially digested food (chyme) passes to the duodenum
PYNE archaic variant of ▶ pine
PYNED ▶ pyne
PYNES ▶ pyne
PYNING ▶ pyne
PYOID adj resembling pus
PYONER old variant of ▶ pioneer
PYONERS ▶ pyoner
PYOSES ▶ pyosis
PYOSIS n formation of pus
PYOT same as ▶ pyat
PYOTS ▶ pyot
PYRAL ▶ pyre
PYRALID n tropical moth
PYRALIS same as ▶ pyralid
PYRAMID n solid figure with a flat base and triangular sides sloping upwards to a point ▷ vb build up or be arranged in the form of a pyramid
PYRAMIS n pyramid-shaped structure
PYRAN n unsaturated heterocyclic compound

having a ring containing five carbon atoms and one oxygen atom and two double bonds
PYRANS ▶ pyran
PYRE n pile of wood for burning a corpse on
PYRENE n solid polynuclear aromatic hydrocarbon extracted from coal tar
PYRENES ▶ pyrene
PYRES ▶ pyre
PYRETIC adj of, relating to, or characterized by fever
PYREX n tradename for any of a variety of borosilicate glasses that have low coefficients of expansion, making them suitable for heat-resistant glassware used in cookery and chemical apparatus
PYREXES ▶ pyrex
PYREXIA technical name for ▶ fever
PYREXIC ▶ pyrexia
PYRIC adj of or relating to burning
PYRIDIC > pyridine
PYRITE n yellow mineral consisting of iron sulphide in cubic crystalline form
PYRITES same as ▶ pyrite
PYRITIC ▶ pyrite
PYRO n pyromaniac
PYROGEN n any of a group of substances that cause a rise in temperature in an animal body
PYROLA n evergreen perennial
PYROLAS ▶ pyrola
PYRONE n type of heterocyclic compound
PYRONES ▶ pyrone
PYROPE n deep yellowish-red garnet that consists of magnesium aluminium silicate and is used as a gemstone
PYROPES ▶ pyrope
PYROPUS same as ▶ pyrope
PYROS ▶ pyro
PYROSES ▶ pyrosis
PYROSIS technical name for > heartburn
PYRRHIC n metrical foot of two short or unstressed syllables ▷ adj of or relating to such a metrical foot
PYRROL same as ▶ pyrrole
PYRROLE n colourless insoluble toxic liquid with a

five-membered ring containing one nitrogen atom
PYRROLS ▶ pyrrol
PYRUVIC *adj as in* **pyruvic acid** colourless pleasant-smelling liquid
PYTHIUM *n* type of fungi
PYTHON *n* large nonpoisonous snake that crushes its prey
PYTHONS ▶ python
PYURIA *n* any condition

characterized by the presence of pus in the urine
PYURIAS ▶ pyuria
PYX *n* any receptacle for the Eucharistic Host ▷ *vb* put (something) in a pyx

> This word can also be spelt **pix**. It's a great word to know as it can earn a good score from a rack that is short of vowels.

PYXED ▶ pyx

PYXES ▶ pyx
PYXIDES ▶ pyxis
PYXIDIA > pyxidium
PYXIE *n* creeping evergreen shrub of the eastern US with small white or pink star-shaped flowers
PYXIES ▶ pyxie
PYXING ▶ pyx
PYXIS *same as* **> pyxidium**
PZAZZ *same as* **▶ pizzazz**
PZAZZES ▶ pzazz

P

Qq

With a value of 10 points, **Q** can help you to some good scores, but it can also be a very awkward tile, making it difficult to get bonus words scoring that extra 50 points, and you will normally want to play it off quickly. Often you will not have a **U** to go with it, so it's a good idea to remember the short words beginning with **Q** that don't need a **U**. This is easy, as there's only one two-letter word starting with **Q**: qi (11 points). There are four three-letter words, only one of which needs a **U**: qua (12). The other three are **qat, qin** and **qis** (12 each). If you do have a **U**, remember **quiz** (22), which is a very useful word, and can take an **S** at the front to make **squiz**. Don't forget **quartz** (24) either, while the useful **suq** (12 points) is easily overlooked.

QABALA *same as*
> **kabbalah**
QABALAH *same as*
> **kabbalah**
QABALAS ▸ **qabala**
QADI *variant spelling of*
▸ **cadi**
QADIS ▸ **qadi**
QAID *n* chief
⎮ An Arabic word, this and
⎮ its variant **qadi** are two
⎮ of the most frequently
⎮ played words in Scrabble.
⎮ There are also alternative
⎮ spellings **cadi, caid, kadi**
⎮ and **kaid**.
QAIDS ▸ **qaid**
QANAT *n* underground
irrigation channel
⎮ This word comes up
⎮ many times as one of the
⎮ words allowing you to
⎮ play the Q without a U.
QANATS ▸ **qanat**
QASIDA *n* Arabic verse form
QASIDAS ▸ **qasida**
QAT *variant spelling of* ▸ **khat**
⎮ The leaves of this shrub
⎮ are chewed as a
⎮ stimulant, and it's
⎮ certainly been a stimulus
⎮ for Scrabble, being one of
⎮ the three three-letter
⎮ words that can be played
⎮ without a U: the others
⎮ are **qin** and **qis**.
QATS ▸ **qat**
QAWWAL *n* qawwali singer
QAWWALI *n* Islamic
religious song, esp in Asia

QAWWALS ▸ **qawwal**
QI *same as* ▸ **ki**
QIBLA *same as* ▸ **kiblah**
⎮ The direction in which
⎮ Muslims turn to pray, a
⎮ useful word allowing the
⎮ Q to be played without
⎮ the U. It can also be spelt
⎮ **keblah, kibla** and
⎮ **kiblah**.
QIBLAS ▸ **qibla**
QIGONG *n* system of
breathing and exercise
designed to benefit both
physical and mental health
QIGONGS ▸ **qigong**
QIN *n* Chinese stringed
instrument related to the
zither
⎮ This Chinese musical
⎮ instrument is another
⎮ indispensable word as,
⎮ like **qat**, it combines Q
⎮ with two of the most
⎮ common letters in the
⎮ game.
QINDAR *n* Albanian
monetary unit worth one
hundredth of a lek
QINDARS ▸ **qindar**
QINS ▸ **qin**
QINTAR *same as* ▸ **qindar**
QINTARS ▸ **qintar**
QIS ▸ **qi**
QIVIUT *n* soft muskox wool
QIVIUTS ▸ **qiviut**
QOPH *same as* ▸ **koph**
⎮ A letter of the Hebrew
⎮ alphabet, also spelt
⎮ **koph**. The Hebrew

⎮ alphabet, like the Greek
⎮ alphabet, is well worth
⎮ studying from the
⎮ Scrabble point of view, as
⎮ it gives us many other
⎮ useful short words like
⎮ **ayin, beth, heth, kaph**
⎮ and **lamedh**.
QOPHS ▸ **qoph**
QORMA *variant spelling of*
▸ **korma**
QORMAS ▸ **qorma**
QUA *prep* in the capacity of
⎮ This is the only
⎮ three-letter word
⎮ beginning with Q that
⎮ needs a U. It is played so
⎮ often that it is well worth
⎮ mastering all the hooks
⎮ to this: it takes A at the
⎮ front to make **aqua** and
⎮ D, G, I, T and Y at the back
⎮ to make **quad, quag,
⎮ quai, quat** and **quay**.
QUACK *vb* (of a duck) utter a
harsh guttural sound ▷ *n*
an unqualified person who
claims medical knowledge
QUACKED ▸ **quack**
QUACKER ▸ **quack**
QUACKLE *same as* ▸ **quack**
QUACKS ▸ **quack**
QUACKY ▸ **quack**
QUAD *n* quadrangle
QUADDED *adj* formed of
multiple quads
QUADRAT *n* area of
vegetation, often one
square metre, marked out
for study of the plants in the

surrounding area

QUADRIC adj having or characterized by an equation of the second degree, usually in two or three variables ▷ n quadric curve, surface, or function

QUADS ▶ quad

QUAERE n query or question ▷ interj ask or inquire: used esp to introduce a question ▷ vb ask

QUAERED ▶ quaere

QUAERES ▶ quaere

QUAFF vb drink heartily or in one draught

QUAFFED ▶ quaff

QUAFFER ▶ quaff

QUAFFS ▶ quaff

QUAG another word for > quagmire

QUAGGA n recently extinct zebra, striped only on the head and shoulders

QUAGGAS ▶ quagga

QUAGGY adj resembling a marsh or quagmire

QUAGS ▶ quag

QUAHAUG same as ▶ quahog

QUAHOG n edible clam

QUAHOGS ▶ quahog

QUAI same as ▶ quay

QUAICH n small shallow drinking cup, usually with two handles

QUAICHS ▶ quaich

QUAIGH same as ▶ quaich

QUAIGHS ▶ quaigh

QUAIL n small game bird of the partridge family ▷ vb shrink back with fear

QUAILED ▶ quail

QUAILS ▶ quail

QUAINT adj attractively unusual, esp in an old-fashioned style

QUAIR n book

QUAIRS ▶ quair

QUAIS ▶ quai

QUAKE vb shake or tremble with or as if with fear ▷ n earthquake

QUAKED ▶ quake

QUAKER ▶ quake

QUAKERS ▶ quake

QUAKES ▶ quake

QUAKIER ▶ quaky

QUAKILY ▶ quaky

QUAKING ▶ quake

QUAKY adj inclined to quake

QUALE n essential property or quality

QUALIA ▶ quale

QUALIFY vb provide or be provided with the abilities necessary for a task, office, or duty

QUALITY n degree or standard of excellence ▷ adj excellent or superior

QUALM n pang of conscience

QUALMS ▶ qualm

QUALMY ▶ qualm

QUAMASH another name for ▶ camass

QUANGO n quasi-autonomous nongovernmental organization: any partly independent official body set up by a government

QUANGOS ▶ quango

QUANNET n flat file with handle at one end

QUANT n long pole for propelling a boat, esp a punt, by pushing on the bottom of a river or lake ▷ vb propel (a boat) with a quant

QUANTA ▶ quantum

QUANTAL adj of or relating to a quantum or an entity that is quantized

QUANTED ▶ quant

QUANTIC n mathematical function

QUANTS ▶ quant

QUANTUM n desired or required amount, esp a very small one ▷ adj of or designating a major breakthrough or sudden advance

QUARE adj remarkable or strange

QUARER ▶ quare

QUAREST ▶ quare

QUARK n subatomic particle thought to be the fundamental unit of matter

This subatomic particle appears in the Scrabble cloud-chamber fairly often, and when it does, remember that you can put an S on the front of it to make **squark**.

QUARKS ▶ quark

QUARREL n angry disagreement ▷ vb have a disagreement or dispute

QUARRY n place where stone is dug from the surface of the earth ▷ vb extract (stone) from a quarry

QUART n unit of liquid measure equal to two pints (1.136 litres)

QUARTAN adj (esp of a malarial fever) occurring every third day ▷ n quartan malaria

QUARTE n fourth of eight basic positions from which a parry or attack can be made in fencing

QUARTER n one of four equal parts of something ▷ vb divide into four equal parts ▷ adj being or consisting of one of four equal parts

QUARTES ▶ quarte

QUARTET n group of four performers

QUARTIC n biquadratic equation

QUARTO n book size in which the sheets are folded into four leaves

QUARTOS ▶ quarto

QUARTS ▶ quart

QUARTZ n hard glossy mineral

QUARTZY ▶ quartz

QUASAR n extremely distant starlike object that emits powerful radio waves

QUASARS ▶ quasar

QUASH vb annul or make void

QUASHED ▶ quash

QUASHEE same as ▶ quashie

QUASHER ▶ quash

QUASHES ▶ quash

QUASHIE n in the Carribbean, an unsophisticated or gullible male Black peasant

QUASI adv as if

QUASS same as ▶ kvass

QUASSES ▶ quass

QUASSIA n tropical American tree, the wood of which yields a substance used in insecticides

QUASSIN n bitter crystalline substance

QUAT n spot

QUATCH vb move

QUATE n fortune

QUATRE n playing card with four pips

QUATRES ▶ quatre

QUATS ▶ quat

QUAVER vb (of a voice) quiver or tremble ▷ n note half the length of a crotchet

QUAVERS ▶ quaver

QUAVERY ▶ quaver

QUAY n wharf built parallel to the shore

QUAYAGE n system of quays

QUAYD archaic past participle of ▶ quail

> a Spenserian word meaning daunted, that makes a surprising hook for **quay**.

QUAYS ▶ quay

QUAZZY adj unwell

QUBIT n quantum bit

QUBITS ▶ qubit

QUBYTE n unit of eight qubits

QUBYTES ▶ qubyte

QUEACH n thicket

QUEACHY adj unwell

QUEAN n boisterous, impudent, or disreputable woman

QUEANS ▶ quean

QUEASY adj having the feeling that one is about to vomit

QUEAZY same as ▶ queasy

QUEBEC n code word for the letter Q

QUEBECS ▶ quebec

QUEECHY same as ▶ queachy

QUEEN n female sovereign who is the official ruler or head of state ▷ vb flaunt one's homosexuality

QUEENED ▶ queen

QUEENIE n scallop

QUEENLY adj resembling or appropriate to a queen ▷ adv in a manner appropriate to a queen

QUEENS ▶ queen

QUEENY adj effeminate

QUEER adj not normal or usual ▷ n derogatory name for a homosexual person ▷ vb spoil or thwart

QUEERED ▶ queer

QUEERER ▶ queer

QUEERLY ▶ queer

QUEERS ▶ queer

QUEEST n wood pigeon

QUEESTS ▶ queest

QUEINT same as ▶ quaint

QUELCH same as ▶ squelch

QUELEA n East African weaver bird

QUELEAS ▶ quelea

QUELL vb suppress

QUELLED ▶ quell

QUELLER ▶ quell

QUELLS ▶ quell

QUEME vb please

QUEMED ▶ queme

QUEMES ▶ queme

QUEMING ▶ queme

QUENA n Andean flute

QUENAS ▶ quena

QUENCH vb satisfy (one's thirst)

QUEP interj expression of derision

QUERIDA n sweetheart

QUERIED ▶ query

QUERIER ▶ query

QUERIES ▶ query

QUERIST n person who makes inquiries or queries

QUERN n stone hand mill for grinding corn

QUERNS ▶ quern

QUERY n question, esp one raising doubt ▷ vb express uncertainty, doubt, or an objection concerning (something)

QUEST n long and difficult search ▷ vb go in search of

QUESTED ▶ quest

QUESTER ▶ quest

QUESTOR same as > quaestor

QUESTS ▶ quest

QUETCH vb move

QUETHE vb say

QUETHES ▶ quethe

QUETSCH n plum brandy

QUETZAL n crested bird of Central and N South America

> This is a great word if you can get the tiles for it, so it's well worth remembering both spellings – it can also be **quezal** – and the four plural forms, which are **quetzals** or **quetzales** and **quezals** or **quezales**.

QUEUE n line of people or vehicles waiting for something ▷ vb form or remain in a line while waiting

QUEUED ▶ queue

QUEUER ▶ queue

QUEUERS ▶ queue

QUEUES ▶ queue

QUEUING ▶ queue

QUEY n young cow

QUEYN n girl

QUEYNIE same as ▶ queyn

QUEYNS ▶ queyn

QUEYS ▶ quey

QUEZAL same as ▶ quetzal

QUEZALS ▶ quezal

QUIBBLE vb make trivial objections ▷ n trivial objection

QUIBLIN same as ▶ quibble

QUICH vb move

QUICHE n savoury flan with an egg custard filling to which vegetables etc are added

QUICHED ▶ quich

QUICHES ▶ quiche

QUICK adj speedy, fast ▷ n area of sensitive flesh under a nail ▷ adv in a rapid manner

QUICKEN vb make or become faster ▷ n rowan tree

QUICKER ▶ quick

QUICKIE n anything done or made hurriedly ▷ adj made or done rapidly

QUICKLY ▶ quick

QUICKS ▶ quick

QUICKY n hastily arranged divorce

QUID n pound (sterling)

QUIDAM n specified person

QUIDAMS ▶ quidam

QUIDDIT same as > quiddity

QUIDDLE vb waste time

QUIDS ▶ quid

QUIESCE vb quieten

QUIET adj with little noise ▷ n quietness ▷ vb make or become quiet

QUIETED ▶ quiet

QUIETEN vb make or become quiet

QUIETER ▶ quiet

QUIETLY ▶ quiet

QUIETS ▶ quiet

QUIETUS n release from life

QUIFF n tuft of hair brushed up above the forehead

QUIFFS ▶ quiff

QUIGHT vb quit

QUIGHTS ▶ quight

QUILL n pen made from the feather of a bird's wing or tail ▷ vb wind (thread, yarn, etc) onto a spool or bobbin

QUILLAI *another name for* > **soapbark**
QUILLED ► **quill**
QUILLET *n* quibble or subtlety
QUILLON *n* either half of the extended crosspiece of a sword or dagger
QUILLS ► **quill**
QUILT *n* padded covering for a bed ▷ *vb* stitch together two layers of (fabric) with padding between them
QUILTED ► **quilt**
QUILTER ► **quilt**
QUILTS ► **quilt**
QUIN *short for* > **quintuplet**
QUINA *n* quinine
QUINARY *adj* consisting of fives or by fives ▷ *n* set of five
QUINAS ► **quina**
QUINATE *adj* arranged in or composed of five parts
QUINCE *n* acid-tasting pear-shaped fruit
QUINCES ► **quince**
QUINCHE *vb* move
QUINE *same as* ► **quean**
QUINELA *same as* > **quinella**
QUINES ► **quine**
QUINIC *adj as in* **quinic acid** white crystalline soluble optically active carboxylic acid
QUINIE *n* girl
QUINIES ► **quinie**
QUININ *same as* ► **quinine**
QUININA *same as* ► **quinine**
QUININE *n* bitter drug used as a tonic and formerly to treat malaria
QUININS ► **quinin**
QUINNAT *n* Pacific salmon
QUINO *same as* ► **keno**
QUINOA *n* type of grain high in nutrients
QUINOAS ► **quinoa**
QUINOID *same as* > **quinonoid**
QUINOL *n* white crystalline soluble phenol used as a photographic developer
QUINOLS ► **quinol**
QUINONE *n* yellow crystalline water-soluble unsaturated ketone
QUINOS ► **quino**
QUINS ► **quin**
QUINSY *n* inflammation of the throat or tonsils
QUINT *same as* ► **quin**
QUINTA *n* Portuguese

vineyard where grapes for wine or port are grown
QUINTAL *n* unit of weight equal to (esp in Britain) 112 pounds (50.85 kg) or (esp in US) 100 pounds (45.36 kg)
QUINTAN *adj* (of a fever) occurring every fourth day ▷ *n* quintan fever
QUINTAR *n* Albanian unit of currency
QUINTAS ► **quinta**
QUINTE *n* fifth of eight basic positions from which a parry or attack can be made in fencing
QUINTES ► **quinte**
QUINTET *n* group of five performers
QUINTIC *adj* of or relating to the fifth degree ▷ *n* mathematical function
QUINTIN *same as* > **quintain**
QUINTS ► **quint**
QUINZE *n* card game with rules similar to those of vingt-et-un, except that the score aimed at is 15 rather than 21

> This card game, deriving from the French word for fifteen, makes a high-scoring word that you may well get to play, and if you can use all of your tiles to form the plural, you'll get a 50-point bonus.

QUINZES ► **quinze**
QUIP *n* witty saying ▷ *vb* make a quip
QUIPO *same as* ► **quipu**
QUIPOS ► **quipo**
QUIPPED ► **quip**
QUIPPER ► **quip**
QUIPPU *same as* ► **quipu**
QUIPPUS ► **quippu**
QUIPPY ► **quip**
QUIPS ► **quip**
QUIPU *n* device of the Incas of Peru used to record information, consisting of an arrangement of variously coloured and knotted cords attached to a base cord
QUIPUS ► **quipu**
QUIRE *n* set of 24 or 25 sheets of paper ▷ *vb* arrange in quires
QUIRED ► **quire**
QUIRES ► **quire**
QUIRING ► **quire**

QUIRK *n* peculiarity of character ▷ *vb* quip
QUIRKED ► **quirk**
QUIRKS ► **quirk**
QUIRKY ► **quirk**
QUIRT *n* whip with a leather thong at one end ▷ *vb* strike with a quirt
QUIRTED ► **quirt**
QUIRTS ► **quirt**
QUIST *n* wood pigeon
QUISTS ► **quist**
QUIT *vb* stop (doing something) ▷ *adj* free (from)
QUITCH *vb* move
QUITE *archaic form of* ► **quit**
QUITED ► **quite**
QUITES ► **quite**
QUITING ► **quite**
QUITS ► **quit**
QUITTAL *n* repayment of an action with a similar action
QUITTED ► **quit**
QUITTER *n* person who lacks perseverance
QUITTOR *n* infection of the cartilages on the side of a horse's foot, characterized by inflammation and the formation of pus
QUIVER *vb* shake with a tremulous movement ▷ *n* shaking or trembling
QUIVERS ► **quiver**
QUIVERY ► **quiver**
QUIXOTE *n* impractical idealist

> Using the Q and X, this word for an impractical dreamer has a reasonable chance of coming up, so keeping an eye open for it is not that quixotic!

QUIZ *n* entertainment in which the knowledge of the players is tested by a series of questions ▷ *vb* investigate by close questioning
QUIZZED ► **quiz**
QUIZZER ► **quiz**
QUIZZES ► **quiz**
QUOAD *adv* as far as
QUOD *n* jail ▷ *vb* say
QUODDED ► **quod**
QUODLIN *n* cooking apple
QUODS ► **quod**
QUOHOG *n* edible clam
QUOHOGS ► **quohog**
QUOIF *vb* arrange (the hair)
QUOIFED ► **quoif**

Q

QUOIFS ▶ **quoif**
QUOIN *n* external corner of a building ▷ *vb* wedge
QUOINED ▶ **quoin**
QUOINS ▶ **quoin**
QUOIST *n* wood pigeon
QUOISTS ▶ **quoist**
QUOIT *n* large ring used in the game of quoits ▷ *vb* throw as a quoit
QUOITED ▶ **quoit**
QUOITER ▶ **quoit**
QUOITS *n* game in which quoits are tossed at a stake in the ground in attempts to encircle it
QUOKKA *n* small Australian wallaby
QUOKKAS ▶ **quokka**
QUOLL *n* Australian catlike carnivorous marsupial
QUOLLS ▶ **quoll**
QUOMODO *n* manner
QUONDAM *adj* of an earlier time
QUONK *vb* make an accidental noise while broadcasting
QUONKED ▶ **quonk**
QUONKS ▶ **quonk**
QUOOKE *archaic past participle of* ▶ **quake**
QUOP *vb* pulsate or throb
QUOPPED ▶ **quop**
QUOPS ▶ **quop**
QUORATE *adj* having or being a quorum
QUORUM *n* minimum number of people required to be present at a meeting before any transactions can take place
QUORUMS ▶ **quorum**
QUOTA *n* share that is due from, due to, or allocated to a group or person
QUOTAS ▶ **quota**
QUOTE *vb* repeat (words) exactly from (an earlier work, speech, or conversation) ▷ *n* quotation ▷ *interj* expression used parenthetically to indicate that the words that follow it form a quotation
QUOTED ▶ **quote**
QUOTER ▶ **quote**
QUOTERS ▶ **quote**
QUOTES ▶ **quote**
QUOTH *vb* said
QUOTHA *interj* expression of mild sarcasm, used in picking up a word or phrase used by someone else
QUOTING ▶ **quote**
QUOTUM *same as* ▶ **quota**
QUOTUMS ▶ **quotum**
QURSH *same as* ▶ **qurush**
QURSHES ▶ **qurush**
QURUSH *n* Saudi Arabian currency unit
QUYTE *same as* ▶ **quit**
QUYTED ▶ **quyte**
QUYTES ▶ **quyte**
QUYTING ▶ **quyte**
QWERTY *n* standard English-language typewriter or computer keyboard
QWERTYS ▶ **qwerty**

Q

Rr

R is one of the most common consonants in Scrabble, along with **N** and **T**. Despite this, however, there is only one two-letter word beginning with **R**: **re** (2 points). This is worth remembering, as you won't need to waste time trying to think of others. There are some good three-letter words with **R**, however, some of which are quite unusual: **raj, rax, rex** (10 each), **rez** and **riz** (12 each). Also, don't forget common words like **raw, ray** and **row** (6 each).

RABANNA n Madagascan woven raffia

RABAT vb rotate so that the plane rotated coincides with another

RABATO n wired or starched collar, often of intricate lace, that stood up at the back and sides: worn in the 17th century

RABATOS ▶ rabato

RABATS ▶ rabat

RABATTE same as ▶ rabat

RABBET n recess, groove, or step, usually of rectangular section, cut into a surface or along the edge of a piece of timber to receive a mating piece ▷ vb cut or form a rabbet in (timber)

RABBETS ▶ rabbet

RABBI n Jewish spiritual leader

RADDIES ▶ rabbi

RABBIN same as ▶ rabbi

RABBINS ▶ rabbin

RABBIS ▶ rabbi

RABBIT n small burrowing mammal with long ears ▷ vb talk too much

RABBITO same as > rabbitoh

RABBITS ▶ rabbit

RABBITY adj rabbitlike

RABBLE n disorderly crowd of noisy people ▷ vb stir, mix, or skim (the molten charge) in a roasting furnace

RABBLED ▶ rabble

RABBLER n iron tool or device for stirring, mixing, or skimming a molten charge in a roasting furnace

RABBLES ▶ rabble

RABBONI n very respectful Jewish title or form of address

RABI n (in Pakistan, India, etc) a crop that is harvested at the end of winter

RABIC ▶ rabies

RABID adj fanatical

RABIDER ▶ rabid

RABIDLY ▶ rabid

RABIES n usu fatal viral disease transmitted by dogs and certain other animals

RABIS ▶ rabi

RACA adj biblical word meaning worthless or empty-headed

RACCOON n small N American mammal with a long striped tail

RACE n contest of speed ▷ vb compete with in a race

RACED ▶ race

RACEME n cluster of flowers along a central stem, as in the foxglove

RACEMED adj with or in racemes

RACEMES ▶ raceme

RACEMIC adj of, concerned with, or being a mixture of equal amounts of enantiomers and consequently having no optical activity

RACER n person, animal, or machine that races

RACERS ▶ racer

RACES ▶ race

RACEWAY n racetrack, esp one for banger racing

RACH n scent hound

RACHE same as ▶ rach

RACHES ▶ rach

RACHET same as ▶ ratchet

RACHETS ▶ rachet

RACHIAL ▶ rachis

RACHIS n main axis or stem of an inflorescence or compound leaf

RACIAL adj relating to the division of the human species into races

RACIER ▶ racy

RACIEST ▶ racy

RACILY ▶ racy

RACING adj denoting or associated with horse races ▷ n practice of engaging horses (or sometimes greyhounds) in contests of speed

RACINGS ▶ racing

RACINO n combined racetrack and casino

RACINOS ▶ racino

RACISM n hostile attitude or behaviour to members of other races, based on a belief in the innate superiority of one's own race

RACISMS ▶ racism

RACIST ▶ racism

RACISTS ▶ racism

RACK n framework for holding particular articles, such as coats or luggage ▷ vb cause great suffering to

RACKED ▶ rack

RACKER ▶ rack

RACKERS ▶ rack

R

RACKET *n* bat with strings stretched in an oval frame, used in tennis etc ▷ *vb* to strike with a racket

RACKETS *n* ball game played in a paved walled court

RACKETT *n* early double-reeded wind instrument

RACKETY *adj* involving noise, commotion and excitement

RACKFUL ▶ rack

RACKING ▶ rack

RACKLE *adj* dialect word meaning rash

RACKS ▶ rack

RACLOIR *n* scraper

RACON *n* radar beacon

RACONS ▶ racon

RACOON *same as* ▶ raccoon

RACOONS ▶ racoon

RACQUET *same as* racket *n*

RACY *adj* slightly shocking

RAD *n* former unit of absorbed ionizing radiation dose equivalent to an energy absorption per unit mass of 0.01 joule per kilogram of irradiated material. 1 rad is equivalent to 0.01 gray ▷ *vb* fear ▷ *adj* slang term for great

RADAR *n* device for tracking distant objects by bouncing high-frequency radio pulses off them

RADARS ▶ radar

RADDED ▶ rad

RADDER ▶ rad

RADDEST ▶ rad

RADDING ▶ rad

RADDLE *same as* ▶ ruddle

RADDLED *adj* (of a person) unkempt or run-down in appearance

RADDLES ▶ raddle

RADE (*in Scots dialect*) *past tense of* ▶ ride

RADGE *adj* angry or uncontrollable ▷ *n* person acting in such a way

RADGER ▶ radge

RADGES ▶ radge

RADGEST ▶ radge

RADIAL *adj* spreading out from a common central point ▷ *n* radial-ply tyre

RADIALE *n* bone in the wrist

RADIALS ▶ radial

RADIAN *n* unit for measuring angles, equal to 57.296°

RADIANS ▶ radian

RADIANT *adj* looking happy ▷ *n* point or object that emits radiation, esp the part of a heater that gives out heat

RADIATA *adj as in* **radiata pine** type of pine tree

RADIATE *vb* spread out from a centre ▷ *adj* having rays or a radial structure

RADICAL *adj* fundamental ▷ *n* person advocating fundamental (political) change

RADICEL *n* very small root

RADICES ▶ radix

RADICLE *n* small or developing root

RADII ▶ radius

RADIO *n* use of electromagnetic waves for broadcasting, communication, etc ▷ *vb* transmit (a message) by radio ▷ *adj* of, relating to, or using radio

RADIOED ▶ radio

RADIOS ▶ radio

RADISH *n* small hot-flavoured root vegetable eaten raw in salads

RADIUM *n* radioactive metallic element

RADIUMS ▶ radium

RADIUS *n* (length of) a straight line from the centre to the circumference of a circle

RADIX *n* any number that is the base of a number system or of a system of logarithms

RADIXES ▶ radix

RADOME *n* protective housing for a radar antenna made from a material that is transparent to radio waves

RADOMES ▶ radome

RADON *n* radioactive gaseous element

RADONS ▶ radon

RADS ▶ rad

RADULA *n* horny tooth-bearing strip on the tongue of molluscs that is used for rasping food

RADULAE ▶ radula

RADULAR ▶ radula

RADULAS ▶ radula

RAFALE *n* burst of artillery fire

RAFALES ▶ rafale

RAFF *n* rubbish

RAFFIA *n* prepared palm fibre for weaving mats etc

RAFFIAS ▶ raffia

RAFFISH *adj* slightly disreputable

RAFFLE *n* lottery with goods as prizes ▷ *vb* offer as a prize in a raffle

RAFFLED ▶ raffle

RAFFLER ▶ raffle

RAFFLES ▶ raffle

RAFFS ▶ raff

RAFT *n* floating platform of logs, planks, etc ▷ *vb* convey on or travel by raft, or make a raft from

RAFTED ▶ raft

RAFTER *n* one of the main beams of a roof ▷ *vb* to fit with rafters

RAFTERS ▶ rafter

RAFTING ▶ raft

RAFTMAN *same as* ▶ raftsman

RAFTMEN ▶ raftman

RAFTS ▶ raft

RAG *n* fragment of cloth ▷ *vb* tease ▷ *adj* (in British universities and colleges) of various events organized to raise money for charity

RAGA *n* any of several conventional patterns of melody and rhythm that form the basis for freely interpreted compositions. Each pattern is associated with different aspects of religious devotion

RAGAS ▶ raga

RAGBAG *n* confused assortment, jumble

RAGBAGS ▶ ragbag

RAGBOLT *n* bolt that has angled projections on it to prevent it working loose once it has been driven home

RAGDE *archaic past form of* ▶ rage

RAGE *n* violent anger or passion ▷ *vb* speak or act with fury

RAGED ▶ rage

RAGEE *same as* ▶ ragi

RAGEES ▶ ragee

RAGEFUL ▶ rage

RAGER ▶ rage
RAGERS ▶ rage
RAGES ▶ rage
RAGG same as > **ragstone**
RAGGA n dance-oriented style of reggae
RAGGAS ▶ ragga
RAGGED ▶ rag
RAGGEDY adj somewhat ragged
RAGGEE same as ▶ ragi
RAGGEES ▶ raggee
RAGGERY n rags
RAGGIER ▶ raggy
RAGGIES ▶ raggy
RAGGING ▶ rag
RAGGLE n thin groove cut in stone or brickwork, esp to hold the edge of a roof ▷ vb cut a raggle in
RAGGLED ▶ raggle
RAGGLES ▶ raggle
RAGGS ▶ ragg
RAGGY adj raglike ▷ n cereal grass cultivated in Africa and Asia for its edible grain
RAGI n cereal grass cultivated in Africa and Asia for its edible grain
RAGING ▶ rage
RAGINGS ▶ rage
RAGINI n Indian musical form related to a raga
RAGINIS ▶ ragini
RAGIS ▶ ragi
RAGLAN adj (of a sleeve) joined to a garment by diagonal seams from the neck to the underarm ▷ n coat with sleeves that continue to the collar instead of having armhole seams
RAGLANS ▶ raglan
RAGMAN n rag-and-bone man
RAGMANS ▶ ragman
RAGMEN ▶ ragman
RAGMENT n statute, roll, or list
RAGOUT n richly seasoned stew of meat and vegetables ▷ vb make into a ragout
RAGOUTS ▶ ragout
RAGS ▶ rag
RAGTAG n disparaging term for common people
RAGTAGS ▶ ragtag
RAGTIME n style of jazz piano music
RAGTOP n informal word

for a car with a folding or removable roof
RAGTOPS ▶ ragtop
RAGU n Italian meat and tomato sauce
RAGULED same as ▶ raguly
RAGULY adj (in heraldry) having toothlike or stublike projections
RAGUS ▶ ragu
RAGWEED n any of several plants regarded as weeds, some of which produce a large amount of hay-fever-causing pollen
RAGWORK n weaving or needlework using rags
RAGWORM n type of worm that lives chiefly in burrows in sand or mud
RAGWORT n plant with ragged leaves and yellow flowers
RAH informal US word for ▶ cheer
RAHED ▶ rah
RAHING ▶ rah
RAHS ▶ rah
RAHUI n Māori prohibition
RAHUIS ▶ rahui
RAI n type of Algerian popular music based on traditional Algerian music influenced by modern Western pop
RAIA same as ▶ rayah
RAIAS ▶ raia
RAID n sudden surprise attack or search ▷ vb make a raid on
RAIDED ▶ raid
RAIDER ▶ raid
RAIDERS ▶ raid
RAIDING ▶ raid
RAIDS ▶ raid
RAIK n wander ▷ vb wander
RAIKED ▶ raik
RAIKING ▶ raik
RAIKS ▶ raik
RAIL n horizontal bar, esp as part of a fence or track ▷ vb complain bitterly or loudly
RAILAGE n cost of transporting goods by rail
RAILBED n ballast layer supporting the sleepers of a railway track
RAILBUS n buslike vehicle for use on railway lines
RAILCAR n passenger-carrying railway vehicle consisting of a single coach with its own power unit

RAILE archaic spelling of ▶ rail
RAILED ▶ rail
RAILER ▶ rail
RAILERS ▶ rail
RAILES ▶ raile
RAILING n fence made of rails supported by posts
RAILLY old word for ▶ mock
RAILMAN n railway employee
RAILMEN ▶ railman
RAILS ▶ rail
RAILWAY n track of iron rails on which trains run
RAIMENT n clothing
RAIN n water falling in drops from the clouds ▷ vb fall or pour down as rain
RAINBOW n arch of colours in the sky
RAINE archaic spelling of ▶ reign
RAINED ▶ rain
RAINES ▶ raine
RAINIER ▶ rainy
RAINILY ▶ rainy
RAINING ▶ rain
RAINOUT n radioactive fallout or atmospheric pollution carried to the earth by rain
RAINS ▶ rain
RAINY adj characterized by a large rainfall
RAIRD same as ▶ reird
RAIRDS ▶ raird
RAIS ▶ rai
RAISE vb lift up ▷ n increase in pay
RAISED ▶ raise
RAISER ▶ raise
RAISERS ▶ raise
RAISES ▶ raise
RAISIN n dried grape
RAISING n rule that moves a constituent from an embedded clause into the main clause
RAISINS ▶ raisin
RAISINY ▶ raisin
RAIT same as ▶ ret
RAITA n Indian dish of chopped cucumber, mint, etc, in yogurt, served with curries
RAITAS ▶ raita
RAITED ▶ rait
RAITING ▶ rait
RAITS ▶ rait
RAIYAT same as ▶ ryot
RAIYATS ▶ raiyat
RAJ n (in India) government

R

This Indian word for rule or empire is one of the essential short words that use a J. Remember that it can extended to **raja**.

RAJA *same as* ▶ **rajah**

RAJAH *n* (in India, formerly) a ruler or landlord: sometimes used as a form of address or as a title preceding a name

RAJAHS ▶ **rajah**

RAJAS ▶ **raja**

RAJES ▶ **raj**

RAKE *n* tool with a long handle and a crosspiece with teeth, used for smoothing earth or gathering leaves, hay, etc ▷ *vb* gather or smooth with a rake

RAKED ▶ **rake**

RAKEE *same as* ▶ **raki**

RAKEES ▶ **rakee**

RAKEOFF *n* share of profits, esp one that is illegal or given as a bribe

RAKER *n* person who rakes

RAKERS ▶ **raker**

RAKERY *n* rakish behaviour

RAKES ▶ **rake**

RAKI *n* strong spirit distilled in Turkey, the former Yugoslavia, etc, from grain, usually flavoured with aniseed or other aromatics

RAKIA *n* strong fruit-based alcoholic drink popular in the Balkans

RAKIAS ▶ **rakia**

RAKIJA ▶ **rakia**

RAKIJAS ▶ **rakia**

RAKING *n* offence committed when a player deliberately scrapes an opponent's leg, arm, etc with the studs of his or her boots

RAKINGS ▶ **raking**

RAKIS ▶ **raki**

RAKISH *adj* dashing or jaunty

RAKSHAS *same as* > **rakshasa**

RAKU *n* type of Japanese pottery

RAKUS ▶ **raku**

RALE *n* abnormal coarse crackling sound heard on auscultation of the chest, usually caused by the accumulation of fluid in the lungs

RALES ▶ **rale**

RALLIED ▶ **rally**

RALLIER ▶ **rally**

RALLIES ▶ **rally**

RALLINE *adj* relating to a family of birds that includes the rails, crakes, and coots

RALLY *n* large gathering of people for a meeting ▷ *vb* bring or come together after dispersal or for a common cause

RALLYE *US variant of* ▶ **rally**

RALLYES ▶ **rallye**

RAM *n* male sheep ▷ *vb* strike against with force

RAMADA *n* outdoor eating area with roof but open sides

RAMADAS ▶ **ramada**

RAMAKIN *same as* ▶ **ramekin**

RAMAL *adj* relating to a branch or branches

RAMATE *adj* with branches

RAMBLA *n* dried-up riverbed

RAMBLAS ▶ **rambla**

RAMBLE *vb* walk without a definite route ▷ *n* walk, esp in the country

RAMBLED ▶ **ramble**

RAMBLER *n* person who rambles

RAMBLES ▶ **ramble**

RAMCAT *n* dialect word for a male cat

RAMCATS ▶ **ramcat**

RAMEAL *same as* ▶ **ramal**

RAMEE *same as* ▶ **ramie**

RAMEES ▶ **ramee**

RAMEKIN *n* small ovenproof dish for a single serving of food

RAMEN *n* Japanese dish consisting of a clear broth containing thin white noodles and sometimes vegetables, meat, etc

RAMENS ▶ **ramen**

RAMENTA > **ramentum**

RAMEOUS *same as* ▶ **ramal**

RAMET *n* any of the individuals in a group of clones

RAMETS ▶ **ramet**

RAMI *same as* ▶ **ramie**

RAMIE *n* woody Asian shrub with broad leaves and a stem that yields a flaxlike fibre

RAMIES ▶ **ramie**

RAMIFY *vb* become complex

RAMILIE *same as* > **ramillie**

RAMIN *n* swamp-growing tree found in Malaysia and Indonesia

RAMINS ▶ **ramin**

RAMIS ▶ **rami**

RAMJET *n* type of jet engine in which fuel is burned in a duct using air compressed by the forward speed of the aircraft

RAMJETS ▶ **ramjet**

RAMMED ▶ **ram**

RAMMEL *n* discarded or waste matter

RAMMELS ▶ **rammel**

RAMMER ▶ **ram**

RAMMERS ▶ **ram**

RAMMIER ▶ **rammish**

RAMMIES ▶ **rammish**

RAMMING ▶ **ram**

RAMMISH *adj* like a ram, esp in being lustful or foul-smelling

RAMMLE *n* collection of items saved in case they become useful

RAMMLES ▶ **rammle**

RAMMY *n* noisy disturbance or free-for-all ▷ *vb* make a rammy

RAMONA *same as* > **sagebrush**

RAMONAS ▶ **ramona**

RAMOSE *adj* having branches

RAMOUS *same as* ▶ **ramose**

RAMP *n* slope joining two level surfaces ▷ *vb* (esp of animals) to rush around in a wild excited manner

RAMPAGE *vb* dash about violently

RAMPANT *adj* growing or spreading uncontrollably

RAMPART *n* mound or wall for defence ▷ *vb* provide with a rampart

RAMPED ▶ **ramp**

RAMPER ▶ **ramp**

RAMPERS ▶ **ramp**

RAMPICK *same as* ▶ **rampike**

RAMPIKE *n* US or dialect word for a dead tree

RAMPING ▶ **ramp**

RAMPION *n* European and Asian plant that has clusters of bluish flowers and an edible white tuberous root used in salads

RAMPIRE *archaic variant of* ▸ **rampart**

RAMPOLE *same as* ▸ **rampike**

RAMPS ▸ **ramp**

RAMROD *n* long thin rod used for cleaning the barrel of a gun or forcing gunpowder into an old-fashioned gun ▸ *adj* (of someone's posture) very straight and upright ▸ *vb* drive

RAMRODS ▸ **ramrod**

RAMS ▸ **ram**

RAMSON *n* type of garlic

RAMSONS ▸ **ramson**

RAMSTAM *adv* headlong ▸ *adj* headlong

RAMTIL *n* African plant grown in India esp for its oil

RAMTILS ▸ **ramtil**

RAMULAR *adj* relating to a branch or branches

RAMULI ▸ **ramulus**

RAMULUS *n* small branch

RAMUS *n* barb of a bird's feather

RAN ▸ **run**

RANA *n* genus of frogs

RANAS ▸ **rana**

RANCE *Scots word for* ▸ **prop**

RANCED ▸ **rance**

RANCEL *vb* (in Shetland and Orkney) carry out a search

RANCELS ▸ **rancel**

RANCES ▸ **rance**

RANCH *n* large cattle farm in the American West ▸ *vb* run a ranch

RANCHED ▸ **ranch**

RANCHER *n* person who owns, manages, or works on a ranch

RANCHES ▸ **ranch**

RANCHO *n* hut or group of huts for housing ranch workers

RANCHOS ▸ **rancho**

RANCID *adj* (of butter, bacon, etc) stale and having an offensive smell

RANCING ▸ **rance**

RANCOR *same as* ▸ **rancour**

RANCORS ▸ **rancor**

RANCOUR *n* deep bitter hate

RAND *n* monetary unit of South Africa; leather strip on the heel of a shoe ▸ *vb* cut into rands

RANDAN *n* boat rowed by three people, in which the person in the middle uses two oars and the people fore and aft use one oar each

RANDANS ▸ **randan**

RANDED ▸ **rand**

RANDEM *adv* with three horses harnessed together as a team ▸ *n* carriage or team of horses so driven

RANDEMS ▸ **randem**

RANDIE *same as* ▸ **randy**

RANDIER ▸ **randy**

RANDIES ▸ **randy**

RANDILY ▸ **randy**

RANDING ▸ **rand**

RANDOM *adj* made or done by chance or without plan ▸ *n* (in mining) the course of a vein of ore

RANDOMS ▸ **random**

RANDON *old variant of* ▸ **random**

RANDONS ▸ **randon**

RANDS ▸ **rand**

RANDY *adj* sexually aroused ▸ *n* rude or reckless person

RANEE *same as* ▸ **rani**

RANEES ▸ **ranee**

RANG ▸ **ring**

RANGE *n* limits of effectiveness or variation ▸ *vb* vary between one point and another

RANGED ▸ **range**

RANGER *n* official in charge of a nature reserve etc

RANGERS ▸ **ranger**

RANGES ▸ **range**

RANGI *n* sky

RANGIER ▸ **rangy**

RANGILY ▸ **rangy**

RANGING ▸ **range**

RANGIS ▸ **rangi**

RANGOLI *n* traditional Indian ground decoration using coloured sand or chalks

RANGY *adj* having long slender limbs

RANI *n* wife or widow of a rajah

RANID *n* frog

RANIDS ▸ **ranid**

RANINE *adj* relating to frogs

RANIS ▸ **rani**

RANK *n* relative place or position ▸ *vb* have a specific rank or position ▸ *adj* complete or absolute

RANKE *archaic variant of* ▸ **rank**

RANKED ▸ **rank**

RANKER *n* soldier in the ranks

RANKERS ▸ **ranker**

RANKES ▸ **ranke**

RANKEST ▸ **rank**

RANKING *adj* prominent ▸ *n* position on a scale

RANKISH *adj* old word meaning rather rank

RANKISM *n* discrimination against people on the grounds of rank

RANKLE *vb* continue to cause resentment or bitterness

RANKLED ▸ **rankle**

RANKLES ▸ **rankle**

RANKLY ▸ **rank**

RANKS ▸ **rank**

RANPIKE *same as* ▸ **rampike**

RANSACK *vb* search thoroughly

RANSEL *same as* ▸ **rancel**

RANSELS ▸ **ransel**

RANSOM *n* money demanded in return for the release of someone who has been kidnapped ▸ *vb* pay money to obtain the release of a captive

RANSOMS ▸ **ransom**

RANT *vb* talk in a loud and excited way ▸ *n* loud excited speech

RANTED ▸ **rant**

RANTER ▸ **rant**

RANTERS ▸ **rant**

RANTING ▸ **rant**

RANTS ▸ **rant**

RANULA *n* saliva-filled cyst that develops under the tongue

RANULAR *adj* of a cyst under the tongue

RANULAS ▸ **ranula**

RANZEL *same as* ▸ **rancel**

RANZELS ▸ **ranzel**

RAOULIA *n* flowering plant of New Zealand

RAP *vb* hit with a sharp quick blow ▸ *n* quick sharp blow

RAPE *vb* force to submit to sexual intercourse ▸ *n* act of raping

RAPED ▸ **rape**

RAPER ▸ **rape**

RAPERS ▸ **rape**

RAPES ▸ **rape**

R

RAPHAE ▸ raphe

RAPHE n elongated ridge of conducting tissue along the side of certain seeds

RAPHES ▸ raphe

RAPHIA same as ▸ raffia

RAPHIAS ▸ raphia

RAPHIDE n any of numerous needle-shaped crystals, usually of calcium oxalate, that occur in many plant cells as a metabolic product

RAPHIS same as ▸ raphide

RAPID adj quick, swift

RAPIDER ▸ rapid

RAPIDLY ▸ rapid

RAPIDS pl n part of a river with a fast turbulent current

RAPIER n fine-bladed sword

RAPIERS ▸ rapier

RAPINE n pillage or plundering

RAPINES ▸ rapine

RAPING ▸ rape

RAPINI pl n type of leafy vegetable

RAPIST n person who commits rape

RAPISTS ▸ rapist

RAPLOCH n Scots word for homespun woollen material ▷ adj Scots word meaning coarse or homemade

RAPPE n Arcadian dish of grated potatoes and pork or chicken

RAPPED ▸ rap

RAPPEE n moist English snuff of the 18th and 19th centuries

RAPPEES ▸ rappee

RAPPEL n (formerly) a drumbeat to call soldiers to arms ▷ vb abseil

RAPPELS ▸ rappel

RAPPEN n Swiss coin equal to one hundredth of a franc

RAPPER n something used for rapping, such as a knocker on a door

RAPPERS ▸ rapper

RAPPES ▸ rappe

RAPPING ▸ rap

RAPPINI same as ▸ rapini

RAPPORT n harmony or agreement

RAPS ▸ rap

RAPT adj engrossed or spellbound

RAPTLY ▸ rapt

RAPTOR n any bird of prey

RAPTORS ▸ raptor

RAPTURE n ecstasy ▷ vb entrance

RARE adj uncommon ▷ vb rear

RAREBIT n as in **Welsh rarebit** dish made from melted cheese and sometimes milk and seasonings and served on toast

RARED ▸ rare

RAREE n as in **raree show** street show or carnival

RAREFY vb make or become rarer or less dense

RARELY adv seldom

RARER ▸ rare

RARES ▸ rare

RAREST ▸ rare

RARIFY same as ▸ rarefy

RARING adj ready

RARITY n something that is valuable because it is unusual

RARK vb as in **rark up** informal New Zealand expression meaning reprimand severely

RARKED ▸ rark

RARKING ▸ rark

RARKS ▸ rark

RAS n headland

RASBORA n often brightly coloured tropical fish

RASCAL n rogue ▷ adj belonging to the mob or rabble

RASCALS ▸ rascal

RASCHEL n type of loosely knitted fabric

RASE same as ▸ raze

RASED ▸ rase

RASER ▸ rase

RASERS ▸ rase

RASES ▸ rase

RASH adj hasty, reckless, or incautious ▷ n eruption of spots or patches on the skin ▷ vb (in old usage) cut

RASHED ▸ rash

RASHER n thin slice of bacon

RASHERS ▸ rasher

RASHES ▸ rash

RASHEST ▸ rash

RASHIE n Australian word for a shirt worn by surfers as protection against sunburn, heat rash, etc

RASHIES ▸ rashie

RASHING ▸ rash

RASHLY ▸ rash

RASING ▸ rase

RASP n harsh grating noise ▷ vb speak in a grating voice

RASPED ▸ rasp

RASPER ▸ rasp

RASPERS ▸ rasp

RASPIER ▸ raspy

RASPING adj (esp of a noise) harsh or grating

RASPISH ▸ rasp

RASPS ▸ rasp

RASPY same as ▸ rasping

RASSE n small S Asian civet

RASSES ▸ rasse

RASSLE dialect variant of ▸ wrestle

RASSLED ▸ rassle

RASSLES ▸ rassle

RAST archaic past form of ▸ race

RASTA adj of a member of a particular Black religious movement

RASTER n image consisting of rows of pixel information, such as a JPEG, GIF etc ▷ vb use web-based technology to turn a digital image into a large picture composed of a grid of black and white dots

RASTERS ▸ raster

RASTRUM n pen for drawing the five lines of a musical stave simultaneously

RASURE n scraping

RASURES ▸ rasure

RAT n small rodent ▷ vb inform (on)

RATA n New Zealand hard-wood forest tree with crimson flowers

RATABLE adj able to be rated or evaluated

RATABLY ▸ ratable

RATAFEE same as ▸ ratafia

RATAFIA n liqueur made from fruit

RATAL n amount on which rates are assessed ▷ adj of or relating to rates (local taxation)

RATALS ▸ ratal

RATAN same as ▸ rattan

RATANS ▸ ratan

RATANY n flowering desert shrub

RATAS ▸ rata

RATATAT n sound of knocking on a door

RATBITE n as in **ratbite**

fever acute infectious disease that can be caught from the bite of an infected rat

RATCH same as ▶ **ratchet**

RATCHED ▶ **ratch**

RATCHES ▶ **ratch**

RATCHET n set of teeth on a bar or wheel allowing motion in one direction only ▷ vb move using or as if using a ratchet system

RATE n degree of speed or progress ▷ vb consider or value

RATED ▶ **rate**

RATEEN same as ▶ **ratine**

RATEENS ▶ **rateen**

RATEL n large African and S Asian musteline mammal

RATELS ▶ **ratel**

RATER ▶ **rate**

RATERS ▶ **rate**

RATES pl n (in some countries) a tax on property levied by a local authority

RATFINK n contemptible or undesirable person

RATFISH n deep-sea fish with a whiplike tail

RATH same as ▶ **rathe**

RATHA n (in India) a four-wheeled carriage drawn by horses or bullocks

RATHAS ▶ **ratha**

RATHE adj blossoming or ripening early in the season

RATHER adv some extent ▷ interj expression of strong affirmation ▷ sentence substitute expression of strong affirmation, often in answer to a question

RATHEST adv dialect or archaic word meaning soonest

RATHOLE n rat's hiding place or burrow

RATHS ▶ **rath**

RATIFY vb give formal approval to

RATINE n coarse loosely woven cloth

RATINES ▶ **ratine**

RATING n valuation or assessment

RATINGS ▶ **rating**

RATIO n relationship between two numbers or amounts expressed as a proportion

RATION n fixed allowance of food etc ▷ vb limit to a

certain amount per person

RATIONS pl n fixed daily allowance of food, esp to military personnel or when supplies are limited

RATIOS ▶ **ratio**

RATITE adj (of flightless birds) having a breastbone that lacks a keel for the attachment of flight muscles ▷ n bird, such as an ostrich, kiwi, or rhea, that belongs to this group

RATITES ▶ **ratite**

RATLIKE ▶ **rat**

RATLIN same as ▶ **ratline**

RATLINE n any of a series of light lines tied across the shrouds of a sailing vessel for climbing aloft

RATLING n young rat

RATLINS ▶ **ratlin**

RATO n rocket-assisted take-off

RATOO same as ▶ **ratu**

RATOON n new shoot that grows from near the root or crown of crop plants, esp the sugar cane, after the old growth has been cut back ▷ vb propagate or cause to propagate by such a growth

RATOONS ▶ **ratoon**

RATOOS ▶ **ratoo**

RATOS ▶ **rato**

RATPACK n members of the press who pursue celebrities and give wide coverage of their private lives

RATS ▶ **rat**

RATTAIL n type of fish

RATTAN n climbing palm with jointed stems used for canes

RATTANS ▶ **rattan**

RATTED ▶ **rat**

RATTEEN same as ▶ **ratine**

RATTEN vb sabotage or steal tools in order to disrupt the work of

RATTENS ▶ **ratten**

RATTER n dog or cat that catches and kills rats

RATTERS ▶ **ratter**

RATTERY n rats' dwelling area

RATTIER ▶ **ratty**

RATTILY ▶ **ratty**

RATTING ▶ **rat**

RATTISH adj of, resembling, or infested with rats

RATTLE vb give out a succession of short sharp sounds ▷ n short sharp sound

RATTLED ▶ **rattle**

RATTLER n something that rattles

RATTLES ▶ **rattle**

RATTLIN same as ▶ **ratline**

RATTLY adj having a rattle

RATTON n dialect word for a little rat

RATTONS ▶ **ratton**

RATTOON same as ▶ **ratoon**

RATTRAP n device for catching rats

RATTY adj bad-tempered, irritable

RATU n title used by Fijian chiefs or nobles

RATUS ▶ **ratu**

RAUCID adj raucous

RAUCITY ▶ **raucous**

RAUCLE adj Scots word for rough or tough

RAUCLER ▶ **raucle**

RAUCOUS adj hoarse or harsh

RAUGHT archaic past form of ▶ **reach**

RAUN n fish roe or spawn

RAUNCH n lack of polish or refinement ▷ vb behave in a raunchy manner

RAUNCHY adj earthy, sexy

RAUNGE archaic word for ▶ **range**

RAUNGED ▶ **raunge**

RAUNGES ▶ **raunge**

RAUNS ▶ **raun**

RAUPATU n confiscation or seizure of land

RAUPO n New Zealand bulrush

RAUPOS ▶ **raupo**

RAURIKI n sow thistle, any of various plants with prickly leaves, milky juice and yellow heads

RAV n Hebrew word for rabbi

RAVAGE vb cause extensive damage to ▷ n destructive action

RAVAGED ▶ **ravage**

RAVAGER ▶ **ravage**

RAVAGES ▶ **ravage**

RAVE vb talk wildly or with enthusiasm ▷ n enthusiastically good review

RAVED ▶ **rave**

RAVEL vb tangle or become

R

entangled ▷ n tangle or complication

RAVELED ▶ **ravel**

RAVELER ▶ **ravel**

RAVELIN n outwork having two embankments at a salient angle

RAVELLY ▶ **ravel**

RAVELS ▶ **ravel**

RAVEN n black bird like a large crow ▷ adj (of hair) shiny black ▷ vb seize or seek (plunder, prey, etc)

RAVENED ▶ **raven**

RAVENER ▶ **raven**

RAVENS ▶ **raven**

RAVER n person who leads a wild or uninhibited social life

RAVERS ▶ **raver**

RAVES ▶ **rave**

RAVIN archaic spelling of ▶ **raven**

RAVINE n narrow steep-sided valley worn by a stream

RAVINED ▶ **ravin**

RAVINES ▶ **ravine**

RAVING adj delirious ▷ n frenzied, irrational, or wildly extravagant talk or utterances

RAVINGS ▶ **raving**

RAVINS ▶ **ravin**

RAVIOLI n small squares of pasta with a savoury filling

RAVISH vb enrapture

RAVS ▶ **rav**

RAW as in **in the raw** without clothes adj uncooked

RAWARU n New Zealand name for blue cod

RAWARUS ▶ **rawaru**

RAWBONE archaic variant of > **rawboned**

RAWER ▶ **raw**

RAWEST ▶ **raw**

RAWHEAD n bogeyman

RAWHIDE n untanned hide ▷ vb whip

RAWIN n monitoring of winds in the upper atmosphere using radar and a balloon

RAWING (in dialect) same as ▶ **rowen**

RAWINGS ▶ **rawing**

RAWINS ▶ **rawin**

RAWISH ▶ **raw**

RAWLY ▶ **raw**

RAWN (in dialect) same as ▶ **rowen**

RAWNESS ▶ **raw**

RAWNS ▶ **rawn**

RAWS ▶ **raw**

RAX vb stretch or extend ▷ n act of stretching or straining

> A dialect word meaning to stretch or strain, and one of the essential short words to know for using the X.

RAXED ▶ **rax**

RAXES ▶ **rax**

RAXING ▶ **rax**

RAY n single line or narrow beam of light ▷ vb (of an object) to emit (light) in rays or (of light) to issue in the form of rays

RAYA same as ▶ **rayah**

RAYAH n (formerly) a non-Muslim subject of the Ottoman Empire

RAYAHS ▶ **rayah**

RAYAS ▶ **raya**

RAYED ▶ **ray**

RAYING ▶ **ray**

RAYLE archaic spelling of ▶ **rail**

RAYLED ▶ **rayle**

RAYLES ▶ **rayle**

RAYLESS adj dark

RAYLET n small ray

RAYLETS ▶ **raylet**

RAYLIKE adj resembling a ray

RAYLING ▶ **rayle**

RAYNE archaic spelling of ▶ **reign**

RAYNES ▶ **rayne**

RAYON n (fabric made of) a synthetic fibre

RAYONS ▶ **rayon**

RAYS ▶ **ray**

RAZE vb destroy (buildings or a town) completely

RAZED ▶ **raze**

RAZEE n sailing ship that has had its upper deck or decks removed ▷ vb remove the upper deck or decks of (a sailing ship)

RAZEED ▶ **razee**

RAZEES ▶ **razee**

RAZER ▶ **raze**

RAZERS ▶ **raze**

RAZES ▶ **raze**

RAZING ▶ **raze**

RAZOO n imaginary coin

RAZOOS ▶ **razoo**

RAZOR n sharp instrument for shaving ▷ vb cut or shave with a razor

RAZORED ▶ **razor**

RAZORS ▶ **razor**

RAZURE same as ▶ **rasure**

RAZURES ▶ **razure**

RAZZ vb make fun of

RAZZED ▶ **razz**

RAZZES ▶ **razz**

RAZZIA n raid for plunder or slaves, esp one carried out by Moors in North Africa

RAZZIAS ▶ **razzia**

RAZZING ▶ **razz**

RAZZLE n as in **on the razzle** out enjoying oneself or celebrating

RAZZLES ▶ **razzle**

RE prep concerning ▷ n the second note of the musical scale

REACH vb arrive at ▷ n distance that one can reach

REACHED ▶ **reach**

REACHER ▶ **reach**

REACHES ▶ **reach**

REACT vb act in response (to)

REACTED ▶ **react**

REACTOR n apparatus in which a nuclear reaction is maintained and controlled to produce nuclear energy

REACTS ▶ **react**

READ vb look at and understand or take in (written or printed matter) ▷ n matter suitable for reading

READAPT vb adapt again

READD vb add again

READDED ▶ **readd**

READDS ▶ **readd**

READER n person who reads

READERS ▶ **reader**

READIED ▶ **ready**

READIER ▶ **ready**

READIES pl n ready money

READILY adv promptly

READING ▶ **read**

README n document which accompanies computer files or software

READMIT vb let (a person, country, etc) back into a place or organization

READOPT vb adopt again

READORN vb adorn again

READOUT n act of retrieving information from a computer memory or storage device

READS ▶ **read**

READY adj prepared for use

or action ▷ vb prepare
REAFFIX vb affix again
REAGENT n chemical substance that reacts with another, used to detect the presence of the other
REAGIN n type of antibody that is formed against an allergen and is attached to the cells of a tissue. The antigen-antibody reaction that occurs on subsequent contact with the allergen causes tissue damage, leading to the release of histamine and other substances responsible for an allergic reaction
REAGINS ▶ **reagin**
REAK same as ▶ **reck**
REAKED ▶ **reak**
REAKING ▶ **reak**
REAKS ▶ **reak**
REAL adj existing in fact ▷ n name of a former small Spanish or Spanish-American silver coin as well as of the standard monetary unit of Brazil
REALER ▶ **real**
REALES ▶ **real**
REALEST ▶ **real**
REALGAR n rare orange-red soft mineral consisting of arsenic sulphide in monoclinic crystalline form
REALIA pl n real-life facts and material used in teaching
REALIGN vb change or put back to a new or former place or position
REALISE same as ▶ **realize**
REALISM n awareness or acceptance of things as they are
REALIST n person who is aware of and accepts the physical universe, events, etc, as they are
REALITY n state of things as they are
REALIZE vb become aware or grasp the significance of
REALLIE old or dialect variant of ▶ **really**
REALLOT vb allot again
REALLY adv very ▷ interj exclamation of dismay, doubt, or surprise ▷ vb (in archaic usage) rally
REALM n kingdom
REALMS ▶ **realm**

REALO n member of the German Green party with moderate views
   A **realo** is a member of the less radical section of the German Green party. It is important to know not because it scores well, but because it provides an easily overlooked 'hook', by allowing you to add O to **real**.
REALOS ▶ **realo**
REALS ▶ **real**
REALTER vb alter again
REALTIE n archaic word meaning sincerity
REALTOR n estate agent
REALTY n immovable property
REAM n twenty quires of paper, generally 500 sheets ▷ vb enlarge (a hole) by use of a reamer
REAME archaic variant of ▶ **realm**
REAMED ▶ **ream**
REAMEND vb amend again
REAMER n steel tool with a cylindrical or tapered shank around which longitudinal teeth are ground, used for smoothing the bores of holes accurately to size
REAMERS ▶ **reamer**
REAMES ▶ **reame**
REAMIER ▶ **reamy**
REAMING ▶ **ream**
REAMS ▶ **ream**
REAMY Scots for ▶ **creamy**
REAN same as ▶ **reen**
REANNEX vb annex again
REANS ▶ **rean**
REAP vb cut and gather (a harvest)
REAPED ▶ **reap**
REAPER n person who reaps or machine for reaping
REAPERS ▶ **reaper**
REAPING ▶ **reap**
REAPPLY vb put or spread (something) on again
REAPS ▶ **reap**
REAR n back part ▷ vb care for and educate (children)
REARED ▶ **rear**
REARER ▶ **rear**
REARERS ▶ **rear**
REARGUE vb argue again
REARING ▶ **rear**
REARISE vb arise again

REARLY old word for ▶ **early**
REARM vb arm again
REARMED ▶ **rearm**
REARMS ▶ **rearm**
REAROSE ▶ **rearise**
REARS ▶ **rear**
REASON n cause or motive ▷ vb think logically in forming conclusions
REASONS ▶ **reason**
REAST same as ▶ **reest**
REASTED ▶ **reast**
REASTS ▶ **reast**
REASTY adj (in dialect) rancid
REATA n lasso
REATAS ▶ **reata**
REATE n type of crowfoot
REATES ▶ **reate**
REAVAIL vb avail again
REAVE vb carry off (property, prisoners, etc) by force
REAVED ▶ **reave**
REAVER ▶ **reave**
REAVERS ▶ **reave**
REAVES ▶ **reave**
REAVING ▶ **reave**
REAVOW vb avow again
REAVOWS ▶ **reavow**
REAWAKE vb awake again
REAWOKE ▶ **reawake**
REB n Confederate soldier in the American Civil War (1861-65)
REBACK vb provide with a new back, backing, or lining
REBACKS ▶ **reback**
REBADGE vb relaunch (a product) under a new name, brand, or logo
REBAIT vb bait again
REBAITS ▶ **rebait**
REBAR n rod providing reinforcement in concrete structures
REBARS ▶ **rebar**
REBATE n discount or refund ▷ vb cut a rabbet in
REBATED ▶ **rebate**
REBATER ▶ **rebate**
REBATES ▶ **rebate**
REBATO same as ▶ **rabato**
REBATOS ▶ **rebato**
REBBE n individual's chosen spiritual mentor
REBBES ▶ **rebbe**
REBEC n medieval stringed instrument resembling the violin but having a lute-shaped body
REBECK same as ▶ **rebec**
REBECKS ▶ **rebeck**

REBECS ▸ rebec
REBEGAN ▸ rebegin
REBEGIN vb begin again
REBEGUN ▸ rebegin
REBEL vb revolt against the ruling power ▷ n person who rebels ▷ adj rebelling
REBELS ▸ rebel
REBID vb bid again
REBIDS ▸ rebid
REBILL vb bill again
REBILLS ▸ rebill
REBIND vb bind again
REBINDS ▸ rebind
REBIRTH n revival or renaissance
REBIT ▸ rebite
REBITE vb (in printing) to give another application of acid in order to cause further cutting of a plate
REBITES ▸ rebite
REBLEND vb blend again
REBLENT same as ▸ reblend
REBLOOM vb bloom again
REBOANT adj resounding or reverberating
REBOARD vb board again
REBODY vb give a new body to
REBOIL vb boil again
REBOILS ▸ reboil
REBOOK vb book again
REBOOKS ▸ rebook
REBOOT vb shut down and then restart (a computer system)
REBOOTS ▸ reboot
REBOP same as ▸ bebop
REBOPS ▸ rebop
REBORE n boring of a cylinder to restore its true shape ▷ vb carry out this process
REBORED ▸ rebore
REBORES ▸ rebore
REBORN adj active again after a period of inactivity
REBOUND vb spring back ▷ n act of rebounding
REBOZO n long wool or linen scarf covering the shoulders and head, worn by Latin American women
REBOZOS ▸ rebozo
REBRACE vb brace again
REBRAND vb change or update the image of (an organization or product)
REBRED ▸ rebreed
REBREED vb breed again
REBS ▸ reb
REBUFF vb reject or snub

▷ n blunt refusal, snub
REBUFFS ▸ rebuff
REBUILD vb build (a building or town) again, after severe damage
REBUILT ▸ rebuild
REBUKE vb scold sternly ▷ n stern scolding
REBUKED ▸ rebuke
REBUKER ▸ rebuke
REBUKES ▸ rebuke
REBURY vb bury again
REBUS n puzzle consisting of pictures and symbols representing words or syllables
REBUSES ▸ rebus
REBUT vb prove that (a claim) is untrue
REBUTS ▸ rebut
REBUY vb buy again
REBUYS ▸ rebuy
REC n short for recreation
RECAL same as ▸ recall
RECALL vb recollect or remember ▷ n ability to remember
RECALLS ▸ recall
RECALS ▸ recall
RECANE vb cane again
RECANED ▸ recane
RECANES ▸ recane
RECANT vb withdraw (a statement or belief) publicly
RECANTS ▸ recant
RECAP vb recapitulate ▷ n recapitulation
RECAPS ▸ recap
RECARRY vb carry again
RECAST vb organize or set out in a different way
RECASTS ▸ recast
RECATCH vb catch again
RECCE vb reconnoitre ▷ n reconnaissance
RECCED ▸ recce
RECCEED ▸ recce
RECCES ▸ recce
RECCIED ▸ reccy
RECCIES ▸ reccy
RECCO same as ▸ recce
RECCOS ▸ recco
RECCY same as ▸ recce
RECEDE vb move to a more distant place
RECEDED ▸ recede
RECEDES ▸ recede
RECEIPT n written acknowledgment of money or goods received ▷ vb acknowledge payment of (a bill), as by marking it

RECEIVE vb take, accept, or get
RECENCY ▸ recent
RECENSE vb revise
RECENT adj having happened lately
RECEPT n idea or image formed in the mind by repeated experience of a particular pattern of sensory stimulation
RECEPTS ▸ recept
RECESS n niche or alcove ▷ vb place or set (something) in a recess
RECHART vb chart again
RECHATE same as ▸ recheat
RECHEAT n (in a hunt) sounding of the horn to call back the hounds ▷ vb sound the horn to call back the hounds
RECHECK vb check again
RECHEW vb chew again
RECHEWS ▸ rechew
RECHIE adj smoky
RECHIP vb put a new chip into (a stolen mobile phone) so it can be reused
RECHIPS ▸ rechip
RECHOSE > rechoose
RECIPE n directions for cooking a dish
RECIPES ▸ recipe
RECIT n narrative
RECITAL n musical performance by a soloist or soloists
RECITE vb repeat (a poem, story, etc) aloud to an audience
RECITED ▸ recite
RECITER ▸ recite
RECITES ▸ recite
RECITS ▸ recit
RECK vb mind or care about (something)
RECKAN adj strained, tormented, or twisted
RECKED ▸ reck
RECKING ▸ reck
RECKON vb consider or think
RECKONS ▸ reckon
RECKS ▸ reck
RECLAD vb cover in a different substance
RECLADS ▸ reclad
RECLAIM vb regain possession of ▷ n act of reclaiming or state of being reclaimed

RECLAME n public acclaim or attention
RECLASP vb clasp again
RECLEAN vb clean again
RECLIMB vb climb again
RECLINE vb rest in a leaning position
RECLOSE vb close again
RECLUSE n person who avoids other people ▷ adj solitary
RECOAL vb supply or be supplied with fresh coal
RECOALS ▶ recoal
RECOAT vb coat again
RECOATS ▶ recoat
RECOCK vb cock again
RECOCKS ▶ recock
RECODE vb put into a new code
RECODED ▶ recode
RECODES ▶ recode
RECOIL vb jerk or spring back ▷ n backward jerk
RECOILS ▶ recoil
RECOIN vb coin again
RECOINS ▶ recoin
RECOLOR vb give a new colour to
RECOMB vb comb again
RECOMBS ▶ recomb
RECON vb to make a preliminary survey
RECONS ▶ recon
RECOOK vb cook again
RECOOKS ▶ recook
RECOPY vb copy again
RECORD n document or other thing that preserves information ▷ vb put in writing
RECORDS ▶ record
RECORK vb cork again
RECORKS ▶ recork
RECOUNT vb tell in detail
RECOUP vb regain or make good (a loss)
RECOUPE vb (in law) keep back or withhold
RECOUPS ▶ recoup
RECOURE archaic variant of ▶ recover
RECOVER vb become healthy again
RECOWER archaic variant of ▶ recover
RECOYLE archaic spelling of ▶ recoil
RECRATE vb crate again
RECROSS vb move or go across (something) again
RECROWN vb crown again
RECRUIT vb enlist (new

soldiers, members, etc) ▷ n newly enlisted soldier
RECS ▶ rec
RECTA ▶ rectum
RECTAL adj of the rectum
RECTI ▶ rectus
RECTIFY vb put right, correct
RECTION n (in grammar) the determination of the form of one word by another word
RECTO n right-hand page of a book
RECTOR n clergyman in charge of a parish
RECTORS ▶ rector
RECTORY n rector's house
RECTOS ▶ recto
RECTRIX n any of the large stiff feathers of a bird's tail, used in controlling the direction of flight
RECTUM n final section of the large intestine
RECTUMS ▶ rectum
RECTUS n straight muscle, esp either of two muscles of the anterior abdominal wall
RECUILE archaic variant of ▶ recoil
RECULE archaic variant of ▶ recoil
RECULED ▶ recule
RECULES ▶ recule
RECUR vb happen again
RECURE vb archaic word for cure or recover
RECURED ▶ recure
RECURES ▶ recure
RECURS ▶ recur
RECURVE vb curve or bend (something) back or down or (of something) to be so curved or bent
RECUSAL n withdrawal of a judge from a case
RECUSE vb (in law) object to or withdraw (a judge)
RECUSED ▶ recuse
RECUSES ▶ recuse
RECUT vb cut again
RECUTS ▶ recut
RECYCLE vb reprocess (used materials) for further use ▷ n repetition of a fixed sequence of events
RED adj of a colour varying from crimson to orange and seen in blood, fire, etc ▷ n red colour
REDACT vb compose or

draft (an edict, proclamation, etc)
REDACTS ▶ redact
REDAN n fortification of two parapets at a salient angle
REDANS ▶ redan
REDATE vb change date of
REDATED ▶ redate
REDATES ▶ redate
REDBACK n small venomous Australian spider
REDBAIT vb harass those with leftwing leanings
REDBAY n type of tree
REDBAYS ▶ redbay
REDBIRD n type of bird, the male of which is distinguished by its bright red plumage and black wings
REDBONE n type of American dog
REDBUD n American leguminous tree with heart-shaped leaves and small budlike pink flowers
REDBUDS ▶ redbud
REDBUG another name for ▶ chigger
REDBUGS ▶ redbug
REDCAP n military policeman
REDCAPS ▶ redcap
REDCOAT n British soldier
REDD vb bring order to ▷ n act or an instance of redding
REDDED ▶ redd
REDDEN vb make or become red
REDDENS ▶ redden
REDDER ▶ redd
REDDERS ▶ redd
REDDEST ▶ red
REDDIER ▶ reddy
REDDING ▶ redd
REDDISH adj somewhat red
REDDLE same as ▶ ruddle
REDDLED ▶ reddle
REDDLES ▶ reddle
REDDS ▶ redd
REDDY adj reddish
REDE n advice or counsel ▷ vb advise
REDEAL vb deal again
REDEALS ▶ redeal
REDEALT ▶ redeal
REDEAR n variety of sunfish with a red flash above the gills
REDEARS ▶ redear

R

REDED ▸ rede
REDEEM vb make up for
REDEEMS ▸ redeem
REDEFY vb defy again
REDENY vb deny again
REDES ▸ rede
REDEYE n inferior whiskey
REDEYES ▸ redeye
REDFIN n any of various small fishes with reddish fins that are popular aquarium fishes
REDFINS ▸ redfin
REDFISH n male salmon that has recently spawned
REDFOOT n fatal disease of newborn lambs of unknown cause in which the horny layers of the feet become separated, exposing the red laminae below
REDHEAD n person with reddish hair
REDIA n parasitic larva of flukes that has simple locomotory organs, pharynx, and intestine and gives rise either to other rediae or to a different larva (the cercaria)
REDIAE ▸ redia
REDIAL vb dial (a telephone number) again
REDIALS ▸ redial
REDIAS ▸ redia
REDID ▸ redo
REDING ▸ rede
REDIP vb dip again
REDIPS ▸ redip
REDIPT archaic past form of ▸ redip
REDLINE vb (esp of a bank or group of banks) to refuse a loan to (a person or country) because of the presumed risks involved
REDLY ▸ red
REDNESS ▸ red
REDO vb do over again in order to improve ▷ n instance of redoing something
REDOCK vb dock again
REDOCKS ▸ redock
REDOES ▸ redo
REDOING ▸ redo
REDON vb don again
REDONE ▸ redo
REDONS ▸ redon
REDOS ▸ redo
REDOUBT n small fort defending a hilltop or pass

▷ vb fear
REDOUND vb cause advantage or disadvantage (to)
REDOUT n reddened vision and other symptoms caused by a rush of blood to the head in response to negative gravitational stresses
REDOUTS ▸ redout
REDOWA n Bohemian folk dance similar to the waltz
REDOWAS ▸ redowa
REDOX n chemical reaction in which one substance is reduced and the other is oxidized
REDOXES ▸ redox
REDPOLL n mostly grey-brown finch with a red crown and pink breast
REDRAFT vb write a second copy of (a letter, proposal, essay, etc) ▷ n second draft
REDRAW vb draw or draw up (something) again or differently
REDRAWN ▸ redraw
REDRAWS ▸ redraw
REDREAM vb dream again
REDRESS vb make amends for ▷ n compensation or amends
REDREW ▸ redraw
REDRIED ▸ redry
REDRIES ▸ redry
REDRILL vb drill again
REDRIVE vb drive again
REDROOT n yellow-flowered bog plant of E North America whose roots yield a red dye
REDROVE ▸ redrive
REDRY vb dry again
REDS ▸ red
REDSEAR same as > redshort
REDTAIL n variety of bird with red colouring on its tail
REDTOP n sensationalist tabloid newspaper
REDTOPS ▸ redtop
REDUB vb fix or repair
REDUBS ▸ redub
REDUCE vb bring down, lower
REDUCED ▸ reduce
REDUCER n chemical solution used to lessen the density of a negative or print by oxidizing some of the blackened silver to

soluble silver compounds
REDUCES ▸ reduce
REDUIT n fortified part from which a garrison may fight on once an enemy has taken outworks
REDUITS ▸ reduit
REDUX adj brought back or returned
REDWARE another name for ▸ kelp
REDWING n small European thrush
REDWOOD n giant Californian conifer with reddish bark
REDYE vb dye again
REDYED ▸ redye
REDYES ▸ redye
REE n Scots word for walled enclosure
REEARN vb earn again
REEARNS ▸ reearn
REEBOK same as ▸ rhebok
REEBOKS ▸ reebok
REECH vb (in dialect) smoke
REECHED ▸ reech
REECHES ▸ reech
REECHIE same as ▸ reechy
REECHO vb echo again
REECHY adj (in dialect) smoky
REED n tall grass that grows in swamps and shallow water
REEDBED n area of wetland with reeds growing in it
REEDE obsolete variant of ▸ red
REEDED ▸ reed
REEDEN adj of or consisting of reeds
REEDER n thatcher
REEDERS ▸ reeder
REEDES ▸ reede
REEDIER ▸ reedy
REEDIFY vb edify again or rebuild
REEDILY ▸ reedy
REEDING n set of small semicircular architectural mouldings
REEDIT vb edit again
REEDITS ▸ reedit
REEDMAN n musician who plays a wind instrument that has a reed
REEDMEN ▸ reedman
REEDS ▸ reed
REEDY adj harsh and thin in tone
REEF n ridge of rock or coral near the surface of the sea

▷ *vb* roll up part of a sail
REEFED ▶ **reef**
REEFER *n* short thick jacket worn esp by sailors
REEFERS ▶ **reefer**
REEFIER ▶ **reefy**
REEFING ▶ **reef**
REEFS ▶ **reef**
REEFY *adj* with reefs
REEJECT *vb* eject again
REEK *vb* smell strongly ▷ *n* strong unpleasant smell
REEKED ▶ **reek**
REEKER ▶ **reek**
REEKERS ▶ **reek**
REEKIE *same as* ▶ **reeky**
REEKIER ▶ **reek**
REEKING ▶ **reek**
REEKS ▶ **reek**
REEKY *adj* steamy or smoky
REEL *n* cylindrical object on which film, tape, thread, or wire is wound ▷ *vb* stagger, sway, or whirl
REELECT *vb* elect again
REELED ▶ **reel**
REELER ▶ **reel**
REELERS ▶ **reel**
REELING ▶ **reel**
REELMAN *n* (formerly) member of a beach life-saving team operating a winch
REELMEN ▶ **reelman**
REELS ▶ **reel**
REEMIT *vb* emit again
REEMITS ▶ **reemit**
REEN *n* ditch, esp a drainage channel
REENACT *vb* enact again
REENDOW *vb* endow again
REENJOY *vb* enjoy again
REENS ▶ **reen**
REENTER *vb* enter again
REENTRY *n* return of a spacecraft into the earth's atmosphere
REEQUIP *vb* equip again
REERECT *vb* erect again
REES ▶ **ree**
REEST *vb* (esp of horses) to be noisily uncooperative
REESTED ▶ **reest**
REESTS ▶ **reest**
REESTY *same as* ▶ **reasty**
REEVE *n* local representative of the king in a shire until the early 11th century ▷ *vb* pass (a rope or cable) through an eye or other narrow opening
REEVED ▶ **reeve**
REEVES ▶ **reeve**

REEVING ▶ **reeve**
REEVOKE *vb* evoke again
REEXPEL *vb* expel again
REF *n* referee in sport ▷ *vb* referee
REFACE *vb* repair or renew the facing of (a wall)
REFACED ▶ **reface**
REFACES ▶ **reface**
REFALL *vb* fall again
REFALLS ▶ **refall**
REFECT *vb* archaic word for restore or refresh with food and drink
REFECTS ▶ **refect**
REFED ▶ **refeed**
REFEED *vb* feed again
REFEEDS ▶ **refeed**
REFEEL *vb* feel again
REFEELS ▶ **refeel**
REFEL *vb* refute
REFELL ▶ **refall**
REFELS ▶ **refel**
REFELT ▶ **refeel**
REFENCE *vb* fence again
REFER *vb* allude (to)
REFEREE *n* umpire in sports, esp soccer or boxing ▷ *vb* act as referee of
REFERS ▶ **refer**
REFFED ▶ **ref**
REFFING ▶ **ref**
REFIGHT *vb* fight again ▷ *n* second or new fight
REFILE *vb* file again
REFILED ▶ **refile**
REFILES ▶ **refile**
REFILL *vb* fill again ▷ *n* second or subsequent filling
REFILLS ▶ **refill**
REFILM *vb* film again
REFILMS ▶ **refilm**
REFIND *vb* find again
REFINDS ▶ **refind**
REFINE *vb* purify
REFINED *adj* cultured or polite
REFINER *n* person, device, or substance that removes impurities, sediment, or other unwanted matter from something
REFINES ▶ **refine**
REFIRE *vb* fire again
REFIRED ▶ **refire**
REFIRES ▶ **refire**
REFIT *vb* make ready for use again by repairing or re-equipping ▷ *n* repair or re-equipping for further use
REFITS ▶ **refit**
REFIX *vb* fix again

REFIXED ▶ **refix**
REFIXES ▶ **refix**
REFLAG *vb* flag again
REFLAGS ▶ **reflag**
REFLATE *vb* inflate or be inflated again
REFLECT *vb* throw back, esp rays of light, heat, etc
REFLET *n* iridescent glow or lustre, as on ceramic ware
REFLETS ▶ **reflet**
REFLEW ▶ **refly**
REFLEX *n* involuntary response to a stimulus or situation ▷ *adj* (of a muscular action) involuntary ▷ *vb* bend, turn, or reflect backwards
REFLIES ▶ **refly**
REFLOAT *vb* float again
REFLOOD *vb* flood again
REFLOW *vb* flow again
REFLOWN ▶ **refly**
REFLOWS ▶ **reflow**
REFLUX *vb* boil or be boiled in a vessel attached to a condenser, so that the vapour condenses and flows back into the vessel ▷ *n* act of refluxing
REFLY *vb* fly again
REFOCUS *vb* focus again or anew
REFOLD *vb* fold again
REFOLDS ▶ **refold**
REFOOT *vb* foot again
REFOOTS ▶ **refoot**
REFORGE *vb* forge again
REFORM *n* improvement ▷ *vb* improve
REFORMS ▶ **reform**
REFOUND *vb* found again
REFRACT *vb* change the course of (light etc) passing from one medium to another
REFRAIN *n* frequently repeated part of a song ▷ *vb* abstain (from action)
REFRAME *vb* support or enclose (a picture, photograph, etc) in a new or different frame
REFRESH *vb* revive or reinvigorate, as through food, drink, or rest
REFRIED ▶ **refry**
REFRIES ▶ **refry**
REFRONT *vb* put a new front on
REFROZE > **refreeze**
REFRY *vb* fry again
REFS ▶ **ref**

R

REFT ▶ reave

REFUEL vb supply or be supplied with fresh fuel

REFUELS ▶ refuel

REFUGE n (source of) shelter or protection ▷ vb take refuge or give refuge to

REFUGED ▶ refuge

REFUGEE n person who seeks refuge, esp in a foreign country

REFUGES ▶ refuge

REFUGIA > **refugium**

REFUND vb pay back ▷ n return of money

REFUNDS ▶ refund

REFUSAL n denial of anything demanded or offered

REFUSE vb decline, deny, or reject ▷ n rubbish or useless matter

REFUSED ▶ refuse

REFUSER ▶ refuse

REFUSES ▶ refuse

REFUTAL n act or process of refuting

REFUTE vb disprove

REFUTED ▶ refute

REFUTER ▶ refute

REFUTES ▶ refute

REG n large expanse of stony desert terrain

REGAIN vb get back or recover ▷ n process of getting something back, esp lost weight

REGAINS ▶ regain

REGAL adj of or like a king or queen ▷ n portable organ equipped only with small reed pipes, popular from the 15th century and recently revived for modern performance

REGALE vb entertain (someone) with stories etc ▷ n feast

REGALED ▶ regale

REGALER ▶ regale

REGALES ▶ regale

REGALIA pl n ceremonial emblems of royalty or high office

REGALLY ▶ regal

REGALS ▶ regal

REGAR same as ▶ regur

REGARD vb consider ▷ n respect or esteem

REGARDS ▶ regard

REGARS ▶ regar

REGATTA n meeting for yacht or boat races

REGAUGE vb gauge again

REGAVE ▶ regive

REGEAR vb readjust

REGEARS ▶ regear

REGENCE old variant of ▶ **regency**

REGENCY n status or period of office of a regent

REGENT n ruler of a kingdom during the absence, childhood, or illness of its monarch ▷ adj ruling as a regent

REGENTS ▶ regent

REGES ▶ rex

REGEST n archaic word for register

REGESTS ▶ regest

REGGAE n style of Jamaican popular music with a strong beat

REGGAES ▶ reggae

REGGO same as ▶ rego

REGGOS ▶ reggo

REGIE n government-directed management or government monopoly

REGIES ▶ regie

REGIFT vb give (a previously received gift) to someone else

REGIFTS ▶ regift

REGILD vb gild again

REGILDS ▶ regild

REGILT archaic past form of ▶ regild

REGIME n system of government

REGIMEN n prescribed system of diet etc

REGIMES ▶ regime

REGINA n queen

REGINAE ▶ regina

REGINAL adj queenly

REGINAS ▶ regina

REGION n administrative division of a country

REGIONS ▶ region

REGIUS adj as in **regius professor** Crown-appointed holder of a university chair

REGIVE vb give again or back

REGIVEN ▶ regive

REGIVES ▶ regive

REGLAZE vb glaze again

REGLET n flat narrow architectural moulding

REGLETS ▶ reglet

REGLOSS vb gloss again or give a new gloss to

REGLOW vb glow again

REGLOWS ▶ reglow

REGLUE vb glue again

REGLUED ▶ reglue

REGLUES ▶ reglue

REGMA n type of fruit with cells that break open and break away when ripe

REGMATA ▶ regma

REGNA ▶ regnum

REGNAL adj of a sovereign, reign, or kingdom

REGNANT adj reigning

REGNUM n reign or rule

REGO n registration of a motor vehicle

REGORGE vb vomit up

REGOS ▶ rego

REGOSOL n type of azonal soil consisting of unconsolidated material derived from freshly deposited alluvium or sands

REGRADE vb grade again

REGRAFT vb graft again

REGRANT vb grant again

REGRATE vb buy up (commodities) in advance so as to raise their price for profitable resale

REGREDE vb go back

REGREEN vb green again

REGREET vb greet again or return greetings of

REGRESS vb revert to a former worse condition ▷ n return to a former and worse condition

REGRET vb feel sorry about ▷ n feeling of repentance, guilt, or sorrow

REGRETS ▶ regret

REGREW ▶ regrow

REGRIND vb grind again

REGROOM vb groom again

REGROUP vb reorganize (military forces) after an attack or a defeat

REGROW vb grow or be grown again after having been cut or having died or withered

REGROWN ▶ regrow

REGROWS ▶ regrow

REGS ▶ reg

REGULA n rule

REGULAE ▶ regula

REGULAR adj normal, customary, or usual ▷ n regular soldier

REGULI ▶ regulus

REGULO n any of a number of temperatures to which a

gas oven may be set
REGULOS ▶ **regulo**
REGULUS n impure metal forming beneath the slag during the smelting of ores
REGUR n black loamy Indian soil
REGURS ▶ **regur**
REH n (in India) salty surface crust on the soil
REHAB vb help (addict, disabled person, prisoner, etc) to readapt to society or a new job ▷ n treatment or help given to an addict, disabled person, or prisoner, etc
REHABS ▶ **rehab**
REHANG vb hang again
REHANGS ▶ **rehang**
REHASH vb rework or reuse ▷ n old ideas presented in a new form
REHEAR vb hear again
REHEARD ▶ **rehear**
REHEARS ▶ **rehear**
REHEAT vb heat or be heated again
REHEATS ▶ **reheat**
REHEEL vb put a new heel or new heels on
REHEELS ▶ **reheel**
REHEM vb hem again
REHEMS ▶ **rehem**
REHINGE vb put a new hinge or new hinges on
REHIRE vb hire again
REHIRED ▶ **rehire**
REHIRES ▶ **rehire**
REHOME vb find a new home for (esp a pet)
REHOMED ▶ **rehome**
REHOMES ▶ **rehome**
REHOUSE vb provide with a new (and better) home
REHS ▶ **reh**
REHUNG ▶ **rehang**
REI n name for a former Portuguese coin, more properly called a real
REIF n Scots word meaning robbery or plunder
REIFIED ▶ **reify**
REIFIER ▶ **reify**
REIFIES ▶ **reify**
REIFS ▶ **reif**
REIFY vb consider or make (an abstract idea or concept) real or concrete
REIGN n period of a sovereign's rule ▷ vb rule (a country)
REIGNED ▶ **reign**

REIGNS ▶ **reign**
REIK Scots word for ▶ **smoke**
REIKI n form of therapy in which the practitioner is believed to channel energy into the patient in order to encourage healing or restore wellbeing
REIKIS ▶ **reiki**
REIKS ▶ **reik**
REIMAGE vb image again
REIN vb check or manage with reins
REINCUR vb incur again
REINDEX vb index again
REINED ▶ **rein**
REINING ▶ **rein**
REINK vb ink again
REINKED ▶ **reink**
REINKS ▶ **reink**
REINS pl n narrow straps attached to a bit to guide a horse
REINTER vb inter again
REIRD Scots word for ▶ **din**
REIRDS ▶ **reird**
REIS ▶ **rei**
REISES ▶ **rei**
REISSUE n book, record, etc, that is published or released again after being unavailable for a time ▷ vb publish or release (a book, record, etc) again after a period of unavailability
REIST same as ▶ **reest**
REISTED ▶ **reist**
REISTS ▶ **reist**
REITBOK same as
> **reedbuck**
REITER n soldier in the German cavalry
REITERS ▶ **reiter**
REIVE vb go on a plundering raid
REIVED ▶ **reive**
REIVER ▶ **reive**
REIVERS ▶ **reive**
REIVES ▶ **reive**
REIVING ▶ **reive**
REJECT vb refuse to accept or believe ▷ n person or thing rejected as not up to standard
REJECTS ▶ **reject**
REJIG vb re-equip (a factory or plant) ▷ n act or process of rejigging
REJIGS ▶ **rejig**
REJOICE vb feel or express great happiness
REJOIN vb join again
REJOINS ▶ **rejoin**

REJON n bullfighting lance
REJONEO n bullfighting activity in which a mounted bullfighter spears the bull with lances
REJONES ▶ **rejon**
REJOURN vb archaic word meaning postpone or adjourn
REJUDGE vb judge again
REKE same as ▶ **reck**
REKED ▶ **reke**
REKES ▶ **reke**
REKEY vb key again
REKEYED ▶ **rekey**
REKEYS ▶ **rekey**
REKING ▶ **reke**
REKNIT vb knit again
REKNITS ▶ **reknit**
REKNOT vb knot again
REKNOTS ▶ **reknot**
RELABEL vb label again
RELACE vb lace again
RELACED ▶ **relace**
RELACES ▶ **relace**
RELACHE n break
RELAID ▶ **relay**
RELAND vb land again
RELANDS ▶ **reland**
RELAPSE vb fall back into bad habits, illness, etc ▷ n return of bad habits, illness, etc
RELATA ▶ **relatum**
RELATE vb establish a relation between
RELATED adj linked by kinship or marriage
RELATER ▶ **relate**
RELATES ▶ **relate**
RELATOR n person who relates a story
RELATUM n one of the objects between which a relation is said to hold
RELAX vb make or become looser, less tense, or less rigid
RELAXED ▶ **relax**
RELAXER n person or thing that relaxes, esp a substance used to straighten curly hair
RELAXES ▶ **relax**
RELAXIN n mammalian polypeptide hormone secreted by the corpus luteum during pregnancy, which relaxes the pelvic ligaments
RELAY n fresh set of people or animals relieving others ▷ vb pass on (a message)

R

RELAYED ▶ **relay**
RELAYS ▶ **relay**
RELEARN vb learn (something previously known) again
RELEASE vb set free ▷ n setting free
RELEND vb lend again
RELENDS ▶ **relend**
RELENT vb give up a harsh intention, become less severe
RELENTS ▶ **relent**
RELET vb let again
RELETS ▶ **relet**
RELEVE n dance move in which heels are off the ground
RELEVES ▶ **releve**
RELIANT > **reliance**
RELIC n something that has survived from the past
RELICS ▶ **relic**
RELICT n relic
RELICTS ◀ **relict**
RELIDE archaic past form of ▶ **rely**
RELIE archaic spelling of ▶ **rely**
RELIED ▶ **rely**
RELIEF n gladness at the end or removal of pain, distress, etc
RELIEFS ▶ **relief**
RELIER ▶ **rely**
RELIERS ▶ **rely**
RELIES ▶ **rely**
RELIEVE vb bring relief to
RELIEVO same as ▶ **relief**
RELIGHT vb ignite or cause to ignite again
RELINE vb line again or anew
RELINED ▶ **reline**
RELINES ▶ **reline**
RELINK vb link again
RELINKS ▶ **relink**
RELIQUE archaic spelling of ▶ **relic**
RELISH vb enjoy, like very much ▷ n liking or enjoyment
RELIST vb list again
RELISTS ▶ **relist**
RELIT ▶ **relight**
RELIVE vb experience (a sensation etc) again, esp in the imagination
RELIVED ▶ **relive**
RELIVER vb deliver up again
RELIVES ▶ **relive**
RELLENO n Mexican dish of stuffed vegetable

RELLIE n relative
RELLIES pl n relatives or relations
RELLISH (in music) same as ▶ **relish**
RELOAD vb put fresh ammunition into (a firearm)
RELOADS ▶ **reload**
RELOAN vb loan again
RELOANS ▶ **reloan**
RELOCK vb lock again
RELOCKS ▶ **relock**
RELOOK vb look again
RELOOKS ▶ **relook**
RELUCT vb struggle or rebel
RELUCTS ▶ **reluct**
RELUME vb light or brighten again
RELUMED ▶ **relume**
RELUMES ▶ **relume**
RELY vb depend (on)
RELYING ▶ **rely**
REM n dose of ionizing radiation that produces the same effect in man as one roentgen of x- or gamma-radiation
REMADE n object that has been reconstructed from original materials
REMADES ▶ **remade**
REMAIL vb mail again
REMAILS ▶ **remail**
REMAIN vb continue
REMAINS pl n relics, esp of ancient buildings
REMAKE vb make again in a different way ▷ n new version of an old film
REMAKER ▶ **remake**
REMAKES ▶ **remake**
REMAN vb man again or afresh
REMAND vb send back into custody or put on bail before trial
REMANDS ▶ **remand**
REMANET n something left over
REMANIE n fragments and fossils of older origin found in a more recent deposit
REMANS ▶ **reman**
REMAP vb map again
REMAPS ▶ **remap**
REMARK vb make a casual comment (on) ▷ n observation or comment
REMARKS ▶ **remark**
REMARRY vb marry again following a divorce or the death of one's previous

husband or wife
REMATCH n second or return game or contest between two players ▷ vb match (two contestants) again
REMATE vb mate again ▷ n finishing pass in bullfighting
REMATED ▶ **remate**
REMATES ▶ **remate**
REMBLAI n earth used for an embankment or rampart
REMBLE dialect word for ▶ **remove**
REMBLED ▶ **remble**
REMBLES ▶ **remble**
REMEAD archaic or dialect word for ▶ **remedy**
REMEADS ▶ **remead**
REMEDE archaic or dialect word for ▶ **remedy**
REMEDED ▶ **remede**
REMEDES ▶ **remede**
REMEDY n means of curing pain or disease ▷ vb put right
REMEET vb meet again
REMEETS ▶ **remeet**
REMEID archaic or dialect word for ▶ **remedy**
REMEIDS ▶ **remeid**
REMELT vb melt again
REMELTS ▶ **remelt**
REMEN n ancient Egyptian measurement unit
REMEND vb mend again
REMENDS ▶ **remend**
REMENS ▶ **remen**
REMERCY vb archaic word for thank
REMERGE vb merge again
REMET ▶ **remeet**
REMEX n any of the large flight feathers of a bird's wing
REMIGES ▶ **remex**
REMIND vb cause to remember
REMINDS ▶ **remind**
REMINT vb mint again
REMINTS ▶ **remint**
REMISE vb give up or relinquish (a right, claim, etc) ▷ n second thrust made on the same lunge after the first has missed
REMISED ▶ **remise**
REMISES ▶ **remise**
REMISS adj negligent or careless
REMIT vb send (money) for

goods, services, etc, esp by post ▷ *n* area of competence or authority

REMITS ▶ **remit**

REMIX *vb* change the relative prominence of each performer's part of (a recording) ▷ *n* remixed version of a recording

REMIXED ▶ **remix**

REMIXES ▶ **remix**

REMIXT *informal past form of* ▶ **remix**

REMNANT *n* small piece, esp of fabric, left over ▷ *adj* remaining

REMODEL *vb* give a different shape or form to ▷ *n* something that has been remodelled

REMOLD *US spelling of* ▶ **remould**

REMOLDS ▶ **remold**

REMORA *n* spiny-finned fish

REMORAS ▶ **remora**

REMORID ▶ **remora**

REMORSE *n* feeling of sorrow and regret for something one did

REMOTE *adj* far away, distant ▷ *n* (in informal usage) remote control

REMOTER ▶ **remote**

REMOTES ▶ **remote**

REMOUD *Spenserian variant of* ▶ **removed**

REMOULD *vb* change completely ▷ *n* renovated tyre

REMOUNT *vb* get on (a horse, bicycle, etc) again ▷ *n* fresh horse, esp (formerly) to replace one killed or injured in battle

REMOVAL *n* removing, esp changing residence

REMOVE *vb* take away or off ▷ *n* degree of difference

REMOVED *adj* very different or distant

REMOVER ▶ **remove**

REMOVES ▶ **remove**

REMS ▶ **rem**

REMUAGE *n* (in the making of sparkling wine) process of turning the bottles to let the sediment out

REMUDA *n* stock of horses enabling riders to change mounts

REMUDAS ▶ **remuda**

REMUEUR *n* (in the making

of sparkling wine) person carrying out remuage, or the turning of bottles

REN *archaic variant of* ▶ **run**

RENAGUE *same as* ▶ **renege**

RENAIL *vb* nail again

RENAILS ▶ **renail**

RENAL *adj* of the kidneys

RENAME *vb* change the name of (someone or something)

RENAMED ▶ **rename**

RENAMES ▶ **rename**

RENAY *vb* archaic word meaning renounce

RENAYED ▶ **renay**

RENAYS ▶ **renay**

REND *vb* tear or wrench apart

RENDED ▶ **rend**

RENDER *vb* cause to become ▷ *n* first thin coat of plaster applied to a surface

RENDERS ▶ **render**

RENDING ▶ **rend**

RENDS ▶ **rend**

RENEGE *vb* go back (on a promise etc)

RENEGED ▶ **renege**

RENEGER ▶ **renege**

RENEGES ▶ **renege**

RENEGUE *same as* ▶ **renege**

RENEST *vb* nest again or form a new nest

RENESTS ▶ **renest**

RENEW *vb* begin again

RENEWAL *n* act of renewing or state of being renewed

RENEWED ▶ **renew**

RENEWER ▶ **renew**

RENEWS ▶ **renew**

RENEY *same as* ▶ **renay**

RENEYED ▶ **reney**

RENEYS ▶ **reney**

RENGA *n* type of collaborative poetry found in Japan

RENGAS ▶ **renga**

RENIED ▶ **reny**

RENIES ▶ **reny**

RENIG *same as* ▶ **renege**

RENIGS ▶ **renig**

RENIN *n* proteolytic enzyme secreted by the kidneys, which plays an important part in the maintenance of blood pressure

RENINS ▶ **renin**

RENK *adj* unpleasant

RENKER ▶ **renk**

RENKEST ▶ **renk**

RENNASE *same as* ▶ **rennin**

RENNE *archaic variant of* ▶ **run**

RENNED ▶ **ren**

RENNES ▶ **renne**

RENNET *n* substance for curdling milk to make cheese

RENNETS ▶ **rennet**

RENNIN *n* enzyme that occurs in gastric juice and is a constituent of rennet. It coagulates milk by converting caseinogen to casein

RENNING ▶ **ren**

RENNINS ▶ **rennin**

RENOWN *n* widespread good reputation ▷ *vb* make famous

RENOWNS ▶ **renown**

RENS ▶ **ren**

RENT *n* payment made by a tenant to a landlord or owner of a property ▷ *vb* grant the right to use one's property for payment

RENTAL *n* sum payable as rent ▷ *adj* of or relating to rent

RENTALS ▶ **rental**

RENTE *n* annual income from capital investment

RENTED ▶ **rent**

RENTER *n* person who lets his property in return for rent, esp a landlord

RENTERS ▶ **renter**

RENTES ▶ **rente**

RENTIER *n* person who lives off unearned income such as rents or interest

RENTING ▶ **rent**

RENTS ▶ **rent**

RENVOI *n* referring of a dispute or other legal question to a jurisdiction other than that in which it arose

RENVOIS ▶ **renvoi**

RENVOY *old variant of* ▶ **renvoi**

RENVOYS ▶ **renvoy**

RENY *same as* ▶ **renay**

RENYING ▶ **reny**

REO *n* a New Zealand language

REOCCUR *vb* happen, take place, or come about again

REOFFER *vb* offer again

REOIL *vb* oil again

REOILED ▶ **reoil**

REOILS ▶ **reoil**

REOPEN *vb* open again after

a period of being closed or suspended

REOPENS ▸ **reopen**

REORDER vb change the order of

REOS ▸ **reo**

REP n sales representative ▹ vb work as a representative

REPACK vb place or arrange (articles) in (a container) again or in a different way

REPACKS ▸ **repack**

REPAID ▸ **repay**

REPAINT vb apply a new or fresh coat of paint

REPAIR vb restore to good condition, mend ▹ n act of repairing

REPAIRS ▸ **repair**

REPAND adj having a wavy margin

REPANEL vb panel again or anew

REPAPER vb paper again or afresh

REPARK vb park again

REPARKS ▸ **repark**

REPASS vb pass again

REPAST n meal ▹ vb feed (on)

REPASTS ▸ **repast**

REPATCH vb patch again

REPAVE vb pave again

REPAVED ▸ **repave**

REPAVES ▸ **repave**

REPAY vb pay back, refund

REPAYS ▸ **repay**

REPEAL vb cancel (a law) officially ▹ n act of repealing

REPEALS ▸ **repeal**

REPEAT vb say or do again ▹ n act or instance of repeating

REPEATS ▸ **repeat**

REPEG vb peg again

REPEGS ▸ **repeg**

REPEL vb be disgusting to

REPELS ▸ **repel**

REPENT vb feel regret for (a deed or omission) ▹ adj lying or creeping along the ground

REPENTS ▸ **repent**

REPERK vb perk again

REPERKS ▸ **reperk**

REPIN vb pin again

REPINE vb fret or complain

REPINED ▸ **repine**

REPINER ▸ **repine**

REPINES ▸ **repine**

REPINS ▸ **repin**

REPIQUE n score of 30 points made from the cards held by a player before play begins ▹ vb score a repique against (someone)

REPLA ▸ **replum**

REPLACE vb substitute for

REPLAN vb plan again

REPLANS ▸ **replan**

REPLANT vb plant again

REPLATE vb plate again

REPLAY n immediate reshowing on TV of an incident in sport, esp in slow motion ▹ vb play (a match, recording, etc) again

REPLAYS ▸ **replay**

REPLEAD vb plead again

REPLED ▸ **replead**

REPLETE adj filled or gorged ▹ vb fill again

REPLEVY vb recover possession of (goods) by replevin

REPLICA n exact copy

REPLIED ▸ **reply**

REPLIER ▸ **reply**

REPLIES ▸ **reply**

REPLOT vb plot again

REPLOTS ▸ **replot**

REPLOW vb plow again

REPLOWS ▸ **replow**

REPLUM n internal separating wall in some fruits

REPLUMB vb plumb again

REPLY vb answer or respond ▹ n answer or response

REPO n act of repossessing

REPOINT vb repair the joints of (brickwork, masonry, etc) with mortar or cement

REPOLL vb poll again

REPOLLS ▸ **repoll**

REPOMAN n informal word for a man employed to repossess goods in cases of non-payment

REPOMEN ▸ **repoman**

REPONE vb restore (someone) to his former status, office, etc

REPONED ▸ **repone**

REPONES ▸ **repone**

REPORT vb give an account of ▹ n account or statement

REPORTS ▸ **report**

REPOS ▸ **repo**

REPOSAL n repose

REPOSE n peace ▹ vb lie or lay at rest

REPOSED ▸ **repose**

REPOSER ▸ **repose**

REPOSES ▸ **repose**

REPOSIT vb put away, deposit, or store up

REPOST vb post again

REPOSTS ▸ **repost**

REPOT vb put (a house plant) into a new usually larger pot

REPOTS ▸ **repot**

REPOUR vb pour back or again

REPOURS ▸ **repour**

REPOWER vb put new engine in

REPP same as ▸ **rep**

REPPED ▸ **rep**

REPPING ▸ **rep**

REPPS ▸ **repp**

REPRESS vb keep (feelings) in check

REPRICE vb price again

REPRIME vb prime again

REPRINT vb print further copies of (a book) ▹ n reprinted copy

REPRISE n repeating of an earlier theme ▹ vb repeat an earlier theme

REPRIVE archaic spelling of ▹ **reprieve**

REPRIZE archaic spelling of ▸ **reprise**

REPRO n imitation or facsimile of a work of art; reproduction

REPROBE vb probe again

REPROOF n severe blaming of someone for a fault ▹ vb treat (a coat, jacket, etc) so as to renew its texture, waterproof qualities, etc

REPROS ▸ **repro**

REPROVE vb speak severely to (someone) about a fault

REPRYVE archaic spelling of ▹ **reprieve**

REPS ▸ **rep**

REPTANT adj creeping, crawling, or lying along the ground

REPTILE n cold-blooded egg-laying vertebrate with horny scales or plates, such as a snake or tortoise ▹ adj creeping, crawling, or squirming

REPUGN vb oppose or conflict (with)

REPUGNS ▸ **repugn**

REPULP vb pulp again

REPULPS ▸ repulp
REPULSE vb be disgusting to ▸ n driving back
REPUMP vb pump again
REPUMPS ▸ repump
REPUNIT n any number that consists entirely of the same repeated digits, such as 111 or 55,555
REPURE vb archaic word meaning make pure again
REPURED ▸ repure
REPURES ▸ repure
REPUTE n reputation ▸ vb consider (a person or thing) to be as specified
REPUTED adj supposed
REPUTES ▸ repute
REQUERE archaic variant of ▸ require
REQUEST vb ask ▸ n asking
REQUIEM n Mass celebrated for the dead
REQUIN vb type of shark
REQUINS ▸ requin
REQUIRE vb want or need
REQUIT vb quit again
REQUITE vb return to someone (the same treatment or feeling as received)
REQUITS ▸ requit
REQUOTE vb quote again
RERACK vb rack again
RERACKS ▸ rerack
RERAIL vb put back on a railway line
RERAILS ▸ rerail
RERAISE vb raise again
RERAN ▸ rerun
REREAD vb read (something) again
REREADS ▸ reread
REREDOS n ornamental screen behind an altar
REREMAI n New Zealand word for the basking shark
RERENT vb rent again
RERENTS ▸ rerent
RERIG vb rig again
RERIGS ▸ rerig
RERISE vb rise again
RERISEN ▸ rerise
RERISES ▸ rerise
REROLL vb roll again
REROLLS ▸ reroll
REROOF vb put a new roof or roofs on
REROOFS ▸ reroof
REROSE ▸ rerise
REROUTE vb send or direct by a different route
RERUN n film or

programme that is broadcast again, repeat ▸ vb put on (a film or programme) again
RERUNS ▸ rerun
RES informal word for > **residence**
RESAID ▸ resay
RESAIL vb sail again
RESAILS ▸ resail
RESALE n selling of something purchased earlier
RESALES ▸ resale
RESAT ▸ resit
RESAW vb saw again
RESAWED ▸ resaw
RESAWN ▸ resaw
RESAWS ▸ resaw
RESAY vb say again or in response
RESAYS ▸ resay
RESCALE vb resize
RESCIND vb annul or repeal
RESCORE vb score afresh
RESCUE vb deliver from danger or trouble, save ▸ n rescuing
RESCUED ▸ rescue
RESCUER ▸ rescue
RESCUES ▸ rescue
RESEAL vb close or secure tightly again
RESEALS ▸ reseal
RESEAT vb show (a person) to a new seat
RESEATS ▸ reseat
RESEAU n mesh background to a lace or other pattern
RESEAUS ▸ reseau
RESEAUX ▸ reseau
RESECT vb cut out part of (a bone, an organ, or other structure or part)
RESECTS ▸ resect
RESEDA n plant that has small spikes of grey-green flowers ▸ adj of a greyish-green colour
RESEDAS ▸ reseda
RESEE vb see again
RESEED vb form seed and reproduce naturally, forming a constant plant population
RESEEDS ▸ reseed
RESEEK vb seek again
RESEEKS ▸ reseek
RESEEN ▸ resee
RESEES ▸ resee
RESEIZE vb seize again
RESELL vb sell (something)

one has previously bought
RESELLS ▸ resell
RESEND vb send again
RESENDS ▸ resend
RESENT vb feel bitter about
RESENTS ▸ resent
RESERVE vb set aside, keep for future use ▸ n something, esp money or troops, kept for emergencies
RESES ▸ res
RESET vb set again (a broken bone, matter in type, a gemstone, etc) ▸ n act or an instance of setting again
RESETS ▸ reset
RESEW vb sew again
RESEWED ▸ resew
RESEWN ▸ resew
RESEWS ▸ resew
RESH n 20th letter of the Hebrew alphabet
RESHAPE vb shape (something) again or differently
RESHAVE vb shave again
RESHES ▸ resh
RESHINE vb shine again
RESHIP vb ship again
RESHIPS ▸ reship
RESHOD ▸ reshoe
RESHOE vb put a new shoe or shoes on
RESHOED ▸ reshoe
RESHOES ▸ reshoe
RESHONE ▸ reshine
RESHOOT vb shoot again
RESHOT ▸ reshoot
RESHOW vb show again
RESHOWN ▸ reshow
RESHOWS ▸ reshow
RESIANT archaic word for > **resident**
RESID n residual oil left over from the petroleum distillation process
RESIDE vb dwell permanently
RESIDED ▸ reside
RESIDER ▸ reside
RESIDES ▸ reside
RESIDS ▸ resid
RESIDUA > residuum
RESIDUE n what is left, remainder
RESIFT vb sift again
RESIFTS ▸ resift
RESIGHT vb sight again
RESIGN vb give up office, a job, etc
RESIGNS ▸ resign

R

RESILE vb spring or shrink back

RESILED ▸ resile

RESILES ▸ resile

RESILIN n substance found in insect bodies

RESIN n sticky substance from plants, esp pines ▷ vb treat or coat with resin

RESINED ▸ resin

RESINER n applier or collector of resin

RESINS ▸ resin

RESINY adj resembling, containing or covered with resin

RESIST vb withstand or oppose ▷ n substance used to protect something, esp a coating that prevents corrosion

RESISTS ▸ resist

RESIT vb take (an exam) again ▷ n exam that has to be taken again

RESITE vb move to a different site

RESITED ▸ resite

RESITES ▸ resite

RESITS ▸ resit

RESIZE vb change size of

RESIZED ▸ resize

RESIZES ▸ resize

RESKEW archaic spelling of ▸ rescue

RESKEWS ▸ reskew

RESKILL vb train (workers) to acquire new skills

RESKUE archaic spelling of ▸ rescue

RESKUED ▸ reskue

RESKUES ▸ reskue

RESLATE vb slate again

RESMELT vb smelt again

RESOAK vb soak again

RESOAKS ▸ resoak

RESOD vb returf

RESODS ▸ resod

RESOJET n type of jet engine

RESOLD ▸ resell

RESOLE vb put a new sole or new soles on

RESOLED ▸ resole

RESOLES ▸ resole

RESOLVE vb decide with an effort of will ▷ n absolute determination

RESORB vb absorb again

RESORBS ▸ resorb

RESORT vb have recourse (to) for help etc ▷ n place for holidays

RESORTS ▸ resort

RESOUND vb echo or ring with sound

RESOW vb sow again

RESOWED ▸ resow

RESOWN ▸ resow

RESOWS ▸ resow

RESPACE vb change the spacing of

RESPADE vb dig over

RESPEAK vb speak further

RESPECT n consideration ▷ vb treat with esteem

RESPELL vb spell again

RESPELT ▸ respell

RESPIRE vb breathe

RESPITE n pause, interval of rest ▷ vb grant a respite to

RESPLIT vb split again

RESPOKE ▸ respeak

RESPOND vb answer ▷ n pilaster or an engaged column that supports an arch or a lintel

RESPOOL vb rewind onto spool

RESPOT vb (in billiards) replace on one of the spots

RESPOTS ▸ respot

RESPRAY n new coat of paint applied to a car, van, etc ▷ vb spray (a car, wheels, etc) with a new coat of paint

REST n freedom from exertion etc ▷ vb take a rest

RESTACK vb stack again

RESTAFF vb staff again

RESTAGE vb produce or perform a new production of (a play)

RESTAMP vb stamp again

RESTART vb commence (something) or set (something) in motion again ▷ n act or an instance of starting again

RESTATE vb state or affirm (something) again or in a different way

RESTED ▸ rest

RESTEM vb stem again

RESTEMS ▸ restem

RESTER ▸ rest

RESTERS ▸ rest

RESTFUL adj relaxing or soothing

RESTIER ▸ resty

RESTIFF same as ▸ restive

RESTING ▸ rest

RESTIVE adj restless or impatient

RESTO n restored antique, vintage car, etc

RESTOCK vb replenish stores or supplies

RESTOKE vb stoke again

RESTORE vb return (a building, painting, etc) to its original condition

RESTOS ▸ resto

RESTS ▸ rest

RESTUDY vb study again

RESTUFF vb put new stuffing in

RESTUMP vb provide with new stumps

RESTY adj restive

RESTYLE vb style again

RESULT n outcome or consequence ▷ vb be the outcome or consequence (of)

RESULTS ▸ result

RESUME vb begin again ▷ n summary

RESUMED ▸ resume

RESUMER ▸ resume

RESUMES ▸ resume

RESURGE vb rise again from or as if from the dead

RET vb moisten or soak (flax, hemp, jute, etc) to promote bacterial action in order to facilitate separation of the fibres from the woody tissue by beating

RETABLE n ornamental screenlike structure above and behind an altar, esp one used as a setting for a religious picture or carving

RETACK vb tack again

RETACKS ▸ retack

RETAG vb tag again

RETAGS ▸ retag

RETAIL n selling of goods individually or in small amounts to the public ▷ adj of or engaged in such selling ▷ adv by retail ▷ vb sell or be sold retail

RETAILS ▸ retail

RETAIN vb keep in one's possession

> Perhaps the most important word in Scrabble, because its letters combine with every other letter apart from A, Q, V, X, Y and Z to form a 7-letter bonus word that will score you an extra 50 points, so if you have these six letters on your rack you know that a bonus is either

available or very close. And if you have an S as well, so much the better, because not only does this rack offer you 11 different words to choose from, but if none of those can be fitted in then RETAINS combines with every other letter except for Q, V, X, Y and Z to form at least one eight-letter word.

RETAINS ▶ retain
RETAKE vb recapture ▷ n act of rephotographing a scene
RETAKEN ▶ retake
RETAKER ▶ retake
RETAKES ▶ retake
RETALLY vb count up again
RETAMA n type of shrub
RETAMAS ▶ retama
RETAPE vb tape again
RETAPED ▶ retape
RETAPES ▶ retape
RETARD vb delay or slow (progress or development) ▷ n offensive term for a retarded person
RETARDS ▶ retard
RETASTE vb taste again
RETAX vb tax again
RETAXED ▶ retax
RETAXES ▶ retax
RETCH vb try to vomit ▷ n involuntary spasm of the stomach
RETCHED ▶ retch
RETCHES ▶ retch
RETE n any network of nerves or blood vessels
RETEACH vb teach again
RETEAM vb team up again
RETEAMS ▶ reteam
RETEAR vb tear again
RETEARS ▶ retear
RETELL vb relate (a story, etc) again or differently
RETELLS ▶ retell
RETEM n type of shrub
RETEMS ▶ retem
RETENE n yellow crystalline hydrocarbon found in tar oils from pine wood and in certain fossil resins
RETENES ▶ retene
RETEST vb test (something) again or differently
RETESTS ▶ retest
RETHINK vb consider again, esp with a view to changing one's tactics ▷ n act or an

instance of thinking again
RETIA ▶ rete
RETIAL ▶ rete
RETIARY adj of, relating to, or resembling a net or web
RETICLE n network of fine lines, wires, etc, placed in the focal plane of an optical instrument to assist measurement of the size or position of objects under observation
RETIE vb tie again
RETIED ▶ retie
RETIES ▶ retie
RETILE vb put new tiles in or on
RETILED ▶ retile
RETILES ▶ retile
RETIME vb time again or alter time of
RETIMED ▶ retime
RETIMES ▶ retime
RETINA n light-sensitive membrane at the back of the eye
RETINAE ▶ retina
RETINAL adj of or relating to the retina ▷ n aldehyde form of the polyene retinol (vitamin A) that associates with the protein opsin to form the visual purple pigment rhodopsin
RETINAS ▶ retina
RETINE n chemical found in body cells that slows cell growth and division
RETINES ▶ retine
RETINOL n another name for vitamin A and rosin oil
RETINT vb tint again or change tint of
RETINTS ▶ retint
RETINUE n band of attendants
RETIRAL n act of retiring from office, one's work, etc
RETIRE vb (cause to) give up office or work, esp through age
RETIRED adj having retired from work etc
RETIREE n person who has retired from work
RETIRER ▶ retire
RETIRES ▶ retire
RETITLE vb give a new title to
RETOLD ▶ retell
RETOOK ▶ retake
RETOOL vb replace, re-equip, or rearrange the

tools in (a factory, etc)
RETOOLS ▶ retool
RETORE ▶ retear
RETORN ▶ retear
RETORT vb reply quickly, wittily, or angrily ▷ n quick, witty, or angry reply
RETORTS ▶ retort
RETOTAL vb add up again
RETOUCH vb restore or improve by new touches, esp of paint ▷ n art or practice of retouching
RETOUR vb (in Scottish law) to return as heir
RETOURS ▶ retour
RETRACE vb go back over (a route etc) again
RETRACK vb track again
RETRACT vb withdraw (a statement etc)
RETRAIN vb train to do a new or different job
RETRAIT archaic form of ▶ retreat
RETRAL adj at, near, or towards the back
RETRATE archaic form of ▶ retreat
RETREAD n remould ▷ vb remould
RETREAT vb move back from a position, withdraw ▷ n act of or military signal for retiring or withdrawal
RETREE n imperfectly made paper
RETREES ▶ retree
RETRIAL n second trial of a case or defendant in a court of law
RETRIED ▶ retry
RETRIES ▶ retry
RETRIM vb trim again
RETRIMS ▶ retrim
RETRO adj associated with or revived from the past ▷ n a retro style of art
RETROD ▶ retread
RETROS ▶ retro
RETRY vb try again (a case already determined)
RETS ▶ ret
RETSINA n Greek wine flavoured with resin
RETTED ▶ ret
RETTERY n flax-retting place
RETTING ▶ ret
RETUND vb weaken or blunt
RETUNDS ▶ retund
RETUNE vb tune (a musical

R

instrument) differently or again

RETUNED ▸ **retune**

RETUNES ▸ **retune**

RETURF vb turf again

RETURFS ▸ **returf**

RETURN vb go or come back ▸ n returning ▸ adj of or being a return

RETURNS ▸ **return**

RETUSE adj having a rounded apex and a central depression

RETWIST vb twist again

RETYING ▸ **retie**

RETYPE vb type again

RETYPED ▸ **retype**

RETYPES ▸ **retype**

REUNIFY vb bring together again something previously divided

REUNION n meeting of people who have been apart

REUNITE vb bring or come together again after a separation

REURGE vb urge again

REURGED ▸ **reurge**

REURGES ▸ **reurge**

REUSE vb use again ▸ n act of using something again

REUSED ▸ **reuse**

REUSES ▸ **reuse**

REUSING ▸ **reuse**

REUTTER vb utter again

REV n revolution (of an engine) ▸ vb increase the speed of revolution of (an engine)

REVALUE vb adjust the exchange value of (a currency) upwards

REVAMP vb renovate or restore ▸ n something that has been renovated or revamped

REVAMPS ▸ **revamp**

REVEAL vb make known ▸ n vertical side of an opening in a wall, esp the side of a window or door between the frame and the front of the wall

REVEALS ▸ **reveal**

REVEL vb take pleasure (in) ▸ n occasion of noisy merrymaking

REVELED ▸ **revel**

REVELER ▸ **revel**

REVELRY n festivity

REVELS ▸ **revel**

REVENGE n retaliation for

wrong done ▸ vb make retaliation for

REVENUE n income, esp of a state

REVERB n electronic device that creates artificial acoustics ▸ vb reverberate

REVERBS ▸ **reverb**

REVERE vb be in awe of and respect greatly

REVERED ▸ **revere**

REVERER ▸ **revere**

REVERES ▸ **revere**

REVERIE n absent-minded daydream

REVERS n turned back part of a garment, such as the lapel

REVERSE vb turn upside down or the other way round ▸ n opposite ▸ adj opposite or contrary

REVERSI n game played on a draughtboard with 64 pieces, black on one side and white on the other. When pieces are captured they are turned over to join the capturing player's forces

REVERSO another name for ▸ **verso**

REVERT vb return to a former state

REVERTS ▸ **revert**

REVERY same as ▸ **reverie**

REVEST vb restore (former power, authority, status, etc, to a person) or (of power, authority, etc) to be restored

REVESTS ▸ **revest**

REVET vb face (a wall or embankment) with stones

REVETS ▸ **revet**

REVEUR n daydreamer

REVEURS ▸ **reveur**

REVEUSE n female daydreamer

REVIE vb archaic cards term meaning challenge by placing a larger stake

REVIED ▸ **revie**

REVIES ▸ **revie**

REVIEW n critical assessment of a book, concert, etc ▸ vb hold or write a review of

REVIEWS ▸ **review**

REVILE vb be abusively scornful of

REVILED ▸ **revile**

REVILER ▸ **revile**

REVILES ▸ **revile**

REVISAL ▸ **revise**

REVISE vb change or alter ▸ n act, process, or result of revising

REVISED ▸ **revise**

REVISER ▸ **revise**

REVISES ▸ **revise**

REVISIT vb visit again

REVISOR ▸ **revise**

REVIVAL n reviving or renewal

REVIVE vb bring or come back to life, vigour, use, etc

REVIVED ▸ **revive**

REVIVER ▸ **revive**

REVIVES ▸ **revive**

REVIVOR n means of reviving a lawsuit that has been suspended owing to the death or marriage of one of the parties

REVOICE vb utter again

REVOKE vb cancel (a will, agreement, etc) ▸ n act of revoking

REVOKED ▸ **revoke**

REVOKER ▸ **revoke**

REVOKES ▸ **revoke**

REVOLT n uprising against authority ▸ vb rise in rebellion

REVOLTS ▸ **revolt**

REVOLVE vb turn round, rotate ▸ n circular section of a stage that can be rotated by electric power to provide a scene change

REVOTE vb decide or grant again by a new vote

REVOTED ▸ **revote**

REVOTES ▸ **revote**

REVS ▸ **rev**

REVUE n theatrical entertainment with topical sketches and songs

REVUES ▸ **revue**

REVUIST ▸ **revue**

REVVED ▸ **rev**

REVVING ▸ **rev**

REVYING ▸ **revie**

REW archaic spelling of ▸ **rue**

REWAKE vb awaken again

REWAKED ▸ **rewake**

REWAKEN vb awaken again

REWAKES ▸ **rewake**

REWAN archaic past form of ▸ **rewin**

REWARD n something given in return for a service ▸ vb pay or give something to (someone) for a service, information, etc

REWARDS ▸ reward
REWARM vb warm again
REWARMS ▸ rewarm
REWASH vb wash again
REWATER vb water again
REWAX vb wax again
REWAXED ▸ rewax
REWAXES ▸ rewax
REWEAR vb wear again
REWEARS ▸ rewear
REWEAVE vb weave again
REWED vb wed again
REWEDS ▸ rewed
REWEIGH vb weigh again
REWELD vb weld again
REWELDS ▸ reweld
REWET vb wet again
REWETS ▸ rewet
REWIDEN vb widen again
REWIN vb win again
REWIND vb wind again
REWINDS ▸ rewind
REWINS ▸ rewin
REWIRE vb provide (a house, engine, etc) with new wiring
REWIRED ▸ rewire
REWIRES ▸ rewire
REWOKE ▸ rewake
REWOKEN ▸ rewake
REWON ▸ rewin
REWORD vb alter the wording of
REWORDS ▸ reword
REWORE ▸ rewear
REWORK vb improve or bring up to date
REWORKS ▸ rework
REWORN ▸ rewear
REWOUND ▸ rewind
REWOVE ▸ reweave
REWOVEN ▸ reweave
REWRAP vb wrap again
REWRAPS ▸ rewrap
REWRAPT ▸ rewrap
REWRITE vb write again in a different way ▷ n something rewritten
REWROTE ▸ rewrite
REWS ▸ rew
REWTH archaic variant of ▸ ruth
REWTHS ▸ rewth
REX n king

> **Rex** is a Latin word for **king**, a very commonly played X word.

REXES ▸ rex
REXINE n tradename for a form of artificial leather
REXINES ▸ rexine
REYNARD n fox
REZ n informal word for an

instance of reserving; reservation

> **Rez** is a short informal word for **reservation**, and is one of the most commonly played Z words.

REZERO vb reset to zero
REZEROS ▸ rezero
REZONE vb zone again
REZONED ▸ rezone
REZONES ▸ rezone
REZZES ▸ rez
RHABDOM n (in insect anatomy) any of many similar rodlike structures found in the eye
RHABDUS n sponge spicule
RHACHIS same as ▸ rachis
RHAMNUS n buckthorn
RHANJA n Indian English word for a male lover
RHANJAS ▸ rhanja
RHAPHAE ▸ rhaphe
RHAPHE same as ▸ raphe
RHAPHES ▸ rhaphe
RHAPHIS same as ▸ raphide
RHATANY n South American leguminous shrub
RHEA n S American three-toed ostrich
RHEAS ▸ rhea
RHEBOK n woolly brownish-grey southern African antelope
RHEBOKS ▸ rhebok
RHEME n constituent of a sentence that adds most new information, in addition to what has already been said in the discourse. The rheme is usually, but not always, associated with the subject
RHEMES ▸ rheme
RHENIUM n silvery-white metallic element with a high melting point
RHESUS n macaque monkey
RHETOR n teacher of rhetoric
RHETORS ▸ rhetor
RHEUM n watery discharge from the eyes or nose
RHEUMED adj rheumy
RHEUMIC adj of or relating to rheum
RHEUMS ▸ rheum
RHEUMY adj of the nature of rheum
RHEXES ▸ rhexis

RHEXIS n rupture
RHIES ▸ rhy
RHIME old spelling of ▸ rhyme
RHIMES ▸ rhime
RHINAL adj of or relating to the nose
RHINE n dialect word for a ditch
RHINES ▸ rhine
RHINO n rhinoceros
RHINOS ▸ rhino
RHIZIC adj of or relating to the root of an equation
RHIZINE same as ▸ rhizoid
RHIZOID n any of various slender hairlike structures that function as roots in the gametophyte generation of mosses, ferns, and related plants
RHIZOMA same as ▸ rhizome
RHIZOME n thick underground stem producing new plants
RHIZOPI > rhizopus
RHO n 17th letter in the Greek alphabet, a consonant transliterated as r or rh

> It's useful to remember words that start with RH, as there are quite a few that can come in useful. If you or someone else plays rho, which is a Greek letter, remember that it could be expanded to, for example, **rhody, rhomb, rhodium, rhombus** or **rhomboid**.

RHODIC adj of or containing rhodium, esp in the tetravalent state
RHODIE same as ▸ rhody
RHODIES ▸ rhody
RHODIUM n hard metallic element
RHODORA n type of shrub
RHODOUS adj of or containing rhodium (but proportionally more than a rhodic compound)
RHODY n rhododendron
RHOMB same as ▸ rhombus
RHOMBI ▸ rhombus
RHOMBIC adj relating to or having the shape of a rhombus
RHOMBOI ▸ rhombos
RHOMBOS n wooden slat attached to a thong that

R

makes a roaring sound when the thong is whirled

RHOMBS ▶ rhomb

RHOMBUS n parallelogram with sides of equal length but no right angles, diamond-shaped figure

RHONCHI > rhonchus

RHONE same as ▶ rone

RHONES ▶ rhone

RHOS ▶ rho

RHOTIC adj denoting or speaking a dialect of English in which postvocalic r s are pronounced

RHUBARB n garden plant of which the fleshy stalks are cooked as fruit ▷ interj noise made by actors to simulate conversation, esp by repeating the word rhubarb ▷ vb simulate conversation in this way

RHUMB n as in **rhumb line** imaginary line on the surface of a sphere, such as the earth, that intersects all meridians at the same angle

RHUMBA same as ▶ rumba

RHUMBAS ▶ rhumba

RHUMBS ▶ rhumb

RHUS n genus of shrubs and small trees, several species of which are cultivated as ornamentals for their colourful autumn foliage

RHUSES ▶ rhus

RHY archaic spelling of ▶ rye
This alternative spelling of **rye** can come in useful when you are short of vowels.

RHYME n sameness of the final sounds at the ends of lines of verse, or in words ▷ vb make a rhyme

RHYMED ▶ rhyme

RHYMER same as > rhymester

RHYMERS ▶ rhymer

RHYMES ▶ rhyme

RHYMING ▶ rhyme

RHYMIST ▶ rhyme

RHYNE same as ▶ rhine

RHYNES ▶ rhyne

RHYTA ▶ rhyton

RHYTHM n any regular movement or beat

RHYTHMI > rhythmus

RHYTHMS ▶ rhythm

RHYTINA n type of sea cow

RHYTON n (in ancient Greece) a horn-shaped drinking vessel with a hole in the pointed end through which to drink

RHYTONS ▶ rhyton

RIA n long narrow inlet of the seacoast, being a former valley that was submerged by a rise in the level of the sea. Rias are found esp on the coasts of SW Ireland and NW Spain

RIAD n traditional Moroccan house with an interior garden

RIADS ▶ riad

RIAL n standard monetary unit of Iran

RIALS ▶ rial

RIALTO n market or exchange

RIALTOS ▶ rialto

RIANCY ▶ riant

RIANT adj laughing

RIANTLY ▶ riant

RIAS ▶ ria

RIATA same as ▶ reata

RIATAS ▶ riata

RIB n one of the curved bones forming the framework of the upper part of the body ▷ vb provide or mark with ribs

RIBA n (in Islam) interest or usury, as forbidden by the Koran

RIBALD adj humorously or mockingly rude or obscene ▷ n ribald person

RIBALDS ▶ ribald

RIBAND n ribbon awarded for some achievement

RIBANDS ▶ riband

RIBAS ▶ riba

RIBAUD archaic variant of ▶ ribald

RIBAUDS ▶ ribaud

RIBBAND same as ▶ riband

RIBBED ▶ rib

RIBBER n someone who ribs

RIBBERS ▶ ribber

RIBBIER ▶ ribby

RIBBING ▶ rib

RIBBON n narrow band of fabric used for trimming, tying, etc ▷ vb adorn with a ribbon or ribbons

RIBBONS ▶ ribbon

RIBBONY ▶ ribbon

RIBBY adj with noticeable ribs

RIBCAGE n bony structure

of ribs enclosing the lungs

RIBES n genus of shrubs that includes currants

RIBEYE n beefsteak cut from the outer side of the rib section

RIBEYES ▶ ribeye

RIBIBE n rebeck

RIBIBES ▶ ribibe

RIBIBLE same as ▶ ribibe

RIBIER n variety of grape

RIBIERS ▶ ribier

RIBLESS ▶ rib

RIBLET n small rib

RIBLETS ▶ riblet

RIBLIKE ▶ rib

RIBOSE n pentose sugar that is an isomeric form of arabinose and that occurs in RNA and riboflavin

RIBOSES ▶ ribose

RIBS ▶ rib

RIBSTON n variety of apple

RIBWORK n work or structure involving ribs

RIBWORT n Eurasian plant with lancelike ribbed leaves and a dense spike of small white flowers

RICE n cereal plant grown on wet ground in warm countries ▷ vb sieve (potatoes or other vegetables) to a coarse mashed consistency

RICED ▶ rice

RICER n kitchen utensil with small holes through which cooked potatoes and similar soft foods are pressed to form a coarse mash

RICERS ▶ ricer

RICES ▶ rice

RICEY adj resembling or containing rice

RICH adj owning a lot of money or property, wealthy ▷ vb (in archaic usage) enrich

RICHED ▶ rich

RICHEN vb enrich

RICHENS ▶ richen

RICHER ▶ rich

RICHES pl n wealth

RICHEST ▶ rich

RICHING ▶ rich

RICHLY adv elaborately

RICHT adj, adv, n, vb right

RICHTED ▶ richt

RICHTER ▶ richt

RICHTS ▶ richt

RICIER ▶ ricy

RICIEST ▶ ricy
RICIN n highly toxic protein, a lectin, derived from castor-oil seeds: used in experimental cancer therapy
RICING ▶ rice
RICINS ▶ ricin
RICINUS n genus of plants
RICK n stack of hay etc ▷ vb wrench or sprain (a joint)
RICKED ▶ rick
RICKER n young kauri tree of New Zealand
RICKERS ▶ ricker
RICKET n mistake
RICKETS n disease of children marked by softening of the bones, bow legs, etc, caused by vitamin D deficiency
RICKETY adj shaky or unstable
RICKEY n cocktail consisting of gin or vodka, lime juice, and soda water, served iced
RICKEYS ▶ rickey
RICKING ▶ rick
RICKLE n unsteady or shaky structure, esp a dilapidated building
RICKLES ▶ rickle
RICKLY adj archaic word for run-down or rickety
RICKS ▶ rick
RICKSHA same as ▶ rickshaw
RICOTTA n soft white unsalted Italian cheese made from sheep's milk
RICRAC same as ▶ rickrack
RICRACS ▶ ricrac
RICTAL ▶ rictus
RICTUS n gape or cleft of an open mouth or beak
RICY same as ▶ ricey
RID vb clear or relieve (of)
RIDABLE ▶ ride
RIDDED ▶ rid
RIDDEN ▶ ride
RIDDER ▶ rid
RIDDERS ▶ rid
RIDDING ▶ rid
RIDDLE n question made puzzling to test one's ingenuity ▷ vb speak in riddles
RIDDLED ▶ riddle
RIDDLER ▶ riddle
RIDDLES ▶ riddle
RIDE vb sit on and control or propel (a horse, bicycle, etc)

▷ n journey on a horse etc, or in a vehicle
RIDENT adj laughing, smiling, or gay
RIDER n person who rides
RIDERED ▶ rider
RIDERS ▶ rider
RIDES ▶ ride
RIDGE n long narrow hill ▷ vb form into a ridge or ridges
RIDGED ▶ ridge
RIDGEL same as ▶ ridgeling
RIDGELS ▶ ridgel
RIDGER n plough used to form furrows and ridges
RIDGERS ▶ ridger
RIDGES ▶ ridge
RIDGIER ▶ ridge
RIDGIL same as ▶ ridgeling
RIDGILS ▶ ridgil
RIDGING ▶ ridge
RIDGY ▶ ridge
RIDING ▶ ride
RIDINGS ▶ ride
RIDLEY n marine turtle
RIDLEYS ▶ ridley
RIDOTTO n entertainment with music and dancing, often in masquerade: popular in 18th-century England
RIDS ▶ rid
RIEL n standard monetary unit of Cambodia, divided into 100 sen
RIELS ▶ riel
RIEM n strip of hide
RIEMPIE n leather thong or lace used mainly to make chair seats
RIEMS ▶ riem
RIEVE n archaic word for rob or plunder
RIEVER n archaic word for robber or plunderer
RIEVERS ▶ riever
RIEVES ▶ rieve
RIEVING ▶ rieve
RIF vb lay off
RIFE adj widespread or common
RIFELY ▶ rife
RIFER ▶ rife
RIFEST ▶ rife
RIFF n short repeated melodic figure ▷ vb play or perform riffs in jazz or rock music
RIFFAGE n (in jazz or rock music) act or an instance of playing a short series of chords

RIFFED ▶ riff
RIFFING ▶ riff
RIFFLE vb flick through (pages etc) quickly ▷ n rapid in a stream
RIFFLED ▶ riffle
RIFFLER n file with a curved face for filing concave surfaces
RIFFLES ▶ riffle
RIFFOLA n use of an abundance of dominant riffs
RIFFS ▶ riff
RIFLE n firearm with a long barrel ▷ vb cut spiral grooves inside the barrel of a gun
RIFLED ▶ rifle
RIFLER ▶ rifle
RIFLERS ▶ rifle
RIFLERY n rifle shots
RIFLES ▶ rifle
RIFLING n cutting of spiral grooves on the inside of a firearm's barrel
RIFLIP n genetic difference between two individuals
RIFLIPS ▶ riflip
RIFS ▶ rif
RIFT n break in friendly relations ▷ vb burst or cause to burst open
RIFTE archaic word for ▶ rift
RIFTED ▶ rift
RIFTIER ▶ rift
RIFTING ▶ rift
RIFTS ▶ rift
RIFTY ▶ rift
RIG vb arrange in a dishonest way ▷ n apparatus for drilling for oil and gas
RIGG n type of fish
RIGGALD same as ▶ ridgeling
RIGGED ▶ rig
RIGGER n workman who rigs vessels, etc
RIGGERS ▶ rigger
RIGGING ▶ rig
RIGGISH adj dialect word meaning wanton
RIGGS ▶ rigg
RIGHT adj just ▷ adv correctly ▷ n claim, title, etc allowed or due ▷ vb bring or come back to a normal or correct state
RIGHTED ▶ right
RIGHTEN vb set right
RIGHTER ▶ right
RIGHTLY adv in accordance

R

with the true facts or justice

RIGHTO *interj* expression of agreement or compliance

RIGHTS ▸ right

RIGHTY *n* informal word for a right-winger

RIGID *adj* inflexible or strict ▷ *adv* completely or excessively ▷ *n* strict and unbending person

RIGIDER ▸ rigid

RIGIDLY ▸ rigid

RIGIDS ▸ rigid

RIGLIN *same as* > **ridgeling**

RIGLING *same as* > **ridgeling**

RIGLINS ▸ riglin

RIGOL *n* (in dialect) ditch or gutter

RIGOLL *same as* ▸ **rigol**

RIGOLLS ▸ rigoll

RIGOLS ▸ rigol

RIGOR *same as* ▸ **rigour**

RIGORS ▸ rigor

RIGOUR *n* harshness, severity, or strictness

RIGOURS ▸ rigour

RIGOUT *n* person's clothing

RIGOUTS ▸ rigout

RIGS ▸ rig

RIKISHA *same as* > **rickshaw**

RIKISHI *n* sumo wrestler

RIKSHAW *same as* > **rickshaw**

RILE *vb* anger or annoy

RILED ▸ rile

RILES ▸ rile

RILEY *adj* cross or irritable

RILIER ▸ riley

RILIEST ▸ riley

RILIEVI ▸ rilievo

RILIEVO *same as* ▸ **relief**

RILING ▸ rile

RILL *n* small stream ▷ *vb* trickle

RILLE *same as* ▸ **rill**

RILLED ▸ rill

RILLES ▸ rille

RILLET *n* little rill

RILLETS ▸ rillet

RILLING ▸ rill

RILLS ▸ rill

RIM *n* edge or border ▷ *vb* put a rim on (a pot, cup, wheel, etc)

RIMA *n* long narrow opening

RIMAE ▸ rima

RIMAYE *n* crevasse at the head of a glacier

RIMAYES ▸ rimaye

RIME *same as* ▸ **rhyme**

RIMED ▸ rime

RIMER *same as* > **rhymester**

RIMERS ▸ rimer

RIMES ▸ rime

RIMFIRE *adj* (of a cartridge) having the primer in the rim of the base ▷ *n* cartridge of this type

RIMIER ▸ rimy

RIMIEST ▸ rimy

RIMING ▸ rime

RIMLAND *n* area situated on the outer edges of a region

RIMLESS ▸ rim

RIMMED ▸ rim

RIMMER *n* tool for shaping the edge of something

RIMMERS ▸ rimmer

RIMMING ▸ rim

RIMOSE *adj* (esp of plant parts) having the surface marked by a network of intersecting cracks

RIMOUS *same as* ▸ **rimose**

RIMPLE *vb* crease or wrinkle

RIMPLED ▸ rimple

RIMPLES ▸ rimple

RIMROCK *n* rock forming the boundaries of a sandy or gravelly alluvial deposit

RIMS ▸ rim

RIMSHOT *n* deliberate simultaneous striking of skin and rim of drum

RIMU *n* New Zealand tree whose wood is used for building and furniture

RIMUS ▸ rimu

RIMY *adj* coated with rime

RIN *Scots variant of* ▸ **run**

RIND *n* tough outer coating of fruits, cheese, or bacon ▷ *vb* take the bark off

RINDED ▸ rind

RINDIER ▸ rindy

RINDING ▸ rind

RINDS ▸ rind

RINDY *adj* with a rind or rindlike skin

RINE *archaic variant of* ▸ **rind**

RINES ▸ rine

RING *vb* give out a clear resonant sound, as a bell ▷ *n* ringing

RINGBIT *n* type of bit worn by a horse

RINGED ▸ ring

RINGENT *adj* (of the corolla of plants such as the snapdragon) consisting of two distinct gaping lips

RINGER *n* person or thing

apparently identical to another

RINGERS ▸ ringer

RINGGIT *n* standard monetary unit of Malaysia, divided into 100 sen

RINGING ▸ ring

RINGLET *n* curly lock of hair

RINGMAN *n* (in dialect) ring finger

RINGMEN ▸ ringman

RINGS ▸ ring

RINGTAW *n* game of marbles in which the aim is to knock other players' marbles out of a ring

RINGWAY *n* bypass

RINK *n* sheet of ice for skating or curling ▷ *vb* skate on a rink

RINKED ▸ rink

RINKING ▸ rink

RINKS ▸ rink

RINNING ▸ rin

RINS ▸ rin

RINSE *vb* remove soap from (washed clothes, hair, etc) by applying clean water ▷ *n* rinsing

RINSED ▸ rinse

RINSER ▸ rinse

RINSERS ▸ rinse

RINSES ▸ rinse

RINSING ▸ rinse

RIOJA *n* red or white Spanish wine with a vanilla bouquet and flavour

RIOJAS ▸ rioja

RIOT *n* disorderly unruly disturbance ▷ *vb* take part in a riot

RIOTED ▸ riot

RIOTER ▸ riot

RIOTERS ▸ riot

RIOTING ▸ riot

RIOTISE *n* archaic word for riotous behaviour and excess

RIOTIZE *same as* ▸ **riotise**

RIOTOUS *adj* unrestrained

RIOTRY *n* riotous behaviour

RIOTS ▸ riot

RIP *vb* tear violently ▷ *n* split or tear

RIPCORD *n* cord pulled to open a parachute

RIPE *adj* ready to be reaped, eaten, etc ▷ *vb* ripen

RIPECK *same as* ▸ **ryepeck**

RIPECKS ▸ ripeck

RIPED ▸ ripe

RIPELY ▸ ripe

RIPEN *vb* grow ripe**

RIPENED ▸ ripen
RIPENER ▸ ripen
RIPENS ▸ ripen
RIPER adj more ripe ▷ n old Scots word meaning plunderer
RIPERS ▸ riper
RIPES ▸ ripe
RIPEST ▸ ripe
RIPIENI ▸ ripieno
RIPIENO n (in baroque concertos and concerti grossi) the full orchestra, as opposed to the instrumental soloists
RIPING ▸ ripe
RIPOFF n grossly overpriced article
RIPOFFS ▸ ripoff
RIPOST same as ▸ riposte
RIPOSTE n verbal retort ▷ vb make a riposte
RIPOSTS ▸ ripost
RIPP n old Scots word for a handful of grain
RIPPED ▸ rip
RIPPER n person who rips
RIPPERS ▸ ripper
RIPPIER n archaic word for fish seller
RIPPING ▸ rip
RIPPLE n slight wave or ruffling of a surface ▷ vb flow or form into little waves (on)
RIPPLED ▸ ripple
RIPPLER ▸ ripple
RIPPLES ▸ ripple
RIPPLET n tiny ripple
RIPPLY ▸ ripple
RIPPS ▸ ripp
RIPRAP vb deposit broken stones in or on
RIPRAPS ▸ riprap
RIPS ▸ rip
RIPSAW n handsaw for cutting along the grain of timber ▷ vb saw with a ripsaw
RIPSAWN ▸ ripsaw
RIPSAWS ▸ ripsaw
RIPSTOP n tear-resistant cloth
RIPT archaic past form of ▸ rip
RIPTIDE n stretch of turbulent water in the sea, caused by the meeting of currents or abrupt changes in depth
RISE vb get up from a lying, sitting, or kneeling position ▷ n rising
RISEN ▸ rise

RISER n person who rises, esp from bed
RISERS ▸ riser
RISES ▸ rise
RISHI n Indian seer or sage
RISHIS ▸ rishi
RISIBLE adj causing laughter, ridiculous
RISIBLY ▸ risible
RISING ▸ rise
RISINGS ▸ rise
RISK n chance of disaster or loss ▷ vb act in spite of the possibility of (injury or loss)
RISKED ▸ risk
RISKER ▸ risk
RISKERS ▸ risk
RISKFUL ▸ risk
RISKIER ▸ risky
RISKILY ▸ risky
RISKING ▸ risk
RISKS ▸ risk
RISKY adj full of risk, dangerous
RISORII > risorius
RISOTTO n dish of rice cooked in stock with vegetables, meat, etc
RISP vb Scots word meaning rasp
RISPED ▸ risp
RISPING ▸ risp
RISPS ▸ risp
RISQUE n risk
RISQUES ▸ risque
RISSOLE n cake of minced meat, coated with breadcrumbs and fried
RISTRA n string of dried chilli peppers
RISTRAS ▸ ristra
RISUS n involuntary grinning expression
RISUSES ▸ risus
RIT vb Scots word for cut or slit
RITARD n (in music) a slowing down
RITARDS ▸ ritard
RITE n formal practice or custom, esp religious
RITES ▸ rite
RITS ▸ rit
RITT same as ▸ rit
RITTED ▸ rit
RITTER n knight or horseman
RITTERS ▸ ritter
RITTING ▸ rit
RITTS ▸ ritt
RITUAL n prescribed order of rites ▷ adj concerning rites

RITUALS ▸ ritual
RITZ modifier as in put on the ritz assume a superior air or make an ostentatious display
RITZES ▸ ritz
RITZIER ▸ ritzy
RITZILY ▸ ritzy
RITZY adj luxurious or elegant
RIVA n rock cleft
RIVAGE n bank, shore, or coast
RIVAGES ▸ rivage
RIVAL n person or thing that competes with or equals another for favour, success, etc ▷ adj in the position of a rival ▷ vb (try to) equal
RIVALED ▸ rival
RIVALRY n keen competition
RIVALS ▸ rival
RIVAS ▸ riva
RIVE vb split asunder
RIVED ▸ rive
RIVEL vb archaic word meaning wrinkle
RIVELS ▸ rivel
RIVEN ▸ rive
RIVER n large natural stream of water
RIVERED adj with a river or rivers
RIVERET n archaic word for rivulet or stream
RIVERS ▸ river
RIVERY adj riverlike
RIVES ▸ rive
RIVET n bolt for fastening metal plates, the end being put through holes and then beaten flat ▷ vb fasten with rivets
RIVETED ▸ rivet
RIVETER ▸ rivet
RIVETS ▸ rivet
RIVIERA n coastline resembling the Mediterranean Riviera
RIVIERE n necklace the diamonds or other precious stones of which gradually increase in size up to a large centre stone
RIVING ▸ rive
RIVLIN n Scots word for rawhide shoe
RIVLINS ▸ rivlin
RIVO interj (in the past) an informal toast
RIVULET n small stream

R

RIYAL n standard monetary unit of Qatar, divided into 100 dirhams

RIYALS ▶ riyal

RIZ (in some dialects) past form of ▶ rise

> This unusual past tense of **rise** is one of the essential Z words.

RIZA n partial icon cover made from precious metal

RIZARD n redcurrant

RIZARDS ▶ rizard

RIZAS ▶ riza

RIZZAR n Scots word for red currant ▷ vb Scots word for sun-dry

RIZZARS ▶ rizzar

RIZZART n Scots word for red currant

RIZZER same as ▶ rizzar

RIZZERS ▶ rizzer

RIZZOR vb dry

RIZZORS ▶ rizzor

ROACH n Eurasian freshwater fish ▷ vb clip (mane) short so that it stands upright

ROACHED adj arched convexly, as the back of certain breeds of dog, such as the whippet

ROACHES ▶ roach

ROAD n way prepared for passengers, vehicles, etc

ROADBED n material used to make a road

ROADEO n competition in which drivers or other road users put their skills on the road to the test

ROADEOS ▶ roadeo

ROADIE n person who transports and sets up equipment for a band

ROADIES ▶ roadie

ROADING n road building

ROADMAN n someone involved in road repair or construction

ROADMEN ▶ roadman

ROADS ▶ road

ROADWAY n part of a road used by vehicles

ROAM vb wander about ▷ n act of roaming

ROAMED ▶ roam

ROAMER ▶ roam

ROAMERS ▶ roam

ROAMING ▶ roam

ROAMS ▶ roam

ROAN adj (of a horse) having a brown or black coat sprinkled with white hairs ▷ n roan horse

ROANS ▶ roan

ROAR vb make or utter a loud deep hoarse sound like that of a lion ▷ n such a sound

ROARED ▶ roar

ROARER ▶ roar

ROARERS ▶ roar

ROARIE Scots word for ▶ noisy

ROARIER ▶ roary

ROARING ▶ roar

ROARS ▶ roar

ROARY adj roarlike or tending to roar

ROAST vb cook by dry heat, as in an oven ▷ n roasted joint of meat ▷ adj roasted

ROASTED ▶ roast

ROASTER n person or thing that roasts

ROASTS ▶ roast

ROATE archaic form of ▶ rote

ROATED ▶ roate

ROATES ▶ roate

ROATING ▶ roate

ROB vb steal from

ROBALO n tropical fish

ROBALOS ▶ robalo

ROBAND n piece of marline used for fastening a sail to a spar

ROBANDS ▶ roband

ROBBED ▶ rob

ROBBER ▶ rob

ROBBERS ▶ rob

ROBBERY n stealing of property from a person by using or threatening to use force

ROBBIN same as ▶ roband

ROBBING ▶ rob

ROBBINS ▶ robbin

ROBE n long loose outer garment ▷ vb put a robe on

ROBED ▶ robe

ROBES ▶ robe

ROBIN n small brown bird with a red breast

ROBING ▶ robe

ROBINGS ▶ robe

ROBINIA n type of leguminous tree

ROBINS ▶ robin

ROBLE n oak tree

ROBLES ▶ roble

ROBOT n automated machine, esp one performing functions in a human manner

ROBOTIC ▶ robot

ROBOTRY ▶ robot

ROBOTS ▶ robot

ROBS ▶ rob

ROBUST adj very strong and healthy

ROBUSTA n species of coffee tree

ROC n monstrous bird of Arabian mythology

ROCH same as ▶ rotch

ROCHES ▶ rotch

ROCHET n white surplice with tight sleeves, worn by bishops, abbots, and certain other Church dignitaries

ROCHETS ▶ rochet

ROCK n hard mineral substance that makes up part of the earth's crust, stone ▷ vb (cause to) sway to and fro ▷ adj of or relating to rock music

ROCKABY same as ▶ rockabye

ROCKED ▶ rock

ROCKER n rocking chair

ROCKERS ▶ rocker

ROCKERY n mound of stones in a garden for rock plants

ROCKET n self-propelling device powered by the burning of explosive contents (used as a firework, weapon, etc) ▷ vb move fast, esp upwards, like a rocket

ROCKETS ▶ rocket

ROCKIER n archaic or dialect word for rock pigeon

ROCKILY ▶ rocky

ROCKING ▶ rock

ROCKLAY same as ▶ rokelay

ROCKOON n rocket carrying scientific equipment for studying the upper atmosphere, fired from a balloon at high altitude

ROCKS ▶ rock

ROCKY adj having many rocks

ROCOCO adj (of furniture, architecture, etc) having much elaborate decoration in an early 18th-century style ▷ n style of architecture and decoration that originated in France in the early 18th century, characterized by elaborate but graceful, light, ornamentation, often containing asymmetrical motifs

ROCOCOS ▶ rococo

ROCQUET n another name for the salad plant rocket

ROCS ▶ roc

ROD n slender straight bar, stick ▷ vb clear with a rod

RODDED ▶ rod

RODDING ▶ rod

RODE vb (of the male woodcock) to perform a display flight at dusk during the breeding season

RODED ▶ rode

RODENT n animal with teeth specialized for gnawing, such as a rat, mouse, or squirrel

RODENTS ▶ rodent

RODEO n display of skill by cowboys, such as bareback riding ▷ vb take part in a rodeo

RODEOED ▶ rodeo

RODEOS ▶ rodeo

RODES ▶ rode

RODEWAY archaic spelling of ▶ roadway

RODING ▶ rode

RODINGS ▶ rode

RODLESS ▶ rod

RODLIKE ▶ rod

RODMAN n someone who uses or fishes with a rod

RODMEN ▶ rodman

RODS ▶ rod

RODSMAN same as ▶ rodman

RODSMEN ▶ rodsman

RODSTER n angler

ROE n mass of eggs in a fish, sometimes eaten as food

ROEBUCK n male of the roe deer

ROED adj with roe inside

ROEMER n drinking glass, typically having an ovoid bowl on a short stem

ROEMERS ▶ roemer

ROES ▶ roe

ROESTI ▶ rosti

ROESTIS ▶ roesti

ROGALLO n flexible fabric delta wing, originally designed as a possible satellite retrieval vehicle but actually developed in the 1960s as the first successful hang-glider

ROGNON n isolated rock

outcrop on a glacier

ROGNONS ▶ rognon

ROGUE n dishonest or unprincipled person ▷ adj (of a wild beast) having a savage temper and living apart from the herd ▷ vb rid (a field or crop) of plants that are inferior, diseased, or of an unwanted variety

ROGUED ▶ rogue

ROGUER n rogue

ROGUERS ▶ roguer

ROGUERY n dishonest or immoral behaviour

ROGUES ▶ rogue

ROGUING ▶ rogue

ROGUISH adj dishonest or unprincipled

ROGUY same as ▶ roguish

ROIL vb make (a liquid) cloudy or turbid by stirring up dregs or sediment

ROILED ▶ roil

ROILIER ▶ roily

ROILING ▶ roil

ROILS ▶ roil

ROILY adj cloudy or muddy

ROIN same as ▶ royne

ROINED ▶ roin

ROINING ▶ roin

ROINISH same as ▶ roynish

ROINS ▶ roin

ROIST archaic variant of ▶ roister

ROISTED ▶ roist

ROISTER vb make merry noisily or boisterously

ROISTS ▶ roist

ROJAK n (in Malaysia) a salad dish served in chilli sauce

ROJAKS ▶ rojak

ROJI n Japanese tea garden or its path of stones

ROJIS ▶ roji

ROK same as ▶ roc

> **Rok** is an alternative spelling of **roc**, the mythical bird. Other spellings are **ruc** and **rukh**.

ROKE vb (in dialect) steam or smoke

ROKED ▶ roke

ROKELAY n type of cloak

ROKER n variety of ray

ROKERS ▶ roker

ROKES ▶ roke

ROKIER ▶ roky

ROKIEST ▶ roky

ROKING ▶ roke

ROKKAKU n hexagonal

Japanese kite

ROKS ▶ rok

ROKY adj (in dialect) steamy or smoky

ROLAG n roll of carded wool ready for spinning

ROLAGS ▶ rolag

ROLE n task or function

ROLES ▶ role

ROLF vb massage following a particular technique

ROLFED ▶ rolf

ROLFER ▶ rolf

ROLFERS ▶ rolf

ROLFING ▶ rolf

ROLFS ▶ rolf

ROLL vb move by turning over and over ▷ n act of rolling over or from side to side

ROLLBAR n bar that reinforces the frame of a car, esp one used for racing, rallying, etc, to protect the driver if the car should turn over

ROLLED ▶ roll

ROLLER n rotating cylinder used for smoothing or supporting a thing to be moved, spreading paint, etc

ROLLERS ▶ roller

ROLLICK vb behave in a carefree, frolicsome, or boisterous manner ▷ n boisterous or carefree escapade or event

ROLLING ▶ roll

ROLLMOP n herring fillet rolled round onion slices and pickled

ROLLOCK same as ▶ rowlock

ROLLOUT n presentation to the public of a new aircraft, product, etc; launch

ROLLS ▶ roll

ROLLTOP n as in **rolltop desk** desk having a slatted wooden panel that can be pulled down over the writing surface when not in use

ROLLWAY n incline down which logs are rolled

ROM n male gypsy

ROMA n gypsy

ROMAGE archaic variant of ▶ rummage

ROMAGES ▶ romage

ROMAIKA n Greek dance

ROMAINE n usual US and

R

Canadian name for 'cos' (lettuce)

ROMAJI n Roman alphabet as used to write Japanese

ROMAJIS ▶ romaji

ROMAL same as ▶ rumal

ROMALS ▶ romal

ROMAN adj in or relating to the vertical style of printing type used for most printed matter ▷ n roman type

ROMANCE n love affair ▷ vb exaggerate or fantasize

ROMANO n hard light-coloured sharp-tasting cheese

ROMANOS ▶ romano

ROMANS ▶ roman

ROMANZA n short instrumental piece of song-like character

ROMAUNT n verse romance

ROMCOM n film or television comedy based around the romantic relationships of the characters

ROMCOMS ▶ romcom

ROMEO n ardent male lover

ROMEOS ▶ romeo

ROMNEYA n bushy type of poppy

ROMP vb play wildly and joyfully ▷ n boisterous activity

ROMPED ▶ romp

ROMPER n playful or boisterous child

ROMPERS pl n child's overalls

ROMPING ▶ romp

ROMPISH ▶ romp

ROMPS ▶ romp

ROMS ▶ rom

RONDE n round dance

RONDEAU n poem consisting of 13 or 10 lines with the opening words of the first line used as a refrain

RONDEL n rondeau consisting of three stanzas of 13 or 14 lines with a two-line refrain appearing twice or three times

RONDELS ▶ rondel

RONDES ▶ ronde

RONDINO n short rondo

RONDO n piece of music with a leading theme continually returned to

RONDOS ▶ rondo

RONDURE n circle or curve

RONE n drainpipe or gutter for carrying rainwater from a roof

RONEO vb duplicate (a document) from a stencil ▷ n document reproduced by this process

RONEOED ▶ roneo

RONEOS ▶ roneo

RONES ▶ rone

RONG archaic past participle of ▶ ring

RONIN n lordless samurai, esp one whose feudal lord had been deprived of his territory

RONINS ▶ ronin

RONIONS ▶ ronion

RONNE archaic form of ▶ run

RONNEL n type of pesticide

RONNELS ▶ ronnel

RONNIE n Dublin slang word for moustache

RONNIES ▶ ronnie

RONNING ▶ ronne

RONT archaic variant of ▶ runt

RONTE archaic variant of ▶ runt

RONTES ▶ ronte

RONTGEN variant spelling of > roentgen

RONTS ▶ ront

RONZ n rest of New Zealand

RONZER n New Zealand word for a New Zealander not from Auckland

RONZERS ▶ ronzer

ROO n kangaroo

ROOD n Cross

ROODS ▶ rood

ROOF n outside upper covering of a building, car, etc ▷ vb put a roof on

ROOFED ▶ roof

ROOFER ▶ roof

ROOFERS ▶ roof

ROOFIE n tablet of sedative drug

ROOFIER ▶ roofy

ROOFIES ▶ roofie

ROOFING n material used to build a roof

ROOFS ▶ roof

ROOFTOP n outside part of the roof of a building

ROOFY adj with roofs

ROOIBOS n tea prepared from the dried leaves of an African plant

ROOIKAT n South African lynx

ROOK n Eurasian bird of the

crow family ▷ vb swindle

ROOKED ▶ rook

ROOKERY n colony of rooks, penguins, or seals

ROOKIE n new recruit

ROOKIER ▶ rooky

ROOKIES ▶ rookie

ROOKING ▶ rook

ROOKISH ▶ rook

ROOKS ▶ rook

ROOKY adj abounding in rooks

ROOM n enclosed area in a building ▷ vb occupy or share a room

ROOMED ▶ room

ROOMER ▶ room

ROOMERS ▶ room

ROOMFUL n number or quantity sufficient to fill a room

ROOMIE n roommate

ROOMIER ▶ roomy

ROOMIES ▶ roomie

ROOMILY ▶ roomy

ROOMING ▶ room

ROOMS ▶ room

ROOMY adj spacious

ROON n Scots word for shred or strip

ROONS ▶ roon

ROOP same as ▶ roup

ROOPED ▶ roop

ROOPIER ▶ roopy

ROOPING ▶ roop

ROOPIT same as ▶ roopy

ROOPS ▶ roop

ROOPY adj (in dialect) hoarse

ROOS ▶ roo

ROOSA n type of grass

ROOSAS ▶ roosa

ROOSE vb flatter

ROOSED ▶ roose

ROOSER ▶ roose

ROOSERS ▶ roose

ROOSES ▶ roose

ROOSING ▶ roose

ROOST n perch for fowls ▷ vb perch

ROOSTED ▶ roost

ROOSTER n domestic cock

ROOSTS ▶ roost

ROOT n part of a plant that grows down into the earth obtaining nourishment ▷ vb establish a root and start to grow

ROOTAGE n root system

ROOTCAP n layer of cells at root tip

ROOTED ▶ root

ROOTER ▶ root

ROOTERS ▶ root

ROOTIER ▶ root

ROOTIES ▶ rooty

ROOTING ▶ root

ROOTKIT n set of programs used to gain unauthorized access to a computer system

ROOTLE same as ▶ **root**

ROOTLED ▶ rootle

ROOTLES ▶ rootle

ROOTLET n small root or branch of a root

ROOTS adj (of popular music) going back to the origins of a style, esp in being unpretentious

ROOTSY ▶ roots

ROOTY adj rootlike ▷ n (in military slang) bread

ROPABLE adj capable of being roped

ROPE n thick cord

ROPED ▶ rope

ROPER n someone who makes ropes

ROPERS ▶ roper

ROPERY n place where ropes are made

ROPES ▶ rope

ROPEWAY n type of aerial lift

ROPEY adj inferior or inadequate

ROPIER ▶ ropy

ROPIEST ▶ ropy

ROPILY ▶ ropey

ROPING ▶ rope

ROPINGS ▶ rope

ROPY same as ▶ **ropey**

ROQUE n game developed from croquet, played on a hard surface with a resilient surrounding border from which the ball can rebound

ROQUES ▶ roque

ROQUET vb drive one's ball against (another person's ball) in order to be allowed to croquet ▷ n act of roqueting

ROQUETS ▶ roquet

RORAL archaic word for ▶ **dewy**

RORE archaic spelling of ▶ **roar**

RORES ▶ rore

RORIC same as ▶ **roral**

RORID same as ▶ **roral**

RORIE same as ▶ **roary**

RORIER ▶ rory

RORIEST ▶ rory

RORQUAL n toothless

whale with a dorsal fin

RORT n dishonest scheme ▷ vb take unfair advantage of something

RORTED ▶ rort

RORTER n small-scale confidence trickster

RORTERS ▶ rorter

RORTIER ▶ rort

RORTING ▶ rort

RORTS ▶ rort

RORTY ▶ rort

RORY adj dewy

ROSACE another name for ▶ **rosette**

ROSACEA n chronic inflammatory disease causing the skin of the face to become abnormally flushed and sometimes pustular

ROSACES ▶ rosace

ROSAKER archaic word for ▶ **realgar**

ROSALIA n melody which is repeated but at a higher pitch each time

ROSARIA > **rosarium**

ROSARY n series of prayers

ROSBIF n term used in France for an English person

ROSBIFS ▶ rosbif

ROSCID adj dewy

ROSCOE slang word for ▶ **gun**

ROSCOES ▶ roscoe

ROSE ▶ rise

ROSEAL adj rosy or roselike

ROSEATE adj rose-coloured

ROSEBAY n as in **rosebay willowherb** perennial plant with spikes of deep pink flowers

ROSEBUD n rose which has not yet fully opened

ROSED ▶ rise

ROSEHIP n berry-like fruit of a rose plant

ROSELLA n type of Australian parrot

ROSELLE n Indian flowering plant

ROSEOLA n feverish condition of young children that lasts for some five days during the last two of which the patient has a rose-coloured rash. It is caused by the human herpes virus

ROSERY n bed or garden of roses

ROSES ▶ rise

ROSET n Scots word meaning rosin ▷ vb rub rosin on

ROSETED ▶ roset

ROSETS ▶ roset

ROSETTE n rose-shaped ornament, esp a circular bunch of ribbons

ROSETTY ▶ roset

ROSETY ▶ roset

ROSHI n teacher of Zen Buddhism

ROSHIS ▶ roshi

ROSIED ▶ rosy

ROSIER archaic word for > **rosebush**

ROSIERE archaic word for > **rosebush**

ROSIERS ▶ rosier

ROSIES ▶ rosy

ROSIEST ▶ rosy

ROSILY ▶ rosy

ROSIN n resin used for treating the bows of violins etc ▷ vb apply rosin to

ROSINED ▶ rosin

ROSINER n strong alcoholic drink

ROSING ▶ rise

ROSINOL n yellowish fluorescent oily liquid obtained from certain resins, used in the manufacture of carbon black, varnishes, and lacquers

ROSINS ▶ rosin

ROSINY ▶ rosin

ROSIT same as ▶ **roset**

ROSITED ▶ rosit

ROSITS ▶ rosit

ROSOLIO n type of cordial

ROSSER n bark-removing machine

ROSSERS ▶ rosser

ROST archaic spelling of ▶ **roast**

ROSTED ▶ rost

ROSTER n list of people and their turns of duty ▷ vb place on a roster

ROSTERS ▶ roster

ROSTI n cheese-topped fried Swiss dish consisting of grated potato and, optionally, onion

ROSTING ▶ rost

ROSTIS ▶ rosti

ROSTRA ▶ rostrum

ROSTRAL adj of or like a beak or snout

ROSTRUM n platform or stage

R

ROSTS ▸ rost

ROSULA *n* rosette

ROSULAS ▸ rosula

ROSY *adj* pink-coloured ▷ *vb* redden or make pink

ROSYING ▸ rosy

ROT *vb* decompose or decay ▷ *n* decay

ROTA *n* list of people who take it in turn to do a particular task

ROTAL *adj* of or relating to wheels or rotation

ROTAN *another name for* ▸ rattan

ROTANS ▸ rotan

ROTARY *adj* revolving ▷ *n* traffic roundabout

ROTAS ▸ rota

ROTATE *vb* (cause to) move round a centre or on a pivot ▷ *adj* designating a corolla the united petals of which radiate from a central point like the spokes of a wheel

ROTATED ▸ rotate

ROTATES ▸ rotate

ROTATOR *n* person, device, or part that rotates or causes rotation

ROTCH *n* little auk

ROTCHE *same as* ▸ rotch

ROTCHES ▸ rotch

ROTCHIE *same as* ▸ rotch

ROTE *n* mechanical repetition ▷ *vb* learn by rote

ROTED ▸ rote

ROTES ▸ rote

ROTGUT *n* alcoholic drink of inferior quality

ROTGUTS ▸ rotgut

ROTHER *dialect word for* ▸ ox

ROTHERS ▸ rother

ROTI *n* (in India and the Caribbean) a type of unleavened bread

ROTIFER *n* minute aquatic multicellular invertebrate

ROTING ▸ rote

ROTIS ▸ roti

ROTL *n* unit of weight used in Muslim countries, varying in value between about one and five pounds

ROTLS ▸ rotl

ROTO *n* printing process using a cylinder etched with many small recesses, from which ink is transferred to a moving web of paper, plastic, etc, in a rotary press

ROTOLO *n* (in Italian cuisine) a roll

ROTOLOS ▸ rotolo

ROTON *n* quantum of vortex motion

ROTONS ▸ roton

ROTOR *n* revolving portion of a dynamo, motor, or turbine

ROTORS ▸ rotor

ROTOS ▸ roto

ROTS ▸ rot

ROTTAN *n* (in dialect) a rat

ROTTANS ▸ rottan

ROTTE *n* ancient stringed instrument

ROTTED ▸ rot

ROTTEN *adj* decaying ▷ *adv* extremely ▷ *n* (in dialect) a rat

ROTTENS ▸ rotten

ROTTER *n* despicable person

ROTTERS ▸ rotter

ROTTES ▸ rotte

ROTTING ▸ rot

ROTULA *n* kneecap

ROTULAE ▸ rotula

ROTULAS ▸ rotula

ROTUND *adj* round and plump ▷ *vb* make round

ROTUNDA *n* circular building or room, esp with a dome

ROTUNDS ▸ rotund

ROUBLE *n* monetary unit of Russia, Belarus, and Tajikistan

ROUBLES ▸ rouble

ROUCHE *same as* ▸ ruche

ROUCHES ▸ rouche

ROUCOU *another name for* ▸ annatto

ROUCOUS ▸ roucou

ROUE *n* man given to immoral living

ROUEN *n* breed of duck

ROUENS ▸ rouen

ROUES ▸ roue

ROUGE *n* red cosmetic used to colour the cheeks ▷ *vb* apply rouge to

ROUGED ▸ rouge

ROUGES ▸ rouge

ROUGH *adj* uneven or irregular ▷ *vb* make rough ▷ *n* rough state or area

ROUGHED ▸ rough

ROUGHEN *vb* make or become rough

ROUGHER *n* person that does the rough preparatory work on something ▷ *adj* more rough

ROUGHIE *n* small food fish found in southern and western Australian waters

ROUGHLY *adv* without being exact or fully authenticated

ROUGHS ▸ rough

ROUGHT *archaic past form of* ▸ reach

ROUGHY *spelling variant of* ▸ roughie

ROUGING ▸ rouge

ROUILLE *n* kind of sauce

ROULADE *n* slice of meat rolled, esp around a stuffing, and cooked

ROULE *archaic form of* ▸ roll

ROULEAU *n* roll of paper containing coins

ROULES ▸ roule

ROULS ▸ roul

ROUM *archaic spelling of* ▸ room

ROUMING *n* pasture given for an animal

ROUMS ▸ roum

ROUNCE *n* handle that is turned to move paper and plates on a printing press

ROUNCES ▸ rounce

ROUNCY *archaic word for* ▸ horse

ROUND *adj* spherical, cylindrical, circular, or curved ▷ *prep* indicating an encircling movement, presence on all sides, etc ▷ *vb* move round ▷ *n* round shape

ROUNDED *adj* round or curved

ROUNDEL *same as* ▸ roundelay

ROUNDER *n* run round all four bases after one hit in rounders

ROUNDLE *same as* ▸ roundel

ROUNDLY *adv* thoroughly

ROUNDS ▸ round

ROUNDUP *n* act of gathering together livestock, people, facts, etc

ROUP *n* any of various chronic respiratory diseases of birds, esp poultry ▷ *vb* sell by auction

ROUPED ▸ roup

ROUPET *adj* Scots word meaning hoarse or croaky

ROUPIER ▶ roup
ROUPILY ▶ roup
ROUPING ▶ roup
ROUPIT same as ▶ roupet
ROUPS ▶ roup
ROUPY ▶ roup
ROUSANT adj (in heraldry) rising
ROUSE same as > reveille
ROUSED ▶ rouse
ROUSER n person or thing that rouses people, such as a stirring speech or compelling rock song
ROUSERS ▶ rouser
ROUSES ▶ rouse
ROUSING adj lively, vigorous
ROUST vb rout or stir, as out of bed
ROUSTED ▶ roust
ROUSTER n unskilled labourer on an oil rig
ROUSTS ▶ roust
ROUT n overwhelming defeat ▷ vb defeat and put to flight
ROUTE n roads taken to reach a destination ▷ vb send by a particular route
ROUTED ▶ route
ROUTER n device that allows data to be moved efficiently between two points on a network
ROUTERS ▶ router
ROUTES ▶ route
ROUTH n abundance ▷ adj abundant
ROUTHIE adj abundant, plentiful, or well filled
ROUTHS ▶ routh
ROUTINE n usual or regular method of procedure ▷ adj ordinary or regular
ROUTING ▶ rout
ROUTOUS ▶ rout
ROUTS ▶ rout
ROUX n fat and flour cooked together as a basis for sauces
ROVE ▶ reeve
ROVED ▶ reeve
ROVEN ▶ reeve
ROVER n wanderer, traveller
ROVERS ▶ rover
ROVES ▶ reeve
ROVING ▶ rove
ROVINGS ▶ rove
ROW n straight line of people or things ▷ vb propel (a boat) by oars

ROWABLE ▶ row
ROWAN n tree producing bright red berries, mountain ash
ROWANS ▶ rowan
ROWBOAT n small boat propelled by one or more pairs of oars
ROWDIER ▶ rowdy
ROWDIES ▶ rowdy
ROWDILY ▶ rowdy
ROWDY adj disorderly, noisy, and rough ▷ n person like this
ROWED ▶ row
ROWEL n small spiked wheel on a spur ▷ vb goad (a horse) using a rowel
ROWELED ▶ rowel
ROWELS ▶ rowel
ROWEN another word for > aftermath
ROWENS ▶ rowen
ROWER ▶ row
ROWERS ▶ row
ROWING ▶ row
ROWINGS ▶ row
ROWLOCK n device on a boat that holds an oar in place
ROWME archaic variant of ▶ room
ROWMES ▶ rowme
ROWND archaic variant of ▶ round
ROWNDED ▶ rownd
ROWNDS ▶ rownd
ROWOVER n act of winning a rowing race unopposed, by rowing the course
ROWS ▶ row
ROWT archaic variant of ▶ rout
ROWTED ▶ rowt
ROWTH same as ▶ routh
ROWTHS ▶ rowth
ROWTING ▶ rowt
ROWTS ▶ rowt
ROYAL adj of, befitting, or supported by a king or queen ▷ n member of a royal family
ROYALET n minor king
ROYALLY ▶ royal
ROYALS ▶ royal
ROYALTY n royal people
ROYNE archaic word for ▶ gnaw
ROYNED ▶ royne
ROYNES ▶ royne
ROYNING ▶ royne
ROYNISH archaic word for ▶ mangy

ROYST same as ▶ roist
ROYSTED ▶ royst
ROYSTER same as ▶ roister
ROYSTS ▶ royst
ROZELLE same as ▶ roselle
ROZET same as ▶ roset
ROZETED ▶ rozet
ROZETS ▶ rozet
ROZIT same as ▶ roset
ROZITED ▶ rozit
ROZITS ▶ rozit
ROZZER n policeman
ROZZERS ▶ rozzer
RUANA n woollen wrap resembling a poncho
RUANAS ▶ ruana
RUB vb apply pressure and friction to (something) with a circular or backwards-and-forwards movement ▷ n act of rubbing
RUBABOO n soup or stew made by boiling pemmican with, if available, flour and vegetables
RUBACE same as ▶ rubasse
RUBACES ▶ rubace
RUBAI n verse form of Persian origin consisting of four-line stanzas
RUBASSE n type of quartz containing red haematite
RUBATI ▶ rubato
RUBATO n (with) expressive flexibility of tempo ▷ adv be played with a flexible tempo
RUBATOS ▶ rubato
RUBBED ▶ rub
RUBBER n strong waterproof elastic material, orig. made from the dried sap of a tropical tree, now usu synthetic ▷ adj made of or producing rubber ▷ vb provide with rubber coating
RUBBERS ▶ rubber
RUBBERY adj having the texture of or resembling rubber, esp in flexibility or toughness
RUBBET old Scots past form of ▶ rob
RUBBIDY same as ▶ rubbity
RUBBIES ▶ rubby
RUBBING ▶ rub
RUBBISH n waste matter ▷ vb criticize
RUBBIT old Scots past form of ▶ rob
RUBBITY n pub

R

RUBBLE n fragments of broken stone, brick, etc ▷ vb turn into rubble

RUBBLED ▶ rubble

RUBBLES ▶ rubble

RUBBLY ▶ rubble

RUBBY n rubbing alcohol, esp when mixed with cheap wine for drinking

RUBDOWN n act of drying or cleaning vigorously

RUBEFY vb make red, esp (of a counterirritant) to make the skin go red

RUBEL n currency unit of Belarus

RUBELLA n mild contagious viral disease characterized by cough, sore throat, and skin rash

RUBELS ▶ rubel

RUBEOLA technical name for ▶ measles

RUBICON n point of no return ▷ vb (in bezique) to beat before the loser has managed to gain as many as 1000 points

RUBIDIC > rubidium

RUBIED ▶ ruby

RUBIER ▶ ruby

RUBIES ▶ ruby

RUBIEST ▶ ruby

RUBIFY same as ▶ rubefy

RUBIGO old Scots word for ▶ penis

RUBIGOS ▶ rubigo

RUBIN archaic word for ▶ ruby

RUBINE archaic word for ▶ ruby

RUBINES ▶ rubine

RUBINS ▶ rubin

RUBIOUS adj of the colour ruby

RUBLE same as ▶ rouble

RUBLES ▶ ruble

RUBOFF n resulting effect on something else; consequences

RUBOFFS ▶ ruboff

RUBOUT n killing or elimination

RUBOUTS ▶ rubout

RUBRIC n set of rules for behaviour ▷ adj written, printed, or marked in red

RUBRICS ▶ rubric

RUBS ▶ rub

RUBUS n fruit-bearing genus of shrubs

RUBY n red precious gemstone ▷ adj deep red

▷ vb redden

RUBYING ▶ ruby

RUC same as ▶ roc

RUCHE n pleat or frill of lace etc as a decoration ▷ vb put a ruche on

RUCHED ▶ ruche

RUCHES ▶ ruche

RUCHING n material used for a ruche

RUCK n rough crowd of common people ▷ vb wrinkle or crease

RUCKED ▶ ruck

RUCKING ▶ ruck

RUCKLE another word for ▶ ruck

RUCKLED ▶ ruckle

RUCKLES ▶ ruckle

RUCKMAN n person who plays in the ruck

RUCKMEN ▶ ruckman

RUCKS ▶ ruck

RUCKUS n uproar

RUCOLA n another name for the salad plant rocket

RUCOLAS ▶ rucola

RUCS ▶ ruc

RUCTION n uproar

RUD n red or redness ▷ vb redden

RUDAS n Scots word for a coarse, rude old woman

RUDASES ▶ rudas

RUDD n European freshwater fish

RUDDED ▶ rud

RUDDER n vertical hinged piece at the stern of a boat or at the rear of an aircraft, for steering

RUDDERS ▶ rudder

RUDDIED ▶ ruddy

RUDDIER ▶ ruddy

RUDDIES ▶ ruddy

RUDDILY ▶ ruddy

RUDDING ▶ rud

RUDDLE n red ochre, used esp to mark sheep ▷ vb mark (sheep) with ruddle

RUDDLED ▶ ruddle

RUDDLES ▶ ruddle

RUDDOCK dialect name for the ▶ robin

RUDDS ▶ rudd

RUDDY adj of a fresh healthy red colour ▷ adv bloody ▷ vb redden

RUDE archaic spelling of ▶ rood

RUDELY ▶ rude

RUDER ▶ rude

RUDERAL n plant that

grows on waste ground ▷ adj growing in waste places

RUDERY ▶ rude

RUDES ▶ rude

RUDESBY n archaic word for rude person

RUDEST ▶ rude

RUDIE n member of a youth movement originating in the 1960s

RUDIES ▶ rudie

RUDISH adj somewhat rude

RUDS ▶ rud

RUE vb feel regret for ▷ n plant with evergreen bitter leaves

RUED ▶ rue

RUEDA n type of Cuban round dance

RUEDAS ▶ rueda

RUEFUL adj regretful or sorry

RUEING ▶ rue

RUEINGS ▶ rue

RUELLE n area between bed and wall, at one time used by French ladies of standing for receiving visitors

RUELLES ▶ ruelle

RUELLIA n genus of plants

RUER ▶ rue

RUERS ▶ rue

RUES ▶ rue

RUFF n circular pleated, gathered, or fluted collar of lawn, muslin, etc, often starched or wired, worn by both men and women in the 16th and 17th centuries ▷ vb trump

RUFFE n European freshwater fish

RUFFED ▶ ruff

RUFFES ▶ ruffe

RUFFIAN n violent lawless person ▷ vb act like a ruffian

RUFFIN archaic name for ▶ ruffe

RUFFING ▶ ruff

RUFFINS ▶ ruffin

RUFFLE vb disturb the calm of ▷ n frill or pleat

RUFFLED ▶ ruffle

RUFFLER n person or thing that ruffles

RUFFLES ▶ ruffle

RUFFLY adj ruffled

RUFFS ▶ ruff

RUFIYAA n standard monetary unit of the Maldives, divided into 100 laari

RUFOUS adj reddish-brown
RUG n small carpet ▷ vb (in dialect) tug
RUGA n fold, wrinkle, or crease
RUGAE ▶ **ruga**
RUGAL adj (in anatomy) with ridges or folds
RUGATE same as ▶ **rugose**
RUGBIES ▶ **rugby**
RUGBY n form of football played with an oval ball which may be handled by the players
RUGGED adj rocky or steep
RUGGER same as ▶ **rugby**
RUGGERS ▶ **rugger**
RUGGIER ▶ **ruggy**
RUGGING ▶ **rug**
RUGGY adj (in dialect) rough or rugged
RUGLIKE ▶ **rug**
RUGOLA n another name for the salad plant rocket
RUGOLAS ▶ **rugola**
RUGOSA n any of various shrubs descended from a particular type of wild rose
RUGOSAS ▶ **rugosa**
RUGOSE adj wrinkled
RUGOUS same as ▶ **rugose**
RUGS ▶ **rug**
RUIN vb destroy or spoil completely ▷ n destruction or decay
RUINATE vb archaic word for bring or come to ruin
RUINED ▶ **ruin**
RUINER ▶ **ruin**
RUINERS ▶ **ruin**
RUING ▶ **rue**
RUINGS ▶ **rue**
RUINING ▶ **ruin**
RUINOUS adj causing ruin
RUINS ▶ **ruin**
RUKH same as ▶ **roc**
RUKHS ▶ **rukh**
RULABLE ▶ **rule**
RULE n statement of what is allowed, for example in a game or procedure ▷ vb govern
RULED ▶ **rule**
RULER n person who governs ▷ vb punish by hitting with a ruler
RULERED ▶ **ruler**
RULERS ▶ **ruler**
RULES ▶ **rule**
RULESSE adj archaic word meaning ruleless or without rules
RULIER ▶ **ruly**

RULIEST ▶ **ruly**
RULING n formal decision ▷ adj controlling or exercising authority
RULINGS ▶ **ruling**
RULLION n Scots word for rawhide shoe
RULLOCK same as ▶ **rowlock**
RULY adj orderly
RUM n alcoholic drink distilled from sugar cane ▷ adj odd, strange
RUMAKI n savoury of chicken liver and sliced water chestnut wrapped in bacon
RUMAKIS ▶ **rumaki**
RUMAL n handkerchief or type of cloth
RUMALS ▶ **rumal**
RUMBA n lively ballroom dance of Cuban origin ▷ vb dance the rumba
RUMBAED ▶ **rumba**
RUMBAS ▶ **rumba**
RUMBLE vb make a low continuous noise ▷ n deep resonant sound
RUMBLED ▶ **rumble**
RUMBLER ▶ **rumble**
RUMBLES ▶ **rumble**
RUMBLY adj rumbling or liable to rumble
RUMBO n rum-based cocktail
RUMBOS ▶ **rumbo**
RUME archaic form of ▶ **rheum**
RUMEN n first compartment of the stomach of ruminants, behind the reticulum, in which food is partly digested before being regurgitated as cud
RUMENS ▶ **rumen**
RUMES ▶ **rume**
RUMINA ▶ **rumen**
RUMINAL ▶ **rumen**
RUMKIN n archaic term for a drinking vessel
RUMKINS ▶ **rumkin**
RUMLY ▶ **rum**
RUMMAGE vb search untidily and at length ▷ n untidy search through a collection of things
RUMMER ▶ **rum**
RUMMERS ▶ **rum**
RUMMEST ▶ **rum**
RUMMIER ▶ **rummy**
RUMMIES ▶ **rummy**

RUMMILY ▶ **rummy**
RUMMISH adj rather strange, peculiar or odd
RUMMY n card game in which players try to collect sets or sequences ▷ adj of or like rum in taste or smell
RUMNESS ▶ **rum**
RUMOR same as ▶ **rumour**
RUMORED ▶ **rumor**
RUMORS ▶ **rumor**
RUMOUR n unproved statement ▷ vb pass around or circulate in the form of a rumour
RUMOURS ▶ **rumour**
RUMP n buttocks ▷ vb turn back on
RUMPED ▶ **rump**
RUMPIES ▶ **rumpy**
RUMPING ▶ **rump**
RUMPLE vb make untidy, crumpled, or dishevelled ▷ n wrinkle, fold, or crease
RUMPLED ▶ **rumple**
RUMPLES ▶ **rumple**
RUMPLY ▶ **rumple**
RUMPS ▶ **rump**
RUMPUS n noisy commotion
RUMPY n tailless Manx cat ▷ adj with a large noticeable rump
RUMS ▶ **rum**
RUN vb move with a more rapid gait than walking ▷ n act or spell of running
RUNANGA n Māori assembly or council
RUNAWAY n person or animal that runs away
RUNBACK n (in tennis) the areas behind the baselines of the court
RUNCH n another name for white charlock
RUNCHES ▶ **runch**
RUND same as ▶ **roon**
RUNDALE n (formerly) the name given, esp in Ireland and earlier in Scotland, to the system of land tenure in which each land-holder had several strips of land that were not contiguous
RUNDLE n rung of a ladder
RUNDLED adj rounded
RUNDLES ▶ **rundle**
RUNDLET n liquid measure, generally about 15 gallons
RUNDOWN adj tired; exhausted ▷ n brief review, résumé, or summary

R

RUNDS ▶ rund
RUNE n any character of the earliest Germanic alphabet
RUNED n with runes on
RUNES ▶ rune
RUNFLAT adj having a safety feature that prevents tyres becoming dangerous or liable to damage when flat
RUNG ▶ ring
RUNGS ▶ ring
RUNIC ▶ rune
RUNKLE vb (in dialect) crease or wrinkle
RUNKLED ▶ runkle
RUNKLES ▶ runkle
RUNLESS ▶ run
RUNLET n cask for wine, beer, etc
RUNLETS ▶ runlet
RUNNEL n small brook
RUNNELS ▶ runnel
RUNNER n competitor in a race
RUNNERS ▶ runner
RUNNET dialect word for ▶ rennet
RUNNETS ▶ runnet
RUNNIER ▶ runny
RUNNING ▶ run
RUNNY adj tending to flow
RUNOFF n extra race to decide the winner after a tie
RUNOFFS ▶ runoff
RUNOUT n dismissal of a batsman by running him out
RUNOUTS ▶ runout
RUNOVER n incident in which someone is run over by a vehicle
RUNRIG same as ▶ rundale
RUNRIGS ▶ runrig
RUNS ▶ run
RUNT n smallest animal in a litter
RUNTED adj stunted
RUNTIER ▶ runt
RUNTISH ▶ runt
RUNTS ▶ runt
RUNTY ▶ runt
RUNWAY n hard level roadway where aircraft take off and land
RUNWAYS ▶ runway
RUPEE n monetary unit of India and Pakistan
RUPEES ▶ rupee
RUPIA n type of skin eruption
RUPIAH n standard monetary unit of Indonesia,

divided into 100 sen
RUPIAHS ▶ rupiah
RUPIAS ▶ rupia
RUPTURE n breaking, breach ▷ vb break, burst, or sever
RURAL adj in or of the countryside ▷ n country dweller
RURALLY ▶ rural
RURALS ▶ rural
RURBAN adj part country, part urban
RURP n very small piton
RURPS ▶ rurp
RURU another name for ▶ mopoke
RURUS ▶ ruru
RUSA n type of deer with a mane
RUSALKA n water nymph or spirit
RUSAS ▶ rusa
RUSCUS n type of shrub
RUSE n stratagem or trick
RUSES ▶ ruse
RUSH vb move or do very quickly ▷ n sudden quick or violent movement ▷ adj done with speed, hasty
RUSHED ▶ rush
RUSHEE n someone interested in gaining fraternity or sorority membership
RUSHEES ▶ rushee
RUSHEN adj made of rushes
RUSHER ▶ rush
RUSHERS ▶ rush
RUSHES pl n (in film-making) the initial prints of a scene or scenes before editing, usually prepared daily
RUSHIER ▶ rushy
RUSHING ▶ rush
RUSHY adj full of rushes
RUSINE adj of or relating to rusa deer
RUSK n hard brown crisp biscuit, used esp for feeding babies
RUSKS ▶ rusk
RUSMA n Turkish depilatory
RUSMAS ▶ rusma
RUSSE adj as in charlotte russe cold dessert made from whipped cream, custard, etc, surrounded by sponge fingers
RUSSEL n type of woollen fabric
RUSSELS ▶ russel

RUSSET adj reddish-brown ▷ n apple with rough reddish-brown skin ▷ vb become russet-coloured
RUSSETS ▶ russet
RUSSETY ▶ russet
RUSSIA n Russia leather
RUSSIAS ▶ russia
RUSSIFY vb cause to become Russian in character
RUSSULA n type of fungus, typically of toadstool shape and often brightly coloured
RUST n reddish-brown coating formed on iron etc that has been exposed to moisture ▷ adj reddish-brown ▷ vb become coated with rust
RUSTED ▶ rust
RUSTIC adj of or resembling country people ▷ n person from the country
RUSTICS ▶ rustic
RUSTIER ▶ rusty
RUSTILY ▶ rusty
RUSTING ▶ rust
RUSTLE n (make) a low whispering sound ▷ vb steal (cattle)
RUSTLED ▶ rustle
RUSTLER n cattle thief
RUSTLES ▶ rustle
RUSTRE n (in heraldry) lozenge with a round hole in the middle showing the background colour
RUSTRED ▶ rustre
RUSTRES ▶ rustre
RUSTS ▶ rust
RUSTY adj coated with rust
RUT n furrow made by wheels ▷ vb be in a period of sexual excitability
RUTH n pity
RUTHFUL adj full of or causing sorrow or pity
RUTHS ▶ ruth
RUTILE n black, yellowish, or reddish-brown mineral
RUTILES ▶ rutile
RUTIN n bioflavonoid found in various plants including rue
RUTINS ▶ rutin
RUTS ▶ rut
RUTTED ▶ rut
RUTTER n (in history) type of cavalry soldier
RUTTERS ▶ rutter
RUTTIER ▶ rutty
RUTTILY ▶ rutty

RUTTING ▶ rut
RUTTISH adj (of an animal) in a condition of rut
RUTTY adj full of ruts or holes
RYA n type of rug originating in Scandinavia
RYAL n one of several old coins
RYALS ▶ ryal
RYAS ▶ rya
RYBAT n polished stone piece forming the side of a window or door
RYBATS ▶ rybat

RYE n kind of grain used for fodder and bread
RYEPECK n punt-mooring pole
RYES ▶ rye
RYFE archaic variant of ▶ rife
RYKE Scots variant of ▶ reach
RYKED ▶ ryke
RYKES ▶ ryke
RYKING ▶ ryke
RYMME same as ▶ rim
RYMMED ▶ rymme
RYMMES ▶ rymme
RYMMING ▶ rymme

RYND n (in milling) crossbar piece forming part of the support structure of the upper millstone
RYNDS ▶ rynd
RYOKAN n traditional Japanese inn
RYOKANS ▶ ryokan
RYOT n (in India) a peasant or tenant farmer
RYOTS ▶ ryot
RYPE n ptarmigan
RYPECK same as ▶ ryepeck
RYPECKS ▶ rypeck
RYPER ▶ rype

R

Ss

S begins only four two-letter words, **sh** (5 points), **si**, **so** and **st** (2 each). These are easy to remember, and it's worth noting that two of them, **sh** and **st**, don't use any vowels. Interestingly, there are quite a few three-letter words beginning with **S** that don't contain vowels, some of which give good scores. These are **shh** (9), **shy** (9), **sky** (10), **sly** (6), **sny** (6), **spy** (8), **sty** (6), **swy** (9) and **syn** (6). **S** also forms a number of three-letter words with **X**. These are easy to remember as they use every vowel except **U**: **sax, sex, six** and **sox** (10 each). When it comes to **Z**, you will find **saz, sez** and **soz** (12 each) very useful, and the same applies to **suq** (12 points).

SAAG n (in Indian cookery) spinach

SAAGS ▶ **saag**

SAB n person engaged in direct action to prevent a targeted activity taking place ▷ vb take part in such action

SABAL n variety of palm tree

SABALS ▶ **sabal**

SABATON n foot covering in suit of armour

SABAYON n dessert or sweet sauce made with egg yolks, sugar, and wine beaten together over heat till thick

SABBAT n midnight meeting of witches

SABBATH n period of rest

SABBATS ▶ **sabbat**

SABBED ▶ **sab**

SABBING ▶ **sab**

SABE n very informal word meaning sense or savvy ▷ vb very informal word meaning know or savvy

SABED ▶ **sabe**

SABEING ▶ **sabe**

SABELLA n marine worm

SABER same as ▶ **sabre**

SABERED ▶ **saber**

SABERS ▶ **saber**

SABES ▶ **sabe**

SABHA n set of Muslim prayer beads

SABHAS ▶ **sabha**

SABIN n unit of acoustic absorption equal to the absorption resulting from one square foot of a perfectly absorbing surface

SABINE same as ▶ **savin**

SABINES ▶ **sabine**

SABINS ▶ **sabin**

SABIR n member of ancient Turkic people

SABIRS ▶ **sabir**

SABKHA n flat coastal plain with a salt crust, common in Arabia

SABKHAH n sabkha

SABKHAS ▶ **sabkha**

SABKHAT n sabkha

SABLE n dark fur from a small weasel-like Arctic animal ▷ adj black

SABLED ▶ **sable**

SABLES ▶ **sable**

SABLING ▶ **sable**

SABOT n wooden shoe traditionally worn by peasants in France

SABOTS ▶ **sabot**

SABRA n native-born Israeli Jew

SABRAS ▶ **sabra**

SABRE n curved cavalry sword ▷ vb injure or kill with a sabre

SABRED ▶ **sabre**

SABRES ▶ **sabre**

SABREUR n person wielding sabre

SABRING ▶ **sabre**

SABS ▶ **sab**

SABURRA n granular deposit

SAC n pouchlike structure in an animal or plant

SACATON n coarse grass of the southwestern US and Mexico, grown for hay and pasture

SACBUT n medieval trombone

SACBUTS ▶ **sacbut**

SACCADE n movement of the eye when it makes a sudden change of fixation, as in reading

SACCATE adj in the form of a sac

SACCOI ▶ **saccos**

SACCOS n bishop's garment in the Orthodox Church

SACCULE n small sac

SACCULI > **sacculus**

SACELLA > **sacellum**

SACHEM same as > **sagamore**

SACHEMS ▶ **sachem**

SACHET n small envelope or bag containing a single portion

SACHETS ▶ **sachet**

SACK n large bag made of coarse material ▷ vb dismiss

SACKAGE n act of sacking a place

SACKBUT n medieval form of trombone

SACKED ▶ **sack**

SACKER ▶ **sack**

SACKERS ▶ **sack**

SACKFUL ▶ **sack**

SACKING n rough woven material used for sacks

SACKS ▶ **sack**

SACLESS adj old word meaning unchallengeable

SACLIKE ▶ **sac**

SACQUE same as ▶ **sack**
SACQUES ▶ **sacque**
SACRA ▶ **sacrum**
SACRAL adj of or associated with sacred rites ▷ n sacral vertebra
SACRALS ▶ **sacral**
SACRED adj holy
SACRIFY vb old form of sacrifice
SACRING n act or ritual of consecration, esp of the Eucharist or of a bishop
SACRIST same as ▷ **sacristan**
SACRUM n wedge-shaped bone at the base of the spine
SACRUMS ▶ **sacrum**
SACS ▶ **sac**
SAD adj sorrowful, unhappy ▷ vb New Zealand word meaning express sadness or displeasure strongly
SADDED ▶ **sad**
SADDEN vb make (someone) sad
SADDENS ▶ **sadden**
SADDER ▶ **sad**
SADDEST ▶ **sad**
SADDHU same as ▶ **sadhu**
SADDHUS ▶ **saddhu**
SADDIE ▶ **saddo**
SADDIES ▶ **saddie**
SADDING ▶ **sad**
SADDISH ▶ **sad**
SADDLE n rider's seat on a horse or bicycle ▷ vb put a saddle on (a horse)
SADDLED ▶ **saddle**
SADDLER n maker or seller of saddles
SADDLES ▶ **saddle**
SADDO vb make sad ▷ n socially inadequate or pathetic person
SADDOES ▶ **saddo**
SADDOS ▶ **saddo**
SADE same as ▶ **sadhe**
SADES ▶ **sade**
SADHANA n one of a number of spiritual practices or disciplines which lead to perfection, these being contemplation, asceticism, worship of a god, and correct living
SADHE n 18th letter in the Hebrew alphabet
SADHES ▶ **sadhe**
SADHU n Hindu wandering holy man
SADHUS ▶ **sadhu**

SADI same as ▶ **sadhe**
SADIRON n heavy iron pointed at both ends, for pressing clothes
SADIS ▶ **sadi**
SADISM n gaining of (sexual) pleasure from inflicting pain
SADISMS ▶ **sadism**
SADIST ▶ **sadism**
SADISTS ▶ **sadism**
SADLY ▶ **sad**
SADNESS ▶ **sad**
SADO same as ▶ **chado**
SADOS ▶ **sado**
SADS ▶ **sad**
SADZA n southern African porridge
SADZAS ▶ **sadza**
SAE Scots word for ▶ **so**
SAETER n upland pasture in Norway
SAETERS ▶ **saeter**
SAFARI n expedition to hunt or observe wild animals, esp in Africa ▷ vb go on safari
SAFARIS ▶ **safari**
SAFE adj secure, protected ▷ n strong lockable container ▷ vb make safe
SAFED ▶ **safe**
SAFELY ▶ **safe**
SAFER ▶ **safe**
SAFES ▶ **safe**
SAFEST ▶ **safe**
SAFETY n state of being safe ▷ vb make safe
SAFFIAN n leather tanned with sumach and usually dyed a bright colour
SAFFRON n orange-coloured flavouring obtained from a crocus ▷ adj orange
SAFING ▶ **safe**
SAFROL n oily liquid obtained from sassafras
SAFROLE n colourless or yellowish oily water-insoluble liquid
SAFROLS ▶ **safrol**
SAFT Scots word for ▶ **soft**
SAFTER ▶ **saft**
SAFTEST ▶ **saft**
SAG vb sink in the middle ▷ n droop
SAGA n legend of Norse heroes
SAGAMAN n person reciting Norse sagas
SAGAMEN ▶ **sagaman**
SAGAS ▶ **saga**

SAGATHY n type of light fabric
SAGBUT n medieval trombone
SAGBUTS ▶ **sagbut**
SAGE n very wise man ▷ adj wise
SAGELY ▶ **sage**
SAGENE n fishing net
SAGENES ▶ **sagene**
SAGER ▶ **sage**
SAGES ▶ **sage**
SAGEST ▶ **sage**
SAGGAR n clay box in which fragile ceramic wares are placed for protection during firing ▷ vb put in a saggar
SAGGARD n saggar
SAGGARS ▶ **saggar**
SAGGED ▶ **sag**
SAGGER same as ▶ **saggar**
SAGGERS ▶ **sagger**
SAGGIER ▶ **saggy**
SAGGING ▶ **sag**
SAGGY adj tending to sag
SAGIER ▶ **sagy**
SAGIEST ▶ **sagy**
SAGITTA n sine of an arc
SAGO n starchy cereal from the powdered pith of the sago palm tree
SAGOIN n South American monkey
SAGOINS ▶ **sagoin**
SAGOS ▶ **sago**
SAGOUIN n South American monkey
SAGRADA adj as in cascara sagrada dried bark of the cascara buckthorn, used as a stimulant and laxative
SAGS ▶ **sag**
SAGUARO n giant cactus of desert regions of Arizona, S California, and Mexico
SAGUIN n South American monkey
SAGUINS ▶ **saguin**
SAGUM n Roman soldier's cloak
SAGY adj like or containing sage
SAHEB same as ▶ **sahib**
SAHEBS ▶ **saheb**
SAHIB n Indian term of address placed after a man's name as a mark of respect
SAHIBA n respectful Indian term of address for woman
SAHIBAH ▶ **sahiba**
SAHIBAS ▶ **sahiba**

S

SAHIBS ▸ sahib
SAHIWAL n breed of cattle in India
SAHUARO same as ▸ saguaro
SAI n South American monkey
SAIC n boat of eastern Mediterranean
SAICE same as ▸ syce
SAICES ▸ saice
SAICK n boat of eastern Mediterranean
SAICKS ▸ saick
SAICS ▸ saic
SAID same as ▸ sayyid
SAIDEST ▸ say
SAIDS ▸ said
SAIDST ▸ say
SAIGA n either of two antelopes of the plains of central Asia
SAIGAS ▸ saiga
SAIKEI n Japanese ornamental miniature landscape
SAIKEIS ▸ saikei
SAIL n sheet of fabric stretched to catch the wind for propelling a sailing boat ▷ vb travel by water
SAILED ▸ sail
SAILER n vessel, esp one equipped with sails, with specified sailing characteristics
SAILERS ▸ sailer
SAILING n practice, art, or technique of sailing a vessel
SAILOR n member of a ship's crew
SAILORS ▸ sailor
SAILS ▸ sail
SAIM Scots word for ▸ lard
SAIMIN n Hawaiian dish of noodles
SAIMINS ▸ saimin
SAIMIRI n South American monkey
SAIMS ▸ saim
SAIN vb make the sign of the cross over so as to bless or protect from evil or sin
SAINE vb old form of say
SAINED ▸ sain
SAINING ▸ sain
SAINS ▸ sain
SAINT n person venerated after death as specially holy ▷ vb canonize
SAINTED adj formally recognized by a Christian Church as a saint

SAINTLY adj behaving in a very good, patient, or holy way
SAINTS ▸ saint
SAIQUE n boat in eastern Mediterranean
SAIQUES ▸ saique
SAIR Scots word for ▸ sore
SAIRED ▸ sair
SAIRER ▸ sair
SAIREST ▸ sair
SAIRING ▸ sair
SAIRS ▸ sair
SAIS ▸ sai
SAIST ▸ say
SAITH form of the present tense (indicative mood) of ▸ say
SAITHE n dark-coloured food fish found in northern seas
SAITHES ▸ saithe
SAITHS ▸ saith
SAIYID n Muslim descended from Mohammed's grandson
SAIYIDS ▸ saiyid
SAJOU n South American monkey
SAJOUS ▸ sajou
SAKAI n Malaysian aborigine
SAKAIS ▸ sakai
SAKE n benefit
SAKER n large falcon of E Europe and central Asia
SAKERET n male saker
SAKERS ▸ saker
SAKES ▸ sake
SAKI same as ▸ sake
SAKIA n water wheel in Middle East
SAKIAS ▸ sakia
SAKIEH n water wheel in Middle East
SAKIEHS ▸ sakieh
SAKIS ▸ saki
SAKIYEH n water wheel in Middle East
SAKKOI ▸ sakkos
SAKKOS n bishop's garment in Orthodox Church
SAKSAUL n Asian tree
SAL pharmacological term for ▸ salt
SALAAM n low bow of greeting among Muslims ▷ vb make a salaam
SALAAMS ▸ salaam
SALABLE same as > saleable
SALABLY > saleably
SALAD n dish of raw vegetables, eaten as a meal

or part of a meal
SALADE same as ▸ sallet
SALADES ▸ salade
SALADS ▸ salad
SALAL n North American shrub
SALALS ▸ salal
SALAMI n highly spiced sausage
SALAMIS ▸ salami
SALAMON n word used in old oaths
SALARY n fixed regular payment, usu monthly, to an employee ▷ vb pay a salary to
SALBAND n coating of mineral
SALCHOW n type of figure-skating jump
SALE n exchange of goods for money
SALEP n dried ground starchy tubers of various orchids, used for food and formerly as drugs
SALEPS ▸ salep
SALES ▸ sale
SALET same as ▸ sallet
SALETS ▸ salet
SALEWD ▸ salue
SALFERN n plant of borage family
SALIC adj (of rocks and minerals) having a high content of silica and alumina
SALICES ▸ salix
SALICET n soft-toned organ stop
SALICIN n colourless or white crystalline water-soluble glucoside
SALIENT adj prominent, noticeable ▷ n projecting part of a front line
SALIFY vb treat, mix with, or cause to combine with a salt
SALIGOT n water chestnut
SALINA n salt marsh, lake, or spring
SALINAS ▸ salina
SALINE adj containing salt ▷ n solution of sodium chloride and water
SALINES ▸ saline
SALIVA n liquid that forms in the mouth, spittle
SALIVAL ▸ saliva
SALIVAS ▸ saliva
SALIX n plant or tree of willow family

SALL *archaic form of* ▶ **shall**
SALLAD *old spelling of* ▶ **salad**
SALLADS ▶ **sallad**
SALLAL *n* North American shrub
SALLALS ▶ **sallal**
SALLE *n* hall
SALLEE *n* SE Australian eucalyptus with a pale grey bark
SALLEES ▶ **sallee**
SALLES ▶ **salle**
SALLET *n* light round helmet extending over the back of the neck
SALLETS ▶ **sallet**
SALLIED ▶ **sally**
SALLIER ▶ **sally**
SALLIES ▶ **sally**
SALLOW *adj* of an unhealthy pale or yellowish colour ▷ *vb* make sallow ▷ *n* any of several small willow trees
SALLOWS ▶ **sallow**
SALLOWY ▶ **sallow**
SALLY *n* violent excursion ▷ *vb* set or rush out
SALMI *n* ragout of game stewed in a rich brown sauce
SALMIS *same as* ▶ **salmi**
SALMON *n* large fish with orange-pink flesh valued as food ▷ *adj* orange-pink
SALMONS ▶ **salmon**
SALMONY *adj* of or like a salmon
SALOL *n* white sparingly soluble crystalline compound with a slight aromatic odour, used as a preservative and to absorb light in sun-tan lotions, plastics, etc
SALOLS ▶ **salol**
SALON *n* commercial premises of a hairdresser, beautician, etc
SALONS ▶ **salon**
SALOON *n* closed car with four or more seats
SALOONS ▶ **saloon**
SALOOP *n* infusion of aromatic herbs or other plant parts formerly used as a tonic or cure
SALOOPS ▶ **saloop**
SALOP *same as* ▶ **saloop**
SALOPS ▶ **salop**
SALP *n* minute animal floating in sea
SALPA *n* any of various

minute floating animals of warm oceans
SALPAE ▶ **salpa**
SALPAS ▶ **salpa**
SALPIAN *n* minute animal floating in sea
SALPID *n* minute animal floating in sea
SALPIDS ▶ **salpid**
SALPINX *n* Fallopian tube or Eustachian tube
SALPS ▶ **salp**
SALS ▶ **sal**
SALSA *n* lively Puerto Rican dance ▷ *vb* dance the salsa
SALSAED ▶ **salsa**
SALSAS ▶ **salsa**
SALSE *n* volcano expelling mud
SALSES ▶ **salse**
SALSIFY *n* Mediterranean plant with a long white edible root
SALT *n* white crystalline substance used to season food ▷ *vb* season or preserve with salt
SALTANT *adj* (of an organism) differing from others of its species because of a saltation ▷ *n* saltant organism
SALTATE *vb* go through saltation
SALTATO *n* saltando
SALTBOX *n* box for salt with a sloping lid
SALTCAT *n* salty medicine for pigeons
SALTED *adj* seasoned, preserved, or treated with salt
SALTER *n* person who deals in or manufactures salt
SALTERN *n* place where salt is obtained from pools of evaporated sea water
SALTERS ▶ **salter**
SALTEST ▶ **salt**
SALTIE *n* saltwater crocodile
SALTIER ▶ **saltire**
SALTIES ▶ **saltie**
SALTILY ▶ **salty**
SALTINE *n* salty biscuit
SALTING *n* area of low ground regularly inundated with salt water
SALTIRE *n* diagonal cross on a shield
SALTISH ▶ **salt**
SALTLY ▶ **salt**
SALTO *n* daring jump ▷ *vb* perform a daring jump

SALTOED ▶ **salto**
SALTOS ▶ **salto**
SALTPAN *n* shallow basin containing salt, gypsum, etc, that was deposited from an evaporated salt lake
SALTS ▶ **salt**
SALTUS *n* break in the continuity of a sequence, esp the omission of a necessary step in a logical argument
SALTY *adj* of, tasting of, or containing salt
SALUE *vb* old word meaning salute
SALUED ▶ **salue**
SALUES ▶ **salue**
SALUING ▶ **salue**
SALUKI *n* type of tall hound with a smooth coat
SALUKIS ▶ **saluki**
SALUTE *n* motion of the arm as a formal military sign of respect ▷ *vb* greet with a salute
SALUTED ▶ **salute**
SALUTER ▶ **salute**
SALUTES ▶ **salute**
SALVAGE *n* saving of a ship or other property from destruction ▷ *vb* save from destruction or waste
SALVE *n* healing or soothing ointment ▷ *vb* soothe or appease
SALVED ▶ **salve**
SALVER *same as* ▶ **salvor**
SALVERS ▶ **salver**
SALVES ▶ **salve**
SALVETE *n* Latin greeting
SALVIA *n* plant with blue or red flowers
SALVIAS ▶ **salvia**
SALVING ▶ **salve**
SALVO *n* simultaneous discharge of guns etc ▷ *vb* attack with a salvo
SALVOED ▶ **salvo**
SALVOES ▶ **salvo**
SALVOR *n* person instrumental in salvaging a vessel or its cargo
SALVORS ▶ **salvor**
SALVOS ▶ **salvo**
SALWAR *n* as in **salwar kameez** long tunic worn over a pair of baggy trousers, usually worn by women, esp in Pakistan
SALWARS ▶ **salwar**
SAM *vb* collect

S

SAMA n Japanese title of respect

SAMAAN n South American tree

SAMAANS ▶ samaan

SAMADHI n state of deep meditative contemplation which leads to higher consciousness

SAMAN n South American tree

SAMANS ▶ saman

SAMARA n dry indehiscent one-seeded fruit with a winglike extension to aid dispersal

SAMARAS ▶ samara

SAMAS ▶ sama

SAMBA n lively Brazilian dance ▷ vb perform such a dance

SAMBAED ▶ samba

SAMBAL n Malaysian dish

SAMBALS ▶ sambal

SAMBAR n S Asian deer with three-tined antlers

SAMBARS ▶ sambar

SAMBAS ▶ samba

SAMBHAR n Indian dish

SAMBHUR n Asian deer

SAMBUCA n Italian liqueur

SAMBUKE n ancient Greek stringed instrument

SAMBUR same as ▶ sambar

SAMBURS ▶ sambur

SAME adj identical, not different, unchanged ▷ n something identical

SAMECH n letter in Hebrew alphabet

SAMECHS ▶ samech

SAMEK same as ▶ samekh

SAMEKH n 15th letter in the Hebrew alphabet, transliterated as s

SAMEKHS ▶ samekh

SAMEKS ▶ samek

SAMEL adj of brick, not sufficiently fired

SAMELY adj the same

SAMEN old Scots form of ▶ same

SAMES ▶ same

SAMEY adj monotonous

SAMFOO n style of casual dress worn by Chinese women, consisting of a waisted blouse and trousers

SAMFOOS ▶ samfoo

SAMFU ▶ samfoo

SAMFUS ▶ samfu

SAMIEL same as ▶ simoom

SAMIELS ▶ samiel

SAMIER ▶ samey

SAMIEST ▶ samey

SAMISEN n Japanese plucked stringed instrument with a long neck, an unfretted fingerboard, and a rectangular soundbox

SAMITE n heavy fabric of silk, often woven with gold or silver threads, used in the Middle Ages for clothing

SAMITES ▶ samite

SAMITHI same as ▶ samiti

SAMITI n (in India) an association, esp one formed to organize political activity

SAMITIS ▶ samiti

SAMLET n young salmon

SAMLETS ▶ samlet

SAMLOR n motor vehicle in Thailand

SAMLORS ▶ samlor

SAMMED ▶ sam

SAMMIES ▶ sammy

SAMMING ▶ sam

SAMMY n (in South Africa) an Indian fruit and vegetable vendor who goes from house to house

SAMOSA n (in Indian cookery) a small fried triangular spiced meat or vegetable pasty

SAMOSAS ▶ samosa

SAMOVAR n Russian tea urn

SAMOYED n Siberian breed of dog of the spitz type, having a dense white or cream coat with a distinct ruff, and a tightly curled tail

SAMP n crushed maize used for porridge

SAMPAN n small boat with oars used in China

SAMPANS ▶ sampan

SAMPI n old Greek number character

SAMPIRE n samphire

SAMPIS ▶ sampi

SAMPLE n part taken as representative of a whole ▷ vb take and test a sample of

SAMPLED ▶ sample

SAMPLER n piece of embroidery showing the embroiderer's skill

SAMPLES ▶ sample

SAMPS ▶ samp

SAMS ▶ sam

SAMSARA n endless cycle of birth, death, and rebirth

SAMSHOO n Chinese alcoholic drink

SAMSHU n alcoholic drink from China that is made from fermented rice and resembles sake

SAMSHUS ▶ samshu

SAMURAI n member of an ancient Japanese warrior caste

SAN n sanatorium

SANCAI n glaze in Chinese pottery

SANCAIS ▶ sancai

SANCHO n African stringed instrument

SANCHOS ▶ sancho

SANCTA ▶ sanctum

SANCTUM n sacred place

SAND n substance consisting of small grains of rock, esp on a beach or in a desert ▷ vb smooth with sandpaper

SANDAL n light shoe consisting of a sole attached by straps ▷ vb put sandals on

SANDALS ▶ sandal

SANDBAG n bag filled with sand, used as protection against gunfire or flood water ▷ vb protect with sandbags

SANDBAR n ridge of sand in a river or sea, often exposed at low tide

SANDBOX n container on a railway locomotive from which sand is released onto the rails to assist the traction

SANDBOY n as in **happy as a sandboy** very happy or high-spirited

SANDBUR n variety of wild grass

SANDDAB n type of small Pacific flatfish

SANDED ▶ sand

SANDEK n man who holds a baby being circumcised

SANDEKS ▶ sandek

SANDER n power tool for smoothing surfaces

SANDERS ▶ sander

SANDFLY n any of various small mothlike dipterous flies: the bloodsucking females transmit diseases including leishmaniasis

SANDHI n modification of the form or sound of a word under the influence of an adjacent word

SANDHIS ▸ sandhi

SANDHOG n person who works in underground or underwater construction projects

SANDIER ▸ sandy

SANDING ▸ sand

SANDLOT n area of vacant ground used by children for playing baseball and other games

SANDMAN n (in folklore) a magical person supposed to put children to sleep by sprinkling sand in their eyes

SANDMEN ▸ sandman

SANDPIT n shallow pit or container holding sand for children to play in

SANDS ▸ sand

SANDY adj covered with sand

SANE adj of sound mind ▸ vb heal

SANED ▸ sane

SANELY ▸ sane

SANER ▸ sane

SANES ▸ sane

SANEST ▸ sane

SANG Scots word for ▸ song

SANGA n Ethiopian ox

SANGAR n breastwork of stone or sods

SANGARS ▸ sangar

SANGAS ▸ sanga

SANGEET n Indian pre-wedding celebration

SANGER n sandwich

SANGERS ▸ sanger

SANGH n Indian union or association

SANGHA n Buddhist monastic order or community

SANGHAS ▸ sangha

SANGHAT n fellowship or assembly, esp a local Sikh community or congregation

SANGHS ▸ sangh

SANGO same as ▸ sanger

SANGOMA n witch doctor or herbalist

SANGOS ▸ sango

SANGRIA n Spanish drink of red wine and fruit

SANGS ▸ sang

SANICLE n type of plant

with clusters of small white flowers and oval fruits with hooked bristles

SANIES n thin greenish foul-smelling discharge from a wound, etc, containing pus and blood

SANIFY vb make healthy

SANING ▸ sane

SANIOUS ▸ sanies

SANITY n state of having a normal healthy mind

SANJAK n (in the Turkish Empire) a subdivision of a vilayet

SANJAKS ▸ sanjak

SANK ▸ sink

SANKO n African stringed instrument

SANKOS ▸ sanko

SANNIE Scots word for ▸ sandshoe

SANNIES ▸ sannie

SANNOP n Native American married man

SANNOPS ▸ sannop

SANNUP n Native American married man

SANNUPS ▸ sannup

SANPAN n sampan

SANPANS ▸ sanpan

SANPRO n sanitary-protection products, collectively

SANPROS ▸ sanpro

SANS archaic word for ▸ without

SANSA n African musical instrument

SANSAR n name of a wind that blows in Iran

SANSARS ▸ sansar

SANSAS ▸ sansa

SANSEI n American whose parents were Japanese immigrants

SANSEIS ▸ sansei

SANT n devout person in India

SANTAL n sandalwood

SANTALS ▸ santal

SANTERA n priestess of santeria

SANTERO n priest of santeria

SANTIMI ▸ santims

SANTIMS n money unit in Latvia

SANTIMU same as ▸ santims

SANTIR n Middle Eastern stringed instrument

SANTIRS ▸ santir

SANTO n saint or representation of one

SANTOL n fruit from Southeast Asia

SANTOLS ▸ santol

SANTON n French figurine

SANTONS ▸ santon

SANTOOR same as ▸ santir

SANTOS ▸ santo

SANTOUR n Middle Eastern stringed instrument

SANTS ▸ sant

SANTUR n Middle Eastern stringed instrument

SANTURS ▸ santur

SANYASI same as ▸ sannyasi

SAOLA n small, very rare bovine mammal of Vietnam and Laos

SAOLAS ▸ saola

SAOUARI n tropical American tree

SAP n moisture that circulates in plants ▸ vb undermine

SAPAJOU n capuchin monkey

SAPAN n tropical tree

SAPANS ▸ sapan

SAPEGO n skin disease

SAPELE n type of W African tree

SAPELES ▸ sapele

SAPFUL adj full of sap

SAPHEAD n simpleton, idiot, or fool

SAPHENA n either of two large superficial veins of the legs

SAPID adj having a pleasant taste

SAPIENS adj relating to or like modern human beings

SAPIENT adj wise, shrewd ▸ n wise person

SAPLESS ▸ sap

SAPLING n young tree

SAPONIN n any of a group of plant glycosides

SAPOR n quality in a substance that is perceived by the sense of taste

SAPORS ▸ sapor

SAPOTA same as ▸ sapodilla

SAPOTAS ▸ sapota

SAPOTE n Central American tree

SAPOTES ▸ sapote

SAPOUR same as ▸ sapor

SAPOURS ▸ sapour

SAPPAN n tropical tree

SAPPANS ▸ sappan

SAPPED ▶ sap

SAPPER n soldier in an engineering unit

SAPPERS ▶ sapper

SAPPHIC adj lesbian ▷ n verse written in a particular form

SAPPIER ▶ sappy

SAPPILY ▶ sappy

SAPPING ▶ sap

SAPPLE vb Scots word meaning wash in water

SAPPLED ▶ sapple

SAPPLES ▶ sapple

SAPPY adj (of plants) full of sap

SAPROBE n organism that lives on decaying organisms

SAPS ▶ sap

SAPSAGO n hard greenish Swiss cheese made with sour skimmed milk and coloured and flavoured with clover

SAPWOOD n soft wood, just beneath the bark in tree trunks, that consists of living tissue

SAR n marine fish ▷ vb Scots word meaning savour

SARAFAN n Russian woman's cloak

SARAN n any one of a class of thermoplastic resins

SARANGI n stringed instrument of India played with a bow

SARANS ▶ saran

SARAPE n serape

SARAPES ▶ sarape

SARCASM n (use of) bitter or wounding ironic language

SARCINA n type of bacterium

SARCODE n material making up living cell

SARCOID adj of, relating to, or resembling flesh ▷ n tumour resembling a sarcoma

SARCOMA n malignant tumour beginning in connective tissue

SARCOUS adj (of tissue) muscular or fleshy

SARD n orange, red, or brown variety of chalcedony, used as a gemstone

SARDANA n Catalan dance

SARDAR n title used before the name of Sikh men

SARDARS ▶ sardar

SARDEL n small fish

SARDELS ▶ sardel

SARDINE n small fish of the herring family, usu preserved tightly packed in tins ▷ vb cram together

SARDIUS same as ▶ sard

SARDS ▶ sard

SARED ▶ sar

SAREE same as ▶ sari

SAREES ▶ saree

SARGE n sergeant

SARGES ▶ sarge

SARGO same as ▶ sargus

SARGOS same as ▶ sargus

SARGUS n species of sea fish

SARI n long piece of cloth draped around the body and over one shoulder, worn by Hindu women

SARIN n chemical used in warfare as a lethal nerve gas producing asphyxia

SARING ▶ sar

SARINS ▶ sarin

SARIS ▶ sari

SARK n shirt or (formerly) chemise

SARKIER ▶ sarky

SARKILY ▶ sarky

SARKING n flat planking supporting the roof cladding of a building

SARKS ▶ sark

SARKY adj sarcastic

SARMENT n thin twig

SARMIE n sandwich

SARMIES ▶ sarmie

SARNEY n sandwich

SARNEYS ▶ sarney

SARNIE n sandwich

SARNIES ▶ sarnie

SAROD n Indian stringed musical instrument that may be played with a bow or plucked

SARODE n Indian stringed instrument

SARODES ▶ sarode

SARODS ▶ sarod

SARONG n long piece of cloth tucked around the waist or under the armpits, worn esp in Malaysia

SARONGS ▶ sarong

SARONIC ▶ saros

SAROS n cycle of about 18 years 11 days in which eclipses of the sun and moon occur in the same sequence

SAROSES ▶ saros

SARS ▶ sar

SARSAR same as ▶ sansar

SARSARS ▶ sarsar

SARSDEN n sarsen

SARSEN n boulder of silicified sandstone found in large numbers in S England

SARSENS ▶ sarsen

SARSNET n type of silk

SARTOR humorous or literary word for ▶ tailor

SARTORS ▶ sartor

SARUS n Indian bird of crane family

SARUSES ▶ sarus

SASER n device for amplifying ultrasound, working on a similar principle to a laser

SASERS ▶ saser

SASH n decorative strip of cloth worn round the waist or over one shoulder ▷ vb furnish with a sash, sashes, or sash windows

SASHAY vb move or walk in a casual or a showy manner

SASHAYS ▶ sashay

SASHED ▶ sash

SASHES ▶ sash

SASHIMI n Japanese dish of thin fillets of raw fish

SASHING ▶ sash

SASIN another name for ▷ blackbuck

SASINE n granting of legal possession of feudal property

SASINES ▶ sasine

SASINS ▶ sasin

SASS n insolent or impudent talk or behaviour ▷ vb talk or answer back in such a way

SASSABY n African antelope of grasslands and semideserts

SASSE n old word meaning canal lock

SASSED ▶ sass

SASSES ▶ sass

SASSIER ▶ sassy

SASSIES ▶ sassy

SASSILY ▶ sassy

SASSING ▶ sass

SASSY adj insolent, impertinent ▷ n W African leguminous tree with poisonous bark

SASTRA same as ▶ shastra

SASTRAS ▶ sastra

SAT ▶ sit

SATAI same as ▶ satay

SATAIS ▷ satai

SATANG n monetary unit of Thailand worth one hundredth of a baht

SATANGS ▷ satang

SATANIC adj of Satan

SATARA n type of cloth

SATARAS ▷ satara

SATAY n Indonesian and Malaysian dish consisting of pieces of chicken, pork, etc, grilled on skewers and served with peanut sauce

SATAYS ▷ satay

SATCHEL n bag, usu with a shoulder strap, for carrying books

SATE vb satisfy (a desire or appetite) fully

SATED ▷ sate

SATEEN n glossy linen or cotton fabric, woven in such a way that it resembles satin

SATEENS ▷ sateen

SATEM adj denoting or belonging to a particular group of Indo-European languages

SATES ▷ sate

SATI n Indian widow suicide

SATIATE vb provide with more than enough, so as to disgust

SATIETY n feeling of having had too much

SATIN n silky fabric with a glossy surface on one side ▷ adj like satin in texture ▷ vb cover with satin

SATINED ▷ satin

SATINET n thin or imitation satin

SATING ▷ sate

SATINS ▷ satin

SATINY ▷ satin

SATIRE n use of ridicule to expose vice or folly

SATIRES ▷ satire

SATIRIC same as > **satirical**

SATIS ▷ sati

SATISFY vb please, content

SATIVE adj old word meaning cultivated

SATORI n state of sudden indescribable intuitive enlightenment

SATORIS ▷ satori

SATRAP n (in ancient Persia) a provincial governor or subordinate ruler

SATRAPS ▷ satrap

SATRAPY n province, office,

or period of rule of a satrap

SATSUMA n kind of small orange

SATYR n woodland god, part man, part goat

SATYRA n female satyr

SATYRAL n mythical beast in heraldry

SATYRAS ▷ satyra

SATYRIC ▷ satyr

SATYRID n butterfly with typically brown or dark wings with paler markings

SATYRS ▷ satyr

SAU archaic past tense of ▷ **see**

SAUBA n South American ant

SAUBAS ▷ sauba

SAUCE n liquid added to food to enhance flavour ▷ vb prepare (food) with sauce

SAUCED ▷ sauce

SAUCER n small round dish put under a cup

SAUCERS ▷ saucer

SAUCES ▷ sauce

SAUCH n sallow or willow

SAUCHS ▷ sauch

SAUCIER n chef who makes sauces

SAUCILY ▷ saucy

SAUCING ▷ sauce

SAUCY adj impudent

SAUGER n small North American pikeperch

SAUGERS ▷ sauger

SAUGH same as ▷ **sauch**

SAUGHS ▷ saugh

SAUGHY adj Scots word meaning made of willow

SAUL Scots word for ▷ **soul**

SAULGE n old word for sage plant

SAULGES ▷ saulge

SAULIE n Scots word meaning professional mourner

SAULIES ▷ saulie

SAULS ▷ saul

SAULT n waterfall in Canada

SAULTS ▷ sault

SAUNA n Finnish-style steam bath ▷ vb have a sauna

SAUNAED ▷ sauna

SAUNAS ▷ sauna

SAUNT Scots form of ▷ **saint**

SAUNTED ▷ saunt

SAUNTER vb walk in a leisurely manner, stroll ▷ n leisurely walk

SAUNTS ▷ saunt

SAUREL n type of mackerel

SAURELS ▷ saurel

SAURIAN n lizard

SAURIES ▷ saury

SAUROID adj like a lizard

SAURY n type of fish of tropical and temperate seas, having an elongated body and long toothed jaws

SAUSAGE n minced meat in an edible tube-shaped skin

SAUT Scots word for ▷ **salt**

SAUTE vb fry quickly in a little fat ▷ n dish of sautéed food ▷ adj sautéed until lightly brown

SAUTED ▷ saut

SAUTEED ▷ saute

SAUTES ▷ saute

SAUTING ▷ saut

SAUTOIR n long necklace or pendant

SAUTS ▷ saut

SAV short for ▷ **saveloy**

SAVABLE ▷ save

SAVAGE adj wild, untamed ▷ n uncivilized person ▷ vb attack ferociously

SAVAGED ▷ savage

SAVAGER ▷ savage

SAVAGES ▷ savage

SAVANNA n open grasslands, usually with scattered bushes or trees, characteristic of much of tropical Africa

SAVANT n learned person

SAVANTE ▷ savant

SAVANTS ▷ savant

SAVARIN n type of cake

SAVATE n form of boxing in which blows may be delivered with the feet as well as the hands

SAVATES ▷ savate

SAVE vb rescue or preserve from harm, protect ▷ n act of preventing a goal ▷ prep except

SAVED ▷ save

SAVELOY n spicy smoked sausage

SAVER ▷ save

SAVERS ▷ save

SAVES ▷ save

SAVEY vb understand

SAVEYED ▷ savey

SAVEYS ▷ savey

SAVIN n small spreading juniper bush of Europe, N Asia, and North America

SAVINE same as ▷ **savin**

S

SAVINES ▸ **savine**
SAVING n economy ▷ prep except ▷ adj tending to save or preserve
SAVINGS ▸ **saving**
SAVINS ▸ **savin**
SAVIOR same as ▸ **saviour**
SAVIORS ▸ **savior**
SAVIOUR n person who rescues another
SAVOR same as ▸ **savour**
SAVORED ▸ **savor**
SAVORER ▸ **savor**
SAVORS ▸ **savor**
SAVORY same as ▸ **savoury**
SAVOUR vb enjoy, relish ▷ n characteristic taste or odour
SAVOURS ▸ **savour**
SAVOURY adj salty or spicy ▷ n savoury dish served before or after a meal
SAVOY n variety of cabbage
SAVOYS ▸ **savoy**
SAVS ▸ **sav**
SAVVEY vb understand
SAVVEYS ▸ **savvey**
SAVVIED ▸ **savvy**
SAVVIER ▸ **savvy**
SAVVIES ▸ **savvy**
SAVVILY ▸ **savvy**
SAVVY vb understand ▷ n understanding, intelligence ▷ adj shrewd
SAW n hand tool for cutting wood and metal ▷ vb cut with a saw
SAWAH n paddyfield
SAWAHS ▸ **sawah**
SAWBILL n type of hummingbird
SAWBUCK n sawhorse, esp one having an X-shaped supporting structure
SAWDER n flattery ▷ vb flatter
SAWDERS ▸ **sawder**
SAWDUST n fine wood fragments made in sawing ▷ vb cover with sawdust
SAWED ▸ **saw**
SAWER ▸ **saw**
SAWERS ▸ **saw**
SAWFISH n fish with a long toothed snout
SAWFLY n any of various hymenopterous insects
SAWING ▸ **saw**
SAWINGS ▸ **saw**
SAWLIKE ▸ **saw**
SAWLOG n log suitable for sawing
SAWLOGS ▸ **sawlog**

SAWMILL n mill where timber is sawn into planks
SAWN past participle of ▸ **saw**
SAWPIT n pit above which a log is sawn into planks
SAWPITS ▸ **sawpit**
SAWS ▸ **saw**
SAWYER n person who saws timber for a living
SAWYERS ▸ **sawyer**
SAX same as > **saxophone**
SAXAUL n Asian tree
SAXAULS ▸ **saxaul**
SAXE adj as in **saxe blue** light greyish-blue colour
SAXES ▸ **sax**
SAXHORN n valved brass instrument used chiefly in brass and military bands
SAXONY n fine 3-ply yarn used for knitting and weaving
SAXTUBA n bass saxhorn
SAY vb speak or utter ▷ n right or chance to speak
SAYABLE ▸ **say**
SAYED same as ▸ **sayyid**
SAYEDS ▸ **sayed**
SAYER ▸ **say**
SAYERS ▸ **say**
SAYEST ▸ **say**
SAYID same as ▸ **sayyid**
SAYIDS ▸ **sayid**
SAYING ▸ **say**
SAYINGS ▸ **say**
SAYNE ▸ **say**
SAYON n type of tunic
SAYONS ▸ **sayon**
SAYS ▸ **say**
SAYST ▸ **say**
SAYYID n Muslim claiming descent from Mohammed's grandson Husain
SAYYIDS ▸ **sayyid**
SAZ n Middle Eastern stringed instrument

This musical instrument is one of the most frequently played Z words.

SAZERAC n mixed drink of whisky, Pernod, syrup, bitters, and lemon
SAZES ▸ **saz**
SAZHEN n Russian measure of length
SAZHENS ▸ **sazhen**
SAZZES ▸ **saz**
SBIRRI ▸ **sbirro**
SBIRRO n Italian police officer
SCAB n crust formed over a

wound ▷ vb become covered with a scab
SCABBED ▸ **scab**
SCABBLE vb shape (stone) roughly
SCABBY adj covered with scabs
SCABIES n itchy skin disease
SCABRID adj having a rough or scaly surface
SCABS ▸ **scab**
SCAD n any of various carangid fishes
SCADS pl n large amount or number
SCAFF n Scots word meaning food
SCAFFIE n Scots word meaning street cleaner
SCAFFS ▸ **scaff**
SCAG n tear in a garment or piece of cloth ▷ vb make a tear in (cloth)
SCAGGED ▸ **scag**
SCAGLIA n type of limestone
SCAGS ▸ **scag**
SCAIL vb Scots word meaning disperse
SCAILED ▸ **scail**
SCAILS ▸ **scail**
SCAITH vb old word meaning injure
SCAITHS ▸ **scaith**
SCALA n passage inside the cochlea
SCALADE short for > **escalade**
SCALADO same as ▸ **scalade**
SCALAE ▸ **scala**
SCALAGE n percentage deducted from the price of goods liable to shrink or leak
SCALAR adj (variable quantity) having magnitude but no direction ▷ n quantity, such as time or temperature, that has magnitude but not direction
SCALARE another name for > **angelfish**
SCALARS ▸ **scalar**
SCALD same as ▸ **skald**
SCALDED ▸ **scald**
SCALDER ▸ **scald**
SCALDIC ▸ **skald**
SCALDS ▸ **scald**
SCALE n one of the thin overlapping plates covering

fishes and reptiles ▷ vb remove scales from

SCALED ▶ **scale**

SCALENE adj (of a triangle) with three unequal sides

SCALENI > **scalenus**

SCALER n person or thing that scales

SCALERS ▶ **scaler**

SCALES ▶ **scale**

SCALEUP n increase

SCALIER ▶ **scaly**

SCALING > **scale** vb

SCALL n disease of the scalp characterized by itching and scab formation

SCALLED ▶ **scall**

SCALLOP n edible shellfish with two fan-shaped shells ▷ vb decorate (an edge) with scallops

SCALLS ▶ **scall**

SCALLY n rascal

SCALP n skin and hair on top of the head ▷ vb cut off the scalp of

SCALPED ▶ **scalp**

SCALPEL n small surgical knife

SCALPER ▶ **scalp**

SCALPS ▶ **scalp**

SCALY adj resembling or covered in scales

SCAM n dishonest scheme ▷ vb swindle (someone) by means of a trick

SCAMBLE vb scramble

SCAMEL n Shakespearian word of uncertain meaning

SCAMELS ▶ **scamel**

SCAMMED ▶ **scam**

SCAMMER n person who perpetrates a scam

SCAMP n mischievous child ▷ vb perform without care

SCAMPED ▶ **scamp**

SCAMPER vb run about hurriedly or in play ▷ n scampering

SCAMPI pl n large prawns

SCAMPIS ▶ **scampi**

SCAMPS ▶ **scamp**

SCAMS ▶ **scam**

SCAMTO n argot of urban South African Blacks

SCAMTOS ▶ **scamto**

SCAN vb scrutinize carefully ▷ n scanning

SCAND ▶ **scan**

SCANDAL n disgraceful action or event ▷ vb disgrace

SCANDIA n scandium oxide

SCANDIC adj of or containing scandium

SCANNED ▶ **scan**

SCANNER n electronic device used for scanning

SCANS ▶ **scan**

SCANT adj barely sufficient, meagre ▷ vb limit in size or quantity ▷ adv scarcely

SCANTED ▶ **scant**

SCANTER ▶ **scant**

SCANTLE vb stint

SCANTLY ▶ **scant**

SCANTS ▶ **scant**

SCANTY adj barely sufficient or not sufficient

SCAPA same as ▶ **scarper**

SCAPAED ▶ **scapa**

SCAPAS ▶ **scapa**

SCAPE n leafless stalk in plants that arises from a rosette of leaves and bears one or more flowers ▷ vb archaic word for escape

SCAPED ▶ **scape**

SCAPES ▶ **scape**

SCAPI ▶ **scapus**

SCAPING ▶ **scape**

SCAPOSE ▶ **scape**

SCAPPLE vb shape roughly

SCAPULA n shoulder blade

SCAPUS n flower stalk

SCAR n mark left by a healed wound ▷ vb mark or become marked with a scar

SCARAB n sacred beetle of ancient Egypt

SCARABS ▶ **scarab**

SCARCE adj insufficient to meet demand

SCARCER ▶ **scarce**

SCARE vb frighten or be frightened ▷ n fright, sudden panic ▷ adj causing (needless) fear or alarm

SCARED ▶ **scare**

SCARER ▶ **scare**

SCARERS ▶ **scare**

SCARES ▶ **scare**

SCAREY adj frightening

SCARF n piece of material worn round the neck, head, or shoulders ▷ vb join in this way

SCARFED ▶ **scarf**

SCARFER ▶ **scarf**

SCARFS ▶ **scarf**

SCARIER ▶ **scary**

SCARIFY vb scratch or cut slightly all over

SCARILY ▶ **scary**

SCARING ▶ **scare**

SCARLET n brilliant red

▷ adj bright red ▷ vb make scarlet

SCARP n steep slope ▷ vb wear or cut so as to form a steep slope

SCARPA vb run away

SCARPAS ▶ **scarpa**

SCARPED ▶ **scarp**

SCARPER vb run away ▷ n hasty departure

SCARPH vb join with scarf joint

SCARPHS ▶ **scarph**

SCARPS ▶ **scarp**

SCARRE n Shakespearian word of unknown meaning

SCARRED ▶ **scar**

SCARRES ▶ **scarre**

SCARRY ▶ **scar**

SCARS ▶ **scar**

SCART vb scratch or scrape ▷ n scratch or scrape

SCARTED ▶ **scart**

SCARTH Scots word for > **cormorant**

SCARTHS ▶ **scarth**

SCARTS ▶ **scart**

SCARVES ▶ **scarf**

SCARY adj frightening

SCAT vb go away ▷ n jazz singing using improvised vocal sounds instead of words

SCATCH same as ▶ **stilt**

SCATH vb old word meaning injure

SCATHE vb attack with severe criticism ▷ n harm

SCATHED ▶ **scathe**

SCATHES ▶ **scathe**

SCATHS ▶ **scath**

SCATOLE n substance found in coal

SCATS ▶ **scat**

SCATT n old word meaning tax ▷ vb tax

SCATTED ▶ **scat**

SCATTER vb throw about in various directions ▷ n scattering

SCATTS ▶ **scatt**

SCATTY adj empty-headed

SCAUD Scots word for ▶ **scald**

SCAUDED ▶ **scaud**

SCAUDS ▶ **scaud**

SCAUP same as ▶ **scalp**

SCAUPED ▶ **scaup**

SCAUPER same as ▶ **scorper**

SCAUPS ▶ **scaup**

SCAUR same as ▶ **scar**

SCAURED ▶ **scaur**

SCAURS ▶ **scaur**

S

SCAURY n young seagull

SCAVAGE n old word meaning toll

SCAW n headland

SCAWS ▶ scaw

SCAZON n metre in poetry

SCAZONS ▶ scazon

SCEAT n Anglo-Saxon coin

SCEATT n Anglo-Saxon coin

SCEDULE old spelling of > schedule

SCENA n scene in an opera, usually longer than a single aria

SCENARY n scenery

SCENAS ▶ scena

SCEND vb (of a vessel) to surge upwards in a heavy sea ▷ n upward heaving of a vessel pitching

SCENDED ▶ scend

SCENDS ▶ scend

SCENE n place of action of a real or imaginary event ▷ vb set in a scene

SCENED ▶ scene

SCENERY n natural features of a landscape

SCENES ▶ scene

SCENIC adj picturesque ▷ n something scenic

SCENICS ▶ scenic

SCENING ▶ scene

SCENT n pleasant smell ▷ vb detect by smell

SCENTED ▶ scent

SCENTS ▶ scent

SCEPSIS n doubt

SCEPTER same as ▶ sceptre

SCEPTIC n person who habitually doubts generally accepted beliefs ▷ adj of or relating to sceptics

SCEPTRE n ornamental rod symbolizing royal power ▷ vb invest with authority

SCEPTRY adj having sceptre

SCERNE vb old word meaning discern

SCERNED ▶ scerne

SCERNES ▶ scerne

SCHANSE n stones heaped to shelter soldiers in battle

SCHANZE same as schanse

SCHAPPE n yarn or fabric made from waste silk

SCHAV n Polish soup

SCHAVS ▶ schav

SCHELLY n freshwater whitefish of the English Lake District

SCHELM n South African word meaning rascal

SCHELMS ▶ schelm

SCHEMA n overall plan or diagram

SCHEMAS ▶ schema

SCHEME n systematic plan ▷ vb plan in an underhand manner

SCHEMED ▶ scheme

SCHEMER ▶ scheme

SCHEMES ▶ scheme

SCHERZI ▶ scherzo

SCHERZO n brisk lively piece of music

SCHISM n (group resulting from) division in an organization

SCHISMA n musical term

SCHISMS ▶ schism

SCHIST n crystalline rock which splits into layers

SCHISTS ▶ schist

SCHLEP vb drag or lug (oneself or an object) with difficulty ▷ n stupid or clumsy person

SCHLEPP vb schlep

SCHLEPS ▶ schlep

SCHLICH n finely crushed ore

SCHLOCK n goods or produce of cheap or inferior quality ▷ adj cheap, inferior, or trashy

SCHLOSS n castle

SCHLUB n coarse or contemptible person

SCHLUBS ▶ schlub

SCHLUMP vb move in lazy way

SCHMALZ same as > schmaltz

SCHMEAR n situation, matter, or affair ▷ vb spread or smear

SCHMECK n taste

SCHMEER same as ▶ schmear

SCHMELZ n ornamental glass

SCHMICK adj (in Australia) excellent, elegant, or stylish

SCHMO n dull, stupid, or boring person

SCHMOCK n stupid person

SCHMOE n stupid person

SCHMOES ▶ schmo

SCHMOOS same as > schmoose

SCHMOOZ n chat

SCHMOS ▶ schmo

SCHMUCK n stupid or contemptible person

SCHNAPS same as > schnapps

SCHNELL adj German word meaning quick

SCHNOOK n stupid or gullible person

SCHNORR vb beg

SCHNOZ n nose

SCHNOZZ n nose

SCHOLAR n learned person

SCHOLIA > scholium

SCHOOL n place where children are taught or instruction is given in a subject ▷ vb educate or train

SCHOOLE n old form of shoal

SCHOOLS ▶ school

SCHORL n type of black tourmaline

SCHORLS ▶ schorl

SCHOUT n council officer in Netherlands

SCHOUTS ▶ schout

SCHRIK same as ▶ skrik

SCHRIKS ▶ schrik

SCHROD n young cod

SCHRODS ▶ schrod

SCHTICK same as ▶ shtick

SCHTIK n schtick

SCHTIKS ▶ schtik

SCHTOOK n trouble

SCHTOOM adj silent

SCHTUCK n trouble

SCHTUM adj silent or dumb

SCHUIT n Dutch boat with flat bottom

SCHUITS ▶ schuit

SCHUL same as ▶ shul

SCHULN ▶ schul

SCHULS ▶ schul

SCHUSS n straight high-speed downhill run ▷ vb perform a schuss

SCHUYT n Dutch boat with flat bottom

SCHUYTS ▶ schuyt

SCHWA n central vowel representing the sound that occurs in unstressed syllables in English

SCHWAS ▶ schwa

SCIARID n small fly

SCIATIC adj of the hip ▷ n sciatic part of the body

SCIENCE n systematic study and knowledge of natural or physical phenomena

SCIENT adj old word meaning scientific

SCILLA n a plant with small bell-shaped flowers

SCILLAS ▶ scilla**

SCIOLTO adv musical direction meaning freely

SCION n descendant or heir

SCIONS ▶ scion

SCIROC n hot Mediterranean wind

SCIROCS ▶ sciroc

SCIRRHI > scirrhus

SCISSEL n waste metal left over from sheet metal after discs have been punched out of it

SCISSIL n scissel

SCISSOR vb cut (an object) with scissors

SCIURID n squirrel or related rodent

SCLAFF vb cause (the club) to hit (the ground behind the ball) when making a stroke ▷ n sclaffing stroke or shot

SCLAFFS ▶ sclaff

SCLATE vb Scots word meaning slate

SCLATES ▶ sclate

SCLAVE n old form of slave

SCLAVES ▶ sclave

SCLERA n tough white substance that forms the outer covering of the eyeball

SCLERAE ▶ sclera

SCLERAL ▶ sclera

SCLERAS ▶ sclera

SCLERE n supporting anatomical structure, esp a sponge spicule

SCLERES ▶ sclere

SCLIFF n Scots word for small piece

SCLIFFS ▶ scliff

SCLIM vb Scots word meaning climb

SCLIMS ▶ sclim

SCODIER ▶ scody

SCODY adj unkempt

SCOFF vb express derision ▷ n mocking expression

SCOFFED ▶ scoff

SCOFFER ▶ scoff

SCOFFS ▶ scoff

SCOG vb shelter

SCOGGED ▶ scog

SCOGS ▶ scog

SCOLD vb find fault with, reprimand ▷ n person who scolds

SCOLDED ▶ scold

SCOLDER ▶ scold

SCOLDS ▶ scold

SCOLEX n headlike part of a tapeworm

SCOLIA ▶ scolion

SCOLION n ancient Greek drinking song

SCOLLOP same as ▶ scallop

SCONCE n bracket on a wall for holding candles or lights ▷ vb challenge (a fellow student) on the grounds of a social misdemeanour to drink a large quantity of beer without stopping

SCONCED ▶ sconce

SCONCES ▶ sconce

SCONE n small plain cake baked in an oven or on a griddle

SCONES ▶ scone

SCOOBY n clue; notion

SCOOCH vb compress one's body into smaller space

SCOOG vb shelter

SCOOGED ▶ scoog

SCOOGS ▶ scoog

SCOOP n shovel-like tool for ladling or hollowing out ▷ vb take up or hollow out with or as if with a scoop

SCOOPED ▶ scoop

SCOOPER ▶ scoop

SCOOPS ▶ scoop

SCOOSH vb squirt ▷ n squirt or rush of liquid

SCOOT vb leave or move quickly ▷ n act of scooting

SCOOTCH same as ▶ scooch

SCOOTED ▶ scoot

SCOOTER n child's vehicle propelled by pushing on the ground with one foot

SCOOTS ▶ scoot

SCOP n (in Anglo-Saxon England) a bard or minstrel

SCOPA n tuft of hairs on the abdomen or hind legs of bees, used for collecting pollen

SCOPAE ▶ scopa

SCOPATE adj having tuft

SCOPE n opportunity for using abilities ▷ vb look at or examine carefully

SCOPED ▶ scope

SCOPES ▶ scope

SCOPING ▶ scope

SCOPS ▶ scop

SCOPULA n small tuft of dense hairs on the legs and chelicerae of some spiders

SCORCH vb burn on the surface ▷ n slight burn

SCORE n points gained in a game or competition ▷ vb gain (points) in a game

SCORED ▶ score

SCORER ▶ score

SCORERS ▶ score

SCORES ▶ score

SCORIA n mass of solidified lava containing many cavities

SCORIAC ▶ scoria

SCORIAE ▶ scoria

SCORIFY vb remove (impurities) from metals by forming scoria

SCORING n act or practice of scoring

SCORN n open contempt ▷ vb despise

SCORNED ▶ scorn

SCORNER ▶ scorn

SCORNS ▶ scorn

SCORPER n kind of fine chisel with a square or curved tip

SCORSE vb exchange

SCORSED ▶ scorse

SCORSER ▶ scorse

SCORSES ▶ scorse

SCOT n payment or tax

SCOTCH vb put an end to ▷ n gash

SCOTER n type of sea duck

SCOTERS ▶ scoter

SCOTIA n deep concave moulding

SCOTIAS ▶ scotia

SCOTOMA n blind spot

SCOTOMY n dizziness

SCOTS ▶ scot

SCOTTIE n type of small sturdy terrier

SCOUG vb shelter

SCOUGED ▶ scoug

SCOUGS ▶ scoug

SCOUP vb Scots word meaning jump

SCOUPED ▶ scoup

SCOUPS ▶ scoup

SCOUR vb clean or polish by rubbing with something rough ▷ n scouring

SCOURED ▶ scour

SCOURER ▶ scour

SCOURGE n person or thing causing severe suffering ▷ vb cause severe suffering to

SCOURIE n young seagull

SCOURS ▶ scour

SCOURSE vb exchange

SCOUSE n stew made from left-over meat

SCOUSER n inhabitant of Liverpool

SCOUSES ▶ scouse

S

SCOUT n person sent out to reconnoitre ▷ vb act as a scout

SCOUTED ▶ scout

SCOUTER ▶ scout

SCOUTH n Scots word meaning plenty of scope

SCOUTHS ▶ scouth

SCOUTS ▶ scout

SCOW n unpowered barge used for carrying freight ▷ vb transport by scow

SCOWDER vb Scots word meaning scorch

SCOWED ▶ scow

SCOWING ▶ scow

SCOWL n, vb (have an) angry or sullen expression

SCOWLED ▶ scowl

SCOWLER n person who scowls

SCOWLS ▶ scowl

SCOWP vb Scots word meaning jump

SCOWPED ▶ scowp

SCOWPS ▶ scowp

SCOWRER n old word meaning hooligan

SCOWRIE n young seagull

SCOWS ▶ scow

SCOWTH n Scots word meaning plenty of scope

SCOWTHS ▶ scowth

SCOZZA n rowdy person, esp one who drinks a lot of alcohol

SCOZZAS ▶ scozza

SCRAB vb scratch

SCRABS ▶ scrab

SCRAE Scots word for ▶ scree

SCRAES ▶ scrae

SCRAG n thin end of a neck of mutton ▷ vb wring the neck of

SCRAGGY adj thin, bony

SCRAGS ▶ scrag

SCRAICH vb Scots word meaning scream

SCRAIGH vb Scots word meaning scream

SCRAM vb go away quickly ▷ n emergency shutdown of a nuclear reactor

SCRAMB vb scratch with nails or claws

SCRAMBS ▶ scramb

SCRAMS ▶ scram

SCRAN n food

SCRANCH vb crunch

SCRANNY adj scrawny

SCRANS ▶ scran

SCRAP n small piece ▷ vb discard as useless

SCRAPE vb rub with something rough or sharp ▷ n act or sound of scraping

SCRAPED ▶ scrape

SCRAPER ▶ scrape

SCRAPES ▶ scrape

SCRAPIE n disease of sheep and goats

SCRAPPY adj fragmentary, disjointed

SCRAPS ▶ scrap

SCRAT vb scratch

SCRATCH vb mark or cut with claws, nails, or anything rough or sharp ▷ n wound, mark, or sound made by scratching ▷ adj put together at short notice

SCRATS ▶ scrat

SCRAUCH vb squawk

SCRAUGH vb squawk

SCRAW n sod from the surface of a peat bog or from a field

SCRAWL vb write carelessly or hastily ▷ n scribbled writing

SCRAWLS ▶ scrawl

SCRAWLY ▶ scrawl

SCRAWM vb dialect word meaning scratch

SCRAWMS ▶ scrawm

SCRAWNY adj thin and bony

SCRAWP vb scratch (the skin) to relieve itching

SCRAWPS ▶ scrawp

SCRAWS ▶ scraw

SCRAY n tern

SCRAYE n tern

SCRAYES ▶ scraye

SCRAYS ▶ scray

SCREAK vb screech or creak ▷ n screech or creak

SCREAKS ▶ screak

SCREAKY ▶ screak

SCREAM vb utter a piercing cry, esp of fear or pain ▷ n shrill piercing cry

SCREAMO n type of emo music featuring screaming vocals

SCREAMS ▶ scream

SCREE n slope of loose shifting stones

SCREECH n (utter) a shrill cry ▷ vb utter a shrill cry

SCREED n long tedious piece of writing ▷ vb rip

SCREEDS ▶ screed

SCREEN n surface of a television set, VDU, etc, on which an image is formed ▷ vb shelter or conceal with or as if with a screen

SCREENS ▶ screen

SCREES ▶ scree

SCREET vb shed tears ▷ n act or sound of crying

SCREETS ▶ screet

SCREEVE vb write

SCREICH same as ▶ screigh

SCREIGH Scots word for ▶ screech

SCREW n metal pin with a spiral ridge along its length, twisted into materials to fasten them together ▷ vb turn (a screw)

SCREWED adj fastened by a screw or screws

SCREWER ▶ screw

SCREWS ▶ screw

SCREWUP n something done badly

SCREWY adj crazy or eccentric

SCRIBAL ▶ scribe

SCRIBE n person who copies documents ▷ vb to score a line with a pointed instrument

SCRIBED ▶ scribe

SCRIBER n pointed steel tool used to score materials as a guide to cutting, etc

SCRIBES ▶ scribe

SCRIECH vb Scots word meaning screech

SCRIED ▶ scry

SCRIENE n old form of screen

SCRIES ▶ scry

SCRIEVE vb Scots word meaning write

SCRIKE vb old word meaning shriek

SCRIKED ▶ scrike

SCRIKES ▶ scrike

SCRIM n open-weave muslin or hessian fabric, used in upholstery, lining, building

SCRIMP vb be very economical

SCRIMPS ▶ scrimp

SCRIMPY ▶ scrimp

SCRIMS ▶ scrim

SCRINE n old form of shrine

SCRINES ▶ scrine

SCRIP n certificate representing a claim to stocks or shares

SCRIPS ▶ scrip

SCRIPT n text of a film, play,

or TV programme ▷ *vb* write a script for

SCRIPTS ▸ **script**

SCRITCH *vb* screech

SCRIVE *Scots word for* ▸ **write**

SCRIVED ▸ **scrive**

SCRIVES ▸ **scrive**

SCROBE *n* groove

SCROBES ▸ **scrobe**

SCROD *n* young cod or haddock, esp one split and prepared for cooking

SCRODS ▸ **scrod**

SCROG *n* Scots word meaning small tree

SCROGGY *same as* > **scroggie**

SCROGS ▸ **scrog**

SCROLL *n* roll of parchment or paper ▷ *vb* move (text) up or down on a VDU screen

SCROLLS ▸ **scroll**

SCROME *vb* crawl or climb, esp using the hands to aid movement

SCROMED ▸ **scrome**

SCROMES ▸ **scrome**

SCROOCH *vb* scratch (the skin) to relieve itching

SCROOGE *same as* ▸ **scrouge**

SCROOP *vb* emit a grating or creaking sound ▷ *n* such a sound

SCROOPS ▸ **scroop**

SCRORP *n* deep scratch or weal

SCRORPS ▸ **scrorp**

SCROTA ▸ **scrotum**

SCROTAL ▸ **scrotum**

SCROTUM *n* pouch of skin containing the testicles

SCROUGE *vb* crowd or press

SCROW *n* scroll

SCROWL *vb* old form of scroll

SCROWLE *vb* old form of scroll

SCROWLS ▸ **scrowl**

SCROWS ▸ **scrow**

SCROYLE *n* old word meaning wretch

SCRUB *vb* clean by rubbing, often with a hard brush and water ▷ *n* scrubbing ▷ *adj* stunted or inferior

SCRUBBY *adj* covered with scrub

SCRUBS ▸ **scrub**

SCRUFF *same as* ▸ **scum**

SCRUFFS ▸ **scruff**

SCRUFFY *adj* unkempt or shabby

SCRUM *n* restarting of play in which opposing packs of forwards push against each other to gain possession of the ball ▷ *vb* form a scrum

SCRUMMY *adj* delicious

SCRUMP *vb* steal (apples) from an orchard or garden

SCRUMPS ▸ **scrump**

SCRUMPY *n* rough dry cider

SCRUMS ▸ **scrum**

SCRUNCH *vb* crumple or crunch or be crumpled or crunched ▷ *n* act or sound of scrunching

SCRUNT *n* Scots word meaning stunted thing

SCRUNTS ▸ **scrunt**

SCRUNTY ▸ **scrunt**

SCRUPLE *n* doubt produced by one's conscience or morals ▷ *vb* have doubts on moral grounds

SCRUTO *n* trapdoor on stage

SCRUTOS ▸ **scruto**

SCRUZE *vb* old word meaning squeeze

SCRUZED ▸ **scruze**

SCRUZES ▸ **scruze**

SCRY *vb* divine, esp by crystal gazing

SCRYDE ▸ **scry**

SCRYER ▸ **scry**

SCRYERS ▸ **scry**

SCRYING ▸ **scry**

SCRYNE *n* old form of shrine

SCRYNES ▸ **scryne**

SCUBA *n* apparatus used in skin diving, consisting of cylinders containing compressed air attached to a breathing apparatus ▷ *vb* dive using scuba equipment

SCUBAED ▸ **scuba**

SCUBAS ▸ **scuba**

SCUCHIN *n* old form of scutcheon

SCUD *vb* move along swiftly ▷ *n* act of scudding

SCUDDED ▸ **scud**

SCUDDER ▸ **scud**

SCUDDLE *vb* scuttle

SCUDI ▸ **scudo**

SCUDLER *n* Scots word meaning leader of festivities

SCUDO *n* any of several former Italian coins

SCUDS ▸ **scud**

SCUFF *vb* drag (the feet)

while walking ▷ *n* mark caused by scuffing

SCUFFED ▸ **scuff**

SCUFFER *n* type of sandal

SCUFFLE *vb* fight in a disorderly manner ▷ *n* disorderly struggle

SCUFFS ▸ **scuff**

SCUFT *n* dialect word meaning nape of neck

SCUFTS ▸ **scuft**

SCUG *vb* shelter

SCUGGED ▸ **scug**

SCUGS ▸ **scug**

SCUL *n* old form of school

SCULCH *n* rubbish

SCULK *vb* old form of skulk

SCULKED ▸ **sculk**

SCULKER ▸ **sculk**

SCULKS ▸ **sculk**

SCULL *n* small oar ▷ *vb* row (a boat) using sculls

SCULLE *n* old form of school

SCULLED ▸ **scull**

SCULLER ▸ **scull**

SCULLES ▸ **sculle**

SCULLS ▸ **scull**

SCULP *same as* > **sculpture**

SCULPED ▸ **sculp**

SCULPIN *n* type of fish of the family which includes bullheads and sea scorpions

SCULPS ▸ **sculp**

SCULPT *same as* > **sculpture**

SCULPTS ▸ **sculpt**

SCULS ▸ **scul**

SCULTCH *same as* ▸ **sculch**

SCUM *n* impure or waste matter on the surface of a liquid ▷ *vb* remove scum from

SCUMBER *vb* old word meaning defecate

SCUMBLE *vb* soften or blend (an outline or colour) with a thin upper coat of opaque colour ▷ *n* upper layer of colour applied in this way

SCUMMED ▸ **scum**

SCUMMER ▸ **scum**

SCUMMY *adj* of, resembling, consisting of, or covered with scum

SCUMS ▸ **scum**

SCUNGE *vb* borrow ▷ *n* dirty or worthless person

SCUNGED ▸ **scunge**

SCUNGES ▸ **scunge**

SCUNGY *adj* sordid or dirty

SCUNNER *vb* feel aversion ▷ *n* strong aversion

SCUP *n* common sparid fish

of American coastal regions of the Atlantic

SCUPPER *vb* defeat or ruin ▷ *n* drain in the side of a ship

SCUPS ▸ **scup**

SCUR *n* small unattached growth of horn at the site of a normal horn in cattle

SCURF *n* flaky skin on the scalp

SCURFS ▸ **scurf**

SCURFY ▸ **scurf**

SCURRED ▸ **scur**

SCURRIL *adj* old word meaning vulgar

SCURRY *vb* move hastily ▷ *n* act or sound of scurrying

SCURS ▸ **scur**

SCURVY *n* disease caused by lack of vitamin C ▷ *adj* mean and despicable

SCUSE *shortened form of* ▸ **excuse**

SCUSED ▸ **scuse**

SCUSES ▸ **scuse**

SCUSING ▸ **scuse**

SCUT *n* short tail of the hare, rabbit, or deer

SCUTA ▸ **scutum**

SCUTAGE *n* payment sometimes exacted by a lord from his vassal in lieu of military service

SCUTAL ▸ **scute**

SCUTATE *adj* (of animals) having or covered with large bony or horny plates

SCUTCH *vb* separate the fibres from the woody part of (flax) by pounding ▷ *n* tool used for this

SCUTE *n* horny or chitinous plate that makes up part of the exoskeleton in armadillos, etc

SCUTES ▸ **scute**

SCUTS ▸ **scut**

SCUTTER *informal word for* ▸ **scurry**

SCUTTLE *n* fireside container for coal ▷ *vb* run with short quick steps

SCUTUM *n* middle of three plates into which the notum of an insect's thorax is divided

SCUZZ *n* dirt

SCUZZES ▸ **scuzz**

SCUZZY *adj* unkempt, dirty, or squalid

SCYBALA > **scybalum**

SCYE *n* Scots word meaning sleeve-hole

SCYES ▸ **scye**

SCYPHI ▸ **scyphus**

SCYPHUS *n* ancient Greek two-handled drinking cup without a footed base

SCYTALE *n* coded message in ancient Sparta

SCYTHE *n* long-handled tool with a curved blade for cutting grass ▷ *vb* cut with a scythe

SCYTHED ▸ **scythe**

SCYTHER ▸ **scythe**

SCYTHES ▸ **scythe**

SDAINE *vb* old form of disdain

SDAINED ▸ **sdaine**

SDAINES ▸ **sdaine**

SDAYN *vb* old form of disdain

SDAYNED ▸ **sdayn**

SDAYNS ▸ **sdayn**

SDEIGN *vb* old form of disdain

SDEIGNE *vb* old form of disdain

SDEIGNS ▸ **sdeign**

SDEIN *vb* old form of disdain

SDEINED ▸ **sdein**

SDEINS ▸ **sdein**

SEA *n* mass of salt water covering three quarters of the earth's surface

SEABAG *n* canvas bag for holding a sailor's belongings

SEABAGS ▸ **seabag**

SEABANK *n* sea shore

SEABED *n* bottom of sea

SEABEDS ▸ **seabed**

SEABIRD *n* bird that lives on the sea

SEABOOT *n* sailor's waterproof boot

SEACOCK *n* valve in the hull of a vessel below the water line for admitting sea water or for pumping out bilge water

SEADOG *another word for* ▸ **fogbow**

SEADOGS ▸ **seadog**

SEAFOLK *n* people who sail sea

SEAFOOD *n* edible saltwater fish or shellfish

SEAFOWL *n* seabird

SEAGIRT *adj* surrounded by the sea

SEAGULL *n* gull

SEAHAWK *n* skua

SEAHOG *n* porpoise

SEAHOGS ▸ **seahog**

SEAKALE *n* European coastal plant

SEAL *n* piece of wax, lead, etc with a special design impressed upon it, attached to a letter or document as a mark of authentication ▷ *vb* close with or as if with a seal

SEALANT *n* any substance used for sealing

SEALCH *Scots word for* ▸ **seal**

SEALCHS ▸ **sealch**

SEALED *adj* (of a road) having a hard surface

SEALER *n* person or thing that seals

SEALERS ▸ **sealer**

SEALERY *n* occupation of hunting seals

SEALGH *Scots word for* ▸ **seal**

SEALGHS ▸ **sealgh**

SEALIFT *vb* transport by ship

SEALINE *n* company running regular sailings

SEALING ▸ **seal**

SEALS ▸ **seal**

SEALWAX *n* sealing wax

SEAM *n* line where two edges are joined, as by stitching ▷ *vb* mark with furrows or wrinkles

SEAMAID *n* mermaid

SEAMAN *n* sailor

SEAMARK *n* aid to navigation, such as a conspicuous object on a shore used as a guide

SEAME *n* old word meaning grease

SEAMED ▸ **seam**

SEAMEN ▸ **seaman**

SEAMER *n* fast bowler who makes the ball bounce on its seam so that it will change direction

SEAMERS ▸ **seamer**

SEAMES ▸ **seame**

SEAMIER ▸ **seamy**

SEAMING ▸ **seam**

SEAMS ▸ **seam**

SEAMSET *n* tool for flattening seams in metal

SEAMY *adj* sordid

SEAN *vb* fish with seine net

SEANCE *n* meeting at which spiritualists attempt to communicate with the dead

SEANCES ▸ **seance**

SEANED ▸ **sean**

SEANING ▸ **sean**
SEANS ▸ **sean**
SEAPORT *n* town or city with a harbour for boats and ships
SEAR *vb* scorch, burn the surface of ▷ *n* mark caused by searing ▷ *adj* dried up
SEARAT *n* pirate
SEARATS ▸ **searat**
SEARCE *vb* sift
SEARCED ▸ **searce**
SEARCES ▸ **searce**
SEARCH *vb* examine closely in order to find something ▷ *n* searching
SEARE *adj* old word meaning dry and withered
SEARED ▸ **sear**
SEARER ▸ **sear**
SEAREST ▸ **sear**
SEARING ▸ **sear**
SEARS ▸ **sear**
SEAS ▸ **sea**
SEASE *vb* old form of seize
SEASED ▸ **sease**
SEASES ▸ **sease**
SEASICK *adj* suffering from nausea caused by the motion of a ship
SEASIDE *n* area, esp a holiday resort, on the coast
SEASING ▸ **sease**
SEASON *n* one of four divisions of the year, each of which has characteristic weather conditions ▷ *vb* flavour with salt, herbs, etc
SEASONS ▸ **season**
SEASURE *n* old form of seizure
SEAT *n* thing designed or used for sitting on ▷ *vb* cause to sit
SEATED ▸ **seat**
SEATER *n* person or thing that seats
SEATERS ▸ **seater**
SEATING *n* supply or arrangement of seats ▷ *adj* of or relating to the provision of places to sit
SEATS ▸ **seat**
SEAWALL *n* wall built to prevent encroachment or erosion by the sea
SEAWAN *n* shell beads, usually unstrung, used by certain North American Indians as money
SEAWANS ▸ **seawan**
SEAWANT *n* Native

American name for silver coins
SEAWARD *same as* > **seawards**
SEAWARE *n* any of numerous large coarse seaweeds
SEAWAY *n* waterway giving access to an inland port, navigable by ocean-going ships
SEAWAYS ▸ **seaway**
SEAWEED *n* plant growing in the sea
SEAWIFE *n* variety of sea fish
SEAWORM *n* marine worm
SEAZE *vb* old form of seize
SEAZED ▸ **seaze**
SEAZES ▸ **seaze**
SEAZING ▸ **seaze**
SEBACIC *adj* derived from sebacic acid, a white crystalline acid
SEBASIC *same as* ▸ **sebacic**
SEBATE *n* salt of sebacic acid
SEBATES ▸ **sebate**
SEBIFIC *adj* producing fat
SEBUM *n* oily substance secreted by the sebaceous glands
SEBUMS ▸ **sebum**
SEBUNDY *n* irregular soldier in India
SEC *same as* ▸ **secant**
SECANT *n* (in trigonometry) the ratio of the length of the hypotenuse to the length of the adjacent side in a right-angled triangle
SECANTS ▸ **secant**
SECCO *n* wall painting done on dried plaster with tempera or pigments ground in limewater
SECCOS ▸ **secco**
SECEDE *vb* withdraw formally from a political alliance or federation
SECEDED ▸ **secede**
SECEDER ▸ **secede**
SECEDES ▸ **secede**
SECERN *vb* (of a gland or follicle) to secrete
SECERNS ▸ **secern**
SECESH *n* secessionist in US Civil War
SECH *n* hyperbolic secant
SECHS ▸ **sech**
SECKEL *same as* ▸ **seckle**
SECKELS ▸ **seckel**
SECKLE *n* type of pear

SECKLES ▸ **seckle**
SECLUDE *vb* keep (a person) from contact with others
SECO *adj* (of wine) dry
SECONAL *n* tradename for secobarbitol
SECOND *adj* coming directly after the first ▷ *n* person or thing coming second ▷ *vb* express formal support for (a motion proposed in a meeting)
SECONDE *n* second of eight positions from which a parry or attack can be made in fencing
SECONDI ▸ **secondo**
SECONDO *n* left-hand part in a piano duet
SECONDS ▸ **second**
SECPAR *n* distance unit in astronomy
SECPARS ▸ **secpar**
SECRECY *n* state of being secret
SECRET *adj* kept from the knowledge of others ▷ *n* something kept secret
SECRETA *n* secretions
SECRETE *vb* (of an organ, gland, etc) produce and release (a substance)
SECRETS ▸ **secret**
SECS ▸ **sec**
SECT *n* often disparaging term for a subdivision of a religious or political group, esp one with extreme beliefs
SECTARY *n* member of a sect
SECTILE *adj* able to be cut smoothly
SECTION *n* part cut off ▷ *vb* cut or divide into sections
SECTOR *n* part or subdivision ▷ *vb* divide into sectors
SECTORS ▸ **sector**
SECTS ▸ **sect**
SECULAR *adj* worldly, as opposed to sacred ▷ *n* member of the secular clergy
SECULUM *n* age in astronomy
SECUND *adj* having or designating parts arranged on or turned to one side of the axis
SECURE *adj* free from danger ▷ *vb* obtain
SECURED ▸ **secure**

S

SECURER ▶ secure
SECURES ▶ secure
SED old spelling of ▶ **said**
SEDAN same as ▶ **saloon**
SEDANS ▶ sedan
SEDARIM ▶ seder
SEDATE adj calm and dignified ▷ vb give a sedative drug to
SEDATED ▶ sedate
SEDATER ▶ sedate
SEDATES ▶ sedate
SEDENT adj seated
SEDER n Jewish ceremonial meal held on the first night or first two nights of Passover
SEDERS ▶ seder
SEDES Latin word for ▶ **seat**
SEDGE n coarse grasslike plant growing on wet ground
SEDGED adj having sedge
SEDGES ▶ sedge
SEDGIER ▶ sedge
SEDGY ▶ sedge
SEDILE n seat for clergy in church
SEDILIA n group of three seats where the celebrant and ministers sit at certain points during High Mass
SEDUCE vb persuade into sexual intercourse
SEDUCED ▶ seduce
SEDUCER n person who entices, allures, or seduces
SEDUCES ▶ seduce
SEDUM n rock plant
SEDUMS ▶ sedum
SEE vb perceive with the eyes or mind ▷ n diocese of a bishop
SEEABLE ▶ see
SEED n mature fertilized grain of a plant ▷ vb sow with seed
SEEDBED n area of soil prepared for the growing of seedlings before they are transplanted
SEEDBOX n part of plant that contains seeds
SEEDED ▶ seed
SEEDER n person or thing that seeds
SEEDERS ▶ seeder
SEEDIER ▶ seedy
SEEDILY ▶ seedy
SEEDING ▶ seed
SEEDLIP n basket holding seeds to be sown
SEEDMAN n seller of seeds

SEEDMEN ▶ seedman
SEEDPOD n carpel enclosing the seeds of a flowering plant
SEEDS ▶ seed
SEEDY adj shabby
SEEING ▶ see
SEEINGS ▶ see
SEEK vb try to find or obtain
SEEKER ▶ seek
SEEKERS ▶ seek
SEEKING ▶ seek
SEEKS ▶ seek
SEEL vb sew up the eyelids of (a hawk or falcon) so as to render it quiet and tame
SEELD adj old word meaning rare
SEELED ▶ seel
SEELIE pl n good benevolent fairies
SEELIER ▶ seely
SEELING ▶ seel
SEELS ▶ seel
SEELY adj old word meaning happy
SEEM vb appear to be
SEEMED ▶ seem
SEEMER ▶ seem
SEEMERS ▶ seem
SEEMING adj apparent but not real ▷ n outward or false appearance
SEEMLY adj proper or fitting ▷ adv properly or decorously
SEEMS ▶ seem
SEEN ▶ see
SEEP vb trickle through slowly, ooze ▷ n small spring or place where water, oil, etc, has oozed through the ground
SEEPAGE n act or process of seeping
SEEPED ▶ seep
SEEPIER ▶ seepy
SEEPING ▶ seep
SEEPS ▶ seep
SEEPY adj tending to seep
SEER n person who sees
SEERESS ▶ seer
SEERS ▶ seer
SEES ▶ see
SEESAW n plank balanced in the middle so that two people seated on either end ride up and down alternately ▷ vb move up and down
SEESAWS ▶ seesaw
SEETHE vb be very agitated ▷ n act or state of seething

SEETHED ▶ seethe
SEETHER ▶ seethe
SEETHES ▶ seethe
SEEWING n suing
SEFER n scrolls of the Law
SEG n metal stud on shoe sole
SEGAR n cigar
SEGARS ▶ segar
SEGETAL adj (of weeds) growing amongst crops
SEGGAR n box in which pottery is baked
SEGGARS ▶ seggar
SEGHOL n pronunciation mark in Hebrew
SEGHOLS ▶ seghol
SEGMENT n one of several sections into which something may be divided ▷ vb divide into segments
SEGNI ▶ segno
SEGNO n sign at the beginning or end of a section directed to be repeated
SEGNOS ▶ segno
SEGO n American variety of lily
SEGOL same as ▶ **seghol**
SEGOLS ▶ segol
SEGOS ▶ sego
SEGS ▶ seg
SEGUE vb proceed from one section or piece of music to another without a break ▷ n practice or an instance of playing music in this way
SEGUED ▶ segue
SEGUES ▶ segue
SEHRI n meal eaten before sunrise by Muslims fasting during Ramadan
SEHRIS ▶ sehri
SEI n type of rorqual
SEICHE n periodic oscillation of the surface of an enclosed or semienclosed body of water
SEICHES ▶ seiche
SEIDEL n vessel for drinking beer
SEIDELS ▶ seidel
SEIF n long ridge of blown sand in a desert
SEIFS ▶ seif
SEIK Scots word for ▶ **sick**
SEIKER ▶ seik
SEIKEST ▶ seik
SEIL vb dialect word meaning strain
SEILED ▶ seil

SEILING ▶ seil

SEILS ▶ seil

SEINE n large fishing net that hangs vertically from floats ▷ vb catch (fish) using this net

SEINED ▶ seine

SEINER ▶ seine

SEINERS ▶ seine

SEINES ▶ seine

SEINING ▶ seine

SEIR n fish of Indian seas

SEIRS ▶ seir

SEIS ▶ sei

SEISE vb put into legal possession of (property, etc)

SEISED ▶ seise

SEISER ▶ seise

SEISERS ▶ seise

SEISES ▶ seise

SEISIN n feudal possession of an estate in land

SEISING ▶ seise

SEISINS ▶ seisin

SEISM n earthquake

SEISMAL adj of earthquakes

SEISMIC adj relating to earthquakes

SEISMS ▶ seism

SEISOR n person who takes seisin

SEISORS ▶ seisor

SEISURE n act of seisin

SEITAN same as ▶ seiten

SEITANS ▶ seitan

SEITEN n gluten from wheat

SEITENS ▶ seiten

SEITIES ▶ seity

SEITY n selfhood

SEIZE vb take hold of forcibly or quickly

SEIZED ▶ seize

SEIZER ▶ seize

SEIZERS ▶ seize

SEIZES ▶ seize

SEIZIN same as ▶ seisin

SEIZING n binding used for holding together two ropes, two spars, etc, esp by lashing with a separate rope

SEIZINS ▶ seizin

SEIZOR n person who takes seisin

SEIZORS ▶ seizor

SEIZURE n sudden violent attack of an illness

SEJANT adj (of a beast) shown seated

SEJEANT same as ▶ sejant

SEKOS n holy place

SEKOSES ▶ sekos

SEKT n German sparkling wine

SEKTS ▶ sekt

SEL Scots word for ▶ self

SELAH n Hebrew word of unknown meaning occurring in the Old Testament psalms, and thought to be a musical direction

SELAHS ▶ selah

SELD adj old word meaning rare

SELDOM adv not often, rarely

SELE n old word meaning happiness

SELECT vb pick out or choose ▷ adj chosen in preference to others

SELECTA n disc jockey

SELECTS ▶ select

SELENIC adj of or containing selenium, esp in the hexavalent state

SELES ▶ sele

SELF n distinct individuality or identity of a person or thing ▷ pron myself, yourself, himself, or herself ▷ vb reproduce by oneself

SELFDOM n selfhood

SELFED ▶ self

SELFING ▶ self

SELFISH adj caring too much about oneself and not enough about others

SELFISM n emphasis on self

SELFIST ▶ selfism

SELFS ▶ self

SELKIE same as ▶ silkie

SELKIES ▶ selkie

SELL vb exchange (something) for money ▷ n manner of selling

SELLA n area of bone in body

SELLAE ▶ sella

SELLAS ▶ sella

SELLE n old word meaning seat

SELLER n person who sells

SELLERS ▶ seller

SELLES ▶ selle

SELLING n the act of providing (e.g. goods or services) to customers in exchange for money

SELLOFF n act of selling cheaply

SELLOUT n performance of a show etc for which all the tickets are sold

SELLS ▶ sell

SELS ▶ sel

SELSYN same as ▶ synchro

SELSYNS ▶ selsyn

SELTZER n natural effervescent water containing minerals

SELVA n dense equatorial forest characterized by tall broad-leaved evergreen trees, lianas, etc

SELVAGE n edge of cloth, woven so as to prevent unravelling ▷ vb edge or border

SELVAS ▶ selva

SELVES ▶ self

SEMATIC adj (of the conspicuous coloration of certain animals) acting as a warning, esp to potential predators

SEMBLE vb seem

SEMBLED ▶ semble

SEMBLES ▶ semble

SEME adj dotted (with)

SEMEE same as ▶ seme

SEMEED adj seme

SEMEIA ▶ semeion

SEMEION n unit of metre in ancient poetry

SEMEME n meaning of a morpheme

SEMEMES ▶ sememe

SEMEMIC ▶ sememe

SEMEN n sperm-carrying fluid produced by male animals

SEMENS ▶ semen

SEMES ▶ seme

SEMI n semidetached house

SEMIDRY adj partly dry

SEMIE n historical name for a student in second year at a Scottish university

SEMIES ▶ semie

SEMIFIT adj not fully fit

SEMILOG adj semilogarithmic

SEMIMAT adj semimatt

SEMINA ▶ semen

SEMINAL adj original and influential

SEMINAR n meeting of a group of students for discussion

SEMIPED n measure in poetic metre

SEMIPRO n semiprofessional

SEMIRAW adj not fully cooked or processed

SEMIS ▶ semi

S

SEMISES ▶ semi
SEMITAR old spelling of > **scimitar**
SEMMIT n vest
SEMMITS ▶ semmit
SEMPER adv Latin word meaning always
SEMPLE adj Scots word meaning simple
SEMPLER ▶ semple
SEMPRE adv (preceding a tempo or dynamic marking) always
SEMSEM n sesame
SEMSEMS ▶ semsem
SEN n monetary unit of Brunei, Cambodia, Indonesia, Malaysia, and formerly of Japan
SENA n (in India) the army: used in the names of certain paramilitary political organizations
SENARII ▶ senarius
SENARY adj of or relating to the number six
SENAS ▶ sena
SENATE n main governing body at some universities
SENATES ▶ senate
SENATOR n member of a senate
SEND vb cause (a person or thing) to go to or be taken or transmitted to a place
SENDAL n fine silk fabric used, esp in the Middle Ages, for ceremonial clothing, etc
SENDALS ▶ sendal
SENDED vb old word meaning sent
SENDER ▶ send
SENDERS ▶ send
SENDING ▶ send
SENDOFF n demonstration of good wishes at a person's departure ▷ vb dispatch (something, such as a letter)
SENDS ▶ send
SENDUP n parody or imitation
SENDUPS ▶ sendup
SENE n money unit in Samoa
SENECA same as ▶ **senega**
SENECAS ▶ seneca
SENECIO n type of plant of the genus which includes groundsels and ragworts
SENEGA n milkwort plant of the eastern US, with small

white flowers
SENEGAS ▶ senega
SENES ▶ sene
SENGI n African shrew
SENHOR n Portuguese term of address for man
SENHORA n Portuguese term of address for woman
SENHORS ▶ senhor
SENILE adj mentally or physically weak because of old age ▷ n senile person
SENILES ▶ senile
SENIOR adj superior in rank or standing ▷ n senior person
SENIORS ▶ senior
SENITI n money unit in Tonga
SENNA n tropical plant
SENNAS ▶ senna
SENNET n fanfare: used as a stage direction in Elizabethan drama
SENNETS ▶ sennet
SENNIT n flat braided cordage used on ships
SENNITS ▶ sennit
SENOPIA n short-sightedness in old age
SENOR n Spanish term of address equivalent to sir or Mr
SENORA n Spanish term of address equivalent to madam or Mrs
SENORAS ▶ senora
SENORES ▶ senor
SENORS ▶ senor
SENRYU n Japanese short poem
SENS ▶ sen
SENSA ▶ sensum
SENSATE adj perceived by the senses ▷ vb make sensate
SENSE n any of the faculties of perception or feeling ▷ vb perceive
SENSED ▶ sense
SENSEI n martial arts teacher
SENSEIS ▶ sensei
SENSES ▶ sense
SENSI same as ▶ **sensei**
SENSILE adj capable of feeling
SENSING ▶ sense
SENSIS ▶ sensi
SENSISM n theory that ideas spring from senses
SENSIST ▶ sensism
SENSOR n device that

detects or measures the presence of something, such as radiation
SENSORS ▶ sensor
SENSORY adj of the senses or sensation
SENSUAL adj giving pleasure to the body and senses rather than the mind
SENSUM n sensation detached from the information it conveys and also from its source in the external world
SENT n former monetary unit of Estonia
SENTE n money unit in Lesotho
SENTED ▶ send
SENTI ▶ sent
SENTIMO n money unit in Philippines
SENTING ▶ send
SENTRY n soldier on watch
SENTS ▶ sent
SENVIES ▶ senvy
SENVY n mustard
SENZA prep without
SEPAD vb suppose
SEPADS ▶ sepad
SEPAL n leaflike division of the calyx of a flower
SEPALED ▶ sepal
SEPALS ▶ sepal
SEPHEN n stingray
SEPHENS ▶ sephen
SEPIA n reddish-brown pigment ▷ adj dark reddish-brown, like the colour of very old photographs
SEPIAS ▶ sepia
SEPIC adj of sepia
SEPIOST n cuttlefish bone
SEPIUM n cuttlefish bone
SEPIUMS ▶ sepium
SEPMAG adj designating a film or television programme for which the sound is recorded on separate magnetic material and run in synchronism with the picture
SEPOY n (formerly) Indian soldier in the service of the British
SEPOYS ▶ sepoy
SEPPUKU n Japanese ritual suicide
SEPS n species of lizard
SEPSES ▶ sepsis
SEPSIS n poisoning caused by pus-forming bacteria

SEPT n clan, esp in Ireland or Scotland

SEPTA ▶ **septum**

SEPTAGE n waste removed from septic tank

SEPTAL adj of or relating to a septum

SEPTATE adj divided by septa

SEPTET n group of seven performers

SEPTETS ▶ **septet**

SEPTIC adj (of a wound) infected ▷ n infected wound

SEPTICS ▶ **septic**

SEPTIME n seventh of eight basic positions from which a parry can be made in fencing

SEPTS ▶ **sept**

SEPTUM n dividing partition between two cavities in the body

SEPTUMS ▶ **septum**

SEPTUOR n group of seven musicians

SEQUEL n novel, play, or film that continues the story of an earlier one

SEQUELA n any abnormal bodily condition or disease related to or arising from a pre-existing disease

SEQUELS ▶ **sequel**

SEQUENT adj following in order or succession ▷ n something that follows

SEQUIN n small ornamental metal disc on a garment ▷ vb apply sequins

SEQUINS ▶ **sequin**

SEQUOIA n giant Californian coniferous tree

| This word for a redwood tree is one of the most frequently played bonuses using the Q, a great one to remember as it also clears out a surplus of vowels.

SER n unit of weight used in India, usually taken as one fortieth of a maund

SERA ▶ **serum**

SERAC n pinnacle of ice among crevasses on a glacier, usually on a steep slope

SERACS ▶ **serac**

SERAFIN n old silver coin of Goa

SERAI n (in the East) a caravanserai or inn

SERAIL same as ▶ **seraglio**

SERAILS ▶ **serail**

SERAIS ▶ **serai**

SERAL ▶ **sere**

SERANG n native captain of a crew of sailors in the East Indies

SERANGS ▶ **serang**

SERAPE n blanket-like shawl often of brightly-coloured wool worn by men in Latin America

SERAPES ▶ **serape**

SERAPH n member of the highest order of angels

SERAPHS ▶ **seraph**

SERDAB n secret chamber in an ancient Egyptian tomb

SERDABS ▶ **serdab**

SERE adj dried up or withered ▷ n series of changes occurring in the ecological succession of a particular community ▷ vb sear

SERED ▶ **sere**

SEREIN n fine rain falling from a clear sky after sunset, esp in the tropics

SEREINS ▶ **serein**

SERENE adj calm, peaceful ▷ vb make serene

SERENED ▶ **serene**

SERENER ▶ **serene**

SERENES ▶ **serene**

SERER ▶ **sere**

SERES ▶ **sere**

SEREST ▶ **sere**

SERF n medieval farm labourer who could not leave the land he worked on

SERFAGE ▶ **serf**

SERFDOM ▶ **serf**

SERFISH ▶ **serf**

SERFS ▶ **serf**

SERGE n strong woollen fabric

SERGED adj with sewn seam

SERGER n sewing machine attachment for finishing seams

SERGERS ▶ **serger**

SERGES ▶ **serge**

SERGING n type of sewing

SERIAL n story or play produced in successive instalments ▷ adj of or forming a series

SERIALS ▶ **serial**

SERIATE adj forming a series

▷ vb form into a series

SERIC adj of silk

SERICIN n gelatinous protein found on the fibres of raw silk

SERICON n solution used in alchemy

SERIEMA n either of two cranelike South American birds

SERIES n group or succession of related things, usu arranged in order

SERIF n small line at the extremities of a main stroke in a type character

SERIFED adj having serifs

SERIFS ▶ **serif**

SERIN n any of various small yellow-and-brown finches

SERINE n sweet-tasting amino acid

SERINES ▶ **serine**

SERING ▶ **sere**

SERINGA n any of several trees that yield rubber

SERINS ▶ **serin**

SERIOUS adj giving cause for concern

SERIPH same as ▶ **serif**

SERIPHS ▶ **seriph**

SERK Scots word for ▶ **shirt**

SERKALI n government in Africa

SERKS ▶ **serk**

SERMON n speech on a religious or moral subject by a clergyman in a church service ▷ vb deliver a sermon

SERMONS ▶ **sermon**

SERON n crate

SERONS ▶ **seron**

SEROON n crate

SEROONS ▶ **seroon**

SEROPUS n liquid consisting of serum and pus

SEROSA n one of the thin membranes surrounding the embryo in an insect's egg

SEROSAE ▶ **serosa**

SEROSAL ▶ **serosa**

SEROSAS ▶ **serosa**

SEROUS adj of, containing, or like serum

SEROVAR n subdivision of species

SEROW n either of two antelopes of mountainous regions of S and SE Asia

SEROWS ▶ **serow**

SERPENT n snake
SERPIGO n any progressive skin eruption, such as ringworm or herpes
SERR vb press close together
SERRA n sawlike part or organ
SERRAE ▶ serra
SERRAN n species of fish
SERRANO n type of Spanish ham
SERRANS ▶ serran
SERRAS ▶ serra
SERRATE adj (of leaves) having a margin of forward pointing teeth ▷ vb make serrate
SERRATI > serratus
SERRE vb press close together
SERRED ▶ serre
SERRES ▶ serre
SERRIED adj in close formation
SERRIES ▶ serry
SERRING ▶ serre
SERRS ▶ serr
SERRY vb close together
SERS ▶ ser
SERUEWE vb old word meaning survey
SERUM n watery fluid left after blood has clotted
SERUMAL ▶ serum
SERUMS ▶ serum
SERVAL n feline African mammal
SERVALS ▶ serval
SERVANT n person employed to do household work for another ▷ vb work as a servant
SERVE vb work for (a person, community, or cause) ▷ n act of serving the ball
SERVED ▶ serve
SERVER n player who serves in racket games
SERVERS ▶ server
SERVERY n room from which food is served
SERVES ▶ serve
SERVEWE vb old word meaning survey
SERVICE n serving ▷ adj serving the public rather than producing goods ▷ vb provide a service or services to
SERVILE adj too eager to obey people, fawning

▷ n servile person
SERVING n portion of food
SERVLET n small program that runs on a web server often accessing databases in response to client input
SERVO n servomechanism ▷ adj of a servomechanism
SERVOS ▶ servo
SESAME n plant cultivated for its seeds and oil, which are used in cooking
SESAMES ▶ sesame
SESE interj exclamation found in Shakespeare
SESELI n garden plant
SESELIS ▶ seseli
SESEY interj exclamation found in Shakespeare
SESH short for ▶ session
SESHES ▶ sesh
SESS n old word meaning tax
SESSA interj exclamation found in Shakespeare
SESSES ▶ sess
SESSILE adj (of flowers or leaves) having no stalk
SESSION n period spent in an activity
SESTET n last six lines of a sonnet
SESTETS ▶ sestet
SESTETT n group of six
SESTINA n elaborate verse form of Italian origin
SESTINE n poem of six lines
SESTON n type of plankton
SESTONS ▶ seston
SET vb put in a specified position or state ▷ n setting or being set ▷ adj fixed or established beforehand
SETA n (in invertebrates and some plants) any bristle or bristle-like appendage
SETAE ▶ seta
SETAL ▶ seta
SETBACK n anything that delays progress
SETLINE n any of various types of fishing line
SETNESS ▶ set
SETOFF n counterbalance
SETOFFS ▶ setoff
SETON n surgical thread inserted below the skin
SETONS ▶ seton
SETOSE adj covered with setae
SETOUS ▶ seta
SETOUT n beginning or outset

SETOUTS ▶ setout
SETS ▶ set
SETT n badger's burrow
SETTEE n couch
SETTEES ▶ settee
SETTER n long-haired gun dog ▷ vb treat with a piece of setterwort
SETTERS ▶ setter
SETTING ▶ set
SETTLE vb arrange or put in order ▷ n long wooden bench with high back and arms
SETTLED ▶ settle
SETTLER n colonist
SETTLES ▶ settle
SETTLOR n person who settles property on someone
SETTS ▶ sett
SETUALE n valerian
SETULE n small bristle
SETULES ▶ setule
SETUP n way in which anything is organized or arranged
SETUPS ▶ setup
SETWALL n valerian
SEVEN n one more than six ▷ adj amounting to seven ▷ determiner amounting to seven
SEVENS n Rugby Union match or series of matches played with seven players on each side
SEVENTH n (of) number seven in a series ▷ adj coming after the sixth and before the eighth ▷ adv after the sixth person, position, event, etc
SEVENTY n ten times seven ▷ adj amounting to seventy ▷ determiner amounting to seventy
SEVER vb cut through or off
SEVERAL adj some, a few ▷ n individual person
SEVERE adj strict or harsh
SEVERED ▶ sever
SEVERER ▶ severe
SEVERS ▶ sever
SEVERY n part of vaulted ceiling
SEVICHE n Mexican fish dish
SEVRUGA n species of sturgeon
SEW vb join with thread repeatedly passed through with a needle
SEWABLE ▶ sew

SEWAGE n waste matter or excrement carried away in sewers

SEWAGES ▶ sewage

SEWAN same as ▶ seawan

SEWANS ▶ sewan

SEWAR n Asian dagger

SEWARS ▶ sewar

SEWED ▶ sew

SEWEL n scarecrow

SEWELS ▶ sewel

SEWEN same as ▶ sewin

SEWENS ▶ sewen

SEWER n drain to remove waste water and sewage ▷ vb provide with sewers

SEWERED ▶ sewer

SEWERS ▶ sewer

SEWIN n sea trout

SEWING ▶ sew

SEWINGS ▶ sew

SEWINS ▶ sewin

SEWN ▶ sew

SEWS ▶ sew

SEX n state of being male or female ▷ vb find out the sex of ▷ adj of sexual matters

SEXED adj having a specified degree of sexuality

SEXER n person checking sex of chickens

SEXERS ▶ sexer

SEXES ▶ sex

SEXFID adj split into six

SEXFOIL n flower with six petals or leaves

SEXIER ▶ sexy

SEXIEST ▶ sexy

SEXILY ▶ sexy

SEXING ▶ sex

SEXINGS ▶ sexing

SEXISM n discrimination on the basis of a person's sex

SEXISMS ▶ sexism

SEXIST ▶ sexism

SEXISTS ▶ sexism

SEXLESS adj neither male nor female

SEXPERT n person who professes a knowledge of sexual matters

SEXPOT n person, esp a young woman, considered as being sexually very attractive

SEXPOTS ▶ sexpot

SEXT n fourth of the seven canonical hours of the divine office or the prayers prescribed for it: originally the sixth hour of the day (noon)

SEXTAIN same as ▶ sestina

SEXTAN adj (of a fever) marked by paroxysms that recur after an interval of five days

SEXTANS n Roman coin

SEXTANT n navigator's instrument for measuring angles to calculate one's position

SEXTET n group of six performers

SEXTETS ▶ sextet

SEXTETT n sextet

SEXTILE n one of five values of a variable dividing its distribution into six groups with equal frequencies

SEXTO same as ▶ sixmo

SEXTON n official in charge of a church and churchyard

SEXTONS ▶ sexton

SEXTOS ▶ sexto

SEXTS ▶ sext

SEXTUOR n sextet

SEXUAL adj of or characterized by sex

SEXY adj sexually exciting or attractive

SEY n Scots word meaning part of cow carcase

SEYEN n old form of scion

SEYENS ▶ seyen

SEYS ▶ sey

SEYSURE n old form of seizure

SEZ vb informal spelling of 'says'

> **Sez** is a short informal form of **says**, very useful for disposing of the Z.

SFERICS same as ▶ spherics

SFUMATO n gradual transition between areas of different colour in painting

SH interj hush

SHA interj be quiet

SHABASH interj (in Indian English) bravo or well done

SHABBLE n Scots word meaning old sword

SHABBY adj worn or dilapidated in appearance

SHACK n rough hut ▷ vb evade (work or responsibility)

SHACKED ▶ shack

SHACKLE n metal ring for securing a person's wrists or ankles ▷ vb fasten with shackles

SHACKO same as ▶ shako

SHACKOS ▶ shacko

SHACKS ▶ shack

SHAD n herring-like fish

SHADE n relative darkness ▷ vb screen from light

SHADED ▶ shade

SHADER ▶ shade

SHADERS ▶ shade

SHADES pl n gathering darkness at nightfall

SHADFLY American name for ▶ mayfly

SHADIER ▶ shady

SHADILY ▶ shady

SHADING n graded areas of tone indicating light and dark in a painting or drawing

SHADOOF n mechanism for raising water, esp as used in Egypt and the Near East

SHADOW n dark shape cast on a surface when something stands between a light and the surface ▷ vb cast a shadow over

SHADOWS ▶ shadow

SHADOWY adj (of a place) full of shadows

SHADS ▶ shad

SHADUF same as ▶ shadoof

SHADUFS ▶ shaduf

SHADY adj situated in or giving shade

SHAFT n long narrow straight handle of a tool or weapon ▷ vb treat badly

SHAFTED ▶ shaft

SHAFTER ▶ shaft

SHAFTS ▶ shaft

SHAGGY adj covered with rough hair or wool

SHAH n formerly, ruler of Iran

SHAHADA n Islamic declaration of faith, repeated daily by Muslims

SHAHDOM ▶ shah

SHAHEED ▶ shahid

SHAHID n Muslim martyr

SHAHIDS ▶ shahid

SHAHS ▶ shah

SHAIKH n sheikh

SHAIKHS ▶ shaikh

SHAIRD n Scots word meaning shred

SHAIRDS ▶ shaird

SHAIRN Scots word for ▶ dung

SHAIRNS ▶ shairn

SHAITAN n (in Muslim countries) an evil spirit

SHAKE vb move quickly up and down or back and forth ▷ n shaking

SHAKED vb old form of shook

SHAKEN ▶ shake

SHAKER n container in which drinks are mixed or from which powder is shaken

SHAKERS ▶ shaker

SHAKES ▶ shake

SHAKEUP n radical reorganization

SHAKIER ▶ shaky

SHAKILY ▶ shaky

SHAKING ▶ shake

SHAKO n tall cylindrical peaked military hat with a plume

SHAKOES ▶ shako

SHAKOS ▶ shako

SHAKT vb old form of shook

SHAKUDO n Japanese alloy of copper and gold

SHAKY adj unsteady

SHALE n flaky sedimentary rock

SHALED ▶ shale

SHALES ▶ shale

SHALEY ▶ shale

SHALIER ▶ shale

SHALING ▶ shale

SHALL vb used as an auxiliary to make the future tense

SHALLI n type of fabric

SHALLIS ▶ shalli

SHALLON n American shrub

SHALLOP n light boat used for rowing in shallow water

SHALLOT n kind of small onion

SHALLOW adj not deep ▷ n shallow place in a body of water ▷ vb make or become shallow

SHALM n old woodwind instrument

SHALMS ▶ shalm

SHALOM n Jewish greeting meaning 'peace be with you'

SHALOMS ▶ shalom

SHALOT n shallot

SHALOTS ▶ shalot

SHALT singular form of the present tense (indicative mood) of ▶ shall

SHALWAR n pair of loose-fitting trousers tapering to a narrow fit around the ankles, worn in the Indian subcontinent, often with a kameez

SHALY ▶ shale

SHAM n thing or person that is not genuine ▷ adj not genuine ▷ vb fake, feign

SHAMA n Indian songbird

SHAMAL n hot northwesterly wind that blows across Iraq and the Persian Gulf

SHAMALS ▶ shamal

SHAMAN n priest of shamanism

SHAMANS ▶ shaman

SHAMAS ▶ shama

SHAMBA n (in E Africa) any field used for growing crops

SHAMBAS ▶ shamba

SHAMBLE vb walk in a shuffling awkward way ▷ n awkward or shuffling walk

SHAMBLY ▶ shamble

SHAME n painful emotion caused by awareness of having done something dishonourable or foolish ▷ vb cause to feel shame

SHAMED ▶ shame

SHAMER n cause of shame

SHAMERS ▶ shame

SHAMES ▶ shame

SHAMINA n wool blend of pashm and shahtoosh

SHAMING ▶ shame

SHAMMAS same as ▶ shammes

SHAMMED ▶ sham

SHAMMER ▶ sham

SHAMMES n official acting as the beadle, sexton, and caretaker of a synagogue

SHAMMOS same as ▶ shammes

SHAMMY n piece of chamois leather ▷ vb rub with a shammy

SHAMOIS n chamois

SHAMOS same as ▶ shammes

SHAMOY n chamois ▷ vb rub with a shamoy

SHAMOYS ▶ shamoy

SHAMPOO n liquid soap for washing hair, carpets, or upholstery ▷ vb wash with shampoo

SHAMS ▶ sham

SHAMUS n police or private detective

SHAN same as ▶ shand

SHAND n old word meaning fake coin

SHANDRY n light horse-drawn cart

SHANDS ▶ shand

SHANDY n drink made of beer and lemonade

SHANK n lower leg ▷ vb (of fruits, roots, etc) to show disease symptoms, esp discoloration

SHANKED ▶ shank

SHANKS ▶ shank

SHANNY n European blenny of rocky coastal waters

SHANS ▶ shan

SHANTEY same as ▶ shanty

SHANTI n peace

SHANTIH same as ▶ shanti

SHANTIS ▶ shanti

SHANTY n shack or crude dwelling

SHAPE n outward form of an object ▷ vb form or mould

SHAPED ▶ shape

SHAPELY adj having an attractive shape

SHAPEN vb old form of shaped

SHAPER ▶ shape

SHAPERS ▶ shape

SHAPES ▶ shape

SHAPEUP n system of hiring dockers for a day's work

SHAPING ▶ shape

SHAPS n leather over-trousers worn by cowboys

SHARD n broken piece of pottery or glass

SHARDED adj old word meaning hidden under dung

SHARDS ▶ shard

SHARE n part of something that belongs to or is contributed by a person ▷ vb give or take a share of (something)

SHARED ▶ share

SHARER ▶ share

SHARERS ▶ share

SHARES ▶ share

SHARIA n body of doctrines that regulate the lives of Muslims

SHARIAH same as ▶ sharia

SHARIAS ▶ sharia

SHARIAT n Islamic religious law

SHARIF same as ▶ sherif

SHARIFS ▶ sharif

SHARING ▶ share

SHARK n large usu predatory sea fish ▷ vb obtain (something) by cheating or deception

SHARKED ▷ **shark**

SHARKER n shark hunter

SHARKS ▷ **shark**

SHARN Scots word for ▷ **dung**

SHARNS ▷ **sharn**

SHARNY ▷ **sharn**

SHARON n as in sharon fruit persimmon

SHARP adj having a keen cutting edge or fine point ▷ adv promptly ▷ n symbol raising a note one semitone above natural pitch ▷ vb make sharp

SHARPED ▷ **sharp**

SHARPEN vb make or become sharp or sharper

SHARPER n person who cheats

SHARPIE n member of a teenage group having short hair and distinctive clothes

SHARPLY ▷ **sharp**

SHARPS ▷ **sharp**

SHARPY n swindler

SHASH vb old form of sash

SHASHED ▷ **shash**

SHASHES ▷ **shash**

SHASLIK n type of kebab

SHASTER same as ▷ **shastra**

SHASTRA n any of the sacred writings of Hinduism

SHATTER vb break into pieces ▷ n fragment

SHAUGH n old word meaning small wood

SHAUGHS ▷ **shaugh**

SHAUL vb old form of shawl

SHAULED ▷ **shaul**

SHAULS ▷ **shaul**

SHAVE vb remove (hair) from (the face, head, or body) (with a razor or shaver ▷ n shaving

SHAVED ▷ **shave**

SHAVEN adj closely shaved or tonsured

SHAVER n electric razor

SHAVERS ▷ **shaver**

SHAVES ▷ **shaul**

SHAVIE n Scots word meaning trick

SHAVIES ▷ **shavie**

SHAVING ▷ **shave**

SHAW n small wood ▷ vb show

SHAWED ▷ **shaw**

SHAWING ▷ **shaw**

SHAWL n piece of cloth worn over a woman's

shoulders or wrapped around a baby ▷ vb cover with a shawl

SHAWLED ▷ **shawl**

SHAWLS ▷ **shawl**

SHAWM n medieval form of the oboe with a conical bore and flaring bell

SHAWMS ▷ **shawm**

SHAWN same as ▷ **shawm**

SHAWS ▷ **shaw**

SHAY dialect word for ▷ **chaise**

SHAYA n Indian plant

SHAYAS ▷ **shaya**

SHAYS ▷ **shay**

SHAZAM interj magic slogan

SHCHI n Russian cabbage soup

SHCHIS ▷ **shchi**

SHE pron female person or animal previously mentioned ▷ n female person or animal

SHEA n tropical African tree

SHEAF n bundle of papers ▷ vb tie into a sheaf

SHEAFED ▷ **sheaf**

SHEAFS ▷ **sheaf**

SHEAFY ▷ **sheaf**

SHEAL vb old word meaning shell

SHEALED ▷ **sheal**

SHEALS ▷ **sheal**

SHEAR vb clip hair or wool from ▷ n breakage caused through strain or twisting

SHEARED ▷ **shear**

SHEARER ▷ **shear**

SHEARS ▷ **shear**

SHEAS ▷ **shea**

SHEATH n close-fitting cover, esp for a knife or sword

SHEATHE vb put into a sheath

SHEATHS ▷ **sheath**

SHEATHY ▷ **sheathe**

SHEAVE vb gather or bind into sheaves ▷ n wheel with a grooved rim, esp one used as a pulley

SHEAVED ▷ **sheave**

SHEAVES ▷ **sheaf**

SHEBANG n situation, matter, or affair

SHEBEAN same as ▷ **shebeen**

SHEBEEN n place where alcohol is sold illegally ▷ vb run a shebeen

SHED n building used for

storage or shelter or as a workshop ▷ vb get rid of

SHEDDED ▷ **shed**

SHEDDER n person or thing that sheds

SHEDFUL n quantity or amount contained in a shed

SHEDS ▷ **shed**

SHEEL vb old word meaning shell

SHEELED ▷ **sheel**

SHEELS ▷ **sheel**

SHEEN n glistening brightness on the surface of something ▷ adj shining and beautiful ▷ vb give a sheen to

SHEENED ▷ **sheen**

SHEENS ▷ **sheen**

SHEEP n ruminant animal bred for wool and meat

SHEEPLE pl n informal derogatory word for people who follow the majority in matters of opinion, taste, etc

SHEEPO n person employed to bring sheep to the catching pen in a shearing shed

SHEEPOS ▷ **sheepo**

SHEEPY ▷ **sheep**

SHEER adj absolute, complete ▷ adv steeply ▷ vb change course suddenly ▷ n any transparent fabric used for making garments

SHEERED ▷ **sheer**

SHEERER ▷ **sheer**

SHEERLY ▷ **sheer**

SHEERS ▷ **sheer**

SHEESH interj exclamation of surprise or annoyance

SHEESHA n Oriental water-pipe for smoking tobacco

SHEET n large piece of cloth used as an inner bed cover ▷ vb provide with, cover, or wrap in a sheet

SHEETED ▷ **sheet**

SHEETER ▷ **sheet**

SHEETS ▷ **sheet**

SHEETY ▷ **sheet**

SHEEVE n part of mine winding gear

SHEEVES ▷ **sheeve**

SHEHITA n slaughter of animal according to Jewish religious law

SHEIK same as ▷ **sheikh**

SHEIKH n Arab chief

SHEIKHA n chief wife of sheikh

SHEIKHS ▶ sheikh

SHEIKS ▶ sheik

SHEILA n girl or woman

SHEILAS ▶ sheila

SHEITAN n Muslim demon

SHEKEL n monetary unit of Israel

SHEKELS ▶ shekel

SHELF n board fixed horizontally for holding things ▷ vb put on a shelf

SHELFED ▶ shelf

SHELFS ▶ shelf

SHELFY ▶ shelf

SHELL n hard outer covering of an egg, nut, or certain animals ▷ vb take the shell from

SHELLAC n resin used in varnishes ▷ vb coat with shellac

SHELLED ▶ shell

SHELLER ▶ shell

SHELLS ▶ shell

SHELLY ▶ shell

SHELTA n secret language used by some traveling people in Britain and Ireland

SHELTAS ▶ shelta

SHELTER n structure providing protection from danger or the weather ▷ vb give shelter to

SHELTIE n small dog similar to a collie

SHELTY same as ▶ sheltie

SHELVE vb put aside or postpone

SHELVED ▶ shelve

SHELVER ▶ shelve

SHELVES ▶ shelf

SHELVY adj having shelves

SHEMALE n male who has acquired female physical characteristics through surgery

SHEND vb put to shame

SHENDS ▶ shend

SHENT ▶ shend

SHEOL n hell

SHEOLS ▶ sheol

SHEQEL same as ▶ shekel

SHEQELS ▶ sheqel

SHERANG n person in charge

SHERBET n fruit-flavoured fizzy powder

SHERD same as ▶ shard

SHERDS ▶ sherd

SHERE old spelling of ▶ sheer

SHEREEF same as ▶ sherif

SHERIA same as ▶ sharia

SHERIAS ▶ sheria

SHERIAT n Muslim religious law

SHERIF n descendant of Mohammed through his daughter Fatima

SHERIFF n (in the US) chief law enforcement officer of a county

SHERIFS ▶ sherif

SHEROOT n cheroot

SHERPA n official who assists at a summit meeting

SHERPAS ▶ sherpa

SHERRIS n old form of sherry

SHERRY n pale or dark brown fortified wine

SHES ▶ she

SHET vb old form of shut

SHETS ▶ shet

SHEUCH n ditch or trough ▷ vb dig

SHEUCHS ▶ sheuch

SHEUGH same as ▶ sheuch

SHEUGHS ▶ sheugh

SHEVA n mark in Hebrew writing

SHEVAS ▶ sheva

SHEW archaic spelling of ▶ show

SHEWED ▶ shew

SHEWEL n old word meaning scarecrow

SHEWELS ▶ shewel

SHEWER ▶ shew

SHEWERS ▶ shew

SHEWING ▶ shew

SHEWN ▶ shew

SHEWS ▶ shew

SHH interj sound made to ask for silence

SHIAI n judo contest

SHIAIS ▶ shiai

SHIATSU n massage in which pressure is applied to the same points of the body as in acupuncture

SHIATZU n shiatzu

SHIBAH n Jewish period of mourning

SHIBAHS ▶ shibah

SHICKER n alcoholic drink

SHIDDER n old word meaning female animal

SHIED ▶ shy

SHIEL vb sheal

SHIELD n piece of armour carried on the arm to protect the body from

blows or missiles ▷ vb protect

SHIELDS ▶ shield

SHIELED ▶ shiel

SHIELS ▶ shiel

SHIER n horse that shies habitually

SHIERS ▶ shier

SHIES ▶ shy

SHIEST ▶ shy

SHIFT vb move ▷ n shifting

SHIFTED ▶ shift

SHIFTER ▶ shift

SHIFTS ▶ shift

SHIFTY adj evasive or untrustworthy

SHIKAR n hunting, esp big-game hunting ▷ vb hunt (game, esp big game)

SHIKARI n (in India) a hunter

SHIKARS ▶ shikar

SHIKKER n Yiddish term for drunk person

SHILL n confidence trickster's assistant ▷ vb act as a shill

SHILLED ▶ shill

SHILLS ▶ shill

SHILPIT adj puny

SHILY ▶ shy

SHIM n thin strip of material placed between two close surfaces to fill a gap ▷ vb fit or fill up with a shim

SHIMAAL n hot Middle Eastern wind

SHIMMED ▶ shim

SHIMMER n (shine with) a faint unsteady light ▷ vb shine with a faint unsteady light

SHIMMEY n chemise

SHIMMY n American ragtime dance with much shaking of the hips and shoulders ▷ vb dance the shimmy

SHIMS ▶ shim

SHIN n front of the lower leg ▷ vb climb by using the hands or arms and legs

SHINDIG n noisy party

SHINDY n quarrel or commotion

SHINDYS ▶ shindy

SHINE vb give out or reflect light; cause to gleam ▷ n brightness or lustre

SHINED ▶ shine

SHINER n black eye

SHINERS ▶ shiner

SHINES ▶ shine

SHINESS ▶ shy
SHINGLE n wooden roof tile ▷ vb cover (a roof) with shingles
SHINGLY ▶ shingle
SHINIER ▶ shiny
SHINIES ▶ shiny
SHINILY ▶ shiny
SHINING ▶ shine
SHINJU n (formerly, in Japan) a ritual double suicide of lovers
SHINJUS ▶ shinju
SHINKIN n worthless person
SHINNE n old form of chin
SHINNED ▶ shin
SHINNES ▶ shinne
SHINNEY vb climb with hands and legs
SHINNY same as ▶ shinty
SHINS ▶ shin
SHINTY n game like hockey ▷ vb play shinty
SHINY adj bright and polished
SHIP n large seagoing vessel ▷ vb send or transport by carrier, esp a ship
SHIPFUL n amount carried by ship
SHIPLAP n method of constructing ship hull
SHIPMAN n master or captain of a ship
SHIPMEN ▶ shipman
SHIPPED ▶ ship
SHIPPEN n dialect word for cattle shed
SHIPPER n person or company that ships
SHIPPIE n prostitute who solicits at a port
SHIPPO n Japanese enamel work
SHIPPON n dialect word for cattle shed
SHIPPOS ▶ shippo
SHIPS ▶ ship
SHIPWAY n structure on which a vessel is built, then launched
SHIR n gathering in material
SHIRE n county ▷ vb refresh or rest
SHIRED ▶ shire
SHIRES ▶ shire
SHIRING ▶ shire
SHIRK vb avoid (duty or work) ▷ n person who shirks
SHIRKED ▶ shirk
SHIRKER ▶ shirk

SHIRKS ▶ shirk
SHIRR vb gather (fabric) into two or more parallel rows to decorate a dress, etc ▷ n series of gathered rows decorating a dress, blouse, etc
SHIRRA old Scots word for ▶ sheriff
SHIRRAS ▶ shirra
SHIRRED ▶ shirr
SHIRRS ▶ shirr
SHIRS ▶ shir
SHIRT n garment for the upper part of the body ▷ vb put a shirt on
SHIRTED ▶ shirt
SHIRTS ▶ shirt
SHIRTY adj bad-tempered or annoyed
SHISH adj as in shish kebab dish of meat and vegetables threaded onto skewers and grilled
SHISHA same as ▶ hookah
SHISHAS ▶ shisha
SHISO n Asian plant with aromatic leaves that are used in cooking
SHISOS ▶ shiso
SHIST n schist
SHISTS ▶ shist
SHITAKE same as > shiitake
SHITTAH n tree mentioned in the Old Testament
SHITTIM ▶ shittah
SHITZU n breed of small dog with long, silky fur
SHITZUS ▶ shitzu
SHIUR n lesson in which a passage of the Talmud is studied together by a group of people
SHIURIM ▶ shiur
SHIV variant spelling of ▶ chiv
SHIVA same as ▶ shivah
SHIVAH n Jewish period of formal mourning
SHIVAHS ▶ shivah
SHIVAS ▶ shiva
SHIVE n flat cork or bung for wide-mouthed bottles
SHIVER vb tremble, as from cold or fear ▷ n shivering
SHIVERS ▶ shiver
SHIVERY adj inclined to shiver or tremble
SHIVES ▶ shive
SHIVITI n Jewish decorative plaque with religious message
SHIVOO n Australian word

meaning rowdy party
SHIVOOS ▶ shivoo
SHIVS ▶ shiv
SHIVVED ▶ shiv
SHLEP vb schlep
SHLEPP vb schlep
SHLEPPS ▶ shlepp
SHLEPS ▶ shlep
SHLOCK n something of poor quality
SHLOCKS ▶ shlock
SHLOCKY ▶ shlock
SHLUB same as ▶ schlub
SHLUBS ▶ shlub
SHLUMP vb move in lazy way
SHLUMPS ▶ shlump
SHLUMPY ▶ shlump
SHMALTZ n schmaltz
SHMATTE n rag
SHMEAR n set of things
SHMEARS ▶ shmear
SHMEK n smell
SHMEKS ▶ shmek
SHMO same as ▶ schmo
SHMOCK n despicable person
SHMOCKS ▶ shmock
SHMOES ▶ shmo
SHMOOSE same as > schmooze
SHMOOZE same as > schmooze
SHMOOZY adj talking casually, gossipy
SHMUCK n despicable person
SHMUCKS ▶ schmuck
SHNAPPS same as > schnapps
SHNAPS n schnaps
SHNOOK n stupid person
SHNOOKS ▶ shnook
SHOAL n large number of fish swimming together ▷ vb make or become shallow ▷ adj (of the draught of a vessel) drawing little water
SHOALED ▶ shoal
SHOALER ▶ shoal
SHOALS ▶ shoal
SHOALY adj shallow
SHOAT n piglet that has recently been weaned
SHOATS ▶ shoat
SHOCHET n (in Judaism) a person who has been specially trained and licensed to slaughter animals and birds in accordance with the laws of shechita**

S

SHOCK vb horrify, disgust, or astonish ▷ n sudden violent emotional disturbance ▷ adj bushy

SHOCKED ▸ shock

SHOCKER n person or thing that shocks or horrifies

SHOCKS ▸ shock

SHOD ▸ shoe

SHODDEN vb old form of shod

SHODDY adj made or done badly ▷ n yarn or fabric made from wool waste or clippings

SHODER n skins used in making gold leaf

SHODERS ▸ shoder

SHOE n outer covering for the foot, ending below the ankle ▷ vb fit with a shoe or shoes

SHOEBOX n cardboard box for shoes

SHOED ▸ shoe

SHOEING ▸ shoe

SHOEPAC n waterproof boot

SHOER n person who shoes horses

SHOERS ▸ shoer

SHOES ▸ shoe

SHOFAR n ram's horn sounded in the synagogue daily during the month of Elul and repeatedly on Rosh Hashanah

SHOFARS ▸ shofar

SHOG vb shake

SHOGGED ▸ shog

SHOGGLE vb shake

SHOGGLY ▸ shoggle

SHOGI n Japanese chess

SHOGIS ▸ shogi

SHOGS ▸ shog

SHOGUN n Japanese chief military commander

SHOGUNS ▸ shogun

SHOJI n Japanese rice-paper screen in a sliding wooden frame

SHOJIS ▸ shoji

SHOLA n Indian plant

SHOLAS ▸ shola

SHOLOM n Hebrew greeting

SHOLOMS ▸ sholom

SHONE ▸ shine

SHONEEN n Irishman who imitates English ways

SHONKY adj unreliable or unsound

SHOO interj go away! ▷ vb

drive away as by saying 'shoo'

SHOOED ▸ shoo

SHOOFLY n as in shoofly pie US dessert similar to treacle tart

SHOOGIE vb Scots word meaning swing

SHOOGLE vb shake, sway, or rock back and forth ▷ n rocking motion

SHOOGLY ▸ shoogle

SHOOING ▸ shoo

SHOOK n set of parts ready for assembly

SHOOKS ▸ shook

SHOOL dialect word for ▸ shovel

SHOOLE dialect word for ▸ shovel

SHOOLED ▸ shool

SHOOLES ▸ shoole

SHOOLS ▸ shool

SHOON plural of ▸ shoe

SHOORA same as ▸ shura

SHOORAS ▸ shoora

SHOOS ▸ shoo

SHOOT vb hit, wound, or kill with a missile fired from a weapon ▷ n new branch or sprout of a plant

SHOOTER n person or thing that shoots

SHOOTS ▸ shoot

SHOP n place for sale of goods and services ▷ vb visit a shop or shops to buy goods

SHOPBOT n price-comparison website

SHOPBOY n boy working in shop

SHOPE n old form of shape

SHOPFUL n amount stored in shop

SHOPHAR same as ▸ shofar

SHOPMAN n man working in shop

SHOPMEN ▸ shopman

SHOPPE old-fashioned spelling of ▸ shop

SHOPPED ▸ shop

SHOPPER n person who buys goods in a shop

SHOPPES ▸ shoppe

SHOPPY adj of a shop

SHOPS ▸ shop

SHORAN n short-range radar system

SHORANS ▸ shoran

SHORE n edge of a sea or lake ▷ vb prop or support

SHORED ▸ shore

SHORER ▸ shore

SHORERS ▸ shore

SHORES ▸ shore

SHORING ▸ shore

SHORL n black mineral

SHORLS ▸ shorl

SHORN past participle of ▸ shear

SHORT adj not long ▷ adv abruptly ▷ n drink of spirits ▷ vb short-circuit

SHORTED ▸ short

SHORTEN vb make or become shorter

SHORTER ▸ short

SHORTIA n American flowering plant

SHORTIE n person or thing that is extremely short

SHORTLY adv soon

SHORTS pl n trousers reaching the top of the thigh or partway to the knee

SHORTY same as ▸ shortie

SHOT vb load with shot

SHOTE same as ▸ shoat

SHOTES ▸ shote

SHOTGUN n gun for firing a charge of shot at short range ▷ adj involving coercion or duress ▷ vb shoot or threaten with or as if with a shotgun

SHOTS ▸ shot

SHOTT n shallow temporary salt lake or marsh in the North African desert

SHOTTE n old form of shoat

SHOTTED ▸ shot

SHOTTEN adj (of fish, esp herring) having recently spawned

SHOTTES ▸ shotte

SHOTTLE n small drawer

SHOTTS ▸ shott

SHOUGH n old word meaning lapdog

SHOUGHS ▸ shough

SHOULD ▸ shall

SHOUSE n toilet ▷ adj unwell or in poor spirits

SHOUSES ▸ shouse

SHOUT n loud cry ▷ vb cry out loudly

SHOUTED ▸ shout

SHOUTER ▸ shout

SHOUTS ▸ shout

SHOUTY adj characterized by or involving shouting

SHOVE vb push roughly ▷ n rough push

SHOVED ▸ shove

SHOVEL *n* tool for lifting or moving loose material ▷ *vb* lift or move as with a shovel

SHOVELS ▶ **shovel**

SHOVER ▶ **shove**

SHOVERS ▶ **shove**

SHOVES ▶ **shove**

SHOVING *n* act of pushing hard

SHOW *vb* make, be, or become noticeable or visible ▷ *n* public exhibition

SHOWBIZ *n* entertainment industry including theatre, films, and TV

SHOWBOX *n* box containing showman's material

SHOWD *vb* rock or sway to and fro ▷ *n* rocking motion

SHOWDED ▶ **showd**

SHOWDS ▶ **showd**

SHOWED ▶ **show**

SHOWER *n* kind of bath in which a person stands while being sprayed with water ▷ *vb* wash in a shower

SHOWERS ▶ **shower**

SHOWERY ▶ **shower**

SHOWGHE *n* old word meaning lapdog

SHOWIER ▶ **showy**

SHOWILY ▶ **showy**

SHOWING ▶ **show**

SHOWMAN *n* man skilled at presenting anything spectacularly

SHOWMEN ▶ **showman**

SHOWN ▶ **show**

SHOWOFF *n* person who makes a vain display of himself or herself

SHOWS ▶ **show**

SHOWY *adj* gaudy

SHOYU *n* Japanese variety of soy sauce

SHOYUS ▶ **shoyu**

SHRANK ▶ **shrink**

SHRED *n* long narrow strip torn from something ▷ *vb* tear to shreds

SHREDDY ▶ **shred**

SHREDS ▶ **shred**

SHREEK *old spelling of* ▶ **shriek**

SHREEKS ▶ **shreek**

SHREIK *old spelling of* ▶ **shriek**

SHREIKS ▶ **shreik**

SHREW *n* small mouselike animal ▷ *vb* curse or damn

SHREWD *adj* clever and perceptive

SHREWED ▶ **shrew**

SHREWS ▶ **shrew**

SHRI *n* Indian title of respect

SHRIECH *old spelling of* ▶ **shriek**

SHRIEK *n* shrill cry ▷ *vb* utter (with) a shriek

SHRIEKS ▶ **shriek**

SHRIEKY ▶ **shriek**

SHRIEVE *archaic word for* ▶ **sheriff**

SHRIFT *n* act or an instance of shriving or being shriven

SHRIFTS ▶ **shrift**

SHRIGHT *n* old word meaning shriek

SHRIKE *n* songbird with a heavy hooked bill ▷ *vb* archaic word for shriek

SHRIKED ▶ **shrike**

SHRIKES ▶ **shrike**

SHRILL *adj* (of a sound) sharp and high-pitched ▷ *vb* utter shrilly

SHRILLS ▶ **shrill**

SHRILLY ▶ **shrill**

SHRIMP *n* small edible shellfish ▷ *vb* fish for shrimps

SHRIMPS ▶ **shrimp**

SHRIMPY ▶ **shrimp**

SHRINAL ▶ **shrine**

SHRINE *n* place of worship associated with a sacred person or object ▷ *vb* enshrine

SHRINED ▶ **shrine**

SHRINES ▶ **shrine**

SHRINK *vb* become or make smaller ▷ *n* psychiatrist

SHRINKS ▶ **shrink**

SHRIS ▶ **shri**

SHRITCH *vb* old word meaning shriek

SHRIVE *vb* hear the confession of (a penitent)

SHRIVED ▶ **shrive**

SHRIVEL *vb* shrink and wither

SHRIVEN ▶ **shrive**

SHRIVER ▶ **shrive**

SHRIVES ▶ **shrive**

SHROFF *n* (in China and Japan) expert employed to separate counterfeit money from the genuine ▷ *vb* test (money) and separate out the counterfeit and base

SHROFFS ▶ **shroff**

SHROOM *n* slang for magic mushroom ▷ *vb* take magic mushrooms

SHROOMS ▶ **shroom**

SHROUD *n* piece of cloth used to wrap a dead body ▷ *vb* conceal

SHROUDS ▶ **shroud**

SHROUDY ▶ **shroud**

SHROVE *vb* dialect word meaning to observe Shrove-tide

SHROVED ▶ **shrove**

SHROVES ▶ **shrove**

SHROW *vb* old form of shrew

SHROWD *adj* old form of shrewd

SHROWED ▶ **shrow**

SHROWS ▶ **shrow**

SHRUB *n* woody plant smaller than a tree ▷ *vb* plant shrubs

SHRUBBY *adj* consisting of, planted with, or abounding in shrubs

SHRUBS ▶ **shrub**

SHRUG *vb* raise and then drop (the shoulders) as a sign of indifference or doubt ▷ *n* shrugging

SHRUGS ▶ **shrug**

SHRUNK ▶ **shrink**

SHTCHI *n* Russian cabbage soup

SHTCHIS ▶ **shtchi**

SHTETEL *n* Jewish community in Eastern Europe

SHTETL *n* (formerly) a small Jewish community in Eastern Europe

SHTETLS ▶ **shtetl**

SHTICK *n* comedian's routine

SHTICKS ▶ **shtick**

SHTICKY ▶ **shtick**

SHTIK *n* shtick

SHTIKS ▶ **shtik**

SHTOOK *n* trouble

SHTOOKS ▶ **shtook**

SHTOOM *adj* silent

SHTUCK *n* trouble

SHTUCKS ▶ **shtuck**

SHTUM *adj* silent

SHTUMM *adj* silent

SHTUP *vb* have sex (with)

SHTUPS ▶ **shtup**

SHUCK *n* outer covering of something ▷ *vb* remove the shucks from

SHUCKED ▶ **shuck**

SHUCKER ▶ **shuck**

SHUCKS *pl n* something of little value ▷ *interj* exclamation of

S

disappointment, annoyance, etc

SHUDDER *vb* shake or tremble violently, esp with horror ▷ *n* shaking or trembling

SHUFFLE *vb* walk without lifting the feet ▷ *n* shuffling

SHUFTI *same as* ▶ **shufty**

SHUFTIS ▶ **shufti**

SHUFTY *n* look

SHUGGY *n* swing, as at a fairground

SHUL *Yiddish word for* > **synagogue**

SHULE *vb* saunter

SHULED ▶ **shule**

SHULES ▶ **shule**

SHULING ▶ **shule**

SHULN ▶ **shul**

SHULS ▶ **shul**

SHUN *vb* avoid

SHUNNED ▶ **shun**

SHUNNER ▶ **shun**

SHUNS ▶ **shun**

SHUNT *vb* move (objects or people) to a different position ▷ *n* shunting

SHUNTED ▶ **shunt**

SHUNTER *n* small railway locomotive used for manoeuvring coaches

SHUNTS ▶ **shunt**

SHURA *n* consultative council or assembly

SHURAS ▶ **shura**

SHUSH *interj* be quiet! ▷ *vb* quiet by saying 'shush'

SHUSHED ▶ **shush**

SHUSHER ▶ **shush**

SHUSHES ▶ **shush**

SHUT *vb* bring together or fold, close

SHUTE *same as* ▶ **chute**

SHUTED ▶ **shute**

SHUTES ▶ **shute**

SHUTEYE *n* sleep

SHUTING ▶ **shute**

SHUTOFF *n* device that shuts something off, esp a machine control

SHUTOUT *n* game in which the opposing team does not score ▷ *vb* keep out or exclude

SHUTS ▶ **shut**

SHUTTER *n* hinged doorlike cover for closing off a window ▷ *vb* close or equip with a shutter

SHUTTLE *n* bobbin-like device used in weaving ▷ *vb* move by or as if by a shuttle

SHWA *same as* ▶ **schwa**

SHWAS ▶ **shwa**

SHY *adj* not at ease in company ▷ *n* start back in fear ▷ *n* throw

SHYER ▶ **shy**

SHYERS ▶ **shy**

SHYEST ▶ **shy**

SHYING ▶ **shy**

SHYISH ▶ **shy**

SHYLOCK *vb* lend money at an exorbitant rate of interest

SHYLY ▶ **shy**

SHYNESS ▶ **shy**

SHYPOO *n* liquor of poor quality

SHYPOOS ▶ **shypoo**

SHYSTER *n* person, esp a lawyer or politician, who uses discreditable or unethical methods

SI *same as* ▶ **te**

SIAL *n* silicon-rich and aluminium-rich rocks of the earth's continental upper crust

SIALIC ▶ **sial**

SIALID *n* species of fly

SIALIDS ▶ **sialid**

SIALOID *adj* resembling saliva

SIALON *n* type of ceramic

SIALONS ▶ **sialon**

SIALS ▶ **sial**

SIAMANG *n* large black gibbon

SIAMESE *same as* ▶ **siameze**

SIAMEZE *vb* join together

SIB *n* blood relative

SIBB *n* sib

SIBBS ▶ **sibb**

SIBLING *n* brother or sister

SIBS ▶ **sib**

SIBSHIP *n* group of children of the same parents

SIBYL *n* (in ancient Greece and Rome) prophetess

SIBYLIC ▶ **sibyl**

SIBYLS ▶ **sibyl**

SIC *adv* thus ▷ *vb* attack

SICCAN *adj* Scots word meaning such

SICCAR *adj* sure

SICCED ▶ **sic**

SICCING ▶ **sic**

SICCITY *n* dryness

SICE *same as* ▶ **syce**

SICES ▶ **syce**

SICH *adj* old form of such

SICHT *Scots word for* ▶ **sight**

SICHTED ▶ **sicht**

SICHTS ▶ **sicht**

SICK *adj* vomiting or likely to vomit ▷ *n* vomit ▷ *vb* vomit

SICKBAY *n* room for the treatment of sick people, for example on a ship

SICKBED *n* bed where sick person lies

SICKED ▶ **sick**

SICKEE *n* person off work through illness

SICKEES ▶ **sickee**

SICKEN *vb* make nauseated or disgusted

SICKENS ▶ **sicken**

SICKER ▶ **sick**

SICKEST ▶ **sick**

SICKIE *n* day of sick leave from work

SICKIES ▶ **sickie**

SICKING ▶ **sick**

SICKISH ▶ **sick**

SICKLE *n* tool with a curved blade for cutting grass or grain ▷ *vb* cut with a sickle

SICKLED ▶ **sickle**

SICKLES ▶ **sickle**

SICKLY *adj* unhealthy, weak ▷ *adv* suggesting sickness ▷ *vb* make sickly

SICKO *n* person who is mentally disturbed or perverted ▷ *adj* perverted or in bad taste

SICKOS ▶ **sicko**

SICKOUT *n* form of industrial action in which all workers in a workplace report sick simultaneously

SICKS ▶ **sick**

SICLIKE *adj* Scots word meaning suchlike

SICS ▶ **sic**

SIDA *n* Australian hemp plant

SIDAS ▶ **sida**

SIDDHA *n* (in Hinduism) person who has achieved perfection

SIDDHAS ▶ **siddha**

SIDDHI *n* (in Hinduism) power attained with perfection

SIDDHIS ▶ **siddhi**

SIDDUR *n* Jewish prayer book

SIDDURS ▶ **siddur**

SIDE *n* line or surface that borders anything ▷ *adj* at or on the side

SIDEARM *n* weapon worn on belt

SIDEBAR *n* small

newspaper article beside larger one

SIDECAR n small passenger car on the side of a motorcycle

SIDED ▶ side

SIDEMAN n member of a dance band or a jazz group other than the leader

SIDEMEN ▶ sideman

SIDER n one who sides with another

SIDERAL adj from the stars

SIDERS ▶ sider

SIDES ▶ side

SIDEWAY same as ▶ sideways

SIDH pl n fairy people

SIDHA n (in Hinduism) person who has achieved perfection

SIDHAS ▶ sidha

SIDHE pl n inhabitants of fairyland

SIDING n short stretch of railway track on which trains are shunted from the main line

SIDINGS ▶ siding

SIDLE vb walk in a furtive manner ▷ n sideways movement

SIDLED ▶ sidle

SIDLER ▶ sidle

SIDLERS ▶ sidle

SIDLES ▶ sidle

SIDLING ▶ sidle

SIECLE n century, period, or era

SIECLES ▶ siecle

SIEGE n surrounding and blockading of a place ▷ vb lay siege to

SIEGED ▶ siege

SIEGER n person who besieges

SIEGERS ▶ sieger

SIEGES ▶ siege

SIEGING ▶ siege

SIELD vb old word meaning given a ceiling

SIEMENS n SI unit of electrical conductance

SIEN n old word meaning scion

SIENITE n type of igneous rock

SIENNA n reddish- or yellowish-brown pigment made from natural earth

SIENNAS ▶ sienna

SIENS ▶ sien

SIENT n old word meaning scion

SIENTS ▶ sient

SIERRA n range of mountains in Spain or America with jagged peaks

SIERRAN ▶ sierra

SIERRAS ▶ sierra

SIES interj in South Africa, an exclamation of disgust

SIESTA n afternoon nap, taken in hot countries

SIESTAS ▶ siesta

SIETH n old form of scythe

SIETHS ▶ sieth

SIEUR n French word meaning lord

SIEURS ▶ sieur

SIEVE n utensil with mesh through which a substance is sifted or strained ▷ vb sift or strain through a sieve

SIEVED ▶ sieve

SIEVERT n derived SI unit of dose equivalent, equal to 1 joule per kilogram

SIEVES ▶ sieve

SIEVING ▶ sieve

SIF adj South African slang for disgusting

SIFAKA n either of two large rare arboreal lemuroid primates

SIFAKAS ▶ sifaka

SIFFLE vb whistle

SIFFLED ▶ siffle

SIFFLES ▶ siffle

SIFREI ▶ sefer

SIFT vb remove the coarser particles from a substance with a sieve

SIFTED ▶ sift

SIFTER ▶ sift

SIFTERS ▶ sift

SIFTING ▶ sift

SIFTS ▶ sift

SIGANID n tropical fish

SIGH n long audible breath expressing sadness, tiredness, relief, or longing ▷ vb utter a sigh

SIGHED ▶ sigh

SIGHER ▶ sigh

SIGHERS ▶ sigh

SIGHFUL ▶ sigh

SIGHING ▶ sigh

SIGHS ▶ sigh

SIGHT n ability to see ▷ vb catch sight of

SIGHTED adj not blind

SIGHTER n any of six practice shots allowed to each competitor in a tournament

SIGHTLY adj pleasing or attractive to see

SIGHTS ▶ sight

SIGIL n seal or signet

SIGILS ▶ sigil

SIGLA n list of symbols used in a book

SIGLAS ▶ sigla

SIGLOI ▶ siglos

SIGLOS n silver coin of ancient Persia worth one twentieth of a daric

SIGLUM n symbol used in book

SIGMA n 18th letter in the Greek alphabet

SIGMAS ▶ sigma

SIGMATE adj shaped like the Greek letter sigma or the Roman S ▷ n sigmate thing ▷ vb add a sigma

SIGMOID adj shaped like the letter S ▷ n S-shaped bend in the final portion of the large intestine

SIGN n indication of something not immediately or outwardly observable ▷ vb write (one's name) on (a document or letter) to show its authenticity or one's agreement

SIGNA pl n symbols

SIGNAGE n signs collectively, esp street signs or signs giving directions

SIGNAL n sign or gesture to convey information ▷ adj very important ▷ vb convey (information) by signal

SIGNALS ▶ signal

SIGNARY n set of symbols

SIGNED ▶ sign

SIGNEE n person signing document

SIGNEES ▶ signee

SIGNER n person who signs something

SIGNERS ▶ signer

SIGNET n small seal used to authenticate documents ▷ vb stamp or authenticate with a signet

SIGNETS ▶ signet

SIGNEUR old spelling of ▶ senior

SIGNIFY vb indicate or suggest

SIGNING n system of communication using hand

and arm movements, such as one used by deaf people

SIGNIOR *same as* ▶ **signor**

SIGNOR *n* Italian term of address equivalent to *sir* or *Mr*

SIGNORA *n* Italian term of address equivalent to *madam* or *Mrs*

SIGNORE *n* Italian man: a title of respect equivalent to *sir*

SIGNORI ▶ **signore**

SIGNORS ▶ **signor**

SIGNORY *same as* ▶ **seigniory**

SIGNS ▶ **sign**

SIJO *n* Korean poem

SIJOS ▶ **sijo**

SIK *adj* excellent

SIKA *n* Japanese forest-dwelling deer

SIKAS ▶ **sika**

SIKE *n* small stream

SIKER *adj* old spelling of sicker

SIKES ▶ **sike**

SILAGE *n* fodder crop harvested while green and partially fermented in a silo ▷ *vb* make silage

SILAGED ▶ **silage**

SILAGES ▶ **silage**

SILANE *n* gas containing silicon

SILANES ▶ **silane**

SILD *n* any of various small young herrings, esp when prepared and canned in Norway

SILDS ▶ **sild**

SILE *vb* pour with rain

SILED ▶ **sile**

SILEN *n* god of woodland

SILENCE *n* absence of noise or speech ▷ *vb* make silent

SILENE *n* type of plant with mostly red or pink flowers, often grown as a garden plant

SILENES ▶ **silene**

SILENI ▶ **silenus**

SILENS ▶ **silen**

SILENT *adj* tending to speak very little ▷ *n* silent film

SILENTS ▶ **silent**

SILENUS *n* woodland deity

SILER *n* strainer

SILERS ▶ **siler**

SILES ▶ **sile**

SILESIA *n* twill-weave fabric of cotton or other fibre

SILEX *n* type of heat-resistant glass made from fused quartz

SILEXES ▶ **silex**

SILICA *n* hard glossy mineral found as quartz and in sandstone

SILICAS ▶ **silica**

SILICIC *adj* of, concerned with, or containing silicon or an acid obtained from silicon

SILICLE *same as* > **silicula**

SILICON *n* brittle nonmetallic element widely used in chemistry and industry ▷ *adj* denoting an area of a country that contains much high-technology industry

SILING ▶ **sile**

SILIQUA *n* long dry dehiscent fruit of cruciferous plants such as the wallflower

SILIQUE *same as* ▶ **siliqua**

SILK *n* fibre made by the larva of a certain moth ▷ *vb* (of maize) develop long hairlike styles

SILKED ▶ **silk**

SILKEN *adj* made of silk ▷ *vb* make like silk

SILKENS ▶ **silken**

SILKIE *n* Scots word for a seal

SILKIER ▶ **silky**

SILKIES ▶ **silkie**

SILKILY ▶ **silky**

SILKING ▶ **silk**

SILKS ▶ **silk**

SILKY *adj* of or like silk

SILL *n* ledge at the bottom of a window or door

SILLER *n* silver ▷ *adj* silver

SILLERS ▶ **siller**

SILLIER ▶ **silly**

SILLIES ▶ **silly**

SILLILY ▶ **silly**

SILLOCK *n* young coalfish

SILLS ▶ **sill**

SILLY *adj* foolish ▷ *n* foolish person

SILO *n* pit or airtight tower for storing silage or grains ▷ *vb* put in a silo

SILOED ▶ **silo**

SILOING ▶ **silo**

SILOS ▶ **silo**

SILPHIA > **silphium**

SILT *n* mud deposited by moving water ▷ *vb* fill or be choked with silt

SILTED ▶ **silt**

SILTIER ▶ **silt**

SILTING ▶ **silt**

SILTS ▶ **silt**

SILTY ▶ **silt**

SILURID *n* type of freshwater fish of the family which includes catfish

SILVA *same as* ▶ **sylva**

SILVAE ▶ **silva**

SILVAN *same as* ▶ **sylvan**

SILVANS ▶ **silvan**

SILVAS ▶ **silva**

SILVER *n* white precious metal ▷ *adj* made of or of the colour of silver ▷ *vb* coat with silver

SILVERN *adj* silver

SILVERS ▶ **silver**

SILVERY *adj* like silver

SILVEX *n* type of weedkiller

SILVICS *n* study of trees

SIM *n* computer game that simulates an activity such as flying or playing a sport

SIMA *n* silicon-rich and magnesium-rich rocks of the earth's oceanic crust

SIMAR *variant spelling of* ▶ **cymar**

SIMARRE *n* woman's loose gown

SIMARS ▶ **simar**

SIMAS ▶ **sima**

SIMATIC ▶ **sima**

SIMBA *E African word for* ▶ **lion**

SIMBAS ▶ **simba**

SIMI *n* East African sword

SIMIAL *adj* of apes

SIMIAN *n* a monkey or ape ▷ *adj* of or resembling a monkey or ape

SIMIANS ▶ **simian**

SIMILAR *adj* alike but not identical

SIMILE *n* figure of speech comparing one thing to another, using 'as' or 'like'

SIMILES ▶ **simile**

SIMILOR *n* alloy used in cheap jewellery

SIMIOID *adj* of apes

SIMIOUS *adj* of apes

SIMIS ▶ **simi**

SIMITAR *same as* > **scimitar**

SIMKIN *word used in India for* > **champagne**

SIMKINS ▶ **simkin**

SIMLIN *n* American variety of squash plant

SIMLINS ▶ **simlin**

SIMMER *vb* cook gently at just below boiling point ▷ *n* state of simmering

SIMMERS ▶ **simmer**

SIMNEL *n* *as in* **simnel cake** fruit cake with marzipan eaten at Easter

SIMNELS ▶ **simnel**

SIMONY *n* practice of buying or selling Church benefits such as pardons

SIMOOM *n* hot suffocating sand-laden desert wind

SIMOOMS ▶ **simoom**

SIMOON *same as* ▶ **simoom**

SIMOONS ▶ **simoon**

SIMORG *n* bird in Persian myth

SIMORGS ▶ **simorg**

SIMP *short for* ▶ **simpleton**

SIMPAI *n* Indonesian monkey

SIMPAIS ▶ **simpai**

SIMPER *vb* smile in a silly or affected way ▷ *n* simpering smile

SIMPERS ▶ **simper**

SIMPKIN *word used in India for* ▶ **champagne**

SIMPLE *adj* easy to understand or do ▷ *n* simpleton ▷ *vb* archaic word meaning to look for medicinal herbs

SIMPLED ▶ **simple**

SIMPLER ▶ **simple**

SIMPLES ▶ **simple**

SIMPLEX *adj* permitting the transmission of signals in only one direction in a radio circuit ▷ *n* simple not a compound word

SIMPLY *adv* in a simple manner

SIMPS ▶ **simp**

SIMS ▶ **sim**

SIMUL *adj* simultaneous ▷ *n* simultaneous broadcast

SIMULAR *n* person or thing that simulates or imitates ▷ *adj* fake

SIMULS ▶ **simul**

SIMURG *n* bird in Persian myth

SIMURGH *n* bird in Persian myth

SIMURGS ▶ **simurg**

SIN *n* offence or transgression ▷ *vb* commit a sin

SINCE *prep* during the period of time after ▷ *adv* from that time

SINCERE *adj* without pretence or deceit

SIND *same as* ▶ **syne**

SINDED ▶ **sind**

SINDING ▶ **sind**

SINDON *n* type of cloth

SINDONS ▶ **sindon**

SINDS ▶ **sind**

SINE ▶ **syne**

SINED ▶ **sine**

SINES ▶ **sine**

SINEW *n* tough fibrous tissue joining muscle to bone ▷ *vb* make strong

SINEWED *adj* having sinews

SINEWS ▶ **sinew**

SINEWY *adj* lean and muscular

SINFUL *adj* guilty of sin

SING *vb* make musical sounds with the voice ▷ *n* act or performance of singing

SINGE *vb* burn the surface of ▷ *n* superficial burn

SINGED ▶ **singe**

SINGER *n* person who sings, esp professionally

SINGERS ▶ **singer**

SINGES ▶ **singe**

SINGING ▶ **sing**

SINGLE *adj* one only ▷ *n* single thing ▷ *vb* pick out from others

SINGLED ▶ **single**

SINGLES *pl n* match played with one person on each side

SINGLET *n* sleeveless vest

SINGLY *adv* one at a time

SINGS ▶ **sing**

SINGULT *n* old word meaning sob

SINH *n* hyperbolic sine

SINHS ▶ **sinh**

SINICAL ▶ **sine**

SINING ▶ **sine**

SINK *vb* submerge (in liquid) ▷ *n* fixed basin with a water supply and drainage pipe

SINKAGE *n* act of sinking or degree to which something sinks or has sunk

SINKER *n* weight for a fishing line

SINKERS ▶ **sinker**

SINKIER ▶ **sinky**

SINKING ▶ **sink**

SINKS ▶ **sink**

SINKY *adj* giving underfoot

SINLESS *adj* free from sin or guilt

SINNED ▶ **sin**

SINNER *n* person that sins ▷ *vb* behave like a sinner

SINNERS ▶ **sin**

SINNET *n* braided rope

SINNETS ▶ **sinnet**

SINNING ▶ **sin**

SINOPIA *n* pigment made from iron ore

SINOPIE ▶ **sinopia**

SINOPIS *n* pigment made from iron ore

SINS ▶ **sin**

SINSYNE *adv* Scots word meaning since

SINTER *n* whitish porous incrustation that is deposited from hot springs ▷ *vb* form large particles from (metal powders or powdery ores) by heating or pressure

SINTERS ▶ **sinter**

SINTERY ▶ **sinter**

SINUATE *vb* wind

SINUOSE *adj* sinuous

SINUOUS *adj* full of turns or curves

SINUS *n* hollow space in a bone, esp an air passage opening into the nose

SINUSES ▶ **sinus**

SIP *vb* drink in small mouthfuls ▷ *n* amount sipped

SIPE *vb* soak

SIPED ▶ **sipe**

SIPES ▶ **sipe**

SIPHON *n* bent tube which uses air pressure to draw liquid from a container ▷ *vb* draw off thus

SIPHONS ▶ **siphon**

SIPING ▶ **sipe**

SIPPED ▶ **sip**

SIPPER ▶ **sip**

SIPPERS ▶ **sip**

SIPPET *n* small piece of toast eaten with soup or gravy

SIPPETS ▶ **sippet**

SIPPING ▶ **sip**

SIPPLE *vb* sip

SIPPLED ▶ **sipple**

SIPPLES ▶ **sipple**

SIPPY *adj* *as in* **sippy cup** infant's drinking cup with a tight-fitting lid and perforated spout

SIPS ▶ **sip**

SIR *n* polite term of address for a man ▷ *vb* call someone 'sir'

SIRCAR *n* government in India

SIRCARS ▶ sircar

SIRDAR *same as* ▶ **sardar**

SIRDARS ▶ sirdar

SIRE *n* male parent of a horse or other domestic animal ▷ *vb* father

SIRED ▶ sire

SIREE *emphasized form of* ▶ **sir**

SIREES ▶ siree

SIREN *n* device making a loud wailing noise as a warning

SIRENIC ▶ siren

SIRENS ▶ siren

SIRES ▶ sire

SIRGANG *n* Asian bird

SIRI *n* betel

SIRIH *n* betel

SIRIHS ▶ sirih

SIRING ▶ sire

SIRINGS ▶ siring

SIRIS ▶ siri

SIRKAR *n* government in India

SIRKARS ▶ sirkar

SIRLOIN *n* prime cut of loin of beef

SIRNAME *vb* old form of surname

SIROC *n* sirocco

SIROCCO *n* hot wind blowing from N Africa into S Europe

SIROCS ▶ siroc

SIROSET *adj* of the chemical treatment of woollen fabrics to give a permanent-press effect

SIRRA *disrespectful form of* ▶ **sir**

SIRRAH *n* contemptuous term used in addressing a man or boy

SIRRAHS ▶ sirrah

SIRRAS ▶ sirra

SIRRED ▶ sir

SIRREE *n* form of 'sir' used for emphasis

SIRREES ▶ sirree

SIRRING ▶ sir

SIRS ▶ sir

SIRTUIN *n* protein that regulates cell metabolism and ageing

SIRUP *same as* ▶ **syrup**

SIRUPED ▶ sirup

SIRUPS ▶ sirup

SIRUPY ▶ sirup

SIS *n* sister

SISAL *n* (fibre of) plant used in making ropes

SISALS ▶ sisal

SISES ▶ sis

SISKIN *n* yellow-and-black finch

SISKINS ▶ siskin

SISS *shortening of* ▶ **sister**

SISSES ▶ siss

SISSIER ▶ sissy

SISSIES ▶ sissy

SISSOO *n* Indian tree

SISSOOS ▶ sissoo

SISSY *n* weak or cowardly (person) ▷ *adj* effeminate, weak, or cowardly

SIST *vb* Scottish law term meaning stop

SISTED ▶ sist

SISTER *n* girl or woman with the same parents as another person ▷ *adj* closely related, similar ▷ *vb* be or be like a sister

SISTERS ▶ sister

SISTING ▶ sist

SISTRA ▶ sistrum

SISTRUM *n* musical instrument of ancient Egypt consisting of a metal rattle

SISTS ▶ sist

SIT *vb* rest one's body upright on the buttocks

SITAR *n* Indian stringed musical instrument

SITARS ▶ sitar

SITCOM *n* situation comedy

SITCOMS ▶ sitcom

SITE *n* place where something is, was, or is intended to be located ▷ *vb* provide with a site

SITED ▶ site

SITELLA *n* type of small generally black-and-white bird

SITES ▶ site

SITFAST *n* sore on a horse's back caused by rubbing of the saddle

SITH *archaic word for* ▶ **since**

SITHE *vb* old form of scythe

SITHED ▶ sithe

SITHEE *interj* look here! listen!

SITHEN *adv* old word meaning since

SITHENS *adv* old word meaning since

SITHES ▶ sithe

SITHING ▶ sithe

SITING ▶ site

SITKA *modifier as in* **sitka spruce** tall North American spruce tree

SITREP *n* military situation report

SITREPS ▶ sitrep

SITS ▶ sit

SITTAR *n* sitar

SITTARS ▶ sittar

SITTEN *adj* dialect word for in the saddle

SITTER *n* baby-sitter

SITTERS ▶ sitter

SITTINE *adj* of nuthatch bird family

SITTING ▶ sit

SITUATE *vb* place ▷ *adj* (now used esp in legal contexts) situated

SITULA *n* bucket-shaped container, usually of metal or pottery and often richly decorated

SITULAE ▶ situla

SITUP *n* exercise in which the body is brought into a sitting position from one lying on the back

SITUPS ▶ situp

SITUS *n* position or location, esp the usual or right position of an organ or part of the body

SITUSES ▶ situs

SITZ *n* as in* **sitz bath** bath in which the buttocks and hips are immersed in hot water

SIVER *same as* ▶ **syver**

SIVERS ▶ siver

SIWASH *vb* (in the Pacific Northwest) to camp out with only natural shelter

SIX *n* one more than five

SIXAIN *n* stanza or poem of six lines

SIXAINE *n* six-line stanza of poetry

SIXAINS ▶ sixain

SIXER *same as* ▶ **six**

SIXERS ▶ sixer

SIXES ▶ six

SIXFOLD *adj* having six times as many or as much ▷ *adv* by six times as many or as much

SIXMO *n* book size resulting from folding a sheet of paper into six leaves or twelve pages, each one sixth the size of the sheet

SIXMOS ▶ sixmo

SIXTE *n* sixth of eight basic positions from which a parry or attack can be made in fencing

SIXTEEN n six and ten ▷ adj amounting to sixteen ▷ determiner amounting to sixteen

SIXTES ▶ sixte

SIXTH n (of) number six in a series ▷ adj coming after the fifth and before the seventh in numbering order ▷ adv after the fifth person, position, etc

SIXTHLY same as ▶ sixth

SIXTHS ▶ sixth

SIXTIES ▶ sixty

SIXTY n six times ten ▷ adj amounting to sixty

SIZABLE adj quite large

SIZABLY ▶ sizable

SIZAR n (at certain universities) an undergraduate receiving a maintenance grant from the college

SIZARS ▶ sizar

SIZE n dimensions, bigness ▷ vb arrange according to size

SIZED adj of a specified size

SIZEISM n discrimination on the basis of a person's size, esp against people considered to be overweight

SIZEIST ▶ sizeism

SIZEL n scrap metal clippings

SIZELS ▶ sizel

SIZER ▶ size

SIZERS ▶ size

SIZES ▶ size

SIZIER ▶ size

SIZIEST ▶ size

SIZING ▶ size

SIZINGS ▶ size

SIZISM n discrimination against people because of weight

SIZISMS ▶ sizism

SIZIST ▶ sizism

SIZISTS ▶ sizism

SIZY ▶ size

SIZZLE vb make a hissing sound like frying fat ▷ n hissing sound

SIZZLED ▶ sizzle

SIZZLER n something that sizzles

SIZZLES ▶ sizzle

SJAMBOK n whip or riding crop made of hide ▷ vb beat with a sjambok

SJOE interj South African exclamation of surprise, admiration, exhaustion, etc

SKA n type of West Indian pop music of the 1960s

SKAG same as ▶ scag

SKAGS ▶ skag

SKAIL vb Scots word meaning disperse

SKAILED ▶ skail

SKAILS ▶ skail

SKAITH vb Scots word meaning injure

SKAITHS ▶ skaith

SKALD n (in ancient Scandinavia) a bard or minstrel

SKALDIC ▶ skald

SKALDS ▶ skald

SKANK n fast dance to reggae music ▷ vb perform this dance

SKANKED ▶ skank

SKANKER ▶ skank

SKANKS ▶ skank

SKANKY adj dirty or unattractive

SKART Scots word for > cormorant

SKARTH Scots word for > cormorant

SKARTHS ▶ skarth

SKARTS ▶ skart

SKAS ▶ ska

SKAT n three-handed card game using 32 cards, popular in German-speaking communities

SKATE n boot with a steel blade or sets of wheels attached to the sole for gliding over ice or a hard surface ▷ vb glide on or as if on skates

SKATED ▶ skate

SKATER n person who skates

SKATERS ▶ skater

SKATES ▶ skate

SKATING ▶ skate

SKATOL n skatole

SKATOLE n white or brownish crystalline solid

SKATOLS ▶ skatol

SKATS ▶ skat

SKATT n dialect word meaning throw

SKATTS ▶ skatt

SKAW same as ▶ scaw

SKAWS ▶ skaw

SKEAN n kind of double-edged dagger formerly used in Ireland and Scotland

SKEANE same as ▶ skein

SKEANES ▶ skeane

SKEANS ▶ skean

SKEAR dialect form of ▶ scare

SKEARED ▶ skear

SKEARS ▶ skear

SKEARY dialect form of ▶ scary

SKEE variant spelling of ▶ ski

SKEED ▶ skee

SKEEF adj, adv South African slang for at an oblique angle

SKEEING ▶ skee

SKEELY adj Scots word meaning skilful

SKEEN n type of ibex

SKEENS ▶ skeen

SKEER dialect form of ▶ scare

SKEERED ▶ skeer

SKEERS ▶ skeer

SKEERY dialect form of ▶ scary

SKEES ▶ skee

SKEET n form of clay-pigeon shooting

SKEETER informal word for > mosquito

SKEETS ▶ skeet

SKEG n reinforcing brace between the after end of a keel and the rudderpost

SKEGG n skeg

SKEGGER n young salmon

SKEGGS ▶ skegg

SKEGS ▶ skeg

SKEIGH adj Scots word meaning shy

SKEIN n yarn wound in a loose coil ▷ vb wind into a skein

SKEINED ▶ skein

SKEINS ▶ skein

SKELDER vb beg

SKELF n splinter of wood, esp when embedded accidentally in the skin

SKELFS ▶ skelf

SKELL n homeless person

SKELLIE adj skelly

SKELLS ▶ skell

SKELLUM n rogue

SKELLY n whitefish of certain lakes in the Lake District ▷ vb look sideways or squint ▷ adj cross-eyed

SKELM n villain or crook

SKELMS ▶ skelm

SKELP vb slap ▷ n slap

SKELPED ▶ skelp

SKELPIT vb Scots word meaning skelped

S

SKELPS ▶ **skelp**

SKELTER vb scurry

SKELUM n Scots word meaning rascal

SKELUMS ▶ **skelum**

SKEN vb squint or stare

SKENE n Scots word meaning dagger

SKENES ▶ **skene**

SKENNED ▶ **sken**

SKENS ▶ **sken**

SKEO n Scots dialect word meaning hut

SKEOS ▶ **skeo**

SKEP n beehive, esp one constructed of straw ▷ vb gather into a hive

SKEPFUL n amount skep will hold

SKEPPED ▶ **skep**

SKEPS ▶ **skep**

SKEPSIS n doubt

SKEPTIC same as ▶ **sceptic**

SKER vb scour

SKERRED ▶ **sker**

SKERRY n rocky island or reef

SKERS ▶ **sker**

SKET vb splash (water)

SKETCH n rough drawing ▷ vb make a sketch (of)

SKETCHY adj incomplete or inadequate

SKETS ▶ **sket**

SKETTED ▶ **sket**

SKEW vb make slanting or crooked ▷ adj slanting or crooked ▷ n slanting position

SKEWED ▶ **skew**

SKEWER n pin to hold meat together during cooking ▷ vb fasten with a skewer

SKEWERS ▶ **skewer**

SKEWEST ▶ **skew**

SKEWING ▶ **skew**

SKEWS ▶ **skew**

SKI n one of a pair of long runners fastened to boots for gliding over snow or water ▷ vb travel on skis

SKIABLE ▶ **ski**

SKIBOB n vehicle made of two short skis for gliding down snow slopes

SKIBOBS ▶ **skibob**

SKID vb (of a moving vehicle) slide sideways uncontrollably ▷ n skidding

SKIDDED ▶ **skid**

SKIDDER ▶ **skid**

SKIDDOO vb go away quickly

SKIDDY ▶ **skid**

SKIDLID n crash helmet

SKIDOO n snowmobile ▷ vb travel on a skidoo

SKIDOOS ▶ **skidoo**

SKIDPAN n area made slippery so that vehicle drivers can practise controlling skids

SKIDS ▶ **skid**

SKIDWAY n platform on which logs ready for sawing are piled

SKIED ▶ **sky**

SKIER ▶ **ski**

SKIERS ▶ **ski**

SKIES ▶ **sky**

SKIEY adj of the sky

SKIEYER ▶ **skiey**

SKIFF n small boat ▷ vb travel in a skiff

SKIFFED ▶ **skiff**

SKIFFLE n style of popular music of the 1950s, played chiefly on guitars and improvised percussion instruments ▷ vb play this style of music

SKIFFS ▶ **skiff**

SKIING ▶ **ski**

SKIINGS ▶ **ski**

SKILFUL adj having or showing skill

SKILL n special ability or expertise

SKILLED adj possessing or demonstrating accomplishment, skill, or special training

SKILLET n small frying pan or shallow cooking pot

SKILLS ▶ **skill**

SKILLY n thin soup or gruel ▷ adj skilled

SKIM vb remove floating matter from the surface of (a liquid) ▷ n act or process of skimming

SKIMMED ▶ **skim**

SKIMMER n person or thing that skims

SKIMMIA n shrub of S and SE Asia grown for its ornamental red berries and evergreen foliage

SKIMP vb not invest enough time, money, material, etc

SKIMPED ▶ **skimp**

SKIMPS ▶ **skimp**

SKIMPY adj scanty or insufficient

SKIMS ▶ **skim**

SKIN n outer covering of the body ▷ vb remove the skin of

SKINFUL n sufficient alcoholic drink to make one drunk

SKINK n type of lizard with reduced limbs and smooth scales ▷ vb serve a drink

SKINKED ▶ **skink**

SKINKER ▶ **skink**

SKINKS ▶ **skink**

SKINNED ▶ **skin**

SKINNER n person who prepares or deals in animal skins

SKINNY adj thin ▷ n information

SKINS ▶ **skin**

SKINT adj having no money

SKINTER ▶ **skint**

SKIO n Scots dialect word meaning hut

SKIOS ▶ **skio**

SKIP vb leap lightly from one foot to the other ▷ n skipping

SKIPPED ▶ **skip**

SKIPPER vb captain ▷ n captain of a ship or aircraft

SKIPPET n small round box for preserving a document or seal

SKIPPY adj in high spirits

SKIPS ▶ **skip**

SKIRL n sound of bagpipes ▷ vb (of bagpipes) to give out a shrill sound

SKIRLED ▶ **skirl**

SKIRLS ▶ **skirl**

SKIRR vb move, run, or fly rapidly ▷ n whirring or grating sound, as of the wings of birds in flight

SKIRRED ▶ **skirr**

SKIRRET n umbelliferous Old World plant

SKIRRS ▶ **skirr**

SKIRT n woman's garment hanging from the waist ▷ vb border

SKIRTED ▶ **skirt**

SKIRTER n man who skirts fleeces

SKIRTS ▶ **skirt**

SKIS ▶ **ski**

SKIT n brief satirical sketch

SKITCH vb (of a dog) to attack

SKITE n, vb boast

SKITED ▶ **skite**

SKITES ▶ **skite**

SKITING ▶ **skite**

SKITS ▶ **skit**

SKITTER vb move or run rapidly or lightly

SKITTLE n bottle-shaped object used as a target in some games ▷ vb play skittles

SKIVE vb evade work or responsibility

SKIVED ▶ skive

SKIVER n tanned outer layer split from a skin ▷ vb cut leather

SKIVERS ▶ skiver

SKIVES ▶ skive

SKIVIE adj old Scots word meaning disarranged

SKIVIER ▶ skivie

SKIVING ▶ skive

SKIVVY n female servant who does menial work ▷ vb work as a skivvy

SKIVY ▶ skive

SKIWEAR n clothes for skiing in

SKLATE Scots word for ▶ slate

SKLATED ▶ sklate

SKLATES ▶ sklate

SKLENT Scots word for ▶ slant

SKLENTS ▶ sklent

SKLIFF n Scots word meaning little piece

SKLIFFS ▶ skliff

SKLIM vb Scots word meaning climb

SKLIMS ▶ sklim

SKOAL same as ▶ skol

SKOALED ▶ skoal

SKOALS ▶ skoal

SKOFF vb eat greedily

SKOFFED ▶ skoff

SKOFFS ▶ skoff

SKOL sentence substitute good health! (a drinking toast) ▷ vb down (an alcoholic drink) in one go

SKOLIA ▶ skolion

SKOLION n ancient Greek drinking song

SKOLLED ▶ skol

SKOLLIE same as ▶ skolly

SKOLLY n hooligan, usually one of a gang

SKOLS ▶ skol

SKOOKUM adj strong or brave

SKOOL ironically illiterate or childish spelling of ▶ school

SKOOLS ▶ skool

SKOOSH vb Scots word meaning squirt

SKORT n pair of shorts with a front panel which gives the appearance of a skirt

SKORTS ▶ skort

SKOSH n little bit

SKOSHES ▶ skosh

SKRAN n food

SKRANS ▶ skran

SKREEGH vb Scots word meaning screech

SKREEN n screen

SKREENS ▶ skreen

SKREIGH vb Scots word meaning screech

SKRIECH vb Scots word meaning screech

SKRIED ▶ skry

SKRIEGH vb Scots word meaning screech

SKRIES ▶ skry

SKRIK n South African word meaning fright

SKRIKE vb cry

SKRIKED ▶ skrike

SKRIKES ▶ skrike

SKRIKS ▶ skrik

SKRIMP vb steal apples

SKRIMPS ▶ skrimp

SKRONK n type of dissonant, grating popular music

SKRONKS ▶ skronk

SKRUMP vb steal apples

SKRUMPS ▶ skrump

SKRY vb try to tell future

SKRYER ▶ skry

SKRYERS ▶ skry

SKRYING ▶ skry

SKUA n large predatory gull

SKUAS ▶ skua

SKUDLER n Scots word meaning leader of festivities

SKUG vb shelter

SKUGGED ▶ skug

SKUGS ▶ skug

SKULK vb move stealthily ▷ n person who skulks

SKULKED ▶ skulk

SKULKER ▶ skulk

SKULKS ▶ skulk

SKULL n bony framework of the head ▷ vb strike on the head

SKULLED ▶ skull

SKULLS ▶ skull

SKULPIN n North American fish

SKUMMER vb defecate

SKUNK n small black-and-white N American mammal which emits a foul-smelling fluid when attacked ▷ vb defeat overwhelmingly in a game

SKUNKED ▶ skunk

SKUNKS ▶ skunk

SKUNKY ▶ skunk

SKURRY vb scurry

SKUTTLE vb scuttle

SKY n upper atmosphere as seen from the earth ▷ vb hit high in the air

SKYBORN adj born in heaven

SKYBOX n luxurious suite high up in the stand of a sports stadium

SKYCAP n luggage porter at American airport

SKYCAPS ▶ skycap

SKYCLAD adj naked

SKYDIVE vb take part in skydiving

SKYDOVE ▶ skydive

SKYED ▶ sky

SKYER n cricket ball hit up into air

SKYERS ▶ skyer

SKYEY adj of the sky

SKYF n South African slang for a cigarette or substance for smoking ▷ vb smoke a cigarette

SKYFED ▶ skyf

SKYFING ▶ skyf

SKYFS ▶ skyf

SKYHOME n Australian slang for a sub-penthouse flat in a tall building

SKYHOOK n hook hung from helicopter

SKYIER ▶ skyey

SKYIEST ▶ skyey

SKYING ▶ sky

SKYISH ▶ sky

SKYJACK vb hijack (an aircraft)

SKYLAB n orbiting space station

SKYLABS ▶ skylab

SKYLARK n lark that sings while soaring at a great height ▷ vb play or frolic

SKYLESS adj having no sky

SKYLIKE ▶ sky

SKYLINE n outline of buildings, trees, etc against the sky

SKYLIT adj having skylight

SKYMAN n paratrooper

SKYMEN ▶ skyman

SKYPHOI ▶ skyphos

SKYPHOS n ancient Greek drinking cup

SKYR n Scandinavian cheese

SKYRE vb Scots word

meaning shine
SKYRED ▶ skyre
SKYRES ▶ skyre
SKYRING ▶ skyre
SKYRS ▶ skyr
SKYSAIL n square sail set above the royal on a square-rigger
SKYSURF vb perform freefall aerobatics
SKYTE vb Scots word meaning slide
SKYTED ▶ skyte
SKYTES ▶ skyte
SKYTING ▶ skyte
SKYWALK n tightrope walk at great height
SKYWARD adj towards the sky ▷ adv towards the sky
SKYWAY n air route
SKYWAYS ▶ skyway
SLAB n broad flat piece ▷ vb cut or make into a slab or slabs
SLABBED ▶ slab
SLABBER vb dribble from the mouth
SLABBY ▶ slab
SLABS ▶ slab
SLACK same as ▶ slake
SLACKED ▶ slack
SLACKEN vb make or become slack
SLACKER n person who evades work or duty
SLACKLY ▶ slack
SLACKS pl n casual trousers
SLADANG n Malayan tapir
SLADE n little valley
SLADES ▶ slade
SLAE Scots word for ▶ sloe
SLAES ▶ slae
SLAG n waste left after metal is smelted ▷ vb criticize
SLAGGED ▶ slag
SLAGGY ▶ slag
SLAGS ▶ slag
SLAID vb Scots word for 'slid'
SLAIN ▶ slay
SLAINTE interj cheers!
SLAIRG Scots word for ▶ spread
SLAIRGS ▶ slairg
SLAKE vb satisfy (thirst or desire)
SLAKED ▶ slake
SLAKER ▶ slake
SLAKERS ▶ slake
SLAKES ▶ slake
SLAKING ▶ slake
SLALOM n skiing or canoeing race over a

winding course ▷ vb take part in a slalom
SLALOMS ▶ slalom
SLAM vb shut, put down, or hit violently and noisily ▷ n act or sound of slamming
SLAMMED ▶ slam
SLAMMER n prison
SLAMS ▶ slam
SLANDER n false and malicious statement about a person ▷ vb utter slander about
SLANE n spade for cutting turf
SLANES ▶ slane
SLANG n very informal language ▷ vb use insulting language to (someone)
SLANGED ▶ slang
SLANGER n street vendor
SLANGS ▶ slang
SLANGY ▶ slang
SLANK dialect word for ▶ lank
SLANT vb lean at an angle, slope ▷ n slope
SLANTED ▶ slant
SLANTER same as ▶ slinter
SLANTLY ▶ slant
SLANTS ▶ slant
SLANTY adj slanting
SLAP n blow with the open hand or a flat object ▷ vb strike with the open hand or a flat object
SLAPPED ▶ slap
SLAPPER ▶ slap
SLAPS ▶ slap
SLART vb spill (something)
SLARTED ▶ slart
SLARTS ▶ slart
SLASH vb cut with a sweeping stroke ▷ n sweeping stroke
SLASHED ▶ slash
SLASHER n tool or tractor-drawn machine used for cutting scrub or undergrowth in the bush
SLASHES ▶ slash
SLAT n narrow strip of wood or metal ▷ vb provide with slats
SLATCH n slack part of rope
SLATE n rock which splits easily into thin layers ▷ vb cover with slates ▷ adj dark grey
SLATED ▶ slate
SLATER n person trained in laying roof slates
SLATERS ▶ slater

SLATES ▶ slate
SLATEY adj slightly mad
SLATHER vb spread quickly or lavishly
SLATIER ▶ slaty
SLATING n act or process of laying slates
SLATS ▶ slat
SLATTED ▶ slat
SLATTER vb be slovenly
SLATY adj consisting of or resembling slate
SLAVE n person owned by another for whom he or she has to work ▷ vb work like a slave
SLAVED ▶ slave
SLAVER n person or ship engaged in the slave trade ▷ vb dribble saliva from the mouth
SLAVERS ▶ slaver
SLAVERY n state or condition of being a slave
SLAVES ▶ slave
SLAVEY n female general servant
SLAVEYS ▶ slavey
SLAVING ▶ slave
SLAVISH adj of or like a slave
SLAW short for > **coleslaw**
SLAWS ▶ slaw
SLAY vb kill
SLAYED ▶ slay
SLAYER ▶ slay
SLAYERS ▶ slay
SLAYING ▶ slay
SLAYS ▶ slay
SLEAVE n tangled thread ▷ vb disentangle (twisted thread, etc)
SLEAVED ▶ sleave
SLEAVES ▶ sleave
SLEAZE n behaviour in public life considered immoral, dishonest, or disreputable
SLEAZES ▶ sleaze
SLEAZO n sleazy person
SLEAZY adj run-down or sordid
SLEB n celebrity
SLEBS ▶ sleb
SLED same as ▶ sledge
SLEDDED ▶ sled
SLEDDER ▶ sled
SLEDED ▶ sled
SLEDGE n carriage on runners for sliding on snow ▷ vb travel by sledge
SLEDGED ▶ sledge
SLEDGER ▶ sledge
SLEDGES ▶ sledge

SLEDS ▶ **sled**
SLEE *Scots word for* ▶ **sly**
SLEECH *n* slippery mud
SLEECHY ▶ **sleech**
SLEEK *adj* glossy, smooth, and shiny ▷ *vb* make smooth and glossy, as by grooming, etc
SLEEKED ▶ **sleek**
SLEEKEN *vb* make sleek
SLEEKER ▶ **sleek**
SLEEKIT *adj* smooth
SLEEKLY ▶ **sleek**
SLEEKS ▶ **sleek**
SLEEKY ▶ **sleek**
SLEEP *n* state of rest characterized by unconsciousness ▷ *vb* be in or as if in a state of sleep
SLEEPER *n* railway car fitted for sleeping in
SLEEPRY *Scots word for* ▶ **sleepy**
SLEEPS ▶ **sleep**
SLEEPY *adj* needing sleep
SLEER ▶ **slee**
SLEEST ▶ **slee**
SLEET *n* rain and snow or hail falling together ▷ *vb* fall as sleet
SLEETED ▶ **sleet**
SLEETS ▶ **sleet**
SLEETY ▶ **sleet**
SLEEVE *n* part of a garment which covers the arm
SLEEVED ▶ **sleeve**
SLEEVER *n* old beer measure
SLEEVES ▶ **sleeve**
SLEEZY *adj* sleazy
SLEIDED *adj* old word meaning separated
SLEIGH *same as* ▶ **sledge**
SLEIGHS ▶ **sleigh**
SLEIGHT *n* skill or cunning
SLENDER *adj* slim
SLENTER *same as* ▶ **slinter**
SLEPT ▶ **sleep**
SLEUTH *n* detective ▷ *vb* track or follow
SLEUTHS ▶ **sleuth**
SLEW *vb* twist sideways, esp awkwardly
SLEWED ▶ **slew**
SLEWING ▶ **slew**
SLEWS ▶ **slew**
SLEY *n* weaver's tool for separating threads
SLEYS ▶ **sley**
SLICE *n* thin flat piece cut from something ▷ *vb* cut into slices
SLICED ▶ **slice**

SLICER ▶ **slice**
SLICERS ▶ **slice**
SLICES ▶ **slice**
SLICING ▶ **slice**
SLICK *adj* persuasive and glib ▷ *n* patch of oil on water ▷ *vb* make smooth or sleek
SLICKED ▶ **slick**
SLICKEN *vb* make smooth
SLICKER *n* sly or untrustworthy person
SLICKLY ▶ **slick**
SLICKS ▶ **slick**
SLID ▶ **slide**
SLIDDEN ▶ **slide**
SLIDDER *vb* slip
SLIDE *vb* slip smoothly along (a surface) ▷ *n* sliding
SLIDED ▶ **slide**
SLIDER ▶ **slide**
SLIDERS ▶ **slide**
SLIDES ▶ **slide**
SLIDING ▶ **slide**
SLIER ▶ **sly**
SLIEST ▶ **sly**
SLIEVE *n* Irish mountain
SLIEVES ▶ **slieve**
SLIGHT *adj* small in quantity or extent ▷ *n* snub ▷ *vb* insult (someone) by behaving rudely
SLIGHTS ▶ **slight**
SLILY ▶ **sly**
SLIM *adj* not heavy or stout, thin ▷ *vb* make or become slim by diet and exercise
SLIME *n* unpleasant thick slippery substance ▷ *vb* cover with slime
SLIMED ▶ **slime**
SLIMES ▶ **slime**
SLIMIER ▶ **slimy**
SLIMILY ▶ **slimy**
SLIMING ▶ **slime**
SLIMLY ▶ **slim**
SLIMMED ▶ **slim**
SLIMMER ▶ **slim**
SLIMPSY *adj* thin and flimsy
SLIMS ▶ **slim**
SLIMSY *adj* frail
SLIMY *adj* of, like, or covered with slime
SLING *n* bandage hung from the neck to support an injured hand or arm ▷ *vb* throw
SLINGER ▶ **sling**
SLINGS ▶ **sling**
SLINK *vb* move furtively or guiltily ▷ *n* animal, esp a calf, born prematurely
SLINKED ▶ **slink**

SLINKER ▶ **slink**
SLINKS ▶ **slink**
SLINKY *adj* (of clothes) figure-hugging
SLINTER *n* dodge, trick, or stratagem
SLIOTAR *n* ball used in hurling
SLIP *vb* lose balance by sliding ▷ *n* slipping
SLIPE *n* wool removed from the pelt of a slaughtered sheep by immersion in a chemical bath ▷ *vb* remove skin
SLIPED ▶ **slipe**
SLIPES ▶ **slipe**
SLIPING ▶ **slipe**
SLIPOUT *n* instance of slipping out
SLIPPED ▶ **slip**
SLIPPER *n* light shoe for indoor wear ▷ *vb* hit or beat with a slipper
SLIPPY *adj* slippery
SLIPS ▶ **slip**
SLIPT *vb* old form of slipped
SLIPUP *n* mistake or mishap
SLIPUPS ▶ **slipup**
SLIPWAY *n* launching slope on which ships are built or repaired
SLISH *n* old word meaning cut
SLISHES ▶ **slish**
SLIT *n* long narrow cut or opening ▷ *vb* make a long straight cut in
SLITHER *vb* slide unsteadily ▷ *n* slithering movement
SLITS ▶ **slit**
SLITTED ▶ **slit**
SLITTER ▶ **slit**
SLITTY ▶ **slit**
SLIVE *vb* slip
SLIVED ▶ **slive**
SLIVEN ▶ **slive**
SLIVER *n* small thin piece ▷ *vb* cut into slivers
SLIVERS ▶ **sliver**
SLIVES ▶ **slive**
SLIVING ▶ **slive**
SLOAN *n* severe telling-off
SLOANS ▶ **sloan**
SLOB *n* lazy and untidy person
SLOBBER *vb* dribble or drool ▷ *n* liquid or saliva spilt from the mouth
SLOBBY ▶ **slob**
SLOBS ▶ **slob**
SLOCKEN *vb* Scots word meaning slake

S

SLOE n sour blue-black fruit
SLOES ▶ sloe
SLOG vb work hard and steadily ▷ n long and exhausting work or walk
SLOGAN n catchword or phrase used in politics or advertising
SLOGANS ▶ slogan
SLOGGED ▶ slog
SLOGGER ▶ slog
SLOGS ▶ slog
SLOID n Swedish woodwork
SLOIDS ▶ sloid
SLOJD n Swedish woodwork
SLOJDS ▶ slojd
SLOKEN vb Scots word meaning slake
SLOKENS ▶ sloken
SLOOM vb slumber
SLOOMED ▶ sloom
SLOOMS ▶ sloom
SLOOMY ▶ sloom
SLOOP n small single-masted ship
SLOOPS ▶ sloop
SLOOSH vb wash with water
SLOOT n ditch for irrigation or drainage
SLOOTS ▶ sloot
SLOP vb splash or spill ▷ n spilt liquid
SLOPE vb slant ▷ n sloping surface
SLOPED ▶ slope
SLOPER ▶ slope
SLOPERS ▶ slope
SLOPES ▶ slope
SLOPIER ▶ slope
SLOPING ▶ slope
SLOPPED ▶ slop
SLOPPY adj careless or untidy
SLOPS ▶ slop
SLOPY ▶ slope
SLORM vb wipe carelessly
SLORMED ▶ slorm
SLORMS ▶ slorm
SLOSH vb pour carelessly ▷ n splashing sound
SLOSHED ▶ slosh
SLOSHES ▶ slosh
SLOSHY ▶ slosh
SLOT n narrow opening for inserting something ▷ vb make a slot or slots in
SLOTH n slow-moving animal of tropical America ▷ vb be lazy
SLOTHED ▶ sloth
SLOTHS ▶ sloth
SLOTS ▶ slot

SLOTTED ▶ slot
SLOTTER ▶ slot
SLOUCH vb sit, stand, or move with a drooping posture ▷ n drooping posture
SLOUCHY adj slouching
SLOUGH n bog ▷ vb (of a snake) shed (its skin)
SLOUGHI n N African breed of dog resembling a greyhound
SLOUGHS ▶ slough
SLOUGHY ▶ slough
SLOVE ▶ slive
SLOVEN n habitually dirty or untidy person
SLOVENS ▶ sloven
SLOW adj taking a longer time than is usual or expected ▷ adv slowly ▷ vb reduce the speed (of)
SLOWED ▶ slow
SLOWER ▶ slow
SLOWEST ▶ slow
SLOWING ▶ slow
SLOWISH ▶ slow
SLOWLY ▶ slow
SLOWS ▶ slow
SLOYD n Swedish woodwork
SLOYDS ▶ sloyd
SLUB n lump in yarn or fabric, often made intentionally to give a knobbly effect ▷ vb draw out and twist (a sliver of fibre) preparatory to spinning ▷ adj (of material) having an irregular appearance
SLUBB same as ▶ slub
SLUBBED ▶ slub
SLUBBER vb smear
SLUBBS ▶ slubb
SLUBBY ▶ slub
SLUBS ▶ slub
SLUDGE n thick mud ▷ vb to convert into sludge
SLUDGED ▶ sludge
SLUDGES ▶ sludge
SLUDGY adj consisting of, containing, or like sludge
SLUE same as ▶ slew
SLUED ▶ slue
SLUEING ▶ slue
SLUES ▶ slue
SLUFF same as ▶ slough
SLUFFED ▶ sluff
SLUFFS ▶ sluff
SLUG n land snail with no shell ▷ vb hit hard
SLUGGED ▶ slug

SLUGGER n (esp in boxing, baseball, etc) a person who strikes hard
SLUGS ▶ slug
SLUICE n channel that carries a rapid current of water ▷ vb drain water by means of a sluice
SLUICED ▶ sluice
SLUICES ▶ sluice
SLUICY ▶ sluice
SLUING ▶ slue
SLUIT n water channel in South Africa
SLUITS ▶ sluit
SLUM n squalid overcrowded house or area ▷ vb temporarily and deliberately experience poorer places or conditions than usual
SLUMBER n sleep ▷ vb sleep
SLUMBRY same as > slumbery
SLUMGUM n material left after wax is extracted from honeycomb
SLUMISM n existence of slums
SLUMMED ▶ slum
SLUMMER ▶ slum
SLUMMY ▶ slum
SLUMP vb (of prices or demand) decline suddenly ▷ n sudden decline in prices or demand
SLUMPED ▶ slump
SLUMPS ▶ slump
SLUMPY adj boggy
SLUMS ▶ slum
SLUNG ▶ sling
SLUNK ▶ slink
SLUR vb pronounce or utter (words) indistinctly ▷ n slurring of words
SLURB n suburban slum
SLURBAN ▶ slurb
SLURBS ▶ slurb
SLURP vb eat or drink noisily ▷ n slurping sound
SLURPED ▶ slurp
SLURPER ▶ slurp
SLURPS ▶ slurp
SLURPY adj making a slurping noise
SLURRED ▶ slur
SLURRY n muddy liquid mixture ▷ vb spread slurry
SLURS ▶ slur
SLUSE same as ▶ sluice
SLUSES ▶ sluice
SLUSH n watery muddy substance ▷ vb make one's

way through or as if through slush

SLUSHED ▶ **slush**

SLUSHES ▶ **slush**

SLUSHY *adj* of, resembling, or consisting of slush ▷ *n* unskilled kitchen assistant

SLUTCH *n* mud

SLUTCHY ▶ **slutch**

SLY *adj* crafty

SLYER ▶ **sly**

SLYEST ▶ **sly**

SLYISH ▶ **sly**

SLYLY ▶ **sly**

SLYNESS ▶ **sly**

SLYPE *n* covered passageway in a church that connects the transept to the chapterhouse

SLYPES ▶ **slype**

SMA *Scots word for* ▶ **small**

SMAAK *vb* South African slang for like or love

SMAAKED ▶ **smaak**

SMAAKS ▶ **smaak**

SMACK *vb* slap sharply ▷ *n* sharp slap ▷ *adv* squarely or directly

SMACKED ▶ **smack**

SMACKER *n* loud kiss

SMACKS ▶ **smack**

SMAIK *n* Scots word meaning rascal

SMAIKS ▶ **smaik**

SMALL *adj* not large in size, number, or amount ▷ *n* narrow part of the lower back ▷ *adv* into small pieces ▷ *vb* make small

SMALLED ▶ **small**

SMALLER ▶ **small**

SMALLS ▶ **small**

SMALM *same as* ▶ **smarm**

SMALMED ▶ **smalm**

SMALMS ▶ **smalm**

SMALMY *same as* ▶ **smarmy**

SMALT *n* type of silica glass coloured deep blue with cobalt oxide

SMALTI ▶ **smalto**

SMALTO *n* coloured glass, etc, used in mosaics

SMALTOS ▶ **smalto**

SMALTS ▶ **smalt**

SMARAGD *n* any green gemstone, such as the emerald

SMARM *vb* bring (oneself) into favour (with) ▷ *n* obsequious flattery

SMARMED ▶ **smarm**

SMARMS ▶ **smarm**

SMARMY *adj* unpleasantly suave or flattering

SMART *adj* well-kept and neat ▷ *vb* feel or cause stinging pain ▷ *n* stinging pain ▷ *adv* in a smart manner

SMARTED ▶ **smart**

SMARTEN *vb* make or become smart

SMARTER ▶ **smart**

SMARTIE *same as* ▶ **smarty**

SMARTLY ▶ **smart**

SMARTS *pl n* know-how, intelligence, or wits

SMARTY *n* would-be clever person

SMASH *vb* break violently and noisily ▷ *n* act or sound of smashing ▷ *adv* with a smash

SMASHED *adj* completely intoxicated with alcohol

SMASHER *n* attractive person or thing

SMASHES ▶ **smash**

SMASHUP *n* bad collision of cars

SMATCH *less common word for* ▶ **smack**

SMATTER *n* smattering ▷ *vb* prattle

SMAZE *n* smoky haze, less damp than fog

SMAZES ▶ **smaze**

SMEAR *vb* spread with a greasy or sticky substance ▷ *n* dirty mark or smudge

SMEARED ▶ **smear**

SMEARER ▶ **smear**

SMEARS ▶ **smear**

SMEARY *adj* smeared, dirty

SMEATH *n* duck

SMEATHS ▶ **smeath**

SMECTIC *adj* (of a substance) existing in state in which the molecules are oriented in layers

SMEDDUM *n* any fine powder

SMEE *n* duck

SMEECH *Southwest English dialect form of* ▶ **smoke**

SMEEK *vb* smoke

SMEEKED ▶ **smeek**

SMEEKS ▶ **smeek**

SMEES ▶ **smee**

SMEETH *n* duck

SMEETHS ▶ **smeeth**

SMEGMA *n* whitish sebaceous secretion that accumulates beneath the prepuce

SMEGMAS ▶ **smegma**

SMEIK ▶ **smeke**

SMEIKED ▶ **smeked**

SMEIKS ▶ **smeik**

SMEKE *n* smoke ▷ *vb* smoke

SMEKED ▶ **smeke** (sense 2)

SMEKES ▶ **smeke**

SMEKING > **smeke** (sense 2)

SMELL *vb* perceive (a scent or odour) by means of the nose ▷ *n* ability to perceive odours by the nose

SMELLED ▶ **smell**

SMELLER ▶ **smell**

SMELLS ▶ **smell**

SMELLY *adj* having a nasty smell

SMELT *vb* extract metal from an ore

SMELTED ▶ **smelt**

SMELTER *n* industrial plant where smelting is carried out

SMELTS ▶ **smelt**

SMERK *same as* ▶ **smirk**

SMERKED ▶ **smerk**

SMERKS ▶ **smerk**

SMEUSE *n* way through hedge

SMEUSES ▶ **smeuse**

SMEW *n* duck of N Europe and Asia

SMEWS ▶ **smew**

SMICKER *vb* look at someone amorously

SMICKET *n* smock

SMICKLY *adv* amorously

SMIDDY *Scots word for* ▶ **smithy**

SMIDGE *n* very small amount or part

SMIDGEN *n* very small amount or part

SMIDGES ▶ **smidge**

SMIDGIN *same as* ▶ **smidgen**

SMIGHT *same as* ▶ **smite**

SMIGHTS ▶ **smight**

SMILAX *n* type of climbing shrub

SMILE *n* turning up of the corners of the mouth to show pleasure or friendliness ▷ *vb* give a smile

SMILED ▶ **smile**

SMILER ▶ **smile**

SMILERS ▶ **smile**

SMILES ▶ **smile**

SMILET *n* little smile

SMILETS ▶ **smilet**

SMILEY *n* symbol depicting a smile or other facial

S

expression, used in e-mail ▷ *adj* cheerful
SMILEYS ▶ **smiley**
SMILIER ▶ **smiley**
SMILING ▶ **smile**
SMIR *n* drizzly rain ▷ *vb* drizzle lightly
SMIRCH *n* stain ▷ *vb* disgrace
SMIRK *n* smug smile ▷ *vb* give a smirk
SMIRKED ▶ **smirk**
SMIRKER ▶ **smirk**
SMIRKS ▶ **smirk**
SMIRKY ▶ **smirk**
SMIRR *same as* ▶ **smir**
SMIRRED ▶ **smirr**
SMIRRS ▶ **smirr**
SMIRRY ▶ **smirr**
SMIRS ▶ **smir**
SMIT ▶ **smite**
SMITE *vb* strike hard
SMITER ▶ **smite**
SMITERS ▶ **smite**
SMITES ▶ **smite**
SMITH *n* worker in metal ▷ *vb* work in metal
SMITHED ▶ **smith**
SMITHS ▶ **smith**
SMITHY *n* blacksmith's workshop ▷ *vb* work as a smith
SMITING ▶ **smite**
SMITS ▶ **smit**
SMITTED ▶ **smit**
SMITTEN ▶ **smite**
SMITTLE *adj* infectious
SMOCK *n* loose overall ▷ *vb* gather (material) by sewing in a honeycomb pattern
SMOCKED ▶ **smock**
SMOCKS ▶ **smock**
SMOG *n* mixture of smoke and fog
SMOGGY ▶ **smog**
SMOGS ▶ **smog**
SMOILE *same as* ▶ **smile**
SMOILED ▶ **smoile**
SMOILES ▶ **smoile**
SMOKE *n* cloudy mass that rises from something burning ▷ *vb* give off smoke or treat with smoke
SMOKED ▶ **smoke**
SMOKEHO *same as* ▶ **smoko**
SMOKER *n* person who habitually smokes tobacco
SMOKERS ▶ **smoker**
SMOKES ▶ **smoke**
SMOKEY *same as* ▶ **smoky**
SMOKIE *n* smoked haddock
SMOKIER ▶ **smoky**

SMOKIES ▶ **smoky**
SMOKILY ▶ **smoky**
SMOKING ▶ **smoke**
SMOKO *n* short break from work for tea or a cigarette
SMOKOS ▶ **smoko**
SMOKY *adj* filled with or giving off smoke, sometimes excessively ▷ *n* haddock that has been smoked
SMOLDER *same as* > **smoulder**
SMOLT *n* young salmon at the stage when it migrates to the sea
SMOLTS ▶ **smolt**
SMOOCH *vb* kiss and cuddle ▷ *n* smooching
SMOOCHY *adj* romantic
SMOODGE *same as* ▶ **smooch**
SMOOGE *same as* ▶ **smooch**
SMOOGED ▶ **smooge**
SMOOGES ▶ **smooge**
SMOOR *vb* Scots word meaning put out fire
SMOORED ▶ **smoor**
SMOORS ▶ **smoor**
SMOOSH *vb* paint to give softened look
SMOOT *vb* work as printer
SMOOTED ▶ **smoot**
SMOOTH *adj* even in surface, texture, or consistency ▷ *vb* make smooth ▷ *adv* in a smooth manner ▷ *n* smooth part of something
SMOOTHS ▶ **smooth**
SMOOTHY *same as* > **smoothie**
SMOOTS ▶ **smoot**
SMORE *same as* ▶ **smoor**
SMORED ▶ **smore**
SMORES ▶ **smore**
SMORING ▶ **smore**
SMOTE ▶ **smite**
SMOTHER *vb* suffocate or stifle ▷ *n* anything, such as a cloud of smoke, that stifles
SMOUCH *vb* kiss
SMOUSE *vb* South African word meaning peddle
SMOUSED ▶ **smouse**
SMOUSER ▶ **smouse**
SMOUSES ▶ **smouse**
SMOUT *n* child or undersized person ▷ *vb* creep or sneak
SMOUTED ▶ **smout**
SMOUTS ▶ **smout**

SMOWT *same as* ▶ **smout**
SMOWTS ▶ **smowt**
SMOYLE *same as* ▶ **smile**
SMOYLED ▶ **smoyle**
SMOYLES ▶ **smoyle**
SMRITI *n* class of Hindu sacred literature derived from the Vedas
SMRITIS ▶ **smriti**
SMUDGE *vb* make or become smeared or soiled ▷ *n* dirty mark
SMUDGED ▶ **smudge**
SMUDGER ▶ **smudge**
SMUDGES ▶ **smudge**
SMUDGY *adj* smeared, blurred, or soiled, or likely to become so
SMUG *adj* self-satisfied ▷ *vb* make neat
SMUGGED ▶ **smug**
SMUGGER ▶ **smug**
SMUGGLE *vb* import or export (goods) secretly and illegally
SMUGLY ▶ **smug**
SMUGS ▶ **smug**
SMUR *same as* ▶ **smir**
SMURRED ▶ **smur**
SMURRY ▶ **smur**
SMURS ▶ **smur**
SMUSH *vb* crush
SMUSHED ▶ **smush**
SMUSHES ▶ **smush**
SMUT *n* obscene jokes, pictures, etc ▷ *vb* mark or become marked or smudged, as with soot
SMUTCH *vb* smudge ▷ *n* mark
SMUTCHY ▶ **smutch**
SMUTS ▶ **smut**
SMUTTED ▶ **smut**
SMUTTY ▶ **smut**
SMYTRIE *n* Scots word meaning collection
ŚNAB *same as* ▶ **snob**
SNABBLE *same as* ▶ **snaffle**
SNABS ▶ **snab**
SNACK *n* light quick meal ▷ *vb* eat a snack
SNACKED ▶ **snack**
SNACKER ▶ **snack**
SNACKS ▶ **snack**
SNAFFLE *n* jointed bit for a horse ▷ *vb* steal
SNAFU *n* confusion or chaos regarded as the normal state ▷ *adj* confused or muddled up, as usual ▷ *vb* throw into chaos
SNAFUED ▶ **snafu**
SNAFUS ▶ **snafu**

S

SNAG n difficulty or disadvantage ▷ vb catch or tear on a point
SNAGGED ▶ snag
SNAGGY adj having sharp protuberances
SNAGS ▶ snag
SNAIL n slow-moving mollusc with a spiral shell ▷ vb move slowly
SNAILED ▶ snail
SNAILS ▶ snail
SNAILY ▶ snail
SNAKE n long thin scaly limbless reptile ▷ vb move in a winding course like a snake
SNAKED ▶ snake
SNAKES ▶ snake
SNAKEY same as ▶ snaky
SNAKIER ▶ snaky
SNAKILY ▶ snaky
SNAKING ▶ snake
SNAKISH ▶ snake
SNAKY adj twisted or winding
SNAP vb break suddenly ▷ n act or sound of snapping ▷ adj made on the spur of the moment ▷ adv with a snap
SNAPPED ▶ snap
SNAPPER n food fish of Australia and New Zealand ▷ vb stumble
SNAPPY adj irritable
SNAPS ▶ snap
SNAPTIN n container for food
SNAR same as ▶ snarl
SNARE n trap with a noose ▷ vb catch in or as if in a snare
SNARED ▶ snare
SNARER ▶ snare
SNARERS ▶ snare
SNARES ▶ snare
SNARF vb eat or drink greedily
SNARFED ▶ snarf
SNARFS ▶ snarf
SNARIER ▶ snare
SNARING ▶ snare
SNARK n imaginary creature in Lewis Carroll's poetry
SNARKS ▶ snark
SNARKY adj unpleasant and scornful
SNARL vb (of an animal) growl with bared teeth ▷ n act or sound of snarling
SNARLED ▶ snarl

SNARLER ▶ snarl
SNARLS ▶ snarl
SNARLY ▶ snarl
SNARRED ▶ snar
SNARS ▶ snar
SNARY ▶ snare
SNASH vb Scots word meaning speak cheekily
SNASHED ▶ snash
SNASHES ▶ snash
SNASTE n candle wick
SNASTES ▶ snaste
SNATCH vb seize or try to seize suddenly ▷ n snatching
SNATCHY adj disconnected or spasmodic
SNATH n handle of a scythe
SNATHE same as ▶ snath
SNATHES ▶ snathe
SNATHS ▶ snath
SNAW Scots variant of ▶ snow
SNAWED ▶ snaw
SNAWING ▶ snaw
SNAWS ▶ snaw
SNAZZY adj stylish and flashy
SNEAD n scythe handle
SNEADS ▶ snead
SNEAK vb move furtively ▷ n cowardly or underhand person ▷ adj without warning
SNEAKED ▶ sneak
SNEAKER n soft shoe
SNEAKS ▶ sneak
SNEAKY ▶ sneak
SNEAP vb nip
SNEAPED ▶ sneap
SNEAPS ▶ sneap
SNEATH same as ▶ snath
SNEATHS ▶ sneath
SNEB same as ▶ snib
SNEBBE same as ▶ snub
SNEBBED ▶ sneb
SNEBBES ▶ snebbe
SNEBS ▶ sneb
SNECK n small squared stone used in a rubble wall to fill spaces between stones ▷ vb fasten (a latch)
SNECKED ▶ sneck
SNECKS ▶ sneck
SNED vb prune or trim
SNEDDED ▶ sned
SNEDS ▶ sned
SNEE vb cut
SNEED ▶ snee
SNEEING ▶ snee
SNEER n contemptuous expression or remark ▷ vb show contempt by a sneer

SNEERED ▶ sneer
SNEERER ▶ sneer
SNEERS ▶ sneer
SNEERY adj contemptuous or scornful
SNEES ▶ snee
SNEESH n Scots word meaning pinch of snuff
SNEEZE vb expel air from the nose suddenly, involuntarily, and noisily ▷ n act or sound of sneezing
SNEEZED ▶ sneeze
SNEEZER ▶ sneeze
SNEEZES ▶ sneeze
SNEEZY ▶ sneeze
SNELL adj biting ▷ vb attach hook to fishing line
SNELLED ▶ snell
SNELLER ▶ snell
SNELLS ▶ snell
SNELLY ▶ snell
SNIB n catch of a door or window ▷ vb bolt or fasten (a door)
SNIBBED ▶ snib
SNIBS ▶ snib
SNICK n (make) a small cut or notch ▷ vb make a small cut or notch in (something)
SNICKED ▶ snick
SNICKER same as ▶ snigger
SNICKET n passageway between walls or fences
SNICKS ▶ snick
SNIDE adj critical in an unfair and nasty way ▷ n sham jewellery ▷ vb fill or load
SNIDED ▶ snide
SNIDELY ▶ snide
SNIDER ▶ snide
SNIDES ▶ snide
SNIDEST ▶ snide
SNIDEY same as ▶ snide
SNIDIER ▶ snidey
SNIDING ▶ snide
SNIES ▶ sny
SNIFF vb inhale through the nose in short audible breaths ▷ n act or sound of sniffing
SNIFFED ▶ sniff
SNIFFER n device for detecting hidden substances such as drugs or explosives, esp by their odour
SNIFFLE vb sniff repeatedly, as when suffering from a cold ▷ n slight cold
SNIFFLY ▶ sniffle
SNIFFS ▶ sniff

S

SNIFFY adj contemptuous or scornful

SNIFT same as ▸ **sniff**

SNIFTED ▸ **snift**

SNIFTER n small quantity of alcoholic drink ▹ vb sniff

SNIFTS ▸ **snift**

SNIFTY adj slang word meaning excellent

SNIG vb drag (a felled log) by a chain or cable

SNIGGED ▸ **snig**

SNIGGER n a sly laugh ▹ vb laugh slyly

SNIGGLE vb fish for eels by dangling or thrusting a baited hook into cavities ▹ n baited hook used for sniggling eels

SNIGLET n invented word

SNIGS ▸ **snig**

SNIP vb cut in small quick strokes with scissors or shears ▹ n bargain ▹ interj representation of the sound of scissors or shears closing

SNIPE n wading bird with a long straight bill ▹ vb shoot at (a person) from cover

SNIPED ▸ **snipe**

SNIPER n person who shoots at someone from cover

SNIPERS ▸ **sniper**

SNIPES ▸ **snipe**

SNIPIER ▸ **snipy**

SNIPING ▸ **snipe**

SNIPPED ▸ **snip**

SNIPPER ▸ **snip**

SNIPPET n small piece

SNIPPY adj scrappy

SNIPS ▸ **snip**

SNIPY adj like a snipe

SNIRT n Scots word meaning suppressed laugh

SNIRTLE vb Scots word meaning snicker

SNIRTS ▸ **snirt**

SNIT n fit of temper

SNITCH vb act as an informer ▹ n informer

SNITCHY adj bad-tempered or irritable

SNITS ▸ **snit**

SNIVEL vb cry in a whining way ▹ n act of snivelling

SNIVELS ▸ **snivel**

SNOB n person who judges others by social rank

SNOBBY ▸ **snob**

SNOBS ▸ **snob**

SNOD vb Scots word meaning make tidy

SNODDED ▸ **snod**

SNODDER ▸ **snod**

SNODDIT ▸ **snod**

SNODS ▸ **snod**

SNOEK n edible marine fish

SNOEKS ▸ **snoek**

SNOEP adj mean or tight-fisted

SNOG vb kiss and cuddle ▹ n act of kissing and cuddling

SNOGGED ▸ **snog**

SNOGS ▸ **snog**

SNOKE same as ▸ **snook**

SNOKED ▸ **snoke**

SNOKES ▸ **snoke**

SNOKING ▸ **snoke**

SNOOD n pouch, often of net, loosely holding a woman's hair at the back ▹ vb hold (the hair) in a snood

SNOODED ▸ **snood**

SNOODS ▸ **snood**

SNOOK n any of several large game fishes ▹ vb lurk

SNOOKED ▸ **snook**

SNOOKER n game played on a billiard table ▹ vb leave (a snooker opponent) in a position such that another ball blocks the target ball

SNOOKS ▸ **snook**

SNOOL vb Scots word meaning dominate

SNOOLED ▸ **snool**

SNOOLS ▸ **snool**

SNOOP vb pry ▹ n snooping

SNOOPED ▸ **snoop**

SNOOPER n person who snoops

SNOOPS ▸ **snoop**

SNOOPY ▸ **snoop**

SNOOT n nose ▹ vb look contemptuously at

SNOOTED ▸ **snoot**

SNOOTS ▸ **snoot**

SNOOTY adj haughty

SNOOZE vb take a brief light sleep ▹ n brief light sleep

SNOOZED ▸ **snooze**

SNOOZER ▸ **snooze**

SNOOZES ▸ **snooze**

SNOOZLE vb cuddle and sleep

SNOOZY ▸ **snooze**

SNORE vb make snoring sounds while sleeping ▹ n sound of snoring

SNORED ▸ **snore**

SNORER ▸ **snore**

SNORERS ▸ **snore**

SNORES ▸ **snore**

SNORING ▸ **snore**

SNORKEL n tube allowing a swimmer to breathe while face down on the surface of the water ▹ vb swim using a snorkel

SNORT vb exhale noisily through the nostrils ▹ n act or sound of snorting

SNORTED ▸ **snort**

SNORTER n person or animal that snorts

SNORTS ▸ **snort**

SNORTY ▸ **snort**

SNOT n mucus from the nose ▹ vb blow one's nose

SNOTRAG n handkerchief

SNOTS ▸ **snot**

SNOTTED ▸ **snot**

SNOTTER vb breathe through obstructed nostrils

SNOTTIE n midshipman

SNOTTY adj covered with mucus from the nose

SNOUT n animal's projecting nose and jaws ▹ vb have or give a snout

SNOUTED ▸ **snout**

SNOUTS ▸ **snout**

SNOUTY ▸ **snout**

SNOW n frozen vapour falling from the sky in flakes ▹ vb fall as or like snow

SNOWCAP n cap of snow on top of a mountain

SNOWCAT n tracked vehicle for travelling over snow

SNOWED adj under the influence of narcotic drugs

SNOWIER ▸ **snowy**

SNOWILY ▸ **snowy**

SNOWING ▸ **snow**

SNOWISH adj like snow

SNOWK same as ▸ **snook**

SNOWKED ▸ **snowk**

SNOWKS ▸ **snowk**

SNOWMAN n figure shaped out of snow

SNOWMEN ▸ **snowman**

SNOWS ▸ **snow**

SNOWY adj covered with or abounding in snow

SNUB vb insult deliberately ▹ n deliberate insult ▹ adj (of a nose) short and blunt

SNUBBE n stub

SNUBBED ▸ **snub**

SNUBBER ▸ **snub**

SNUBBES ▸ **snubbe**

SNUBBY ▸ **snub**

SNUBFIN adj as in snubfin dolphin Australian dolphin with a small dorsal fin

SNUBS ▸ **snub**

S

SNUCK *past tense and past participle of* ▶ **sneak**

SNUDGE *vb* be miserly

SNUDGED ▶ **snudge**

SNUDGES ▶ **snudge**

SNUFF *n* powdered tobacco for sniffing up the nostrils ▷ *vb* extinguish (a candle)

SNUFFED ▶ **snuff**

SNUFFER ▶ **snuff**

SNUFFLE *vb* breathe noisily or with difficulty ▷ *n* act or the sound of snuffling

SNUFFLY ▶ **snuffle**

SNUFFS ▶ **snuff**

SNUFFY *adj* of, relating to, or resembling snuff

SNUG *adj* warm and comfortable ▷ *n* (in Britain and Ireland) small room in a pub ▷ *vb* make or become comfortable and warm

SNUGGED ▶ **snug**

SNUGGER ▶ **snug**

SNUGGLE *vb* nestle into a person or thing for warmth or from affection ▷ *n* act of snuggling

SNUGLY ▶ **snug**

SNUGS ▶ **snug**

SNUSH *vb* take snuff

SNUSHED ▶ **snush**

SNUSHES ▶ **snush**

SNUZZLE *vb* root in ground

SNY *same as* ▶ **snye**

> A side channel of a river, that can be useful when you are short of vowels. And note that it can be extended to form **snye**.

SNYE *n* side channel of a river

SNYES ▶ **snye**

SO *adv* such an extent ▷ *interj* exclamation of surprise, triumph, or realization ▷ *n* the fifth note of the musical scale

SOAK *vb* make wet ▷ *n* soaking

SOAKAGE *n* process or a period in which a permeable substance is soaked in a liquid

SOAKED ▶ **soak**

SOAKEN ▶ **soak**

SOAKER ▶ **soak**

SOAKERS ▶ **soak**

SOAKING ▶ **soak**

SOAKS ▶ **soak**

SOAP *n* compound of alkali and fat, used with water as a cleaning agent ▷ *vb* apply soap to

SOAPBOX *n* crate used as a platform for speech-making ▷ *vb* deliver a speech from a soapbox

SOAPED ▶ **soap**

SOAPER *n* soap opera

SOAPERS ▶ **soaper**

SOAPIE *n* soap opera

SOAPIER ▶ **soapy**

SOAPIES ▶ **soapie**

SOAPILY ▶ **soapy**

SOAPING ▶ **soap**

SOAPS ▶ **soap**

SOAPY *adj* covered with soap

SOAR *vb* rise or fly upwards ▷ *n* act of soaring

SOARE *n* young hawk

SOARED ▶ **soar**

SOARER ▶ **soar**

SOARERS ▶ **soar**

SOARES ▶ **soare**

SOARING ▶ **soar**

SOARS ▶ **soar**

SOAVE *n* dry white Italian wine

SOAVES ▶ **soave**

SOB *vb* weep with convulsive gasps ▷ *n* act or sound of sobbing

SOBA *n* (in Japanese cookery) noodles made from buckwheat flour

SOBAS ▶ **soba**

SOBBED ▶ **sob**

SOBBER ▶ **sob**

SOBBERS ▶ **sob**

SOBBING ▶ **sob**

SOBEIT *conj* provided that

SOBER *adj* not drunk ▷ *vb* make or become sober

SOBERED ▶ **sober**

SOBERER ▶ **sober**

SOBERLY ▶ **sober**

SOBERS ▶ **sober**

SOBFUL *adj* tearful

SOBOLE *n* creeping underground stem that produces roots and buds

SOBOLES ▶ **sobole**

SOBS ▶ **sob**

SOC *n* feudal right to hold court

SOCA *n* mixture of soul and calypso music popular in the E Caribbean

SOCAGE *n* tenure of land by certain services, esp of an agricultural nature

SOCAGER ▶ **socage**

SOCAGES ▶ **socage**

SOCAS ▶ **soca**

SOCCAGE *same as* ▶ **socage**

SOCCER *n* football played by two teams of eleven kicking a spherical ball

SOCCERS ▶ **soccer**

SOCIAL *adj* living in a community ▷ *n* informal gathering

SOCIALS ▶ **social**

SOCIATE *n* associate

SOCIETY *n* human beings considered as a group

SOCK *n* knitted covering for the foot ▷ *vb* hit hard

SOCKED ▶ **sock**

SOCKET *n* hole or recess into which something fits ▷ *vb* furnish with or place into a socket

SOCKETS ▶ **socket**

SOCKEYE *n* Pacific salmon with red flesh

SOCKING ▶ **sock**

SOCKMAN *same as* ▶ **socman**

SOCKMEN ▶ **sockman**

SOCKO *adj* excellent

SOCKS ▶ **sock**

SOCLE *another name for* ▶ **plinth**

SOCLES ▶ **socle**

SOCMAN *n* tenant holding land by socage

SOCMEN ▶ **socman**

SOCS ▶ **soc**

SOD *n* (piece of) turf ▷ *vb* cover with sods

SODA *n* compound of sodium

SODAIC *adj* containing soda

SODAIN *same as* ▶ **sudden**

SODAINE *same as* ▶ **sudden**

SODAS ▶ **soda**

SODDED ▶ **sod**

SODDEN *adj* soaked ▷ *vb* make or become sodden

SODDENS ▶ **sodden**

SODDIER ▶ **soddy**

SODDIES ▶ **soddy**

SODDING ▶ **sod**

SODDY *adj* covered with turf

SODGER *dialect variant of* ▶ **soldier**

SODGERS ▶ **sodger**

SODIC *adj* containing sodium

SODIUM *n* silvery-white metallic element

SODIUMS ▶ **sodium**

SODOM *n* person who performs sodomy

SODOMS ▶ **sodom**

SODOMY *n* anal intercourse

S

SODS ▶ **sod**

SOEVER *adv* in any way at all

SOFA *n* couch

SOFABED *n* sofa that converts into a bed

SOFAR *n* system for determining a position at sea

SOFARS ▶ **sofar**

SOFAS ▶ **sofa**

SOFFIT *n* underside of a part of a building or a structural component

SOFFITS ▶ **soffit**

SOFT *adj* easy to shape or cut ▷ *adv* softly ▷ *vb* soften

SOFTA *n* Muslim student of divinity and jurisprudence, esp in Turkey

SOFTAS ▶ **softa**

SOFTED ▶ **soft**

SOFTEN *vb* make or become soft or softer

SOFTENS ▶ **soften**

SOFTER ▶ **soft**

SOFTEST ▶ **soft**

SOFTIE *n* person who is easily upset

SOFTIES ▶ **softy**

SOFTING ▶ **soft**

SOFTISH ▶ **soft**

SOFTLY ▶ **soft**

SOFTS ▶ **soft**

SOFTY *same as* ▶ **softie**

SOG *vb* soak

SOGER *same as* ▶ **sodger**

SOGERS ▶ **soger**

SOGGED ▶ **sog**

SOGGIER ▶ **soggy**

SOGGILY ▶ **soggy**

SOGGING ▶ **sog**

SOGGY *adj* soaked

SOGS ▶ **sog**

SOH *n* (in tonic sol-fa) fifth degree of any major scale

SOHO *interj* exclamation announcing the sighting of a hare

SOHS ▶ **soh**

SOHUR ▶ **suhur**

SOHURS ▶ **sohur**

SOIGNE *adj* well-groomed, elegant

SOIGNEE *same as* ▶ **soigne**

SOIL *n* top layer of earth ▷ *vb* make or become dirty

SOILAGE *n* green fodder, esp when freshly cut and fed to livestock in a confined area

SOILED ▶ **soil**

SOILIER ▶ **soil**

SOILING ▶ **soil**

SOILS ▶ **soil**

SOILURE *n* act of soiling or the state of being soiled

SOILY ▶ **soil**

SOIREE *n* evening party or gathering

SOIREES ▶ **soiree**

SOJA *same as* ▶ **soya**

SOJAS ▶ **soja**

SOJOURN *n* temporary stay ▷ *vb* stay temporarily

SOKAH *same as* ▶ **soca**

SOKAHS ▶ **sokah**

SOKAIYA *n* Japanese extortionist

SOKE *n* right to hold a local court

SOKEMAN *same as* ▶ **socman**

SOKEMEN ▶ **sokeman**

SOKEN *n* feudal district

SOKENS ▶ **soken**

SOKES ▶ **soke**

SOKOL *n* Czech gymnastic association

SOKOLS ▶ **sokol**

SOL *n* liquid colloidal solution

SOLA ▶ **solum**

SOLACE *vb* comfort in distress ▷ *n* comfort in misery or disappointment

SOLACED ▶ **solace**

SOLACER ▶ **solace**

SOLACES ▶ **solace**

SOLAH *n* Indian plant

SOLAHS ▶ **solah**

SOLAN *archaic name for* ▶ **gannet**

SOLAND *n* solan goose

SOLANDS ▶ **soland**

SOLANIN *same as* > **solanine**

SOLANO *n* hot wind in Spain

SOLANOS ▶ **solano**

SOLANS ▶ **solan**

SOLANUM *n* any plant of the mainly tropical genus that includes the potato, aubergine, and certain nightshades

SOLAR *adj* of the sun

SOLARIA > **solarium**

SOLARS ▶ **solum**

SOLAS ▶ **solum**

SOLATE *vb* change from gel to liquid

SOLATED ▶ **solate**

SOLATES ▶ **solate**

SOLATIA > **solatium**

SOLD *n* obsolete word for salary

SOLDADO *n* soldier

SOLDAN *archaic word for* ▶ **sultan**

SOLDANS ▶ **soldan**

SOLDE *n* wages

SOLDER *n* soft alloy used to join two metal surfaces ▷ *vb* join with solder

SOLDERS ▶ **solder**

SOLDES ▶ **solde**

SOLDI ▶ **soldo**

SOLDIER *n* member of an army ▷ *vb* serve in an army

SOLDO *n* former Italian copper coin worth one twentieth of a lira

SOLDS ▶ **sold**

SOLE *adj* one and only ▷ *n* underside of the foot ▷ *vb* provide (a shoe) with a sole

SOLED ▶ **sole**

SOLEI ▶ **soleus**

SOLEIN *same as* ▶ **sullen**

SOLELY *adv* only, completely

SOLEMN *adj* serious, deeply sincere

SOLER *same as* ▶ **sole**

SOLERA *n* system for aging sherry and other fortified wines

SOLERAS ▶ **solera**

SOLERET *n* armour for foot

SOLERS ▶ **soler**

SOLES ▶ **sole**

SOLEUS *n* muscle in calf of leg

SOLFEGE *same as* > **solfeggio**

SOLGEL *adj* changing between sol and gel

SOLI *adv* (of a piece or passage) to be performed by or with soloists

SOLICIT *vb* request

SOLID *adj* (of a substance) keeping its shape ▷ *n* three-dimensional shape

SOLIDER ▶ **solid**

SOLIDI ▶ **solidus**

SOLIDLY ▶ **solid**

SOLIDS ▶ **solid**

SOLIDUM *n* part of pedestal

SOLIDUS *same as* ▶ **slash**

SOLING ▶ **sole**

SOLION *n* amplifier used in chemistry

SOLIONS ▶ **solion**

SOLIPED *n* animal whose hooves are not cloven

SOLITO *adv* musical instruction meaning play in usual manner

SOLITON *n* type of isolated particle-like wave

SOLIVE *n* type of joist

SOLIVES ▸ solive

SOLLAR *n* archaic word meaning attic

SOLLARS ▸ sollar

SOLLER *same as* ▸ **sollar**

SOLLERS ▸ soller

SOLO *n* music for one performer ▷ *adj* done alone ▷ *adv* by oneself, alone ▷ *vb* undertake a venture alone, esp to operate an aircraft alone or climb alone

SOLOED ▸ solo

SOLOING ▸ solo

SOLOIST *n* person who performs a solo

SOLON *n* US congressman

SOLONS ▸ solon

SOLOS ▸ solo

SOLS ▸ sol

SOLUBLE *adj* able to be dissolved ▷ *n* soluble substance

SOLUBLY ▸ soluble

SOLUM *n* upper layers of the soil profile, affected by climate and vegetation

SOLUMS ▸ solum

SOLUNAR *adj* relating to sun and moon

SOLUS *adj* alone

SOLUTAL *adj* relating to a solute

SOLUTE *n* substance in a solution that is dissolved ▷ *adj* loose or unattached

SOLUTES ▸ solute

SOLVATE *vb* undergo, cause to undergo, or partake in solvation

SOLVE *vb* find the answer to (a problem)

SOLVED ▸ solve

SOLVENT *adj* having enough money to pay one's debts ▷ *n* liquid capable of dissolving other substances

SOLVER ▸ solve

SOLVERS ▸ solve

SOLVES ▸ solve

SOLVING ▸ solve

SOM *n* currency of Kyrgyzstan and Uzbekistan

SOMA *n* body of an organism, esp an animal, as distinct from the germ cells

SOMAN *n* organophosphorus compound developed as a nerve gas in Germany during World War II

SOMANS ▸ soman

SOMAS ▸ soma

SOMATA ▸ soma

SOMATIC *adj* of the body, as distinct from the mind

SOMBER *adj* (in the US) sombre ▷ *vb* (in the US) make sombre

SOMBERS ▸ somber

SOMBRE *adj* dark, gloomy ▷ *vb* make sombre

SOMBRED ▸ sombre

SOMBRER ▸ sombre

SOMBRES ▸ sombre

SOME *adj* unknown or unspecified ▷ *pron* certain unknown or unspecified people or things ▷ *adv* approximately ▷ *determiner* (a) certain unknown or unspecified

SOMEDAY *adv* at some unspecified time in the future

SOMEHOW *adv* in some unspecified way

SOMEONE *pron* somebody ▷ *n* significant or important person

SOMEWAY *adv* in some unspecified manner

SOMEWHY *adv* for some reason

SOMITAL ▸ somite

SOMITE *n* any of a series of dorsal paired segments of mesoderm occurring along the notochord in vertebrate embryos

SOMITES ▸ somite

SOMITIC ▸ somite

SOMNIAL *adj* of dreams

SOMONI *n* monetary unit of Tajikistan

SOMS ▸ som

SOMY ▸ som

SON *n* male offspring

SONANCE ▸ sonant

SONANCY ▸ sonant

SONANT *n* voiced sound able to form a syllable or syllable nucleus ▷ *adj* denoting a voiced sound like this

SONANTS ▸ sonant

SONAR *n* device for detecting underwater objects by the reflection of sound waves

SONARS ▸ sonar

SONATA *n* piece of music in several movements for one instrument with or without piano

SONATAS ▸ sonata

SONCE *n* Scots word meaning good luck

SONCES ▸ sonce

SONDAGE *n* deep trial trench for inspecting stratigraphy

SONDE *n* rocket, balloon, or probe used for observing in the upper atmosphere

SONDELI *n* Indian shrew

SONDER *n* yacht category

SONDERS ▸ sonder

SONDES ▸ sonde

SONE *n* subjective unit of loudness

SONERI *n* Indian cloth of gold

SONERIS ▸ soneri

SONES ▸ sone

SONG *n* music for the voice

SONGFUL *adj* tuneful

SONGKOK *n* (in Malaysia and Indonesia) a kind of oval brimless hat, resembling a skull

SONGMAN *n* singer

SONGMEN ▸ songman

SONGS ▸ song

SONHOOD ▸ son

SONIC *adj* of or producing sound

SONICS *n* study of mechanical vibrations in matter

SONLESS ▸ son

SONLIKE ▸ son

SONLY *adj* like a son

SONNE *same as* ▸ **son**

SONNES ▸ sonne

SONNET *n* fourteen-line poem with a fixed rhyme scheme ▷ *vb* compose sonnets

SONNETS ▸ sonnet

SONNIES ▸ sonny

SONNY *n* term of address to a boy

SONOVOX *n* device used to alter sound of human voice in music recordings

SONS ▸ son

SONSE *same as* ▸ **sonce**

SONSES ▸ sonse

SONSHIP ▸ son

SONSIE *same as* ▸ **sonsy**

SONSIER ▸ sonsy

SONSY *adj* plump

SONTAG *n* type of knitted women's cape

SONTAGS ▸ sontag

S

SONTIES n Shakespearian oath

SOOEY interj call used to summon pigs

SOOGEE vb clean ship using a special solution

SOOGEED ▶ soogee

SOOGEES ▶ soogee

SOOGIE ▶ soogie

SOOGIED ▶ soogie

SOOGIES ▶ soogie

SOOJEY same as ▶ soogee

SOOJEYS ▶ soojey

SOOK n baby ▷ vb suck

SOOKED ▶ sook

SOOKING ▶ sook

SOOKS ▶ sook

SOOL vb incite (a dog) to attack

SOOLE same as ▶ sool

SOOLED ▶ sool

SOOLES ▶ soole

SOOLING ▶ sool

SOOLS ▶ sool

SOOM Scots word for ▶ swim

SOOMED ▶ soom

SOOMING ▶ soom

SOOMS ▶ soom

SOON adv in a short time

SOONER adv rather ▷ n an idler or shirker

SOONERS ▶ sooner

SOONEST adv as soon as possible

SOOP Scots word for ▶ sweep

SOOPED ▶ soop

SOOPING ▶ soop

SOOPS ▶ soop

SOOT n black powder formed by the incomplete burning of an organic substance ▷ vb cover with soot

SOOTE n sweet

SOOTED ▶ soot

SOOTES ▶ soot

SOOTH n truth or reality ▷ adj true or real

SOOTHE vb make calm

SOOTHED ▶ soothe

SOOTHER vb flatter

SOOTHES ▶ soothe

SOOTHLY ▶ sooth

SOOTHS ▶ sooth

SOOTIER ▶ sooty

SOOTILY ▶ sooty

SOOTING ▶ soot

SOOTS ▶ soot

SOOTY adj covered with soot

SOP n concession to pacify someone ▷ vb mop up or absorb (liquid)

SOPH shortened form of ▶ sophomore

SOPHIES ▶ sophy

SOPHISM n argument that seems reasonable but is actually false and misleading

SOPHIST n person who uses clever but invalid arguments

SOPHS ▶ soph

SOPHY n title of the Persian monarchs

SOPITE vb lull to sleep

SOPITED ▶ sopite

SOPITES ▶ sopite

SOPOR n abnormally deep sleep

SOPORS ▶ sopor

SOPPED ▶ sop

SOPPIER ▶ soppy

SOPPILY ▶ soppy

SOPPING ▶ sop

SOPPY adj oversentimental

SOPRA adv musical instruction meaning above

SOPRANI ▶ soprano

SOPRANO n singer with the highest female or boy's voice ▷ adj of a musical instrument that is the highest or second highest pitched in its family

SOPS ▶ sop

SORA n North American rail with a yellow bill

SORAGE n first year in hawk's life

SORAGES ▶ sorage

SORAL ▶ sorus

SORAS ▶ sora

SORB n any of various related trees, esp the mountain ash ▷ vb absorb or adsorb

SORBATE n salt of sorbic acid

SORBED ▶ sorb

SORBENT ▶ sorb

SORBET same as ▶ sherbet

SORBETS ▶ sorbet

SORBIC ▶ sorb

SORBING ▶ sorb

SORBITE n mineral found in steel

SORBO n as in sorbo rubber spongy form of rubber

SORBOSE n sweet-tasting hexose sugar derived from the berries of the mountain ash

SORBS ▶ sorb

SORBUS n rowan or related tree

SORCERY n witchcraft or magic

SORD n flock of mallard ducks

SORDA n deaf woman

SORDES pl n dark incrustations on the lips and teeth of patients with prolonged fever

SORDID adj dirty, squalid

SORDINE same as ▶ sordino

SORDINI ▶ sordino

SORDINO n mute for a stringed or brass musical instrument

SORDO n deaf man

SORDOR n sordidness

SORDORS ▶ sordor

SORDS ▶ sord

SORE adj painful ▷ n painful area on the body ▷ adv greatly ▷ vb make sore

SORED ▶ sore

SOREDIA > soredium

> This is the plural of **soredium**, a reproductive body in lichens. It is a very frequently played bonus, and it has a 'twin' **roadies**. It is a good idea to become familiar with at least the higher probability twin sevens and eights, since the thought of one will often prompt the other, and it may well be that one twin will fit on the board where the other would not.

SOREE same as ▶ sora

SOREES ▶ soree

SOREHON n old Irish feudal right

SOREL same as ▶ sorrel

SORELL same as ▶ sorrel

SORELLS ▶ sorell

SORELS ▶ sorel

SORELY adv greatly

SORER ▶ sore

SORES ▶ sore

SOREST ▶ sore

SOREX n shrew or related animal

SOREXES ▶ sorex

SORGHOS same as ▶ sorgo

SORGHOS ▶ sorgho

SORGHUM n kind of grass cultivated for grain

SORGO n any of several varieties of sorghum that have watery sweet juice

SORGOS ▶ sorgo
SORI ▶ sorus
SORING ▶ sore
SORINGS ▶ sore
SORITES n polysyllogism in which the premises are arranged so that intermediate conclusions are omitted, being understood, and only the final conclusion is stated
SORITIC ▶ sorites
SORN vb obtain food, lodging, etc, from another person by presuming on his or her generosity
SORNED ▶ sorn
SORNER ▶ sorn
SORNERS ▶ sore
SORNING ▶ sorn
SORNS ▶ sorn
SOROBAN n Japanese abacus
SOROCHE n altitude sickness
SORORAL adj of sister
SOROSES ▶ sorosis
SOROSIS n fleshy multiple fruit
SORRA Irish word for ▶ sorrow
SORRAS ▶ sorra
SORREL n bitter-tasting plant
SORRELS ▶ sorrel
SORRIER ▶ sorry
SORRILY ▶ sorry
SORROW n grief or sadness ▷ vb grieve
SORROWS ▶ sorrow
SORRY adj feeling pity or regret ▷ interj exclamation expressing apology or asking someone to repeat what he or she has said
SORT n group all sharing certain qualities or characteristics ▷ vb arrange according to kind
SORTA adv phonetic representation of 'sort of'
SORTAL n type of logical or linguistic concept
SORTALS ▶ sortal
SORTED interj exclamation of satisfaction, approval, etc ▷ adj possessing the desired recreational drugs
SORTER ▶ sort
SORTERS ▶ sort
SORTES n divination by opening book at random
SORTIE n relatively short

return trip ▷ vb make a sortie
SORTIED ▶ sortie
SORTIES ▶ sortie
SORTING ▶ sort
SORTS ▶ sort
SORUS n cluster of sporangia on the undersurface of certain fern leaves
SOS ▶ so
SOSATIE n skewer of curried meat pieces
SOSS vb make dirty or muddy
SOSSED ▶ soss
SOSSES ▶ soss
SOSSING ▶ soss
SOT n habitual drunkard ▷ adv indeed: used to contradict a negative statement ▷ vb be a drunkard
SOTH archaic variant of ▶ sooth
SOTHS ▶ soth
SOTOL n American plant related to agave
SOTOLS ▶ sotol
SOTS ▶ sot
SOTTED ▶ sot
SOTTING ▶ sot
SOTTISH ▶ sot
SOU n former French coin
SOUARI n tree of tropical America
SOUARIS ▶ souari
SOUBISE n purée of onions mixed into a thick white sauce and served over eggs, fish, etc
SOUCAR n Indian banker
SOUCARS ▶ soucar
SOUCE same as ▶ souse
SOUCED ▶ souce
SOUCES ▶ souce
SOUCING ▶ souce
SOUCT ▶ souce
SOUDAN obsolete variant of ▶ sultan
SOUDANS ▶ soudan
SOUFFLE n light fluffy dish made with beaten egg whites and other ingredients ▷ adj made light and puffy, as by beating and cooking
SOUGH vb (of the wind) make a sighing sound ▷ n soft continuous murmuring sound
SOUGHED ▶ sough
SOUGHS ▶ sough

SOUGHT ▶ seek
SOUK same as ▶ sook
SOUKED ▶ souk
SOUKING ▶ souk
SOUKOUS n style of African popular music characterized by syncopated rhythms and intricate contrasting guitar melodies
SOUKS ▶ souk
SOUL n spiritual and immortal part of a human being
SOULDAN same as ▶ soldan
SOULED adj having soul
SOULFUL adj full of emotion
SOULS ▶ soul
SOUM vb decide how many animals can graze particular pasture
SOUMED ▶ soum
SOUMING ▶ soum
SOUMS ▶ soum
SOUND n something heard, noise ▷ vb make or cause to make a sound ▷ adj in good condition ▷ adv soundly
SOUNDED ▶ sound
SOUNDER n electromagnetic device formerly used in telegraphy to convert electric signals into audible sounds
SOUNDLY ▶ sound
SOUNDS ▶ sound
SOUP n liquid food made from meat, vegetables, etc ▷ vb give soup to
SOUPCON n small amount
SOUPED ▶ soup
SOUPER n person dispensing soup
SOUPERS ▶ souper
SOUPFIN n Pacific requiem shark valued for its fins
SOUPIER ▶ soupy
SOUPING ▶ soup
SOUPLE same as ▶ supple
SOUPLED ▶ souple
SOUPLES ▶ souple
SOUPS ▶ soup
SOUPY adj having the appearance or consistency of soup
SOUR adj sharp-tasting ▷ vb make or become sour
SOURCE n origin or starting point ▷ vb establish a supplier of (a product, etc)
SOURCED ▶ source
SOURCES ▶ source
SOURED ▶ sour

S

SOURER ▷ sour
SOUREST ▷ sour
SOURING ▷ sour
SOURISH ▷ sour
SOURLY ▷ sour
SOUROCK n Scots word for sorrel plant
SOURS ▷ sour
SOURSE same as ▷ source
SOURSES ▷ sourse
SOURSOP n small West Indian tree
SOUS ▷ sou
SOUSE vb plunge (something) into liquid ▷ n liquid used in pickling
SOUSED ▷ souse
SOUSES ▷ souse
SOUSING ▷ souse
SOUSLIK same as ▷ suslik
SOUT same as ▷ soot
SOUTANE n Roman Catholic priest's cassock
SOUTAR same as ▷ souter
SOUTARS ▷ soutar
SOUTER n shoemaker or cobbler
SOUTERS ▷ souter
SOUTH n direction towards the South Pole, opposite north ▷ adj or in the south ▷ adv in, to, or towards the south ▷ vb turn south
SOUTHED ▷ south
SOUTHER n strong wind or storm from the south ▷ vb turn south
SOUTHS ▷ south
SOUTS ▷ sout
SOV shortening of ▷ sovereign
SOVIET n formerly, elected council at various levels of government in the USSR ▷ adj of the former USSR
SOVIETS ▷ soviet
SOVKHOZ n (in the former Soviet Union) a large mechanized farm owned by the state
SOVRAN literary word for ▷ sovereign
SOVRANS ▷ sovran
SOVS ▷ sov
SOW vb scatter or plant (seed) in or on (the ground) ▷ n female adult pig
SOWABLE ▷ sow
SOWANS same as ▷ sowens
SOWAR n Indian cavalryman
SOWARRY same as ▷ sowarree
SOWARS ▷ sowar

SOWBACK another name for ▷ hogback
SOWCAR same as ▷ soucar
SOWCARS ▷ sowcar
SOWCE same as ▷ souse
SOWCED ▷ sowce
SOWCES ▷ sowce
SOWCING ▷ sowce
SOWDER ▷ sawder n
SOWDERS ▷ sowder
SOWED ▷ sow
SOWENS n pudding made from oatmeal husks steeped and boiled
SOWER ▷ sow
SOWERS ▷ sow
SOWF same as ▷ sowth
SOWFED ▷ sowf
SOWFF same as ▷ sowth
SOWFFED ▷ sowff
SOWFFS ▷ sowff
SOWFING ▷ sowf
SOWFS ▷ sowf
SOWING ▷ sow
SOWINGS ▷ sow
SOWL same as ▷ sole
SOWLE same as ▷ sole
SOWLED ▷ sowl
SOWLES ▷ sowle
SOWLING ▷ sowl
SOWLS ▷ sowl
SOWM same as ▷ soum
SOWMED ▷ sowm
SOWMING ▷ sowm
SOWMS ▷ sowm
SOWN ▷ sow
SOWND vb wield
SOWNDED ▷ sownd
SOWNDS ▷ sownd
SOWNE same as ▷ sound
SOWNES ▷ sowne
SOWP n spoonful
SOWPS ▷ sowp
SOWS ▷ sow
SOWSE same as ▷ souse
SOWSED ▷ sowse
SOWSES ▷ sowse
SOWSING ▷ sowse
SOWSSE same as ▷ souse
SOWSSED ▷ sowsse
SOWSSES ▷ sowsse
SOWTER same as ▷ souter
SOWTERS ▷ sowter
SOWTH vb Scots word meaning whistle
SOWTHED ▷ sowth
SOWTHS ▷ sowth
SOX pl n informal spelling of 'socks'

> This informal word for **socks** is one of the key short words to remember for using the X.

SOY n as in **soy sauce** salty dark brown sauce made from soya beans, used in Chinese and Japanese cookery
SOYA n plant whose edible bean is used for food and as a source of oil
SOYAS ▷ soya
SOYBEAN n soya bean
SOYLE n body
SOYLES ▷ soyle
SOYMILK n milk substitute made from soya
SOYS ▷ soy
SOYUZ n Russian spacecraft used to ferry crew to and from space stations
SOYUZES ▷ soyuz
SOZ interj (slang) sorry
SOZIN n form of protein
SOZINE same as ▷ sozin
SOZINES ▷ sozine
SOZINS ▷ sozin
SOZZLE vb make wet
SOZZLED adj drunk
SOZZLES ▷ sozzle
SOZZLY adj wet
SPA n resort with a mineral-water spring ▷ vb visit a spa
SPACE n unlimited expanse in which all objects exist and move ▷ vb place at intervals
SPACED ▷ space
SPACER n piece of material used to create or maintain a space between two things
SPACERS ▷ spacer
SPACES ▷ space
SPACEY adj vague and dreamy, as if under the influence of drugs
SPACIAL same as ▷ spatial
SPACIER ▷ spacey
SPACING n arrangement of letters, words, etc, on a page in order to achieve legibility
SPACKLE vb fill holes in plaster
SPACY same as ▷ spacey
SPADE n tool for digging
SPADED ▷ spade
SPADER ▷ spade
SPADERS ▷ spade
SPADES ▷ spade
SPADGER n sparrow
SPADING ▷ spade
SPADIX n spike of small flowers on a fleshy stem
SPADO n neutered animal

SPADOES ▶ spado
SPADOS ▶ spado
SPAE vb foretell (the future)
SPAED ▶ spae
SPAEING ▶ spae
SPAEMAN n man who foretells future
SPAEMEN ▶ spaeman
SPAER ▶ spae
SPAERS ▶ spae
SPAES ▶ spae
SPAG vb (of a cat) to scratch (a person) with the claws ▷ n Australian offensive slang for an Italian
SPAGGED ▶ spag
SPAGS ▶ spag
SPAHEE same as ▶ spahi
SPAHEES ▶ spahee
SPAHI n (formerly) an irregular cavalryman in the Turkish armed forces
SPAHIS ▶ spahi
SPAIL Scots word for ▶ spall
SPAILS ▶ spail
SPAIN same as ▶ spane
SPAINED ▶ spain
SPAING ▶ spa
SPAINGS ▶ spa
SPAINS ▶ spain
SPAIRGE Scots word for ▶ sparge
SPAIT same as ▶ spate
SPAITS ▶ spait
SPAKE past tense of ▶ speak
SPALD same as ▶ spauld
SPALDS ▶ spald
SPALE Scots word for ▶ spall
SPALES ▶ spale
SPALL n splinter or chip of ore, rock, or stone ▷ vb split or cause to split into such fragments
SPALLE same as ▶ spauld
SPALLED ▶ spall
SPALLER ▶ spall
SPALLES ▶ spalle
SPALLS ▶ spall
SPALT vb split
SPALTED ▶ spalt
SPALTS ▶ spalt
SPAM vb send unsolicited e-mail simultaneously to a number of newsgroups on the internet ▷ n unsolicited electronic mail or text messages sent in this way
SPAMBOT n computer programme that identifies email addresses to send spam to
SPAMMED ▶ spam
SPAMMER ▶ spam

SPAMMIE n love bite
SPAMMY adj bland
SPAMS ▶ spam
SPAN n space between two points ▷ vb stretch or extend across
SPANCEL n length of rope for hobbling an animal, esp a horse or cow ▷ vb hobble (an animal) with a loose rope
SPANDEX n type of synthetic stretch fabric made from polyurethane fibre
SPANE vb Scots word meaning wean
SPANED ▶ spane
SPANES ▶ spane
SPANG adv exactly, firmly, or straight ▷ vb dash
SPANGED ▶ spang
SPANGLE n small shiny metallic ornament ▷ vb decorate with spangles
SPANGLY ▶ spangle
SPANGS ▶ spang
SPANIEL n dog with long ears and silky hair
SPANING ▶ spane
SPANK vb slap with the open hand, on the buttocks or legs ▷ n such a slap
SPANKED ▶ spank
SPANKER n fore and aft sail or a mast that is aftermost in a sailing vessel
SPANKS ▶ spank
SPANNED ▶ span
SPANNER n tool for gripping and turning a nut or bolt
SPANS ▶ span
SPAR n pole used as a ship's mast, boom, or yard ▷ vb box or fight using light blows for practice
SPARD ▶ spare
SPARE adj extra ▷ n duplicate kept in case of damage or loss ▷ vb refrain from punishing or harming
SPARED ▶ spare
SPARELY ▶ spare
SPARER ▶ spare
SPARERS ▶ spare
SPARES ▶ spare
SPAREST ▶ spare
SPARGE vb sprinkle or scatter (something)
SPARGED ▶ sparge
SPARGER ▶ sparge
SPARGES ▶ sparge

SPARID n type of marine percoid fish ▷ adj of or belonging to this family of fish
SPARIDS ▶ sparid
SPARING adj economical
SPARK n fiery particle thrown out from a fire or caused by friction ▷ vb give off sparks
SPARKE n weapon
SPARKED ▶ spark
SPARKER ▶ spark
SPARKES ▶ sparke
SPARKIE n electrician
SPARKLE vb glitter with many points of light ▷ n sparkling points of light
SPARKLY adj sparkling ▷ n sparkling thing
SPARKS n electrician
SPARKY adj lively
SPAROID same as ▶ sparid
SPARRE same as ▶ spar
SPARRED ▶ spar
SPARRER ▶ spar
SPARRES ▶ sparre
SPARROW n small brownish bird
SPARRY adj (of minerals) containing, relating to, or resembling spar
SPARS ▶ spar
SPARSE adj thinly scattered
SPARSER ▶ sparse
SPART n esparto
SPARTAN adj strict and austere ▷ n disciplined or brave person
SPARTH n type of battle-axe
SPARTHE same as ▶ sparth
SPARTHS ▶ sparth
SPARTS ▶ spart
SPAS ▶ spa
SPASM n involuntary muscular contraction ▷ vb go into spasm
SPASMED ▶ spasm
SPASMIC ▶ spasm
SPASMS ▶ spasm
SPAT vb have a quarrel
SPATE n large number of things happening within a period of time
SPATES ▶ spate
SPATHAL ▶ spathe
SPATHE n large sheathlike leaf enclosing a flower cluster
SPATHED ▶ spathe
SPATHES ▶ spathe
SPATHIC adj (of minerals) resembling spar, esp in

S

having good cleavage

SPATIAL adj of or in space

SPATS ▶ spat

SPATTED ▶ spat

SPATTEE n type of gaiter

SPATTER vb scatter or be scattered in drops over (something) ▷ n spattering sound

SPATULA n utensil with a broad flat blade for spreading or stirring

SPATULE n spatula

SPATZLE same as > spaetzle

SPAUL same as ▶ spauld

SPAULD n shoulder

SPAULDS ▶ spauld

SPAULS ▶ spaul

SPAVIE Scots variant of ▶ spavin

SPAVIES ▶ spavie

SPAVIET adj Scots word meaning spavined

SPAVIN n enlargement of the hock of a horse by a bony growth

SPAVINS ▶ spavin

SPAW same as ▶ spa

SPAWL vb spit

SPAWLED ▶ spawl

SPAWLS ▶ spawl

SPAWN n jelly-like mass of eggs of fish, frogs, or molluscs ▷ vb (of fish, frogs, or molluscs) lay eggs

SPAWNED ▶ spawn

SPAWNER ▶ spawn

SPAWNS ▶ spawn

SPAWNY adj like spawn

SPAWS ▶ spaw

SPAY vb remove the ovaries from (a female animal)

SPAYAD n male deer

SPAYADS ▶ spayad

SPAYD same as ▶ spayad

SPAYDS ▶ spayd

SPAYED ▶ spay

SPAYING ▶ spay

SPAYS ▶ spay

SPAZA adj as in spaza shop South African slang for a small shop in a township

SPEAK vb say words, talk

SPEAKER n person who speaks, esp at a formal occasion

SPEAKS ▶ speak

SPEAL same as ▶ spule

SPEALS ▶ speal

SPEAN same as ▶ spane

SPEANED ▶ spean

SPEANS ▶ spean

SPEAR n weapon consisting

of a long shaft with a sharp point ▷ vb pierce with or as if with a spear

SPEARED ▶ spear

SPEARER ▶ spear

SPEARS ▶ spear

SPEARY ▶ spear

SPEAT same as ▶ spate

SPEATS ▶ speat

SPEC vb set specifications

SPECCED ▶ spec

SPECCY n person wearing spectacles

SPECIAL adj distinguished from others of its kind ▷ n product, programme, etc which is only available at a certain time ▷ vb advertise and sell (an item) at a reduced price

SPECIE n coins as distinct from paper money

SPECIES n group of plants or animals that are related closely enough to interbreed naturally

SPECIFY vb refer to or state specifically

SPECK n small spot or particle ▷ vb mark with specks or spots

SPECKED ▶ speck

SPECKLE n small spot ▷ vb mark with speckles

SPECKS ▶ speck

SPECKY same as ▶ speccy

SPECS pl n spectacles

SPECTER same as ▶ spectre

SPECTRA > spectrum

SPECTRE n ghost

SPECULA > speculum

SPED ▶ speed

SPEECH n act, power, or manner of speaking ▷ vb make a speech

SPEED n swiftness ▷ vb go quickly

SPEEDED ▶ speed

SPEEDER ▶ speed

SPEEDO n speedometer

SPEEDOS ▶ speedo

SPEEDS ▶ speed

SPEEDUP n acceleration

SPEEDY adj prompt

SPEEL n splinter of wood ▷ vb Scots word meaning climb

SPEELED ▶ speel

SPEELER ▶ speel

SPEELS ▶ speel

SPEER same as ▶ speir

SPEERED ▶ speer

SPEERS ▶ speer

SPEIL dialect word for ▶ climb

SPEILED ▶ speil

SPEILS ▶ speil

SPEIR vb ask

SPEIRED ▶ speir

SPEIRS ▶ speir

SPEISE same as ▶ speiss

SPEISES ▶ speise

SPEISS n arsenides and antimonides that form when ores containing arsenic or antimony are smelted

SPEK n bacon, fat, or fatty pork used for larding venison or other game

SPEKS ▶ spek

SPELD vb Scots word meaning spread

SPELDED ▶ speld

SPELDER same as ▶ speld

SPELDIN n fish split and dried

SPELDS ▶ speld

SPELEAN same as > spelaean

SPELK n splinter of wood

SPELKS ▶ spelk

SPELL vb give in correct order the letters that form (a word) ▷ n formula of words supposed to have magic power

SPELLED ▶ spell

SPELLER n person who spells words in the manner specified

SPELLS ▶ spell

SPELT ▶ spell

SPELTER n impure zinc, usually containing about 3 per cent of lead and other impurities

SPELTS ▶ spell

SPELTZ n wheat variety

SPELUNK vb explore caves

SPENCE n larder or pantry

SPENCER n short fitted coat or jacket

SPENCES ▶ spence

SPEND vb pay out (money)

SPENDER n person who spends money in a manner specified

SPENDS ▶ spend

SPENDY adj expensive

SPENSE same as ▶ spence

SPENSES ▶ spense

SPENT ▶ spend

SPEOS n (esp in ancient Egypt) a temple or tomb cut into a rock face

SPEOSES ▶ speos

SPERM *n* male reproductive cell released in semen during ejaculation

SPERMIC same as > spermatic

SPERMS ▶ sperm

SPERRE *vb* bolt

SPERRED ▶ sperre

SPERRES ▶ sperre

SPERSE *vb* disperse

SPERSED ▶ sperse

SPERSES ▶ sperse

SPERST ▶ sperse

SPERTHE same as ▶ sparth

SPET same as ▶ spit

SPETCH *n* piece of animal skin

SPETS ▶ spet

SPEUG *n* sparrow

SPEUGS ▶ speug

SPEW *vb* vomit ▷ *n* something ejected from the mouth

SPEWED ▶ spew

SPEWER ▶ spew

SPEWERS ▶ spew

SPEWIER ▶ spewy

SPEWING ▶ spew

SPEWS ▶ spew

SPEWY *adj* marshy

SPHAER same as ▶ sphere

SPHAERE same as ▶ sphere

SPHAERS ▶ sphaere

SPHEAR same as ▶ sphere

SPHEARE same as ▶ sphere

SPHEARS ▶ sphear

SPHENE *n* brown, yellow, green, or grey lustrous mineral

SPHENES ▶ sphene

SPHENIC *adj* having the shape of a wedge

SPHERAL *adj* of or shaped like a sphere

SPHERE *n* perfectly round solid object ▷ *vb* surround or encircle

SPHERED ▶ sphere

SPHERES ▶ sphere

SPHERIC same as > spherical

SPHERY *adj* resembling a sphere

SPHINX *n* one of the huge statues built by the ancient Egyptians, with the body of a lion and the head of a man

SPHYNX *n* breed of cat

SPIAL *n* observation

SPIALS ▶ spial

SPICA *n* spiral bandage formed by a series of overlapping figure-of-eight turns

SPICAE ▶ spica

SPICAS ▶ spica

SPICATE *adj* having, arranged in, or relating to spikes

SPICE *n* aromatic substance used as flavouring ▷ *vb* flavour with spices

SPICED ▶ spice

SPICER ▶ spice

SPICERS ▶ spice

SPICERY *n* spices collectively

SPICES ▶ spice

SPICEY same as ▶ spicy

SPICIER ▶ spicy

SPICILY ▶ spicy

SPICING ▶ spice

SPICULA > spiculum

SPICULE *n* small slender pointed structure or crystal

SPICY *adj* flavoured with spices

SPIDER *n* small eight-legged creature which spins a web to catch insects for food

SPIDERS ▶ spider

SPIDERY *adj* thin and angular like a spider's legs

SPIE same as ▶ spy

SPIED ▶ spy

SPIEGEL *n* manganese-rich pig iron

SPIEL *n* speech made to persuade someone to do something ▷ *vb* deliver a prepared spiel

SPIELED ▶ spiel

SPIELER ▶ spiel

SPIELS ▶ spiel

SPIER same as ▶ speir

SPIERED ▶ spier

SPIERS ▶ spier

SPIES ▶ spy

SPIF *n* postage stamp perforated with the initials of a firm to avoid theft by employees

SPIFF *vb* make smart

SPIFFED ▶ spiff

SPIFFS ▶ spiff

SPIFFY *adj* smart ▷ *n* smart thing or person ▷ *vb* to smarten

SPIFS ▶ spif

SPIGHT same as ▶ spite

SPIGHTS ▶ spight

SPIGNEL *n* European umbelliferous plant

SPIGOT *n* stopper for, or tap fitted to, a cask

SPIGOTS ▶ spigot

SPIKE *n* sharp point ▷ *vb* put spikes on

SPIKED ▶ spike

SPIKER ▶ spike

SPIKERS ▶ spike

SPIKERY *n* High-Church Anglicanism

SPIKES ▶ spike

SPIKEY same as ▶ spiky

SPIKIER ▶ spiky

SPIKILY ▶ spiky

SPIKING ▶ spike

SPIKY *adj* resembling a spike

SPILE *n* heavy timber stake or pile ▷ *vb* provide or support with a spile

SPILED ▶ spile

SPILES ▶ spile

SPILING ▶ spile

SPILITE *n* type of igneous rock

SPILL *vb* pour from or as if from a container ▷ *n* fall

SPILLED ▶ spill

SPILLER ▶ spill

SPILLS ▶ spill

SPILT ▶ spill

SPILTH *n* something spilled

SPILTHS ▶ spilth

SPIM *n* unsolicited commercial communications received on a computer via an instant-messaging system

SPIMS ▶ spim

SPIN *vb* revolve or cause to revolve rapidly ▷ *n* revolving motion

SPINA *n* spine

SPINACH *n* dark green leafy vegetable

SPINAE ▶ spina

SPINAGE same as ▶ spinach

SPINAL *adj* of the spine ▷ *n* anaesthetic administered in the spine

SPINALS ▶ spinal

SPINAR *n* fast-spinning star

SPINARS ▶ spinar

SPINAS ▶ spina

SPINATE *adj* having a spine

SPINDLE *n* rotating rod that acts as an axle ▷ *vb* form into a spindle or equip with spindles

SPINDLY *adj* long, slender, and frail

SPINE *n* backbone

SPINED ▶ spine

SPINEL *n* any of a group of hard glassy minerals of variable colour

S

SPINELS ▶ **spinel**
SPINES ▶ **spine**
SPINET *n* small harpsichord
SPINETS ▶ **spinet**
SPINIER ▶ **spiny**
SPINK *n* finch
SPINKS ▶ **spink**
SPINNER *n* bowler who specializes in spinning the ball to make it change direction when it bounces or strikes the bat
SPINNET *same as* ▶ **spinet**
SPINNEY *n* small wood
SPINNY *same as* ▶ **spinney**
SPINODE *another name for* ▶ **cusp**
SPINOFF *n* development derived incidentally from an existing enterprise
SPINONE *n as in* **Italian spinone** wiry-coated gun dog
SPINONI ▶ **spinone**
SPINOR *n* type of mathematical object
SPINORS ▶ **spinor**
SPINOSE *adj* (esp of plants) bearing many spines
SPINOUS *adj* resembling a spine or thorn
SPINOUT *n* spinning skid that causes a car to run off the road
SPINS ▶ **spin**
SPINTO *n* lyrical singing voice
SPINTOS ▶ **spinto**
SPINULA *n* small spine
SPINULE *n* very small spine, thorn, or prickle
SPINY *adj* covered with spines
SPIRAEA *n* plant with small white or pink flowers
SPIRAL *n* continuous curve formed by a point winding about a central axis at an ever-increasing distance from it ▷ *vb* move in a spiral ▷ *adj* having the form of a spiral
SPIRALS ▶ **spiral**
SPIRANT *n* fricative consonant
SPIRE *n* pointed part of a steeple ▷ *vb* assume the shape of a spire
SPIREA *same as* ▶ **spiraea**
SPIREAS ▶ **spirea**
SPIRED ▶ **spire**
SPIREM *same as* ▶ **spireme**
SPIREME *n* tangled mass of

chromatin threads into which the nucleus of a cell is resolved at the start of mitosis
SPIREMS ▶ **spirem**
SPIRES ▶ **spire**
SPIRIC *n* type of curve
SPIRICS ▶ **spiric**
SPIRIER ▶ **spire**
SPIRING ▶ **spire**
SPIRIT *n* nonphysical aspect of a person concerned with profound thoughts ▷ *vb* carry away mysteriously
SPIRITS ▶ **spirit**
SPIRITY *adj* spirited
SPIROID *adj* resembling a spiral or displaying a spiral form
SPIRT *same as* ▶ **spurt**
SPIRTED ▶ **spirt**
SPIRTLE *same as* ▶ **spurtle**
SPIRTS ▶ **spirt**
SPIRULA *n* tropical cephalopod mollusc
SPIRY ▶ **spire**
SPIT *vb* eject (saliva or food) from the mouth ▷ *n* saliva
SPITAL *n* hospital, esp for the needy sick
SPITALS ▶ **spital**
SPITE *n* deliberate nastiness ▷ *vb* annoy or hurt from spite
SPITED ▶ **spite**
SPITES ▶ **spite**
SPITING ▶ **spite**
SPITS ▶ **spit**
SPITTED ▶ **spit**
SPITTEN ▶ **spit**
SPITTER ▶ **spit**
SPITTLE *n* fluid produced in the mouth, saliva
SPITZ *n* stockily built dog with a pointed face, erect ears, and a tightly curled tail
SPITZES ▶ **spitz**
SPIV *n* smartly dressed man who makes a living by shady dealings
SPIVS ▶ **spiv**
SPIVVY ▶ **spiv**
SPLAKE *n* type of hybrid trout bred by Canadian zoologists
SPLAKES ▶ **splake**
SPLASH *vb* scatter liquid on (something) ▷ *n* splashing sound
SPLASHY *adj* having irregular marks
SPLAT *n* wet slapping sound

▷ *vb* make wet slapping sound
SPLATCH *vb* splash
SPLATS ▶ **splat**
SPLAY *vb* spread out, with ends spreading in different directions ▷ *adj* spread out ▷ *n* surface of a wall that forms an oblique angle to the main flat surfaces
SPLAYED ▶ **splay**
SPLAYS ▶ **splay**
SPLEEN *n* abdominal organ which filters bacteria from the blood
SPLEENS ▶ **spleen**
SPLEENY ▶ **spleen**
SPLENIA > **splenium**
SPLENIC *adj* of, relating to, or in the spleen
SPLENII > **splenius**
SPLENT *same as* ▶ **splint**
SPLENTS ▶ **splent**
SPLICE *vb* join by interweaving or overlapping ends
SPLICED ▶ **splice**
SPLICER ▶ **splice**
SPLICES ▶ **splice**
SPLIFF *n* cannabis, used as a drug
SPLIFFS ▶ **spliff**
SPLINE *n* type of narrow key around a shaft that fits into a corresponding groove ▷ *vb* provide (a shaft, part, etc) with splines
SPLINED ▶ **spline**
SPLINES ▶ **spline**
SPLINT *n* rigid support for a broken bone ▷ *vb* apply a splint to (a broken arm, etc)
SPLINTS ▶ **splint**
SPLISH *vb* splash
SPLIT *vb* break into separate pieces ▷ *n* splitting
SPLITS ▶ **split**
SPLODGE *n* large uneven spot or stain ▷ *vb* mark (something) with a splodge or splodges
SPLODGY ▶ **splodge**
SPLOG *n* spam blog
SPLOGS ▶ **splog**
SPLOOSH *vb* splash or cause to splash about uncontrollably ▷ *n* instance or sound of splooshing
SPLORE *n* revel
SPLORES ▶ **splore**
SPLOSH *vb* scatter (liquid) vigorously about in blobs

▷ *n* instance or sound of sploshing

SPLOTCH *vb* splash, daub

SPLURGE *vb* spend money extravagantly ▷ *n* bout of extravagance

SPLURGY ▷ **splurge**

SPOD *adj* boring, unattractive, or overstudious

SPODDY ▷ **spod**

SPODE *n* type of English china or porcelain

SPODES ▷ **spode**

SPODIUM *n* black powder

SPODS ▷ **spod**

SPOFFY *same as* ▷ **spoffish**

SPOIL *vb* damage

SPOILED ▷ **spoil**

SPOILER *n* device on an aircraft or car to increase drag

SPOILS ▷ **spoil**

SPOILT ▷ **spoil**

SPOKE *n* radial member of a wheel ▷ *vb* equip with spokes

SPOKED ▷ **spoke**

SPOKEN ▷ **speak**

SPOKES ▷ **spoke**

SPOKING ▷ **spoke**

SPONDEE *n* metrical foot of two long syllables

SPONDYL *n* vertebra

SPONGE *n* sea animal with a porous absorbent skeleton ▷ *vb* wipe with a sponge

SPONGED ▷ **sponge**

SPONGER *n* person who sponges on others

SPONGES ▷ **sponge**

SPONGIN *n* fibrous horny protein that forms the skeletal framework of the bath sponge and related sponges

SPONGY *adj* of or resembling a sponge

SPONSAL *n* marriage

SPONSON *n* outboard support for a gun enabling it to fire fore and aft

SPONSOR *n* person who promotes something ▷ *vb* act as a sponsor for

SPOOF *n* mildly satirical parody ▷ *vb* fool (a person) with a trick or deception

SPOOFED ▷ **spoof**

SPOOFER ▷ **spoof**

SPOOFS ▷ **spoof**

SPOOFY ▷ **spoof**

SPOOK *n* ghost ▷ *vb* frighten

SPOOKED ▷ **spook**

SPOOKS ▷ **spook**

SPOOKY *adj* ghostly or eerie

SPOOL *n* cylinder round which something can be wound ▷ *vb* wind or be wound onto a spool or reel

SPOOLED ▷ **spool**

SPOOLER ▷ **spool**

SPOOLS ▷ **spool**

SPOOM *vb* sail fast before wind

SPOOMED ▷ **spoom**

SPOOMS ▷ **spoom**

SPOON *n* shallow bowl attached to a handle for eating, stirring, or serving food ▷ *vb* lift with a spoon

SPOONED ▷ **spoon**

SPOONEY *same as* ▷ **spoony**

SPOONS ▷ **spoon**

SPOONY *adj* foolishly or stupidly amorous ▷ *n* fool or silly person, esp one in love

SPOOR *n* trail of an animal ▷ *vb* track (an animal) by following its trail

SPOORED ▷ **spoor**

SPOORER ▷ **spoor**

SPOORS ▷ **spoor**

SPOOT *n* razor shell

SPOOTS ▷ **spoot**

SPORAL ▷ **spore**

SPORE *n* minute reproductive body of some plants ▷ *vb* produce, carry, or release spores

SPORED ▷ **spore**

SPORES ▷ **spore**

SPORING ▷ **spore**

SPORK *n* spoon-shaped piece of cutlery with tines like a fork

SPORKS ▷ **spork**

SPOROID *adj* of or like a spore

SPORRAN *n* pouch worn in front of a kilt

SPORT *n* activity for pleasure, competition, or exercise ▷ *vb* wear proudly

SPORTED ▷ **sport**

SPORTER ▷ **sport**

SPORTIF *adj* sporty

SPORTS *adj* of or used in sports ▷ *n* meeting held at a school or college for competitions in athletic events

SPORTY *adj* (of a person) interested in sport ▷ *n* young person who typically wears sportswear, is competitive about sport, and takes an interest in his or her fitness

SPORULE *n* spore, esp a very small spore

SPOSH *n* slush

SPOSHES ▷ **sposh**

SPOSHY ▷ **sposh**

SPOT *n* small mark on a surface ▷ *vb* notice

SPOTLIT ▷ **spotlight**

SPOTS ▷ **spot**

SPOTTED ▷ **spot**

SPOTTER *n* person whose hobby is watching for and noting numbers or types of trains or planes

SPOTTIE *n* young deer of up to three months of age

SPOTTY *adj* with spots

SPOUSAL *n* marriage ceremony ▷ *adj* of or relating to marriage

SPOUSE *n* husband or wife ▷ *vb* marry

SPOUSED ▷ **spouse**

SPOUSES ▷ **spouse**

SPOUT *vb* pour out in a stream or jet ▷ *n* projecting tube or lip for pouring liquids

SPOUTED ▷ **spout**

SPOUTER ▷ **spout**

SPOUTS ▷ **spout**

SPOUTY ▷ **spout**

SPRACK *adj* vigorous

SPRAD ▷ **spread**

SPRAG *n* chock or steel bar used to prevent a vehicle from running backwards on an incline ▷ *vb* use sprag to prevent vehicle from moving

SPRAGS ▷ **sprag**

SPRAID *adj* chapped

SPRAIN *vb* injure (a joint) by a sudden twist ▷ *n* such an injury

SPRAINS ▷ **sprain**

SPRAINT *n* piece of otter's dung

SPRANG *n* branch

SPRANGS ▷ **sprang**

SPRAT *n* small sea fish

SPRATS ▷ **sprat**

SPRAWL *vb* lie or sit with the limbs spread out ▷ *n* part of a city that has spread untidily over a large area

S

SPRAWLS ▶ sprawl
SPRAWLY ▶ sprawl
SPRAY n (device for producing) fine drops of liquid ▷ vb scatter in fine drops
SPRAYED ▶ spray
SPRAYER ▶ spray
SPRAYEY ▶ spray
SPRAYS ▶ spray
SPREAD vb open out or be displayed to the fullest extent ▷ n spreading ▷ adj extended or stretched out, esp to the fullest extent
SPREADS ▶ spread
SPREAGH n cattle raid
SPREAZE same as > **spreathe**
SPRED same as ▶ **spread**
SPREDD same as ▶ **spread**
SPREDDE same as ▶ **spread**
SPREDDS ▶ spredd
SPREDS ▶ spred
SPREE n session of overindulgence, usu in drinking or spending money ▷ vb go on a spree
SPREED ▶ spree
SPREES ▶ spree
SPREEZE same as > **spreathe**
SPRENT ▶ sprinkle
SPREW same as ▶ **sprue**
SPREWS ▶ sprew
SPRIER ▶ spry
SPRIEST ▶ spry
SPRIG n twig or shoot ▷ vb fasten or secure with sprigs
SPRIGGY ▶ sprig
SPRIGHT same as ▶ **sprite**
SPRIGS ▶ sprig
SPRING vb move suddenly upwards or forwards in a single motion, jump ▷ n season between winter and summer
SPRINGE n type of snare for catching small wild animals or birds ▷ vb set such a snare
SPRINGS ▶ spring
SPRINGY adj elastic
SPRINT n short race run at top speed ▷ vb run a short distance at top speed
SPRINTS ▶ sprint
SPRIT n small spar set diagonally across a sail to extend it
SPRITE n elf
SPRITES ▶ sprite
SPRITS ▶ sprit

SPRITZ vb spray liquid
SPROD n young salmon
SPRODS ▶ sprod
SPROG n child
SPROGS ▶ sprog
SPRONG ▶ spring
SPROUT vb put forth shoots ▷ n shoot
SPROUTS ▶ sprout
SPRUCE n kind of fir ▷ adj neat and smart
SPRUCED ▶ spruce
SPRUCER ▶ spruce
SPRUCES ▶ spruce
SPRUCY ▶ spruce
SPRUE n vertical channel in a mould through which plastic or molten metal is poured
SPRUES ▶ sprue
SPRUG n sparrow
SPRUGS ▶ sprug
SPRUIK vb speak in public (used esp of a showman or salesman)
SPRUIKS ▶ spruik
SPRUIT n small tributary stream or watercourse
SPRUITS ▶ spruit
SPRUNG ▶ spring
SPRUSH Scots form of ▶ **spruce**
SPRY adj active or nimble
SPRYER ▶ spry
SPRYEST ▶ spry
SPRYLY ▶ spry
SPUD n potato ▷ vb remove (bark) or eradicate (weeds) with a spud
SPUDDED ▶ spud
SPUDDER same as ▶ **spud**
SPUDDLE n feeble movement
SPUDDY adj short and fat
SPUDS ▶ spud
SPUE same as ▶ **spew**
SPUED ▶ spue
SPUEING ▶ spue
SPUER ▶ spue
SPUERS ▶ spue
SPUES ▶ spue
SPUG same as ▶ **spuggy**
SPUGGY n house sparrow
SPUGS ▶ spug
SPUING ▶ spue
SPULE Scots word for > **shoulder**
SPULES ▶ spule
SPULYE same as > **spuilzie**
SPULYED ▶ spulye
SPULYES ▶ spulye
SPULYIE same as > **spuilzie**
SPULZIE same as > **spuilzie**

SPUME vb froth ▷ n foam or froth on the sea
SPUMED ▶ spume
SPUMES ▶ spume
SPUMIER ▶ spumy
SPUMING ▶ spume
SPUMONE n creamy Italian ice cream
SPUMONI same as ▶ **spumone**
SPUMOUS ▶ spume
SPUMY ▶ spume
SPUN ▶ spin
SPUNGE same as ▶ **sponge**
SPUNGES ▶ spunge
SPUNK n courage, spirit ▷ vb catch fire
SPUNKED ▶ spunk
SPUNKIE n will-o'-the-wisp
SPUNKS ▶ spunk
SPUNKY ▶ spunk
SPUR n stimulus or incentive ▷ vb urge on, incite (someone)
SPURGE n plant with milky sap
SPURGES ▶ spurge
SPURIAE n type of bird feathers
SPURN vb reject with scorn ▷ n instance of spurning
SPURNE vb spur
SPURNED ▶ spurn
SPURNER ▶ spurn
SPURNES ▶ spurne
SPURNS ▶ spurn
SPURRED ▶ spur
SPURRER ▶ spur
SPURREY n any of several low-growing European plants
SPURRY n spurrey ▷ adj resembling a spur
SPURS ▶ spur
SPURT vb gush or cause to gush out in a jet ▷ n short sudden burst of activity or speed
SPURTED ▶ spurt
SPURTER ▶ spurt
SPURTLE n wooden spoon for stirring porridge
SPURTS ▶ spurt
SPURWAY n path used by riders
SPUTA ▶ sputum
SPUTNIK n early Soviet artificial satellite
SPUTTER n splutter ▷ vb splutter
SPUTUM n spittle, usu mixed with mucus
SPY n person employed to

obtain secret information ▷ *vb* act as a spy

SPYAL *n* spy

SPYALS ▸ **spyal**

SPYCAM *n* camera used for covert surveillance

SPYCAMS ▸ **spycam**

SPYHOLE *n* small hole in a door, etc through which one may watch secretly

SPYING ▸ **spy**

SPYINGS ▸ **spy**

SPYRE *same as* ▸ **spire**

SPYRES ▸ **spyre**

SPYWARE *n* software installed via the internet on a computer without the user's knowledge and used to gain information about the user

SQUAB *n* young bird yet to leave the nest ▷ *adj* (of birds) recently hatched and still unfledged ▷ *vb* fall

SQUABBY ▸ **squab**

SQUABS ▸ **squab**

SQUACCO *n* S European heron

SQUAD *n* small group of people working or training together ▷ *vb* set up squads

SQUADDY *same as* > **squaddie**

SQUADS ▸ **squad**

SQUAIL *vb* throw sticks at

SQUAILS ▸ **squail**

SQUALID *adj* dirty and unpleasant

SQUALL *n* sudden strong wind ▷ *vb* cry noisily, yell

SQUALLS ▸ **squall**

SQUALLY ▸ **squall**

SQUALOR *n* disgusting dirt and filth

SQUAMA *n* scale or scalelike structure

SQUAMAE ▸ **squama**

SQUAME *same as* ▸ **squama**

SQUAMES ▸ **squame**

SQUARE *n* geometric figure with four equal sides and four right angles ▷ *adj* square in shape ▷ *vb* multiply (a number) by itself ▷ *adv* squarely, directly

SQUARED ▸ **square**

SQUARER ▸ **square**

SQUARES ▸ **square**

SQUARK *n* hypothetical boson partner of a quark

SQUARKS ▸ **squark**

SQUASH *vb* crush flat ▷ *n*

sweet fruit drink diluted with water

SQUASHY *adj* soft and easily squashed

SQUAT *vb* crouch with the knees bent and the weight on the feet ▷ *n* place where squatters live ▷ *adj* short and broad

SQUATLY ▸ **squat**

SQUATS ▸ **squat**

SQUATTY *adj* short and broad

SQUAWK *n* loud harsh cry ▷ *vb* utter a squawk

SQUAWKS ▸ **squawk**

SQUAWKY ▸ **squawk**

SQUEAK *n* short shrill cry or sound ▷ *vb* make or utter a squeak

SQUEAKS ▸ **squeak**

SQUEAKY ▸ **squeak**

SQUEAL *n* long shrill cry or sound ▷ *vb* make or utter a squeal

SQUEALS ▸ **squeal**

SQUEEZE *vb* grip or press firmly ▷ *n* squeezing

SQUEEZY ▸ **squeeze**

SQUEG *vb* oscillate

SQUEGS ▸ **squeg**

SQUELCH *vb* make a wet sucking sound, as by walking through mud ▷ *n* squelching sound

SQUIB *n* small firework that hisses before exploding

SQUIBS ▸ **squib**

SQUID *n* sea creature with a long soft body and ten tentacles ▷ *vb* (of a parachute) to assume an elongated squidlike shape owing to excess air pressure

SQUIDGE *vb* squash

SQUIDGY *adj* soft, moist, and squashy

SQUIDS ▸ **squid**

SQUIER *same as* ▸ **squire**

SQUIERS ▸ **squier**

SQUIFF *same as* ▸ **squiffy**

SQUIFFY *adj* slightly drunk

SQUILL *n* Mediterranean plant of the lily family

SQUILLA *n* type of mantis shrimp

SQUILLS ▸ **squill**

SQUINCH *n* small arch across an internal corner of a tower, used to support a superstructure such as a spire ▷ *vb* squeeze

SQUINNY *vb* squint ▷ *adj* squint

SQUINT *vb* have eyes which face in different directions ▷ *n* squinting condition of the eye ▷ *adj* crooked

SQUINTS ▸ **squint**

SQUINTY ▸ **squint**

SQUINY *same as* ▸ **squinny**

SQUIRE *n* country gentleman, usu the main landowner in a community ▷ *vb* (of a man) escort (a woman)

SQUIRED ▸ **squire**

SQUIRES ▸ **squire**

SQUIRM *vb* wriggle, writhe ▷ *n* wriggling movement

SQUIRMS ▸ **squirm**

SQUIRMY *adj* moving with a wriggling motion

SQUIRR *same as* ▸ **skirr**

SQUIRRS ▸ **squirr**

SQUIRT *vb* force (a liquid) or (of a liquid) be forced out of a narrow opening ▷ *n* jet of liquid

SQUIRTS ▸ **squirt**

SQUISH *n* (make) a soft squelching sound ▷ *vb* crush (something) with a soft squelching sound

SQUISHY *adj* soft and yielding to the touch

SQUIT *n* insignificant person

SQUITCH *n* couch grass

SQUITS ▸ **squit**

SQUIZ *n* look or glance, esp an inquisitive one

> The word **quiz** comes up surprisingly often, so it is useful to remember that you can put an S on the front of it to form this Australian slang word for a quick look.

SQUOOSH *vb* squash

SQUUSH *same as* ▸ **squoosh**

SRADDHA *n* Hindu offering to ancestor

SRADHA *same as* ▸ **sraddha**

SRADHAS ▸ **sradha**

SRI *n* title of respect used when addressing a Hindu

SRIS ▸ **sri**

ST *interj* exclamation to attract attention

STAB *vb* pierce with something pointed ▷ *n* stabbing

STABBED ▸ **stab**

STABBER ▸ **stab**

STABILE n stationary abstract construction, usually of wire, metal, wood, etc ▷ adj fixed

STABLE n building in which horses are kept ▷ vb put or keep (a horse) in a stable ▷ adj firmly fixed or established

STABLED ▶ stable

STABLER n stable owner

STABLES ▶ stable

STABLY ▶ stable

STABS ▶ stab

STACHYS n type of plant of the genus which includes lamb's ears and betony

STACK n ordered pile ▷ vb pile in a stack

STACKED ▶ stack

STACKER ▶ stack

STACKET n fence of wooden posts

STACKS ▶ stack

STACKUP n number of aircraft waiting to land

STACTE n one of several sweet-smelling spices used in incense

STACTES ▶ stacte

STADDA n type of saw

STADDAS ▶ stadda

STADDLE n type of support or prop

STADE same as ▶ stadium

STADES ▶ stade

STADIA n instrument used in surveying

STADIAL n stage in development of glacier

STADIAS ▶ stadia

STADIUM n sports arena with tiered seats for spectators

STAFF n people employed in an organization ▷ vb supply with personnel

STAFFED ▶ staff

STAFFER n member of staff, esp, in journalism, of editorial staff

STAFFS ▶ staff

STAG n adult male deer ▷ adv without a female escort ▷ vb apply for (shares in a new issue) with the intention of selling them for a quick profit

STAGE n step or period of development ▷ vb put (a play) on stage

STAGED ▶ stage

STAGER n person of experience

STAGERS ▶ stager

STAGERY n theatrical effects or techniques

STAGES ▶ stage

STAGEY same as ▶ stagy

STAGGED ▶ stag

STAGGER vb walk unsteadily ▷ n staggering

STAGGIE n little stag

STAGGY ▶ stag

STAGIER ▶ stagy

STAGILY ▶ stagy

STAGING n temporary support used in building

STAGS ▶ stag

STAGY adj too theatrical or dramatic

STAID adj sedate, serious, and rather dull

STAIDER ▶ staid

STAIDLY ▶ staid

STAIG Scots variant of ▶ stag

STAIGS ▶ staig

STAIN vb discolour, mark ▷ n discoloration or mark

STAINED ▶ stain

STAINER ▶ stain

STAINS ▶ stain

STAIR n one step in a flight of stairs

STAIRED adj having stairs

STAIRS pl n flight of steps between floors, usu indoors

STAITH same as ▶ staithe

STAITHE n wharf

STAITHS ▶ staith

STAKE n pointed stick or post driven into the ground as a support or marker ▷ vb support or mark out with stakes

STAKED ▶ stake

STAKES ▶ stake

STAKING ▶ stake

STALAG n German prisoner-of-war camp in World War II

STALAGS ▶ stalag

STALE adj not fresh ▷ vb make or become stale ▷ n urine of horses or cattle

STALED ▶ stale

STALELY ▶ stale

STALER ▶ stale

STALES ▶ stale

STALEST ▶ stale

STALING ▶ stale

STALK n plant's stem ▷ vb follow or approach stealthily

STALKED ▶ stalk

STALKER ▶ stalk

STALKO n idle gentleman

STALKS ▶ stalk

STALKY adj like a stalk

STALL n small stand for the display and sale of goods ▷ vb stop (a motor vehicle or engine) or (of a motor vehicle or engine) stop accidentally

STALLED ▶ stall

STALLS ▶ stall

STAMEN n pollen-producing part of a flower

STAMENS ▶ stamen

STAMINA n enduring energy and strength

STAMMEL n coarse woollen cloth in former use for undergarments

STAMMER vb speak or say with involuntary pauses or repetition of syllables ▷ n tendency to stammer

STAMNOI ▶ stamnos

STAMNOS n ancient Greek jar

STAMP n piece of gummed paper stuck to an envelope or parcel to show that the postage has been paid ▷ vb bring (one's foot) down forcefully

STAMPED ▶ stamp

STAMPER ▶ stamp

STAMPS ▶ stamp

STANCE n attitude

STANCES ▶ stance

STANCH vb stem the flow of (a liquid, esp blood) ▷ adj loyal and dependable

STANCK adj faint

STAND vb be in, rise to, or place in an upright position ▷ n stall for the sale of goods

STANDBY n person or thing that is ready for use

STANDEE n person who stands, esp when there are no vacant seats

STANDEN ▶ stand

STANDER ▶ stand

STANDS ▶ stand

STANDUP n comedian who performs solo

STANE Scots word for ▶ stone

STANED ▶ stane

STANES ▶ stane

STANG vb sting

STANGED ▶ stang

STANGS ▶ stang

STANIEL n kestrel

STANINE n scale of nine levels

STANING ▶ stane

STANK vb dam

STANKED ▶ stink

STANKS ▶ stink

STANNEL same as ▶ staniel

STANNIC adj of or containing tin, esp in the tetravalent state

STANNUM n tin (the metal)

STANOL n drug taken to prevent heart disease

STANOLS ▶ stanol

STANYEL same as ▶ staniel

STANZA n verse of a poem

STANZAS ▶ stanza

STANZE same as ▶ stanza

STANZES ▶ stanze

STANZO same as ▶ stanza

STANZOS ▶ stanzo

STAP same as ▶ stop

STAPES n stirrup-shaped bone that is the innermost of three small bones in the middle ear of mammals

STAPH n staphylococcus

STAPHS ▶ staph

STAPLE n U-shaped piece of metal used to fasten papers or secure things ▷ vb fasten with staples ▷ adj of prime importance, principal

STAPLED ▶ staple

STAPLER n small device for fastening papers together

STAPLES ▶ staple

STAPPED ▶ stap

STAPPLE same as ▶ stopple

STAPS ▶ stap

STAR n hot gaseous mass in space, visible in the night sky as a point of light ▷ vb feature or be featured as a star ▷ adj leading, famous

STARCH n carbohydrate forming the main food element in bread, potatoes, etc, and used mixed with water for stiffening fabric ▷ vb stiffen (fabric) with starch ▷ adj (of a person) formal

STARCHY adj containing starch

STARDOM n status of a star in the entertainment or sports world

STARE vb look or gaze fixedly (at) ▷ n fixed gaze

STARED ▶ stare

STARER ▶ stare

STARERS ▶ stare

STARES ▶ stare

STARETS n Russian holy man

STARETZ same as ▶ starets

STARING ▶ stare

STARK adj harsh, unpleasant, and plain ▷ adv completely ▷ vb stiffen

STARKED ▶ stark

STARKEN vb become or make stark

STARKER ▶ stark

STARKLY ▶ stark

STARKS ▶ stark

STARLET n young actress presented as a future star

STARLIT same as > starlight

STARN same as ▶ stern

STARNED ▶ starn

STARNIE n Scots word for little star

STARNS ▶ starn

STARR n (in Judaism) release from a debt

STARRED ▶ star

STARRS ▶ starr

STARRY adj full of or like stars

STARS ▶ star

START vb take the first step, begin ▷ n first part of something

STARTED ▶ start

STARTER n first course of a meal

STARTLE vb slightly surprise or frighten

STARTLY same as > startlish

STARTS ▶ start

STARTSY ▶ starets

STARTUP n business enterprise that has been launched recently

STARVE vb die or suffer or cause to die or suffer from hunger

STARVED ▶ starve

STARVER ▶ starve

STARVES ▶ starve

STASES ▶ stasis

STASH vb store in a secret place ▷ n secret store

STASHED ▶ stash

STASHES ▶ stash

STASHIE same as ▶ stushie

STASIMA > stasimon

STASIS n stagnation in the normal flow of bodily fluids, such as the blood or urine

STAT n statistic

STATAL adj of a federal state

STATANT adj (of an animal) in profile with all four feet on the ground

STATE n condition of a person or thing ▷ adj of or concerning the State ▷ vb express in words

STATED adj (esp of a sum) determined by agreement

STATELY adj dignified or grand ▷ adv in a stately manner

STATER n any of various usually silver coins of ancient Greece

STATERS ▶ stater

STATES ▶ state

STATIC adj stationary or inactive ▷ n crackling sound or speckled picture caused by interference in radio or television reception

STATICE n plant name formerly used for both thrift and sea lavender

STATICS n branch of mechanics dealing with the forces producing a state of equilibrium

STATIM adv right away

STATIN n type of drug that lowers the levels of low-density lipoproteins in the blood

STATING ▶ state

STATINS ▶ statin

STATION n place where trains stop for passengers ▷ vb assign (someone) to a particular place

STATISM n theory or practice of concentrating economic and political power in the state

STATIST n advocate of statism ▷ adj of, characteristic of, advocating, or relating to statism

STATIVE adj denoting a verb describing a state rather than an activity, act, or event ▷ n stative verb

STATOR n stationary part of a rotary machine or device, esp of a motor or generator

STATORS ▶ stator

STATS ▶ stat

STATTO n person preoccupied with the facts and figures of a subject

STATTOS ▶ statto

STATUA same as ▶ statue

S

STATUAS ▶ **statua**
STATUE n large sculpture of a human or animal figure
STATUED adj decorated with or portrayed in a statue or statues
STATUES ▶ **statue**
STATURE n person's height
STATUS n social position
STATUSY adj conferring or having status
STATUTE n written law
STAUN Scots word for ▶ **stand**
STAUNCH same as ▶ **stanch**
STAUNS ▶ **staun**
STAVE same as ▶ **staff**
STAVED ▶ **stave**
STAVES ▶ **stave**
STAVING ▶ **stave**
STAW Scots form of ▶ **stall**
STAWED ▶ **staw**
STAWING ▶ **staw**
STAWS ▶ **staw**
STAY vb remain in a place or condition ▷ n period of staying in a place
STAYED ▶ **stay**
STAYER n person or thing that stays
STAYERS ▶ **stayer**
STAYING ▶ **stay**
STAYNE same as ▶ **stain**
STAYNED ▶ **stayne**
STAYNES ▶ **stayne**
STAYRE same as ▶ **stair**
STAYRES ▶ **stayre**
STAYS pl n old-fashioned corsets with bones in them
STEAD n place or function that should be taken by another ▷ vb help or benefit
STEADED ▶ **stead**
STEADS ▶ **stead**
STEADY adj not shaky or wavering ▷ vb make steady ▷ adv in a steady manner
STEAK n thick slice of meat, esp beef
STEAKS ▶ **steak**
STEAL vb take unlawfully or without permission
STEALE n handle
STEALED ▶ **steal**
STEALER n person who steals something
STEALES ▶ **steale**
STEALS ▶ **steal**
STEALT ▶ **steal**
STEALTH n moving carefully and quietly ▷ adj (of technology) able to render

an aircraft almost invisible to radar ▷ vb approach undetected
STEAM n vapour into which water changes when boiled ▷ vb give off steam
STEAMED ▶ **steam**
STEAMER n steam-propelled ship ▷ vb travel by steamer
STEAMIE n public wash house
STEAMS ▶ **steam**
STEAMY adj full of steam
STEAN n earthenware vessel
STEANE same as ▶ **steen**
STEANED ▶ **steane**
STEANES ▶ **steane**
STEANS ▶ **stean**
STEAR same as ▶ **steer**
STEARD ▶ **stear**
STEARE same as ▶ **steer**
STEARED ▶ **steare**
STEARES ▶ **steare**
STEARIC adj of or relating to suet or fat
STEARIN n colourless crystalline ester of glycerol and stearic acid
STEARS ▶ **stear**
STED same as ▶ **stead**
STEDD same as ▶ **stead**
STEDDE same as ▶ **stead**
STEDDED ▶ **sted**
STEDDES ▶ **stedde**
STEDDS ▶ **stedd**
STEDDY same as ▶ **steady**
STEDE same as ▶ **stead**
STEDED ▶ **stede**
STEDES ▶ **stede**
STEDING ▶ **stede**
STEDS ▶ **sted**
STEED same as ▶ **stead**
STEEDED ▶ **steed**
STEEDS ▶ **steed**
STEEDY same as ▶ **steady**
STEEK vb Scots word meaning shut
STEEKED ▶ **steek**
STEEKIT ▶ **steek**
STEEKS ▶ **steek**
STEEL n hard malleable alloy of iron and carbon ▷ vb prepare (oneself) for something unpleasant
STEELD ▶ **steel**
STEELED ▶ **steel**
STEELIE n steel ball bearing used as marble
STEELS pl n shares and bonds of steel companies
STEELY ▶ **steel**

STEEM same as ▶ **esteem**
STEEMED ▶ **steem**
STEEMS ▶ **steem**
STEEN vb line with stone
STEENED ▶ **steen**
STEENS ▶ **steen**
STEEP adj sloping sharply ▷ vb soak or be soaked in liquid ▷ n instance or the process of steeping or the condition of being steeped
STEEPED ▶ **steep**
STEEPEN vb become or cause (something) to become steep or steeper
STEEPER ▶ **steep**
STEEPLE same as ▶ **spire**
STEEPLY ▶ **steep**
STEEPS ▶ **steep**
STEEPUP adj very steep
STEEPY same as ▶ **steep**
STEER vb direct the course of (a vehicle or ship) ▷ n castrated male ox
STEERED ▶ **steer**
STEERER ▶ **steer**
STEERS ▶ **steer**
STEERY n commotion
STEEVE n spar having a pulley block at one end, used for stowing cargo on a ship ▷ vb stow (cargo) securely in the hold of a ship
STEEVED ▶ **steeve**
STEEVER ▶ **steeve**
STEEVES ▶ **steeve**
STEIL same as ▶ **steal**
STEILS ▶ **steil**
STEIN same as ▶ **steen**
STEINED ▶ **stein**
STEINS ▶ **stein**
STELA same as ▶ **stele**
STELAE ▶ **stele**
STELAI ▶ **stele**
STELAR ▶ **stele**
STELE n upright stone slab or column decorated with figures or inscriptions
STELENE ▶ **stele**
STELES ▶ **stele**
STELIC ▶ **stele**
STELL n shelter for cattle or sheep built on moorland or hillsides ▷ vb position or place
STELLA n star or something star-shaped
STELLAR adj of stars
STELLAS ▶ **stella**
STELLED ▶ **stell**
STELLIO n as in **stellio lizard** denoting type of lizard

S

STELLS ▶ **stell**
STEM vb stop (the flow of something) ▷ n main axis of a plant, which bears the leaves, axillary buds, and flowers
STEMBOK same as > **steenbok**
STEME same as ▶ **steam**
STEMED ▶ **steme**
STEMES ▶ **steme**
STEMING ▶ **steme**
STEMLET n little stem
STEMMA n family tree
STEMMAS ▶ **stemma**
STEMME archaic variant of ▶ **stem**
STEMMED ▶ **stem**
STEMMER ▶ **stem**
STEMMES ▶ **stemme**
STEMMY adj (of wine) young and raw
STEMPEL n timber support
STEMPLE same as ▶ **stempel**
STEMS ▶ **stem**
STEMSON n curved timber scarfed into or bolted to the stem and keelson at the bow of a wooden vessel
STEN vb stride
STENCH n foul smell ▷ vb cause to smell
STENCHY ▶ **stench**
STENCIL n thin sheet with cut-out pattern through which ink or paint passes to form the pattern on the surface below ▷ vb make (a pattern) with a stencil
STEND vb Scots word meaning bound
STENDED ▶ **stend**
STENDS ▶ **stend**
STENGAH same as ▶ **stinger**
STENNED ▶ **sten**
STENO n stenographer
STENOKY n life and survival that is dependent on conditions remaining within a narrow range of variables
STENOS ▶ **steno**
STENS ▶ **sten**
STENT n surgical implant used to keep an artery open ▷ vb assess
STENTED ▶ **stent**
STENTOR n person with an unusually loud voice
STENTS ▶ **stent**
STEP vb move and set down the foot, as when walking

▷ n stepping
STEPNEY n spare wheel
STEPPE n extensive grassy plain usually without trees
STEPPED ▶ **step**
STEPPER n person who or animal that steps, esp a horse or a dancer
STEPPES ▶ **steppe**
STEPS ▶ **step**
STEPSON n son of one's husband or wife by an earlier relationship
STEPT ▶ **step**
STERE n unit used to measure volumes of stacked timber
STEREO n stereophonic record player ▷ adj (of a sound system) using two or more separate microphones to feed two or more loudspeakers through separate channels ▷ vb make stereophonic
STEREOS ▶ **stereo**
STERES ▶ **stere**
STERIC adj of or caused by the spatial arrangement of atoms in a molecule
STERILE adj free from germs
STERLET n small sturgeon of seas and rivers in N Asia and E Europe
STERN adj severe, strict ▷ n rear part of a ship ▷ vb row boat backward
STERNA ▶ **sternum**
STERNAL ▶ **sternum**
STERNED ▶ **stern**
STERNER ▶ **stern**
STERNLY ▶ **stern**
STERNS ▶ **stern**
STERNUM n long flat bone in the front of the body, to which the collarbone and most of the ribs are attached
STEROID n organic compound containing a carbon ring system, such as many hormones
STEROL n natural insoluble alcohol such as cholesterol and ergosterol
STEROLS ▶ **sterol**
STERTOR n laborious or noisy breathing caused by obstructed air passages
STERVE same as ▶ **starve**
STERVED ▶ **sterve**
STERVES ▶ **sterve**
STET interj instruction to

ignore an alteration previously made by a proofreader ▷ vb indicate to a printer that certain deleted matter is to be kept ▷ n word or mark indicating that certain deleted written matter is to be retained
STETS ▶ **stet**
STETSON n cowboy hat
STETTED ▶ **stet**
STEVEN n voice
STEVENS ▶ **steven**
STEW n food cooked slowly in a closed pot ▷ vb cook slowly in a closed pot
STEWARD n person who looks after passengers on a ship or aircraft ▷ vb act as a steward (of)
STEWBUM n drunkard
STEWED adj (of food) cooked by stewing
STEWER ▶ **stew**
STEWERS ▶ **stew**
STEWIER ▶ **stew**
STEWING ▶ **stew**
STEWPAN n pan used for making stew
STEWPOT n pot used for making stew
STEWS ▶ **stew**
STEWY ▶ **stew**
STEY adj Scots word meaning steep
STEYER ▶ **stey**
STEYEST ▶ **stey**
STHENIA n abnormal strength
STHENIC adj abounding in energy or bodily strength
STIBBLE Scots form of ▶ **stubble**
STIBIAL ▶ **stibium**
STIBINE n colourless slightly soluble poisonous gas
STIBIUM obsolete name for > **antimony**
STICH n line of poetry
STICHIC ▶ **stich**
STICHOI ▶ **stichos**
STICHOS n line of poem
STICHS ▶ **stich**
STICK n long thin piece of wood ▷ vb push (a pointed object) into (something)
STICKED ▶ **stick**
STICKER n adhesive label or sign ▷ vb put stickers on
STICKIT Scots form of ▶ **stuck**
STICKLE vb dispute

S

stubbornly, esp about minor points
STICKS ▸ stick
STICKUM n adhesive
STICKUP n robbery at gun-point
STICKY adj covered with an adhesive substance ▷ vb make sticky ▷ n inquisitive look or stare
STIDDIE same as ▸ **stithy**
STIE same as ▸ **sty**
STIED ▸ sty
STIES ▸ sty
STIEVE same as ▸ **steeve**
STIEVER ▸ stieve
STIFF adj not easily bent or moved ▷ n corpse ▷ adv completely or utterly ▷ vb fail completely
STIFFED ▸ stiff
STIFFEN vb make or become stiff
STIFFER ▸ stiff
STIFFLY ▸ stiff
STIFFS ▸ stiff
STIFFY n erection of the penis
STIFLE vb suppress ▷ n joint in the hind leg of a horse, dog, etc, between the femur and tibia
STIFLED ▸ stifle
STIFLER ▸ stifle
STIFLES ▸ stifle
STIGMA n mark of social disgrace
STIGMAL adj of part of insect wing
STIGMAS ▸ stigma
STIGME n dot in Greek punctuation
STIGMES ▸ stigme
STILB n unit of luminance equal to 1 candela per square centimetre.
STILBS ▸ stilb
STILE same as ▸ **style**
STILED ▸ stile
STILES ▸ stile
STILET same as ▸ **stylet**
STILETS ▸ stilet
STILING ▸ stile
STILL adv now or in the future as before ▷ adj motionless ▷ n calmness; apparatus for distillation ▷ vb make still
STILLED ▸ still
STILLER ▸ still
STILLS ▸ still
STILLY adv quietly or calmly ▷ adj still, quiet, or calm

STILT n either of a pair of long poles with footrests for walking raised from the ground ▷ vb raise or place on or as if on stilts
STILTED adj stiff and formal in manner
STILTER ▸ stilt
STILTS ▸ stilt
STILTY ▸ stilt
STIM n very small amount
STIME same as ▸ **styme**
STIMED ▸ stime
STIMES ▸ stime
STIMIE same as ▸ **stymie**
STIMIED ▸ stimie
STIMIES ▸ stimie
STIMING ▸ stime
STIMS ▸ stim
STIMULI > stimulus
STIMY same as ▸ **stymie**
STING vb (of certain animals or plants) wound by injecting with poison ▷ n wound or pain caused by or as if by stinging
STINGED ▸ sting
STINGER n person, plant, animal, etc, that stings or hurts
STINGO n strong alcohol
STINGOS ▸ stingo
STINGS ▸ sting
STINGY adj mean or miserly ▷ n stinging nettle
STINK n strong unpleasant smell ▷ vb give off a strong unpleasant smell
STINKER n difficult or unpleasant person or thing
STINKO adj drunk
STINKS ▸ stink
STINKY adj having a foul smell
STINT vb be miserly with (something) ▷ n allotted amount of work
STINTED ▸ stint
STINTER ▸ stint
STINTS ▸ stint
STINTY ▸ stint
STIPA n variety of grass
STIPAS ▸ stipa
STIPE n stalk in plants that bears reproductive structures
STIPED same as > **stipitate**
STIPEL n small paired leaflike structure at the base of certain leaflets
STIPELS ▸ stipel
STIPEND n regular allowance or salary, esp

that paid to a clergyman
STIPES n second maxillary segment in insects and crustaceans
STIPPLE vb paint, draw, or engrave using dots ▷ n technique of stippling or a picture produced by or using stippling
STIPULE n small paired usually leaflike outgrowth occurring at the base of a leaf or its stalk
STIR vb mix up (a liquid) by moving a spoon etc around in it ▷ n stirring
STIRE same as ▸ **steer**
STIRED ▸ stire
STIRES ▸ stire
STIRING ▸ stire
STIRK n heifer of 6 to 12 months old
STIRKS ▸ stirk
STIRP same as ▸ **stirps**
STIRPES ▸ stirps
STIRPS n line of descendants from an ancestor
STIRRA same as ▸ **sirra**
STIRRAH same as ▸ **sirrah**
STIRRAS ▸ stirra
STIRRE same as ▸ **steer**
STIRRED ▸ stir
STIRRER n person who deliberately causes trouble
STIRRES ▸ stirre
STIRRUP n metal loop attached to a saddle for supporting a rider's foot
STIRS ▸ stir
STISHIE same as ▸ **stushie**
STITCH n link made by drawing thread through material with a needle ▷ vb sew
STITHY n forge or anvil ▷ vb forge on an anvil
STIVE vb stifle
STIVED ▸ stive
STIVER n former Dutch coin worth one twentieth of a guilder
STIVERS ▸ stiver
STIVES ▸ stive
STIVIER ▸ stivy
STIVING ▸ stive
STIVY adj stuffy
STOA n covered walk that has a colonnade on one or both sides, esp as used in ancient Greece
STOAE ▸ stoa
STOAI ▸ stoa

STOAS ▶ stoa
STOAT n small mammal of the weasel family, with brown fur that turns white in winter
STOATS ▶ stoat
STOB same as ▶ stab
STOBBED ▶ stob
STOBIE adj as in **stobie pole** steel and concrete pole for supporting electricity wires
STOBS ▶ stob
STOCK n total amount of goods available for sale in a shop ▷ adj kept in stock, standard ▷ vb keep for sale or future use
STOCKED ▶ stock
STOCKER ▶ stock
STOCKS pl n instrument of punishment consisting of a heavy wooden frame with holes in which the feet, hands, or head of an offender were locked
STOCKY adj (of a person) broad and sturdy
STODGE n heavy starchy food ▷ vb stuff (oneself or another) with food
STODGED ▶ stodge
STODGER n dull person
STODGES ▶ stodge
STODGY adj (of food) heavy and starchy
STOEP n verandah
STOEPS ▶ stoep
STOGEY same as ▶ stogy
STOGEYS ▶ stogey
STOGIE same as ▶ stogy
STOGIES ▶ stogy
STOGY n any long cylindrical inexpensive cigar
STOIC n person who suffers hardship without showing his or her feelings ▷ adj suffering hardship without showing one's feelings
STOICAL adj suffering great difficulties without showing one's feelings
STOICS ▶ stoic
STOIT vb bounce
STOITED ▶ stoit
STOITER vb stagger
STOITS ▶ stoit
STOKE vb feed and tend (a fire or furnace)
STOKED adj very pleased
STOKER n person employed to tend a furnace on a ship or train powered by steam

STOKERS ▶ stoker
STOKES n cgs unit of kinematic viscosity
STOKING ▶ stoke
STOKVEL n (in S Africa) informal savings pool or syndicate
STOLE n long scarf or shawl
STOLED adj wearing a stole
STOLEN ▶ steal
STOLES ▶ stole
STOLID adj showing little emotion or interest
STOLLEN n rich sweet bread containing nuts, raisins, etc
STOLN ▶ steal
STOLON n long horizontal stem that grows along the surface of the soil and propagates by producing roots and shoots at the nodes or tip
STOLONS ▶ stolon
STOMA n pore in a plant leaf that controls the passage of gases into and out of the plant
STOMACH n organ in the body which digests food ▷ vb put up with
STOMACK n as in **have a stomack** (in E Africa) be pregnant
STOMAL ▶ stoma
STOMAS ▶ stoma
STOMATA ▶ stoma
STOMATE n opening on leaf through which water evaporates
STOMIA ▶ stomium
STOMIUM n part of the sporangium of ferns that ruptures to release the spores
STOMP vb tread heavily ▷ n rhythmic stamping jazz dance
STOMPED ▶ stomp
STOMPER n rock or jazz song with a particularly strong and danceable beat
STOMPIE n cigarette butt
STOMPS ▶ stomp
STOND same as ▶ stand
STONDS ▶ stond
STONE n material of which rocks are made ▷ vb throw stones at
STONED adj under the influence of alcohol or drugs
STONEN adj of stone
STONER n device for

removing stones from fruit
STONERN same as ▶ stonen
STONERS ▶ stoner
STONES ▶ stone
STONEY same as ▶ stony
STONG ▶ sting
STONIED ▶ stony
STONIER ▶ stony
STONIES ▶ stony
STONILY ▶ stony
STONING ▶ stone
STONISH same as > astonish
STONK vb bombard (soldiers, buildings, etc) with artillery ▷ n concentrated bombardment by artillery
STONKED ▶ stonk
STONKER vb destroy
STONKS ▶ stonk
STONN same as ▶ stun
STONNE same as ▶ stun
STONNED ▶ stonne
STONNES ▶ stonne
STONNS ▶ stonn
STONY adj of or like stone ▷ vb astonish
STOOD ▶ stand
STOODEN ▶ stand
STOOGE n actor who feeds lines to a comedian or acts as the butt of his jokes ▷ vb act as a stooge
STOOGED ▶ stooge
STOOGES ▶ stooge
STOOK n number of sheaves set upright in a field to dry with their heads together ▷ vb set up (sheaves) in stooks
STOOKED ▶ stook
STOOKER ▶ stook
STOOKIE n stucco
STOOKS ▶ stook
STOOL n chair without arms or back ▷ vb (of a plant) send up shoots from the base of the stem
STOOLED ▶ stool
STOOLIE n police informer
STOOLS ▶ stool
STOOP vb bend forward and downward
STOOPE same as ▶ stoup
STOOPED ▶ stoop
STOOPER ▶ stoop
STOOPES ▶ stoope
STOOPS ▶ stoop
STOOR same as ▶ stour
STOORS ▶ stoor
STOOZE vb borrow money at 0% interest rate on a

S

credit card then invest it to make a profit

STOOZED ▷ stooze

STOOZER n person who borrows money at 0% interest rate on a credit card then invests it to make a profit

STOOZES ▷ stooze

STOP vb cease or cause to cease from doing (something) ▷ n stopping or being stopped

STOPE n steplike excavation made in a mine to extract ore ▷ vb mine (ore, etc) by cutting stopes

STOPED ▷ stope

STOPER n drill used in mining

STOPERS ▷ stoper

STOPES ▷ stope

STOPGAP n temporary substitute

STOPING n process by which country rock is broken up and engulfed by the upward movement of magma

STOPOFF n break in a journey

STOPPED ▷ stop

STOPPER n plug for closing a bottle etc ▷ vb close or fit with a stopper

STOPPLE same as ▷ **stopper**

STOPS ▷ stop

STOPT ▷ stop

STORAGE n storing

STORAX n type of tree or shrub with drooping showy white flowers

STORE vb collect and keep (things) for future use ▷ n shop

STORED ▷ store

STORER ▷ store

STORERS ▷ store

STORES pl n supply or stock of food and other essentials for a journey

STOREY n floor or level of a building

STOREYS ▷ storey

STORGE n affection

STORGES ▷ storge

STORIED ▷ story

STORIES ▷ story

STORING ▷ store

STORK n large wading bird

STORKS ▷ stork

STORM n violent weather with wind, rain, or snow

▷ vb attack or capture (a place) suddenly

STORMED ▷ storm

STORMER n outstanding example of its kind

STORMS ▷ storm

STORMY adj characterized by storms

STORY n narration of a chain of events ▷ vb decorate with scenes from history

STOSS adj (of the side of a hill) facing the onward flow of a glacier ▷ n hillside facing glacier flow

STOSSES ▷ stoss

STOT n bullock ▷ vb bounce or cause to bounce

STOTIN n monetary unit of Slovenia, worth one hundredth of a tolar

STOTINS ▷ stotin

STOTS ▷ stot

STOTT same as ▷ **stot**

STOTTED ▷ stot

STOTTER same as ▷ **stot**

STOTTIE n wedge of bread cut from a flat round loaf that has been split and filled with meat, cheese, etc

STOTTS ▷ stott

STOTTY n type of flat, round loaf made in NE England

STOUN same as ▷ **stun**

STOUND n short while ▷ vb ache

STOUNDS ▷ stound

STOUNS ▷ stoun

STOUP n small basin for holy water

STOUPS ▷ stoup

STOUR n turmoil or conflict

STOURE same as ▷ **stour**

STOURES ▷ stoure

STOURIE same as ▷ **stoury**

STOURS ▷ stour

STOURY adj dusty

STOUSH vb hit or punch (someone) ▷ n fighting or violence

STOUT adj fat ▷ n strong dark beer

STOUTEN vb make or become stout

STOUTER ▷ stout

STOUTH n Scots word meaning theft

STOUTHS ▷ stouth

STOUTLY ▷ stout

STOUTS ▷ stout

STOVE n apparatus for cooking or heating ▷ vb

process (ceramics, metalwork, etc) by heating in a stove

STOVED ▷ stove

STOVER n fodder

STOVERS ▷ stover

STOVES ▷ stove

STOVIES pl n potatoes stewed with onions

STOVING ▷ stove

STOW vb pack or store

STOWAGE n space or charge for stowing goods

STOWED ▷ stow

STOWER ▷ stow

STOWERS ▷ stow

STOWING ▷ stow

STOWN ▷ steal

STOWND same as ▷ **stound**

STOWNDS ▷ stownd

STOWP same as ▷ **stoup**

STOWPS ▷ stowp

STOWRE same as ▷ **stour**

STOWRES ▷ stowre

STOWS ▷ stow

STRACK vb archaic past tense form of strike

STRAD n violin made by Stradivarius

STRADS ▷ strad

STRAE Scots form of ▷ **straw**

STRAES ▷ strae

STRAFE vb attack (an enemy) with machine guns from the air ▷ n act or instance of strafing

STRAFED ▷ strafe

STRAFER ▷ strafe

STRAFES ▷ strafe

STRAFF same as ▷ **strafe**

STRAFFS ▷ straff

STRAG n straggler

STRAGS ▷ strag

STRAIK Scots word for ▷ **stroke**

STRAIKS ▷ straik

STRAIN vb subject to mental tension ▷ n tension or tiredness

STRAINS ▷ strain

STRAINT n pressure

STRAIT n narrow channel connecting two areas of sea ▷ adj (of spaces, etc) affording little room ▷ vb tighten

STRAITS ▷ strait

STRAK vb archaic past tense form of strike

STRAKE n curved metal plate forming part of the metal rim on a wooden wheel

STRAKED adj having a strake

STRAKES ▶ strake

STRAMP Scots variant of ▶ tramp

STRAMPS ▶ stramp

STRAND vb run aground ▷ n shore

STRANDS ▶ strand

STRANG dialect variant of ▶ strong

STRANGE adj odd or unusual ▷ n odd or unfamiliar person or thing

STRAP n strip of flexible material for lifting or holding in place ▷ vb fasten with a strap or straps

STRAPPY adj having straps

STRAPS ▶ strap

STRASS another word for ▶ paste

STRATA ▶ stratum

STRATAL ▶ stratum

STRATAS ▶ stratum

STRATH n flat river valley

STRATHS ▶ strath

STRATI ▶ stratus

STRATUM n layer, esp of rock

STRATUS n grey layer cloud

STRAW n dried stalks of grain ▷ vb spread around

STRAWED ▶ straw

STRAWEN adj of straw

STRAWN ▶ strew

STRAWS ▶ straw

STRAWY adj containing straw, or like straw in colour or texture

STRAY vb wander ▷ adj having strayed ▷ n stray animal

STRAYED ▶ stray

STRAYER ▶ stray

STRAYS ▶ stray

STRAYVE vb wander aimlessly

STREAK n long band of contrasting colour or substance ▷ vb mark with streaks

STREAKS ▶ streak

STREAKY adj marked with streaks

STREAM n small river ▷ vb flow steadily

STREAMS ▶ stream

STREAMY adj (of an area, land, etc) having many streams

STREEK Scots word for ▶ stretch

STREEKS ▶ streek

STREEL n slovenly woman ▷ vb trail

STREELS ▶ streel

STREET n public road, usu lined with buildings ▷ vb lay out a street or streets

STREETS ▶ street

STREETY adj of streets

STRENE same as ▶ strain

STRENES ▶ strene

STREP n streptococcus

STREPS ▶ strep

STRESS n tension or strain ▷ vb emphasize

STRETCH vb extend or be extended ▷ n stretching

STRETTA same as ▶ stretto

STRETTE ▶ stretta

STRETTI ▶ stretto

STRETTO n (in a fugue) the close overlapping of two parts or voices

STREW vb scatter (things) over a surface

STREWED ▶ strew

STREWER ▶ strew

STREWN ▶ strew

STREWS ▶ strew

STREWTH interj expression of surprise or alarm

STRIA n scratch or groove on the surface of a rock crystal

STRIAE ▶ stria

STRIATA > striatum

STRIATE adj marked with striae ▷ vb mark with striae

STRICH n screech owl

STRICK n any bast fibres preparatory to being made into slivers

STRICKS ▶ strick

STRICT adj stern or severe

STRIDE vb walk with long steps ▷ n long step

STRIDER ▶ stride

STRIDES ▶ stride

STRIDOR n high-pitched whistling sound made during respiration

STRIFE n conflict, quarrelling

STRIFES ▶ strife

STRIFT n struggle

STRIFTS ▶ strift

STRIG vb remove stalk from

STRIGA same as ▶ stria

STRIGAE ▶ striga

STRIGIL n curved blade used by the ancient Romans and Greeks to scrape the body after bathing

STRIGS ▶ strig

STRIKE vb cease work as a protest ▷ n stoppage of work as a protest

STRIKER n striking worker

STRIKES ▶ strike

STRIM vb cut (grass) using a strimmer

STRIMS ▶ strim

STRING n thin cord used for tying ▷ vb provide with a string or strings

STRINGS ▶ string

STRINGY adj like string

STRIP vb take (the covering or clothes) off ▷ n act of stripping

STRIPE n long narrow band of contrasting colour or substance ▷ vb mark (something) with stripes

STRIPED adj marked or decorated with stripes

STRIPER n officer who has a stripe or stripes on his uniform, esp in the navy

STRIPES ▶ stripe

STRIPEY same as ▶ stripy

STRIPS ▶ strip

STRIPT ▶ strip

STRIPY adj marked by or with stripes

STRIVE vb make a great effort

STRIVED ▶ strive

STRIVEN ▶ strive

STRIVER ▶ strive

STRIVES ▶ strive

STROAM vb wander

STROAMS ▶ stroam

STROBE n high intensity flashing beam of light ▷ vb give the appearance of slow motion by using a strobe

STROBED ▶ strobe

STROBES ▶ strobe

STROBIC adj spinning or appearing to spin

STROBIL n scaly multiple fruit

STRODE ▶ stride

STRODLE same as > straddle

STROKE vb touch or caress lightly with the hand ▷ n light touch or caress with the hand

STROKED ▶ stroke

STROKEN ▶ strike

STROKER ▶ stroke

STROKES ▶ stroke

STROLL vb walk in a leisurely manner ▷ n

S

leisurely walk

STROLLS ▷ stroll

STROMA n gel-like matrix of chloroplasts and certain cells

STROMAL ▷ stroma

STROMB n shellfish like a whelk

STROMBS ▷ stromb

STROND same as ▷ **strand**

STRONDS ▷ strond

STRONG adj having physical power

STROOK ▷ strike

STROOKE n stroke

STROP n leather strap for sharpening razors ▷ vb sharpen (a razor, etc) on a strop

STROPHE n first of two movements made by a chorus during the performance of a choral ode

STROPPY adj angry or awkward

STROPS ▷ strop

STROUD n coarse woollen fabric

STROUDS ▷ stroud

STROUP Scots word for ▷ **spout**

STROUPS ▷ stroup

STROUT vb bulge

STROUTS ▷ strout

STROVE ▷ strive

STROW archaic variant of ▷ **strew**

STROWED ▷ strow

STROWER ▷ strow

STROWN ▷ strow

STROWS ▷ strow

STROY archaic variant of ▷ **destroy**

STROYED ▷ stroy

STROYER ▷ stroy

STROYS ▷ stroy

STRUCK ▷ strike

STRUDEL n thin sheet of filled dough rolled up and baked, usu with an apple filling

STRUM vb play (a guitar or banjo) by sweeping the thumb or a plectrum across the strings

STRUMA n abnormal enlargement of the thyroid gland

STRUMAE ▷ struma

STRUMAS ▷ struma

STRUMS ▷ strum

STRUNG ▷ string

STRUNT Scots word for ▷ **strut**

STRUNTS ▷ strunt

STRUT vb walk pompously, swagger ▷ n bar supporting a structure

STRUTS ▷ strut

STUB n short piece left after use ▷ vb strike (the toe) painfully against an object

STUBBED ▷ stub

STUBBIE same as ▷ **stubby**

STUBBLE n short stalks of grain left in a field after reaping

STUBBLY ▷ stubble

STUBBY adj short and broad ▷ n small bottle of beer

STUBS ▷ stub

STUCCO n plaster used for coating or decorating walls ▷ vb apply stucco to (a building)

STUCCOS ▷ stucco

STUCK n thrust

STUCKS ▷ stuck

STUD n small piece of metal attached to a surface for decoration ▷ vb set with studs

STUDDED ▷ stud

STUDDEN ▷ stand

STUDDIE Scots word for ▷ **anvil**

STUDDLE n post

STUDE vb past tense and past participle of staun (Scots form of stand)

STUDENT n person who studies a subject, esp at university

STUDIED adj carefully practised

STUDIER ▷ study

STUDIES ▷ study

STUDIO n workroom of an artist or photographer

STUDIOS ▷ studio

STUDLY adj strong and virile

STUDS ▷ stud

STUDY vb be engaged in learning (a subject) ▷ n act or process of studying

STUFF n substance or material ▷ vb pack, cram, or fill completely

STUFFED ▷ stuff

STUFFER ▷ stuff

STUFFS ▷ stuff

STUFFY adj lacking fresh air

STUGGY adj stout

STUIVER same as ▷ **stiver**

STULL n timber prop or

platform in a stope

STULLS ▷ stull

STULM n shaft

STULMS ▷ stulm

STUM n partly fermented wine added to fermented wine as a preservative ▷ vb preserve (wine) by adding stum

STUMBLE vb trip and nearly fall ▷ n stumbling

STUMBLY adj tending to stumble

STUMER n forgery or cheat

STUMERS ▷ stumer

STUMM same as ▷ **shtoom**

STUMMED ▷ stum

STUMMEL n bowl of pipe

STUMP n base of a tree left when the main trunk has been cut away ▷ vb baffle

STUMPED ▷ stump

STUMPER ▷ stump

STUMPS ▷ stump

STUMPY adj short and thick ▷ n stumpy thing

STUMS ▷ stum

STUN vb shock or overwhelm ▷ n state or effect of being stunned

STUNG ▷ sting

STUNK ▷ stink

STUNNED ▷ stun

STUNNER n beautiful person or thing

STUNS ▷ stun

STUNT vb prevent or impede the growth of ▷ n acrobatic or dangerous action

STUNTED ▷ stunt

STUNTS ▷ stunt

STUPA n domed edifice housing Buddhist or Jain relics

STUPAS ▷ stupa

STUPE n hot damp cloth applied to the body to relieve pain ▷ vb treat with a stupe

STUPED ▷ stupe

STUPEFY vb make insensitive or lethargic

STUPENT adj astonished

STUPES ▷ stupe

STUPID adj lacking intelligence ▷ n stupid person

STUPIDS ▷ stupid

STUPING ▷ stupe

STUPOR n dazed or unconscious state

STUPORS ▷ stupor

STURDY *adj* healthy and robust ▷ *n* disease of sheep

STURE *same as* ▶ **stoor**

STURMER *n* type of eating apple with pale green skin

STURNUS *n* bird of starling family

STURT *vb* bother

STURTED ▶ **sturt**

STURTS ▶ **sturt**

STUSHIE *n* commotion, rumpus, or row

STUTTER *vb* speak with repetition of initial consonants ▷ *n* tendency to stutter

STY *vb* climb

STYE *n* inflammation at the base of an eyelash

STYED ▶ **stye**

STYES ▶ **stye**

STYGIAN *adj* dark, gloomy, or hellish

STYING ▶ **sty**

STYLAR ▶ **stylus**

STYLATE *adj* having style

STYLE *n* shape or design ▷ *vb* shape or design

STYLED ▶ **style**

STYLEE ▶ **style**

STYLEES ▶ **stylee**

STYLER ▶ **style**

STYLERS ▶ **style**

STYLES ▶ **style**

STYLET *n* wire for insertion into a flexible cannula or catheter to maintain its rigidity during passage

STYLETS ▶ **stylet**

STYLI ▶ **stylus**

STYLIE *adj* fashion-conscious

STYLIER ▶ **stylie**

STYLING ▶ **style**

STYLISE *same as* ▶ **stylize**

STYLISH *adj* smart, elegant, and fashionable

STYLIST *n* hairdresser

STYLITE *n* one of a class of recluses who in ancient times lived on the top of high pillars

STYLIZE *vb* cause to conform to an established stylistic form

STYLO *n* type of fountain pen

STYLOID *adj* resembling a stylus ▷ *n* spiny growth

STYLOPS *n* type of insect that lives as a parasite in other insects

STYLOS ▶ **stylo**

STYLUS *n* needle-like device on a record player that rests in the groove of the record and picks up the sound signals

STYME *vb* peer

STYMED ▶ **styme**

STYMES ▶ **styme**

STYMIE *vb* hinder or thwart

STYMIED ▶ **stymy**

STYMIES ▶ **stymy**

STYMING ▶ **styme**

STYMY *same as* ▶ **stymie**

STYPSIS *n* action, application, or use of a styptic

STYPTIC *adj* (drug) used to stop bleeding ▷ *n* styptic drug

STYRAX *n* type of tropical or subtropical tree

STYRE *same as* ▶ **stir**

STYRED ▶ **styre**

STYRENE *n* colourless oily volatile flammable water-insoluble liquid

STYRES ▶ **styre**

STYRING ▶ **styre**

STYTE *vb* bounce

STYTED ▶ **styte**

STYTES ▶ **styte**

STYTING ▶ **styte**

SUABLE *adj* liable to be sued in a court

SUABLY ▶ **suable**

SUASION *n* persuasion

SUASIVE ▶ **suasion**

SUASORY ▶ **suasion**

SUAVE *adj* smooth and sophisticated in manner

SUAVELY ▶ **suave**

SUAVER ▶ **suave**

SUAVEST ▶ **suave**

SUAVITY ▶ **suave**

SUB *n* subeditor ▷ *vb* act as a substitute

SUBA *n* shepherd's cloak

SUBACID *adj* (esp of some fruits) moderately acid or sour

SUBACT *vb* subdue

SUBACTS ▶ **subact**

SUBADAR *n* (formerly) the chief native officer of a company of Indian soldiers in the British service

SUBAH *same as* ▶ **subadar**

SUBAHS ▶ **subah**

SUBALAR *adj* below a wing

SUBAQUA *adj* of or relating to underwater sport

SUBAREA *n* area within a larger area

SUBARID *adj* receiving slightly more rainfall than arid regions

SUBAS ▶ **suba**

SUBATOM *n* part of an atom

SUBBASE *same as* ▶ **subbass**

SUBBASS *another name for* ▶ **bourdon**

SUBBED ▶ **sub**

SUBBIE *n* subcontractor

SUBBIES ▶ **subbie**

SUBBING ▶ **sub**

SUBBY *same as* ▶ **subbie**

SUBCELL *n* cell within a larger cell

SUBCLAN *n* clan within a larger clan

SUBCODE *n* computer tag identifying data

SUBCOOL *vb* make colder

SUBCULT *n* cult within larger cult

SUBDEAN *n* deputy of dean

SUBDEB *n* young woman who is not yet a debutante

SUBDEBS ▶ **subdeb**

SUBDEW *same as* ▶ **subdue**

SUBDEWS ▶ **subdew**

SUBDUAL ▶ **subdue**

SUBDUCE *vb* withdraw

SUBDUCT *vb* draw or turn (the eye, etc) downwards

SUBDUE *vb* overcome

SUBDUED *adj* cowed, passive, or shy

SUBDUER ▶ **subdue**

SUBDUES ▶ **subdue**

SUBECHO *n* echo resonating more quietly than another echo

SUBEDAR *same as* ▶ **subadar**

SUBEDIT *vb* edit and correct (written or printed material)

SUBER *n* cork

SUBERIC *same as* > **suberose**

SUBERIN *n* fatty or waxy substance that is present in the walls of cork cells

SUBERS ▶ **suber**

SUBFEU *vb* grant feu to vassal

SUBFEUS ▶ **subfeu**

SUBFILE *n* file within another file

SUBFIX *n* suffix

SUBFUSC *adj* devoid of brightness or appeal ▷ *n* (at Oxford University) formal academic dress

SUBFUSK same as
▶ **subfusc**
SUBGOAL n secondary goal
SUBGUM n Chinese dish
SUBGUMS ▶ **subgum**
SUBHA n string of beads
used in praying and
meditating
SUBHAS ▶ **subha**
SUBHEAD n heading of a
subsection in a printed
work
SUBIDEA n secondary idea
SUBITEM n item that is less
important than another
item
SUBITO adv (preceding or
following a dynamic
marking, etc) suddenly
SUBJECT n person or thing
being dealt with or studied
▷ adj being under the rule of
a monarch or government
▷ vb cause to undergo
SUBJOIN vb add or attach at
the end of something
spoken, written, etc
SUBLATE vb deny
SUBLET vb rent out
(property rented from
someone else) ▷ n sublease
SUBLETS ▶ **sublet**
SUBLIME adj of high moral,
intellectual, or spiritual
value ▷ vb change from a
solid to a vapour without
first melting
SUBLINE n secondary
headline
SUBLOT n subdivision of a
lot
SUBLOTS ▶ **sublot**
SUBMAN n primitive form
of human
SUBMEN ▶ **subman**
SUBMENU n further list of
options within computer
menu
SUBMISS adj docile
SUBMIT vb surrender
SUBMITS ▶ **submit**
SUBNET n part of network
SUBNETS ▶ **subnet**
SUBORAL adj not quite oral
SUBORN vb bribe or incite
(a person) to commit a
wrongful act
SUBORNS ▶ **suborn**
SUBOVAL adj not quite oval
SUBPAR adj not up to
standard
SUBPART n part within
another part

SUBPENA same as
> **subpoena**
SUBPLOT n secondary plot
in a novel, play, or film
SUBRACE n race of people
considered to be inferior
SUBRENT n rent paid to
renter who rents to another
SUBRING n mathematical
ring that is a subset of
another ring
SUBRULE n rule within
another rule
SUBS ▶ **sub**
SUBSALE n sale carried out
within the process of a
larger sale
SUBSEA adj undersea
SUBSECT n sect within a
larger sect
SUBSERE n secondary sere
arising when the progress
of a sere towards its climax
has been interrupted
SUBSET n mathematical set
contained within a larger
set
SUBSETS ▶ **subset**
SUBSIDE vb become less
intense
SUBSIDY n financial aid
SUBSIST vb manage to live
SUBSITE n location within a
website
SUBSOIL n earth just below
the surface soil ▷ vb plough
(land) to a depth below the
normal ploughing level
SUBSONG n subdued form
of birdsong modified from
the full territorial song
SUBSUME vb include (an
idea, case, etc) under a
larger classification or
group
SUBTACK Scots word for
> **sublease**
SUBTASK n task that is part
of a larger task
SUBTAXA > **subtaxon**
SUBTEEN n young person
who has not yet become a
teenager
SUBTEND vb be opposite
(an angle or side)
SUBTEST n test that is part
of larger test
SUBTEXT n underlying
theme in a piece of writing
SUBTIL same as ▶ **subtle**
SUBTILE rare spelling of
▶ **subtle**
SUBTLE adj not

immediately obvious
SUBTLER ▶ **subtle**
SUBTLY ▶ **subtle**
SUBTONE n subdivision of a
tone
SUBTYPE n secondary or
subordinate type or genre
SUBUNIT n distinct part or
component of something
larger
SUBURB n residential area
on the outskirts of a city
SUBURBS ▶ **suburb**
SUBVENE vb happen in such
a way as to be of assistance,
esp in preventing
something
SUBVERT vb overthrow the
authority of
SUBWAY n passage under a
road or railway ▷ vb travel
by subway
SUBWAYS ▶ **subway**
SUBZERO adj lower than
zero
SUBZONE n subdivision of a
zone
SUCCADE n piece of
candied fruit
SUCCAH same as ▶ **sukkah**
SUCCAHS ▶ **succah**
SUCCEED vb accomplish an
aim
SUCCES French word for
▶ **success**
SUCCESS n achievement of
something attempted
SUCCI ▶ **succus**
SUCCISE adj ending
abruptly, as if cut off
SUCCOR same as ▶ **succour**
SUCCORS ▶ **succor**
SUCCORY another name for
▶ **chicory**
SUCCOS same as ▶ **succoth**
SUCCOSE ▶ **succus**
SUCCOT same as ▶ **sukkoth**
SUCCOTH same as ▶ **sukkoth**
SUCCOUR n help in distress
▷ vb give aid to (someone in
time of difficulty)
SUCCOUS ▶ **succus**
SUCCUBA same as
> **succubus**
SUCCUBI > **succubus**
SUCCUMB vb give way (to
something overpowering)
SUCCUS n fluid
SUCCUSS vb shake (a
patient) to detect the
sound of fluid in the
thoracic or another bodily
cavity

SUCH *adj* of the kind specified ▷ *pron* such things

SUCK *vb* draw (liquid or air) into the mouth ▷ *n* sucking

SUCKED ▶ **suck**

SUCKEN *Scots word for* > **district**

SUCKENS ▶ **sucken**

SUCKER *n* person who is easily deceived or swindled ▷ *vb* strip off the suckers from (a plant)

SUCKERS ▶ **sucker**

SUCKET *same as* ▶ **succade**

SUCKETS ▶ **sucket**

SUCKIER ▶ **sucky**

SUCKING *adj* not yet weaned

SUCKLE *vb* feed at the breast

SUCKLED ▶ **suckle**

SUCKLER ▶ **suckle**

SUCKLES ▶ **suckle**

SUCKS *interj* expression of disappointment

SUCKY *adj* despicable

SUCRASE *another name for* > **invertase**

SUCRE *n* former standard monetary unit of Ecuador

SUCRES ▶ **sucre**

SUCRIER *n* small container for sugar at table

SUCROSE *same as* ▶ **sugar**

SUCTION *n* sucking ▷ *vb* subject to suction

SUD *singular of* ▶ **suds**

SUDAMEN *n* small cavity in the skin

SUDARIA > **sudarium**

SUDARY *same as* > **sudarium**

SUDATE *vb* sweat

SUDATED ▶ **sudate**

SUDATES ▶ **sudate**

SUDD *n* floating masses of reeds and weeds that occur on the White Nile

SUDDEN *adj* done or occurring quickly and unexpectedly

SUDDENS ▶ **sudden**

SUDDER *n* supreme court in India

SUDDERS ▶ **sudder**

SUDDS ▶ **sudd**

SUDOR *technical name for* ▶ **sweat**

SUDORAL ▶ **sudor**

SUDORS ▶ **sudor**

SUDS *pl n* froth of soap and water, lather ▷ *vb* wash in suds

SUDSED ▶ **suds**

SUDSER *n* soap opera

SUDSERS ▶ **sudser**

SUDSES ▶ **suds**

SUDSIER ▶ **suds**

SUDSING ▶ **suds**

SUDSY ▶ **suds**

SUE *vb* start legal proceedings against

SUEABLE ▶ **sue**

SUED ▶ **sue**

SUEDE *n* leather with a velvety finish on one side ▷ *vb* give a suede finish to

SUEDED ▶ **suede**

SUEDES ▶ **suede**

SUEDING ▶ **suede**

SUENT *adj* smooth

SUER ▶ **sue**

SUERS ▶ **sue**

SUES ▶ **sue**

SUET *n* hard fat obtained from sheep and cattle, used in cooking

SUETIER ▶ **suet**

SUETS ▶ **suet**

SUETTY ▶ **suet**

SUETY ▶ **suet**

SUFFARI *same as* ▶ **safari**

SUFFECT *adj* additional

SUFFER *vb* undergo or be subjected to

SUFFERS ▶ **suffer**

SUFFETE *n* official in ancient Carthage

SUFFICE *vb* be enough for a purpose

SUFFIX *n* letter or letters added to the end of a word to form another word ▷ *vb* add (a letter or letters) to the end of a word to form another word

SUFFUSE *vb* spread through or over (something)

SUG *vb* sell a product while pretending to conduct market research

SUGAN *n* straw rope

SUGANS ▶ **sugan**

SUGAR *n* sweet crystalline carbohydrate used to sweeten food and drinks ▷ *vb* sweeten or cover with sugar

SUGARED *adj* made sweeter or more appealing with or as with sugar

SUGARER ▶ **sugar**

SUGARS ▶ **sugar**

SUGARY *adj* of, like, or containing sugar

SUGGED ▶ **sug**

SUGGEST *vb* put forward (an idea) for consideration

SUGGING *n* practice of selling products under the pretence of conducting market research

SUGH *same as* ▶ **sough**

SUGHED ▶ **sugh**

SUGHING ▶ **sugh**

SUGHS ▶ **sugh**

SUGO *n* Italian pasta sauce

SUGOS ▶ **sugo**

SUGS ▶ **sug**

SUHUR *n* meal eaten before sunrise by Muslims fasting during Ramadan

SUHURS ▶ **suhur**

SUI *adj* of itself

SUICIDE *n* killing oneself intentionally ▷ *vb* commit suicide

SUID *n* pig or related animal

SUIDIAN ▶ **suid**

SUIDS ▶ **suid**

SUING ▶ **sue**

SUINGS ▶ **sue**

SUINT *n* water-soluble substance found in the fleece of sheep

SUINTS ▶ **suint**

SUIPLAP *n* South African slang for a drunkard

SUIT *n* set of clothes designed to be worn together ▷ *vb* be appropriate for

SUITE *n* set of connected rooms in a hotel

SUITED ▶ **suit**

SUITER *n* piece of luggage for carrying suits and dresses

SUITERS ▶ **suiter**

SUITES ▶ **suite**

SUITING *n* fabric used for suits

SUITOR *n* man who is courting a woman ▷ *vb* act as a suitor

SUITORS ▶ **suitor**

SUITS ▶ **suit**

SUIVEZ *vb* musical direction meaning follow

SUJEE *same as* ▶ **soogee**

SUJEES ▶ **sujee**

SUK *same as* ▶ **souk**

SUKH *same as* ▶ **souk**

SUKHS ▶ **sukh**

SUKKAH *n* temporary structure with a roof of branches in which orthodox Jews eat and, if possible, sleep during the

S

festival of Sukkoth

SUKKAHS ▸ sukkah

SUKKOS same as ▸ sukkoth

SUKKOT same as ▸ sukkoth

SUKKOTH n eight-day Jewish harvest festival

SUKS ▸ suk

SUKUK n financial certificate conforming to Islam lending principles

SUKUKS ▸ sukuk

SULCAL ▸ sulcus

SULCATE adj marked with longitudinal parallel grooves

SULCI ▸ sulcus

SULCUS n linear groove, furrow, or slight depression

SULDAN same as ▸ sultan

SULDANS ▸ suldan

SULFA same as ▸ sulpha

SULFAS ▸ sulfa

SULFATE same as ▸ sulphate

SULFID same as ▸ sulphide

SULFIDE same as ▸ sulphide

SULFIDS ▸ sulfid

SULFITE same as ▸ sulphite

SULFO same as ▸ sulphonic

SULFONE same as ▸ sulphone

SULFUR same as ▸ sulphur

SULFURS ▸ sulfur

SULFURY ▸ sulfur

SULK vb be silent and sullen because of resentment or bad temper ▷ n resentful or sullen mood

SULKED ▸ sulk

SULKER same as ▸ sulk

SULKERS ▸ sulker

SULKIER ▸ sulky

SULKIES ▸ sulky

SULKILY ▸ sulky

SULKING ▸ sulk

SULKS ▸ sulk

SULKY adj moody or silent because of anger or resentment ▷ n light two-wheeled vehicle for one person, usually drawn by one horse

SULLAGE n filth or waste, esp sewage

SULLEN adj unwilling to talk or be sociable ▷ n sullen mood

SULLENS ▸ sullen

SULLIED ▸ sully

SULLIES ▸ sully

SULLY vb ruin (someone's reputation) ▷ n stain

SULPH n amphetamine sulphate

SULPHA n any of a group of sulphonamides that prevent the growth of bacteria

SULPHAS ▸ sulpha

SULPHID same as ▸ sulphide

SULPHS ▸ sulph

SULPHUR n pale yellow nonmetallic element ▷ vb treat with sulphur

SULTAN n sovereign of a Muslim country

SULTANA n kind of raisin

SULTANS ▸ sultan

SULTRY adj (of weather or climate) hot and humid

SULU n type of sarong worn in Fiji

SULUS ▸ sulu

SUM n result of addition, total ▷ vb add or form a total of (something)

SUMAC same as ▸ sumach

SUMACH n type of temperate or subtropical shrub or small tree

SUMACHS ▸ sumach

SUMACS ▸ sumac

SUMATRA n violent storm blowing from the direction of Sumatra

SUMLESS adj uncountable

SUMMA n compendium of theology, philosophy, or canon law, or sometimes of all three together

SUMMAE ▸ summa

SUMMAND n number or quantity forming part of a sum

SUMMAR Scots variant of ▸ summer

SUMMARY n brief account giving the main points of something ▷ adj done quickly, without formalities

SUMMAS ▸ summa

SUMMAT pron something ▷ n impressive or important person or thing

SUMMATE vb add up

SUMMATS ▸ summat

SUMMED ▸ sum

SUMMER n warmest season of the year, between spring and autumn ▷ vb spend the summer (at a place)

SUMMERS ▸ summer

SUMMERY ▸ summer

SUMMING ▸ sum

SUMMIST n writer of summae

SUMMIT n top of a mountain or hill ▷ vb reach summit

SUMMITS ▸ summit

SUMMON vb order (someone) to come

SUMMONS n command summoning someone ▷ vb order (someone) to appear in court

SUMO n Japanese style of wrestling

SUMOIST ▸ sumo

SUMOS ▸ sumo

SUMP n container in an internal-combustion engine into which oil can drain

SUMPH n stupid person

SUMPHS ▸ sumph

SUMPIT n Malay blowpipe

SUMPITS ▸ sumpit

SUMPS ▸ sump

SUMPTER n packhorse, mule, or other beast of burden

SUMS ▸ sum

SUMY pl n the monetary units of Uzbekistan

SUN n star around which the earth and other planets revolve ▷ vb expose (oneself) to the sun's rays

SUNBACK adj (of dress) cut low at back

SUNBAKE vb sunbathe, esp in order to become tanned ▷ n period of sunbaking

SUNBATH n exposure of the body to the sun to get a suntan

SUNBEAM n ray of sun

SUNBEAT adj exposed to sun

SUNBED n machine for giving an artificial tan

SUNBEDS ▸ sunbed

SUNBELT n southern states of the US

SUNBIRD n type of small songbird with a bright plumage in the males

SUNBOW n bow of prismatic colours similar to a rainbow, produced when sunlight shines through spray

SUNBOWS ▸ sunbow

SUNBURN n painful reddening of the skin caused by overexposure to the sun ▷ vb become sunburnt

SUNDAE n ice cream topped with fruit etc
SUNDAES ▸ **sundae**
SUNDARI n Indian tree
SUNDECK n upper open deck on a passenger ship
SUNDER vb break apart
SUNDERS ▸ **sunder**
SUNDEW n type of bog plant with leaves covered in sticky hairs that trap and digest insects
SUNDEWS ▸ **sundew**
SUNDIAL n device showing the time by means of a pointer that casts a shadow on a marked dial
SUNDOG n small rainbow or halo near the horizon
SUNDOGS ▸ **sundog**
SUNDOWN same as ▸ **sunset**
SUNDRA same as ▸ **sundari**
SUNDRAS ▸ **sundra**
SUNDRI same as ▸ **sundari**
SUNDRIS ▸ **sundri**
SUNDRY adj several, various
SUNFAST adj not fading in sunlight
SUNFISH n large sea fish with a rounded body
SUNG ▸ **sing**
SUNGAR same as ▸ **sangar**
SUNGARS ▸ **sungar**
SUNGLOW n pinkish glow often seen in the sky before sunrise or after sunset
SUNHAT n hat that shades the face and neck from the sun
SUNHATS ▸ **sunhat**
SUNI n S African dwarf antelope
SUNIS ▸ **suni**
SUNK n bank or pad
SUNKEN adj unhealthily hollow
SUNKET n something good to eat
SUNKETS ▸ **sunket**
SUNKIE n little stool
SUNKIES ▸ **sunkie**
SUNKS ▸ **sunk**
SUNLAMP n lamp that generates ultraviolet rays
SUNLAND n sunny area
SUNLESS adj without sun or sunshine
SUNLIKE ▸ **sun**
SUNLIT ▸ **sunlight**
SUNN n leguminous plant of the East Indies, having

yellow flowers
SUNNA n body of traditional Islamic law
SUNNAH same as ▸ **sunna**
SUNNAHS ▸ **sunnah**
SUNNAS ▸ **sunna**
SUNNED ▸ **sun**
SUNNIER ▸ **sunny**
SUNNIES pl n pair of sunglasses
SUNNILY ▸ **sunny**
SUNNING ▸ **sun**
SUNNS ▸ **sunn**
SUNNY adj full of or exposed to sunlight
SUNRAY n ray of light from the sun
SUNRAYS ▸ **sunray**
SUNRISE n daily appearance of the sun above the horizon
SUNROOF n panel in the roof of a car that opens to let in air
SUNROOM n room or glass-enclosed porch designed to display beautiful views
SUNS ▸ **sun**
SUNSET n daily disappearance of the sun below the horizon
SUNSETS ▸ **sunset**
SUNSPOT n dark patch appearing temporarily on the sun's surface
SUNSTAR n type of starfish with up to 13 arms radiating from a central disc
SUNSUIT n child's outfit consisting of a brief top and shorts or a short skirt
SUNTAN n browning of the skin caused by exposure to the sun
SUNTANS ▸ **suntan**
SUNTRAP n very sunny sheltered place
SUNUP same as ▸ **sunrise**
SUNUPS ▸ **sunup**
SUNWARD same as ▸ **sunwards**
SUNWISE adv moving in the same direction as the sun
SUP same as ▸ **supine**
SUPAWN same as ▸ **suppawn**
SUPAWNS ▸ **supawn**
SUPE n superintendent
SUPER adj excellent ▷ n superannuation ▷ interj enthusiastic expression of approval or assent ▷ vb

work as superintendent
SUPERB adj excellent, impressive, or splendid
SUPERED ▸ **super**
SUPERS ▸ **super**
SUPES ▸ **supe**
SUPINE adj lying flat on one's back ▷ n noun form derived from a verb in Latin
SUPINES ▸ **supine**
SUPLEX n wrestling hold in which a wrestler grasps his opponent round the waist from behind and carries him backwards
SUPPAWN n kind of porridge
SUPPED ▸ **sup**
SUPPER n light evening meal ▷ vb eat supper
SUPPERS ▸ **supper**
SUPPING ▸ **sup**
SUPPLE adj (of a person) moving and bending easily and gracefully ▷ vb make or become supple
SUPPLED ▸ **supple**
SUPPLER ▸ **supple**
SUPPLES ▸ **supple**
SUPPLY vb provide with something required ▷ n supplying ▷ adj acting as a temporary substitute ▷ adv in a supple manner
SUPPORT vb bear the weight of ▷ n supporting
SUPPOSE vb presume to be true
SUPRA adv above, esp referring to earlier parts of a book etc
SUPREMA > **supremum**
SUPREME adj highest in authority, rank, or degree ▷ n rich velouté sauce made with a base of veal or chicken stock, with cream or egg yolks added
SUPREMO n person in overall authority
SUPS ▸ **sup**
SUQ same as ▸ **souk**
│ This unusual word for an Arab market-place is easy to overlook because we tend not to think of words ending in Q. It can also be spelt **sook, souk, suk** or **sukh**.
SUQS ▸ **suq**
SUR prep above
SURA n any of the 114 chapters of the Koran

S

SURAH n twill-weave fabric of silk or rayon, used for dresses, blouses, etc

SURAHS ▶ surah

SURAL adj of or relating to the calf of the leg

SURAMIN n drug used in treating sleeping sickness

SURANCE same as > assurance

SURAS ▶ sura

SURAT n (formerly) a cotton fabric from the Surat area of India

SURATS ▶ surat

SURBASE n uppermost part, such as a moulding, of a pedestal, base, or skirting

SURBATE vb make feet sore through walking

SURBED vb put something on its edge

SURBEDS ▶ surbed

SURBET ▶ surbate

SURCOAT n tunic worn by a knight over his armour during the Middle Ages

SURCULI > surculus

SURD n number that cannot be expressed in whole numbers ▷ adj of or relating to a surd

SURDITY n deafness

SURDS ▶ surd

SURE adj free from uncertainty or doubt ▷ interj certainly ▷ vb archaic form of sewer

SURED ▶ sure

SURELY adv it must be true that

SURER ▶ sure

SURES ▶ sure

SUREST ▶ sure

SURETY n person who takes responsibility for the fulfilment of another's obligation ▷ vb be surety for

SURF n foam caused by waves breaking on the shore ▷ vb take part in surfing

SURFACE n outside or top of an object ▷ vb become apparent

SURFED ▶ surf

SURFEIT n excessive amount ▷ vb supply or feed excessively

SURFER ▶ surfing

SURFERS ▶ surfing

SURFIE n young person

whose main interest is in surfing

SURFIER ▶ surf

SURFIES ▶ surfie

SURFING n sport of riding towards the shore on a surfboard on the crest of a wave

SURFMAN n sailor skilled in sailing through surf

SURFMEN ▶ surfman

SURFS ▶ surf

SURFY ▶ surf

SURGE n sudden powerful increase ▷ vb increase suddenly

SURGED ▶ surge

SURGENT ▶ surge

SURGEON n doctor who specializes in surgery

SURGER ▶ surge

SURGERS ▶ surge

SURGERY n treatment in which the patient's body is cut open in order to treat the affected part

SURGES ▶ surge

SURGIER ▶ surge

SURGING ▶ surge

SURGY ▶ surge

SURIMI n blended seafood product made from precooked fish, restructured into stick shapes

SURIMIS ▶ surimi

SURING ▶ sure

SURLIER ▶ surly

SURLILY ▶ surly

SURLOIN same as ▶ sirloin

SURLY adj ill-tempered and rude

SURMISE n guess, conjecture ▷ vb guess (something) from incomplete or uncertain evidence

SURNAME n family name ▷ vb furnish with or call by a surname

SURPASS vb be greater than or superior to

SURPLUS n amount left over in excess of what is required ▷ adj extra ▷ vb be left over in excess of what is required

SURRA n tropical febrile disease of animals

SURRAS ▶ surra

SURREAL adj bizarre ▷ n atmosphere or qualities evoked by surrealism

SURREY n light four-wheeled horse-drawn carriage having two or four seats

SURREYS ▶ surrey

SURTAX n extra tax on incomes above a certain level ▷ vb assess for liability to surtax

SURTOUT n man's overcoat resembling a frock coat, popular in the late 19th century

SURVEIL same as > surveille

SURVEY vb view or consider in a general way ▷ n surveying

SURVEYS ▶ survey

SURVIEW vb survey

SURVIVE vb continue to live or exist after (a difficult experience)

SUS same as ▶ suss

SUSES ▶ sus

SUSHI n Japanese dish of small cakes of cold rice with a topping of raw fish

SUSHIS ▶ sushi

SUSLIK n central Eurasian ground squirrel

SUSLIKS ▶ suslik

SUSPECT vb believe (someone) to be guilty without having any proof ▷ adj not to be trusted ▷ n person who is suspected

SUSPEND vb hang from a high place

SUSPENS same as > suspense

SUSPIRE vb sigh or utter with a sigh

SUSS vb attempt to work out (a situation, etc), using one's intuition ▷ n sharpness of mind

SUSSED ▶ suss

SUSSES ▶ suss

SUSSING ▶ suss

SUSTAIN vb maintain or prolong ▷ n prolongation of a note, by playing technique or electronics

SUSU n (in the Caribbean) savings fund shared by friends

SUSUS ▶ susu

SUTILE adj involving sewing

SUTLER n (formerly) a merchant who accompanied an army in order to sell provisions to the soldiers

SUTLERS ▶ sutler
SUTLERY ▶ sutler
SUTOR n cobbler
SUTORS ▶ sutor
SUTRA n Sanskrit sayings or collections of sayings
SUTRAS ▶ sutra
SUTTA n Buddhist scripture
SUTTAS ▶ sutta
SUTTEE n former Hindu custom whereby a widow burnt herself to death on her husband's funeral pyre
SUTTEES ▶ suttee
SUTTLE vb work as sutler
SUTTLED ▶ suttle
SUTTLES ▶ suttle
SUTTLY ▶ subtle
SUTURAL ▶ suture
SUTURE n stitch joining the edges of a wound ▷ vb join (the edges of a wound, etc) by means of sutures
SUTURED ▶ suture
SUTURES ▶ suture
SVARAJ same as ▶ swaraj
SVELTE adj attractively or gracefully slim
SVELTER ▶ svelte
SWAB n small piece of cotton wool used to apply medication, clean a wound, etc ▷ vb clean (a wound) with a swab
SWABBED ▶ swab
SWABBER n person who uses a swab
SWABBIE same as ▶ swabby
SWABBY n seaman
SWABS ▶ swab
SWACK adj flexible
SWACKED adj in a state of intoxication, stupor, or euphoria induced by drugs or alcohol
SWAD n loutish person
SWADDIE same as ▶ swaddy
SWADDLE vb wrap (a baby) in swaddling clothes ▷ n swaddling clothes
SWADDY n private soldier
SWADS ▶ swaddle
SWAG n stolen property ▷ vb sway from side to side
SWAGE n shaped tool or die used in forming cold metal by hammering ▷ vb form (metal) with a swage
SWAGED ▶ swage
SWAGER ▶ swage
SWAGERS ▶ swage
SWAGES ▶ swage

SWAGGED ▶ swag
SWAGGER vb walk or behave arrogantly ▷ n arrogant walk or manner ▷ adj elegantly fashionable
SWAGGIE same as ▶ swagger
SWAGING ▶ swage
SWAGMAN n tramp who carries his belongings in a bundle on his back
SWAGMEN ▶ swagman
SWAGS ▶ swag
SWAIL same as ▶ swale
SWAILS ▶ swail
SWAIN n suitor
SWAINS ▶ swain
SWALE n moist depression in a tract of land, usually with rank vegetation ▷ vb sway
SWALED ▶ swale
SWALES ▶ swale
SWALIER ▶ swale
SWALING ▶ swale
SWALLET n hole where water goes underground
SWALLOW vb cause to pass down one's throat ▷ n swallowing
SWALY ▶ swale
SWAM ▶ swim
SWAMI n Hindu religious teacher
SWAMIES ▶ swami
SWAMIS ▶ swami
SWAMP n watery area of land, bog ▷ vb cause (a boat) to fill with water and sink
SWAMPED ▶ swamp
SWAMPER n person who lives or works in a swampy region, esp in the southern US
SWAMPS ▶ swamp
SWAMPY ▶ swamp
SWAMY same as ▶ swami
SWAN n large usu white water bird with a long graceful neck ▷ vb wander about idly
SWANG ▶ swing
SWANK vb show off or boast ▷ n showing off or boasting
SWANKED ▶ swank
SWANKER ▶ swank
SWANKEY same as ▶ swanky
SWANKIE same as ▶ swanky
SWANKS ▶ swank

SWANKY adj expensive and showy, stylish ▷ n lively person
SWANNED ▶ swan
SWANNIE n (in NZ) type of all-weather heavy woollen shirt
SWANNY adj swanlike
SWANPAN n Chinese abacus
SWANS ▶ swan
SWAP vb exchange (something) for something else ▷ n exchange
SWAPPED ▶ swap
SWAPPER ▶ swap
SWAPS ▶ swap
SWAPT ▶ swap
SWARAJ n (in British India) self-government
SWARD n stretch of short grass ▷ vb cover or become covered with grass
SWARDED ▶ sward
SWARDS ▶ sward
SWARDY adj covered with sward
SWARE ▶ swear
SWARF n material removed by cutting tools in the machining of metals, stone, etc ▷ vb faint
SWARFED ▶ swarf
SWARFS ▶ swarf
SWARM n large group of bees or other insects ▷ vb move in a swarm
SWARMED ▶ swarm
SWARMER ▶ swarm
SWARMS ▶ swarm
SWART adj swarthy
SWARTH same as ▶ swart
SWARTHS ▶ swarth
SWARTHY adj dark-complexioned
SWARTY ▶ swart
SWARVE same as ▶ swarf
SWARVED ▶ swarf
SWARVES ▶ swarf
SWASH n rush of water up a beach following each break of the waves ▷ vb (esp of water or things in water) to wash or move with noisy splashing
SWASHED ▶ swash
SWASHER n braggart
SWASHES ▶ swash
SWASHY adj slushy
SWAT vb strike or hit sharply ▷ n swatter
SWATCH n sample of cloth
SWATH n width of one

S

sweep of a scythe or of the blade of a mowing machine

SWATHE vb bandage or wrap completely ▷ n bandage or wrapping

SWATHED ▶ swathe

SWATHER ▶ swathe

SWATHES ▶ swathe

SWATHS ▶ swath

SWATHY ▶ swath

SWATS ▶ swat

SWATTED ▶ swat

SWATTER n device for killing insects, esp a meshed flat attached to a handle ▷ vb splash

SWATTY ▶ swotty

SWAY vb swing to and fro or from side to side ▷ n power or influence

SWAYED ▶ sway

SWAYER ▶ sway

SWAYERS ▶ sway

SWAYFUL ▶ sway

SWAYING ▶ sway

SWAYL same as ▶ sweal

SWAYLED ▶ swayl

SWAYLS ▶ swayl

SWAYS ▶ sway

SWAZZLE n small metal instrument used to produce a shrill voice

SWEAL vb scorch

SWEALED ▶ sweal

SWEALS ▶ sweal

SWEAR vb use obscene or blasphemous language

SWEARD same as ▶ sword

SWEARDS ▶ sweard

SWEARER ▶ swear

SWEARS ▶ swear

SWEARY adj inclined to swear or characterized by swear-words

SWEAT n salty liquid given off through the pores of the skin ▷ vb have sweat coming through the pores

SWEATED adj made by exploited labour

SWEATER n (woollen) garment for the upper part of the body

SWEATS ▶ sweat

SWEATY adj covered with sweat

SWEDE n kind of turnip

SWEDES ▶ swede

SWEDGER n Scots dialect word for sweet

SWEE vb sway

SWEED ▶ swee

SWEEING ▶ swee

SWEEL same as ▶ sweal

SWEELED ▶ sweel

SWEELS ▶ sweel

SWEENEY n police flying squad

SWEENY n wasting of the shoulder muscles of a horse

SWEEP vb remove dirt from (a floor) with a broom ▷ n sweeping

SWEEPER n device used to sweep carpets, consisting of a long handle attached to a revolving brush

SWEEPS ▶ sweep

SWEEPY ▶ sweep

SWEER same as ▶ sweir

SWEERED ▶ sweer

SWEERS ▶ sweer

SWEERT ▶ sweer

SWEES ▶ swee

SWEET adj tasting of or like sugar ▷ n shaped piece of food consisting mainly of sugar ▷ vb sweeten

SWEETED ▶ sweet

SWEETEN vb make (food or drink) sweet or sweeter

SWEETER ▶ sweet

SWEETIE n lovable person

SWEETLY ▶ sweet

SWEETS ▶ sweet

SWEETY same as ▶ sweetie

SWEIR vb swear ▷ adj lazy

SWEIRED ▶ sweir

SWEIRER ▶ sweir

SWEIRS ▶ sweir

SWEIRT ▶ sweir

SWELL vb expand or increase ▷ n swelling or being swollen ▷ adj excellent or fine

SWELLED ▶ swell

SWELLER ▶ swell

SWELLS ▶ swell

SWELT vb die

SWELTED ▶ swelt

SWELTER vb feel uncomfortably hot ▷ n hot and uncomfortable condition

SWELTRY adj sultry

SWELTS ▶ swelt

SWEPT ▶ sweep

SWERF same as ▶ swarf

SWERFED ▶ swerf

SWERFS ▶ swerf

SWERVE vb turn aside from a course sharply or suddenly ▷ n swerving

SWERVED ▶ swerve

SWERVER ▶ swerve

SWERVES ▶ swerve

SWEVEN n vision or dream

SWEVENS ▶ sweven

SWEY same as ▶ swee

SWEYED ▶ swey

SWEYING ▶ swey

SWEYS ▶ swey

SWIDDEN n area of land where slash-and-burn techniques have been used to prepare it for cultivation

SWIES ▶ swy

SWIFT adj moving or able to move quickly ▷ n fast-flying bird with pointed wings ▷ adv swiftly or quickly ▷ vb make tight

SWIFTED ▶ swift

SWIFTER n line run around the ends of capstan bars to prevent their falling out of their sockets

SWIFTIE n trick, ruse, or deception

SWIFTLY ▶ swift

SWIFTS ▶ swift

SWIFTY same as ▶ swiftie

SWIG n large mouthful of drink ▷ vb drink in large mouthfuls

SWIGGED ▶ swig

SWIGGER ▶ swig

SWIGS ▶ swig

SWILER n (in Newfoundland) a seal hunter

SWILERS ▶ swiler

SWILL vb drink greedily ▷ n sloppy mixture containing waste food, fed to pigs

SWILLED ▶ swill

SWILLER ▶ swill

SWILLS ▶ swill

SWIM vb move along in water by movements of the limbs ▷ n act or period of swimming

SWIMMER ▶ swim

SWIMMY adj dizzy

SWIMS ▶ swim

SWINDGE same as ▶ swinge

SWINDLE vb cheat (someone) out of money ▷ n instance of swindling

SWINE n contemptible person

SWINERY n pig farm

SWINES ▶ swine

SWING vb move to and fro, sway ▷ n swinging

SWINGBY n act of spacecraft passing close to planet

SWINGE *vb* beat, flog, or punish

SWINGED ▸ **swinge**

SWINGER *n* person regarded as being modern and lively

SWINGES ▸ **swinge**

SWINGLE *n* flat-bladed wooden instrument used for beating and scraping flax ▷ *vb* use a swingle on

SWINGS ▸ **swing**

SWINGY *adj* lively and modern

SWINISH ▸ **swine**

SWINK *vb* toil or drudge ▷ *n* toil or drudgery

SWINKED ▸ **swink**

SWINKER ▸ **swink**

SWINKS ▸ **swink**

SWINNEY *same as* ▸ **sweeny**

SWIPE *vb* strike (at) with a sweeping blow ▷ *n* hard blow

SWIPED ▸ **swipe**

SWIPER ▸ **swipe**

SWIPERS ▸ **swipe**

SWIPES *pl n* beer, esp when poor or weak

SWIPEY *adj* drunk

SWIPIER ▸ **swipey**

SWIPING ▸ **swipe**

SWIPLE *same as* ▸ **swipple**

SWIPLES ▸ **swiple**

SWIPPLE *n* part of a flail that strikes the grain

SWIRE *n* neck

SWIRES ▸ **swire**

SWIRL *vb* turn with a whirling motion ▷ *n* whirling motion

SWIRLED ▸ **swirl**

SWIRLS ▸ **swirl**

SWIRLY ▸ **swirl**

SWISH *vb* move with a whistling or hissing sound ▷ *n* whistling or hissing sound ▷ *adj* fashionable, smart

SWISHED ▸ **swish**

SWISHER ▸ **swish**

SWISHES ▸ **swish**

SWISHY *adj* moving with a swishing sound

SWISS *n* type of muslin

SWISSES ▸ **swiss**

SWITCH *n* device for opening and closing an electric circuit ▷ *vb* change abruptly

SWITCHY ▸ **switch**

SWITH *adv* swiftly

SWITHE *same as* ▸ **swith**

SWITHER *vb* hesitate or be indecisive ▷ *n* state of hesitation or uncertainty

SWITHLY ▸ **swith**

SWITS *same as* ▸ **switch**

SWITSES ▸ **swits**

SWIVE *vb* have sexual intercourse with (a person)

SWIVED ▸ **swive**

SWIVEL *vb* turn on a central point ▷ *n* coupling device that allows an attached object to turn freely

SWIVELS ▸ **swivel**

SWIVES ▸ **swive**

SWIVET *n* nervous state

SWIVETS ▸ **swivet**

SWIVING ▸ **swive**

SWIZ *n* swindle or disappointment

SWIZZ *same as* ▸ **swiz**

SWIZZED ▸ **swizz**

SWIZZES ▸ **swizz**

SWIZZLE *n* unshaken cocktail ▷ *vb* stir a swizzle stick in (a drink)

SWOB *less common word for* ▸ **swab**

SWOBBED ▸ **swob**

SWOBBER ▸ **swob**

SWOBS ▸ **swob**

SWOFFER > **swoffing**

SWOLLEN ▸ **swell**

SWOLN ▸ **swell**

SWOON *n* faint ▷ *vb* faint because of shock or strong emotion

SWOONED ▸ **swoon**

SWOONER ▸ **swoon**

SWOONS ▸ **swoon**

SWOONY *adj* romantic or sexy

SWOOP *vb* sweep down or pounce on suddenly ▷ *n* swooping

SWOOPED ▸ **swoop**

SWOOPER ▸ **swoop**

SWOOPS ▸ **swoop**

SWOOPY ▸ **swoop**

SWOOSH *vb* make a swirling or rustling sound when moving or pouring out ▷ *n* swirling or rustling sound or movement

SWOP *same as* ▸ **swap**

SWOPPED ▸ **swop**

SWOPPER ▸ **swop**

SWOPS ▸ **swop**

SWOPT ▸ **swop**

SWORD *n* weapon with a long sharp blade ▷ *vb* bear a sword

SWORDED ▸ **sword**

SWORDER *n* fighter with sword

SWORDS ▸ **sword**

SWORE ▸ **swear**

SWORN ▸ **swear**

SWOT *vb* study (a subject) intensively ▷ *n* person who studies hard

SWOTS ▸ **swot**

SWOTTED ▸ **swot**

SWOTTER *same as* ▸ **swot**

SWOTTY *adj* given to studying hard, esp to the exclusion of other activities

SWOUN *same as* ▸ **swoon**

SWOUND *same as* ▸ **swoon**

SWOUNDS *less common spelling of* ▸ **zounds**

SWOUNE *same as* ▸ **swoon**

SWOUNED ▸ **swoune**

SWOUNES ▸ **swoune**

SWOUNS ▸ **swoun**

SWOWND *same as* ▸ **swoon**

SWOWNDS ▸ **swownd**

SWOWNE *same as* ▸ **swoon**

SWOWNES ▸ **swowne**

SWOZZLE *same as* ▸ **swazzle**

SWUM ▸ **swim**

SWUNG ▸ **swing**

SWY *n* Australian gambling game involving two coins

A type of card-game, that can be useful in helping you to clear a difficult rack.

SYBBE *same as* ▸ **sib**

SYBBES ▸ **sybbe**

SYBIL *same as* ▸ **sibyl**

SYBILS ▸ **sybil**

SYBO *n* spring onion

SYBOE *same as* ▸ **sybo**

SYBOES ▸ **syboe**

SYBOTIC *adj* of a swineherd

SYBOW *same as* ▸ **sybo**

SYBOWS ▸ **sybow**

SYCE *n* (formerly, in India) a servant employed to look after horses, etc

SYCEE *n* silver ingots formerly used as a medium of exchange in China

SYCEES ▸ **sycee**

SYCES ▸ **syce**

SYCONIA > **syconium**

SYCOSES ▸ **sycosis**

SYCOSIS *n* chronic inflammation of the hair follicles

SYE *vb* strain

SYED ▸ **sye**

SYEING ▸ **sye**

S

SYEN same as ▶ **scion**
SYENITE n light-coloured coarse-grained plutonic igneous rock
SYENS ▶ **syen**
SYES ▶ **sye**
SYKE same as ▶ **sike**
SYKER adv surely
SYKES ▶ **syke**
SYLI n Finnish unit of volume
SYLIS ▶ **syli**
SYLLABI > **syllabus**
SYLLOGE n collection or summary
SYLPH n slender graceful girl or woman
SYLPHIC ▶ **sylph**
SYLPHID n little sylph
SYLPHS ▶ **sylph**
SYLPHY ▶ **sylph**
SYLVA n trees growing in a particular region
SYLVAE ▶ **sylva**
SYLVAN adj relating to woods and trees ▷ n inhabitant of the woods, esp a spirit
SYLVANS ▶ **sylvan**
SYLVAS ▶ **sylva**
SYLVIA n songbird
SYLVIAS ▶ **sylvia**
SYLVIN same as ▶ **sylvite**
SYLVINE same as ▶ **sylvite**
SYLVINS ▶ **sylvin**
SYLVITE n soluble colourless, white, or coloured mineral
SYMAR same as ▶ **cymar**
SYMARS ▶ **symar**
SYMBION same as > **symbiont**
SYMBIOT same as > **symbiont**
SYMBOL n sign or thing that stands for something else ▷ vb be a symbol
SYMBOLE same as ▶ **cymbal**
SYMBOLS ▶ **symbol**
SYMITAR same as > **scimitar**
SYMPTOM n sign indicating the presence of an illness
SYN Scots word for ▶ **since**
SYNAGOG same as > **synagogue**
SYNANON n type of therapy given to drug addicts
SYNAPSE n gap where nerve impulses pass between two nerve cells ▷ vb create a synapse
SYNAPTE n litany in Greek Orthodox Church

SYNAXES ▶ **synaxis**
SYNAXIS n early Christian meeting
SYNC n synchronization ▷ vb synchronize
SYNCARP n fleshy multiple fruit
SYNCED ▶ **sync**
SYNCH same as ▶ **sync**
SYNCHED ▶ **synch**
SYNCHRO n type of electrical device
SYNCHS ▶ **synch**
SYNCING ▶ **sync**
SYNCOM n communications satellite in stationary orbit
SYNCOMS ▶ **syncom**
SYNCOPE n omission of one or more sounds or letters from the middle of a word
SYNCS ▶ **sync**
SYND same as ▶ **syne**
SYNDED ▶ **synd**
SYNDET n synthetic detergent
SYNDETS ▶ **syndet**
SYNDIC n business or legal agent of some universities or other institutions
SYNDICS ▶ **syndic**
SYNDING ▶ **synd**
SYNDS ▶ **synd**
SYNE vb rinse ▷ n rinse ▷ adv since
SYNED ▶ **syne**
SYNERGY n working together of two or more people, substances, or things to produce an effect greater than the sum of their individual effects
SYNES ▶ **syne**
SYNESES ▶ **synesis**
SYNESIS n grammatical construction in which the inflection or form of a word is conditioned by the meaning rather than the syntax
SYNFUEL n synthetic fuel
SYNGAMY n sexual reproduction
SYNGAS n mixture of carbon monoxide and hydrogen
SYNING ▶ **syne**
SYNOD n church council
SYNODAL adj of or relating to a synod ▷ n money paid to a bishop by less senior members of the clergy at a synod

SYNODIC adj relating to or involving a conjunction or two successive conjunctions of the same star, planet, or satellite
SYNODS ▶ **synod**
SYNONYM n word with the same meaning as another
SYNOVIA n clear thick fluid that lubricates the body joints
SYNROC n titanium-ceramic substance that can incorporate nuclear waste in its crystals
SYNROCS ▶ **synroc**
SYNTAGM same as > **syntagma**
SYNTAN n synthetic tanning substance
SYNTANS ▶ **syntan**
SYNTAX n way in which words are arranged to form phrases and sentences
SYNTENY n presence of two or more genes on the same chromosome
SYNTH n type of electrophonic musical instrument operated by a keyboard and pedals
SYNTHON n molecule used in synthesis
SYNTHS ▶ **synth**
SYNTONY n matching of frequencies
SYNURA n variety of microbe
SYNURAE ▶ **synura**
SYPE same as ▶ **sipe**
SYPED ▶ **sype**
SYPES ▶ **sype**
SYPH shortening of > **syphilis**
SYPHER vb lap (a chamfered edge of one plank over that of another) in order to form a flush surface
SYPHERS ▶ **sypher**
SYPHON same as ▶ **siphon**
SYPHONS ▶ **syphon**
SYPHS ▶ **syph**
SYPING ▶ **sype**
SYRAH n type of French red wine
SYRAHS ▶ **syrah**
SYREN same as ▶ **siren**
SYRENS ▶ **syren**
SYRETTE n small disposable syringe
SYRINGA n mock orange or lilac
SYRINGE n device for withdrawing or injecting

fluids, consisting of a hollow cylinder, a piston, and a hollow needle ▷ *vb* wash out or inject with a syringe

SYRINX *n* vocal organ of a bird, which is situated in the lower part of the trachea

SYRPHID *n* type of fly

SYRTES ▶ **syrtis**

SYRTIS *n* area of quicksand

SYRUP *n* solution of sugar in water ▷ *vb* bring to the consistency of syrup

SYRUPED ▶ **syrup**

SYRUPS ▶ **syrup**

SYRUPY *adj* thick and sweet

SYSOP *n* person who runs a system or network

SYSOPS ▶ **sysop**

SYSTEM *n* method or set of methods

SYSTEMS ▶ **system**

SYSTOLE *n* regular contraction of the heart as it pumps blood

SYSTYLE *n* building with different types of columns

SYTHE *same as* ▶ **sith**

SYTHES ▶ **sythe**

SYVER *n* street drain or the grating over it

SYVERS ▶ **syver**

SYZYGAL ▶ **syzygy**

SYZYGY *n* either of the two positions of a celestial body when sun, earth, and the body lie in a straight line

S

Tt

T is one of the most common consonants in Scrabble. There are only four two-letter words that begin with **T**, but they are easy to remember as there is one for every vowel except **U**. Like **S**, **T** begins a number of three-letter words that don't use vowels, which are well worth remembering. These are: **thy** (6 points), **try** (6), **tsk** (7), **twp** (8) and **tyg** (7). There are also some useful three-letter words using **X**: **tax**, **tex**, **tix** and **tux** (10 each). If you have an **X** during a game, remember words like **text** (11), **texts** (12), **textile** (14), **textual** (14) and **texture** (14). The last three of these have seven letters, and so will earn you 50-point bonuses if you use all your tiles to form them. Other threes well worth remembering are **taj** (10) and **tik** (7).

TA *interj* thank you ▷ *n* thank you

TAAL *n* language: usually, by implication, Afrikaans

TAALS ▶ **taal**

TAATA *child's word for* ▶ **father**
> This East African word for a father is one of those short words that can help you dispose of a surplus of As.

TAATAS ▶ **taata**

TAB *n* small flap or projecting label ▷ *vb* supply with a tab

TABANID *n* stout-bodied fly, the females of which have mouthparts specialized for sucking blood

TABARD *n* short sleeveless tunic decorated with a coat of arms, worn in medieval times

TABARDS ▶ **tabard**

TABARET *n* hard-wearing fabric of silk or similar cloth with stripes of satin or moire, used esp for upholstery

TABBED ▶ **tab**

TABBIED ▶ **tabby**

TABBIES ▶ **tabby**

TABBING ▶ **tab**

TABBIS *n* silken cloth

TABBY *vb* make (eg a material) appear wavy ▷ *n* female domestic cat

TABEFY *vb* emaciate or become emaciated

TABER *old variant of* ▶ **tabor**

TABERD *same as* ▶ **tabard**

TABERDS ▶ **taberd**

TABERED ▶ **taber**

TABERS ▶ **taber**

TABES *n* wasting of a bodily organ or part

TABETIC ▶ **tabes**

TABI *n* thick-soled Japanese sock, worn with sandals

TABID *adj* emaciated

TABINET *n* type of tabbied fabric

TABLA *n* one of a pair of Indian drums played with the hands

TABLAS ▶ **tabla**

TABLE *n* piece of furniture with a flat top supported by legs ▷ *vb* submit (a motion) for discussion by a meeting

TABLEAU *n* silent motionless group arranged to represent some scene

TABLED ▶ **table**

TABLES ▶ **table**

TABLET *n* medicinal pill ▷ *vb* make (something) into a tablet

TABLETS ▶ **tablet**

TABLIER *n* (formerly) part of a dress resembling an apron

TABLING ▶ **table**

TABLOID *n* small-sized newspaper with many photographs and a concise, usu sensational style

TABOO *n* prohibition resulting from religious or social conventions ▷ *adj* forbidden by a taboo ▷ *vb* place under a taboo

TABOOED ▶ **taboo**

TABOOS ▶ **taboo**

TABOR *vb* play the tabor

TABORED ▶ **tabor**

TABORER ▶ **tabor**

TABORET *n* low stool, originally in the shape of a drum

TABORIN *same as* ▶ **taboret**

TABORS ▶ **tabor**

TABOULI *same as* > **tabbouleh**

TABOUR *same as* ▶ **tabor**

TABOURS ▶ **tabour**

TABRERE *same as* ▶ **tabor**

TABRET *n* smaller version of a tabor

TABRETS ▶ **tabret**

TABS ▶ **tab**

TABU *same as* ▶ **taboo**

TABUED ▶ **tabu**

TABUING ▶ **tabu**

TABULA *n* tablet for writing on

TABULAE ▶ **tabula**

TABULAR *adj* arranged in a table

TABULI *same as* > **tabbouleh**

TABULIS ▶ **tabuli**

TABUN *n* organic compound used in chemical warfare as a lethal nerve gas

TABUNS ▶ **tabun**

TABUS ▶ **tabu**

TACAN *n* electronic ultrahigh-frequency navigation system for aircraft which gives a continuous indication of bearing and distance from a transmitting station

TACANS ▸ **tacan**

TACE same as ▸ **tasset**

TACES ▸ **tace**

TACET n direction on a musical score indicating that a particular instrument or singer does not take part in a movement or part of a movement

TACH n device for measuring speed

TACHE n buckle, clasp, or hook

TACHES ▸ **tache**

TACHINA n as in **tachina fly** bristly fly

TACHISM same as > **tachisme**

TACHIST ▸ **tachism**

TACHO same as > **tachogram**

TACHOS ▸ **tacho**

TACHS ▸ **tach**

TACHYON n hypothetical elementary particle capable of travelling faster than the velocity of light

TACIT adj implied but not spoken

TACITLY ▸ **tacit**

TACK n short nail with a large head ▷ vb fasten with tacks

TACKED ▸ **tack**

TACKER ▸ **tack**

TACKERS ▸ **tack**

TACKET n nail, esp a hobnail

TACKETS ▸ **tacket**

TACKETY ▸ **tacket**

TACKEY same as ▸ **tacky**

TACKIER ▸ **tacky**

TACKIES pl n tennis shoes or plimsolls

TACKIFY vb give (eg rubber) a sticky feel

TACKILY ▸ **tacky**

TACKING ▸ **tack**

TACKLE vb deal with (a task) ▷ n act of tackling an opposing player

TACKLED ▸ **tackle**

TACKLER ▸ **tackle**

TACKLES ▸ **tackle**

TACKS ▸ **tack**

TACKY adj slightly sticky

TACNODE n in maths, point at which two branches of a curve have a common

tangent, each branch extending in both directions of the tangent

TACO n tortilla fried until crisp, served with a filling

TACOS ▸ **taco**

TACRINE n drug used to treat Alzheimer's disease

TACT n skill in avoiding giving offence

TACTFUL ▸ **tact**

TACTIC n method or plan to achieve an end

TACTICS n art of directing military forces in battle

TACTILE adj of or having the sense of touch

TACTION n act of touching

TACTISM another word for ▸ **taxis**

TACTS ▸ **tact**

TACTUAL adj caused by touch

TAD n small bit or piece

TADDIE short for ▸ **tadpole**

TADDIES ▸ **taddie**

TADPOLE n limbless tailed larva of a frog or toad

TADS ▸ **tad**

TAE Scots form of the verb ▸ **toe**

TAED ▸ **tae**

TAEDIUM archaic spelling of ▸ **tedium**

TAEING ▸ **tae**

TAEL n unit of weight, used in the Far East, having various values between one to two and a half ounces

TAELS ▸ **tael**

TAENIA n (in ancient Greece) a narrow fillet or headband for the hair

TAENIAE ▸ **taenia**

> This is the plural of **taenia**, a kind of hairband worn in ancient Greece. It's difficult to see on your rack, but those letters come up so often that it is well worth making the effort to master it.

TAENIAS ▸ **taenia**

TAES ▸ **tae**

TAFFETA n shiny silk or rayon fabric

TAFFETY same as ▸ **taffeta**

TAFFIA same as ▸ **tafia**

TAFFIAS ▸ **taffia**

TAFFIES ▸ **taffy**

TAFFY same as ▸ **toffee**

TAFIA n type of rum, esp

from Guyana or the Caribbean

TAFIAS ▸ **tafia**

TAG n label bearing information ▷ vb attach a tag to

TAGETES n any of a genus of plants with yellow or orange flowers, including the French and African marigolds

TAGGANT n microscopic material added to substance to identify it

TAGGED ▸ **tag**

TAGGEE n one who has been made to wear a tag

TAGGEES ▸ **taggee**

TAGGER n one who marks with a tag

TAGGERS ▸ **tagger**

TAGGIER ▸ **taggy**

TAGGING ▸ **tag**

TAGGY adj (of wool, hair, etc) matted

TAGINE n large, heavy N African cooking pot with a conical lid

TAGINES ▸ **tagine**

TAGLESS adj having no tag

TAGLIKE adj resembling a tag

TAGLINE n funny line of joke

TAGMA n distinct region of the body of an arthropod, such as the head, thorax, or abdomen of an insect

TAGMATA ▸ **tagma**

TAGMEME n class of speech elements all of which may fulfil the same grammatical role in a sentence

TAGRAG same as ▸ **ragtag**

TAGRAGS ▸ **tagrag**

TAGS ▸ **tag**

TAGUAN n large nocturnal flying squirrel of high forests in the East Indies that uses its long tail as a rudder

TAGUANS ▸ **taguan**

TAHA n type of South African bird

TAHAS ▸ **taha**

TAHINA same as ▸ **tahini**

TAHINAS ▸ **tahina**

TAHINI n paste made from ground sesame seeds, used esp in Middle Eastern cookery

TAHINIS ▸ **tahini**

TAHR n goatlike bovid mammal of mountainous

regions of S and SW Asia, having a shaggy coat and curved horns

TAHRS ▶ tahr

TAHSIL *n* administrative division of a zila in certain states in India

TAHSILS ▶ tahsil

TAI *n* a type of sea bream

TAIAHA *n* carved weapon in the form of a staff, now used in Māori ceremonial oratory

TAIAHAS ▶ taiaha

TAIGA *n* belt of coniferous forest extending across much of subarctic North America, Europe, and Asia

TAIGAS ▶ taiga

TAIGLE *vb* entangle or impede

TAIGLED ▶ taigle

TAIGLES ▶ taigle

TAIHOA *interj* hold on! no hurry!

TAIKO *n* large Japanese drum

TAIKOS ▶ taiko

TAIL *n* rear part of an animal's body, usu forming a flexible appendage ▷ *adj* at the rear ▷ *vb* follow (someone) secretly

TAILARD *n* one having a tail

TAILED ▶ tail

TAILER *n* one that tails

TAILERS ▶ tailer

TAILFAN *n* fanned structure at the hind end of a lobster or related crustacean, formed from the telson and uropods

TAILFIN *n* decorative projection at back of car

TAILFLY *n* in angling, the lowest fly on a wet-fly cast

TAILING *n* part of a beam, rafter, projecting brick or stone, etc, embedded in a wall

TAILLE *n* (in France before 1789) a tax levied by a king or overlord on his subjects

TAILLES ▶ taille

TAILLIE *n* (in law) the limitation of an estate or interest to a person and the heirs of his body

TAILOR *n* person who makes men's clothes ▷ *vb* cut or style (a garment) to specific requirements

TAILORS ▶ tailor

TAILS *adv* with the side of a coin that does not have a portrait of a head on it uppermost

TAILYE *same as* **▶ taillie**

TAILYES ▶ tailye

TAILZIE *same as* **▶ taillie**

TAIN *n* tinfoil used in backing mirrors

TAINS ▶ tain

TAINT *vb* spoil with a small amount of decay, contamination, or other bad quality ▷ *n* something that taints

TAINTED ▶ taint

TAINTS ▶ taint

TAIPAN *n* large poisonous Australian snake

TAIPANS ▶ taipan

TAIRA *same as* **▶ tayra**

TAIRAS ▶ taira

TAIS ▶ tai

TAISCH *n* (in Scotland) apparition of a person whose death is imminent

TAISH *same as* **▶ taisch**

TAISHES ▶ taish

TAIT *same as* **▶ tate**

TAITS ▶ tait

TAIVER *same as* **▶ taver**

TAIVERS ▶ taiver

TAIVERT *adj* Scots word meaning confused or bewildered

TAJ *n* tall conical cap worn as a mark of distinction by Muslims

This word for a Muslim's cap is one of the key words to remember for using the J.

TAJES ▶ taj

TAJINE *same as* **▶ tagine**

TAJINES ▶ tajine

TAK *Scots variant spelling of* **▶ take**

TAKA *n* standard monetary unit of Bangladesh, divided into 100 paise

TAKABLE ▶ take

TAKAHE *n* very rare flightless New Zealand bird

TAKAHES ▶ takahe

TAKAS ▶ taka

TAKE *vb* remove from a place ▷ *n* one of a series of recordings from which the best will be used

TAKEN ▶ take

TAKEOFF *n* act or process of making an aircraft airborne

TAKEOUT *n* shop or

restaurant that sells such food

TAKER *n* person who agrees to take something that is offered

TAKERS ▶ taker

TAKES ▶ take

TAKEUP *n* the claiming or acceptance of something, esp a state benefit, that is due or available

TAKEUPS ▶ takeup

TAKHI *n* type of wild Mongolian horse

TAKHIS ▶ takhi

TAKI ▶ takhi

TAKIER ▶ taky

TAKIEST ▶ taky

TAKIN *n* massive bovid mammal of mountainous regions of S Asia, having a shaggy coat, short legs, and horns that point backwards and upwards

TAKING ▶ take

TAKINGS ▶ take

TAKINS ▶ takin

TAKIS ▶ taki

TAKKIES *same as* **▶ tackies**

TAKS ▶ tak

TAKY *adj* appealing

TALA *n* standard monetary unit of Samoa, divided into 100 sene

TALAK *same as* **▶ talaq**

TALAKS ▶ talak

TALANT *old variant of* **▶ talon**

TALANTS ▶ talant

TALAQ *n* Muslim form of divorce

In Islamic law, a word for divorce: easy to miss because one tends not to think of words ending in Q.

TALAQS ▶ talaq

TALAR *n* ankle-length robe

TALARIA *pl n* winged sandals, such as those worn by Hermes

TALARS ▶ talar

TALAS ▶ tala

TALAUNT *old variant of* **▶ talon**

TALAYOT *n* ancient Balearic stone tower

TALBOT *n* (formerly) an ancient breed of large hound, usually white or light-coloured, having pendulous ears and strong powers of scent

TALBOTS ▸ **talbot**
TALC n talcum powder ▷ vb apply talc to ▷ adj of, or relating to, talc
TALCED ▸ **talc**
TALCIER ▸ **talcy**
TALCING ▸ **talc**
TALCKED ▸ **talcky**
TALCKY same as ▸ **talcy**
TALCOSE ▸ **talc**
TALCOUS ▸ **talc**
TALCS ▸ **talc**
TALCUM n white, grey, brown, or pale green mineral, found in metamorphic rocks. It is used in the manufacture of talcum powder and electrical insulators
TALCUMS ▸ **talcum**
TALCY adj like, containing, or covered in talc
TALE n story
TALEA n rhythmic pattern in certain mediaeval choral compositions
TALEAE ▸ **talea**
TALEFUL adj having many tales
TALENT n natural ability
TALENTS ▸ **talent**
TALER same as ▸ **thaler**
TALERS ▸ **taler**
TALES n group of persons summoned from among those present in court or from bystanders to fill vacancies on a jury panel
TALI ▸ **talus**
TALION n system or legal principle of making the punishment correspond to the crime
TALIONS ▸ **talion**
TALIPAT same as ▸ **talipot**
TALIPED adj having a club foot ▷ n club-footed person
TALIPES n congenital deformity of the foot by which it is twisted in any of various positions
TALIPOT n palm tree of the East Indies, having large leaves that are used for fans, thatching houses, etc
TALK vb express ideas or feelings by means of speech ▷ n speech or lecture
TALKBOX n voice box
TALKED ▸ **talk**
TALKER ▸ **talk**
TALKERS ▸ **talk**

TALKIE n early film with a soundtrack
TALKIER ▸ **talky**
TALKIES ▸ **talkie**
TALKING n speech; the act of speaking
TALKS ▸ **talk**
TALKY adj containing too much dialogue or inconsequential talk
TALL adj higher than average
TALLAGE n tax levied by the Norman and early Angevin kings on their Crown lands and royal towns ▷ vb levy a tax (upon)
TALLAT same as ▸ **tallet**
TALLATS ▸ **tallat**
TALLBOY n high chest of drawers
TALLENT n plenty
TALLER ▸ **tall**
TALLEST ▸ **tall**
TALLET n loft
TALLETS ▸ **tallet**
TALLIED ▸ **tally**
TALLIER ▸ **tally**
TALLIES ▸ **tally**
TALLIS same as ▸ **tallith**
TALLISH adj quite tall
TALLIT same as ▸ **tallith**
TALLITH n white shawl with fringed corners worn over the head and shoulders by Jewish males during religious services
TALLITS ▸ **tallit**
TALLOL n oily liquid used for making soaps, lubricants, etc
TALLOLS ▸ **tallol**
TALLOT same as ▸ **tallet**
TALLOTS ▸ **tallot**
TALLOW n hard animal fat used to make candles ▷ vb cover or smear with tallow
TALLOWS ▸ **tallow**
TALLOWY ▸ **tallow**
TALLS ▸ **tall**
TALLY vb (of two things) correspond ▷ n record of a debt or score
TALLYHO n cry of a participant at a hunt to encourage the hounds when the quarry is sighted ▷ vb to make the cry of tallyho
TALMA n short cloak
TALMAS ▸ **talma**
TALMUD n primary source of Jewish religious law,

consisting of the Mishnah and the Gemara
TALMUDS ▸ **talmud**
TALON n bird's hooked claw
TALONED ▸ **talon**
TALONS ▸ **talon**
TALOOKA same as ▸ **taluk**
TALPA n sebaceous cyst
TALPAE ▸ **talpa**
TALPAS ▸ **talpa**
TALUK n subdivision of a district
TALUKA same as ▸ **taluk**
TALUKAS ▸ **taluka**
TALUKS ▸ **taluk**
TALUS n bone of the ankle that articulates with the leg bones to form the ankle joint
TALUSES ▸ **talus**
TALWEG same as ▸ **thalweg**
TALWEGS ▸ **talweg**
TAM n type of hat
TAMABLE ▸ **tame**
TAMAL same as ▸ **tamale**
TAMALE n Mexican dish made of minced meat mixed with crushed maize and seasonings, wrapped in maize husks and steamed
TAMALES ▸ **tamale**
TAMALS ▸ **tamal**
TAMANDU same as ▸ **tamandua**
TAMANU n poon tree
TAMANUS ▸ **tamanu**
TAMARA n powder consisting of cloves, cinnamon, fennel, coriander, etc, used in certain cuisines
TAMARAO same as ▸ **tamarau**
TAMARAS ▸ **tamara**
TAMARAU n small rare member of the cattle tribe of lowland areas of Mindoro in the Philippines
TAMARI n Japanese variety of soy sauce
TAMARIN n small monkey of South and Central American forests
TAMARIS ▸ **tamari**
TAMASHA n (in India) a show
TAMBAC same as ▸ **tombac**
TAMBACS ▸ **tambac**
TAMBAK same as ▸ **tombac**
TAMBAKS ▸ **tambak**
TAMBALA n unit of Malawian currency

T

TAMBER *same as* ▸ **timbre**

TAMBERS ▸ **tamber**

TAMBOUR *n* embroidery frame, consisting of two hoops over which the fabric is stretched while being worked ▷ *vb* embroider (fabric or a design) on a tambour

TAMBUR *n* old Turkish stringed instrument

TAMBURA *n* Middle-Eastern stringed instrument with a long neck, related to the tambur

TAMBURS ▸ **tambur**

TAME *adj* (of animals) brought under human control ▷ *vb* make tame

TAMED ▸ **tame**

TAMEIN *n* Burmese skirt

TAMEINS ▸ **tamein**

TAMELY ▸ **tame**

TAMER ▸ **tame**

TAMERS ▸ **tame**

TAMES ▸ **tame**

TAMEST ▸ **tame**

TAMIN *n* thin woollen fabric

TAMINE *same as* ▸ **tamin**

TAMINES ▸ **tamine**

TAMING *n* act of making (something) tame

TAMINGS ▸ **taming**

TAMINS ▸ **tamin**

TAMIS *same as* ▸ **tammy**

TAMISE *n* type of thin cloth

TAMISES ▸ **tamis**

TAMMAR *n* small scrub wallaby of Australia, with a thick dark-coloured coat

TAMMARS ▸ **tammar**

TAMMIE *n* short for tam-o'shanter, a traditional Scottish hat

TAMMIED ▸ **tammy**

TAMMIES ▸ **tammy**

TAMMY *n* glazed woollen or mixed fabric, used for linings, undergarments, etc ▷ *vb* (esp formerly) to strain (sauce, soup, etc) through a tammy

TAMP *vb* pack down by repeated taps

TAMPALA *n* Asian plant (Amaranthus tricolor), eaten as food

TAMPAN *n* biting mite

TAMPANS ▸ **tampan**

TAMPED ▸ **tamp**

TAMPER *vb* interfere ▷ *n* person or thing that tamps, esp an instrument for packing down tobacco in a pipe

TAMPERS ▸ **tamper**

TAMPING *adj* very angry ▷ *n* act or instance of tamping

TAMPION *n* plug placed in a gun's muzzle when the gun is not in use to keep out moisture and dust

TAMPON *n* absorbent plug of cotton wool inserted into the vagina during menstruation ▷ *vb* use a tampon

TAMPONS ▸ **tampon**

TAMPS ▸ **tamp**

TAMS ▸ **tam**

TAN *n* brown coloration of the skin from exposure to sunlight ▷ *vb* (of skin) go brown from exposure to sunlight ▷ *adj* yellowish-brown

TANA *n* small Madagascan lemur

TANADAR *n* commanding officer of an Indian police station

TANAGER *n* American songbird with a short thick bill and a brilliantly coloured male plumage

TANAGRA *n* type of tanager

TANAS ▸ **tana**

TANBARK *n* bark of certain trees, esp the oak and hemlock, used as a source of tannin

TANDEM *n* bicycle for two riders, one behind the other

TANDEMS ▸ **tandem**

TANDOOR *n* type of Indian clay oven

TANE *old Scottish variant of* ▸ **taken**

TANG *n* strong taste or smell ▷ *vb* cause to ring

TANGA *n* triangular loincloth worn by indigenous peoples in tropical America

TANGAS ▸ **tanga**

TANGED ▸ **tang**

TANGELO *n* hybrid produced by crossing a tangerine tree with a grapefruit tree

TANGENT *n* line that touches a curve without intersecting it

TANGHIN *n* strong poison formerly used in Madagascar to determine the guilt or otherwise of crime suspects

TANGI *n* Māori funeral ceremony

TANGIE *n* water spirit of Orkney, appearing as a figure draped in seaweed, or as a seahorse

TANGIER ▸ **tangy**

TANGIES ▸ **tangie**

TANGING ▸ **tang**

TANGIS ▸ **tangi**

TANGLE *n* confused mass or situation ▷ *vb* twist together in a tangle

TANGLED ▸ **tangle**

TANGLER ▸ **tangle**

TANGLES ▸ **tangle**

TANGLY ▸ **tangle**

TANGO *n* S American dance ▷ *vb* dance a tango

TANGOED ▸ **tango**

TANGOS ▸ **tango**

TANGRAM *n* Chinese puzzle in which a square, cut into a parallelogram, a square, and five triangles, is formed into figures

TANGS ▸ **tang**

TANGUN *n* small and sturdy Tibetan pony

TANGUNS ▸ **tangun**

TANGY *adj* having a pungent, fresh, or briny flavour or aroma

TANH *n* hyperbolic tangent

TANHS ▸ **tanh**

TANIST *n* heir apparent of a Celtic chieftain chosen by election during the chief's lifetime: usually the worthiest of his kin

TANISTS ▸ **tanist**

TANIWHA *n* mythical Māori monster that lives in water

TANK *n* container for liquids or gases ▷ *vb* put or keep in a tank

TANKA *n* Japanese verse form consisting of five lines, the first and third having five syllables, the others seven

TANKAGE *n* capacity or contents of a tank or tanks

TANKARD *n* large beer-mug, often with a hinged lid

TANKAS ▸ **tanka**

TANKED ▸ **tank**

TANKER *n* ship or truck for carrying liquid in bulk

TANKERS ▸ **tanker**

TANKFUL n quantity contained in a tank

TANKIA n type of boat used in Canton

TANKIAS ▸ **tankia**

TANKIES ▸ **tanky**

TANKING n heavy defeat

TANKINI n woman's two-piece swimming costume consisting of a vest or camisole top and bikini briefs

TANKS ▸ **tank**

TANKY n die-hard communist

TANLING n suntanned person

TANNA n Indian police station or army base

TANNAGE n act or process of tanning

TANNAH same as ▸ **tanna**

TANNAHS ▸ **tannah**

TANNAS ▸ **tanna**

TANNATE n any salt or ester of tannic acid

TANNED ▸ **tan**

TANNER ▸ **tan**

TANNERS ▸ **tan**

TANNERY n place where hides are tanned

TANNEST ▸ **tan**

TANNIC adj of, containing, or produced from tannin or tannic acid

TANNIE n in S Africa, title of respect used to refer to an elderly woman

TANNIES ▸ **tannie**

TANNIN n vegetable substance used in tanning

TANNING ▸ **tan**

TANNINS ▸ **tannin**

TANNISH ▸ **tan**

TANNOY n sound-amplifying apparatus used as a public-address system esp in a large building, such as a university ▷ vb announce (something) using a Tannoy system

TANNOYS ▸ **tannoy**

TANREC same as ▸ **tenrec**

TANRECS ▸ **tanrec**

TANS ▸ **tan**

TANSIES ▸ **tansy**

TANSY n yellow-flowered plant

TANTARA n blast, as on a trumpet or horn

TANTI adj old word for worthwhile

TANTIVY adv at full speed ▷ interj hunting cry, esp at full gallop

TANTO adv too much

TANTONY n runt

TANTRA n sacred books of Tantrism, written between the 7th and 17th centuries AD, mainly in the form of a dialogue between Siva and his wife

TANTRAS ▸ **tantra**

TANTRIC ▸ **tantra**

TANTRUM n childish outburst of temper

TANUKI n animal similar to a raccoon, found in Japan

TANUKIS ▸ **tanuki**

TANYARD n part of a tannery

TAO n (in Confucian philosophy) the correct course of action

TAONGA n treasure

TAONGAS ▸ **taonga**

TAOS ▸ **tao**

TAP vb knock lightly and usu repeatedly ▷ n light knock

TAPA n inner bark of the paper mulberry

TAPALO n Latin American scarf, often patterned and brightly coloured

TAPALOS ▸ **tapalo**

TAPAS pl n (in Spanish cookery) light snacks or appetizers, usually eaten with drinks

TAPE n narrow long strip of material ▷ vb record on magnetic tape

TAPED ▸ **tape**

TAPEN adj made of tape

TAPER ▸ **tape**

TAPERED ▸ **tape**

TAPERER ▸ **tape**

TAPERS ▸ **tape**

TAPES ▸ **tape**

TAPET n example of tapestry

TAPETA ▸ **tapetum**

TAPETAL ▸ **tapetum**

TAPETI n forest rabbit of Brazil

TAPETIS ▸ **tapeti**

TAPETS ▸ **tapet**

TAPETUM n layer of nutritive cells in the sporangia of ferns and anthers of flowering plants that surrounds developing spore cells

TAPHOLE n hole in a furnace for running off molten metal or slag

TAPING ▸ **tape**

TAPIOCA n beadlike starch made from cassava root, used in puddings

TAPIR n piglike mammal of tropical America and SE Asia, with a long snout

TAPIRS ▸ **tapir**

TAPIS n tapestry or carpeting, esp as formerly used to cover a table in a council chamber

TAPISES ▸ **tapis**

TAPIST n person who records (read out) printed matter in an audio format for the benefit of visually impaired people

TAPISTS ▸ **tapist**

TAPLASH n dregs of beer

TAPPA same as ▸ **tapa**

TAPPAS ▸ **tappa**

TAPPED ▸ **tap**

TAPPER n person who taps

TAPPERS ▸ **tapper**

TAPPET n short steel rod in an engine, transferring motion from one part to another

TAPPETS ▸ **tappet**

TAPPICE vb hide

TAPPING ▸ **tap**

TAPPIT adj crested; topped

TAPROOM n public bar in a hotel or pub

TAPROOT n main root of a plant, growing straight down

TAPS ▸ **tap**

TAPSMAN n old word for a barman

TAPSMEN ▸ **tapsman**

TAPSTER n barman

TAPSTRY adj relating to tapestry

TAPU adj sacred ▷ n Māori religious or superstitious restriction on something ▷ vb put a tapu on something

TAPUED ▸ **tapu**

TAPUING ▸ **tapu**

TAPUS ▸ **tapu**

TAR n thick black liquid distilled from coal etc ▷ vb coat with tar

TARA same as ▸ **taro**

TARAIRE n type of New Zealand tree

TARAMA n cod roe

TARAMAS ▸ **tarama**

TARAMEA *n* variety of New Zealand speargrass

TARAND *n* northern animal of legend, now supposed to have been the reindeer

TARANDS ▶ **tarand**

TARAS ▶ **tara**

TARBOY *n* boy who applies tar to the skin of sheep cut during shearing

TARBOYS ▶ **tarboy**

TARBUSH *same as* > **tarboosh**

TARCEL *same as* ▶ **tarsel**

TARCELS ▶ **tarcel**

TARDIED ▶ **tardy**

TARDIER ▶ **tardy**

TARDIES ▶ **tardy**

TARDILY ▶ **tardy**

TARDIVE *adj* tending to develop late

TARDO *adj* (of music) slow; to be played slowly

TARDY *adj* slow or late ▷ *vb* delay or impede (something or someone)

TARDYON *n* particle travelling slower than the speed of light

TARE *n* weight of the wrapping or container of goods ▷ *vb* weigh (a package, etc) in order to calculate the amount of tare

TARED ▶ **tare**

TARES ▶ **tare**

TARGA *n as in* **targa top** denotes removable hard roof on a car

TARGE *vb* interrogate

TARGED ▶ **targe**

TARGES ▶ **targe**

TARGET *n* object or person a missile is aimed at ▷ *vb* aim or direct

TARGETS ▶ **target**

TARGING ▶ **targe**

TARIFF *n* tax levied on imports ▷ *vb* impose punishment for a criminal offence

TARIFFS ▶ **tariff**

TARING ▶ **tare**

TARINGS ▶ **tare**

TARMAC *See also* ▶ **macadam**

TARMACS ▶ **tarmac**

TARN *n* small mountain lake

TARNAL *adj* damned ▷ *adv* extremely

TARNISH *vb* make or become stained or less

bright ▷ *n* discoloration or blemish

TARNS ▶ **tarn**

TARO *n* plant with a large edible rootstock

TAROC *old variant of* ▶ **tarot**

TAROCS ▶ **taroc**

TAROK *old variant of* ▶ **tarot**

TAROKS ▶ **tarok**

TAROS ▶ **taro**

TAROT *n* special pack of cards used mainly in fortune-telling ▷ *adj* relating to tarot cards

TAROTS ▶ **tarot**

TARP *informal word for* > **tarpaulin**

TARPAN *n* European wild horse common in prehistoric times but now extinct

TARPANS ▶ **tarpan**

TARPON *n* large silvery clupeoid game fish found in warm Atlantic waters

TARPONS ▶ **tarpon**

TARPS ▶ **tarp**

TARRAS *same as* ▶ **trass**

TARRE *vb* old word meaning to provoke or goad

TARRED ▶ **tar**

TARRES ▶ **tarre**

TARRIED ▶ **tarry**

TARRIER ▶ **tarry**

TARRIES ▶ **tarry**

TARRING ▶ **tar**

TARROCK *n* seabird

TARROW *vb* exhibit reluctance

TARROWS ▶ **tarrow**

TARRY *vb* linger or delay ▷ *n* stay ▷ *adj* covered in or resembling tar

TARS ▶ **tar**

TARSAL *adj* of the tarsus or tarsi ▷ *n* tarsal bone

TARSALS ▶ **tarsal**

TARSEAL *n* bitumen surface of a road

TARSEL *same as* ▶ **tercel**

TARSELS ▶ **tarsel**

TARSI ▶ **tarsus**

TARSIA *another term for* > **intarsia**

TARSIAS ▶ **tarsia**

TARSIER *n* small nocturnal primate of the E Indies, which has very large eyes

TARSUS *n* bones of the heel and ankle collectively

TART *n* pie or flan with a sweet filling ▷ *adj* sharp or bitter ▷ *adj* (of a flavour,

food, etc) sour, acid, or astringent ▷ *vb* (of food, drink, etc) become tart (sour)

TARTAN *n* design of straight lines crossing at right angles, esp one associated with a Scottish clan

TARTANA *n* small Mediterranean sailing boat

TARTANE *same as* ▶ **tartana**

TARTANS ▶ **tartan**

TARTAR *n* hard deposit on the teeth

TARTARE *n* mayonnaise sauce mixed with hard-boiled egg yolks, chopped herbs, capers, and gherkins

TARTARS ▶ **tartar**

TARTED ▶ **tart**

TARTER ▶ **tart**

TARTEST ▶ **tart**

TARTIER ▶ **tarty**

TARTILY ▶ **tarty**

TARTINE *n* slice of bread with butter or jam spread on it

TARTING ▶ **tart**

TARTISH ▶ **tart**

TARTLET *n* individual pastry case with a filling of fruit or other sweet or savoury mixture

TARTLY ▶ **tart**

TARTS ▶ **tart**

TARTUFE *same as* > **tartuffe**

TARTUFO *n* Italian mousse-like chocolate dessert

TARTY *adj* resembling a promiscuous woman; provocative in a cheap and bawdy way

TARWEED *n* resinous Californian plant with a pungent scent

TARZAN *n* man with great physical strength, agility, and virility

TARZANS ▶ **tarzan**

TAS ▶ **ta** *n*

TASAR *same as* ▶ **tussore**

TASARS ▶ **tasar**

TASBIH *n* form of Islamic prayer

TASBIHS ▶ **tasbih**

TASER *vb* use a Taser (trademark) stun gun on (someone)

TASERED ▶ **taser**

TASERS ▶ **taser**

TASH *vb* stain or besmirch

TASHED ▶ **tash**
TASHES ▶ **tash**
TASHING ▶ **tash**
TASK n piece of work to be done ▷ vb give someone a task to do
TASKBAR n area of computer screen showing what programs are running
TASKED ▶ **task**
TASKER ▶ **task**
TASKERS ▶ **task**
TASKING ▶ **task**
TASKS ▶ **task**
TASLET same as ▶ **tasset**
TASLETS ▶ **taslet**
TASS n cup, goblet, or glass
TASSE same as ▶ **tasset**
TASSEL n decorative fringed knot of threads ▷ vb adorn with a tassel or tassels
TASSELL same as ▶ **tassel**
TASSELS ▶ **tassel**
TASSES ▶ **tasse**
TASSET n piece of armour consisting of one or more plates fastened on to the bottom of a cuirass to protect the thigh
TASSETS ▶ **tasset**
TASSIE same as ▶ **tass**
TASSIES ▶ **tassie**
TASTE n sense by which the flavour of a substance is distinguished in the mouth ▷ vb distinguish the taste of (a substance)
TASTED ▶ **taste**
TASTER n person employed to test the quality of food or drink by tasting it
TASTERS ▶ **taster**
TASTES ▶ **taste**
TASTIER ▶ **tasty**
TASTILY ▶ **tasty**
TASTING ▶ **taste**
TASTY adj pleasantly flavoured
TAT n tatty or tasteless article(s) ▷ vb make (something) by tatting
TATAMI n thick rectangular mat of woven straw, used as a standard to measure a Japanese room
TATAMIS ▶ **tatami**
TATAR n brutal person
TATARS ▶ **tatar**
TATE n small tuft of fibre
TATER n potato
TATERS ▶ **tater**
TATES ▶ **tate**

TATH vb (of cattle) to defecate
TATHED ▶ **tath**
TATHING ▶ **tath**
TATHS ▶ **tath**
TATIE same as ▶ **tattie**
TATIES ▶ **tatie**
TATLER old variant of ▶ **tattler**
TATLERS ▶ **tatler**
TATOU n armadillo
TATOUAY n large armadillo of South America
TATOUS ▶ **tatou**
TATS ▶ **tat**
TATSOI n variety of Chinese cabbage
TATSOIS ▶ **tatsoi**
TATT same as ▶ **tat**
TATTED ▶ **tat**
TATTER vb make or become torn
TATTERS ▶ **tatter**
TATTERY same as > **tattered**
TATTIE Scots or dialect word for ▶ **potato**
TATTIER ▶ **tatty**
TATTIES ▶ **tattie**
TATTILY ▶ **tatty**
TATTING ▶ **tat**
TATTLE n gossip or chatter ▷ vb gossip or chatter
TATTLED ▶ **tattle**
TATTLER n person who tattles
TATTLES ▶ **tattle**
TATTOO n pattern made on the body by pricking the skin and staining it with indelible inks ▷ vb make such a pattern on the skin
TATTOOS ▶ **tattoo**
TATTOW old variant of ▶ **tattoo**
TATTOWS ▶ **tattow**
TATTS ▶ **tatt**
TATTY adj worn out, shabby, tawdry, or unkempt
TATU old variant of ▶ **tattoo**
TATUED ▶ **tatu**
TATUING ▶ **tatu**
TATUS ▶ **tatu**
TAU n 19th letter in the Greek alphabet
TAUBE n type of German aeroplane
TAUBES ▶ **taube**
TAUGHT ▶ **teach**
TAUHINU New Zealand name for ▶ **poplar**
TAUHOU same as > **silvereye**
TAUHOUS ▶ **tauhou**

TAUIWI n Māori term for the non-Māori people of New Zealand
TAUIWIS ▶ **tauiwi**
TAULD vb old Scots variant of told
TAUNT vb tease with jeers ▷ n jeering remark ▷ adj (of the mast or masts of a sailing vessel) unusually tall
TAUNTED ▶ **taunt**
TAUNTER ▶ **taunt**
TAUNTS ▶ **taunt**
TAUON n negatively charged elementary particle
TAUONS ▶ **tauon**
TAUPATA n New Zealand shrub or tree, with shiny dark green leaves
TAUPE adj brownish-grey ▷ n brownish-grey colour
TAUPES ▶ **taupe**
TAUPIE same as ▶ **tawpie**
TAUPIES ▶ **taupie**
TAUREAN adj born under or characteristic of Taurus
TAURIC same as ▶ **taurean**
TAURINE adj of, relating to, or resembling a bull ▷ n derivative of the amino acid, cysteine, obtained from the bile of animals
TAUS ▶ **tau**
TAUT adj drawn tight ▷ vb Scots word meaning to tangle
TAUTAUG same as ▶ **tautog**
TAUTED ▶ **taut**
TAUTEN vb make or become taut
TAUTENS ▶ **tauten**
TAUTER ▶ **taut**
TAUTEST ▶ **taut**
TAUTING ▶ **taut**
TAUTIT adj Scots word meaning tangled
TAUTLY ▶ **taut**
TAUTOG n large dark-coloured wrasse, used as a food fish
TAUTOGS ▶ **tautog**
TAUTS ▶ **taut**
TAV n 23rd and last letter in the Hebrew alphabet
TAVA n thick Indian frying pan
TAVAH same as ▶ **tava**
TAVAHS ▶ **tavah**
TAVAS ▶ **tava**
TAVER vb wander about
TAVERED ▶ **taver**
TAVERN n pub

T

TAVERNA n (in Greece) a guesthouse that has its own bar
TAVERNS ▶ **tavern**
TAVERS ▶ **taver**
TAVERT adj bewildered or confused
TAVS ▶ **tav**
TAW vb convert skins into leather
TAWA n tall timber tree from New Zealand, with edible purple berries
TAWAI n New Zealand beech
TAWAIS ▶ **tawai**
TAWAS ▶ **tawa**
TAWDRY adj cheap, showy, and of poor quality ▷ n gaudy finery of poor quality
TAWED ▶ **taw**
TAWER ▶ **taw**
TAWERS ▶ **taw**
TAWERY n place where tawing is carried out
TAWHAI same as ▶ **tawai**
TAWHAIS ▶ **tawhai**
TAWHIRI n small New Zealand tree with wavy green glossy leaves
TAWIE adj easily persuaded or managed
TAWIER ▶ **tawie**
TAWIEST ▶ **tawie**
TAWING ▶ **taw**
TAWINGS ▶ **taw**
TAWNEY same as ▶ **tawny**
TAWNEYS ▶ **tawney**
TAWNIER ▶ **tawny**
TAWNIES ▶ **tawny**
TAWNILY ▶ **tawny**
TAWNY adj yellowish-brown ▷ n light brown to brownish-orange colour
TAWPIE n foolish or maladroit girl
TAWPIES ▶ **tawpie**
TAWS same as ▶ **tawse**
TAWSE n leather strap with one end cut into thongs, formerly used by schoolteachers to hit children who had misbehaved ▷ vb punish (someone) with or as if with a tawse
TAWSED ▶ **tawse**
TAWSES ▶ **tawse**
TAWSING ▶ **tawse**
TAWT same as ▶ **taut**
TAWTED ▶ **tawt**
TAWTIE ▶ **tawt**
TAWTIER ▶ **tawt**

TAWTING ▶ **tawt**
TAWTS ▶ **tawt**
TAX n compulsory payment levied by a government on income, property, etc to raise revenue ▷ vb levy a tax on
TAXA ▶ **taxon**
TAXABLE adj capable of being taxed ▷ n person, income, property, etc, that is subject to tax
TAXABLY ▶ **taxable**
TAXED ▶ **tax**
TAXEME n any element of speech that may differentiate one utterance from another with a different meaning
TAXEMES ▶ **taxeme**
TAXEMIC ▶ **taxeme**
TAXER ▶ **tax**
TAXERS ▶ **tax**
TAXES ▶ **tax**
TAXI n car with a driver that may be hired to take people to any specified destination ▷ vb (of an aircraft) run along off or after landing
TAXICAB same as ▶ **taxi**
TAXIED ▶ **taxi**
TAXIES ▶ **taxis**
TAXIING ▶ **taxi**
TAXIMAN n taxi driver
TAXIMEN ▶ **taximan**
TAXING adj demanding, onerous
TAXINGS ▶ **tax**
TAXIS n movement of a cell or organism in a particular direction in response to an external stimulus ▷ n ancient Greek army unit
TAXITE n type of volcanic rock
TAXITES ▶ **taxite**
TAXITIC ▶ **taxite**
TAXIWAY n marked path along which aircraft taxi to or from a runway, parking area, etc
TAXLESS ▶ **tax**
TAXMAN n collector of taxes
TAXMEN ▶ **taxman**
TAXOL n trademarked anti-cancer drug
TAXOLS ▶ **taxol**
TAXON n any taxonomic group or rank
TAXONS ▶ **taxon**
TAXOR ▶ **tax**

TAXORS ▶ **tax**
TAXPAID adj (of taxable products, esp wine) having had the applicable tax paid already
TAXUS n genus of conifers
TAXWISE adv regarding tax
TAXYING ▶ **taxi**
TAY Irish dialect word for ▶ **tea**
TAYRA n large arboreal musteline mammal, of Central and South America, with a dark brown body and paler head
TAYRAS ▶ **tayra**
TAYS ▶ **tay**
TAZZA n wine cup with a shallow bowl and a circular foot
TAZZAS ▶ **tazza**
TAZZE ▶ **tazza**
TCHICK vb make a click by creating a vacuum in the mouth with the tongue pressed against the palate then suddenly breaking the seal by withdrawing part of the tongue from the palate
TCHICKS ▶ **tchick**
TE n (in tonic sol-fa) seventh degree of any major scale
TEA n drink made from infusing the dried leaves of an Asian bush in boiling water ▷ vb take tea
TEABAG n porous bag of tea leaves for infusion
TEABAGS ▶ **teabag**
TEABOWL n small bowl used (instead of a teacup) for serving tea
TEABOX n box for storing tea
TEACAKE n flat bun, usually eaten toasted and buttered
TEACART n trolley from which tea is served
TEACH vb tell or show (someone) how to do something
TEACHER n person who teaches, esp in a school
TEACHES ▶ **teach**
TEACHIE old form of ▶ **tetchy**
TEACUP n cup out of which tea may be drunk
TEACUPS ▶ **teacup**
TEAD old word for ▶ **torch**
TEADE same as ▶ **tead**
TEADES ▶ **teade**
TEADS ▶ **tead**

TEAED ▶ tea

TEAGLE vb raise or hoist using a tackle

TEAGLED ▶ teagle

TEAGLES ▶ teagle

TEAING ▶ tea

TEAK n very hard wood of an E Indian tree

TEAKS ▶ teak

TEAL n kind of small duck

TEALIKE adj resembling tea

TEALS ▶ teal

TEAM n group of people forming one side in a game ▷ vb make or cause to make a team

TEAMED ▶ team

TEAMER ▶ team

TEAMERS ▶ team

TEAMING ▶ team

TEAMS ▶ team

TEAPOT n container with a lid, spout, and handle for making and serving tea

TEAPOTS ▶ teapot

TEAPOY n small table or stand with a tripod base

TEAPOYS ▶ teapoy

TEAR n drop of fluid appearing in and falling from the eye ▷ vb rip a hole in ▷ vb shed tears

TEARED ▶ tear

TEARER ▶ tear

TEARERS ▶ tear

TEARFUL adj weeping or about to weep

TEARGAS n gas or vapor that makes the eyes smart and water ▷ vb deploy teargas against

TEARIER ▶ teary

TEARILY ▶ teary

TEARING ▶ tear

TEAROOM same as ▶ teashop

TEARS ▶ tear

TEARY adj characterized by, covered with, or secreting tears

TEAS ▶ tea

TEASE vb make fun of (someone) in a provoking or playful way ▷ n person who teases

TEASED ▶ tease

TEASEL n plant with prickly leaves and flowers ▷ vb tease (a fabric)

TEASELS ▶ teasel

TEASER n annoying or difficult problem

TEASERS ▶ teaser

TEASES ▶ tease

TEASHOP n restaurant where tea and light refreshments are served

TEASING ▶ tease

TEAT n nipple of a breast or udder

TEATED ▶ teat

TEATIME n late afternoon

TEATS ▶ teat

TEAWARE n implements and vessels for brewing and serving tea

TEAZE old variant of ▶ tease

TEAZED ▶ teaze

TEAZEL same as ▶ teasel

TEAZELS ▶ teazel

TEAZES ▶ teaze

TEAZING ▶ teaze

TEAZLE same as ▶ teasel

TEAZLED ▶ teazle

TEAZLES ▶ teazle

TEBBAD n sandstorm

TEBBADS ▶ tebbad

TEC short for ▶ detective

TECH n technical college

TECHED adj showing slight insanity

TECHIE n person who is skilled in the use of technology ▷ adj relating to or skilled in the use of technology

TECHIER ▶ techy

TECHIES ▶ techie

TECHILY ▶ techy

TECHNIC another word for ▶ technique

TECHNO n type of electronic dance music with a very fast beat

TECHNOS ▶ techno

TECHS ▶ tech

TECHY same as ▶ techie

TECKEL n dachshund

TECKELS ▶ teckel

TECS ▶ tec

TECTA ▶ tectum

TECTAL ▶ tectum

TECTITE same as ▶ tektite

TECTRIX another name for ▶ covert

TECTUM n any roof-like structure in the body, esp the dorsal area of the midbrain

TECTUMS ▶ tectum

TED vb shake out (hay), so as to dry it

TEDDED ▶ ted

TEDDER n machine equipped with a series of small rotating forks for tedding hay

TEDDERS ▶ tedder

TEDDIE same as ▶ teddy

TEDDIES ▶ teddy

TEDDING ▶ ted

TEDDY n teddy bear

TEDIER ▶ tedy

TEDIEST ▶ tedy

TEDIOUS adj causing fatigue or boredom

TEDIUM n monotony

TEDIUMS ▶ tedium

TEDS ▶ ted

TEDY same as ▶ tedious

TEE n small peg from which a golf ball can be played at the start of each hole ▷ vb position (the ball) ready for striking, on or as if on a tee

TEED ▶ tee

TEEING ▶ tee

TEEK adj in Indian English, well

TEEL same as ▶ sesame

TEELS ▶ teel

TEEM vb be full of

TEEMED ▶ teem

TEEMER ▶ teem

TEEMERS ▶ teem

TEEMFUL ▶ teem

TEEMING ▶ teem

TEEMS ▶ teem

TEEN n affliction or woe ▷ n teenager ▷ vb set alight

TEENAGE adj (of a person) aged between 13 and 19 ▷ n this period of time

TEEND same as ▶ tind

TEENDED ▶ teend

TEENDS ▶ teend

TEENE same as ▶ teen

TEENED ▶ teen

TEENER ▶ teen

TEENERS ▶ teen

TEENES ▶ teene

TEENFUL ▶ teen

TEENIER ▶ teeny

TEENING ▶ teen

TEENS ▶ teen

TEENSY same as ▶ teeny

TEENTSY same as ▶ teeny

TEENTY same as ▶ teeny

TEENY adj extremely small

TEEPEE same as ▶ tepee

TEEPEES ▶ teepee

TEER vb smear; daub

TEERED ▶ teer

TEERING ▶ teer

TEERS ▶ teer

TEES ▶ tee

TEETER vb wobble or move unsteadily

T

TEETERS ▶ teeter
TEETH ▶ tooth
TEETHE vb (of a baby) grow his or her first teeth
TEETHED ▶ teethe
TEETHER n object for an infant to bite on during teething
TEETHES ▶ teethe
TEF n annual grass, of NE Africa, grown for its grain
TEFF same as ▶ tef
TEFFS ▶ teff
TEFLON n a trademark for polytetrafluoroethylene when used in nonstick cooking vessels
TEFLONS ▶ teflon
TEFS ▶ tef
TEG n two-year-old sheep
TEGG same as ▶ teg
TEGGS ▶ tegg
TEGMEN n either of the leathery forewings of the cockroach and related insects
TEGMINA ▶ tegmen
TEGS ▶ teg
TEGU n large South American lizard
TEGUA n type of moccasin
TEGUAS ▶ tegua
TEGULA n one of a pair of coverings of the forewings of certain insects
TEGULAE ▶ tegula
TEGULAR adj of, relating to, or resembling a tile or tiles
TEGUMEN same as ▶ tegmen
TEGUS ▶ tegu
TEHR same as ▶ tahr
TEHRS ▶ tehr
TEHSIL n administrative region in some S Asian countries
TEHSILS ▶ tehsil
TEIID n member of the Teiidae family of lizards
TEIIDS ▶ teiid
TEIL n lime tree
TEILS ▶ teil
TEIN n monetary unit of Kazakhstan
TEIND Scots and northern English word for ▶ tithe
TEINDED ▶ teind
TEINDS ▶ teind
TEINS ▶ tein
TEKKIE same as ▶ techie
TEKKIES ▶ tekkie
TEKTITE n small dark glassy object found in several

areas around the world, thought to be a product of meteorite impact
TEL same as ▶ tell
TELA n any delicate tissue or weblike structure
TELAE ▶ tela
TELAMON n column in the form of a male figure, used to support an entablature
TELARY adj capable of spinning a web
TELCO n telecommunications company
TELCOS ▶ telco
TELD same as ▶ tauld
TELE same as ▶ telly
TELECOM n telecommunications
TELEDU n badger of SE Asia and Indonesia, having dark brown hair with a white stripe along the back and producing a fetid secretion from the anal glands when attacked
TELEDUS ▶ teledu
TELEFAX another word for ▶ fax
TELEGA n rough four-wheeled cart used in Russia
TELEGAS ▶ telega
TELEMAN n noncommissioned officer in the US navy, usually charged with communications duties
TELEMEN ▶ teleman
TELEOST n bony fish with rayed fins and a swim bladder ▷ adj of, relating to, or belonging to this type of fish
TELEPIC n feature-length film made for television
TELERAN n electronic navigational aid in which the image of a ground-based radar system is televised to aircraft in flight so that a pilot can see the position of his aircraft in relation to others
TELERGY n name for the form of energy supposedly transferred during telepathy
TELES ▶ tele
TELESES ▶ telesis
TELESIS n purposeful use of natural and social

processes to obtain specific social goals
TELESM n talisman
TELESMS ▶ telesm
TELETEX n international means of communicating text between a variety of terminals
TELEX n international communication service using teleprinters ▷ vb transmit by telex
TELEXED ▶ telex
TELEXES ▶ telex
TELFER n an overhead transport system
TELFERS ▶ telfer
TELFORD n road built using a method favoured by Thomas Telford (1757-1834)
TELIA ▶ telium
TELIAL ▶ telium
TELIC adj directed or moving towards some goal
TELIUM n spore-producing body of some rust fungi in which the teliospores are formed
TELL vb make known in words ▷ n large mound resulting from the accumulation of rubbish on a long-settled site, esp one with mudbrick buildings, particularly in the Middle East
TELLAR same as ▶ tiller
TELLARS ▶ tellar
TELLEN same as ▶ tellin
TELLENS ▶ tellen
TELLER n narrator ▷ vb (of a plant) to produce tillers
TELLERS ▶ teller
TELLIES ▶ telly
TELLIN n slim marine bivalve molluscs that live in intertidal sand
TELLING ▶ tell
TELLINS ▶ tellin
TELLS ▶ tell
TELLUS n earth
TELLY n television
TELLYS ▶ telly
TELNET n computer system allowing one user to access remotely other computers on the same network ▷ vb use a telnet system
TELNETS ▶ telnet
TELOI ▶ telos
TELOME n fundamental unit of a plant's structure

TELOMES ▶ telome
TELOMIC ▶ telome
TELOS *n* objective; ultimate purpose
TELPHER *same as* > telferage
TELS ▶ tel
TELSON *n* last segment or an appendage on the last segment of the body of crustaceans and arachnids
TELSONS ▶ telson
TELT *same as* ▶ tauld
TEMBLOR *n* earthquake or earth tremor
TEME *old variant of* ▶ team
TEMED ▶ teme
TEMENE ▶ temenos
TEMENOS *n* sacred area, esp one surrounding a temple
TEMES ▶ teme
TEMP *same as* > temporary
TEMPED ▶ temp
TEMPEH *n* fermented soya beans
TEMPEHS ▶ tempeh
TEMPER *n* outburst of anger ▷ *vb* make less extreme
TEMPERA *n* painting medium for powdered pigments
TEMPERS ▶ temper
TEMPEST *n* violent storm ▷ *vb* agitate or disturb violently
TEMPI ▶ tempo
TEMPING ▶ temp
TEMPLAR *n* lawyer, esp a barrister, who lives or has chambers in the Inner or Middle Temple in London
TEMPLE *n* building for worship
TEMPLED ▶ temple
TEMPLES ▶ temple
TEMPLET *same as* > template
TEMPO *n* rate or pace
TEMPORE *adv* in the time of
TEMPOS ▶ tempo
TEMPS ▶ temp
TEMPT *vb* entice (a person) to do something wrong
TEMPTED ▶ tempt
TEMPTER ▶ tempt
TEMPTS ▶ tempt
TEMPURA *n* Japanese dish of seafood or vegetables dipped in batter and deep-fried, often at the table

TEMS *same as* ▶ temse
TEMSE *vb* sieve
TEMSED ▶ temse
TEMSES ▶ temse
TEMSING ▶ temse
TEN *n* one more than nine ▷ *adj* amounting to ten
TENABLE *adj* able to be upheld or maintained
TENABLY ▶ tenable
TENACE *n* holding of two nonconsecutive high cards of a suit, such as the ace and queen
TENACES ▶ tenace
TENAIL *same as* > tenaille
TENAILS ▶ tenail
TENANCY *n* temporary possession or use of lands or property owned by somebody else, in return for payment
TENANT *n* person who rents land or a building ▷ *vb* hold (land or property) as a tenant
TENANTS ▶ tenant
TENCH *n* freshwater game fish of the carp family
TENCHES ▶ tench
TEND *vb* be inclined
TENDED ▶ tend
TENDENZ *same as* > tendency
TENDER *adj* not tough ▷ *vb* offer ▷ *n* such an offer
TENDERS ▶ tender
TENDING ▶ tend
TENDON *n* strong tissue attaching a muscle to a bone
TENDONS ▶ tendon
TENDRE *n* care
TENDRES ▶ tendre
TENDRIL *n* slender stem by which a climbing plant clings
TENDRON *n* shoot
TENDS ▶ tend
TENDU *n* position in ballet
TENDUS ▶ tendu
TENE *same as* ▶ teen
TENES ▶ tene
TENET *n* doctrine or belief
TENETS ▶ tenet
TENFOLD *n* one tenth
TENGE *n* standard monetary unit of Kazakhstan, divided into 100 tiyn
TENGES ▶ tenge
TENIA *same as* ▶ taenia
TENIAE ▶ tenia

This plural of **tenia**, a kind of hair-ribbon, is another of those 6-letter words which come in useful for dumping a surplus of vowels.

TENIAS ▶ tenia
TENIOID ▶ tenia
TENNE *n* tawny colour
TENNER *n* ten-pound note
TENNERS ▶ tenner
TENNES ▶ tenne
TENNIES ▶ tenny
TENNIS *n* game in which players use rackets to hit a ball back and forth over a net
TENNIST *n* tennis player
TENNO *n* formal title of the Japanese emperor, esp when regarded as a divine religious leader
TENNOS ▶ tenno
TENNY *same as* ▶ tenne
TENON *n* projecting end on a piece of wood fitting into a slot in another ▷ *vb* form a tenon on (a piece of wood)
TENONED ▶ tenon
TENONER ▶ tenon
TENONS ▶ tenon
TENOR *n* (singer with) the second highest male voice ▷ *adj* (of a voice or instrument) between alto and baritone
TENORS ▶ tenor
TENOUR *old variant of* ▶ tenor
TENOURS ▶ tenour
TENPIN *n* one of the pins used in tenpin bowling
TENPINS ▶ tenpin
TENREC *n* small mammal resembling hedgehogs or shrews
TENRECS ▶ tenrec
TENS ▶ ten
TENSE *adj* emotionally strained ▷ *vb* make or become tense ▷ *n* form of a verb showing the time of action
TENSED ▶ tense
TENSELY ▶ tense
TENSER ▶ tense
TENSES ▶ tense
TENSEST ▶ tense
TENSILE *adj* of tension
TENSING ▶ tense
TENSION *n* hostility or suspense ▷ *vb* tighten

TENSITY *rare word for* ▶ **tension**

TENSIVE *adj* of or causing tension or strain

TENSON *n* type of French lyric poem

TENSONS ▶ **tenson**

TENSOR *n* any muscle that can cause a part to become firm or tense

TENSORS ▶ **tensor**

TENT *n* portable canvas shelter ▷ *vb* camp in a tent

TENTAGE *n* tents collectively

TENTED ▶ **tent**

TENTER ▶ **tent**

TENTERS ▶ **tent**

TENTFUL *n* number of people or objects that can fit in a tent

TENTH *n* (of) number ten in a series ▷ *adj* coming after the ninth in numbering or counting order, position, time, etc ▷ *adv* after the ninth person, position, event, etc

TENTHLY *same as* ▶ **tenth**

TENTHS ▶ **tenth**

TENTIE *adj* wary

TENTIER ▶ **tentie**

TENTIGO *n* morbid preoccupation with sex

TENTING ▶ **tent**

TENTS ▶ **tent**

TENTY *same as* ▶ **tentie**

TENUE *n* deportment

TENUES ▶ **tenuis**

TENUIS *n* (in the grammar of classical Greek) any of the voiceless stops as represented by kappa, pi, or tau (k, p, t)

TENUITY ▶ **tenuous**

TENUOUS *adj* slight or flimsy

TENURE *n* (period of) the holding of an office or position ▷ *vb* to assign a tenured position to

TENURED *adj* having tenure of office

TENURES ▶ **tenure**

TENUTI ▶ **tenuto**

TENUTO *adv* (of a note) to be held for or beyond its full time value ▷ *vb* note sustained thus

TENUTOS ▶ **tenuto**

TENZON *same as* ▶ **tenson**

TENZONS ▶ **tenzon**

TEOPAN *n* enclosure

surrounding a teocalli

TEOPANS ▶ **teopan**

TEPA *n* type of tree native to South America

TEPAL *n* any of the subdivisions of a perianth that is not clearly differentiated into calyx and corolla

TEPALS ▶ **tepal**

TEPAS ▶ **tepa**

TEPEE *n* cone-shaped tent, formerly used by Native Americans

TEPEES ▶ **tepee**

TEPEFY *vb* make or become tepid

TEPHRA *n* solid matter ejected during a volcanic eruption

TEPHRAS ▶ **tephra**

TEPID *adj* slightly warm

TEPIDER ▶ **tepid**

TEPIDLY ▶ **tepid**

TEPOY *same as* ▶ **teapoy**

TEPOYS ▶ **tepoy**

TEQUILA *n* Mexican alcoholic drink

TERAI *n* felt hat with a wide brim worn in subtropical regions

TERAIS ▶ **terai**

TERAOHM *n* unit of resistance equal to 10^{12} ohms

TERAPH *n* any of various small household gods or images venerated by ancient Semitic peoples

TERAS *n* monstrosity; teratism

TERATA ▶ **teras**

TERBIA *n* amorphous white insoluble powder

TERBIAS ▶ **terbia**

TERBIC ▶ **terbium**

TERBIUM *n* rare metallic element

TERCE *n* third of the seven canonical hours of the divine office, originally fixed at the third hour of the day, about 9 am

TERCEL *n* male falcon or hawk, esp as used in falconry

TERCELS ▶ **tercel**

TERCES ▶ **terce**

TERCET *n* group of three lines of verse that rhyme together or are connected by rhyme with adjacent groups of three lines

TERCETS ▶ **tercet**

TERCIO *n* regiment of Spanish or Italian infantry

TERCIOS ▶ **tercio**

TEREBIC *adj as in* **terebic acid** white crystalline carboxylic acid produced by the action of nitric acid on turpentin

TEREBRA *n* ancient Roman device used for boring holes in defensive walls

TEREDO *n* marine mollusc that bores into and destroys submerged timber

TEREDOS ▶ **teredo**

TEREFA *same as* ▶ **tref**

TEREFAH *same as* ▶ **tref**

TEREK *n* type of sandpiper

TEREKS ▶ **terek**

TERES *n* shoulder muscle

TERETE *adj* (esp of plant parts) smooth and usually cylindrical and tapering

TERETES ▶ **terete**

TERF *old variant of* ▶ **turf**

TERFE *old variant of* ▶ **turf**

TERFES ▶ **terfe**

TERFS ▶ **terf**

TERGA ▶ **tergum**

TERGAL ▶ **tergum**

TERGITE *n* constituent part of a tergum

TERGUM *n* cuticular plate covering the dorsal surface of a body segment of an arthropod

TERM *n* word or expression ▷ *vb* name or designate

TERMED ▶ **term**

TERMER *same as* ▶ **termor**

TERMERS ▶ **termer**

TERMING ▶ **term**

TERMINI > **terminus**

TERMITE *n* white antlike insect that destroys timber

TERMLY *n* publication issued once a term

TERMOR *n* person who holds an estate for a term of years or until he dies

TERMORS ▶ **termor**

TERMS ▶ **term**

TERN *n* gull-like sea bird with a forked tail and pointed wings

TERNAL ▶ **tern**

TERNARY *adj* consisting of three parts ▷ *n* group of three

TERNATE *adj* (esp of a leaf) consisting of three leaflets or other parts

TERNE *n* alloy of lead containing tin (10–20 per cent) and antimony (1.5–2 per cent) ▷ *vb* coat with this alloy
TERNED ▶ **terne**
TERNES ▶ **terne**
TERNING ▶ **terne**
TERNION *n* group of three
TERNS ▶ **tern**
TERPENE *n* any one of a class of unsaturated hydrocarbons, such as the carotenes, that are found in the essential oils of many plants
TERRA *n* (in legal contexts) earth or land
TERRACE *n* row of houses built as one block ▷ *vb* form into or provide with a terrace
TERRAE ▶ **terra**
TERRAIN *same as* ▶ **terrane**
TERRANE *n* series of rock formations, esp one having a prevalent type of rock
TERRAS *same as* ▶ **trass**
TERREEN *old variant of* ▶ **tureen**
TERRENE *adj* of or relating to the earth ▷ *n* land
TERRET *n* either of the two metal rings on a harness saddle through which the reins are passed
TERRETS ▶ **terret**
TERRIER *n* any of various breeds of small active dog
TERRIES ▶ **terry**
TERRIFY *vb* fill with fear
TERRINE *n* earthenware dish with a lid
TERRIT *same as* ▶ **terret**
TERRITS ▶ **territ**
TERROIR *n* combination of factors, including soil, climate, and environment, that gives a wine its distinctive character
TERROR *n* great fear
TERRORS ▶ **terror**
TERRY *n* fabric with small loops covering both sides, used esp for making towels
TERSE *adj* neat and concise
TERSELY ▶ **terse**
TERSER ▶ **terse**
TERSEST ▶ **terse**
TERSION *n* action of rubbing off or wiping
TERTIA *same as* ▶ **tercio**
TERTIAL *same as* > **tertiary**

TERTIAN *adj* (of a fever or the symptoms of a disease, esp malaria) occurring every other day ▷ *n* tertian fever or symptoms
TERTIAS ▶ **tertia**
TERTIUM *adj as in* **tertium quid** unknown or indefinite thing related in some way to two known or definite things, but distinct from both
TERTIUS *n* third (in a group)
TERTS *n* card game using 32 cards
TES ▶ **te**
TESLA *n* derived SI unit of magnetic flux density equal to a flux of 1 weber in an area of 1 square metre.
TESLAS ▶ **tesla**
TESSERA *n* small square tile used in mosaics
TEST *vb* try out to ascertain the worth, capability, or endurance of ▷ *n* critical examination
TESTA *n* hard outer layer of a seed
TESTACY ▶ **testate**
TESTAE ▶ **testa**
TESTATE *adj* having left a valid will ▷ *n* person who dies and leaves a legally valid will
TESTE *n* witness
TESTED ▶ **test**
TESTEE *n* person subjected to a test
TESTEES ▶ **testee**
TESTER *n* person or thing that tests or is used for testing
TESTERN *vb* give (someone) a teston
TESTERS ▶ **tester**
TESTES ▶ **testis**
TESTIER ▶ **testy**
TESTIFY *vb* give evidence under oath
TESTILY ▶ **testy**
TESTING ▶ **test**
TESTIS *same as* > **testicle**
TESTON *n* French silver coin of the 16th century
TESTONS ▶ **teston**
TESTOON *same as* ▶ **teston**
TESTRIL *same as* > **testrill**
TESTS ▶ **test**
TESTUDO *n* form of shelter used by the ancient Roman Army for protection against attack from above,

consisting either of a mobile arched structure or of overlapping shields held by the soldiers over their heads
TESTY *adj* irritable or touchy
TET *same as* ▶ **teth**
TETANAL ▶ **tetanus**
TETANIC *adj* of, relating to, or producing tetanus or the spasms of tetanus ▷ *n* tetanic drug or agent
TETANUS *n* acute infectious disease producing muscular spasms and convulsions
TETANY *n* abnormal increase in the excitability of nerves and muscles resulting in spasms of the arms and legs, caused by a deficiency of parathyroid secretion
TETCHED *same as* ▶ **teched**
TETCHY *adj* cross and irritable
TETE *n* elaborate hairstyle
TETES ▶ **tete**
TETH *n* ninth letter of the Hebrew alphabet transliterated as t and pronounced more or less like English t with pharyngeal articulation
TETHER *n* rope or chain for tying an animal to a spot ▷ *vb* tie up with rope
TETHERS ▶ **tether**
TETHS ▶ **teth**
TETOTUM *same as* > **teetotum**
TETRA *n* brightly coloured tropical freshwater fish
TETRACT *n* sponge spicule with four rays
TETRAD *n* group or series of four
TETRADS ▶ **tetrad**
TETRAS ▶ **tetra**
TETRI *n* currency unit of Georgia
TETRIS ▶ **tetri**
TETRODE *n* electronic valve having four electrodes, namely a cathode, control grid, screen grid, and anode
TETRYL *n* yellow crystalline explosive solid used in detonators
TETRYLS ▶ **tetryl**
TETS ▶ **tet**
TETTER *n* blister or pimple ▷ *vb* cause a tetter to erupt (on)

TETTERS ▸ tetter
TETTIX *n* cicada
TEUCH *Scots variant of* ▸ **tough**
TEUCHAT *Scots variant of* ▸ **tewit**
TEUCHER ▸ teuch
TEUGH *same as* ▸ **teuch**
TEUGHER ▸ teugh
TEUGHLY ▸ teugh
TEW *vb* work hard
TEWART *same as* ▸ **tuart**
TEWARTS ▸ tewart
TEWED ▸ tew
TEWEL *n* horse's rectum
TEWELS ▸ tewel
TEWHIT *same as* ▸ **tewit**
TEWHITS ▸ tewhit
TEWING ▸ tew
TEWIT *n* lapwing
TEWITS ▸ tewit
TEWS ▸ tew
TEX *n* unit of weight used to measure yarn density
TEXAS *n* structure on the upper deck of a paddle-steamer containing the officers' quarters and the wheelhouse
TEXASES ▸ texas
TEXES ▸ tex
TEXT *n* main body of a book as distinct from illustrations etc ▷ *vb* send a text message to (someone)
TEXTED ▸ text
TEXTER *n* person who communicates by text messaging
TEXTERS ▸ texter
TEXTILE *n* fabric or cloth, esp woven ▷ *adj* of (the making of) fabrics
TEXTING ▸ text
TEXTS ▸ text
TEXTUAL *adj* of, based on, or relating to, a text or texts
TEXTURE *n* structure, feel, or consistency ▷ *vb* give a distinctive texture to (something)
THACK *Scots word for* ▸ **thatch**
THACKED ▸ thack
THACKS ▸ thack
THAE *Scots word for* ▸ **those**
THAGI *same as* ▸ **thuggee**
THAGIS ▸ thagi
THAIM *Scots variant of* ▸ **them**
THAIRM *n* catgut
THAIRMS ▸ thairm
THALAMI > thalamus

THALE *n as in* **thale cress** a cruciferous wall plant
THALER *n* former German, Austrian, or Swiss silver coin
THALERS ▸ thaler
THALI *n* meal consisting of several small meat or vegetable dishes accompanied by rice, bread, etc, and sometimes by a starter or a sweet
THALIAN *adj* of or relating to comedy
THALIS ▸ thali
THALLI ▸ thallus
THALLIC *adj* of or containing thallium, esp in the trivalent state
THALLUS *n* undifferentiated vegetative body of algae, fungi, and lichens
THALWEG *n* longitudinal outline of a riverbed from source to mouth
THAN *prep* used to introduce the second element of a comparison ▷ *n* old variant of "then" (that time)
THANA *same as* ▸ **tana**
THANAGE *n* state of being a thane
THANAH *same as* ▸ **tana**
THANAHS ▸ thanah
THANAS ▸ thana
THANE *n* Anglo-Saxon or medieval Scottish nobleman
THANES ▸ thane
THANG *n* thing
THANGKA *n* (in Tibetan Buddhism) a religious painting on a scroll
THANGS ▸ thang
THANK *vb* express gratitude to
THANKED ▸ thank
THANKEE *interj* thank you
THANKER ▸ thank
THANKIT *adj as in* **be thankit** thank God
THANKS *pl n* words of gratitude ▷ *interj* polite expression of gratitude
THANNA *same as* ▸ **tana**
THANNAH *same as* ▸ **tana**
THANNAS ▸ thanna
THANS ▸ than
THAR *same as* ▸ **tahr**
THARM *n* stomach
THARMS ▸ tharm

THARS ▸ thar
THAT *pron* used to refer to something already mentioned or familiar, or further away
THATCH *n* roofing material of reeds or straw ▷ *vb* roof (a house) with reeds or straw
THATCHT *old variant of* > **thatched**
THATCHY ▸ thatch
THAW *vb* make or become unfrozen ▷ *n* thawing
THAWED ▸ thaw
THAWER ▸ thaw
THAWERS ▸ thaw
THAWIER ▸ thawy
THAWING ▸ thaw
THAWS ▸ thaw
THAWY *adj* tending to thaw
THE *determiner* definite article, used before a noun
THEATER *same as* ▸ **theatre**
THEATRE *n* place where plays etc are performed
THEAVE *n* young ewe
THEAVES ▸ theave
THEBE *n* inner satellite of Jupiter discovered in 1979
THEBES ▸ thebe
THECA *n* enclosing organ, cell, or spore case, esp the capsule of a moss
THECAE ▸ theca
THECAL ▸ theca
THECATE ▸ theca
THEE *pron* refers to the person addressed: used mainly by members of the Society of Friends ▷ *vb* use the word "thee"
THEED ▸ thee
THEEING ▸ thee
THEEK *Scots variant of* ▸ **thatch**
THEEKED ▸ theek
THEEKS ▸ theek
THEELIN *trade name for* ▸ **estrone**
THEELOL *n* estriol
THEES ▸ thee
THEFT *n* act or an instance of stealing
THEFTS ▸ theft
THEGN *same as* ▸ **thane**
THEGNLY ▸ thegn
THEGNS ▸ thegn
THEIC *n* person who drinks excessive amounts of tea
THEICS ▸ theic
THEIN *old variant of* ▸ **thane**
THEINE *another name for*

> **caffeine**
THEINES ▶ **theine**
THEINS ▶ **thein**
THEIR *determiner* of, belonging to, or associated in some way with them
THEIRS *pron* (thing or person) belonging to them
THEISM *n* belief in a God or gods
THEISMS ▶ **theism**
THEIST ▶ **theism**
THEISTS ▶ **theism**
THELF *n* old contraction of "the element"
THELVES ▶ **thelf**
THEM *pron* refers to people or things other than the speaker or those addressed
THEMA *n* theme
THEMATA ▶ **thema**
THEME *n* main idea or subject being discussed ▷ *vb* design, decorate, arrange, etc, in accordance with a theme
THEMED ▶ **theme**
THEMES ▶ **theme**
THEMING ▶ **theme**
THEN *adv* at that time ▷ *pron* that time ▷ *adj* existing or functioning at that time ▷ *n* that time
THENAGE old variant of ▶ **thanage**
THENAL *adj* of or relating to the thenar
THENAR *n* palm of the hand ▷ *adj* of or relating to the palm or the region at the base of the thumb
THENARS ▶ **thenar**
THENCE *adv* from that place or time
THENS ▶ **then**
THEOCON *n* person who believes that religion should play a greater role in politics
THEOLOG same as > **theologue**
THEORBO *n* obsolete form of the lute, having two necks, one above the other, the second neck carrying a set of unstopped sympathetic bass strings
THEOREM *n* proposition that can be proved by reasoning
THEORIC *n* theory; conjecture
THEORY *n* set of ideas to explain something
THEOW *n* slave in Anglo-Saxon Britain
THEOWS ▶ **theow**
THERAPY *n* curing treatment
THERE *adv* in or to that place ▷ *n* that place
THEREAT *adv* at that point or time
THEREBY *adv* by that means
THEREIN *adv* in or into that place or thing
THEREOF *adv* of or concerning that or it
THEREON *archaic word for* > **thereupon**
THERES ▶ **there**
THERETO *adv* that or it
THERIAC *n* ointment or potion of varying composition, used as an antidote to a poison
THERIAN *n* animal of the class Theria, a subclass of mammals
THERM *n* unit of measurement of heat ▷ *n* public bath
THERMAE *pl n* public baths or hot springs, esp in ancient Greece or Rome
THERMAL *adj* of heat ▷ *n* rising current of warm air
THERME *old variant of* ▶ **therm**
THERMEL *n* type of thermometer measuring temperature by means of thermoelectic current
THERMES ▶ **therme**
THERMIC same as ▶ **thermal**
THERMIT same as > **thermite**
THERMOS *n* trademark term for a type of stoppered vacuum flask used to preserve the temperature of its contents
THERMS ▶ **therm**
THEROID *adj* of, relating to, or resembling a beast
THESE *determiner* form of this used before a plural noun
THESES ▶ **thesis**
THESIS *n* written work submitted for a degree
THESP *short for* > **thespian**
THESPS ▶ **thesp**
THETA *n* eighth letter of the Greek alphabet
THETAS ▶ **theta**
THETCH *old variant spelling of* ▶ **thatch**
THETE *n* member of the lowest order of freeman in ancient Athens
THETES ▶ **thete**
THETHER *old variant of* ▶ **thither**
THETIC *adj* (in classical prosody) of, bearing, or relating to a metrical stress
THEURGY *n* intervention of a divine or supernatural agency in the affairs of man
THEW *n* muscle, esp if strong or well-developed
THEWED *adj* strong; muscular
THEWES ▶ **thew**
THEWIER ▶ **thew**
THEWS ▶ **thew**
THEWY ▶ **thew**
THEY *pron* people or things other than the speaker or people addressed
THIAMIN same as > **thiamine**
THIASUS *n* congregation of people who have gathered to sing and dance in honour of a god
THIAZIN same as > **thiazine**
THIAZOL same as > **thiazole**
THIBET *n* coloured woollen cloth
THIBETS ▶ **thibet**
THIBLE *n* stick for stirring porridge
THIBLES ▶ **thible**
THICK *adj* of great or specified extent from one side to the other ▷ *vb* thicken
THICKED ▶ **thick**
THICKEN *vb* make or become thick or thicker
THICKER ▶ **thick**
THICKET *n* dense growth of small trees
THICKLY ▶ **thick**
THICKS ▶ **thick**
THIEF *n* person who steals
THIEVE *vb* steal
THIEVED ▶ **thieve**
THIEVES ▶ **thieve**
THIG *vb* beg
THIGGER ▶ **thig**
THIGGIT *Scots inflection of* ▶ **thig**
THIGH *n* upper part of the human leg

T

THIGHED adj having thighs

THIGHS ▶ thigh

THIGS ▶ thig

THILK pron that same

THILL another word for ▶ **shaft**

THILLER n horse that goes between the thills of a (cart

THILLS ▶ thill

THIMBLE n cap protecting the end of the finger (when sewing ▷ vb use a thimble

THIN adj not thick ▷ vb make or become thin ▷ adv in order to produce something thin

THINE adj (something) of or associated with you (thou) ▷ pron something belonging to you (thou) ▷ determiner of, belonging to, or associated in some way with you (thou)

THING n material object

THINGS ▶ thing

THINGY adj existing in reality; actual

THINK vb consider, judge, or believe

THINKER ▶ think

THINKS ▶ think

THINLY ▶ thin

THINNED ▶ thin

THINNER ▶ thin

THINS ▶ thin

THIO adj of, or relating to, sulphur

THIOL n any of a class of sulphur-containing organic compounds with the formula RSH, where R is an organic group

THIOLIC ▶ thiol

THIOLS ▶ thiol

THIONIC adj of, relating to, or containing sulphur

THIONIN same as > **thionine**

THIONYL n of, consisting of, or containing the divalent group SO

THIR Scots word for ▶ **these**

THIRAM n antifungal agent

THIRAMS ▶ thiram

THIRD adj of number three in a series ▷ n one of three equal parts ▷ adv in the third place ▷ vb divide (something) by three

THIRDED ▶ third

THIRDLY ▶ third

THIRDS ▶ third

THIRL vb bore or drill

THIRLED ▶ thirl

THIRLS ▶ thirl

THIRST n desire to drink ▷ vb feel thirst

THIRSTS ▶ thirst

THIRSTY adj feeling a desire to drink

THIRTY n three times ten ▷ adj amounting to thirty ▷ determiner amounting to thirty

THIS pron used to refer to a thing or person nearby, just mentioned, or about to be mentioned ▷ adj used to refer to the present time

THISTLE n prickly plant with dense flower heads

THISTLY ▶ thistle

THITHER adv or towards that place

THIVEL same as ▶ **thible**

THIVELS ▶ thivel

THO short for ▶ **though**

THOFT n bench (in a boat) upon which a rower sits

THOFTS ▶ thoft

THOLE n wooden pin set in the side of a rowing boat to serve as a fulcrum for rowing ▷ vb bear or put up with

THOLED ▶ thole

THOLES ▶ thole

THOLI ▶ tholus

THOLING ▶ thole

THOLOI ▶ tholos

THOLOS n dry-stone beehive-shaped tomb associated with the Mycenaean culture of Greece in the 16th to the 12th century BC

THOLUS n domed tomb

THON Scots word for ▶ **yon**

THONDER Scots word for ▶ **yonder**

THONG n thin strip of leather etc

THONGED adj fastened with a thong

THONGS ▶ thong

THORAX n part of the body between the neck and the abdomen

THORIA ▶ thorium

THORIAS ▶ thorium

THORIC ▶ thorium

THORITE n yellow, brownish, or black radioactive mineral consisting of tetragonal thorium silicate. It occurs in coarse granite and is a source of thorium

THORIUM n radioactive metallic element

THORN n prickle on a plant ▷ vb jag or prick (something) as if with a thorn

THORNED ▶ thorn

THORNS ▶ thorn

THORNY adj covered with thorns

THORO (nonstandard) variant spelling of > **thorough**

THORON n radioisotope of radon that is a decay product of thorium

THORONS ▶ thoron

THORP n small village

THORPE same as ▶ **thorp**

THORPES ▶ thorpe

THORPS ▶ thorp

THOSE determiner form of that used before a plural noun

THOTHER pron old contraction of the other

THOU pron used when talking to one person ▷ n one thousandth of an inch ▷ vb use the word thou

THOUED ▶ thou

THOUGH adv nevertheless

THOUGHT ▶ think

THOUING ▶ thou

THOUS ▶ thou

THOWEL old variant of ▶ **thole**

THOWELS ▶ thowel

THOWL old variant of ▶ **thole**

THOWLS ▶ thowel

THRAE same as ▶ **frae**

THRALL n state of being in the power of another person ▷ vb enslave or dominate

THRALLS ▶ thrall

THRANG n throng ▷ vb throng ▷ adj crowded

THRANGS ▶ thrang

THRASH vb beat, esp with a stick or whip ▷ n party

THRAVE n twenty-four sheaves of corn

THRAVES ▶ thrave

THRAW vb twist (something); make something thrawn

THRAWED ▶ thraw

THRAWN adj crooked or twisted

THRAWS ▶ thraw

THREAD n fine strand or

yarn ▷ vb pass thread through

THREADS slang word for ▶ **clothes**

THREADY adj of, relating to, or resembling a thread or threads

THREAP vb scold

THREAPS ▶ **threap**

THREAT n declaration of intent to harm

THREATS ▶ **threat**

THREAVE same as ▶ **thrave**

THREE n one more than two ▷ adj amounting to three ▷ determiner amounting to three

THREEP same as ▶ **threap**

THREEPS ▶ **threep**

THREES ▶ **three**

THRENE n dirge; threnody

THRENES ▶ **threne**

THRENOS n threnody; lamentation

THRESH vb beat (wheat etc) to separate the grain from the husks and straw ▷ n act of threshing

THRETTY nonstandard variant of ▶ **thirty**

THREW ▶ **throw**

THRICE adv three times

THRID old variant of ▶ **thread**

THRIDS ▶ **thrid**

THRIFT n wisdom and caution with money

THRIFTS ▶ **thrift**

THRIFTY adj not wasteful with money

THRILL n sudden feeling of excitement ▷ vb (cause to) feel a thrill

THRILLS ▶ **thrill**

THRILLY adj causing thrills

THRIMSA same as ▶ **thrymsa**

THRIP same as ▶ **thrips**

THRIPS n small slender-bodied insect with piercing mouthparts that feeds on plant sap

THRIST old variant of ▶ **thirst**

THRISTS ▶ **thrist**

THRISTY ▶ **thrist**

THRIVE vb flourish or prosper

THRIVED ▶ **thrive**

THRIVEN ▶ **thrive**

THRIVER ▶ **thrive**

THRIVES ▶ **thrive**

THRO same as ▶ **through**

THROAT n passage from the mouth and nose to the stomach and lungs ▷ vb vocalize in the throat

THROATS ▶ **throat**

THROATY adj (of the voice) hoarse

THROB vb pulsate repeatedly ▷ n throbbing

THROBS ▶ **throb**

THROE n pang or pain ▷ n endure throes

THROED ▶ **throe**

THROES pl n violent pangs or pains

THROMBI > **thrombus**

THRONE n ceremonial seat of a monarch or bishop ▷ vb place or be placed on a throne

THRONED ▶ **throne**

THRONES ▶ **throne**

THRONG vb crowd ▷ n great number of people or things crowded together ▷ adj busy

THRONGS ▶ **throng**

THROUGH prep from end to end or side to side of ▷ adj finished

THROVE ▶ **thrive**

THROW vb hurl through the air ▷ n throwing

THROWE old variant of ▶ **throe**

THROWER ▶ **throw**

THROWES ▶ **throwe**

THROWN ▶ **throw**

THROWS ▶ **throw**

THRU same as ▶ **through**

THRUM vb strum rhythmically but without expression on (a musical instrument) ▷ n in textiles, unwoven ends of wap thread

THRUMMY adj made of thrums

THRUMS ▶ **thrum**

THRUPUT n quantity of raw material or information processed in a given period

THRUSH n brown songbird

THRUST vb push forcefully ▷ n forceful stab

THRUSTS ▶ **thrust**

THRUTCH n narrow, fast-moving stream ▷ vb thrust

THRUWAY n thoroughfare

THRYMSA n gold coin used in Anglo-Saxon England

THUD n dull heavy sound ▷ vb make such a sound

THUDDED ▶ **thud**

THUDS ▶ **thud**

THUG n violent man, esp a criminal

THUGGEE n methods and practices of the thugs of India

THUGGO n tough and violent person

THUGGOS ▶ **thuggo**

THUGS ▶ **thug**

THUJA n coniferous tree of North America and East Asia, with scalelike leaves, small cones, and an aromatic wood

THUJAS ▶ **thuja**

THULIA n oxide of thulium

THULIAS ▶ **thulia**

THULITE n rose-coloured zoisite sometimes incorporated into jewellery

THULIUM n malleable ductile silvery-grey element

THUMB n short thick finger set apart from the others ▷ vb touch or handle with the thumb

THUMBED ▶ **thumb**

THUMBS ▶ **thumb**

THUMBY adj clumsy; uncoordinated

THUMP n (sound of) a dull heavy blow ▷ vb strike heavily

THUMPED ▶ **thump**

THUMPER ▶ **thump**

THUMPS ▶ **thump**

THUNDER n loud noise accompanying lightning ▷ vb rumble with thunder

THUNK another word for ▶ **thud**

THUNKED ▶ **thunk**

THUNKS ▶ **thunk**

THURIFY vb burn incense near or before an altar, shrine, etc

THURL same as ▶ **thirl**

THURLS ▶ **thurl**

THUS adv in this manner ▷ n aromatic gum resin

THUSES ▶ **thus**

THUSLY adv in such a way; thus

THUYA same as ▶ **thuja**

THUYAS ▶ **thuya**

THWACK n whack ▷ vb beat with something flat ▷ interj exclamation imitative of this sound

THWACKS ▶ **thwack**

T

THWAITE n piece of land cleared from forest or reclaimed from wasteland

THWART vb foil or frustrate ▷ n seat across a boat ▷ adj passing or being situated across ▷ adv across

THWARTS ▶ thwart

THY adj of or associated with you (thou) ▷ determiner belonging to or associated in some way with you (thou)

THYINE adj of relating to the sandarac tree

THYLOSE old variant of ▶ tylosis

THYME n aromatic herb

THYMES ▶ thyme

THYMEY ▶ thyme

THYMI ▶ thymus

THYMIC adj of or relating to the thymus

THYMIER ▶ thyme

THYMINE n white crystalline pyrimidine base found in DNA

THYMOL n substance obtained from thyme, used as an antiseptic

THYMOLS ▶ thymol

THYMUS n small gland at the base of the neck

THYMY ▶ thyme

THYROID n (of) a gland in the neck controlling body growth ▷ adj of or relating to the thyroid gland

THYRSE n type of inflorescence, occurring in the lilac and grape, in which the main branch is racemose and the lateral branches cymose

THYRSES ▶ thyrse

THYRSI ▶ thyrsus

THYRSUS same as ▶ thyrse

THYSELF pron reflexive form of thou

TI same as ▶ te

TIAN n traditional French vegetable stew or earthenware dish it is cooked in

TIANS ▶ tian

TIAR same as ▶ tiara

TIARA n semicircular jewelled headdress

TIARAED ▶ tiara

TIARAS ▶ tiara

TIARS ▶ tiar

TIBIA n inner bone of the lower leg

TIBIAE ▶ tibia

TIBIAL ▶ tibia

TIBIAS ▶ tibia

TIC n spasmodic muscular twitch

TICAL n former standard monetary unit of Thailand, replaced by the baht in 1928

TICALS ▶ tical

TICCA adj (of a thing or the services of a person) having been acquired for temporary use in exchange for payment

TICCED ▶ tic

TICCING ▶ tic

TICE vb tempt or allure; entice

TICED ▶ tice

TICES ▶ tice

TICH same as ▶ titch

TICHES ▶ tich

TICHIER ▶ tichy

TICHY same as ▶ titchy

TICING ▶ tice

TICK n mark (✓) used to check off or indicate the correctness of something ▷ vb mark with a tick

TICKED ▶ tick

TICKEN same as ▶ ticking

TICKENS ▶ ticken

TICKER n heart

TICKERS ▶ ticker

TICKET n card or paper entitling the holder to admission, travel, etc ▷ vb attach or issue a ticket to

TICKETS pl n death or ruin

TICKEY n South African threepenny piece, which was replaced by the five-cent coin in 1961

TICKEYS ▶ tickey

TICKIES ▶ ticky

TICKING n strong material for mattress covers

TICKLE vb touch or stroke (a person) to produce laughter ▷ n tickling

TICKLED ▶ tickle

TICKLER n difficult or delicate problem

TICKLES ▶ tickle

TICKLY ▶ tickle

TICKS ▶ tick

TICKY same as ▶ tickey

TICS ▶ tic

TICTAC same as > ticktack

TICTACS ▶ tictac

TICTOC same as > ticktock

TICTOCS ▶ tictoc

TID n girl

TIDAL adj (of a river, lake, or sea) having tides

TIDALLY ▶ tidal

TIDBIT same as ▶ titbit

TIDBITS ▶ tidbit

TIDDIER ▶ tiddy

TIDDIES ▶ tiddy

TIDDLE vb busy oneself with inconsequential tasks

TIDDLED ▶ tiddle

TIDDLER n very small fish

TIDDLES ▶ tiddle

TIDDLEY same as ▶ tiddly

TIDDLY adj tiny ▷ n alcoholic beverage

TIDDY n four of trumps in the card game gleek

TIDE n rise and fall of the sea caused by the gravitational pull of the sun and moon ▷ vb carry or be carried with or as if with the tide

TIDED ▶ tide

TIDERIP same as ▶ riptide

TIDES ▶ tide

TIDEWAY n strong tidal current or its channel, esp the tidal part of a river

TIDIED ▶ tidy

TIDIER ▶ tidy

TIDIERS ▶ tidy

TIDIES ▶ tidy

TIDIEST ▶ tidy

TIDILY ▶ tidy

TIDING ▶ tide

TIDINGS pl n news

TIDS ▶ tid

TIDY adj neat and orderly ▷ vb put in order ▷ n small container for odds and ends

TIDYING ▶ tidy

TIE vb fasten or be fastened with string, rope, etc ▷ n long narrow piece of material worn knotted round the neck

TIEBACK n length of cord, ribbon, or other fabric used for tying a curtain to one side

TIED ▶ tie

TIEING same as ▶ tie

TIELESS ▶ tie

TIEPIN n ornamental pin used to pin the two ends of a tie to a shirt

TIEPINS ▶ tiepin

TIER n one of a set of rows placed one above and behind the other ▷ vb be or arrange in tiers

TIERCE same as ▶ terce

TIERCED adj (of a shield)

divided into three sections of similar size but different colour

TIERCEL same as ▸**tercel**

TIERCES ▸**tierce**

TIERCET same as ▸**tercet**

TIERED ▸**tier**

TIERING ▸**tier**

TIERS ▸**tier**

TIES ▸**tie**

TIETAC n fastener for holding a tie in place

TIETACK same as ▸**tietac**

TIETACS ▸**tietac**

TIFF n petty quarrel ▷ vb have or be in a tiff

TIFFANY n sheer fine gauzy fabric

TIFFED ▸**tiff**

TIFFIN n (in India) a light meal, esp at midday ▷ vb take tiffin

TIFFING ▸**tiff**

TIFFINS ▸**tiffin**

TIFFS ▸**tiff**

TIFOSI ▸**tifoso**

TIFOSO n fanatical fan (esp an Italian F1 fan)

TIFT Scots variant of ▸**tiff**

TIFTED ▸**tift**

TIFTING ▸**tift**

TIFTS ▸**tift**

TIG n child's game

TIGE n trunk of an architectural column

TIGER n large yellow-and-black striped Asian cat

TIGERLY adj of or like a tiger

TIGERS ▸**tiger**

TIGERY ▸**tiger**

TIGES ▸**tige**

TIGGED ▸**tig**

TIGGING ▸**tig**

TIGHT adj stretched or drawn taut ▷ adv in a close, firm, or secure way

TIGHTEN vb make or become tight or tighter

TIGHTER ▸**tight**

TIGHTLY ▸**tight**

TIGHTS pl n one-piece clinging garment covering the body from the waist to the feet

TIGLIC adj as in **tiglic acid** syrupy liquid or crystalline colourless unsaturated carboxylic acid

TIGLON same as ▸**tigon**

TIGLONS ▸**tiglon**

TIGON n hybrid offspring of a male tiger and a female lion

TIGONS ▸**tigon**

TIGRESS n female tiger

TIGRINE adj of, characteristic of, or resembling a tiger

TIGRISH ▸**tiger**

TIGROID adj resembling a tiger

TIGS ▸**tig**

TIK n South African slang term for crystal meth

TIKA same as ▸**tikka**

TIKANGA n Māori ways or customs

TIKAS ▸**tika**

TIKI n small carving of a grotesque person worn as a pendant ▷ vb take a scenic tour around an area

TIKIED ▸**tiki**

TIKIING ▸**tiki**

TIKIS ▸**tiki**

TIKKA adj marinated in spices and dry-roasted ▷ n act of marking a tikka on the forehead

TIKKAS ▸**tikka**

TIKS ▸**tik**

TIL another name for ▸**sesame**

TILAK n coloured spot or mark worn by Hindus, esp on the forehead, often indicating membership of a religious sect, caste, etc, or (in the case of a woman) marital status

TILAKS ▸**tilak**

TILAPIA n type of fish

TILBURY n light two-wheeled horse-drawn open carriage, seating two people

TILDE n mark (~) used in Spanish to indicate that the letter 'n' is to be pronounced in a particular way

TILDES ▸**tilde**

TILE n flat piece of ceramic, plastic, etc used to cover a roof, floor, or wall ▷ vb cover with tiles

TILED ▸**tile**

TILER ▸**tile**

TILERS ▸**tile**

TILERY n place where tiles are produced

TILES ▸**tile**

TILING n tiles collectively

TILINGS ▸**tiling**

TILL prep until ▷ vb cultivate (land) ▷ n drawer for money, usu in a cash

register ▷ n unstratified glacial deposit consisting of rock fragments of various sizes

TILLAGE n act, process, or art of tilling

TILLED ▸**till**

TILLER n on boats, a handle fixed to the top of a rudderpost to serve as a lever in steering ▷ vb use a tiller

TILLERS ▸**till**

TILLIER ▸**till**

TILLING ▸**till**

TILLITE n rock formed from hardened till

TILLS ▸**till**

TILLY ▸**till**

TILS ▸**til**

TILT vb slant at an angle ▷ n slope

TILTED ▸**tilt**

TILTER ▸**tilt**

TILTERS ▸**tilt**

TILTH n (condition of) land that has been tilled

TILTHS ▸**tilth**

TILTING ▸**tilt**

TILTS ▸**tilt**

TIMARAU same as ▸**tamarau**

TIMBAL n type of kettledrum

TIMBALE n mixture of meat, fish, etc, in a rich sauce, cooked in a mould lined with potato or pastry

TIMBALS ▸**timbal**

TIMBER n wood as a building material ▷ adj made out of timber ▷ vb provide with timbers ▷ interj lumberjack's shouted warning when a tree is about to fall

TIMBERS ▸**timber**

TIMBERY ▸**timber**

TIMBO n Amazonian vine from which a useful insecticide can be derived

TIMBOS ▸**timbo**

TIMBRAL adj relating to timbre

TIMBRE n distinctive quality of sound of a voice or instrument

TIMBREL n tambourine

TIMBRES ▸**timbre**

TIME n past, present, and future as a continuous whole ▷ vb note the time taken by

T

TIMED ▶ **time**

TIMELY *adj* at the appropriate time ▷ *adv* at the right or an appropriate time

TIMEOUS *adj* in good time

TIMEOUT *n* in sport, interruption in play during which players rest, discuss tactics, or make substitutions

TIMER *n* device for measuring time, esp a switch or regulator that causes a mechanism to operate at a specific time

TIMERS ▶ **timer**

TIMES ▶ **time**

TIMID *adj* easily frightened

TIMIDER ▶ **timid**

TIMIDLY ▶ **timid**

TIMING *n* ability to judge when to do or say something so as to make the best effect

TIMINGS ▶ **timing**

TIMIST *n* one concerned with time

TIMISTS ▶ **timist**

TIMOLOL *n* relaxant medicine used (for example) to reduce blood pressure

TIMON *n* apparatus by which a vessel is steered

TIMONS ▶ **timon**

TIMOTHY *n as in* **timothy grass** perennial grass of temperate regions, having erect stiff stems and cylindrical flower spikes: grown for hay and pasture

TIMOUS *same as* ▶ **timeous**

TIMPANA *n* traditional Maltese baked pasta and pastry dish

TIMPANI *pl n* set of kettledrums

TIMPANO *n* kettledrum

TIMPS *same as* ▶ **timpani**

TIN *n* soft metallic element ▷ *vb* put (food) into tins

TINA *n* (slang) crystal meth

TINAJA *n* large jar for cooling water

TINAJAS ▶ **tinaja**

TINAMOU *n* type of bird of Central and S America, with small wings, a heavy body, and an inconspicuous plumage

TINAS ▶ **tina**

TINCAL *another name for*
▶ **borax**

TINCALS ▶ **tincal**

TINCHEL *n* in Scotland, a circle of deer hunters who gradually close in on their quarry

TINCT *vb* tint ▷ *adj* tinted or coloured

TINCTED ▶ **tinct**

TINCTS ▶ **tinct**

TIND *vb* set alight

TINDAL *n* petty officer

TINDALS ▶ **tindal**

TINDED ▶ **tind**

TINDER *n* dry easily-burning material used to start a fire

TINDERS ▶ **tinder**

TINDERY ▶ **tinder**

TINDING ▶ **tind**

TINDS ▶ **tind**

TINE *n* prong of a fork or antler ▷ *vb* lose

TINEA *n* any fungal skin disease, esp ringworm

TINEAL ▶ **tinea**

TINEAS ▶ **tinea**

TINED ▶ **tine**

TINEID *n* type of moth of the family which includes the clothes moths

TINEIDS ▶ **tineid**

TINES ▶ **tine**

TINFOIL *n* paper-thin sheet of metal, used for wrapping foodstuffs

TINFUL *n* contents of a tin or the amount a tin will hold

TINFULS ▶ **tinful**

TING *same as* ▶ **thing**

TINGE *n* slight tint ▷ *vb* give a slight tint or trace to

TINGED ▶ **tinge**

TINGES ▶ **tinge**

TINGING ▶ **tinge**

TINGLE *n* (feel) a prickling or stinging sensation ▷ *vb* feel a mild prickling or stinging sensation, as from cold or excitement

TINGLED ▶ **tingle**

TINGLER ▶ **tingle**

TINGLES ▶ **tingle**

TINGLY ▶ **tingle**

TINGS ▶ **ting**

TINHORN *n* cheap pretentious person, esp a gambler with extravagant claims ▷ *adj* cheap and showy

TINIER ▶ **tiny**

TINIES *pl n* small children

TINIEST ▶ **tiny**

TINILY ▶ **tiny**

TINING ▶ **tine**

TINK shortened form of
▶ **tinker**

TINKED ▶ **tink**

TINKER *n* derogatory term for travelling mender of pots and pans ▷ *vb* fiddle with (an engine etc) in an attempt to repair it

TINKERS ▶ **tinker**

TINKING ▶ **tink**

TINKLE *vb* ring with a high tinny sound like a small bell ▷ *n* this sound or action

TINKLED ▶ **tinkle**

TINKLER *same as* ▶ **tinker**

TINKLES ▶ **tinkle**

TINKLY ▶ **tinkle**

TINKS ▶ **tink**

TINLIKE ▶ **tin**

TINMAN *n* one who works with tin or tin plate

TINMEN ▶ **tinman**

TINNED ▶ **tin**

TINNER *n* tin miner

TINNERS ▶ **tinner**

TINNIE *same as* ▶ **tinny**

TINNIER ▶ **tinny**

TINNIES ▶ **tinny**

TINNILY ▶ **tinny**

TINNING ▶ **tin**

TINNY *adj* (of sound) thin and metallic ▷ *n* can of beer

TINPOT *adj* worthless or unimportant ▷ *n* pot made of tin

TINPOTS ▶ **tinpot**

TINS ▶ **tin**

TINSEL *n* decorative metallic strips or threads ▷ *adj* made of or decorated with tinsel ▷ *vb* decorate with or as if with tinsel

TINSELS ▶ **tinsel**

TINSEY *old variant of* ▶ **tinsel**

TINSEYS ▶ **tinsey**

TINT *n* (pale) shade of a colour ▷ *vb* give a tint to

TINTACK *n* tin-plated tack

TINTED ▶ **tint**

TINTER ▶ **tint**

TINTERS ▶ **tint**

TINTIER ▶ **tinty**

TINTING ▶ **tint**

TINTS ▶ **tint**

TINTY *adj* having many tints

TINTYPE *another name for*
> **ferrotype**

TINWARE *n* objects made of tin plate

TINWORK *n* objects made of tin

TINY adj very small

TIP n narrow or pointed end of anything ▷ vb put a tip on

TIPCART n cart that can be tipped to empty out its contents

TIPCAT n game in which a short sharp-ended piece of wood (the cat) is tipped in the air with a stick

TIPCATS ▶ **tipcat**

TIPI variant spelling of ▶ **tepee**

TIPIS ▶ **tipi**

TIPLESS ▶ **tip**

TIPOFF n warning or hint, esp given confidentially and based on inside information

TIPOFFS ▶ **tipoff**

TIPPED ▶ **tip**

TIPPEE n person who receives a tip, esp regarding share prices

TIPPEES ▶ **tippee**

TIPPER n person who gives or leaves a tip

TIPPERS ▶ **tipper**

TIPPET n scarflike piece of fur, often made from a whole animal skin, worn, esp formerly, round a woman's shoulders

TIPPETS ▶ **tippet**

TIPPIER ▶ **tippy**

TIPPING ▶ **tip**

TIPPLE vb drink alcohol habitually, esp in small quantities ▷ n alcoholic drink

TIPPLED ▶ **tipple**

TIPPLER ▶ **tipple**

TIPPLES ▶ **tipple**

TIPPY adj extremely fashionable or stylish

TIPS ▶ **tip**

TIPSIER ▶ **tipsy**

TIPSIFY vb make tipsy

TIPSILY ▶ **tipsy**

TIPSTER n person who sells tips about races

TIPSY adj slightly drunk

TIPT ▶ **tip**

TIPTOE vb walk quietly with the heels off the ground

TIPTOED ▶ **tiptoe**

TIPTOES ▶ **tiptoe**

TIPTOP adj of the highest quality or condition ▷ adv of the highest quality or condition ▷ n best in quality ▷ n very top; pinnacle

TIPTOPS ▶ **tiptop**

TIPULA n crane fly

TIPULAS ▶ **tipula**

TIPUNA n ancestor

TIPUNAS ▶ **tipuna**

TIRADE n long angry speech

TIRADES ▶ **tirade**

TIRAGE n drawing of wine from a barrel prior to bottling

TIRAGES ▶ **tirage**

TIRASSE n mechanism in an organ connecting two pedals, so that both may be depressed at once

TIRE vb reduce the energy of, as by exertion

TIRED adj exhausted

TIREDER ▶ **tired**

TIREDLY ▶ **tired**

TIRES ▶ **tire**

TIRING ▶ **tire**

TIRINGS ▶ **tire**

TIRITI n another name for the Treaty of Waitangi

> A Maori word for treaty. Any 6-letter word that lets you get rid of three Is can't be bad!

TIRITIS ▶ **tiriti**

TIRL vb turn

TIRLED ▶ **tirl**

TIRLING ▶ **tirl**

TIRLS ▶ **tirl**

TIRO same as ▶ **tyro**

TIROES ▶ **tiro**

TIRONIC same as ▶ **tyronic**

TIROS ▶ **tiro**

TIRR vb strip or denude

TIRRED ▶ **tirr**

TIRRING ▶ **tirr**

TIRRIT n panic; scare

TIRRITS ▶ **tirrit**

TIRRS ▶ **tirr**

TIS ▶ **ti**

TISANE n infusion of dried or fresh leaves or flowers, as camomile

TISANES ▶ **tisane**

TISICK n splutter; cough

TISICKS ▶ **tisick**

TISSUAL adj relating to tissue

TISSUE n substance of an animal body or plant ▷ vb weave into tissue

TISSUED ▶ **tissue**

TISSUES ▶ **tissue**

TISSUEY ▶ **tissue**

TISWAS n state of anxiety or excitement

TIT n any of various small songbirds; informal term for a female breast ▷ vb jerk or tug

TITAN n person who is huge, strong, or very important

TITANIA > **titanium**

TITANIC adj huge or very important

TITANIS n large predatory flightless prehistoric bird

TITANS ▶ **titan**

TITBIT n tasty piece of food

TITBITS ▶ **titbit**

TITCH n small person

TITCHES ▶ **titch**

TITCHY adj very small

TITE adj immediately

TITELY adv immediately

TITER same as ▶ **titre**

TITERS ▶ **titer**

TITFER n hat

TITFERS ▶ **titfer**

TITHE n esp formerly, one tenth of one's income or produce paid to the church as a tax ▷ vb charge or pay a tithe

TITHED ▶ **tithe**

TITHER ▶ **tithe**

TITHERS ▶ **tithe**

TITHES ▶ **tithe**

TITHING ▶ **tithe**

TITI n small omnivorous New World monkey of South America, with long beautifully coloured fur and a long nonprehensile tail

TITIAN n reddish gold colour

TITIANS ▶ **titian**

TITIS ▶ **titi**

TITLARK another name for ▶ **pipit**

TITLE n name of a book, film, etc ▷ vb give a title to

TITLED adj aristocratic

TITLER n one who writes titles

TITLERS ▶ **title**

TITLES ▶ **title**

TITLING ▶ **title**

TITLIST n titleholder

TITMAN n (of pigs) the runt of a litter

TITMEN ▶ **titman**

TITMICE > **titmouse**

TITMOSE old spelling of > **titmouse**

TITOKI n New Zealand evergreen tree with a spreading crown and glossy green leaves

TITOKIS ▶ **titoki**

TITRANT n solution in a titration that is added from

a burette to a measured quantity of another solution

TITRATE vb measure the volume or concentration of (a solution) by titration

TITRE n concentration of a solution as determined by titration

TITRES ▸ titre

TITS ▸ tit

TITTED ▸ tit

TITTER vb laugh in a suppressed way ▷ n suppressed laugh

TITTERS ▸ titter

TITTIE n sister; young woman

TITTIES ▸ tittie

TITTING ▸ tit

TITTISH adj testy

TITTLE n very small amount ▷ vb chatter; tattle

TITTLED ▸ tittle

TITTLES ▸ tittle

TITTUP vb prance or frolic ▷ n caper

TITTUPS ▸ tittup

TITTUPY adj spritely; lively

TITTY same as ▸ tittie

TITULAR adj in name only ▷ n bearer of a title

TITULE same as ▸ title

TITULED ▸ titule

TITULES ▸ titule

TITULI ▸ titulus

TITULUS n (in crucifixion) a sign attached to the top of the cross on which were written the condemned man's name and crime

TITUP same as ▸ tittup

TITUPED ▸ titup

TITUPS ▸ titup

TITUPY same as ▸ tittupy

TIVY same as ▸ tantivy

TIX pl n tickets

> **Tix** is an informal word for **tickets**, and of of the key short words for using the X.

TIYIN n monetary unit of Uzbekistan and Kyrgyzstan

TIYINS ▸ tiyin

TIZWAS same as ▸ tiswas

TIZZ same as ▸ tizzy

TIZZES ▸ tizz

TIZZIES ▸ tizzy

TIZZY n confused or agitated state

TMESES ▸ tmesis

TMESIS n interpolation of a

word or group of words between the parts of a compound word

TO prep indicating movement towards, equality or comparison, etc ▷ adv a closed position

TOAD n animal like a large frog

TOADIED ▸ toady

TOADIES ▸ toady

TOADISH ▸ toad

TOADS ▸ toad

TOADY n ingratiating person ▷ vb be ingratiating

TOAST n sliced bread browned by heat ▷ vb brown (bread) by heat

TOASTED ▸ toast

TOASTER ▸ toast

TOASTIE same as ▸ toasty

TOASTS ▸ toast

TOASTY n toasted sandwich ▷ adj tasting or smelling like toast

TOAZE variant spelling of ▸ toze

TOAZED ▸ toaze

TOAZES ▸ toaze

TOAZING ▸ toaze

TOBACCO n plant with large leaves dried for smoking

TOBIES ▸ toby

TOBY n water stopcock at the boundary of a street and house section

TOC n in communications code, signal for letter t

TOCCATA n rapid piece of music for a keyboard instrument

TOCCATE ▸ toccata

TOCHER n dowry ▷ vb give a dowry to

TOCHERS ▸ tocher

TOCK n sound made by a clock ▷ vb (of a clock) make such a sound

TOCKED ▸ tock

TOCKIER ▸ tocky

TOCKING ▸ tock

TOCKS ▸ tock

TOCKY adj muddy

TOCO n punishment

TOCOS ▸ toco

TOCS ▸ toc

TOCSIN n warning signal

TOCSINS ▸ tocsin

TOD n unit of weight, used for wool, etc, usually equal to 28 pounds ▷ vb produce a tod

TODAY n this day ▷ adv on this day

TODAYS ▸ today

TODDE same as ▸ tod

TODDED ▸ tod

TODDES ▸ todde

TODDIES ▸ toddy

TODDING ▸ tod

TODDLE vb walk with short unsteady steps ▷ n act or an instance of toddling

TODDLED ▸ toddle

TODDLER n child beginning to walk

TODDLES ▸ toddle

TODDY n sweetened drink of spirits and hot water

TODIES ▸ tody

TODS ▸ tod

TODY n small bird of the Caribbean, with a red-and-green plumage and long straight bill

TOE n digit of the foot ▷ vb touch or kick with the toe

TOEA n monetary unit of Papua New Guinea, worth one-hundredth of a kina

> This monetary unit of Papua New Guinea is very often played to rid the rack of a surplus of vowels.

TOEAS ▸ toea

TOEBIE n South African slang for sandwich

TOEBIES ▸ toebie

TOECAP n strengthened covering for the toe of a shoe

TOECAPS ▸ toecap

TOECLIP n clip on a bicycle pedal into which the toes are inserted to prevent the foot from slipping

TOED ▸ toe

TOEHOLD n small space on a mountain for supporting the toe of the foot in climbing

TOEIER ▸ toey

> This is the comparative of **toey**, Australian slang for nervous or edgy, and can come in useful for dumping a surplus of vowels.

TOEIEST ▸ toey

TOEING ▸ toe

TOELESS adj not having toes

TOELIKE ▸ toe

TOENAIL n thin hard clear

plate covering part of the upper surface of the end of each toe ▷ vb join (beams) by driving nails obliquely

TOES ▸ toe

TOESHOE n ballet pump with padded toes

TOETOE same as ▸ toitoi

TOETOES ▸ toetoe

TOEY adj (of a person) nervous or anxious

TOFF n well-dressed or upper-class person

TOFFEE n chewy sweet made of boiled sugar

TOFFEES ▸ toffee

TOFFIER ▸ toffy

TOFFIES ▸ toffy

TOFFISH adj belonging to or characteristic of the upper class

TOFFS adj like a toff

TOFFY same as ▸ toffee

TOFORE prep before

TOFT n homestead

TOFTS ▸ toft

TOFU n soft food made from soya-bean curd

TOFUS ▸ tofu

TOFUTTI n tradename for any of a variety of nondairy, soya-based food products, esp frozen desserts

TOG n unit for measuring the insulating power of duvets ▷ vb dress oneself, esp in smart clothes

TOGA n garment worn by citizens of ancient Rome ▷ vb wear a toga

TOGAE ▸ toga

TOGAED ▸ toga

TOGAS ▸ toga

TOGATE adj clad in a toga

TOGATED same as ▸ togate

TOGE old variant of ▸ toga

TOGED ▸ toge

TOGES ▸ toge

TOGGED ▸ tog

TOGGER vb play football ▷ n football player

TOGGERS ▸ togger

TOGGERY n clothes

TOGGING ▸ tog

TOGGLE n small bar-shaped button inserted through a loop for fastening ▷ vb supply or fasten with a toggle or toggles

TOGGLED ▸ toggle

TOGGLER ▸ toggle

TOGGLES ▸ toggle

TOGS ▸ tog

TOGUE n large North American freshwater game fish

TOGUES ▸ togue

TOHEROA n large edible mollusc of New Zealand with a distinctive flavour

TOHO n (to a hunting dog) an instruction to stop

TOHUNGA n Māori priest

TOIL n hard work ▷ vb work hard

TOILE n transparent linen or cotton fabric

TOILED ▸ toil

TOILER ▸ toil

TOILERS ▸ toil

TOILES ▸ toile

TOILET n a bowl connected to a drain for receiving and disposing of urine and faeces ▷ vb go to the toilet

TOILETS ▸ toilet

TOILFUL same as > toilsome

TOILING ▸ toil

TOILS ▸ toil

TOING n as in toing and froing state of going back and forth

TOINGS ▸ toing

TOISE n obsolete French unit of length roughly equal to 2m

TOISECH same as > toiseach

TOISES ▸ toise

TOISON n fleece

TOISONS ▸ toison

TOIT vb walk or move in an unsteady manner, as from old age

TOITED ▸ toit

TOITING ▸ toit

TOITOI n tall grasses with feathery fronds

TOITOIS ▸ toitoi

TOITS ▸ toit

TOKAMAK n reactor used in thermonuclear experiments

TOKAY n small gecko of S and SE Asia, having a retractile claw at the tip of each digit

TOKAYS ▸ tokay

TOKE n draw on a cannabis cigarette ▷ vb take a draw on a cannabis cigarette

TOKED ▸ toke

TOKEN n sign or symbol ▷ adj nominal or slight

TOKENED ▸ token

TOKENS ▸ token

TOKER ▸ toke

TOKERS ▸ toke

TOKES ▸ toke

TOKING ▸ toke

TOKO same as ▸ toco

TOKOMAK variant spelling of ▸ tokamak

TOKOS ▸ toko

TOLA n unit of weight, used in India, equal to 180 ser or 180 grains

TOLAN n white crystalline derivative of acetylene

TOLANE same as ▸ tolan

TOLANES ▸ tolane

TOLANS ▸ tolan

TOLAR n standard monetary unit of Slovenia, divided into 100 stotin

TOLARJI ▸ tolar

TOLARS ▸ tolar

TOLAS ▸ tola

TOLD ▸ tell

TOLE same as ▸ toll

TOLED ▸ tole

TOLEDO n type of sword originally made in Toledo

TOLEDOS ▸ toledo

TOLES ▸ tole

TOLIDIN same as > tolidine

TOLING ▸ tole

TOLINGS ▸ tole

TOLL vb ring (a bell) slowly and regularly, esp to announce a death ▷ n tolling

TOLLAGE same as ▸ toll

TOLLBAR n bar blocking passage of a thoroughfare, raised on payment of a toll

TOLLED ▸ toll

TOLLER ▸ toll

TOLLERS ▸ toller

TOLLEY n large shooting marble used in a game of marbles

TOLLEYS ▸ tolley

TOLLIE same as ▸ tolly

TOLLIES ▸ tolly

TOLLING ▸ toll

TOLLMAN n man who collects tolls

TOLLMEN ▸ tollman

TOLLS ▸ toll

TOLLWAY n road on which users must pay tolls to travel

TOLLY n castrated calf

TOLSEL n tolbooth

TOLSELS ▸ tolsel

TOLSEY n tolbooth

TOLSEYS > tolbooth

TOLT n type of obsolete English writ

T

TOLTER *vb* struggle or move with difficulty, as in mud

TOLTERS ▸ **tolter**

TOLTS ▸ **tolt**

TOLU *n* sweet-smelling balsam obtained from a South American tree, used in medicine and perfume

TOLUATE *n* any salt or ester of any of the three isomeric forms of toluic acid

TOLUENE *n* colourless volatile flammable liquid obtained from petroleum and coal tar

TOLUIC *adj as in* **toluic acid** white crystalline derivative of toluene existing in three isomeric forms

TOLUID *n* white crystalline derivative of glycocoll

TOLUIDE *same as* ▸ **toluid**

TOLUIDS ▸ **toluid**

TOLUOL *another name for* ▸ **toluene**

TOLUOLE *another name for* ▸ **toluene**

TOLUOLS ▸ **toluol**

TOLUS ▸ **tolu**

TOLUYL *n* of, consisting of, or containing any of three isomeric groups $CH_3C_6H_4CO-$, derived from a toluic acid by removal of the hydroxyl group

TOLUYLS ▸ **toluyl**

TOLYL *n* of, consisting of, or containing any of three isomeric groups, $CH_3C_6H_4-$, derived from toluene

TOLYLS ▸ **tolyl**

TOLZEY *n* tolbooth

TOLZEYS ▸ **tolzey**

TOM *n* male cat ▷ *adj* (of an animal) male ▷ *vb* prostitute oneself

TOMAN *n* gold coin formerly issued in Persia

TOMANS ▸ **toman**

TOMATO *n* red fruit used in salads and as a vegetable

TOMB *n* grave

TOMBAC *n* any of various brittle alloys containing copper and zinc and sometimes tin and arsenic: used for making cheap jewellery, etc

TOMBACK *variant spelling of* ▸ **tombac**

TOMBACS ▸ **tombac**

TOMBAK *same as* ▸ **tombac**

TOMBAKS ▸ **tombak**

TOMBAL *adj* like or relating to a tomb

TOMBED ▸ **tomb**

TOMBIC *adj* of or relating to tombs

TOMBING ▸ **tomb**

TOMBOC *n* weapon

TOMBOCS ▸ **tomboc**

TOMBOLA *n* lottery with tickets drawn from a revolving drum

TOMBOLO *n* narrow sand or shingle bar linking a small island with another island or the mainland

TOMBOY *n* girl who acts or dresses like a boy

TOMBOYS ▸ **tomboy**

TOMBS ▸ **tomb**

TOMCAT *vb* (of a man) to be promiscuous

TOMCATS ▸ **tomcat**

TOMCOD *n* small fish resembling the cod

TOMCODS ▸ **tomcod**

TOME *n* large heavy book

TOMENTA ▸ **tomentum**

TOMES ▸ **tome**

TOMFOOL *n* fool ▷ *vb* act the fool

TOMIA ▸ **tomium**

TOMIAL ▸ **tomium**

TOMIUM *n* sharp edge of a bird's beak

TOMMIED ▸ **tommy**

TOMMIES ▸ **tommy**

TOMMY *n* private in the British Army ▷ *vb* (formerly) to exploit workers by paying them in goods rather than in money

TOMO *n* shaft formed by the action of water on limestone or volcanic rock

TOMOS ▸ **tomo**

TOMPION *same as* ▸ **tampion**

TOMPON *same as* ▸ **tampon**

TOMPONS ▸ **tompon**

TOMS ▸ **tom**

TOMTIT *n* small European bird that eats insects and seeds

TOMTITS ▸ **tomtit**

TON *n* unit of weight equal to 2240 pounds or 1016 kilograms (long ton) or, in the US, 2000 pounds or 907 kilograms (short ton); style, distinction

TONAL *adj* written in a key

TONALLY ▸ **tonal**

TONANT *adj* very loud

TONDI ▸ **tondo**

TONDINI ▸ **tondino**

TONDINO *n* small tondo

TONDO *n* circular easel painting or relief carving

TONDOS ▸ **tondo**

TONE *n* sound with reference to its pitch, volume, etc ▷ *vb* harmonize (with)

TONEARM *same as* ▸ **pickup**

TONED ▸ **tone**

TONEME *n* phoneme that is distinguished from another phoneme only by its tone

TONEMES ▸ **toneme**

TONEMIC ▸ **toneme**

TONEPAD *n* keypad used to transmit information by generating tones that can be recognised by a central system as corresponding to particular digits

TONER *n* cosmetic applied to the skin to reduce oiliness

TONERS ▸ **toner**

TONES ▸ **tone**

TONETIC *adj* (of a language) distinguishing words semantically by distinction of tone as well as by other sounds

TONETTE *n* small musical instrument resembling a recorder

TONEY *variant spelling of* ▸ **tony**

TONG *n* (formerly) a secret society of Chinese Americans ▷ *vb* gather or seize with tongs ▷ *n* (formerly) a Chinese secret society

TONGA *n* light two-wheeled vehicle used in rural areas of India

TONGAS ▸ **tonga**

TONGED ▸ **tong**

TONGER *n* one who uses tongs to gather oysters

TONGERS ▸ **tonger**

TONGING ▸ **tong**

TONGMAN *another word for* ▸ **tonger**

TONGMEN ▸ **tongman**

TONGS *pl n* large pincers for grasping and lifting

TONGUE *n* muscular organ in the mouth, used in speaking and tasting ▷ *vb*

use the tongue
TONGUED ▶ **tongue**
TONGUES ▶ **tongue**
TONIC n medicine to improve body tone ▷ adj invigorating
TONICS ▶ **tonic**
TONIER ▶ **tony**
TONIES ▶ **tony**
TONIEST ▶ **tony**
TONIGHT n (in or during) the night or evening of this day ▷ adv in or during the night or evening of this day
TONING ▶ **tone**
TONINGS ▶ **tone**
TONISH ▶ **ton**
TONITE n explosive used in quarrying
TONITES ▶ **tonite**
TONK vb strike with a heavy blow ▷ n effete or effeminate man
TONKA n as in **tonka bean** tall leguminous tree of tropical America, having fragrant black almond-shaped seeds
TONKED ▶ **tonk**
TONKER ▶ **tonk**
TONKERS ▶ **tonk**
TONKING ▶ **tonk**
TONKS ▶ **tonk**
TONLET n skirt of a suit of armour, consisting of overlapping metal bands
TONLETS ▶ **tonlet**
TONNAG n type of (usually tartan) shawl
TONNAGE n weight capacity of a ship
TONNAGS ▶ **tonnag**
TONNE same as ▶ **ton**
TONNEAU n detachable cover to protect the rear part of an open car when it is not carrying passengers
TONNELL old spelling of ▶ **tunnel**
TONNER n something, for example a vehicle, that weighs one ton
TONNERS ▶ **tonne**
TONNES ▶ **tonne**
TONNISH ▶ **ton**
TONS ▶ **ton**
TONSIL n small gland in the throat
TONSILS ▶ **tonsil**
TONSOR n barber
TONSORS ▶ **tonsor**
TONSURE n shaving of all or the top of the head as a

religious or monastic practice ▷ vb shave the head of
TONTINE n annuity scheme by which several subscribers accumulate and invest a common fund out of which they receive an annuity that increases as subscribers die until the last survivor takes the whole
TONUS n normal tension of a muscle at rest
TONUSES ▶ **tonus**
TONY adj stylish or distinctive ▷ n stylish or distinctive person
TOO adv also, as well
TOOART variant spelling of ▶ **tuart**
TOOARTS ▶ **tooart**
TOOK ▶ **take**
TOOL n implement used by hand ▷ vb work on with a tool
TOOLBAG n bag for storing or carrying tools
TOOLBAR n horizontal row or vertical column of selectable buttons displayed on a computer screen, allowing the user to select a variety of functions
TOOLBOX n box for storing or carrying tools
TOOLED ▶ **tool**
TOOLER ▶ **tool**
TOOLERS ▶ **tool**
TOOLIE n adult who gatecrashes schools to make advances to the students
TOOLIES ▶ **toolie**
TOOLING n any decorative work done with a tool, esp a design stamped onto a book cover, piece of leatherwork, etc
TOOLKIT n set of tools designed to be used together or for a particular purpose
TOOLMAN n person who works with tools
TOOLMEN ▶ **toolman**
TOOLS ▶ **tool**
TOOLSET n set of predefined tools associated with a particular computer application
TOOM vb empty (something) ▷ adj empty
TOOMED ▶ **toom**

TOOMER ▶ **toom**
TOOMEST ▶ **toom**
TOOMING ▶ **toom**
TOOMS ▶ **toom**
TOON n large meliaceous tree of the East Indies and Australia, having clusters of flowers from which a dye is obtained
TOONIE n Canadian two-dollar coin
TOONIES ▶ **toonie**
TOONS ▶ **toon**
TOORIE n tassel or bobble on a bonnet
TOORIES ▶ **toorie**
TOOSHIE adj angry
TOOT n short hooting sound ▷ vb (cause to) make such a sound
TOOTED ▶ **toot**
TOOTER ▶ **toot**
TOOTERS ▶ **toot**
TOOTH n bonelike projection in the jaws of most vertebrates for biting and chewing
TOOTHED adj having a tooth or teeth
TOOTHS ▶ **tooth**
TOOTHY adj having or showing numerous, large, or prominent teeth
TOOTING ▶ **toot**
TOOTLE vb hoot softly or repeatedly ▷ n soft hoot or series of hoots
TOOTLED ▶ **tootle**
TOOTLER ▶ **tootle**
TOOTLES ▶ **tootle**
TOOTS Scots version of ▶ **tut**
TOOTSED ▶ **toots**
TOOTSES ▶ **toots**
TOOTSIE same as ▶ **tootsy**
TOOTSY same as ▶ **toots**
TOP n highest point or part ▷ adj at or of the top ▷ vb form a top on
TOPARCH n ruler of a small state or realm
TOPAZ n semiprecious stone in various colours
TOPAZES ▶ **topaz**
TOPCOAT n overcoat
TOPE vb drink alcohol regularly ▷ n small European shark
TOPED ▶ **tope**
TOPEE n lightweight hat worn in tropical countries
TOPEES ▶ **topee**
TOPEK same as ▶ **tupik**
TOPEKS ▶ **topek**

T

TOPER ▶ tope

TOPERS ▶ tope

TOPES ▶ tope

TOPFUL variant spelling of ▶ topfull

TOPFULL adj full to the top

TOPH n variety of sandstone

TOPHE variant spelling of ▶ toph

TOPHES ▶ tophe

TOPHI ▶ tophus

TOPHS ▶ toph

TOPHUS n deposit of sodium urate in the helix of the ear or surrounding a joint

TOPI same as ▶ topee

TOPIARY n art of trimming trees and bushes into decorative shapes ▷ adj of or relating to topiary

TOPIC n subject of a conversation, book, etc

TOPICAL adj relating to current events

TOPICS ▶ topic

TOPING ▶ tope

TOPIS ▶ topi

TOPKICK n (formerly) sergeant

TOPKNOT n crest, tuft, decorative bow, etc, on the top of the head

TOPLESS adj (of a costume or woman) with no covering for the breasts

TOPLINE vb headline; be the main focus of a newspaper story

TOPMAN n sailor positioned in the rigging of the topsail

TOPMAST n mast next above a lower mast on a sailing vessel

TOPMEN ▶ topman

TOPMOST adj highest or best

TOPO n picture of a mountain with details of climbing routes superimposed on it

TOPOI ▶ topo

TOPONYM n name of a place

TOPOS ▶ topo

TOPPED ▶ top

TOPPER n top hat

TOPPERS ▶ topper

TOPPIER ▶ toppy

TOPPING ▶ top

TOPPLE vb (cause to) fall over

TOPPLED ▶ topple

TOPPLES ▶ topple

TOPPY adj (of audio reproduction) having too many high-frequency sounds

TOPS ▶ top

TOPSAIL n square sail carried on a yard set on a topmast

TOPSIDE n lean cut of beef from the thigh containing no bone

TOPSMAN n chief drover

TOPSMEN ▶ topsman

TOPSOIL n surface layer of soil ▷ vb spread topsoil on (land)

TOPSPIN n spin imparted to make a ball bounce or travel exceptionally far, high, or quickly, as by hitting it with a sharp forward and upward stroke

TOPWORK vb graft shoots or twigs onto the main branches of (for example, a fruit tree) to modify its yield

TOQUE same as ▶ tuque

TOQUES ▶ toque

TOQUET same as ▶ toque

TOQUETS ▶ toquet

TOR n high rocky hill

TORA variant spelling of ▶ torah

TORAH n whole body of traditional Jewish teaching, including the Oral Law

TORAHS ▶ torah

TORAN n (in Indian architecture) an archway, usually wooden and often ornately carved

TORANA same as ▶ toran

TORANAS ▶ torana

TORANS ▶ toran

TORAS ▶ tora

TORC same as ▶ torque

TORCH n small portable battery-powered lamp ▷ vb deliberately set (a building) on fire

TORCHED ▶ torch

TORCHER ▶ torch

TORCHES ▶ torch

TORCHON n as in torchon lace coarse linen or cotton lace with a simple openwork pattern

TORCHY adj sentimental; maudlin; characteristic of a torch song

TORCS ▶ torc

TORDION n old triple-time dance for two people

TORE same as ▶ torus

TORERO n bullfighter, esp one on foot

TOREROS ▶ torero

TORES ▶ tore

TORGOCH n type of char

TORI ▶ torus

TORIC adj of, relating to, or having the form of a torus

TORICS ▶ toric

TORIES ▶ tory

TORII n gateway, esp one at the entrance to a Japanese Shinto temple

TORMENT vb cause (someone) great suffering ▷ n great suffering

TORMINA n complaints

TORN ▶ tear

TORNADE same as ▶ tornado

TORNADO n violent whirlwind

TORO n bull

TOROID n surface generated by rotating a closed plane curve about a coplanar line that does not intersect the curve

TOROIDS ▶ toroid

TOROS ▶ toro

TOROSE adj (of a cylindrical part) having irregular swellings

TOROT ▶ torah

TOROTH ▶ torah

TOROUS same as ▶ torose

TORPEDO n self-propelled underwater missile ▷ vb attack or destroy with or as if with torpedoes

TORPEFY n make torpid

TORPID adj sluggish and inactive

TORPIDS n series of boat races held at Oxford University during Lent

TORPOR n torpid state

TORPORS ▶ torpor

TORQUE n force causing rotation ▷ vb apply torque to (something)

TORQUED ▶ torque

TORQUER ▶ torque

TORQUES n distinctive band of hair, feathers, skin, or colour around the neck of an animal

TORR n unit of pressure equal to one millimetre of mercury (133.3 newtons per square metre)

TORREFY vb dry (drugs, ores, etc) by subjection to intense heat

TORRENT n rushing stream ▷ adj like or relating to a torrent

TORRET same as ▶ terret

TORRETS ▶ torret

TORRID adj very hot and dry

TORRIFY same as ▶ torrefy

TORRS ▶ torr

TORS ▶ tor

TORSADE n ornamental twist or twisted cord, as on hats

TORSE same as ▶ torso

TORSEL n wooden beam along the top of a wall for distributing the weight of something laid upon it

TORSELS ▶ torsel

TORSES ▶ torse

TORSI ▶ torso

TORSION n twisting of a part by equal forces being applied at both ends but in opposite directions

TORSIVE adj twisted

TORSK n fish with a single long dorsal fin

TORSKS ▶ torsk

TORSO n trunk of the human body

TORSOS ▶ torso

TORT n civil wrong or injury for which damages may be claimed

TORTA n (in mining) a flat circular pile of silver ore

TORTAS ▶ torta

TORTE n rich cake, originating in Austria, usually decorated or filled with cream, fruit, nuts, and jam

TORTEN ▶ torte

TORTES ▶ torte

TORTILE adj twisted or coiled

TORTIVE adj twisted

TORTONI n rich ice cream often flavoured with sherry

TORTRIX n type of moth

TORTS ▶ tort

TORTURE vb cause (someone) severe pain or mental anguish ▷ n severe physical or mental pain

TORULA n species of fungal microorganisms

TORULAE ▶ torula

TORULAS ▶ torula

TORULI ▶ torulus

TORULIN n vitamin found in yeast

TORULUS n socket in an insect's head in which its antenna is attached

TORUS n large convex moulding approximately semicircular in cross section, esp one used on the base of a classical column

TORY n ultraconservative or reactionary person ▷ adj ultraconservative or reactionary

TOSA n large reddish dog, originally bred for fighting

TOSAS ▶ tosa

TOSE same as ▶ toze

TOSED ▶ tose

TOSES ▶ tose

TOSH n nonsense ▷ vb tidy or trim

TOSHACH n military leader of a clan

TOSHED ▶ tosh

TOSHER ▶ tosh

TOSHERS ▶ tosh

TOSHES ▶ tosh

TOSHIER ▶ toshy

TOSHING ▶ tosh

TOSHY adj neat; trim

TOSING ▶ tose

TOSS vb throw lightly ▷ n tossing

TOSSED ▶ toss

TOSSEN old past participle of ▶ toss

TOSSES ▶ toss

TOSSIER ▶ tossy

TOSSILY ▶ tossy

TOSSING ▶ toss

TOSSUP n an instance of tossing up a coin

TOSSUPS ▶ tossup

TOSSY adj impudent

TOST old past participle of ▶ toss

TOSTADA n crispy deep-fried tortilla topped with meat, cheese, and refried beans

TOSTADO same as ▶ tostada

TOT n small child ▷ vb total

TOTABLE ▶ tote

TOTAL n whole, esp a sum of parts ▷ adj complete ▷ vb amount to

TOTALED ▶ total

TOTALLY ▶ total

TOTALS ▶ total

TOTANUS another name for

> **redshank**

TOTARA n tall coniferous forest tree of New Zealand, with a hard durable wood

TOTARAS ▶ totara

TOTE vb carry (a gun etc) ▷ n act of or an instance of toting

TOTED ▶ tote

TOTEM n tribal badge or emblem

TOTEMIC ▶ totem

TOTEMS ▶ totem

TOTER ▶ tote

TOTERS ▶ tote

TOTES ▶ tote

TOTHER n other

TOTIENT n quantity of numbers less than, and sharing no common factors with, a given number

TOTING ▶ tote

TOTS ▶ tot

TOTTED ▶ tot

TOTTER vb move unsteadily ▷ n act or an instance of tottering

TOTTERS ▶ totter

TOTTERY ▶ totter

TOTTIE adj very small

TOTTIER ▶ totty

TOTTIES ▶ totty

TOTTING ▶ tot

TOTTY n people, esp women, collectively considered as sexual objects ▷ adj very small

TOUCAN n tropical American bird with a large bill

TOUCANS ▶ toucan

TOUCH vb come into contact with ▷ n sense by which an object's qualities are perceived when they come into contact with part of the body ▷ adj of a non-contact version of particular sport

TOUCHE interj acknowledgment of the striking home of a remark or witty reply

TOUCHED adj emotionally moved

TOUCHER ▶ touch

TOUCHES ▶ touch

TOUCHUP n renovation or retouching, as of a painting

TOUCHY adj easily offended

TOUGH adj strong or resilient ▷ n rough violent person

T

TOUGHED ▶ tough
TOUGHEN vb make or become tough or tougher
TOUGHER ▶ tough
TOUGHIE n person who is tough
TOUGHLY ▶ tough
TOUGHS ▶ tough
TOUGHY same as ▶ toughie
TOUK same as ▶ tuck
TOUKED ▶ touk
TOUKING ▶ touk
TOUKS ▶ touk
TOUN n town
TOUNS ▶ toun
TOUPEE n small wig
TOUPEED adj wearing a toupee
TOUPEES ▶ toupee
TOUPET same as ▶ toupee
TOUPETS ▶ toupet
TOUR n journey visiting places of interest along the way ▷ vb make a tour (of)
TOURACO n brightly coloured crested arboreal African bird
TOURED ▶ tour
TOURER n large open car with a folding top, usually seating a driver and four passengers
TOURERS ▶ tourer
TOURIE same as ▶ toorie
TOURIES ▶ tourie
TOURING ▶ tour
TOURISM n tourist travel as an industry
TOURIST n person travelling for pleasure ▷ adj of or relating to tourists or tourism
TOURNEY n knightly tournament ▷ vb engage in a tourney
TOURS ▶ tour
TOUSE vb tangle, ruffle, or disarrange; treat roughly
TOUSED ▶ touse
TOUSER ▶ touse
TOUSERS ▶ touse
TOUSES ▶ touse
TOUSIER ▶ tousy
TOUSING ▶ touse
TOUSLE vb make (hair or clothes) ruffled and untidy ▷ n disorderly, tangled, or rumpled state
TOUSLED ▶ tousle
TOUSLES ▶ tousle
TOUSTIE adj irritable; testy
TOUSY adj tousled

TOUT vb seek business in a persistent manner ▷ n person who sells tickets for a popular event at inflated prices
TOUTED ▶ tout
TOUTER ▶ tout
TOUTERS ▶ tout
TOUTIE adj childishly irritable or sullen
TOUTIER ▶ toutie
TOUTING ▶ tout
TOUTS ▶ tout
TOUZE variant spelling of ▶ touse
TOUZED ▶ touze
TOUZES ▶ touze
TOUZIER ▶ touzy
TOUZING ▶ touze
TOUZLE rare spelling of ▶ tousle
TOUZLED ▶ touzle
TOUZLES ▶ touzle
TOUZY variant spelling of ▶ tousy
TOW vb drag, esp by means of a rope ▷ n towing
TOWABLE ▶ tow
TOWAGE n charge made for towing
TOWAGES ▶ towage
TOWARD same as ▶ towards
TOWARDS prep in the direction of
TOWAWAY n vehicle which has been towed away (because, for example, it was illegally parked)
TOWBAR n metal bar on a car for towing vehicles
TOWBARS ▶ towbar
TOWBOAT n another word for tug (the boat)
TOWED ▶ tow
TOWEL n cloth for drying things ▷ vb dry or wipe with a towel
TOWELED ▶ towel
TOWELS ▶ towel
TOWER n tall structure, often forming part of a larger building ▷ vb to be or rise like a tower; loom
TOWERED adj having a tower or towers
TOWERS ▶ tower
TOWERY adj with towers
TOWHEAD n often disparaging term for a person with blond or yellowish hair
TOWHEE n N American

brownish-coloured sparrow
TOWHEES ▶ towhee
TOWIE n truck used for towing
TOWIER ▶ tow
TOWIES ▶ towie
TOWIEST ▶ tow
TOWING ▶ tow
TOWINGS ▶ tow
TOWKAY n sir
TOWKAYS ▶ towkay
TOWLINE same as ▶ towrope
TOWMON same as ▶ towmond
TOWMOND n old word for year
TOWMONS ▶ towmon
TOWMONT same as ▶ towmond
TOWN n group of buildings larger than a village
TOWNEE same as ▶ townie
TOWNEES ▶ townee
TOWNIE n often disparaging term for a resident in a town, esp as distinct from country dwellers
TOWNIER ▶ towny
TOWNIES ▶ towny
TOWNISH ▶ town
TOWNLET n small town
TOWNLY adj characteristic of a town
TOWNS ▶ town
TOWNY adj characteristic of a town
TOWPATH n path beside a canal or river, originally for horses towing boats
TOWROPE n rope or cable used for towing a vehicle or vessel
TOWS ▶ tow
TOWSACK n sack made from tow
TOWSE same as ▶ touse
TOWSED ▶ towse
TOWSER ▶ towse
TOWSERS ▶ towse
TOWSES ▶ towse
TOWSIER ▶ towsy
TOWSING ▶ towse
TOWSY same as ▶ tousy
TOWT vb sulk
TOWTED ▶ towt
TOWTING ▶ towt
TOWTS ▶ towt
TOWY ▶ tow
TOWZE same as ▶ touse
TOWZED ▶ towze

TOWZES ▶ **towze**
TOWZIER ▶ **towzy**
TOWZING ▶ **towze**
TOWZY same as ▶ **tousy**
TOXEMIA same as > **toxaemia**
TOXEMIC > **toxaemia**
TOXIC adj poisonous ▷ n toxic substance
TOXICAL adj toxic
TOXICS ▶ **toxic**
TOXIN n poison of bacterial origin
TOXINE nonstandard variant spelling of ▶ **toxin**
TOXINES ▶ **toxine**
TOXINS ▶ **toxin**
TOXOID n toxin that has been treated to reduce its toxicity and is used in immunization to stimulate production of antitoxins
TOXOIDS ▶ **toxoid**
TOY n something designed to be played with ▷ adj designed to be played with ▷ vb play, fiddle, or flirt
TOYED ▶ **toy**
TOYER ▶ **toy**
TOYERS ▶ **toy**
TOYETIC adj (of a film or television franchise) able to generate revenue via spin-off toy products
TOYING ▶ **toy**
TOYINGS ▶ **toy**
TOYISH adj resembling a toy
TOYLESS ▶ **toy**
TOYLIKE ▶ **toy**
TOYLSOM old spelling of > **toilsome**
TOYMAN n man who sells toys
TOYMEN ▶ **toyman**
TOYO n Japanese straw-like material made out of rice paper and used to make hats
TOYON n shrub related to the rose
TOYONS ▶ **toyon**
TOYOS ▶ **toyo**
TOYS ▶ **toy**
TOYSHOP n shop selling toys
TOYSOME adj playful
TOYTOWN adj having an unreal and picturesque appearance
TOZE vb tease out; (of wool, etc) card
TOZED ▶ **toze**
TOZES ▶ **toze**

TOZIE n type of shawl
TOZIES ▶ **tozie**
TOZING ▶ **toze**
TRABS pl n training shoes
TRACE vb locate or work out (the cause of something) ▷ n track left by something
TRACED ▶ **trace**
TRACER n projectile which leaves a visible trail
TRACERS ▶ **tracer**
TRACERY n pattern of interlacing lines
TRACES ▶ **trace**
TRACEUR n parkour participant
TRACHEA n windpipe
TRACHLE vb (of hair, clothing, etc) make untidy; dishevel; rumple
TRACING n traced copy
TRACK n rough road or path ▷ vb follow the trail or path of
TRACKED ▶ **track**
TRACKER ▶ **track**
TRACKS ▶ **track**
TRACT n wide area ▷ vb track
TRACTED ▶ **tract**
TRACTOR n motor vehicle with large rear wheels for pulling farm machinery
TRACTS ▶ **tract**
TRACTUS n anthem sung in some RC masses
TRAD n traditional jazz, as revived in the 1950s
TRADE n buying, selling, or exchange of goods ▷ vb buy and sell ▷ adj intended for or available only to people in industry or business
TRADED ▶ **trade**
TRADER n person who engages in trade
TRADERS ▶ **trader**
TRADES ▶ **trade**
TRADING ▶ **trade**
TRADS ▶ **trad**
TRADUCE vb slander
TRAFFIC n vehicles coming and going on a road ▷ vb trade, usu illicitly
TRAGAL ▶ **tragus**
TRAGEDY n shocking or sad event
TRAGI ▶ **tragus**
TRAGIC adj of or like a tragedy ▷ n tragedian
TRAGICS ▶ **tragic**
TRAGULE n mouse deer
TRAGUS n cartilaginous

fleshy projection that partially covers the entrance to the external ear
TRAIK vb trudge; trek with difficulty
TRAIKED ▶ **traik**
TRAIKIT ▶ **traik**
TRAIKS ▶ **traik**
TRAIL n path, track, or road ▷ vb drag along the ground
TRAILED ▶ **trail**
TRAILER n vehicle designed to be towed by another vehicle ▷ vb use a trailer to advertise (something)
TRAILS ▶ **trail**
TRAIN vb instruct in a skill ▷ n line of railway coaches or wagons drawn by an engine
TRAINED ▶ **train**
TRAINEE n person being trained ▷ adj (of a person) undergoing training
TRAINER n person who trains an athlete or sportsman
TRAINS ▶ **train**
TRAIPSE vb walk wearily ▷ n long or tiring walk
TRAIT n characteristic feature
TRAITOR n person guilty of treason or treachery
TRAITS ▶ **trait**
TRAJECT vb transport or transmit
TRAM same as ▶ **trammel**
TRAMCAR same as ▶ **tram**
TRAMEL variant spelling of ▶ **trammel**
TRAMELL variant spelling of ▶ **trammel**
TRAMELS ▶ **tramel**
TRAMMED ▶ **tram**
TRAMMEL n hindrance to free action or movement ▷ vb hinder or restrain
TRAMMIE n conductor or driver of a tram
TRAMP vb travel on foot, hike ▷ n homeless person who travels on foot
TRAMPED ▶ **tramp**
TRAMPER n person who tramps
TRAMPET variant spelling of > **trampette**
TRAMPLE vb tread on and crush ▷ n action or sound of trampling
TRAMPS ▶ **tramp**
TRAMPY adj (of woman)

T

disreputable

TRAMS ▶ **tram**

TRAMWAY same as
▶ **tramline**

TRANCE n unconscious or
dazed state ▷ vb put into or
as into a trance

TRANCED ▶ **trance**

TRANCES ▶ **trance**

TRANCEY adj (of music)
characteristic of the trance
sub-genre

TRANCHE n portion of
something large, esp a sum
of money

TRANECT n ferry

TRANGAM n bauble or
trinket

TRANGLE n (in heraldry) a
small fesse

TRANK n short form of
tranquillizer: drug that
calms a person

TRANKS ▶ **trank**

TRANKUM same as
▶ **trangam**

TRANNIE n transistor radio

TRANNY same as ▶ **trannie**

TRANQ same as ▶ **trank**

> Short for tranquilliser;
> another of those useful
> words allowing you to
> play the Q without a U.

TRANQS ▶ **tranq**

TRANS n short from of
translation

TRANSE n way through;
passage

TRANSES ▶ **transe**

TRANSIT n passage or
conveyance of goods or
people ▷ vb make transit

TRANSOM n horizontal bar
across a window

TRANT vb travel from place
to place selling goods

TRANTED ▶ **trant**

TRANTER ▶ **trant**

TRANTS ▶ **trant**

TRAP n device for catching
animals ▷ vb catch

TRAPAN same as ▶ **trepan**

TRAPANS ▶ **trapan**

TRAPE same as ▶ **traipse**

TRAPED ▶ **trape**

TRAPES same as ▶ **traipse**

TRAPEZE n horizontal bar
suspended from two ropes,
used by circus acrobats ▷ vb
swing on a trapeze

TRAPING ▶ **trape**

TRAPPED ▶ **trap**

TRAPPER n person who

traps animals for their fur

TRAPPY adj having many
traps

TRAPS ▶ **trap**

TRAPT old past participle of
▶ **trap**

TRASH n anything
worthless ▷ vb attack or
destroy maliciously

TRASHED adj drunk

TRASHER ▶ **trash**

TRASHES ▶ **trash**

TRASHY adj cheap,
worthless, or badly made

TRASS n variety of the
volcanic rock tuff, used to
make a hydraulic cement

TRASSES ▶ **trass**

TRAT n type of fishing line
holding a series of baited
hooks

TRATS ▶ **trat**

TRATT short for ▶ **trattoria**

TRATTS ▶ **tratt**

TRAUMA n emotional
shock

TRAUMAS ▶ **trauma**

TRAVAIL n labour or toil
▷ vb suffer or labour
painfully, esp in childbirth

TRAVE n stout wooden
cage in which difficult
horses are shod

TRAVEL vb go from one
place to another, through
an area, or for a specified
distance ▷ n travelling, esp
as a tourist

TRAVELS ▶ **travel**

TRAVES ▶ **trave**

TRAVIS same as ▶ **treviss**

TRAVOIS n sled used for
dragging logs

TRAWL n net dragged at
deep levels behind a fishing
boat ▷ vb fish with such a
net

TRAWLED ▶ **trawl**

TRAWLER n trawling boat

TRAWLEY same as ▶ **trolley**

TRAWLS ▶ **trawl**

TRAY n flat board, usu with
a rim, for carrying things

TRAYBIT n threepenny bit

TRAYFUL n as many or as
much as will fit on a tray

TRAYNE old spelling of
▶ **train**

TRAYNED ▶ **trayne**

TRAYNES ▶ **trayne**

TRAYS ▶ **tray**

TREACLE n thick dark syrup
produced when sugar is

refined ▷ vb add treacle to

TREACLY ▶ **treacle**

TREAD vb set one's foot on
▷ n way of walking or
dancing

TREADED ▶ **tread**

TREADER ▶ **tread**

TREADLE n lever worked by
the foot to turn a wheel
▷ vb work (a machine) with
a treadle

TREADS ▶ **tread**

TREAGUE n agreement to
stop fighting

TREASON n betrayal of
one's sovereign or country

TREAT vb deal with or
regard in a certain manner
▷ n pleasure,
entertainment, etc given or
paid for by someone else

TREATED ▶ **treat**

TREATER ▶ **treat**

TREATS ▶ **treat**

TREATY n signed contract
between states

TREBLE adj triple ▷ n
(singer with or part for) a
soprano voice ▷ vb increase
three times

TREBLED ▶ **treble**

TREBLES ▶ **treble**

TREBLY ▶ **treble**

TRECK same as ▶ **trek**

TRECKED ▶ **treck**

TRECKS ▶ **treck**

TREDDLE variant spelling of
▶ **treadle**

TREE n large perennial plant
with a woody trunk

TREED ▶ **tree**

TREEING ▶ **tree**

TREEN adj made of wood
▷ n art of making
treenware

TREENS ▶ **treen**

TREES ▶ **tree**

TREETOP n top of a tree

TREEWAX n yellowish wax
secreted by an oriental
scale insect

TREF adj in Judaism, ritually
unfit to be eaten

TREFA same as ▶ **tref**

TREFAH same as ▶ **tref**

TREFOIL n plant, such as
clover, with a three-lobed
leaf

TREHALA n edible sugary
substance obtained from
the pupal cocoon of an
Asian weevil

TREIF same as ▶ **tref**

TREIFA same as ▸ **tref**
TREILLE another word for
▸ **trellis**
TREK n long difficult
journey, esp on foot ▸ vb
make such a journey
TREKKED ▸ **trek**
TREKKER ▸ **trek**
TREKS ▸ **trek**
TRELLIS n framework of
horizontal and vertical
strips of wood ▸ vb
interweave (strips of wood,
etc) to make a trellis
TREMA n mark consisting of
two dots placed over the
second of two adjacent
vowels to indicate it is to be
pronounced separately
rather than forming a
diphthong with the first
TREMAS ▸ **trema**
TREMBLE vb shake or quiver
▸ n trembling
TREMBLY ▸ **tremble**
TREMIE n large metal
hopper and pipe used to
distribute freshly mixed
concrete over an
underwater site.
TREMIES ▸ **tremie**
TREMOLO n quivering
effect in singing or playing
TREMOR n involuntary
shaking ▸ vb tremble
TREMORS ▸ **tremor**
TRENAIL same as > **treenail**
TRENCH n long narrow
ditch, esp one used as a
shelter in war ▸ adj of or
involving military trenches
▸ vb make a trench in (a
place)
TREND n general tendency
or direction ▸ vb take a
certain trend
TRENDED ▸ **trend**
TRENDS ▸ **trend**
TRENDY n consciously
fashionable (person) ▸ adj
consciously fashionable
TRENISE n one of the figures
in a quadrille
TRENTAL n mass said in
remembrance of a person
30 days after his or her
death
TREPAN same as > **trephine**
TREPANG n any of various
large sea cucumbers of
tropical Oriental seas, the
body walls of which are
used as food by the

Japanese and Chinese
TREPANS ▸ **trepan**
TREPID adj trembling
TRES adj very
TRESS n lock of hair, esp a
long lock of woman's hair
▸ vb arrange in tresses
TRESSED adj having a tress
or tresses as specified
TRESSEL variant spelling of
▸ **trestle**
TRESSES ▸ **tress**
TRESSY ▸ **tress**
TREST old variant of
▸ **trestle**
TRESTLE n board fixed on
pairs of spreading legs,
used as a support
TRESTS ▸ **trest**
TRET n (formerly) an
allowance according to
weight granted to
purchasers for waste due to
transportation
TRETS ▸ **tret**
TREVET same as ▸ **trivet**
TREVETS ▸ **trevet**
TREVIS variant spelling of
▸ **treviss**
TREVISS n partition in a
stable for keeping animals
apart
TREW old variant spelling of
▸ **true**
TREWS pl n close-fitting
tartan trousers
TREY n any card or dice
throw with three spots
TREYBIT same as ▸ **traybit**
TREYS ▸ **trey**
TREZ same as ▸ **trey**
TREZES ▸ **trez**
TRIABLE adj liable to be
tried judicially
TRIAC n device for
regulating the amount of
electric current allowed to
reach a circuit
TRIACID adj (of a base)
capable of reacting with
three molecules of a
monobasic acid
TRIACS ▸ **triac**
TRIACT adj having three
rays
TRIAD n group of three
TRIADIC n something that
has the characteristics of a
triad
TRIADS ▸ **triad**
TRIAGE n (in a hospital) the
principle or practice of
sorting emergency patients

into categories of priority
for treatment ▸ vb sort
(patients) into categories of
priority for treatment
TRIAGED ▸ **triage**
TRIAGES ▸ **triage**
TRIAL n investigation of a
case before a judge
TRIALS ▸ **trial**
TRIARCH n one of three
rulers of a triarchy
TRIATIC n rope between a
ship's mastheads
TRIAXON another name for
> **triaxial**
TRIAZIN same as > **triazine**
TRIBADE n lesbian, esp one
who practises tribadism
TRIBADY another word for
> **tribadism**
TRIBAL adj of or denoting a
tribe or tribes ▸ n member
of a tribal community
TRIBALS > **tribal** n
TRIBBLE n frame for drying
paper
TRIBE n group of clans or
families believed to have a
common ancestor
TRIBES ▸ **tribe**
TRIBLET n spindle or
mandrel used in making
rings, tubes, etc
TRIBUNE n people's
representative, esp in
ancient Rome
TRIBUTE n sign of respect or
admiration
TRICAR n car with three
wheels
TRICARS ▸ **tricar**
TRICE n moment ▸ vb haul
up or secure
TRICED ▸ **trice**
TRICEP same as ▸ **triceps**
TRICEPS n muscle at the
back of the upper arm
TRICES ▸ **trice**
TRICING ▸ **trice**
TRICK n deceitful or
cunning action or plan ▸ vb
cheat or deceive
TRICKED ▸ **trick**
TRICKER ▸ **trick**
TRICKIE Scots form of
▸ **tricky**
TRICKLE vb (cause to) flow
in a thin stream or drops ▸ n
gradual flow
TRICKLY ▸ **trickle**
TRICKS ▸ **trick**
TRICKSY adj playing tricks
habitually

T

TRICKY adj difficult, needing careful handling

TRICLAD n type of worm having a tripartite intestine

TRICORN n cocked hat with opposing brims turned back and caught in three places ▷ adj having three horns or corners

TRICOT n thin rayon or nylon fabric knitted or resembling knitting, used for dresses, etc

TRICOTS ▶ tricot

TRIDARN n sideboard with three levels

TRIDE old spelling of the past tense of ▶ try

TRIDENT n three-pronged spear ▷ adj having three prongs

TRIDUAN adj three days long

TRIDUUM n period of three days for prayer before a feast

TRIE old spelling of ▶ try

TRIED ▶ try

TRIELLA n three nominated horse races in which the punter bets on selecting the three winners

TRIENE n chemical compound containing three double bonds

TRIENES ▶ triene

TRIENS n Byzantine gold goin worth one third of a solidus

TRIER n person or thing that tries

TRIERS ▶ trier

TRIES ▶ try

TRIFF adj terrific; very good indeed

TRIFFER ▶ triff

TRIFFIC adj terrific; very good indeed

TRIFFID n any of a species of fictional plants that supposedly grew to a gigantic size, were capable of moving about, and could kill humans

TRIFID adj divided or split into three parts or lobes

TRIFLE n insignificant thing or amount ▷ vb deal (with) as if worthless

TRIFLED ▶ trifle

TRIFLER ▶ trifle

TRIFLES ▶ trifle

TRIFOLD less common word for ▶ triple

TRIFOLY same as ▶ trefoil

TRIFORM adj having three parts

TRIG adj neat or spruce ▷ vb make or become spruce

TRIGAMY n condition of having three spouses

TRIGGED ▶ trig

TRIGGER n small lever releasing a catch on a gun or machine ▷ vb set (an action or process) in motion

TRIGLOT n person who can speak three languages

TRIGLY ▶ trig

TRIGO n wheat field

TRIGON n (in classical Greece or Rome) a triangular harp or lyre

TRIGONS ▶ trigon

TRIGOS ▶ trigo

TRIGRAM n three-letter inscription

TRIGS ▶ trig

TRIJET n jet with three engines

TRIJETS ▶ trijet

TRIKE n tricycle

TRIKES ▶ trike

TRILBY n man's soft felt hat

TRILBYS ▶ trilby

TRILD old past tense of ▶ trill

TRILITH same as > trilithon

TRILL n rapid alternation between two notes ▷ vb play or sing a trill

TRILLED ▶ trill

TRILLER ▶ trill

TRILLO n (in music) a trill

TRILLS ▶ trill

TRILOBE n three-lobed thing

TRILOGY n series of three related books, plays, etc

TRIM adj neat and smart ▷ vb cut or prune into good shape ▷ n decoration

TRIMER n polymer or a molecule of a polymer consisting of three identical monomers

TRIMERS ▶ trimer

TRIMIX n gas mixture of nitrogen, helium and oxygen used by deep-sea divers

TRIMLY ▶ trim

TRIMMED ▶ trim

TRIMMER ▶ trim

TRIMS ▶ trim

TRIMTAB n small control surface attached to the trailing edge of a main control surface to enable the pilot to balance an aircraft

TRIN n triplet

TRINAL ▶ trine

TRINARY adj made up of three parts

TRINDLE vb move heavily on (or as if on) wheels

TRINE n aspect of 120° between two planets, an orb of 8° being allowed ▷ adj of or relating to a trine ▷ vb put in a trine aspect

TRINED ▶ trine

TRINES ▶ trine

TRINGLE n slim rod

TRINING ▶ trine

TRINITY n group of three

TRINKET n small or worthless ornament or piece of jewellery ▷ vb ornament with trinkets

TRINKUM n trinket or bauble

TRINS ▶ trin

TRIO n group of three

TRIODE n electronic valve having three electrodes, a cathode, an anode, and a grid

TRIODES ▶ triode

TRIOL n any of a class of alcohols that have three hydroxyl groups per molecule

TRIOLET n verse form of eight lines

TRIOLS ▶ triol

TRIONES n seven stars of the constellation Ursa Major

TRIONYM another name for > trinomial

TRIOR old form of ▶ trier

TRIORS ▶ trior

TRIOS ▶ trio

TRIOSE n simple monosaccharide produced by the oxidation of glycerol

TRIOSES ▶ triose

TRIOXID same as > trioxide

TRIP n journey to a place and back, esp for pleasure ▷ vb (cause to) stumble

TRIPACK n pack of three

TRIPART adj composed of three parts

TRIPE n stomach of a cow used as food

TRIPERY n place where tripe is prepared

TRIPES ▸ tripe
TRIPEY ▸ tripe
TRIPIER ▸ tripe
TRIPLE adj having three parts ▷ vb increase three times ▷ n something that is, or contains, three times as much as normal
TRIPLED ▸ triple
TRIPLES ▸ triple
TRIPLET n one of three babies born at one birth
TRIPLEX n building divided into three separate dwellings
TRIPLY vb give a reply to a duply
TRIPOD n three-legged stand, stool, etc
TRIPODS ▸ tripod
TRIPODY n metrical unit consisting of three feet
TRIPOLI n lightweight porous siliceous rock derived by weathering and used in a powdered form as a polish, filter, etc
TRIPOS n final examinations for an honours degree at Cambridge University
TRIPPED ▸ trip
TRIPPER n tourist
TRIPPET n any mechanism that strikes or is struck at regular intervals, as by a cam
TRIPPLE vb canter
TRIPPY adj suggestive of or resembling the effect produced by a hallucinogenic drug
TRIPS ▸ trip
TRIPSES ▸ tripsis
TRIPSIS n act of kneading the body to promote circulation, suppleness, etc
TRIPTAN n drug used to treat migraine
TRIPY ▸ tripe
TRIREME n ancient Greek warship with three rows of oars on each side
TRISECT vb divide into three parts, esp three equal parts
TRISEME n metrical foot of a length equal to three short syllables
TRISHAW another name for > rickshaw
TRISMIC ▸ trismus
TRISMUS n state of being unable to open the mouth

because of sustained contractions of the jaw muscles, caused by tetanus
TRISOME n chromosome occurring three times (rather than twice) in a cell
TRISOMY n condition of having one chromosome of the set represented three times in an otherwise diploid organism, cell, etc
TRIST variant spelling of ▸ triste
TRISTE adj sad
TRISUL n trident symbol of Siva
TRISULA same as ▸ trisul
TRISULS ▸ trisul
TRITE adj (of a remark or idea) commonplace and unoriginal ▷ n (on a lyre) the third string from the highest in pitch
TRITELY ▸ trite
TRITER ▸ trite
TRITES ▸ trite
TRITEST ▸ trite
TRITIDE n tritium compound
TRITIUM n radioactive isotope of hydrogen
TRITOMA another name for > kniphofia
TRITON n any of various chiefly tropical marine gastropod molluscs, having large beautifully-coloured spiral shells
TRITONE n musical interval consisting of three whole tones
TRITONS ▸ triton
TRIUMPH n (happiness caused by) victory or success ▷ vb be victorious or successful
TRIUNE adj constituting three in one, esp the three persons in one God of the Trinity ▷ n group of three
TRIUNES ▸ triune
TRIVET n metal stand for a pot or kettle
TRIVETS ▸ trivet
TRIVIA pl n trivial things or details
TRIVIAL adj of little importance
TRIVIUM n (in medieval learning) the lower division of the seven liberal arts, consisting of grammar, rhetoric, and logic

TRIZONE n area comprising three zones
TROAD same as ▸ trod
TROADE same as ▸ trod
TROADES ▸ troade
TROADS ▸ troad
TROAK old form of ▸ truck
TROAKED ▸ troak
TROAKS ▸ troak
TROAT vb (of a rutting buck) to call or bellow
TROATED ▸ troat
TROATS ▸ troat
TROCAR n surgical instrument for removing fluid from bodily cavities, consisting of a puncturing device situated inside a tube
TROCARS ▸ trocar
TROCHAL adj shaped like a wheel
TROCHAR old variant spelling of ▸ trocar
TROCHE another name for ▸ lozenge
TROCHEE n metrical foot of one long and one short syllable
TROCHES ▸ troche
TROCHI ▸ trochus
TROCHIL same as ▸ trochilus
TROCHUS n hoop (used in exercise)
TROCK same as ▸ truck
TROCKED ▸ trock
TROCKEN adj dry (used of wine, esp German wine)
TROCKS ▸ trock
TROD vb past participle of tread ▷ n path
TRODDEN ▸ tread
TRODE same as ▸ trod
TRODES ▸ trode
TRODS ▸ trod
TROELIE same as ▸ troolie
TROELY same as ▸ troolie
TROFFER n trough-like fixture for holding in place and reflecting light from a fluorescent tube
TROG vb walk, esp aimlessly or heavily
TROGGED ▸ trog
TROGGS n loyalty; fidelity
TROGON n bird of tropical and subtropical regions of America, Africa, and Asia. They have a brilliant plumage, short hooked bill, and long tail
TROGONS ▸ trogon

T

TROGS ▸ trog

TROIKA n Russian vehicle drawn by three horses abreast

TROIKAS ▸ troika

TROILUS n type of large butterfly

TROIS Scots form of ▸ troy

TROKE same as ▸ truck

TROKED ▸ troke

TROKES ▸ troke

TROKING ▸ troke

TROLAND n unit of light intensity in the eye

TROLL n giant or dwarf in Scandinavian folklore ▷ vb fish by dragging a lure through the water

TROLLED ▸ troll

TROLLER ▸ troll

TROLLEY n small wheeled table for food and drink ▷ vb transport on a trolley

TROLLS ▸ troll

TROLLY same as ▸ trolley

TROMINO n shape made from three squares, each joined to the next along one full side

TROMMEL n revolving cylindrical sieve used to screen crushed ore

TROMP vb trample

TROMPE n apparatus for supplying the blast of air in a forge, consisting of a thin column down which water falls, drawing in air through side openings

TROMPED ▸ tromp

TROMPES ▸ trompe

TROMPS ▸ tromp

TRON n public weighing machine

TRONA n greyish mineral that consists of hydrated sodium carbonate and occurs in salt deposits

TRONAS ▸ trona

TRONC n pool into which waiters, waitresses, hotel workers, etc, pay their tips

TRONCS ▸ tronc

TRONE same as ▸ tron

TRONES ▸ trone

TRONK n jail

TRONKS ▸ tronk

TRONS ▸ tron

TROOLIE n large palm leaf

TROOP n large group ▷ vb move in a crowd

TROOPED ▸ troop

TROOPER n cavalry soldier

TROOPS ▸ troop

TROOZ same as ▸ trews

TROP adv too, too much

TROPE n figure of speech ▷ vb use tropes (in speech or writing)

TROPED ▸ trope

TROPES ▸ trope

TROPHI pl n collective term for the mandibles and other parts of an insect's mouth

TROPHIC adj of or relating to nutrition

TROPHY n cup, shield, etc given as a prize ▷ adj regraded as a highly desirable symbol of wealth or success ▷ vb award a trophy to (someone)

TROPIC n either of two lines of latitude at $23\frac{1}{2}°$N (tropic of Cancer) or $23\frac{1}{2}°$S (tropic of Capricorn)

TROPICS ▸ tropic

TROPIN n adrenal androgen

TROPINE n white crystalline poisonous hygroscopic alkaloid obtained by heating atropine or hyoscyamine with barium hydroxide

TROPING ▸ trope

TROPINS ▸ tropin

TROPISM n tendency of a plant or animal to turn or curve in response to an external stimulus

TROPIST ▸ tropism

TROPPO adv too much ▷ adj mentally affected by a tropical climate

TROT vb (of a horse) move at a medium pace, lifting the feet in diagonal pairs ▷ n trotting

TROTH n pledge of devotion, esp a betrothal ▷ vb promise to marry (someone)

TROTHED ▸ troth

TROTHS ▸ troth

TROTS ▸ trot

TROTTED ▸ trot

TROTTER n pig's foot

TROTYL n trinitrotoluene; a yellow solid: used chiefly as a high explosive and is also an intermediate in the manufacture of dyestuffs

TROTYLS ▸ trotyl

TROUBLE n (cause of) distress or anxiety ▷ vb (cause to) worry

TROUCH n rubbish

TROUGH n long open container, esp for animals' food or water ▷ vb eat, consume, or take greedily

TROUGHS ▸ trough

TROULE old variant of ▸ troll

TROULED ▸ troule

TROULES ▸ troule

TROUNCE vb defeat utterly

TROUPE n company of performers ▷ vb (esp of actors) to move or travel in a group

TROUPED ▸ troupe

TROUPER n member of a troupe

TROUPES ▸ troupe

TROUSE pl n close-fitting breeches worn in Ireland

TROUSER adj of trousers ▷ vb take (something, esp money), often surreptitiously or unlawfully ▷ n of or relating to trousers

TROUSES ▸ trouse

TROUT n game fish related to the salmon ▷ vb fish for trout

TROUTER ▸ trout

TROUTS ▸ trout

TROUTY ▸ trout

TROVE n as in treasure-trove valuable articles, such as coins, bullion, etc, found hidden in the earth or elsewhere and of unknown ownership

TROVER n (formerly) the act of wrongfully assuming proprietary rights over personal goods or property belonging to another

TROVERS ▸ trover

TROVES ▸ trove

TROW vb think, believe, or trust

TROWED ▸ trow

TROWEL n hand tool with a wide blade for spreading mortar, lifting plants, etc ▷ vb use a trowel on (plaster, soil, etc)

TROWELS ▸ trowel

TROWING ▸ trow

TROWS ▸ trow

TROWTH variant spelling of ▸ troth

TROWTHS ▸ trowth

TROY n as in troy weight system of weights used for

precious metals and gemstones, based on the grain, which is identical to the avoirdupois grain

TROYS ▷ **troy**

TRUANCY ▷ **truant**

TRUANT n pupil who stays away from school without permission ▷ adj being or relating to a truant ▷ vb play truant

TRUANTS ▷ **truant**

TRUCAGE n art forgery

TRUCE n temporary agreement to stop fighting ▷ vb make a truce

TRUCED ▷ **truce**

TRUCES ▷ **truce**

TRUCIAL ▷ **truce**

TRUCING ▷ **truce**

TRUCK n railway goods wagon ▷ vb exchange (goods); barter

TRUCKED ▷ **truck**

TRUCKER n truck driver

TRUCKIE n truck driver

TRUCKLE vb yield weakly or give in ▷ n small wheel

TRUCKS ▷ **truck**

TRUDGE vb walk heavily or wearily ▷ n long tiring walk

TRUDGED ▷ **trudge**

TRUDGEN n type of swimming stroke that uses overarm action, as in the crawl, and a scissors kick

TRUDGER ▷ **trudge**

TRUDGES ▷ **trudge**

TRUE adj in accordance with facts

TRUED ▷ **true**

TRUEING ▷ **true**

TRUEMAN n honest person

TRUEMEN ▷ **trueman**

TRUER ▷ **true**

TRUES ▷ **true**

TRUEST ▷ **true**

TRUFFE rare word for ▷ **truffle**

TRUFFES ▷ **truffle**

TRUFFLE n edible underground fungus ▷ vb hunt for truffles

TRUG n long shallow basket used by gardeners

TRUGO n game similar to croquet, originally improvised in Victoria from the rubber discs used as buffers on railway carriages

TRUGOS ▷ **trugo**

TRUGS ▷ **trug**

TRUING ▷ **true**

TRUISM n self-evident truth

TRUISMS ▷ **truism**

TRULL n prostitute

TRULLS ▷ **trull**

TRULY adv in a true manner

TRUMEAU n section of a wall or pillar between two openings

TRUMP adj (card) of the suit outranking the others ▷ vb play a trump card on (another card) ▷ pl n suit outranking the others

TRUMPED ▷ **trump**

TRUMPET n valved brass instrument with a flared tube ▷ vb proclaim loudly

TRUMPS ▷ **trump**

TRUNCAL adj of or relating to the trunk

TRUNDLE vb move heavily on wheels ▷ n act or an instance of trundling

TRUNK n main stem of a tree ▷ vb lop or truncate

TRUNKED ▷ **trunk**

TRUNKS pl n shorts worn by a man for swimming

TRUNNEL same as ▷ **treenail**

TRUSS vb tie or bind up ▷ n device for holding a hernia, etc in place

TRUSSED ▷ **truss**

TRUSSER ▷ **truss**

TRUSSES ▷ **truss**

TRUST vb believe in and rely on ▷ n confidence in the truth, reliability, etc of a person or thing ▷ adj of or relating to a trust or trusts

TRUSTED ▷ **trust**

TRUSTEE n person holding property on another's behalf ▷ vb act as a trustee

TRUSTER ▷ **trust**

TRUSTOR n person who sets up a trust

TRUSTS ▷ **trust**

TRUSTY adj faithful or reliable ▷ n trustworthy convict to whom special privileges are granted

TRUTH n state of being true

TRUTHS ▷ **truth**

TRUTHY adj truthful

TRY vb make an effort or attempt ▷ n attempt or effort

TRYE adj very good; select

TRYER same as ▷ **trier**

TRYERS ▷ **tryer**

TRYING ▷ **try**

TRYINGS ▷ **try**

TRYKE variant spelling of ▷ **trike**

TRYKES ▷ **tryke**

TRYMA n drupe produced by the walnut and similar plants, in which the endocarp is a hard shell and the epicarp is dehiscent

TRYMATA ▷ **tryma**

TRYOUT n a trial or test, as of an athlete or actor

TRYOUTS ▷ **tryout**

TRYP n parasitic protozoan

TRYPAN modifier as in **trypan blue** dye obtained from tolidine that is absorbed by the macrophages of the reticuloendothelial system and is therefore used for staining cells in biological research

TRYPS ▷ **tryp**

TRYPSIN n enzyme occurring in pancreatic juice

TRYPTIC ▷ **trypsin**

TRYSAIL n small fore-and-aft sail set on a sailing vessel to help keep her head to the wind in a storm

TRYST n arrangement to meet ▷ vb meet at or arrange a tryst

TRYSTE variant spelling of ▷ **tryst**

TRYSTED ▷ **tryst**

TRYSTER ▷ **tryst**

TRYSTES ▷ **tryste**

TRYSTS ▷ **tryst**

TSADDIK same as ▷ **zaddik**

TSADDIQ same as ▷ **zaddik**

TSADE variant spelling of ▷ **sadhe**

TSADES ▷ **tsade**

TSADI same as ▷ **sadhe**

TSADIS ▷ **tsadi**

TSAMBA n Tibetan dish made from roasted barley and tea

TSAMBAS ▷ **tsamba**

TSANTSA n (among the Shuar subgroup of the Jivaro people of Ecuador) shrunken head of an enemy kept as a trophy

TSAR n Russian emperor

TSARDOM ▷ **tsar**

TSARINA n wife of a Russian tsar

TSARISM n system of

government by a tsar, esp in Russia until 1917

TSARIST ▸ **tsarism**

TSARS ▸ **tsar**

TSATSKE same as > **tchotchke**

TSETSE n any of various bloodsucking African dipterous flies which transmit the pathogens of various diseases

TSETSES ▸ **tsetse**

TSIGANE same as ▸ **tzigane**

TSIMMES variant spelling of ▸ **tzimmes**

TSK vb utter the sound "tsk", usu in disapproval

> This can occasionally be useful because it enables you to play K without using vowels.

TSKED ▸ **tsk**

TSKING ▸ **tsk**

TSKS ▸ **tsk**

TSKTSK same as ▸ **tsk**

TSKTSKS ▸ **tsktsk**

TSOORIS same as ▸ **tsuris**

TSORES same as ▸ **tsuris**

TSORIS same as ▸ **tsuris**

TSOTSI n Black street thug or gang member

TSOTSIS ▸ **tsotsi**

TSOURIS same as ▸ **tsuris**

TSUBA n sword guard of a Japanese sword

TSUBAS ▸ **tsuba**

TSUNAMI n tidal wave, usu caused by an earthquake under the sea

TSURIS n grief or strife

TUAN n lord

TUANS ▸ **tuan**

TUART n eucalyptus tree of Australia, yielding a very durable light-coloured timber

TUARTS ▸ **tuart**

TUATARA n large lizard-like New Zealand reptile

TUATERA variant spelling of ▸ **tuatara**

TUATH n territory of an ancient Irish tribe

TUATHS ▸ **tuath**

TUATUA n edible marine bivalve of New Zealand waters

TUATUAS ▸ **tuatua**

TUB n open, usu round container ▷ vb wash (oneself or another) in a tub

TUBA n valved low-pitched brass instrument

TUBAE ▸ **tuba**

TUBAGE n insertion of a tube

TUBAGES ▸ **tubage**

TUBAIST ▸ **tuba**

TUBAL adj of or relating to a tube

TUBAR another word for ▸ **tubular**

TUBAS ▸ **tuba**

TUBATE less common word for ▸ **tubular**

TUBBED ▸ **tub**

TUBBER ▸ **tub**

TUBBERS ▸ **tub**

TUBBIER ▸ **tubby**

TUBBING ▸ **tub**

TUBBISH adj fat

TUBBY adj (of a person) short and fat

TUBE n hollow cylinder

TUBED ▸ **tube**

TUBEFUL n quantity (of something) that a tube can hold

TUBER n fleshy underground root of a plant such as a potato

TUBERS ▸ **tuber**

TUBES ▸ **tube**

TUBFAST n period of fasting and sweating in a tub, intended as a cure for disease

TUBFISH another name for ▸ **gurnard**

TUBFUL n amount a tub will hold

TUBFULS ▸ **tubful**

TUBIFEX n type of small reddish freshwater worm

TUBING n length of tube

TUBINGS ▸ **tubing**

TUBIST ▸ **tuba**

TUBISTS ▸ **tuba**

TUBLIKE ▸ **tub**

TUBS ▸ **tub**

TUBULAR adj of or shaped like a tube

TUBULE n any small tubular structure, esp in an animal or plant

TUBULES ▸ **tubule**

TUBULIN n protein forming the basis of microtubules

TUCHUN n (formerly) a Chinese military governor or warlord

TUCHUNS ▸ **tuchun**

TUCK vb push or fold into a small space ▷ n stitched fold ▷ vb touch or strike

TUCKED ▸ **tuck**

TUCKER n food ▷ vb weary or tire completely

TUCKERS ▸ **tucker**

TUCKET n flourish on a trumpet

TUCKETS ▸ **tucket**

TUCKING ▸ **tuck**

TUCKS ▸ **tuck**

TUFA n porous rock formed as a deposit from springs

TUFAS ▸ **tufa**

TUFF n porous rock formed from volcanic dust or ash

TUFFE old form of ▸ **tuft**

TUFFES ▸ **tuffe**

TUFFET n small mound or seat

TUFFETS ▸ **tuffet**

TUFFS ▸ **tuff**

TUFOLI n type of tubular pasta

TUFT n bunch of feathers, grass, hair, etc held or growing together at the base ▷ vb provide or decorate with a tuft or tufts

TUFTED adj having a tuft or tufts

TUFTER ▸ **tuft**

TUFTERS ▸ **tuft**

TUFTIER ▸ **tuft**

TUFTILY ▸ **tuft**

TUFTING ▸ **tuft**

TUFTS ▸ **tuft**

TUFTY ▸ **tuft**

TUG vb pull hard ▷ n hard pull

TUGBOAT same as ▸ **tug**

TUGGED ▸ **tug**

TUGGER ▸ **tug**

TUGGERS ▸ **tug**

TUGGING ▸ **tug**

TUGHRA n Turkish Sultan's official emblem

TUGHRAS ▸ **tughra**

TUGHRIK same as ▸ **tugrik**

TUGLESS ▸ **tug**

TUGRA same as ▸ **tughra**

TUGRAS ▸ **tugra**

TUGRIK n standard monetary unit of Mongolia, divided into 100 möngös

TUGRIKS ▸ **tugrik**

TUGS ▸ **tug**

TUI n New Zealand honeyeater that mimics human speech and the songs of other birds

TUILLE n (in a suit of armour) hanging plate protecting the thighs

TUILLES ▸ **tuille**

TUILYIE vb fight

TUILZIE *variant form of* ▶**tuilyie**

TUINA *n* form of massage originating in China

TUINAS ▶**tuina**

TUIS ▶**tui**

TUISM *n* practice of putting the interests of another before one's own

TUISMS ▶**tuism**

TUITION *n* instruction, esp received individually or in a small group

TUKTOO *same as* ▶**tuktu**

TUKTOOS ▶**tuktoo**

TUKTU *(in Canada) another name for* ▶**caribou**

TUKTUS ▶**tuktu**

TULADI *n* large trout found in Canada and northern areas of the US

TULADIS ▶**tuladi**

TULBAN *old form of* ▶**turban**

TULBANS ▶**tulban**

TULCHAN *n* skin of a calf placed next to a cow to induce it to give milk

TULE *n* type of bulrush found in California

TULES ▶**tule**

TULIP *n* plant with bright cup shaped flowers

TULIPS ▶**tulip**

TULLE *n* fine net fabric of silk etc

TULLES ▶**tulle**

TULPA *n* being or object created through willpower and visualization techniques

TULPAS ▶**tulpa**

TULWAR *n* Indian sabre

TULWARS ▶**tulwar**

TUM *informal or childish word for* ▶**stomach**

TUMBLE *vb* (cause to) fall, esp awkwardly or violently ▷ *n* fall

TUMBLED ▶**tumble**

TUMBLER *n* stemless drinking glass

TUMBLES ▶**tumble**

TUMBREL *n* farm cart for carrying dung, esp one that tilts backwards to deposit its load

TUMBRIL *same as* ▶**tumbrel**

TUMEFY *vb* make or become tumid

TUMESCE *vb* swell

TUMID *adj* (of an organ or part of the body) enlarged or swollen

TUMIDLY ▶**tumid**

TUMMIES ▶**tummy**

TUMMLER *n* comedian or other entertainer employed to encourage audience participation or to encourage guests at a resort to take part in communal activities

TUMMY *n* stomach

TUMOR *same as* ▶**tumour**

TUMORAL ▶**tumour**

TUMORS ▶**tumor**

TUMOUR *n* abnormal growth in or on the body

TUMOURS ▶**tumour**

TUMP *n* small mound or clump ▷ *vb* make a tump around

TUMPED ▶**tump**

TUMPHY *n* dolt; fool

TUMPIER ▶**tump**

TUMPING ▶**tump**

TUMPS ▶**tump**

TUMPY ▶**tump**

TUMS ▶**tum**

TUMSHIE *n* turnip

TUMULAR *adj* of, relating to, or like a mound

TUMULI ▶**tumulus**

TUMULT *n* uproar or commotion ▷ *vb* stir up a commotion

TUMULTS ▶**tumult**

TUMULUS *n* burial mound

TUN *n* large beer cask ▷ *vb* put into or keep in tuns

TUNA *n* large marine food fish

TUNABLE *adj* able to be tuned

TUNABLY ▶**tunable**

TUNAS ▶**tuna**

TUND *vb* beat; strike

TUNDED ▶**tund**

TUNDING ▶**tund**

TUNDISH *n* type of funnel

TUNDRA *n* vast treeless Arctic region with permanently frozen subsoil

TUNDRAS ▶**tundra**

TUNDS ▶**tund**

TUNDUN *n* wooden instrument used by Native Australians in religious rites

TUNDUNS ▶**tundun**

TUNE *n* (pleasing) sequence of musical notes ▷ *vb* adjust (a musical instrument) so that it is in tune

TUNED ▶**tune**

TUNEFUL *adj* having a pleasant tune

TUNER *n* part of a radio or television receiver for selecting channels

TUNERS ▶**tuner**

TUNES ▶**tune**

TUNEUP *n* adjustments made to an engine to improve its performance

TUNEUPS ▶**tuneup**

TUNG *n* *as in* **tung oil** fast-drying oil obtained from the seeds of a central Asian euphorbiaceous tree, used in paints, varnishes, etc, as a drying agent and to give a water-resistant finish

TUNGS ▶**tung**

TUNIC *n* close-fitting jacket forming part of some uniforms

TUNICA *n* tissue forming a layer or covering of an organ or part, such as any of the tissue layers of a blood vessel wall

TUNICAE ▶**tunica**

TUNICIN *n* cellulose-like substance found in tunicates

TUNICLE *n* liturgical vestment worn by the subdeacon and bishops at High Mass and other religious ceremonies

TUNICS ▶**tunic**

TUNIER ▶**tuny**

TUNIEST ▶**tuny**

TUNING *n* set of pitches to which the open strings of a guitar, violin, etc, are tuned

TUNINGS ▶**tuning**

TUNNAGE *same as* ▶**tonnage**

TUNNED ▶**tun**

TUNNEL *n* underground passage ▷ *vb* make a tunnel (through)

TUNNELS ▶**tunnel**

TUNNIES ▶**tunny**

TUNNING ▶**tun**

TUNNY *same as* ▶**tuna**

TUNS ▶**tun**

TUNY *adj* having an easily discernable melody

TUP *n* male sheep ▷ *vb* cause (a ram) to mate with a ewe, or (of a ram) to mate with (a ewe)

TUPEK *same as* ▶**tupik**

TUPEKS ▶ **tupek**

TUPELO *n* large tree of deep swamps and rivers of the southern US

TUPELOS ▶ **tupelo**

TUPIK *n* tent of seal or caribou skin used for shelter by the Inuit in summer

TUPIKS ▶ **tupik**

TUPLE *n* row of values in a relational database

TUPLES ▶ **tuple**

TUPPED ▶ **tup**

TUPPING ▶ **tup**

TUPS ▶ **tup**

TUPUNA *same as* ▶ **tipuna**

TUPUNAS ▶ **tupuna**

TUQUE *n* knitted cap with a long tapering end

TUQUES ▶ **tuque**

TURACIN *n* red pigment found in touraco feathers

TURACO *same as* ▶ **touraco**

TURACOS ▶ **turaco**

TURACOU *same as* ▶ **touraco**

TURBAN *n* Muslim, Hindu, or Sikh man's head covering, made by winding cloth round the head

TURBAND *old variant of* ▶ **turban**

TURBANS ▶ **turban**

TURBANT *old variant of* ▶ **turban**

TURBARY *n* land where peat or turf is cut or has been cut

TURBETH *same as* ▶ **turpeth**

TURBID *adj* muddy, not clear

TURBINE *n* machine or generator driven by gas, water, etc turning blades

TURBIT *n* crested breed of domestic pigeon

TURBITH *same as* ▶ **turpeth**

TURBITS ▶ **turbit**

TURBO *n* compressor in an engine

TURBOND *old variant of* ▶ **turban**

TURBOS ▶ **turbo**

TURBOT *n* large European edible flatfish

TURBOTS ▶ **turbot**

TURDINE *adj* of, relating to, or characteristic of thrushes

TURDION *same as* ▶ **tordion**

TURDOID *same as* ▶ **turdine**

TUREEN *n* serving dish for soup

TUREENS ▶ **tureen**

TURF *n* short thick even grass ▷ *vb* cover with turf

TURFED ▶ **turf**

TURFEN *adj* made of turf

TURFIER ▶ **turfy**

TURFING ▶ **turf**

TURFITE *same as* ▶ **turfman**

TURFMAN *n* person devoted to horse racing

TURFMEN ▶ **turfman**

TURFS ▶ **turf**

TURFSKI *n* ski down a grassy hill on skis modified with integral wheels

TURFY *adj* of, covered with, or resembling turf

TURGENT *obsolete word for* ▶ **turgid**

TURGID *adj* (of language) pompous

TURGITE *n* red or black mineral consisting of hydrated ferric oxide

TURGOR *n* normal rigid state of a cell, caused by pressure of the cell contents against the cell wall or membrane

TURGORS ▶ **turgor**

TURION *n* perennating bud produced by many aquatic plants

TURIONS ▶ **turion**

TURISTA *n* traveller's diarrhoea

TURKEY *n* large bird bred for food

TURKEYS ▶ **turkey**

TURKIES *old form of* ▷ **turquoise**

TURKIS *old form of* ▷ **turquoise**

TURKOIS *old form of* ▷ **turquoise**

TURM *n* troop of horsemen

TURME *same as* ▶ **turm**

TURMES ▶ **turme**

TURMOIL *n* agitation or confusion ▷ *vb* make or become turbulent

TURMS ▶ **turm**

TURN *vb* change the position or direction (of) ▷ *n* turning

TURNDUN *another name for* ▶ **tundun**

TURNED ▶ **turn**

TURNER *n* person or thing that turns, esp a person

who operates a lathe

TURNERS ▶ **turner**

TURNERY *n* objects made on a lathe

TURNING *n* road or path leading off a main route

TURNIP *n* root vegetable with orange or white flesh ▷ *vb* sow (a field) with turnips

TURNIPS ▶ **turnip**

TURNIPY *adj* like a turnip

TURNKEY *n* jailer ▷ *adj* denoting a project, as in civil engineering, in which a single contractor has responsibility for the complete job from the start to the time of installation or occupancy

TURNOFF *n* road or other way branching off from the main

TURNON *n* something sexually exciting

TURNONS ▶ **turnon**

TURNOUT *n* number of people appearing at a gathering

TURNS ▶ **turn**

TURNUP *n* the turned-up fold at the bottom of some trouser legs

TURNUPS ▶ **turnup**

TURPETH *n* convolvulaceous plant of the East Indies, having roots with purgative properties

TURPS *n* colourless, flammable liquid

TURRET *n* small tower

TURRETS ▶ **turret**

TURTLE *n* sea tortoise

TURTLED ▶ **turtle**

TURTLER ▶ **turtle**

TURTLES ▶ **turtle**

TURVES ▶ **turf**

TUSCHE *n* substance used in lithography for drawing the design and as a resist in silk-screen printing and lithography

TUSCHES ▶ **tusche**

TUSH *interj* exclamation of disapproval or contempt ▷ *n* small tusk ▷ *vb* utter the interjection "tush"

TUSHED ▶ **tush**

TUSHERY *n* use of affectedly archaic language in novels, etc

TUSHES ▶ **tush**

TUSHIE n pair of buttocks
TUSHIES ▶ tushie
TUSHING ▶ tush
TUSHKAR same as
▶ tuskar
TUSHKER same as ▶ tuskar
TUSHY same as ▶ tushie
TUSK n long pointed tooth of an elephant, walrus, etc ▷ vb stab, tear, or gore with the tusks
TUSKAR n peat-cutting spade
TUSKARS ▶ tuskar
TUSKED ▶ tusk
TUSKER n any animal with prominent tusks, esp a wild boar or elephant
TUSKERS ▶ tusker
TUSKIER ▶ tusk
TUSKING ▶ tusk
TUSKS ▶ tusk
TUSKY ▶ tusk
TUSSAC modifier as in **tussac grass** kind of grass
TUSSAH same as ▶ tussore
TUSSAHS ▶ tussah
TUSSAL ▶ tussis
TUSSAR same as ▶ tussore
TUSSARS ▶ tussar
TUSSEH same as ▶ tussore
TUSSEHS ▶ tusseh
TUSSER same as ▶ tussore
TUSSERS ▶ tusser
TUSSES ▶ tussis
TUSSIS technical name for a ▶ cough
TUSSIVE ▶ tussis
TUSSLE vb fight or scuffle ▷ n energetic fight, struggle, or argument
TUSSLED ▶ tussle
TUSSLES ▶ tussle
TUSSOCK n tuft of grass
TUSSOR same as ▶ tussore
TUSSORE n strong coarse brownish Indian silk obtained from the cocoons of an Oriental saturniid silkworm
TUSSORS ▶ tussor
TUSSUCK same as ▶ tussock
TUSSUR same as ▶ tussore
TUSSURS ▶ tussur
TUT interj an exclamation of mild reprimand, disapproval, or surprise ▷ vb express disapproval by the exclamation of "tut-tut." ▷ n payment system based on measurable work done

rather that time spent doing it
TUTANIA n alloy of low melting point containing tin, antimony, copper and used mostly for decorative purposes
TUTEE n one who is tutored, esp in a university
TUTEES ▶ tutee
TUTELAR same as
> tutelary
TUTENAG n zinc alloy
TUTMAN n one who does tutwork
TUTMEN ▶ tutman
TUTOR n person teaching individuals or small groups ▷ vb act as a tutor to
TUTORED ▶ tutor
TUTORS ▶ tutor
TUTOYED adj addressed in a familiar way
TUTOYER vb speak to someone on familiar terms
TUTRESS same as > tutoress
TUTRIX n female tutor; tutoress
TUTS Scots version of ▶ tut
TUTSAN n woodland shrub of Europe and W Asia
TUTSANS ▶ tutsan
TUTSED ▶ tuts
TUTSES ▶ tuts
TUTSING ▶ tuts
TUTTED ▶ tut
TUTTI adv be performed by the whole orchestra or choir ▷ n piece of tutti music
TUTTIES ▶ tutty
TUTTING ▶ tut
TUTTIS ▶ tutti
TUTTY n finely powdered impure zinc oxide obtained from the flues of zinc-smelting furnaces and used as a polishing powder
TUTU n short stiff skirt worn by ballerinas
TUTUED adj wearing tutu
TUTUS ▶ tutu
TUTWORK n work paid using a tut system
TUX short for ▶ tuxedo

Tux is a short form of **tuxedo**, and is a very commonly played X word.

TUXEDO n dinner jacket
TUXEDOS ▶ tuxedo
TUXES ▶ tux
TUYER same as ▶ tuyere

TUYERE n water-cooled nozzle through which air is blown into a cupola, blast furnace, or forge
TUYERES ▶ tuyere
TUYERS ▶ tuyer
TUZZ n tuft or clump of hair
TUZZES ▶ tuzz
TWA Scots word for ▶ two
TWADDLE n silly or pretentious talk or writing ▷ vb talk or write in a silly or pretentious way
TWADDLY ▶ twaddle
TWAE same as ▶ twa
TWAES ▶ twae
TWAFALD Scots variant of ▶ twofold
TWAIN n two
TWAINS ▶ twain
TWAITE n herring-like food fish
TWAITES ▶ twaite
TWAL n twelve
TWALS ▶ twal
TWANG n sharp ringing sound ▷ vb (cause to) make a twang
TWANGED ▶ twang
TWANGER ▶ twang
TWANGLE vb make a continuous loose twanging sound (on a musical instrument, for example)
TWANGS ▶ twang
TWANGY ▶ twang
TWANK vb make an sharply curtailed twang
TWANKAY n variety of Chinese green tea
TWANKS ▶ twank
TWANKY same as
▶ twankay
TWAS ▶ twa
TWASOME same as
▶ twosome
TWATTLE rare word for
▶ twaddle
TWAY old variant of ▶ twain
TWAYS ▶ tway
TWEAK vb pinch or twist sharply ▷ n tweaking
TWEAKED ▶ tweak
TWEAKER n engineer's small screwdriver, used for fine adjustments
TWEAKS ▶ tweak
TWEAKY ▶ tweak
TWEE adj too sentimental, sweet, or pretty
TWEED n thick woollen cloth
TWEEDLE vb improvise

T

aimlessly on a musical instrument

TWEEDS ▶ tweed

TWEEDY adj of or made of tweed

TWEEL same as ▶ twill

TWEELED ▶ tweel

TWEELS ▶ tweel

TWEELY ▶ twee

TWEEN same as ▶ between

TWEENER same as > tweenager

TWEENIE same as ▶ tweeny

TWEENS ▶ tween

TWEENY n maid who assists both cook and housemaid

TWEER same as ▶ twire

TWEERED ▶ tweer

TWEERS ▶ tweer

TWEEST ▶ twee

TWEET vb chirp ▷ interj imitation of the thin chirping sound made by small birds

TWEETED ▶ tweet

TWEETER n loudspeaker reproducing high-frequency sounds

TWEETS ▶ tweet

TWEEZE vb take hold of or pluck (hair, small objects, etc) with or as if with tweezers

TWEEZED ▶ tweeze

TWEEZER same as > tweezers

TWEEZES ▶ tweeze

TWELFTH n (of) number twelve in a series ▷ adj of or being number twelve in a series

TWELVE n two more than ten ▷ adj amounting to twelve ▷ determiner amounting to twelve

TWELVES ▶ twelve

TWENTY n two times ten ▷ adj amounting to twenty ▷ determiner amounting to twenty

TWERP n silly person

TWERPS ▶ twerp

TWERPY ▶ twerp

TWIBIL same as ▶ twibill

TWIBILL n mattock with a blade shaped like an adze at one end and like an axe at the other

TWIBILS ▶ twibil

TWICE adv two times

TWICER n someone who does something twice

TWICERS ▶ twicer

TWIDDLE vb fiddle or twirl in an idle way ▷ n act or instance of twiddling

TWIDDLY ▶ twiddle

TWIER same as ▶ tuyere

TWIERS ▶ twier

TWIFOLD same as ▶ twofold

TWIG n small branch or shoot ▷ vb realize or understand

TWIGGED ▶ twig

TWIGGEN adj made of twigs

TWIGGER ▶ twig

TWIGGY adj of or relating to a twig or twigs

TWIGHT old variant of ▶ twit

TWIGHTS ▶ twight

TWIGLET n small twig

TWIGLOO n temporary shelter made from twigs, branches, leaves, etc

TWIGS ▶ twig

TWILIT > twilight

TWILL n fabric woven to produce parallel ridges ▷ adj (in textiles) of or designating a weave in which the weft yarns are worked around two or more warp yarns to produce an effect of parallel diagonal lines or ribs ▷ vb weave in this fashion

TWILLED ▶ twill

TWILLS ▶ twill

TWILLY n machine having a system of revolving spikes for opening and cleaning raw textile fibres

TWILT same as ▶ quilt

TWILTED ▶ twilt

TWILTS ▶ twilt

TWIN n one of a pair, esp of two children born at one birth ▷ vb pair or be paired

TWINE n string or cord ▷ vb twist or coil round

TWINED ▶ twine

TWINER ▶ twine

TWINERS ▶ twine

TWINES ▶ twine

TWINGE n sudden sharp pain or emotional pang ▷ vb have or cause to have a twinge

TWINGED ▶ twinge

TWINGES ▶ twinge

TWINIER ▶ twine

TWINING ▶ twine

TWINJET n jet aircraft with two engines

TWINK n white correction fluid for deleting written text ▷ vb twinkle

TWINKED ▶ twink

TWINKIE n stupid person

TWINKLE vb shine brightly but intermittently ▷ n flickering brightness

TWINKLY ▶ twinkle

TWINKS ▶ twink

TWINNED ▶ twin

TWINS ▶ twin

TWINSET n matching jumper and cardigan

TWINTER n animal that is 2 years old

TWINY ▶ twine

TWIRE vb look intently at with (or as if with) difficulty

TWIRED ▶ twire

TWIRES ▶ twire

TWIRING ▶ twire

TWIRL vb turn or spin around quickly ▷ n whirl or twist

TWIRLED ▶ twirl

TWIRLER ▶ twirl

TWIRLS ▶ twirl

TWIRLY ▶ twirl

TWIRP same as ▶ twerp

TWIRPS ▶ twirp

TWIRPY ▶ twirp

TWISCAR same as ▶ tuskar

TWIST vb turn out of the natural position ▷ n twisting

TWISTED ▶ twist

TWISTER n swindler

TWISTOR n variable corresponding to the coordinates of a point in space and time

TWISTS ▶ twist

TWISTY ▶ twist

TWIT vb poke fun at (someone) ▷ n foolish person

TWITCH vb move spasmodically ▷ n nervous muscular spasm

TWITCHY adj nervous, worried, and ill-at-ease

TWITE n N European finch with a brown streaked plumage

TWITES ▶ twite

TWITS ▶ twit

TWITTED ▶ twit

TWITTEN n narrow alleyway

TWITTER vb (of birds) utter chirping sounds ▷ n act or sound of twittering

TWIXT *same as* ▶ **betwixt**
TWIZZLE *vb* spin around
TWO *n* one more than one
TWOCCER > **twoccing**
TWOCKER > **twoccing**
TWOER *n* (in a game) something that scores two
TWOERS ▶ **twoer**
TWOFER *n* single ticket allowing the buyer entrance to two events, attractions, etc, for substantially less than the cost were he or she to pay for each individually
TWOFERS ▶ **twofer**
TWOFOLD *adj* having twice as many or as much ▷ *adv* by twice as many or as much ▷ *n* folding piece of theatrical scenery
TWONESS *n* state or condition of being two
TWONIE *same as* ▶ **toonie**
TWONIES ▶ **twonie**
TWOONIE *same as* ▶ **toonie**
TWOS ▶ **two**
TWOSOME *n* group of two people
TWP *adj* stupid

> This Welsh word for stupid is useful because it contains no vowels, and can thus help when you have an awkward rack full of consonants.

TWYER *same as* ▶ **tuyere**
TWYERE *same as* ▶ **tuyere**
TWYERES ▶ **twyere**
TWYERS ▶ **twyer**
TWYFOLD *adj* twofold
TYCHISM *n* theory that chance is an objective reality at work in the universe, esp in evolutionary adaptations
TYCOON *n* powerful wealthy businessman; shogun
TYCOONS ▶ **tycoon**
TYDE *old variant of the past participle of* ▶ **tie**
TYE *n* trough used in mining to separate valuable material from dross ▷ *vb* (in mining) isolate valuable material from dross using a tye
TYED ▶ **tye**
TYEE *n* large northern Pacific salmon
TYEES ▶ **tyee**
TYEING ▶ **tye**

TYER ▶ **tye**
TYERS ▶ **tye**
TYES ▶ **tye**
TYG *n* mug with two handles

> This old word for a two-handled drinking cup is another key word to know for situations when you are short of vowels.

TYGS ▶ **tyg**
TYIN *same as* ▶ **tyiyn**
TYING ▶ **tie**
TYIYN *n* money unit of Kyrgyzstan
TYIYNS ▶ **tyiyn**
TYLER *same as* ▶ **tiler**
TYLERS ▶ **tyler**
TYLOPOD *n* mammal with padded feet, such as a camel or llama
TYLOSES ▶ **tylosis**
TYLOSIN *n* broad spectrum antibiotic
TYLOSIS *n* bladder-like outgrowth from certain cells in woody tissue that extends into and blocks adjacent conducting xylem cells
TYLOTE *n* knobbed sponge spicule
TYLOTES ▶ **tylote**
TYMBAL *same as* ▶ **timbal**
TYMBALS ▶ **tymbal**
TYMP *n* blast furnace outlet through which molten metal flows
TYMPAN *same as* > **tympanum**
TYMPANA ▶ **tympanum**
TYMPANI *same as* ▶ **timpani**
TYMPANO ▶ **tympani**
TYMPANS ▶ **tympan**
TYMPANY *n* distention of the abdomen
TYMPS ▶ **tymp**
TYND *same as* ▶ **tind**
TYNDE *same as* ▶ **tind**
TYNE *same as* ▶ **tine**
TYNED *same as* ▶ **tyne**
TYNES ▶ **tyne**
TYNING ▶ **tyne**
TYPABLE ▶ **type**
TYPAL *rare word for* ▶ **typical**
TYPE *n* class or category ▷ *vb* print with a typewriter or word processor
TYPEBAR *n* one of the bars in a typewriter that carry

the type and are operated by keys
TYPED ▶ **type**
TYPES ▶ **type**
TYPESET *vb* set (text for printing) in type
TYPEY *same as* ▶ **typy**
TYPHOID *adj* of or relating to typhoid fever
TYPHON *n* whirlwind
TYPHONS ▶ **typhon**
TYPHOON *n* violent tropical storm
TYPHOSE *adj* relating to typhoid
TYPHOUS ▶ **typhus**
TYPHUS *n* infectious feverish disease
TYPIC *same as* ▶ **typical**
TYPICAL *adj* true to type, characteristic
TYPIER ▶ **typy**
TYPIEST ▶ **typy**
TYPIFY *vb* be typical of
TYPING *n* work or activity of using a typewriter or word processor
TYPINGS ▶ **typing**
TYPIST *n* person who types with a typewriter or word processor
TYPISTS ▶ **typist**
TYPO *n* typographical error
TYPOS ▶ **typo**
TYPP *n* unit of thickness of yarn
TYPPS ▶ **typp**
TYPTO *vb* learn Greek conjugations
TYPTOED ▶ **typto**
TYPTOS ▶ **typto**
TYPY *adj* (of an animal) typifying the breed
TYRAN *vb* act as a tyrant
TYRANED ▶ **tyran**
TYRANNE *same as* ▶ **tyran**
TYRANNY *n* tyrannical rule
TYRANS ▶ **tyran**
TYRANT *n* oppressive or cruel ruler ▷ *vb* act the tyrant
TYRANTS ▶ **tyrant**
TYRE *n* rubber ring, usu inflated, over the rim of a vehicle's wheel to grip the road ▷ *vb* fit a tyre or tyres to (a wheel, vehicle, etc)
TYRED ▶ **tyre**
TYRES ▶ **tyre**
TYRING ▶ **tyre**
TYRO *n* novice or beginner
TYROES ▶ **tyro**
TYRONES ▶ **tyro**

T

TYRONIC ▶ tyro
TYROS ▶ tyro
TYSTIE n black guillemot
TYSTIES ▶ tystie
TYTE variant spelling of ▶ tite
TYTHE same as ▶ tithe
TYTHED ▶ tythe
TYTHES ▶ tythe
TYTHING ▶ tythe
TZADDI ▶ sadhe
TZADDIK same as ▶ zaddik
TZADDIQ same as ▶ zaddik

An unlikely word from Judaism, meaning a person of great piety, but offering a great score played as a bonus.

TZADDIS ▶ tzaddi
TZAR same as ▶ tsar
TZARDOM ▶ tzar
TZARINA same as ▶ tsarina
TZARISM same as ▶ tsarism
TZARIST ▶ tzarism
TZARS ▶ tzar

TZETSE same as ▶ tsetse
TZETSES ▶ tzetse
TZETZE same as ▶ tsetse
TZETZES ▶ tzetze
TZIGANE n type of Gypsy music
TZIGANY same as ▶ tzigane
TZIMMES n traditional Jewish stew
TZITZIS same as > tsitsith
TZITZIT same as > tsitsith
TZURIS same as ▶ tsuris**

T

Uu

U can be a difficult tile to use effectively. Although there are quite a few two-letter words beginning with **U**, most of them are quite unusual, and so difficult to remember. Only **up** (4 points) and **us** (2) are immediately obvious, so it's well worth learning words like **ug** (3), **uh** (5), **um** (4), and **un, ur** and **ut** (2 each). Three-letter words beginning with **U** can also be difficult to remember. If you are trying to use a **Q, X** or **Z**, bear in mind that there aren't any valid three-letter words with these letters that start with **U**. Knowing this can save you valuable time. It's also helpful to remember that there aren't any particularly high-scoring two- or three-letter words starting with **U**, the best being **uke** (7 points) and **uva** (6 points). If you have a surplus of **U**s, it is well worth remembering **ulu, umu** and **utu**, which score only 3 points but should improve your rack.

UAKARI n type of monkey
UAKARIS ▶ uakari
UBEROUS adj abundant
UBERTY n abundance
UBIETY n condition of being in a particular place
UBIQUE adv everywhere
UBUNTU n quality of compassion and humanity
UBUNTUS ▶ ubuntu
UCKERS n type of naval game
UDAL n form of freehold possession of land existing in northern Europe before the introduction of the feudal system and still used in Orkney and Shetland
UDALLER n person possessing a udal
UDALS ▶ udal
UDDER n large baglike milk-producing gland of cows, sheep, or goats
UDDERED ▶ udder
UDDERS ▶ udder
UDO n stout perennial plant of Japan and China with berry-like black fruits and young shoots that are edible when blanched
UDON n (in Japanese cookery) large noodles made of wheat flour
UDONS ▶ udon
UDOS ▶ udo
UDS interj God's or God save
UEY n u-turn

UEYS ▶ uey
UFO n flying saucer
UFOLOGY n study of UFOs
UFOS ▶ ufo
UG vb hate
UGALI n type of stiff porridge made by mixing corn meal with boiling water: the basic starch constituent of a meal
UGALIS ▶ ugali
UGGED ▶ ug
UGGING ▶ ug
UGH interj exclamation of disgust ▷ n sound made to indicate disgust

> Together with **uke**, this is the highest-scoring three-letter word starting with U.

UGHS ▶ ugh
UGLIED ▶ ugly
UGLIER ▶ ugly
UGLIES ▶ ugly
UGLIEST ▶ ugly
UGLIFY vb make or become ugly or more ugly
UGLILY ▶ ugly
UGLY adj of unpleasant appearance ▷ vb make ugly
UGLYING ▶ ugly
UGS ▶ ug
UGSOME adj loathsome
UH interj used to express hesitation
UHLAN n member of a body of lancers first employed in the Polish army and later in

W European armies
UHLANS ▶ uhlan
UHURU n national independence

> You won't often have three Us on your rack, but when you do this Swahili word for freedom may get you out of trouble. The only other 5-letter word containing three Us is **urubu**, a kind of vulture.

UHURUS ▶ uhuru
UILLEAN adj as in **uillean pipes** bagpipes developed in Ireland and operated by squeezing bellows under the arm
UJAMAA n as in **ujamaa village** communally organized village in Tanzania
UJAMAAS ▶ ujamaa
UKASE n (in imperial Russia) a decree from the tsar
UKASES ▶ ukase
UKE short form of ▶ **ukulele**

> Together with ugh, this is the highest-scoring three-letter word starting with U.

UKELELE same as ▶ **ukulele**
UKES ▶ uke
UKULELE n small guitar with four strings
ULAMA n body of Muslim

U

scholars or religious leaders
ULAMAS ▶ ulama
ULAN *same as* ▶ uhlan
ULANS ▶ ulan
ULCER *n* open sore on the surface of the skin or mucous membrane. ▷ *vb* make or become ulcerous
ULCERED ▶ ulcer
ULCERS ▶ ulcer
ULE *n* rubber tree
ULEMA *same as* ▶ ulama
ULEMAS ▶ ulema
ULES ▶ ule
ULEX *n* variety of shrub
ULEXES ▶ ulex
ULEXITE *n* type of mineral
ULICES ▶ ulex
ULICON *same as* > **eulachon**
ULICONS ▶ ulicon
ULIKON *same as* > **eulachon**
ULIKONS ▶ ulikon
ULITIS *n* gingivitis
ULLAGE *n* volume by which a liquid container falls short of being full ▷ *vb* create ullage in
ULLAGED ▶ ullage
ULLAGES ▶ ullage
ULLING *n* process of filling
ULLINGS ▶ ulling
ULMIN *n* substance found in decaying vegetation
ULMINS ▶ ulmin
ULNA *n* inner and longer of the two bones of the human forearm
ULNAD *adv* towards the ulna
ULNAE ▶ ulna
ULNAR ▶ ulna
ULNARE *n* bone in the wrist
ULNARIA ▶ ulnare
ULNAS ▶ ulna
ULOSES ▶ ulosis
ULOSIS *n* formation of a scar
ULPAN *n* Israeli study centre
ULPANIM ▶ ulpan
ULSTER *n* man's heavy double-breasted overcoat
ULSTERS ▶ ulster
ULTIMA *n* final syllable of a word
ULTIMAS ▶ ultima
ULTIMO *adv* in or during the previous month
ULTION *n* vengeance
ULTIONS ▶ ultion
ULTRA *n* person who has extreme or immoderate beliefs or opinions ▷ *adj* extreme or immoderate,

esp in beliefs or opinions
ULTRAS ▶ ultra
ULU *n* type of knife
ULULANT ▶ ululate
ULULATE *vb* howl or wail
ULUS ▶ ulu
ULVA *n* genus of seaweed
ULYIE *Scots variant of* ▶ **oil**
ULYIES ▶ ulyie
ULZIE *Scots variant of* ▶ **oil**
ULZIES ▶ ulzie
UM *interj* representation of a common sound made when hesitating in speech ▷ *vb* hesitate while speaking
UMAMI *n* savoury flavour
UMAMIS ▶ umami
UMBEL *n* umbrella-like flower cluster with the stalks springing from the central point
UMBELED *same as* > **umbelled**
UMBELS ▶ umbel
UMBER *adj* dark brown to reddish-brown ▷ *n* type of dark brown earth containing ferric oxide (rust) ▷ *vb* stain with umber
UMBERED ▶ umber
UMBERS ▶ umber
UMBERY ▶ umber
UMBLE *adj as in* **umble pie** (formerly) a pie made from the heart, entrails, etc, of a deer
UMBLES *another term for* ▶ **numbles**
UMBO *n* small hump projecting from the centre of the cap in certain mushrooms
UMBONAL ▶ umbo
UMBONES ▶ umbo
UMBONIC ▶ umbo
UMBOS ▶ umbo
UMBRA *n* shadow, esp the shadow cast by the moon onto the earth during a solar eclipse
UMBRAE ▶ umbra
UMBRAGE *n* displeasure or resentment ▷ *vb* shade
UMBRAL ▶ umbra
UMBRAS ▶ umbra
UMBRE *same as* > **umbrette**
UMBREL *n* umbrella
UMBRELS ▶ umbrel
UMBRERE *n* helmet visor
UMBRES ▶ umbre

UMBRIL *same as* ▶ **umbrere**
UMBRILS ▶ umbril
UMBROSE *same as* ▶ **umbrous**
UMBROUS *adj* shady
UMFAZI *n* African married woman
UMFAZIS ▶ umfazi
UMIAC *same as* ▶ **umiak**
UMIACK *same as* ▶ **umiak**
UMIACKS ▶ umiack
UMIACS ▶ umiac
UMIAK *n* Inuit boat made of skins
UMIAKS ▶ umiak
UMIAQ *same as* ▶ **umiak**

> An Inuit word for a type of canoe: easy to miss because one tends automatically to put the Q with the U and not think of a word ending in Q. The many variant spellings of this word include **umiac** and **umiak**.

UMIAQS ▶ umiaq
UMLAUT *n* mark (¨) placed over a vowel, esp in German, to indicate a change in its sound ▷ *vb* modify by umlaut
UMLAUTS ▶ umlaut
UMLUNGU *n* White man: used esp as a term of address
UMM *same as* ▶ **um**
UMMA *n* Muslim community
UMMAH ▶ umma
UMMAHS ▶ ummah
UMMAS ▶ umma
UMMED ▶ um
UMMING ▶ um *vb*
UMP *short for* ▶ **umpire**
UMPED ▶ ump
UMPH *same as* ▶ **humph**
UMPIE *informal word for* ▶ **umpire**
UMPIES ▶ umpy
UMPING ▶ ump
UMPIRE *n* official who rules on the playing of a game ▷ *vb* act as umpire in (a game)
UMPIRED ▶ umpire
UMPIRES ▶ umpire
UMPS ▶ ump
UMPTEEN *adj* very many ▷ *determiner* very many
UMPTY *same as* ▶ **umpteen**
UMPY *same as* ▶ **umpie**
UMRA *n* pilgrimage to

Mecca that can be made at any time of the year
UMRAH ▸ umra
UMRAHS ▸ umrah
UMRAS ▸ umra
UMS ▸ um
UMU n type of oven
UMUS ▸ umu
UMWELT n environmental factors, collectively, that are capable of affecting the behaviour of an animal or individual
UMWELTS ▸ umwelt
UMWHILE same as
> umquhile
UN pron spelling of 'one' intended to reflect a dialectal or informal pronunciation
UNABLE adj lacking the necessary power, ability, or authority (to do something)
UNACTED adj not acted or performed
UNADDED adj not added
UNADEPT adj not adept
UNADULT adj not mature
UNAGED adj not old
UNAGILE adj not agile
UNAGING same as
> unageing
UNAI same as ▸ unau
UNAIDED adv without any help or assistance ▷ adj without having received any help
UNAIMED adj not aimed or specifically targeted
UNAIRED adj not aired
UNAIS ▸ unai
UNAKIN adj not related
UNAKING Shakespearean form of > unaching
UNAKITE n type of mineral
UNALIKE adj not similar
UNALIST n priest holding only one benefice
UNALIVE adj unaware
UNAPT adj not suitable or qualified
UNAPTLY ▸ unapt
UNARM less common word for
▸ disarm
UNARMED adj without weapons
UNARMS ▸ unarm
UNARY adj consisting of, or affecting, a single element or component
UNASKED adv without being asked to do

something ▷ adj (of a question) not asked, although sometimes implied
UNAU n two-toed sloth
UNAUS ▸ unau
UNAWAKE adj not awake
UNAWARE adj not aware or conscious ▷ adv by surprise
UNAWED adj not awed
UNAXED adj not axed
UNBAG vb take out of a bag
UNBAGS ▸ unbag
UNBAKED adj not having been baked
UNBALE vb remove from bale
UNBALED ▸ unbale
UNBALES ▸ unbale
UNBAN vb stop banning or permit again
UNBANS ▸ unban
UNBAR vb take away a bar or bars from
UNBARE vb expose
UNBARED ▸ unbare
UNBARES ▸ unbare
UNBARK vb strip bark from
UNBARKS ▸ unbark
UNBARS ▸ unbar
UNBASED adj not having a base
UNBATED adj (of a sword, lance etc) not covered with a protective button
UNBE vb make non-existent
UNBEAR vb release (horse) from the bearing rein
UNBEARS ▸ unbear
UNBED vb remove from bed
UNBEDS ▸ unbed
UNBEEN ▸ unbe
UNBEGET vb deprive of existence
UNBEGOT adj unbegotten
UNBEGUN adj not commenced
UNBEING n non-existence
UNBELT vb unbuckle the belt of (a garment)
UNBELTS ▸ unbelt
UNBEND vb become less strict or more informal in one's attitudes or behaviour
UNBENDS ▸ unbend
UNBENT adj not bent or bowed
UNBIAS vb free from prejudice
UNBID same as > unbidden
UNBIND vb set free from bonds or chains
UNBINDS ▸ unbind

UNBITT vb remove (cable) from the bitts
UNBITTS ▸ unbitt
UNBLENT same as
> unblended
UNBLESS vb deprive of a blessing
UNBLEST same as
> unblessed
UNBLIND vb rid of blindness
UNBLOCK vb remove a blockage from
UNBLOWN adj (of a flower) still in the bud
UNBOLT vb unfasten a bolt of (a door)
UNBOLTS ▸ unbolt
UNBONE vb remove bone from
UNBONED adj (of meat, fish, etc) not having had the bones removed
UNBONES ▸ unbone
UNBOOT vb remove boots from
UNBOOTS ▸ unboot
UNBORE adj unborn
UNBORN adj not yet born
UNBORNE adj not borne
UNBOSOM vb relieve (oneself) of (secrets or feelings) by telling someone
UNBOUND adj (of a book) not bound within a cover
UNBOWED adj not giving in or submitting
UNBOX vb empty a box
UNBOXED ▸ unbox
UNBOXES ▸ unbox
UNBRACE vb remove tension or strain from
UNBRAID vb remove braids from
UNBRAKE vb stop reducing speed by releasing brake
UNBRED adj not taught or instructed
UNBROKE same as
> unbroken
UNBUILD vb destroy
UNBUILT ▸ unbuild
UNBULKY adj not bulky
UNBURNT adj not burnt
UNBURY vb unearth
UNBUSY adj not busy
UNCAGE vb release from a cage
UNCAGED adj at liberty
UNCAGES ▸ uncage
UNCAKE vb remove compacted matter from
UNCAKED ▸ uncake
UNCAKES ▸ uncake

U

UNCANNY adj weird or mysterious

UNCAP vb remove a cap or top from (a container)

UNCAPE vb remove the cape from

UNCAPED ▷ uncape

UNCAPES ▷ uncape

UNCAPS ▷ uncap

UNCARED adj as in uncared for not cared (for)

UNCART vb remove from a cart

UNCARTS ▷ uncart

UNCASE vb display

UNCASED ▷ uncase

UNCASES ▷ uncase

UNCAST adj not cast

UNCATE same as > uncinate

UNCE same as ▷ ounce

UNCEDED adj not ceded

UNCES ▷ unce

UNCHAIN vb remove a chain or chains from

UNCHAIR vb unseat from chair

UNCHARM vb disenchant

UNCHARY adj not cautious

UNCHECK vb remove check mark from

UNCHIC adj not chic

UNCHILD vb deprive of children

UNCHOKE vb unblock

UNCI ▷ uncus

UNCIA n twelfth part

UNCIAE ▷ uncia

UNCIAL adj of or written in letters that resemble modern capitals, as used in Greek and Latin manuscripts of the third to ninth centuries ▷ n uncial letter or manuscript

UNCIALS ▷ uncial

UNCINAL same as > uncinate

UNCINI ▷ uncinus

UNCINUS n small hooked structure, such as any of the hooked chaetae of certain polychaete worms

UNCITED adj not quoted

UNCIVIL adj impolite, rude or bad-mannered

UNCLAD adj having no clothes on

UNCLAMP vb remove clamp from

UNCLASP vb unfasten the clasp of (something)

UNCLE n brother of one's father or mother ▷ vb refer to as uncle

UNCLEAN adj lacking moral, spiritual, or physical cleanliness

UNCLEAR adj confusing or hard to understand

UNCLED ▷ uncle

UNCLEFT adj not cleft

UNCLES ▷ uncle

UNCLEW vb undo

UNCLEWS ▷ unclew

UNCLING ▷ uncle

UNCLIP vb remove clip from

UNCLIPS ▷ unclip

UNCLIPT archaic past form of ▷ unclip

UNCLOAK vb remove cloak from

UNCLOG vb remove an obstruction from (a drain, etc)

UNCLOGS ▷ unclog

UNCLOSE vb open or cause to open

UNCLOUD vb clear clouds from

UNCO adj awkward ▷ n awkward or clumsy person

UNCOCK vb remove from a cocked position

UNCOCKS ▷ uncock

UNCODED adj not coded

UNCOER ▷ unco

UNCOES ▷ unco

UNCOEST ▷ unco

UNCOIL vb unwind or untwist

UNCOILS ▷ uncoil

UNCOLT vb divest of a horse

UNCOLTS ▷ uncolt

UNCOMFY adj not comfortable

UNCOMIC adj not comical

UNCOOL adj unsophisticated

UNCOPE vb unmuzzle

UNCOPED ▷ uncope

UNCOPES ▷ uncope

UNCORD vb release from cords

UNCORDS ▷ uncord

UNCORK vb remove the cork from (a bottle)

UNCORKS ▷ uncork

UNCOS ▷ unco

UNCOUTH adj lacking in good manners, refinement, or grace

UNCOVER vb reveal or disclose

UNCOWL vb remove hood from

UNCOWLS ▷ uncowl

UNCOY adj not modest

UNCRATE vb remove from a crate

UNCRAZY adj not crazy

UNCROSS vb cease to cross

UNCROWN vb take the crown from

UNCTION n act of anointing with oil in sacramental ceremonies

UNCUFF vb remove handcuffs from

UNCUFFS ▷ uncuff

UNCURB vb remove curbs from (a horse)

UNCURBS ▷ uncurb

UNCURED adj not cured

UNCURL vb move or cause to move out of a curled or rolled up position

UNCURLS ▷ uncurl

UNCURSE vb remove curse from

UNCUS n hooked part or process, as in the human cerebrum

UNCUT adj not shortened or censored

UNCUTE adj not cute

UNDAM vb free from a dam

UNDAMS ▷ undam

UNDATE vb remove date from

UNDATED adj (of a manuscript, letter, etc) not having an identifying date

UNDE same as ▷ undee

UNDEAD adj alive

UNDEAF vb restore hearing to

UNDEAFS ▷ undeaf

UNDEALT adj not dealt (with)

UNDEAR adj not dear

UNDECK vb remove decorations from

UNDECKS ▷ undeck

UNDEE adj wavy

UNDEIFY vb strip of the status of a deity

UNDER adv indicating movement to or position beneath the underside or base ▷ prep less than

UNDERDO vb do (something) inadequately

UNDERGO vb experience, endure, or sustain

UNDERN n time between sunrise and noon

UNDERNS ▷ undern

UNDID ▷ undo

UNDIES pl n underwear, esp women's
UNDIGHT vb remove
UNDINE n female water spirit
UNDINES ▶ undine
UNDO vb open, unwrap
UNDOCK vb take out of a dock
UNDOCKS ▶ undock
UNDOER ▶ undo
UNDOERS ▶ undo
UNDOES ▶ undo
UNDOING n cause of someone's downfall
UNDONE adj not done or completed
UNDRAPE vb remove drapery from
UNDRAW vb open (curtains)
UNDRAWN ▶ undraw
UNDRAWS ▶ undraw
UNDRESS vb take off clothes from (oneself or another) ▷ n partial or complete nakedness ▷ adj characterized by or requiring informal or normal working dress or uniform
UNDREST same as
▷ **undressed**
UNDREW ▶ undraw
UNDRIED adj not dried
UNDRUNK adj not drunk
UNDUE adj greater than is reasonable; excessive
UNDUG adj not having been dug
UNDULAR > undulate
UNDULY adv excessively
UNDY same as ▶ **undee**
UNDYED adj not dyed
UNDYING adj never ending, eternal
UNEAGER adj nonchalant
UNEARED adj not ploughed
UNEARTH vb reveal or discover by searching
UNEASE ▶ uneasy
UNEASES ▶ uneasy
UNEASY adj (of a person) anxious or apprehensive
UNEATEN adj (of food) not having been consumed
UNEATH adv not easily
UNEDGE vb take the edge off
UNEDGED ▶ unedge
UNEDGES ▶ unedge
UNENDED adj without end
UNEQUAL adj not equal in

quantity, size, rank, value, etc ▷ n person who is not equal
UNETH same as ▶ **uneath**
UNEVEN adj not level or flat
UNEYED adj unseen
UNFACT n event or thing not provable
UNFACTS ▶ unfact
UNFADED adj not faded
UNFAIR adj not right, fair, or just ▷ vb disfigure
UNFAIRS ▶ unfair
UNFAITH n lack of faith
UNFAKED adj not faked
UNFAMED adj not famous
UNFANCY vb consider (a sportsperson or team) unlikely to win or succeed
UNFAZED adj not disconcerted
UNFED adj not fed
UNFEED adj unpaid
UNFELT adj not felt
UNFENCE vb remove a fence from
UNFEUED adj not feued
UNFILDE archaic form of
▶ **unfiled**
UNFILED adj not filed
UNFINE adj not fine
UNFIRED adj not fired
UNFIRM adj soft or unsteady
UNFIT adj unqualified or unsuitable ▷ vb make unfit
UNFITLY adv in an unfit way
UNFITS ▶ unfit
UNFIX vb unfasten, detach, or loosen
UNFIXED adj not fixed
UNFIXES ▶ unfix
UNFIXT same as ▶ **unfixed**
UNFLESH vb remove flesh from
UNFLUSH vb lose the colour caused by flushing
UNFOLD vb open or spread out from a folded state
UNFOLDS ▶ unfold
UNFOND adj not fond
UNFOOL vb undeceive
UNFOOLS ▶ unfool
UNFORM vb make formless
UNFORMS ▶ unform
UNFOUND adj not found
UNFREE vb remove freedom from
UNFREED ▶ unfree
UNFREES ▶ unfree
UNFROCK vb deprive (a priest in holy orders) of his or her priesthood

UNFROZE > unfreeze
UNFUMED adj not fumigated
UNFUNNY adj not funny
UNFURL vb unroll or unfold
UNFURLS ▶ unfurl
UNFUSED adj not fused
UNFUSSY adj not characterized by overelaborate detail
UNGAG vb restore freedom of speech to
UNGAGS ▶ ungag
UNGAIN adj inconvenient
UNGATED adj without gate
UNGAZED adj as in **ungazed at/ungazed upon** not gazed (at or upon)
UNGEAR vb disengage
UNGEARS ▶ ungear
UNGET vb get rid of
UNGETS ▶ unget
UNGILD vb remove gilding from
UNGILDS ▶ ungild
UNGILT ▶ ungild
UNGIRD vb remove belt from
UNGIRDS ▶ ungird
UNGIRT adj not belted
UNGIRTH vb release from a girth
UNGLAD adj not glad
UNGLOVE vb remove glove(s)
UNGLUE vb remove adhesive from
UNGLUED ▶ unglue
UNGLUES ▶ unglue
UNGOD vb remove status of being a god from
UNGODLY adj unreasonable or outrageous
UNGODS ▶ ungod
UNGORD same as
▶ **ungored**
UNGORED adj not gored
UNGOT same as > **ungotten**
UNGOWN vb remove gown (from)
UNGOWNS ▶ ungown
UNGREEN adj not environmentally friendly
UNGROWN adj not fully developed
UNGUAL adj of, relating to, or affecting the fingernails or toenails
UNGUARD vb expose (to attack)
UNGUENT n ointment
UNGUES ▶ unguis
UNGUIS n nail, claw, or

hoof, or the part of the digit giving rise to it

UNGULA n truncated cone, cylinder, etc

UNGULAE ▶ **ungula**

UNGULAR ▶ **ungula**

UNGULED adj hoofed

UNGUM vb remove adhesive from

UNGUMS ▶ **ungum**

UNGYVE vb release from shackles

UNGYVED ▶ **ungyve**

UNGYVES ▶ **ungyve**

UNHABLE same as ▶ **unable**

UNHAIR vb remove the hair from (a hide)

UNHAIRS ▶ **unhair**

UNHAND vb release from one's grasp

UNHANDS ▶ **unhand**

UNHANDY adj not skilful with one's hands

UNHANG vb take down from hanging position

UNHANGS ▶ **unhang**

UNHAPPY adj sad or depressed ▷ vb make unhappy

UNHARDY adj fragile

UNHASP vb unfasten

UNHASPS ▶ **unhasp**

UNHASTY adj not speedy

UNHAT vb doff one's hat

UNHATS ▶ **unhat**

UNHEAD vb remove the head from

UNHEADS ▶ **unhead**

UNHEAL vb expose

UNHEALS ▶ **unheal**

UNHEARD adj not listened to

UNHEART vb discourage

UNHEEDY adj not heedful

UNHELE same as ▶ **unheal**

UNHELED ▶ **unhele**

UNHELES ▶ **unhele**

UNHELM vb remove the helmet of (oneself or another)

UNHELMS ▶ **unhelm**

UNHERST archaic past form of ▷ **unhearse**

UNHEWN adj not hewn

UNHINGE vb derange or unbalance (a person or his or her mind)

UNHIP adj not at all fashionable or up to date

UNHIRED adj not hired

UNHITCH vb unfasten or detach

UNHIVE vb remove from a hive

UNHIVED ▶ **unhive**

UNHIVES ▶ **unhive**

UNHOARD vb remove from a hoard

UNHOLY adj immoral or wicked

UNHOOD vb remove hood from

UNHOODS ▶ **unhood**

UNHOOK vb unfasten the hooks of (a garment)

UNHOOKS ▶ **unhook**

UNHOOP vb remove hoop(s) from

UNHOOPS ▶ **unhoop**

UNHOPED adj unhoped-for

UNHORSE vb knock or throw from a horse

UNHOUSE vb remove from a house

UNHUMAN adj inhuman or not human

UNHUNG ▶ **unhang**

UNHURT adj not injured in an accident, attack, etc

UNHUSK vb remove the husk from

UNHUSKS ▶ **unhusk**

UNI n (in informal English) university

UNIBODY adj of a vehicle in which frame and body are one unit

UNIBROW n informal word for eyebrows that meet above the nose

UNICITY n oneness

UNICORN n imaginary horselike creature with one horn growing from its forehead

UNIDEAL adj not ideal

UNIFACE n type of tool

UNIFIC adj unifying

UNIFIED ▶ **unify**

UNIFIER ▶ **unify**

UNIFIES ▶ **unify**

UNIFORM n special identifying set of clothes for the members of an organization, such as soldiers ▷ adj regular and even throughout, unvarying ▷ vb fit out (a body of soldiers, etc) with uniforms

UNIFY vb make or become one

UNION n uniting or being united ▷ adj of a trade union

UNIONS ▶ **union**

UNIPED n person or thing with one foot

UNIPEDS ▶ **uniped**

UNIPOD n one-legged support, as for a camera

UNIPODS ▶ **unipod**

UNIQUE n person or thing that is unique

UNIQUER ▶ **unique**

UNIQUES ▶ **unique**

UNIS ▶ **uni**

UNISEX adj designed for use by both sexes ▷ n condition of seeming not to belong obviously either to one sex or the other from the way one behaves or dresses

UNISIZE adj in one size only

UNISON n complete agreement

UNISONS ▶ **unison**

UNIT n single undivided entity or whole

UNITAGE ▶ **unit**

UNITAL ▶ **unit**

UNITARD n all-in-one skintight suit

UNITARY adj consisting of a single undivided whole

UNITE vb make or become an integrated whole ▷ n English gold coin minted in the Stuart period, originally worth 20 shillings

UNITED adj produced by two or more people or things in combination

UNITER ▶ **unite**

UNITERS ▶ **unite**

UNITES ▶ **unite**

UNITIES ▶ **unity**

UNITING ▶ **unite**

UNITION n joining

UNITISE same as ▶ **unitize**

UNITIVE adj tending to unite or capable of uniting

UNITIZE vb convert (an investment trust) into a unit trust

UNITS ▶ **unit**

UNITY n state of being one

UNJADED adj not jaded

UNJAM vb remove blockage from

UNJAMS ▶ **unjam**

UNJOINT vb disjoint

UNJUST adj not fair or just

UNKED adj alien

UNKEMPT adj (of the hair) not combed

UNKEND same as ▷ **unkenned**

UNKENT *same as*
> **unkenned**

UNKEPT *adj* not kept

UNKET *same as* ▶ **unked**

UNKID *same as* ▶ **unked**

UNKIND *adj* unsympathetic
or cruel

UNKING *vb* strip of
sovereignty

UNKINGS ▶ **unking**

UNKINK *vb* straighten out

UNKINKS ▶ **unkink**

UNKISS *vb* cancel (a
previous action) with a kiss

UNKNIT *vb* make or become
undone, untied, or
unravelled

UNKNITS ▶ **unknit**

UNKNOT *vb* disentangle or
undo a knot or knots in

UNKNOTS ▶ **unknot**

UNKNOWN *adj* not known
▷ *n* unknown person,
quantity, or thing

UNLACE *vb* loosen or undo
the lacing of (shoes,
garments, etc)

UNLACED *adj* not laced

UNLACES ▶ **unlace**

UNLADE *less common word
for* ▶ **unload**

UNLADED ▶ **unlade**

UNLADEN *adj* not laden

UNLADES ▶ **unlade**

UNLAID ▶ **unlay**

UNLASH *vb* untie or
unfasten

UNLAST *archaic variant of*
▶ **unlaced**

UNLASTE *archaic variant of*
▶ **unlaced**

UNLATCH *vb* open or
unfasten or come open or
unfastened by the lifting or
release of a latch

UNLAW *vb* penalize

UNLAWED ▶ **unlaw**

UNLAWS ▶ **unlaw**

UNLAY *vb* untwist (a rope
or cable) to separate its
strands

UNLAYS ▶ **unlay**

UNLEAD *vb* strip off lead

UNLEADS ▶ **unlead**

UNLEAL *adj* treacherous

UNLEARN *vb* try to forget
something learnt or to
discard accumulated
knowledge

UNLEASH *vb* set loose or
cause (something bad)

UNLED *adj* not led

UNLESS *conj* except under

the circumstances that
▷ *prep* except

UNLET *adj* not rented

UNLEVEL *adj* not level ▷ *vb*
make unbalanced

UNLICH *Spenserian form of*
▶ **unlike**

UNLID *vb* remove lid from

UNLIDS ▶ **unlid**

UNLIKE *adj* dissimilar or
different ▷ *prep* not like or
typical of ▷ *n* person or
thing that is unlike another

UNLIKED *adj* not liked

UNLIKES ▶ **unlike**

UNLIME *vb* detach

UNLIMED ▶ **unlime**

UNLIMES ▶ **unlime**

UNLINE *vb* remove the
lining from

UNLINED *adj* not having any
lining

UNLINES ▶ **unline**

UNLINK *vb* undo the link or
links between

UNLINKS ▶ **unlink**

UNLIT *adj* (of a fire,
cigarette, etc) not lit and
therefore not burning

UNLIVE *vb* live so as to
nullify, undo, or live down
(past events or times)

UNLIVED ▶ **unlive**

UNLIVES ▶ **unlive**

UNLOAD *vb* remove (cargo)
from (a ship, truck, or
plane)

UNLOADS ▶ **unload**

UNLOBED *adj* without lobes

UNLOCK *vb* unfasten (a lock
or door)

UNLOCKS ▶ **unlock**

UNLOOSE *vb* set free or
release

UNLORD *vb* remove from
position of being lord

UNLORDS ▶ **unlord**

UNLOST *adj* not lost

UNLOVE *vb* stop loving

UNLOVED *adj* not loved by
anyone

UNLOVES ▶ **unlove**

UNLUCKY *adj* having bad
luck, unfortunate

UNMACHO *adj* not macho

UNMADE *adj* (of a bed) with
the bedclothes not
smoothed and tidied

UNMAKE *vb* undo or
destroy

UNMAKER ▶ **unmake**

UNMAKES ▶ **unmake**

UNMAN *vb* cause to lose

courage or nerve

UNMANLY *adj* not
masculine or virile

UNMANS ▶ **unman**

UNMARD *same as*
> **unmarred**

UNMARRY *vb* divorce

UNMASK *vb* remove the
mask or disguise from

UNMASKS ▶ **unmask**

UNMATED *adj* not mated

UNMEANT *adj*
unintentional

UNMEEK *adj* not
submissive

UNMEET *adj* not meet

UNMERRY *adj* not merry

UNMESH *vb* release from
mesh

UNMET *adj* unfulfilled

UNMETED *adj* unmeasured

UNMEW *vb* release from
confinement

UNMEWED ▶ **unmew**

UNMEWS ▶ **unmew**

UNMINED *adj* not mined

UNMIRY *adj* not swampy

UNMITER *same as*
▶ **unmitre**

UNMITRE *vb* divest of a
mitre

UNMIX *vb* separate

UNMIXED ▶ **unmix**

UNMIXES ▶ **unmix**

UNMIXT *same as* ▶ **unmix**

UNMOLD *same as*
▶ **unmould**

UNMOLDS ▶ **unmold**

UNMOOR *vb* weigh the
anchor or drop the mooring
of (a vessel)

UNMOORS ▶ **unmoor**

UNMORAL *adj* outside
morality

UNMOULD *vb* change
shape of

UNMOUNT *vb* dismount

UNMOVED *adj* not affected
by emotion, indifferent

UNMOWN *adj* not mown

UNNAIL *vb* unfasten by
removing nails

UNNAILS ▶ **unnail**

UNNAMED *adj* not
mentioned by name

UNNEATH *adj* archaic word
for underneath

UNNERVE *vb* cause to lose
courage, confidence, or
self-control

UNNEST *vb* remove from a
nest

UNNESTS ▶ **unnest**

U

UNNOBLE *vb* strip of nobility

UNNOISY *adj* quiet

UNNOTED *adj* not noted

UNOAKED *adj* (of wine) not matured in an oak barrel

UNOFTEN *adv* infrequently

UNOILED *adj* not lubricated with oil

UNOPEN *adj* not open

UNORDER *vb* cancel an order

UNOWED *same as* ▶**unowned**

UNOWNED *adj* not owned

UNPACED *adj* without the aid of a pacemaker

UNPACK *vb* remove the contents of (a suitcase, trunk, etc)

UNPACKS ▶**unpack**

UNPAGED *adj* (of a book) having no page numbers

UNPAID *adj* without a salary or wage

UNPAINT *vb* remove paint from

UNPANEL *vb* unsaddle

UNPAPER *vb* remove paper from

UNPARED *adj* not pared

UNPAVED *adj* not covered in paving

UNPAY *vb* undo

UNPAYS ▶**unpay**

UNPEG *vb* remove the peg or pegs from, esp to unfasten

UNPEGS ▶**unpeg**

UNPEN *vb* release from a pen

UNPENS ▶**unpen**

UNPENT *archaic past form of* ▶**unpen**

UNPERCH *vb* remove from a perch

UNPICK *vb* undo (the stitches) of (a piece of sewing)

UNPICKS ▶**unpick**

UNPILE *vb* remove from a pile

UNPILED ▶**unpile**

UNPILES ▶**unpile**

UNPIN *vb* remove a pin or pins from

UNPINKT *same as* >**unpinked**

UNPINS ▶**unpin**

UNPLACE *same as* >**displace**

UNPLAIT *vb* remove plaits from

UNPLUG *vb* disconnect (a piece of electrical equipment) by taking the plug out of the socket

UNPLUGS ▶**unplug**

UNPLUMB *vb* remove lead from

UNPLUME *vb* remove feathers from

UNPOPE *vb* strip of popedom

UNPOPED ▶**unpope**

UNPOPES ▶**unpope**

UNPOSED *adj* not posed

UNPRAY *vb* withdraw (a prayer)

UNPRAYS ▶**unpray**

UNPROP *vb* remove support from

UNPROPS ▶**unprop**

UNPURE *same as* ▶**impure**

UNPURSE *vb* relax (lips) from pursed position

UNQUEEN *vb* depose from the position of queen

UNQUIET *adj* anxious or uneasy ▷*n* state of unrest ▷*vb* disquiet

UNQUOTE *interj* expression used to indicate the end of a quotation that was introduced with the word 'quote' ▷*vb* close (a quotation), esp in printing

UNRACED *adj* not raced

UNRAKE *vb* unearth through raking

UNRAKED *adj* not raked

UNRAKES ▶**unrake**

UNRATED *adj* not rated

UNRAVEL *vb* reduce (something knitted or woven) to separate strands

UNRAZED *adj* not razed

UNREAD *adj* (of a book or article) not yet read

UNREADY *adj* not ready or prepared

UNREAL *adj* (as if) existing only in the imagination

UNREAVE *vb* unwind

UNRED *same as* ▶**unread**

UNREDY *same as* ▶**unready**

UNREEL *vb* unwind from a reel

UNREELS ▶**unreel**

UNREEVE *vb* withdraw (a rope) from a block, thimble, etc

UNREIN *vb* free from reins

UNREINS ▶**unrein**

UNRENT *adj* not torn

UNREST *n* rebellious state

of discontent

UNRESTS ▶**unrest**

UNRID *adj* unridden

UNRIG *vb* strip (a vessel) of standing and running rigging

UNRIGHT *n* wrong

UNRIGS ▶**unrig**

UNRIMED *same as* >**unrhymed**

UNRIP *vb* rip open

UNRIPE *adj* not fully matured

UNRIPER ▶**unripe**

UNRIPS ▶**unrip**

UNRISEN *adj* not risen

UNRIVEN *adj* not torn apart

UNRIVET *vb* remove rivets from

UNROBE *same as* ▶**disrobe**

UNROBED ▶**unrobe**

UNROBES ▶**unrobe**

UNROLL *vb* open out or unwind (something rolled or coiled) or (of something rolled or coiled) become opened out or unwound

UNROLLS ▶**unroll**

UNROOF *vb* remove the roof from

UNROOFS ▶**unroof**

UNROOST *vb* remove from a perch

UNROOT *less common word for* ▶**uproot**

UNROOTS ▶**unroot**

UNROPE *vb* release from a rope

UNROPED ▶**unrope**

UNROPES ▶**unrope**

UNROUGH *adj* not rough

UNROUND *vb* release (lips) from a rounded position

UNROVE ▶**unreeve**

UNROVEN ▶**unreeve**

UNROYAL *adj* not royal

UNRUDE *adj* not rude

UNRUFFE *same as* ▶**unrough**

UNRULE *n* lack of authority

UNRULED *adj* not ruled

UNRULES ▶**unrule**

UNRULY *adj* difficult to control or organize

UNS ▶**un**

UNSAFE *adj* dangerous

UNSAFER ▶**unsafe**

UNSAID *adj* not said or expressed

UNSAINT *vb* remove status of being a saint from

UNSATED *adj* not sated

UNSAVED *adj* not saved

UNSAWED *same as* ▸ **unsawn**

UNSAWN *adj* not cut with a saw

UNSAY *vb* retract or withdraw (something said or written)

UNSAYS ▸ **unsay**

UNSCALE *same as* ▸ **descale**

UNSCARY *adj* not scary

UNSCREW *vb* loosen (a screw or lid) by turning it

UNSEAL *vb* remove or break the seal of

UNSEALS ▸ **unseal**

UNSEAM *vb* open or undo the seam of

UNSEAMS ▸ **unseam**

UNSEAT *vb* throw or displace from a seat or saddle

UNSEATS ▸ **unseat**

UNSEEL *vb* undo seeling

UNSEELS ▸ **unseel**

UNSEEN *adj* hidden or invisible ▷ *adv* without being seen ▷ *n* passage which is given to students for translation without them having seen it in advance

UNSEENS ▸ **unseen**

UNSELF *vb* remove self-centredness from ▷ *n* lack of self

UNSELFS ▸ **unself**

UNSELL *vb* speak unfavourably and off-puttingly of (something or someone)

UNSELLS ▸ **unsell**

UNSENSE *vb* remove sense from

UNSENT *adj* not sent

UNSET *adj* not yet solidified or firm ▷ *vb* displace

UNSETS ▸ **unset**

UNSEW *vb* undo stitching of

UNSEWED ▸ **unsew**

UNSEWN ▸ **unsew**

UNSEWS ▸ **unsew**

UNSEX *vb* deprive (a person) of the attributes of his or her sex, esp to make a woman more callous

UNSEXED ▸ **unsex**

UNSEXES ▸ **unsex**

UNSEXY *adj* not sexually attractive

UNSHALE *vb* expose

UNSHAPE *vb* make shapeless

UNSHARP *adj* not sharp

UNSHED *adj* not shed

UNSHELL *vb* remove from a shell

UNSHENT *adj* undamaged

UNSHEWN *adj* unshown

UNSHIFT *vb* release the shift key on a keyboard

UNSHIP *vb* be or cause to be unloaded, discharged, or disembarked from a ship

UNSHIPS ▸ **unship**

UNSHOD *adj* not wearing shoes

UNSHOE *vb* remove shoes from

UNSHOED *same as* ▸ **unshod**

UNSHOES ▸ **unshoe**

UNSHOOT *Shakespearean variant of* ▸ **unshout**

UNSHORN *adj* not cut

UNSHOT *adj* not shot

UNSHOUT *vb* revoke (an earlier statement) by shouting a contrary one

UNSHOWN *adj* not shown

UNSHOWY *adj* not showy

UNSHUT *vb* open

UNSHUTS ▸ **unshut**

UNSIGHT *vb* obstruct vision of

UNSINEW *vb* weaken

UNSIZED *adj* not made or sorted according to size

UNSLAIN *adj* not killed

UNSLICK *adj* not slick

UNSLING *vb* remove or release from a slung position

UNSLUNG ▸ **unsling**

UNSMART *adj* not smart

UNSMOTE *same as* ▸ **unsmitten**

UNSNAG *vb* remove snags from

UNSNAGS ▸ **unsnag**

UNSNAP *vb* unfasten (the snap or catch) of (something)

UNSNAPS ▸ **unsnap**

UNSNARL *vb* free from a snarl or tangle

UNSNECK *vb* unlatch

UNSOBER *adj* not sober

UNSOD *same as* ▸ **unsodden**

UNSOFT *adj* hard

UNSOLD *adj* not sold

UNSOLID *adj* not solid

UNSONCY *same as* ▸ **unsonsy**

UNSONSY *adj* unfortunate

UNSOOTE *adj* not sweet

UNSOUL *vb* cause to be soulless

UNSOULS ▸ **unsoul**

UNSOUND *adj* unhealthy or unstable

UNSOWED *same as* ▸ **unsown**

UNSOWN *adj* not sown

UNSPAR *vb* open

UNSPARS ▸ **unspar**

UNSPEAK *obsolete word for* ▸ **unsay**

UNSPED *adj* not achieved

UNSPELL *vb* release from a spell

UNSPENT *adj* not spent

UNSPIDE *same as* ▸ **unspied**

UNSPIED *adj* unnoticed

UNSPILT *adj* not spilt

UNSPLIT *adj* not split

UNSPOKE ▸ **unspeak**

UNSPOOL *vb* unwind from spool

UNSPUN *adj* not spun

UNSTACK *vb* remove from a stack

UNSTAID *adj* not staid

UNSTATE *vb* deprive of state

UNSTEEL *vb* make (the heart, feelings, etc) more gentle or compassionate

UNSTEP *vb* remove (a mast) from its step

UNSTEPS ▸ **unstep**

UNSTICK *vb* free or loosen (something stuck)

UNSTOCK *vb* remove stock from

UNSTOP *vb* remove the stop or stopper from

UNSTOPS ▸ **unstop**

UNSTOW *vb* remove from storage

UNSTOWS ▸ **unstow**

UNSTRAP *vb* undo the straps fastening (something) in position

UNSTRIP *vb* strip

UNSTUCK *adj* freed from being stuck, glued, fastened, etc

UNSTUFT *same as* ▸ **unstuffed**

UNSTUNG *adj* not stung

UNSUIT *vb* make unsuitable

UNSUITS ▸ **unsuit**

UNSUNG *adj* not acclaimed or honoured

UNSUNK *adj* not sunken

UNSUNNY *adj* not sunny

UNSURE *adj* lacking assurance or self-confidence

U

UNSURED adj not assured

UNSURER ▶ unsure

UNSWEAR vb retract or revoke (a sworn oath)

UNSWEET adj not sweet

UNSWEPT adj not swept

UNSWORE ▶ unswear

UNSWORN ▶ unswear

UNTACK vb remove saddle and harness, etc, from

UNTACKS ▶ untack

UNTAKEN adj not taken

UNTAME vb undo the taming of

UNTAMED adj not brought under human control

UNTAMES ▶ untame

UNTAX vb stop taxing

UNTAXED adj not subject to taxation

UNTAXES ▶ untax

UNTEACH vb cause to disbelieve (teaching)

UNTEAM vb disband a team

UNTEAMS ▶ unteam

UNTENT vb remove from a tent

UNTENTS ▶ untent

UNTENTY adj inattentive

UNTHAW same as ▶ thaw

UNTHAWS ▶ unthaw

UNTHINK vb reverse one's opinion about

UNTIDY adj messy and disordered ▷ vb make untidy

UNTIE vb open or free (something that is tied)

UNTIED ▶ untie

UNTIES ▶ untie

UNTIL prep in or throughout the period before

UNTILE vb strip tiles from

UNTILED ▶ untile

UNTILES ▶ untile

UNTIMED adj not timed

UNTIN vb remove tin from

UNTINS ▶ untin

UNTIRED adj not tired

UNTO prep to

UNTOLD adj incapable of description

UNTOMB vb exhume

UNTOMBS ▶ untomb

UNTONED adj not toned

UNTORN adj not torn

UNTRACE vb remove traces from

UNTRACK vb remove from track

UNTREAD vb retrace (a course, path, etc)

UNTRIDE same as ▶ untried

UNTRIED adj not yet used, done, or tested

UNTRIM vb deprive of elegance or adornment

UNTRIMS ▶ untrim

UNTROD ▶ untread

UNTRUE adj incorrect or false

UNTRUER ▶ untrue

UNTRULY ▶ untrue

UNTRUSS vb release from or as if from a truss

UNTRUST n mistrust

UNTRUTH n statement that is not true, lie

UNTUCK vb become or cause to become loose or not tucked in

UNTUCKS ▶ untuck

UNTUNE vb make out of tune

UNTUNED ▶ untune

UNTUNES ▶ untune

UNTURF vb remove turf from

UNTURFS ▶ unturf

UNTURN vb turn in a reverse direction

UNTURNS ▶ unturn

UNTWINE vb untwist, unravel, and separate

UNTWIST vb twist apart and loosen

UNTYING ▶ untie

UNURGED adj not urged

UNUSED adj not being or never having been used

UNUSUAL adj uncommon or extraordinary

UNVAIL same as ▶ unveil

UNVAILE same as ▶ unveil

UNVAILS ▶ unvail

UNVEIL vb ceremonially remove the cover from (a new picture, plaque, etc)

UNVEILS ▶ unveil

UNVEXED adj not annoyed

UNVEXT same as ▶ unvexed

UNVISOR vb remove visor from

UNVITAL adj not vital

UNVOCAL adj not vocal

UNVOICE vb pronounce without vibration of the vocal cords

UNWAGED adj (of a person) not having a paid job

UNWAKED same as > unwakened

UNWARE same as ▶ unaware

UNWARES same as > unawares

UNWARIE same as ▶ unwary

UNWARY adj not careful or cautious and therefore likely to be harmed

UNWATER vb dry out

UNWAXED adj not treated with wax, esp of oranges or lemons, not sprayed with a protective coating of wax

UNWAYED adj having no routes

UNWEAL n ill or sorrow

UNWEALS ▶ unweal

UNWEARY adj not weary

UNWEAVE vb undo (weaving)

UNWED adj not wed

UNWELDY same as > unwieldy

UNWELL adj not healthy, ill

UNWEPT adj not wept for or lamented

UNWET adj not wet

UNWHIPT same as > unwhipped

UNWHITE adj not white

UNWILL vb will the reversal of (something that has already occurred)

UNWILLS ▶ unwill

UNWIND vb relax after a busy or tense time

UNWINDS ▶ unwind

UNWIPED adj not wiped

UNWIRE vb remove wiring from

UNWIRED ▶ unwire

UNWIRES ▶ unwire

UNWISE adj foolish

UNWISER ▶ unwise

UNWISH vb retract or revoke (a wish)

UNWIST adj unknown

UNWIT vb divest of wit

UNWITCH vb release from witchcraft

UNWITS ▶ unwit

UNWITTY adj not clever and amusing

UNWIVE vb remove a wife from

UNWIVED ▶ unwive

UNWIVES ▶ unwive

UNWOMAN vb remove womanly qualities from

UNWON adj not won

UNWONT adj unaccustomed

UNWOOED adj not wooed

UNWORK vb destroy (work previously done)

UNWORKS ▶ unwork

UNWORN adj not having deteriorated through use or age

UNWORTH n lack of value

UNWOUND past tense and past participle of ▶ **unwind**

UNWOVE ▶ unweave

UNWOVEN ▶ unweave

UNWRAP vb remove the wrapping from (something)

UNWRAPS ▶ unwrap

UNWRITE vb cancel (what has been written)

UNWROTE ▶ unwrite

UNWRUNG adj not twisted

UNYOKE vb release (an animal, etc) from a yoke

UNYOKED ▶ unyoke

UNYOKES ▶ unyoke

UNYOUNG adj not young

UNZIP vb unfasten the zip of (a garment) or (of a zip or a garment with a zip) to become unfastened

UNZIPS ▶ unzip

UNZONED adj not divided into zones

UP adv indicating movement to or position at a higher place ▷ adj of a high or higher position ▷ vb increase or raise

UPAS n large Javan tree with whitish bark and poisonous milky sap

UPASES ▶ upas

UPBEAR vb sustain

UPBEARS ▶ upbear

UPBEAT adj cheerful and optimistic ▷ n unaccented beat

UPBEATS ▶ upbeat

UPBIND vb bind up

UPBINDS ▶ upbind

UPBLEW ▶ upblow

UPBLOW vb inflate

UPBLOWN ▶ upblow

UPBLOWS ▶ upblow

UPBOIL vb boil up

UPBOILS ▶ upboil

UPBORE ▶ upbear

UPBORNE adj held up

UPBOUND adj travelling upwards

UPBOW n stroke of the bow from its tip to its nut on a stringed instrument

UPBOWS ▶ upbow

UPBRAID vb scold or reproach

UPBRAST same as ▶ upburst

UPBRAY vb shame

UPBRAYS ▶ upbray

UPBREAK vb escape upwards

UPBRING vb rear

UPBROKE ▶ upbreak

UPBUILD vb build up

UPBUILT ▶ upbuild

UPBURST vb burst upwards

UPBY same as ▶ upbye

UPBYE adv yonder

UPCAST n material cast or thrown up ▷ adj directed or thrown upwards ▷ vb throw or cast up

UPCASTS ▶ upcast

UPCATCH vb catch up

UPCHEER vb cheer up

UPCHUCK vb vomit

UPCLIMB vb ascend

UPCLOSE vb close up

UPCOAST adv up the coast

UPCOIL vb make into a coil

UPCOILS ▶ upcoil

UPCOME vb come up

UPCOMES ▶ upcome

UPCOURT adv up basketball court

UPCURL vb curl up

UPCURLS ▶ upcurl

UPCURVE vb curve upwards

UPDART vb dart upwards

UPDARTS ▶ updart

UPDATE vb bring up to date ▷ n act of updating or something that is updated

UPDATED ▶ update

UPDATER ▶ update

UPDATES ▶ update

UPDIVE vb leap upwards

UPDIVED ▶ updive

UPDIVES ▶ updive

UPDO n type of hairstyle

UPDOS ▶ updo

UPDOVE ▶ updive

UPDRAFT n upwards air current

UPDRAG vb drag up

UPDRAGS ▶ updrag

UPDRAW vb draw up

UPDRAWN ▶ updraw

UPDRAWS ▶ updraw

UPDREW ▶ updraw

UPDRIED ▶ updry

UPDRIES ▶ updry

UPDRY vb dry up

UPEND vb turn or set (something) on its end

UPENDED ▶ upend

UPENDS ▶ upend

UPFIELD adj in sport, away from the defending team's goal

UPFILL vb fill up

UPFILLS ▶ upfill

UPFLING vb throw upwards

UPFLOW vb flow upwards

UPFLOWS ▶ upflow

UPFLUNG ▶ upfling

UPFOLD vb fold up

UPFOLDS ▶ upfold

UPFRONT adj open and frank ▷ adv (of money) paid out at the beginning of a business arrangement

UPFURL vb roll up

UPFURLS ▶ upfurl

UPGANG n climb

UPGANGS ▶ upgang

UPGAZE vb gaze upwards

UPGAZED ▶ upgaze

UPGAZES ▶ upgaze

UPGIRD vb belt up

UPGIRDS ▶ upgird

UPGIRT ▶ upgird

UPGO vb ascend

UPGOES ▶ upgo

UPGOING ▶ upgo

UPGONE ▶ upgo

UPGRADE vb promote (a person or job) to a higher rank

UPGREW ▶ upgrow

UPGROW vb grow up

UPGROWN ▶ upgrow

UPGROWS ▶ upgrow

UPGUSH vb flow upwards

UPHAND adj lifted by hand

UPHANG vb hang up

UPHANGS ▶ uphang

UPHAUD Scots variant of ▶ uphold

UPHAUDS ▶ uphaud

UPHEAP vb computing term

UPHEAPS ▶ upheap

UPHEAVE vb heave or rise upwards

UPHELD ▶ uphold

UPHILD archaic past form of ▶ uphold

UPHILL adj sloping or leading upwards ▷ adv up a slope ▷ n difficulty

UPHILLS ▶ uphill

UPHOARD vb hoard up

UPHOIST vb raise

UPHOLD vb maintain or defend against opposition

UPHOLDS ▶ uphold

UPHOORD vb heap up

UPHOVE ▶ upheave

UPHROE variant spelling of ▶ euphroe

UPHROES ▶ uphroe

UPHUNG ▶ uphang

UPHURL vb throw upwards

U

UPHURLS ▶ uphurl

UPJET *vb* stream upwards

UPJETS ▶ upjet

UPKEEP *n* act, process, or cost of keeping something in good repair

UPKEEPS ▶ upkeep

UPKNIT *vb* bind

UPKNITS ▶ upknit

UPLAID ▶ uplay

UPLAND *adj* of or in an area of high or relatively high ground ▷ *n* area of high or relatively high ground

UPLANDS ▶ upland

UPLAY *vb* stash

UPLAYS ▶ uplay

UPLEAD *vb* lead upwards

UPLEADS ▶ uplead

UPLEAN *vb* lean on something

UPLEANS ▶ uplean

UPLEANT ▶ uplean

UPLEAP *vb* jump upwards

UPLEAPS ▶ upleap

UPLEAPT ▶ upleap

UPLED ▶ uplead

UPLIFT *vb* raise or lift up ▷ *n* act or process of improving moral, social, or cultural conditions ▷ *adj* (of a bra) designed to lift and support the breasts

UPLIFTS ▶ uplift

UPLIGHT *n* lamp or wall light designed or positioned to cast its light upwards ▷ *vb* light in an upward direction

UPLINK *n* transmitter on the ground that sends signals up to a communications satellite ▷ *vb* send (data) to a communications satellite

UPLINKS ▶ uplink

UPLIT ▶ uplight

UPLOAD *vb* transfer (data or a program) from one's own computer into the memory of another computer

UPLOADS ▶ upload

UPLOCK *vb* lock up

UPLOCKS ▶ uplock

UPLOOK *vb* look up

UPLOOKS ▶ uplook

UPLYING *adj* raised

UPMAKE *vb* make up

UPMAKER ▶ upmake

UPMAKES ▶ upmake

UPMOST *another word for* > uppermost

UPO *prep* upon

UPON *prep* on

UPPED ▶ up

UPPER *adj* higher or highest in physical position, wealth, rank, or status ▷ *n* part of a shoe above the sole

UPPERS ▶ upper

UPPILE *vb* pile up

UPPILED ▶ uppile

UPPILES ▶ uppile

UPPING ▶ up

UPPINGS ▶ up

UPPISH *adj* snobbish, arrogant, or presumptuous

UPPITY *adj* snobbish, arrogant, or presumptuous

UPPROP *vb* support

UPPROPS ▶ upprop

UPRAISE *vb* lift up

UPRAN ▶ uprun

UPRATE *vb* raise the value, rate, or size of, upgrade

UPRATED ▶ uprate

UPRATES ▶ uprate

UPREACH *vb* reach up

UPREAR *vb* lift up

UPREARS ▶ uprear

UPREST *n* uprising

UPRESTS ▶ uprest

UPRIGHT *adj* vertical or erect ▷ *adv* vertically or in an erect position ▷ *n* vertical support, such as a post ▷ *vb* make upright

UPRISAL ▶ uprise

UPRISE *vb* rise up

UPRISEN ▶ uprise

UPRISER ▶ uprise

UPRISES ▶ uprise

UPRIST *same as* ▶ uprest

UPRISTS ▶ uprist

UPRIVER *adv* towards or near the source of a river ▷ *n* area located upstream

UPROAR *n* disturbance characterized by loud noise and confusion ▷ *vb* cause an uproar

UPROARS ▶ uproar

UPROLL *vb* roll up

UPROLLS ▶ uproll

UPROOT *vb* pull up by or as if by the roots

UPROOTS ▶ uproot

UPROSE ▶ uprise

UPROUSE *vb* rouse or stir up

UPRUN *vb* run up

UPRUNS ▶ uprun

UPRUSH *n* upward rush, as of consciousness ▷ *vb* rush upwards

UPRYST *same as* ▶ uprest

UPS ▶ up

UPSCALE *adj* of or for the upper end of an economic or social scale ▷ *vb* upgrade

UPSEE *n* drunken revel

UPSEES ▶ upsee

UPSELL *vb* persuade a customer to buy a more expensive or additional item

UPSELLS ▶ upsell

UPSEND *vb* send up

UPSENDS ▶ upsend

UPSENT ▶ upsend

UPSET *adj* emotionally or physically disturbed or distressed ▷ *vb* tip over ▷ *n* unexpected defeat or reversal

UPSETS ▶ upset

UPSEY *same as* ▶ upsee

UPSEYS ▶ upsey

UPSHIFT *vb* move up (a gear)

UPSHOOT *vb* shoot upwards

UPSHOT *n* final result or conclusion

UPSHOTS ▶ upshot

UPSIDE *n* upper surface or part

UPSIDES ▶ upside

UPSIES ▶ upsy

UPSILON *n* 20th letter in the Greek alphabet

UPSIZE *vb* increase in size

UPSIZED ▶ upsize

UPSIZES ▶ upsize

UPSKILL *vb* improve the aptitude for work of (a person) by additional training

UPSLOPE *adv* up a or the slope

UPSOAR *vb* soar up

UPSOARS ▶ upsoar

UPSOLD ▶ upsell

UPSPAKE ▶ upspeak

UPSPEAK *vb* speak with rising intonation

UPSPEAR *vb* grow upwards in a spear-like manner

UPSPOKE ▶ upspeak

UPSTAGE *adj* at the back half of the stage ▷ *vb* draw attention to oneself from (someone else) ▷ *adv* on, at, or to the rear of the stage ▷ *n* back half of the stage

UPSTAIR *same as* > upstairs

UPSTAND *vb* rise

UPSTARE *vb* stare upwards

UPSTART n person who has risen suddenly to a position of power and behaves arrogantly ▷ vb start up, as in surprise, etc

UPSTATE adv towards, in, from, or relating to the outlying or northern sections of a state, esp of New York State ▷ n outlying, esp northern, sections of a state

UPSTAY vb support

UPSTAYS ▶ upstay

UPSTEP n type of vocal intonation

UPSTEPS ▶ upstep

UPSTIR vb stir up ▷ n commotion

UPSTIRS ▶ upstir

UPSTOOD ▶ upstand

UPSURGE n rapid rise or swell ▷ vb surge up

UPSWAY vb swing in the air

UPSWAYS ▶ upsway

UPSWEEP n curve or sweep upwards ▷ vb sweep, curve, or brush be swept, curved, or brushed upwards

UPSWELL vb swell up or cause to swell up

UPSWEPT ▶ upsweep

UPSWING n recovery period in the trade cycle ▷ vb swing or move up

UPSWUNG ▶ upswing

UPSY same as ▶ upsee

UPTA same as ▶ upter

UPTAK same as ▶ uptake

UPTAKE n numbers taking up something such as an offer or the act of taking it up ▷ vb take up

UPTAKEN ▶ uptake

UPTAKES ▶ uptake

UPTAKS ▶ uptak

UPTALK n style of speech in which every sentence ends with a rising tone, as if the speaker is always asking a question ▷ vb talk in this manner

UPTALKS ▶ uptalk

UPTEAR vb tear up

UPTEARS ▶ uptear

UPTEMPO adj fast ▷ n uptempo piece

UPTER adj of poor quality

UPTHREW ▶ upthrow

UPTHROW n upward movement of rocks on one side of a fault plane relative to rocks on the other side

▷ vb throw upwards

UPTICK n rise or increase

UPTICKS ▶ uptick

UPTIE vb tie up

UPTIED ▶ uptie

UPTIES ▶ uptie

UPTIGHT adj nervously tense, irritable, or angry

UPTILT vb tilt up

UPTILTS ▶ uptilt

UPTIME n time during which a machine, such as a computer, actually operates

UPTIMES ▶ uptime

UPTOOK ▶ uptake

UPTORE ▶ uptear

UPTORN ▶ uptear

UPTOSS vb throw upwards

UPTOWN adv towards, in, or relating to some part of a town that is away from the centre ▷ n such a part of town, esp a residential part

UPTOWNS ▶ uptown

UPTRAIN vb train up

UPTREND n upward trend

UPTURN n upward trend or improvement ▷ vb turn or cause to turn over or upside down

UPTURNS ▶ upturn

UPTYING ▶ uptie

UPVALUE vb raise the value of

UPWAFT vb waft upwards

UPWAFTS ▶ upwaft

UPWARD same as ▶ upwards

UPWARDS adv from a lower to a higher place, level, condition, etc

UPWELL vb well up

UPWELLS ▶ upwell

UPWENT ▶ upgo

UPWHIRL vb spin upwards

UPWIND adv into or against the wind ▷ adj going against the wind ▷ vb wind up

UPWINDS ▶ upwind

UPWOUND ▶ upwind

UPWRAP vb wrap up

UPWRAPS ▶ upwrap

UR interj hesitant utterance used to fill gaps in talking

URACHI ▶ urachus

URACHUS n cord of tissue connected to the bladder

URACIL n pyrimidine present in all living cells, usually in a combined form, as in RNA

URACILS ▶ uracil

URAEI ▶ uraeus

This plural of **uraeus**, an Egyptian symbol of kingship, is very useful for dumping a surplus of vowels.

URAEMIA n accumulation of waste products, normally excreted in the urine, in the blood: causes severe headaches, vomiting, etc

URAEMIC ▶ uraemia

URAEUS n sacred serpent represented on the headdresses of ancient Egyptian kings and gods

URALI n type of plant

URALIS ▶ urali

URALITE n amphibole mineral, similar to hornblende, that replaces pyroxene in some igneous and metamorphic rocks

URANIA n uranium dioxide

URANIAN adj heavenly

URANIAS ▶ urania

URANIC adj of or containing uranium, esp in a high valence state

URANIDE n any element having an atomic number greater than that of protactinium

URANIN n type of alkaline substance

URANINS ▶ uranin

URANISM n homosexuality

URANITE n any of various minerals containing uranium, esp torbernite or autunite

URANIUM n radioactive silvery-white metallic element, used chiefly as a source of nuclear energy

URANOUS adj of or containing uranium, esp in a low valence state

URANYL n of, consisting of, or containing the divalent ion UO_2^{2+} or the group $-UO_2$

URANYLS ▶ uranyl

URAO n type of mineral

URAOS ▶ urao

URARE same as ▶ urali

URARES ▶ urare

URARI same as ▶ urali

URARIS ▶ urari

URASE same as ▶ urease

URASES ▶ urase

URATE n any salt or ester of uric acid

URATES ▸ urate
URATIC ▸ urate
URB n urban area
URBAN adj of or living in a city or town
URBANE adj characterized by courtesy, elegance, and sophistication
URBANER ▸ urbane
URBIA n urban area
URBIAS ▸ urbia
URBS ▸ urb
URCEOLI > urceolus
URCHIN n mischievous child
URCHINS ▸ urchin
URD n type of plant with edible seeds
URDE adj (in heraldry) having points
URDEE ▸ urde
URDS ▸ urd
URDY n heraldic line pattern
URE same as ▸ aurochs
UREA n white soluble crystalline compound found in urine
UREAL ▸ urea
UREAS ▸ urea
UREASE n enzyme occurring in many plants, esp fungi, that converts urea to ammonium carbonate
UREASES ▸ urease
UREDIA ▸ uredium
UREDIAL ▸ uredium
UREDINE ▸ uredo
UREDIUM n spore-producing body of some rust fungi in which uredospores are formed
UREDO less common name for > urticaria
UREDOS ▸ uredo
UREIC ▸ urea
UREIDE n any of a class of organic compounds derived from urea by replacing one or more of its hydrogen atoms by organic groups
UREIDES ▸ ureide
UREMIA same as ▸ uraemia
UREMIAS ▸ uremia
UREMIC ▸ uremia
URENA n plant genus
URENAS ▸ urena
URENT adj burning
URES ▸ ure
URESES ▸ uresis
URESIS n urination
URETER n tube that conveys urine from the kidney to the bladder
URETERS ▸ ureter
URETHAN same as > urethane
URETHRA n canal that carries urine from the bladder out of the body
URETIC adj of or relating to the urine
URGE n strong impulse, inner drive, or yearning ▷ vb plead with or press (a person to do something)
URGED ▸ urge
URGENCE ▸ urgent
URGENCY ▸ urgent
URGENT adj requiring speedy action or attention
URGER ▸ urge
URGERS ▸ urge
URGES ▸ urge
URGING ▸ urge
URGINGS ▸ urge
URIAL n type of sheep
URIALS ▸ urial
URIC adj of or derived from urine
URICASE n type of enzyme
URIDINE n nucleoside present in all living cells in a combined form, esp in RNA
URINAL n sanitary fitting used by men for urination
URINALS ▸ urinal
URINANT adj having the head downwards
URINARY adj of urine or the organs that secrete and pass urine ▷ n reservoir for urine
URINATE vb discharge urine
URINE n pale yellow fluid excreted by the kidneys to the bladder and passed as waste from the body ▷ vb urinate
URINED ▸ urine
URINES ▸ urine
URINING ▸ urine
URINOSE same as ▸ urinous
URINOUS adj of, resembling, or containing urine
URITE n part of the abdomen
URITES ▸ urite
URMAN n forest
URMANS ▸ urman
URN n vase used as a container for the ashes of the dead ▷ vb put in an urn
URNAL ▸ urn

URNED ▸ urn
URNFUL n capacity of an urn
URNFULS ▸ urnful
URNING n homosexual man
URNINGS ▸ urning
URNLIKE ▸ urn
URNS ▸ urn
URODELE n amphibian of the order which includes the salamanders and newts
UROLITH n calculus in the urinary tract
UROLOGY n branch of medicine concerned with the urinary system and its diseases
UROMERE n part of the abdomen
UROPOD n paired appendage that arises from the last segment of the body in lobsters and related crustaceans and forms part of the tail fan
UROPODS ▸ uropod
UROSES ▸ urosis
UROSIS n urinary disease
UROSOME n abdomen of arthropods
URP dialect word for ▸ vomit
URPED ▸ urp
URPING ▸ urp
URPS ▸ urp
URSA n she-bear
URSAE ▸ ursa
URSID n meteor
URSIDS ▸ ursid
URSINE adj of or like a bear
URSON n type of porcupine
URSONS ▸ urson
URTEXT n earliest form of a text as established by linguistic scholars as a basis for variants in later texts still in existence
URTEXTS ▸ urtext
URTICA n type of nettle
URTICAS ▸ urtica
URUBU n type of bird
URUBUS ▸ urubu
URUS another name for the ▸ aurochs
URUSES ▸ urus
URVA n Indian mongoose
URVAS ▸ urva
US pron refers to the speaker or writer and another person or other people
USABLE adj able to be used
USABLY ▸ usable
USAGE n regular or constant use

USAGER *n* person who has the use of something in trust

USAGERS ▶ usager

USAGES ▶ usage

USANCE *n* period of time permitted by commercial usage for the redemption of foreign bills of exchange

USANCES ▶ usance

USAUNCE same as ▶ usance

USE *vb* put into service or action ▷ *n* using or being used

USEABLE same as ▶ usable

USEABLY ▶ usable

USED *adj* second-hand

USEFUL *adj* able to be used advantageously or for several different purposes ▷ *n* odd-jobman or general factotum

USEFULS ▶ useful

USELESS *adj* having no practical use

USER *n* continued exercise, use, or enjoyment of a right, esp in property

USERS ▶ user

USES ▶ use

USHER *n* official who shows people to their seats, as in a church ▷ *vb* conduct or escort

USHERED ▶ usher

USHERS ▶ usher

USING ▶ use

USNEA *n* type of lichen

USNEAS ▶ usnea

USQUE *n* whisky

USQUES ▶ usque

USTION *n* burning

USTIONS ▶ ustion

USUAL *adj* of the most normal, frequent, or regular type ▷ *n* ordinary or commonplace events

USUALLY *adv* most often, in most cases

USUALS ▶ usual

USUCAPT > usucapion

USURE *vb* be involved in usury

USURED ▶ usure

USURER *n* person who lends funds at an exorbitant rate of interest

USURERS ▶ usurer

USURES ▶ usure

USURESS *n* female usurer

USURIES ▶ usury

USURING ▶ usure

USUROUS ▶ usury

USURP *vb* seize (a position or power) without authority

USURPED ▶ usurp

USURPER ▶ usurp

USURPS ▶ usurp

USURY *n* practice of lending money at an extremely high rate of interest

USWARD *adv* towards us

USWARDS same as ▶ usward

UT *n* syllable used in the fixed system of solmization for the note C

UTA *n* side-blotched lizard

UTAS *n* eighth day of a festival

UTASES ▶ utas

UTE same as ▶ utility

UTENSIL *n* tool or container for practical use

UTERI ▶ uterus

UTERINE *adj* of or affecting the womb

UTERUS *n* womb

UTES ▶ ute

UTILE *obsolete word for* ▶ useful

UTILISE same as ▶ utilize

UTILITY *n* usefulness ▷ *adj* designed for use rather than beauty

UTILIZE *vb* make practical use of

UTIS *n* uproar

UTISES ▶ utis

UTMOST *n* the greatest possible degree or amount ▷ *adj* of the greatest possible degree or amount

UTMOSTS ▶ utmost

UTOPIA *n* real or imaginary society, place, state, etc, considered to be perfect or ideal

UTOPIAN *adj* of or relating to a perfect or ideal existence ▷ *n* idealistic social reformer

UTOPIAS ▶ utopia

UTOPISM ▶ utopia

UTOPIST ▶ utopia

UTRICLE *n* larger of the two parts of the membranous labyrinth of the internal ear

UTS ▶ ut

UTTER *vb* express (something) in sounds or words ▷ *adj* total or absolute

UTTERED ▶ utter

UTTERER ▶ utter

UTTERLY *adv* extrremely

UTTERS ▶ utter

UTU *n* reward

UTUS ▶ utu

UVA *n* grape or fruit resembling this

UVAE ▶ uva

UVAS ▶ uva

UVEA *n* part of the eyeball consisting of the iris, ciliary body, and choroid

UVEAL ▶ uvea

UVEAS ▶ uvea

UVEITIC ▶ uveitis

UVEITIS *n* inflammation of the uvea

UVEOUS ▶ uvea

UVULA *n* small fleshy part of the soft palate that hangs in the back of the throat

UVULAE ▶ uvula

UVULAR *adj* of or relating to the uvula ▷ *n* uvular consonant

UVULARS ▶ uvular

UVULAS ▶ uvula

UXORIAL *adj* of or relating to a wife

U

Vv

If you have a **V** on your rack, the first thing to remember is that there are no valid two-letter words beginning with **V**. In fact, there are no two-letter words that end in **V** either, so you can't form any two-letter words using **V**. Remembering this will stop you wasting time trying to think of some. While **V** is useless for two-letter words, it does start some good three-letter words. **Vex** and **vox** (13 points each) are the best of these, while **vaw**, **vow** and **vly** (9 each) are also useful.

VAC *vb* clean with a vacuum cleaner

> Meaning to clean with a vacuum cleaner, this can be a useful short word for dealing with that awkward letter V.

VACANCE *n* vacant period
VACANCY *n* unfilled job
VACANT *adj* (of a toilet, room, etc) unoccupied
VACATE *vb* cause (something) to be empty by leaving
VACATED ▶ **vacate**
VACATES ▶ **vacate**
VACATUR *n* annulment
VACCINA *same as* > **vaccinia**
VACCINE *n* substance designed to cause a mild form of a disease to make a person immune to the disease itself
VACKED ▶ **vac**
VACKING ▶ **vac**
VACS ▶ **vac**
VACUA ▶ **vacuum**
VACUATE *vb* empty
VACUIST *n* person believing in the existence of vacuums in nature
VACUITY *n* absence of intelligent thought or ideas
VACUOLE *n* fluid-filled cavity in the cytoplasm of a cell
VACUOUS *adj* not expressing intelligent thought
VACUUM *n* empty space from which all or most air or gas has been removed ▷ *vb* clean with a vacuum cleaner

VACUUMS ▶ **vacuum**
VADE *vb* fade
VADED ▶ **vade**
VADES ▶ **vade**
VADING ▶ **vade**
VADOSE *adj* of or derived from water occurring above the water table
VAE *same as* ▶ **voe**
VAES ▶ **vae**
VAG *n* vagrant
VAGAL *adj* of, relating to, or affecting the vagus nerve
VAGALLY ▶ **vagal**
VAGARY *n* unpredictable change
VAGGED ▶ **vag**
VAGGING ▶ **vag**
VAGI ▶ **vagus**
VAGILE *adj* able to move freely
VAGINA *n* (in female mammals) passage from the womb to the external genitals
VAGINAE ▶ **vagina**
VAGINAL ▶ **vagina**
VAGINAS ▶ **vagina**
VAGITUS *n* new-born baby's cry
VAGRANT *n* person with no settled home ▷ *adj* wandering
VAGROM *same as* ▶ **vagrant**
VAGS ▶ **vag**
VAGUE *adj* not clearly explained ▷ *vb* wander
VAGUED ▶ **vague**
VAGUELY ▶ **vague**
VAGUER ▶ **vague**
VAGUES ▶ **vague**
VAGUEST ▶ **vague**

VAGUING ▶ **vague**
VAGUS *n* tenth cranial nerve, which supplies the heart, lungs, and viscera
VAHANA *n* vehicle
VAHANAS ▶ **vahana**
VAHINE *n* Polynesian woman
VAHINES ▶ **vahine**
VAIL *vb* lower (something, such as a weapon), esp as a sign of deference or submission
VAILED ▶ **vail**
VAILING ▶ **vail**
VAILS ▶ **vail**
VAIN *adj* excessively proud, esp of one's appearance
VAINER ▶ **vain**
VAINEST ▶ **vain**
VAINLY ▶ **vain**
VAIR *n* fur, probably Russian squirrel, used to trim robes in the Middle Ages
VAIRE *adj* of Russian squirrel fur
VAIRIER ▶ **vair**
VAIRS ▶ **vair**
VAIRY ▶ **vair**
VAIVODE *n* European ruler
VAKAS *n* Armenian priestly garment
VAKASES ▶ **vakas**
VAKEEL *n* ambassador
VAKEELS ▶ **vakeel**
VAKIL *same as* ▶ **vakeel**
VAKILS ▶ **vakil**
VALANCE *n* piece of drapery round the edge of a bed ▷ *vb* provide with a valance
VALE *n* valley ▷ *sentence substitute* farewell
VALENCE *same as* ▶ **valency**

V

VALENCY n power of an atom to make molecular bonds

VALERIC adj of, relating to, or derived from valerian

VALES ▶ vale

VALET n man's personal male servant ▷ vb act as a valet (for)

VALETA n old-time dance in triple time

VALETAS ▶ valeta

VALETE n farewell

VALETED ▶ valet

VALETES ▶ valete

VALETS ▶ valet

VALGOID ▶ valgus

VALGOUS same as ▶ valgus

VALGUS adj denoting a deformity of a limb ▷ n abnormal position of a limb

VALI n Turkish civil governor

VALIANT adj brave or courageous ▷ n brave person

VALID adj soundly reasoned

VALIDER ▶ valid

VALIDLY ▶ valid

VALINE n essential amino acid

VALINES ▶ valine

VALIS ▶ vali

VALISE n small suitcase

VALISES ▶ valise

VALIUM n as in valium picnic refers to a day on the New York Stock Exchange when business is slow

VALKYR same as ▶ valkyrie

VALKYRS ▶ valkyr

VALLAR adj pertaining to a rampart

VALLARY ▶ vallar

VALLATE adj surrounded with a wall

VALLEY n low area between hills, often with a river running through it

VALLEYS ▶ valley

VALLUM n Roman rampart or earthwork

VALLUMS ▶ vallum

VALONEA same as ▶ valonia

VALONIA n acorn cups and unripe acorns of a particular oak

VALOR same as ▶ valour

VALORS ▶ valor

VALOUR n bravery ▷ n courageous person

VALOURS ▶ valour

VALSE another word for ▶ waltz

VALSED ▶ valse

VALSES ▶ valse

VALSING ▶ valse

VALUATE vb value or evaluate

VALUE n importance, usefulness ▷ vb assess the worth or desirability of

VALUED ▶ value

VALUER ▶ value

VALUERS ▶ value

VALUES ▶ value

VALUING ▶ value

VALUTA n value of one currency in terms of its exchange rate with another

VALUTAS ▶ valuta

VALVAL same as ▶ valvular

VALVAR same as ▶ valvular

VALVATE adj furnished with a valve or valves

VALVE n device to control the movement of fluid through a pipe ▷ vb provide with a valve

VALVED ▶ valve

VALVES ▶ valve

VALVING ▶ valve

VALVULA same as ▶ valvule

VALVULE n small valve or a part resembling one

VAMOOSE vb leave a place hurriedly

VAMOSE same as ▶ vamoose

VAMOSED ▶ vamose

VAMOSES ▶ vamose

VAMP n sexually attractive woman who seduces men ▷ vb (of a woman) to seduce (a man)

VAMPED ▶ vamp

VAMPER ▶ vamp

VAMPERS ▶ vamp

VAMPIER ▶ vamp

VAMPING ▶ vamp

VAMPIRE n (in folklore) corpse that rises at night to drink the blood of the living ▷ vb assail

VAMPISH ▶ vamp

VAMPS ▶ vamp

VAMPY ▶ vamp

VAN n motor vehicle for transporting goods ▷ vb send in a van

VANADIC adj of or containing vanadium, esp in a trivalent or pentavalent state

VANDA n type of orchid

VANDAL n person who deliberately damages property

VANDALS ▶ vandal

VANDAS ▶ vanda

VANDYKE n short pointed beard ▷ vb cut with deep zigzag indentations

VANE n flat blade on a rotary device such as a weathercock or propeller

VANED ▶ vane

VANES ▶ vane

VANESSA n type of butterfly

VANG n type of rope or tackle on a sailing ship

VANGS ▶ vang

VANILLA n seed pod of a tropical climbing orchid, used for flavouring ▷ adj flavoured with vanilla

VANISH vb disappear suddenly or mysteriously ▷ n second and weaker of the two vowels in a falling diphthong

VANITAS n type of Dutch painting

VANITY n (display of) excessive pride

VANLOAD n amount van will carry

VANMAN n man in control of a van

VANMEN ▶ vanman

VANNED ▶ van

VANNER n horse used to pull delivery vehicles

VANNERS ▶ vanner

VANNING ▶ van

VANPOOL n van-sharing group

VANS ▶ van

VANT archaic word for ▶ vanguard

VANTAGE n state, position, or opportunity offering advantage ▷ vb benefit

VANTS ▶ vant

VANWARD adv in or towards the front

VAPID adj lacking character, dull

VAPIDER ▶ vapid

VAPIDLY ▶ vapid

VAPOR same as ▶ vapour

VAPORED ▶ vapor

VAPORER ▶ vapor

VAPORS ▶ vapor

VAPORY ▶ vapor

VAPOUR n moisture suspended in air as steam or mist ▷ vb evaporate

VAPOURS ▶ vapour

V

VAPOURY ▶ vapour

VAQUERO n cattlehand

VAR n unit of reactive power of an alternating current

VARA n unit of length used in Spain, Portugal, and South America

VARAN n type of lizard

VARANS ▶ varan

VARAS ▶ vara

VARDIES ▶ vardy

VARDY n verdict

VARE n rod

VAREC n ash obtained from kelp

VARECH same as ▶ varec

VARECHS ▶ varech

VARECS ▶ varec

VARES ▶ vare

VAREUSE n type of coat

VARIA n collection or miscellany, esp of literary works

VARIANT adj differing from a standard or type ▷ n something that differs from a standard or type

VARIAS ▶ varia

VARIATE n random variable or a numerical value taken by it ▷ vb vary

VARICES ▶ varix

VARIED ▶ vary

VARIER n person who varies

VARIERS ▶ varier

VARIES ▶ vary

VARIETY n state of being diverse or various

VARIOLA n smallpox

VARIOLE n any of the rounded masses that make up the rock variolite

VARIOUS adj of several kinds

VARIX n tortuous dilated vein

VARLET n menial servant

VARLETS ▶ varlet

VARMENT same as ▶ varmint

VARMINT n irritating or obnoxious person or animal

VARNA n any of the four Hindu castes

VARNAS ▶ varna

VARNISH n solution of oil and resin, put on a surface to make it hard and glossy ▷ vb apply varnish to

VAROOM same as ▶ vroom

VAROOMS same as ▶ varoom

VARROA n small parasite

VARROAS ▶ varroa

VARS ▶ var

VARSAL adj universal

VARSITY n university

VARUS adj denoting a deformity of a limb ▷ n abnormal position of a limb

VARUSES ▶ varus

VARVE n typically thin band of sediment deposited annually in glacial lakes

VARVED adj having layers of sedimentary deposit

VARVEL n piece of falconry equipment

VARVELS ▶ varvel

VARVES ▶ varve

VARY vb change

VARYING ▶ vary

VAS n vessel or tube that carries a fluid

VASA ▶ vas

VASAL ▶ vas

VASCULA > vasculum

VASE n ornamental jar, esp for flowers

VASES ▶ vase

VASSAIL archaic variant of ▶ vassal

VASSAL n man given land by a lord in return for military service ▷ adj of or relating to a vassal ▷ vb vassalize

VASSALS ▶ vassal

VAST adj extremely large ▷ n immense or boundless space

VASTER ▶ vast

VASTEST ▶ vast

VASTIER ▶ vasty

VASTITY ▶ vast

VASTLY ▶ vast

VASTS ▶ vast

VASTY archaic or poetic word for ▶ vast

VAT n large container for liquids ▷ vb place, store, or treat in a vat

VATABLE adj subject to VAT

VATFUL n amount enough to fill a vat

VATFULS ▶ vatful

VATIC adj of, relating to, or characteristic of a prophet

VATICAL same as ▶ vatic

VATMAN n Customs and Excise employee

VATMEN ▶ vatman

VATS ▶ vat

VATTED ▶ vat

VATTER n person who works with vats; blender

VATTERS ▶ vatter

VATTING ▶ vat

VATU n standard monetary unit of Vanuatu

VATUS ▶ vatu

VAU same as ▶ vav

VAUCH vb move fast

VAUCHED ▶ vauch

VAUCHES ▶ vauch

VAUDOO same as ▶ voodoo

VAUDOOS ▶ vaudoo

VAUDOUX same as ▶ voodoo

VAULT n secure room for storing valuables ▷ vb jump over (something) by resting one's hand(s) on it.

VAULTED ▶ vault

VAULTER ▶ vault

VAULTS ▶ vault

VAULTY adj arched

VAUNCE ▶ advance

VAUNCED ▶ vaunce

VAUNCES ▶ vaunce

VAUNT vb describe or display (success or possessions) boastfully ▷ n boast

VAUNTED ▶ vaunt

VAUNTER ▶ vaunt

VAUNTIE same as ▶ vaunty

VAUNTS ▶ vaunt

VAUNTY adj proud

VAURIEN n rascal

VAUS ▶ vau

VAUT same as ▶ vault

VAUTE same as ▶ vault

VAUTED ▶ vaute

VAUTES ▶ vaute

VAUTING ▶ vaut

VAUTS ▶ vaut

VAV n sixth letter of the Hebrew alphabet

It is surprising how often one wants to get rid of two Vs, and when one does, this word, the name of a Hebrew letter, fits the bill nicely. It has an equally useful variant **vaw**.

VAVASOR n (in feudal society) vassal who also has vassals himself

VAVS ▶ vav

VAW n Hebrew letter

VAWARD n vanguard

VAWARDS ▶ vaward

VAWNTIE ▶ vaunty

VAWS ▶ vaw

VAWTE same as ▶ vault

VAWTED ▶ vawte

VAWTES ▶ vawte

VAWTING ▶ vawte

VEAL n calf meat ▷ vb cover with a veil

VEALE same as ▶ **veil**

VEALED ▶ **veal**

VEALER n young bovine animal of up to 14 months old grown for veal

VEALERS ▶ **vealer**

VEALES ▶ **veale**

VEALIER ▶ **veal**

VEALING ▶ **veal**

VEALS ▶ **veal**

VEALY ▶ **veal**

VECTOR n quantity that has size and direction, such as force ▷ vb direct or guide (a pilot) by directions transmitted by radio

VECTORS ▶ **vector**

VEDALIA n Australian ladybird which is a pest of citrus fruits

VEDETTE n small patrol vessel

VEDUTA n painting of a town or city

VEDUTE ▶ **veduta**

VEE n letter 'v'

VEEJAY n video jockey

VEEJAYS ▶ **veejay**

VEENA same as ▶ **vina**

VEENAS ▶ **veena**

VEEP n vice president

VEEPEE n vice president

VEEPEES ▶ **veepee**

VEEPS ▶ **veep**

VEER vb change direction suddenly ▷ n change of course or direction

VEERED ▶ **veer**

VEERIES ▶ **veery**

VEERING ▶ **veer**

VEERS ▶ **veer**

VEERY n tawny brown North American thrush

VEES ▶ **vee**

VEG n vegetable or vegetables ▷ vb relax

> Veg is a short form of **vegetable**. If someone plays this, remember that you can add an A or O to it to form **vega** or **vego**.

VEGA n tobacco plantation

VEGAN n person who eats no meat, fish, eggs, or dairy products ▷ adj suitable for a vegan

VEGANIC adj farmed without the use of animal products or byproducts

VEGANS ▶ **vegan**

VEGAS ▶ **vega**

VEGES ▶ **veg**

VEGETAL adj of or relating to plant life ▷ n vegetable

VEGETE adj lively

VEGGED ▶ **veg**

VEGGES ▶ **veg**

VEGGIE n vegetable ▷ adj vegetarian

VEGGIES ▶ **veggie**

VEGGING ▶ **veg**

VEGIE same as ▶ **veggie**

VEGIES ▶ **vegie**

VEGO adj vegetarian ▷ n vegetarian

VEGOS ▶ **vego**

VEHICLE n machine for carrying people or objects

VEHM n type of medieval German court

VEHME ▶ **vehm**

VEHMIC ▶ **vehm**

VEIL n piece of thin cloth covering the head or face ▷ vb cover with or as if with a veil

VEILED adj disguised

VEILER ▶ **veil**

VEILERS ▶ **veil**

VEILIER ▶ **veil**

VEILING n veil or the fabric used for veils

VEILS ▶ **veil**

VEILY ▶ **veil**

VEIN n tube that takes blood to the heart ▷ vb diffuse over or cause to diffuse over in streaked patterns

VEINAL ▶ **vein**

VEINED ▶ **vein**

VEINER n wood-carving tool

VEINERS ▶ **veiner**

VEINIER ▶ **vein**

VEINING n pattern or network of veins or streaks

VEINLET n any small vein or venule

VEINOUS ▶ **vein**

VEINS ▶ **vein**

VEINULE less common spelling of ▶ **venule**

VEINY ▶ **vein**

VELA ▶ **velum**

VELAMEN n thick layer of dead cells that covers the aerial roots of certain orchids

VELAR n of, relating to, or attached to a velum ▷ n velar sound

VELARIA > **velarium**

VELARIC ▶ **velar**

VELARS ▶ **velar**

VELATE adj having or covered with velum

VELATED same as ▶ **velate**

VELCRO n tradename for a fastening consisting of two strips of nylon fabric that form a strong bond when pressed together

VELCROS ▶ **velcro**

VELD n high grassland in southern Africa

VELDS ▶ **veld**

VELDT same as ▶ **veld**

VELDTS ▶ **veldt**

VELE same as ▶ **veil**

VELES ▶ **vele**

VELETA same as ▶ **valeta**

VELETAS ▶ **veleta**

VELIGER n free-swimming larva of many molluscs

VELITES pl n light-armed troops in ancient Rome, drawn from the poorer classes

VELL vb cut turf

VELLET n velvet

VELLETS ▶ **vellet**

VELLON n silver and copper alloy used in old Spanish coins

VELLONS ▶ **vellon**

VELLS ▶ **vell**

VELLUM n fine caltskin parchment ▷ adj made of or resembling vellum

VELLUMS ▶ **vellum**

VELLUS n as in **vellus hair** short fine unpigmented hair covering the human body

VELOCE adv be played rapidly

VELOUR n fabric similar to velvet

VELOURS same as ▶ **velour**

VELOUTE n rich white sauce or soup made from stock, egg yolks, and cream

VELUM n any of various membranous structures

VELURE n velvet or a similar fabric ▷ vb cover with velure

VELURED ▶ **velure**

VELURES ▶ **velure**

VELVET n fabric with a thick soft pile ▷ vb cover with velvet

VELVETS ▶ **velvet**

VELVETY ▶ **velvet**

VENA n vein in the body

V

VENAE ▸ vena
VENAL adj easily bribed
VENALLY ▸ venal
VENATIC adj of, relating to, or used in hunting
VENATOR n hunter
VEND vb sell
VENDACE n either of two small whitefish occurring in lakes in Scotland and NW England
VENDAGE n vintage
VENDED ▸ vend
VENDEE n person to whom something, esp real property, is sold
VENDEES ▸ vendee
VENDER same as ▸ vendor
VENDERS ▸ vender
VENDING ▸ vend
VENDIS same as ▸ vendace
VENDISS same as
▸ vendace
VENDOR n person who sells goods such as newspapers or hamburgers from a stall or cart
VENDORS ▸ vendor
VENDS ▸ vend
VENDUE n public sale
VENDUES ▸ vendue
VENEER n thin layer of wood etc covering a cheaper material ▷ vb cover (a surface) with a veneer
VENEERS ▸ veneer
VENEFIC adj having poisonous effects
VENENE n medicine from snake venom
VENENES ▸ venene
VENERER n hunter
VENERY n pursuit of sexual gratification
VENEWE same as ▸ venue
VENEWES ▸ venewe
VENEY n thrust
VENEYS ▸ veney
VENGE vb avenge
VENGED ▸ venge
VENGER ▸ venge
VENGERS ▸ venge
VENGES ▸ venge
VENGING ▸ venge
VENIAL adj (of a sin or fault) easily forgiven
VENIN n any of the poisonous constituents of animal venoms
VENINE same as ▸ venin
VENINES ▸ venine
VENINS ▸ venin

VENIRE n list from which jurors are selected
VENIRES ▸ venire
VENISON n deer meat
VENITE n musical setting for the 95th psalm
VENITES ▸ venite
VENNEL n lane
VENNELS ▸ vennel
VENOM n malice or spite ▷ vb poison
VENOMED ▸ venom
VENOMER ▸ venom
VENOMS ▸ venom
VENOSE adj having veins
VENOUS adj of veins
VENT n outlet releasing fumes or fluid ▷ vb express (an emotion) freely
VENTAGE n small opening
VENTAIL n (in medieval armour) a covering for the lower part of the face
VENTANA n window
VENTED ▸ vent
VENTER ▸ vent
VENTERS ▸ vent
VENTIGE same as ▸ ventage
VENTIL n valve on a musical instrument
VENTILS ▸ ventil
VENTING ▸ vent
VENTOSE adj full of wind
VENTRAL adj relating to the front of the body ▷ n ventral fin
VENTRE same as ▸ venture
VENTRED ▸ ventre
VENTRES ▸ ventre
VENTS ▸ vent
VENTURE n risky undertaking, esp in business ▷ vb do something risky
VENTURI n tube used to control the flow of fluid
VENUE n place where an organized gathering is held
VENUES ▸ venue
VENULAR ▸ venule
VENULE n any of the small branches of a vein
VENULES ▸ venule
VENUS n type of marine bivalve mollusc
VENUSES ▸ venus
VERA adj as in aloe vera plant substance used in skin and hair preparations
VERANDA n porch or portico along the outside of a building
VERB n word that expresses

the idea of action, happening, or being
VERBAL adj spoken ▷ n abuse or invective ▷ vb implicate (someone) in a crime by quoting alleged admission of guilt in court
VERBALS ▸ verbal
VERBENA n plant with sweet-smelling flowers
VERBID n any nonfinite form of a verb or any nonverbal word derived from a verb
VERBIDS ▸ verbid
VERBIFY another word for
> verbalize
VERBILE n person who is best stimulated by words
VERBING n use of nouns as verbs
VERBOSE adj speaking at tedious length
VERBS ▸ verb
VERD adj as in verd antique dark green mottled impure variety of serpentine marble
VERDANT adj covered in green vegetation
VERDET n type of verdigris
VERDETS ▸ verdet
VERDICT n decision of a jury
VERDIN n small W North American tit having grey plumage with a yellow head
VERDINS ▸ verdin
VERDIT same as ▸ verdict
VERDITE n type of rock used in jewellery
VERDITS ▸ verdit
VERDOY n floral or leafy shield decoration
VERDURE n flourishing green vegetation
VERGE n grass border along a road ▷ vb move in a specified direction
VERGED ▸ verge
VERGER n church caretaker
VERGERS ▸ verger
VERGES ▸ verge
VERGING ▸ verge
VERGLAS n thin film of ice on rock
VERIDIC same as > veridical
VERIER ▸ very
VERIEST ▸ very
VERIFY vb check the truth or accuracy of
VERILY adv in truth
VERISM n extreme

naturalism in art or literature

VERISMO n school of composition that originated in Italian opera

VERISMS ▶ verism

VERIST ▶ verism

VERISTS ▶ verism

VERITAS n truth

VERITE adj involving a high degree of realism or naturalism ▷ n this kind of realism in film

VERITES ▶ verite

VERITY n true statement or principle

VERLAN n variety of French slang in which the syllables are inverted

VERLANS ▶ verlan

VERLIG adj enlightened

VERMAL ▶ vermis

VERMEIL n gilded silver, bronze, or other metal, used esp in the 19th century ▷ vb decorate with vermeil ▷ adj vermilion

VERMELL same as ▶ vermeil

VERMES ▶ vermis

VERMIAN ▶ vermis

VERMIL same as ▶ vermeil

VERMILS ▶ vermeil

VERMILY ▶ vermeil

VERMIN pl n animals, esp insects and rodents, that spread disease or cause damage

VERMINS ▶ vermin

VERMINY ▶ vermin

VERMIS n middle lobe connecting the two halves of the cerebellum

VERMUTH same as > **vermouth**

VERNAL adj occurring in spring

VERNANT ▶ vernal

VERNIER n movable scale on a graduated measuring instrument for taking readings in fractions

VERNIX n white substance covering the skin of a foetus

VERONAL n a long-acting barbiturate used medicinally

VERRA Scots word for ▶ very

VERREL n ferrule

VERRELS ▶ verrel

VERREY same as ▶ vair

VERRUCA n wart, usu on the foot

VERRUGA same as

▶ **verruca**

VERRY same as ▶ vair

VERS n verse

VERSAL n embellished letter

VERSALS ▶ versal

VERSANT n side or slope of a mountain or mountain range

VERSE n group of lines forming part of a song or poem ▷ vb write verse

VERSED adj thoroughly knowledgeable (about)

VERSER n versifier

VERSERS ▶ verser

VERSES ▶ verse

VERSET n short, often sacred, verse

VERSETS ▶ verset

VERSIFY vb write in verse

VERSIN same as ▶ versine

VERSINE n mathematical term

VERSING ▶ verse

VERSINS ▶ versin

VERSION n form of something, such as a piece of writing, with some differences from other forms

VERSO n left-hand page of a book

VERSOS ▶ verso

VERST n unit of length used in Russia

VERSTE same as ▶ verst

VERSTES ▶ verste

VERSTS ▶ verst

VERSUS prep in opposition to or in contrast with

VERSUTE adj cunning

VERT n right to cut green wood in a forest ▷ vb turn

VERTED ▶ vert

VERTEX n point on a geometric figure where the sides form an angle

VERTIGO n dizziness, usu when looking down from a high place

VERTING ▶ vert

VERTS ▶ vert

VERTU same as ▶ virtu

VERTUE same as ▶ virtu

VERTUES ▶ vertue

VERTUS ▶ vertu

VERVAIN n plant with spikes of blue, purple, or white flowers

VERVE n enthusiasm or liveliness

VERVEL same as ▶ varvel

VERVELS ▶ vervel

VERVEN same as ▶ vervain

VERVENS ▶ verven

VERVES ▶ verve

VERVET n variety of a South African guenon monkey

VERVETS ▶ vervet

VERY adv more than usually, extremely ▷ adj absolute, exact

VESICA n bladder

VESICAE ▶ vesica

VESICAL adj of or relating to a vesica, esp the urinary bladder

VESICLE n sac or small cavity, esp one containing fluid

VESPA n type of wasp

VESPAS ▶ vespa

VESPER n evening prayer, service, or hymn

VESPERS pl n service of evening prayer

VESPID n insect of the family that includes the common wasp and hornet ▷ adj of or belonging to this family

VESPIDS ▶ vespid

VESPINE adj of, relating to, or resembling a wasp or wasps

VESPOID adj like a wasp

VESSAIL archaic variant of ▶ vessel

VESSEL n container or ship ▷ adj contained in a vessel

VESSELS ▶ vessel

VEST n undergarment worn on the top half of the body ▷ vb give (authority) to (someone)

VESTA n short friction match, usually of wood

VESTAL adj pure, chaste ▷ n chaste woman

VESTALS ▶ vestal

VESTAS ▶ vesta

VESTED adj having an existing right to the immediate or future possession of property

VESTEE n person having a vested interest something

VESTEES ▶ vestee

VESTIGE n small amount or trace

VESTING ▶ vest

VESTRAL ▶ vestry

VESTRY n room in a church used as an office by the priest or minister

V

VESTS ▶ vest

VESTURE *n* garment or something that seems like a garment ▷ *vb* clothe

VET *vb* check the suitability of ▷ *n* military veteran

VETCH *n* climbing plant with a beanlike fruit used as fodder

VETCHES ▶ vetch

VETCHY *adj* consisting of vetches

VETERAN *n* person with long experience in a particular activity, esp military service ▷ *adj* long-serving

VETIVER *n* tall hairless grass of tropical and subtropical Asia

VETKOEK *n* South African cake

VETO *n* official power to cancel a proposal ▷ *vb* enforce a veto against

VETOED ▶ veto

VETOER ▶ veto

VETOERS ▶ veto

VETOES ▶ veto

VETOING ▶ veto

VETS ▶ vet

VETTED ▶ vet

VETTER ▶ vet

VETTERS ▶ vet

VETTING *n as in* **positive vetting** checking a person's background to assess their suitability of an important post

VETTURA *n* Italian mode of transport

VEX *vb* frustrate, annoy

VEXED *adj* annoyed and puzzled

VEXEDLY ▶ vexed

VEXER ▶ vex

VEXERS ▶ vex

VEXES ▶ vex

VEXIL *same as* ▶ **vexillum**

VEXILLA > **vexillum**

VEXILS ▶ vexil

VEXING ▶ vex

VEXINGS ▶ vex

VEXT *same as* ▶ **vexed**

VEZIR *same as* ▶ **vizier**

VEZIRS ▶ vezir

VIA *prep* by way of ▷ *n* road

VIABLE *adj* able to be put into practice

VIABLY ▶ viable

VIADUCT *n* bridge over a valley

VIAE ▶ via

VIAL *n* small bottle for liquids ▷ *vb* put into a vial

VIALED ▶ vial

VIALFUL ▶ vial

VIALING ▶ vial

VIALLED ▶ vial

VIALS ▶ vial

VIAND *n* type of food, esp a delicacy

VIANDS ▶ viand

VIAS ▶ via

VIATIC *same as* > **viatical**

VIATICA > **viaticum**

VIATOR *n* traveller

VIATORS ▶ viator

VIBE *n* feeling or flavour of the kind specified

VIBES *pl n* vibrations

VIBEX *n* mark under the skin

VIBEY *adj* lively and vibrant

VIBICES ▶ vibex

VIBIER ▶ vibey

VIBIEST ▶ vibey

VIBIST *n* person who plays a vibraphone in a jazz band or group

VIBISTS ▶ vibist

VIBRANT *adj* vigorous in appearance, energetic ▷ *n* trilled or rolled speech sound

VIBRATE *vb* move back and forth rapidly

VIBRATO *n* rapid fluctuation in the pitch of a note

VIBRIO *n* curved or spiral rodlike bacterium

VIBRION *same as* ▶ **vibrio**

VIBRIOS ▶ vibrio

VIBS *pl n* type of climbing shoes

VICAR *n* member of the clergy in charge of a parish

VICARLY ▶ vicar

VICARS ▶ vicar

VICARY *n* office of a vicar

VICE *n* immoral or evil habit or action ▷ *adj* serving in place of ▷ *vb* grip (something) with or as if with a vice ▷ *prep* instead of

VICED ▶ vice

VICEROY *n* governor of a colony who represents the monarch

VICES ▶ vice

VICHIES ▶ vichy

VICHY *n* French mineral water

VICIATE *same as* ▶ **vitiate**

VICINAL *adj* neighbouring

VICING ▶ vice

VICIOUS *adj* cruel and violent

VICOMTE *n* French nobleman

VICTIM *n* person or thing harmed or killed

VICTIMS ▶ victim

VICTOR *n* person who has defeated an opponent, esp in war or in sport

VICTORS ▶ victor

VICTORY *n* winning of a battle or contest

VICTRIX *same as* > **victress**

VICTUAL *vb* supply with or obtain victuals

VICUGNA *same as* ▶ **vicuna**

VICUNA *n* S American animal like the llama

VICUNAS ▶ vicuna

VID *same as* ▶ **video**

VIDAME *n* French nobleman

VIDAMES ▶ vidame

VIDE *interj* look

VIDENDA > **videndum**

VIDEO *vb* record (a TV programme or event) on video ▷ *adj* relating to or used in producing television images ▷ *n* recording and showing of films and events using a television set, video tapes, and a video recorder

VIDEOED ▶ video

VIDEOS ▶ video

VIDETTE *same as* ▶ **vedette**

VIDICON *n* small television camera tube used in closed-circuit television

VIDIMUS *n* inspection

VIDS ▶ vid

VIDUAGE *n* widows collectively

VIDUAL *adj* widowed

VIDUITY *n* widowhood

VIDUOUS *adj* empty

VIE *vb* compete (with someone)

VIED ▶ vie

VIELLE *n* stringed musical instrument

VIELLES ▶ vielle

VIENNA *n as in* **vienna loaf, vienna steak** associated with Vienna

VIER ▶ vie

VIERS ▶ vie

VIES ▶ vie

VIEW *n* opinion or belief ▷ *vb* think of (something) in a particular way

VIEWED ▶ view

VIEWER n person who watches television

VIEWERS ▶ viewer

VIEWIER ▶ viewy

VIEWING n act of watching television

VIEWLY adj pleasant on the eye

VIEWS ▶ view

VIEWY adj having fanciful opinions or ideas

VIFDA same as ▶ vivda

VIFDAS ▶ vifda

VIG n interest on a loan that is paid to a moneylender

VIGA n rafter

VIGAS ▶ viga

VIGIA n navigational hazard marked on a chart although its existence has not been confirmed

VIGIAS ▶ vigia

VIGIL n night-time period of staying awake to look after a sick person, pray, etc

VIGILS ▶ vigil

VIGOR same as ▶ vigour

VIGORO n women's game similar to cricket

VIGOROS ▶ vigoro

VIGORS ▶ vigor

VIGOUR n physical or mental energy

VIGOURS ▶ vigour

VIGS ▶ vig

VIHARA n type of Buddhist temple

VIHARAS ▶ vihara

VIHUELA n obsolete plucked stringed instrument of Spain, related to the guitar

VIKING n Dane, Norwegian, or Swede who raided by sea most of N and W Europe between the 8th and 11th centuries

VIKINGS ▶ viking

VILAYET n major administrative division of Turkey

VILD same as ▶ vile

VILDE same as ▶ vile

VILDLY ▶ vild

VILE adj very wicked

VILELY ▶ vile

VILER ▶ vile

VILEST ▶ vile

VILIACO n scoundrel

VILIAGO same as ▶ viliaco

VILIFY vb attack the character of

VILL n township

VILLA n large house with gardens

VILLAE ▶ villa

VILLAGE n small group of houses in a country area

VILLAIN n wicked person

VILLAN same as ▶ villein

VILLANS ▶ villan

VILLANY same as > villainy

VILLAR ▶ vill

VILLAS ▶ villa

VILLEIN n peasant bound in service to his lord

VILLI ▶ villus

VILLOSE same as ▶ villous

VILLOUS adj (of plant parts) covered with long hairs

VILLS ▶ vill

VILLUS n one of the finger-like projections in the small intestine of many vertebrates

VIM n force, energy

This word can be helpful when you're stuck with unpromising letters, and gives a reasonable score for a three-letter word.

VIMANA n Indian mythological chariot of the gods

VIMANAS ▶ vimana

VIMEN n long flexible shoot that occurs in certain plants

VIMINA ▶ vimen

VIMINAL ▶ vimen

VIMS ▶ vim

VIN n French wine

VINA n stringed musical instrument related to the sitar

VINAL n type of manmade fibre

VINALS ▶ vinal

VINAS ▶ vina

VINASSE n residue left in a still after distilling spirits, esp brandy

VINCA n type of trailing plant with blue flowers

VINCAS ▶ vinca

VINCULA > vinculum

VINE n climbing plant, esp one producing grapes ▷ vb form like a vine

VINEAL adj relating to wines

VINED ▶ vine

VINEGAR n acid liquid made from wine, beer, or cider ▷ vb apply vinegar to

VINER n vinedresser

VINERS ▶ viner

VINERY n hothouse for growing grapes

VINES ▶ vine

VINEW vb become mouldy

VINEWED ▶ vinew

VINEWS ▶ vinew

VINIC adj of, relating to, or contained in wine

VINIER ▶ vine

VINIEST ▶ vine

VINIFY vb convert into wine

VINING ▶ vine

VINO n wine

VINOS ▶ vino

VINOUS adj of or characteristic of wine

VINS ▶ vin

VINT vb sell (wine)

VINTAGE n wine from a particular harvest of grapes ▷ adj best and most typical ▷ vb gather (grapes) or make (wine)

VINTED ▶ vint

VINTING ▶ vint

VINTNER n dealer in wine

VINTRY n place where wine is sold

VINTS ▶ vint

VINY ▶ vine

VINYL n type of plastic, used in mock leather and records ▷ adj of or containing a particular group of atoms

VINYLIC ▶ vinyl

VINYLS ▶ vinyl

VIOL n early stringed instrument preceding the violin

VIOLA n stringed instrument lower in pitch than a violin

VIOLAS ▶ viola

VIOLATE vb break (a law or agreement) ▷ adj violated or dishonoured

VIOLD archaic or poetic past form of ▶ vial

VIOLENT adj using or involving physical force with the intention of causing injury or destruction ▷ vb coerce

VIOLER n person who plays the viol

VIOLERS ▶ violer

VIOLET n plant with bluish-purple flowers ▷ adj bluish-purple

VIOLETS ▶ violet

VIOLIN n small four-stringed musical

V

instrument played with a bow

VIOLINS ▶ **violin**

VIOLIST n person who plays the viola

VIOLONE n double-bass member of the viol family

VIOLS ▶ **viol**

VIPER n poisonous snake

VIPERS ▶ **viper**

VIRAGO n aggressive woman

VIRAGOS ▶ **virago**

VIRAL adj of or caused by a virus

VIRALLY ▶ **viral**

VIRANDA same as ▶ **veranda**

VIRANDO same as ▶ **veranda**

VIRE vb turn

VIRED ▶ **vire**

VIRELAI same as ▶ **virelay**

VIRELAY n old French verse form

VIREMIA same as > **viraemia**

VIREMIC ▶ **viremia**

VIRENT adj green

VIREO n American songbird

VIREOS ▶ **vireo**

VIRES ▶ **vire**

VIRETOT n as in **on the viretot** in a rush

VIRGA n wisps of rain or snow that evaporate before reaching the earth

VIRGAS ▶ **virga**

VIRGATE adj long, straight, and thin ▷ n obsolete measure of land area, usually taken as equivalent to 30 acres

VIRGE n rod

VIRGER n rod-bearer

VIRGERS ▶ **virger**

VIRGES ▶ **virge**

VIRGIN n person, esp a woman, who has not had sexual intercourse ▷ adj not having had sexual intercourse ▷ vb behave like a virgin

VIRGINS ▶ **virgin**

VIRGULE another name for ▶ **slash**

VIRID adj verdant

VIRILE adj having the traditional male characteristics of physical strength and a high sex drive

VIRING ▶ **vire**

VIRINO n entity postulated to be the causative agent of BSE

VIRINOS ▶ **virino**

VIRION n virus in infective form, consisting of an RNA particle within a protein covering

VIRIONS ▶ **virion**

VIRL same as ▶ **ferrule**

VIRLS ▶ **virl**

VIROID n any of various infective RNA particles

VIROIDS ▶ **viroid**

VIROSE adj poisonous

VIROSES ▶ **virosis**

VIROSIS n viral disease

VIROUS same as ▶ **virose**

VIRTU n taste or love for curios or works of fine art

VIRTUAL adj having the effect but not the form of

VIRTUE n moral goodness

VIRTUES ▶ **virtue**

VIRTUS ▶ **virtu**

VIRUS n microorganism that causes disease in humans, animals, and plants

VIRUSES ▶ **virus**

VIS n power, force, or strength

VISA n permission to enter a country, shown by a stamp on the passport ▷ vb enter a visa into (a passport)

VISAED ▶ **visa**

VISAGE n face

VISAGED ▶ **visage**

VISAGES ▶ **visage**

VISAING ▶ **visa**

VISARD same as ▶ **vizard**

VISARDS ▶ **visard**

VISAS ▶ **visa**

VISCERA pl n large abdominal organs

VISCID adj sticky

VISCIN n sticky substance found on plants

VISCINS ▶ **viscin**

VISCOID adj (of a fluid) somewhat viscous

VISCOSE same as ▶ **viscous**

VISCOUS adj thick and sticky

VISCUM n shrub genus

VISCUMS ▶ **viscum**

VISCUS n internal organ

VISE vb advise or award a visa to ▷ n (in US English) vice

VISED ▶ **vise**

VISEED ▶ **vise**

VISEING ▶ **vise**

VISES ▶ **vise**

VISHING n telephone scam

used to gain access to credit card numbers or bank details

VISIBLE adj able to be seen ▷ n visible item of trade

VISIBLY ▶ **visible**

VISIE same as ▶ **vizy**

VISIED ▶ **visie**

VISIER ▶ **visie**

VISIERS ▶ **visie**

VISIES ▶ **visie**

VISILE n person best stimulated by vision

VISILES ▶ **visile**

VISING ▶ **vise**

VISION n ability to see ▷ vb see or show in or as if in a vision

VISIONS ▶ **vision**

VISIT vb go or come to see ▷ n instance of visiting

VISITE n type of cape

VISITED ▶ **visit**

VISITEE n person who is visited

VISITER same as ▶ **visitor**

VISITES ▶ **visite**

VISITOR n person who visits a person or place

VISITS ▶ **visit**

VISIVE adj visual

VISNE n neighbourhood

VISNES ▶ **visne**

VISNOMY n method of judging character from facial features

VISON n type of mink

VISONS ▶ **vison**

VISOR n transparent part of a helmet that pulls down over the face ▷ vb cover, provide, or protect with a visor

VISORED ▶ **visor**

VISORS ▶ **visor**

VISTA n (beautiful) extensive view ▷ vb make into vistas

VISTAED ▶ **vista**

VISTAL ▶ **vista**

VISTAS ▶ **vista**

VISTO same as ▶ **vista**

VISTOS ▶ **visto**

VISUAL adj done by or used in seeing ▷ n sketch to show the proposed layout of an advertisement, as in a newspaper

VISUALS ▶ **visual**

VITA n curriculum vitae

VITAE ▶ **vita**

VITAL adj essential or highly important ▷ n bodily

organs that are necessary to maintain life

VITALLY ▶ **vital**

VITALS ▶ **vital**

VITAMER n type of chemical

VITAMIN n one of a group of substances that are essential in the diet for specific body processes

VITAS ▶ **vita**

VITE adv musical direction

VITELLI > **vitellus**

VITESSE n speed

VITEX n type of herb

VITEXES ▶ **vitex**

VITIATE vb spoil the effectiveness of

VITIOUS adj mistaken

VITRAGE n light fabric

VITRAIL n stained glass

VITRAIN n type of coal occurring as horizontal glassy bands of a nonsoiling friable material

VITRAUX ▶ **vitrail**

VITREUM n vitreous body

VITRIC adj of, relating to, resembling, or having the nature of glass

VITRICS n glassware

VITRIFY vb change or be changed into glass or a glassy substance

VITRINE n glass display case or cabinet for works of art, curios, etc

VITRIOL n language expressing bitterness and hatred ▷ vb attack or injure with or as if with vitriol

VITTA n tubelike cavity containing oil that occurs in the fruits of certain plants

VITTAE ▶ **vitta**

VITTATE ▶ **vitta**

VITTLE obsolete or dialect spelling of ▶ **victual**

VITTLED ▶ **vittle**

VITTLES obsolete or dialect spelling of > **victuals**

VITULAR same as > **vituline**

VIVA interj long live (a person or thing) ▷ n examination in the form of an interview ▷ vb examine (a candidate) in a spoken interview

VIVACE adj, adv (to be performed) in a lively manner ▷ n piece of music to be performed in this way

VIVACES ▶ **vivace**

VIVAED ▶ **viva**

VIVAING ▶ **viva**

VIVARIA > **vivarium**

VIVARY same as > **vivarium**

VIVAS ▶ **viva**

VIVAT interj long live ▷ n expression of acclamation

VIVATS ▶ **vivat**

VIVDA n method of drying meat

VIVDAS ▶ **vivda**

VIVE interj long live

VIVELY adv in a lively manner

VIVENCY n physical or mental energy

VIVER n fish pond

VIVERRA n civet genus

VIVERS ▶ **viver**

VIVES n disease found in horses

VIVID adj very bright

VIVIDER ▶ **vivid**

VIVIDLY ▶ **vivid**

VIVIFIC adj giving life

VIVIFY vb animate, inspire

VIVO adv with life and vigour

VIVRES n provisions

VIXEN n female fox

VIXENLY ▶ **vixen**

VIXENS ▶ **vixen**

VIZARD n means of disguise ▷ vb conceal by means of a disguise

VIZARDS ▶ **vizard**

VIZIED ▶ **vizy**

VIZIER n high official in certain Muslim countries

VIZIERS ▶ **vizier**

VIZIES ▶ **vizy**

VIZIR same as ▶ **vizier**

VIZIRS ▶ **vizir**

VIZOR same as ▶ **visor**

VIZORED ▶ **vizor**

VIZORS ▶ **vizor**

VIZSLA n breed of Hungarian hunting dog with a smooth rusty-gold coat

VIZSLAS ▶ **vizsla**

VIZY vb look

VIZYING ▶ **vizy**

VIZZIE same as ▶ **vizy**

VIZZIED ▶ **vizzie**

VIZZIES ▶ **vizzie**

VLEI n area of low marshy ground, esp one that feeds a stream

VLEIS ▶ **vlei**

VLIES ▶ **vly**

VLOG n video weblog

VLOGGER n person who keeps a video blog

VLOGS ▶ **vlog**

VLY same as ▶ **vlei**
This word for low-lying wet ground can be useful when you are short of vowels. It can also be spelt **vlei**.

VOAR n spring

VOARS ▶ **voar**

VOCAB n vocabulary

VOCABLE n word regarded simply as a sequence of letters or spoken sounds ▷ adj capable of being uttered

VOCABLY ▶ **vocable**

VOCABS ▶ **vocab**

VOCAL adj relating to the voice ▷ n piece of jazz or pop music that is sung

VOCALIC adj of, relating to, or containing a vowel or vowels

VOCALLY ▶ **vocal**

VOCALS ▶ **vocal**

VOCES ▶ **vox**

VOCODER n type of synthesizer that uses the human voice as an oscillator

VOCULAR ▶ **vocule**

VOCULE n faint noise made when articulating certain sounds

VOCULES ▶ **vocule**

VODCAST vb podcast with video

VODDIES ▶ **voddy**

VODDY n vodka

VODKA n (Russian) spirit distilled from potatoes or grain

VODKAS ▶ **vodka**

VODOU same as ▶ **voodoo**
This West Indian word for a kind of black magic may indeed work magic on an unpromising rack. And it has a host of variants, though few people will remember them all: **vaudoo, vaudoux, vodoun, vodun, voudon, voudou** and **voudoun**!

VODOUN same as ▶ **vodun**

VODOUNS ▶ **vodoun**

VODOUS ▶ **vodou**

VODUN n voodoo

VODUNS ▶ **vodun**

VOE n (in Orkney and Shetland) a small bay or narrow creek

VOEMA n vigour or energy

V

VOEMAS ▷ voema
VOES ▷ voe
VOGIE adj conceited
VOGIER ▷ vogie
VOGIEST ▷ vogie
VOGUE n popular style ▷ adj popular or fashionable ▷ vb bring into vogue
VOGUED ▷ vogue
VOGUER ▷ vogue
VOGUERS ▷ vogue
VOGUES ▷ vogue
VOGUEY ▷ vogue
VOGUIER ▷ vogue
VOGUING same as > vogueing
VOGUISH ▷ vogue
VOICE n (quality of) sound made when speaking or singing ▷ vb express verbally
VOICED adj articulated with accompanying vibration of the vocal cords
VOICER ▷ voice
VOICERS ▷ voice
VOICES ▷ voice
VOICING ▷ voice
VOID adj not legally binding ▷ n feeling of deprivation ▷ vb make invalid
VOIDED adj (of a design) with a hole in the centre of the same shape as the design
VOIDEE n light meal eaten before bed
VOIDEES ▷ voidee
VOIDER ▷ void
VOIDERS ▷ void
VOIDING ▷ void
VOIDS ▷ void
VOILA interj word used to express satisfaction
VOILE n light semitransparent fabric
VOILES ▷ voile
VOIP n voice-over internet protocol
VOIPS ▷ voip
VOITURE n type of vehicle
VOIVODE n type of military leader
VOL n heraldic wings
VOLA n palm of hand or sole of foot
VOLABLE adj quick-witted
VOLAE ▷ vola
VOLAGE adj changeable
VOLANT adj in a flying position
VOLANTE n Spanish horse carriage

VOLAR adj of or relating to the palm of the hand or the sole of the foot
VOLARY n large bird enclosure
VOLATIC adj flying
VOLCANO n mountain with a vent through which lava is ejected
VOLE n small rodent ▷ vb to win by taking all the tricks in a deal
VOLED ▷ vole
VOLENS adj as in nolens volens whether willing or unwilling
VOLERY same as ▷ volary
VOLES ▷ vole
VOLET n type of veil
VOLETS ▷ volet
VOLING ▷ vole
VOLK n people or nation, esp the nation of Afrikaners
VOLKS ▷ volk
VOLLEY n simultaneous discharge of ammunition ▷ vb discharge (ammunition) in a volley
VOLLEYS ▷ volley
VOLOST n (in the former Soviet Union) a rural soviet
VOLOSTS ▷ volost
VOLPINO n Italian breed of dog
VOLS ▷ vol
VOLT n unit of electric potential ▷ vb (in fencing) make a quick movement to avoid a thrust
VOLTA n quick-moving Italian dance popular during the 16th and 17th centuries
VOLTAGE n electric potential difference expressed in volts
VOLTAIC adj producing an electric current
VOLTE same as ▷ volt
VOLTED ▷ volt vb
VOLTES ▷ volte
VOLTI adv musical direction
VOLTING > volt vb
VOLTS ▷ volt
VOLUBIL same as ▷ voluble
VOLUBLE adj talking easily and at length
VOLUBLY ▷ voluble
VOLUME n size of the space occupied by something ▷ vb billow or surge in volume
VOLUMED ▷ volume

VOLUMES ▷ volume
VOLUSPA n Icelandic mythological poem
VOLUTE n spiral or twisting turn, form, or object ▷ adj having the form of a volute
VOLUTED ▷ volute
VOLUTES ▷ volute
VOLUTIN n granular substance found in cells
VOLVA n cup-shaped structure that sheathes the base of the stalk of certain mushrooms
VOLVAE ▷ volva
VOLVAS ▷ volva
VOLVATE ▷ volva
VOLVE vb turn over
VOLVED ▷ volve
VOLVES ▷ volve
VOLVING ▷ volve
VOLVOX n freshwater protozoan
VOLVULI > volvulus
VOMER n thin flat bone forming part of the separation between the nasal passages in mammals
VOMERS ▷ vomer
VOMICA n pus-containing cavity
VOMICAE ▷ vomica
VOMICAS ▷ vomica
VOMIT vb eject (the contents of the stomach) through the mouth ▷ n matter vomited
VOMITED ▷ vomit
VOMITER ▷ vomit
VOMITO n form of yellow fever
VOMITOS ▷ vomito
VOMITS ▷ vomit
VOMITUS n matter that has been vomited
VONGOLE pl n (in Italian cookery) clams
VOODOO n religion involving ancestor worship and witchcraft ▷ adj of or relating to voodoo ▷ vb affect by or as if by the power of voodoo
VOODOOS ▷ voodoo
VOR vb (in dialect) warn
VORAGO n chasm
VORANT adj devouring
VORLAGE n skiing position
VORPAL adj sharp
VORRED ▷ vor
VORRING ▷ vor
VORS ▷ vor
VORTEX n whirlpool

VOSTRO *adj as in* **vostro account** bank account held by a foreign bank with a British bank

VOTABLE ▶ **vote**

VOTARY *n* person dedicated to religion or to a cause ▷ *adj* ardently devoted to the services or worship of God

VOTE *n* choice made by a participant in a shared decision ▷ *vb* make a choice by a vote

VOTED ▶ **vote**

VOTEEN *n* devotee

VOTEENS ▶ **voteen**

VOTER *n* person who can or does vote

VOTERS ▶ **voter**

VOTES ▶ **vote**

VOTING ▶ **vote**

VOTINGS ▶ **vote**

VOTIVE *adj* done or given to fulfil a vow ▷ *n* votive offering

VOTIVES ▶ **votive**

VOTRESS > **votaress**

VOUCH *vb* give personal assurance ▷ *n* act of vouching

VOUCHED ▶ **vouch**

VOUCHEE *n* person summoned to court to defend a title

VOUCHER *n* ticket used instead of money to buy specified goods ▷ *vb* summon someone to court as a vouchee

VOUCHES ▶ **vouch**

VOUDON *same as* ▶ **voodoo**

VOUDONS ▶ **voudon**

VOUDOU *same as* ▶ **voodoo**

VOUDOUN *same as* ▶ **voodoo**

VOUDOUS ▶ **voudou**

VOUGE *n* form of pike used by foot soldiers in the 14th century and later

VOUGES ▶ **vouge**

VOULGE *n* type of medieval weapon

VOULGES ▶ **voulge**

VOULU *adj* deliberate

VOUVRAY *n* dry white French wine

VOW *n* solemn and binding promise ▷ *vb* promise solemnly

VOWED ▶ **vow**

VOWEL *n* speech sound made without obstructing the flow of breath ▷ *vb* say as a vowel

VOWELLY ▶ **vowel**

VOWELS ▶ **vowel**

VOWER ▶ **vow**

VOWERS ▶ **vow**

VOWESS *n* nun

VOWING ▶ **vow**

VOWLESS ▶ **vow**

VOWS ▶ **vow**

VOX *n* voice or sound

Along with **vex**, this Latin word for voice is the highest-scoring three-letter word beginning with V.

VOXEL *n* term used in computing imaging

VOXELS ▶ **voxel**

VOYAGE *n* long journey by sea or in space ▷ *vb* make a voyage

VOYAGED ▶ **voyage**

VOYAGER ▶ **voyage**

VOYAGES ▶ **voyage**

VOYEUR *n* person who obtains pleasure from watching people undressing or having sex

VOYEURS ▶ **voyeur**

VOZHD *n* Russian leader

This unlikely looking word is Russian for a chief or leader, and may provide a great score from an apparently difficult rack.

VOZHDS ▶ **vozhd**

VRAIC *n* type of seaweed

VRAICS ▶ **vraic**

VRIL *n* life force

VRILS ▶ **vril**

VROOM *interj* exclamation imitative of a car engine revving up ▷ *vb* move noisily and at high speed

VROOMED ▶ **vroom**

VROOMS ▶ **vroom**

VROT *adj* South African slang for rotten

VROU *n* Afrikaner woman, esp a married woman

VROUS ▶ **vrou**

VROUW *n* woman

The heart of any Scrabble player sinks to see a combination of U, V and W on the rack, as there are relatively few words that use even two of these letters. But **vrouw**, a word of Dutch origin for a woman or goodwife, may get you out of the mess.

VROUWS ▶ **vrouw**

VROW *same as* ▶ **vrouw**

VROWS ▶ **vrow**

VUG *n* small cavity in a rock or vein, usually lined with crystals

This unusual word of Cornish origin, meaning a cavity in rock, is another that can be useful when you have an uninspiring combination of letters. And it has a variant **vugh** and can be extended to **vuggy** or **vughy.**

VUGG *same as* ▶ **vug**

VUGGIER ▶ **vug**

VUGGS ▶ **vugg**

VUGGY ▶ **vug**

VUGH *same as* ▶ **vug**

VUGHIER ▶ **vugh**

VUGHS ▶ **vugh**

VUGHY ▶ **vugh**

VUGS ▶ **vug**

VULCAN *n* blacksmith

VULCANS ▶ **vulcan**

VULGAR *adj* showing lack of good taste, decency, or refinement ▷ *n* common and ignorant person

VULGARS ▶ **vulgar**

VULGATE *n* commonly recognized text or version ▷ *adj* generally accepted

VULGO *adv* generally

VULGUS *n* the common people

VULN *vb* wound

VULNED ▶ **vuln**

VULNING ▶ **vuln**

VULNS ▶ **vuln**

VULPINE *adj* of or like a fox

VULTURE *n* large bird that feeds on the flesh of dead animals

VULTURN *n* type of turkey

VULVA *n* woman's external genitals

VULVAE ▶ **vulva**

VULVAL ▶ **vulva**

VULVAR ▶ **vulva**

VULVAS ▶ **vulva**

VULVATE ▶ **vulva**

VUM *vb* swear

VUMMED ▶ **vum**

VUMMING ▶ **vum**

VUMS ▶ **vum**

VUTTIER ▶ **vutty**

VUTTY *adj* dirty

VYING ▶ **vie**

VYINGLY ▶ **vie**

VYINGS ▶ **vie**

Ww

W, like V, can be an awkward tile to handle, but at least there are two two-letter words that begin with **W**: **we** and **wo** (5 points each) and two that end with **W**: **aw** and **ow** (5 points each). There are lots of everyday three-letter words that earn good scores: **wiz** (15), **wax** (13) with its two old-fashioned variants **wex** and **wox** (also 13 each) and **way, who, why, wow** and **wry** (9 each). Don't forget **wok** (10) either, which can be as useful on the Scrabble board as in the kitchen!

WAAC n (formerly) member of the Women's Auxiliary Army Corp
WAACS ▶ waac
WAB ▶ web n
WABAIN same as ▷ ouabain
WABAINS ▶ wabain
WABBIT adj weary
WABBLE same as ▶ wobble
WABBLED ▶ wabble
WABBLER ▶ wabble
WABBLES ▶ wabble
WABBLY ▶ wabble
WABOOM another word for > **wagenboom**
WABOOMS ▶ waboom
WABSTER Scots form of ▶ webster
WACK n friend
WACKE n any of various soft earthy rocks that resemble or are derived from basaltic rocks
WACKER same as ▶ wack
WACKERS ▶ wacker
WACKES ▶ wacke
WACKEST ▶ wack
WACKIER ▶ wacky
WACKILY ▶ wacky
WACKO adj mad or eccentric ▷ n mad or eccentric person
WACKOS ▶ wacko
WACKS ▶ wack
WACKY adj eccentric or funny
WAD n black earthy ore of manganese ▷ n small mass of soft material ▷ vb form (something) into a wad
WADABLE ▶ wade
WADD same as ▶ wad
WADDED ▶ wad

WADDER ▶ wad
WADDERS ▶ wad
WADDIE same as ▶ waddy
WADDIED ▶ waddy
WADDIES ▶ waddy
WADDING ▶ wad
WADDLE vb walk with short swaying steps ▷ n swaying walk
WADDLED ▶ waddle
WADDLER ▶ waddle
WADDLES ▶ waddle
WADDLY ▶ waddle
WADDS ▶ wadd
WADDY n heavy wooden club used by Australian Aborigines ▷ vb hit with a waddy
WADE vb walk with difficulty through water or mud ▷ n act or an instance of wading
WADED ▶ wade
WADER n long-legged water bird
WADERS pl n long waterproof boots which completely cover the legs, worn by anglers for standing in water
WADES ▶ wade
WADI n (in N Africa and Arabia) river which is dry except in the wet season
WADIES ▶ wady
WADING ▶ wade
WADINGS ▶ wade
WADIS ▶ wadi
WADMAAL same as ▶ wadmal
WADMAL n coarse thick woollen fabric, formerly woven esp in Orkney and

Shetland, for outer garments
WADMALS ▶ wadmal
WADMEL same as ▶ wadmal
WADMELS ▶ wadmel
WADMOL same as ▶ wadmal
WADMOLL same as ▶ wadmal
WADMOLS ▶ wadmol
WADS ▶ wad
WADSET vb pledge or mortgage
WADSETS ▶ wadset
WADSETT same as ▶ wadset
WADT same as ▶ wad
WADTS ▶ wadt
WADY same as ▶ wadi
WAE old form of ▶ woe
WAEFUL old form of ▶ woeful
WAENESS n sorrow
WAES ▶ wae
WAESOME adj sorrowful
WAESUCK interj alas
WAFER n thin crisp biscuit ▷ vb seal, fasten, or attach with a wafer
WAFERED ▶ wafer
WAFERS ▶ wafer
WAFERY ▶ wafer
WAFF n gust or puff of air ▷ vb flutter or cause to flutter
WAFFED ▶ waff
WAFFIE n person regarded as having little worth to society
WAFFIES ▶ waffie
WAFFING ▶ waff
WAFFLE vb speak or write in

W

a vague wordy way ▷ *n* vague wordy talk or writing
WAFFLED ▶ **waffle**
WAFFLER ▶ **waffle**
WAFFLES ▶ **waffle**
WAFFLY ▶ **waffle**
WAFFS ▶ **waff**
WAFT *vb* drift or carry gently through the air ▷ *n* something wafted
WAFTAGE ▶ **waft**
WAFTED ▶ **waft**
WAFTER *n* device that causes a draught
WAFTERS ▶ **wafter**
WAFTING ▶ **waft**
WAFTS ▶ **waft**
WAFTURE *n* act of wafting or waving
WAG *vb* move rapidly from side to side ▷ *n* wagging movement
WAGE *n* payment for work done, esp when paid weekly ▷ *vb* engage in (an activity)
WAGED ▶ **wage**
WAGER *vb* bet on the outcome of something ▷ *n* bet on the outcome of an event or activity
WAGERED ▶ **wager**
WAGERER ▶ **wager**
WAGERS ▶ **wager**
WAGES ▶ **wage**
WAGGA *n* blanket or bed covering made out of sacks stitched together
WAGGAS ▶ **wagga**
WAGGED ▶ **wag**
WAGGER ▶ **wag**
WAGGERS ▶ **wag**
WAGGERY *n* quality of being humorous
WAGGING ▶ **wag**
WAGGISH *adj* jocular or humorous
WAGGLE *vb* move with a rapid shaking or wobbling motion ▷ *n* rapid shaking or wobbling motion
WAGGLED ▶ **waggle**
WAGGLER *n* float only the bottom of which is attached to the fishing line
WAGGLES ▶ **waggle**
WAGGLY ▶ **waggle**
WAGGON *same as* ▶ **wagon**
WAGGONS ▶ **waggon**
WAGING ▶ **wage**
WAGON *n* four-wheeled vehicle for heavy loads ▷ *vb* transport by wagon

WAGONED ▶ **wagon**
WAGONER *n* person who drives a wagon
WAGONS ▶ **wagon**
WAGS ▶ **wag**
WAGSOME *another word for* ▶ **waggish**
WAGTAIL *n* small long-tailed bird
WAGYU *n* Japanese breed of beef cattle
WAGYUS ▶ **wagyu**
WAHINE *n* Māori woman, esp a wife
WAHINES ▶ **wahine**
WAHOO *n* food and game fish of tropical seas
WAHOOS ▶ **wahoo**
WAI *n* in New Zealand, water
WAIATA *n* Māori song
WAIATAS ▶ **waiata**
WAID ▶ **weigh**
WAIDE ▶ **weigh**
WAIF *n* young person who is, or seems, homeless or neglected ▷ *vb* treat as a waif
WAIFED ▶ **waif**
WAIFING ▶ **waif**
WAIFISH ▶ **waif**
WAIFS ▶ **waif**
WAIFT *n* piece of lost property found by someone other than the owner
WAIFTS ▶ **waift**
WAIL *vb* cry out in pain or misery ▷ *n* mournful cry
WAILED ▶ **wail**
WAILER ▶ **wail**
WAILERS ▶ **wail**
WAILFUL ▶ **wail**
WAILING ▶ **wail**
WAILS ▶ **wail**
WAIN *vb* transport ▷ *n* farm wagon
WAINAGE *n* carriages, etc, for transportation of goods
WAINED ▶ **wain**
WAINING ▶ **wain**
WAINS ▶ **wain**
WAIR *vb* spend
WAIRED ▶ **wair**
WAIRING ▶ **wair**
WAIRS ▶ **wair**
WAIRSH *variant spelling of* ▶ **wersh**
WAIRUA *n* in New Zealand, spirit or soul
WAIRUAS ▶ **wairua**
WAIS ▶ **wai**
WAIST *n* part of the trunk

between the ribs and the hips
WAISTED *adj* having a waist or waistlike part
WAISTER *n* sailor performing menial duties
WAISTS ▶ **waist**
WAIT *vb* remain inactive in expectation (of something) ▷ *n* act or period of waiting
WAITE *old form of* ▶ **wait**
WAITED ▶ **wait**
WAITER *n* man who serves in a restaurant etc ▷ *vb* serve at table
WAITERS ▶ **waiter**
WAITES ▶ **waite**
WAITING ▶ **wait**
WAITRON *n* waiter or waitress
WAITS ▶ **wait**
WAIVE *vb* refrain from enforcing (a law, right, etc)
WAIVED ▶ **waive**
WAIVER *n* act or instance of voluntarily giving up a claim, right, etc
WAIVERS ▶ **waiver**
WAIVES ▶ **waive**
WAIVING ▶ **waive**
WAIVODE *same as* ▶ **voivode**
WAIWODE *same as* ▶ **voivode**
WAKA *n* Māori canoe
WAKAME *n* edible seaweed
WAKAMES ▶ **wakame**
WAKANDA *n* supernatural quality said by Native American people to be held by natural objects
WAKAS ▶ **waka**
WAKE *vb* rouse from sleep or inactivity ▷ *n* vigil beside a corpse the night before the funeral
WAKED ▶ **wake**
WAKEFUL *adj* unable to sleep
WAKEMAN *n* watchman
WAKEMEN ▶ **wakeman**
WAKEN *vb* wake
WAKENED ▶ **waken**
WAKENER ▶ **waken**
WAKENS ▶ **waken**
WAKER ▶ **wake**
WAKERS ▶ **wake**
WAKES ▶ **wake**
WAKF *same as* ▶ **waqf**
WAKFS ▶ **wakf**
WAKIKI *n* Melanesian shell currency
WAKIKIS ▶ **wakiki**

W

WAKING ▸ **wake**
WAKINGS ▸ **wake**
WALD *Scots form of* ▸ **weld**
WALDO *n* gadget for manipulating objects by remote control
WALDOES ▸ **waldo**
WALDOS ▸ **waldo**
WALDS ▸ **wald**
WALE *same as* ▸ **weal**
WALED ▸ **wale**
WALER ▸ **wale**
WALERS ▸ **wale**
WALES ▸ **wale**
WALI *same as* ▸ **vali**
WALIER ▸ **waly**
WALIES ▸ **waly**
WALIEST ▸ **waly**
WALING ▸ **wale**
WALIS ▸ **wali**
WALISE *same as* ▸ **valise**
WALISES ▸ **walise**
WALK *vb* move on foot with at least one foot always on the ground ▷ *n* short journey on foot, usu for pleasure
WALKED ▸ **walk**
WALKER *n* person who walks
WALKERS ▸ **walker**
WALKIES *pl n as in* **go walkies** a walk
WALKING *adj* (of a person) considered to possess the qualities of something inanimate as specified ▷ *n* act of walking
WALKOUT *n* strike
WALKS ▸ **walk**
WALKUP *n* building with stairs to upper floors
WALKUPS ▸ **walkup**
WALKWAY *n* path designed for use by pedestrians
WALL *n* structure of brick, stone, etc used to enclose, divide, or support ▷ *vb* enclose or seal with a wall or walls
WALLA *same as* ▸ **wallah**
WALLABA *n* type of S American tree
WALLABY *n* marsupial like a small kangaroo
WALLAH *n* person involved with or in charge of a specified thing
WALLAHS ▸ **wallah**
WALLAS ▸ **walla**
WALLED ▸ **wall**
WALLER ▸ **wall**
WALLERS ▸ **wall**

WALLET *n* small folding case for paper money, documents, etc
WALLETS ▸ **wallet**
WALLEYE *n* fish with large staring eyes
WALLIE *same as* ▸ **wally**
WALLIER ▸ **wally**
WALLIES ▸ **wally**
WALLING ▸ **wall**
WALLOP *vb* hit hard ▷ *n* hard blow
WALLOPS ▸ **wallop**
WALLOW *vb* revel in an emotion ▷ *n* act or instance of wallowing
WALLOWS ▸ **wallow**
WALLS ▸ **wall**
WALLY *n* stupid person ▷ *adj* fine, pleasing, or splendid
WALNUT *n* edible nut with a wrinkled shell ▷ *adj* made from the wood of a walnut tree
WALNUTS ▸ **walnut**
WALRUS *n* large sea mammal with long tusks
WALTIER ▸ **walty**
WALTY *adj* (of a ship) likely to roll over
WALTZ *n* ballroom dance ▷ *vb* dance a waltz
WALTZED ▸ **waltz**
WALTZER *n* person who waltzes
WALTZES ▸ **waltz**
WALY *same as* ▸ **wally**
WAMBLE *vb* move unsteadily ▷ *n* unsteady movement
WAMBLED ▸ **wamble**
WAMBLES ▸ **wamble**
WAMBLY ▸ **wamble**
WAME *n* belly, abdomen, or womb
WAMED ▸ **wame**
WAMEFOU *Scots variant of* ▸ **wameful**
WAMEFUL *n* bellyful
WAMES ▸ **wame**
WAMMUL *n* dog
WAMMULS ▸ **wammul**
WAMMUS *same as* ▸ **wamus**
WAMPEE *n* type of Asian fruit tree
WAMPEES ▸ **wampee**
WAMPISH *vb* wave
WAMPUM *n* shells woven together, formerly used by Native Americans for money and ornament

WAMPUMS ▸ **wampum**
WAMPUS *same as* ▸ **wamus**
WAMUS *n* type of cardigan or jacket
WAMUSES ▸ **wamus**
WAN *adj* pale and sickly looking ▷ *vb* make or become wan
WAND *n* thin rod, esp one used in performing magic tricks
WANDER *vb* move about without a definite destination or aim ▷ *n* act or instance of wandering
WANDERS ▸ **wander**
WANDLE *adj* supple
WANDOO *n* eucalyptus tree of W Australia, having white bark and durable wood
WANDOOS ▸ **wandoo**
WANDS ▸ **wand**
WANE *vb* decrease gradually in size or strength
WANED ▸ **wane**
WANES ▸ **wane**
WANEY ▸ **wane**
WANG *n* cheekbone
WANGAN *same as* ▸ **wanigan**
WANGANS ▸ **wangan**
WANGLE *vb* get by devious methods ▷ *n* act or an instance of wangling
WANGLED ▸ **wangle**
WANGLER ▸ **wangle**
WANGLES ▸ **wangle**
WANGS ▸ **wang**
WANGUN *same as* ▸ **wanigan**
WANGUNS ▸ **wangun**
WANHOPE *n* delusion
WANIER ▸ **wany**
WANIEST ▸ **wany**
WANIGAN *n* provisions for camp
WANING ▸ **wane**
WANINGS ▸ **wane**
WANION *n* vehemence
WANIONS ▸ **wanion**
WANKLE *adj* unstable
WANLE *same as* ▸ **wandle**
WANLY ▸ **wan**
WANNA *vb* spelling of **want to** intended to reflect a dialectal or informal pronunciation
WANNABE *adj* wanting to be, or be like, a particular person or thing ▷ *n* person who wants to be, or be like, a particular person or thing

WANNED ▶ wan
WANNEL *same as* ▶ wandle
WANNER ▶ wan
WANNESS ▶ wan
WANNEST ▶ wan
WANNING ▶ wan
WANNION ▶ wanion
WANNISH *adj* rather wan
WANS ▶ wan
WANT *vb* need or long for ▷ *n* act or instance of wanting
WANTAGE *n* shortage
WANTED ▶ want
WANTER ▶ want
WANTERS ▶ want
WANTIES ▶ wanty
WANTING *adj* lacking ▷ *prep* without
WANTON *adj* without motive, provocation, or justification ▷ *n* sexually unrestrained or immodest woman ▷ *vb* behave in a wanton manner
WANTONS ▶ wanton
WANTS ▶ want
WANTY *adj* belt
WANY ▶ wane
WANZE *vb* wane
WANZED ▶ wanze
WANZES ▶ wanze
WANZING ▶ wanze
WAP *vb* strike
WAPITI *n* large N American deer, now also common in New Zealand
WAPITIS ▶ wapiti
WAPPED ▶ wap
WAPPEND *adj* tired
WAPPER *vb* blink
WAPPERS ▶ wapper
WAPPING ▶ wap
WAPS ▶ wap
WAQF *n* endowment in Muslim law

> An Arabic word meaning the donation of land, property or money for charitable purposes. As one of the Q words without a U, this comes up surprisingly often. It can also be spelt **wakf**.

WAQFS ▶ waqf
WAR *n* fighting between nations ▷ *adj* of, like, or caused by war ▷ *vb* conduct a war
WARAGI *n* Ugandan alcoholic drink made from bananas
WARAGIS ▶ waragi

WARATAH *n* Australian shrub with crimson flowers
WARB *n* dirty or insignificant person
WARBIER ▶ warb
WARBIRD *n* vintage military aeroplane
WARBLE *vb* sing in a trilling voice ▷ *n* act or an instance of warbling
WARBLED ▶ warble
WARBLER *n* any of various small songbirds
WARBLES ▶ warble
WARBS ▶ warb
WARBY ▶ warb
WARD *n* room in a hospital for patients needing a similar kind of care ▷ *vb* guard or protect
WARDED ▶ ward
WARDEN *n* person in charge of a building and its occupants ▷ *vb* act as a warden
WARDENS ▶ warden
WARDER *vb* guard ▷ *n* prison officer
WARDERS ▶ warder
WARDIAN *n as in* **wardian case** type of glass container for housing delicate plants
WARDING ▶ ward
WARDOG *n* veteran warrior
WARDOGS ▶ wardog
WARDROP *obsolete form of* > wardrobe
WARDS ▶ ward
WARE *n* articles of a specified type or material ▷ *vb* spend or squander
WARED ▶ ware
WAREHOU *n* any of several edible saltwater New Zealand fish
WARES *pl n* goods for sale
WAREZ *pl n* illegally copied computer software which has had its protection codes de-activated
WARFARE *vb* engage in war ▷ *n* fighting or hostilities
WARHEAD *n* explosive front part of a missile
WARIER ▶ wary
WARIEST ▶ wary
WARILY ▶ wary
WARING ▶ ware
WARISON *n* (esp formerly) a bugle note used as an order to a military force to attack
WARK *Scots form of* ▶ work
WARKED ▶ wark

WARKING ▶ wark
WARKS ▶ wark
WARLESS ▶ war
WARLIKE *adj* of or relating to war
WARLING *n* one who is not liked
WARLOCK *n* man who practises black magic
WARLORD *n* military leader of a nation or part of a nation
WARM *adj* moderately hot ▷ *vb* make or become warm ▷ *n* warm place or area
WARMAN *n* one experienced in warfare
WARMED ▶ warm
WARMEN ▶ warman
WARMER ▶ warm
WARMERS ▶ warm
WARMEST ▶ warm
WARMING ▶ warm
WARMISH ▶ warm
WARMLY ▶ warm
WARMS ▶ warm
WARMTH *n* mild heat
WARMTHS ▶ warmth
WARMUP *n* preparatory exercise routine
WARMUPS ▶ warmup
WARN *vb* make aware of possible danger or harm
WARNED ▶ warn
WARNER ▶ warn
WARNERS ▶ warn
WARNING *n* something that warns ▷ *adj* giving or serving as a warning
WARNS ▶ warn
WARP *vb* twist out of shape ▷ *n* state of being warped
WARPAGE ▶ warp
WARPATH *n* route taken by Native Americans on a warlike expedition
WARPED ▶ warp
WARPER ▶ warp
WARPERS ▶ warp
WARPING ▶ warp
WARPS ▶ warp
WARRAN *same as* ▶ warrant
WARRAND *same as* ▶ warrant
WARRANS ▶ warran
WARRANT *n* (document giving) official authorization ▷ *vb* make necessary
WARRAY *vb* wage war on
WARRAYS ▶ warray
WARRE *same as* ▶ war

W

WARRED ▶ **war**
WARREN *n* series of burrows in which rabbits live
WARRENS ▶ **warren**
WARREY *same as* ▶ **warray**
WARREYS ▶ **warrey**
WARRING ▶ **war**
WARRIOR *n* person who fights in a war
WARS ▶ **war**
WARSAW *n* type of grouper fish
WARSAWS ▶ **warsaw**
WARSHIP *n* ship designed and equipped for naval combat
WARSLE *dialect word for* ▶ **wrestle**
WARSLED ▶ **warsle**
WARSLER ▶ **warsle**
WARSLES ▶ **warsle**
WARST *obsolete form of* ▶ **worst**
WARSTLE *dialect form of* ▶ **wrestle**
WART *n* small hard growth on the skin
WARTED ▶ **wart**
WARTHOG *n* wild African pig with heavy tusks, wartlike lumps on the face, and a mane of coarse hair
WARTIER ▶ **wart**
WARTIME *n* time of war ▷ *adj* of or in a time of war
WARTS ▶ **wart**
WARTY ▶ **wart**
WARWOLF *n* Roman engine of war
WARWORK *n* work contributing to war effort
WARWORN *adj* worn down by war
WARY *adj* watchful or cautious
WARZONE *n* area where a war is taking place or there is some other violent conflict
WAS ▶ **be**
WASABI *n* Japanese cruciferous plant cultivated for its thick green pungent root
WASABIS ▶ **wasabi**
WASE *n* pad to relieve pressure of load carried on head
WASES ▶ **wase**
WASH *vb* clean (oneself, clothes, etc) with water and usu soap ▷ *n* act or

process of washing
WASHDAY *n* day on which clothes and linen are washed, often the same day each week
WASHED ▶ **wash**
WASHEN ▶ **wash**
WASHER *n* ring put under a nut or bolt or in a tap as a seal ▷ *vb* fit with a washer
WASHERS ▶ **washer**
WASHERY *n* plant at a mine where water or other liquid is used to remove dirt from a mineral, esp coal
WASHES ▶ **wash**
WASHIER ▶ **washy**
WASHILY ▶ **washy**
WASHIN *n* increase in the angle of attack of an aircraft wing towards the wing tip
WASHING *n* clothes to be washed
WASHINS ▶ **washin**
WASHOUT *n* complete failure
WASHPOT *n* pot for washing things in
WASHRAG *same as* > **washcloth**
WASHTUB *n* tub or large container used for washing anything, esp clothes
WASHUP *n* outcome of a process
WASHUPS ▶ **washup**
WASHY *adj* overdiluted or weak
WASP *n* stinging insect with a slender black-and-yellow striped body
WASPIE *n* tight-waisted corset
WASPIER ▶ **wasp**
WASPIES ▶ **waspie**
WASPILY ▶ **wasp**
WASPISH *adj* bad-tempered
WASPS ▶ **wasp**
WASPY ▶ **wasp**
WASSAIL *n* formerly, festivity when much drinking took place ▷ *vb* drink health of (a person) at a wassail
WASSUP *sentence substitute* what is happening?
WAST *singular form of the past tense of* ▶ **be**
WASTAGE *n* loss by wear or waste
WASTE *vb* use pointlessly or thoughtlessly ▷ *n* act of

wasting or state of being wasted ▷ *adj* rejected as worthless or surplus to requirements
WASTED ▶ **waste**
WASTEL *n* fine bread or cake
WASTELS ▶ **wastel**
WASTER *vb* waste ▷ *n* layabout
WASTERS ▶ **waster**
WASTERY *n* extravagance
WASTES ▶ **waste**
WASTING *adj* reducing the vitality and strength of the body
WASTREL *n* lazy or worthless person
WASTRIE *same as* ▶ **wastery**
WASTRY *n* wastefulness
WASTS ▶ **wast**
WAT *adj* wet; drunken
WATAP *n* stringy thread made by Native Americans from the roots of conifers
WATAPE *same as* ▶ **watap**
WATAPES ▶ **watape**
WATAPS ▶ **watap**
WATCH *vb* look at closely ▷ *n* portable timepiece for the wrist or pocket
WATCHED ▶ **watch**
WATCHER *n* person who watches
WATCHES ▶ **watch**
WATCHET *n* shade of blue
WATE ▶ **wit**
WATER *n* clear colourless tasteless liquid that falls as rain and forms rivers etc ▷ *vb* put water on or into
WATERED ▶ **water**
WATERER ▶ **water**
WATERS ▶ **water**
WATERY *adj* of, like, or containing water
WATS ▶ **wat**
WATT *n* unit of power
WATTAGE *n* electrical power expressed in watts
WATTAPE *same as* ▶ **watap**
WATTER ▶ **wat**
WATTEST ▶ **wat**
WATTLE *n* branches woven over sticks to make a fence ▷ *adj* made of, formed by, or covered with wattle ▷ *vb* construct from wattle
WATTLED ▶ **wattle**
WATTLES ▶ **wattle**
WATTS ▶ **watt**
WAUCHT *same as* ▶ **waught**
WAUCHTS ▶ **waucht**

WAUFF *same as* ▸ **waff**
WAUFFED ▸ **wauff**
WAUFFS ▸ **wauff**
WAUGH *vb* bark
WAUGHED ▸ **waugh**
WAUGHS ▸ **waugh**
WAUGHT *vb* drink in large amounts
WAUGHTS ▸ **waught**
WAUK *vb* full (cloth)
WAUKED ▸ **wauk**
WAUKER ▸ **wauk**
WAUKERS ▸ **wauk**
WAUKING ▸ **wauk**
WAUKS ▸ **wauk**
WAUL *vb* cry or wail plaintively like a cat
WAULED ▸ **waul**
WAULING ▸ **waul**
WAULK *same as* ▸ **wauk**
WAULKED ▸ **waulk**
WAULKER ▸ **waulk**
WAULKS ▸ **waulk**
WAULS ▸ **waul**
WAUR *obsolete form of* ▸ **war**
WAURED ▸ **waur**
WAURING ▸ **waur**
WAURS ▸ **waur**
WAURST ▸ **waur**
WAVE *vb* move the hand to and fro as a greeting or signal ▷ *n* moving ridge on water
WAVED ▸ **wave**
WAVELET *n* small wave
WAVEOFF *n* signal or instruction to an aircraft not to land
WAVER *vb* hesitate or be irresolute ▷ *n* act or an instance of wavering
WAVERED ▸ **waver**
WAVERER ▸ **waver**
WAVERS ▸ **waver**
WAVERY *adj* lacking firmness
WAVES ▸ **wave**
WAVESON *n* goods floating on waves after shipwreck
WAVEY *n* snow goose or other wild goose
WAVEYS ▸ **wavey**
WAVICLE *n* origin of wave
WAVIER ▸ **wavy**
WAVIES ▸ **wavy**
WAVIEST ▸ **wavy**
WAVILY ▸ **wavy**
WAVING ▸ **wave**
WAVINGS ▸ **wave**
WAVY *adj* having curves ▷ *n* snow goose or other wild goose
WAW *another name for* ▸ **vav**

WAWA *n* speech ▷ *vb* speak
WAWAED ▸ **wawa**
WAWAING ▸ **wawa**
WAWAS ▸ **wawa**
WAWE *same as* ▸ **waw**
WAWES ▸ **wawe**
WAWL *same as* ▸ **waul**
WAWLED ▸ **wawl**
WAWLING ▸ **wawl**
WAWLS ▸ **wawl**
WAWS ▸ **waw**
WAX *n* solid shiny fatty or oily substance used for sealing, making candles, etc ▷ *vb* coat or polish with wax
WAXABLE ▸ **wax**
WAXBILL *n* any of various chiefly African finchlike weaverbirds
WAXED ▸ **wax**
WAXEN *adj* made of or like wax
WAXER ▸ **wax**
WAXERS ▸ **wax**
WAXES ▸ **wax**
WAXEYE *n* small New Zealand bird with a white circle round its eye
WAXEYES ▸ **waxeye**
WAXIER ▸ **waxy**
WAXIEST ▸ **waxy**
WAXILY ▸ **waxy**
WAXING ▸ **wax**
WAXINGS ▸ **wax**
WAXLIKE ▸ **wax**
WAXWEED *n* type of wild flower
WAXWING *n* type of songbird
WAXWORK *n* lifelike wax model of a (famous) person
WAXWORM *n* waxmoth larva
WAXY *adj* resembling wax in colour, appearance, or texture
WAY *n* manner or method ▷ *vb* travel
WAYBILL *n* document stating the nature, origin, and destination of goods being transported
WAYED ▸ **way**
WAYFARE *vb* travel
WAYGONE *adj* travel-weary
WAYING ▸ **way**
WAYLAID ▸ **waylay**
WAYLAY *vb* lie in wait for and accost or attack
WAYLAYS ▸ **waylay**
WAYLESS ▸ **way**
WAYMARK *n* symbol or

signpost marking the route of a footpath ▷ *vb* mark out with waymarks
WAYMENT *vb* express grief
WAYPOST *n* signpost
WAYS ▸ **way**
WAYSIDE *n* side of a road
WAYWARD *adj* erratic, selfish, or stubborn
WAYWODE *n* Slavonic governor
WAYWORN *adj* worn or tired by travel
WAZIR *another word for* ▸ **vizier**
WAZIRS ▸ **wazir**
WAZZOCK *n* foolish or annoying person
WE *pron* speaker or writer and one or more others
WEAK *adj* lacking strength
WEAKEN *vb* make or become weak
WEAKENS ▸ **weaken**
WEAKER ▸ **weak**
WEAKEST ▸ **weak**
WEAKISH ▸ **weak**
WEAKLY *adv* feebly ▷ *adj* weak or sickly
WEAKON *n* subatomic particle
WEAKONS ▸ **weakon**
WEAL *n* raised mark left on the skin by a blow
WEALD *n* open or forested country
WEALDS ▸ **weald**
WEALS ▸ **weal**
WEALTH *n* state of being rich
WEALTHS ▸ **wealth**
WEALTHY *adj* possessing wealth
WEAMB *same as* ▸ **wame**
WEAMBS ▸ **weamb**
WEAN *vb* accustom (a baby or young mammal) to food other than mother's milk
WEANED ▸ **wean**
WEANEL *n* recently-weaned child or animal
WEANELS ▸ **weanel**
WEANER *n* person or thing that weans
WEANERS ▸ **weaner**
WEANING ▸ **wean**
WEANS ▸ **wean**
WEAPON *vb* arm ▷ *n* object used in fighting
WEAPONS ▸ **weapon**
WEAR *vb* have on the body as clothing or ornament ▷ *n* clothes suitable for a

W

particular time or purpose
WEARED ▷ **wear**
WEARER ▷ **wear**
WEARERS ▷ **wear**
WEARIED ▷ **weary**
WEARIER ▷ **weary**
WEARIES ▷ **weary**
WEARILY ▷ **weary**
WEARING *adj* tiring ▷ *n* act of wearing
WEARISH *adj* withered
WEARS ▷ **wear**
WEARY *adj* tired or exhausted ▷ *vb* make or become weary
WEASAND *former name for the* ▷ **trachea**
WEASEL *n* small carnivorous mammal with a long body and short legs ▷ *vb* use ambiguous language to avoid speaking directly or honestly
WEASELS ▷ **weasel**
WEASELY ▷ **weasel**
WEASON *Scots form of* ▷ **weasand**
WEASONS ▷ **weason**
WEATHER *n* day-to-day atmospheric conditions of a place ▷ *vb* (cause to) be affected by the weather
WEAVE *vb* make (fabric) by interlacing (yarn) on a loom
WEAVED ▷ **weave**
WEAVER *n* person who weaves, esp as a means of livelihood
WEAVERS ▷ **weaver**
WEAVES ▷ **weave**
WEAVING ▷ **weave**
WEAZAND *same as* ▷ **weasand**
WEAZEN *same as* ▷ **wizen**
WEAZENS ▷ **weazen**
WEB *n* net spun by a spider ▷ *vb* cover with or as if with a web
WEBBED ▷ **web**
WEBBIE *n* person who is well versed in the use of the World Wide Web
WEBBIER ▷ **webby**
WEBBIES ▷ **webbie**
WEBBING *n* anything that forms a web
WEBBY *adj* of, relating to, resembling, or consisting of a web
WEBCAM *n* camera that transmits images over the internet
WEBCAMS ▷ **webcam**

WEBCAST *n* broadcast of an event over the internet ▷ *vb* make such a broadcast
WEBER *n* SI unit of magnetic flux
WEBERS ▷ **weber**
WEBFED *adj* (of printing press) printing from rolls of paper
WEBFEET ▷ **webfoot**
WEBFOOT *n* foot having the toes connected by folds of skin
WEBHEAD *n* person who uses the Internet a lot
WEBIFY *vb* convert (information) to a format capable of being displayed on the Internet
WEBINAR *n* interactive seminar conducted over the World Wide Web
WEBLESS ▷ **web**
WEBLIKE ▷ **web**
WEBLISH *n* shorthand form of English that is used in text messaging, chat rooms, etc
WEBLOG *n* person's online journal
WEBLOGS ▷ **weblog**
WEBMAIL *n* system of electronic mail that allows account holders to access their mail via an internet site rather than downloading it
WEBPAGE *n* page on website
WEBRING *n* group of websites organized in a circular structure
WEBS ▷ **web**
WEBSITE *n* group of connected pages on the World Wide Web
WEBSTER *archaic word for* ▷ **weaver**
WEBWORK *n* work done using the World Wide Web
WEBWORM *n* type of caterpillar
WEBZINE *n* magazine published on the Internet
WECHT *n* agricultural tool
WECHTS ▷ **wecht**
WED *vb* marry
WEDDED ▷ **wed**
WEDDER *dialect form of* ▷ **weather**
WEDDERS ▷ **wedder**
WEDDING ▷ **wed**
WEDEL *same as* ▷ **wedeln**

WEDELED ▷ **wedel**
WEDELN *n* succession of high-speed turns performed in skiing ▷ *vb* perform a wedeln
WEDELNS ▷ **wedeln**
WEDELS ▷ **wedel**
WEDGE *n* piece of material thick at one end and thin at the other ▷ *vb* fasten or split with a wedge
WEDGED ▷ **wedge**
WEDGES ▷ **wedge**
WEDGIE *n* wedge-heeled shoe
WEDGIER ▷ **wedge**
WEDGIES ▷ **wedgie**
WEDGING ▷ **wedge**
WEDGY ▷ **wedge**
WEDLOCK *n* marriage
WEDS ▷ **wed**
WEE *adj* small or short ▷ *n* instance of urinating ▷ *vb* urinate
WEED *n* plant growing where undesired ▷ *vb* clear of weeds
WEEDED ▷ **weed**
WEEDER ▷ **weed**
WEEDERS ▷ **weed**
WEEDERY *n* weed-ridden area
WEEDIER ▷ **weedy**
WEEDILY ▷ **weedy**
WEEDING ▷ **weed**
WEEDS *pl n* widow's mourning clothes
WEEDY *adj* (of a person) thin and weak
WEEING ▷ **wee**
WEEK *n* period of seven days, esp one beginning on a Sunday ▷ *adv* seven days before or after a specified day
WEEKDAY *n* any day of the week except Saturday or Sunday
WEEKE *same as* ▷ **wick**
WEEKEND *n* Saturday and Sunday ▷ *vb* spend or pass a weekend
WEEKES ▷ **weeke**
WEEKLY *adv* happening, done, etc once a week ▷ *n* newspaper or magazine published once a week ▷ *adj* happening once a week or every week
WEEKS ▷ **week**
WEEL *Scots word for* ▷ **well**
WEELS ▷ **weel**
WEEM *n* underground home

WEEMS ▶ weem
WEEN *vb* think or imagine (something)
WEENED ▶ ween
WEENIE *adj* very small ▷ *n* wiener
WEENIER ▶ weeny
WEENIES ▶ weenie
WEENING ▶ ween
WEENS ▶ ween
WEENSY *same as* ▶ weeny
WEENY *adj* very small
WEEP *vb* shed tears ▷ *n* spell of weeping
WEEPER *n* person who weeps, esp a hired mourner
WEEPERS ▶ weeper
WEEPIE ▶ weepy
WEEPIER ▶ weepy
WEEPIES ▶ weepy
WEEPILY ▶ weepy
WEEPING *adj* (of plants) having slender hanging branches
WEEPS ▶ weep
WEEPY *adj* liable to cry ▷ *n* sentimental film or book
WEER ▶ wee
WEES ▶ wee
WEEST ▶ wee
WEET *dialect form of* ▶ wet
WEETE *same as* ▶ wit
WEETED ▶ weete
WEETEN *same as* ▶ wit
WEETER ▶ weet
WEETEST ▶ weet
WEETING ▶ weet
WEETS ▶ weet
WEEVER *n* type of small fish
WEEVERS ▶ weever
WEEVIL *n* small beetle that eats grain etc
WEEVILS ▶ weevil
WEEVILY *another word for* ▶ weevilled
WEEWEE *vb* urinate
WEEWEED ▶ weewee
WEEWEES ▶ weewee
WEFT *n* cross threads in weaving ▷ *vb* form weft
WEFTAGE *n* texture
WEFTE *n* forsaken child
WEFTED ▶ weft
WEFTES ▶ wefte
WEFTING ▶ weft
WEFTS ▶ weft
WEID *n* sudden illness
WEIDS ▶ weid
WEIGELA *n* type of shrub
WEIGH *vb* have a specified weight
WEIGHED ▶ weigh
WEIGHER ▶ weigh

WEIGHS ▶ weigh
WEIGHT *n* heaviness of an object ▷ *vb* add weight to
WEIGHTS ▶ weight
WEIGHTY *adj* important or serious
WEIL *n* whirlpool
WEILS ▶ weil
WEINER *same as* ▶ wiener
WEINERS ▶ weiner
WEIR *vb* ward off ▷ *n* river dam
WEIRD *adj* strange or bizarre ▷ *vb* warn beforehand
WEIRDED ▶ weird
WEIRDER ▶ weird
WEIRDIE *same as* ▶ weirdo
WEIRDLY ▶ weird
WEIRDO *n* peculiar person
WEIRDOS ▶ weirdo
WEIRDS ▶ weird
WEIRDY *n* weird person
WEIRED ▶ weir
WEIRING ▶ weir
WEIRS ▶ weir
WEISE *same as* ▶ wise
WEISED ▶ weise
WEISES ▶ weise
WEISING ▶ weise
WEIZE *same as* ▶ wise
WEIZED ▶ weize
WEIZES ▶ weize
WEIZING ▶ weize
WEKA *n* flightless New Zealand rail
WEKAS ▶ weka
WELAWAY *same as* > wellaway
WELCH *same as* ▶ welsh
WELCHED ▶ welch
WELCHER ▶ welch
WELCHES ▶ welch
WELCOME *vb* greet with pleasure ▷ *n* kindly greeting ▷ *adj* received gladly
WELD *vb* join (pieces of metal or plastic) by softening with heat ▷ *n* welded joint
WELDED ▶ weld
WELDER ▶ weld
WELDERS ▶ weld
WELDING ▶ weld
WELDOR ▶ weld
WELDORS ▶ weldor
WELDS ▶ weld
WELFARE *n* wellbeing
WELK *vb* wither; dry up
WELKE *obsolete form of* ▶ welk
WELKED ▶ welk

WELKES ▶ welke
WELKIN *n* sky, heavens, or upper air
WELKING ▶ welk
WELKINS ▶ welkin
WELKS ▶ welk
WELKT *adj* twisted
WELL *adv* satisfactorily ▷ *adj* in good health ▷ *interj* exclamation of surprise, interrogation, etc ▷ *n* hole sunk into the earth to reach water, oil, or gas ▷ *vb* flow upwards or outwards
WELLED ▶ well
WELLIE *n* wellington boot
WELLIES ▶ welly
WELLING ▶ well
WELLS ▶ well
WELLY *n* energy or commitment
WELS *n* type of catfish
WELSH *vb* fail to pay a debt or fulfil an obligation
WELSHED ▶ welsh
WELSHER ▶ welsh
WELSHES ▶ welsh
WELT *same as* ▶ weal
WELTED ▶ welt
WELTER *n* jumbled mass ▷ *vb* roll about, writhe, or wallow
WELTERS ▶ welter
WELTING ▶ welt
WELTS ▶ welt
WEM *same as* ▶ wame
WEMB *same as* ▶ wame
WEMBS ▶ wemb
WEMS ▶ wem
WEN *n* cyst on the scalp
WENA *pron* South African word for you
WENCH *n* young woman ▷ *vb* frequent the company of prostitutes
WENCHED ▶ wench
WENCHER ▶ wench
WENCHES ▶ wench
WEND *vb* go or travel
WENDED ▶ wend
WENDIGO *n* evil spirit or cannibal
WENDING ▶ wend
WENDS ▶ wend
WENGE *n* type of tree found in central and West Africa
WENGES ▶ wenge
WENNIER ▶ wen
WENNISH ▶ wen
WENNY ▶ wen
WENS ▶ wen
WENT *n* path
WENTS ▶ went

W

WEPT ▷ **weep**

WERE *vb* form of the past tense of **be** used after *we, you, they,* or a plural noun

WERGELD *same as* ▷ **wergild**

WERGELT *same as* ▷ **wergeld**

WERGILD *n* price set on a man's life in successive Anglo-Saxon and Germanic law codes, to be paid as compensation by his slayer

WERO *n* challenge made by an armed Māori warrior to a visitor to a marae

WEROS ▷ **wero**

WERSH *adj* tasteless

WERSHER ▷ **wersh**

WERT *singular form of the past tense of* ▷ **be**

WERWOLF *same as* > **werewolf**

WESAND *same as* ▷ **weasand**

WESANDS ▷ **wesand**

WESKIT *informal word for* > **waistcoat**

WESKITS ▷ **weskit**

WESSAND *same as* ▷ **weasand**

WEST *n* part of the horizon where the sun sets ▷ *adj* or in the west ▷ *adv* in, to, or towards the west ▷ *vb* move in westerly direction

WESTED ▷ **west**

WESTER *vb* move or appear to move towards the west ▷ *n* strong wind or storm from the west

WESTERN *adj* of or in the west ▷ *n* film or story about cowboys in the western US

WESTERS ▷ **wester**

WESTING *n* movement, deviation, or distance covered in a westerly direction

WESTLIN *Scots word for* ▷ **western**

WESTS ▷ **west**

WET *adj* covered or soaked with water or another liquid ▷ *n* moisture or rain ▷ *vb* make wet

WETA *n* type of wingless insect

WETAS ▷ **weta**

WETHER *n* male sheep, esp a castrated one

WETHERS ▷ **wether**

WETLAND *n* area of marshy land

WETLY ▷ **wet**

WETNESS ▷ **wet**

WETS ▷ **wet**

WETSUIT *n* body suit for diving

WETTED ▷ **wet**

WETTER ▷ **wet**

WETTERS ▷ **wet**

WETTEST ▷ **wet**

WETTIE *n* wetsuit

WETTIES ▷ **wettie**

WETTING ▷ **wet**

WETTISH ▷ **wet**

WETWARE *n* humorous term for the brain

WEX *obsolete form of* ▷ **wax**

> Wex is an old word for **wax**, in the sense of grow. It gives a very good score for a three-letter word, and can be extended to **wexe**.

WEXE *obsolete form of* ▷ **wax**

WEXED ▷ **wex**

WEXES ▷ **wex**

WEXING ▷ **wex**

WEY *n* measurement of weight

WEYARD *obsolete form of* ▷ **weird**

WEYS ▷ **wey**

WEYWARD *obsolete form of* ▷ **weird**

WEZAND *obsolete form of* ▷ **weasand**

WEZANDS ▷ **wezand**

WHA *Scots word for* ▷ **who**

WHACK *vb* strike with a resounding blow ▷ *n* such a blow

WHACKED ▷ **whack**

WHACKER ▷ **whack**

WHACKO *n* mad person

WHACKOS ▷ **whacko**

WHACKS ▷ **whack**

WHACKY *variant spelling of* ▷ **wacky**

WHAE *same as* ▷ **wha**

WHAISLE *Scots form of* ▷ **wheeze**

WHAIZLE *same as* ▷ **whaisle**

WHALE *n* large fish-shaped sea mammal ▷ *vb* hunt for whales

WHALED ▷ **whale**

WHALER *n* ship or person involved in whaling

WHALERS ▷ **whaler**

WHALERY *n* whaling

WHALES ▷ **whale**

WHALING *n* hunting of whales for food and oil ▷ *adv* extremely

WHALLY *adj* (of eyes) with light-coloured irises

WHAM *interj* expression indicating suddenness or forcefulness ▷ *n* forceful blow or impact or the sound produced by such a blow or impact ▷ *vb* strike or cause to strike with great force

WHAMMED ▷ **wham**

WHAMMO *n* sound of a sudden collision

WHAMMOS ▷ **whammo**

WHAMMY *n* devastating setback

WHAMO *same as* ▷ **whammo**

WHAMPLE *n* strike

WHAMS ▷ **wham**

WHANAU *n* (in Māori societies) a family, esp an extended family

WHANAUS ▷ **whanau**

WHANG *vb* strike or be struck so as to cause a resounding noise ▷ *n* resounding noise produced by a heavy blow

WHANGAM *n* imaginary creature

WHANGED ▷ **whang**

WHANGEE *n* tall woody grass grown for its stems, which are used for bamboo canes

WHANGS ▷ **whang**

WHAP *same as* ▷ **whop**

WHAPPED ▷ **whap**

WHAPPER *same as* ▷ **whopper**

WHAPS ▷ **whap**

WHARE *n* Māori hut or dwelling place

WHARES ▷ **whare**

WHARF *n* platform at a harbour for loading and unloading ships ▷ *vb* put (goods, etc) on a wharf

WHARFED ▷ **wharf**

WHARFIE *n* person employed to load and unload ships

WHARFS ▷ **wharf**

WHARVE *n* wooden disc or wheel on a shaft serving as a flywheel or pulley

WHARVES ▷ **wharve**

WHAT *pron* which thing ▷ *interj* exclamation of anger, surprise, etc ▷ *adv* in which way, how much ▷ *n* part; portion

WHATA n building on stilts or a raised platform for storing provisions

WHATAS ▶ whata

WHATEN adj what; what kind of

WHATNA another word for ▶ whaten

WHATNOT n similar unspecified thing

WHATS ▶ what

WHATSIS US form of ▶ whatsit

WHATSIT n person or thing the name of which is unknown, temporarily forgotten, or deliberately overlooked

WHATSO n of whatever kind

WHATTEN same as ▶ whaten

WHAUP n curlew

WHAUPS ▶ whaup

WHAUR Scots word for ▶ where

WHAURS ▶ whaur

WHEAL same as ▶ weal

WHEALS ▶ wheal

WHEAR obsolete variant of ▶ where

WHEARE obsolete variant of ▶ where

WHEAT n grain used in making flour, bread, and pasta

WHEATEN n type of dog ▷ adj made of the grain or flour of wheat

WHEATS ▶ wheat

WHEATY adj having a wheat-like taste

WHEE interj exclamation of joy, thrill, etc

WHEECH vb move quickly

WHEECHS ▶ wheech

WHEEDLE vb coax or cajole

WHEEL n disc that revolves on an axle ▷ vb push or pull (something with wheels)

WHEELED adj having or equipped with a wheel or wheels

WHEELER n horse or other draught animal nearest the wheel

WHEELIE n manoeuvre on a bike in which the front wheel is raised off the ground

WHEELS ▶ wheel

WHEELY adj resembling a wheel

WHEEN n few

WHEENGE Scots form of ▶ whinge

WHEENS ▶ wheen

WHEEP vb fly quickly and lightly

WHEEPED ▶ wheep

WHEEPLE vb whistle weakly

WHEEPS ▶ wheep

WHEESH vb silence (a person, noise, etc) or be silenced

WHEESHT same as ▶ wheesh

WHEEZE vb breathe with a hoarse whistling noise ▷ n wheezing sound

WHEEZED ▶ wheeze

WHEEZER ▶ wheeze

WHEEZES ▶ wheeze

WHEEZLE vb make hoarse breathing sound

WHEEZY ▶ wheeze

WHEFT same as ▶ waft

WHEFTS ▶ wheft

WHELK n edible snail-like shellfish

WHELKED adj having or covered with whelks

WHELKS ▶ whelk

WHELKY ▶ whelk

WHELM vb engulf entirely with or as if with water

WHELMED ▶ whelm

WHELMS ▶ whelm

WHELP n pup or cub ▷ vb (of an animal) give birth

WHELPED ▶ whelp

WHELPS ▶ whelp

WHEMMLE vb overturn

WHEN adv at what time? ▷ pron at which time ▷ n question of when

WHENAS conj while; inasmuch as

WHENCE n point of origin ▷ adv from what place or source ▷ pron from what place, cause, or origin

WHENCES ▶ whence

WHENS ▶ when

WHENUA n land

WHENUAS ▶ whenua

WHENWE n White immigrant from Zimbabwe, caricatured as being tiresomely over-reminiscent of happier times

WHENWES ▶ whenwe

WHERE adv in, at, or to what place? ▷ pron in, at, or to which place ▷ n question

as to the position, direction, or destination of something

WHEREAS n testimonial introduced by whereas

WHEREAT adv at or to which place

WHEREBY pron by which ▷ adv how? by what means?

WHEREIN adv in what place or respect? ▷ pron in which place or thing

WHEREOF adv of what or which person or thing? ▷ pron of which person or thing

WHEREON adv on what thing or place? ▷ pron on which thing, place, etc

WHERES ▶ where

WHERESO adv in or to unspecified place

WHERETO adv towards what (place, end, etc)? ▷ pron which

WHERRET vb strike (someone) a blow ▷ n blow, esp a slap on the face

WHERRIT vb worry or cause to worry

WHERRY n any of certain kinds of half-decked commercial boats, such as barges, used in Britain ▷ vb travel in a wherry

WHERVE same as ▶ wharve

WHERVES ▶ wherve

WHET vb sharpen (a tool) ▷ n act of whetting

WHETHER conj used to introduce any indirect question

WHETS ▶ whet

WHETTED ▶ whet

WHETTER ▶ whet

WHEUGH same as ▶ whew

WHEUGHS ▶ wheugh

WHEW interj exclamation expressing relief, delight, etc ▷ vb express relief

WHEWED ▶ whew

WHEWING ▶ whew

WHEWS ▶ whew

WHEY n watery liquid that separates from the curd when milk is clotted

WHEYEY ▶ whey

WHEYIER ▶ whey

WHEYISH ▶ whey

WHEYS ▶ whey

WHICH pron used to request or refer to a choice from different possibilities ▷ adj

W

used with a noun in requesting that the particular thing being referred to is further identified or distinguished

WHICKER vb (of a horse) to whinny or neigh

WHID vb move quickly

WHIDAH same as ▶ **whydah**

WHIDAHS ▶ **whidah**

WHIDDED ▶ **whid**

WHIDDER vb move with force

WHIDS ▶ **whid**

WHIFF n puff of air or odour ▷ vb come, convey, or go in whiffs

WHIFFED ▶ **whiff**

WHIFFER ▶ **whiff**

WHIFFET n insignificant person

WHIFFLE vb think or behave in an erratic or unpredictable way

WHIFFS ▶ **whiff**

WHIFFY adj smelly

WHIFT n brief emission of air

WHIFTS ▶ **whift**

WHIG vb go quickly

WHIGGED ▶ **whig**

WHIGS ▶ **whig**

WHILE n period of time

WHILED ▶ **while**

WHILERE adv a while ago

WHILES adv at times

WHILING ▶ **while**

WHILK archaic and dialect word for ▶ **which**

WHILLY vb influence by flattery

WHILOM adv formerly ▷ adj one-time

WHILST same as ▶ **while**

WHIM n sudden fancy ▷ vb have a whim

WHIMMED ▶ **whim**

WHIMMY adj having whims

WHIMPER vb cry in a soft whining way ▷ n soft plaintive whine

WHIMPLE same as ▶ **wimple**

WHIMS ▶ **whim**

WHIMSEY same as ▶ **whimsy**

WHIMSY n capricious idea ▷ adj quaint, comical, or unusual, often in a tasteless way

WHIN n gorse

WHINE n high-pitched plaintive cry ▷ vb make

such a sound

WHINED ▶ **whine**

WHINER ▶ **whine**

WHINERS ▶ **whine**

WHINES ▶ **whine**

WHINEY same as ▶ **whiny**

WHINGE vb complain ▷ n complaint

WHINGED ▶ **whinge**

WHINGER ▶ **whinge**

WHINGES ▶ **whinge**

WHINGY adj complaining peevishly, whining

WHINIER ▶ **whiny**

WHINING ▶ **whine**

WHINNY vb neigh softly ▷ n soft neigh ▷ adj covered in whin

WHINS ▶ **whin**

WHINY adj high-pitched and plaintive

WHIO n New Zealand mountain duck with blue plumage

WHIOS ▶ **whio**

WHIP n cord attached to a handle, used for beating animals or people ▷ vb strike with a whip, strap, or cane

WHIPCAT n tailor

WHIPPED ▶ **whip**

WHIPPER ▶ **whip**

WHIPPET n racing dog like a small greyhound

WHIPPY adj springy

WHIPRAY n stingray

WHIPS ▶ **whip**

WHIPSAW n any saw with a flexible blade, such as a bandsaw ▷ vb saw with a whipsaw

WHIPT old past tense of ▶ **whip**

WHIR n prolonged soft swish or buzz, as of a motor working or wings flapping ▷ vb make or cause to make a whir

WHIRL vb spin or revolve ▷ n whirling movement

WHIRLED ▶ **whirl**

WHIRLER ▶ **whirl**

WHIRLS ▶ **whirl**

WHIRLY adj characterized by whirling

WHIRR same as ▶ **whir**

WHIRRED ▶ **whir**

WHIRRET vb strike with sharp blow

WHIRRS ▶ **whirr**

WHIRRY vb move quickly

WHIRS ▶ **whir**

WHIRTLE same as ▶ **wortle**

WHISH less common word for ▶ **swish**

WHISHED ▶ **whish**

WHISHES ▶ **whish**

WHISHT interj hush! be quiet! ▷ adj silent or still ▷ vb make or become silent

WHISHTS ▶ **whisht**

WHISK vb move or remove quickly ▷ n quick movement

WHISKED ▶ **whisk**

WHISKER n any of the long stiff hairs on the face of a cat or other mammal

WHISKET same as ▶ **wisket**

WHISKEY n Irish or American whisky

WHISKS ▶ **whisk**

WHISKY n spirit distilled from fermented cereals

WHISPER vb speak softly, without vibration of the vocal cords ▷ n soft voice

WHISS vb hiss

WHISSED ▶ **whiss**

WHISSES ▶ **whiss**

WHIST same as ▶ **whisht**

WHISTED ▶ **whist**

WHISTLE vb produce a shrill sound, esp by forcing the breath through pursed lips ▷ n whistling sound

WHISTS ▶ **whist**

WHIT n smallest particle

WHITE adj of the colour of snow ▷ n colour of snow

WHITED adj as in **whited sepulchre** hypocrite

WHITELY ▶ **white**

WHITEN vb make or become white or whiter

WHITENS ▶ **whiten**

WHITER ▶ **white**

WHITES pl n white clothes, as worn for playing cricket

WHITEST ▶ **white**

WHITHER same as ▶ **wuther**

WHITING n edible sea fish

WHITISH ▶ **white**

WHITLOW n inflamed sore on a finger or toe, esp round a nail

WHITRET n same as > **whittret**

WHITS ▶ **whit**

WHITTAW same as > **whittawer**

WHITTER variant spelling of ▶ **witter**

WHITTLE vb cut or carve

W

(wood) with a knife ▷ *n* knife, esp a large one
WHIZ *same as* ▶ **whizz**
WHIZZ *vb* make a loud buzzing sound ▷ *n* loud buzzing sound
WHIZZED ▶ **whizz**
WHIZZER ▶ **whizz**
WHIZZES ▶ **whizz**
WHIZZO ▶ **whizzy**
WHIZZY *adj* using sophisticated technology to produce vivid effects
WHO *pron* which person
WHOA *interj* command used, esp to horses, to stop or slow down
WHOEVER *pron* any person who
WHOLE *adj* containing all the elements or parts ▷ *n* complete thing or system
WHOLES ▶ **whole**
WHOLISM *same as* ▶ **holism**
WHOLIST *same as* ▶ **holist**
WHOLLY *adv* completely or totally
WHOM *pron* objective form of *who*
WHOMBLE *same as* ▶ **whemmle**
WHOMMLE *same as* ▶ **whemmle**
WHOMP *vb* strike; thump
WHOMPED ▶ **whomp**
WHOMPS ▶ **whomp**
WHOMSO *pron* whom; whomever
WHOOBUB *same as* ▶ **hubbub**
WHOOF *same as* ▶ **woof**
WHOOFED ▶ **whoof**
WHOOFS ▶ **whoof**
WHOOP *n* shout or cry to express excitement ▷ *vb* emit a whoop
WHOOPED ▶ **whoop**
WHOOPEE *n* cry of joy
WHOOPER *n* type of swan
WHOOPIE *same as* ▶ **whoopee**
WHOOPLA *n* commotion; fuss
WHOOPS *interj* exclamation of surprise or of apology
WHOOSH *n* hissing or rushing sound ▷ *vb* make or move with a hissing or rushing sound
WHOOSIS *n* thingamajig
WHOOT *obsolete variant of* ▶ **hoot**
WHOOTED ▶ **whoot**

WHOOTS ▶ **whoot**
WHOP *vb* strike, beat, or thrash ▷ *n* heavy blow or the sound made by such a blow
WHOPPED ▶ **whop**
WHOPPER *n* anything unusually large
WHOPS ▶ **whop**
WHORE *n* prostitute ▷ *vb* be or act as a prostitute
WHORED ▶ **whore**
WHORES ▶ **whore**
WHORING ▶ **whore**
WHORISH ▶ **whore**
WHORL *n* ring of leaves or petals
WHORLED ▶ **whorl**
WHORLS ▶ **whorl**
WHORT *n* small shrub bearing blackish edible sweet berries
WHORTLE *n* whortleberry
WHORTS ▶ **whort**
WHOSE *pron* of whom or of which ▷ *determiner* of whom? belonging to whom?
WHOSIS *n* thingamajig
WHOSO *archaic word for* ▶ **whoever**
WHOT *obsolete variant of* ▶ **hot**
WHOW *interj* wow
WHUMMLE *vb same as* ▶ **whemmle**
WHUMP *vb* make a dull thud ▷ *n* dull thud
WHUMPED ▶ **whump**
WHUMPS ▶ **whump**
WHUP *vb* defeat totally
WHUPPED ▶ **whup**
WHUPS ▶ **whup**
WHY *adv* for what reason ▷ *pron* because of which ▷ *n* reason, purpose, or cause of something
WHYDAH *n* type of black African bird
WHYDAHS ▶ **whydah**
WHYEVER *adv* for whatever reason
WHYS ▶ **why**
WIBBLE *vb* wobble
WIBBLED ▶ **wibble**
WIBBLES ▶ **wibble**
WICCA *n* cult or practice of witchcraft
WICCAN *n* member of wicca
WICCANS ▶ **wiccan**
WICCAS ▶ **wicca**
WICE *Scots form of* ▶ **wise**
WICH *n* variant of wych

WICHES ▶ **wich**
WICK *n* cord through a lamp or candle which carries fuel to the flame ▷ *adj* lively or active ▷ *vb* (of a material) draw in (water, fuel, etc)
WICKAPE *same as* ▶ **wicopy**
WICKED *adj* morally bad ▷ *n* wicked person
WICKEDS ▶ **wicked**
WICKEN *same as* ▶ **quicken**
WICKENS ▶ **wicken**
WICKER *adj* made of woven cane ▷ *n* slender flexible twig or shoot, esp of willow
WICKERS ▶ **wicker**
WICKET *n* set of three cricket stumps and two bails
WICKETS ▶ **wicket**
WICKIES ▶ **wicky**
WICKING ▶ **wick**
WICKIUP *n* crude shelter made of brushwood, mats, or grass and having an oval frame
WICKS ▶ **wick**
WICKY *same as* ▶ **quicken**
WICKYUP *same as* ▶ **wickiup**
WICOPY *n* any of various North American trees, shrubs, or herbaceous plants
WIDDER *same as* ▶ **widow**
WIDDERS ▶ **widder**
WIDDIE *same as* ▶ **widdy**
WIDDIES ▶ **widdy**
WIDDLE *vb* urinate ▷ *n* urine
WIDDLED ▶ **widdle**
WIDDLES ▶ **widdle**
WIDDY *vb* rope made of twigs
WIDE *adj* large from side to side ▷ *adv* the full extent ▷ *n* (in cricket) a bowled ball ruled to be outside a batsman's reach
WIDELY ▶ **wide**
WIDEN *vb* make or become wider
WIDENED ▶ **widen**
WIDENER ▶ **widen**
WIDENS ▶ **widen**
WIDEOUT *n* footballer who catches passes from the quarterback
WIDER ▶ **wide**
WIDES ▶ **wide**
WIDEST ▶ **wide**
WIDGEON *same as* ▶ **wigeon**

W

WIDGET n any small device, the name of which is unknown or forgotten
WIDGETS ▶ widget
WIDGIE n female larrikin or bodgie
WIDGIES ▶ widgie
WIDISH ▶ wide
WIDOW n woman whose husband is dead and who has not remarried ▷ vb cause to become a widow
WIDOWED ▶ widow
WIDOWER n man whose wife is dead and who has not remarried
WIDOWS ▶ widow
WIDTH n distance from side to side
WIDTHS ▶ width
WIEL same as ▶ weel
WIELD vb hold and use (a weapon)
WIELDED ▶ wield
WIELDER ▶ wield
WIELDS ▶ wield
WIELDY adj easily handled, used, or managed
WIELS ▶ wiel
WIENER n kind of smoked beef or pork sausage, similar to a frankfurter
WIENERS ▶ wiener
WIENIE same as ▶ wiener
WIENIES ▶ wienie
WIFE n woman to whom a man is married ▷ vb marry
WIFED ▶ wife
WIFEDOM n state of being a wife
WIFELY ▶ wife
WIFES ▶ wife
WIFEY n wife
WIFEYS ▶ wifey
WIFIE n woman
WIFIES ▶ wifie
WIFING ▶ wife
WIFTIER ▶ wifty
WIFTY adj scatterbrained
WIG n artificial head of hair ▷ vb furnish with a wig
WIGAN n stiff fabric
WIGANS ▶ wigan
WIGEON n duck found in marshland
WIGEONS ▶ wigeon
WIGGED ▶ wig
WIGGERY n wigs
WIGGIER ▶ wiggy
WIGGING ▶ wig
WIGGLE vb move jerkily from side to side ▷ n wiggling movement

WIGGLED ▶ wiggle
WIGGLER ▶ wiggle
WIGGLES ▶ wiggle
WIGGLY ▶ wiggle
WIGGY adj eccentric
WIGHT vb blame ▷ n human being ▷ adj strong and brave
WIGHTED ▶ wight
WIGHTLY adv swiftly
WIGHTS ▶ wight
WIGLESS ▶ wig
WIGLET n small wig
WIGLETS ▶ wiglet
WIGLIKE ▶ wig
WIGS ▶ wig
WIGWAG vb move (something) back and forth ▷ n system of communication by flag semaphore
WIGWAGS ▶ wigwag
WIGWAM n Native American's tent
WIGWAMS ▶ wigwam
WIKI n website consisting mainly of user-generated content
WIKIS ▶ wiki
WIKIUP same as ▶ wickiup
WIKIUPS ▶ wikiup
WILCO interj expression in telecommunications etc, indicating that the message just received will be complied with
WILD same as ▶ wield
WILDCAT n European wild animal like a large domestic cat ▷ adj risky and financially unsound ▷ vb drill for petroleum or natural gas in an area having no known reserves
WILDED ▶ wild
WILDER vb lead or be led astray
WILDERS ▶ wilder
WILDEST ▶ wild
WILDING n uncultivated plant, esp the crab apple, or a cultivated plant that has become wild
WILDISH ▶ wild
WILDLY ▶ wild
WILDS ▶ wild
WILE n trickery, cunning, or craftiness ▷ vb lure, beguile, or entice
WILED ▶ wile
WILEFUL adj deceitful
WILES ▶ wile
WILFUL adj headstrong or obstinate

WILGA n small drought-resistant tree of Australia
WILGAS ▶ wilga
WILI n spirit
WILIER ▶ wily
WILIEST ▶ wily
WILILY ▶ wily
WILING ▶ wile
WILIS ▶ wili
WILJA ▶ wiltja
WILJAS ▶ wilja
WILL vb used as an auxiliary to form the future tense or to indicate intention, ability, or expectation ▷ n strong determination
WILLED adj having a will as specified
WILLER ▶ will
WILLERS ▶ will
WILLEST ▶ will
WILLET n large American shore bird
WILLETS ▶ willet
WILLEY same as ▶ willy
WILLEYS ▶ willey
WILLFUL same as ▶ wilful
WILLIAM n as in **sweet william** flowering plant
WILLIE n informal word for a penis
WILLIED ▶ willy
WILLIES ▶ willy
WILLING adj ready or inclined (to do something)
WILLOW n tree with thin flexible branches ▷ vb (of raw textile fibres) to open and clean in a machine having a system of rotating spikes
WILLOWS ▶ willow
WILLOWY adj slender and graceful
WILLS ▶ will
WILLY vb clean in willowing-machine
WILT vb (cause to) become limp or lose strength ▷ n act of wilting or state of becoming wilted
WILTED ▶ wilt
WILTING ▶ wilt
WILTJA n Aboriginal shelter
WILTJAS ▶ wiltja
WILTS ▶ wilt
WILY adj crafty or sly
WIMBLE n any of a number of hand tools, such as a brace and bit or a gimlet, used for boring holes ▷ vb bore (a hole) with or as if with a wimble

WIMBLED ▶ wimble
WIMBLES ▶ wimble
WIMBREL *same as*
> **whimbrel**
WIMMIN *n* common intentional literary misspelling of 'women'
WIMP *n* feeble ineffectual person ▷ *vb as in* **wimp out** fail to complete something through fear
WIMPED ▶ wimp
WIMPIER ▶ wimp
WIMPING ▶ wimp
WIMPISH ▶ wimp
WIMPLE *n* garment framing the face, worn by medieval women and now by nuns ▷ *vb* ripple or cause to ripple or undulate
WIMPLED ▶ wimple
WIMPLES ▶ wimple
WIMPS ▶ wimp
WIMPY ▶ wimp
WIN *vb* come first in (a competition, fight, etc) ▷ *n* victory, esp in a game
WINCE *vb* draw back, as if in pain ▷ *n* wincing
WINCED ▶ wince
WINCER ▶ wince
WINCERS ▶ wince
WINCES ▶ wince
WINCEY *n* plain- or twill-weave cloth, usually having a cotton or linen warp and a wool filling
WINCEYS ▶ wincey
WINCH *n* machine for lifting or hauling using a cable or chain wound round a drum ▷ *vb* lift or haul using a winch
WINCHED ▶ winch
WINCHER ▶ winch
WINCHES ▶ winch
WINCING ▶ wince
WIND *n* current of air ▷ *vb* render short of breath
WINDAC *same as* ▶ **windas**
WINDACS ▶ windac
WINDAGE *n* deflection of a projectile as a result of the effect of the wind
WINDAS *n* windlass
WINDBAG *n* person who talks much but uninterestingly
WINDED ▶ wind
WINDER *n* person or device that winds, as an engine for hoisting the cages in a mine shaft

WINDERS ▶ winder
WINDGUN *n* air gun
WINDIER ▶ windy
WINDIGO *same as* ▶ **wendigo**
WINDILY ▶ windy
WINDING ▶ wind
WINDLE *vb* wind something round continuously
WINDLED ▶ windle
WINDLES ▶ windle
WINDOCK *same as* ▶ **winnock**
WINDORE *n* window
WINDOW *n* opening in a wall to let in light or air ▷ *vb* furnish with windows
WINDOWS ▶ window
WINDOWY ▶ window
WINDROW *n* long low ridge or line of hay or a similar crop, designed to achieve the best conditions for drying or curing ▷ *vb* put (hay or a similar crop) into windrows
WINDS ▶ wind
WINDSES *pl n* ventilation shafts within mines
WINDUP *n* prank or hoax
WINDUPS ▶ windup
WINDWAY *n* part of wind instrument
WINDY *adj* denoting a time or conditions in which there is a strong wind
WINE *n* alcoholic drink made from fermented grapes ▷ *adj* of a dark purplish-red colour ▷ *vb* give wine to
WINED ▶ wine
WINERY *n* place where wine is made
WINES ▶ wine
WINESAP *n* variety of apple
WINESOP *n* old word for an alcoholic
WINEY *adj* having the taste or qualities of wine
WING *n* one of the limbs or organs of a bird, insect, or bat that are used for flying ▷ *vb* fly
WINGBOW *n* distinctive band of colour marking the wing of a bird
WINGE *same as* ▶ **whinge**
WINGED *adj* furnished with wings
WINGER *n* player positioned on a wing
WINGERS ▶ winger

WINGES ▶ winge
WINGIER ▶ wingy
WINGING ▶ wing
WINGLET *n* small wing
WINGMAN *n* player in the wing position in Australian Rules
WINGMEN ▶ wingman
WINGS ▶ wing
WINGTIP *n* outermost edge of a wing
WINGY *adj* having wings
WINIER ▶ winy
WINIEST ▶ winy
WINING ▶ wine
WINISH ▶ wine
WINK *vb* close and open (an eye) quickly as a signal ▷ *n* winking
WINKED ▶ wink
WINKER *n* person or thing that winks
WINKERS ▶ winker
WINKING ▶ wink
WINKLE *n* shellfish with a spiral shell ▷ *vb* extract or prise out
WINKLED ▶ winkle
WINKLER *n* one who forces person or thing out
WINKLES ▶ winkle
WINKS ▶ wink
WINLESS *adj* not having won anything
WINN *n* penny
WINNA *vb* will not
WINNARD *n* heron
WINNED ▶ win
WINNER *n* person or thing that wins
WINNERS ▶ winner
WINNING *adj* (of a person) charming, attractive, etc
WINNLE *same as* ▶ **windle**
WINNLES ▶ winnle
WINNOCK *n* window
WINNOW *vb* separate (chaff) from (grain) ▷ *n* device for winnowing
WINNOWS ▶ winnow
WINNS ▶ winn
WINO *n* destitute person who habitually drinks cheap wine
WINOES ▶ wino
WINOS ▶ wino
WINS ▶ win
WINSEY *same as* ▶ **wincey**
WINSEYS ▶ winsey
WINSOME *adj* charming or winning
WINTER *n* coldest season ▷ *vb* spend the winter

W

WINTERS ▸ winter
WINTERY same as ▸ wintry
WINTLE vb reel; stagger
WINTLED ▸ wintle
WINTLES ▸ wintle
WINTRY adj of or like winter
WINY same as ▸ winey
WINZE n steeply inclined shaft, as for ventilation between levels
WINZES ▸ winze
WIPE vb clean or dry by rubbing ▸ n wiping
WIPED ▸ wipe
WIPEOUT n instance of wiping out
WIPER n any piece of cloth, such as a handkerchief, towel, etc, used for wiping
WIPERS ▸ wiper
WIPES ▸ wipe
WIPING ▸ wipe
WIPINGS ▸ wipe
WIPPEN n part of hammer action in piano
WIPPENS ▸ wippen
WIRABLE adj that can be wired
WIRE n thin flexible strand of metal ▸ vb fasten with wire
WIRED adj excited or nervous
WIREMAN n person who installs and maintains electric wiring, cables, etc
WIREMEN ▸ wireman
WIRER n person who sets or uses wires to snare rabbits and similar animals
WIRERS ▸ wirer
WIRES ▸ wire
WIRETAP vb make a connection to a telegraph or telephone wire in order to obtain information secretly
WIREWAY n tube for electric wires
WIRIER ▸ wiry
WIRIEST ▸ wiry
WIRILDA n SE Australian acacia tree with edible seeds
WIRILY ▸ wiry
WIRING n system of wires ▸ adj used for wiring
WIRINGS ▸ wiring
WIRRA interj exclamation of sorrow or deep concern
WIRRAH n Australian saltwater fish with bright blue spots

WIRRAHS ▸ wirrah
WIRY adj lean and tough
WIS vb know or suppose (something)
WISARD obsolete spelling of ▸ wizard
WISARDS ▸ wisard
WISDOM n good sense and judgment
WISDOMS ▸ wisdom
WISE vb guide ▸ adj having wisdom ▸ n manner
WISEASS n person who thinks he or she is being witty or clever
WISED ▸ wise
WISEGUY n person who wants to seem clever
WISELY ▸ wise
WISENT n European bison
WISENTS ▸ wisent
WISER ▸ wise
WISES ▸ wise
WISEST ▸ wise
WISH vb want or desire ▸ n expression of a desire
WISHA interj expression of surprise
WISHED ▸ wish
WISHER ▸ wish
WISHERS ▸ wish
WISHES ▸ wish
WISHFUL adj too optimistic
WISHING ▸ wish
WISHT same as ▸ whisht
WISING ▸ wise
WISKET n basket
WISKETS ▸ wisket
WISP n light delicate streak ▸ vb move or act like a wisp
WISPED ▸ wisp
WISPIER ▸ wispy
WISPILY ▸ wispy
WISPING ▸ wisp
WISPISH ▸ wisp
WISPS ▸ wisp
WISPY adj thin, fine, or delicate
WISS vb urinate
WISSED ▸ wis
WISSES ▸ wis
WISSING ▸ wis
WIST vb know
WISTED ▸ wist
WISTFUL adj sadly longing
WISTING ▸ wist
WISTITI n marmoset
WISTLY adv intently
WISTS ▸ wist
WIT vb detect ▸ n ability to use words or ideas in a clever and amusing way
WITAN n assembly of higher

ecclesiastics and important laymen, including king's thegns, that met to counsel the king on matters such as judicial problems
WITANS ▸ witan
WITCH n person, usu female, who practises (black) magic ▸ vb cause or change by or as if by witchcraft
WITCHED ▸ witch
WITCHEN n rowan tree
WITCHES ▸ witch
WITCHY adj like a witch
WITE vb blame
WITED ▸ wite
WITES ▸ wite
WITGAT n type of S African tree
WITGATS ▸ witgat
WITH prep indicating presence alongside, possession, means of performance, characteristic manner, etc ▸ n division between flues in chimney
WITHAL adv as well
WITHE n strong flexible twig, esp of willow, suitable for binding things together ▸ vb bind with withes
WITHED ▸ withe
WITHER vb wilt or dry up
WITHERS pl n ridge between a horse's shoulder blades
WITHES ▸ withe
WITHIER ▸ withy
WITHIES ▸ withy
WITHIN adv in or inside ▸ prep in or inside ▸ n something that is within
WITHING ▸ withe
WITHINS ▸ within
WITHOUT prep not accompanied by, using, or having ▸ adv outside ▸ n person who is without
WITHS ▸ with
WITHY n willow tree, esp an osier ▸ adj (of people) tough and agile
WITING ▸ wite
WITLESS adj foolish
WITLING n person who thinks himself witty
WITLOOF n chicory
WITNESS n person who has seen something happen ▸ vb see at first hand
WITNEY n type of blanket; heavy cloth

WITNEYS ▶ witney
WITS ▶ wit
WITTED adj having wit
WITTER vb chatter pointlessly or at unnecessary length ▷ n pointless chat
WITTERS ▶ witter
WITTIER ▶ witty
WITTILY ▶ witty
WITTING adj deliberate
WITTOL n man who tolerates his wife's unfaithfulness
WITTOLS ▶ wittol
WITTY adj clever and amusing
WITWALL n golden oriole
WIVE vb marry (a woman)
WIVED ▶ wive
WIVER another word for ▶ wivern
WIVERN same as ▶ wyvern
WIVERNS ▶ wivern
WIVERS ▶ wiver
WIVES ▶ wife
WIVING ▶ wive
WIZ shortened form of ▶ wizard

> **Wiz** is a short form of **wizard**. This is the highest-scoring three-letter word beginning with W, and can be especially useful when there isn't much room to manoeuvre.

WIZARD n magician ▷ adj superb
WIZARDS ▶ wizard
WIZEN vb make or become shrivelled ▷ n archaic word for 'weasand' (the gullet)
WIZENED adj shrivelled or wrinkled
WIZENS ▶ wizen
WIZES ▶ wiz
WIZIER same as ▶ vizier
WIZIERS ▶ wizier
WIZZEN same as ▶ wizen
WIZZENS ▶ wizen
WIZZES ▶ wiz
WO archaic spelling of ▶ woe
WOAD n blue dye obtained from a plant, used by the ancient Britons as a body dye
WOADED adj coloured blue with woad
WOADS ▶ woad
WOADWAX n small Eurasian leguminous shrub
WOALD same as ▶ weld

WOALDS ▶ woald
WOBBLE vb move unsteadily ▷ n wobbling movement or sound
WOBBLED ▶ wobble
WOBBLER ▶ wobble
WOBBLES ▶ wobble
WOBBLY adj unsteady ▷ n temper tantrum
WOCK same as ▶ wok
WOCKS ▶ wock
WODGE n thick lump or chunk
WODGES ▶ wodge
WOE n grief
WOEFUL adj extremely sad
WOENESS ▶ woe
WOES ▶ woe
WOESOME adj woeful
WOF n fool
WOFS ▶ wof
WOFUL same as ▶ woeful
WOFULLY ▶ woful
WOGGLE n ring of leather through which a Scout neckerchief is threaded
WOGGLES ▶ woggle
WOIWODE same as ▶ voivode
WOK n bowl-shaped Chinese cooking pan, used for stir-frying
WOKE ▶ wake
WOKEN ▶ wake
WOKKA modifier as in **wokka board** wobble board: a piece of fibreboard used as a musical instrument
WOKS ▶ wok
WOLD same as ▶ weld
WOLDS ▶ wold
WOLF n wild predatory canine mammal ▷ vb eat ravenously
WOLFED ▶ wolf
WOLFER same as ▶ wolver
WOLFERS ▶ wolfer
WOLFING ▶ wolf
WOLFISH ▶ wolf
WOLFKIN n young wolf
WOLFRAM another name for ▶ tungsten
WOLFS ▶ wolf
WOLLIES ▶ wolly
WOLLY n pickled cucumber or olive
WOLVE vb hunt for wolves
WOLVED ▶ wolve
WOLVER n person who hunts wolves
WOLVERS ▶ wolver
WOLVES ▶ wolf

WOLVING ▶ wolve
WOLVISH same as ▶ wolfish
WOMAN n adult human female ▷ adj female ▷ vb provide with a woman or women
WOMANED ▶ woman
WOMANLY adj having qualities traditionally associated with a woman
WOMANS ▶ woman
WOMB vb enclose ▷ n hollow organ in female mammals where babies are conceived and develop
WOMBAT n small heavily-built burrowing Australian marsupial
WOMBATS ▶ wombat
WOMBED ▶ womb
WOMBIER ▶ womby
WOMBING ▶ womb
WOMBS ▶ womb
WOMBY adj hollow; spacious
WOMEN ▶ woman
WOMERA same as ▶ woomera
WOMERAS ▶ womera
WOMMERA same as ▶ woomera
WOMMIT n foolish person
WOMMITS ▶ wommit
WOMYN same as ▶ woman
WON n standard monetary unit of North Korea, divided into 100 chon ▷ vb live or dwell
WONDER vb be curious about ▷ n wonderful thing ▷ adj spectacularly successful
WONDERS ▶ wonder
WONDRED adj splendid
WONGA n money
WONGAS ▶ wonga
WONGI vb talk informally
WONGIED ▶ wongi
WONGIS ▶ wongi
WONING ▶ won
WONINGS ▶ won
WONK n person who is obsessively interested in a specified subject
WONKIER ▶ wonky
WONKS ▶ wonk
WONKY adj shaky or unsteady
WONNED ▶ won
WONNER ▶ won
WONNERS ▶ won
WONNING ▶ won
WONS ▶ won

W

WONT *adj* accustomed ▷ *n* custom ▷ *vb* become or cause to become accustomed

WONTED *adj* accustomed or habituated (to doing something)

WONTING ▶ **wont**

WONTON *n* dumpling filled with spiced minced pork

WONTONS ▶ **wonton**

WONTS ▶ **wont**

WOO *vb* seek the love or affection of (a woman)

WOOBUT *same as* ▶ **woubit**

WOOBUTS ▶ **woobut**

WOOD *n* substance trees are made of, used in carpentry and as fuel ▷ *adj* made of or using wood ▷ *vb* (of land) plant with trees

WOODBIN *n* box for firewood

WOODBOX *n* box for firewood

WOODCUT *n* (print made from) an engraved block of wood

WOODED *adj* covered with trees

WOODEN *adj* made of wood ▷ *vb* fell or kill (a person or animal)

WOODENS ▶ **wooden**

WOODHEN *another name for* ▶ **weka**

WOODIE *n* gallows rope

WOODIER ▶ **woody**

WOODIES ▶ **woodie**

WOODING ▶ **wood**

WOODLOT *n* area restricted to the growing of trees

WOODMAN *same as* > **woodsman**

WOODMEN ▶ **woodman**

WOODRAT *n* pack-rat

WOODS *pl n* closely packed trees forming a forest or wood

WOODSIA *n* type of small fern with tufted rhizomes and wiry fronds

WOODSY *adj* of, reminiscent of, connected with woods

WOODWAX *same as* > **woodwaxen**

WOODY *adj* (of a plant) having a very hard stem

WOOED ▶ **woo**

WOOER ▶ **woo**

WOOERS ▶ **woo**

WOOF *vb* (of dogs) bark or growl

WOOFED ▶ **woof**

WOOFER *n* loudspeaker reproducing low-frequency sounds

WOOFERS ▶ **woofer**

WOOFIER ▶ **woofy**

WOOFING ▶ **woof**

WOOFS ▶ **woof**

WOOFY *adj* with close, dense texture

WOOHOO *interj* expression of joy, approval, etc

WOOING ▶ **woo**

WOOINGS ▶ **woo**

WOOL *n* soft hair of sheep, goats, etc

WOOLD *vb* wind (rope)

WOOLDED ▶ **woold**

WOOLDER *n* stick for winding rope

WOOLDS ▶ **woold**

WOOLED *same as* ▶ **woolled**

WOOLEN *same as* ▶ **woollen**

WOOLENS ▶ **woolen**

WOOLER *same as* ▶ **woolder**

WOOLERS ▶ **wooler**

WOOLFAT *same as* ▶ **lanolin**

WOOLHAT *n* poor white person in S States

WOOLIE *n* wool garment

WOOLIER ▶ **wooly**

WOOLIES ▶ **wooly**

WOOLLED *adj* (of animals) having wool

WOOLLEN *adj* relating to or consisting partly or wholly of wool ▷ *n* garment or piece of cloth made wholly or partly of wool, esp a knitted one

WOOLLY *adj* of or like wool ▷ *n* knitted woollen garment

WOOLMAN *n* wool trader

WOOLMEN ▶ **woolman**

WOOLS ▶ **wool**

WOOLSEY *n* cotton and wool blend

WOOLY *same as* ▶ **woolly**

WOOMERA *n* notched stick used by Australian Aborigines to aid the propulsion of a spear

WOON *same as* ▶ **won**

WOONED ▶ **woon**

WOONING ▶ **woon**

WOONS ▶ **woon**

WOOPIE *n* well-off older person

WOOPIES ▶ **woopie**

WOOPS *vb* (esp of small child) vomit

WOOPSED ▶ **woops**

WOOPSES ▶ **woops**

WOORALI *less common name for* ▶ **curare**

WOORARA *same as* ▶ **wourali**

WOORARI *same as* ▶ **wourali**

WOOS ▶ **woo**

WOOSE *same as* ▶ **wuss**

WOOSEL *same as* ▶ **ouzel**

WOOSELL *same as* ▶ **ouzel**

WOOSELS ▶ **woosel**

WOOSES ▶ **woose**

WOOSH *same as* ▶ **whoosh**

WOOSHED ▶ **woosh**

WOOSHES ▶ **woosh**

WOOT *vb* wilt thou?

WOOTZ *n* Middle-Eastern steel

WOOTZES ▶ **wootz**

WOOZIER ▶ **woozy**

WOOZILY ▶ **woozy**

WOOZY *adj* weak, dizzy, and confused

WOPPED ▶ **wop**

WOPPING ▶ **wop**

WORD *n* smallest single meaningful unit of speech or writing ▷ *vb* express in words

WORDAGE *n* words considered collectively, esp a quantity of words

WORDED ▶ **word**

WORDIER ▶ **wordy**

WORDILY ▶ **wordy**

WORDING *n* choice and arrangement of words

WORDISH *adj* talkative

WORDS ▶ **word**

WORDY *adj* using too many words

WORE ▶ **wear**

WORK *n* physical or mental effort directed to making or doing something ▷ *adj* of or for work ▷ *vb* (cause to) do work

WORKBAG *n* container for implements, tools, or materials, esp sewing equipment

WORKBOX *same as* ▶ **workbag**

WORKDAY *another word for* > **workaday**

WORKED *adj* made or decorated with evidence of workmanship

WORKER n person who works in a specified way
WORKERS ▶ **worker**
WORKFUL adj hardworking
WORKING n operation or mode of operation of something ▷ adj relating to or concerned with a person or thing that works
WORKMAN n manual worker
WORKMEN ▶ **workman**
WORKOUT n session of physical exercise for training or fitness
WORKS ▶ **work**
WORKSHY adj not inclined to work
WORKTOP n surface in a kitchen, used for food preparation
WORKUP n medical examination
WORKUPS ▶ **workup**
WORLD n planet earth ▷ adj of the whole world
WORLDED adj incorporating worlds
WORLDLY adj not spiritual ▷ adv in a worldly manner
WORLDS ▶ **world**
WORM n small limbless invertebrate animal ▷ vb rid of worms
WORMED ▶ **worm**
WORMER ▶ **worm**
WORMERS ▶ **worm**
WORMERY n piece of apparatus, having a glass side or sides, in which worms are kept for study
WORMFLY n type of lure dressed on a double hook, the barbs of which sit one above the other and back-to-back
WORMIER ▶ **wormy**
WORMIL n burrowing larva of type of fly
WORMILS ▶ **wormil**
WORMING ▶ **worm**
WORMISH ▶ **worm**
WORMS n disease caused by parasitic worms living in the intestines
WORMY adj infested with or eaten by worms
WORN ▶ **wear**
WORRAL n type of lizard
WORRALS ▶ **worral**
WORREL same as ▶ **worral**
WORRELS ▶ **worrel**
WORRIED ▶ **worry**

WORRIER ▶ **worry**
WORRIES ▶ **worry**
WORRIT vb tease or worry
WORRITS ▶ **worrit**
WORRY vb (cause to) be anxious or uneasy ▷ n (cause of) anxiety or concern
WORSE vb defeat
WORSED ▶ **worse**
WORSEN vb make or grow worse
WORSENS ▶ **worsen**
WORSER archaic or nonstandard word for ▶ **worse**
WORSES ▶ **worse**
WORSET n worsted fabric
WORSETS ▶ **worset**
WORSHIP vb show religious devotion to ▷ n act or instance of worshipping
WORSING ▶ **worse**
WORST n worst thing ▷ vb defeat
WORSTED n type of woollen yarn or fabric
WORSTS ▶ **worst**
WORT n any of various unrelated plants, esp ones formerly used to cure diseases
WORTH prep having a value of ▷ n value or price ▷ vb happen or betide
WORTHED ▶ **worth**
WORTHS ▶ **worth**
WORTHY adj deserving admiration or respect ▷ n notable person ▷ vb make worthy
WORTLE n plate with holes for drawing wire through
WORTLES ▶ **wortle**
WORTS ▶ **wort**
WOS ▶ **wo**
WOSBIRD n illegitimate child
WOST vb wit, to know
WOT vb wit, to know
WOTCHA ▶ **wotcher**
WOTCHER sentence substitute slang term of greeting
WOTS ▶ **wot**
WOTTED ▶ **wot**
WOTTEST ▶ **wot**
WOTTETH ▶ **wot**
WOTTING ▶ **wot**
WOUBIT n type of caterpillar
WOUBITS ▶ **woubit**

WOULD ▶ **will**
WOULDS same as ▶ **wouldst**
WOULDST singular form of the past tense of ▶ **will**
WOUND vb injure ▷ n injury
WOUNDED adj suffering from wounds
WOUNDER ▶ **wound**
WOUNDS ▶ **wound**
WOUNDY adj extreme
WOURALI n plant from which curare is obtained
WOVE ▶ **weave**
WOVEN n article made from woven cloth
WOVENS ▶ **woven**
WOW interj exclamation of astonishment ▷ n astonishing person or thing ▷ vb be a great success with
WOWED ▶ **wow**
WOWEE stronger form of ▶ **wow**
WOWF adj mad

> This is a Scots word meaning crazy: you are not likely to get the chance to play this very often but if your opponent plays **wow** and you have an F you would be wowf to miss the opportunity of the hook!

WOWFER ▶ **wowf**
WOWFEST ▶ **wowf**
WOWING ▶ **wow**
WOWS ▶ **wow**
WOWSER n puritanical person
WOWSERS ▶ **wowser**
WOX ▶ **wax**

> **Wox** is an old past tense of the verb **wax**, to grow, and is another of the key words using X.

WOXEN ▶ **wax**
WRACK n seaweed ▷ vb strain or shake (something) violently
WRACKED ▶ **wrack**
WRACKS ▶ **wrack**
WRAITH n ghost
WRAITHS ▶ **wraith**
WRANG Scots word for ▶ **wrong**
WRANGED ▶ **wrang**
WRANGLE vb argue noisily ▷ n noisy argument
WRANGS ▶ **wrang**
WRAP vb fold (something)

W

round (a person or thing) so as to cover ▷ *n* garment wrapped round the shoulders

WRAPPED ▶ **wrap**

WRAPPER *vb* cover with wrapping ▷ *n* cover for a product

WRAPS ▶ **wrap**

WRAPT *same as* ▶ **rapt**

WRASSE *n* colourful sea fish

WRASSES ▶ **wrasse**

WRASSLE *same as* ▶ **wrestle**

WRAST *same as* ▶ **wrest**

WRASTED ▶ **wrast**

WRASTLE *same as* ▶ **wrestle**

WRASTS ▶ **wrast**

WRATE ▶ **write**

WRATH *n* intense anger ▷ *adj* incensed ▷ *vb* make angry

WRATHED ▶ **wrath**

WRATHS ▶ **wrath**

WRATHY *same as* > **wrathful**

WRAWL *vb* howl

WRAWLED ▶ **wrawl**

WRAWLS ▶ **wrawl**

WRAXLE *vb* wrestle

WRAXLED ▶ **wraxle**

WRAXLES ▶ **wraxle**

WREAK *vb* inflict (vengeance, etc) or to cause (chaos, etc)

WREAKED ▶ **wreak**

WREAKER ▶ **wreak**

WREAKS ▶ **wreak**

WREATH *n* twisted ring or band of flowers or leaves used as a memorial or tribute

WREATHE *vb* form into or take the form of a wreath by intertwining or twisting together

WREATHS ▶ **wreath**

WREATHY *adj* twisted into wreath

WRECK *vb* destroy ▷ *n* remains of something that has been destroyed or badly damaged, esp a ship

WRECKED *adj* in a state of intoxication, stupor, or euphoria, induced by drugs or alcohol

WRECKER *n* formerly, person who lured ships onto the rocks in order to plunder them

WRECKS ▶ **wreck**

WREN *n* small brown songbird

WRENCH *vb* twist or pull violently ▷ *n* violent twist or pull

WRENS ▶ **wren**

WREST *vb* twist violently ▷ *n* act or an instance of wresting

WRESTED ▶ **wrest**

WRESTER ▶ **wrest**

WRESTLE *vb* fight, esp as a sport, by grappling with and trying to throw down an opponent ▷ *n* act of wrestling

WRESTS ▶ **wrest**

WRETCH *n* despicable person

WRETHE *same as* ▶ **wreathe**

WRETHED ▶ **wrethe**

WRETHES ▶ **wrethe**

WRICK *variant spelling* (*chiefly Brit*) *of* ▶ **rick**

WRICKED ▶ **wrick**

WRICKS ▶ **wrick**

WRIED ▶ **wry**

WRIER ▶ **wry**

WRIES ▶ **wry**

WRIEST ▶ **wry**

WRIGGLE *vb* move with a twisting action ▷ *n* wriggling movement

WRIGGLY ▶ **wriggle**

WRIGHT *n* maker

WRIGHTS ▶ **wright**

WRING *vb* twist, esp to squeeze liquid out of

WRINGED ▶ **wring**

WRINGER *same as* ▶ **mangle**

WRINGS ▶ **wring**

WRINKLE *n* slight crease, esp one in the skin due to age ▷ *vb* make or become slightly creased

WRINKLY ▶ **wrinkle**

WRIST *n* joint between the hand and the arm

WRISTS ▶ **wrist**

WRISTY *adj* (of a player's style of hitting the ball in cricket, tennis, etc) characterized by considerable movement of the wrist

WRIT *n* written legal command

WRITE *vb* mark paper etc with symbols or words

WRITER *n* author

WRITERS ▶ **writer**

WRITES ▶ **write**

WRITHE *vb* twist or squirm in or as if in pain ▷ *n* act or an instance of writhing

WRITHED ▶ **writhe**

WRITHEN *adj* twisted

WRITHER ▶ **writhe**

WRITHES ▶ **writhe**

WRITING ▶ **write**

WRITS ▶ **writ**

WRITTEN ▶ **write**

WRIZLED *adj* wrinkled

WROATH *n* unforeseen trouble

WROATHS ▶ **wroath**

WROKE ▶ **wreak**

WROKEN ▶ **wreak**

WRONG *adj* incorrect or mistaken ▷ *adv* in a wrong manner ▷ *n* something immoral or unjust ▷ *vb* treat unjustly

WRONGED ▶ **wrong**

WRONGER ▶ **wrong**

WRONGLY ▶ **wrong**

WRONGS ▶ **wrong**

WROOT *obsolete form of* ▶ **root**

WROOTED ▶ **wroot**

WROOTS ▶ **wroot**

WROTE ▶ **write**

WROTH *adj* angry

WROUGHT *adj* (of metals) shaped by hammering or beating

WRUNG ▶ **wring**

WRY *adj* drily humorous ▷ *vb* twist or contort

WRYBILL *n* New Zealand plover whose bill is bent to one side enabling it to search for food beneath stones

WRYER ▶ **wry**

WRYEST ▶ **wry**

WRYING ▶ **wry**

WRYLY ▶ **wry**

WRYNECK *n* woodpecker that has a habit of twisting its neck round

WRYNESS ▶ **wry**

WRYTHEN *adj* twisted

WUD *Scots form of* ▶ **wood**

W and U are a horrible combination to have on your rack, so this Scots word for wood can be a godsend. And remember that it can also be a verb, meaning to load with wood, so you have **wuds, wudding** and **wudded**.

WUDDED ▶ wud
WUDDING ▶ wud
WUDJULA *n* Australian word for a non-Aboriginal person
WUDS ▶ wud
WUDU *n* practice of ritual washing before daily prayer
WUDUS ▶ wudu
WULL *obsolete form of* ▶ will
WULLED ▶ will
WULLING ▶ will
WULLS ▶ will
WUNNER *same as* ▶ oner
WUNNERS ▶ wunner
WURLEY *n* Aboriginal hut
WURLEYS ▶ wurley
WURLIE *same as* ▶ wurley
WURLIES ▶ wurlie
WURST *n* large sausage, esp of a type made in Germany, Austria, etc
WURSTS ▶ wurst
WURZEL *n* root
WURZELS ▶ wurzel
WUS *n* casual term of address
WUSES ▶ wus
WUSHU *n* Chinese martial arts

WUSHUS ▶ wushu
WUSS *n* feeble or effeminate person
WUSSES ▶ wuss
WUSSIER ▶ wussy
WUSSIES ▶ wussy
WUSSY *adj* feeble or effeminate ▷ *n* feeble person
WUTHER *vb* (of wind) blow and roar
WUTHERS ▶ wuther
WUXIA *n* genre of Chinese fiction and film, concerning the adventures of sword-wielding chivalrous heroes

> This Chinese word for a genre of fiction may get you a decent score from a very difficult-looking rack.

WUXIAS ▶ wuxia
WUZZLE *vb* mix up
WUZZLED ▶ wuzzle
WUZZLES ▶ wuzzle
WYCH *n* type of tree having flexible branches
WYCHES ▶ wych
WYE *n* y-shaped pipe

> If you have W and Y on your rack, look for an E on the board that will allow you to play this name for the letter Y, especially if you can land on a bonus square as a result.

WYES ▶ wye
WYLE *vb* entice
WYLED ▶ wyle
WYLES ▶ wyle
WYLING ▶ wyle
WYN *n* rune equivalent to English 'w'
WYND *n* narrow lane or alley
WYNDS ▶ wynd
WYNN *same as* ▶ wyn
WYNNS ▶ wynn
WYNS ▶ wyn
WYTE *vb* blame
WYTED ▶ wyte
WYTES ▶ wyte
WYTING ▶ wyte
WYVERN *n* heraldic beast having a serpent's tail and a dragon's head and a body with wings and two legs
WYVERNS ▶ wyvern

W

Xx

Worth 8 points on its own, **X** is one of the best tiles in the game. It doesn't, however, start many two- and three-letter words. There are only two valid two-letter words, **xi** and **xu** (9 points each) beginning with **X**, and only one three-letter word, **xis**. Therefore, if you have an **X** on your rack and need to play short words, you're probably better off thinking of words that end in **X** or have **X** in them rather than those that start with **X**. Particularly good to remember are **zax**, **zex** (19 points each) and **kex** (14 points).

XANTHAM n acacia gum

XANTHAN same as ▸ xantham

XANTHIC adj of, containing, or derived from xanthic acid

XANTHIN n any of a group of yellow or orange carotene derivatives that occur in the fruit and flowers of certain plants

XEBEC n small three-masted Mediterranean vessel with both square and lateen sails, formerly used by Algerian pirates and later used for commerce

> A kind of small boat, and a good high-scoring word that can easily be missed, as we tend to be slow to consider words beginning with X.

XEBECS ▸ xebec

XENIA n influence of pollen upon the form of the fruit developing after pollination

XENIAL ▸ xenia

XENIAS ▸ xenia

XENIC adj denoting the presence of bacteria

XENIUM n diplomatic gift

XENON n colourless odourless gas found in very small quantities in the air

XENONS ▸ xenon

XENOPUS n African frog

XERAFIN n Indian coin

XERARCH adj (of a sere) having its origin in a dry habitat

XERASIA n dryness of the hair

XERIC adj of, relating to, or growing in dry conditions

XEROMA n excessive dryness of the cornea

XEROMAS ▸ xeroma

XEROSES ▸ xerosis

XEROSIS n abnormal dryness of bodily tissues, esp the skin, eyes, or mucous membranes

XEROTES same as ▸ xerosis

XEROTIC ▸ xerosis

XEROX n tradename for a machine employing a xerographic copying process ▷ vb produce a copy (of a document, etc) using such a machine

XEROXED ▸ xerox

XEROXES ▸ xerox

XERUS n ground squirrel

XERUSES ▸ xerus

XI n 14th letter in the Greek alphabet

XIPHOID adj shaped like a sword ▷ n part of the sternum

XIS ▸ xi

XOANA ▸ xoanon

XOANON n primitive image of a god, carved, esp originally, in wood, and supposed to have fallen from heaven

> One of the few words starting with X, this means a kind of primitive statue. But be careful: the plural is **xoana** not **xoanons**.

XRAY n code word for the letter X

XRAYS ▸ xray

XU n Vietnamese currency unit

XYLAN n yellow polysaccharide consisting of xylose units: occurs in straw husks and other woody tissue

XYLANS ▸ xylan

XYLEM n plant tissue that conducts water and minerals from the roots to all other parts

XYLEMS ▸ xylem

XYLENE n type of hydrocarbon

XYLENES ▸ xylene

XYLENOL n synthetic resin made from xylene

XYLIC ▸ xylem

XYLIDIN same as > xylidine

XYLITOL n crystalline alcohol used as sweetener

XYLOGEN same as ▸ xylem

XYLOID adj of, relating to, or resembling wood

XYLOL another name (not in technical usage) for ▸ xylene

XYLOLS ▸ xylol

XYLOMA n hard growth in fungi

XYLOMAS ▸ xyloma

XYLONIC adj denoting an acid formed from xylose

XYLOSE n white crystalline dextrorotatory sugar found in the form of xylan in wood and straw

XYLOSES ▸ xylose

X

XYLYL *n* group of atoms
XYLYLS ▶ xylyl
XYST *n* long portico, esp one used in ancient Greece for athletics

A kind of court used by ancient Greek athletes for exercises, this is a lovely high-scoring word to play. And if your opponent plays it, remember that you can put an I on it to make **xysti**, as well as an S to make **xysts**.

XYSTER *n* surgical instrument for scraping bone
XYSTERS ▶ xyster
XYSTI ▶ xystus
XYSTOI ▶ xystos
XYSTOS *same as* **▶ xyst**
XYSTS ▶ xyst
XYSTUS *same as* **▶ xyst**

X

Yy

Y can be a useful tile to have on your rack, particularly if you are short of vowels, but it can make it difficult to find bonus words scoring that extra 50 points, and you will normally want to play it off as soon as a good score offers itself. There are only four two-letter words beginning with Y, but these are easy to remember as there's one for every vowel except I: **ya**, **ye**, **yo** and **yu** (5 points each). There are quite a few useful three-letter words: **yew** (9) and **yob** (8) and remember that **yob** was originally **boy** backwards: if you can't fit in **yob**, you may be able to use **boy** instead. And while his half-brother the **zo** (or **dzo** or **dso** or **zho**) gets all the attention, don't forget that the **yak** (10) earns quite a decent score!

YA pron you

YAAR n in informal Indian English, a friend

YAARS ▶ yaar

YABA n informal word for 'yet another bloody acronym'

YABAS ▶ yaba

YABBA n form of methamphetamine

YABBAS ▶ yabba

YABBER vb talk or jabber ▷ n talk or jabber

YABBERS ▶ yabber

YABBIE same as ▶ yabby

YABBIED ▶ yabby

YABBIES ▶ yabby

YABBY n small freshwater crayfish ▷ vb go out to catch yabbies

YACCA n Australian plant with a woody stem, stiff grasslike leaves, and a spike of small white flowers

YACCAS ▶ yacca

YACHT n large boat with sails or an engine, used for racing or pleasure cruising ▷ vb sail in a yacht

YACHTED ▶ yacht

YACHTER ▶ yacht

YACHTIE n yachtsman

YACHTS ▶ yacht

YACK same as ▶ yak

YACKA same as ▶ yacca

YACKAS ▶ yacka

YACKED ▶ yack

YACKER same as ▶ yakka

YACKERS ▶ yacker

YACKING ▶ yack

YACKS ▶ yack

YAD n hand-held pointer used for reading the sefer torah

YADS ▶ yad

YAE same as ▶ ae

YAFF vb bark

YAFFED ▶ yaff

YAFFING ▶ yaff

YAFFLE n woodpecker with a green back and wings, and a red crown

YAFFLES ▶ yaffle

YAFFS ▶ yaff

YAG n artificial crystal

YAGER same as ▶ jaeger

YAGERS ▶ yager

YAGGER n pedlar

YAGGERS ▶ yagger

YAGI n type of highly directional aerial

YAGIS ▶ yagi

YAGS ▶ yag

YAH interj exclamation of derision or disgust ▷ n affected upper-class person

YAHOO n crude coarse person

YAHOOS ▶ yahoo

YAHS ▶ yah

YAIRD Scots form of ▶ yard

YAIRDS ▶ yaird

YAK n Tibetan ox with long shaggy hair ▷ vb talk continuously about unimportant matters

YAKHDAN n box for carrying ice on a pack animal

YAKKA n work

YAKKAS ▶ yakka

YAKKED ▶ yak

YAKKER same as ▶ yakka

YAKKERS ▶ yakker

YAKKING ▶ yak

YAKOW n animal bred from a male yak and a domestic cow

YAKOWS ▶ yakow

YAKS ▶ yak

YAKUZA n Japanese criminal organization involved in illegal gambling, extortion, gun-running, etc

YALD adj vigorous

YALE n mythical beast with the body of an antelope (or similar animal) and swivelling horns

YALES ▶ yale

YAM n tropical root vegetable

YAMALKA same as > yarmulke

YAMEN n (in imperial China) the office or residence of a public official

YAMENS ▶ yamen

YAMMER vb whine in a complaining manner ▷ n yammering sound

YAMMERS ▶ yammer

YAMPIES ▶ yampy

YAMPY n foolish person

YAMS ▶ yam

YAMULKA same as > yarmulke

YAMUN same as ▶ yamen

YAMUNS ▶ yamun

YANG n (in Chinese

philosophy) one of two complementary principles maintaining harmony in the universe

YANGS ▶ yang

YANK vb pull or jerk suddenly ▷ n sudden pull or jerk

YANKED ▶ yank

YANKEE n code word for the letter Y

YANKEES ▶ yankee

YANKER ▶ yank

YANKERS ▶ yank

YANKIE n shrewish woman

YANKIES ▶ yankie

YANKING ▶ yank

YANKS ▶ yank

YANQUI n slang word for American

YANQUIS ▶ yanqui

YANTRA n diagram used in meditation

YANTRAS ▶ yantra

YAOURT n yoghurt

YAOURTS ▶ yaourt

YAP vb bark with a high-pitched sound ▷ n high-pitched bark ▷ interj imitation or representation of the sound of a dog yapping or people jabbering

YAPOCK same as ▶ yapok

YAPOCKS ▶ yapock

YAPOK n type of opossum

YAPOKS ▶ yapok

YAPON same as ▶ yaupon

YAPONS ▶ yapon

YAPP n type of book binding

YAPPED ▶ yap

YAPPER ▶ yap

YAPPERS ▶ yap

YAPPIE n young aspiring professional

YAPPIER ▶ yap

YAPPIES ▶ yappie

YAPPING ▶ yap

YAPPS ▶ yapp

YAPPY ▶ yap

YAPS ▶ yap

YAPSTER ▶ yap

YAQONA n Polynesian shrub

YAQONAS ▶ yaqona

YAR adj nimble

YARD n unit of length equal to 36 inches or about 91.4 centimetres ▷ vb draft (animals), esp to a saleyard

YARDAGE n length measured in yards

YARDANG n ridge formed by wind erosion

YARDARM n outer end of a ship's yard

YARDED ▶ yard

YARDER ▶ yard

YARDERS ▶ yard

YARDING n group of animals displayed for sale

YARDMAN n farm overseer

YARDMEN ▶ yardman

YARDS ▶ yard

YARE adj ready, brisk, or eager ▷ adv readily or eagerly

YARELY ▶ yare

YARER ▶ yare

YAREST ▶ yare

YARFA n peat

YARFAS ▶ yarfa

YARK vb make ready

YARKED ▶ yark

YARKING ▶ yark

YARKS ▶ yark

YARN n thread used for knitting or making cloth ▷ vb thread with yarn

YARNED ▶ yarn

YARNER ▶ yarn

YARNERS ▶ yarn

YARNING ▶ yarn

YARNS ▶ yarn

YARPHA n peat

YARPHAS ▶ yarpha

YARR n wild white flower

YARRAN n type of small hardy tree of inland Australia

YARRANS ▶ yarran

YARROW n wild plant with flat clusters of white flowers

YARROWS ▶ yarrow

YARRS ▶ yarr

YARTA Shetland word for ▶ heart

YARTAS ▶ yarta

YARTO same as ▶ yarta

YARTOS ▶ yarto

YASHMAC same as ▶ yashmak

YASHMAK n veil worn by a Muslim woman to cover her face in public

YASMAK same as ▶ yashmak

YASMAKS ▶ yashmak

YATAGAN same as > yataghan

YATE n type of small eucalyptus tree yielding a very hard timber

YATES ▶ yate

YATTER vb talk at length ▷ n continuous chatter

YATTERS ▶ yatter

YAUD Scots word for ▶ mare

YAUDS ▶ yaud

YAULD adj alert, spritely, or nimble

YAUP variant spelling of ▶ yawp

YAUPED ▶ yaup

YAUPER ▶ yaup

YAUPERS ▶ yaup

YAUPING ▶ yaup

YAUPON n southern US evergreen holly shrub with spreading branches, scarlet fruits, and oval leaves

YAUPONS ▶ yaupon

YAUPS ▶ yaup

YAUTIA n Caribbean plant cultivated for its edible leaves and underground stems

YAUTIAS ▶ yautia

YAW vb (of an aircraft or ship) turn to one side or from side to side while moving ▷ n act or movement of yawing

YAWED ▶ yaw

YAWEY ▶ yaws

YAWING ▶ yaw

YAWL n two-masted sailing boat ▷ vb howl, weep, or scream harshly

YAWLED ▶ yawl

YAWLING ▶ yawl

YAWLS ▶ yawl

YAWN vb open the mouth wide and take in air deeply, often when sleepy or bored ▷ n act of yawning

YAWNED ▶ yawn

YAWNER ▶ yawn

YAWNERS ▶ yawn

YAWNIER ▶ yawn

YAWNING ▶ yawn

YAWNS ▶ yawn

YAWNY ▶ yawn

YAWP vb gape or yawn, esp audibly ▷ n shout, bark, yelp, or cry

YAWPED ▶ yawp

YAWPER ▶ yawp

YAWPERS ▶ yawp

YAWPING ▶ yawp

YAWPS ▶ yawp

YAWS n infectious tropical skin disease

YAWY ▶ yaws

YAY interj exclamation indicating approval, congratulation, or triumph ▷ n cry of approval

YAYS ▶ yay

Y

YBET archaic past participle of ▸ **beat**

YBLENT archaic past participle of ▸ **blend**

YBORE archaic past participle of ▸ **bear**

YBOUND archaic past participle of ▸ **bind**

YBRENT archaic past participle of ▸ **burn**

YCLAD archaic past participle of ▸ **clothe**

YCLED archaic past participle of ▸ **clothe**

YCLEEPE archaic form of ▸ **clepe**

YCLEPED same as ▸ **yclept**

YCLEPT adj having the name of

YCOND archaic past participle of ▸ **con**

YDRAD archaic past participle of ▸ **dread**

YDRED archaic past participle of ▸ **dread**

YE pron you ▷ adj the

YEA interj yes ▷ adv indeed or truly ▷ sentence substitute aye ▷ n cry of agreement

YEAD vb proceed

YEADING ▸ **yead**

YEADS ▸ **yead**

YEAH n positive affirmation

YEAHS ▸ **yeah**

YEALDON n fuel

YEALING n person of the same age as oneself

YEALM vb prepare for thatching

YEALMED ▸ **yealm**

YEALMS ▸ **yealm**

YEAN vb (of a sheep or goat) to give birth to (offspring)

YEANED ▸ **yean**

YEANING ▸ **yean**

YEANS ▸ **yean**

YEAR n time taken for the earth to make one revolution around the sun, about 365 days

YEARD vb bury

YEARDED ▸ **yeard**

YEARDS ▸ **yeard**

YEAREND n end of the year

YEARLY adv (happening) every year or once a year ▷ adj occurring, done, or appearing once a year or every year ▷ n publication, event, etc, that occurs once a year

YEARN vb want (something) very much

YEARNED ▸ **yearn**

YEARNER ▸ **yearn**

YEARNS ▸ **yearn**

YEARS ▸ **year**

YEAS ▸ **yea**

YEAST n fungus used to make bread rise and to ferment alcoholic drinks ▷ vb froth or foam

YEASTED ▸ **yeast**

YEASTS ▸ **yeast**

YEASTY adj of, resembling, or containing yeast

YEBO interj yes ▷ sentence substitute expression of affirmation

YECCH same as ▸ **yech**

YECCHS ▸ **yecch**

YECH n expression of disgust

YECHIER ▸ **yechy**

YECHS ▸ **yech**

YECHY ▸ **yech**

YEDE same as ▸ **yead**

YEDES ▸ **yede**

YEDING ▸ **yede**

YEED same as ▸ **yead**

YEEDING ▸ **yeed**

YEEDS ▸ **yeed**

YEELIN n person of the same age as oneself

YEELINS ▸ **yeelin**

YEGG n burglar or safe-breaker

YEGGMAN same as ▸ **yegg**

YEGGMEN ▸ **yeggman**

YEGGS ▸ **yegg**

YEH same as ▸ **yeah**

YELD adj (of an animal) barren or too young to bear young

YELK n yolk of an egg

YELKS ▸ **yelk**

YELL vb shout or scream in a loud or piercing way ▷ n loud cry of pain, anger, or fear

YELLED ▸ **yell**

YELLER ▸ **yell**

YELLERS ▸ **yell**

YELLING ▸ **yell**

YELLOCH vb yell

YELLOW n colour of gold, a lemon, etc ▷ adj of this colour ▷ vb make or become yellow

YELLOWS n any of various fungal or viral diseases of plants, characterized by yellowish discoloration and stunting

YELLOWY ▸ **yellow**

YELLS ▸ **yell**

YELM same as ▸ **yealm**

YELMED ▸ **yelm**

YELMING ▸ **yelm**

YELMS ▸ **yelm**

YELP n a short sudden cry ▷ vb utter a sharp or high-pitched cry of pain

YELPED ▸ **yelp**

YELPER ▸ **yelp**

YELPERS ▸ **yelp**

YELPING ▸ **yelp**

YELPS ▸ **yelp**

YELT n young sow

YELTS ▸ **yelt**

YEMMER southwest English form of ▸ **ember**

YEMMERS ▸ **yemmer**

YEN n monetary unit of Japan ▷ vb have a longing

YENNED ▸ **yen**

YENNING ▸ **yen**

YENS ▸ **yen**

YENTA n meddlesome woman

YENTAS ▸ **yenta**

YENTE same as ▸ **yenta**

YENTES ▸ **yente**

YEOMAN n farmer owning and farming his own land

YEOMEN ▸ **yeoman**

YEP n affirmative statement

YEPS ▸ **yep**

YERBA n stimulating South American drink made from dried leaves

YERBAS ▸ **yerba**

YERD vb bury

YERDED ▸ **yerd**

YERDING ▸ **yerd**

YERDS ▸ **yerd**

YERK vb tighten stitches

YERKED ▸ **yerk**

YERKING ▸ **yerk**

YERKS ▸ **yerk**

YES interj expresses consent, agreement, or approval ▷ n answer or vote of yes ▷ sentence substitute used to express acknowledgment, affirmation, consent, agreement, or approval or to answer when one is addressed ▷ vb reply in the affirmative

YESES ▸ **yes**

YESHIVA n traditional Jewish school devoted chiefly to the study of rabbinic literature and the Talmud

YESK vb hiccup

YESKED ▸ **yesk**

YESKING ▸ **yesk**
YESKS ▸ **yesk**
YESSED ▸ **yes**
YESSES ▸ **yes**
YESSING ▸ **yes**
YEST *archaic form of* ▸ **yeast**
YESTER *adj* of or relating to yesterday
YESTERN *same as* ▸ **yester**
YESTS ▸ **yest**
YESTY *archaic form of* ▸ **yeasty**
YET *adv* up until then or now
YETI *n* large legendary manlike creature alleged to inhabit the Himalayan Mountains
YETIS ▸ **yeti**
YETT *n* gate or door
YETTIE *n* young, entrepreneurial, and technology-based (person)
YETTIES ▸ **yettie**
YETTS ▸ **yett**
YEUK *vb* itch
YEUKED ▸ **yeuk**
YEUKIER ▸ **yeuky**
YEUKING ▸ **yeuk**
YEUKS ▸ **yeuk**
YEUKY ▸ **yeuk**
YEVE *vb* give
YEVEN ▸ **yeve**
YEVES ▸ **yeve**
YEVING ▸ **yeve**
YEW *n* evergreen tree with needle-like leaves and red berries
YEWEN *adj* made of yew
YEWS ▸ **yew**
YEX *vb* hiccup

> This word meaning to hiccup gives you a good score, and the verb forms offer the chance to expand it if someone else plays it, or if you get the chance later on.

YEXED ▸ **yex**
YEXES ▸ **yex**
YEXING ▸ **yex**
YFERE *adv* together
YGO *archaic past participle of* ▸ **go**
YGOE *archaic past participle of* ▸ **go**
YIBBLES *adv* perhaps
YICKER *vb* squeal or squeak
YICKERS ▸ **yicker**
YIDAKI *n* long wooden wind instrument played by the Aboriginal peoples of Arnhem Land
YIDAKIS ▸ **yidaki**

YIELD *vb* produce or bear ▹ *n* amount produced
YIELDED ▸ **yield**
YIELDER ▸ **yield**
YIELDS ▸ **yield**
YIKE *n* argument, squabble, or fight ▹ *vb* argue, squabble, or fight
YIKED ▸ **yike**
YIKES *interj* expression of surprise, fear, or alarm
YIKING ▸ **yike**
YIKKER *vb* squeal or squeak
YIKKERS ▸ **yikker**
YILL *n* ale
YILLS ▸ **yill**
YIN *Scots word for* ▸ **one**
YINCE *Scots form of* ▸ **once**
YINDIE *n* person who combines a lucrative career with non-mainstream tastes
YINDIES ▸ **yindie**
YINS ▸ **yin**
YIP *n* emit a high-pitched bark
YIPE *same as* ▸ **yipes**
YIPES *interj* expression of surprise, fear, or alarm
YIPPED ▸ **yip**
YIPPEE *interj* exclamation of joy or pleasure
YIPPER *n* golfer who suffers from a failure of nerve
YIPPERS ▸ **yipper**
YIPPIE *n* young person sharing hippy ideals
YIPPIES ▸ **yippie**
YIPPING ▸ **yip**
YIPPY *same as* ▸ **yippie**
YIPS ▸ **yip**
YIRD *vb* bury
YIRDED ▸ **yird**
YIRDING ▸ **yird**
YIRDS ▸ **yird**
YIRK *same as* ▸ **yerk**
YIRKED ▸ **yirk**
YIRKING ▸ **yirk**
YIRKS ▸ **yirk**
YIRR *vb* snarl, growl, or yell
YIRRED ▸ **yirr**
YIRRING ▸ **yirr**
YIRRS ▸ **yirr**
YIRTH *n* earth
YIRTHS ▸ **yirth**
YITE *n* European bunting with a yellowish head and body and brown streaked wings and tail
YITES ▸ **yite**
YITIE *same as* ▸ **yite**
YITIES ▸ **yitie**
YITTEN *adj* frightened

YLEM *n* original matter from which the basic elements are said to have been formed following the explosion postulated in the big bang theory of cosmology
YLEMS ▸ **ylem**
YLIKE *Spenserian form of* ▸ **alike**
YLKE *archaic spelling of* ▸ **ilk**
YLKES ▸ **ylke**
YMOLT *Spenserian past participle of* ▸ **melt**
YMOLTEN *Spenserian past participle of* ▸ **melt**
YMPE *Spenserian form of* ▸ **imp**
YMPES ▸ **ympe**
YMPING ▸ **ympe**
YMPT ▸ **ympe**
YNAMBU *n* South American bird
YNAMBUS ▸ **ynambu**
YO *interj* expression used as a greeting or to attract someone's attention ▹ *sentence substitute* expression used as a greeting, to attract someone's attention, etc
YOB *n* bad-mannered aggressive youth
YOBBERY *n* behaviour typical of aggressive surly youths
YOBBISH *adj* typical of aggressive surly youths
YOBBISM ▸ **yob**
YOBBO *same as* ▸ **yob**
YOBBOES ▸ **yobbo**
YOBBOS ▸ **yobbo**
YOBS ▸ **yob**
YOCK *vb* chuckle
YOCKED ▸ **yock**
YOCKING ▸ **yock**
YOCKS ▸ **yock**
YOD *n* tenth letter in the Hebrew alphabet
YODE ▸ **yead**
YODEL *vb* sing with abrupt changes between a normal and a falsetto voice ▹ *n* act or sound of yodelling
YODELED ▸ **yodel**
YODELER ▸ **yodel**
YODELS ▸ **yodel**
YODH *same as* ▸ **yod**
YODHS ▸ **yodh**
YODLE *variant spelling of* ▸ **yodel**
YODLED ▸ **yodle**
YODLER ▸ **yodle**

Y

YODLERS ▷ **yodle**
YODLES ▷ **yodle**
YODLING ▷ **yodle**
YODS ▷ **yod**
YOGA *n* Hindu method of exercise and discipline aiming at spiritual, mental, and physical wellbeing
YOGAS ▷ **yoga**
YOGEE *same as* ▷ **yogi**
YOGEES ▷ **yogee**
YOGH *n* character used in Old and Middle English to represent a palatal fricative
YOGHS ▷ **yogh**
YOGHURT *same as* ▷ **yogurt**
YOGI *n* person who practises yoga
YOGIC ▷ **yoga**
YOGIN *same as* ▷ **yogi**
YOGINI ▷ **yogi**
YOGINIS ▷ **yogi**
YOGINS ▷ **yogin**
YOGIS ▷ **yogi**
YOGISM ▷ **yogi**
YOGISMS ▷ **yogi**
YOGURT *n* slightly sour custard-like food made from milk that has had bacteria added to it, often sweetened and flavoured with fruit
YOGURTS ▷ **yogurt**
YOHIMBE *n* bark used in herbal medicine
YOICK *vb* urge on foxhounds
YOICKED ▷ **yoick**
YOICKS *interj* cry used by huntsmen to urge on the hounds to the fox ▷ *vb* urge on foxhounds
YOJAN *n* Indian unit of distance
YOJANA *same as* ▷ **yojan**
YOJANAS ▷ **yojana**
YOJANS ▷ **yojan**
YOK *vb* chuckle

| A useful short word meaning to laugh, with an alternative spelling **yuk**.

YOKE *n* wooden bar put across the necks of two animals to hold them together ▷ *vb* put a yoke on
YOKED ▷ **yoke**
YOKER *vb* spit
YOKERED ▷ **yoker**
YOKERS ▷ **yoke**
YOKES ▷ **yoke**
YOKING ▷ **yoke**
YOKINGS ▷ **yoke**
YOKKED ▷ **yok**

YOKKING ▷ **yok**
YOKS ▷ **yok**
YOKUL *Shetland word for* ▷ **yes**
YOLD *archaic past participle of* ▷ **yield**
YOLK *n* yellow part of an egg that provides food for the developing embryo
YOLKED ▷ **yolk**
YOLKIER ▷ **yolk**
YOLKS ▷ **yolk**
YOLKY ▷ **yolk**
YOM *n* day
YOMIM ▷ **yom**
YOMP *vb* walk or trek laboriously, esp heavily laden and over difficult terrain
YOMPED ▷ **yomp**
YOMPING ▷ **yomp**
YOMPS ▷ **yomp**
YON *adj* that or those over there ▷ *adv* yonder ▷ *pron* that person or thing
YOND *same as* ▷ **yon**
YONDER *adv* over there ▷ *adj* situated over there ▷ *determiner* being at a distance, either within view or as if within view ▷ *n* person
YONDERS ▷ **yonder**
YONI *n* female genitalia, regarded as a divine symbol of sexual pleasure
YONIC *adj* resembling a vulva
YONIS ▷ **yoni**
YONKER *same as* ▷ **younker**
YONKERS ▷ **yonker**
YONKS *pl n* very long time
YONNIE *n* stone
YONNIES ▷ **yonnie**
YONT *same as* ▷ **yon**
YOOF *n* non-standard spelling of youth, used humorously or facetiously
YOOFS ▷ **yoof**
YOOP *n* sob
YOOPS ▷ **yoop**
YORE *n* time long past ▷ *adv* in the past
YORES ▷ **yore**
YORK *vb* bowl or try to bowl (a batsman) by pitching the ball under or just beyond the bat
YORKED ▷ **york**
YORKER *n* ball that pitches just under the bat
YORKERS ▷ **yorker**
YORKIE *n* Yorkshire terrier

YORKIES ▷ **yorkie**
YORKING ▷ **york**
YORKS ▷ **york**
YORLING *n as in* **yellow yorling** yellowhammer
YORP *vb* shout
YORPED ▷ **yorp**
YORPING ▷ **yorp**
YORPS ▷ **yorp**
YOU *pron* person or people addressed ▷ *n* personality of the person being addressed
YOUK *vb* itch
YOUKED ▷ **youk**
YOUKING ▷ **youk**
YOUKS ▷ **youk**
YOUNG *adj* in an early stage of life or growth ▷ *n* young people in general; offspring
YOUNGER ▷ **young**
YOUNGLY *adv* youthfully
YOUNGS ▷ **young**
YOUNGTH *n* youth
YOUNKER *n* young man
YOUPON *same as* ▷ **yaupon**
YOUPONS ▷ **youpon**
YOUR *adj* of, belonging to, or associated with you
YOURN *dialect form of* ▷ **yours**
YOURS *pron* something belonging to you
YOURT *same as* ▷ **yurt**
YOURTS ▷ **yourt**
YOUS *pron* refers to more than one person including the person or persons addressed but not including the speaker
YOUSE *same as* ▷ **yous**
YOUTH *n* time of being young
YOUTHEN *vb* render more youthful-seeming
YOUTHLY *adv* young
YOUTHS ▷ **youth**
YOUTHY *Scots word for* ▷ **young**
YOW *vb* howl
YOWE *Scots word for* ▷ **ewe**
YOWED ▷ **yow**
YOWES ▷ **yowe**
YOWIE *n* legendary Australian apelike creature
YOWIES ▷ **yowie**
YOWING ▷ **yow**
YOWL *n* loud mournful cry ▷ *vb* produce a loud mournful wail or cry
YOWLED ▷ **yowl**
YOWLER ▷ **yowl**
YOWLERS ▷ **yowl**

Y

YOWLEY n yellowhammer (bird)
YOWLEYS ▶ yowley
YOWLING ▶ yowl
YOWLS ▶ yowl
YOWS ▶ yow
YPERITE n mustard gas
YPIGHT archaic past participle of ▶ pitch
YPLAST archaic past participle of ▶ place
YPLIGHT archaic past participle of ▶ plight
YPSILON same as ▶ upsilon
YRAPT Spenserian form of ▶ rapt
YRENT archaic past participle of ▶ rend
YRIVD archaic past participle of ▶ rive
YRNEH n unit of reciprocal inductance
YRNEHS ▶ yrneh
YSAME Spenserian word for > together
YSHEND Spenserian form of ▶ shend
YSHENDS ▶ yshend
YSHENT ▶ yshend
YSLAKED archaic past participle of ▶ slake
YTOST archaic past participle of ▶ toss
YTTRIA n insoluble solid used mainly in incandescent mantles
YTTRIAS ▶ yttria
YTTRIC ▶ yttrium
YTTRIUM n silvery metallic element used in various alloys
YU n jade
YUAN n standard monetary unit of the People's Republic of China
YUANS ▶ yuan
YUCA same as ▶ yucca
YUCAS ▶ yuca
YUCCA n tropical plant with spikes of white leaves
YUCCAS ▶ yucca
YUCCH interj expression of disgust
YUCH interj expression of disgust

YUCK interj exclamation indicating contempt, dislike, or disgust ▷ vb chuckle
YUCKED ▶ yuck
YUCKER ▶ yuck
YUCKERS ▶ yuck
YUCKIER ▶ yucky
YUCKING ▶ yuck
YUCKO adj disgusting ▷ interj exclamation of disgust
YUCKS ▶ yuck
YUCKY adj disgusting, nasty
YUFT n Russia leather
YUFTS ▶ yuft
YUG same as ▶ yuga
YUGA n (in Hindu cosmology) one of the four ages of mankind
YUGARIE variant spelling of ▶ eugarie
YUGAS ▶ yuga
YUGS ▶ yug
YUK same as ▶ yuck
YUKATA n light kimono
YUKATAS ▶ yukata
YUKE vb itch
YUKED ▶ yuke
YUKES ▶ yuke
YUKIER ▶ yuky
YUKIEST ▶ yuky
YUKING ▶ yuke
YUKKED ▶ yuk
YUKKIER ▶ yukky
YUKKING ▶ yuk
YUKKY same as ▶ yucky
YUKO n score of five points in judo
YUKOS ▶ yuko
YUKS ▶ yuk
YUKY adj itchy
YULAN n Chinese magnolia often cultivated for its showy white flowers
YULANS ▶ yulan
YULE n Christmas, the Christmas season, or Christmas festivities
YULES ▶ yule
YUM interj expression of delight
YUMMIER ▶ yummy
YUMMIES ▶ yummy

YUMMO adj tasty ▷ interj exclamation of delight or approval
YUMMY adj delicious ▷ interj exclamation indicating pleasure or delight, as in anticipation of delicious food ▷ n delicious food item
YUMP vb leave the ground when driving over a ridge
YUMPED ▶ yump
YUMPIE n young upwardly mobile person
YUMPIES ▶ yumpie
YUMPING ▶ yump
YUMPS ▶ yump
YUNX n wryneck
YUNXES ▶ yunx
YUP n informal affirmative statement
YUPON same as ▶ yaupon
YUPONS ▶ yupon
YUPPIE n young highly-paid professional person, esp one who has a materialistic way of life ▷ adj typical of or reflecting the values of yuppies
YUPPIES ▶ yuppy
YUPPIFY vb make yuppie in nature
YUPPY same as ▶ yuppie
YUPS ▶ yup
YUPSTER ▶ yindie
YURT n circular tent consisting of a framework of poles covered with felt or skins, used by Mongolian and Turkic nomads of E and central Asia
YURTA same as ▶ yurt
YURTAS ▶ yurt
YURTS ▶ yurt
YUS ▶ yu
YUTZ n Yiddish word meaning fool
YUTZES ▶ yutz
YUZU n type of citrus fruit
YUZUS ▶ yuzu
YWIS adv certainly
YWROKE archaic past participle of ▶ wreak

Y

Zz

Scoring the same as **Q** but easier to use, **Z** is normally a good tile to have, but it is not the best when it comes to making bonus words scoring that extra 50 points, so you will normally want to play it off as soon as a good score offers itself. There are only two two-letter words beginning with **Z**, **za** and **zo** (11 points), but remembering this will save you wasting time looking for others. There some very good three-letter words starting with **Z**, however. These include another variant of **zo**, **zho** (15), as well as **zax** and **zex**, (19 each) **zap**, (14) **zep**, (14) **zip**, (14) and **zoo** (12).

ZA n pizza
ZABETA n tariff
ZABETAS ▶ zabeta
ZABRA n small sailing vessel
ZABRAS ▶ zabra
ZABTIEH n Turkish police officer
ZACATON n coarse grass
ZACK n Australian five-cent piece
ZACKS ▶ zack
ZADDICK adj righteous
ZADDIK n Hasidic Jewish leader
ZADDIKS ▶ zaddik
ZAFFAR same as ▶ zaffer
ZAFFARS ▶ zaffar
ZAFFER n impure cobalt oxide, used to impart a blue colour to enamels
ZAFFERS ▶ zaffer
ZAFFIR same as ▶ zaffer
ZAFFIRS ▶ zaffir
ZAFFRE same as ▶ zaffer
ZAFFRES ▶ zaffre
ZAFTIG adj ripe or curvaceous
ZAG vb change direction sharply
ZAGGED ▶ zag
ZAGGING ▶ zag
ZAGS ▶ zag
ZAIKAI n Japanese business community
ZAIKAIS ▶ zaikai
ZAIRE n currency used in the former Zaïre
ZAIRES ▶ zaire
ZAITECH n investment in financial markets by a company to supplement its main income

ZAKAT n annual tax on Muslims to aid the poor in the Muslim community
ZAKATS ▶ zakat
ZAKUSKA ▶ zakuski
ZAKUSKI pl n hors d'oeuvres, consisting of tiny open sandwiches spread with caviar, smoked sausage, etc
ZAMAN n tropical tree
ZAMANG same as ▶ zaman
ZAMANGS ▶ zamang
ZAMANS ▶ zaman
ZAMARRA n sheepskin coat
ZAMARRO same as ▶ zamarra
ZAMBUCK n St John ambulance attendant, esp at a sports meeting
ZAMBUK same as ▶ zambuck
ZAMBUKS ▶ zambuk
ZAMIA n type of plant of tropical and subtropical America, with a short thick trunk, palmlike leaves, and short stout cones
ZAMIAS ▶ zamia
ZAMOUSE n West African buffalo
ZAMPONE n sausage made from pig's trotters
ZAMPONI ▶ zampone
ZANANA same as ▶ zenana
ZANANAS ▶ zanana
ZANDER n European freshwater pikeperch, valued as a food fish
ZANDERS ▶ zander
ZANELLA n twill fabric
ZANIED ▶ zany

ZANIER ▶ zany
ZANIES ▶ zany
ZANIEST ▶ zany
ZANILY ▶ zany
ZANJA n irrigation canal
┃ An irrigation canal in Spanish America, notable for combining the J and Z.
ZANJAS ▶ zanja
ZANJERO n irrigation supervisor
┃ Someone who supervises the distribution of water in a **zanja** or irrigation canal. This has a fair chance of coming up in actual play, and would make a great bonus.
ZANTE n type of wood
ZANTES ▶ zante
ZANY adj comical in an endearing way ▷ n clown or buffoon, esp one in old comedies who imitated other performers with ludicrous effect ▷ vb clown
ZANYING ▶ zany
ZANYISH ▶ zany
ZANYISM ▶ zany
ZANZA same as ▶ zanze
ZANZAS ▶ zanza
ZANZE n African musical instrument
ZANZES ▶ zanze
ZAP vb kill (by shooting) ▷ n energy, vigour, or pep ▷ interj exclamation used to express sudden or swift action
ZAPATA adj (of a

moustache) drooping
ZAPATEO n Cuban folk dance
ZAPPED ▶ zap
ZAPPER n remote control for a television etc
ZAPPERS ▶ zapper
ZAPPIER ▶ zappy
ZAPPING ▶ zap
ZAPPY adj energetic
ZAPS ▶ zap
ZAPTIAH same as ▶ zaptieh
ZAPTIEH n Turkish police officer

Watch out for this Turkish policeman, who can also be spelt **zabtieh** or **zaptiah**.

ZARAPE n blanket-like shawl
ZARAPES ▶ zarape
ZAREBA n stockade or enclosure of thorn bushes around a village or campsite
ZAREBAS ▶ zareba
ZAREEBA same as ▶ zareba
ZARF n (esp in the Middle East) a holder, usually ornamental, for a hot coffee cup
ZARFS ▶ zarf
ZARI n thread made from fine gold or silver wire
ZARIBA same as ▶ zareba
ZARIBAS ▶ zariba
ZARIS ▶ zari
ZARNEC n sulphide of arsenic
ZARNECS ▶ zarnec
ZARNICH same as ▶ zarnec
ZAS ▶ za
ZATI n type of macaque
ZATIS ▶ zati
ZAX same as ▶ sax

A chopper for trimming slate, and a great word combining X and Z. It has a variant **zex**.

ZAXES ▶ zax
ZAYIN n seventh letter of the Hebrew alphabet
ZAYINS ▶ zayin
ZAZEN n (in Zen Buddhism) deep meditation undertaken whilst sitting upright with legs crossed
ZAZENS ▶ zazen
ZEA n corn silk
ZEAL n great enthusiasm or eagerness
ZEALANT archaic variant of ▶ zealot

ZEALFUL ▶ zeal
ZEALOT n fanatic or extreme enthusiast
ZEALOTS ▶ zealot
ZEALOUS adj extremely eager or enthusiastic
ZEALS ▶ zeal
ZEAS ▶ zeal
ZEATIN n cytokinin derived from corn
ZEATINS ▶ zeatin
ZEBEC variant spelling of ▶ xebec
ZEBECK same as ▶ zebec
ZEBECKS ▶ zebeck
ZEBECS ▶ zebec
ZEBRA n black-and-white striped African animal of the horse family
ZEBRAIC adj like a zebra
ZEBRANO n type of striped wood
ZEBRAS ▶ zebra
ZEBRASS n offspring of a male zebra and a female ass
ZEBRINA n trailing herbaceous plant
ZEBRINE ▶ zebra
ZEBROID ▶ zebra
ZEBRULA n offspring of a male zebra and a female horse
ZEBRULE same as ▶ zebrula
ZEBU n Asian ox with a humped back and long horns
ZEBUB n large African fly
ZEBUBS ▶ zebub
ZEBUS ▶ zebu
ZECCHIN same as > zecchino
ZECHIN same as > zecchino
ZECHINS ▶ zechin
ZED n British and New Zealand spoken form of the letter z

A name for the letter Z, and one of the most commonly played Z words.

ZEDOARY n dried rhizome of a tropical Asian plant, used as a stimulant and a condiment
ZEDS ▶ zed
ZEE the US word for ▶ zed

This word can be very useful because E is the most common tile in Scrabble, so keep it in mind if you draw a Z. Zee scores 12 points.

ZEES ▶ zee

ZEIN n protein occurring in maize and used in the manufacture of plastics
ZEINS ▶ zein
ZEK n Soviet prisoner
ZEKS ▶ zek
ZEL n Turkish cymbal
ZELANT alternative form of ▶ zealant
ZELANTS ▶ zelant
ZELATOR same as > zelatrix
ZELKOVA n type of elm tree
ZELOSO adv with zeal
ZELS ▶ zel
ZEMSTVA ▶ zemstvo
ZEMSTVO n (in tsarist Russia) an elective provincial or district council established in most provinces of Russia by Alexander II in 1864 as part of his reform policy
ZENAIDA n dove
ZENANA n (in the East, esp in Muslim and Hindu homes) part of a house reserved for the women and girls of a household
ZENANAS ▶ zenana
ZENDIK n unbeliever or heretic
ZENDIKS ▶ zendik
ZENITH n highest point of success or power
ZENITHS ▶ zenith
ZEOLITE n any of a large group of glassy secondary minerals
ZEP n type of long sandwich
ZEPHYR n soft gentle breeze
ZEPHYRS ▶ zephyr
ZEPPOLE n Italian fritter
ZEPPOLI ▶ zeppole
ZEPS ▶ zep
ZERDA n fennec
ZERDAS ▶ zerda
ZEREBA same as ▶ zareba
ZEREBAS ▶ zereba
ZERIBA same as ▶ zareba
ZERIBAS ▶ zeriba
ZERK n grease fitting
ZERKS ▶ zerk
ZERO n (symbol representing) the number 0 ▷ adj having no measurable quantity or size ▷ vb adjust (an instrument or scale) so as to read zero ▷ determiner no (thing) at all
ZEROED ▶ zero
ZEROES ▶ zero
ZEROING ▶ zero

ZEROS ▸ zero

ZEROTH adj denoting a term in a series that precedes the term otherwise regarded as the first term

ZEST n enjoyment or excitement ▷ vb give flavour, interest, or piquancy to

ZESTED ▸ zest

ZESTER n kitchen utensil used to scrape fine shreds of peel from citrus fruits

ZESTERS ▸ zester

ZESTFUL ▸ zest

ZESTIER ▸ zest

ZESTILY ▸ zest

ZESTING ▸ zest

ZESTS ▸ zest

ZESTY ▸ zest

ZETA n sixth letter in the Greek alphabet, a consonant, transliterated as z

ZETAS ▸ zeta

ZETETIC adj proceeding by inquiry ▷ n investigation

ZEUGMA n figure of speech in which a word is used to modify or govern two or more words although appropriate to only one of them or making a different sense with each

ZEUGMAS ▸ zeugma

ZEUXITE n ferriferous mineral

> This mineral, a kind of tourmaline, makes an excellent bonus.

ZEX n tool for cutting roofing slate

ZEXES ▸ zex

ZEZE n stringed musical instrument

ZEZES ▸ zeze

ZHO same as ▸ zo

> A cross between a yak and a cow; the other forms are **dso, dzo** and **zo,** and it's worth remembering all of them.

ZHOMO n female zho

ZHOMOS ▸ zhomo

ZHOS ▸ zho

ZIBET n large civet of S and SE Asia, having tawny fur marked with black spots and stripes

ZIBETH same as ▸ zibet

ZIBETHS ▸ zibeth

ZIBETS ▸ zibet

ZIFF n beard

ZIFFIUS n sea monster

ZIFFS ▸ ziff

ZIG same as ▸ zag

ZIGAN n gypsy

ZIGANKA n Russian dance

ZIGANS ▸ zigan

ZIGGED ▸ zig

ZIGGING ▸ zig

ZIGS ▸ zig

ZIGZAG n line or course having sharp turns in alternating directions ▷ vb move in a zigzag ▷ adj formed in or proceeding in a zigzag ▷ adv in a zigzag manner

ZIGZAGS ▸ zigzag

ZIKURAT same as > ziggurat

ZILA n administrative district in India

ZILAS ▸ zila

ZILCH n nothing

ZILCHES ▸ zilch

ZILL n finger cymbal

ZILLA same as ▸ zila

ZILLAH same as ▸ zila

ZILLAHS ▸ zillah

ZILLAS ▸ zilla

ZILLION n extremely large but unspecified number

ZILLS ▸ zill

ZIMB same as ▸ zebub

ZIMBI n cowrie shell used as money

ZIMBIS ▸ zimbi

ZIMBS ▸ zimb

ZIMOCCA n bath sponge

ZIN short form of > zinfandel

ZINC n bluish-white metallic element used in alloys and to coat metal ▷ vb coat with zinc

ZINCATE n any of a class of salts derived from the amphoteric hydroxide of zinc

ZINCED ▸ zinc

ZINCIC ▸ zinc

ZINCIER ▸ zinc

ZINCIFY vb coat with zinc

ZINCING ▸ zinc

ZINCITE n red or yellow mineral consisting of zinc oxide in hexagonal crystalline form

ZINCKED ▸ zinc

ZINCKY ▸ zinc

ZINCO n printing plate made from zincography

ZINCODE n positive electrode

ZINCOID ▸ zinc

ZINCOS ▸ zinco

ZINCOUS ▸ zinc

ZINCS ▸ zinc

ZINCY ▸ zinc

ZINE n magazine or fanzine

ZINEB n organic insecticide

ZINEBS ▸ zineb

ZINES ▸ zine

ZING n quality in something that makes it lively or interesting ▷ vb make or move with or as if with a high-pitched buzzing sound

ZINGANI ▸ zingano

ZINGANO n gypsy

ZINGARA same as ▸ zingaro

ZINGARE ▸ zingara

ZINGARI ▸ zingaro

ZINGARO n Italian Gypsy

ZINGED ▸ zing

ZINGEL n small freshwater perch

ZINGELS ▸ zingel

ZINGER ▸ zing

ZINGERS ▸ zing

ZINGIER ▸ zingy

ZINGING ▸ zing

ZINGS ▸ zing

ZINGY adj vibrant

ZINKE n cornett

ZINKED ▸ zinc

ZINKES ▸ zinke

ZINKIER ▸ zinc

ZINKIFY vb coat with zinc

ZINKING ▸ zinc

ZINKY ▸ zinc

ZINNIA n plant of tropical and subtropical America, with solitary heads of brightly coloured flowers

ZINNIAS ▸ zinnia

ZINS ▸ zin

ZIP same as ▸ zipper

ZIPLESS ▸ zip

ZIPLOCK adj fastened with interlocking plastic strips ▷ vb seal (a ziplock storage bag)

ZIPPED ▸ zip

ZIPPER n fastening device operating by means of two parallel rows of metal or plastic teeth on either side of a closure that are interlocked by a sliding tab ▷ vb fasten with a zipper

ZIPPERS ▸ zipper

ZIPPIER ▸ zippy

ZIPPING ▸ zip

ZIPPO n nothing

ZIPPOS ▸ zippo

ZIPPY adj full of energy

ZIPS ▷ zip
ZIPTOP adj (of a bag) closed with a zip
ZIRAM n industrial fungicide
ZIRAMS ▷ ziram
ZIRCON n mineral used as a gemstone and in industry
ZIRCONS ▷ zircon
ZIT n spot or pimple

> This little word for a pimple can be very useful for disposing of the Z.

ZITE same as ▷ ziti
ZITHER n musical instrument consisting of strings stretched over a flat box and plucked to produce musical notes
ZITHERN same as ▷ zither
ZITHERS ▷ zither
ZITI n type of pasta

> Another very useful word for disposing of the Z, **ziti** is a type of pasta. It has a variant **zite**. Remember that **ziti** takes an S to form **zitis**, but **zite** does not take an S.

ZITIS ▷ ziti
ZITS ▷ zit
ZIZ same as ▷ zizz
ZIZANIA n aquatic grass
ZIZEL n chipmunk
ZIZELS ▷ zizel
ZIZIT same as ▷ zizith
ZIZITH variant spelling of ▷ tsitsith
ZIZZ n short sleep ▷ vb take a short sleep, snooze
ZIZZED ▷ zizz
ZIZZES ▷ zizz
ZIZZING ▷ zizz
ZIZZLE vb sizzle
ZIZZLED ▷ zizzle
ZIZZLES ▷ zizzle
ZLOTE ▷ zloty
ZLOTIES ▷ zloty
ZLOTY n monetary unit of Poland
ZLOTYCH same as ▷ zloty
ZLOTYS ▷ zloty
ZO n Tibetan breed of cattle, developed by crossing the yak with common cattle
ZOA ▷ zoon
ZOAEA same as ▷ zoea
ZOAEAE ▷ zoaea
ZOAEAS ▷ zoaea
ZOARIA ▷ zoarium
ZOARIAL ▷ zoarium
ZOARIUM n colony of zooids

ZOBO same as ▷ zo
ZOBOS ▷ zobo
ZOBU same as ▷ zo
ZOBUS ▷ zobu
ZOCALO n plaza in Mexico
ZOCALOS ▷ zocalo
ZOCCO n plinth
ZOCCOLO same as ▷ zocco
ZOCCOS ▷ zocco
ZODIAC n imaginary belt in the sky within which the sun, moon, and planets appear to move, divided into twelve equal areas, called signs of the zodiac, each named after a constellation
ZODIACS ▷ zodiac
ZOEA n free-swimming larva of a crab or related crustacean, which has well-developed abdominal appendages and may bear one or more spines

> A larval stage in certain crustaceans, and one of the most frequently played words in Scrabble, along with its friends **zoaea** and **zooea** and the various inflections: remember that these words can take an E in the plural as well as S, giving **zoeaa**, **zoacae** and **zooeae**.

ZOEAE ▷ zoea
ZOEAL ▷ zoea
ZOEAS ▷ zoea
ZOECIA ▷ zoecium
ZOECIUM same as ▷ zooecium
ZOEFORM ▷ zoea
ZOETIC adj pertaining to life
ZOFTIG adj ripe or curvaceous
ZOIC adj relating to or having animal life
ZOISITE n grey, brown, or pink mineral
ZOISM n belief in magical animal powers
ZOISMS ▷ zoism
ZOIST ▷ zoism
ZOISTS ▷ zoism
ZOL n South African slang for a cannabis cigarette
ZOLS ▷ zol
ZOMBI same as ▷ zombie
ZOMBIE n person who appears to be lifeless, apathetic, or totally lacking in independent judgment

ZOMBIES ▷ zombie
ZOMBIFY vb turn into a zombie
ZOMBIS ▷ zombi
ZONA n zone or belt
ZONAE ▷ zona
ZONAL adj of, relating to, or of the nature of a zone
ZONALLY ▷ zonal
ZONARY same as ▷ zonal
ZONATE adj marked with, divided into, or arranged in zones
ZONATED same as ▷ zonate
ZONDA n South American wind
ZONDAS ▷ zonda
ZONE n area with particular features or properties ▷ vb divide into zones
ZONED ▷ zone
ZONER n something which divides other things into zones
ZONERS ▷ zoner
ZONES ▷ zone
ZONING ▷ zone
ZONINGS ▷ zone
ZONK vb strike resoundingly
ZONKED adj highly intoxicated with drugs or alcohol
ZONKING ▷ zonk
ZONKS ▷ zonk
ZONOID adj resembling a zone
ZONULA n small zone or belt
ZONULAE ▷ zonula
ZONULAR ▷ zonule
ZONULAS ▷ zonula
ZONULE n small zone, band, or area
ZONULES ▷ zonule
ZONULET n small belt
ZONURE n lizard with ringed tail
ZONURES ▷ zonure
ZOO n place where live animals are kept for show
ZOOEA same as ▷ zoea
ZOOEAE ▷ zooea
ZOOEAL ▷ zooea
ZOOEAS ▷ zooea
ZOOECIA > zooecium
ZOOEY ▷ zoo
ZOOGAMY n sexual reproduction in animals
ZOOGENY n doctrine of formation of animals
ZOOGLEA same as > zoogloea
ZOOGONY same as ▷ zoogeny

ZOOID n any independent animal body, such as an individual of a coral colony

ZOOIDAL ▸ zooid

ZOOIDS ▸ zooid

ZOOIER ▸ zoo

ZOOIEST ▸ zoo

ZOOKS short form of > gadzooks

ZOOLITE n fossilized animal

ZOOLITH n fossilized animal

ZOOLOGY n study of animals

ZOOM vb move or rise very rapidly ▷ n sound or act of zooming

ZOOMED ▸ zoom

ZOOMING ▸ zoom

ZOOMS ▸ zoom

ZOON ▸ zoon

ZOONAL ▸ zoon

ZOONED ▸ zoon

ZOONIC adj concerning animals

ZOONING ▸ zoon

ZOONITE n segment of an articulated animal

ZOONOMY n science of animal life

ZOONS ▸ zoon

ZOOPERY n experimentation on animals

ZOOS ▸ zoo

ZOOT n as in **zoot suit** man's suit consisting of baggy trousers with tapered bottoms and a long jacket with wide padded shoulders

ZOOTAXY n science of the classification of animals

> The science of classifying animals. An unlikely word to appear on your rack, but you never know, and it would make an impressive bonus!

ZOOTIER ▸ zooty

ZOOTOMY n branch of zoology concerned with the dissection and anatomy of animals

ZOOTY adj showy

ZOOTYPE n animal figure used as a symbol

ZOOZOO n wood pigeon

ZOOZOOS ▸ zoozoo

ZOPPA adj syncopated

ZOPPO same as ▸ zoppa

ZORBING n activity of travelling downhill inside a large air-cushioned hollow ball

ZORGITE n copper-lead selenide

ZORI n Japanese sandal

ZORIL same as ▸ zorilla

ZORILLA n skunk-like African musteline mammal having a long black-and-white coat

ZORILLE same as ▸ zorilla

ZORILLO same as ▸ zorille

ZORILS ▸ zoril

ZORINO n skunk fur

ZORINOS ▸ zorino

ZORIS ▸ zori

ZORRO n hoary fox

ZORROS ▸ zorro

ZOS ▸ zo

ZOSTER n shingles; herpes zoster

ZOSTERS ▸ zoster

ZOUAVE n (formerly) member of a body of French infantry composed of Algerian recruits

ZOUAVES ▸ zouave

ZOUK n style of dance music that combines African and Latin American rhythms and uses electronic instruments and modern studio technology

ZOUKS ▸ zouk

ZOUNDS interj mild oath indicating surprise or indignation

ZOWIE interj expression of pleasurable surprise

ZOYSIA n type of grass with short stiffly pointed leaves, often used for lawns

ZOYSIAS ▸ zoysia

ZUFFOLI ▸ zuffolo

ZUFFOLO same as ▸ zufolo

ZUFOLI ▸ zufolo

ZUFOLO n small flute

ZULU n (in the NATO phonetic alphabet) used to represent z

ZULUS ▸ zulu

ZUPA n confederation of Serbian villages

ZUPAN n head of a zupa

ZUPANS ▸ zupan

ZUPAS ▸ zupa

ZURF same as ▸ zarf

ZURFS ▸ zurf

ZUZ n ancient Hebrew silver coin

ZUZIM ▸ zuz

ZUZZIM ▸ zuz

ZYDECO n type of Black Cajun music

ZYDECOS ▸ zydeco

ZYGA ▸ zygon

ZYGAL ▸ zygon

ZYGOID same as ▸ diploid

ZYGOMA n slender arch of bone that forms a bridge between the cheekbone and the temporal bone on each side of the skull of mammals

ZYGOMAS ▸ zygoma

ZYGON n brain fissure

ZYGOSE ▸ zygosis

ZYGOSES ▸ zygosis

ZYGOSIS n (in bacteria) the direct transfer of DNA between two cells that are temporarily joined

ZYGOTE n fertilized egg cell

ZYGOTES ▸ zygote

ZYGOTIC ▸ zygote

ZYMASE n mixture of enzymes that is obtained as an extract from yeast and ferments sugars

ZYMASES ▸ zymase

ZYME n ferment

ZYMES ▸ zyme

ZYMIC ▸ zyme

ZYMITE n priest who uses leavened bread during communion

ZYMITES ▸ zymite

ZYMOGEN n any of a group of compounds that are inactive precursors of enzymes and are activated by a kinase

ZYMOID adj relating to a ferment

ZYMOME n glutinous substance that is insoluble in alcohol

ZYMOMES ▸ zymome

ZYMOSAN n insoluble carbohydrate found in yeast

ZYMOSES ▸ zymosis

ZYMOSIS same as > zymolysis

ZYMOTIC adj of, relating to, or causing fermentation ▷ n disease

ZYMURGY n branch of chemistry concerned with fermentation processes in brewing, etc

ZYTHUM n Ancient Egyptian beer

ZYTHUMS ▸ zythum

ZYZZYVA n American weevil

ZZZ n informal word for sleep

ZZZS ▸ zzz

Z